AN EXEGETICAL SUMMARY OF
ROMANS 1–8

AN EXEGETICAL SUMMARY OF ROMANS 1–8

Second Edition

David Abernathy

SIL International

Second Edition
© 2006, 2008 by SIL International

Library of Congress Catalog Card Number: 2008923533
ISBN: 978-155671-207-4

Printed in the United States of America

All Rights Reserved
No part of this publication may be reproduced, stored in a retrieval system, or transmitted in any form or by any means without the express permission of SIL International. However, brief excerpts, generally understood to be within the limits of fair use, may be quoted without written permission.

Copies of this and other publications
of SIL International may be obtained from

International Academic Bookstore
SIL International
7500 West Camp Wisdom Road
Dallas, TX 75236-5699, USA

Voice: 972-708-7404
Fax: 972-708-7363
academic_books@sil.org
www.ethnologue.com

PREFACE

Exegesis is concerned with the interpretation of a text. Exegesis of the New Testament involves determining the meaning of the Greek text. Translators must be especially careful and thorough in their exegesis of the New Testament in order to accurately communicate its message in the vocabulary, grammar, and literary devices of another language. Questions occurring to translators as they study the Greek text are answered by summarizing how scholars have interpreted the text. This is information that should be considered by translators as they make their own exegetical decisions regarding the message they will communicate in their translations.

The Semi-Literal Translation

As a basis for discussion, a semi-literal translation of the Greek text is given so that the reasons for different interpretations can best be seen. When one Greek word is translated into English by several words, these words are joined by hyphens. There are a few times when clarity requires that a string of words joined by hyphens have a separate word, such as "not" (μή), inserted in their midst. In this case, the separate word is surrounded by spaces between the hyphens. When alternate translations of a Greek word are given, these are separated by slashes.

The Text

Variations in the Greek text are noted under the heading TEXT. The base text for the summary is the text of the fourth revised edition of *The Greek New Testament,* published by the United Bible Societies, which has the same text as the twenty-sixth edition of the *Novum Testamentum Graece* (Nestle-Aland). The versions that follow different variations are listed without evaluating their choices.

The Lexicon

The meaning of a key word in context is the first question to be answered. Words marked with a raised letter in the semi-literal translation are treated separately under the heading LEXICON. First, the lexicon form of the Greek word is given. Within the parentheses following the Greek word is the location number where, in the author's judgment, this word is defined in the *Greek-English Lexicon of the New Testament Based on Semantic Domains* (Louw and Nida 1988). When a semantic domain includes a translation of the particular verse being treated, **LN** in bold type indicates that specific translation. If the specific reference for the verse is listed in *A Greek-English Lexicon of the New Testament and Other Early Christian Literature* (Bauer, Arndt, Gingrich, and Danker 1979), the outline location and page number is given. Then English equivalents of the Greek word are given to show how it is translated by commentators who offer their own translations of the whole text and, after a semicolon, all the versions in the list of abbreviations for translations. When reference is made to "all versions," it refers to only the versions in the list of translations. Sometimes further comments are made about the meaning of the word or the significance of a verb's tense, voice, or mood.

The Questions

Under the heading QUESTION, a question is asked that comes from examining the Greek text under consideration. Typical questions concern the identity of an implied actor or object of an event word, the antecedent of a pronominal reference, the connection indicated by a relational word, the meaning of a genitive construction, the meaning of figurative language, the function of a rhetorical question, the identification of an ambiguity, and the presence of implied information that is needed to understand the passage correctly. Background information is also considered for a proper understanding of a passage. Although not all implied information and background information is made explicit in a translation, it is important to consider it so that the translation will not be stated in such a way that prevents a reader from arriving at the proper interpretation. The question is answered with a summary of what commentators have said. If there are contrasting differences of opinion, the different interpretations are numbered and the commentaries that support each are listed. Differences that are not treated by many of the commentaries often are not numbered, but are introduced with a contrastive 'Or' at the beginning of the sentence. No attempt has been made to select which interpretation is best.

In listing support for various statements of interpretation, the author is often faced with the difficult task of matching the different terminologies used in commentaries with the terminology he has adopted. Sometimes he can only infer the position of a commentary from incidental remarks. This book, then, includes the author's interpretation of the views taken in the various commentaries. General statements are followed by specific statements, which indicate the author's understanding of the pertinent relationships, actors, events, and objects implied by that interpretation.

The Use of This Book

This book does not replace the commentaries that it summarizes. Commentaries contain much more information about the meaning of words and passages. They often contain arguments for the interpretations that are taken and they may have important discussions about the discourse features of the text. In addition, they have information about the historical, geographical, and cultural setting. Translators will want to refer to at least four commentaries as they exegete a passage. However, since no one commentary contains all the answers translators need, this book will be a valuable supplement. It makes more sources of exegetical help available than most translators have access to. Even if they had all the books available, few would have the time to search through all of them for the answers.

When many commentaries are studied, it soon becomes apparent that they frequently disagree in their interpretations. That is the reason why so many answers in this book are divided into two or more interpretations. The reader's initial reaction may be that all of these different interpretations complicate exegesis rather than help it. However, before translating a passage, a translator needs to know exactly where there is a problem of interpretation and what the exegetical options are.

Acknowledgments

Like many other works, this one was the result of a team effort. Harold Greenlee did the initial translation, and framed the lexicon. Andrew Sims did most of the research and much of the writing for chapters 1–3. Jean Goddard assisted with the lexicon in several chapters. I greatly appreciate their contributions, without which this volume would not be what it is.

Special thanks goes to Richard Blight, who edited all the chapters and made numerous helpful suggestions, and who has been an encouragement to me for all the years that I have worked for him.

ABBREVIATIONS

COMMENTARIES AND REFERENCE BOOKS

AB — Fitzmyer, Joseph A. *Romans*. The Anchor Bible, edited by W. F. Albright and D. N. Freedman. Garden City, N.Y.: Doubleday, 1993.

BAGD — Bauer, Walter. *A Greek–English Lexicon of the New Testament and Other Early Christian Literature*. Translated and adapted from the 5th ed., 1958 by William F. Arndt and F. Wilbur Gingrich. 2d English ed. revised and augmented by F. Wilbur Gingrich and Frederick W. Danker. Chicago: University of Chicago Press, 1979.

BECNT — Schreiner, Thomas R. *Romans*. Baker Exegetical Commentary on the New Testament. Grand Rapids: Baker, 1998.

Gdt — Godet, F. *Commentary on the Epistle to the Romans*. Tr. by A. Cusin, revised and edited by Talbot W. Chambers, 1883. Grand Rapids: Zondervan, 1969.

HNTC — Barrett, C. K. *A Commentary on the Epistle to the Romans*. Harper's New Testament Commentaries, edited by Henry Chadwick. New York: Harper & Row, 1957.

Ho — Hodge, Charles. *Commentary on the Epistle to the Romans*. 1886. Reprint. Grand Rapids: Eerdmans, 1953.

ICC1 — Sanday, William, and Arthur C. Headlam. *A Critical and Exegetical Commentary on the Epistle to the Romans*. The International Critical Commentary, edited by S. R. Driver, A. Plummer, and C. A. Briggs. 1902. Reprint. Edinburgh: T. & T. Clark, 1971.

ICC2 — Cranfield, C. E. B. *A Critical and Exegetical Commentary on the Epistle to the Romans*. Vol. 1. The International Critical Commentary, edited by J. A. Emerton and C. E. B. Cranfield. Edinburgh: T. & T. Clark, 1975.

LN — Louw, Johannes P., and Eugene A. Nida. *Greek–English Lexicon of the New Testament Based on Semantic Domains*. New York: United Bible Societies, 1988.

Mor — Morris, Leon. *The Epistle to the Romans*. Grand Rapids: Eerdmans, 1988.

Mu — Murray, John. *The Epistle to the Romans. The English Text with Introduction, Exposition and Notes*. Grand Rapids: Eerdmans, 1968.

NAC — Mounce, Robert H. *Romans*. New American Commentary, edited by E. Ray Clendenen. Nashville: Broadman and Holman, 2001.

NICNT — Moo, Douglas J. *The Epistle to the Romans*. The New International Commentary on the New Testament, edited by Gordon D. Fee. Grand Rapids: Eerdmans, 1996.

ABBREVIATIONS

NTC	Hendricksen, William. *Exposition of Paul's Epistle to the Romans*, vol 1, chapters 1–8. New Testament Commentary. Grand Rapids: Baker, 1980.
SSA	Deibler, Ellis W. Jr. *A Semantic and Structural Analysis of Romans.* Dallas: Summer Institute of Linguistics, 1998.
St	Stott, John. *Romans. God's Good News for the World.* Downers Grove, Ill.: InterVarsity Press, 1994.
TH	Newman, Barclay M. and Eugene A. Nida. *A Translator's Handbook on Paul's Letter to the Romans.* Helps for Translators. London: United Bible Societies, 1973.
TNTC	Bruce F. F. *The Epistle of Paul to the Romans An Introduction and Commentary.* Revised edition. The Tyndale New Testament Commentaries. Grand Rapids: Eerdmans, 1985.
WBC	Dunn, James D. G. *Romans 1–8.* Word Biblical Commentary, Vol. 38a. Waco, Texas: Word, 1988.

Some of the commentaries that have been reviewed for this summary are very thorough and have dealt with the subject exhaustively. Moo's commentary (NICNT) is particularly useful, in that it not only gives a very comprehensive review of other scholarship, but is also structured and arranged in a very reader-friendly way. Moo and Schreiner (BECNT), who both write from the perspective of Reformed theology, are the most up to date and comprehensive of the ones I have used. They were also the ones I relied on the most to identify and address the various exegetical issues involved, especially Moo.

Much could be said about the two-volume *Word Biblical Commentary* (WBC) by James D. G. Dunn, who has, along with E. P. Sanders, charted a new trajectory in Pauline scholarship that raises a serious challenge to the way Protestants since the time of the Reformation have interpreted Paul's understanding of justification, and even to the basic premises of the Reformation itself. Whether or not one agrees with Sanders and Dunn, they cannot be ignored, particularly in studies of Galatians or Romans.

One of Dunn's main premises is that Paul's emphasis on faith was not so much a matter of combating works-righteousness, but that Paul is trying to free God's law and promises from the narrow constraints of Jewish ethnicity. Dunn holds that Paul's discussions of circumcision are principally about the law in its social function as a boundary marker distinguishing Jew from Gentile, not about salvation by merit. That is, Paul's concern has as much to do with how the Jews and Gentiles stand in relation to each other as with how one is made right with God. Dunn's writing and premises can be complex and at times ambiguous, and, in certain important instances, well outside the stream of conservative Protestant exegesis.

I also found the *International Critical Commentary* by Cranford (ICC2) to be very good. Others also have their merits, particularly the classic work by Murray (Mu). But the four by Moo, Schreiner, Dunn, and Cranford are the ones most likely to identify and discuss exegetical issues relevant to the translation task.

GREEK TEXT AND TRANSLATIONS

GNT	The Greek New Testament. Edited by B. Aland, K Aland, J. Karavidopoulos, C. Martini, and B. Metzger. 4th ed. London, New York: United Bible Societies, 1993.
CEV	The Holy Bible, Contemporary English Version. New York: American Bible Society, 1995.
GW	God's Word. World Publishing: Grand Rapids, 1995.
KJV	The Holy Bible. Authorized (or King James) Version. 1611.
NASB	The New American Standard Bible. Nashville, Tennessee: Holman, 1977.
NCV	The Holy Bible, New Century Version. Word Publishing: Dallas, 1991.
NET	The Net Bible, New English Translation. Biblical Studies Press: Dallas, 1999.
NIV	The Holy Bible, New International Version. Grand Rapids: Zondervan, 1984.
NLT	The Holy Bible, New Living Translation. Wheaton, Ill.: Tyndale House Publishers, 1996.
NRSV	The Holy Bible, New Revised Standard Version. Nashville: Thomas Nelson Publishers, 1989.
REB	The Revised English Bible. Oxford: Oxford University Press and Cambridge University Press, 1989.
TEV	Good News Bible, Today's English Version. New York: American Bible Society, 1976.

GRAMMATICAL TERMS

act.	active	mid.	middle
fut.	future	opt.	optative
impera	imperative	pass.	passive
imperf.	imperfect	perf.	perfect
indic.	indicative	pres.	present
infin.	infinitive	subj.	subjunctive

MISCELLANEOUS

LXX	Septuagint
TR	Textus Receptus
OT	Old Testament
NT	New Testament

EXEGETICAL SUMMARY OF ROMANS 1–8

DISCOURSE UNIT: 1:1–17 [BECNT, NAC, NICNT, St, WBC; CEV]. The topic is the letter opening [NICNT], the introduction [NAC], introduction, greetings, and statement of the letter's theme [WBC], Paul and the message of good news [CEV], God's uprightness revealed through the gospel [BECNT], the gospel and Paul's desire to share it [St].

DISCOURSE UNIT: 1:1–15 [AB, Gdt, ICC1, Mor, TNTC; REB, TEV]. The topic is introduction [AB, ICC1, Mor], introduction and theme [TEV], preface [Gdt], prologue [TNTC], the gospel of Christ [REB].

DISCOURSE UNIT: 1:1–7 [AB, BECNT, GNT, Ho, ICC1, ICC2, Mor, Mu, NTC, SSA, St, TNTC, WBC; CEV, GW, NET, NIV, NLT, TEV]. The topic is salutation [GNT, Ho, ICC1, Mor, Mu, NAC, NTC, TNTC, WBC; NET], salutation; the gospel concerning his son [BECNT], the Apostolic salutation [ICC1], prescript [NICNT], superscription, address, and salutation [ICC2], address and greetings [AB], introduction and greetings [WBC], greeting [GW], address and salutation [ICC2], the address [Gdt, HNTC], opening and blessing [SSA], greetings from Paul [NLT], Paul and the gospel [St], this division with no heading given [CEV, NIV, TEV].

1:1 **Paul, a-slave[a] of-Christ Jesus,**

TEXT—Instead of Χριστοῦ Ἰησοῦ 'Christ Jesus', some manuscripts have Ἰησοῦ Χριστοῦ 'Jesus Christ'. GNT selects the reading Χριστοῦ Ἰησοῦ 'Christ Jesus' with a B rating, indicating that the text is almost certain. The reading Ἰησοῦ Χριστοῦ 'Jesus Christ' is read by KJV, NLT, and NRSV.

LEXICON—a. δοῦλος (LN **87.76**) (BAGD 4. p. 206): 'slave' [AB, BAGD, BECNT, HNTC, ICC2, LN, NICNT, WBC; NET, NLT], 'servant' [NTC; CEV, GW, KJV, NCV, NIV, NRSV, REB], 'bond servant' [NASB].

QUESTION—What is the significance of the word order Χριστοῦ Ἰησοῦ 'Christ Jesus'?

1. The order 'Christ Jesus' is a reference to Jesus' role as Messiah [BECNT, Gdt, ICC2, NICNT, NTC, WBC]. When using both terms, Paul prefers 'Christ Jesus' (80 times) much more than 'Jesus Christ' (25 times), and uses it more than other NT writers. For Paul, the order highlights the fact that Jesus is the Messiah [NICNT].
2. Paul uses the combination as a proper name, not a title [AB, Mor].

QUESTION—What is meant by δοῦλος 'slave'?

The use of the term is probably patterned on the Old Testament phrase 'servant of Yahweh' [AB, BECNT, HNTC, Ho, ICC2, Mu, NAC, NICNT, NTC, TH, WBC]. Paul may be affirming that he stands in the true succession of the prophets, since this term was applied to Abraham, Moses, and the OT prophets from the time of Amos on [Mor]. The term carries some sense of special office, service, and authority [HNTC, Ho, ICC2]. It indicates a special ministry, though one that exhibits the submission that all believers owe the Lord [Gdt]. It expresses Paul's absolute submission to the authority of Christ [Ho]. The term emphasizes total submission, commitment, obedience, and humility [AB, Ho, ICC2, NICNT], complete and utter devotion [Mor], as well as God's absolute ownership [ICC2].

(a) called[a] apostle[b]

LEXICON—a. κλητός (LN **33.314**, 33.312) (BAGD p. 436): 'called' [**LN**, NTC], 'called (to be)' [AB, BAGD, BECNT, LN, NICNT, WBC; GW, KJV, NASB, NET, NIV, NRSV], 'called (as)' [NASB], 'called by God (to be)' [BECNT; REB], 'God called me (to be)' [NCV] 'God chose me (to be)' [CEV], 'chosen by God (to be)' [NLT]. The phrase κλητὸς ἀπόστολος 'a called apostle' is translated 'by divine call an apostle' [HNTC], 'apostle by God's calling' [ICC2], 'an apostle chosen (to preach)' [TEV].
    b. ἀπόστολος (LN **53.74**) (BAGD 3. p. 99): 'apostle' [AB, BAGD, BECNT, HNTC, ICC2, **LN**, NICNT, NTC, WBC; all versions].

QUESTION—Who κλητὸς 'called' Paul?

God called Paul [AB, Gdt, HNTC, Ho, ICC1, ICC2, Mor, NAC, NICNT, NTC, TH]. It means that Paul's appointment to be an apostle took place at God's initiative, and thus his teachings bear the authority of God [AB, HNTC, ICC1, NAC, NICNT]. He was called, chosen, and appointed by God, not by men, to this sacred office [Ho, NTC]. This word is used by Paul of those whose lives and purposes have been determined by the power of God's summons [WBC]. It expresses God's initiative and choosing as opposed to self-appointment or choice by other men [Gdt, Ho, ICC1, ICC2, Mor, NAC]. In Galatians 1:1, Paul says that he was sent be both by Jesus Christ and God the Father. Some commentaries relate the calling to Jesus' appearance to Paul on the road to Damascus [Ho, St, WBC]. Paul was set apart and commissioned by virtue of his conversion on the Damascus road and the agent is presumably Christ whom he saw then [WBC].

QUESTION—What is meant by ἀπόστολος 'apostle'?

The word is used to designate someone sent to deliver a message or to act as an authorized representative [AB, BAGD, NTC]. It designates those commissioned by Christ [AB, ICC2], sent to bear witness or preach in his name [AB]. It is someone chosen and commissioned by Christ himself to proclaim in his name the message of salvation [Ho]. Apostles are those appointed by Christ to be his messengers or witnesses [Ho, NICNT, NTC, St, TH, WBC]. It is sometimes used elsewhere to designate a larger group of ministers of the gospel [ICC1, ICC2, NICNT, NTC, TH, WBC].

having-been-set-apart[a] for[b] (the) gospel[c] of-God,

LEXICON—a. perf. pass. participle of ἀφορίζω (LN 37.97) (BAGD 2. p. 127): 'to be set apart' [AB, BAGD, BECNT, HNTC, ICC2, LN, NICNT, NTC, WBC; NASB, NET, NIV, NRSV, REB], 'to be appointed' [BAGD, LN; CEV, GW], 'to be separated' [KJV], 'to be sent out' [NLT], 'to be called'

[TEV]. This passive participle is translated as an active verb phrase: 'God chose me' [NCV].
b. εἰς (LN 89.57) (BAGD 4.d. p. 229): 'for' [BAGD, BECNT, HNTC, ICC2, NICNT, NTC, WBC; NASB, NET, NIV, NRSV, REB], 'unto' [KJV], 'for the purpose of' [LN], 'for the service of' [REB], 'to preach' [CEV, NLT, TEV], 'to tell' [NCV], 'to spread' [GW].
c. εὐαγγέλιον (LN 33.217) (BAGD 2.b.β. p. 318): 'gospel' [AB, BAGD, BECNT, LN, NICNT, NTC, WBC; KJV, NASB, NET, NIV, NRSV, REB], 'good news' [BAGD, LN; CEV, GW, NCV, NLT], 'Good News' [HNTC; NLT, TEV], 'message of good news' [ICC2]. The phrase εἰς εὐαγγέλιον 'for the gospel' is translated 'for the work of proclaiming the gospel' [ICC2].

QUESTION—What is the relationship between the phrase ἀφωρισμένος εἰς 'set apart for' and the term κλητὸς 'called'?

This phrase 'set apart for' functions as a further definition and explanation of what it means to be called [BECNT, Ho, Mu, NICNT, WBC]. These two phrases are parallel and belong inseparably together since as an apostle it was Paul's task to proclaim the gospel [ICC2, Mu, St]. There is perhaps an allusion to the calling of the OT prophets [BECNT, HNTC], or to the separating of Israel from among the nations [AB, ICC2, Mor, NICNT, St]. By the use of ἀφωρισμένος 'having been set apart' Paul may be alluding to his being chosen for this task 'from the womb' (Gal 1:5) [Gdt, HNTC, Ho, ICC1, ICC2, Mor, NAC, NTC, TNTC, WBC].

QUESTION—What is meant by being set apart εἰς 'for' the gospel?

It indicates the purpose for which Paul was set apart, namely the special purpose and activity of proclaiming the gospel [AB, BECNT, Gdt, HNTC, Ho, ICC1, ICC2, Mor, NAC, NICNT, NTC, SSA, St, TH, TNTC, WBC; NCV], the good news about salvation made possible through the death and resurrection of Jesus Christ [TH]. The word 'gospel' here may mean more than just a message proclaimed, that the gospel itself is part of the event or operation through which God brings salvation [HNTC]. Paul is saying that he is dedicated to a life of believing in, obeying, and proclaiming God's act of sending his son for the salvation of the world [NICNT], that he is called to a way of life, not just proclaiming a message [Mor], that the gospel was the dominant focus of his life [WBC].

QUESTION—What is the meaning of the genitive phrase εὐαγγέλιον θεοῦ 'gospel of God'?

It indicates that God is the source of the gospel [AB, Gdt, HNTC, Ho, ICC1, ICC2, Mor, Mu, NAC, NICNT, SSA, St, TH, WBC]. It is the gospel revealed by God [St], set forth by God [HNTC], sent by God [NICNT]. It is God's good news, and it is revealed and entrusted to the apostles by God himself [St]. The source of the gospel is God's eternal purpose and his concern for his people, and his will to save them [Mor]. It speaks of the divine origin and character of the gospel, God's message of salvation to lost men [Mu]. Or, the gospel is both from God and about him [BECNT]. It is the gospel about what God has done [Mor, NTC]. It is about God and how he has revealed himself in his son [BECNT].

1:2 which he-promised-beforehand[a] through[b] his prophets in[c] holy[d] Scriptures[e]

LEXICON—a. aorist mid. (deponent = act.) indic. of προεπαγγέλλομαι (LN 33.287) (BAGD p. 705): 'to promise beforehand' [BAGD, BECNT, ICC2, LN, NTC; NASB, NET, NIV, NRSV], 'to promise already' [GW], 'to promise long ago' [AB; CEV, NCV], 'to promise in the past' [HNTC], 'to promise afore' [KJV], 'to announce beforehand' [REB]. This active voice is also translated as a passive: 'promised long ago by God' [NLT, TEV], 'which was promised beforehand' [NICNT, WBC].

b. διά with genitive object (LN 90.4) (BAGD A.III.2.a. p. 180): 'through' [AB, BECNT, HNTC, ICC2, LN, NICNT, NTC, WBC; all versions except CEV, KJV], 'by' [BAGD, LN; KJV], 'by (what his prophets said)' [CEV], 'by means of' [LN].

c. ἐν with dative object (LN 83.13): 'in' [AB, BECNT, HNTC, ICC2, LN, NICNT, NTC, WBC; all versions except TEV], 'as written in' [TEV]

d. ἁγίαις (LN 88.24) (BAGD 1.A.α. p. 9): 'holy' [BECNT, HNTC, ICC2, NICNT, WBC; all versions except REB], 'sacred' [AB, BAGD, NTC; REB]. This term emphasizes the divine origin and authority and trustworthiness of these writings [Gdt, ICC1, Mor, Mu, TH].

e. γραφαῖς 'Scriptures' (LN 33.54) (BAGD 2.b.α. p. 166): 'the Scriptures' [AB, BECNT, ICC2, NICNT, NTC, WBC; all versions], 'the sacred writings of the OT' [LN], 'writ' [HNTC].

QUESTION—What is the point of reference in time indicated by 'promised beforehand'?

Paul means that the gospel was promised in the OT [Ho, ICC2, Mor, Mu, NAC, NICNT, TH], and the gospel is a fulfillment of OT promises [BECNT, ICC2].

QUESTION—Who were the prophets referred to here?

The prophets are all those whom we would normally designate by that term [AB, BECNT, Ho, ICC2, Mor, Mu, NICNT, NTC, St, TH], and also men like David and Moses [ICC2, Mor, Mu, NICNT, NTC, TH]. It refers to all OT writers and not just those strictly designated prophets [Ho, Mor]. The use of this phrase may indicate Paul's wish to emphasize God's personal involvement and authority behind the message of these prophets [WBC], and the close relation between a prophet and God [Gdt].

QUESTION—What are the writings being referred to by the phrase γραφαῖς ἁγίαις 'holy scriptures'?

The phrase 'holy scriptures' is meant to designate all of the OT Scriptures [BAGD, ICC2, Mor, NICNT, St, TH, WBC]. Paul wants to stress that the gospel is the fulfillment of those scriptures [AB, Gdt, HNTC, Ho, ICC2, Mor, Mu, NAC, NICNT, NTC, St, WBC]. These scriptures should not be limited to some specific portion of the OT, but understood to mean that all of the OT is prophetic [NICNT]. Paul may have been particularly thinking of passages dealing with the glorious future of Israel since he uses the term εὐαγγέλιον 'gospel' to refer to the promises of salvation to Israel in the OT being fulfilled in the gospel [BECNT].

1:3 concerning[a] his Son

LEXICON—a. περί with genitive object (LN 90.24): 'concerning' [AB, ICC2, LN, NICNT, NTC; KJV, NASB, NET, NRSV], 'it concerns' [WBC], 'regarding' [NIV], 'about' [BECNT, HNTC, LN; CEV, GW, NCV, NLT, REB, TEV]. This verse begins a new sentence in BECNT, WBC; CEV, GW, NCV, NLT, REB, TEV.

QUESTION—To what does the phrase περὶ τοῦ υἱοῦ αὐτοῦ 'concerning his son' relate?
1. It refers to the gospel [AB, HNTC, ICC2, Mor, NAC, NTC, SSA, St, TH, TNTC, WBC; CEV, GW, KJV, NCV, NLT, NRSV, REB, TEV]: it is the gospel concerning his son.
2. It refers to God's promise [Gdt, Ho]: he promised beforehand concerning his son.

QUESTION—Is there particular significance to the use of the term τοῦ υἱοῦ αὐτοῦ 'his son' here?
The use of the term is a reference to Jesus' preexistence [AB, BECNT, Gdt, ICC2, NICNT, NTC]. The use of this phrase is meant to focus primarily on Jesus' relationship to the Father [AB, ICC2, NICNT, SSA]. The term is messianic [Mor, NICNT]. It indicates a real community of nature between Christ and God [ICC2, Mor], that the son has the same nature and essence as God [SSA].

the (one) having-come[a] from[b] (the) seed[c] of-David according-to[d] (the) flesh,[e]

LEXICON—a. aorist mid. (deponent = act.) participle of γίνομαι (LN 13.80) (BAGD I.1.a. p. 158): 'to come' [BAGD, LN, NICNT], 'to be' [BAGD, LN; CEV, GW, NET, NIV, NRSV, REB], 'to be born' [AB, BAGD, BECNT, HNTC, ICC2, NTC; NASB, NCV, NLT, TEV], 'to be made' [KJV]. The use of this word, as opposed to the more commonly used verb 'to be born', suggests that something more than a simple birth took place, perhaps signaling a change in existence [NICNT].

b. ἐκ with genitive object (LN 90.16) (BAGD 3.b. p. 235): 'from' [BAGD LN, NICNT, WBC; CEV, NCV, NRSV], 'of' [AB, BECNT, HNTC, ICC2, NTC; KJV, NASB, NET, NIV, REB, TEV], 'into (the line of)' [NLT], not explicit [GW]. This preposition is used to denote origin as to family [BAGD].

c. σπέρμα (LN 10.29) (BAGD 1.b. p. 761; 2.b. p. 762): 'seed' [BAGD, BECNT, ICC2, LN, NICNT, NTC, WBC; KJV, NASB], 'descendants' [BAGD (2.b.), LN; NIV, NRSV, REB, TEV], 'descendant' [GW], 'posterity' [BAGD, LN], 'family' [CEV, NCV], 'offspring' [LN] 'children' [BAGD], 'stock' [AB]. The phrase ἐκ σπέρματος 'from the seed' is translated 'a descendant of' [NET, NIV, REB, TEV], 'descended from' [BAGD, WBC; NRSV], 'born into King David's royal family line' [NLT]. To come from the seed is a dead metaphor signifying that Jesus was a descendant of David [SSA].

d. κατά (LN **89.4**) (BAGD II.6. p. 407): 'according to' [BECNT, ICC2, NICNT, NTC; KJV, NASB, NRSV], 'with respect to' [BAGD; NET], 'with regard to' [**LN**], 'in relation to' [BAGD, LN], 'in' [GW], 'as to' [NIV, TEV], 'as' [CEV, NCV], 'in terms of' [WBC], 'by' [AB], 'in the sphere of' [HNTC], 'on the (human) level' [REB], not explicit [NLT].

e. σάρξ (LN 58.10) (BAGD 4. p. 744): 'flesh' [LN], 'human nature' [BAGD, LN], 'physical nature' [LN], 'earthly or physical descent' [BAGD]. This noun, which lacks the definite article here, is translated 'the flesh' [BECNT, HNTC, ICC2, LN, NICNT, NTC, WBC; KJV, NASB, NET, NRSV], 'his human nature' [NIV], 'natural descent' [AB]. The phrase κατά σάρκα 'according to (the) flesh' is translated 'as a human' [CEV], 'as a man' [NCV], 'as to his humanity' [TEV], 'on the human level' [REB], 'in his human nature' [GW], 'who came as a man' [NLT], 'according to the human side of his nature, as far as his physical descent is concerned' [BAGD].

QUESTION—What is the significance of the phrase ἐκ σπέρματος Δαυὶδ 'from the seed of David'?

This is a clear reference to the messianic promise to David of an eternal reign for his seed or descendents, an expectation found in both the OT and early Judaism, and this indicates Jesus' messianic status [BECNT, Gdt, HNTC, Ho, ICC1, ICC2, Mor, Mu, NICNT, NTC, St, WBC; NLT]. Paul asserts that his gospel tells of the fulfillment of those promises [BECNT]. Davidic descent is important in understanding the significance of Jesus' status as Messiah [Mor].

QUESTION—What is meant by κατά σάρκα 'according to the flesh'?

It refers to the natural or human descent of Jesus [AB, BECNT, Gdt, HNTC, ICC1, ICC2, Mor, Mu, NAC, NICNT, NTC, SSA, St, TH, TNTC, WBC]. It speaks of his human nature in its entirety [Gdt, Mu]. There is an undertone of weakness or frailty implied in the term [St]. Jesus' physical descent had a role in God's saving purpose, though not as important a role as his status 'according to spirit' to which this phrase is set in contrast [WBC]. The words 'according to the flesh' imply that there is more to be said, that he was more than just human [Mor], that other aspects of his being must be taken into account to get the complete picture [NICNT]. This connection to David is not limited only to Christ's earthly life, as he still possesses in his resurrection state the same human nature, though it is now glorified [ICC2].

1. The phrase refers to the human nature of Jesus as distinguished from his divine nature [Ho, NAC, SSA]. Verse 1:3 proclaims his humanity and 1:4 proclaims his deity [NAC].

2. The phrase refers to his human body as distinguished from his human spirit, although the holiness which characterizes his spirit is something more than merely human [ICC1].

1:4 the-(one) having-been-appointed/declared[a] Son of-God in[b] power[c]

LEXICON—a. aorist pass. participle of ὁρίζω (LN 37.96) (BAGD 1.b. p. 581): 'to be appointed' [BECNT, HNTC, ICC2, NTC, WBC; NCV, NET], 'to be designated' [LN, NICNT], 'to be established as' [AB], 'to be declared' [BAGD; GW, KJV, NASB, NIV], 'to be declared to be' [NRSV], 'to be proclaimed' [REB], 'to be proved' [CEV], 'to be shown to be' [NLT, TEV].

b. ἐν with dative object (LN 13.8, 89.80) (BAGD III.2. p. 261): 'in' [HNTC, ICC2, LN (13.8), NICNT, WBC; GW, NET], 'with' [AB, BAGD, LN (13.8, 89.80); KJV, NASB, NCV, NIV, NRSV, TEV], 'invested with' [NTC], 'by' [REB], not explicit [CEV].

c. δύναμις (LN 76.1) (BAGD 1. p. 207): 'power' [AB, BAGD, HNTC, ICC2, LN, NICNT, NTC, WBC; KJV, NASB, NET, NIV, NRSV, TEV], 'great power' [NCV, TEV], 'an act of power' [REB]. The phrase ἐν δυνάμει 'in/with power' is translated 'in a powerful way' [GW], 'by an act of power' [REB], 'when God powerfully raised him' [NLT], '(proved that Jesus) is the powerful Son of God' [CEV], 'invested with power' [NTC]. God is the implied agent of this passive participle [AB, NICNT].

QUESTION—What is meant by ὁρισθέντος υἱοῦ θεοῦ ἐν δυνάμει 'having been appointed/declared Son of God in power'?

1. It means that Jesus was appointed to a new position as Son of God [AB, BECNT, Gdt, HNTC, ICC2, Mu, NAC, NICNT, NTC, St, TNTC, WBC; NCV, NET]. In the NT this verb consistently means 'to appoint' [AB, BECNT, HNTC, ICC2, Mu, NICNT] and there is no example in first century Greek literature or earlier of it being used in the sense 'declare' [ICC2]. However, Paul is not saying that Jesus became the Son of God only after the resurrection, or because of it [AB, BECNT, HNTC, ICC1, ICC2, Mu, NTC, St, TNTC]. Christ, already the eternal Son of God, was appointed 'Son of God in power' at his resurrection [ICC2, NICNT, St, WBC]. The prepositional phrase 'in power' modifies the title 'Son of God', meaning 'Son-of-God-in-power', and reflects a new level of power and authority as compared with the pre-resurrection period [AB, BECNT, HNTC, ICC2, Mor, Mu, NAC, NICNT, NTC, St, TNTC, WBC; CEV, NET]. Before his resurrection he was Son of God in weakness and in lowliness, but after it he was Son of God in power [ICC2, St], being then invested with power [ICC2]. He more fully shared in God's power [WBC]. It means that he was established in power and is the source of power for granting life to human beings [AB]. He existed and reigned with God eternally as the Son, but it was because of his incarnation and atoning work that he was appointed Son of God in power as one who is now both God and man [BECNT].

2. It means that Jesus was declared or shown to others to be God's Son [Gdt, Ho, ICC1, Mor, SSA; CEV, GW, KJV, NASB, NIV, NLT, NRSV, REB, TEV]. The alternative meaning that Jesus was 'appointed' to be Son of God by means of his resurrection is contrary to Paul's theology in the rest of his writings [SSA]. It means 'to be declared' in reference to the understanding of men [Ho]. Christ did not become the Son of God by his resurrection, but was manifested to be God's Son at that time [ICC1].
  2.1 Jesus was shown to be God's Son in powerful way [Gdt, Ho, ICC1, SSA; GW, NIV, NLT, REB, TEV]. The prepositional phrase 'in power' modifies adverbially the participle 'having been designated', meaning that he was powerfully or decisively designated, or was designated by a mighty, powerful act [Gdt, Ho, ICC1, SSA; NIV, NLT, REB, TEV]. God's power was shown in a striking or powerful manner when he raised Christ from the dead [Gdt].
  2.2 Jesus was shown to be God's powerful Son [CEV].

according-to[a] (the) Spirit/spirit[b] of-holiness[c]
LEXICON—a. κατά with accusative object (LN 89.8) (BAGD II.6. p. 407): 'according to' [BECNT, Gdt, ICC2, NICNT; KJV, NASB, NET, NRSV], 'in accordance with' [LN], 'through' [NCV, NIV], 'by' [AB], 'by means of' [NLT], 'by virtue of' [NTC], 'on the level of' [REB]. The phrase κατὰ πνεῦμα ἁγιωσύνης is translated 'as to his divine holiness' [TEV], 'in his spiritual, holy nature' [GW], 'in the sphere of the Holy Spirit' [HNTC], 'the Holy Spirit proved that' [CEV].
  b. πνεῦμα (LN 12.18, **26.9**) (BAGD 2. p. 675): 'the Spirit' [BECNT, ICC2, LN (12.18), NICNT, NTC; KJV, NASB, NCV, NIV, NLT], 'spirit' [AB, WBC; NRSV], 'spiritual being' [**LN** (26.9)]. The phrase πνεῦμα ἁγιωσύνης 'spirit of holiness' is translated 'his holy spiritual being' [**LN** (26.9)], 'his divine being' [see LN 88.25 (next entry)], 'his spiritual, holy nature' [GW], 'his divine holiness' [LN (**26.9**); TEV], 'the spirit—the Holy Spirit' [REB], 'the Holy Spirit' [HNTC; CEV, NET].
  c. ἁγιωσύνη (LN **88.25**) (BAGD p. 10): 'holiness' [AB, BAGD, BECNT, ICC2, LN, NICNT, NTC, WBC; CEV, KJV, NCV, NET, NIV, NRSV, TEV], 'divine quality' [LN]. This noun in the genitive case is also translated as an adjective: 'holy' [GW, NET, NLT, REB].
QUESTION—What is meant by πνεῦμα ἁγιωσύνης 'the spirit of holiness'?
  1. It refers to the Holy Spirit [BECNT, Gdt, HNTC, ICC2, Mor, NICNT, NTC, St, TNTC, WBC; CEV, NASB, NCV, NIV, NLT, REB]. It probably reflects the Hebrew for 'Holy Spirit' [BECNT, NICNT, St, TNTC, WBC]. The noun ἁγιωσύνης is a qualitative genitive, making the phrase more or less the same as 'the Holy Spirit' [BECNT, HNTC, TNTC; NET, NLT, REB].
  1.1 It is a reference to the power of the Holy Spirit as shown in Christ's resurrection and subsequent designation as the powerful Son of God [Mor]. It was through the Holy Spirit that God raised Christ from the

dead, and Christ now lives in the power of the Spirit and has poured out that Spirit on the church [NTC]. Not only is the Holy Spirit linked to the resurrection of Christ from the dead, but the risen and exalted Christ demonstrated his power and authority by pouring out the Holy Spirit, beginning the new era of the Spirit [St]. The fact that he has poured out the Holy Spirit manifests the exalted Christ's power and majesty and demonstrates that he really is the son of God in power [ICC2, TNTC]. This refers to the action or influence of the Holy Spirit in the life of Christ producing holiness, and the new resurrected life of Jesus is consistent with or agreeable to that same spirit of holiness and consecration [Gdt].
  1.2 In Paul's concept of salvation history, in which spirit and flesh refers to two contrasting aeons, it speaks of the eschatological gift of the Holy Spirit which characterizes the new era [BECNT, NICNT]. The two contrasting ages are also two contrasting spheres, so this term also refers to the sphere of the Holy Spirit as distinct from the sphere of the flesh [HNTC].
  1.3 The new, resurrection phase of Christ's role and existence was characterized by the Holy Spirit just as the previous, earthly phase was characterized by the flesh, that is, by weakness and mortality [WBC]. It refers to the new phase of sovereignty in Jesus' existence in which he is endowed with power for exercising his mediatorial lordship, and in which he is so endowed with and in control of the Holy Spirit that Paul can say that he was made a life-giving Spirit in 1 Cor. 15:45, and can be identified with the Holy Spirit in 2 Cor. 3:18 [Mu].
2. It refers to Jesus' own spirit [ICC1, NAC]. This phrase refers to the human spirit of Jesus, although distinguished from ordinary humans by exceptional holiness [ICC1]. It refers to Jesus' own inner spirit, that he lived in complete and perfect holiness [NAC].
3. This phrase refers to the divine nature of Jesus [Ho, LN (26.9), SSA, TH; GW, TEV].
4. In the OT, the term 'Spirit' spoke of God's being present to his people to create, to speak prophetically, or to renew, and it could also refer to an apocalyptic manifestation of the end time. In a similar way, it refers here to the fact that the risen Christ is now present and active in the Christian community, having become the transcendent and dynamic source of holiness, and having power to quicken and renew life for human beings [AB].

QUESTION—What contrast is being drawn by the parallelism or antithesis of the two phrases 'according to the flesh' and 'according to the spirit of holiness'?
  1. The contrast is between the two natures of Jesus, the human and divine [Ho, NAC, SSA]. It contrasts his human nature and descent from David with his spiritual or divine nature [SSA].

2. It draws a distinction between Jesus' human body and his human spirit, that is, between the physical and spiritual aspects of his human nature [ICC1, NAC]. In addition to contrasting his two natures, his humanity and his deity, there is also contrast drawn between his natural, physical descent and the holiness of his inner spirit [NAC].
3. This contrasts the two stages of Jesus' ministry [AB, Gdt, HNTC, St]. It is a contrast between the natural Davidic form of his earthly life and the exalted state which he entered at the end of his earthly ministry [Gdt, HNTC]. 'Flesh' and 'Spirit' also represent the two spheres of the two stages of Christ's existence, the natural or human, with its weakness and humility, and in which he is characterized as the son of David, and the supernatural sphere of the Spirit, in which he is characterized as the son of God [HNTC]. It is a contrast between Christ's pre-resurrection, earthly life, when he was Son of God in weakness, and his post-resurrection existence when he became the Son of God in power [AB, St], which is a contrast between frailty and exaltation [St]. The natural Jewish and Davidic form of his earthly appearance is contrasted with the more exalted state he entered at the resurrection, and which is in accord with the holy consecration worked in Christ's human nature by the Holy Spirit during his earthly life [Gdt].
4. The contrast is between two ages of redemptive history represented by the flesh and the Holy Spirit respectively; Jesus participated in the old age of weakness through his incarnation as son of David in order to inaugurate the new age characterized by the Holy Spirit and power [BECNT, Mu, NICNT, TNTC]. The contrast is between the old phase of Jesus' life characterized by 'flesh', with its mortality and weakness, and the new resurrection phase characterized by 'Spirit' [WBC]. The contrast has to do with the disjunction between the two ages in Paul's redemptive-historical understanding; the old age, which was dominated by the flesh, is the eon of weakness, but the age of the Spirit is an age of power [BECNT].

by[a] (the) resurrection[b] (from among)[c] dead-ones,[d]

LEXICON—a. ἐκ with genitive object (LN 89.25): 'by' [KJV, NASB, NCV, NET, NIV, NRSV, TEV], 'by means of' [LN, NTC], 'because of' [LN; CEV], 'on the basis of' [NICNT], 'as of' [AB], 'as from' [WBC], 'from' [ICC2, LN], 'at' [BECNT], 'when' [GW, NLT], 'after (his resurrection)' [HNTC].

b. ἀνάστασις (LN 23.93) (BAGD 2.a. p. 60): 'resurrection' [AB, BAGD, BECNT, HNTC, ICC2, LN, NICNT, NTC, WBC; KJV, NASB, NET, NIV, NRSV]. This abstract noun is also translated by a verb phrase: 'by rising' [NCV], 'by being raised from death' [TEV], 'he was raised from death' [CEV], 'he came back to life' [GW]. The phrase ἐξ ἀναστάσεως 'by resurrection' is translated with an agent supplied: 'God...raised him from the dead' [NLT], 'by an act of power that raised him' [REB].

c. There is no lexical entry in the Greek text for this phrase, the relationship between 'resurrection' and 'dead ones' being indicated by the genitive case of νεκρῶν 'dead ones'. This relation is translated 'from' [AB, BECNT, HNTC, NTC; NASB, NCV, NET, NIV, NRSV, REB, TEV], 'of' [ICC2, NICNT, WBC], not explicit [GW, NLT].
   d. νεκρός (LN 23.121) (BAGD 2.a. p. 535): 'the dead' [AB, BAGD, BECNT, HNTC, ICC2, LN, NICNT, NTC, WBC; KJV, NASB, NCV, NET, NIV, NLT, NRSV, REB], 'death' [CEV, TEV], not explicit [GW].

QUESTION—What relationship is indicated by ἐξ 'from/by' ?
   1. It has a temporal sense [AB, BECNT, HNTC, ICC2, WBC; NLT]: he was appointed or declared Son of God when he was resurrected. The resurrection was the event which marked the beginning of Jesus' exalted life [ICC2]. That event begins the new era and inaugurates the general resurrection [BECNT]. However, the temporal sense intended here does not completely exclude causality [AB].
   2. It indicates causality or means [Gdt, Ho, ICC1, Mor, Mu, NAC, NICNT, NTC, SSA, St, TH, TNTC; CEV, KJV, NET, NIV, NLT, NRSV, REB, TEV]: he was appointed or declared Son of God by being resurrected. The resurrection was the powerful means by which Jesus was shown to be God's own son [Gdt, Ho, Mor, NAC, SSA]. By means of his resurrection, Jesus' power and glory were enhanced and began to be more fully apparent [NTC]. It is by the resurrection that he was proved or evidenced to be the Son of God [Ho]. The resurrection authenticates Jesus' deity [NAC].

QUESTION—What is meant by genitive construction ἀναστάσεως νεκρῶν 'resurrection from among the dead'?
   1. It refers to Jesus' resurrection from death or from among the dead [AB, BECNT, Gdt, HNTC, ICC1, ICC2, Mor, NAC, NICNT, NTC, SSA, St, TH, TNTC; all versions]: the resurrection from the dead. Christ's resurrection signals that the new age has begun, and indicates that God has begun to fulfill his covenant promises to Israel through Jesus [BECNT].
   2. It refers in general to the resurrection of the dead, which the resurrection of Jesus inaugurates. This is part of the general resurrection prior to final judgment [WBC].

Jesus Christ our Lord,

TEXT—Some versions have transposed this phrase from here at the end of 1:4 and inserted it following 'Son' in 1:3 [CEV, KJV, NLT, TEV]: 'concerning his Son, Jesus Christ our Lord'. In the Greek text, the position of this title at the end of 1:4 gives it emphasis [NAC].

QUESTION—What is the significance of the position of this phrase Ἰησοῦ Χριστοῦ τοῦ κυρίου ἡμῶν 'Jesus Christ our Lord'?
   The phrase stands in apposition to τοῦ υἱοῦ αὐτοῦ 'his son' of 1:3 [Ho, ICC2, SSA]. Identifying Jesus in this way builds on the Christological

formula of 1:3b–4 [BECNT, NICNT, WBC]. Paul frames his description of the gospel with the phrases 'of his Son' and 'Jesus Christ our Lord' [NICNT, WBC]. In 1:3 he uses the phrase 'his Son' to describe the inner content of the gospel, and now with the phrase 'Jesus Christ our Lord' he identifies that content finally and climactically, expressing the true significance of Jesus for the believer [NICNT]. Here he gives the full title of the one who is the content of the gospel [ICC2]. This title concludes his explication of the gospel in 1:3–4; Jesus' lordship as Messiah flows naturally from what he has just said [BECNT]. It stands in apposition to the phrase 'concerning his son' and highlights the importance of Christology in the faith of the early church [WBC]. It identifies the person who is himself the gospel; 'Jesus' speaks of his historical identity and of his being savior, 'Christ' points to his office as the anointed one, and 'Lord' indicates his exaltation by which he exercises all authority in heaven and earth [Ho, Mu]. 'Jesus' speaks of the historical person, 'Christ' sums up what is said in 1:3 about him being the son of David, and 'Lord' tells us that he represents the divine sovereignty [Gdt]. Because the term 'Lord' was used of Yahweh in the OT, Paul's use of it as a title for Christ indicates his belief in Christ's deity [AB, Ho, ICC2, Mor].

QUESTION—Who is the referent of the first person plural pronoun 'our' in this phrase?

The first person plural 'our' is inclusive of Paul and his readers [Gdt, SSA]. Jesus is ours in the sense that we belong to him and we are completely under his authority [Ho].

1:5 through^a whom we-received grace^b and apostleship^c

LEXICON—a. διά with genitive object (LN 90.4) (BAGD A.III.2.b.γ. p. 180): 'through' [AB, BAGD, BECNT, HNTC, ICC2, LN, NICNT, NTC, WBC; all versions except CEV, KJV], 'by' [LN; KJV], not explicit [CEV]. NTC and NIV have transposed the phrase ὑπὲρ τοῦ ὀνόματος αὐτοῦ 'for the sake of his name' from the end of verse 5 and placed it here: 'through whom and for whose sake' [NTC], 'through him and for his name's sake' [NIV].

b. χάρις (LN 88.66) (BAGD 4 p.878): 'grace' [AB, BAGD, HNTC, ICC2, LN, NICNT, WBC; KJV, NASB, NET, NIV, NRSV], 'kindness' [LN], 'God's kindness' [GW], 'favor' [LN]. This noun is translated as part of a phrase: 'the privilege (of being an apostle)' [TEV], 'the privilege (of an apostolic commission)' [REB], 'the privilege (to tell what God has done)' [NLT], 'the grace (of apostleship)' [AB], 'the gift of (apostleship)' [NTC], 'the special (work of an apostle)' [NCV]. This noun is also translated as an adjective: 'gracious' [BECNT]. The phrase 'we received grace' is translated 'Jesus was kind to me' [CEV]. This refers to exceptional effects produced by God's grace [BAGD].

c. ἀποστολή (LN **53.73**) (BAGD p. 99) 'apostleship' [AB, BAGD, BECNT, Gdt, ICC2, LN, NICNT, WBC; KJV, NET, NIV, NRSV], 'apostolic commission' [HNTC; REB]. This word is translated as a phrase: 'to be an apostle' [**LN**; CEV, TEV], 'the privilege of being apostles' [GW], 'the (special) work of an apostle' [NCV], 'authority to tell what God has done for them' [NLT]. It is the role of one commissioned and sent as a special messenger [LN].

QUESTION—What relationship is indicated by διά 'through'?
1. It indicates that Jesus Christ is the intermediate agent through whom God gave grace and apostleship [ICC2, Mu, NICNT, SSA, St, TH, TNTC, WBC; NLT, TEV]: through Jesus Christ we received from God grace and apostleship. The relationship with reference to Christ is one of means: by means of Christ revealing himself to Paul, God appointed Paul to be an apostle [SSA]. Christ is the active agent and participant in the process of salvation [WBC].
2. It indicates that Jesus was the source of this action [AB, Gdt, HNTC, Ho, ICC1, NAC, NTC; CEV]: from Jesus Christ we received grace and apostleship. Although this preposition usually indicates instrumentality, here it is used in a more general sense of source [Ho].

QUESTION—Who is the referent of the first person plural 'we' in the verb ἐλάβομεν 'we have received'?
1. Paul is most likely using the literary or editorial plural and is actually referring only to himself [AB, BECNT, Gdt, Ho, ICC2, Mor, Mu, NICNT, NTC, SSA, St, TH; CEV, NCV, REB, TEV]: I received grace and apostleship. This is a plural of category [Gdt, Mu], which may be used as a means of putting the focus on the work to which one is charged rather than on the person himself [Gdt].
2. The reference here is to Paul and also other apostles [ICC1, NAC, WBC]: we apostles received grace and apostleship. Paul links himself with others, sensitive to the fact that he is not to be considered the only apostle to the Gentiles [WBC], that he was not alone in ministering to the Gentiles [NAC].
3. Speaking both as a Christian and as an apostle he says 'we received', because he has received grace along with all other Christians [HNTC].

QUESTION—How are the nouns related in the phrase χάριν καὶ ἀποστολὴν 'grace and apostleship'?
1. This is a hendiadys, one semantic concept expressed by two nouns connected by 'and', in this case meaning the grace of apostleship, the divine gift of being an apostle [AB, BECNT, ICC2, NICNT, NTC, SSA, St, TH, TNTC, WBC; CEV, NCV, NLT, REB, TEV]. Since salvation is not in focus here, grace is not to be taken in the sense of God's favor in granting salvation, but of God graciously appointing Paul to ministry [SSA]. He has received the special gift or privilege of being an apostle [NICNT, St, TH]. It is a gift that enables Paul's ministry [AB]. It is God's grace that makes it possible to minister as an apostle [NAC]. Paul's apostleship was not conferred on him because of any merit of his own [ICC2]. It is the privilege of being an apostle [REB, TEV]. Paul has

received a special gift or grace that enables him to fulfill his ministry of evangelizing people [AB].
2. Paul is saying that he has received two things: God's unmerited favor in common with other Christians, and also the office of apostleship [BECNT, Gdt, HNTC, Ho, ICC1, Mu, St]. Grace is God's undeserved favor which all Christians share [ICC1, Mu], the undeserved favor of God for sinful men [HNTC]. Paul has received apostleship as well as the grace that made it possible to carry out this task [NAC]. In Paul's case his conversion and calling to apostleship coincide in one event, and should not be thought of as separate from one another [Gdt, Mu]. The grace that installed Paul as an apostle should not be understood as separate from the grace given in his conversion, as they occurred in the same event [BECNT].

for[a] (the) obedience[b] of-faith[c] among[d] all the Gentiles[e] for-the-sake-of[f] his name,

LEXICON—a. εἰς (LN 89.57): 'for' [NICNT; KJV], 'for the purpose of' [LN], 'so that' [CEV, NLT], 'in order to' [ICC2, LN, NTC; TEV], 'with a view to' [WBC]. This preposition is also translated as an infinitive verb phrase: 'to bring about' [BECNT; NET, NRSV], 'to bring to' [REB], 'to lead to' [TEV], 'to lead people to' [NCV], 'to bring people to' [GW], 'to bring about' [NASB], 'to promote' [AB], 'to win' [HNTC], 'to call to' [NIV]. The preposition εἰς expresses intent and often has the implication of expected result [LN].

b. ὑπακοή (LN 36.15) (BAGD 1.b. p. 837): 'obedience' [BAGD, HNTC, ICC2, LN, NTC; KJV, NIV, REB], 'the obedience' [BECNT, NICNT, WBC; GW, NASB, NET, NRSV], 'a commitment (of faith)' [AB]. This noun is also translated as a verb: 'to obey' [CEV, NCV, NLT, TEV].

c. πίστις (LN 31.102, 31.85) (BAGD 2.d.α. p. 663; 3. p. 664): 'faith' [AB, BAGD, BECNT, ICC2, LN (31.85), NICNT, NTC, WBC; GW, NASB, NET, NIV, NRSV, REB], 'the faith' [KJV], 'Christian faith' [LN (31.102)]. This noun is also translated as a verb: 'to believe' [NCV, NLT, TEV], 'to have faith' [CEV], 'to be a Christian' [BAGD]; as an adjective: 'believing (obedience)' [HNTC].

d. ἐν with dative object (LN 83.9): 'among' [AB, BECNT, HNTC, ICC2, LN, NICNT, NTC, WBC; KJV, NASB, NET, NIV, NRSV], 'of' [NCV], '(bring people) from (every nation)' [GW], not explicit [CEV, NLT, REB, TEV].

e. ἔθνος (LN 11.37, 11.55): 'nation, people' [LN (11.55)], 'heathen, pagans' [LN (11.37)]. This plural noun is translated 'Gentiles' [AB, BECNT, HNTC, ICC2, NICNT, NTC; NASB, NET, NIV, NLT, NRSV], 'nations' [WBC; CEV, KJV, NCV, REB, TEV], 'all nations' [NCV], 'people from every nation' [GW], 'people of all nations' [CEV, NCV, REB, TEV].

f. ὑπέρ with genitive object (LN 90.36) (BAGD 1.b. p. 838): 'for the sake of' [BECNT, LN, NICNT, WBC; NRSV, TEV], 'for' [LN; GW, KJV,

NASB, NCV], 'in behalf of' [BAGD], 'on behalf of' [AB, LN; NET], not explicit [CEV]. The phrase ὑπὲρ τοῦ ὀνόματος αὐτοῦ 'for the sake of his name' is translated: 'for his name's sake' [ICC2; NASB, NIV], 'for whose sake' [NTC], 'on his behalf' [HNTC], 'bringing glory to his name' [NLT], 'for the honor of his name' [GW], 'in his name' [REB], 'to spread his name' [BAGD], 'for the sake of Christ' [TEV].

QUESTION—What relationship is indicated by εἰς 'for' in the prepositional phrase εἰς ὑπακοὴν πίστεως 'for the obedience of faith'?

This indicates the purpose for which grace and apostleship were given to Paul, and the goal and purpose of his ministry [AB, Gdt, HNTC, Ho, ICC1, Mor, Mu, NAC, NICNT, NTC, SSA, St, TH, TNTC]. The aim of Paul's apostleship is to win believing obedience [HNTC], to bring Gentiles to faith in the Lord Jesus Christ [BECNT].

QUESTION—How are the nouns related in the genitive phrase ὑπακοὴν πίστεως 'obedience of faith'?

1. Obedience is brought about by faith; faith is the source and motivating force of obedience [AB, Ho, Mor, NAC, NTC, SSA, St, TH, TNTC]. Because there is no definite article, 'faith' here means the act of belief itself, and not the doctrine or a body of teaching which is believed and to which the faith is directed [Mor, NAC, TNTC]. It is noteworthy that this is an obedience of faith as distinct from an obedience to law [NICNT, St]. Paul seeks to stir up a commitment that flows from faith, which is not only expressed as obedience, but is also a commitment to the service of God in Christ through the Spirit [AB]. Obedience and faith are inseparable [NAC, NTC]. The gospel demands the response of faith [Mor].
2. Faith is in apposition to obedience; Paul speaks of the obedience which is faith [Gdt, Ho, ICC1, ICC2, Mu, St]. Faith consists in obedience [ICC1, ICC2]. Responding to the gospel in faith is the essence of true obedience to God [ICC2]. Obedience consists in faith [Gdt, Ho, Mu, St]. Accepting the gospel in faith is itself an act of obedience [ICC2, Mu], and true faith includes a sincere desire to obey [ICC1]. Faith is the controlling principle of this obedience [Ho].
3. Paul may have intended both of the meanings listed above [BECNT, St, WBC]. It is both the obedience that springs from faith and the obedience that is faith [BECNT, WBC].
4. The two nouns are mutually interpreting; faith is always inseparable from obedience and obedience can never be divorced from faith [NICNT]. Paul calls men to believing obedience; that is, that they become obedient to Christ and put their faith in him [HNTC].

QUESTION—To whom does τοῖς ἔθνεσιν 'all the Gentiles' refer?

1. It refers to those who are non-Jews, the Gentiles [AB, BECNT, Gdt, HNTC, ICC1, ICC2, Mor, Mu, NICNT, NTC, SSA, St, TNTC, WBC; NET, NIV, NLT, NRSV]. No people, nation, or ethnic group was to be excluded [BECNT]. The gospel is for the whole world [WBC]. It is

universal in its scope, it is for everybody without exception or distinction [St].
2. It refers to the nations [Ho, NAC, TH; CEV, KJV, REB, TEV]. The apostle's commission was a general one to all nations [Ho, TH], to the entire world [NAC].

QUESTION—What is meant by the phrase ὑπὲρ τοῦ ὀνόματος αὐτοῦ 'for the sake of his name'?

'Name' speaks of the person in his true character and significance [NICNT]. It signifies the character and being of a person [BECNT]. Paul ministers for the glory of Christ [BECNT, NICNT]. His primary motivation in ministry was a zeal for Christ's glory, which is more important even than concern for the lost [BECNT, Mu, St]. It means that Paul ministers for the glory and benefit of Jesus Christ [NICNT]. Paul ministers for the benefit of Christ's reputation, that Christ would be known as the one who fulfills God's purpose in bringing Gentiles to the obedience of faith and that God and Christ may be known in their true character and accorded their due honor [WBC]. Paul ministers to serve the cause of Christ [AB]. It is an idiomatic expression involving metonymy, 'name' standing for the person and specifically the person's reputation, here meaning that non-Jews would give honor to Christ as a response to hearing the good news [SSA]. To do something for his name is to do it for his glory [Gdt, ICC1, St] and for his honor [St]. Paul does what he does to serve Christ, to help or benefit him [TH]. Paul was given the apostolic ministry in order to proclaim Christ's name and promote his cause [NTC]. Since 'name' stands for the whole person, Paul's obedience was to all that Christ represents [Mor]. 'For his name' means to act or do something in Christ's behalf, in this case, to win believing obedience among the Gentiles [HNTC].

QUESTION—To what is the phrase ὑπὲρ τοῦ ὀνόματος αὐτοῦ 'for the sake of his name' attached?

Note that there is a certain amount of overlap possible between the positions listed below, and one does not necessarily rule out the other.

1. Grace and apostleship are for the sake of his name [NICNT, NTC, SSA; TEV]. That is, Paul ministers for the glory of Christ and for his benefit [NICNT]. Paul's call as an apostle is for the sake of Christ, to serve him [TH]. The aim of Paul's ministry is the honor of Christ and to further the revelation of God made in Christ [ICC1]. God graciously made Paul an apostle so that non-Jewish people would honor Christ [SSA].
2. Bringing about the obedience of faith among the Gentiles would be for the sake of his name [AB, BECNT, HNTC, ICC2, Mu, NAC, St; NLT]. Paul is called to win believing obedience on Christ's behalf [HNTC]. The goal of preaching the gospel and winning people to faith is the glory of God and Christ [ICC2]. Christ's name will be honored when people from all nations profess faith in Christ and demonstrate their faith through obedience [NAC].

3. The phrase attaches to the whole preceding verse [Gdt, Ho, WBC]. Grace and apostleship for the obedience of faith among the Gentiles are for the sake of his name [WBC]. The knowledge of Christ and his glory was the final end or goal of the apostleship, and of Paul's labor to make the nations obedient to the gospel [Ho]. The purpose of Paul's apostolic ministry is to bring greater glory to Christ's name and increase the number of people who call upon him as Lord [Gdt].

1:6 among[a] whom you also are called-ones[b] of Jesus Christ,

LEXICON—a. ἐν with dative object (LN 83.9): 'among' [BECNT, ICC2, LN, NICNT, WBC; GW, KJV, NASB, NET, NIV, NLT], not explicit [CEV, NCV, NRSV, REB, TEV].

b. κλητός (LN 33.314) (BAGD p. 436): 'called' [BAGD, BECNT, ICC2, LN, NICNT, NTC, WBC; NET], 'the called' [KJV, NASB]. This nominal adjective is also translated as a passive verb: 'to be called' [NIV, NLT, NRSV], 'to be called to belong to' [GW, NCV], 'to be chosen' [CEV]; as an active verb with God as the subject: 'to call' [TEV]. This clause is translated 'you who have heard the call and belong to Jesus Christ' [REB].

QUESTION—What does the phrase ἐν οἷς ἐστε καὶ ὑμεῖς 'among whom you also are' imply about the ethnicity of the Roman Christians?

1. The Roman Christians are mostly Gentiles [AB, BECNT, Gdt, HNTC, ICC1, Mor, NAC, NICNT, NTC, TNTC, WBC]. As such they fall within the sphere of Paul's apostolic ministry and are under his authority [BECNT, Gdt, NICNT]. They were Gentiles by race, and had been Gentiles by religion [NTC]. Paul's use of καὶ 'also' is a subtle way of indicating that although he is apostle to the Gentiles, the Roman church is not a result of his direct efforts, nor are they the only Gentiles to have responded to the gospel [WBC].

2. Paul is simply saying that the Roman Christians live in the midst of Gentiles, implying nothing definitive about their ethnicity [ICC2]. Even a predominantly Jewish church situated in the center of the Roman empire would have been regarded by Paul as within his sphere of ministry [ICC2]. This phrase alone does not settle the issue of the church's ethnic makeup [ICC2].

3. This probably means both that Rome was geographically situated within a Gentile area and that the Christians there were mostly Gentiles by origin [ICC1, TNTC,].

QUESTION—What is the meaning of the genitive phrase κλητοί Ἰησοῦ Χριστοῦ 'called ones of Jesus Christ'?

The word 'call' is used by Paul to express the 'effectual call', which is the irresistible call of God in grace to bring people into his kingdom and service [BECNT, Ho, ICC2, NAC, NICNT, NTC, TNTC]. This is the same word used by Paul in 1:1 of his own call to apostleship [BECNT, Gdt, Mor, NAC].

1. They are called by God to belong to Jesus Christ [AB, HNTC, ICC1, Mor, Mu, NICNT, NTC, SSA, TH, WBC; GW, NCV, NET, NIV, NLT, NRSV, REB, TEV]. God is the one who initiates the call [HNTC, Ho, Mor, SSA, TH, WBC].
2. They are called by Jesus Christ [BAGD, BECNT, Gdt, ICC2; CEV]. It means that Jesus Christ chose them [CEV].
3. They are called people who belong to Jesus Christ [Ho, ICC1]. It is the genitive of possession [ICC1].

1:7 to-all the-(ones) being in Rome, loved[a] (ones) of God, called[b] (ones), saints,[c]

LEXICON—a. ἀγαπητός (LN 25.45) (BAGD 2. p. 6): 'loved' [BAGD, BECNT, LN; NET, NIV, REB], 'beloved' [AB, HNTC, ICC2, LN (25.45), NICNT, NTC, WBC; KJV, NASB, NRSV], 'dear' [BAGD, LN]. The phrase ἀγαπητοῖς θεοῦ 'loved ones of God' is translated 'whom God loves' [GW, NCV, TEV], 'God loves you' [CEV], 'God loves you dearly' [NLT], 'you who are loved by God' [BECNT; REB].

b. κλητός (LN 33.314) (BAGD p. 436): 'called' [BAGD, LN; KJV, NASB]. This adjective is translated as a passive participle with the implied infinitive εἶναι 'to be': 'called to be' [AB, BECNT, NICNT, WBC; GW, KJV, NASB, NCV, NET, NIV, NRSV, REB]; as an active verb with the implied infinitive εἶναι 'to be' or γίνομαι 'to become': '(whom God) has called to be' [NCV, TEV], '(whom God) has called to become' [GW], '(God) has called you to be' [NLT]. It is translated as a verb phrase: '(God) has chosen (you)' [CEV]. The phrase κλητοῖς ἁγίοις is translated 'by divine call, saints' [HNTC], 'saints by God's calling' [ICC2], 'saints by virtue of having been called' [NTC].

c. ἅγιος (LN 11.27, 88.24) (BAGD 2.d.β. p. 10): This plural noun is translated 'saints' [BAGD; KJV, NASB, NET, NIV, NRSV], 'God's people' [LN (11.27)], 'his very own people' [CEV, NLT], 'his own people' [TEV], 'his holy people' [GW, NCV], 'his people' [REB], 'holy' [LN 88.24)]. The word ἁγίοις 'saints' ought to be understood in the OT sense of being dedicated to, consecrated to, or set apart for God [AB, HNTC, ICC1, ICC2, Mor, Mu, NAC, TH, TNTC, WBC]. While it may imply ethical and moral behavior, this is not the primary emphasis [AB, HNTC, Mor, Mu].

QUESTION—How are the words related in the phrase κλητοῖς ἁγίοις 'called ones, saints'?

Note that there is a certain amount of overlap possible between the positions listed below, and one does not rule out the other.

1. They were called to be saints [Ho, ICC1, NAC, NICNT, SSA; GW, KJV, NCV, NET, NIV, NLT, NRSV, REB, TEV], or called to be dedicated people [AB], or called to be holy and pure [Ho]. Being called to be saints means that they were chosen so they would become his people [SSA].

1.1 They were called to be holy in the sense of being set apart or dedicated to God [AB, TH], and thus separated from the profane aspects of life [AB].
1.2 They were called to be set apart for God and also to be holy in the moral and ethical sense, just as God is holy [Ho, ICC1, NAC]. All Christians are called by God to belong to Jesus Christ and to be his holy people [St].
2. They are saints as a result of being called; that is, they are called and thus are saints [Gdt, HNTC, ICC2, Mor, Mu, NTC, TNTC, WBC]. By virtue of their effectual call they have already become people set apart and consecrated to live in service to God and for the glory of God [Gdt, ICC2, Mu, NTC, WBC]. They are called to be God's [Mor]. They are saints by virtue of God's calling, but they are also called to be holy [HNTC, Mu, NTC].

grace[a] to-you and peace[b] from[c] God our Father and (the) Lord Jesus Christ.

LEXICON—a. χάρις (LN 25.89, 88.66) (BAGD 2.c. p. 877): 'grace' [AB, BAGD, BECNT, HNTC, ICC2, LN (88.66), NICNT, NTC, WBC; all versions except CEV, GW], 'kindness' [LN (88.66)], 'favor' [BAGD, LN (25.89)], 'good will' [BAGD, LN (25.89); GW]. This noun is also translated as a verb: 'to be kind' [CEV].

b. εἰρήνη (LN 22.42) (BAGD 2. p. 227): 'peace' [AB, BAGD, BECNT, HNTC, ICC2, LN, NICNT, NTC, WBC; all versions].

c. ἀπό (LN 90.15) (BAGD V.4. p. 88): 'from' [AB, BAGD, BECNT, HNTC, ICC2, LN, NICNT, NTC, WBC; all versions except CEV, TEV]. The phrase χάρις ὑμῖν καὶ εἰρήνη ἀπὸ θεοῦ πατρὸς ἡμῶν 'grace to you and peace from God our Father' is translated 'I pray that God our Father…will be kind to you and bless you with peace' [CEV], 'may God our Father…give you grace and peace' [TEV].

QUESTION—What is meant by χάρις 'grace'?

Paul changes the standard Hellenistic greeting of χαίρειν 'greetings' to χάρις 'grace', since this is a key concept of his gospel [AB, BECNT, Gdt, WBC]. As it is used here it is God's spontaneous, unmerited favor in action, such as bestowing salvation on sinners [Gdt, Ho, Mu, NTC, TNTC]. Addressed to Christians, it is a request for God to bestow his undeserved kindness on them [SSA]. It is God's love and mercy expressed towards those who do not deserve it [TH].

QUESTION—What is meant by εἰρήνη 'peace'?

Note that there is a certain amount of overlap possible between the positions listed below, and one does not rule out the other.
1. It signifies the holistic well being and completeness of those under God's care and favor, thus echoing the Hebrew *shalom* [AB, BECNT, Ho, Mor, WBC], and includes not only spiritual and personal or individual well being, but also material benefit and harmonious social relations [Ho,

WBC]. It is the well being that believers enjoy through the grace of God [TNTC]. This expresses an inner peace and positive blessing, not necessarily an absence of hostilities among people [Mor, SSA].

2. This reflects both a state of reconciliation with God and a condition of consequent well being that results [ICC1, ICC2, Mu, NAC, NTC, TH], including harmony with God and the resultant peace of mind [ICC1]. The uppermost thought is that of peace with God, although the blessings which result from this reconciliation may also have been in mind [ICC2]. It refers to profound calm or inward quiet resulting from reconciliation [Gdt]. It refers to favor with God based on reconciliation through Christ [Mu]. Peace is what we experience as a result of receiving God's grace [NAC].

DISCOURSE UNIT: 1:8–17 [Ho; GW, NCV, NIV, NLT]. The topic is the introduction [Ho], Paul's longing to visit Rome [NIV], Paul's prayer and desire to visit Rome [GW], God's good news [NLT], a prayer of thanks [NCV].

DISCOURSE UNIT: 1:8–15 [BECNT, Gdt, GNT, HNTC, ICC1, ICC2, Mor, Mu, NAC, NICNT, NTC, TNTC, WBC; CEV, NET, TEV]. The topic is the introduction [Mu, TNTC], thanksgiving and prayer for an Apostolic visit [BECNT], Paul's thanksgiving and desire to visit Rome [NTC], God's good news [NLT], Paul's desire to visit Rome [GNT, NAC; NET, NIV], thanksgiving and personal explanations [WBC], a prayer of thanksgiving [CEV, TEV], prayer [Mor], thanksgiving and occasion; Paul and the Romans [NICNT], Paul and Rome [HNTC, ICC1, ICC2], Paul's interest in the Roman Christians [Gdt].

1:8 First[a] I-thank my God through[b] Jesus Christ for[c] you all

LEXICON—a. adverb πρῶτον (LN 60.46, 65.52): 'first' (in a series) [LN (60.46)], 'first' [ICC2, NICNT; CEV, GW, KJV, NASB, NIV, NRSV, TEV], 'first of all' [AB, BECNT, HNTC, WBC; NET, NLT] 'to begin with' [NTC], 'let me begin by' [REB], 'first I want to say' [NCV], 'most importantly' [LN (65.52)].

b. διά with genitive object (LN 90.4) (BAGD A.III.2.a. p. 180): 'through' [AB, BAGD, BECNT, HNTC, ICC2, LN, NICNT, NTC, WBC; all versions except CEV], 'in the name of' [CEV], 'through the agency of' [BAGD].

c. περί with genitive object (LN 89.6): 'for' [AB, BECNT, HNTC, ICC2, NICNT, NTC, WBC; all versions], 'in relation to, with regard to, concerning' [LN].

QUESTION—What is meant by πρῶτον 'first'?

1. It means first in a series [AB, HNTC, Ho, ICC2, Mor, NTC, SSA, TH, WBC]. The later points in the letter are not explicitly enumerated [BECNT, Gdt, HNTC, Ho, ICC2, SSA, TH]. It is a way of beginning what he wants to say [NTC, SSA, TH; NCV]. The second idea is in 1:10, but it is not explicitly stated so [Gdt].

2. The word indicates something of primary importance [Mu, NAC, NICNT]. Thanksgiving and praise were central to Paul, as ten of his thirteen epistles open with some form of thanks [NAC]. Thanksgiving for their faith was uppermost in his mind [Mu]. It draws special attention to his thanksgiving [NICNT].

QUESTION—What is meant by the use of the personal pronoun 'my' in the phrase τῷ θεῷ μου 'my God'?

This indicates the personal devotion, intimacy and feeling of Paul towards God [Gdt, Ho, SSA, WBC]. It is a note of personal piety [NICNT]. This does not indicate any kind of exclusiveness [ICC2].

QUESTION—What is the significance of Paul's offering thanks διὰ Ἰησοῦ Χριστοῦ 'through Jesus Christ'?

It emphasizes the mediation of Christ in our access to God and as our intercessor in heaven [AB, Gdt, Ho, ICC2, Mor, Mu, TH, WBC]. Christ is the one who creates the access to God that such thanks may be given [Ho, NICNT]. Jesus is the one who makes this thanksgiving possible [TH]. This connects with the thought of 1:4–6 that blessings have been received through Christ, so thanks should be given through him [NTC]. Christ is the mediator of God's approach to men and their response to him in gratitude or worship [ICC2, TNTC]. This reflects the clear emphasis of Scripture that in all our approaches to God we must come in the name of Christ, because he is the grounds of our acceptance [Ho]. Christ is the one who makes it possible to give thanks for the Romans because of what he has done for them [NAC, SSA].

because[a] your faith[b] is-being-proclaimed[c] in[d] all the world.

LEXICON—a. ὅτι (LN 89.33, 90.21): 'because' [AB, BECNT, HNTC, LN (89.33), NICNT, NTC, WBC; all versions except KJV, NLT], 'since, for, in view of the fact that' [LN (89.33)], 'that' [LN (90.21); KJV].

  b. πίστις (LN **31.102**) (BAGD 2.d.α. p.663): 'faith' [AB, BAGD, BECNT, HNTC, ICC2, **LN**, NICNT, NTC, WBC; all versions].

  c. pres. pass. indic. of καταγγέλλω (LN **33.204**) (BAGD 1. p. 409): 'to be proclaimed' [AB, BAGD, BECNT, **LN**, NICNT; NET, NRSV], 'to be reported' [NIV], 'to be spoken about' [LN], 'to be spoken of' [HNTC, WBC; KJV], 'to be talked of' [NTC], 'to be told' [REB], 'to be well known' [BAGD], 'to become known' [NLT], 'to be published abroad' [ICC2]. The phrase ἡ πίστις ὑμῶν καταγγέλλεται 'your faith is being proclaimed' is translated 'people...are talking about your faith' [CEV], 'the news of your faith is spreading' [GW], 'the story of your faith is being told' [REB], 'people everywhere are talking about your faith' [NCV]. This entire clause is translated 'because the whole world is hearing about your faith' [TEV], 'the news of your faith is being published abroad in all the world' [ICC2].

  d. ἐν with dative object (LN 83.13): 'in' [AB, BECNT, HNTC, ICC2, LN, NICNT; CEV, NCV], 'throughout' [NTC; GW, KJV, NASB, NET, NLT,

NRSV]. The phrase ἐν ὅλῳ τῷ κόσμῳ 'in all the world' [AB, ICC2, NICNT] is also translated 'everywhere in the world' [CEV, NCV], 'in the entire world' [BECNT], 'throughout the world' [NLT, NRSV], 'throughout the whole world' [GW, KJV, NASB, NET], 'throughout the entire world' [NTC], 'all over the world' [WBC; NIV, REB], 'the whole world' [HNTC; TEV].

QUESTION—What relationship is indicated by ὅτι 'because'?
1. It indicates Paul's reason for giving thanks [AB, BECNT, Gdt, HNTC, Ho, ICC2, Mor, NAC, NICNT, NTC, St, TH, TNTC, WBC]: I thank God because your faith, etc.
2. It indicates the content of his thanksgiving [KJV]: I thank God that your faith, etc.

QUESTION—What is meant by the phrase ἡ πίστις ὑμῶν 'your faith'?
1. It refers to the fact of their having accepted the gospel message [BECNT, Gdt, ICC2, Mor, Mu, NAC, NICNT, NTC, St, WBC].
2. This refers to the particular quality of the faith of the Romans, not just the fact that they had faith [HNTC, Ho, TH]. He is thankful for the understanding and constancy with which they believed [HNTC]. Their faith was of such a quality as to be widely spoken of and recognized [Ho].

QUESTION—What is meant by the phrase ἐν ὅλῳ τῷ κόσμῳ 'in all the world'?
This is hyperbole [AB, BECNT, Gdt, HNTC, Ho, ICC2, Mor, NAC, NICNT, SSA, St, WBC]. It means 'throughout the Roman empire' [SSA]. Paul means that other Christians in many other places knew about their faith [NICNT, TNTC], or that other churches which he himself had established knew about it [BECNT]. Wherever the gospel was being spread, the churches knew about the faith of the Roman Christians [Mu, St]. Rome was the principle city of the world as Paul knew it, so many people would become aware that there were Christians in Rome [AB, NTC].

1:9 For my witness[a] is God,

LEXICON—a. μάρτυς (LN 33.270) (BAGD 2.a. p. 494): 'witness' [AB, BAGD, BECNT, HNTC, ICC2, LN, NICNT, NTC, WBC; GW, KJV, NASB, NET, NIV, NRSV, REB, TEV], 'one who testifies' [LN]. This clause is translated 'God…knows' [NCV, NLT], 'God has seen' [CEV].

QUESTION—What relationship is indicated by γάρ 'for'?
It introduces further remarks concerning his prayers and concerns for the Roman believers for their spiritual growth [NICNT]. It introduces his next major theme, which is his prayer and desire to visit them [BECNT].

QUESTION—What is the significance of the phrase μάρτυς γάρ μού ἐστιν ὁ θεός 'God is my witness'?
Paul uses this formula to emphasize the truth that he is particularly eager for them to know of his concern for them, and that he regularly prayed for an opportunity to visit them [BECNT, ICC2, Mu, NAC, NICNT, NTC]. He appeals to the all-knowing God, who cannot lie and who judges all hearts

[NTC]. Paul's assertions in this section are something the Roman Christians could not verify for themselves, so he wants to emphasize the certainty of his dedication to God and his concern for them, as well as the truth of the statement [AB, Gdt, ICC2, Mor]. Paul appeals to God who cannot lie and who judges human hearts as a means of confirming what he says [NTC]. It is a reverent appeal to the God who searches all hearts [Ho]. Paul is concerned that he might be misunderstood or not be heard sympathetically [Mu, WBC].

whom I-serve[a] in[b] my spirit[c] in[d] the gospel of-his Son,

LEXICON—a. pres. act. indic. of λατρεύω (LN 53.14) (BAGD p. 467): 'to serve' [BAGD, BECNT, ICC2, NICNT, NTC, WBC; all versions except REB], 'to worship' [AB, LN], 'to carry out religious duties' [BAGD], 'to offer service' [REB], 'to render service' [HNTC].
  b. ἐν with dative object (LN 83.13, 90.10): 'in' [BECNT, ICC2, LN (83.13), NICNT; NASB, NET], 'within' [LN (83.13)], 'with' [AB, LN (90.10), WBC; CEV, KJV, NCV, NIV, NLT, NRSV, TEV], 'from' [NTC], '(I offer the service) of' [REB], not explicit [HNTC; GW].
  c. πνεῦμα (LN 26.9) (BAGD 3.b. p. 675): 'spirit' [AB, BAGD, BECNT, ICC2, LN, NICNT, WBC; KJV, NASB, NET, NRSV, REB], 'spiritual nature' [LN], 'inner being' [BAGD, LN], 'heart' [NTC; CEV, NIV, NLT, TEV], 'whole heart' [NCV], not explicit [GW]. This word is also translated as an adjective modifying 'service': 'spiritual' [HNTC]. The phrase ἐν τῷ πνεύματί μου is translated 'in my spirit' [BECNT, ICC2, NICNT; NASB, NET], 'with my spirit' [AB, WBC; KJV, NRSV], 'from the heart' [NTC], 'with all my heart' [CEV, NLT, TEV], 'with my whole heart' [NCV, NIV], '(the service) of my spirit' [REB], 'spiritual (service)' [HNTC].
  d. ἐν with dative object (LN 83.13, 89.5): 'in' [AB, BECNT, HNTC, ICC2, LN (83.13, 89.5), NICNT, NTC, WBC; KJV, NET], 'with regard to' [LN (89.5)]. This is also translated as 'in' or 'by' in conjunction with a verb having to do with disseminating or telling the gospel added for clarity: 'by announcing' [NRSV], 'by preaching' [REB, TEV], 'by spreading' [GW], 'by telling others' [NLT], 'in preaching' [NIV], 'in the preaching' [NASB], 'in proclaiming' [HNTC, ICC2]. The phrase 'in the gospel of his Son' is translated 'and tell the good news about his Son' [CEV].

QUESTION—What is the relationship between the word λατρεύω 'I serve' and the phrase ἐν τῷ εὐαγγελίῳ 'in the gospel of his son'?
  1. It indicates means; Paul serves God by preaching the gospel [SSA, TH; GW, NCV]. Paul expresses worship by evangelizing [AB]. This could also be considered a relationship of circumstance, that he serves while or as he proclaims the gospel, though this is not very different from a means relationship [SSA]. Preaching the gospel is the sphere in which Paul's service of devotion was expressed [Mu].

2. The gospel itself is the sphere in which Paul's service is offered [BECNT, Mor], not just the preaching of it, for the gospel is central to how the Christian life is to be lived out [Mor].

QUESTION—What is the significance of the use of the term λατρευω 'to serve' in this verse?

This is a cultic term, used even in classical Greek of service to a deity [BECNT, ICC1], but here designating service in the gospel [BECNT]. It focuses on the vertical aspect of Paul's ministry as an offering of worship to God [NICNT]. Paul applies it to all activity expressing commitment to the gospel of Christ [WBC], indicating that his service is itself an act of worship [ICC2, NAC, NICNT]. In the LXX this verb is used regularly for Israel's worship of Yahweh, and Paul's worship is expressed by his evangelistic ministry [AB]. In the NT it is always used regarding religious service, usually to God [Ho]. This points to the fact that his prayer for them is an integral part of his service to God [ICC2]. Paul's preaching is a service of devotion [Mu]. As in 15:16, he sees his ministry in priestly and cultic terms [BECNT, WBC].

QUESTION—What is meant by ἐν τῷ πνεύματί μου 'in my spirit' in this context?

Note that there is a certain amount of overlap possible between the positions listed below, and one does not rule out the other.

1. This refers to Paul's spirit [AB, BAGD, Gdt, NICNT, WBC]: I serve him in my spirit. It is that part of Paul by which his soul communicates with God [AB, Gdt], and he serves God [Gdt]. It is an aspect of Paul's human nature, the organ of his service to God [Gdt, ICC1], and is thought of as being permeated with God's Spirit [Gdt]. It is that aspect of Paul most open to God's Spirit [AB]. Paul contrasts the worship appropriate to the gospel with worship that is external and ritually oriented [WBC]. The deepest inward part of Paul's being is the instrument of his service [NICNT].

2. This refers to the spiritual character of Paul's service [HNTC, ICC2]. Paul uses his spirit to engage in activities that pertain to the spiritual aspect of his nature to offer spiritual service to God [HNTC]. The phrase may denote prayer, the inward or spiritual aspect of Paul's ministry, or service such as would be contrasted with the outward service of preaching the gospel [ICC2].

3. This refers to Paul's sincerity and wholeheartedness in his service [BECNT, Ho, Mor, Mu, NAC, NTC, SSA, TH; CEV, NCV, NIV, NLT, TEV]. He serves God wholeheartedly [NAC], with depth and sincerity [Mu], with all his might and with his innermost being and not merely in a superficial or external service [Mor]. This is contrasted with an insincere or merely external service [Ho].

QUESTION—What is meant by ἐν τῷ εὐαγγελίῳ τοῦ υἱοῦ αὐτοῦ 'in the gospel of his Son'?
1. The phrase 'the gospel of his Son' refers to preaching the gospel about or concerning his Son [AB, Gdt, Ho, ICC2, Mu, NICNT, SSA, TH, WBC; CEV, GW, NCV, NIV, NLT]. A verb such as 'preach' or 'proclaim' should be understood here since ἐν 'in' is not to be understood in its primary locative sense [SSA].
2. Paul serves in the gospel of God's Son, which means that the gospel is central to how Paul sees the Christian life being lived, and involves a complete change in one's life [Mor].

that[a] constantly[b] I-make mention[c] of-you
LEXICON—a. ὡς (LN 90.21, 89.86) (BAGD IV.4. p. 899): 'that' [AB, BAGD, HNTC, LN (90.21), NICNT; GW, KJV, NCV, NET, NRSV, REB, TEV], 'how' [BECNT, ICC2, LN (89.86), NTC, WBC; CEV, NIV, NLT], 'as to how' [NASB]. After verbs of knowing or saying, the word means 'that' [BAGD].
b. ἀδιαλείπτως (LN 68.55) (BAGD p. 17): 'constantly' [AB, BAGD, BECNT, WBC; NIV], 'continuously' [LN; NET], 'continually' [REB], 'unceasingly' [BAGD, HNTC, ICC2, LN, NTC; NASB], 'without ceasing' [NICNT; KJV, NRSV], 'always' [GW, NCV], 'often…day and night' [NLT], not explicit [TEV]. This word is translated as a phrase: 'I never stop (praying)' [CEV].
c. μνεία (LN **29.18**) (BAGD 2. p. 524): 'mention' [BAGD, LN]. The phrase 'to make mention' [KJV, NASB, REB] is also translated 'to mention' [AB, BAGD, BECNT, HNTC, ICC2, NTC, WBC; GW, NCV], 'to remember to mention' [**LN**], 'to remember' [NICNT; NET, NIV, NRSV, TEV] 'to pray' [CEV]. The phrase 'constantly I make mention of you always in my prayers' is translated 'I pray for you. Day and night I bring you and your needs in prayer to God' [NLT], 'I never stop praying for you' [CEV]. In the NT this is used almost exclusively of remembering someone in prayer [AB, ICC2, Mor].

QUESTION—What is meant by ἀδιαλείπτως 'constantly' in this phrase?
He speaks of prayer that is frequently and regularly offered [BECNT, Mor, Mu, NICNT], or that occurs every time he prays [ICC1, SSA]. Paul uses hyperbole here [AB, SSA, WBC]. He wants to emphasize that he has not let up in his habit of praying for the Romans [NTC].

1:10 always[a] in[b] my prayers[c]
TEXT—This phrase is included at the end of 1:9 by KJV, NLT, NRSV, REB.
LEXICON—a. πάντοτε (LN 67.88) (BAGD p. 609): 'always' [AB, BAGD, BECNT, HNTC, ICC2, LN, NICNT, WBC; KJV, NASB, NET, NLT, NRSV], 'at all times' [BAGD, LN, NTC; NIV], 'every time' [GW, NCV, TEV].
b. ἐπί with genitive object (LN 67.136) (BAGD I.2. p. 286): 'in' [AB, BAGD, BECNT, HNTC, ICC2, NICNT, NTC, WBC; CEV, KJV, NASB,

NET, NIV, NRSV, REB], 'during, in the course of' [LN], not explicit [GW, NCV, NLT, TEV].
  c. προσευχή (LN 33.178) (BAGD 1. p. 713): 'prayer' [AB, BAGD, BECNT, HNTC, ICC2, LN, NICNT, NTC, WBC; all versions except GW, NCV, TEV]. The phrase 'always in my prayers' is translated as a verb phrase: 'every time I pray' [GW, NCV, TEV].

QUESTION—What is the connection between 1:9 and 1:10?

Verse nine is a somewhat unspecified prayer and verse ten gives the specific content, which is Paul's desire to visit Rome [BECNT, Mu, NICNT, SSA, St]. Paul's unceasing desire is to visit them and to minister to them [NICNT].

QUESTION—With what is the phrase πάντοτε ἐπὶ τῶν προσευχῶν μου 'on every occasion in my prayers' connected?

1. It is connected with what precedes [ICC2, NTC, SSA, St, TH; GW, KJV, NCV, NIV, NRSV]: I constantly make mention of you always in my prayers. 'Constantly' and 'always' may be considered a doublet and somewhat hyperbolic, meaning 'each time I pray' [SSA].
2. It is connected with what follows [AB, BECNT, Gdt, HNTC, ICC1, Mu, NICNT, WBC; CEV, NASB, NET, NLT, REB]: Always in my prayers I ask that I may come to you.

QUESTION—What is meant by πάντοτε 'always'?

It means that Paul prays this frequently and regularly, not that he prays without ever stopping [BECNT, ICC2, Mu, NICNT, SSA]. Paul presumably maintained times of regular prayer [WBC]. The adverbs ἀδιαλείπτως 'constantly' and πάντοτε 'always' are nearly synonymous [HNTC, SSA]. The change from the word ἀδιαλείπτως 'constantly' of verse nine is merely stylistic, so he is not intending to be more precise here than in verse nine [BECNT].

asking[a] if[b] somehow[c] now at-some-time[d]

LEXICON—a. pres. mid. (deponent = act.) participle of δέομαι (LN 33.170) (BAGD 4. p. 175): 'to ask' [BAGD, BECNT, ICC2, NTC, WBC; CEV, GW, NET, NRSV, REB, TEV], 'to make request' [KJV, NASB], 'to make a petition' [HNTC], 'to pray' [NICNT; NCV, NIV, NLT], 'to beg' [AB, LN].
  b. εἰ (LN 90.26) (BAGD VI.12.b. p. 220): 'if' [ICC2, LN, NICNT, NTC; KJV, NASB, NET], 'that' [AB, BECNT, HNTC, LN, WBC; GW, NIV, NRSV, REB, TEV], not explicit [CEV, NCV, NLT].
  c. πως (LN 92.17) (BAGD 732): 'somehow' [AB, BAGD LN, NICNT, WBC; GW, NRSV], 'in some way' [BAGD], 'perhaps' [BAGD, NTC; NASB, NET], 'by any means' [ICC2; KJV], 'somehow or other' [REB], not explicit [NCV, NIV, TEV]. The phrase εἴ πως 'if somehow' is translated 'to make it possible' [CEV].
  d. ποτέ (LN 67.9, **67.40**) (BAGD 1. p. 695): 'at some time, at any time' [LN (67.9)]. The idiom ἤδη ποτέ 'now at some time' is translated 'now at last'

[BAGD, ICC2, **LN** (67.40), NICNT, NTC, WBC; GW, NASB, NET, NIV], 'now at length' [LN (67.40); KJV], 'at length' [AB], 'finally' [BECNT], 'already now' [LN (67.40)], 'in the end' [HNTC], 'at last' [NLT, NRSV, TEV], 'at long last' [REB], not explicit [CEV, NCV].

I-shall-succeed^a by^b the will^c of-God to-come^d to you.
 LEXICON—a. fut. pass. (deponent = act.) indic. of εὐοδόομαι (LN **68.30**) (BAGD p. 323): 'to succeed' [AB, BAGD, HNTC, LN, NICNT, WBC; NASB, NET, NRSV, REB]. This active verb is translated as passive: 'to be allowed' [BECNT; NCV], 'the way may be opened for me' [NTC; NIV]. It is translated as a phrase: '(to ask God) to make it possible' [CEV, GW], 'to have a prosperous journey' [KJV].
 b. ἐν with dative object (LN 89.76, 90.6): 'by' [AB, BECNT, LN (89.76, 90.6) NTC, WBC; KJV, NASB, NIV, NRSV, REB], 'by means of' [LN (89.76); KJV], 'through' [LN (89.76)], 'in' [NET, NICNT; TEV], 'if it be' [ICC2], not explicit [GW, NCV].
 c. θέλημα (LN 30.59) (BAGD 2.b. p. 354): 'will' [AB, BAGD, BECNT, HNTC, ICC2, LN, NICNT, NTC, WBC; KJV, NASB, NET, NIV, NRSV, REB], 'good will' [TEV], 'purpose, plan' [LN], not explicit [CEV, GW]. The phrase 'by the will of God' is translated 'God willing' [NLT], 'if God wants it' [NCV], 'God will make it possible' [GW].
 d. aorist act. infin. of ἔρχομαι (LN 15.7); 'to come' [BECNT, LN, NTC, WBC; KJV, NCV, NIV, NLT]. The phrase ἐλθεῖν πρός 'to come to' is translated 'to visit' [CEV, GW, NET, TEV], 'in visiting' [NET], 'in coming to visit' [REB], 'in coming to' [AB, HNTC, ICC2, NICNT; NASB, NRSV].

QUESTION—What is the significance of Paul's using somewhat hypothetical language in reference to the timing of his going to visit the Roman church?
 This communicates some uncertainty on Paul's part regarding the outcome of his request [Gdt, Mu, NICNT, NTC, SSA, WBC], and perhaps some impatience about the delay in carrying out the visit [Gdt, NICNT]. This phrasing clearly indicates eagerness on Paul's part to make the visit, and the forefronting indicates prominence [SSA]. It indicates submission to God's will [Ho, ICC2, Mor]. His concern is to do God's will, not his own, so he wants to go to Rome only if God so allows [Mor]. There is some reserve on Paul's part since he neither planted the church nor had he visited it [BECNT, HNTC], and would arrive there only if God willed it [BECNT]. Paul has a strong sense of the risks involved and is perhaps doubtful that what he intends will be accomplished [ICC1].

QUESTION—What is the significance of the phrase ἐν τῷ θελήματι τοῦ θεοῦ 'by the will of God' in this verse?
 This frequent expression of Paul's communicates humility in that Paul is not presuming on the will of God nor imposing his own will and desire on God's [Ho, ICC1, Mor, Mu, SSA, St, TH, WBC], he realizes that this trip depends on factors beyond his control [AB, Gdt], and is an expression of his constant

submission to God's sovereign intentions [NTC]. As God's servant he worked within the framework of God's will [NAC]. This may also indicate Paul's persuasion that such a visit was in agreement with the will of God and his own apostolic commission [Mu].

1:11 **For[a] I-long[b] to-see you,**
LEXICON—a. γάρ (LN 89.23) (BAGD p. 151) 'for' [BAGD, BECNT, HNTC, ICC2, LN, NICNT, NTC, WBC; all versions except CEV, GW, NCV], 'because' [LN], not explicit [AB; CEV, GW, NCV].
  b. pres. act. indic. of ἐπιποθέω (LN 25.18) (BAGD p.297): 'to long' [BAGD, BECNT, HNTC, ICC2, NICNT, WBC; all versions except CEV, NCV, TEV], 'to desire' [BAGD], 'to desire deeply' [BAGD, LN], 'to want very much' [NCV, TEV], 'to want' [CEV], 'to yearn' [AB, NTC].
QUESTION—What relationship is indicated by γάρ 'for'?
  This conjunction introduces one of several reasons why Paul wants to visit the Roman church [BECNT, Mor, NICNT].

in-order-that[a] I-may-impart[b] some spiritual[c] gift[d] to-you
LEXICON—a. ἵνα (LN 89.59) (BAGD I.1.a. p. 376) 'in order that' [BAGD, HNTC, ICC2, LN, NTC, WBC; KJV, NASB], 'in order to' [AB; TEV], 'to' [BECNT; GW, NCV], 'that' [BAGD], 'so that' [LN, NICNT; NET, NIV, NRSV], 'so' [NLT], 'for the purpose of' [LN]. This conjunction is also translated as a verb phrase: 'I want to (bring)' [REB].
  b. aorist act. subj. of μεταδίδωμι (LN 57.96) (BAGD p. 511): 'to impart' [BAGD, BECNT, HNTC, ICC2, NTC; KJV, NASB, NET, NIV], 'to give' [BAGD LN; NCV], 'to bring' [REB], 'to share' [BAGD LN, NICNT, WBC; CEV, GW, NLT, NRSV, TEV], 'to pass on' [AB].
  c. πνευματικός (LN **12.21**) (BAGD 2.a.β. p. 679): 'spiritual' [AB, BAGD, BECNT, HNTC, **LN**, NICNT, NTC, WBC; all versions except CEV], 'from the Spirit' [LN], 'pertaining to the spirit' [BAGD]. The phrase χάρισμα...πνευματικόν 'spiritual gift' is translated 'gift of the Spirit' [HNTC], 'blessings that God's Spirit has given me' [CEV].
  d. χάρισμα (LN **57.103**) (BAGD 1.a. p. 879): 'gift' [AB, BAGD, BECNT, HNTC, **LN**, NICNT, NTC, WBC; KJV, NASB, NCV, NET, NIV, NRSV, REB], 'gracious gift' [LN], 'favor bestowed' [BAGD], 'blessing' [CEV, GW, NLT, TEV].
QUESTION—What relationship is expressed by the conjunction ἵνα 'in order that' in this clause?
  This indicates one of the specific reasons for Paul's proposed visit [BECNT, Ho, Mor, St]. The particular aim of his longing to visit was to impart some spiritual gift to them [Mu].
QUESTION—What is meant by τι χάρισμα...πνευματικόν 'some spiritual gift'?
  1. This likely refers to some spiritual blessing or benefit that Paul hopes will result from his visit [AB, Ho, ICC2, Mor, Mu, NAC, NTC, SSA, St, WBC]. The gift Paul wants to impart is that of strengthening them

spiritually [NTC, SSA], that is, to strengthen their faith [AB], to build up their spiritual life [Mor], to help them grow in their knowledge, grace, and power [Ho]. Paul would minister to them in teaching and exhortation [St]. He is being somewhat indefinite here because he does not yet know what the spiritual needs of the Roman Christians are [ICC2, NICNT, St]. Paul expects that God's grace will work through him in some way to benefit the Roman Christians, though he does not know exactly how [WBC]. Paul wants to share some insight, gift, or ability that he himself has from the Spirit [NAC, NICNT].
2. It refers to the charismatic gifts described in Romans 12 and 1 Corinthians 12–14 [HNTC, ICC1], which Paul himself possessed and felt sure he could use for the benefit and blessing of the church during his visit there [ICC1].
3. The gift he wishes to impart is the gift of understanding his apostolic message, a message that declares the union of Jews and Gentiles in Christ and which would edify and strengthen them to endure in their faith, be freed of their own divisions, and be able to support him in his quest for evangelizing Spain [BECNT].

in-order-for[a] you to-be-strengthened,[b]
LEXICON—a. εἰς (LN 89.57): 'in order to' [LN], 'for the purpose of' [LN], 'that' [AB; NASB], 'so that' [BECNT, ICC2, NTC, WBC; GW], 'for' [HNTC], 'to the end that' [KJV], 'then' [CEV], 'to' [NICNT; NCV, NET, NIV, NRSV, REB, TEV], not explicit [NLT].
  b. aorist pass. infin. of στηρίζω (LN 74.19) (BAGD 2. p. 768): 'to be strengthened' [AB, BAGD, BECNT, ICC2, LN, NTC, WBC], 'to be established' [BAGD; KJV], 'to be made more firm' [LN], 'to make strong' [NCV, NIV, REB, TEV], 'to strengthen' [NICNT; NET, NRSV]. This entire phrase is translated 'for your strengthening' [HNTC], 'that will help you grow strong in the Lord' [NLT], 'then you will grow stronger in your faith' [CEV].
QUESTION—What relationship is indicated by εἰς 'in order for'?
This indicates the purpose of Paul's wanting to impart the gift [BECNT, Mor, Mu, NAC, NICNT].

1:12 that-is[a] to-be-encouraged-together[b] (while) among[c] you
LEXICON—a. τοῦτο δέ ἐστιν. This phrase is translated 'that is' [NICNT; KJV, NASB, NET, NIV], 'or rather that' [AB, HNTC, ICC2, WBC; NRSV, REB], 'what I am saying is that' [CEV], 'what I mean is that' [GW, TEV], 'I mean that' [NTC; NCV], 'or rather what I wish is that' [HNTC], 'in this way' [NLT], 'I also expect' [BECNT].
  b. aorist pass. infin. of συμπαρακαλέω (LN **25.151**) (BAGD p. 779): 'to be encouraged together' [LN; NASB], 'to receive encouragement together' [BAGD], 'to be encouraged at the same time' [**LN**], 'to be mutually encouraged' [AB, BECNT, HNTC, NICNT, NTC, WBC; NET, NIV, NRSV], 'to receive comfort together' [BAGD], 'to be comforted together

with' [ICC2; KJV], 'to be helped at the same time' [TEV]. This is also translated 'we can encourage each other' [CEV], 'to be encouraged by one another's (faith)' [GW, REB], 'both you and I will be helped at the same time' [TEV], 'to help each other' [NCV], 'I'm eager to encourage you…, but I also want to be encouraged' [NLT]. In addition to the notion of being encouraged, this verb also has connotations of being comforted [ICC2, NICNT] and consoled [HNTC]. This word is found only here in the NT.

c. ἐν with dative object (LN 83.9): 'among, with' [LN]. The phrase ἐν ὑμῖν '(while) among you' is translated 'when I am with you' [REB], 'among you' [BECNT, NICNT, WBC], 'when I am among you' [HNTC], 'while I am among you' [NTC], 'in your midst' [ICC2], 'at the same time' [TEV], not explicit [AB; CEV, GW, KJV, NCV, NET, NIV, NLT, NRSV].

QUESTION—What is the function of the phrase τοῦτο δέ ἐστιν 'that is', and to what does it relate?

Note that there is a certain amount of overlap possible between the positions listed below, and one does not rule out the other.

1. The phrase implies that what follows, in some sense, qualifies or corrects what was just said [AB, BECNT, HNTC, ICC1, NICNT, TNTC]. Paul wishes to expand the thought to the mutual encouragement or strengthening that he expects to take place [NICNT]. In an effort to avoid misunderstanding, he affirms that the edification and encouragement would be mutual [BECNT]. Paul does not want to insist on his apostolic authority in relation to the Roman church nor on any superiority over them [AB], so he corrects himself somewhat to stress the mutual profit to be gained through this visit [AB, ICC1, Mor]. This corrects any possible wrong impression that the benefit would have been only in one direction, not mutual [TNTC].

2. This may be seen as an elaboration or clarification by Paul of his previous statement in 1:11 [Gdt, Ho, ICC2, Mor, Mu, NAC, SSA, St, TH, WBC]. This restatement is more an amplification than a correction [SSA]. Paul is not taking back what he said earlier, but he qualifies it [NAC]. Perhaps sensing the one-sidedness of the previous comment Paul quickly modifies or explains what he has said [Gdt, Mu, St]. His purpose was not only to do them good but also to be benefited himself [Ho]. This is an elaboration of what spirit-empowered ministry and community involve; Paul is emphasizing the mutual interdependence that is fundamental to the exercise of the gifts and to Christian community, especially the gift of mutual encouragement [WBC]. The phrase amends the effect of everything that follows ἐπιποθῶ γάρ 'for I long' in 1:11 by expressing a complementary truth, thus making clear that he desires to see them in order to be mutually encouraged together with them [ICC2].

QUESTION—With what is the passive infinitive συμπαρακληθῆναι 'to be encouraged together' to be taken?
- 1. It is connected with ἐπιποθῶ ἰδεῖν ὑμᾶς 'I long to see you'; Paul wants to visit them in order that they might encourage and strengthen one another [BECNT, ICC1, ICC2, NICNT, SSA].
- 2. It is coordinate with στηριχθῆναι 'to be strengthened' and both are dependent on μεταδῶ 'that I may impart'; Paul wants to impart some spiritual gift so that the Roman believers may be strengthened and both he and they may be encouraged together [Ho].
- 3. It is loosely connect with all of 1:11, indicating the purpose of the various verbs there and qualifying the statement he makes [AB].

through[a] the faith[b] (which is) in[c] one-another both yours and mine.
LEXICON—a. διά with genitive object (LN 89.76) (BAGD A.III.1.d. p. 180): 'through' [BAGD, BECNT, ICC2, LN, NICNT, WBC], 'by' [AB, BAGD, HNTC, LN, NTC; all versions except NCV], 'with' [NCV], 'by means of' [LN].
- b. πίστις (LN 31.102) (BAGD 2.d.α. p.663): 'faith' [AB, BAGD, BECNT, HNTC, ICC2, LN, NICNT, NTC, WBC; all versions].
- c. ἐν with dative object (LN 13.8) (BAGD I.4.a. p. 259): 'in' [BECNT, LN, NICNT]. The phrase ἐν ἀλλήλοις 'in one another' is translated 'mutual' [HNTC; KJV], 'mutually' [BAGD; NIV], 'each other's (faith)' [AB, ICC2, NTC, WBC; GW, NIV, NRSV], 'one another's' [NICNT; NET, REB], 'that is ours' [CEV], 'that we have' [NCV], 'you by my faith and I by yours' [TEV], 'both yours and mine' [NASB].

QUESTION—What relationship is indicated by διά 'through'?
It indicates the means by which the encouragement will take place [BECNT, Ho, ICC2, NAC, NICNT, SSA, TH]. It is faith that strengthens and encourages other believers [BECNT]. The medium of this mutual encouragement is their shared faith [Mu].

QUESTION—What is meant by πίστις 'faith'?
It is their trust in Christ [TH]. It is trusting in God in the course of everyday life [BECNT]. Here it refers to what they believe, their convictions, and how their faith expresses itself in daily life [WBC]. In this epistle faith is equivalent to obedience to God, responding to the good news, and a sincere desire to obey God in all things [ICC2]. Their faith is their trust in Jesus, and Paul is implying that they will mutually encourage one another by sharing the results of this faith in Jesus, as opposed to the content of it [SSA].

QUESTION—What is meant by the phrase 'both yours and mine'?
The phrase suggests both the commonality of a shared faith as well as the distinctives of perspective and gifts that, when shared, result in mutual strengthening or edification [NICNT]. When believers perceive faith in others in the course of everyday life it reminds them that God is faithful, and they are inspired and strengthened in their faith and are encouraged to trust God themselves [BECNT]. There is a mutual interdependence involved in

the exercise of the gifts of the Spirit, especially in the area of mutual encouragement [WBC]. Paul is speaking of the reciprocal blessings that come from Christian fellowship [Mor, St]. The faith that he and the believers share in common acts and reacts reciprocally for mutual strengthening and consolation [Mu]. This also shows Paul's modesty and humility [ICC2, Mor, NAC, NTC]. He truly expected to be benefited by the faith of other believers [NAC]. The stress is on the mutuality of the shared faith; both he and the Roman believers will have something to share [HNTC, Ho].

1:13 Now[a] I-do- not –want[b] you to-be-unaware,[c] brothers,[d]

LEXICON—a. δέ (LN 89.94, 89.124): 'now' [NICNT; KJV], 'indeed' [HNTC], 'and' [LN (89.94); NASB], 'but' [ICC2, LN (89.124)], not explicit [AB, BECNT, NTC, WBC; all versions except KJV, NASB].

b. pres. act. indic. of θέλω (LN 25.1) (BAGD 1. p. 355): 'to want' [AB, BAGD, BECNT, ICC2, LN, NTC, WBC; CEV, GW, NASB, NCV, NET, NIV, NLT, NRSV], 'to desire' [BAGD, LN], 'to wish' [BAGD, LN, NICNT], 'to like' [REB], 'to have' [KJV], not explicit [TEV].

c. pres. act. infin. of ἀγνοεῖν (LN 28.13) (BAGD 1. p. 11): 'to be unaware of' [AB, BECNT, HNTC, LN, NTC, WBC; NASB, NET, NIV], 'to not know' [LN], 'to be ignorant of' [ICC2, LN, NICNT; KJV]. Some translate this as a positive statement 'I want you to know' [BAGD; CEV, GW, NASB, NLT, NRSV], 'I should like you to know' [REB], 'you must remember' [TEV]. The phrase 'of the fact (that)' is added for stylistic reasons by ICC2, WBC.

d. ἀδελφός (LN 11.23) (BAGD 2. p. 16): 'brother' [AB, BAGD, NTC, WBC; NASB, NIV], 'fellow believer' [LN], 'Christian brother' [LN]. This term refers specifically to fellow believers in Christ, so the masculine form may include both men and women [LN]. This plural noun is translated 'brothers and sisters' [BECNT, NICNT; GW, NCV, NET, NRSV, REB], 'my brothers' [WBC], 'brethren' [HNTC, ICC2; KJV, NASB], 'my friends' [CEV, TEV], 'dear friends' [NLT].

QUESTION—What is the function and meaning of the double negative in the clause 'I do not want you to be unaware'?

This is litotes, a device in which something is expressed and emphasized by the negation of its opposite, functioning here as an emphatic positive statement [NTC, SSA, TH]. Frequently used by Paul, the emphatic function of the litotes is translated 'I certainly want you to know' [SSA]. Paul wants them to take special note of what he is about to say [NTC]. He uses this formula to introduce something of particular importance [AB, ICC2, Mu, NAC]. This characteristically Pauline phrase carries solemnity [NICNT, WBC] or gives additional weight to what follows [WBC]. It conveys something important the reader might not know [Mor]. It is used by Paul to assure readers or to call particular attention to something [Ho]. This formula, which Paul also uses again in 11:25 and five times in other epistles, is always followed by the term 'brothers' [AB].

that often[a] I-have-planned[b] to-come to[c] you,
LEXICON—a. πολλάκις (LN 67.11) (BAGD p. 686): 'often' [BAGD, BECNT, HNTC, ICC2, LN, NICNT, WBC; CEV, GW, NASB, NET, NRSV, REB], 'how often' [AB], 'many times' [BAGD, LN, NTC; NCV, NIV, NLT, TEV], 'frequently' [BAGD], 'oftentimes' [KJV].
  b. aorist mid. (deponent = act.) indic. of προτίθεμαι (LN **30.62**) (BAGD 2.b. p. 722): 'to plan' [BAGD, **LN,** NTC, WBC; CEV, GW, NASB, NCV, NIV, NLT, REB, TEV], 'to plan beforehand' [LN], 'to intend' [BAGD, BECNT, HNTC, LN; NET, NRSV], 'to propose' [AB, BAGD], 'to purpose' [ICC2, LN; KJV], 'to want to' [NICNT].
  c. πρός with accusative object (LN 84.18): 'to' [AB, HNTC, ICC2, LN, NICNT, NTC, WBC; NASB, NCV, NET, NIV, NRSV], 'unto' [KJV], not explicit [REB]. The phrase ἐλθεῖν πρός ὑμᾶς 'to come to you' is translated 'to come for a visit' [CEV], 'to visit you' [BECNT; GW, NLT, TEV].
QUESTION—What is meant by πολλάκις προεθέμην 'often I have planned'?
  It means that this is a longstanding intent of his [AB, NICNT], and its lack of fulfillment of is not caused by indifference [AB] or by intentional neglect [NAC]. He has had interest in them and a love for them for some time [NTC]. He seems to regard this visit as a clear duty and had made definite plans for such a trip [ICC2]. It shows that this is no new resolve on his part [ICC1], and that he has tried hard to make the trip [Mor]. The forefronting of πολλάκις 'often' gives it emphasis [SSA]. 'Often' indicates that the Roman church has been in existence for some time [Mor]. Paul would have considered a strong Christian group in Rome to be significant, and naturally would have desired to have contact with them [WBC].

but/and[a] I-was-hindered[b] until now,[c]
LEXICON—a. καί (LN 89.92) (BAGD I.2.i. p. 393): 'but' [BAGD, BECNT, ICC2, NICNT, NTC, WBC; CEV, KJV, NCV, NIV, NLT, NRSV, TEV], 'and' [LN; NASB, NET], 'though' [AB; REB], 'however' [GW], 'only' [HNTC]. The conjunction introduces a parenthesis [HNTC, Ho, ICC2, NICNT, NTC], and gives the reason that Paul's plans have not been fulfilled [SSA, TH].
  b. aorist pass. indic. of κωλύω (LN 13.146) (BAGD 1. p. 461): 'to be hindered' [AB, BAGD, LN, NICNT], 'to be prevented (from doing something)' [BAGD, BECNT, HNTC, ICC2, LN, NTC, WBC; NASB, NET, NIV, NLT, NRSV], 'to be kept from (doing something)' [CEV, GW, TEV]. The phrase καὶ ἐκωλύθην 'and I have been hindered' is translated 'but so far I have been prevented' [BAGD], 'but something has always kept me from doing it' [CEV, GW, TEV], 'but was let hitherto' [KJV], 'though so far without success' [REB], 'but this has not been possible' [NCV]. Use of the aorist tense implies that the hindrance is now over [AB].

c. δεῦρο (LN **67.43**) (BAGD 2. p. 176): 'now' [BAGD, **LN,** NICNT, NTC; GW, NET, NIV, NLT], 'up to now' [AB], 'the present time' [BECNT, HNTC, LN], not explicit [NCV]. The phrase ἄχρι τοῦ δεῦρο 'until now' is translated 'up to the present' [HNTC], 'until the present time' [BECNT], 'up til the present' [ICC2], 'thus far' [BAGD; NASB, NRSV], 'so far' [REB], 'hitherto' [WBC; KJV].

QUESTION—What was the nature of the hindrances Paul mentions here?
1. This was probably the ministry demands on Paul in the eastern Mediterranean referred to in 15:19ff [AB, NICNT, NTC, St]. This may be taken as referring to busyness with ministries elsewhere [AB, Ho, ICC2, WBC], or to fresh opportunities and the demands of already established churches, along with other duties [WBC]. The passive may be taken as a theological passive, indicating that God had prevented him from coming due to using him in ministries elsewhere [HNTC, Ho, ICC2, TH, WBC]. Probably God had prevented it because it was not yet time [Mor].
2. There are no specific agents mentioned, but the passive suggests forces which were hostile to his desires to visit [SSA]. One possible hindrance could have been the imperial edict of A.D. 49 expelling Jews from Rome [TNTC, WBC].

in-order-that[a] I-may-have some fruit[b] among[c] you also

LEXICON—a. ἵνα (LN 89.59) (BAGD I.1.a. p. 376) 'in order that' [BECNT, ICC2, LN, NTC, WBC; NASB, NIV, NRSV], 'in order to' [AB, LN], 'that' [BAGD, HNTC; KJV] 'so that' [LN, NICNT; NCV, NET], 'in the hope of' [REB], not explicit [CEV, GW, NLT, TEV].

b. καρπός (LN 43.15) (BAGD 2.b. p. 405): 'fruit' [AB, BAGD, BECNT, HNTC, ICC2, LN, NTC, WBC; KJV, NASB, NET], 'harvest' [LN, NICNT; NIV, NRSV], 'results' [GW, NLT]. The phrase ἵνα τινὰ καρπὸν σχῶ 'in order that I may have some fruit' is translated 'in order to reap some fruit' [AB], 'in order that I may reap some harvest' [NRSV], 'that I might get some fruit' [HNTC], 'I want to work…and see good results' [NLT], 'I want to enjoy some of the results' [GW], 'in the hope of achieving something' [REB], 'I want to win converts' [TEV], 'I want to win followers to Christ in Rome' [CEV], 'I wanted to come so that I could help you grow spiritually' [NCV].

c. ἐν (LN 83.9): 'among' [AB, BECNT, HNTC, ICC2, LN, NICNT, NTC, WBC; all versions except NCV], not explicit [NCV].

QUESTION—What relationship is indicated by ἵνα 'so that'?
This expresses Paul's purpose for wanting to come to the Rome [AB, ICC2, Mor, Mu, NAC, NTC, SSA]. Winning converts is Paul's third reason for wanting to make the visit [St].

QUESTION—What is meant by the figurative use of 'fruit' in the phrase τινὰ καρπὸν σχῶ καὶ ἐν ὑμῖν 'some fruit among you also'?
This expresses Paul's desire to win converts among the Romans [Gdt, Mor, NAC, NTC, St, TH; CEV, TEV], an appropriate desire for him as apostle to

the Gentiles in the capital city of the Gentiles [St]. Paul wants to evangelize the unsaved in Rome and also to strengthen the existing believers in the church [AB, BECNT, HNTC, Ho, ICC2, NICNT, SSA]. This dead metaphor in Greek should be taken broadly to refer to his helping them to grow spiritually [SSA].

QUESTION—What is implied by the phrase 'among you also just as among the other Gentiles also'?

Paul had an extensive ministry among Gentiles and anticipated the same kinds of results among those in Rome [Mor]. Paul expected a continuation of the harvest he had experienced elsewhere among Gentiles, expecting to see converts through evangelism in Rome as well [BECNT, NAC, St]. Paul expects to see the results in Rome that he has seen elsewhere [Gdt]. It indicates that the make-up of the church in Rome was mostly Gentile [Gdt, Mu, NTC].

just-as[a] among[b] the other Gentiles[c] also.

LEXICON—a. καθώς (LN 64.14) (BAGD 1. p. 391) 'just as' [BAGD, LN, NTC, WBC; NET, NIV, NLT], 'as' [AB, BAGD, BECNT; GW, NCV, NRSV, REB, TEV], 'even as' [ICC2, NICNT; KJV, NASB]. An explanatory helping verb is added for clarity and style: 'I have' [GW, NRSV, REB, TEV], 'I already have' [NET], 'I have (helped)' [NCV], 'I have done' [ICC2; CEV, NLT], or 'I have had' [NICNT, NTC; NIV].
  b. ἐν (LN 83.9): 'among' [BECNT, HNTC, LN, NICNT, NTC, WBC; CEV, GW, KJV, NET, NIV, NLT, NRSV, TEV], 'in' [ICC2; CEV, REB], not explicit [NCV].
  c. ἔθνος (LN 11.37): 'Gentile' [AB, HNTC, ICC2, NICNT, NTC, WBC; KJV, NET, NIV, NLT, NRSV, TEV], 'gentile' [NLT, REB]. The plural form τὰ ἔθνη is translated 'heathen, pagans' [LN], 'the rest of the gentile world' [REB], 'the rest of the nations' [GW], 'the rest of the Gentile world' [ICC2], 'the rest of the Gentiles' [BECNT, NICNT, NTC, WBC; NASB, NET, NRSV], 'the rest of the non-Jewish people' [NCV], 'many other places' [CEV].

QUESTION—Who are the other Gentiles?

Paul would particularly be thinking of churches he established in Greece, Macedonia, and Asia [WBC]. As apostle to the Gentiles Paul had already traveled through a large amount of the Gentile territory [ICC2]. They are non-Jewish peoples other than those in Rome [TH]. Paul had engaged in an extensive ministry in the Gentile world [Mor].

1:14 Both to-Greeks[a] and to-barbarians,[b] both to-wise[c] and to foolish,[d]

LEXICON—a. Ἕλλην (LN 11.40, **11.90**) (BAGD 1. p. 251, 2. p. 252): 'Greek' [AB, BAGD (1.), BECNT, HNTC, ICC2, LN (11.40), NICNT, NTC, WBC; KJV, NASB, NCV, NET, NIV, NRSV, REB], 'civilized' [**LN (11.90)**; CEV, GW, TEV], 'Gentile, non-Jew' [LN (11.40)]. This refers to a person of Greek language and culture [BAGD (1.)] or in the broad sense, a person under the influence of Greek culture [BAGD (2.)].

b. βάρβαρος (LN **11.95**) (BAGD 2.b. p. 133): 'barbarian' [AB, BAGD, BECNT, HNTC, ICC2, NICNT, NTC, WBC; KJV, NASB, NET, NRSV], 'foreigner' [BAGD], 'uncivilized' [**LN**; CEV], 'non-Greek' [LN; NIV, REB], 'non-Greek person' [BAGD], 'those who are not Greeks' [NCV], 'person in another culture' [NLT], 'savage' [TEV], 'those who aren't (civilized)' [GW].

c. σοφός (LN 32.33) (BAGD 2. p. 760): 'wise' [AB, BAGD, BECNT, HNTC, ICC2, LN NICNT, WBC; GW, KJV, NET, NIV, NRSV], 'learned' [BAGD, NTC; REB], 'educated' [CEV, NLT, TEV], 'understanding, prudent' [LN].

d. ἀνόητος (LN **32.50**) (BAGD 1. p. 70): 'foolish' [BAGD, BECNT, HNTC, ICC2, **LN**, WBC; NASB, NCV, NET, NIV, NRSV], 'unwise' [KJV], 'uneducated' [CEV, NLT], 'unlearned' [AB, NICNT, NTC], 'ignorant' [TEV], 'simple' [REB], 'those who aren't (wise)' [GW], 'without understanding' [LN].

QUESTION—What is meant by the phrase Ἕλλησίν τε καὶ βαρβάροις 'both to Greeks and barbarians'?

The Ἕλλησίν would be all Gentiles united by Greek language and culture, including non-Greek people who came to speak Greek and shared to some degree in that culture [AB, BECNT, HNTC, ICC2, NTC, WBC]. The term βάρβαρος 'barbarian' was widely used of non-Greek speaking peoples, and by connotation refers to their supposedly inferior cultures [AB, NAC, NICNT, NTC]. They were looked down upon due to their unfamiliarity with Greek language and culture [BECNT]. It is a contrast between the cultured Greeks and all non-Greek peoples [SSA], between those who partook of Greco-Roman culture and those who did not [ICC2]. Greeks had used this contrasted pair to describe the cultured and the non-cultured [WBC], but Paul simply uses it to describe all races and classes of the Gentile world [NAC, WBC]. The contrast describes the civilized and the uncivilized [LN (11.95)]. 'Greeks' would be those in the city-states of the inner Mediterranean world, and barbarians would be those outside that cultivated circle [HNTC]. The distinction is not one of race or nation, but of culture, classifying people as being either within or outside civilized society [TH]. Greeks and non-Greeks is equivalent to all nations, and wise and unwise equates to all classes, so Paul is speaking of all men first in relation to national origins, and secondly with regard to culture [Gdt, Ho], or with reference to language and culture [NICNT]. This contrasted pair refers to all Gentiles, according to divisions of language and degrees of culture [ICC1]. Since 'Greeks' lacks the definite article, it is used generally here to describe a quality rather than the Greek people specifically [Mor].

QUESTION—Does this contrasted pair include or exclude the Jews?

1. It describes all Gentiles [AB, BECNT, ICC1, NAC, NICNT, St, WBC], that is, the non-Jewish world [AB], the whole of Gentile humanity [ICC2, St].

2. The pair of terms is used to sum up the whole of mankind [Ho, Mor], which would include Jews [Mor]. Greeks and non-Greeks means all nations [Ho].

QUESTION—What is meant by the contrasted pair σοφοῖς τε καὶ ἀνοήτοις 'both to wise and to foolish'?

It is a reference to those who might pride themselves on educational or intellectual attainment as compared with those who could not make such a claim [NAC, NICNT, St], meaning the educated and the uneducated [SSA]. The distinction is not of intellectual capacity, but of degree of learning [TH], those having intelligence and education and those not having those advantages [ICC2, Mor]. Paul is under obligation to preach the gospel to all without distinction of nationality or cultural development [Mu]. In using these two phrases together 'Greek and barbarian, wise and foolish', Paul encompasses all peoples in terms of extremes of culture and education [TH].

QUESTION—Do the two sets of contrasting pairs describe the same groups of people?

1. The same groups of people are intended in the second pair as in the first pair, but are seen here from a slightly different perspective, that of intellect or education [BECNT, ICC1, NAC, NTC]. The second pair further describes the first: he is debtor to Greeks and barbarians, which is to say, to both learned and unlearned [NTC].
2. The two sets of contrasted pairs are not necessarily equivalent [AB, ICC2, Mor, Mu, WBC]. Since it is possible that there would be foolish or wise people among either the cultured or uncultured, this division is not an identical match-up with the first [ICC2, Mor, Mu]. 'Wise' and 'foolish' denotes a wider, less restricted group of humanity than the first contrasted pair, which is more culturally defined [AB]. Since Greeks held a certain disdain for those without similar education and culture, the two categories were the same to them, but Paul simply uses the two pairs as a way of designating all Gentile humanity [WBC].

I-am debtor,[a]

LEXICON—a. ὀφειλέτης (LN 71.27) (BAGD 2.a., 2.b. p. 598): 'debtor' [BAGD (2.a., 2.b.), ICC2, NICNT, NTC, WBC; KJV, NET, NRSV], 'one who is obligated to' [BAGD (2.a.), BECNT, HNTC, LN; NIV, REB, TEV]. This phrase is translated 'I have an obligation to' [GW, REB], 'I have a great sense of obligation to' [NLT], 'I am under obligation' [HNTC; NASB], 'I am indebted' [AB], 'I have a duty' [NCV]. This clause plus εὐαγγελίσασθαι 'to preach the gospel' in the following verse is translated 'I must tell the good news to everyone' [CEV].

QUESTION—What is meant by the clause ὀφειλέτης εἰμί 'I am a debtor'?

This means that he is obligated to do something, and in this context, he is obligated to proclaim the gospel [Ho, SSA]. It expresses Paul's deep sense of missionary obligation by virtue of his divine calling as apostle to the Gentiles [AB, BECNT, Gdt, HNTC, ICC2, Mor, Mu, WBC]. He had a sense of obligation both to God and to people to carry the gospel to people everywhere regardless of ethnicity, culture, or intellectual sophistication [NAC]. Paul has a deep sense of obligation and calling [NICNT]. Paul's sense of obligation came from receiving God's commission as well as from the gracious way in which the Lord had saved him despite his having been a persecutor [NTC]. This was not a joyless burden but grew out of Paul's own personal transforming experience and a sense of privilege to share the gospel [NAC]. It refers to Paul's sense that Jesus has entrusted the gospel to him as something of great importance and value that must be passed on, and in his case to pass it on particularly to the Gentile world [St]. Paul is indebted to the non-Jewish world for that which has been gained from his Hellenistic education, his Roman citizenship, and his missionary experience among the Gentiles, but he also has a sense of obligation as apostle to the Gentiles and to Christ who died for him [AB]. Paul had a sense of obligation from the fact of God's having called him, but also because through his many travels he was a cosmopolitan man of his age, and he came to feel a sense of indebtedness to all types and conditions of people, whether cultured or not [WBC].

1:15 hence[a] with-regard-to[b] me (I am) eager[c] to-preach-the-gospel[d] also to-you the-ones in Rome.

LEXICON—a. οὕτως (LN 61.9) (BAGD 1.b. p. 597): 'hence' [AB, BAGD, NTC, WBC; NRSV, REB], 'so' [BAGD, ICC2, LN, NICNT; KJV, NASB, NET, NLT], 'so, then' [TEV], 'that is why' [HNTC; CEV, GW, NCV, NIV], 'therefore' [BECNT].

b. κατά (LN 89.4) (BAGD II.7.b. p. 408): 'with regard to' [LN], 'in relation to' [LN], not explicit [AB, BAGD, BECNT, HNTC, ICC2, NICNT, NTC, WBC; all versions except KJV, NASB]. The phrase τὸ κατ' ἐμέ 'with regard to me' is translated 'as much as in me is' [KJV], 'for my part' [NASB].

c. πρόθυμος (LN **25.69**) (BAGD p. 706): 'eager' [BAGD, BECNT, ICC2, **LN**; CEV, GW, NASB, NET, NIV, NLT, TEV], 'willing' [LN], not explicit [HNTC]. This adjective is also translated as an noun: '(my) eagerness' [AB, BAGD, NTC, WBC; NRSV, REB]; as a verb: 'I must' [CEV], 'I desire' [HNTC], 'I want so much' [NCV], 'I am ready' [KJV]. Here Paul, as is his custom, uses a neuter adjective as a substantive: 'my desire is' [NICNT], 'my eager desire is' [ICC2].

d. aorist mid. infin. of εὐαγγελίζω (LN 33.215) (BAGD 2.a.γ. p. 317): 'to preach the gospel' [AB, BAGD BECNT, HNTC, ICC2, NICNT, NTC, WBC; KJV, NASB, NET, NIV], 'to tell the good news' [LN; CEV, GW], 'to announce the gospel' [LN], 'to proclaim the gospel' [BAGD; NRSV], 'to declare the gospel' [REB], 'to preach the Good News' [NCV, TEV], 'to preach God's Good News' [NLT].

ROMANS 1:15

QUESTION—What relationship is indicated by οὕτως 'hence'?
This introduces an inference based on what has preceded it [AB, BAGD, BECNT, Gdt, Ho, ICC2, Mor, NICNT, SSA]. Paul's eagerness to preach in Rome arises from his sense of general obligation spoken of in the previous verse [Gdt, Ho, ICC2, Mor]. Having spoken of his general obligation to preach to Gentiles, Paul then applies that specifically to the Romans [NICNT].

QUESTION—What is the function of the phrase τὸ κατ' ἐμέ 'with regard to me' in this sentence?

1. It is used as a possessive pronoun modifying πρόθυμον 'eagerness', with the verb 'is' implied, and the rest of the sentence forming a predicate [AB, ICC2, NICNT, NTC, WBC; NRSV, REB]: my eagerness is to preach to you in Rome. In Hellenistic Greek κατ' ἐμέ was used as an equivalent of the genitive possessive pronoun μου 'my' [NICNT].
2. It has the connotation of 'as far as I'm concerned' [Gdt, HNTC, ICC1, Mor, Mu, SSA]. Paul is saying that so far as it rests with him he would do this, meaning he would if God allowed [ICC1], or if circumstances did not prevent it [Gdt].

QUESTION—Is Paul saying that he is eager to preach the gospel there, or that he previously had been eager to do so?

1. The implied verb would be in the present tense: he is eager to preach there [AB, BECNT, HNTC, ICC2, Mor, Mu, NICNT, TNTC, WBC; CEV, GW, KJV, NASB, NCV, NET, NIV, NLT, TEV]. 1:15 is tied to 1:14, which uses a present tense verb, indicating that Paul still wants to preach in Rome [NICNT].
2. The implied verb would be in the past tense; because of what he had been called to do, he wanted to preach [SSA].

QUESTION—Who is the referent of the plural pronoun ὑμῖν 'you' and in what sense are the Romans Christians included among those to whom Paul desires to 'preach the gospel'?

1. The pronoun 'you' refers to the Roman Christians [AB, ICC2, NICNT, WBC]. The meaning of the verb includes more than just evangelism, it encompasses the whole range of Paul's ministry including his explanation of the gospel contained in this letter [WBC]. Paul desires to teach and to disciple Roman believers, building upon their earlier evangelization, because for Paul preaching the gospel includes the entire process from initial preaching on through to the point of having an established church [NICNT]. Paul preaching in Rome would be brief, while he is passing through on his way to Spain [AB].
2. The pronoun 'you' refers to people in Rome generally and indicates Paul's desire to evangelize in Rome [BECNT, Gdt, Mor, SSA]. Paul desired to use all opportunities to evangelize and to win more converts [BECNT]. This refers to what Paul had planned to do among the Romans in the past [SSA]. It is to unbelievers in Rome that Paul wants to preach the gospel [Gdt, Mor], and so increase the church there [Gdt].

DISCOURSE UNIT: 1:16–17 [AB, BECNT, Gdt, GNT, HNTC, ICC1, ICC2, Mor, Mu, NAC, NICNT, NTC, SSA, TNTC, WBC; CEV, NET, TEV]. The topic is the theme of the letter [AB, BECNT, Gdt, ICC2, Mor, Mu, NICNT, NTC, WBC], the gospel of God's righteousness [BECNT], the gospel is the source of salvation for all [AB], the gospel [HNTC], the power of the Gospel [GNT; CEV, NET, TEV], righteousness from God [NAC], the righteousness of God revealed [TNTC], righteousness obtained by God's gift through faith [ICC1].

1:16 For[a] **I-am- not -ashamed-of**[b] **the gospel,**[c]

TEXT—Some manuscripts add τοῦ Χριστοῦ 'of Christ' following εὐαγγέλιον 'gospel'. GNT does not mention this variant. The reading τοῦ Χριστοῦ is taken by KJV, where it is translated 'of Christ', and NLT, where it is translated 'about Christ' [NLT].

LEXICON—a. γάρ (LN 89.23) (BAGD 1.b. p. 152): 'for' [BAGD, BECNT, HNTC, ICC2, LN, NICNT, NTC, WBC; KJV, NASB, NET, NLT, NRSV, REB], 'now' [AB], not explicit [CEV, GW, NCV, NIV, TEV].

b. pres. mid. (deponent = act.) indic. of ἐπαισχύνομαι (LN 25.193) (BAGD 1. p. 282): 'to be ashamed of' [AB, BAGD, BECNT, HNTC, ICC2, LN, NICNT, NTC, WBC; GW, KJV, NASB, NET, NIV, NLT, NRSV, REB]. The phrase οὐ...ἐπαισχύνομαι 'I am not ashamed of' is translated by a positive statement, 'I am proud of' [CEV, NCV], 'I have complete confidence in' [TEV].

c. εὐαγγέλιον (LN **33.217**) (BAGD 1.a. p. 318): 'gospel' [AB, BAGD, BECNT, HNTC, ICC2, **LN**, NICNT, NTC, WBC; KJV, NASB, NET, NIV, NRSV, REB, TEV], 'good news' [BAGD, LN; CEV], 'Good News' [GW, NCV, NLT].

QUESTION—What relationship is indicated by γάρ 'for'?

It introduces the reason for Paul's eagerness to preach in Rome [BECNT, Ho, ICC2, Mor, Mu, NICNT, NTC, SSA, St]. This and the γάρ that follows introduce the main thrust and direction for the rest of the letter, explaining the reason for the very existence of Paul's ministry and giving an outline of what he will begin arguing until the end of chapter 15 [WBC]. It signals a tail-head link to a transitional paragraph consisting of 1:16–17, and which states the theme for 1:18–11:36. The tail of this link is 'proclaim the good news' in 1:15 and 'good news' in 1:16 is the head. It also introduces the claim made in 1:16 about Paul's confidence in the power of the gospel message, for which the justification is given in 1:17 [SSA].

QUESTION—How does the grammar of this verse (and verse 17) affect its interpretation as being the theme of the letter?

Greek clauses which are grammatically subordinate may actually have prominence and emphasis because of their content, which is the case here; despite the subordinate clause construction, these verses are the theme statement of the letter [BECNT, NICNT]. 1:16–17 contain the central theme of this epistle, which is that the righteousness of God is revealed in the gospel; Paul's desire to preach, which he discusses in 1:15, is directly tied to what the gospel is, and it is that content of the gospel that gives him the boldness to preach it [BECNT]. The verses both continue the thought of 1:8–15 as well as begin that of 1:18–32, and they represent a summary of Paul's theology as a whole [HNTC].

QUESTION—What is the significance of the negative form of Paul's assertion in this verse?

1. Paul is speaking of his own confidence and employs the literary device known as litotes, which is the negation of an already negative word, constituting an understatement for rhetorical effect and used in order to make an emphatic positive statement [SSA, TH, TNTC]. The meaning is that Paul counts it a great honor to proclaim the gospel [TNTC], that he is proud and overjoyed to have the opportunity to preach the gospel [NTC], that he has complete confidence in the gospel [TH].
2. Paul is speaking of the psychological state of shame and fear, and of hesitancy to suffer harm because of the gospel [BECNT], and he is saying that he does not have such shame about the gospel message [Ho, NAC, St]. Some degree of embarrassment about the gospel would have been natural in the capital of the Roman world [AB, Gdt, HNTC, ICC1, Mu, NAC, NICNT, St]. This reflects a sober recognition that because of this world's hostility to it, the gospel is by its very nature something about which Christians may be tempted to be ashamed [ICC2]. It reflects Jesus' warning against being afraid to acknowledge him publicly (Mark 8:28, Luke 9:26) and which Paul repeats to Timothy in 2 Tim. 1:8 [AB, St]. It is the negative equivalent of 'confess' in those passages; Paul is ready and even proud to proclaim the gospel despite the hostility it can arouse [AB]. Although Paul has suffered for preaching the gospel he is not afraid to continue preaching nor is he ashamed of the message, because it has proven adequate to meet the needs of Paul and those who listened to him [Mor]. He would have been ashamed if it was found that he was acting on a misplaced confidence in the message [WBC]. Paul is both confident in the efficacy of the gospel as well as unashamed to proclaim it, even in the capital of the empire [Mu]. Paul is expressing both his willingness to confess the gospel publicly as well as the fact that he was not afraid to do so [BECNT]. The gospel is foolishness to some and a stumbling block to others, so whenever the gospel is preached opposition and ridicule may result [St]. It can be understood both socially and psychologically in that he comes to the capital of Rome to proclaim a gospel considered foolishness to some and a stumbling block to others, and could expect criticism and condescension as a result [AB, Mu, NAC].

for[a] it-is (the) power[b] of-God for[c] salvation[d] to everyone believing,[e]

LEXICON—a. γάρ (LN 89.23) (BAGD p. 152): 'for', [BAGD, BECNT, ICC2, LN, NICNT, NTC; KJV, NET], 'since' [HNTC, WBC], 'because' [NCV, NIV], not explicit [AB; CEV, GW, NASB, NLT, NRSV, REB, TEV].

b. δύναμις (LN 76.1) (BAGD 1. p. 207): 'power' [AB, BAGD, BECNT, HNTC, ICC2, LN, NICNT, NTC, WBC; all versions except CEV, NLT], 'power...at work' [NLT]. The phrase 'for it is the power of God' is translated 'it is the operation of God's power working' [HNTC], 'it is the power God uses' [NCV], 'it is God's powerful way' [CEV].

c. εἰς (LN 89.57) (BAGD 4.e. p. 229): 'for' [AB, NICNT, NTC, WBC; NASB, NET, NIV, NRSV], 'unto' [KJV], 'resulting in' [BECNT], 'towards' [HNTC], 'at work (saving)' [NLT], not explicit [GW, NCV, TEV].

d. σωτηρία (LN 21.26) (BAGD 2. p. 801): 'salvation' [AB, BAGD, BECNT, HNTC, LN, NICNT, NTC, WBC; KJV, NASB, NET, NIV, NRSV]. The phrase εἰς σωτηρίαν 'for salvation' is translated 'to save' [GW, NCV, TEV], 'saving' [ICC2; NLT, REB], 'of saving' [CEV].

e. pres. act. participle of πιστεύω (LN **31.102,** 31.85) (BAGD 2.b. p. 661): 'to believe (in)' [AB, BAGD BECNT, ICC2, LN (31.85), NICNT, WBC; GW, KJV, NASB, NCV, NET, NIV, NLT, TEV], 'to be a believer, to be a Christian' [LN (31.102)], 'to have confidence in' [LN (31.85)], 'to have faith (in)' [HNTC, LN (31.85), NTC; CEV, NRSV, REB], 'to exercise faith' [NTC], 'to trust' [BAGD, LN (31.85)]. The phrase παντὶ τῷ πιστεύοντι 'to everyone believing' is translated 'to everyone who is a believer' [**LN** (31.102)].

QUESTION—What relationship is indicated by γάρ 'for'?

This introduces the reason for Paul's statement that he is not ashamed of the gospel, which is that it mediates the power of God that leads to salvation [BECNT, Gdt, Ho, ICC2, Mor, Mu, NAC, NICNT, NTC, SSA, St]. Only those who have experienced the effects of the gospel in their own lives can overcome the temptation to be ashamed of it [St]. This γάρ and the one that follow it introduce two reasons that Paul is not ashamed of the gospel, which is that it is God's power to save, and that it reveals a righteousness from God [NAC]. This γάρ and the one that precedes it introduce what Paul will argue overall in the letter and why Paul ministers as an apostle [WBC]. Paul glories in the gospel and sees it as a great honor to be able to preach it [TNTC].

QUESTION—What is meant by δύναμις γὰρ θεοῦ ἐστιν εἰς σωτηρίαν 'it is the power of God for salvation'?

When the gospel is preached, the power of God is at work, resulting in salvation [AB, BECNT, Ho, ICC2, Mor, Mu, NAC, NICNT]. This refers to the effective and transforming power that accompanies the preaching of the gospel, which is effective in calling believers to salvation [BECNT, WBC]. God is the one who makes the gospel efficacious [Ho]. 'Power' means that the message has a dynamic quality to it, one in which God is actively at work reaching out to the hearts of people [NAC]. The message of the gospel is a power that is now unleashed in human history, directly related to the power of Jesus Christ himself, through whom God has unleashed his own power [AB]. The gospel is a force that has all of the omnipotence of God behind it

[ICC1]. The gospel is the means by which God utilizes his power to save people; his saving power attends the proclamation of the gospel, and the word εἰς 'unto' also signals a means-result relationship. Furthermore, 'power' is an attributive concept and may best be expressed as modifying a verb form of the Greek noun σωτηρίαν 'salvation' and having the sense 'God powerfully saves' [SSA].

QUESTION—What is meant by σωτηρία 'salvation'?
Salvation focuses on deliverance from eschatological judgment and from the wrath of God [BECNT, HNTC, ICC2, Mor, NICNT, WBC]. The future sense of salvation should be understood here [AB, BECNT, HNTC], as it is a deliverance from judgment that is only fully realized at the last day [NICNT]. The blessing of eschatological salvation can also be enjoyed in this life [AB, WBC]. It expresses generally God's provision for the spiritual needs of people including restoring them to a share of God's glory [NICNT]. It refers to deliverance from the power of sin [TH]. It has both negative and positive content [Gdt, Ho, ICC1, ICC2, Mor, Mu, NICNT, NTC]. Negatively, it is deliverance from sin and punishment [Ho, Mu, NTC], and divine wrath [Gdt, HNTC, ICC1, ICC2, Mor], the bondage of sin [Mor], guilt, pollution, slavery, alienation from God [NTC]. Positively, it is being admitted to eternal life [HNTC, Ho, ICC1], being brought to righteousness and life [Mu], God's blessings [Mor], the restoration of the glory of God which is already beginning to reflect its splendor into the present experience of those who will one day experience it in full [ICC2]. Salvation has an already-not-yet quality about it, touching both the future and the past, because it not only means being delivered from future judgment, but also represents the fulfillment of God's promises in the past to Israel [BECNT], eternal life in fellowship with God [Gdt], a state of freedom, righteousness, holiness, fellowship with God, and everlasting life [NTC], forgiveness and deliverance from the results of sin, including justification, sanctification, and ultimately glorification [NAC]. It brings reconciliation, forgiveness, the privilege of becoming God's child, having his Spirit, the beginning of personal transformation, and becoming a part of God's new community [St].

QUESTION—What is meant by the preposition εἰς in the phrase εἰς σωτηρίαν 'for salvation'?

1. The preposition indicates result [BECNT, Gdt, HNTC, Mor, NAC, SSA, TH, WBC]. The gospel is the means by which God utilizes his power to save [SSA]. Paul equates the gospel with God's power to save those who believe; that is, by means of the gospel, God saves [TH].
2. The preposition indicates purpose [AB, NTC].

QUESTION—What is meant by the participle πιστεύοντι 'believing'?
It means to put one's full trust in Christ [NICNT, SSA], and not simply giving assent to the truth of something [Ho, SSA]. It involves commitment and trust in God [BECNT]. While intellectual assent is not excluded, Paul's emphasis is on surrender to God as an act of the will, and on trust in a person, not simply in a set of doctrines [NICNT]. It is to believe and trust,

and to receive and confide in Christ as the gospel presents him [Ho]. Faith is believing obedience, entrusting oneself totally to God's grace and wisdom [HNTC]. It is simply accepting the salvation offered in the preaching of the gospel [Gdt]. People must react to the gospel by placing their faith in the message and in Christ Jesus whom it announces, as well as in God from whom it originates [AB, ICC2]. It is to accept the gospel [AB, ICC2], and to surrender to the judgment and mercy of God [ICC2]. This faith is a trusting acceptance of and commitment to the gospel message, as well as on ongoing orientation and motivation in a believer's life [WBC]. It implies confidence and trust, as well as being persuaded of a truth [Ho]. It is the simple acceptance of what is offered; if the gospel is God laying hold of someone, faith is the act of allowing God to do so [Gdt].

QUESTION—What is the significance of the present tense of the participle πιστεύοντι 'believing'?

Paul's use of the present tense shows that his focus is not solely on an initial act of faith, but a continuing commitment that provides the access for God's saving power in human life [NAC, WBC].

QUESTION—What is the significance of the phrase παντὶ τῷ πιστεύοντι 'to everyone believing'?

A recurring theme of Romans is that God's salvation is available to all, being a fulfillment of the OT promise of the universal reign of God, and has particular reference in this epistle to the removal of barriers between Jews and Gentiles [NICNT]. Here he emphasizes the universal reach of the gospel, that it is extended to Gentiles as well as Jews, and that God's saving promises to the Jews are now being fulfilled among Gentiles [BECNT], it is efficacious for all those who believe whether Jew or Gentile [Ho]. This shows that the gospel is aimed at all of humanity [AB, Gdt, Mor]. The word 'every' emphasizes a point made throughout the book that the gospel is God's effective power for salvation without exception for all who accept it [ICC2]. The gospel is universal in that it is for all, and it is free, being offered to those who believe [Gdt, HNTC]. This means that salvation comes to all only by faith, and faith is the condition without which God does not save [AB, Mu, NAC, WBC]. This is the one significant qualification to the statement that salvation is for everyone [Mor, NTC].

both to-(the)-Jew first and to-(the)-Greek.[a]

LEXICON—a. Ἕλλην (LN 11.40, 11.90) (BAGD 2.a. p. 252): 'Greek' [AB, LN (11.40, 11.90); KJV, NET, NRSV, REB], 'the Greek' [BECNT, ICC2, NICNT, NTC; KJV, NASB, NET, NRSV, REB], 'Greeks' [GW]. 'Gentile' [BAGD, HNTC, LN (11.40), WBC; NIV], 'non-Jew' [LN (11.40)], 'those who are not Jews' [NCV]. This singular noun is translated as a plural: 'Gentiles' [CEV, NLT, TEV].

QUESTION—In what sense is the word πρῶτον 'first' to be understood in the phrase Ἰουδαίῳ τε πρῶτον καὶ Ἕλληνι 'to the Jew first and to the Greek'?
1. While Paul asserts the universalism of the gospel and the underlying equality of all men as regards response to the gospel, he also speaks of particularism in reference to the priority of the Jews in God's overall plan of salvation [AB, BECNT, HNTC, ICC1, ICC2, Mor, Mu, NICNT, NTC, WBC]. Although all people have equal access to the gospel, Paul believes that the gospel has a special relevance for the Jew [Mu, NICNT], since the Jews were the ones through whom God's oracles and the promise of the gospel came [Mu]. The Jews were privileged to have had the gospel revealed to them first, but when they rejected it, the apostles took it to the Gentiles [NTC]. Because of their election the Jews were the first to hear the gospel [HNTC, Mor, Mu]. Paul acknowledges that the Jews have a privileged status in God's plan of salvation, and their priority is expressed not only in the fact that the gospel was preached to them first, but also in that it had been promised long before in their own sacred scriptures [AB]. The meaning of πρῶτον is theological in that God first chose the Jews, but also historical in that the gospel was preached among them first of all [St]. The Jews do have a certain priority in God's saving purpose, though that does not change the terms of salvation at all, since it is by faith for all [WBC]. Paul concedes the Jewish claim of priority and is anxious to conciliate them [ICC1]. Paul's missionary practice of beginning in the local synagogue as a starting point for preaching is rooted in his belief that the Jews were specially God's chosen people [BECNT].
2. This refers to their being first in historical sequence [Gdt, Ho, NAC, SSA, TH]. This refers to the fact of the gospel having been first preached to the Jews [Gdt, Ho, TH]. The promise of the gospel had been communicated via the Jewish Scriptures and prophets, and Paul went first to Jews before going on to Gentiles [Gdt]. Historically God worked through Israel first, and now the message goes to all people [NAC]. This means priority in time, not in a more general overall priority since that seems contrary to the thrust of the book in promoting oneness between Jews and Greeks [Gdt, SSA].

QUESTION—What is meant by Ἕλλην 'Greek' in this phrase and context?
Since it stands in contrast to 'Jews', it is equivalent to Gentiles, all non-Jews [AB, BECNT, Gdt, HNTC, Ho, ICC1, ICC2, Mor, Mu, NAC, NICNT, NTC, SSA, TH, WBC], and would include the 'barbarians' of 1:14 [AB, Mu]. It refers to any person influenced by Greek culture, that is, the Gentiles [NTC]. All humanity is summed up in the phrase 'Jew and Greek', for salvation is open to all [AB, Mor, NAC].

1:17 For[a] (the) righteousness[b] of-God is-revealed[c] in[d] it

LEXICON—a. γάρ (LN 89.23) (BAGD p. 152): 'for', [AB, BAGD, BECNT, HNTC, ICC2, LN, WBC; KJV, NASB, NET, NIV, NRSV, TEV], 'because' [REB], not explicit [CEV, GW, NCV, NLT].

b. δικαιοσύνη (LN **34.46**) (BAGD 3. p. 197): 'righteousness' [BAGD, BECNT, HNTC, ICC2, NICNT, NTC, WBC; KJV, NASB, NET, NIV, NRSV, REB], 'uprightness' [AB]. The phrase δικαιοσύνη...θεοῦ 'righteousness of God' is translated 'how God puts people right with himself' [**LN;** TEV], 'how God makes people right with himself' [NCV], 'how God makes us right in his sight' [NLT], 'how God accepts everyone' [CEV], 'God's approval' [GW].
  c. pres. pass. indic. of ἀποκαλύπτω (LN 28.38) (BAGD 1. p. 92): 'to be revealed' [AB, BAGD, BECNT, HNTC, ICC2, LN, NICNT, NTC, WBC; GW, KJV, NASB, NET, NIV, NRSV], 'to be made fully known' [LN], 'to be disclosed' [BAGD, LN], 'to be brought to light' [BAGD], 'to be seen at work' [REB]. The phrase ἐν αὐτῷ ἀποκαλύπτεται 'is revealed in it' is translated 'this Good News tells us how' [NLT], 'the good news tells how' [CEV] 'the Good News shows how' [NCV], 'the gospel reveals how' [TEV].
  d. ἐν (LN 83.13): 'in' [BECNT, LN, NICNT, NTC, WBC; GW, NASB, NET, NIV, NRSV, REB], 'therein is' [KJV], not explicit [CEV, NCV, NLT, TEV].

QUESTION—What relationship is indicated by γάρ 'for'?

This indicates the reason why the gospel is the power of God that leads to salvation, which is that the righteousness of God is revealed in it [BECNT, HNTC, Ho, ICC2, Mu, NICNT, NTC, St]. It introduces grounds for the claim in 1:16 [Mor, SSA]. It introduces an explanation for why the gospel brings salvation, which is that it offers the righteousness of God [Gdt]. It introduces a second reason why he is not ashamed of the gospel, which is that it reveals a righteousness from God [NAC].

QUESTION—What is the meaning of the genitive construction δικαιοσύνη...θεοῦ 'righteousness of God'?

In the history of interpretation there have primarily been three meanings assigned to the phrase 'the righteousness of God': one is the attribute of righteousness which characterizes God, another is the saving activity of God, and a third is the status of right relationship with himself that God grants. These definitions are not mutually exclusive, and many interpreters understand the phrase as involving more than one of these areas of meaning [NICNT]. Note that there is a considerable amount of overlap possible between the positions listed below, and one does not rule out the other.

  1. It is a righteousness or righteous status that comes as a gift from God, because of what he has done [Gdt, Ho, ICC2, Mor, NTC, SSA, TH]. The genitive indicates origin, that the righteous status comes from God [ICC2]. While Paul primarily meant to focus on righteousness as a status granted by God and not God's righteous activity, a direct reference to either one inherently carries an indirect reference to the other [ICC2]. It is God's action of declaring people righteous [Gdt, SSA], meaning that their guilt for sin is ended [SSA]. It is the saving activity of God whereby he puts men in right relationship with himself [TH]. It is the righteousness

freely imputed to a sinner by God's sovereign grace because of Christ's substitutionary atonement [NTC].
2. It is both the saving action of God, whereby he makes righteous, as well as the status of righteousness that he grants through that saving intervention [NICNT]. It is primarily God's action to create, restore, or sustain his people in covenant relation with himself; there is a dynamic relationship between the subjective aspect of God's saving activity and the objective aspect of the status of right standing, and neither is to be excluded [WBC].
3. This is a combination of God's own quality of righteousness, and of his action in making people right before him through the gift of righteousness [AB, HNTC, ICC1, Mu, TNTC]. This is a subjective genitive which speaks of God's attribute of uprightness, both in his being as well as his activity, an uprightness that is dynamic and which is expressed in his saving and acquitting activity [AB]. It is God's personal righteousness as well as the righteousness with which the sinner is justified through faith [TNTC]. God's righteousness issues in his saving and vindicating work [HNTC]. God attributes righteousness to the believer because he is righteousness himself [ICC1].
4. It is a divine quality, an activity, and a gift [BECNT, Mu, NAC, St]. It is God's righteous initiative in putting sinful people right with himself and granting them his righteousness as their own [St]. The righteousness of God is God's righteousness, but it is also a gift and a power; God grants his own righteousness as a gift to those who have faith in Jesus Christ, but his righteousness also expresses itself as divine activity in which God saves his people and judges all others [BECNT]. It is primarily the righteous status that results from God's saving work, although the other aspects of attribute and saving activity are not to be excluded [NAC]. It is God's saving activity, as God's righteousness and salvation are used as parallel expressions, and the revelation of God's righteousness is his salvation actively working to bring redemption into the realm of human sin and ruin. But it is also a God-righteousness, a property of deity and characterized by divine qualities and by the perfection belonging to all that God is and does. Finally, it is also a righteousness of which God is the author [Mu].

QUESTION—What is the relation between an imputed forensic righteousness and the righteousness that is a matter of a changed character?

Imputed righteousness is offered to man, that is, forensically, as opposed to an internally communicated righteousness by the gift of the Holy Spirit [Gdt, Ho], a status that is granted to the believer [NICNT]. Righteousness is not simply something that one has on his or her own as a measure of ethical norms, but is a matter of one's relationships as a social being; here the revealing of God's righteousness is God's creating or restoring a covenant relationship with himself, such that it would be right to say not that only does God count people righteous in the forensic sense, but that he also makes them righteous in the relational sense [WBC]. This righteousness is a righteous status that is granted as a divine gift, but sanctification and justification, though distinguished, should not be separated as though someone could receive righteousness from Christ without also laying hold of sanctification [ICC2]. God's righteousness is forensic, but it is also his saving power that transforms people [BECNT].

QUESTION—In what sense is the righteousness of God being revealed?
1. It is revealed in the sense that the gospel explains how people can have righteousness [AB, Ho, ICC2, SSA, TH]. It is revealed in the sense that God's plan of salvation is now enunciated and disclosed as the gospel is spread [AB]. The gospel message reveals something new that was not known previously, and which God must reveal for anyone to know it [Mor], because it is a radical departure from conventional wisdom about how righteousness is to be had [NAC]. It is revealed in the preaching of the gospel message, wherever and whenever it is preached [ICC2].
2. It is also revealed is a dynamic and active sense [BECNT, Mu, NICNT, WBC]. It is revealed in the sense that through the preaching of the gospel the righteousness of God is being unfolded or manifested in the plane of human history in eschatological fullness [NICNT]. God's saving power and activity are revealed as an eschatological event that has invaded history [BECNT]. It is manifested not just to human apprehension or recognition, but in action and operation, in its saving efficacy [Mu]. It is revealed not just as something being announced, but as something that is having an impact in the lives of people and which is taking effect in their conversion [WBC].
3. It was revealed in what Christ suffered on the cross in man's place [HNTC].

QUESTION—What is the antecedent of 'it'?
It is the gospel, mentioned in 1:16 [AB, BECNT, HNTC, Ho, ICC2, Mor, Mu, NAC, NICNT, SSA, St; CEV, GW, NCV, NET, NIV, NLT, TEV].

from^a faith to faith,

LEXICON—a. ἐκ (LN **78.48**) (BAGD 6.d. p. 236): 'from' [ICC2, **LN**, NICNT, NTC, WBC; KJV, NET], 'beginning in' [REB], 'begins with' [GW], 'by' [BECNT; NIV], 'through' [AB; NRSV, TEV], 'on the basis of' [HNTC], 'this is accomplished from' [NLT]. The phrase ἐκ πίστεως εἰς πίστιν '(is revealed) from faith to faith' [ICC2, NTC, WBC; KJV, NASB, NET] is also translated 'from faith for faith' [NICNT], 'through faith and for faith' [AB], '(righteousness is revealed) on the basis of nothing but faith' [HNTC], 'as a matter of faith from beginning to end' [**LN**], '(a righteousness) that is by faith from first to last' [NIV], '(this approval) begins and ends with faith' [GW], '(shows how) God makes people right with himself—that it begins and ends with faith' [NCV], '(the righteous of God is seen at work), beginning in faith and ending in faith' [REB], 'it is through faith from beginning to end' [TEV], '(a righteousness) that is by faith from first to last' [BECNT], '(this is accomplished) from start to finish by faith' [NLT], 'from faith for faith' [NICNT], '(is revealed) through faith for faith' [NRSV], '(God accepts) everyone who has faith, but only those who have faith' [CEV]. The repetition of 'faith' gives this expression special emphasis [BAGD].

QUESTION—What is meant by ἐκ πίστεως εἰς πίστιν 'from faith to faith'?

1. The phrase is emphatic in nature, highlighting the centrality or importance of faith that salvation is completely by faith [BECNT, Gdt, HNTC, Ho, ICC1, ICC2, LN, Mor, Mu, NICNT, NTC, SSA, TH, TNTC; CEV, GW, NCV, NIV, NLT, REB, TEV]. It is faith and only faith that can put us in right relation to God [NICNT]. God's gift of righteousness is altogether by faith [ICC2]. It is intensive, meaning that it is entirely by faith [Ho]. The idiomatic expression stresses that the Christian life is by faith from beginning to end [SSA], from faith from start to finish [HNTC]. 'From faith' indicates that it is only by faith that anyone is the beneficiary of God's righteousness, and 'to faith' indicates that every believer is such a beneficiary [Mu]. In this righteousness faith is everything [Gdt].
2. This refers to the growth or development of faith and means 'from one degree of faith to another' [AB, NAC]. Righteousness is received by faith and leads to continually increasing faith [NAC]. The preposition ἐκ is used instrumentally, meaning that salvation is 'through' faith, but the preposition εἰς indicates purpose, meaning 'for' faith in the sense of progressing in the intensity of one's faith as devotion to God [AB].
3. While it mainly speaks of the centrality of faith, it also refers to a faith that grows and moves forward. Both the deepening of the faith of the individual and the spread of faith in the world at large are meant, and one sense should not be focused on to the exclusion of the other [ICC1].
4. 'From...to' is an idiom indicating progression and probably involves a word play on the ambiguity of the word faith and faithfulness; here it has the sense of movement from God's faithfulness to his covenant promises to man's response of faith [WBC].

QUESTION—With what element in the sentence does the phrase 'from faith to faith' refer?

1. It is linked to the verb: it is revealed from faith to faith, revelation is made known only through faith [Gdt, HNTC, ICC1, Mu, WBC; perhaps KJV, NASB, NET, NRSV]. Perhaps it means that righteousness is obtained by faith because it was designed for faith [NET].
2. It is linked to the phrase δικαιοσύνη θεοῦ 'a righteousness from God' [BECNT, Ho, ICC2, Mor, NAC, NICNT, NTC, SSA, St; GW, NCV, NIV, NLT, TEV]. That is, it is a righteousness from God that is obtained altogether by faith or which is by faith from first to last.

just-as it-is-written,[a]

LEXICON—a. perf. pass. indic. of γράφω (LN 33.61) (BAGD 2.c. p. 166): 'to be written' [AB, BAGD, BECNT, HNTC, LN, NTC, WBC; KJV, NASB,

NET, NIV, NRSV]. This is used as a formula for introducing OT quotations [BAGD]. This is translated 'as the Scriptures say' [CEV, NLT], 'as the scripture says' [NCV, TEV], 'as Scripture says' [GW, REB].

QUESTION—What is the significance of the phrase καθὼς γέγραπται 'just as it is written'?

Paul quotes Habakkuk 2:4 to support his argument [AB, BECNT, Gdt, HNTC, Ho, Mor, Mu, NAC, NICNT, NTC, St, TNTC, WBC]. He uses this quote to support the theme of this epistle [AB, BECNT, Gdt, WBC]. This introduces supporting evidence from the OT regarding the statement that righteousness is attained only on the basis of faith [BECNT, Ho, ICC2, NAC, NICNT, St, TH, TNTC]. He uses it to support the theme of the letter, which is that the upright finds life through faith [AB], that the saving righteousness of God is by faith from first to last [BECNT]. He uses it to support his assertion that the righteousness of God that results in justification is made known only through faith [Mu]. It supports his theme statement that the salvation being revealed in the gospel is a result of the outreach of God's faithfulness to the faith of believers [WBC].

But the righteous[b] (person) by[c] faith[d] will-live.[e]

LEXICON—a. δέ (LN 89.124): 'but' [LN, NTC; NASB, NCV], not explicit [AB, BECNT, HNTC, ICC2, NICNT, WBC; all versions except NASB, NCV].

b. δίκαιος (LN **34.47**, 88.12) (BAGD 1.b. p. 195): 'the righteous' [BAGD, BECNT, HNTC, ICC2, LN (34.47, 88.12), NICNT, NTC, WBC; NASB, NET, NIV, NLT, NRSV], 'the just' [LN (88.12); KJV], 'the people God accepts' [CEV], 'he who has been put right with God' [**LN** (34.47); TEV], 'he who is in a right relation with God' [**LN** (34.47)], 'those who are right with God' [NCV], 'the one who is upright' [AB], 'whoever is justified' [REB], 'he who is righteous' [ICC2], 'the one who is righteous' [NRSV], 'the person who has God's approval' [GW].

c. ἐκ (LN 89.77, 89.25): 'by' [BECNT, HNTC, ICC2, NICNT, NTC, WBC; KJV, NASB, NCV, NET, NIV, NRSV], 'by means of' [LN (89.77)], 'through' [AB; NLT, REB, TEV], 'because of' [LN (89.25); CEV, GW].

d. πίστις (LN **31.85**, 31.102): 'faith' [AB, BECNT, HNTC, ICC2, LN (31.85, 31.102), NICNT, NTC, WBC; all versions except NCV], 'trusting in him' [NCV].

e. fut. mid. indic. of ζάω (LN 23.88) (BAGD 2.b.β. p. 336): 'to live' [BECNT, HNTC, ICC2, LN, NICNT, NTC, WBC; all versions except NLT, REB], 'to have life' [BAGD; NLT], 'to be alive' [LN], 'to gain life' [REB], 'to find life' [AB].

QUESTION—Is there as difference in the meaning of the quotation here as compared with the Habakkuk passage?

The original text of Hob. 2:4 is uncertain, with the Hebrew text and the various Greek translations differing from one another in some details, mainly with regard to whether a personal pronoun should be included and with regard to what it modifies: 'his faith' (Heb text, Aquila), 'his own faith' (Symmachus), 'my faith' (LXX), 'my righteous one' (some LXX manuscripts) [NICNT]. Note that the difference in emphasis between the positions listed below is not great.

1. Paul uses the quotation with a slightly different nuance of meaning here [ICC2, NAC, NICNT, TH, TNTC]. Paul's quotation does not agree precisely either in form or meaning [TH]. The meaning in the Habakkuk passage is that the righteous are preserved through difficulties by their faithfulness or loyalty to God, but Paul uses the quote to make the somewhat different point that those who are righteous by faith will live [ICC2, NAC, TH, TNTC]. Habakkuk's statement originally addresses the person who is righteous but who is facing difficulties along with apparent contradictions between the promises of God and historical events, whereas in Romans Paul uses the quote to explain how one can attain right standing with God, and so live eternally. However, these differences should not be magnified, because in Habakkuk faith and faithfulness are inseparable and the key point in both passages is that faith is the key to a person's relationship with God [NICNT]. Although Paul has a somewhat different meaning than the original, the terms of what Habakkuk says are general enough to allow for Paul's application here [NAC, TNTC].
2. The sense and meaning is basically the same in the present context as in Habakkuk [AB, BECNT, Gdt, Ho, ICC1, Mor, Mu, NTC, St, WBC]. The OT depicts the righteous as being those who are faithful in obedience to the covenant obligations by keeping the commands of God; Paul's emphasis here is on trust and reliance on God for righteousness and life, since his conception of authentic faith involves obedience, nevertheless we should not see too great a distinction between 'faithfulness' in Habakkuk and 'faith' in Paul, since in both Habakkuk and Paul there is a vital connection between faith and faithfulness [BECNT]. The Hebrew word *emunah*, here translated 'faith', can also refer to one's fidelity or constancy, but the two concepts are not so far apart considering that one may only exercise constancy by trusting in God, and both Paul and Habakkuk speak of a humble dependence on God [Mor]. The wording of what Habakkuk says is general enough to allow for Paul's application here [Mor, NAC, TNTC]. Paul's use of Hab. 2:4 generally supports Habakkuk's oracle rather than doing violence to it [Mor, TNTC]. The sense both in Habakkuk and here is that the righteous shall live through faith [AB, Gdt, NTC]. Because Paul's comment 'from faith to faith' can be taken to mean God's faithfulness reaching out to man's faith, including both the initial reception of the gospel and the continuing process towards salvation, the Hab. 2:4 passage serves particularly well as Paul's proof text here, which he may have cited in a deliberately ambiguous manner in order to extend the meaning; that is, someone who has a saving relationship to God because of the outreach of God's faithfulness to his or her

faith will experience the fullness of life that God intended [WBC]. Both Paul and Habakkuk affirm that faith is essential and that the righteous shall live [St].

QUESTION—With what is the prepositional phrase ἐκ πίστεως 'by faith' connected, and what then is the meaning?

Note that there is a certain amount of overlap possible between the positions listed below, and one does not necessarily rule out the other.

1. It is connected with the noun δίκαιος 'righteous' and the sense is 'the one who by faith is righteous shall live' [BAGD, Ho, ICC2, Mor, NAC, NICNT, TH, TNTC; CEV, NET, REB, TEV]. It is translated 'the righteous by faith will live' [NET], 'the person who is put right with God through faith shall live' [TEV], 'whoever is justified through faith shall gain life' [REB], 'the people God accepts because of their faith will live' [CEV]. The context favors this meaning since Paul's concern at this point in the letter is how sinners become righteous, not how righteous people live [ICC2, Mor, SSA, St]. Several times in the early chapters of the epistle Paul connects righteousness with faith, but never righteousness with living by faith [SSA]. Paul consistently links faith with righteousness and his emphasis is that life is the result of that righteousness. However, the differences between the two options should not be over emphasized since both OT and NT concepts of 'faith' share the notion of absolute reliance on God rather than on human abilities or activities [NICNT]. Either construction is possible and the sense is largely the same [Ho].

2. It is connected with the verb ζήσεται 'shall live' and the sense is 'the righteous shall live by faith' [AB, BECNT, Gdt, ICC1, Mu, NAC, NTC; GW, KJV, NASB, NCV, NIV, NLT, NRSV]. It is translated 'the just/righteous shall live by faith' [KJV, NIV], 'the righteous man shall live by faith' [NASB], 'the one who is righteous will live by faith' [NRSV], 'those who are right with God will live by trusting in him' [NCV], 'the person who has God's approval will live because of faith' [GW], 'it is through faith that a righteous person has life' [NLT]. While it is more likely that this prepositional phrase modifies the verb, it may be that Paul did not intend to distinguish clearly between the two options [BECNT].

3. There is probably a connection both to the verb and to the noun [HNTC, St, WBC]. Paul may have dropped the personal possessive pronouns of the Heb and LXX texts in order to extend the connection of the phrase 'by faith' to both the noun and the verb [HNTC, WBC]. Paul drops the pronouns, perhaps to bring out his own characteristic phrase emphasizing 'faith all the time'; that is, if one is righteous at all, it is by faith, and also it is by faith that one will live [HNTC]. Paul drops the personal pronouns 'my' and 'his' from the older texts perhaps due to a wish to avoid choosing between them, and to broaden and extend the meaning to what he was particularly concerned with at this point, thus allowing 'by faith' to be associated with either the verb or with the noun [WBC]. Whichever

way one understands the sentence, either rendering indicates that the righteous will live and also affirms the essential nature of faith [St].

QUESTION—What is meant by ζήσεται 'will live' here?
1. It refers to eternal life [AB, BAGD, BECNT, Gdt, Ho, ICC2, NICNT, SSA, TNTC, WBC]. It denotes salvation [AB, NAC, NICNT, NTC, WBC], which is eschatological [AB, NICNT, WBC] and is equivalent to life with or in Christ [AB, WBC]. It refers to eschatological life [BECNT]. It is life with God, not only which is enjoyed here and now, but also in its fullness in the eschatological future [ICC2]. It represents deliverance from perdition and having eternal life [Gdt]. It is the everlasting life that Christ gives, a life that is blessed and spiritual [Ho]. It is salvation, which includes justification and sanctification, and which is consummated in eternal glory [TNTC].
2. The emphasis in this passage is on the quality of life, with the sense 'shall truly live' or 'shall really live', as opposed to mere continued existence [TH].

DISCOURSE UNIT: 1:18–5:21 [ICC1, Mor, WBC]. The topic is righteousness in the sight of God [ICC1], the way of deliverance [Mor], the righteousness of God [WBC].

DISCOURSE UNIT: 1:18–4:25 [ICC2, NICNT]. The topic is righteousness from God by faith alone [ICC2], justification by faith [NICNT].

DISCOURSE UNIT: 1:18–3:20 [AB, BECNT, Gdt, ICC1, ICC2, Mor, Mu, NAC, NICNT, SSA, St]. The topic is God's righteousness in his wrath against sinners [BECNT], God's wrath manifested against all human beings [AB], the wrath of God resting on the whole world [Gdt], righteousness not yet attained [ICC1], righteousness before God by faith alone [ICC2], universal sinfulness [Mor], universality of sin and condemnation [Mu], the unrighteousness of all humankind [NAC], the universal reign of sin [NICNT], the wrath of God against all humankind [St], sin and retribution: the universal need diagnosed [TNTC].

DISCOURSE UNIT: 1:18–2:16 [REB]. The topic is God's judgment on sin.

DISCOURSE UNIT: 1:18–32 [AB, BECNT, Gdt, GNT, HNTC, Ho, ICC1, ICC2, Mor, Mu, NAC, NICNT, NTC, SSA, St, TNTC, WBC; CEV, GW, NCV, NET, NIV, NLT, TEV]. The topic is the unrighteousness of Gentiles [BECNT], God's wrath manifested against pagans [Gdt], Gentiles exposed to condemnation [Ho], judgment and the Gentile [HNTC], failure of the Gentile [ICC1], man under the judgment of the gospel [ICC2], the condemnation of the Gentile world [Mor], the universality of sin and condemnation: the Gentiles [Mu], the unrighteousness of all humankind [NAC], all people have done wrong [NCV], everyone accountable to God for sin [NICNT], the Gentiles need this justification [NTC], God's wrath against depraved Gentile society [St], the pagan world [TNTC], God's wrath on humankind from a Jewish perspective [WBC], God's anger against sinful humanity [GW], human guilt [TEV], the guilt of mankind [GNT], everyone is guilty [CEV], the condemnation of the unrighteous [NET], God's wrath against mankind [NIV], God's anger at sin [NLT].

1:18 For^a (the) wrath^b of-God is-revealed^c from^d heaven

LEXICON—a. γάρ (LN 89.23) (BAGD p. 152): 'for' [AB, BAGD, BECNT, HNTC, ICC2, LN, NICNT, NTC, WBC; KJV, NASB, NET, NIV, NRSV, TEV], 'because' [REB], not explicit [CEV, GW, NCV, NIV, NLT, REB, TEV]. The connection between this verse and the previous one is translated 'but' [NLT].

b. ὀργή (LN 88.173) (BAGD 2.a. p. 579): 'wrath' [AB, BAGD, BECNT, HNTC, ICC2, NICNT, NTC, WBC; KJV, NASB, NET, NIV, NRSV], 'anger' [LN; CEV, GW, NCV, NLT, TEV], 'retribution' [REB].

c. pres. pass. indic. of ἀποκαλύπτω (LN 28.38) (BAGD 1. p. 92): 'to be revealed' [AB, BAGD, BECNT, HNTC, ICC2, LN, NICNT, NTC, WBC; GW, KJV, NASB, NET, NIV, NRSV, TEV], 'to be shown' [NCV], 'to be seen at work' [REB], 'to show' [CEV, NLT]. The phrase ἀποκαλύπτεται...ὀργὴ θεοῦ 'the wrath of God is revealed' is translated 'God shows his anger' [NLT], 'God shows how angry he is' [CEV], 'God's anger is revealed' [TEV], 'God's wrath is revealed' [KJV, NET, NRSV], 'God's wrath is being revealed' [NIV], 'Divine retribution is to be seen at work' [REB].

d. ἀπό with genitive object (LN 84.3): 'from' [AB, BECNT, HNTC, ICC2, LN, NICNT, NTC, WBC; all versions except REB], 'falling from' [REB].

QUESTION—What relationship is indicated by γάρ 'for'?

1. This introduces a reason or grounds for the preceding verse. The reason that the righteousness of God is being revealed is that the wrath of God is coming against the sinfulness of men [Gdt, Ho, Mor, St, TNTC]. It introduces 1:18 as a grounds for what is said in 1:17; that is, since the wrath of God rests on man by nature, man cannot save himself and there is no other way to be saved than by accepting the gospel by faith [NTC]. It introduces 1:18 as evidence for 1:17; a clear signal that his righteousness is being revealed is the fact that his wrath is being revealed [HNTC]. The reason it was necessary for the gospel to reveal a righteousness from God as God's way of justifying sinners is that the wrath of God is being revealed against human wickedness which suppresses the knowledge of God [St]. It introduces 1:18 as the grounds to an implied statement that follows logically from 1:17: the reason we need the saving righteousness of God is that the wrath of God is being revealed against all people who have sinned against his glory [BECNT]. This word relates this section to the previous one in that the revelation of God's wrath against men's sins makes it clear that apart from faith there is no other way that men may have a status of righteousness before God [ICC2]. The fact of God's wrath is what makes the gospel necessary, as the gospel of salvation by grace is the only deliverance from it [Mor].

2. It introduces the whole argument of 1:18–3:20 as the answer to an implied question that would naturally follow from 1:17, which is, Why has God revealed his righteousness and why can it only be appropriated by faith? [NICNT].
   3. It indicates a contrast [AB, WBC]. It links the section 1:18–3:20 to 1:17 as a contrast between God's righteousness, described in 1:17, and his wrath, described in the next section, and as a contrast between the human condition without the gospel and the human condition under the revelation of God's righteousness which is by faith [AB]. It links 1:17 and 1:18, in which the righteousness of God granted to faith is contrasted with the wrath of God toward human wickedness [WBC].

QUESTION—What is meant by the phrase ὀργὴ θεοῦ 'wrath of God'?

It is God's action in judging and punishing men for sin [TH], his holy disapproval of what is evil [Gdt]. It is the response of God's holiness to human wickedness and rebellion that suppresses the knowledge of God and embraces a lie instead, the retribution that must operate in a moral universe [TNTC]. It is God's settled and righteous antagonism to evil [Mu, NAC], his settled indignation [NTC], his holy hostility to evil [St], his determination and firm resolve to punish sin and destroy evil [Gdt, Ho]. Here it is not so much God's final judgment as his response to unfolding events and relationships, both individually and in society [WBC]. This wrath is not merely an attitude of God, but is something God does in response to human transgression [Mu, WBC]. God, who is perfectly loving and good, expresses indignation against injustice, cruelty, corruption, and human evil [ICC2]. It is God's vigorous and personal opposition to every evil [Mor], his divine displeasure with sin [NAC]. God's wrath is not malicious [HNTC, Ho, NAC, St], vengeful [WBC], spiteful, or vindictive [St], although it is personal [HNTC]. God's anger is not capricious or irrational, but thoroughly rational [ICC2]. This could be considered metonymy, representing not only the anger of God but also the outcome of it, the punishment of those deserving it [SSA].

QUESTION—How should the present indicative form of the verb ἀποκαλύπτω 'is revealed' be understood?

The verb should be understood as a present tense [BECNT, HNTC, ICC2, Mor, Mu, NAC, NICNT, WBC]. 1:17 says that God's righteousness is currently being revealed, and the same form of the same verb in this verse indicates that his wrath is also being revealed at present [AB, BECNT, Gdt, HNTC, Mor, Mu, WBC]. We should understand the wrath in eschatological terms, but should also not overlook its present reality [BECNT, HNTC, ICC1, Mor, NAC, St]. The eventual revelation of God's wrath at the end-time is anticipated by the same principle of his wrath being revealed in the world here and now [BECNT, HNTC, NAC, TNTC, WBC].

QUESTION—In what sense is the wrath of God revealed?
   1. God's wrath is being manifested in action in human history [AB, BECNT, HNTC, Ho, Mu, NAC, NICNT, NTC, TH, TNTC, WBC]. The object of

the revealing is the sinfulness of people, and although God's wrath will be manifest in a final fashion at the end of time, its anticipatory workings can be seen already in handing people over to their sinful choices and their consequences as in 1:24–28 [NICNT, St]. It is revealed in the current condition of the world, but will also be revealed at the final judgment [ICC1]. The moral desolation of human society throughout history, which is referred to by the use of past tenses for 'handed over' in verses 24–28, is an evidence of God's judgment and wrath, anticipating what will happen on judgment day [BECNT, Gdt]. God's wrath is revealed in the fact of his abandoning sinners to their own ways, allowing them to degenerate morally, socially, and spiritually [AB, St]. God establishes a connection between sin and misery through specific punishments for sin, through the inherent tendency of moral evil to produce evil, and through conviction felt in the conscience, none of which depend on special revelation [Ho].

2. God's wrath is communicated to human understanding in the message of the gospel as well as through the events of the gospel, that is, the crucifixion, where God's wrath against sin was shown [ICC2, Mor]. The cross shows us the measure of God's wrath [Mor].

QUESTION—What is the significance of the phrase ἀπ' οὐρανοῦ 'from heaven'?

This is essentially a metonymy for 'God', meaning that the manifestations of God's wrath have their origin in heaven in the sense that it is God himself who expresses his wrath on ungodly people [AB, HNTC, Ho, NTC, TH]. 'Heaven' is a reverent way of referring to God; the wrath is God's wrath [Mor]. It God's wrath in its cosmic dimension, God's own reaction to the sins of the human race [AB]. It conveys the idea of a revelation that has its source in God [Ho, WBC]. This emphasizes the utter seriousness of the wrath as being God's own wrath [ICC2]. It adds weight to what Paul is saying, speaking as it does of the majesty of the one who is angry, of his ability to see everything, and of the wide extent of His wrath [NICNT]. It implies the place of God's rule and judgment [SSA]. 'Heaven' is an expression for the invisible residence of God, the seat of perfect order, indicating that God is the source of the judgment [Gdt].

against[a] all[b] godlessness[c] and unrighteousness[d] of-people[e]

LEXICON—a. ἐπί with accusative object (LN 90.34): 'against' [AB, BECNT, HNTC, ICC2, LN, NICNT, NTC, WBC; all versions except CEV, REB], 'with' [CEV], '(falling) on' [REB]. The phrase ἐπὶ πᾶσαν ἀσέβειαν 'against all ungodliness' is translated '(how angry he is) with all the wicked and evil things' [CEV]

b. πᾶς (LN 59.23. 58.28) (BAGD 1.a.β. p. 631): 'all' [AB, BECNT, HNTC, LN (59.23), NICNT, NTC, WBC; all versions except GW], 'every' [LN (59.23); GW], 'every kind of' [BAGD, ICC2, LN (58.28)].

c. ἀσέβεια (LN 53.10) (BAGD p. 114): 'godlessness' [AB, BAGD, LN; NIV], 'ungodliness' [BECNT, HNTC, ICC2, NICNT, NTC; KJV, NASB, NET, NRSV], 'impiety' [BAGD, WBC; REB], 'sin' [TEV], '(every) ungodly thing' [GW], 'wicked things' [CEV], 'evil things' [NCV], 'sinful...people' [NLT].

d. ἀδικία (LN 88.21) (BAGD p. 18): 'unrighteousness' [BAGD, BECNT, HNTC, ICC2, LN, NICNT, NTC, WBC; KJV, NASB, NET], 'unjust deed' [LN], 'injustice' [BAGD], 'wickedness' [AB, BAGD; NIV, NRSV, REB], 'immoral thing' [GW], 'evil' [TEV], 'wrong things' [NCV], 'evil things' [CEV]. The phrase ἀσέβειαν καὶ ἀδικίαν ἀνθρώπων 'godlessness and unrighteousness of men' is translated 'all sinful, wicked people' [NLT], 'all the wicked and evil things that sinful people do' [CEV], 'all the evil and wrong things people do' [NCV].

e. ἄνθρωπος (LN 9.1): 'people' [BECNT, LN, NTC; CEV, GW, NCV, NET, NLT], 'mankind' [LN], 'man' [KJV, NIV], 'persons' [LN]. This plural noun is translated 'men' [HNTC, ICC2, WBC; KJV, NASB, NIV], 'men and women' [REB], 'people' [NET, TEV], 'human beings' [AB, NICNT], 'sinful people' [CEV], 'of those who' [NRSV].

QUESTION—How distinct are the meanings of the two nouns ἀσέβειαν 'ungodliness' and ἀδικίαν 'unrighteousness'?

1. The words should be distinguished [Gdt, Ho, NAC, SSA, St, TH]. The first term refers to sins of a religious nature such as transgressing one's duty towards God, or to sin and impiety against God, and the latter term refers to sins of a moral nature, regarding one's responsibility to other people, to sins and injustice against others [Gdt, Ho, ICC1, NAC, St, TH]. They sin against morals and religion [ICC1]. This is also reflected in the sequence of 1:19–27 where he speaks of the rejection of God by people, followed by 1:28–32 which speak of the problems in human relations that follow as a result [Gdt]. Lack of respect for God is always followed by injustice and a loss of concern for the rights of other people [NAC]. The two categories may also be understood as the sin within the heart and the evil things that people do [TH]. Ungodliness refers to perversity that is religious in nature, as illustrated by idolatry, and the second refers to what is moral, as illustrated by immorality. The order is significant in that impiety is the precursor of immorality [Mu]. The two words, which should not be considered a doublet, describe the sins of the Gentiles, and could be translated 'godless and wicked non-Jewish people' [SSA].

2. The distinction in the meanings of the words should not be pressed [AB, BECNT, ICC2, Mor, NICNT, NTC, WBC]. In Paul the two words are often used together, and a distinction is not strictly maintained; ἀδικία 'unrighteousness' may often refer to sin in the widest sense [NICNT]. It is unlikely that Paul intends a distinction between the two words, but the phrase taken together is all-embracing, referring to the violation of accepted religious practice as well as to unlawful actions toward other people [WBC]. The words should be understood to express one thought,

the sinfulness of humans [BECNT, ICC2, Mor, NTC]. Paul is using the two terms together to indicate the variety of evil, not to specify different aspects of evil; God's wrath is revealed against every wrong [Mor]. These words do not represent completely separate thoughts, for while it may be said that the first may view sin as lack of reverence for God and the second as a lack of reverence for his law, together they represent sin as a rebellion against God [NTC]. For Paul this is hendiadys, both nouns being governed by πᾶσαν 'all', and it sums up the total sinfulness of pagan humanity [AB]. Two names for the same thing are combined to give a more rounded description than either is able to give alone [ICC2].

QUESTION—Does the description of sin that follows refer to that of Gentiles or does he include Jews as well?

    1. The description from here to the end of the chapter refers to the Gentiles' sins [Gdt, HNTC, Ho, Mu, NTC, SSA, St, TNTC, WBC].

        1.1 1:18–32 refers to Gentiles, and 2:1 through 3:20 refers to Jews [Gdt, Ho, NTC].

        1.2 1:18–32 refers to decadent Gentile society, in 2:1–16 he addresses moralizers, whether Jew or Gentile, in 2:17–3:8 he addresses Jews who are confident of their righteousness, and in 3:9–20 he addresses the whole human race as guilty before God [HNTC, Mu, St, TNTC].

    2. 1:18–32 refers primarily, though not exclusively, to the Gentiles [BECNT, ICC2, Mor, NAC, NICNT, NTC]. In 1:18 he addresses all people, in 1:19–32 he is primarily speaking about the Gentiles, in 2:1–11 he addresses the moral person, but implicitly means the Jew, and in 2:17–29 he is plainly speaking of the Jew [NICNT]. Beginning in chapter 2 the Jewish reader would begin to realize that he was not exempt from the sins charged in chapter 1 [BECNT]. While referring primarily to Gentiles, he describes all people as being under the judgment of the gospel, and in 2:1–3:20 he shows that Jewish people are no exception [ICC2, NAC]

    3. It speaks of humanity in general apart from the influence of the gospel [AB].

the (ones) suppressing[a] the truth[b] in[c] unrighteousness,[d]

LEXICON—a. pres. act. participle of κατέχω (LN **13.150**) (BAGD 1.a.β. p. 422): 'to suppress' [BAGD, BECNT, ICC2, NICNT, WBC; GW, NASB, NET, NIV, NRSV, REB], 'to hinder, to restrain' [LN], 'to hold back, to hold down' [BAGD], 'to hide' [NCV], 'to keep…from being known' [**LN**], 'to prevent (from being known)' [**LN**; TEV], 'to hold' [KJV], 'to crush' [CEV], 'to push away…from oneself' [NLT]. This entire phrase is translated 'whose evil ways prevent the truth from being known' [TEV], 'the people whose evil ways keep the truth from being known' [**LN**], 'human beings who by such wickedness stifle the truth' [AB], 'men who try to suppress the truth by their unrighteousness' [ICC2], 'people who are constantly attempting to suppress the truth' [NTC], 'men who by their unrighteousness hold the truth imprisoned'

[HNTC], 'men who hold the truth in unrighteousness' [KJV], '(sinful, wicked) people who push the truth away from themselves' [NLT].
b. ἀλήθεια (LN 72.2) (BAGD 2.b. p. 36) 'the truth' [BECNT, HNTC, ICC2, NICNT, NTC, WBC; all versions], 'truth' [AB, LN].
c. ἐν (LN 13.8, 89.76): 'in' [LN (13.8), NICNT, WBC; KJV, NASB, REB], 'in a state of' [LN (13.8)], 'by' [AB, HNTC, ICC2, LN (89.76), NTC; GW, NCV, NET, NIV, NRSV].
d. ἀδικία (LN 88.21) (BAGD 2. p. 18): 'unrighteousness' [BAGD, HNTC, ICC2, LN, NICNT, NTC, WBC; KJV, NASB, NET], 'wickedness' [AB, BAGD; NIV, NRSV, REB], 'immoral living' [GW], 'their own evil lives' [NCV]. The phrase ἐν ἀδικίᾳ 'in unrighteousness' is translated 'unrighteously' [BECNT], 'by their unrighteousness' [HNTC, ICC2, NTC; NET], 'evil things that sinful people do' [CEV], 'whose evil ways...' [TEV], not explicit [NLT].

QUESTION—What is the meaning of the participle κατεχόντων 'suppressing', and how is it that the truth is suppressed by the unrighteousness of men?

1. The term refers to preventing, restraining, or hindering someone from doing something, and in this passage, to keep the truth from being known [LN (13.50), SSA, TH]. The truth is concealed or stifled by these people's sinful lives [HNTC, NAC]. The truth is hindered or thwarted in its free and expansive operation [ICC1]. It refers to suppressing the effects of the truth on oneself and others by unrighteous behavior [Gdt, SSA]. The meaning of 'restraining' or 'holding back' is well suited to the context since Paul is speaking of the truth that can be derived from observing God's handiwork in creation [Mu]. It is to repress, hinder, or oppose the truth through unrighteous acts [Gdt, Ho].
2. This means that by their unrighteous acts and rebellion against God's just rule, people actually hinder or suppress the effect the truth would otherwise have had on their religious and moral state [NICNT]. Suppressing the truth implies willfulness on the part of those doing it, but also that the truth would have had its effects had it not been so suppressed [WBC].
3. The truth that the one true God is to be honored and worshipped is suppressed as people unrighteously refuse to do this [BECNT]. People who have some knowledge of God's truth through the created order deliberately suppress it in order to pursue their own self-centeredness, choosing to live for themselves rather than for God and others, and they deliberately stifle any truth which challenges that kind of self-centeredness [St]. Some knowledge of God is accessible but men have closed their minds to it [TNTC]. Human wickedness holds the truth about God captive by rebelling against him and against the truth about him, thus in effect stifling it [AB].
4. This should be understood to have a conative force, expressing will or intent; although people try or intend to hold down or hinder the truth, they are ultimately unable to thwart God's purposes. This inherent futility of

sin is repeatedly emphasized in Paul's argument [ICC2]. A verb suggesting effort when used in a context implying action in progress suggests an action being attempted; the immediate context here shows that these ungodly ones do not actually succeed in holding back the truth [NTC]. These people do not like the truth and do what they can to hinder it; Paul is speaking here of what sinners attempt to do, not of what they are actually able to do [Mor].
  5. This verb may be taken in the sense of 'to possess' instead of 'to suppress', and it speaks of those who, although they possess the truth, act unrighteously [Ho].

QUESTION—How should τὴν ἀλήθειαν 'the truth' be understood in this context?

It is the knowledge of God which is available to all people through observing the natural order; the creation is a visible disclosure of the invisible God [Mu, St]. The truth that has been suppressed is that God should be honored, worshipped, and esteemed as God, and the fundamental sin is the refusal to worship God and give him proper sovereignty in one's life [BECNT]. What has been suppressed is the fundamental truth that God is Creator, Judge, and Redeemer [HNTC, ICC2]. It is truth about God [AB, TH, TNTC], about his eternal power and nature [NAC]. It is truth about the reality of God such as pagans would be aware of [AB]. It is the truth about God, especially that God is creator and is reliable and trustworthy, but also includes truth about God in relation to man and man in relation to God and other men [WBC]. In the NT, truth is something to be obeyed, not just to give mental assent to, and acting sinfully is to rebel against God's rule and what he has said should be done [NICNT]. It is general truth, such as is open to all people, not revealed truth [Mor]. It is moral and religious truth, that is, true religion, our knowing what is true and right relative to God and to our duty to him [Ho]. They suppress what they know about God [SSA]. It is knowledge about God that is derived from general revelation [NTC]. It is God's revelation to the consciences of the Gentiles [Gdt]. They will stifle any truth which challenges their self-centeredness [St].

QUESTION—How should the phrase ἐν ἀδικίᾳ 'in unrighteousness' be understood in this verse?
  1. It should be understood as adverbial; they unrighteously suppress the truth [BECNT, Gdt, TNTC].
  2. It should be understood as instrumental; they suppress the truth through or by unrighteous acts [AB, HNTC, Ho, ICC2, Mu, NAC, NICNT, NTC, St, TH; CEV, GW, NCV, NET, NIV, NRSV, TEV].
  3. This phrase is translated literally, 'in unrighteousness' [WBC; KJV, NASB, NLT, REB], possibly indicating either the sinful state or condition of those who suppress the truth or their motivation for doing so.

1:19 because[a] what-can-be-known[b] of God is clear[c] to/among/within[d] them;

LEXICON—a. διότι (LN 89.26) (BAGD 3. p. 199) 'because' [BAGD, LN, NTC, WBC; KJV, NASB, NCV, NET, TEV], 'for' [BAGD, BECNT, HNTC, ICC2, NICNT; NLT, NRSV, REB], 'since' [NIV], not explicit [AB; CEV, GW]. The phrase 'Justly so,' is added at the beginning of this verse by HNTC. The clause 'God punishes them' is added at the beginning of this verse by TEV.

b. γνωστός (LN **28.57**) (BAGD 2. p. 164): 'what can be known' [AB, BAGD, BECNT, HNTC, **LN**, NICNT, NTC, WBC; GW, NET, NRSV, TEV], 'what may be known' [NIV], 'that which may be known' [KJV], 'all that can be known' [REB], 'everything that can be known' [CEV], 'that which is known' [BECNT; NASB], 'what is knowable' [ICC2], 'what is evident, what can be clearly seen' [LN], '(God,) to the extent that he can be known' [BAGD], 'some knowledge' [NCV], 'the truth about God' [NLT], 'capable of being known' [BAGD].

c. φανερός (LN **28.58**, 24.20) (BAGD 1. p. 852): 'clear' [BAGD, LN (28.58, 24.20); GW, NCV], 'plain' [BAGD, **LN** (25.58), NTC; NET, NIV, NRSV, REB, TEV], 'clearly known' [LN (28.58)], 'evident' [BAGD, LN (25.58, 24.20), WBC; NASB], 'manifest' [AB, BECNT, HNTC, ICC2, NICNT; KJV], 'know everything' [CEV], 'known… instinctively' [NLT]. This is also translated 'lies plain before their eyes' [REB].

d. ἐν (LN 90.56, 83.9, 83.13) (BAGD IV.4.a. p. 261): 'to' [AB, BECNT, LN (90.56), NTC, WBC; GW, NCV, NET, NIV, NLT, NRSV, TEV], 'among' [HNTC, LN (83.9), NICNT], 'in' [LN (83.13); KJV], 'within' [LN (83.13); NASB], not explicit [CEV]. The phrase ἐν αὐτοῖς 'to/among/within them' is translated 'before their eyes' [REB], 'in their midst' [ICC2].

QUESTION—What relationship is signaled by the use of the conjunction διότι 'because' and to what does it refer?

1. It introduces what follows as the reason that God's wrath is being revealed, which is that people suppress the truth [HNTC, Ho, NAC, NICNT, SSA, TH]. It introduces 1:19–32 as the justification for the claim in 1:18 that God is angry with people [SSA]. Their opposition to the truth cannot be excused on the basis of ignorance because God has manifest the knowledge of himself among them [Ho]. God punishes people because even though they know the truth about God they sin anyway [TH].
2. It introduces what follows as the reason that people suppress the truth; they suppress the truth because it has been revealed to them [AB, Gdt].
3. It introduces what follows as the grounds for his assertion that people hinder the truth [ICC2, Mor, Mu, NTC]. People really do have enough knowledge of the truth to justify the charge that they try to suppress it [ICC2, NTC]. He can say that people hinder the truth because God made

the truth known to them, and they can't claim ignorance as an excuse for their idolatry [Mor].
   4. It introduces what follows as the object clause stating what it is that has been suppressed; that is, the truth that they stifle is the fact that what can be known about God is manifest to them [AB].

QUESTION—What is meant by τὸ γνωστόν 'what can be known'?
   1. It means 'what can be known' [AB, Gdt, HNTC, ICC1, ICC2, Mor, NAC, NICNT, NTC, St; CEV, GW, KJV, NET, NIV, NRSV, REB, TEV]. It speaks of the knowability of God [AB], the extent to which God can be known [ICC2, WBC]. There is a strong implicit conviction that, although God is not knowable in himself, he has made himself known to some extent [WBC]. Although there are things about God which cannot be made known through observing the natural order, God has made known that which can be made known [Mor]. What can be known of God is perfectly clear [NAC].
   2. It means 'that which is known of God' [BECNT, Ho, Mu; NASB]. It is manifest in them because God has manifested it unto them [Mu]. The rendering 'what may be known' implies too much since Paul is not saying that everything that might possibly be known was in fact revealed; he is only discussing what actually is known about his nature and power, and his eternal power and deity [Ho].

QUESTION—What is the nature of the knowledge of God that has been made known?
   This refers to what may be known of God by observing the creation [AB, BECNT, ICC2, Mu, NAC, St], namely his power and deity as 1:20 states [BECNT, Gdt, HNTC, Ho, St, TH]. The emphasis here is on whatever in the area of nature or creation can be made known about him [NTC]. It is the revelation of the creator in what he has made [ICC2]. The visible creation discloses the invisible and otherwise unknown God [St]. Through the creation God has provided sufficient evidence of himself to hold all people who reject that revelation accountable [Ho, NAC]. That creation is the work of a creator is a fact which cannot be doubted [NAC]. Observing created life tells us that creation does not provide the key to its own existence [HNTC, WBC]. God is not knowable in himself unless he makes himself known, which he has done to some extent in creation, but the question of whether this is a saving knowledge is not addressed here by Paul [WBC]. This is certainly not a saving knowledge [BECNT, Mor], for faith becomes a reality only through the preached word [BECNT]. Paul is not establishing a natural theology [HNTC, St], for people cannot know God fully or savingly through nature [St].

QUESTION—What is meant by ἐν in the phrase ἐν αὐτοῖς 'to/among/within them'?
   1. It is equivalent to the dative of indirect object αὐτοῖς that follows in the next phrase, meaning 'to them' [AB, BECNT, Mor, NTC, SSA, St; CEV, GW, NCV, NET, NIV, NLT, NRSV, TEV].

2. It should be understood to mean 'within them' [Ho, ICC1, Mu; NASB]. That is, it is in their minds, for any revelation must pass through the human conscience [ICC1]. It is not mere external revelation, but revelation to that part of every man's being and nature by virtue of which he is able to apprehend the manifestations of God in what he does [Ho]. Paul writes as one who has had revelations, and so uses the language of his own experiences [ICC1].
3. It means 'among', and refers to God's making himself known among people through his works of creation [HNTC, ICC2, NICNT]. The whole of God's creation declares him, and this knowledge is in their midst and all around them, even in the fact of their own existence as creatures [ICC2]. This knowledge was available in their midst or among them through the creation, in which God had made it manifest, but they did not in fact actually possess this knowledge within them [HNTC].
4. It means 'to' as well as 'in', because revelation to them is also, by necessity, a revelation in them; manifestations of truth always presuppose the inner realities of mind and consciousness [Mu].
5. It may be understood as any of the previous three alternatives, and the ambiguity may reflect the common belief in a direct continuity between human rationality and that rationality evident in the created order [WBC].

for[a] God has-made- (it) -manifest[b] to-them.

LEXICON—a. γάρ (LN 89.23) (BAGD p. 152): 'for', [AB, BAGD, BECNT, HNTC, ICC2, LN, NICNT, NTC, WBC; KJV, NASB, TEV], 'because' [LN; CEV, GW, NET, NIV, NRSV], 'since' [HNTC], 'indeed' [REB], not explicit [NCV, NLT].

b. aorist act. indic. of φανερόω (LN 28.36) (BAGD 1.a. p. 852): 'to make manifest' [BECNT, HNTC, ICC2, NICNT], 'to make plain' [LN, NTC; NET, NIV, TEV], 'to make evident' [AB; NASB], 'to make clear' [GW], 'to make known' [BAGD, LN], 'to show' [BAGD, WBC; CEV, KJV, NCV, NRSV], 'to disclose' [LN; REB], 'to reveal' [BAGD, LN]. This clause is translated 'for God has made it manifest to them' [BECNT, ICC2, NICNT], 'God himself made it manifest among them' [HNTC], 'for God has made it plain to them' [NTC; NIV], 'God himself made it plain' [TEV], 'indeed God himself has disclosed it to them' [REB], 'because God has shown it all to them' [CEV], 'God has shown them what can be known about him' [BAGD], 'God has put this knowledge in their hearts' [NLT]. This aorist verb is translated as a simple past tense [HNTC; NASB, TEV]; as a perfect tense [AB, BAGD, BECNT, ICC2, NICNT, NTC, WBC; CEV, GW, KJV, NCV, NET, NIV, NLT, NRSV, REB].

QUESTION—What relationship is signaled by the word γάρ 'for' in this clause?

It introduces the reason or grounds for the assertion of the first half of the verse; what may be known of God is 'clear' because God has made it clear [AB, Mor, NICNT, SSA, St].

QUESTION—In what way does the word order of this clause affect its meaning?

The subject of the clause, God, is given some prominence by its position before the verb. This primary emphasis on the agent may be expressed by the translation 'God himself' [HNTC, NAC, SSA]. The position of γάρ 'for' after ὁ θεὺς 'God' puts a bit more emphasis on θεὺς 'God' than would have been the case if the more normal order was followed [Mor].

QUESTION—What is the meaning and significance of the word ἐφανέρωσεν 'made manifest'?

It signals a revealing that God willed and caused to happen [AB, Gdt, ICC2, Mor, St, WBC]. The word means to make something evident or perceptible so that it can be grasped, as something that is made plain to them through creation itself apart from any special revelation or miracle [AB]. This knowledge is a revelation, the manifestation by God of himself in his works and in the constitution of man's nature such that his rational creatures are bound to acknowledge him [Ho]. There is no suggestion here that this requires careful deduction or reasoning, for Paul states that it is a reality for all people; God has created people in such a way that his existence and power are instinctively recognized when they view the created world [BECNT]. Or, it is a divine revelation, because only by a revelation from above can people understand God as he is [NICNT]. This revelation is one that is willed and effected by God and given through the created order to all people throughout history, and is not simply a happenstance of creation [WBC]. This emphasizes that God's being manifest in creation is a result of his own deliberate self-disclosure [ICC2]. God has freely chosen to make himself manifest [AB, Gdt]. God has taken the initiative to make this plain or open to man [Mor, St], and he is only known as he chooses to make himself known [Mor].

1:20 For[a] the invisible[b] (things) of-him since[c] (the) creation[d] of-(the)-world[e]

LEXICON—a. γάρ (LN 89.23) (BAGD p. 152): 'for', [AB, BAGD, BECNT, ICC2, NICNT, NTC, WBC; KJV, NASB, NET, NIV], 'because' [LN], not explicit [AB, HNTC; CEV, GW, NCV, NLT, NRSV, REB, TEV].

b. ἀόρατος (LN 24.4) (BAGD p.79): 'invisible, what cannot be seen' [LN], 'unseen' [BAGD]. This adjective is translated 'invisible things' [KJV], 'invisible attributes' [BAGD, BECNT, HNTC, ICC2, NICNT, WBC; KJV, NASB, NET, REB], 'invisible qualities' [AB, NTC; GW, NIV, NLT, TEV], 'things that people cannot see' [NCV], 'invisible though they

are' [NRSV], '(God's eternal power and character) cannot be seen' [CEV].
c. ἀπό (LN 67.131) (BAGD II.2.a. p.87): 'since' [BAGD, ICC2, LN, NICNT, NTC; NASB, NCV, NET, NIV], 'ever since' [AB; NRSV, REB, TEV], 'from' [BAGD, BECNT, HNTC, LN, WBC; CEV, GW, KJV, NLT].
d. κτίσις (LN 42.35) (BAGD 1.a. p.455): 'creation' [AB, BAGD, HNTC, ICC2, LN, NICNT, NTC, WBC; CEV, GW, KJV, NASB, NET, NIV, NRSV]. The phrase ἀπὸ κτίσεως κόσμου 'since the creation of the world' [BAGD, NICNT, NTC; NET, NIV] is also translated 'from the creation of the world' [WBC; KJV], 'from the time the world was created' [BECNT; NLT], 'from the creation of the world onwards' [HNTC], 'ever since the creation of the world' [NRSV], 'ever since God created the world' [TEV], 'since the beginning of the world' [NCV], 'from the beginning of creation' [CEV], 'ever since the world began' [REB].
e. κόσμος (LN 1.1, 1.39) (BAGD 2. p. 445): 'world' [AB, BAGD, BECNT, HNTC, ICC2, LN (1.39), NICNT, NTC, WBC; all versions except CEV], 'earth' [LN (1.39)], 'universe, cosmos' [BAGD, LN (1.1)].

QUESTION—What relationship is indicated by the use of γάρ 'for' in this verse?

This expresses grounds for what has just been stated in 1:19 [NICNT]. Paul maintains the chain of reasoning begun in 1:19; having asserted that what can be known of God is visible to people because God has chosen to manifest himself, he now gives the explanation that God has disclosed himself through the created order [NICNT]. It expands upon what he has just said in 1:19; God has made it plain in that his invisible qualities have been seen [Mor]. This verse further amplifies the grounds given in 1:19b for what was said in 1:19a [SSA]. This marks 1:20 as providing an explanation of what is said in the latter half of 1:19 [HNTC, ICC2, Mu], but more generally it also relates 1:20 and what follows to 1:18–19 [ICC2]. It introduces 1:20 as a continuation and amplification of what precedes, giving proof that God does in fact manifest himself to men leaving them inexcusable for their impiety [Ho]. The word is not simply continuative, but also supportive, showing that the assertion of 1:19 is in fact true, and gives further reason why God's wrath is being revealed, which is that the wickedness is inexcusable [NTC].

QUESTION—To what does the phrase τὰ...ἀόρατα αὐτοῦ 'the invisible things of him' refer?

This refers to his eternal power and divinity mentioned later in the verse [BECNT, HNTC, Ho, ICC1, ICC2, Mor, Mu, NAC, NICNT, NTC, TH, TNTC; all versions]. The invisible things refer to his nature, the essence of God, which is then further specified in the following clauses [Gdt, Ho, Mor, SSA]. 'The invisible things of him' refers to the essence of God and the many attributes which manifest it, and which are summed up in the phrase 'eternal power and divinity' [Gdt]. In distinction from 'power', the word for 'divine nature' summarizes all other attributes that constitute his divinity [ICC1, Mor]. The invisible qualities are the sum of his divine being, two examples of which are given in the verse [AB].

QUESTION—Does ἀπό κτίσεως have a temporal meaning, 'since the time of creation', or a causal meaning 'from the fact of creation'?

It is temporal [AB, BECNT, Gdt, HNTC, Ho, ICC1, ICC2, Mor, Mu, NICNT, NTC, SSA, TH; CEV, NASB, NCV, NET, NIV, NLT, NRSV, REB, TEV]: it has been known since the creation of the world. The idea is that the revelation has been made since the time of creation of the world, not by the fact of its creation [Ho]. This self-revelation of God has been continuous ever since creation [Gdt, ICC2]. The universe has always shown the imprint of God's handiwork [Mor].

QUESTION—What is meant by κόσμος 'world'?

Most translate this noun as 'world' [AB, BAGD, BECNT, HNTC, ICC2, LN (1.39), NICNT, NTC, WBC; all versions except CEV], A few take it to refer to the whole created universe [Mor, NAC]. For people the most important part of the universe is the earth; however, order in the heavens as well as that on earth bear testimony of God [Mor].

(by)[a] the things-made[b] being-understood[c] are-clearly-seen,[d]

LEXICON—a. There is no lexical entry for the word 'by' in the Greek text, but it is supplied in translation to express the relation indicated by the dative case of the phrase τοῖς ποιήμασιν 'the things made'. This relation is translated 'by' [CEV, KJV, NCV], 'by means of' [ICC2], 'by reflection on' [AB], 'through' [BECNT, NICNT, NTC; NASB, NET, NRSV], 'in' [HNTC, WBC; GW, REB, TEV], 'from' [NIV], not explicit [NLT].

b. ποίημα (LN 42.30) (BAGD p. 683): 'things made' [LN; KJV], 'things he has made' [HNTC, ICC2, NICNT; NRSV, REB], 'things God has made' [TEV], 'what he made' [GW], 'what he has made' [AB], 'what God has made' [NCV], 'what is made' [BAGD, LN], 'what has been made' [BECNT; NASB, NET, NIV], 'things which have been made' [WBC], 'things that God has made' [TEV], 'things (one) has created' [BAGD], '(his) works' [NTC], 'the earth and sky and all that God made' [NLT].

c. pres. pass. participle of νοέω (LN 32.2) (BAGD 1.a. p. 540): 'to be understood' [BAGD, BECNT, LN, NICNT, NTC; KJV, NASB, NET, NIV, NRSV], 'to be perceived' [AB, BAGD, ICC2, LN, WBC; TEV], 'to be comprehended' [LN], 'to be apprehended, to be given insight into' [BAGD], not explicit [CEV]. This passive verb is translated as an active verb: 'they understood' [BECNT], 'the mind can grasp (them)' [HNTC], 'people have seen' [NLT].

d. pres. pass. indic. of καθοράω (LN **27.7**) (BAGD p. 391): 'to be seen clearly' [BECNT, HNTC, ICC2, NTC; KJV, NASB, NET, NIV, NLT, TEV], 'to be perceived clearly' [**LN**], 'to be perceived' [BAGD], 'to be learned about' [LN]. This passive verb is also translated actively: 'they can clearly see' [NLT], '(by) reflection on' [AB], 'God has shown what (these) are like' [CEV]. The phrase νοούμενα καθοράται 'being understood are clearly seen' is translated 'have been clearly observed' [GW], 'have been easy to understand' [NCV], 'are perceived rationally' [WBC], 'have been visible to the eye of reason' [REB], 'are perceived with the eye of reason' [BAGD]. This word occurs only here in the NT.

QUESTION—To what action is the plural noun τοῖς ποιήμασιν 'by the things made' connected?
1. It is connected to the action of the participle νοούμενα 'being understood' [BECNT, HNTC, Ho, ICC2, Mu, NICNT, NTC; KJV, NASB, NET, NIV, TEV]. The whole phrase 'by the things made being understood' modifies the main verb 'seen'. That is, his invisible attributes are seen, being understood through the things he has made.
2. It is connected to both the participial phrase and the verb, which are conflated to express one action, with νοούμενα 'being understood' functioning adverbially to modify καθοράται 'are seen' to indicate that the 'seeing' is mental or conceptual [AB, SSA, TH, WBC; CEV, GW, NCV, NRSV, REB]. Through the created order God's attributes are spiritually contemplated [Gdt], clearly revealed [SSA], 'clearly observed' [GW], 'easy to understand' [NCV], 'perceived by reflection' [AB], 'perceived rationally' [WBC], 'understood and seen' [NRSV], 'visible to the eye of reason' [REB], or 'shown' [CEV].

QUESTION—How does the verb καθοράται 'are clearly seen' correspond in meaning with the participle νοούμενα 'being understood'?
1. Καθοράται refers to physical sight, while νοούμενα refers to the mental comprehension that is based on what has been seen physically [Gdt, HNTC, Ho, Mor, NICNT]. By seeing visible things, invisible things are perceived or understood [Ho, Mor, NICNT]. These two forms of 'seeing', one by the eye and the other by the mind, become a single act of spiritual contemplation, whereby what presents itself to the eye becomes a revelation to the conscience [Gdt]. Paul appeals to a commonly used contrast between perception by the eye and perception by the mind, and uses it in a line of reasoning that was common both in Stoic literature and in Hellenistic Judaism [HNTC].
2. Both refer to physical sight, but the statement is a paradoxical assertion, meaning that God's invisible attributes are actually seen in the visible creation [ICC2].
3. The two ideas are combined and speak of a single concept of 'seeing' that is mental or conceptual [AB, Mu, NTC, SSA, TH, WBC; CEV, GW, NCV, NRSV, REB]. Both refer to mental comprehension; what is not physically visible can be clearly seen or apprehended mentally [Mu].

QUESTION—How can God's invisible or unseen attributes be said to be clearly seen?
This is an example of the rhetorical device known as an oxymoron, the effect being achieved by asserting something that is apparently contradictory [AB, Mu, NICNT, NTC]. It is a paradoxical statement and means that God's

invisible attributes may be seen in and through his creation [ICC2]. God is not able to be seen with human senses, but his power and character may be perceived in his work of creation through reflection on it by the human mind [AB, Ho, WBC] or soul [NTC]. Although God in his essence is hidden from human sight, there is much about him which can be known through what he has made [NICNT]. Outward things that we see are the means by which we perceive invisible things [Gdt, Mor]. Certain attributes of God are clearly perceived by viewing what God has made [NAC]. The creation is a visible disclosure of the invisible God [St]. Through the creation he has made himself knowable [TH]. A clear perception or comprehension of God's invisible perfections is derived from seeing what is visible to the senses [Mu].

QUESTION—What is meant that people 'see' and 'understand' something about God from creation?

Paul asserts that people actually do come to understand clearly something about God's nature and existence from the evidence of the natural order around them, and that this knowledge is available to all people, as he makes clear in 3:9 and 3:19–20 [NICNT]. The knowledge gained is mediated through observation of the created world [BECNT]. God's power, skill and goodness are displayed in the balance and intricacy of creation [NTC, St]. Although God himself is invisible, his qualities are mirrored in his works of creation and can be discerned through the power of reason [AB, Gdt, WBC]. On contemplating God's works, people can grasp enough about His nature to prevent them from confusing the created things with the Creator and committing the sin of idolatry [TNTC].

QUESTION—What does this passage say regarding the creation as a means to a saving knowledge of God?

Paul speaks of people coming to know God's power and deity, not his saving grace through Christ, and states that this results in condemnation, not in salvation, because they suppress that knowledge instead of living in accord with it [NICNT, St]. God reveals himself in nature in such a way as to hold all people responsible, since disbelief requires rebellion against common sense [NAC]. Though God's self-revelation through creation is sufficient to render people without excuse, it does not follow that it is sufficient to lead them to a saving knowledge of him [Ho]. What is clearly seen is that God is God, not man, and he stands infinitely above his creatures; moreover, he is not even saying that they denied the existence of God, but that they failed to give him the honor and praise he is due [HNTC]. God's power and deity can be known through observing the created world, but this does not convey the knowledge of his mercy and love, nor does it bring people to salvation [BECNT].

both/that-is-to-say[a] his eternal[b] power[c] and[a] divinity,[d]

LEXICON—a. τε…καί (LN 89.102): 'both…and' [ICC2, LN, WBC; TEV], 'even both…and' [ICC2], 'even… and' [KJV], 'that is to say…and'

[REB], 'namely...and' [BECNT], 'by (his invisible attributes) I mean' [HNTC]. This construction is translated simply as a coordinate noun phrase using 'and' [AB, NICNT; CEV, GW, KJV, NASB, NCV, NET, NIV, NLT, NRSV, REB]: his eternal power and divinity.
- b. ἀΐδιος (LN **67.96**) (BAGD p. 22): 'eternal' [AB, BAGD, BECNT, HNTC, ICC2, LN, NICNT, NTC; all versions except REB], 'everlasting' [REB].
- c. δύναμις (LN 76.1) (BAGD 1. p. 207): 'power' [AB, BAGD, BECNT, HNTC, ICC2, LN, NICNT, NTC; all versions], 'might' [BAGD].
- d. θειότης (LN **12.13**) (BAGD p. 354): 'divinity' [AB, BAGD, ICC2], 'divine nature' [BAGD, NTC; GW, NASB, NET, NIV, NLT, NRSV, TEV], 'divine being' [LN], 'deity' [BECNT, **LN,** NICNT; REB], 'Godhead' [HNTC; KJV], '(God's) character' [CEV], 'all the things that make him God' [NCV]. This word occurs only here in the NT.

QUESTION—What is meant by θειότης 'divinity'?

It is a summary term for all those attributes constituting divinity [ICC1, Mor, Mu]. It is a collective term for all the divine perfections [Ho], the divine nature and properties [ICC2], the sum total of the moral attributes of God the creator [Gdt]. It is the sum of his attributes, and in this context particularly the power, wisdom, and goodness exhibited in the creation [NTC]. It means that he is God, wholly other from his creation [HNTC, NAC, SSA].

QUESTION—What does the word 'eternal' modify?
1. It modifies δύναμις 'power' [Gdt, HNTC, ICC1, Mu, NICNT, NTC, SSA, TH; NCV]: his eternal power and his divinity. The attribute of eternity is predicated of God's power, but of course that also implies the eternity of God himself [Mu]. 'Power' is defined as eternal in order to describe it as the first or uncaused cause, and to distinguish it from all secondary causes observed in nature; the term divinity did not need such a qualification [Gdt].
2. It modifies the phrase δύναμις καὶ θειότης 'power and divinity' [BECNT, ICC2; GW, NLT, REB, TEV].

so-that[a] they-(are)-without-excuse,[b]

LEXICON—a. εἰς (LN **89.48**) (BAGD 4.e. p. 229): 'so that' [BAGD, ICC2, NICNT, NTC; KJV, NASB, NIV], 'as a result' [GW], 'so that as a result' [**LN**], 'so' [NET, NLT, NRSV, TEV], 'that' [HNTC], 'the result is that' [BECNT], 'consequently' [AB], 'that's why' [CEV], 'therefore' [REB], not explicit [NCV].
- b. ἀναπολόγητος (LN 33.438) (BAGD p. 60): '(to be) without excuse' [AB, BAGD, BECNT, HNTC, ICC2, LN, NICNT, NTC; KJV, NASB, NET, NIV, NRSV], 'to have no excuse' [LN; CEV, GW, NCV, NLT, TEV], 'to be left with no defense' [LN], 'indefensible (conduct)' [REB].

QUESTION—Is the phrase εἰς τό 'so that' to be understood as expressing result or purpose?
1. It indicates result [AB, BECNT, Ho, ICC2, NICNT, NTC, St, WBC; CEV, GW, KJV, NASB, NIV], or conclusion [AB, ICC1, SSA; CEV, REB]. It is not God's design that by revealing himself he makes the opposition of men inexcusable, but rather that because he has so revealed himself, they have no excuse for ignorance or neglect of God [Ho]. They ought to have recognized him since they have been constantly surrounded by evidences of God's nature [ICC2].
2. It indicates purpose, not merely result [Gdt, HNTC, ICC2, Mor, Mu, NAC, NICNT]. God has made the universe in such a way that people are responsible and culpable if they reject the light given them [Mor]. One of God's purposes in providing this revelation is to make all people responsible for their own condemnation [NAC, NICNT]. The design of God was to give such a clear disclosure of his power and divinity through creation that men who reject it are without excuse [Mu]. It is not God's intent that people sin, but if they do sin, he intends that they will be without excuse since he has done what was necessary to give them sufficient knowledge of himself [ICC1].

QUESTION—What is it that people have no excuse for?

They are without excuse for their failure to respond appropriately to the revelation of God in creation [WBC]. People have no excuse for not acknowledging him as their God and worshipping him [AB, Mu, NTC], for not acknowledging him as the powerful creator who exists above the natural order [NAC]. They have no excuse for rejecting the knowledge of God which was available to them through creation [HNTC, NICNT]. They have no excuse for their ignorance of the existence of God [BECNT, Gdt, Ho, ICC2, Mor, SSA], nor for neglecting him [Ho]. They have no excuse for being ignorant of God's character [Gdt], or of his power [BECNT]. They have no excuse for their sinning [ICC1, TH] and their rebellion against what they can know about God's power, deity, and glory through creation [St].

1:21 because[a], knowing[b] God, did-they-did not -glorify[c] (him) as[d] God nor did-they-give-thanks,[e]

LEXICON—a. διότι (LN 89.26) (BAGD 3. p. 199) 'because' [AB, BAGD, BECNT, HNTC, ICC2, LN, NICNT, WBC; KJV, TEV], 'for' [BAGD, NTC; NASB, NET, NIV, NRSV], 'since' [NIV], not explicit [CEV, GW, NCV, NLT, REB, TEV].

b. aorist act. participle of γινώσκω (LN **28.1**) (BAGD 1.b. p. 160): 'to know' [AB, BAGD, BECNT, HNTC, LN, NTC, WBC; all versions except CEV], 'to know about' [**LN**; CEV], 'to have knowledge of' [ICC2, LN, NICNT]. The phrase 'because knowing God' is translated concessively: 'since, although they knew about God' [**LN**], 'because though they knew God' [AB, HNTC, WBC], 'for though they knew God'

[NRSV], 'because though they have known God' [ICC2], 'for although they knew God' [NTC; NET, NIV].
   c. aorist act. indic. of δοξάζω (LN 87.24) (BAGD 1. p. 204): 'to glorify' [AB, BECNT, HNTC, ICC2, LN, NICNT, NTC, WBC; KJV, NET, NIV], 'to give glory to' [NCV], 'to praise' [BAGD; GW], 'to honor' [BAGD; CEV, NASB, NRSV, REB], 'to give (him) the honor' [TEV], 'to worship' [NLT].
   d. ὡς (LN 64.12) (BAGD III.1.a. p. 898): 'as' [AB, BAGD, BECNT, HNTC, ICC2, LN, NICNT, NTC, WBC; KJV, NASB, NET, NIV, NLT, NRSV, REB], not explicit [CEV, NCV]. The phrase ὡς θεόν 'as God' is translated 'for being God' [GW], 'that belongs to him' [TEV].
   e. aorist act. indic. of εὐχαριστέω (LN 25.100, 33.349) (BAGD 2. p. 328): 'to give thanks' [BAGD, BECNT, HNTC, ICC2, NICNT, NTC, WBC; NASB, NET, NIV, NLT, NRSV], 'to render thanks' [BAGD; REB], 'to thank' [AB, LN (33.349); CEV, GW, NCV, TEV], 'to be thankful' [LN (25.100); KJV], 'to be grateful' [LN (25.100)].

QUESTION—What relationship is expressed by the conjunction διότι 'because', and what is the relationship of this verse to the preceding material?
   1. This expresses reason. The revelation of God in nature leads to condemnation because people refuse to acknowledge and worship God [Gdt, Ho, Mu, NICNT]. The conjunction has a weak causal force [NICNT]. The verse gives the grounds for the conclusion reached in 1:20 that people are without excuse [Gdt, SSA].
   2. It introduces 1:21 as a clarification and amplification of the last clause of 1:18 regarding how people suppress the truth by their wickedness, and of 1:20 [NTC]. It introduces 1:21–23 as an explanation of what was just said in the last clause of 1:20 and also to clarify the last part of 1:18 [ICC2]. The word is used to carry on the argument in a logical sequence, introducing 1:21–23 as an explanation of what was just said in 1:20 [Mor]. It introduces a more detailed explanation of the ungodliness described in 1:18; that is, people are ungodly in abandoning the worship of God for the worship of idols [BECNT].

QUESTION—What relationship is expressed by the participle γνόντες 'knowing'?
   Note that there is a considerable amount of overlap possible between the positions listed below, and one does not rule out the other.
   1. It expresses concession [AB, BECNT, HNTC, Ho, ICC1, ICC2, LN (28.1), NICNT, NTC, SSA, TH, WBC; NET, NIV, NRSV]: although they knew, they did not honor.
   2. It expresses a contrast with the following clause [Mor; CEV, NLT, TEV]: they knew but did not honor. They had the knowledge but reacted the wrong way; they refused to glorify or honor God [Mor].
   3. It is expressed as a temporal relation [Gdt; KJV]: when they knew they did not honor.

QUESTION—Of what significance is the aorist tense of the participle γνόντες 'knowing'?
1. The aorist is important in that knowing God precedes the refusal to revere him [ICC2, NICNT]. Their experience of God always goes before the failure to recognize its significance and then to act accordingly [ICC2]. This shows that their knowledge preceded their failure and makes it more worthy of blame [Mor].
2. The aorist tense verb forms used in this and the following two verses are gnomic, which means they describe what is always true about what the pagans do [NAC]. The force of the Greek aorist in this passage is to indicate what men have typically done throughout history [TH].

QUESTION—In what sense did they know God?

It is limited to what can be known of God through the created order [Ho, Mu, NICNT, NTC], but this is not sufficient to establish a relationship with him [NICNT]. It refers to knowing about God, but not to having an intimate relationship with him [TH]. God made himself known through creation in such a way that they should have acknowledged his great splendor and power as creator [WBC]. This cannot be understood absolutely since elsewhere Paul states that people outside Christ do not know God, but refers only to that limited knowledge of God's power available to all people through observing creation [St]. They had some experience of God through awareness of the created order, but failed to see the significance of it or act accordingly [ICC2]. This refers to a vague, inceptive, unformulated knowledge about God which never developed as it should into a proper recognition expressed in worship and love [AB].

QUESTION—What is the reason Paul gives in this verse for people being without excuse?

All acts of sin are all rooted in the most fundamental human sin, which is the rejection of God as God by failing to glorify him and give him thanks, that is, to give him proper worship [BECNT]. Paul emphasizes that the sin is not ignorance but failure to show reverence to God [AB, Gdt, ICC1, NTC, TH], or to have gratitude for one's existence and the good things which have been experienced [AB, NTC]. They did not give God the glory and thanks that the knowledge they actually had ought to have prompted [Mu]. They did not thank him or give him glory, but chose to ignore him instead [NAC]. God's self revelation calls for a human response of acknowledgment of his splendor and power as creator, with the humble gratitude of a creature to a creator, yet they refused to do this [WBC]. They failed to recognize him as the creator and source of all the good things they enjoy, and to thank him for his goodness and generosity [ICC2]. Men should have recognized his lordship and lived in thankful obedience, but have not done so; their fault is in their rebellion, not a lack of knowledge [HNTC]. They did not act on the knowledge of God they had, but instead failed to give him honor or willing obedience [Mor].

But[a] they-became-futile[b] in[c] their reasonings[d]

LEXICON—a. ἀλλά (LN 89.125) 'but' [ICC2, NICNT, NTC, WBC; KJV, NASB, NET, NIV, NRSV], 'instead' [AB, BECNT, HNTC; GW, TEV], not explicit [CEV, NCV]. It is translated as coordinate: 'and' [NLT]; as result: 'hence' [REB], 'the result was that' [NLT].
  b. aorist pass. (deponent = act.) indic. of ματαιόομαι (LN **65.38**) (BAGD p. 495): 'to become futile' [BECNT, ICC2, LN, NTC, WBC; NASB, NET, NIV, NRSV], 'to become foolish' [NICNT], 'to be become useless' [NCV], 'to be reduced to futile thinking' [AB], 'to become nonsense' [**LN**; TEV], 'to grow vain (in thinking)' [HNTC], 'to become vain (in their imaginations)' [KJV]. The phrase ἐν τοῖς διαλογισμοῖς αὐτῶν 'in their reasonings' is translated as the subject of this verb: 'their reasoning became futile' [**LN**], 'their thoughts have become complete nonsense' [TEV], 'their thoughts are useless' [CEV], 'all their thinking has ended in futility' [REB], 'their thoughts were total nonsense' [GW], 'their thoughts became directed to worthless things' [BAGD], 'their thinking became useless' [NCV], 'they began to think up foolish ideas of what God was like' [NLT]. This aorist is probably ingressive [NICNT]. This would mean that it the action is viewed in terms of a beginning, that their thoughts began being futile.
  c. ἐν with dative object (LN 83.13): 'in' [BECNT, HNTC, ICC2, LN, NICNT, NTC, WBC; KJV, NASB, NET, NRSV], not explicit [AB; CEV, GW, NCV, NIV, NLT, REB, TEV].
  d. διαλογισμός (LN **30.10**) (BAGD 1. p. 186): 'reasoning' [BAGD, BECNT, ICC2, LN, NICNT; NET], 'thinking' [AB, HNTC, WBC; NCV, NIV, NRSV, REB], 'thoughts' [BAGD, **LN**; CEV, GW, NET, TEV], 'imaginations' [KJV], 'speculations' [NTC; NASB].

QUESTION—What is meant by ἐματαιώθησαν ἐν τοῖς διαλογισμοῖς αὐτῶν 'they became futile in their reasonings'?

In the NT this word for 'reasoning' is usually used in a negative sense [Gdt, Ho, ICC1, ICC2, Mor, Mu], reflecting reasonings that are perverse and self-willed [ICC1], or destitute of any fruitful content [Mu]. It is the reasoning of an unregulated mind serving a corrupt heart [Gdt]. The phrase means that their natural capacity to reason accurately about God has been damaged permanently [NICNT]. In this context this refers specifically to a futility in their thinking about God, not necessarily in their thinking in general [SSA]. It refers to useless and vain speculation [AB]. In their futile arguing and speculation they ignored what God has revealed to be true through nature, history, conscience, and Scripture [NTC]. Their thoughts became perverted, corrupt, evil, and foolish [Ho]. There is a disconnection from reality involved in failing to recognize and glorify the true God [ICC2]. Worship of idols is futile and pointless, causing people to be out of touch with divine reality [Mor]. Because they closed their understanding and refused to respond properly to what revelation they had, they began fumbling with

and their foolish^a heart^b was-darkened.^c

LEXICON—a. ἀσύνετος (LN **32.49**) (BAGD 2. p. 118): 'foolish' [BAGD, BECNT, **LN**, NTC, WBC; KJV, NASB, NCV, NIV], 'senseless' [BAGD, HNTC, LN; NET, NRSV], 'lacking understanding' [NICNT], 'uncomprehending' [ICC2], 'misguided' [AB; GW, REB], 'stupid' [CEV], 'empty' [TEV], not explicit [NLT]. This clause is translated 'and their minds became dark and confused' [NLT].

b. καρδία (LN 26.3) (BAGD 1.b.β. p. 403): 'heart' [BECNT, HNTC, ICC2, LN, NICNT, NTC, WBC; KJV, NASB, NET, NIV], 'mind' [AB, BAGD, LN; CEV, GW, NCV, NLT, NRSV, REB, TEV]. This word represents the faculty of thought or the thoughts themselves [BAGD].

c. aorist pass. indic. of σκοτίζω (LN **32.44**) (BAGD 2. p. 757): 'to be darkened' [BAGD, BECNT, HNTC, ICC2, **LN**, NICNT, NTC, WBC; KJV, NASB, NET, NIV, NRSV], 'to be filled with darkness' [NCV, TEV], 'to be plunged into darkness' [GW, REB], 'to be steeped in darkness' [AB]. This verb is translated as active: 'to become dark' [BAGD; NLT], 'to be in the dark' [CEV].

QUESTION—What is meant by καρδία 'heart'?

The meaning is very comprehensive, including elements of rational thinking, volition, and emotion [AB, Gdt, Mor, NICNT, WBC]. It is the responding, feeling actions of the thinking and willing self [AB]. For Paul it is the mainspring of all one's thoughts, word, deeds, and motives [NTC]. It is the center of the inner life [Mor, WBC], from which all of a person's direction and commitments are shaped [Mor]. It is the center of rational and spiritual faculties [SSA], the most comprehensive term of human faculties, the seat of feelings, thoughts, and will [ICC1, Mu], the whole soul [Ho]. For Paul, it represents man's inward self as thinking, willing, and feeling, but here it focuses especially on the intellectual aspect [ICC2], on human reasoning [BECNT]. It is the inner faculty of thought and feeling [HNTC], the mind [AB, TH]. The word 'heart' is similar in Paul's usage to 'mind', referring to one's capacity for conscious, intelligent, and critical reflection and understanding; it is also that which grieves, craves, doubts or believes, or which is stubborn [AB].

QUESTION—In what sense has the heart been 'darkened'?

At the very center of the person where the knowledge of God must be embraced if it is to be effective, there has been a loss of ability to reason accurately regarding God [NICNT]. It means that they can no longer reason straight, their emotions cannot function properly, and their wills no longer desire to live in harmony with the law of God [NTC]. They are unable to comprehend the truth about what God wants them to know [SSA], incapable of truly rational thought about God [HNTC, NAC]. As a qualifier of 'thoughts' this figurative use of 'darkened' does not mean ignorance, but refers to a failure to think rightly or correctly concerning moral issues [TH]. Because they willingly refused God's self-revelation their whole intellectual and emotional life became clouded, their capacity respond to God was diminished, and they were less able to function as rational human beings [WBC]. They have lost the light of divine knowledge, which is it is not simply intellectual darkness, but darkness of the whole moral state, resulting in moral depravity and causing more such depravity [Ho].

1:22 Claiming[a] to-be wise[b] they-became-fools[c]

LEXICON—a. pres. act. participle of φάσκω (LN 33.218) (BAGD p. 854): 'to claim' [BAGD, NTC, WBC; CEV, GW, NET, NIV, NLT, NRSV], 'to assert' [BAGD, LN], 'to say' [BAGD; NCV, TEV], 'to boast of' [REB], 'to pretend to be' [AB, ICC2], 'to make oneself out to be' [HNTC], 'to profess to be' [BECNT; KJV, NASB] 'to suppose oneself to be' [NICNT]. This participle is translated concessively: 'even though' [BECNT], 'although' [NTC; NET, NIV].
  b. σοφός (LN 32.33) (BAGD 2. p. 760): 'wise' [AB, BAGD, BECNT, HNTC, ICC2, LN, NICNT, NTC, WBC; all versions except REB]. This adjective is translated as a noun: '(their) wisdom' [REB].
  c. aorist pass. (deponent = act.) indic. of μωραίνομαι (LN **32.56**) (BAGD 1. p. 531): 'to become a fool' [AB, BAGD, BECNT, **LN,** NICNT, NTC, WBC; GW, KJV, NASB, NCV, NET, NIV, NLT, NRSV], 'to become an utter fool' [NLT], 'to become foolish' [**LN**], 'to be turned into a fool' [HNTC], 'to be a fool' [CEV, TEV], 'to make a fool of oneself' [REB], 'to show oneself to be a fool' [BAGD, ICC2]. This aorist is probably ingressive [NICNT]. This would mean that the action is viewed in terms of a beginning, that they began being fools.

QUESTION—In what sense were they becoming foolish?

Their folly was their idolatry [BECNT, Gdt, HNTC, Ho, NICNT, NTC, St]. It refers specifically to idolatry, in which the glory of God is abandoned for the worship of the creature [BECNT]. They became foolish by not worshipping and honoring God as they should have, as well as by turning to false gods and idolatry [NICNT]. Polytheism could be viewed as a mental disorder or permanent hallucination [Gdt]. Their folly was in worshipping created beasts rather than God [Ho]. The rejection of truth marks one as a fool, and exchanging what is immortal for what is in the process of decay shows abysmal ignorance [NAC]. Their folly was their rejection of God's revelation [Mor]. This refers to moral obtuseness rather than any deficiency in intellectual capacity [TNTC]. By creating other gods they sought to attain a higher status than what God appointed to them, but they actually fell far below their God-given place [HNTC]. They sought to rise above their own creatureliness, but actually they became less capable of directing their own lives [WBC].

QUESTION—What relationship is indicated by the participle φάσκοντες 'claiming'?

1. It expresses a contrast with the following clause; they claimed to be wise, but became fools [AB, ICC2, NICNT, WBC; CEV, KJV, NCV, NRSV, REB, TEV]. The contrast is concessive; although they claimed to be wise they became fools [BECNT, NAC, NTC, TH; NET, NIV, NLT].
2. It expresses an instrumental relation; that is, by pretending to be wise they became fools [Mu].

1:23 and they-exchanged[a] the glory[b] of-the immortal[c] God

LEXICON—a. aorist act. indic. of ἀλλάσσω (LN **57.142**) (BAGD 2. p. 39): 'to exchange' [AB, BAGD, BECNT, HNTC, ICC2, **LN,** NICNT, NTC; GW, NASB, NET, NIV, NRSV, REB], 'to substitute' [LN], 'to trade' [NCV], 'to change' [WBC; KJV]. The phrase καὶ ἤλλαξαν... ἐν 'they exchanged...into' is translated 'instead of worshiping...they worship' [NLT, TEV], 'they don't worship...Instead, they worship' [CEV]. The phrase 'in that' is added at the beginning of this verse: 'in that they exchanged' [BECNT].

b. δόξα (LN 33.357, 79.18, 87.23) (BAGD 1.a. p. 203): 'glory' [AB, BECNT, HNTC, ICC2, LN (79.18, 87.23), NICNT, NTC, WBC; GW, KJV, NASB, NCV, NET, NIV, NRSV, REB] 'splendor' [LN (79.18)], 'majesty' [BAGD], 'greatness' [LN (87.23)], not explicit [TEV]. This noun is translated as an adjective: 'glorious' [CEV, NLT].

c. ἄφθαρτος (LN 23.128) (BAGD p. 125): 'immortal' [AB, BAGD, ICC2, LN, NICNT, NTC; GW, NET, NIV, NRSV, REB, TEV], 'imperishable' [BAGD, LN], 'incorruptible' [BAGD, BECNT, HNTC, WBC; NASB, NET], 'eternal' [CEV], 'ever-living' [NLT], 'who lives forever' [NCV], 'uncorruptible' [KJV].

QUESTION—What is meant here by δόξα 'glory'?

It refers to the splendor and majesty that intrinsically belong to God, his awesome presence [NICNT]. It is the splendor of his perfections that are revealed in the heart of his thinking human creation, producing within them an image forming the ideal of all that is good [Gdt]. It refers to the radiant manifestations of God's presence in the tabernacle, in all the splendor of his presence, and the force of his self-manifestation [AB]. It refers to God's existence and being, which should be praised, honored, and worshipped [TH]. It is the sum total of God's marvelous attributes, perfection, and splendor [NTC], a collective term for all God's perfections [Ho]. It is the self-manifestation of the majesty of the true God spoken of in 1:19 and 1:20 [ICC2, Mu]. It is his manifest perfections [ICC1]. It speaks of God's greatness and majesty [Mor]. Here it refers to his self-revelation in nature in 1:19–22 [NAC].

for[a] (the) likeness[b] of-(the)-form[c] of-(a)-mortal[d] human-being[e] and birds and four-footed-animals[f] and reptiles.[g]

LEXICON—a. ἐν (LN 84.22) (BAGD IV.5. p. 261): 'for' [AB, BAGD, BECNT, HNTC, ICC2, NICNT, NTC, WBC; GW, NASB, NCV, NET, NIV, NRSV, REB], 'into' [LN; KJV], not explicit [CEV, NLT, TEV].

b. ὁμοίωμα (LN **64.3**) (BAGD 2. p. 567): 'likeness' [BECNT, ICC2, **LN,** NICNT, WBC], 'copy' [BAGD], 'image' [AB, BAGD, NTC; KJV, NASB, NET, NIV, NRSV, REB, TEV], 'statue' [GW], 'idol' [CEV, NCV, NLT]. The phrase ὁμοιώματι εἰκόνος 'the likeness of the form' is translated 'the likeness of' [**LN**], 'the mere likeness of' [WBC], 'the mere shadowy image of' [HNTC].

c. εἰκών (LN **6.96**, 58.35) (BAGD 2. p. 222): 'form' [BAGD, ICC2; NASB], 'likeness' [LN (**6.96**, 58.35)], 'same form as' [LN (58.35)], 'image' [BECNT, NICNT; KJV], 'idols' [NLT]. The phrase 'of the form' is translated 'shaped like' [AB; REB], 'in the shape of' [NTC], 'made like to' [KJV], 'made to look like' [CEV, NCV, NIV, NLT, TEV], 'that looked like' [GW], 'resembling' [NET, NRSV].

d. φθαρτός (LN **23.125**) (BAGD p. 857): 'mortal' [AB, BAGD, ICC2, **LN,** NICNT, NTC; GW, NET, NIV, NRSV, REB], 'corruptible' [BECNT, HNTC, WBC; KJV, NASB, NET], 'perishable' [LN], 'who cannot live forever' [CEV], 'earthly' [NCV]. The phrase φθαρτοῦ ἀνθρώπου 'a mortal human being' [BAGD, **LN**] is also translated 'mere people' [NLT], 'mortals' [TEV].

e. ἄνθρωπος (LN 9.1): 'human being' [AB, BECNT, LN (9.1); NET, NRSV], 'man' [HNTC, ICC2, LN (9.24), NICNT, NTC, WBC; KJV, NASB, NIV, REB]. This singular noun is translated as a plural: 'people' [NCV, NLT], 'human beings' [AB, BECNT; NRSV], 'humans' [CEV, GW], 'mortals' [TEV].

f. τετράπουν (LN 4.4) (BAGD p. 814). This plural noun is translated 'four-footed animals' [BAGD, ICC2, LN, NTC; NASB, NET, NRSV], 'animals' [HNTC, LN, NICNT; CEV, GW, NCV, NIV, NLT, TEV], 'four-footed beasts' [KJV], 'beasts' [BECNT, WBC; REB], 'four-footed creatures' [AB], 'quadrupeds' [BAGD, LN]. This word occurs only here in the NT.

g. ἑρπετόν (LN 4.51) (BAGD p. 310): 'reptile' [AB, BAGD, BECNT, ICC2, LN, NICNT, NTC, WBC; CEV, NET, NIV, NRSV, REB, TEV], 'snake' [HNTC, LN; GW, NCV, NLT], 'creeping thing' [LN; KJV], 'crawling creature' [NASB].

QUESTION—What does it mean to exchange the glory of God for images?

They exchanged the worship of God for the worship of idols [BECNT, Mor, NTC, SSA, WBC]. They substituted the indirect and shadowy experience found in idolatry for direct contact with the glorious presence of God [NICNT]. The idea of exchange means that instead of doing one thing, they did another [SSA]. To exchange his glory is to give up acknowledging, honoring, and worshipping the true God, whose existence and being are revealed in his glory, and worshipping idols instead [TH]. In so doing they exchanged something of genuine worth, God's glory, for an image with no value at all [Mor].

QUESTION—What is the significance of using both the words ὁμοιώματι 'likeness' and εἰκόνος 'form' in the phrase ἐν ὁμοιώματι εἰκόνος 'for the likeness of the form of'?

1. The words are very similar in meaning, both being used frequently of idolatry [AB, BECNT, Mor, NICNT]. The two terms are essentially synonymous and together simply denote idol worship [BECNT, TH]. The significant semantic overlap means that the second word could be understood as epexegetic, or added for clarification, and has the effect of stressing the inferior nature of idolatry [NICNT]. Use of the two words together indicate that they worshipped not just the created thing, but an imperfect copy of the created thing, instead of God who created them [WBC]. Perhaps using both terms emphasizes the inferior character and utter unreality of what was substituted for God [HNTC, Mor].
2. The first word 'likeness' refers to what is crafted to represent something, and the second means the actual thing which is being copied, that which the idol seeks to reproduce [ICC2].
3. The first term applies to the material likeness, and the second to the mental image the artist has as he conceives of what sort of god he wants to represent [Gdt].

QUESTION—Are the words used for the classification of creatures a direct reference to the creation account or other OT passages?

It echoes language used in Ps. 106:20 [AB, BECNT, HNTC, Ho, ICC1, ICC2, Mor, NAC, NICNT, NTC, TNTC, WBC], and Jer. 2:11 [AB, BECNT, ICC1, ICC2, Mor, NICNT, NTC, WBC], as well as in Deut. 4:16–18 [AB, BECNT, ICC2, Mor], in Gen. 1:22–25 [BECNT, NICNT], and in Ex. 32 [AB, ICC2, WBC]. Paul may be alluding to the creation story, with its threefold division of the animal kingdom [NAC, NICNT, TNTC]. He may also be referring to Ps. 106:20 which comments on how Israel exchanged its glory for an image of a bull, and Jer. 2:11 which charges God's people with having exchanged their glory, and uses these as a paradigm to illustrate how all people tend to corrupt what knowledge of God they have [NICNT]. There may be some allusion to Ps. 106:20, but what is important about the designation of creatures is not so much the specifics of the categories, but the all-inclusive nature of them [TH]. The description of what they worshipped indicates a downhill progression [SSA].

1. Paul also seems to have the account of the fall in mind [NAC, TNTC, WBC].
2. It is unlikely that he is alluding to the account of the fall in Genesis 1 [AB, NICNT].

1:24 Therefore[a] God gave- them -over[b] in[c] the lusts[d] of-their hearts[e] to[f] impurity[g]

LEXICON—a. διό (LN 89.47) (BAGD p. 198) 'therefore' [BAGD, BECNT, LN, NICNT, NTC; NASB, NET, NIV, NRSV], 'wherefore' [ICC2, WBC; KJV], 'for this reason' [AB, LN; GW, REB], 'so' [HNTC; CEV, NLT], 'and so' [TEV], 'because they did these things' [NCV]. This word is a relatively emphatic marker of result [LN].
  b. aorist act. indic. of παραδίδωμι (LN 57.77) (BAGD 1.b. p. 615): 'to give (them) over to' [BAGD, LN, NTC; NASB, NET, NIV, TEV], 'to deliver over for' [AB], 'to deliver up' [ICC2], 'to hand (them) over to' [BAGD, BECNT, HNTC, LN, NICNT, WBC], 'to give (them) up to' [BAGD; KJV, NRSV, REB], 'to abandon' [BAGD], 'to allow (their lusts) to control them' [GW], 'to let (them) go ahead and do whatever…' [NLT], 'to leave (them) and let them go their sinful way' [NCV]. 'letting (them) follow…gave them over' [NTC], 'to let (these people) go their own way' [CEV].
  c. ἐν with dative object (LN 13.8) (BAGD III.3.a. p. 261): 'in' [BECNT, ICC2, LN, NICNT, WBC; NASB, NET, NIV, NRSV], 'to' [AB; REB], 'through' [KJV], 'by' [HNTC], 'letting them follow' [NTC], not explicit [CEV, GW, NCV, NLT, TEV].
  d. ἐπιθυμία (LN 25.20, 25.12) (BAGD 3. p. 293): 'lust' [HNTC, ICC2, LN (25.20); GW, KJV, NRSV], 'evil desire' [BAGD, LN (25.20)], 'desire' [BAGD, BECNT, LN (25.12), WBC; NET], 'vile desire' [REB], 'longing' [BAGD, LN (25.12)], 'craving' [AB, BAGD], 'sinful craving' [NTC], 'passion' [NICNT], 'sinful desire' [NIV]. The phrase ἐν ταῖς ἐπιθυμίαις τῶν καρδιῶν 'in the lusts of their hearts' is translated 'wanting only to do evil' [NCV], '(allowed) their lusts to control them' [GW]. The phrase ἐν ταῖς ἐπιθυμίαις τῶν καρδιῶν εἰς ἀκαθαρσίαν 'in the lust of their hearts to impurity' is translated 'they did what they wanted to do, and their filthy thoughts (made them do…)' [CEV], 'do the filthy things their hearts desire' [TEV], 'do whatever shameful things their hearts desired' [NLT], 'their own vile desires' [REB].
  e. καρδία (LN 26.3) (BAGD 1.b.ε. p. 404): 'heart' [AB, BAGD, BECNT, HNTC, ICC2, LN, NICNT, NTC, WBC; KJV, NASB, NET, NIV, NLT, NRSV, TEV], not explicit [CEV, GW, NCV, REB].
  f. εἰς with accusative object (LN 89.57): 'to' [NICNT, NTC, WBC; KJV, NASB, NET, NIV, NRSV], 'in order to, for the purpose of' [LN (89.57)], 'for' [AB], 'to…so that' [BECNT, ICC2], 'to…that by' [HNTC], 'as a result' [NCV], not explicit [CEV, GW, NLT, REB, TEV]. This word marks intent, often with the implication of expected result [LN].
  g. ἀκαθαρσία (LN **88.261**) (BAGD 2. p. 28): 'impurity' [AB, LN; NASB, NET, NRSV], 'uncleanness' [BECNT, ICC2, NICNT, WBC; KJV], 'unclean life' [HNTC], 'filthiness' [LN], 'filthy thoughts' [CEV], 'sexual immorality' [NTC], 'immorality' [LN], 'immoral things' [**LN**], 'sexual impurity' [NIV], 'to go their sinful way' [NCV], not explicit [CEV, GW,

NLT, REB, TEV]. This noun is also translated as a verb phrase: 'they became full of sexual sin' [NCV]. This represents a state of moral impurity, especially in relation to sexual sin [LN].

QUESTION—What relationship is indicated by the use of διό 'therefore'?

Paul now begins to speak of the consequences of refusing to worship God and of choosing sin [AB, BECNT, Gdt, Ho, ICC2, Mor, NAC, NICNT, SSA, TH]. God did this because they rejected the knowledge of God that was available to them and worshipped idols [BECNT, Mor, NICNT, SSA, TH], because they forsook him [Ho]. Immorality is a consequence of idolatry [AB, BECNT, NTC, St]. This particle links what follows to what has preceded [ICC2, Mor]. The conjunction is an inferential one, but the content of the verses following indicate that Paul presents the first in a set of consequences resulting from the rejection of the knowledge of God [SSA].

QUESTION—What is meant by παρέδωκεν αὐτοὺς ὁ θεός 'God gave them over'?

1. God is seen as taking an active role in this process [BECNT, Gdt, HNTC, Ho, ICC2, Mor, NTC, WBC]. This in not an impersonal working out of moral law, but it involves an active personal decision and response by God [BECNT]. God was not merely passive in the sense of abstaining from something, he actively withdrew the force of his restraining hand [Gdt, NAC]. God does not compel men to do evil [Gdt, ICC2], but he does withhold his help, which is the only thing that would prevent such a thing [ICC2]. God withdraws his blessings and restraints, allowing moral degradation to pursue its course; moral perversion is a result of God's wrath [AB]. God abandons them to their sin, letting them go their own way [TH]. He removes the restraints of his providence and grace, abandoning them to be dominated by sin [Ho].

2. God does even more than remove his restraint, he actively delivers them up to ever increasing wickedness [ICC1, Mu, NICNT]. Their being handed over is not merely a matter of God passively withdrawing his influence, but his taking an active role as the initiator of the process, handing them over to the terrible cycle of ever increasing sin [NICNT]. Although there is a natural law of consequence at work here, God's consigning them to retribution means that they are actively abandoned to a more intense and aggravated cultivation of their own lusts, with the result that they reap an even greater retribution for their sin [Mu].

QUESTION—Is the intent of this 'giving over' reformative, to bring about repentance, or is it punitive, to bring judgment?

1. It is retributive or punitive [AB, HNTC, Ho, ICC1, Mu, NAC, NICNT, NTC, TH, TNTC]. It is the judgment of letting people have their own way [NAC, TH]. They are enslaved by the very freedom they demanded and received [TNTC].

2. It is intended to bring about repentance [Gdt, ICC2, Mor]. Some people can only come to their senses by the very excesses of their own corruption [Gdt]. God, who smites in order to heal, gave them over as an act of

judgment as well as of mercy, so that they might learn to hate the futility of a life lived apart from the truth of God [ICC2]. God allows people to experience the consequences of their sin so they will repent and seek his mercy [Mor].
3. While it is punitive, it is also at least potentially redemptive if it causes people to recoil from the degeneracy to which their sins lead [WBC].

QUESTION—What relationship is indicated by the preposition ἐν in the phrase 'in the evil desires of their hearts'?
1. It indicates the existing moral condition of these people [Ho, ICC2, Mu, NICNT, SSA, TH]. The phrase expresses the condition or circumstances of these people, showing that they were already immersed in sin prior to being given over by God [Ho, Mu, NICNT]. This is their actual condition and character of life [ICC2].
2. It indicates that the lusts are the instrument of punishment [Gdt, HNTC, Mor]: they are punished through or by their sinful lusts.
3. It indicates that the lusts are the consequential punishment of God's handing them over [AB, ICC1]: he gave them over to their sinful lusts.

QUESTION—What is meant by ἀκαθαρσία 'impurity'?
All Pauline uses of this word refer generally to immorality and especially of sexual immorality [ICC2, Mu, NICNT]. In many places where Paul uses this word he is referring to illicit sexual activity, which is what it means here [BECNT, St]. It is moral depravity [TH], sexual immorality [SSA], the implications and specifics of which are further elaborated in the following verses [BECNT, NICNT, SSA]. This is a broad and general term, usually implying sexual immorality, as is hinted at here, but not limited to that [Mor]. It includes, but is not limited to, the sexual immorality committed in pagan religious practices [ICC2]. It is lust, perversion, and moral degradation [AB].

the dishonoring[a] their bodies among[b] themselves;

TEXT—Instead of ἐν αὐτοῖς 'among themselves', some manuscripts have ἐν ἑαυτοῖς 'with each other'. GNT does not mention this alternative. This phrase is translated 'with each other' [TEV], 'with each other's bodies' [NLT], 'with one another' [NIV], though this may be for stylistic reasons only.

LEXICON—a. pres. mid. or pass. infin. of ἀτιμάζω (LN 88.127) (BAGD p. 120): 'to be dishonored, to be treated shamefully' [BAGD, LN], 'to be degraded' [AB, BAGD]. The phrase τοῦ ἀτιμάζεσθαι τὰ σώματα αὐτῶν 'the dishonoring their bodies' is translated 'made them do shameful things with their bodies' [CEV], 'as a result they dishonor their bodies by sexual perversion' [GW], 'as a result they did vile and degrading things with (each other's) bodies' [NLT], 'and the consequent degradation of their bodies' [REB], 'so that their bodies would be dishonored' [BECNT; NASB], 'so that their bodies were dishonored' [NTC], 'so that their bodies are dishonored' [ICC2], 'that their bodies

might be dishonored' [HNTC], 'using their bodies wrongly' [NCV], 'for the degrading of their bodies' [NIV], 'to dishonor their bodies' [NET], 'to dishonor their own bodies' [KJV], 'to the degrading of their bodies' [NRSV], 'and they do shameful things (with each other)' [TEV].
- b. ἐν with dative object (LN 83.9): 'among' [AB, BECNT, LN, NICNT, NTC, WBC; NASB, NET, NRSV], 'with' [LN; CEV, GW, NCV, NIV, NLT, TEV]. The phrase ἐν αὐτοῖς is translated 'among them' [AB, ICC2; NASB], 'among themselves' [BECNT, NTC, WBC; NET, NRSV], 'by their own activities' [HNTC], 'with their (bodies)' [CEV], 'with one another' [NIV], 'with each other' [GW, NCV, TEV], 'between themselves' [KJV], not explicit [REB].

QUESTION—How should the genitive particular infinitive construction τοῦ ἀτιμάζεσθαι 'for dishonoring' be understood?

1. It indicates result or consequence [AB, ICC1, ICC2, Mor, NTC, SSA, St, TH; CEV, GW, NCV, NLT, REB]. Though it generally denotes purpose in Greek literature, here we should understand it as result [Mor]. This indicates the result of God's having handed these people over [ICC2]. Sexual sin is a consequence or outworking of these people rejecting God [St, TH]. It was God's purpose that the consequence of humans being delivered over to sexual immorality would be dishonoring their bodies [BECNT].
2. This is epexegetical, explaining and further elaborating the word 'impurity' [HNTC, Mu, NICNT]. This clause defines the 'uncleanness' to which they were abandoned [Mu].
3. It indicates the purpose for which God handed these people over [Gdt; NASB].

QUESTION—Should the verb ἀτιμάζεσθαι 'to dishonor' be understood as middle or passive?

1. It should be understood as passive [BECNT, HNTC, ICC1, ICC2, Mor, Mu, NTC; NASB]: that their bodies should be dishonored.
2. It should be understood in this context as middle [Gdt, Ho, NICNT, WBC]: they dishonored their bodies. The punishment consists not only of being dishonored, but of dishonoring oneself [Gdt]. It is translated here as middle by GW, KJV, NET, NIV, NRSV, though possibly for stylistic reasons.

QUESTION—To what does the phrase τοῦ ἀτιμάζεσθαι τὰ σώματα αὐτῶν ἐν αὐτοῖς 'dishonoring their bodies among themselves' refer?

1. This is in reference to the content of verses 1:26–27 and specifically of homosexual activity both for men and women [BECNT, Mu, NAC, NTC, TH]. The present tense indicates a continuing practice of dishonoring the body [NAC].
2. It speaks generally of sexual license [WBC].
3. Paul was referring to ritual prostitution which was nearly universal in idolatrous systems of the first century [Mor].

QUESTION—How should the phrase ἐν αὐτοῖς 'among themselves' be understood?
1. The phrase should be understood reflexively [AB, BECNT, Gdt, ICC1, ICC2, Mu, NICNT, NTC, WBC; NASB, NET, NRSV]: dishonoring their bodies among themselves. They now carry the seal of their infamy within their own personalities [Gdt]. Their lust brings about the degrading of their own bodies [AB]. The result of their having been delivered up to uncleanness is that among them, their bodies are dishonored [ICC2].
2. The phrase should be understood reciprocally [SSA, TH; GW, KJV, NCV, NIV, NLT, TEV]: with one another.

1:25 who[a] exchanged[b] the truth of God for[c] the lie[d]

LEXICON—a. ὅστις (LN 92.18) (BAGD 2.b. p. 587): 'who' [LN; KJV], 'they' [BAGD, BECNT, ICC2, NICNT, NTC, WBC; all versions except GW, NET], 'these people' [AB; GW], 'men who' [HNTC], 'such people who' [BAGD; NET].
b. aorist act. indic. of μεταλλάσσω (LN 57.142, 68.50) (BAGD p. 511): 'to exchange' [AB, BAGD, BECNT, HNTC, ICC2, LN (**57.142**, 68.50), NICNT, NTC, WBC; GW, NASB, NET, NIV, NRSV, REB, TEV], 'to trade' [NCV], 'to change' [KJV], 'to give up' [CEV], 'to substitute' [LN (57.142)]. This entire phrase is translated 'instead of believing what they knew was the truth about God, they deliberately chose to believe lies' [NLT]. This word occurs only here and in the next verse in the NT.
c. ἐν (LN 84.22) (BAGD IV.5. p. 261): 'for' [AB, BAGD, BECNT, HNTC, ICC2, NICNT, NTC, WBC; all versions except KJV, NLT], 'into' [LN; KJV], not explicit [NLT].
d. ψεῦδος (LN 33.254) (BAGD p. 892): 'lie' [AB, BAGD, BECNT, HNTC, ICC2, LN, NICNT, NTC; all versions], 'falsehood' [BAGD, LN, WBC]. This noun, which has the definite article, is translated as having the article: 'the lie' [BECNT, ICC2; KJV]; as not having the article: 'a lie' [AB, HNTC, NICNT, NTC; CEV, KJV, NET, NIV, NRSV, REB, TEV]; as a plural: 'lies' [NLT]; as an abstract noun: 'falsehood' [WBC].

QUESTION—What is the relationship between this verse and the context?
1. The first clause of 1:25 continues the thought of 1:24 and implies a causal relation; that is, God gave them over to impurity because they exchanged the truth of God for a lie [Gdt, HNTC, Ho, ICC1, Mu, NTC; NRSV], because they abandoned the true God and worshipped idols [BECNT]. Οἵτινες 'who' also has a qualitative nuance here, meaning 'being such a kind as that' or 'such people' [Gdt, Ho, ICC1, Mu, NAC], describing what it is that people of that sort do [Gdt, NAC]. Describing what kind of people they were explains why they merited what happened to them [Mu].
2. This verse summarizes what has been said in the previous verses and gives the root cause for the state of corruption and degradation that he has been describing, which is that people had turned away from what they

knew to be the truth of God for a lie, and worshipped the creature instead of the creator [WBC].
3. This verse begins a new sentence [ICC2, NICNT; CEV, GW, NCV, NIV, NLT, REB, TEV]. It introduces a new sentence that provides, just as 1:23 does for 1:24, the basis for God's judicial handing over of people to the consequences of their sinful choices described in 1:26 [NICNT]. This verse repeats and describes more fully what was already said in 1:22–24 [ICC2].

QUESTION—What is meant by the compound verb form μεταλλάσσω 'to exchange'?
1. This has the same meaning as the simple verb form ἀλλάσσω in 1:23, which is 'to exchange' [AB, BECNT, HNTC, Ho, ICC1, ICC2, Mor, NAC, NICNT, NTC, St, WBC].
2. The addition of the preposition μετά intensifies or strengthens the force of the verb [Gdt].

QUESTION—What is the meaning of the genitive phrase τὴν ἀλήθειαν τοῦ θεοῦ 'the truth of God'?
1. It is the truth about God, what is true about God [AB, Gdt, Ho, SSA, TH; CEV, NLT, NRSV, TEV]. It is the reality of God or the fact of God as he has revealed himself [NICNT]. It is the reality consisting of God himself and his self-revelation [ICC2, Mor]. It is the truth that God has made known [Mor, Mu], and which belongs to him [Mu]. This is God's self-revelation through creation [NAC]. This refers to the true conception of his being, which he has given through his self-revelation [Gdt]. This means the reality revealed about God in the gospel and manifested in creation [AB].
2. It is a periphrasis for 'the true God' [BECNT, Ho, ICC1], God himself as true [BECNT, Ho].
3. The phrase τοῦ θεοῦ 'of God' stands in apposition to τὴν ἀλήθειαν 'the truth', and the entire phrase refers to the fact that God himself is the truth [NTC]; that is, they exchanged God, who is the truth, for an idol, which is a lie.
4. 'The truth of God' is his invisible nature and power, but it also speaks of God's reliability and trustworthiness [WBC].

QUESTION—What is meant by the phrase τῷ ψεύδει 'the lie' for which the truth of God has been exchanged?
1. It refers to idolatry [AB, BECNT, Gdt, Ho, ICC1, ICC2, Mor, NAC, NICNT, NTC, SSA, St, WBC]. It refers to the second clause of the verse, that these people worship and serve the creature rather than the creator; putting any created thing in the place of God is the essence of idolatry [NICNT]. They turned away from what they knew was true about God, their creator, who alone was worthy of worship, and consequently turned their worship toward a created thing that was inferior and unworthy of worship [WBC]. The idol is a lie because it promises much but delivers little [NTC]. They have exchanged a true God for a false one [Ho, ICC1].

The lie is the idea that idols are real gods [SSA]. It is the whole futility of idolatry [ICC2]. The definite article indicates that this is more than just any lie, idolatry is 'the' lie [Mor, NAC, SSA], the ultimate lie [St]. Idolatry is the big lie, the deception that smothers the truth [AB]. Idolatrous heathen religion is the lie that leads people away from the truth of God [Mor]. It is that which contradicts God's truth [TNTC].

2. It refers to what is not true, in this case, about God [TH]. It is that truth that God has made known, particularly about himself, and conversely the lie is the contradiction of that truth about God, of which idolatry is but the concrete expression [Mu].

and worshiped[a] and served[b] what-has-been-created[c] instead-of[d] the-(one) having-created,[e]

LEXICON—a. aorist pass. (deponent = act.) indic. of σεβάζομαι (LN **53.53**) (BAGD p. 745): 'to worship' [BAGD, BECNT, HNTC, ICC2, **LN**, NTC, WBC; all versions except GW, REB], 'to reverence' [AB, BAGD] 'to offer reverence to' [REB], not explicit [GW]. This word is translated as a present participle: 'worshipping' [NICNT]. This clause is translated as beginning a new sentence: 'So they...' [GW, NLT]. This word occurs only here in the NT.

b. aorist act. indic. of λατρεύω (LN 53.14) (BAGD p. 467): 'to serve' [BAGD, BECNT, HNTC, ICC2, NTC, WBC; GW, KJV, NASB, NCV, NET, NIV, NRSV, TEV], 'to worship' [AB], 'to offer worship to' [REB], not explicit [CEV, NLT]. This finite verb is translated as a present participle: 'serving' [NICNT]. This word translates the most general Greek term for religious activity in honor of deity [TH].

c. κτίσις (LN **42.38**) (BAGD 1.b.β. p. 456): 'what has been created' [LN; NCV], 'what was created' [BAGD], 'what is created' [GW], 'creature' [AB, BECNT, ICC2, LN, NICNT, NTC, WBC; KJV, NASB, NRSV], 'creation' [BAGD, HNTC, LN; NET], 'created things' [NIV, REB], 'what God has created' [TEV], 'God's creation' [CEV], 'the things God made' [NLT].

d. παρά with accusative object (LN **89.132**, 78.29) (BAGD III.3. p. 611): 'instead of' [ICC2, LN (**89.132**); CEV, NCV, REB, TEV], 'rather than' [AB, BAGD, BECNT, HNTC, LN (89.132), NICNT, NTC, WBC; GW, NASB, NET, NIV, NRSV], 'more than' [BAGD, LN (78.29); KJV], 'but not' [NLT].

e. aorist act. participle of κτίζω (LN 42.35) (BAGD p.455): 'to create' [BAGD, LN]. The phrase τὸν κτίσαντα 'the one having created' is translated 'the creator' [AB, BAGD, BECNT, HNTC, ICC2, NICNT, NTC, WBC; GW, KJV, NASB, NET, NIV, NRSV, REB], 'the creator himself' [NLT, TEV], 'the God who created those things' [NCV], 'God' [CEV].

QUESTION—What is the meaning of the preposition παρά 'instead of' followed by the accusative?

1. It means 'instead of' [BAGD, ICC1, ICC2, Mor, Mu, NICNT, SSA, TH; CEV, NCV, REB, TEV] or 'rather than' [AB, NICNT, NTC, WBC; GW, NASB, NET, NIV, NRSV]. It expresses preference for one thing over another [AB]. When a comparison is being made, one member or element of the comparison may receive so little attention as to pass from consideration entirely, such that 'more than' becomes 'instead of', 'rather than', or 'to the exclusion of' [BAGD]. By a natural extension of its comparative force 'more than' it can mean 'instead of', as it does here [BAGD, ICC2], and this sense better fits Paul's emphasis on the exchange that idolaters are making [NICNT]. It means passing by and neglecting one thing for the sake of another [Ho, ICC1], leaving something aside with contempt so as to worship something else [Gdt]. Worshipping the creature means not worshipping the creator [Mu, NTC].
2. It is translated 'more than' [KJV].

QUESTION—What is the meaning of the two verbs σεβάζομαι 'worship' and λατρεύω 'serve' in this verse?

1. The two verbs are mutually interpreting and together sum up all that is involved in the worship of idols [NICNT]. It is a combination of two expressions, in which the first indicates in a general way what is defined more precisely in the second [ICC2]. The two words are used together to emphasize worship in the fullest sense [Mor].
2. The first refers to worship and the second to service [Gdt, Ho, SSA]. The first represents religious veneration and the second speaks of positive acts of worship or service [Gdt]. The first connotes adoring or revering and the second refers to cultic service [NTC]. The first word denotes general religious veneration, and the second denotes formal cultic worship [AB]. The words are often synonymous and both may express inward reverence as well as outward worship. However, the former properly expresses the feeling and the latter the outward service [Ho].

who is blessed[a] to the ages,[b] amen.[c]

LEXICON—a. εὐλογητός (LN 33.362) (BAGD p. 322): 'is blessed' [BAGD, BECNT, ICC2, NICNT, NTC, WBC; GW, KJV, NET, NRSV, REB], 'be blest' [AB], 'blessed be' [HNTC], 'is praised' [BAGD; NIV], 'is to be praised' [LN; NLT, TEV], 'should be praised' [LN; NCV], 'will be praised' [CEV].

b. εἰς τοὺς αἰῶνας (LN 67.95) (BAGD 1.b. p. 27): The idiom 'to the ages' is translated 'forever' [AB, BECNT, ICC2, LN, NICNT, NTC, WBC; all versions], 'eternally, always' [LN].

c. ἀμήν (LN **72.6**) (BAGD 1. p. 45): 'amen' [AB, BAGD, BECNT, HNTC, ICC2, NICNT, NTC, WBC; all versions], 'indeed, this is true' [**LN**], 'indeed' [LN], 'so let it be' [BAGD], 'truly' [BAGD, LN]. This word gives a strong affirmation of what is declared [LN].

QUESTION—What is the significance of Paul's use of this doxology or blessing form here?

This was a common Jewish blessing or doxology [AB, HNTC, ICC1, NTC, WBC], especially common at the mention of God's name [NTC]. Here it is a spontaneous doxology [AB, Mu, St], declaring that God is worthy of adoration [St]. It is a reaction against the dishonor just described in preceding clauses, affirming the intrinsic blessedness that belongs to God, and from which the dishonor done by men cannot detract [Mu]. It repudiates the dishonor directed toward God by heathenism [Gdt]. Paul adds this blessing formula to emphasize how foolish it is to worship created things instead of God [NICNT]. Although this appears as a doxology and semantically has emotive elements, in fact it serves as a concession to verse 25d–e; that is, although God deserves to be praised forever, these people worshiped and served the creation [SSA]. This phrase expresses the kind of worship that people should offer to God, and also functions as the conclusion to Paul's argument, with what follows from here to 1:32 being a series of illustrations of what he has been saying [TH].

QUESTION—What is the significance of the word ἀμήν 'amen' here?

This is the usual Jewish conclusion to a prayer or doxology [AB]. This word functions to affirm the truthfulness of what has just been said [Ho, TH]. It is a strong affirmation [Gdt], which in this case would be Paul's own assent of heart and mind [Ho, Mor, Mu, NTC], affirming what was just said [Mu, WBC]. It ends the doxology on a solemn note [Mor].

1:26 Because-of[a] this God gave- them -over[b] to[c] passions[d] of-dishonor,[e]

LEXICON—a. διά with accusative object (LN 89.26): 'because of, on account of' [LN]. The phrase διὰ τοῦτο 'because of this' [NICNT, NTC; NIV] is also translated 'for this reason' [AB, BECNT, WBC; GW, NASB, NET, NRSV], 'for this cause' [KJV], 'that is why' [NLT], 'wherefore' [ICC2], 'as a result' [REB], 'so' [HNTC], 'because they do this' [TEV], 'because people did those things' [NCV], not explicit [CEV].

b. aorist act. indic. of παραδίδωμι (LN 57.77) (BAGD 1.b. p. 615): 'to give (them) over to' [AB, BAGD, LN, NTC; NASB, NET, NIV, TEV], 'to give (them) up to' [BAGD; KJV, NRSV, REB], 'to abandon (them) to' [BAGD; NLT], 'to deliver (them) up to' [ICC2], 'to hand (them) over to' [BAGD, BECNT, HNTC, LN, NICNT, WBC]. This clause is translated 'God let them follow their own evil desires' [CEV], 'God allowed their shameful passions to control them' [GW], 'God left them and let them do the shameful things they wanted to do' [NCV].

c. εἰς with accusative object (LN 13.62): 'to' [AB, BECNT, HNTC, ICC2, LN, NICNT, NTC, WBC; NASB, NET, NIV, NLT, NRSV, REB, TEV], 'unto' [KJV], not explicit [CEV, GW, NCV].

d. πάθος (LN **25.30**) (BAGD 2. p. 603): 'passion' [AB, BAGD, BECNT, HNTC, ICC2, **LN,** NICNT, NTC, WBC; GW, NASB, NET, NRSV, REB,

TEV], 'lust' [LN; NIV], 'lustful desire' [LN], 'desire' [CEV, NLT], 'affections' [KJV], '(shameful) things they wanted to do' [NCV].
e. ἀτιμία (LN 87.71) (BAGD p. 120): 'dishonor' [BAGD, ICC2, LN, NTC], 'disgrace, shame' [BAGD]. This genitive noun is translated as an adjective: 'dishonorable' [BECNT, HNTC, NICNT; NET], 'disgraceful' [AB, WBC], 'shameful' [BAGD; GW, NCV, NIV, NLT, REB, TEV], 'evil' [CEV], 'vile' [KJV], 'degrading' [NASB, NRSV].

QUESTION—What relationship is indicated by the phrase διὰ τοῦτο 'because of this'?

It is inferential, relating a cause, stated in 1:25, with the effect, stated in 1:26 [Gdt, Ho, ICC1, ICC2, Mor, Mu, NICNT, NTC]. It introduces the result of what was described in 1:25, just as διό 'therefore' introduces 1:24 as expressing the result of what was described in 1:22–23 [Gdt, ICC2, NICNT, NTC]; that is, their exchanging the true God for idols is the cause of their being handed over to dishonorable passions [Gdt, Ho, Mor, NAC, NICNT]. Sexual immorality is a consequence of rejecting God and of idolatry [AB, BECNT]. Because they exchanged the true God for a false one, they also exchanged true natural functions for ones that are perverted [AB].

QUESTION—How are the nouns related in the genitive phrase πάθη ἀτιμίας 'passions of dishonor'?

1. The genitive noun ἀτιμία 'dishonor' is qualitative, describing the dishonorable, disgraceful, or evil nature of the passions [AB, BECNT, Gdt, HNTC, ICC1, Mor, Mu, NICNT, SSA, WBC; CEV, GW, KJV, NCV, NET, NIV, NLT, REB, TEV].
2. The genitive noun ἀτιμία 'dishonor' describes the degrading result of the passions [Ho, ICC2, NAC]. The passions bring dishonor [ICC2, NTC]. Indulging them covers a person with ignominy [Ho].

QUESTION—How should the phrase πάθη ἀτιμίας 'passions of dishonor' be understood?

The phrase πάθη ἀτιμίας 'passions of dishonor' corresponds to the 'uncleanness' of verse 24 [Mu, NICNT], and clearly refers to illicit sexual desires and behaviors as the following clauses make clear [NICNT]. It refers to homosexual activity [AB, Mor, Mu, St]. Here it has the connotation of a lust that is unnatural [NAC]. This echoes 1:24b about the dishonoring of their bodies [Gdt, NAC, NTC]. The acts as well as the passions are dishonoring [WBC]. This term represents something more ignoble than ἐπιθυμία, the word normally used in the NT for lust, and conveys the idea of a greater moral passivity and shameful bondage [Gdt].

for even[a] their women[b] exchanged[c] the natural[d] function[e]

LEXICON—a. τε...τε (LN 89.102): 'both...and' [LN]. This construction marks a closely related coordinate set [LN], which in this case would be his comments about women in 1:26 and men in 1:27. The phrase τε γάρ is translated 'for even' [KJV], 'for both' [ICC2], 'for' [NICNT, WBC; NASB, NET], 'even' [NIV, NLT, TEV], 'for as well as' [NTC], 'that is'

[BECNT], 'for example' [HNTC], not explicit [AB; CEV, GW, NCV, NRSV, REB].
b. θῆλυς (LN **79.103**) (BAGD p. 360): 'woman' [AB, BAGD, BECNT, HNTC, **LN,** NICNT, NTC; all versions], 'female' [ICC2, LN, NTC, WBC]. The phrase αἵ θήλειαι αὐτῶν 'their women' [AB, BECNT; GW, KJV, NASB, NET, NIV, NRSV] is also translated 'the women' [NLT, TEV], 'women' [NICNT; CEV, NCV], 'the women among them' [HNTC], 'among them, women' [REB], 'their females' [ICC2, NTC, WBC].
c. aorist act. indic. of μεταλλάσσω (LN 57.142, **68.50**) (BAGD p. 511): 'to exchange' [AB, BAGD, BECNT, HNTC, ICC2, LN (57.142, 68.50), NICNT, NTC; GW, NASB, NET, NIV, NRSV, REB], 'to substitute' [LN (57.142)], 'to change' [WBC; KJV], 'to pervert' [TEV], 'to cease...and to start' [LN (**68.50**)]. This entire clause is translated 'women no longer wanted to have sex in a natural way, and they did things with each other that were not natural' [CEV], 'women turned against the natural way to have sex and instead indulged in sex with each other' [NLT], 'women stopped having natural sex and started having sex with other women' [NCV].
d. φυσικός (LN **58.9**): 'natural' [AB, BECNT, HNTC, ICC2, LN, NICNT, NTC, WBC; all versions], 'in accordance with nature' [**LN**].
e. χρῆσις (LN **23.65**) (BAGD 3. p. 886): 'function' [BAGD; NASB], 'relations' [BAGD, WBC; NIV], 'sexual function' [**LN**], 'use' [KJV], 'sexual use' [LN], 'intercourse' [AB, HNTC, ICC2, NTC; NRSV, REB], 'sex' [NCV], 'the way to have sex' [NLT], 'use of their sex' [TEV], 'use of their bodies' [BECNT, NICNT], 'kind of intercourse' [HNTC], 'sexual relations' [GW, NET, REB], 'to have sex' [CEV].

QUESTION—What relationship is indicated by γάρ 'for'?

This connecting conjunction introduces the clause that follows as an explanation of what is meant by 'dishonorable passions' [NICNT].

QUESTION—What is the significance of repeating the verb μεταλλάσσω 'exchange' which was also used in 1:23 and 1:25?

There is a correspondence between this exchange and that described in 1:23 and 1:25 [AB, Gdt, ICC2, NICNT, NTC]. The meaning is essentially the same in each case and the repetition of this term clearly indicates Paul's condemnation of this conduct because of its association with idolatry and the rejection of God described earlier in the passage [AB, WBC]. Repetition of this word insinuates that this conduct is guilty [AB]. The repetition of the phrase 'God handed them over' intensifies the seriousness and solemnity of the sinful state that Paul is describing [WBC].

for[a] the (function) contrary-to[b] nature,[c]

LEXICON—a. εἰς (LN 13.62) (BAGD 4.b. p. 229): 'for' [AB, BECNT, HNTC, ICC2, LN (13.62), NICNT, NTC; GW, NASB, NET, NIV, NRSV, REB], 'into' [WBC; KJV], not explicit [CEV, NCV, NLT, TEV].

b. παρά with accusative object (LN **89.137**) (BAGD III.6. p. 611): 'contrary to' [BAGD, BECNT, ICC2, **LN,** NTC, WBC], 'against' [AB, BAGD, NICNT; KJV, NLT], 'not in accordance' [LN], not explicit [HNTC; NCV, NLT]. The phrase παρὰ φύσιν 'against nature' corresponds with παρὰ τὸν κτίσαντα 'instead of the creator' in 1:25 [Gdt].

c. φύσις (LN 58.8) (BAGD 3. p. 869): 'nature' [LN], 'the regular natural order' [BAGD]. The phrase παρὰ φύσιν 'contrary to nature' [ICC2, NTC, WBC] is also translated 'against nature' [AB, NICNT; KJV], 'that which is unnatural' [NASB], 'unnatural' [HNTC; NRSV, REB], 'unnatural ones' [GW, NET, NIV], 'unnatural acts' [TEV], 'not natural' [CEV], 'the way people should not act' [**LN**], 'the way in which people were not made to behave' [**LN**].

QUESTION—What is referred to by the phrase τὴν παρὰ φύσιν 'the (function) contrary to nature' in this verse?

It refers to lesbian behaviors and relationships [AB, BECNT, ICC2, Mor, Mu, NAC, NICNT, NTC, SSA, St, TH, WBC]. This is also strongly suggested by the use of 'likewise' in the following verse which more specifically details the homosexual vice among men [AB, ICC2]. The use of the word χρῆσις 'function' is well established as a periphrasis for sexual intercourse [ICC2, Mor]. Paul condemns homosexual practices as unnatural, indecent, shameful, and perverted [NAC].

QUESTION—What is the significance of the words φύσις 'nature' and φυσικός 'natural' in these verses in regards to homosexuality being a violation of God's created order and will?

These terms refer to God's original intent when he created men and women [BECNT, St]. The term φύσις 'nature' signifies God's created order [AB, HNTC, NICNT, St, WBC], and sins that are against nature are sins against God and against his created order [NICNT]. It is that which is in accord with the creator's intention and is manifest in nature, and men have no excuse for failing to recognize and respect it [ICC2]. That which is according to nature is in harmony with the natural order of things [AB]. Homosexuality is unnatural and is worthy of no respect [WBC]. Paul condemns homosexual partnerships and behaviors as always being illegitimate, so 'nature' cannot refer to an individual's personal nature or what seems right to him or her [St]. There is no indication that only specific kinds of homosexuality are prohibited; rather, all such conduct is forbidden as sinful and contrary to what God intended [BECNT, St]. Homosexuality is an abandonment of a divinely constituted order and is unnatural, on a lower level of degeneracy and perversion even than other sexual sin [Mu].

1:27 and likewise[a] also[b] the males[c]

LEXICON—a. ὁμοίως (LN 64.1) (BAGD p. 568): 'likewise' [AB, BAGD, BECNT, ICC2, LN, NICNT, NTC, WBC; GW, KJV, NET], 'similarly' [BAGD, LN], 'in the same way' [BAGD, HNTC; CEV, NASB, NCV, NIV, NRSV, TEV], 'so likewise' [NTC], not explicit [NLT, REB].

b. τε...καί (LN 89.103, 89.102): 'and...also' [ICC2; KJV, NASB, NET, NRSV], 'also' [BECNT, WBC; NIV], 'so...also' [NTC], 'and' [AB; NLT], 'and...too' [REB], 'both...and' [LN (89.102)], 'as...so also', 'not only...but also' [LN (89.103)], 'too' [REB], 'even' [TEV], not explicit [HNTC, NICNT; CEV, GW, NCV, TEV].
c. ἄρσην (LN **79.102**) (BAGD p. 109): 'male' [BAGD, **LN**], 'man' [LN; CEV, NET, NIV, NLT, NRSV, REB, TEV]. This plural form οἱ ἄρσενες 'the males' [ICC2, NTC, WBC] is also translated 'the men' [BECNT, HNTC; KJV, NASB, NET, NIV, NLT, NRSV, TEV], 'men' [NICNT, NTC; CEV, NCV, REB].

QUESTION—What is the significance of the connector ὁμοίως 'likewise' at the beginning of this verse?

This sin was not limited just to women [Mor]. This connects the two verses and shows that the same passions leading women into sexual perversion were also at work among men and have the same effect [NICNT]. It describes something that is equally dishonoring as what has just been described [Gdt]. Males engaged in behavior that was just as evil [Mor].

QUESTION—Is there any significance to the order and the use of the words θήλειαι 'females' and ἄρσενες 'males' instead of using 'men and women' in these verses?

1. Using the terms 'male and female' rather than 'men and women' emphasizes the element of sexual distinction or differentiation [BECNT, ICC2, Mor, Mu, NICNT, NTC]. He is thinking of the sexual relationship and compatibility [WBC]. The emphasis here is on sex [Mu]. Paul's use of these words probably draws on the LXX Genesis account of creation which uses the same words, and emphasizes how homosexual relations violate the distinctions God intended when he created them male and female [BECNT, NICNT]. Perhaps Paul mentions females first because he want to end the discussion with males, whose homosexuality was more prevalent, and with which he intended to deal in more detail [ICC2, Mor, NTC, WBC]. He could have used the terms 'men' and 'women' but the terms 'male' and 'female' emphasize not only the distinction between the sexes, but also allow for the fact that at times these sins were committed by boys and girls, and not just by men and women [NTC]. Paul may also have chosen to use the word ἄρσενες 'males' because it is used in passages in the LXX that condemn homosexuality [NICNT].
2. Paul mentions females first for the purpose of accentuating the grossness of the evil [Ho, Mu]. The delicacy of women makes more apparent the degeneracy of homosexuality in their case, which is brought out by translating 'even their women' [Mu]. They are mentioned first because as morals decay they are the last to be affected, and their corruption proves that all virtue has been lost [Ho].

having-abandoned[a] **the natural**[b] **sexual-function**[c] **of-the female**[d]

LEXICON—a. aorist act. participle of ἀφίημι (LN 68.43) (BAGD 3.b. p. 126): 'to abandon' [AB, BAGD, ICC2, NTC; NASB, NET, NIV], 'to give up' [BAGD, LN, WBC; GW, NRSV, REB, TEV], 'to forsake' [BECNT, HNTC], 'to leave' [NICNT; KJV], 'to stop' [LN; NCV], 'to stop having' [NCV], 'to stop wanting' [CEV], 'to quit' [LN], not explicit [NLT]. This participle is translated 'instead of having' [NLT].

b. φυσικός (LN 58.9) (BAGD 1. p. 869): 'natural' [AB, BAGD, BECNT, HNTC, ICC2, LN, NICNT, NTC, WBC; all versions except CEV, NLT], 'in accordance with nature' [BAGD], 'normal' [NLT], not explicit [CEV]. See this word at 1:26.

c. χρῆσις (LN **23.65**) (BAGD 3. p. 886): 'sexual function' [BAGD, **LN**], 'function' [NASB]. This word is translated 'sexual relations' [GW, TEV], 'relations' [BAGD, WBC; NET, NIV, REB], 'sexual relationships' [NLT], 'intercourse with' [HNTC, ICC2, NTC; NRSV], 'use (of women)' [BECNT], 'use of (the woman)' [NICNT; KJV], 'sex' [NCV]. The phrase τὴν φυσικὴν χρῆσιν τῆς θηλείας 'the natural sexual function of the female' is translated 'to have sex with women' [CEV], 'having natural sex' [NCV]. See this word at 1.26.

d. θῆλυς (LN 79.103) (BAGD p. 360): 'female' [BAGD, HNTC, ICC2, LN, NTC, WBC], 'female partner' [HNTC], 'woman' [BAGD, LN, NICNT, NTC; KJV, NASB], not explicit [NCV]. This genitive singular noun is translated as a plural: 'women' [AB, BECNT; CEV, GW, NET, NIV, NLT, NRSV, REB, TEV].

they-became-inflamed[a] **in**[b] **their desire**[c] **for**[d] **one-another,**[e]

LEXICON—a. aorist pass. indic. of ἐκκαίω (LN **25.16**) (BAGD p. 240): 'to be inflamed' [WBC], 'to be inflamed with passion for' [**LN**; NET, NIV], 'to have a strong lust for' [LN], 'to be inflamed with lust' [LN; NIV], 'to be inflamed with sensual desire' [BAGD], 'to be consumed' [HNTC, NTC; NRSV]. This passive verb is translated as an active intransitive verb: 'to burn' [AB, BECNT, ICC2, NICNT; GW, KJV, NASB, NLT, REB, TEV]. This entire phrase is translated '(they) began wanting each other' [NCV]. This word occurs only here in the NT.

b. ἐν with dative object (LN 13.8, 89.5): 'in' [BECNT, HNTC, ICC2, LN (13.8, 89.5), NICNT; KJV, NASB, NET], 'with' [AB, LN (13.8), WBC; GW, NIV, NLT, NRSV, REB, TEV], 'with regard to' [LN (89.5)], 'by' [NTC], not explicit [NCV].

c. ὄρεξις (LN **25.16**) (BAGD p. 580): 'desire' [BAGD, BECNT, NICNT, WBC; CEV, NASB], 'lust' [AB, HNTC, ICC2, **LN**; GW, KJV, NIV, NLT, REB], 'passion for' [LN, NTC; NET, NRSV, TEV], 'flaming passion' [NTC], 'intense desire for' [LN]. This noun is translated as a verb: '(they) began wanting' [NCV]. This word occurs only here in the NT.

d. εἰς with genitive object (LN 90.23): 'for' [BECNT, HNTC, ICC2, NICNT, NTC, WBC; GW, NET, NIV, NLT, NRSV, REB, TEV], 'towards' [NASB], 'toward' [KJV], 'with' [CEV], 'concerning' [LN], not explicit [NCV].

e. ἀλλήλων (LN 92.26): 'one another' [AB, BECNT, HNTC, ICC2, LN, NICNT, NTC, WBC; KJV, NET, NIV, NRSV, REB], 'each other' [LN; NLT, TEV]. The phrase εἰς ἀλλήλους 'for one another' is translated 'with other men' [CEV].

QUESTION—What is meant by ἐξεκαύθησαν ἐν τῇ ὀρέξει 'inflamed with desire'?

It is inordinate sexual desire or lust [NTC, WBC], an intense passion [Mu], a powerful but unnatural passion [Mor]. The implication is of something immoderate and ultimately self-destructive [WBC]. It is a strong sexual desire [SSA].

men with[a] men committing[b] the shameful-deed[c]

LEXICON—a. ἐν with dative object (LN, 90.56): 'with' [AB, BECNT, HNTC, ICC2, NICNT, NTC, WBC; all versions]. The phrase ἄρσενες ἐν ἄρσεσιν 'men with men' [HNTC, NICNT; GW, KJV, NASB, NRSV] is also translated 'men...with other men' [BECNT; NCV, NIV, NLT], 'with each other' [CEV, TEV].

b. pres. mid. (deponent = indic.) participle of κατεργάζομαι (LN **90.47**) (BAGD 1. p. 421): 'to commit' [AB, BAGD, BECNT, WBC; GW, NASB, NET, NIV, NRSV], 'to do' [BAGD, **LN,** NICNT; CEV, NCV, NLT, TEV], 'to perform' [LN], 'to perpetrate' [ICC2, NTC], 'to work' [KJV], 'to behave' [REB], 'wrought' [HNTC].

c. ἀσχημοσύνη (LN **88.149**) (BAGD 1. p. 119): 'shameful deed' [**LN**], 'shameless deed' [BAGD], 'shameless acts' [AB; NET, NRSV], 'that which was/is shameful' [BECNT, NICNT], 'what is shameless' [WBC], 'shameful things' [CEV, NCV, NLT, TEV], 'shamelessness' [ICC2, NTC], 'indecent behavior' [LN], 'obscenity' [HNTC], 'indecent acts' [GW, NASB, NIV], 'indecently' [REB], 'that which is unseemly' [KJV].

QUESTION—What is the ἀσχημοσύνην 'shameful deed' referred to here?

It is homosexual activity between men [AB, BECNT, HNTC, ICC2, Mor, Mu, NAC, NICNT, NTC, SSA, WBC].

and receiving-back[a] in[b] themselves the recompense[c] of-their error[d] which was-necessary.[e]

LEXICON—a. pres. act. participle of ἀπολαμβάνω (LN 90.63) (BAGD 1. p. 94): 'to receive back' [WBC], 'to receive' [BAGD, BECNT, HNTC, ICC2, **LN,** NICNT, NTC; KJV, NASB, NCV, NET, NIV, NRSV], 'to suffer' [NLT], 'to bring upon oneself' [TEV]. This active participle is translated as passive: 'to be paid' [REB], 'being paid in turn' [AB]. The phrase ἣν ἔδει...ἀπολαμβάνοντες 'receiving back...which was necessary' is translated 'what has happened to them is punishment' [CEV]. The phrase 'and receiving back in themselves the recompense' is

rendered so as to express a relationship of result or consequence by inserting the phrase 'as a result' at the beginning of the clause [NLT, TEV].
b. ἐν (LN 83.13, 83.9): 'in' [AB, BECNT, HNTC, ICC2, LN (83.13), NICNT, NTC, WBC; KJV, NASB, NCV, NET, NIV, NRSV, REB], 'within' [NLT], 'among' [LN (83.9); GW], 'upon' [TEV]. The phrase ἐν ἑαυτοῖς 'in themselves' is also translated 'in their own persons' [AB, HNTC, ICC2, NTC; NASB, NRSV, REB], 'within themselves' [NLT], 'in their bodies' [NCV], 'to them' [CEV], '(bring) upon themselves' [TEV].
c. ἀντιμισθία (LN **38.15**) (BAGD p. 75): 'recompense' [**LN**; KJV], 'penalty' [BAGD, BECNT, NICNT, WBC; NASB, NET, NIV, NLT, NRSV], '(due) reward' [HNTC], 'wage' [AB, ICC2; REB], '(due) return' [NTC], 'punishment' [CEV, GW, NCV, TEV].
d. πλάνη (LN **88.262**) (BAGD p. 665): 'error' [BAGD, BECNT, NICNT, WBC; KJV, NASB, NET, NRSV], 'folly' [HNTC], 'wrongdoing' [TEV], 'wrongs' [NCV], 'foolish deeds' [CEV], 'perversion' [ICC2, **LN**; GW, NIV, REB], 'deviation' [AB, NTC], not explicit [NLT].
e. imperf. act. indic. of δεῖ (LN 71.34) (BAGD 1. p. 172): 'to be necessary' [BAGD, LN, NICNT], '(it) must (be)' [BAGD, LN], 'to be suited to' [AB], 'appropriate' [BECNT, WBC], 'due' [HNTC, ICC2, NTC; NASB, NET, NIV, NRSV], 'fitting' [REB], not explicit [CEV, NCV]. The phrase ἣν ἔδει 'which was necessary' is translated 'which was meet' [KJV], 'they deserve' [GW, TEV], 'they so richly deserved' [NLT], not explicit [CEV].

QUESTION—What is the ἀντιμισθία 'recompense' or 'penalty' which people receive ἐν ἑαυτοῖς 'in themselves'?
1. The penalty is being handed over to the sin of sexual perversion [AB, BECNT, Gdt, Ho, ICC2, Mor, Mu, NAC, WBC]. Homosexuality is a perversion of God's intended relationship between men and women and carries its own destructive penalty [NAC]. Abandonment to immorality was the judicial consequence of apostasy [Ho, Mu]. Rejecting God ends in the ruin of self; the punishment of idolatry is immorality and unnatural impurity [Gdt]. Sexual perversion becomes its own penalty, and comes as a result of wandering from God [WBC]. They experience the ever-unsatisfied lust of sexual perversion, along with the terrible physical and moral consequences of such debauchery [Mu].
2. It is the guilty conscience, emotional stress, sleeplessness, and depression that result from such immoral acts, along with all the negative effects those have on the body [NTC].
3. It is probably eternal punishment, since he says in 1 Cor 6:9–10 that those who practice homosexuality will not inherit God's kingdom [NICNT].

QUESTION—What is the πλάνη 'error' that is referred to in this verse?
The term πλάνη 'error' should be taken in the strongest possible sense as a thorough turning away from truth in one's thinking as well as in one's

conduct [ICC2]. By using the word 'error' Paul is not minimizing the seriousness of the offense [NICNT].
1. This refers to the sin of homosexual relations [AB, Mor, NAC, NICNT, NTC, TH, WBC]. By the use of this word Paul clearly shows that he regards homosexual activity to be a perversion [AB], and a deviation from what is right [AB, Mor].
2. It is primarily or fundamentally the rejection of the true God for idols [BECNT, Gdt, Ho, ICC2, Mu]. The context shows that their error was forsaking the true God [Ho]. It is the apostasy from worship of God as described in verses 21–23, and 25 [Mu]. It is thinking wrongly about God [SSA]. It is voluntarily choosing the lie of idolatry [Gdt].

QUESTION—In what sense is the punishment ἔδει 'necessary'?

It is necessary in the sense that it is the punishment that they deserve [Gdt, TH; GW, NLT, TEV]. God will not allow his created order to be violated without imposing a just punishment [NICNT]. The indignant expression of God's wrath and desire for justice is well merited or deserved [Gdt]. Because these people have rejected God and scorned his glory, they had to be handed over to punishment [BECNT]. The punishment is decreed by God [Mor, WBC], and is not simply a natural result of people's actions [Mor]. In his wording he is adopting a legal formulation [AB]. In a moral universe there is a principle of retribution such that moral sin necessarily has a penalty [NAC, TNTC]. People will reap what they sow [NTC].

1:28 And just-as[a] they-thought-(it)- not -worthwhile[b] to-have[c] God in knowledge,[d]

LEXICON—a. καθώς (LN 89.34) (BAGD 3. p. 391): 'just as' [BECNT; NASB, NET], 'as' [AB, HNTC, ICC2, WBC], 'even as' [NICNT; KJV], 'since' [BAGD, ICC2, NTC; CEV, NIV, NRSV], 'because' [GW, TEV], 'thus, because' [REB], 'when' [NLT], not explicit [NCV].
  b. aorist act. indic. of δοκιμάζω (LN **30.98, 30.114**) (BAGD 2.b. p. 202): 'to think worthwhile' [**LN** (30.98); NIV], 'to regard as worthwhile' [LN (30.98)], 'to deem worthwhile' [NTC], 'to see fit' [AB, BAGD, HNTC, ICC2, NICNT; NASB, NET, NRSV, REB], 'to think important' [NCV], 'to think...fit' [BECNT], 'to think (God) qualified (for)' [WBC], 'to approve of' [BAGD, **LN** (30.114)], 'to think of as appropriate' [LN (30.98)], 'to like' [KJV]. The phrase οὐκ ἐδοκίμασαν 'they did not think worthwhile' is translated 'they thought it was worthless' [GW], 'they refused' [NLT], 'these people refused' [CEV], 'those people refuse' [TEV].
  c. pres. act. infin. of ἔχω (LN **31.28**) (BAGD I.7.a. p. 333): 'to acknowledge' [AB, BAGD, LN], 'to have' [BAGD], 'to hold' [BAGD], 'to retain' [NICNT, NTC; KJV, NIV], 'to keep in mind' [TEV].
  d. ἐπίγνωσις (LN **28.2, 31.28**) (BAGD p. 291): 'knowledge (about)' [LN (28.2)], The idiom ἔχειν ἐν ἐπιγνώσει 'to have in knowledge' is translated 'to think about' [**LN** (28.2)], 'to acknowledge (God)' [AB,

BAGD, **LN** (31.28); GW, NASB, NET, NLT, NRSV, REB]. The phrase τὸν θεὸν ἔχειν ἐν ἐπιγνώσει 'to have God in knowledge' is translated 'to retain God in knowledge' [NICNT; KJV], 'to retain the knowledge of God' [NTC; NIV], 'to have a true knowledge of God' [NCV], 'to keep in mind the true knowledge about God' [TEV], 'to take cognizance of God' [HNTC], 'to take God into account' [ICC2], 'even to think about God' [CEV], 'to think God qualified for continued recognition' [WBC]. This entire clause is translated 'they did not think God was fit to be known' [BECNT].

QUESTION—What relationship is indicated by καθώς 'just as' at the beginning of this verse?

Note that the positions listed below are not mutually exclusive, and one does not necessarily rule out the other.

1. It indicates a causal relation, meaning 'because' or 'since' [AB, BAGD, BECNT, ICC2, NTC, SSA, St, WBC; CEV, GW, NCV, NIV, NRSV, REB, TEV]. There is a direct link between humanity having rejected God and its being in such a disordered condition [WBC].
2. It indicates a correlative relation, meaning 'as', 'just as', or 'even as' [Gdt, HNTC, Ho, Mor, Mu, NICNT; KJV, NET]. It continues the thought from the previous two sections that there is a close correspondence between sin and divine retribution, and emphasizes it in this verse [NICNT]. It indicates that the cases are parallel; these people have deserted God and God has abandoned them [Ho, Mor]. There is a correlation between the offense and the punishment [Gdt, Mu].
3. It is translated as indicating a temporal relation, 'when', although this could also imply a causal relation [NLT].

QUESTION—What is meant by the statement οὐκ ἐδοκίμασαν τὸν θεὸν ἔχειν ἐν ἐπιγνώσει 'they did not think it worthwhile to have God in knowledge'?

They did not acknowledge God [AB, NICNT]. They considered it unimportant to pay any attention to God and his revelation [NTC]. They rejected the knowledge about God [TH]. They refused to retain or respond properly to the knowledge about God that was available through nature [NICNT]. They deliberately refused to know God, preferring other things to him, and put him out of their circle of acquaintance [Mor]. They did not keep him in mind by praising and thanking him [AB], or take him seriously into account by glorifying and thanking him [ICC2]. They were unwilling to retain any accurate or practical knowledge of God, considering religion to be useless and not worth the trouble [Ho]. They refused to keep alive within their thinking a sufficient recognition of God's holy being such that they would contemplate his will for human conduct [Gdt]. They did not see God as being fit for them to have in their knowledge, nor see him as being worthy of such thought and attention [Mu]. As one of life's most basic presuppositions they concluded that God was not necessary [NAC].

QUESTION—What is the significance here of the compound form ἐπίγνωσις 'knowledge'?
1. In the NT this is used with regard to religious or moral knowledge [ICC2, WBC]. It is a more advanced or fuller knowledge [Ho, ICC1]. Here the sense is accurate or practical knowledge, which in this case is the knowledge of God who has revealed himself in his works [Ho]. It refers to what men may know is true about God, the true knowledge of God [TH]. The expression 'to have in knowledge' is stronger than the word 'know', and the forefronting of 'God' gives emphasis; it was no less than God that they rejected [Mor]. It requires a strong sense here and goes beyond the knowing spoken of in 1:19 [ICC2]. Used with δοκιμάζω it has an intensive sense of knowledge deliberately gained in order to serve as a guide for daily living [WBC].
2. It is used with an object of what is known [Gdt, NICNT]. God should have been the object of distinct knowledge [Gdt]. The prefix ἐπι- indicates direction, not intensity, and is normally used along with an object of the knowing, which in this case is God. Since the compound word may be used to connote practical knowledge as distinct from theoretical knowledge, it may be possible to make the distinction between the theoretical knowledge given to Gentiles in 3:19 and 3:21 with the more experiential knowledge of God (which they rejected having) that would be involved in glorifying and thanking him [NICNT].

God gave- them -over[a] to[b] (a) worthless[c] mind,[d]

LEXICON—a. aorist act. indic. of παραδίδωμι (LN 37.111) (BAGD 1.b. p. 615): 'to give over' [LN, NTC, WBC; KJV, NASB, NET, NIV, TEV], 'to give up' [BAGD; NRSV, REB], 'to hand over' [BAGD, BECNT, HNTC, LN, NICNT], 'to turn over' [BAGD, LN], 'to deliver up' [ICC2], 'to deliver over to' [AB]. The phrase παρέδωκεν αὐτοῖς ὁ θεὸς εἰς 'God abandoned them to' is translated 'he let…rule over them' [CEV], 'he abandoned them…and let them' [NLT], 'God allowed…to control them' [GW], 'God allowed them to have' [NCV]. See this word also at 1:24, 1:26.
b. εἰς (LN 89.48): 'to' [AB, BECNT, HNTC, LN (84.16), NICNT, NTC, WBC; KJV, NASB, NET, NIV, NLT, NRSV, TEV], not explicit [GW, NCV]. The aspect of result this word implies is made explicit: 'that's why' [CEV], 'and this leads them to' [REB], 'so that' [TEV].
c. ἀδόκιμος (LN **88.111**) (BAGD p. 18): 'worthless' [BAGD, NICNT, NTC; NCV], 'useless' [CEV], 'corrupted' [**LN**; TEV], 'depraved' [NASB, NET, NIV, REB], 'debased' [NRSV], 'base' [AB, BAGD], 'unfit' [BECNT, HNTC], 'reprobate' [ICC2; KJV], 'disqualified' [WBC], 'immoral' [GW], 'evil' [NLT]. There is a wordplay here with the verb δοκιμάζω 'to think (it) worthwhile' [AB, Gdt, ICC1, ICC2, Mor, NICNT, NTC, St, TH].

d. νοῦς (LN 26.14, 30.5) (BAGD 3.a. p. 544): 'mind' [BECNT, HNTC, ICC2, LN (26.14), NICNT, WBC; all versions except NCV, REB], 'thinking' [NCV], 'way of thinking' [LN (30.5); REB], 'mentality' [AB], 'manner of thought, attitude' [LN (30.5)], 'disposition' [LN (30.5), NTC], 'thoughts' [BAGD]. This clause is translated 'he let their useless minds rule over them' [CEV], 'God allowed their immoral minds to control them' [GW], 'God allowed them to have their own worthless thinking' [NCV].

QUESTION—What is meant by νοῦς 'mind'?

It refers to the center for moral reasoning and willful choice, not just to intellectual capacity [NICNT]. It is the seat of both thought and action [Mu], the faculty of thinking and the intellectual part of the conscience [ICC1, Mor]. The mind is capable of and in need of renewal, and is sometimes related to conscience in Romans [HNTC]. It is the disposition or attitude, and which results in deeds [NTC]. It is that which guides moral decisions [ICC2, NAC].

QUESTION—What is meant by 'a worthless mind'?

Note that there is a certain amount of overlap possible between the positions listed below, and one does not rule out the other.

1. It refers to a mind that no longer functions properly in its capacity of thinking about moral and spiritual truths [TH]. Their minds are so debilitated as to be untrustworthy in moral discernment and decisions [Gdt, ICC2, Mor], and unable to think clearly about moral issues [NAC]. It is a deep-seated blindness and perversity with regard to understanding and acknowledging God's will or comprehending and practicing biblical ethical principles [NICNT]. It is an evil disposition out of which evil deeds arise [NTC]. Their reasoning has become counterfeit [TNTC]. Having a mind that is unfit comes as a result of esteeming God as unfit [BECNT].

2. That which is ἀδόκιμος is something that has not passed the test, and is therefore worthless [AB], rejected, not worthy of acceptance [HNTC, Ho, ICC1], reprobate [Ho]. It means that their thoughts are worthless and depraved [SSA]. Their minds are deemed worthless and thus rejected by God and are unfit for any worthwhile activity [Mu]. Their minds are rejected as worthless and useless for their intended purpose [ICC2]. The mind that leaves God out of consideration diminishes its own ability to function and will itself degenerate and fail the test [WBC].

to-do[a] the (things) not being-proper,[b]

LEXICON—a. pres. act. infin. of ποιέω (LN 42.7, 90.45, 41.7) (BAGD I.1.c.γ. p. 682): 'to do' [BAGD, BECNT, HNTC, ICC2, LN (42.7, 90.45), NICNT, NTC, WBC; CEV, KJV, NCV, NET, NIV, NLT, TEV], 'to commit' [GW, NASB], 'to be guilty of' [BAGD], 'to perform' [LN (42.7)], not explicit [NRSV]. This entire phrase is translated 'to improper conduct' [AB], 'and this leads them to break all rules of conduct' [REB].

The word is the exegetical infinitive having the sense 'so that they did' and expresses the consequence of the moral dereliction and reprobate mind just described [Ho].

   b. pres. act. participle of καθήκω (LN 66.1) (BAGD p. 389): 'to be proper' [BAGD], 'to be right' [LN], 'to be fitting' [BAGD, LN]. The phrase μὴ καθήκοντα 'not being proper' is translated 'not proper' [NASB], 'improper' [AB, BAGD, NTC, WBC], 'indecent' [CEV, GW], 'unseemly' [HNTC], 'morally wrong' [ICC2], 'not fitting' [BECNT], 'not right' [NICNT], 'not convenient' [KJV], 'ought not to be done' [NIV], 'should not be done' [NET, NRSV], 'should never be done' [NLT], '(they) should not do' [NCV, TEV], 'break all rules of conduct' [REB].

QUESTION—What is meant by τὰ μὴ καθήκοντα 'things that are not proper'?

It refers to actions that are morally wrong [NICNT]. It represents offensive conduct that human society considers vicious and wrong [Mor, NAC]. It means those things that are not proper in God's sight or judgment [SSA]. The improper things he is referring to are spelled out in the next four verses [BECNT, Ho, NAC, NTC, St]. Such behavior is unseemly, not because it is antisocial, but because it indicates rebellion against God [HNTC]. This phrase was very similar to a technical term used in Stoic ethics [AB, BECNT, HNTC, ICC1, ICC2, NAC, NICNT, TNTC, WBC], and by using it Paul appeals to a broader sense of ethics than just Jewish standards [NAC, WBC]. It is that which is inappropriate to the basic nature and duties of human beings [Ho]. In general it speaks of what is morally wrong [ICC2], disgraceful [ICC1], not morally fitting [ICC1, WBC], or is unnatural and improper [WBC]. It refers to such antisocial practices as those listed here, which taken together describe the breakdown and disintegration of human community and society [St]. It is conduct that is morally incongruous and should be revolting to any mind capable of moral discernment [Gdt].

1:29 **filled[a] (with) all[b] unrighteousness,[c] wickedness,[d] greediness,[e] malice,[f]**

TEXT—Instead of πονηρία 'wickedness', some manuscripts read πορνεία 'fornication' either in this word order or in a different word order; and some manuscripts read both πονηρία 'wickedness' and πορνεία 'fornication'. GNT selects the reading πονηρία 'wickedness' with a C rating, indicating difficulty in deciding which variant to place in the text. The reading πορνεία is taken by GW and translated 'sexual sins'. KJV reads both πορνεία 'fornication' and πονηρία 'wickedness'.

LEXICON—a. perf. pass. participle of πληρόω (LN 59.37) (BAGD 1.b. p. 671): 'to be filled' [AB, BAGD, BECNT, ICC2, LN, NICNT, NTC, WBC; all versions except CEV, NLT], 'to be full' [BAGD], 'to be replete with' [HNTC], 'their lives became full of' [NLT]. The phrase 'filled with all unrighteousness' is translated 'they are evil' [CEV].

   b. πᾶς (LN 58.28) (BAGD 1.a.β. p. 631): 'all' [NASB], 'every kind of' [BAGD, HNTC, LN, NTC; NCV, NET, NIV, NLT, NRSV, REB], 'all kinds of' [BAGD, BECNT; GW, TEV], 'all sorts of' [BAGD, LN], 'every sort of' [AB], 'all manner of' [ICC2, NICNT], not explicit [CEV].

c. ἀδικία (LN 88.21) (BAGD 2. p. 18): 'unrighteousness' [BAGD, BECNT, HNTC, ICC2, LN, NICNT, NTC, WBC; KJV, NASB, NET], 'wickedness' [BAGD; NIV, NLT, NRSV, REB, TEV], 'sin' [NCV], 'injustice' [BAGD], 'unjust deed, what is unjust' [BAGD, LN]. This noun is translated as a predicate adjective: '(they are) evil' [CEV].

d. πονηρία (LN 88.108) (BAGD p. 690): 'wickedness' [BAGD, BECNT, HNTC, ICC2, LN NTC, WBC; GW, KJV, NASB, NET], 'evil' [AB, NICNT; NCV, NIV, NRSV, TEV], 'sin' [NLT], 'villainy' [REB]. This noun is translated as an adjective: '(they are) wicked' [CEV].

e. πλεονεξία (LN 25.22) (BAGD p. 667): 'greediness' [BAGD, WBC], 'greed' [AB, LN, NICNT, NTC; GW, NASB, NIV, NLT, REB, TEV], 'covetousness' [BAGD, BECNT, HNTC, LN; KJV, NET, NRSV], 'avarice' [BAGD, LN], 'selfishness' [NCV], 'ruthlessness' [ICC2]. This noun is translated as an adjective: '(they are) greedy' [CEV]. It describes a strong desire to acquire and possess more and more things [BAGD, LN], regardless of need [LN]. It is the unlimited selfishness characterizing a person who has total disregard for others [Mor]. It is a ruthless self-assertion of one who has no regard for others' rights [ICC2].

f. κακία (LN 88.105) (BAGD 1.b. p. 397): 'malice' [AB, BECNT, HNTC; NASB, NET, NRSV, REB], 'maliciousness' [KJV], 'wickedness' [LN, NICNT], 'evil' [BAGD, LN], 'badness' [LN, WBC], 'depravity' [ICC2, NTC; NIV], 'hatred' [NCV], 'hate' [NLT], 'vice' [TEV]. This noun is translated '(they are) mean' [GW], '(they are) mean in every possible way' [CEV].

QUESTION—Is it possible to definitively characterize the structure of the list of vices in 1:29–31 into certain clear groupings?

The vice list has three very general groups of traits [BECNT, Ho, ICC2, Mor, Mu, NAC, NICNT, NTC], divided into groups of four, five, and twelve [BECNT, ICC2, Mor, Mu, NAC, NICNT, NTC]. The first group begins with πεπληρωμένους 'having been filled', and lists four very general nouns in the dative case, each ending in -ία, concluding with κακία 'wickedness'. The second part, beginning with μεστούς 'full', lists five nouns in the genitive which modify it, all of which speak of broken human relationships. The last section of twelve words or phrases are all in the accusative plural and describe sins that even Gentiles would view as dangerous to society [NAC]. The second group, consisting of five vices following μεστούς 'full', speaks of ills that are related to envy [ICC2, NAC]. The last four vices all begin with α-privative, which has a negating function like the English prefix 'un-' or the suffix '-less'. The similar endings lend some assonance and rhetorical force [BECNT, Ho, Mor, SSA]. Throughout the list Paul focuses on social ills, and the harm that people of corrupted minds are doing to others [NICNT]. The literary form of vice lists is widespread in secular as well as NT writings, but has no rigid logical order or structure [NICNT, St,

WBC]. As is common in Paul, such lists are a general and wide ranging catalogue of human sinfulness [BECNT]. One must not force a logical ordering [Gdt, Mu], though some groupings are noticeable [Gdt, ICC1]. This list is not necessarily reflective of specific ethical problems in the Roman church [BECNT].

QUESTION—How precisely can the individual terms of this list of sins in 1:29–32 be defined?

These terms do not necessarily all represent distinctly separate qualities, and some are clearly synonymous [BECNT, NICNT, TH]. Paul's concern is to make the point that people who reject God are given over to all kinds of evil [Mor, Mu], and we should not attempt to delimit the words in the list too closely, although there is certainly significance in the words he chooses [Mor]. The total effect is to emphasize the comprehensiveness of human sin [BECNT, Mu], and it is not possible to draw precise distinctions between many of these overlapping terms [BECNT]. Despite the completeness of this list it is selective, and does not list some of the vices he mentions in other epistles [Mu].

QUESTION—What is the relationship of the word ἀδικία 'unrighteousness' to the list of vices which follows?

1. It is a comprehensive general term which includes the following concepts, some of which specify in more detail what is included in the word [Gdt, ICC1, Mu, NAC]. The first term is the generic word of which the other vices are specific examples [Mu]. Its position at the head of the list implies that the vices that follow characterize people as having forgotten the creator's claim on them as creatures [WBC].
2. This first term does encompass a great variety of evils, though it may not be so comprehensive as to include all of the following terms [Mor].

QUESTION—What is the difference, if any, between πονηρία 'wickedness' and κακία 'malice'?

1. There is little difference between the two [AB, ICC2, Mor, NICNT, TH]. Both indicate evil, not only of the inner disposition but also as expressed outwardly in actions that harm others [Mor].
2. There is some distinction to be made between the two [Gdt, Ho, ICC1]. Where πονηρία denotes a perverse instinct of the heart, κακία is the deliberate wickedness that enjoys hurting others [Gdt]. Κακία 'malice' indicates more of an inward viciousness of disposition [ICC1], a disposition to inflict evil on others [Ho].

full-of[a] envy,[b] murder,[c] strife,[d] deceit,[e] malice,[f]

LEXICON—a. μεστός (LN 68.77) (BAGD 2.a. p. 508): '(to be) full of' [BAGD, HNTC, LN, NICNT; NLT], '(to be) filled with' [AB, BECNT, ICC2, NTC, WBC; GW, KJV, NASB, NCV, NIV, NRSV, TEV], 'rife with' [NET], 'to be constantly engaged in' [LN], not explicit [CEV, NLT]. This word is translated as a phrase: '(they) are one mass of' [REB].

b. φθόνος (LN 88.160) (BAGD p. 857): 'envy' [AB, BAGD, BECNT, HNTC, ICC2, LN, NICNT, NTC; all versions except CEV, NCV, TEV], 'jealousy' [BAGD, LN, WBC; NCV, TEV]. The phrase μεστούς φθόνου 'full of envy' is translated 'they want what others have' [CEV].

c. φόνος (LN 20.82) (BAGD p. 864): 'murder' [AB, BAGD, BECNT, HNTC, ICC2, LN, NICNT, NTC, WBC; all versions except CEV], 'killing' [BAGD]. This noun is translated as a verb: 'they murder' [CEV].

d. ἔρις (LN 33.447, 39.22) (BAGD p. 309): 'strife' [AB, BAGD, BECNT, HNTC, LN (39.22), NICNT, NTC; NASB, NET, NIV, NRSV], 'fighting' [NCV, NLT, TEV], 'rivalry' [ICC2, WBC; REB], 'debate' [KJV] 'quarreling' [GW], 'contention' [BAGD], 'discord' [BAGD, LN (39.22)], 'dispute' [LN (33.447)]. The noun is translated as a verb: 'to argue' [LN (33.447); CEV].

e. δόλος (LN 88.154) (BAGD p. 203): 'deceit' [BAGD, BECNT, HNTC, NICNT, NTC, WBC; GW, KJV, NASB, NET, NIV, NRSV, TEV], 'treachery' [BAGD, ICC2, LN; REB], 'lying' [NCV], 'deception' [NLT], 'cunning' [BAGD], 'craftiness' [AB]. This noun is also translated as a verb: 'to cheat' [CEV].

f. κακοήθεια (LN **88.113**) (BAGD p. 397): 'malice' [BAGD, ICC2, **LN,** NICNT, NTC; NASB, NIV, TEV], 'viciousness' [GW], 'evil disposition' [LN], 'malicious behavior' [NLT], 'malevolence' [REB], 'ill will' [BECNT], 'evil constructions' [HNTC], 'craftiness' [BAGD; NRSV], 'spite' [AB, WBC], 'hostility' [NET], 'malignity' [BAGD; KJV, NET]. This noun is translated as a phrase: 'thinking the worst about each other' [NCV], '(they are) hard to get along with' [CEV]. This word denotes being intentionally and consciously wicked [Mor]. It occurs only here in the NT.

QUESTION—What correspondence is there between πεπληρωμένους 'having been filled with' at the beginning of 1:29 and μεστούς 'full of' in this clause?

Both are used figuratively to describe a condition that is habitual [SSA]. Both refer to αὐτούς 'them' in 1:28 and explicate τὰ μὴ καθήκοντα 'things that are not proper', and both indicate an existing state [NICNT]. There is probably little difference in meaning between the adjective and the participle, both indicating that the people being described were not half-hearted about their sin, rather they were wholly given over to it [Mor].

(they are)[a] gossips,[b]

LEXICON—a. There is no lexical entry for this phrase. It is translated in this way as an implied verb by GW, NASB, NET, NIV, NRSV. The plural noun ψιθυριστάς is translated 'they (gossip)' [CEV, NCV, TEV].

b. ψιθυριστής (LN **33.405**) (BAGD p. 893): 'gossip' [BECNT, NICNT, NTC; CEV, GW, NASB, NET, NIV, NLT, NRSV, REB], 'gossiper' [**LN**], 'gossiping whisperer' [HNTC], 'whisperer' [BAGD, ICC2; KJV], 'tale-bearer' [AB, BAGD], 'rumor monger' [WBC]. This noun is translated as a verb: 'to gossip' [CEV, NCV, TEV]. This word occurs only here in the NT and is not found in any literature prior to its use here.

1:30 **slanderers,**[a] **God-haters/hated,**[b] **insolent**[c] **(persons),**

LEXICON—a. κατάλαλος (LN **33.388**) (BAGD p. 412): 'slanderer' [AB, BAGD, BECNT, HNTC, ICC2, **LN,** NTC, WBC; GW, NASB, NET, NIV, NRSV], 'one who insults' [LN], 'scandalmonger' [REB], 'backstabber' [NLT], 'backbiter' [KJV], 'maligners' [NICNT]. This noun is translated as a phrase: 'they say cruel things about others' [CEV], 'they…say evil things about each other' [NCV], 'they speak evil of one another' [LN; TEV].

b. θεοστυγής (LN **88.205**) (BAGD p. 358): 'God-hater' [AB, WBC; NIV, NRSV], 'hater of God' [BECNT, ICC2, **LN,** NICNT, NTC; GW, KJV, NASB, NET, NLT], 'one who hates God' [LN], 'blasphemer' [REB]. This noun is translated 'they hate God' [CEV, NCV]. This is also translated with God being the one who is the subject of the action instead of the object: 'God-hated' [HNTC], 'hateful to God' [TEV]. This word occurs only here in the NT.

c. ὑβριστής (LN **88.132**) (BAGD p. 832): 'insolent' [AB, BECNT, HNTC, ICC2, **LN,** NTC, WBC; NASB, NET, NIV, NLT, NRSV, REB, TEV], 'haughty' [GW], 'despiteful' [KJV], 'proud' [CEV], 'overbearing' [NICNT], 'rude' [NCV], 'insolent and violent' [LN], 'violent, insolent man' [BAGD]. This word implies an attitude of superiority which results in mistreatment of and violence against others [LN]. It is contempt expressed in violence [ICC2]. There is an element of cruelty as well as pride [NAC].

QUESTION—Is there any distinction between the words ψιθυριστής 'gossip(s)' in 1:29, and κατάλαλος 'slanderer(s)' in this verse?

1. The word ψιθυριστής refers more to something done in private [Gdt, Ho, ICC1, ICC2, Mor, NICNT]. The first denotes whispering [AB, Gdt, ICC2, SSA], and the second is a more general term [ICC2, NICNT]. The idea of secrecy is contained in the first word ψιθυριστής 'gossip(s)', but not in the second word κατάλαλος 'slanderer(s)' [ICC1]. Both refer to those who destroy the reputations of others by misrepresentation, but the former denotes those who do so privately, and the latter those who do so quite publicly [Gdt, Ho, ICC2]. The first is more vicious and dangerous since there is virtually no defense against it [ICC2]. Both refer to slander, but the first refers to whispering what one does not want to be heard saying openly, as contrasted with the second word which denotes the open slandering of others [Mor].

2. The two words are substantially the same and mean that they say bad things about one another [TH].

QUESTION—Does the word θεοστυγής mean that they hate God or that God hates them?
1. It is active and means 'those who hate God' [AB, BAGD, BECNT, Gdt, Ho, ICC1, ICC2, NICNT, NTC, SSA, St, WBC; all versions except TEV]. The emphasis in this section is on the sinful behavior and attitudes of people [AB, BECNT, Ho, ICC1, ICC2, Mor, NICNT, NTC].
2. It is passive and means 'those who are hated by God' [HNTC; TEV]. It functions as an adjective qualifying κατάλαλος: 'God-hated slanderers' [HNTC]. Or, it is a separate description [TEV].

arrogant,[a] boasters,[b] contrivers[c] of-evil,[d] disobedient[e] to-parents,
LEXICON—a. ὑπερήφανος (LN 88.214) (BAGD p. 841): 'arrogant' [BAGD, BECNT, ICC2, LN, NICNT, NTC, WBC; GW, NASB, NET, NIV, REB], 'proud' [BAGD, HNTC; KJV, NLT, TEV], 'haughty' [AB, BAGD, LN; NRSV], 'conceited' [CEV, NCV], 'contemptuous' [LN].
b. ἀλαζών (LN 88.220) (BAGD p. 34): 'boaster' [BAGD; KJV], 'braggart' [BAGD, BECNT, LN, WBC], 'arrogant person' [LN]. This noun is translated as an adjective: 'boastful' [AB, HNTC, ICC2, NTC; all versions except KJV, NCV], 'proud' [ICC1]; as a phrase: 'they brag about themselves' [NCV].
c. ἐφευρετής (LN **30.69**) (BAGD p. 330): 'contriver' [AB, BAGD, LN, WBC; NET], 'inventor' [BECNT, HNTC, LN, NTC; KJV, NASB, NRSV], 'deviser' [NICNT]. This noun is also translated as a verb: 'to invent' [HNTC, NICNT; NCV, NIV, NLT, REB], 'to think of' [TEV], 'to think up' [GW]; as an adjective: 'inventive' [ICC2]. This word occurs only here in the NT.
d. κακός (LN 88.106) (BAGD 1.c. p. 397): 'evil' [AB, BAGD, BECNT, HNTC, LN, NICNT, NTC, WBC; CEV, NASB, NET, NIV, NRSV, TEV], 'evil deeds' [BAGD], 'evil things' [KJV], 'vice' [REB], '(novel) forms of evil' [ICC2], 'all sorts of evil' [NET], 'ways of doing evil' [NCV], '(new) ways of sinning' [NLT], '(new) kinds of vice' [REB], '(new) ways to be cruel' [GW]. The phrase ἐφευρετὰς κακῶν 'contrivers of evil' implies an ingenuity and eagerness in devising new ways to do what is wrong [Mor], of being inventive in finding ever more hateful ways of hurting other people [Gdt, ICC2]. It may have a political connotation [AB].
e. ἀπειθής (LN 36.24) (BAGD 1. p. 82): 'disobedient' [BAGD, BECNT, HNTC, ICC2, LN, NICNT, NTC, WBC; KJV, NET, NLT], 'rebellious (toward)' [NRSV]. This adjective is translated as a verb: 'they disobey' [NIV, TEV], 'they don't obey' [GW], 'these people don't respect' [CEV], 'they show no respect to' [REB]; as a noun: 'rebels (against)' [AB]. The noun γονεύς 'parents' is translated as having a possessive pronoun: 'their parents' [CEV, GW, NCV, NIV, NLT, TEV].

QUESTION—What are the distinctions between the three words ὑβριστής 'insolent', ὑπερήφανος 'arrogant', and ἀλαζών 'boasters'?

The first focuses on actions, the second on attitudes, and the last on speech [Gdt, NICNT, TH], although the distinctions are not entirely absolute [NICNT]. The first has the sense of 'those who insult others'; the second, 'proud', has to do with personal attitudes; the third, 'boastful', has to do with the outward behavior of expressing that attitude [TH]. The first two are similar; the first denotes someone with such a sense of personal superiority that all others are treated as inferiors, and the second is not much different, referring to one who exhibits a contempt for all but oneself. The third, 'boastful', refers to making extravagant claims that cannot be substantiated, but with the implication of doing so with harmful intent [Mor].

QUESTION—What is implied by the denunciation of those disobedient to parents?

It shows a lack of gratitude along with a contempt for family authority, which was considered to be a grievous offense at that time [Mor]. It is related to the arrogance mentioned in 1:30 [NICNT]. This fault would be particularly offensive to Jews [WBC].

1:31 senseless,[a] faithless,[b] loveless,[c] merciless;[d]

TEXT—Some manuscripts include ἀσπόνδους 'implacable' after ἀστόργους 'unloving'. It is omitted by GNT with an A rating, indicating that the text is certain. It is included only by KJV.

LEXICON—a. ἀσύνετος (LN 32.49) (BAGD 1. p. 118): 'senseless' [BAGD, BECNT, HNTC, LN, NTC, WBC; NET, NIV], 'foolish' [AB, LN; NCV, NRSV], 'without understanding' [ICC2, LN, NICNT; KJV, NASB], 'without sense' [REB], 'stupid' [CEV]. This is translated as a clause: 'they refuse to understand' [NLT], 'they don't have any sense' [GW], 'they have no conscience' [TEV].

b. ἀσύνθετος (LN **34.45**) (BAGD p. 118): 'faithless' [AB, BAGD, BECNT, HNTC, NTC, WBC; NIV, NRSV], 'untrustworthy' [NASB], 'unreliable' [CEV], 'undutiful' [BAGD], 'without loyalty' [ICC2], 'without…fidelity' [REB], 'without faithfulness' [NICNT], 'not keeping one's promises' [**LN**], 'covenant-breaker' [KJV, NET], 'covenant breaking' [BAGD; NET]. This adjective is translated as a clause: 'they feel no obligation to keep their agreements' [**LN**], 'they do not feel bound to do what they have promised to do' [**LN**], 'they don't keep promises' [GW], 'they do not keep their promises' [NCV, TEV], 'they…break their promises' [NLT]. This word occurs only here in the NT.

c. ἄστοργος (LN 25.42) (BAGD p. 118): 'loveless' [BECNT, HNTC, NTC, WBC], 'unloving' [BAGD; NASB], 'without affection' [NICNT], 'without natural affection' [ICC2; KJV, REB], 'without normal human affection' [LN], 'without love for others' [LN], 'uncaring' [AB], 'heartless' [NET, NIV, NLT, NRSV]. This word is translated as a clause: 'they don't have any love…for others' [CEV], 'they don't show love to

their own families' [GW], 'they show no kindness…to/for others' [NCV, TEV]. This refers to a lack of the bonds of love and affection that are natural in family relationships [Mor, NICNT].
  d. ἀνελεήμων (LN 88.82) (BAGD p. 64): 'merciless' [AB, BECNT, **LN**, WBC], 'without mercy' [NICNT], 'unmerciful' [BAGD; KJV, NASB], 'ruthless' [NET, NIV, NRSV], 'without pity' [ICC2; REB], 'pitiless' [HNTC, NTC], 'unforgiving' [NLT]. This word is translated as a clause: 'they don't have any…pity for others' [CEV], 'they show no…pity for others' [TEV], 'they show no mercy to others' [NCV], 'they don't show mercy to others' [GW]. This word occurs only here in the NT.

QUESTION—What is meant by ἀσύνετος 'foolish'?
  This is not merely mental weakness, but denotes moral blemish, an unwillingness to listen to God; they are stupid [NTC]. This means one who is incapable of listening to wise counsel [Gdt]. It refers more to a lack of conscience than of common sense, and describes those who act stupidly and wickedly because they have rejected God [Mor]. This denotes those who, having rejected God, can no longer comprehend the will of God [NICNT]. They are without insight into moral or religious things [Ho]. Such people are devoid of conscience [NAC; TEV].

QUESTION—What is meant by ἀσύνθετος 'faithless'?
  This denotes those who refuse to abide by covenants or treaties [NICNT], who are not to be trusted with regard to covenants [NTC], who are unfaithful to a covenantal agreement [AB], who are unreliable and treacherous [ICC2]. It denotes those who break agreements [Gdt, ICC1, Mor] and cannot be trusted to keep their word [Mor, NAC, TH].

QUESTION—What is meant by ἄστοργος 'unloving'?
  Since the root word often refers to the love of relatives for each other, it may be best understood to mean lack of affection for family members, and shows that the moral corruption is so deep that it affects even this natural affection [NICNT]. Among the Greek words for love this was the one particularly denoting affection for family, so the sense here is that they lack natural affection [Ho, ICC2]. In the ancient world it was expressed in the infanticide of unwanted babies [ICC2, NTC]. It denotes the love that naturally binds people in groups, particularly the family, and those who lack it are without natural affection [Gdt, Mor, NAC]. It also speaks of the hardness of heart of the kind of people who would be entertained by the dying agonies of the gladiators [Gdt].

1:32 who,[a] having-known-fully[b] the just-requirements[c] of-God,
LEXICON—a. ὅστις (LN 92.18) (BAGD 2.b. p. 587): 'who' [BAGD, LN; KJV], 'such people' [BAGD], 'they' [CEV, GW, NASB, NCV, NET, NIV, NLT, NRSV, REB, TEV]. The word is used to emphasize a characteristic quality by which a preceding statement is confirmed [BAGD].

b. aorist act. participle of ἐπιγινώσκω (LN 32.16) (BAGD 1.a. p. 291): 'to know fully' [NET], 'to know' [BAGD, BECNT, HNTC, ICC2, NICNT, NTC, WBC; CEV, GW, KJV, NASB, NCV, NIV, NRSV, TEV], 'to know full well' [AB], 'to know well enough' [REB], 'to be fully aware of' [NLT], 'to perceive, to comprehend' [LN]. This word implies a complete or full knowledge [BAGD]. The function of this participle is translated as a concessive or contrary to expectation relationship: 'though (they knew)' [AB], 'they knew…yet' [HNTC], 'they know…nonetheless' [BECNT], 'they know… yet' [ICC2; NRSV, REB, TEV], 'they know…but' [NCV], 'although they know' [NTC, WBC; GW, NASB, NET, NIV], 'fully aware…yet' [NLT].
c. δικαίωμα (LN **33.334**) (BAGD 1. p. 198): 'just-requirement' [AB, BAGD, LN], 'regulation' [BAGD, LN] 'commandment' [BAGD], 'righteous decree' [ICC2, NICNT; NET, NIV], 'just decree' [WBC; REB], 'decree' [NRSV], 'ordinance' [BECNT, HNTC, NTC; NASB], 'law' [NCV, TEV], 'judgment' [GW, KJV], 'penalty' [NLT]. The phrase τὸ δικαίωμα τοῦ θεοῦ 'the just requirements of God' is translated 'God has said' [CEV], 'God's law says' [NCV, TEV], 'God's…penalty' [NLT].

QUESTION—Who are the referents of the plural pronoun οἵτινες 'who'?

The people in view are those who practice the evil just described in previous verses [BECNT, Gdt, HNTC, Ho, NICNT, NTC, St]. This pronoun emphasizes the character of the people referred to, meaning 'they are of such a character that' [Gdt, Ho, ICC1, Mu, NICNT].

QUESTION—What relationship is indicated between the relative clause 'who having known…are deserving of death', and the main clause '(they) not only do them but also approve of the ones doing them'?

The relationship is that of concession and contra-expectation [AB, BECNT, HNTC, ICC2, NTC, SSA, St, WBC; CEV, GW, NASB, NCV, NET, NIV, NRSV, REB, TEV]. The first clause is explicitly translated as concessive [AB, NTC, WBC; GW, NASB, NET, NIV]: although they know. The second clause is explicitly translated as contra-expectation [BECNT, HNTC, ICC2; CEV, NCV, NLT, NRSV, REB, TEV]: they know, nevertheless they continue to engage in these sins.

QUESTION—What is the requirement or decree referred to by the phrase τὸ δικαίωμα τοῦ θεοῦ 'the just requirements of God'?

It refers to the following clause which specifies the requirement or decree, which is that those who indulge in such behaviors are worthy of death [BECNT, Gdt, HNTC, Ho, ICC2, Mu, NTC, St]. This includes Gentiles, who though not having the Mosaic law, are aware of its moral requirements [BECNT]. This is not a reference to the Law in a formal sense, but rather to what all people can know of God's just judgments, whether or not they have access to special revelation [NICNT]. The point Paul stresses throughout the passage is that God has revealed enough of himself for people to be able to know enough to realize that they are doing wrong; there is a recognizable divine order [Mor]. It is a knowledge of God and his righteous requirements which is attested to by conscience [Gdt, Mu]. It is a declaration by God of what is right and just, which is written on the human heart by virtue of our nature as moral beings [Ho]. It is an objective knowledge of God's righteousness and thus his hostility to evil, and therefore of the penalty for evil doing [ICC2]. It is the moral sense which even Gentiles have about right and wrong, and they also know, either in fact or in effect, that such is God's requirement [WBC]. The word means that which is required by what is right [AB], a declaration of what is right [ICC1, Mor].

that the-(ones) doing[a] such[b] (things) are worthy[c] of-death,

LEXICON—a. pres. act. participle of πράσσω (LN 42.8) (BAGD 1.a. p. 698): 'to do' [AB, BAGD, LN, NICNT; GW, NIV, NLT], 'to carry out' [LN], 'to perform' [LN], 'to commit' [BAGD; KJV], 'to practice' [BECNT, HNTC, ICC2, NTC, WBC; NASB, NET, NRSV], 'to act' [CEV], 'to behave' [REB], 'to live (in this way)' [TEV], 'to live (like this)' [NCV].

   b. τοιοῦτος (LN 64.2, 92.31) (BAGD 3.a.β. p. 821): 'such things' [AB, BAGD, BECNT, ICC2, NICNT, NTC, WBC; GW, KJV, NASB, NET, NIV, NRSV], 'such' [BAGD, LN (64.2); KJV, NET, NIV, NRSV], 'such things as these' [HNTC], 'these things' [NLT], '(things) like that' [BAGD, LN (64.2)], 'similar things' [BAGD], 'this' [NLT], '(behave) like this' [REB], '(acts) this way' [CEV], '(live) in this way' [TEV], '(live) like this' [NCV], 'of a kind such as this' [LN (92.31)].

   c. ἄξιος (LN 66.6) (BAGD 2.b. p. 78): 'worthy of' [HNTC, LN, NICNT; KJV, NASB], 'deserving of' [BAGD, BECNT]. The phrase ἄξιοι θανάτου εἰσίν 'worthy of death' [HNTC, NICNT, NTC; KJV, NASB] is also translated 'deserve(s) to die' [AB; CEV, GW, NET, NRSV, REB], 'should die' [NCV], 'deserve death' [BECNT, ICC2, WBC; NIV, TEV] '(they are fully aware of) God's death penalty' [NLT].

QUESTION—What is meant by 'death' here?

   1. It is the death of eternal punishment [AB, BECNT, Gdt, ICC2, Mu, NTC]. It is the death referred to in 6:23 [AB, BECNT]. It is the exclusion from the kingdom of God that is the lot of all sinners [AB]. It is the penalty of death as only God can inflict it, the pains of Hades, which even the Gentiles recognized [Gdt]. It refers to the pains of hell [Mu]. This is not the penalty of physical death for specific wrongdoings, since some in the list would be very unlikely to carry that punishment in any code of law known to pagans [AB, ICC2].
   2. He is alluding to the sentence of death pronounced on Adam in the Genesis account of the fall [HNTC, NICNT, WBC].
   3. He is speaking in general terms [Ho, Mor, SSA]. The key thought is that sin deserves death, but Paul is not defining this term closely in this context, only that it is a horror [Mor]. Neither spiritual nor physical death is specifically in view since the focus is on punishment [SSA]. It is punishment in the general sense [Ho].

QUESTION—What is the significance of the present tenses of the verbs of this verse?

This emphasizes that Paul is not just speaking about what has been true in past times, but that people generally have an awareness that moral degeneration of the types mentioned deserve to be punished by God [NICNT]. These show that those people being described retain some knowledge of God and his requirements even while at the same time being involved in the vices listed here [Mu, NICNT]. This emphasizes the habitual attitudes and behaviors of these sinners [Mor].

not only do them but also approve-of[a] the (ones) doing[b] (them).

LEXICON—a. pres. act. indic. of συνευδοκέω (LN 31.17) (BAGD p. 788): 'to approve of' [BAGD, HNTC, NTC, WBC; GW, NET, NIV, REB, TEV], 'to give approval' [AB, BECNT], 'to give hearty approval' [NASB], 'to agree to' [LN], 'to agree with' [BAGD], 'to consent to' [BAGD, LN], 'to sympathize with' [BAGD], 'to applaud' [ICC2; NCV, NRSV], 'to commend' [NICNT], 'to encourage (others to do)' [CEV, NLT], 'to have pleasure in' [KJV].

b. pres. act. participle of πράσσω (LN 42.8) (BAGD 1.a. p. 698): 'to do' [BAGD, LN, NICNT, NTC; CEV, GW, KJV, NCV, NLT, TEV], 'to commit' [BAGD], 'to practice' [HNTC, ICC2, WBC; NASB, NET, NIV, NRSV]. The phrase τοῖς πράσσουσιν 'the ones doing (them)' is translated 'such conduct in others' [REB], 'those who so act' [AB], 'those who live this way' [BECNT].

QUESTION—What is the force of the construction οὐ μόνον...ἀλλὰ καί 'not only...but also'?

This shows that the depth of the evil of these persons is very great in that they know full well that these evil behaviors deserve God's punishment of death, yet they defiantly continue in them and commend them to others, indicating the extent of their rejection of God [WBC]. This statement accentuates the enormity of the offense [Mor]. It indicates an increase in the offense [TH], that this is the climax of depravity [Gdt, Mu]. Their rejection and hatred of God is so great that they knowingly accept the risk of future judgment in order to pursue evil [BECNT].

QUESTION—What is Paul saying here?

1. Encouraging others in evil is a more serious sin than merely doing it oneself [BECNT, Gdt, Ho, ICC1, ICC2, Mor, Mu, NAC, NTC, St]. Together with practicing these things themselves, they support and encourage others to do the same, while knowing that these acts issue in damnation [ICC1, Mu, NICNT, NTC]. Even though the actions of one doing evil are not excusable, such people may be acting on the passion of the moment, but those condoning and encouraging others to evil do so out of a settled disposition and contribute to the corruption of a number of people [BECNT, ICC2]. To influence public opinion in favor of wrong is worse than yielding for a moment to temptation [ICC1], since it suggests a

settled choice, contributes to others accepting it, and adds to a firmer entrenchment of evil with an appearance of respectability [ICC2]. This level of degradation, the corrupt conscience, is the last stage in the corruption of moral sensibility, wherein men approve what they should have condemned and prevented [Gdt]. It is the climax of perversity [NTC]. Wickedness has sunk to the lowest possible level when the rebel delights in the sinfulness of other people [NAC]. It shows a definite preference and set purpose for evil such that they delight in the sins of others [Ho]. It is less reprehensible to sin under temptation than to dispassionately agree with and encourage sin in others [NICNT].
2. Doing evil is just as bad as encouraging others to sin, and it cannot be regarded as worse to approve of sin than to actually do it; Paul is saying that both those who do such things as well as those who approve of them are all under the same condemnation and are hateful to God [HNTC].

DISCOURSE UNIT: 2:1–3:20 [AB, ICC2]. The topic is God's judgment manifested against Jews [AB], the Jewish man is no exception [ICC2].

DISCOURSE UNIT: 2:1–3:18 [SSA]. The topic is the world under God's condemnation for sin; here with focus on the Jews.

DISCOURSE UNIT: 2:1–3:8 [BECNT, NAC, NICNT, NTC, WBC]. The topic is the unrighteousness of Jews [BECNT, NAC], the Jews are accountable to God for sin [NICNT], the Jews also need justification by faith [NTC], God's wrath on Jew first as well as Gentile [WBC].

DISCOURSE UNIT: 2:1–29 [Gdt]. The topic is the wrath of God suspended over Jews.

DISCOURSE UNIT: 2:1–24 [SSA]. The topic is God will recompense all people for the evil they have done, including the Jews.

DISCOURSE UNIT: 2:1–16 [GNT, Ho, ICC1, Mor, Mu, NAC, NICNT, St, TNTC; CEV, NCV, NET, NIV, NLT, TEV]. The topic is God's righteous judgment [Mor, Mu, NAC; NIV], the Jews and the judgment of God [NICNT], future judgment without respect of persons [ICC1], the condemnation of the Jew [Mor], universality of sin and condemnation in respect to the Jews [Mu], you people also are sinful [NCV], God's wrath against critical moralizers [St], the moralist [TNTC], God's judgment [TEV], God's judgment of sin [NLT], the righteous judgment of God [GNT], God's judgment is fair [CEV], the condemnation of the moralist [NET].

DISCOURSE UNIT: 2:1–13 [GW]. The topic is God will judge everyone.

DISCOURSE UNIT: 2:1–11 [AB, HNTC]. The topic is discernment at God's judgment [AB], judgment and the critic [HNTC].

2:1 Therefore[a] you-are without-excuse,[b] O man,[c] every (one) judging;[d]

LEXICON—a. διό 'therefore' (LN 89.47) (BAGD p. 198) 'therefore' [BAGD, BECNT, LN, NICNT, NTC; NASB, NCV, NET, NIV, NRSV], 'for this reason' [AB, BAGD, LN, WBC; REB], 'for this very reason, so then' [LN], 'then' [REB], 'so' [AB], 'that means that' [HNTC], 'wherefore' [ICC2, WBC; KJV], not explicit [CEV, GW, NLT, TEV].

  b. ἀναπολόγητος (LN **33.438**) (BAGD p. 60): 'to be without excuse' [AB, BAGD, BECNT, HNTC, LN, NICNT, WBC; NASB, NET], 'to have no excuse' [ICC2, **LN**; CEV, GW, NIV, NLT, NRSV, TEV], 'to be inexcusable' [BAGD; KJV], 'to have no defense' [REB], 'to be wrong' [NCV]. The word refers to not being able to defend oneself or to justify one's actions [LN]. See this word also at 1:20.

  c. ἄνθρωπος (LN 9.1, 9.24) (BAGD 1.a.γ, p. 68): 'man' [BAGD, BECNT, ICC2, LN (9.24), NTC; KJV], 'person' [LN (9.1), NICNT], not explicit [GW, NCV]. The word has a reproachful implication [BAGD]. The vocative phrase ὦ ἄνθρωπε πᾶς ὁ 'oh man every (one)' is translated 'Oh man, everyone who' [BECNT], 'O man, whosoever' [KJV], 'my good man…whoever you are' [HNTC], 'man, whoever thou art' [ICC2, NTC], 'my friend, whoever you are' [TEV], 'whoever you are' [AB; NET, NRSV], 'whoever you may be' [REB], 'O person' [NICNT], 'you sir, each one of you' [WBC], 'some of you' [CEV], 'every man of you who' [NASB], 'you' [NIV, NLT].

  d. pres. act. participle of κρίνω (LN 30.108, 56.30) (BAGD 6.b. p. 452): 'to judge' [AB, BECNT, HNTC, ICC2, LN (30.108), NICNT; GW, KJV, NCV, NET, NRSV, TEV], 'to pass judgment' [NTC, WBC; NASB, NIV], 'to sit in judgment' [AB; REB], 'to accuse of doing wrong' [CEV], 'to say someone is wicked and should be punished' [NLT], 'to condemn' [BAGD, LN (56.30)], 'to act as judge' [HNTC].

QUESTION—What relationship is indicated by διό 'therefore'?

  1. It indicates a conclusion to what precedes [AB, Gdt, HNTC, Ho, ICC1, NAC, NICNT, SSA, WBC].
     1.1 It draws a conclusion from what has been stated in 1:18–20 [AB, NICNT, SSA]. Because God's wrath is being revealed against all people who suppress the truth, anyone who would presume to judge others is without excuse [AB, NICNT, SSA]. Those who judge recognize God's requirements and are, like everyone else, without excuse [AB].
     1.2 It draws a conclusion from 1:18–32 [BECNT, ICC2, WBC]. Since the immorality of the Gentiles is an abomination to God, therefore anyone else who does the same thing is equally without excuse [NTC]. Paul challenges those who would have thought themselves exempt from the previous indictment [WBC]. Although Paul has in mind especially the sins of Gentiles in 1:18–32, his focus is not exclusively on them, but rather the sins of all men are in view. Thus he can now turn to the Jews in chapter 2 and deal with their false assumption that they would be differently judged than other men [ICC2].

1.3 It draws a conclusion from 1:32 [Gdt, HNTC, Ho, ICC1, NAC]. Those who are sinning themselves, and yet are condemning others for these same sins, are even more deserving of condemnation than those of 1:32 who simply sin and commend it to others, and who at least are in agreement in thought and action [Gdt]. All men know that sinners are worthy of death, thus those who commit sin are without excuse, even those whose self-conceit leads them to censor the behavior of others and consider themselves exempt [Ho]. This links best with 1:32 though the use of 'without excuse' indicates a link with 1:20 as well [ICC1]. Men know God's verdict regarding sinners such as those just described, therefore one who judges shows himself to be without excuse since he sins, and by judging others proves that he knows what is right [NAC]. It connects 1:32a with what follows; the man who judges also sins, and in the act of judging shows that he knows what is right, so he proves that he too is without excuse [HNTC].
2. The conjunction points forward, and indicates the conclusion of the argument Paul is making in the first two verses of this chapter, which can be summarized as follows: (a) you judge others for doing things; (b) you do the same things yourself; (c) therefore you condemn yourself and are without excuse [Mu].
3. This is used as a transitional particle only [TH; CEV, NLT, TEV].

QUESTION—What is the significance of the use of second person singular forms in the verbs and pronouns of this verse?

Paul is making use of a literary form known as the diatribe [AB, BECNT, HNTC, NAC, NICNT, St, TH, TNTC, WBC], in which an imaginary dialogue takes place between himself and another person, and which may include questions, objections, and direct address [NICNT]. Paul is not necessarily accusing the readers of these particular things, but such points do reflect real-life situations and points of view [NICNT]. The line of argument may be the same as what he had already engaged in during the course of preaching and debating in synagogue and marketplace [WBC]. Although addressing a group, Paul uses the second person singular [SSA], a device which is used for vividness [ICC2]. The use of ὦ 'O' with ἄνθρωπε 'man' expresses emotion [AB, Mor].

QUESTION—Whom is Paul primarily addressing in this section?

1. Paul is primarily referring to Jews [AB, BECNT, Gdt, Ho, ICC1, ICC2, Mor, Mu, NAC, NICNT, NTC, SSA, TNTC, WBC]. Although 2:1–3 may apply to anyone, 2:4 and 2:6–11 show the position of the Jew relative to the Gentile, and the Jew is specifically identified in 2:17 [NICNT]. The Jews are his specific target audience all along, and he is concerned that they realize they are not somehow excused from God's judgments [BECNT, ICC2, Mu, NICNT]. The propensity of the Jews to judge Gentiles for immoral behavior, the argument that special privilege does not exempt anyone from judgment, and the explicit address to the Jews in 2:17 indicate that the Jew is primarily in focus [Mu]. Paul primarily has

the Jew in mind, but his statements could be applied to anyone [Mor]. Paul begins stating the arguments generally in terms to which Jews would certainly assent before becoming aware of how they apply directly to themselves; further, the argument as a whole and the explicit mention of the Jews in 2:17 show that they are primarily being addressed [Gdt, Ho]. Much as Nathan did with David by the use of a parable, Paul addresses the Jew under the cover of a general statement, and then says 'you are the man' [ICC1].
2. Paul is addressing anyone who judges [HNTC, St, TH]. Paul primarily addresses anyone, whether Jew or Gentile, who would presume to judge others, as there were at least some Gentiles with high moral standards [St]. Paul's argument is that the self-righteous person, regardless of his nationality, finds himself under the same judgment as do pagans [TH]. Paul is arguing that this is true even if a person does not necessarily commit all the same specific sins outlined in 1:18–29; the self-righteous person who judges others is guilty of the same sin underlying them all, which is idolatry, because in making himself judge he has put himself in the place of God [HNTC].

QUESTION—What is meant by κρίνω 'to judge'?

In this context the word means 'to condemn' and is not distinct from the word κατακρίνω 'to condemn' later in the verse [AB, Ho, NICNT]. It is a strong condemnation [TH]. The word has the connotation of condemning, of passing a negative judgment or sentence [AB, SSA]. The word is used in its normal judicial sense of judging or passing judgment on someone or something [WBC].

for[a] in[b] that-which you-judge the other (person) you-condemn[c] yourself;

LEXICON—a. γάρ (LN 89.23): 'for' [BECNT, HNTC, ICC2, LN, NICNT, NTC, WBC; KJV, NASB, NCV, NET, NIV, NRSV, REB, TEV], not explicit [AB; CEV, GW, NLT].
  b. ἐν (LN 89.5, 67.33) (BAGD IV.6.a. p. 261): 'in' [AB, HNTC, LN, NICNT, WBC; NRSV, REB], 'wherein' [BAGD, ICC2; KJV], 'with regard to, about, in the case of' [LN], 'when' [CEV, NLT, TEV], 'whenever' [HNTC], 'while' [BECNT], 'at whatever point' [NTC; NIV], 'on whatever grounds' [NET], 'in (judging others)' [REB].
  c. pres. act. indic. of κατακρίνω (LN 56.31) (BAGD p. 412): 'to condemn' [AB, BAGD, BECNT, HNTC, ICC2, LN, NICNT, NTC, WBC; all versions except NCV], 'to judge yourself guilty' [NCV].

QUESTION—What relationship is indicated by γάρ 'for'?
1. It indicates grounds for the previous statement [BECNT, NICNT]: you are without excuse because you condemn yourself.
2. This section begins an amplification of what precedes it [SSA]: I mean that when you condemn others, you condemn yourself.

QUESTION—What relationship is indicated by ἐν ᾧ 'in that which'?
Note that there is a certain amount of overlap possible between the positions listed below, and one does not rule out the other.
1. It indicates equivalence [AB, HNTC, ICC1, NTC, WBC]: in condemning others you condemn yourselves. The sense of the word is 'in that you judge another', that is, by the fact of your judging, you condemn yourself, as opposed to condemning yourself in and by the action of judging [WBC]. By the fact of your judging you show that you know right and wrong [ICC1]. Passing judgment on another means to condemn oneself [Mor].
2. It indicates circumstance [BECNT, HNTC; CEV, NLT, TEV]: when you condemn others, you condemn yourself.
3. It indicates means [Gdt, NAC]: by condemning another for what you yourself are doing, you thereby condemn yourself and take away any excuse for yourself [Gdt]. In the very act of judging you condemn yourself [NAC, NICNT].

QUESTION—What is it that Paul is criticizing here?
He is focusing on the inconsistency and self-deception of the Jews in that they practiced evil but hoped to escape God's judgment [BECNT]. He is not condemning objective evaluation as such [NAC], but the hypocritical condemnation of another [NAC, St]. The Jew is indicted not for judging people for sins, but for judging people for the same sins of which he is himself guilty [Mu]. In the act of judging, the judge condemns himself, since he too is doing these same things [Gdt].

QUESTION—In what way does one condemn himself by judging others?
1. The condemnation comes from condemning others for the very same things a person is guilty of himself [AB, BECNT, Gdt, Ho, ICC2, Mu, NAC, NICNT, NTC, WBC]. The argument is that such a person is condemned because, despite having a moral understanding superior to that of the pagans, he does not actually live according to what that moral understanding says [AB]. The critic passes judgment on himself because by criticizing he demonstrates that he has a knowledge of right and wrong, and yet his own conduct is the same as what is being condemned [ICC1]. The statement that the one judging is condemned by his own judgment according to the principle of 'measure for measure' shows the influence of the Jesus tradition, especially Matt. 7:1–2, on Paul's thinking [WBC]. Many of the specific sins were committed by both Jew and Gentile, each in their own way [NTC].
2. By condemning Gentiles, the Jew was taking on a position of superiority and to putting himself in the position of God [HNTC, Mor].

for[a] the same-(things) you-do[b], the-(one) judging.
LEXICON—a. γάρ (LN 89.23) (BAGD 1.a. p. 151): 'for' [BAGD, BECNT, ICC2, LN, NICNT, WBC; KJV, NASB, NLT], 'because' [LN, NTC; CEV, NCV, NET, NIV, NRSV], 'since' [AB, HNTC; GW, REB].

b. pres. act. indic. of πράσσω (LN 42.8) (BAGD 1.a. p. 698): 'to do' [AB, BAGD, ICC2, LN, NICNT; CEV, GW, KJV, NCV, NIV, NLT, NRSV, TEV], 'to practice' [BECNT, HNTC, NTC, WBC; NASB, NET]. The phrase τὰ...αὐτὰ πράσσεις 'the same things you do' is translated 'you...are equally guilty' [REB], 'you are guilty of doing the very same things' [CEV]. The word is used mostly of committing actions that are not praiseworthy [BAGD].

QUESTION—What relationship is indicated by γάρ 'for'?

It indicates the grounds for the preceding accusation [BECNT, NICNT, SSA]: you condemn yourself since you do the same things. The one who judges is without excuse before God because he himself is guilty of the same things he is judging [NICNT, St]. It is not the act of judging others that is blameworthy, but rather that those who judge are guilty of the same things, which is what the next phrase asserts [BECNT].

QUESTION—What is meant by τὰ...αὐτά 'the same things'?

1. This refers to the sins listed in 1:28–31 [BECNT, NAC, NICNT, TH, WBC]. The sins of this list would be equally common among both Jews and Gentiles [BECNT, NICNT, WBC]. He is speaking more specifically of the anti-social vices listed in 1:28–31, and which are more general and widespread [WBC]. While it is true that idolatry and homosexual sin were not common among Jews, the other vices mentioned are easy for anyone to fall into, Jews included [NAC].
2. This does not mean the specific sins earlier mentioned, but rather as seen in principle or essence, as inner motives, rather than explicit actions [Gdt, HNTC, ICC2, Mor, NTC, TNTC]. While it is true that the moral lifestyles of Jews and Gentiles were quite different, in a sense the same sins were committed in different ways; for example, Jewish self-righteousness made an idol of self, and refusal to repent was common to both groups. This is the type of reasoning used by Jesus as well in Matt. 7:1–4 [NTC]. While not all pagans or Jews were as immoral as the previous passage describes, Paul is saying that in principle people do the same kinds of things that they judge in others, and are thereby self-condemned [TNTC]. Though he is certainly speaking of actual sins, Paul may not have had the vices of 1:21–32 specifically in mind, but rather a conception of sin involving the inner motives rather than the outward actions [NAC]. While there was a difference between the moral state of the Jews and that of the pagans, the difference was only relative [Gdt].

2:2 Now[a] we-know that the judgment[b] of God is according-to[c] truth[d] upon[e] the-(ones) doing[f] the such-(things).

LEXICON—a. δέ (LN 89.94, 89.124): 'now' [HNTC, NICNT, NTC; NET, NIV], 'but' [ICC2, LN (89.124); KJV], 'yet' [AB], 'and' [BECNT, LN (89.94), WBC; NASB, NLT], not explicit [CEV, GW, NCV, NRSV, REB, TEV].

b. κρίμα (LN 30.110, 56.24, 56.30) (BAGD 4.b. p. 450): 'judgment' [AB, BECNT, HNTC, ICC2, LN (56.24, 30.110), NICNT, NTC; GW, KJV, NASB, NET, NIV, NRSV, REB], 'verdict, sentence' [LN (56.24)], 'condemnation' [BAGD, LN (56.30), WBC]. This noun is also translated as a verb: 'to judge' [CEV, NCV, TEV], 'to punish' [NLT]. The word is mainly used in the unfavorable sense of the sentence of condemnation [BAGD].

c. κατά with accusative object (LN 89.8) (BAGD II.5.a.β. p. 407): 'according to' [BAGD, BECNT, NICNT; KJV], 'in accordance with' [BAGD, LN, WBC; NET, NRSV], 'in conformity with, corresponding to' [BAGD], 'based on' [NIV], 'in' [AB; NLT], not explicit [ICC2; CEV, GW, NASB, NCV, REB, TEV]. This indicates the norm according to which a judgment is rendered, or rewards and punishments are given [BAGD].

d. ἀλήθεια (LN **70.4**, 72.2) (BAGD 3. p.36): 'truth' [AB, BECNT, LN (72.2, 70.4), NICNT, WBC; KJV, NET, NIV, NRSV]. This noun is also translated as an adverb modifying the act of judging: 'rightly' [BAGD; NASB], 'justly' [ICC2, NTC]; as an adjective describing the judgment: 'just' [REB], 'right' [CEV, GW, NCV], 'fair' [HNTC]. The phrase ἐστιν κατὰ ἀλήθειαν 'is according to truth' is translated 'in his justice' [NLT]. This clause is translated 'the judgment of God is upon those who actually did such things' [**LN** (70.4)].

e. ἐπί with accusative object (LN 90.34, 83.46) (BAGD III.1.b.γ. p. 289): 'against' [ICC2, LN (90.34), NTC, WBC; KJV, NET, NIV], 'on' [AB, BAGD, BECNT, HNTC, LN (83.46); NRSV, REB], 'upon' [BAGD, LN (83.46), NICNT], 'falls upon' [NASB], not explicit [CEV, GW, NCV, NLT, TEV].

f. pres. act. participle of πράσσω: 'to do'. See this word at 2:1.

QUESTION—What relationship is indicated by δὲ 'now'?

1. It has a continuative sense [BECNT, Gdt, HNTC, NICNT, NTC, WBC; NASB, NET, NIV, NLT]: and, now. It is used to introduce a syllogism [Gdt, SSA]. This word is not translated by CEV, GW, NCV, NRSV, REB, TEV, but it presumably is taken as having the continuative sense in those versions.

2. It indicates contrast [AB, ICC2; KJV]: but, yet.

QUESTION—What is meant by οἴδαμεν 'we know'?

1. This introduces a general statement or principle, that which would be generally recognized [AB, Gdt, Ho, ICC2, Mor, Mu, NICNT, TH, WBC]. This frequently used formula introduces a fact which is generally accepted [WBC]. This truth is ingrained on the human conscience, and plain common sense, free of bias, compels all to accept it [Gdt].

2. Paul is speaking to Jews in particular and knows that they would agree with this point [BECNT, HNTC, NAC]: we Jews know. Paul identifies himself with what he knows to be the opinion of his Jewish audience that those engaged in evil will be judged [BECNT]. This introduces the

objection of a Jewish critic, or Paul as representing the Jewish perspective, concerning the sins he has just discussed: 'but Paul, we know that God will judge people who sin like that!' [HNTC].

QUESTION—What is meant by κρίμα τοῦ θεοῦ 'the judgment of God'?

The word κρίμα 'judgment' means the judicial verdict of condemnation, [ICC2, Mu, NAC, NICNT, SSA, WBC], and in this case refers to the judgment rendered by God on those guilty of these things [NAC, NICNT]. In this instance it is not the act of judging, but the sentence of condemnation [Gdt, Mu]. Strictly speaking the word denotes the sentence rather than the process of judging, but the two are not sharply distinguished [Mor].

QUESTION—To what element in the sentence is the phrase κατὰ ἀλήθειαν 'according to truth' grammatically related?

1. The phrase is related to the verb ἐστιν 'is' [BECNT, HNTC, Ho, ICC2, Mor, Mu, NAC, NICNT, NTC; KJV, NET, NIV, NRSV, REB, TEV]: the judgment of God is according to truth, that is, in accordance with the facts of the case. God's judgment on these people will be without favoritism [HNTC] or respect of persons [Ho, Mu].
2. It is related to the following prepositional phrase [AB, HNTC, ICC2, LN, NAC; CEV, NLT]: it is right for God's judgment to fall on people who do such things.

QUESTION—What is meant by κατὰ ἀλήθειαν 'according to truth' in relation to God's judgments?

It means that God's judgments are fair, just, right, and impartial [BECNT, Gdt, HNTC, Ho, ICC1, ICC2, Mor, Mu, NAC, NICNT, NTC; CEV, GW, NCV, REB]. In this context Paul asserts the fairness of God's judgments and means that God will impartially assess the works of every individual person fully in accord with the facts of each case, so that his judgment is just and fair [Ho, Mu, NAC, NICNT]. Some of his Jewish audience may have believed that the special relationship God has with Israel would afford them preferential treatment [ICC1, NICNT]. God's judgments on evil doers are just, and it is right and proper for him to judge evil acts [BECNT]. His judgment is without respect of persons [AB, HNTC, Ho, Mu]. The Jews did not dispute the fact of God's judgment, but felt that somehow they would enjoy certain immunities due to their special relationship with God and that they would not be judged impartially according to the same standards as other people [Gdt].

2:3 And[a] do-you-think[b] this,

LEXICON—a. δέ (LN 89.94, 89.124): 'and' [ICC2, LN (89.94), NTC; KJV, NET, REB], 'but' [HNTC, LN (89.124); TEV], 'now' [BECNT], 'or' [NICNT], 'then' [WBC], 'so' [NIV], not explicit [AB, WBC; CEV, GW, NASB, NCV, NLT, NRSV].

b. pres. mid. (deponent = act.) indic. of λογίζομαι (LN 31.1) (BAGD 3. p.476): 'to think' [BECNT, HNTC; CEV, GW, KJV, NCV, NET, NIV, NLT, TEV], 'to really think' [AB; CEV], 'to reckon' [ICC2, NICNT], 'to consider, to be of the opinion' [LN], 'to suppose' [WBC; NASB], 'to imagine' [BAGD, NTC; NRSV, REB].

QUESTION—What is the function of the shift back to second person singular in this verse?

Paul shifts back to confronting the presumed opponent [ICC2, NICNT], and the use of the nominative personal pronoun σύ 'you' in the phrase 'that you will escape' is emphatic [AB, HNTC, Ho, ICC1, ICC2, Mu, NAC, NICNT, TH]. This is meant to counteract the conviction of Jews that they are secure from judgment due to their descent from Abraham [AB, Ho].

QUESTION—To whom is Paul addressing the question by using the second person singular 'you', and the vocative 'O man' in this and the following phrases?

1. The reference is primarily to the Jew [AB, BECNT, Gdt, HNTC, Ho, ICC1, ICC2, Mu, NICNT, WBC]. This question would be legitimate for the Gentile moralist who believes he can please God by a good life, but it is particularly appropriate to the Jew, who might falsely assume that at least some degree of righteous living in accord with the Mosaic law might exempt him from judgment [NICNT]. Paul uses this expression to summon the Jew's attention [Mu].
2. The question would be addressed to anyone in the situation described who presumes to judge another [TH].

QUESTION—What is the function of the rhetorical question posed in this verse?

The rhetorical question implies an emphatic negative answer [AB, Gdt, Ho, ICC1, Mu, NAC, SSA, TH]. The rhetorical question here is equivalent to an emphatic negative statement such as 'you should certainly not think that' [SSA]. It serves to enlighten the objector who may have supposed that God's wrath did not apply to him since he had not been turned over to the same reprobation as the Gentiles [HNTC].

oh man[a] the-(one) judging the-(ones) doing[b] such-(things) and (you) doing[c] them,

LEXICON—a. ἄνθρωπος: 'man'. See this word in 2:1.
  b. pres. act. participle of πράσσω: 'to do'. See this word at 2:1, 2.
  c. pres. act. participle of ποιέω (LN 42.7) (BAGD I.1.b.ε. p. 681): 'to do' [AB, BAGD, BECNT, HNTC, ICC2, LN, NICNT, NTC, WBC; GW, KJV, NASB, NET, NIV, NLT, NRSV, TEV], 'to perform' [LN], 'to carry out' [LN], 'to behave' [CEV], 'to commit' [REB]. The phrase '(you) doing them' is translated 'do wrong yourselves' [NCV].

that you will-escape[a] the judgment of God?

LEXICON—a. fut. mid. indic. of ἐκφεύγω (LN **21.14**) (BAGD 2.b.β. p. 247): 'to escape' [AB, BAGD, BECNT, HNTC, ICC2, LN, NICNT, NTC, WBC; all versions except CEV, NLT], 'to be able to escape' [**LN**]. This entire clause is translated 'God won't punish you?' [CEV], 'and (God will) not judge you…?' [NLT].

2:4 Or the wealth[a] of-his kindness[b] and the forbearance[c] and the patience[d] do-you-despise,[e]

LEXICON—a. πλοῦτος (LN 57.30, 78.15) (BAGD 2. p. 674): 'wealth' [BAGD, HNTC, ICC2, LN (57.30), WBC; NET, REB], 'riches' [BECNT, LN (57.30), NICNT, NTC; KJV, NASB, NIV, NRSV], 'abundance' [AB, BAGD, LN (57.30)], not explicit [NLT]. This noun is also translated as an adjective modifying 'kindness': 'great' [LN (78.15); TEV], 'very great' [LN (78.15)], 'wonderful' [CEV]. The phrase 'wealth of his kindness' is translated 'very kind' [GW, NCV]. This entire clause is translated 'Don't you realize how kind, tolerant, and patient God is with you? Or don't you care?' [NLT].

  b. χρηστότης (LN 88.67) (BAGD 2.b. p. 886): 'kindness' [BAGD, BECNT, HNTC, ICC2, LN, NTC; NET, NIV, NRSV, REB, TEV], 'goodness' [AB, BAGD, NICNT, WBC; CEV, KJV], 'generosity' [BAGD]. This noun is also translated as an adjective: 'kind' [GW, NCV, NLT].

  c. ἀνοχή (LN **25.171**) (BAGD 2. p. 72): 'forbearance' [AB, BAGD, BECNT, HNTC, ICC2, NICNT, NTC, WBC; KJV, NASB, NET, NRSV], 'patience' [**LN;** CEV], 'tolerance' [NIV, REB, TEV]. This noun is also translated as an adjective: 'tolerant' [NLT], 'patient' [NCV]; as a phrase: 'puts up with you' [GW].

  d. μακροθυμία (LN 25.167) (BAGD 2.b.α. p. 488): 'patience' [BAGD, BECNT, ICC2, LN, NICNT, NTC, WBC; NASB, NET, NIV, NRSV, REB, TEV], 'forbearance' [BAGD], 'long-suffering' [AB, HNTC; KJV], 'willingness to put up with someone' [CEV]. This noun is also translated as an adjective: 'patient' [NCV, NLT]; as a phrase: 'deals patiently with you' [GW].

  e. pres. act. indic. of καταφρονέω (LN **88.192**) (BAGD 1. p. 420): 'to despise' [BAGD, HNTC, ICC2, LN; KJV, NRSV, REB, TEV], 'to scorn' [BAGD, LN], 'to have contempt for' [**LN;** GW, NET], 'to treat with contempt' [BAGD], 'to pour contempt on' [BECNT], 'to show contempt for' [NICNT; NIV], 'to look down on' [BAGD, LN, NTC], 'to not think much of' [CEV], 'to think nothing of' [NCV], 'to think lightly of' [WBC; NASB], 'to make light of' [AB], 'to not care' [NLT].

QUESTION—What is the function of ἤ 'or' here?

  It introduces a restatement of the point being made in the preceding passage [ICC2, Mor, Mu, NICNT], this time with greater intensity [BECNT, ICC2, Mu]. It introduces another possibility which is even worse, which is that they are actually guilty of contempt [Gdt].

QUESTION—What is the function of the rhetorical question in this verse?

  The rhetorical question has the effect of calling the reader to pay special attention to a statement which ought to be regarded as true [NAC, SSA]. The question highlights the inconsistency and self-deception of the Jews [BECNT, NAC]. This question exposes the false assumptions of the opponent addressed in 2:3, namely that anyone who is guilty of the same things that he condemns other for doing, and yet supposes that he will avoid judgment for what he does, is in fact showing contempt for God's mercy [NICNT]. Paul wants to press upon the hard-hearted Jew that he is actually guilty of impiety and perversity [Mu]. God's delay in punishing sin ought to lead one to repentance, but to make light of it is not simply delusion but is actually contempt and culpable negligence [AB]. He is making a point, similar to that in the preceding verse, that anyone who thinks he will escape God's judgment is treating God's kindness as if it were nothing [ICC2, Mor]. He is making the statement that by condemning in others the same sins of which they were also guilty, they were showing contempt for God's kindness by which he intended to lead them to repentance [NAC]. It calls the reader to conclude that God's kindness and patience are not a sign that he does not need to be converted, but are what make possible the opportunity for him to do so [NTC]. Paul raises the possibility that they are guilty of something even worse than illusion, that they are guilty of contempt for God's kindness [Gdt].

QUESTION—What is meant by καταφρονέω 'despise'?

It means to underestimate [WBC], to take lightly [TH], to make light of something [AB]. The word means to have contempt for something [ICC2, NAC], to treat it as being of no account [Mor]. Here it is to underestimate or fail to esteem the significance of the revelation of grace in Christ [Mu]. The word means to form a low estimate of something and thus to reach a false conclusion about it, which in this case would be that God's goodness towards Jews is so great that he will not punish them as he will others [Ho]. It means to presume upon the goodness, forbearance, and patience with which God delays punishment [ICC1].

QUESTION—To what does the noun πλοῦτος 'wealth' relate in this context?

All of the three terms which follow this noun, kindness, forbearance, and patience, are dependent on it, and all describe God's mercy [ICC2, Mor, Mu, NICNT]. It implies the abundance or magnitude of these qualities [AB, Mu]. This word has the effect of intensifying the attribute or event expressed by the noun that follows it [SSA]. These qualities of God are not in short supply [Mor].

QUESTION—What is meant by χρηστότης 'kindness'?

This refers to the actions of God [Mu, NAC]. It refers to his benevolent acts on behalf of sinners [NAC]. This term embraces all of God's benefits to Israel in the past and the privileged position they enjoyed [Gdt]. It is God's patiently withholding the punishment that a sinner rightly deserves [NICNT]. Or, it refers to God's kindness of disposition [ICC1, Mu], as well as his restraint in inflicting wrath as punishment for sin [Mu]. It is a benevolent goodness of heart [Mor]. This refers to kindness in general, especially in giving favors [Ho]. The term 'kindness' sums up the other three qualities just mentioned [NTC].

QUESTION—Is there any significant difference between the meaning of ἀνοχή 'forbearance' and μακροθυμία 'patience'?
1. There is no significant difference [ICC2, Mu, NICNT, SSA, TH]. Used together they express the fact that God is slow to execute his wrath by inflicting punishment [Mu]. These words are more or less synonymous [ICC2, NICNT, SSA] and refer to God's goodness as shown by his patience in withholding the judgment that sinners merit [ICC2, NICNT].
2. There is some distinction [Gdt, Ho, ICC1, Mor].
2.1 The first term ἀνοχή 'forbearance' means the delay of wrath and the second μακροθυμία means 'patience' [ICC1, Mor, WBC]. God shows forbearance in that he delays punishing sinners to give them time to repent, and patience in that he is not short-tempered but patiently endures the continuing failure of sinners [Mor]. The first word, ἀνοχή 'patience', refers to what may be awakened in a benefactor when his goodness is met by ingratitude, and the second, μακροθυμία 'long-suffering', refers to God's incomprehensible prolonging of Israel's existence despite their many years of resistance to him [Gdt].
2.2 The first word, ἀνοχή, speaks of his patience and the second word, μακροθυμία, to his slowness in inflicting punishment [Ho].

not-knowing[a] that the kind[b] (nature) of God leads[c] you to[d] repentance?[e]
LEXICON—a. pres. act. participle of ἀγνοέω (LN 28.13, 30.38, 32.7) (BAGD 1. p. 11): 'to not know' [BAGD, BECNT, LN (28.13); CEV, KJV, NASB, NET], 'to not realize' [AB, NTC; NIV, NLT, NRSV], 'to fail to see' [REB], 'to be unaware of' [LN (28.13)], 'to not understand' [LN (32.7); NCV], 'to be ignorant of' [BAGD, LN (28.13), NICNT], 'to ignore' [HNTC, LN (30.38)], 'to pay no attention to' [LN (32.7)], 'to refuse to see that' [ICC2], 'to disregard' [WBC]. The phrase ἀγνοῶν ὅτι 'not knowing that' is translated 'don't you realize' [GW], 'don't you realize…can't you see that' [NLT], 'and yet you do not know that' [NET], 'surely you know that' [TEV].
b. χρηστός (LN **88.68**) (BAGD 2. p. 886): 'kind' [**LN**; NLT], 'gracious' [LN]. The adjectival phrase τὸ χρηστόν 'the kind nature' is translated as a substantive: 'kindness' [BAGD, BECNT, HNTC, ICC2, NTC, WBC; GW, NASB, NET, NIV, NRSV, REB], 'goodness' [NICNT; KJV]. The phrase τὸ χρηστὸν τοῦ θεοῦ 'the kind nature of God' is translated 'God is kind' [**LN**; NCV, TEV], 'how kind he has been' [NLT], 'God is good to you' [CEV], 'what is good about God' [AB].
c. pres. act. indic. of ἄγω (LN 15.165) (BAGD 1.c. p. 14): 'to lead' [BAGD, BECNT, HNTC, ICC2, LN, NICNT, WBC; KJV, NASB, NET, NIV], 'to bring' [LN], 'to be meant to lead' [AB, ICC2; NRSV, REB], 'is intended to lead (you) to' [BECNT, HNTC], 'is to lead you to' [WBC], 'seeks to bring you to' [NTC], 'he is trying to lead' [GW, TEV], 'he wants you to' [CEV], 'to give you time' [NLT], not explicit [NCV].

d. εἰς (LN **89.48**) (BAGD 4.a. p. 229): 'to' [AB, BAGD, BECNT, HNTC, ICC2, NICNT, NTC, WBC; CEV, KJV, NASB, NET, NLT, NRSV, REB, TEV], not explicit [GW, NCV]. It is also possible to translate 'leads you to repentance' as 'it causes you to repent' [LN], with εἰς marking a resulting event or state [LN].

e. μετάνοια (LN **41.52**) (BAGD p. 512): 'repentance' [AB, BECNT, HNTC, ICC2, LN, NICNT, WBC; KJV, NASB, NET, NIV, NRSV, REB], 'conversion' [NTC]. This noun is translated as a verb or verb phrase: 'to repent' [**LN**; TEV], 'to change one's way' [LN], 'to turn to him' [CEV], 'to turn from your sin' [NLT], 'to change your hearts and lives' [NCV], 'to change the way you think and act' [GW]. The word means to change one's way of life as a result of a complete change of thought and attitude with regard to sin and righteousness [LN], a change of mind [BAGD].

QUESTION—What is meant by ἀγνοῶν 'not knowing'?

1. It means to ignore or to disregard [Gdt, Mor, Mu, NICNT, WBC]. Their refusal to consider the kindness of God, the purpose of which was so clear, is inexcusable [Mu]. He addresses the person who willfully ignores or refuses to recognize the truth [ICC2, NICNT], who ignores what he does not wish to see [Gdt]. They disregard the fact that God's kindness is intended to lead them to repentance [WBC]. This ignorance is culpable, since they have no excuse for no knowing [Mor].
2. They scorned the kindness and patience of God [BECNT].
3. They failed to comprehend the true nature or intent of God's kindness [AB, Ho].
4. They forgot God's gracious dealings with them, by which they should have learned of his kindness and patience [NAC].

QUESTION—What is the significance of the present tense of the verb ἄγω 'leads' in the phrase μετάνοιάν σε ἄγει 'leads you to repentance'?

The present tense is used in the conative sense, referring to what God intends by this action [AB, BECNT, Gdt, HNTC, ICC1, ICC2, Mor, Mu, NAC, NICNT, St, TH, TNTC, WBC]. It means to bring about or to induce repentance [ICC2, Mu]. God's kindness is calculated to induce repentance, not simply to point towards repentance; however, not all who benefit from God's kindness actually repent, as the example of the Jews in this context demonstrates [Mu]. The intent of God's longsuffering is to induce people to repent [ICC1]. Repentance is the goal of God's kindness [St]. God's goodness affords an opportunity to repent as well as summoning people to do so [ICC2]. The word implies the power of man to resist as well as to yield to the influences on him [Gdt].

QUESTION—What is meant by μετάνοια 'repentance'?

It means to have a change of mind [AB, Gdt, Mor, Mu, TH]. There is a change of mind about sin such that the person turns away from it, but in the NT it means turning to a new life in Christ, not simply having remorse for sin [Mor]. It means a transformation of consciousness in which people turn from sin to God, doing so in mind, in feeling, and in will [Mu]. It means to go back on one's former views and to change one's standpoint and feelings [Gdt]. The word focuses on a change of heart or mind, or of behavior as in to turning away from sins [TH]. Paul uses this term to refer to conversion [WBC]. Sorrow for sin is a part of what Paul has in mind, but the concept of conversion is more to the point, focusing on the positive aspect of turning to God in trust and wholehearted surrender, a complete turnabout from sin to holiness [NTC]. This change of mind also includes the idea of remorse, repentance, or conversion in the religious sense [AB].

2:5 But[a] in-accordance-with/because-of/by[b] your stubbornness[c] and unrepentant[d] heart[e]

LEXICON—a. δέ (LN 89.124): 'but' [BECNT, ICC2, LN, NTC; CEV, KJV, NASB, NCV, NET, NIV, NRSV, TEV], 'but no' [NLT], not explicit [AB, HNTC, NICNT, WBC; GW, REB].
- b. κατά with accusative object (LN 89.8) (BAGD II.5.a.δ. p. 407): 'in accordance with' [BAGD, LN], 'according to' [BAGD; KJV], 'on the basis of' [BAGD], 'in relation to' [LN], 'in' [REB], 'by' [NTC; NRSV], 'with' [AB, HNTC], 'yes, with' [HNTC], 'after' [KJV], 'as a result of' [BAGD, WBC], 'based on' [NIV], 'on account of' [ICC2], 'because of' [BAGD, BECNT, NICNT; NCV, NET, NIV, NLT], not explicit [CEV, GW, NCV, NLT].
- c. σκληρότης (LN **88.223**) (BAGD p. 756): 'stubbornness' [BAGD, **LN**; NASB, NET, NIV, NLT], 'hardness' [BAGD, HNTC, WBC; KJV, NRSV], 'obstinacy' [ICC2]. This noun is also translated as an adjective: 'stubborn (heart)' [AB], 'hard (heart)' [BECNT, NICNT, NTC; NRSV, TEV], 'obstinate (impenitence)' [REB], '(you are) stubborn' [CEV, GW, NCV]. This word is found only here in the NT.
- d. ἀμετανόητος (LN **41.54**) (BAGD p. 45): 'unrepentant' [BAGD, BECNT, HNTC, ICC2, **LN**, NICNT; NASB, NET, NIV], 'impenitent' [AB, WBC; KJV, NRSV], 'unconverted' [NTC], 'stubborn (heart)' [TEV]. This adjective is also translated as a noun: 'impenitence' [REB]; as a verb phrase: 'to refuse to turn to God' [LN; CEV], 'to refuse to repent' [LN], 'to refuse to turn from sin' [NLT], 'to refuse to change' [NCV], 'to not want to change' [GW]. This word is found only here in the NT.
- e. καρδία (LN 26.3) (BAGD 1.b.δ p. 404): 'heart' [AB, BECNT, HNTC, ICC2, LN, NICNT, NTC, WBC; KJV, NET, NIV, NRSV, REB, TEV], 'inner self, mind' [LN], not explicit [CEV, NCV, NLT]. The phrase 'unrepentant heart' is translated '(you) don't want to change the way you think and act' [GW]. Καρδία 'heart' represents the center and source of thinking, feeling, and volition, especially with regard to the moral life [BAGD].

QUESTION—What relationship is indicated by κατά 'in accordance with/ because of/by'?

Note that there is a considerable amount of overlap possible between the positions listed below, and one does not rule out the other.
1. It indicates the standard by which a judgment is made or meted out [AB, Gdt, HNTC, Ho]: in accordance with or corresponding to. The Jews will receive the judgment that might be expected from their hardness of heart [Ho]. It implies a line of conduct that has long been followed [Gdt]. This not only denotes the norm according to which a judgment is rendered, but at the same time gives the reason for it [BAGD].
2. It indicates reason [BAGD, BECNT, ICC2, Mor, Mu, NICNT, TH; TEV]: because of your stubbornness and unrepentant hearts, you are storing up wrath. It is related as cause and effect; that is, 'because you have a hard and stubborn heart' [TH].
3. It indicates means [ICC1, SSA, WBC]: by your stubbornly refusing to repent you are storing up wrath.

QUESTION—What is meant by σκληρότης 'stubbornness'?

The word denotes spiritual hardness and rebellion [NICNT]. A judgmental attitude towards Gentiles and a readiness to discount similar sins among the Jews is evidence that this hardness has already taken hold [WBC]. It speaks of an insensibility of heart to divine favor [Gdt], of callousness [ICC1]. A sure sign of this stubbornness is to presume on God's patience by interpreting it as a license to sin instead of repenting of sin [St]. In the OT these terms were used primarily with reference to Israel [ICC2]. The concept of 'hardness' and 'unrepentant heart' are a figurative doublet and signify stubborn refusal to repent [SSA]. Σκληρότης should be understood as modifying 'heart' [AB, BECNT, Mor, Mu, NAC, NICNT, NTC, WBC; NRSV, TEV], meaning that the Jews' hearts were stubborn [AB, NAC], or hard and unconverted [NTC].

you-are-storing-up[a] for-yourself wrath[b]

LEXICON—a. pres. act. indic. of θησαυρίζω (LN **13.135**) (BAGD 2.b. p. 361): 'to store up' [BAGD, BECNT, HNTC, ICC2, NICNT, NTC, WBC; NASB, NET, NIV, NLT, NRSV], 'to lay up a store' [REB], 'to treasure up' [KJV], 'to amass' [AB], 'to accumulate even more' [LN], 'to make even worse' [CEV], 'to make even greater' [NCV, TEV], 'to add to' [GW].

b. ὀργή (LN 38.10, 88.173) (BAGD 2.b. p. 579): 'wrath' [AB, BAGD, BECNT, HNTC, ICC2, NICNT, NTC, WBC; KJV, NASB, NET, NIV, NRSV], 'anger' [BAGD, LN (88.173)], 'fury' [LN (88.173)], 'indignation' [BAGD], 'punishment' [LN (38.10); NCV, TEV], 'terrible punishment' [NLT], 'retribution' [REB]. This word is translated 'the anger God will have against you' [GW]. This denotes God's reaction towards evil, as opposed to an emotion [BAGD].

QUESTION—What is meant by θησαυρίζεις σεαυτῷ 'you are storing up for yourself'?

The normal meaning of the metaphor is to store up something good for oneself, so this is an ironical use of the metaphor [AB, BECNT, Gdt, ICC2, NAC, NICNT, St]. What is being stored in this case is not blessing but wrath [AB, BECNT, Gdt, ICC2, NICNT, St, WBC]. The phrase is a metaphor; just as rich people store up wealth, so you are causing God's anger to increase. In addition, the noun 'anger' is an experience type event which is an example of metonymy in which the cause, which is anger, stands for the effect, which is punishment [SSA]. The phrase means to store up or accumulate something little by little, which in this case is wrath because of abusing God's goodness [Ho]. This has a negative connotation, meaning that the storing up is against oneself, that is, to one's own disadvantage [NICNT, NTC]. The person addressed is himself represented as being the agent in piling up wrath for himself [Mu]. There is an ironic parallel between 'riches of goodness' in 2:4 and 'treasure up' in 2:5 [Gdt].

QUESTION—What is to be understood as the time period during which one is 'storing up wrath'?

One who refuses to repent is now accumulating the wrath that will later be revealed at the end of history [AB, BECNT, HNTC, ICC1, ICC2, Mor, Mu, NAC, NICNT, NTC, St, TNTC]. Every favor being trampled underfoot adds to the accumulation of wrath [Gdt]. There will be a climactic outpouring of wrath at the end of history [NICNT]. In contrast to the wrath spoken of as being revealed in 1:18, this wrath is eschatological [NAC].

on[a] (the) day[b] of-wrath and of-(the)-revelation[c] of-(the)-righteous-judgment[d] of God,

LEXICON—a. ἐν (LN 67.33): 'on' [AB, NICNT; CEV, GW, NCV, NRSV, TEV], 'in' [BECNT, HNTC, ICC2, NTC, WBC; NASB, NET], 'at the time of, when' [LN], 'against' [KJV, REB], 'for' [NIV], not explicit [NLT].

b. ἡμέρα (LN 67.142, 67.178) (BAGD 3.b.β. p. 347): 'day' [AB, BAGD, BECNT, HNTC, ICC2, LN (67.178), NICNT, NTC, WBC; all versions except TEV], 'the Day' [TEV], 'time' [LN (67.142)].

c. ἀποκάλυψις (LN 28.38) (BAGD 3. p. 92): 'revelation' [BAGD, BECNT, ICC2, LN, NICNT, NTC; KJV, NASB]. This noun is also translated as a verb: 'to show' [CEV, NCV], 'to be revealed' [NET, NIV, NRSV, REB, TEV], 'to come' [NLT], 'to vent' [GW].

d. δικαιοκρισία (LN **56.27**) (BAGD p. 195): 'righteous judgment' [BAGD, BECNT, ICC2, NICNT, NTC, WBC; KJV, NASB, NET, NIV, NRSV], 'right judgment' [LN; NCV], 'just judgment' [AB, HNTC; REB], 'right verdict' [**LN**], 'just verdict' [LN]. This singular noun is also translated as a plural: 'righteous judgments' [TEV], 'right judgments' [NCV]; as a verb phrase: 'to judge the world with fairness' [CEV]; as a noun phrase modifying God: 'God, the just judge' [NLT]. The phrase 'revelation of the righteous judgment of God' is translated 'God will reveal that his decisions are fair' [GW]. This word is found only here in the NT.

QUESTION—What relationship is indicated by ἐν 'on'?

It has the temporal sense here, meaning 'on the day of wrath', or at the time of the day of wrath [AB, BECNT, Gdt, Ho, ICC1, ICC2, Mor, Mu, NICNT, NTC, St, TH, TNTC, WBC].

QUESTION—What is the time or event referred to by the phrase ἐν ἡμέρᾳ ὀργῆς 'on (the) day of wrath'?

Paul refers to an outpouring of God's wrath at the end of history, the final judgment [Gdt, HNTC, ICC2, Mor, Mu, NICNT, NTC, TH, TNTC, WBC]. This refers to eschatological wrath that will come on the day of the Lord [AB, BECNT, ICC1]. This is the day identified in 2:16 as the time when God will judge the secrets of men, namely, the final judgment at which time the wicked will be judged and the aspirations of righteous people will be realized [Mu]. This will be a public event on the last day, the time when God's judgments will be announced and vindicated [St]. It also includes God's judgments within history in the form of great national catastrophes [Gdt]. On that day God's settled opposition to evil will come to consummation [Mor].

QUESTION—What is meant by δικαιοκρισίας τοῦ θεοῦ 'the righteous judgment of God'?

This refers to the final judgment and means that it will be just and in accord with the facts of each person's life [AB, Gdt, NICNT, NTC, St, TH]. This connotes God's condemnatory judgment and stresses the fairness of the sentence to be passed [AB]. This phrase recalls that of 2:2 'according to truth' and removes the false hope the Jews held of immunity from judgment by virtue of special relationship with God, since it is clear from what follows that its measure will be the moral life of each individual [Gdt]. Paul states that the principle on which this judgment is based is 'according to what one has done', the principle of exact retribution, and is a sentence that is made public and verifiable by the evidence of one's works [St]. It also implies something about the righteous character of God, the judge [BECNT, ICC1, WBC]. God's righteousness includes the truth of his righteous judgments, and is not limited to his saving righteousness [BECNT]. Wrath may be seen as an expression of God's righteousness as creator [WBC]. God will be revealed in his character as a righteous judge [ICC1].

QUESTION—How is the word ἀποκάλυψις 'revelation' to be understood in relation to 'the righteous judgment of God'?

The word 'revelation' has its fullest eschatological sense here, since it is only at the end that it will be clear that the current human condition is the result of the outworking of God's wrath [WBC]. The word points to the fact that the full manifestation and execution of God's judgments are reserved for a future day [Mu]. The righteous judgment of God is still veiled so far as the Jews are concerned, but will be fully revealed in relation to them on that day [Gdt]. God will reveal or show his anger and judge sin rightly [TH].

2:6 who will-render[a] to-each (person) according-to[b] his works:[c]

LEXICON—a. fut. act. indic. of ἀποδίδωμι (LN **38.16**) (BAGD 3. p. 90): 'to render' [BAGD, HNTC, NICNT, NTC, WBC; KJV, NASB, NET], 'to repay' [AB, BECNT; NRSV], 'to recompense' [BAGD, ICC2, **LN**], 'to pay' [REB], 'to pay back' [GW], 'to reward' [BAGD, LN; CEV, NET, TEV], 'to reward or punish' [NCV], 'to give' [NIV], 'to judge' [NLT].
  b. κατά with accusative object (LN 89.8) (BAGD II.5.a.β. p. 407): 'according to' [AB, BAGD, BECNT, HNTC, ICC2, NICNT, NTC; KJV, NASB, NET, NIV, NLT, NRSV, TEV], 'in accordance with' [BAGD, LN, WBC], 'corresponding to, in conformity with' [BAGD], 'in relation to' [LN], 'for' [CEV, GW, NCV, REB]. See this word also in 2:5.
  c. ἔργον (LN 42.11) (BAGD 1.c.β. p. 308): 'works' [BECNT, HNTC, NICNT, WBC; NET], 'deed' [AB, BAGD, ICC2, LN, NTC; KJV, NASB, NRSV], 'act' [LN], 'what (one) has done' [CEV, GW, NCV, NIV, NLT, REB, TEV]. It refers collectively to the deeds of men exhibiting a consistent moral character [BAGD].

QUESTION—How does the structure of 2:6–11, indicate that it is a unit?

These verses are a self-contained thought unit which is indicated by the chiastic arrangement [AB, BECNT, NAC, NICNT, SSA]. This chiasm may be represented as follows [AB, NICNT]:

> A. God will judge everyone equitably   v. 6
>   B. Those who do good will attain eternal life   v. 7
>   C. Those who do evil will suffer wrath   v. 8
>   C'. Wrath for those who do evil   v. 9
>   B'. Glory for those who do good   v.10
> A'. God judges impartially   v.11

The main point, which is that God will judge all impartially by the standard of their works, is stated at the beginning and end rather than in the middle of the paragraph as with some chiastic passages [NAC, NICNT], and the two possible outcomes of judgment are given in the middle of the paragraph [NICNT]. In the context of God's punishment for evildoers, the prominence is in the central elements describing sinful actions and God's punishment of them. The outer elements, which also have some prominence, express the universality of God's rewards and impartiality [SSA].

QUESTION—How does the statement of this verse relate to the truth of salvation by grace alone?
  1. This statement has to do with judgment according to works, not about the method of salvation, so there is no contradiction here [Gdt, Ho, ICC1, Mor, Mu, NAC, NICNT, NTC, St, TH, TNTC]. Although salvation is by grace, judgment will be on the basis of works [Ho, Mor, Mu, TH, TNTC], because works are the expression of what a person is deep down; this judgment will be impartial, and not based on being a member of a favored group [Mor]. There is no real antithesis between faith and works, since works are the evidence and the necessary outcome of faith [Ho, ICC1, St].

In the present passage Paul is not speaking of how one is made right with God, but about how God judges the reality of a person's faith by the difference it makes in how he or she lives; only those who have put their trust in God through Jesus Christ are even capable of seeking godliness [NAC]. Justification by free grace applies to the entrance into salvation by faith, after which God expects responsibility from the believer to manifest the fruits of faith, without which that faith is declared to be dead [Gdt]. In stating that good works are necessary for salvation Paul is talking about eschatological salvation, and is saying that Christians can and will keep the Law by the power of the Holy Spirit [BECNT]. The reward of eternal life goes to those who see their good works not as an achievement but as an expression of their hope in God [HNTC, NAC]. These works do not earn salvation, but arise out of a right relationship with God that has already been established by faith [TH]. God saves by his sovereign grace, but man must always respond in faithfulness to the responsibilities and tasks which God assigns, and for which he gives strength; it is faithfulness to these responsibilities that will be the basis for judgment [NTC].

2. Paul would understand the principle stated in this verse as the simpler and more universal work of trusting in God through Christ, and so challenges the typical Jewish assumption that faithfulness to covenant obligations, including works of charity and observance of ritual law, were the works in question. However, to assert that Paul is here denying a rabbinic 'works theology' is to miss the point, and forces Paul's dialectic between grace and judgment into an antithesis that confuses his theology about these issues [WBC].

QUESTION—What is the significance of the shift from second person singular to third person plural beginning in this verse?

The 'diatribe' style of accusation of and dialogue with an imaginary person is interrupted here for the sake of an explanation which is given in the third person plural, the basic principle of which is that God will treat all people the same with regard to judgment, whether Jew or Gentile [NICNT].

2:7 on-the-one-hand,[a] to-the-ones (who) by[b] perseverance[c] in[d] good[e] work[f]

LEXICON—a. μέν (...δέ) (LN 89.136) 'on the one hand...(but on the other hand)' [LN, NICNT], not explicit [AB, BECNT, HNTC, ICC2, NTC, WBC; CEV, GW, KJV, NASB, NET, NIV, NLT, NRSV, REB]. In conjunction with the first word of 2:8 (δέ) this is rendered 'some people...(other people)' [NCV, TEV]. This construction marks a set of elements which are in contrast with one another [LN].

b. κατά with accusative object (LN 89.8) (BAGD II.5.a.δ. p. 407): 'by' [AB, BECNT, ICC2, NICNT, NTC, WBC; GW, KJV, NASB, NCV, NET, NIV, NRSV, REB], 'with' [HNTC], 'in accordance with, in relation to' [LN], 'on the basis of, because of, or as a result of' [BAGD], 'to everyone who has...done' [CEV], not explicit [NLT]. See this word also in 2:5.

c. ὑπομονή (LN 25.174) (BAGD 1. p. 846): 'perseverance' [BAGD, NTC, WBC; NASB, NET], 'endurance' [BAGD, LN], 'steadfastness' [BAGD], 'persistence' [NICNT; NIV], 'steady persistence' [REB], 'steadfast perseverance' [ICC2], 'patient continuance' [KJV], 'patient endurance' [HNTC]. This noun is also translated as an adverb: 'patiently (doing good)' [AB; CEV, NRSV]; as a participle: 'persevering' [BECNT], 'persisting' [GW], 'always continuing' [NCV]; as a verb: 'to persist in' [NLT].

d. There is no lexical entry for this word in the Greek text, it is supplied to express the relationship indicated by the genitive case of the phrase 'good works'. This relationship is translated 'in' [BECNT, ICC2, NICNT, NTC, WBC; GW, KJV, NASB, NET, NIV, REB], not explicit [AB, HNTC; CEV, NCV, NRSV, TEV].

e. ἀγαθός (LN 88.1) (BAGD 1.b.β. p. 3): 'good' [AB, BECNT, ICC2, LN, NICNT, WBC; NASB, NCV, NET, NIV, NRSV, TEV], 'goodness, good act' [LN], 'what is right' [BAGD, NTC], 'what is good' [CEV, GW, NLT], 'well doing' [HNTC; KJV, REB].

f. ἔργον (LN 42.11) (BAGD 1.c.β. p. 308): 'work' [BECNT, ICC2, NICNT; NET], 'deed' [BAGD, LN]. This noun is translated as a verb: 'to do' [CEV, NCV], 'doing' [AB, HNTC, NTC, WBC; GW, NASB, NLT, NRSV, TEV]. The phrase 'good works' is translated 'well-doing' [KJV, REB], 'doing what is good' [NLT]. See this word at 2:6.

QUESTION—What relationship is indicated by κατά 'by'?

Note that there is a certain amount of overlap possible between the positions listed below, and one does not rule out the other.

1. It indicates the means by which they seek glory, honor, and immortality [AB, BECNT, ICC2, NICNT, NTC, WBC; KJV, NET, NIV, NRSV, REB]: by means of perseverance in good works, they seek glory, honor, and immortality. It also has a causal nuance [NICNT].

2. It indicates the cause or reason that God will given eternal life [CEV, NLT, TEV]: because they persist in doing good works and seek glory, honor, and immortality, God will them eternal life. The word has a causal nuance [BAGD, NICNT].

3. It is normative, and means according to a norm or standard [BAGD, Gdt]. In this case the standard is patiently continuing in well doing [Gdt]. Here it combines a normative as well as a causative sense [BAGD].

4. It indicates accompanying circumstance [HNTC; NLT]: seeking with patient endurance.

QUESTION—What is meant by ἔργου ἀγαθοῦ 'good work'?

1. This refers to the good deeds they have done [Gdt, HNTC, ICC1, ICC2, Mu, NICNT, NTC, St, TH]. Because 'works' is plural in 2:6, the singular form is somewhat unexpected here, unless it is understood as having a collective sense summing up all the good works of a person's life [ICC1, NICNT]. It is the sum total of a person's actions, referring especially to one's kindness toward other people [TH]. It is our actions done in the

service of others [St]. It refers to goodness of life, though not as meriting the favor of God, but as an expression of faith [ICC2]. The many good works of a believer's life are here summarized in terms of the one deep principle from which they spring, which is the permanent determination to realize goodness [Gdt]. The reward of eternal life is promised to those who see their good works not as human achievements but as marks of hope in God [HNTC]. It is glorifying God by doing what is right in his eyes [NTC].
2. Paul would see the principle stated in 2:6 in a more general sense as the work of trusting God through Christ [WBC].

seek[a] glory[b] and honor[c] and immortality,[d] (he will give)[e] life eternal;

LEXICON—a. pres. act. participle of ζητέω (LN 25.9) (BAGD 2.a. p. 339): 'to seek' [BECNT, ICC2, NICNT, NTC, WBC; KJV, NET, NIV, TEV], 'to seek for' [KJV, NASB, NRSV], 'to seek after' [NLT], 'to strive for' [AB], 'to pursue' [REB], 'to search' [GW], 'to live for' [NCV], 'to desire to (have, or experience)' [LN], 'to desire to possess' [BAGD, LN], 'to try to obtain' [BAGD], 'to hope to receive' [CEV], 'to look beyond...to' [HNTC]. The word has the implication of making an attempt to realize this desire [LN].

b. δόξα (LN 33.357, 87.4) (BAGD 1.a. p. 203): 'glory' [AB, BECNT, HNTC, ICC2, NICNT, NTC, WBC; all versions], 'praise' [LN (33.357)], 'honor, respect' [LN (87.4)].

c. τιμή (LN 87.4) (BAGD 2.b. p. 817): 'honor' [AB, BAGD, BECNT, HNTC, ICC2, LN, NICNT, NTC, WBC; all versions], 'respect' [BAGD, LN], 'status' [LN].

d. ἀφθαρσία (LN 23.127) (BAGD p. 125): 'immortality' [AB, BAGD, ICC2, LN, NICNT, NTC, WBC; GW, KJV, NASB, NET, NIV, NLT, NRSV, REB], 'incorruptibility' [BAGD, BECNT], 'incorruption' [HNTC], 'immortal life' [TEV], 'life that lasts forever' [CEV], 'life that has no end' [NCV]. The word is referring to a quality of the future life [BAGD].

e. There is no lexical entry for the phrase 'he will give' in the Greek text, but it is implied from the context and is added for considerations of English style. This is represented in translation as 'he will give' [NTC; CEV, GW, NIV, NLT, NRSV, REB], 'he will grant' [BECNT], 'he will render' [HNTC, NICNT], 'God will give' [NCV, TEV], not explicit [AB, ICC2, WBC; KJV, NASB, NET]. The object of the verb ζητέω 'seek' is 'glory, honor, and immortality' [AB, BECNT, HNTC, ICC2, NICNT, NTC, WBC; all versions].

QUESTION—How does the syntax of this verse aid in its understanding?

The fact that the phrase 'glory and honor and immortality' is enclosed on the one side by the article τοῖς 'to the ones' and on the other by the participle ζητοῦσιν 'seeking' strongly favors the understanding that it is by their persistence in good works that these people are seeking these three blessings, and that as a result, God will give them eternal life [NICNT].

QUESTION—What is meant by ζητέω 'seek'?

The word implies striving to obtain something [ICC1, SSA]. The verb in the present continuous tense used in conjunction with the phrase 'by patient persistence' implies that this goal requires lifelong, sustained, and deliberate perseverance, not a casual or occasional effort [WBC]. The word 'seek' is closely connected with the phrase 'patient continuance in well doing', since the seeking must be in a certain direction, and 'perseverance' indicates that this is more than just intermittent moral efforts [Gdt]. It means they look beyond their own works to the greater goal of glory, honor, and immortality [HNTC]. It is worth noting that Paul speaks of those who seek glory, honor, and incorruption, not of those who deserve them [ICC2]. It speaks of the believer's aspiration for the highest goals that he hopes for [Mu]. It is the orientation of one's life [Mor], how a person directs his or her life [NAC].

QUESTION—When will those who are seeking glory, honor, and immortality receive them?

These three nouns represent blessings that the righteous can hope to receive in the eschatological future [AB, BECNT, HNTC, Ho, ICC2, Mor, Mu, NICNT, NTC, TH, WBC]. These are three qualities of the eternal life which will be the destiny of Christians in the age to come [AB]. These three point to the transformation which will be realized when believers will be completely conformed to the image of God's son and will reflect God's glory [Mu]. These are direct gifts from God and are qualities of the eternal life which God will give at the end of time [TH].

QUESTION—What is meant by the terms δόξα, τιμή, ἀφθαρσία 'glory, honor, and immortality'?

'Glory' is the manifestation of God himself; 'honor' refers to the approval of God; 'immortality' is the never changing joy of being in God's presence [St]. 'Glory' refers to the excellence of the saints' future condition, a condition that is worthy of 'honor', and the endless nature of this condition is expressed by 'immortality' [Ho]. 'Glory' is an existence with no weakness or defilement, and characterized by the divine holiness and power; 'honor' is God's approval; and 'immortality' indicates the fact that this state of being cannot be interrupted or wounded [Gdt]. Immortality is a quality of the eternal life that God gives [TH], it is the state of incorruption [HNTC, ICC2]. The first two, 'glory' and 'honor', frequently occur together and are probably a doublet with the effect of intensifying 'honor', while the third means 'life which will not end' [SSA]. 'Glory', which is closely associated in Paul's writings with 'honor', denotes God's majesty or loftiness, and often denotes the final blessedness of the believer, while 'immortality' means not being subject to corruption [Mor]. 'Glory' speaks of the transformation that will occur when the believer is conformed to the image of God's son and then reflects God's own glory; 'honor' is God's approval, and stands in contrast to the reproach given by unbelievers and the disgrace which the unbelievers will receive; 'immortality' refers to the hope of the resurrection that God's people have [Mu]. They are eschatological blessings associated with the resurrection life [ICC2]. Together they represent the unending bliss of the resurrection life, a life that is indestructible and incorruptible [NTC]. These qualities describe the 'eternal life' [BECNT, Ho].

2:8 on-the-other-hand,[a] to the-(ones who) out-of[b] selfish-ambition[c] (are) even disobeying[d] the truth[e]

LEXICON—a. (μέν...) δέ: 'but' [AB, BECNT, ICC2, NTC, WBC; CEV, KJV, NASB, NCV, NET, NLT, REB], 'but on the other hand' [NICNT], 'while' [NRSV]. In conjunction with the first word of 2:7 (μέν) this is rendered '(some people)...other people' [NCV, TEV], not explicit [HNTC; GW]. See the first part of this construction in 2:7.

  b. ἐκ with genitive object (LN 89.25, 90.16) (BAGD 3.d. p. 235): 'out of' [WBC], 'from' [LN (90.16)], 'because of' [LN (89.25)], 'in' [GW], not explicit [AB, ICC2; CEV, KJV, NIV, NRSV, TEV]. This preposition is also translated by a verb phrase: 'to act out of' [BECNT], 'to be characterized by' [NICNT], 'to be' [NASB, NCV], 'to be governed by' [REB], 'to be out for' [HNTC], 'to be filled with' [NTC], 'to live in' [NET], 'to live for' [NLT].

  c. ἐριθεία (LN **88.167**) (BAGD p. 309 twice): 'selfish ambition' [BAGD, BECNT, LN, NTC, WBC; NET, REB], 'selfishness' [BAGD, NICNT], 'selfish pride' [GW], 'quick and selfish profit' [HNTC], 'rivalry, resentfulness' [LN]. This noun is also translated as an adjective describing such people: 'selfish' [CEV, NCV, TEV], 'selfishly ambitious' [**LN**; NASB], 'self-seeking' [ICC2; NIV, NRSV], 'contentious' [KJV]; as an adverb: 'selfishly' [AB]; as a verb phrase: 'to live for oneself' [NLT].

  d. pres. act. participle of ἀπειθέω (LN 31.107, 36.23) (BAGD 1. or 3. p. 82): 'to disobey' [AB, BAGD, BECNT, HNTC, ICC2, LN (36.23), NICNT, NTC, WBC], 'to be disobedient' [BAGD], 'to not obey' [KJV, NASB, NET, NRSV], 'to refuse to obey' [NLT], 'to refuse obedience' [REB], 'to refuse to follow' [NCV], 'to reject' [LN (31.107); CEV, NIV, TEV], 'to refuse to believe' [LN (31.107); GW].

  e. ἀλήθεια (LN 72.2) (BAGD 2.b. p. 36): 'truth' [AB, BAGD, BECNT, HNTC, ICC2, LN, NICNT, NTC, WBC; all versions except TEV], 'what is right' [TEV]. It pertains especially to the content of Christianity as the absolute truth [BAGD]. This noun, which has the definite article in the Greek text, is translated with the definite article: 'the truth' [AB, BECNT, HNTC, ICC2, NICNT, NTC, WBC; CEV, GW, KJV, NASB, NET, NIV, NLT, NRSV]; without the definite article: 'truth' [NCV, REB].

QUESTION—What relationship is indicated by ἐκ 'out of' in the phrase ἐξ ἐριθείας '(those who) out-of selfishness'?

  Note that there is a certain amount of overlap possible between the positions listed below, and one does not rule out the other.

1. Here the word denotes the origin of their behavior [BECNT, HNTC, Mor, NICNT, WBC; NET, NLT, REB]: people whose conduct has its roots in or comes from selfishness. It is the motivating principle out of which they live and act [BECNT, HNTC, ICC1, NICNT]. These actions are described as arising out of the quality just described, namely those who have the characteristics and mind of a hireling who is out for quick and selfish profit [HNTC]. The people themselves have their root in factiousness [Mor].
2. It indicates a quality or characteristic of the people who disobey the truth [AB, Gdt, Ho, ICC2, Mu, NICNT, NTC, SSA; CEV, KJV, NIV, NRSV, TEV]: the ones who are selfish disobey the truth. They are of mutinous spirits, that is, they are characterized by an unwillingness to submit [ICC1]. These people are filled with selfish ambition [NTC]. It is used in a way that is similar to 'those of faith' in Gal 3:7, 'those of the circumcision' in Rom 4:12 [Gdt, Ho, Mu].

QUESTION—What is meant by ἐριθεία 'selfishness'?

Note that there is a certain amount of overlap possible between the positions listed below, and one does not rule out the other.

1. It means 'selfishness' [AB, ICC2, NICNT; CEV, NCV, NIV, NLT, NRSV, TEV], or 'selfish ambition' [BAGD, BECNT, HNTC, LN, NAC, NTC, St, TNTC, WBC; NASB, NET, REB]. The word ἐριθεία was used by Aristotle of those who were self-seeking in their pursuit of political office by unfair means, and thus denotes selfishness or selfish ambition here [St, WBC].
2. It means 'factiousness' or 'contentiousness' [Gdt, Ho, ICC1, Mor, Mu; KJV]. It relates to lack of subjection to God as evidenced by the phrase that coordinates with it, 'who obey not the truth but obey unrighteousness' [Ho, Mu]. It is malicious opposition to God and his requirements [Ho]. It is a spirit of faction or contention, here used of those who are in factious opposition to the kingdom of heaven instead of offering loyal and willing obedience [ICC1]. Here the word denotes the kind of contentious attitude that seeks the victory of a given side not out of a desire for truth or right, but out of self-interest [Gdt].

and/but[a] (are) obeying[b] unrighteousness,[c] (there will be)[d] wrath[e] and anger;[f]

LEXICON—a. δέ: 'and' [AB, BECNT, HNTC, ICC2, LN (89.94); CEV, GW, NCV, NIV, NLT, REB], 'but' [LN (89.124), NTC; KJV, NASB, NET, NRSV], 'while' [NICNT], not explicit [WBC; TEV].

b. pres. mid. (deponent = act.) participle of πείθομαι (LN 36.12) (BAGD 3.b. p. 639): 'to obey' [BAGD, HNTC, ICC2, LN, NICNT, NTC; KJV, NASB, NRSV], 'to follow' [BAGD; GW, NCV, NET, NIV, TEV], 'to want to do' [CEV], 'to practice' [NLT], 'to follow' [TEV], 'to take for one's guide' [REB], 'to be won over to' [AB], 'to be persuaded to' [WBC], 'to submit to' [BECNT].

c. ἀδικία (LN 88.21) (BAGD 2. p. 18): 'unrighteousness' [BAGD, BECNT, HNTC, ICC2, LN, NICNT, NTC, WBC; KJV, NASB, NET], 'wickedness' [AB, BAGD; NRSV], 'evil' [NCV, NIV, REB], 'what is unjust' [LN], 'what is wrong' [GW, TEV], 'the wrong' [BAGD].
d. There is no lexical entry for the phrase 'there will be' in the Greek text, but it is implied from the context and is added for considerations of English style. This is represented in translation as 'there will be' [ICC2, NICNT, NTC; NRSV], 'he will show' [CEV], 'he will pour out' [NLT], 'God will pour out' [TEV], 'God will give' [NCV], 'he will bring' [GW], 'he will render' [HNTC], '(the retribution of his wrath) awaits' [REB], 'he will inflict' [BECNT], not explicit [AB, WBC; KJV, NASB, NET].
e. ὀργή: 'wrath'. See this word at 2:5.
f. θυμός (LN **88.178**) (BAGD 2. p. 365): 'anger' [BAGD, BECNT, HNTC, **LN,** NTC, WBC; NCV, NET, NIV], 'fury' [AB, ICC2, LN, NICNT; GW, NRSV, TEV], 'wrath' [BAGD, LN; KJV, NLT, REB], 'indignation' [NASB]. This noun is also translated as an adjective: 'furious' [CEV]. It is a state of intense anger, and when used together with ὀργή 'wrath' as in this context, each of the two words heightens the intensity or significance of the other [LN]. The two words are often used together [BAGD].

QUESTION—Is there a significant distinction between the terms ὀργή 'wrath' and θυμός 'anger' in this context?

1. The words are synonymous or nearly so [BAGD, ICC2, Mor, Mu, NICNT, SSA, TH, WBC]. These two words are a doublet and intensify the one idea of severe punishment [SSA]. The words are essentially synonymous and describe God's attitude towards those he condemns [TH]. The meaning is simply God's wrath, and here the two nouns are synonyms; the second has the effect of emphasizing the first [ICC2]. They reinforce each other and emphasize the intensity and reality of God's anger [Mor, Mu]. The phrase 'wrath and anger' stand in contrast to 'eternal life', and are the response of a just God to the violation of the order he has established [NICNT]. While θυμός 'indignation' is not much different than ὀργή 'wrath', it reflects on the violence of the wrath [Mu]. θυμός reflects God's deeply felt indignation at injustice [WBC].
2. There is some useful distinction between the words [Gdt, Ho, ICC1, NAC, NTC]. The first, ὀργή 'wrath', denotes the settled feeling and the second, θυμός 'anger', the outward manifestation of it [Gdt, ICC1, NAC]. The first word denotes a deep-seated permanent anger or antagonism, and the second usually describes a sudden impulse of anger [Ho, NAC, NTC]. The first word, ὀργή 'wrath', reflects a settled disposition, and θυμός 'anger', expresses the outpouring of that wrath [ICC1, NTC]. When ὀργή 'wrath' and θυμός 'anger' are used together, as in this context, each word heightens the intensity or significance of the other [Ho, LN (88.178)].

2:9 (there will be)[a] affliction[b] and distress[c] for[d] every soul[e] of man[f] the-(one) doing[g] the evil,[h]

LEXICON—a. There is no lexical entry for the phrase 'there will be' in the Greek text, but it is implied from the context and is added for considerations of English style. It is represented in translation as 'there will be' [AB, ICC2, NICNT, NTC; GW, NASB, NET, NIV, NLT, NRSV, REB, TEV], 'there shall be' [BECNT], 'he will give' [NCV], 'will be punished with' [CEV], 'will fall upon' [HNTC].

b. θλῖψις (LN 22.2) (BAGD 1. p. 362): 'affliction' [BAGD, NTC, WBC; NET, REB], 'tribulation' [BAGD, BECNT, HNTC, ICC2, NICNT; KJV, NASB], 'trouble' [LN; CEV, NCV, NIV, NLT], 'suffering' [LN; GW, TEV], 'distress' [AB], 'anguish' [NRSV]. The word denotes trouble that involves direct suffering [LN], distress brought about by outward circumstances [BAGD].

c. στενοχωρία (LN **22.10**) (BAGD p. 766): 'distress' [BAGD, BECNT, ICC2, **LN,** NICNT, NTC, WBC; GW, NASB, NET, NIV, NRSV, REB], 'difficulty' [BAGD, LN], 'anguish' [AB, BAGD, HNTC; KJV], 'trouble' [BAGD], 'pain' [TEV], 'suffering' [CEV, NCV], 'calamity' [NLT], 'difficult circumstances' [LN].

d. ἐπί with accusative object (LN 83.46) (BAGD III.1.b.γ. p. 289): 'for' [AB, BECNT, NICNT, NTC; GW, NCV, NIV, NLT, NRSV, REB, TEV], 'upon' [BAGD, HNTC, LN; KJV], 'on' [BAGD, LN, WBC; NET], 'to' [BAGD; NCV], 'will fall upon' [HNTC], 'to be punished with' [CEV], 'as the lot of' [ICC2].

e. ψυχή (LN **9.20**) (BAGD 1.b.γ. p. 893; 2. p. 894): 'soul' [BAGD, HNTC, NICNT; KJV, NASB], 'person' [BECNT, **LN**; GW], 'human being' [AB], 'human soul' [HNTC], 'individual' [ICC2], not explicit [NTC; CEV, NCV, NET, NIV, NLT, NRSV, REB, TEV]. This word is used as a figurative extension of the meaning of ψυχή 'inner self' meaning a person as a living being [LN].

f. ἄνθρωπος (LN 9.1) (BAGD 1.a.α. p. 68): 'man' [BAGD, ICC2; KJV], 'person' [LN, NICNT, WBC], 'human being' [AB, BAGD, LN, NTC; NIV], 'human' [HNTC], 'individual' [LN], not explicit [BECNT; NLT, NRSV, TEV]. The phrase πᾶσαν ψυχὴν ἀνθρώπου 'every soul of man' is translated 'every human being' [AB, NTC; NIV, REB], 'everyone' [BAGD; NCV, NET, NLT, NRSV], 'every person' [BECNT, **LN**; GW], 'every individual man' [ICC2], 'every soul of a person' [NICNT], 'every human soul' [HNTC], 'every soul of man' [KJV, NASB], 'every living person' [WBC], 'all those who' [TEV], 'all who are' [CEV]. See this word at 2:3.

g. pres. mid. (deponent = act.) participle of κατεργάζομαι (LN **90.47**) (BAGD 1. p. 421): 'to do' [AB, BAGD, BECNT, **LN,** NICNT; GW, KJV, NASB, NCV, NET, NIV, NRSV, TEV], 'to perform' [LN], 'to work' [HNTC, ICC2], 'to bring about' [WBC], 'to be' [NTC; CEV, REB], 'to keep on (sinning)' [NLT].

h. κακός (LN 88.106) (BAGD 1.c. p. 397): 'evil' [AB, BAGD, BECNT, HNTC, ICC2, LN, NICNT, NTC, WBC; all versions except CEV, NLT, REB], 'evil deeds' [BAGD], 'bad' [LN], 'wicked' [CEV], 'wrongdoer' [REB]. This adjective is also translated as a verb: 'to sin' [NLT].

QUESTION—What is meant by θλῖψις 'affliction'?

In this context, it is used of the suffering that comes from eschatological condemnation [NICNT]. This denotes the effects of the wrath of God [ICC2]. This word denotes the punishment itself, the external state of the one on whom wrath comes [Gdt]. The affliction is outward [ICC2, NAC, NICNT, NTC].

QUESTION—Is there a significant difference in meaning between θλῖψις 'affliction' and στενοχωρία 'distress'?

1. 'Distress' refers to the inner anguish experienced by a person in difficult circumstances [Gdt, Ho, ICC2, NICNT, NTC, WBC]. Although the meaning of the two words is close, 'distress' may focus more on the subjective suffering caused by the external or objective affliction [NICNT]. Στενοχωρία 'distress' is the stronger of the two terms [Ho, ICC2, WBC]. Judgment is compared to those life experiences in which outward circumstances or affliction create pressure and stress, and causing personal distress to the individual [WBC]. 'Tribulation' is the objective punishment itself, and 'distress' describes the anguish and wringing of heart which it causes [Gdt].

2. This words are more or less synonymous, and are used together for intensity of effect [ICC1, Mor, SSA]. Distress comes as the result of affliction, and the two used together form a nearly synonymous doublet indicating the intensity of the one event [SSA]. When these two words, which are nearly synonymous, are used together it has the effect of emphasizing the severity of the trouble [Mor]. Using the two words together intensifies the effect [ICC1, Mor, SSA]. Although στενοχωρία 'distress' is the stronger of the two terms, the distinction has probably been lost here, and the two words are used together to indicate galling, crushing pain [ICC1].

QUESTION—What is meant by ἐπὶ πᾶσαν ψυχὴν ἀνθρώπου 'for every soul of man'?

This is a Semitic way of saying every living person [AB, Ho, ICC2, NTC], every human being [Mor, Mu, St], all mankind [TH]. It means every single person, and reflects the Semitic understanding of man as a living being, not just having a soul but being a soul [WBC]. 'Soul' as used in scripture is often synonymous for 'person' [AB, Ho, ICC2, Mu], and this is an emphatic way of asserting the universality of the judgment just mentioned [Mu]. Paul is not saying that punishment affects only the soul of a person [AB, ICC2, Mor]. In using this phrase Paul emphasizes that God's judgment is totally impartial [Gdt, NICNT], and that it is universal [Gdt]. The soul is mentioned as representing the seat of feeling [Gdt].

ROMANS 2:9

of-(the) Jew first[a] and-also[b] of-(the) Greek;[c]

LEXICON—a. πρῶτον (LN 60.46) (BAGD 2.c. p. 726), 'first' [AB, BECNT, HNTC, ICC2, LN, NICNT, NTC, WBC; all versions except CEV], not explicit [CEV].

b. καί (LN 89.93): 'and also' [AB, BECNT, ICC2, LN; KJV, NASB, NCV, NET, NLT, NRSV, TEV], 'and…also' [REB], 'and' [LN], 'also' [LN, NTC], 'and…too' [HNTC], 'and…as well' [WBC; GW], 'and then' [NICNT], 'then' [NIV], not explicit [CEV].

c. Ἕλλην (LN 11.40, 11.90) (BAGD 2.a. p. 252): 'Greek' [AB, BECNT, ICC2, LN (11.40, 11.90), NICNT, NTC; NET, NRSV, REB], 'Gentile' [BAGD, HNTC, LN (11.40), WBC; CEV, KJV, NIV, NLT, TEV], 'non-Jew' [LN (11.40)], 'those who are not Jews' [NCV]. This is a person who participates in Greek culture and in so doing speaks the Greek language, but is not necessarily a person of Greek ethnic background [LN (11.90)].

QUESTION—What is meant by the Jew being πρῶτος 'first'?

When Paul affirms the priority of the Jew in salvation as well as judgment, he is affirming that God's judgment will be absolutely impartial [Mor, St]. The Jews have a certain priority both for good as well as for ill, though that is not necessarily enviable [HNTC].

1. It means that the Jews are first in priority and responsibility due to having greater privilege [AB, BECNT, Ho, ICC2, Mu, NAC, NICNT, SSA, St, TH, WBC], though not implying a difference in the timing of judgment [SSA]. It is an ironic twist from what many Jews would have expected, who believed they would be first in salvation and last in judgment [NICNT]. The Jew is singled out in priority due to his position of privilege and advantage in having the Mosaic law and knowing God's will [AB]. Priority in blessing results in priority in judgment [Mu, NAC, WBC]. It indicates preeminence, especially since in scripture there seems to be little or no evidence for temporal sequence of judgment according to racial groups [SSA]. It emphasizes God's priority in dealing with people, not a chronology of timing with respect to judgment [TH]. Because of the privilege the Jew has had, his responsibility is that much greater [Mu]. It intensifies with reference to the Jews what is stated generally about the judgment of all people; that is, what is true for all men is especially true of the Jews, to whom God gave special revelation [Ho].

2. It refers to priority in time as well as to the principle that the one with greatest benefits has also the heaviest responsibility [Gdt, Mor]. At the judgment God will take into account the fact that the Jews were the first to be offered the gospel and that they had been far more privileged than the Gentiles [NTC]. The Jews expected to escape the judgment that would fall on the Gentiles, but Paul is saying that judgment will be universal [Mor].

2:10 but^a **(there will be)^b glory^c and honor^d and peace^e to-everyone doing the good,^f**

LEXICON—a. δέ (LN 89.124): 'but' [AB, BECNT, ICC2, LN, NICNT, NTC, WBC; all versions], not explicit [HNTC].
  b. There is no lexical entry for the phrase 'there will be' in the Greek text, but it is implied from the context and is added for considerations of English style. It is represented in translation as 'there will be' [AB, NICNT; GW, NLT, REB], 'there shall be' [BECNT], 'there will be…from God' [NLT], 'God will give' [TEV], 'he will give' [NCV], 'will be rewarded with' [CEV], not explicit [HNTC, ICC2, NTC, WBC; KJV, NASB, NET, NIV, NRSV].
  c. δόξα: 'glory'. See this word at 2:7.
  d. τιμή: 'honor'. See this word at 2:7.
  e. εἰρήνη (LN 22.42, 25.248) (BAGD 3. p. 227): 'peace' [AB, BAGD, BECNT, HNTC, ICC2, LN (22.42, 25.248), NICNT, NTC, WBC; all versions].
  f. ἀγαθός (LN 88.1) (BAGD 2.a.α. p. 3): 'good' [AB, BAGD, BECNT, HNTC, LN, NICNT, NTC, WBC; KJV, NASB, NCV, NET, NIV, NLT, NRSV, TEV], 'right' [BAGD; CEV, REB], 'what is good' [BECNT, ICC2, NTC; GW], 'that which is good' [HNTC], 'good act' [LN]. See this word at 2:7.

QUESTION—What is said about 'glory and honor' in this verse that differs from 2:7?

Both verses describe the personal benefits of those who experience eternal life [BECNT]. Though partly a repetition of 2:7, these terms are used here in reference to the final eschatological state of the good individual [WBC]. The words describe the qualities of life forever with the Lord [AB]. Not meant to be taken separately here, these describe the rich spiritual blessings awaiting the believer [SSA]. In 2:7 these are what God's people are seeking, and here it is what they will receive [NICNT, NTC, St]. They are used in basically the same way as in 2:7 [ICC2, Mor].

QUESTION—What is being described by the phrase δόξα δὲ καὶ τιμὴ καὶ εἰρήνη 'glory, honor and peace' in this verse?

The three nouns are probably not meant to be understood separately, but rather as a unit denoting the richness of the blessings awaiting believers [Mor, SSA]. These are qualities of the eternal life which God will give at the end of time [AB, St, TH]. It speaks of the glorious reconciliation between God and people that will be universally recognized when eternity dawns [NAC]. These refer to the rewards of the righteous [Mu]. These terms describe eternal life; it is a life that is glorious, something that is an object of honor and regard by others, and which is a source of blessedness or peace [Ho]. The combination of these words describes complete bliss and blessing, the first two having to do with status and what is outward, and the last with the inward state as well as the relationship with God [Mor].

QUESTION—What is meant by εἰρήνη 'peace'?
1. It is eschatological [Mu, NICNT, NTC]. It denotes the state of perfect well being to be brought about by God's intervention at the end of time and which the righteous will enjoy [NICNT]. The word should be understood in the broadest sense, indicating the fullness of salvation and a never ending participation in fellowship with God and all the redeemed in all the blessings of the new heaven and earth; it is nearly synonymous with 'immortality' [NTC]. It is the highest realization of the fruits of reconciliation, including peace with God and inner peace of heart, along with the full enjoyment of God eternally [Mu].
2. It relates to the inward experience of the believer [Gdt, ICC1, Mor]. The word refers to the subjective feeling of profound peace produced by deliverance from wrath and the reception of blessedness which is unchanging, and which is experienced by the saved person at that time when glory and honor are conferred on him [Gdt]. It refers to an inward state, although the external reconciliation with God is also in mind [Mor]. It is the bliss that comes from being reconciled to God [ICC1].
3. It describes restored relationships [ICC2, St]. It refers to peace with God through reconciliation, and is similar in meaning to 'salvation' [ICC2]. This word is a comprehensive one for the reconciled relationships of believers with God and with each other [St].

to-(the) Jew first and-also to-(the) Greek;[a]
LEXICON—a. Ἕλλην (LN 11.40, 11.90) (BAGD 2.a. p. 252): 'Greek' [AB, BECNT, ICC2, LN (11.40, 11.90), NICNT, NTC; GW, NASB, NET, NRSV, REB], 'Gentile' [BAGD, HNTC, LN (11.40), WBC; CEV, KJV, NIV, NLT, TEV], 'non-Jew' [LN (11.40)], 'those who are not Jews' [NCV], 'pagan, heathen' [BAGD]. This entire phrase is translated 'whether they are Jews or Gentiles' [CEV]. See this word in a similarly worded phrase at 2:9.

2:11 for[a] there-is not (any) partiality[b] with[c] God.
LEXICON—a. γάρ (LN 89.23) (BAGD p. 152): 'for' [AB, BAGD, BECNT, HNTC, ICC2, LN, NICNT, NTC, WBC; KJV, NASB, NCV, NET, NIV, NLT, NRSV, TEV], not explicit [CEV, GW, REB].
b. προσωπολημψία (LN **88.238**) (BAGD p. 720): 'partiality' [AB, BAGD, BECNT, ICC2, LN, NICNT, NTC, WBC; NASB, NET, NRSV], 'favoritism' [HNTC, **LN**; NIV, NLT], 'respect of persons' [KJV]. This entire clause is translated 'God doesn't have any favorites' [CEV], 'God has no favorites' [REB], 'God does not play favorites' [GW], 'God judges everyone by the same standard' [TEV], 'God judges all people in the same way' [NCV]. This idiom literally means 'to accept a face' and refers to giving preferential treatment [LN].
c. παρά with dative object (LN 89.111) (BAGD II.2.d. p. 610): 'with' [BAGD, BECNT, LN, NICNT, WBC; KJV, NASB, NET], 'in' [AB, BAGD], not explicit [CEV, GW, NCV, REB, TEV].

QUESTION—What relationship is indicated by γάρ 'for'?
   It indicate the grounds for 2:6–10 [BECNT, Gdt, Ho, ICC2, Mor, Mu, NICNT, TH]. It indicates the grounds for the inclusion of the Jews in his description God's judgment of the world [HNTC]. It introduces the statement that God is impartial as the grounds for 2:6–10, which asserts that God will reward those who do good and punish those who do evil [BECNT]. It provides the grounds for the statement in 2:6 that God will recompense all people according to what they do [SSA]. This expresses the ground of assurance that God will judge all, whether Jew or Gentile, according to their works [Ho]. It introduces 2:11 as a conclusion to the thought of 2:6; the fact that God judges all by the same standard indicates his impartiality towards all men of whatever race [TH]. It connects this verse with what precedes, reasserting that God's judgment is impartial, as well as with what follows [Mu].

QUESTION—What is the main point of this statement regarding God's impartiality?
   The primary point is that God's impartiality demands that he judges all people on the same basis [AB, BECNT, HNTC, Ho, Mu, NAC, NTC, TH, WBC]. Paul has stated positively in 2:6–10 that God judges all people equally, and now makes the same point negatively by denying that there is any partiality with God [NICNT]. God will judge all people fairly without regard to their ethnicity, status, or wealth [Mor, SSA]. God has no favorites and looks on Jew and Gentile equally alike [AB]. Ethnicity and race will not be a factor when God judges [NAC]. To those Jews who had come to be self-confident in their election by God, Paul says that God has no favorites [WBC]. The basis of judgment will be works, not privilege or position [Mu].

DISCOURSE UNIT: 2:12–16 [AB, HNTC]. The topic is the law and its observance [AB], conscience [HNTC].

2:12 For as-many-as have-sinned[a] without-law,[b] also without-law shall-perish;[c]

LEXICON—a. aorist act. indic. of ἁμαρτάνω (LN 88.289) (BAGD 3. p. 42): 'to sin' [AB, BAGD, BECNT, HNTC, ICC2, LN, NICNT, NTC, WBC; all versions except CEV, NCV], 'to do wrong' [BAGD]. The phrase 'as many as have sinned' is translated 'people who are sinners' [NCV]. This entire clause is translated 'those people who don't know about God's Law will still be punished for what they do wrong' [CEV]. This aorist verb is translated as a perfect tense: 'have sinned' [AB, HNTC, ICC2, NTC, WBC; KJV, NASB, NET, NRSV, REB]; as a past tense: 'sinned' [BECNT], as a present tense: 'sin' [NICNT; NIV, NLT, TEV], 'sins' [GW].

   b. ἀνόμως (LN **33.57**) (BAGD p. 72): 'without the Law' [LN, WBC; NASB], 'without the law' [BAGD, BECNT, NICNT], 'apart from the law' [AB; NET, NIV, NRSV], 'in ignorance of the law' [ICC2, NTC], 'outside the pale of the law of Moses' [REB], 'outside the sphere of the law' [HNTC], 'without law' [KJV]. This word is also translated a verb phrase: 'who do not have the law' [NCV], 'do not have the Law of Moses' [TEV], 'without having laws from God' [GW], 'never had God's written law' [NLT], 'don't know about God's law' [CEV]. In this verse this word refers to being without the Law, specifically the first five books of the OT, and in this context it refers to those who are ignorant of the Law and thus are not bound by it [LN]. This word is found only in this verse in the NT.

c. fut. mid.(deponent = act.) indic. of ἀπόλλυμι (LN 21.32, 23.106) (BAGD 2.a.α. p. 95): 'to perish' [AB, BAGD, BECNT, HNTC, ICC2, LN (21.32, 23.106), NICNT, NTC, WBC; KJV, NASB, NET, NIV, NRSV, REB], 'to die' [BAGD, LN (23.106)], 'to be lost' [NCV, TEV], 'to be punished' [CEV], 'to be condemned to destruction' [GW]. This verb is also translated with God as the subject: 'God will punish' [NLT].

QUESTION—What relationship is indicated by γάρ 'for'?

It explains the preceding section [BECNT, NTC]. It provides an illustration or further explanation of God's impartiality asserted in 2:11 [BECNT]. It introduces 2:12 as confirming and illustrating what was said in 2:11 that God shows no favoritism, because in executing judgment God deals with people according to the light they have had [Ho, Mu]. It introduces this section to clarify his assertion that every person will be judged according to his or her deeds, and which he does by stating that what counts is not whether one has possessed or heard the law, but whether he or she has conducted life in accordance with its requirements [NTC]. It introduces a justification for what would be the answer to the challenge that could naturally be raised to what is stated in 2:11; that is, there is no partiality with God and he is not unjust to judge the Gentiles, despite the fact that the Gentiles did not have the law to guide them, because (γάρ) their condemnation does not come from the fact that they did not have the law, but from their actions [Gdt].

QUESTION—What law is being referred to in this verse?

The law in question is the law of Moses [AB, BECNT, Gdt, HNTC, ICC2, Mor, NAC, NICNT, SSA, St, TH, WBC]. The term is first used somewhat generically, but it soon becomes clear that he is referring to the Mosaic Law [AB]. It is a supernaturally revealed, written law [Ho]. This is the law of Moses, specifically the commandments given by God through Moses to the Israelites on Mt. Sinai, the Torah [NICNT]. Paul is referring to the Pentateuch and even more precisely the Ten Commandments [NTC]. The law referred to throughout 2:12–16 is the Mosaic law, and specifically what is commanded therein, since Paul refers to sinning as a failure to obey the law or as a transgression of the law [BECNT].

QUESTION—What is meant by ἀνόμως ἥμαρτον, 'have sinned without law'?

1. It means to sin, but as one who does not possess the law of Moses [BECNT, Gdt, Ho, Mor, NICNT, TH] or as one who is not subject to that law [SSA]. Those who do not have the Mosaic law or know its requirements nevertheless sin, and their condemnation is not derived from

the prescriptions of the law, but is due to their own evil and sinfulness [AB]. The referents are the Gentiles [AB, BECNT, Gdt, HNTC, Mor, NAC, NICNT, NTC, SSA, St, TH, TNTC, WBC; NLT, TEV]. It means to sin in ignorance of the law [ICC2, NTC]. It means to sin while lacking the law [WBC]. It is to sin outside the sphere of the law of Moses, though not outside the sphere of law altogether [HNTC].

2. It means to be lawless; the heathen rejected the law of Moses as well as the ordinances God gave through Noah [ICC1].

QUESTION—What is meant by ἀπόλλυμι 'perish'?

It denotes eternal punishment, of perishing in the eschatological judgment [BECNT]. This word is often used in Scriptures to denote the results of a negative verdict in the eschatological judgment [NICNT]. The word means that these will be condemned in the final judgment [ICC2]. It is the ultimate fate of the wicked of eternal and unending loss [Mor], the ultimate destiny of unbelievers [NAC]. 'Perish' does not mean that the person ceases to exist [Mor, NICNT]. This future tense verb expresses the outcome of a life characterized by sin [AB]. This refers to what earlier verses have mentioned, namely suffering God's wrath and enduring tribulation and anguish, as contrasted with those who will know glory, honor, and incorruption as recipients of eternal life [Mu]. It is to be eternally separated from God [SSA]. It is the final outcome of a life determined by sin [WBC]. The word refers to eternal death, not physical death [SSA].

QUESTION—What is meant by ἀνόμως καὶ ἀπολοῦνται 'also without law shall perish'?

It means to be judged guilty of transgression and to perish, but without knowing of or having had the Mosaic law [AB, BECNT, Gdt, ICC2, Mor, NAC, NICNT, NTC, St, TH]. The Gentiles will not be judged by a standard they have not known, but will perish because of their sin [Gdt, Mor, NTC, St, TNTC]. The Gentiles will not be judged according to the Mosaic ordinances [Gdt]. They perish even though they did not have the law [TH]. It means to perish without consideration of whether or not they had the law [SSA]. This also alludes to the degree of the severity of the judgment, which is based on the light or knowledge that one has [Mu]. The punishment they receive will not be determined in reference to the written law, so they will be treated less severely than those who did have written revelation, but they will still perish [Ho]. Judgment will be based on what people have done, and the standard of judgment will be whatever knowledge they had [Ho, St]. All will be judged according to whatever revelation and light God had given them [Mor, NAC, TNTC].

and as-many-as have-sinned[a] in[b] (the) law, by[c] (the) law will-be-judged;[d]

LEXICON—a. aorist act. indic. of ἁμαρτάνω (LN 88.289) (BAGD 3. p. 42): 'to sin' [AB, BAGD, BECNT, ICC2, LN, NICNT, NTC, WBC; all versions except CEV, NCV], 'to do wrong' [BAGD], 'to engage in wrongdoing' [LN], not explicit [CEV]. The phrase καὶ ὅσοι...ἥμαρτον 'and as many as have sinned' is translated 'those who are sinners' [NCV], 'the Jews when they sin' [NLT], 'the Jews (have the law); they sin' [TEV].

b. ἐν with dative object (LN 89.5, 89.119) (BAGD I.5.d. p. 260): 'in' [LN (89.5, 89.119), NICNT; KJV], 'under' [AB; NASB, NET, NIV, NRSV, REB], 'under the domination of' [BAGD], 'within the realm of' [BECNT], 'within the sphere of' [HNTC], 'within' [WBC]. The phrase 'in the law' is translated 'knowing the law' [ICC2, NTC], 'have the law' [NCV, NLT, TEV], 'has laws from God' [GW], '(who) knows what it (the law) says' [CEV].

d. διά with genitive object (LN 89.76): 'by' [AB, BECNT, LN, NTC; GW, KJV, NASB, NCV, NET, NIV, NRSV, REB, TEV], 'by means of' [HNTC, LN], 'on the basis of' [ICC2], 'through' [LN, NICNT, WBC], not explicit [NLT]. The phrase διὰ νόμου 'by (the) Law' is translated 'the Law will be used (to judge)' [CEV].

f. fut. pass. indic. of κρίνω (LN 56.20, 56.30) (BAGD 4.b.α. p. 452): 'to be judged' [AB, BAGD, BECNT, HNTC, ICC2, LN (56.20), NICNT, NTC; all versions except NLT], 'to be condemned' [BAGD, LN (56.30), WBC], 'to be punished' [BAGD], 'to be tried' [LN (56.20)]. This passive verb is also translated actively with God as the subject: 'God will punish' [NLT].

QUESTION—What is meant by ἐν νόμῳ ἥμαρτον 'have sinned in the law'?

The Jews have sinned despite having knowledge of the law [Ho, NAC, NTC, SSA, St, TH], despite having had the privilege of possessing, knowing, and living within the sphere or domain of the Mosaic Law [NICNT, WBC]. They sinned despite living within the boundaries defined by the law [NICNT]. Those who live by the guidance of the Mosaic Law will be judged for their sins according to it [AB]. Those who had the law and still sinned will be judged by that law [Gdt]. This denotes the circumstances of their sinning and means they sinned while knowing the law [ICC2].

QUESTION—Who are the referents of those who have sinned ἐν νόμῳ 'in the law'?

The reference is to the Jews [AB, BECNT, Gdt, HNTC, Ho, ICC1, Mor, NAC, NICNT, NTC, SSA, St, TH, WBC].

QUESTION—What is indicated by the use of the aorist form ἥμαρτον 'have sinned'?

The aorist form of the word expresses the summation of a person's life as it will be seen at the time of the judgment [AB, Gdt, NAC, St]. At the judgment, the whole of one's life, and the character of that life, may be summed up as one past event [WBC]. This could be called an historical collective aorist such that as viewed from the point of the last judgment, the sins are thought of as together constituting a past event [ICC2]. The word used in the aorist tense connotes indefinite past action, which in English is often communicated by the perfect tense [NICNT]. This is a collective aorist, in which all the sins are viewed as an aggregate constituting a past fact as viewed from the speaker's perspective, but not necessarily as viewed from the last judgment [ICC1]. The aorist expresses a fact that is true for all times rather than as a specific past action [TH].

QUESTION—What is meant by διὰ νόμου κριθήσονται 'by (the) law will be judged'?
1. It means that judgment will be by the standard of, or on the basis of, the law [AB, Gdt, HNTC, ICC2, Mor, NAC, SSA, TH, WBC]. It means to be judged on the basis of what is written in the law [TH]. The law will be the standard by which a negative verdict of condemnation will be given [NAC, WBC]. The law is the means God uses to judge these people, and they are judged as to whether or not they obeyed it, not just whether they had or knew it [SSA]. Paul is not saying that the law itself judges, but that it is the means God uses to judge those who have received it, but have not obeyed it [Mor]. The law is an instrument of judgment, especially for those who sin within the sphere of the law [HNTC].
2. This indicates a judgment of greater severity for those having had the law [Ho, Mu]. The final judgment of these who have had the specially revealed law will be aggravated in correspondence with their sin, which is greater since they have had the revealed law, and which now for them will be the criterion of a judgment that implies destruction [Mu]. The ground of judgment is one's works, and the rule of judgment is one's knowledge, for God will judge all according to the light they have had. Those who have had written revelation will be judged by it and their punishment will be more severe than for those without that advantage [Ho].

QUESTION—What distinction, if any, is there between the words ἀπολοῦνται 'shall perish' and κριθήσονται 'will be judged'?

The sense of both is condemnation [BECNT, ICC2, NICNT, SSA, WBC]. Condemnation is the outcome for everyone who sins, and perishing is the result of this negative judgment [NICNT]. The parallelism of the two clauses shows that both the judgment and the perishing are eternal [BECNT]. Regarding the final outcome, there is no distinction between those without the law and those under the law, since both will be judged and perish [AB, St]. Judgment is the negative verdict of condemnation, and perish designates the ultimate destiny [NAC].

2:13 for[a] not the hearers[b] of-(the)-Law (are) righteous[c] in the sight of[d] God,

LEXICON—a. γάρ (LN 89.23) (BAGD 1.b. p. 152): 'for' [AB, BAGD, BECNT, HNTC, ICC2, LN, NICNT, NTC, WBC; KJV, NASB, NET, NIV, NLT, NRSV, TEV], not explicit [CEV, GW, NCV, REB].
    b. ἀκροατής (LN **24.56**) (BAGD p. 33): 'hearer' [BAGD, BECNT, ICC2, LN, NICNT, NTC, WBC; KJV, NASB, NRSV]. The phrase οἱ ἀκροαταί 'the hearers' is translated 'the ones who hear' [NET], 'those who hear' [NET, NIV], 'those who listen to' [AB, HNTC], 'those who simply hear (it)' [CEV], 'people who merely listen' [GW]. This noun is also translated as a verb: 'to hear' [REB, TEV], 'hearing' [NCV], 'to know' [NLT].

c. δίκαιος (LN 34.47, 88.12) (BAGD 1.b. p. 195): 'righteous' [BAGD, BECNT, HNTC, ICC2, LN (34.47, 88.12), NTC, WBC; NET, NIV, NRSV], 'just' [LN (88.12), NICNT; KJV, NASB], 'upright' [AB], 'right (with God)' [NCV], 'justified' [REB], '(God's) approval' [GW, NLT]. This adjective is also translated as a passive verb: 'to be in a right relation with, to be put right with' [LN (34.47)], 'to be put right (with God)' [TEV]; as a verb with God as the actor: 'God accepts' [CEV].

e. παρά with dative object (LN **90.20**) (BAGD II.2.b. p. 610): 'in the sight of' [BAGD, **LN**, NTC; NIV, NLT, NRSV], 'before' [AB, BECNT, NICNT, WBC; KJV, NASB, NET, REB], 'with' [HNTC, ICC2; NCV, TEV], 'in the opinion of' [LN], 'in the judgment of' [BAGD, LN], not explicit [CEV, GW].

QUESTION—What relationship is indicated by γάρ 'for'?

1. It introduces the grounds for the claim made in 2:12 that those who have sinned will be punished because only the doers of the Law will be justified [BECNT, Ho, Mor, NICNT, SSA]. Those who have the law will be condemned when they sin, because it is only when the law is obeyed that it could justify [Ho, NICNT]. The reason that Jews should not be deceived by thinking that merely possessing the law exempts them from judgment is that hearing the law does not constitute righteousness, rather it is obedience to the law that enables one to be declared righteous [BECNT]. It is a justification of the claim made in 2:12, that all will be condemned for sin, the justification being that only those who have continually obeyed the Mosaic law will be justified, but none have done so [SSA].
2. It introduces the grounds for the claim made in 2:12 that the law will be the means of condemnation for all those who have sinned under it [ICC2, Mu]. It introduces the grounds for his claim that possession of the law does not insure that a Jew will escape condemnation [WBC].

QUESTION—What is meant by οἱ ἀκροαταὶ νόμου 'the hearers of (the) Law' in this verse?

It refers it those who merely hear it [ICC2, Mor, NAC], or merely know it [Ho, SSA], or merely possess it [Ho, Mu, TH]. Paul is speaking of the Jews [Gdt, Ho, Mu, NICNT], who had the false hope that having the law, or intending to obey the law, would be enough to avoid severe judgment and lead to final salvation [NICNT]. Devout Jews understood 'hearing' in the positive sense of attentive or heedful hearing, so for them being hearers of the law and being righteous were concepts that complemented and overlapped one another; yet Paul contrasts even these aspects of Jewish self-understanding, for he has in mind a different kind of doing of the law [WBC]. In that era most people were exposed to the law by hearing it read [AB, Ho, Mor, Mu, SSA]. The Jewish people heard it read each Sabbath in the synagogue [HNTC].

but[a] the doers[b] of-(the)-law will-be-justified.[c]

LEXICON—a. ἀλλά (LN 89.125) 'but' [BECNT, ICC2, LN, NICNT, NTC, WBC; CEV, KJV, NASB, NET, NIV, NRSV, REB, TEV], 'rather' [AB; GW], 'no' [HNTC], 'instead, on the contrary' [LN], not explicit [NCV, NLT].

b. ποιητής (LN **42.20**) (BAGD 2. p. 683): 'doer' [BAGD, BECNT, ICC2, LN, NICNT, NTC, WBC; KJV, NASB, NRSV], 'one who does' [BAGD], 'the ones who do' [NET], 'these who do (what the Law requires)' [**LN**], 'those who do' [HNTC; NET], 'people who do' [GW], 'those who obey' [CEV, NCV, NIV, NLT], 'those who observe' [AB], 'by doing it' [REB], 'by doing (what the Law commands)' [TEV].

c. fut. pass. indic. of δικαιόω (LN 34.46, 56.34) (BAGD 3.a. p. 197): 'to be justified' [AB, BAGD, HNTC, NICNT; KJV, NASB, NRSV, REB], 'to be declared righteous' [BECNT; NET, NIV], 'to be declared right in God's sight' [NLT], 'to be put right with God' [LN (34.46); NCV, TEV], 'to be pronounced righteous' [ICC2, NTC], 'to be counted righteous' [WBC], 'to be accepted (by God)' [CEV], 'to have God's approval' [GW], 'to be acquitted' [LN (56.34)], 'to have one's guilt removed' [LN (56.34)]. This passive verb is translated 'God accepts' [CEV].

QUESTION—What is meant by δικαιωθήσονται 'justified'?

This refers to a favorable verdict of acquittal at the last judgment [AB, Gdt, HNTC, Ho, ICC1, ICC2, WBC]. It describes a status in relation to God, not the moral quality of the person [HNTC, ICC2, TH]. It refers to being acquitted or declared not guilty, not to being made righteous or virtuous [HNTC, Ho, Mor, SSA]. This word denotes God's judicial decision to regard the sinner as innocent before him, and is used here of salvation in its broadest sense; Paul's intent here is to set out the standard that would have to be met if God were to give a verdict of justification [NICNT]. God will declare these persons to be righteous [BECNT]. It means to be recognized as righteous and declared as such in the day of judgment, a time when no one will be made righteous, morally speaking [Gdt]. It means to be pronounced righteous in the sight of God [NTC]. It is being declared not guilty, as opposed to being condemned [SSA].

QUESTION—Is there any difference in meaning between δίκαιοι παρὰ [τῷ] θεῷ 'righteous in the sight of God' and δικαιωθήσονται 'will be justified'?

There is little or no difference [BECNT, HNTC, ICC2, Mu, SSA, TH]. They are similar in that the first means to be declared innocent before God and the second refers to the forensic justification expected at the final judgment [AB, WBC]. There are those who are called righteous here and now, but 'will be justified' refers to being acquitted on the day of judgment [WBC]. 'Righteous' is a relation of favor and peace with God, and being made righteous is a verdict of acquittal [HNTC]. The first refers to a status of righteousness before God, not a moral quality, and the second refers to the final verdict on judgment day [ICC2]. The terms are synonymous forensic terms referring to their state rather than to their character; the just are those

who have done what the law requires and are therefore regarded as free from condemnation and entitled to God's favor [Ho].
QUESTION—Who are the 'doers of the law' who will be justified in the judgment on that basis, and what have they done?
1. No one will actually be justified by obedience to the law [AB, Ho, Mor, Mu, NAC, NICNT, SSA, St, TH, TNTC]. Paul only makes this statement to argue against someone thinking that he will be justified merely by knowing the law [AB]. Paul later claims that no one can succeed in obeying the law perfectly, so no one is actually justified by works of the law [NICNT]. Paul is not saying that anyone actually is justified by law-keeping, only laying down the principle in order to deny that people are justified by merely having or hearing the law [Mor, Mu, TH]. He is not telling how people are actually justified, he is stating the principles of justice that will apply to those who expect to be justified by the law [Ho]. The statement is hypothetical in the sense that there is no possibility of salvation by obeying the law, since no human has ever fully done so; here Paul is writing about judgment, not salvation, and is emphasizing that possession of the law is no guarantee of immunity from judgment, since obedience is the standard of judgment [St]. Paul states that doing the law is necessary for justification, but his main concern here is to question the prevailing Jewish understanding of who is righteous and on what grounds they might hope for final justification, as well as to bring into question the presupposition that membership in the covenant people accorded one favored status with God [WBC]. This verse reiterates the principle of 2:6, that those who do the required works will be rewarded with justification, but only in verses 26–29 does Paul clarify whether he thinks justification can be truly obtained in this way [BECNT].
2. He is speaking of Christians [BECNT, Gdt, ICC2, NTC]. The believer's initial imputed righteousness eventually must lead to the fruit of actual righteousness, the fulfilling of the law [Gdt]. Paul is speaking of Christians here, and this refers to a grateful obedience to God found in believers, which, although not meriting justification, is pleasing to him [ICC2]. Believers, who have been delivered from the law's curse, are motivated even more to hear and obey the gospel, and show by their good deeds done in gratitude that they are God's people [NTC].

DISCOURSE UNIT: 2:14–15 [GW]. God will judge people who are not Jewish.

2:14 For[a] when[b] Gentiles[c] the-(ones) not having (the) law
LEXICON—a. γάρ (LN 89.23) (BAGD 1.b. p. 152): 'for' [BAGD, BECNT, HNTC, ICC2, LN, NICNT, NTC, WBC; KJV, NASB, NET], 'thus' [AB], 'indeed' [NIV], 'even' [NLT], 'for example' [GW], not explicit [CEV, NCV, NRSV, REB, TEV].

b. ὅταν (LN 67.31): 'when' [BECNT, HNTC, ICC2, LN, NTC, WBC; KJV, NASB, NCV, NIV, NLT, NRSV, REB], 'whenever' [AB, LN, NICNT; GW, NET, TEV], not explicit [CEV].
c. ἔθνος (LN 11.37). This plural noun is translated 'Gentiles' [AB, BECNT, HNTC, ICC2, NICNT, NTC, WBC; KJV, NASB, NET, NIV, NLT, NRSV, REB, TEV], 'non-Jews' [GW], 'those who are not Jews' [NCV], 'some people' [CEV].

QUESTION—What relationship is indicated by γάρ 'for'?

1. It introduces an explanation or illustration of 2:12 [Ho, Mu, NICNT]. It is an explanation and qualification of the phrase 'without the law' from 2:12a since the Gentiles, from the Jewish perspective, were without the Law of Moses [Mu, NICNT]. It introduces an answer to the question raised by 2:12 concerning how it is that the Gentiles can be regarded as sinning if they don't have the law, the answer being that the law actually is brought to bear upon them, though in a different way than for the Jews [Mu]. The logical connection is with 2:12 since Paul's purpose is to lay out the principles by which God will judge the world, in which connection he states that those with the law will be judged by it, and those without the law will be judged without reference to it, because even the Gentiles have a form of law, one by which they will be judged [Ho].
2. It continues the argument of 2:13 with the case of the Gentiles, that what is important is not just having or hearing the Mosaic law, but doing what is right, and even Gentiles have enough knowledge about what is right to be judged by it [Mor]. In this verse the principle from 2:13 of being judged for what one has done according to the standard of whatever knowledge he had is more fully applied to the Gentiles, who also have knowledge of the law, 'hearing it' via what is written in their hearts [St].
3. It indicates the grounds for the assertion in 2:13b that the doers of the law will be justified [ICC2, WBC]. Verses 2:14–15 give further justification to the assertion that 'the doers of the law' will include Gentiles as well as Jews, by alluding to the fact that man by nature knows what is right in conduct [WBC].
4. It introduces an amplification of the premise of 2:13b that only those who obey all the laws of Moses will be declared righteous [SSA].
5. It indicates the grounds for 2:13a, the point being that just hearing or having the law is not enough for salvation, because even Gentiles appear to have some knowledge of the law, as indicated by the fact that sometimes some of them keep it, so having the Mosaic Law is not an advantage and not having it is not a disadvantage [BECNT].

QUESTION—Who are the Gentiles that he is referring to in this verse?

1. Paul is referring generally to Gentiles without reference to whether or not they are believers.
    1.1 This refers to some but not all Gentiles [AB, Gdt, Mor, NAC, St]. The lack of the definite article indicates that he not making a universal claim about all Gentiles, but about some Gentiles: sometimes there are

Gentiles who sometimes do what the law requires [AB, Gdt, Mor, NAC, St].
1.2 The reference is to Gentiles generally [Mu, NTC, TH, TNTC]. They are people who are Gentiles, who generally or collectively do not have the specially revealed law but who have a sense of right and wrong within them functioning for them as the law [Mu]. He is saying that all people, including Gentiles, have a sense of right and wrong [NTC].
2. They are unbelieving Gentiles who, though they may do some parts of the law, are not saved [BECNT, Ho, NICNT, WBC]. The number of Gentiles who do the things the law requires is left indefinite; he is not saying either that there are only a very few exceptional Gentiles, or that most of them would fit this category [NICNT]. There are some Gentiles who at least part of the time live in accordance with what the law says through their own innate sense of right and wrong even though they have no direct knowledge of the Mosaic law [WBC]. They are Gentiles, but Paul's object is to show that the occasionally moral conduct of all men only proves that they have a knowledge of right and wrong and that there is a rule of duty written on men's hearts, not that their conduct saves them [Ho]. That these are unbelieving Gentiles is indicated by the fact that the obedience of the Gentiles mentioned is inconsistent and insufficient, that the testimony of their conscience is mainly accusatory, and that what is innate to them is said to constitute a 'law to themselves' instead of speaking of the Holy Spirit's enabling, as would be expected if they were Christians [BECNT].
3. They are Gentile Christians whose works of obedience, though imperfect and not deserving of God's favor, are still the expression of their faith [ICC2].
4. They are Gentiles who have realized and accepted the fact that a relationship with the creator must be based on obedience and faith, and by responding in this way, are doing what is in fact required by the law [HNTC].

QUESTION—What law is it that the Gentiles do not have?

They lack the Mosaic Law [AB, BECNT, Gdt, HNTC, Ho, ICC2, Mor, NAC, NICNT, NTC, SSA, St, TH, TNTC, WBC]. While it is true that non-Christian Gentiles are without the Law of Moses, they are not without any law in the more generic sense, since they have some knowledge of God's moral demands [NICNT]. The reference is to the Law of Moses, but the lack of the article indicates that what is in focus is more its nature or quality as law, not a distinction between this particular law and any other [Mor].

do[a] by-nature[b] the-things of-the law,[c]

LEXICON—a. pres. act. subj. of ποιέω (LN 90.45) (BAGD I.1.c.α. p. 682): 'to do' [BAGD, BECNT, HNTC, ICC2, LN, NICNT, NTC, WBC; GW, KJV, NASB, NCV, NET, NIV, NRSV, TEV], 'to obey' [CEV], 'to keep'

[BAGD], 'to follow' [NLT], 'to carry out' [BAGD; REB], 'to observe' [AB], 'to practice' [BAGD, LN].

b. φύσις (LN 58.8) (BAGD 3. p. 869). This noun in the dative case is translated 'by nature' [AB, BECNT, HNTC, ICC2, LN, NICNT, NTC, WBC; GW, KJV, NET, NIV], 'naturally' [CEV], 'freely' [NCV], 'instinctively' [NASB, NLT, NRSV], 'by instinct' [TEV], 'by the light of nature' [REB].

c. νόμος (LN 33.333, 33.55): 'law' [LN (33.333)], 'the Law' [LN (33.55)]. The phrase τὰ τοῦ νόμου is translated 'the things of the law' [NASB], 'precepts of the law' [AB], 'its precepts' [REB], 'what the law says' [BECNT; NLT], 'what the law requires' [WBC; NRSV], 'things which the law requires' [HNTC, ICC2], 'things required by the law' [NTC; NET, NIV], 'the things contained in the law' [KJV], 'the things Moses' teachings contain' [GW], 'the Law's commands' [CEV], 'what the Law commands' [NCV, TEV].

QUESTION—What is meant by τὰ τοῦ νόμου 'the things of the law' which these Gentiles do by nature?

1. The phrase is to be understood generically, and means moral behaviors which happen to also be included in the written law [BECNT, Gdt, Ho, Mor, Mu, NAC, NICNT, NTC, St]. It means those occasions when Gentiles do something that is also prescribed in the law [Gdt, Mor]. Paul is thinking of things which exemplify the moral dimensions of the law like obeying parents, being honest, telling the truth, not committing murder, theft, and so forth [Mor, Mu, NAC, NTC, St]. They do certain specific things stipulated by the law, but Paul is not saying that they fulfill the whole law [AB, Ho, Mu]. The phrase means the moral norms of the Mosaic law [BECNT]. Paul is not asserting the existence of a 'natural law', but rather that some Gentiles, despite ignorance of the law, show moral sensitivity in their behavior [WBC].

2. Paul does not mean the detailed precepts of the Mosaic Law, the ritual law or the moral law, nor moral or ceremonial conformity; rather this is in reference to what is really required by the law and the basis of any relationship with God, which is believing obedience or obedient faith, [HNTC].

3. Gentile Christians, who were not were not brought up possessing God's law, now know it and earnestly desire to obey it [ICC2].

QUESTION—To what should the word φύσει 'by nature' be linked?

1. It should be linked with the verb ποιέω 'do', referring to the fact that these Gentiles instinctively or naturally do some things required by the law [AB, Gdt, HNTC, Ho, Mor, Mu, NAC, NICNT, NTC, SSA, St, TH, TNTC, WBC; CEV, KJV, NET, NIV, NLT, NRSV, REB, TEV]. The Gentiles have an innate sense of right and wrong, and at times do by nature certain things required by God's law [NTC].

2. It should be linked with the preceding words, μὴ νόμον χοντα 'not having the law' [BECNT, ICC2]. The Gentiles simply do not have the

Mosaic law by virtue of their birth [BECNT]. It describes the Gentiles who by virtue of birth did not have the Mosaic Law, but who, after conversion as Christians, do have some knowledge of the moral law of God [ICC2].
3. It should be linked with the verb, but the meaning is 'obedience and faith'. The only basis of relationship between man and Creator is one of obedience and faith, and when one recognizes this and accepts it, he may be said to do what the law requires 'by nature' [HNTC].

these (persons) not having (the) law are (a) law^a to-themselves;

LEXICON—a. νόμος (LN 33.333): 'law' [LN (33.333), WBC; REB, TEV], 'a law' [AB, BECNT, HNTC, ICC2, NICNT, NTC; GW, KJV, NASB, NET, NIV, NRSV] 'the law' [NCV], '(their own) law' [REB, TEV], not explicit [NLT]. Also see this word above in 2:14.

QUESTION—What relationship is indicated by the participial phrase μὴ ἔχοντες 'not having'?
1. It is concessive [AB, BECNT, ICC2, NAC, NICNT, NTC, SSA, WBC; CEV, GW, NCV, NIV, NRSV, REB, TEV]: although the Gentiles do not have the law, they are a law to themselves.
2. It is descriptive [HNTC, WBC; KJV, NASB, NET, NLT]: the Gentiles, who do not have the law, are a law to themselves.

QUESTION—Is there any distinction in the sense in which νόμος 'law' is used in its two occurrences in this particular section of this verse?
1. There is a difference between the law of Moses and the law they are to themselves [AB, BECNT, Gdt, HNTC, Ho, Mu, NAC, NICNT, NTC, SSA, St, TH].
1.1 The first occurrence means the Law of Moses [AB, BECNT, Gdt, Mu, NAC, NICNT, NTC, St]. The second occurrence denotes the moral standards or demands of God in a more extended or generic sense [NICNT], the moral norms of that law [BECNT]. The second refers to the fact that God has created people as self-conscious moral beings who show by their behaviors that God has put into their hearts knowledge of some of the requirements of the law [St]. It is the testimony written on their hearts about right and wrong [NTC], and they know what should and should not be done [TH]. Pagans do know some of the things prescribed in the Mosaic Law [AB]. While the first reference is to the law of Moses, the emphasis is on its quality as law generally, not on the Mosaic law as distinct from all others, and as the self-imposed disciplines of the Gentiles indicate, they are not outside the sphere of such law [Mor]. They don't have the Mosaic law as such, but they fulfill its contents, doing instinctively according to the moral law written on their hearts what the Jew does by precepts [Gdt]. The first is the law of Moses and the second is metaphorical; Paul is not arguing for how much of the Mosaic Law Gentiles know and obey, but simply that everyone has standards which they obey inconsistently [SSA].

1.2 The first is the law of Moses and the second is the 'natural law' rooted in one's nature; this usage reflects Stoic-Jewish thinking and is further clarified by verse 15 as 'the effects of the law' which are written on their hearts [HNTC].
2. There is a sense in which it is the same law, the Torah [Mu, WBC]. Gentiles are *the* law, that is, the Torah, for themselves, not *a* law unto themselves. Paul's is attempting to undercut the Jewish assumption that the law is only known and able to be followed within Israel, and to remove any grounds for Jewish boasting or sense of privilege with regard to it [WBC]. The law is the same, although in the case of the Gentiles the method of being confronted by it and the degree of detail to which it is known are different than in the case of the Jews [Mu].
3. In both occurrences he is referring to the law of Moses; although as Gentiles they were not brought up having the law of Moses, they know it now and have the earnest desire in their hearts to follow it [ICC2].

QUESTION—What is meant by οὗτοι...ἑαυτοῖς εἰσιν νόμος 'these...are (a) law to themselves'?

1. God has created human beings with an innate moral sense and an inherent knowledge of some of the requirements of the law in their hearts [BECNT, Ho, Mor, Mu, NICNT, NTC, St, TH, WBC]. It refers to their knowledge of moral right and wrong, and this knowledge is counted as a 'law' they are subject to; the fact that they are at least conscious of the moral norms of the law is shown by their occasionally keeping some of these commands and by the fact that their consciences both accuse and excuse them [BECNT, NTC, St]. God created man with a sense of moral obligation which encourages conduct that at some points overlaps with the law given to Israel [NAC]. There is an innate sense of right and wrong written on human hearts, giving the knowledge of right and wrong, and which for the Gentiles functions in the place of the external or written law [Ho]. God is sufficiently at work in the Gentiles that they have enough of a sense of right and wrong to be guilty when they sin [Mor]. Gentiles know by instinct some of the things that are prescribed in the Mosaic Law and their conscience testifies as to whether they are acting accordingly [AB]. Their own consciences inform them of things that the Torah teaches and in that sense they also have the Torah [WBC]. The moral instinct of the Gentiles is to be identified with the contents of the Mosaic law, and its existence as written on their hearts is evidenced or proved by their behavior [Gdt].
2. It refers to the Law of Moses that they learned after their conversion; Gentiles who did not by virtue of birth possess God's law now have it and know it, and after conversion they desire in their hearts to obey it [ICC2].

2:15 such-(persons)-who[a] show[b] the work[c] of-the law written in[d] their hearts,[e]

LEXICON—a. ὅστις. The plural of this relative pronoun (οἵτινες) is translated 'they' [AB, BECNT, HNTC, ICC2, NICNT, WBC; GW, NCV, NET, NLT, NRSV, REB], 'since they' [NIV], 'which' [KJV], 'in that' [NASB], 'their conduct' [TEV], 'this (proves)' [CEV]. It indicates a causal relationship [Ho, ICC1, Mu, NTC; NASB, NIV].
- b. pres. mid. indic. of ἐνδείκνυμι (LN 28.51) (BAGD 1. p. 262): 'to show' [AB, BAGD, HNTC, LN, NICNT, NTC; all versions except CEV, NLT], 'to show forth' [BECNT], 'to demonstrate' [BAGD, LN, WBC; NLT], 'to give proof (of the fact that)' [ICC2], 'to prove' [CEV], 'to cause to be known' [LN].
- c. ἔργον (LN 42.12, 42.42) (BAGD 1.b. p. 308): 'work' [BECNT, ICC2, LN (42.42), NICNT, NTC; KJV, NASB, NET], 'effect' [HNTC], 'business' [WBC], 'manifestation or proof' [BAGD], not explicit [CEV, GW, NCV, NLT]. This singular noun is translated as a plural: 'requirements' [NIV]. The phrase τὸ ἔργον τοῦ νόμου 'the work of the law' is translated: 'what the law prescribes' [AB], 'what the law requires' [NRSV, REB], 'what the Law commands' [TEV], 'the work which the law requires' [ICC2], 'the work required by the law' [NTC].
- d. ἐν (LN 83.13): 'in' [BECNT, HNTC, LN, WBC; CEV, GW, KJV, NASB, NCV, NET, TEV], 'on' [AB, ICC2, NICNT, NTC; NIV, NRSV, REB], 'within' [LN; NLT].
- e. καρδία (LN 26.3) (BAGD 1.b.γ. p. 404): 'heart' [AB, BAGD, BECNT, HNTC, ICC2, LN, NICNT, NTC, WBC; all versions except NLT], 'mind' [BAGD, LN], '(within) them' [NLT].

QUESTION—What is meant by τὸ ἔργον τοῦ νόμου 'the work of the law'?
1. It is the work or deeds that the law commands to be done [AB, BECNT, Ho, ICC1, ICC2, Mor, Mu, NICNT, NTC, SSA, St; NRSV, REB, TEV].
   1.1 God has put a knowledge of what the law commands within the heart by creating conscience within people [AB, BECNT, Ho, ICC1, Mor, Mu, NICNT, NTC, SSA, St; NRSV, REB, TEV]. It is parallel to the phrase 'the things of the law' in 2:14 and refers to doing what the law demands or conduct that is consistent with the law [AB, BECNT, NICNT], particularly the moral norms of the Mosaic law [BECNT]. It is the course of conduct that would be in accordance with the law [ICC1]. It is the work that the law commands [SSA]. The singular form is a collective singular referring to the deeds or conduct that the law prescribes and demands [AB, NICNT]. Paul says these people sometimes do some of what the law requires, showing that these requirements are written on their hearts, but he is not saying that the law itself is written there or that they fulfilled the law [Mor, Mu]. It speaks of the totality of the moral law written on the heart, the whole content of the law [Gdt].

1.2 God has created within the hearts of Gentile Christians a desire to do the same things that the law prescribes and requires [ICC2].
2. It is the work or effect of the law upon the heart. As these Gentiles do things required by the law, they show that its effects are written in their hearts and that its stamp is the conscience [HNTC].
3. It is the 'business' of the law, the work or deeds that the law is supposed to effect on the heart. Paul allows the possibility of a certain religiosity among the Gentiles that produces the kind of effect that the law was concerned with, and which is to be contrasted with the 'works of the law', which are outward and lacking depth [WBC].

QUESTION—In what sense is the work of the law written in their hearts?
1. God has put into the hearts of all people a basic moral sense of right and wrong [BECNT, Gdt, Mor, NAC, NICNT, St]. What God commands is intuitively known by all people [SSA]. This is not what Jeremiah 31 refers to, where God's law is to be written on people's hearts [BECNT, HNTC, Mor, NICNT, St]. Paul has borrowed wording from Jeremiah 31 [AB, WBC], and uses it here to describe the awareness of right and wrong that Gentiles have [AB], the moral sensibility that exists within so many Gentiles [WBC]. The prescriptions of the law are written on that which is deepest and most determinative of the moral and spiritual being of people [Mu].
2. It is the fulfillment of the promise of the new covenant in Jeremiah 31, in which God has given Gentile Christians the earnest desire to obey his law [ICC2].

their conscience[a] bearing-witness-with[b] (it)

LEXICON—a. συνείδησις (LN 26.13) (BAGD 2. p. 786 twice): 'conscience' [AB, BAGD, BECNT, HNTC, ICC2, LN, NICNT, NTC, WBC; all versions], 'moral consciousness' [BAGD], 'moral sensitivity' [LN].
b. pres. act. participle of συμμαρτυρέω (LN **33.266**) (BAGD p. 778): 'to bear witness with' [BAGD, HNTC], 'to bear witness' [AB, NICNT, NTC, WBC; KJV, NASB, NET, NIV, NRSV], 'to join in bearing witness' [BECNT], 'to give supporting witness' [LN; REB], 'to testify' [BAGD, ICC2], 'to testify in support of' [BAGD, **LN**], 'to speak (to them)' [GW], 'to confirm' [BAGD], 'to tell' [NLT], 'to show' [NCV], 'show that this is true' [TEV], 'it will show whether' [CEV]. The prefix συμ- (from the preposition σύν 'with') is translated as indicating a witness given in addition to another witness: 'also bearing witness' [NTC, WBC; NIV, NRSV], 'also show' [TEV], 'joins in bearing witness' [BECNT], 'gives supporting witness' [REB], 'bears witness with the law' [HNTC].

QUESTION—What is meant by συνείδησις 'conscience'?
It means the moral faculty by which people judge their own actions to be right or wrong [BECNT, Gdt, HNTC, Ho, ICC1, ICC2, Mor, Mu, NAC, NICNT, NTC, TNTC]. The conscience is not the source of moral norms but is rather the faculty which judges whether one has done right or wrong with

respect to the norms [BECNT, Gdt, Mu, NAC, NICNT]. In this case the norm is the law and each person's conscience reveals to them the extent to which they follow it [NICNT]. It is an evidence of our moral nature and that God has written his law in the heart [Mu]. Man has the ability to detach from himself and view his own character and actions independently [HNTC].
1. Conscience is the capacity by which one may judge his or her past actions [BECNT, Ho, ICC1, Mu], whereas 'the work of the law' in the heart is the capacity by which one may judge his or her future actions [Mu].
2. It is the human capacity to judge one's own past actions or contemplated future actions [AB, NICNT, NTC].

QUESTION—To whom is the witness borne?

The witness is borne to these persons themselves [AB, BECNT, Gdt, HNTC, Ho, ICC1, ICC2, Mor, Mu, NAC, NICNT, NTC, St, TH, TNTC, WBC]. This refers to an internal dialogue within a person involving their hearts on which God has written these standards, their thoughts which accuse or excuse them, and the conscience which prods and rebukes [St]. The witness is to the individuals themselves, but in view of 2:16 the term 'witness' may also be used in a secondary sense to describe what will occur at the judgment seat [NICNT].

QUESTION—What relationship is implied by the prefixed preposition σύν 'with' in the word συμμαρτυρούσης 'bearing witness with'?
1. The prefix indicates that the conscience bears witness along with something else [BECNT, Gdt, HNTC, Ho, ICC1, Mu, NTC, WBC; NLT, NRSV, REB, TEV].
1.1 The witness of conscience comes in addition to or in conjunction with the law written on their hearts [BECNT, Gdt, HNTC, Mu, NTC, WBC; NLT, NRSV, REB, TEV]. Here the prefix shows that the Gentiles without the written law have a two-fold witness, one being the law written on their hearts and the other being the testimony of conscience to the truth of these moral norms and the degree to which one has complied with them [BECNT]. Conscience joins its testimony to the testimony of the heart which dictated whatever virtuous actions have been done [Gdt]. Conscience is not the same as the work of the law, but adds its witness to it [WBC].
1.2 The witness of conscience comes in addition to their actions [Ho, ICC1, TH]. The quality of the acts themselves provides one witness and the reflective judgment on them by conscience is another [ICC1]. The conscience joins witness with the moral acts of people and testifies to the fact that they are a law for themselves [Ho]. The conduct, the conscience, and the thoughts of a person all give witness as evidence that God's law is written in the heart and that Gentiles are a law to themselves [TH].
2. The prefix simply strengthens the verb [AB, ICC2]. Although the form of the word could imply that there is some other witness along with conscience, there is no accompanying dative, thus the sense is simply

'testifying or bearing witness' and the implication is that it is to these Gentiles themselves [AB].

and between[a] one-another their thoughts[b] accusing[c] or even defending[d] (them),

LEXICON—a. μεταξύ (LN 89.115) (BAGD 2.b. p. 513): 'between' [LN, NTC], 'among' [BAGD, BECNT, ICC2, NICNT, WBC], 'with' [BAGD], 'in mutual debate' [HNTC], 'sometimes...sometimes' [NCV], 'on one occasion...on another' [GW], 'alternately' [NASB], not explicit [AB; CEV, KJV, NIV, NLT, NRSV, REB, TEV]. The word denotes a reciprocal relationship [BAGD].
  b. λογισμός (LN **30.9**) (BAGD 1. p. 476): 'thought' [AB, BAGD, BECNT, HNTC, ICC2, NICNT, NTC, WBC; all versions except CEV, NLT], 'reasoning' [BAGD, **LN**], 'reflection' [BAGD], not explicit [CEV, NLT].
  c. pres. act. participle of κατηγορέω (LN **33.427**) (BAGD 2. p. 423): 'to accuse' [AB, BAGD, HNTC, ICC2, LN, NICNT, NTC; GW, KJV, NASB, NET, NIV, NLT, NRSV, TEV], 'to bring accusation' [BECNT], 'to argue the case...against (them)' [REB], 'to tell them they did wrong' [NCV], 'to show we are condemned' [CEV]. This verb is also translated as a noun: 'accusation' [BECNT, WBC].
  d. pres. mid. (deponent = act.) participle of ἀπολογέομαι (LN 33.435) (BAGD p. 95): 'to defend' [AB, NTC; GW, NASB, NET, NIV, TEV], 'to defend oneself' [BAGD, LN], 'to speak in one's own defense' [BAGD], 'to excuse' [HNTC, ICC2, NICNT; KJV, NRSV], 'to tell (them they) are doing what is right' [NLT], 'to tell them they did right' [NCV], 'to argue the case for (them)' [REB], 'to show we are forgiven' [CEV]. This participle is also translated as a noun: 'defense' [WBC], 'self-defense' [BECNT].

QUESTION—What relationship is indicated by καί 'and'?
1. This clause further explains what is meant by the witness of the conscience [AB, HNTC, Ho, ICC2, NAC, NICNT, SSA]. The witness of conscience is, or consists in, one's own thoughts rendering mixed verdicts of accusation or defense [ICC2, NICNT]. The second clause clarifies the first, describing how the conscience functions [NAC].
2. This clause speaks of yet another witness [Mor, Mu, St, WBC]. The law written on the heart precedes conscience and is the cause of its operations, but the operations of conscience bears witness to the work of the law written in the heart [Mu]. This speaks of a witness other than one's conscience and describes a sense of self contradiction and some moral confusion similar to what is found in 7:14–25 [WBC].
3. These clauses describe two different processes, the first regarding the action of one's own conscience, and this one regarding the actions of others [ICC1].

QUESTION—What is meant by μεταξὺ ἀλλήλων 'between one another' and what is its referent?
1. It is the internal debate of a person's own thoughts [AB, BECNT, Gdt, HNTC, Ho, Mor, NAC, NICNT, NTC, SSA, St, TH, WBC; GW, NASB, NCV]. The context is primarily speaking of the way a person's thoughts in continual debate within himself back up or accuse the witness of his actions and conscience [Mor].
2. It refers to a contrasting process between people, namely, thoughts which people have in their dealing with other people that are either critical of them or in defense of them [ICC1, Mu]. The conscience and the thoughts belong to the same person, but the first is exercised with respect to oneself and the second focuses on other people [ICC1]. Though coordinate with conscience, this is another respect in which evidence of conscience is given, and in which there is proof of the work of the law being written in a person's heart [Mu].
3. It is the internal debate of a person's thoughts that will occur at the last judgment, when believing Gentiles will recognize that their lives fell far short of the perfection demanded by the law, but also that they had believed and had begun to be obedient [ICC2].

QUESTION—What is meant by ἢ καί 'or even'?
This phrase indicates that accusing thoughts predominate and that defending thoughts are the exception [BECNT, Gdt, ICC1, ICC2, Mor, NICNT, NTC]. Even that which is thought to be defensible in one's behavior contributes to culpability since it demonstrates knowledge of the standard, and that only a portion of one's behavior is in accord with it [NICNT].

QUESTION—When is it that this process of accusing or defending occurs?
1. This process takes place during this life on earth [BECNT, Gdt, Ho, Mu, NAC, NICNT, NTC, SSA].
2. It will take place on the day of judgment [ICC2; CEV].
3. It takes place during life on earth, but it also describes what will take place at the time of God's final judgment [AB, HNTC, Mor]. Whatever the conscience does inwardly, what ultimately will matter is the witness that it will bear on the day of judgment when God judges [HNTC]. Whatever else the consciences of sinners might be doing in the meantime, they will certainly be a witness against them on the day of judgment [Mor]. Paul does not mean that one's conscience only functions on judgment day, but that it will especially bear witness on that day [AB].

2:16 on[a] (the) day[b] when God judges[c] the hidden[d] (things) of people[e]
LEXICON—a. ἐν (LN 67.33): 'on' [AB, BECNT, ICC2, NICNT, NTC; CEV, NASB, NCV, NET, NIV, NRSV, REB, TEV], 'in' [HNTC, ICC2, NTC, WBC; KJV, NET], 'at the time of' [LN], 'when' [LN; CEV], 'against' [KJV, REB]. The phrase 'on the day' is translated 'this happens as they face the day' [GW], 'the day will come' [NLT].
b. ἡμέρα: 'day'. See this word at 2:5.

c. pres. act. indic. of κρίνω: 'to judge'. See this word at 2:12.
d. κρυπτός (LN 28.69, 28.75) (BAGD 2.a. p. 454): 'hidden, secret' [LN (28.69)], 'secret knowledge or information' [LN (28.75)], 'secret plans or purposes' [BAGD]. The phrase τὰ κρυπτά 'the hidden things' is translated 'the secrets' [AB, BECNT, ICC2, LN (28.75), NTC, WBC; KJV, NASB, NET, NIV, REB], 'secret thoughts' [BAGD; CEV, GW, NCV, NRSV, TEV], 'the secret things' [HNTC, NICNT], 'secret life' [NLT].
e. ἄνθρωπος (LN **9.1**): 'person' [**LN**]. This plural noun is translated 'people' [GW, NCV], 'men' [HNTC, ICC2, NTC; KJV, NASB, NIV], 'mankind' [LN, WBC], 'human' [AB; NET, REB], 'human beings' [BECNT], 'everyone' [CEV, NLT], 'all' [NRSV, TEV].

QUESTION—What is the relationship between this verse and the preceding context?

1. 2:16 is connected with the entire preceding passage [AB, Gdt, HNTC, Ho, ICC1, Mu, NTC, SSA, St, WBC; NCV, NIV].

   1.1 Verses 2:14–15 are parenthetical and 2:16 resumes or summarizes the thought of the larger passage [Gdt, HNTC, Ho, ICC1, St, WBC; NCV, NIV]. This verse expresses and sums up the idea of the entire passage beginning in 2:6, which is the final judgment, with 2:14–15 forming somewhat of a parenthesis [Gdt]. 2:16 resumes the phrase 'the doers of the law will be justified' from 2:13, which will happen on the day when God judges the hidden things of men [Gdt, HNTC, ICC1]. 2:13–15 explains how the Gentiles can be judged without having the law, which is that they have something similar, though inferior to the law, and will be judged by that [ICC1]. 2:16 concludes the section by returning to the theme of judgment and adding three further truths about that judgment [St]. The doing of the law by Gentiles mentioned in 2:13–14, both in conduct as well as in the inward workings of the heart, conscience and thoughts, will be made evident in the day of judgment, and when the inner secrets of all people are revealed many Gentiles will fare better than many Jews [WBC].

   1.2 Verse 2:16 is linked to the main verbs of the preceding sections; the verbs 'will be revealed' (2:5), 'will be judged' (2:12), and 'declared righteous' (2:13) are all events which will all take place on the day of judgment [NTC]. 2:16 may be readily connected with 2:12, 13 or with the entire passage, all of which deals with the judgment of God [Mu]. This verse forms a conclusion for the whole paragraph, and echoes the thought of 'on the day of wrath' of 2:5 [AB]. It relates to the entire preceding context which deals with God's final judgment of both Jews and Gentiles [SSA].

2. Verses 2:14–15 are closely linked with 2:16 and refer to the fact that the conscience will bear witness on the day of judgment [BECNT, Mor, NAC, NICNT]. His focus in this section is on the standard of judgment; just as the Jews will be judged according to their conformity to the written

law, the Gentiles will be judged according to their conformity to the standard of law they possess, and in all cases the conscience and even the hidden thoughts will be part of the evidence at final judgment, when the continual self-criticism of conscience will find its ultimate meaning [NICNT]. 2:15 describes the work of the conscience of accusing and defending that goes on during this present life, and which will reach its full validity and consummation in the final climactic and comprehensive judgment described in 2:16 [BECNT]. Whatever else it does in the meantime, conscience will certainly be a witness on judgment day [Mor].
3. Verse 2:16 is a continuation of 2:15; the convicting work of conscience described in 2:15 will occur on judgment day [ICC2; CEV, NET, NRSV]. Verses 2:15–16 form one Greek sentence and the phrase 'this is how it will be' refers back to the total content of 2:15 [TH]. The 'testimony' mentioned in 2:15 that will occur on the day of judgment will demonstrate that even in the present time they have the work of the law written on their hearts [ICC2].
4. Verses 2:13–15 are parenthetical [Ho; KJV]: on the day when God judges, Gentiles without the law will perish and Jews with the law will be judged. Verses 2:13–15 are somewhat parenthetical and this verse best relates to 2:12 in that the heathen will be judged without the law and the Jew by the law, all of which takes place on the day when God judges the secrets of men [Ho].

QUESTION—What is the time period or event referred to by the phrase ἐν ἡμέρᾳ ὅτε κρίνει ὁ θεὸς 'on the day when God judges'?

The verb may be taken as having a future reference [Ho, ICC1, ICC2, Mor, WBC], and refers to the final judgment [AB, BECNT, Gdt, Ho, ICC1, ICC2, Mor, NAC, NICNT, NTC, SSA, St, TH, WBC]. This is the same day as described in 2:5 [Mu]. Paul's use of words like 'accusing' and 'defending', which are words connoting the kind of activity characteristic of a court of law, emphasizes that the ultimate significance of the continual evaluation of conscience will be at the final judgment [NICNT]. Although the verb 'judges' is in the present tense, it should be taken as having a future meaning because Paul's customary use of the word ἡμέρᾳ 'day' points to an eschatological day of the Lord [BECNT]. The context requires a future meaning for the present tense of 'judges', and refers to the time when the living and the dead will stand before God's tribunal [AB]. All of what has just been discussed will become clear on judgment day [NTC]. Although in Paul's writings there is a continuity between the present and future with regard to both justification and judgment [WBC], this is undoubtedly a reference to the final judgment [ICC2, WBC].

QUESTION—What is meant by τὰ κρυπτὰ τῶν ἀνθρώπων 'the hidden things of men'?

On the day of judgment God will take into account even the secrets of the heart [ICC2, NAC, NICNT, NTC, WBC], their secret thoughts [BECNT, Mu, NTC, TH], motivations [BECNT, Mu, NTC], intents [Mu], their secret deeds [Mu]. This refers to the fact that God's judgment will take into account not only the outward and visible actions of men, but also the inner witness of conscience, and the secrets of men's hearts and whatever has been done in secret, all of which are known to God and will be revealed on the day of judgment [NICNT]. The reference is to the surest criteria of character, the hidden deeds of heart and life [Ho]. God will judge people not only for known sins, but also for those which are hidden, whether in thought or action [SSA]. It refers to the hidden workings of conscience that leave behind their own marks that God will see on judgment day [ICC1]. It stands in contrast to the external legal and ceremonial works in which Jews were inclined to put their confidence [Gdt].

according-to[a] my gospel[b] through[c] Christ Jesus.

TEXT—Instead of Χριστοῦ Ἰησοῦ 'Christ Jesus' some manuscripts read Ἰησοῦ Χριστοῦ 'Jesus Christ', and others read Ἰησοῦ Χριστοῦ τοῦ κυρίου ἡμῶν 'Jesus Christ our Lord'. GNT reads Χριστοῦ Ἰησοῦ 'Christ Jesus' with a C rating, indicating difficulty in deciding which variant to place in the text. The reading Χριστοῦ Ἰησοῦ 'Christ Jesus' is taken by AB, BECNT, NICNT, WBC; GW, NASB, NCV, NET, REB. The reading Ἰησοῦ Χριστοῦ 'Jesus Christ' is read by HNTC, ICC2, NTC; CEV, KJV, NIV, NLT, NRSV, TEV.

LEXICON—a. κατά with accusative object (LN 89.8) (BAGD II.5.a.α. p. 407): 'according to' [AB, BECNT, HNTC, ICC2, NICNT, NTC; KJV, NASB, NET, NRSV, REB, TEV], 'in accordance with' [BAGD, LN, WBC]. The phrase κατὰ τὸ εὐαγγέλιόν μου 'according to my gospel' is translated 'just as my message says' [CEV], 'as my gospel declares' [NIV], 'this is my message' [NLT], 'the Good News that I preach says this' [NCV], 'he will use the Good News that I am spreading to make that judgment' [GW].

b. εὐαγγέλιον (LN 33.217) (BAGD 2.b.β. p. 318): 'gospel' [AB, BAGD, BECNT, ICC2, LN, NICNT, NTC, WBC; KJV, NASB, NET, NIV, NRSV, REB], 'Gospel' [HNTC], 'good news' [BAGD, ICC2, LN; CEV, GW, NCV, NLT], 'Good News' [HNTC; NLT, TEV], 'message' [CEV, NLT]. The phrase τὸ εὐαγγέλιόν μου 'my gospel' is translated 'the gospel which I preach' [ICC2], 'the Good News I preach' [TEV].

c. διά with genitive object (LN 90.4) (BAGD A.III.2.a. p. 180): 'through' [AB, BAGD, BECNT, HNTC, ICC2, LN, NICNT, NTC, WBC; all versions except CEV, KJV, NLT], 'by' [BAGD, LN; KJV, NLT]. The phrase ὅτε κρίνει ὁ θεός...διὰ Χριστοῦ Ἰησοῦ 'when God judges...through Christ Jesus' is translated 'when God has Jesus Christ judge' [CEV].

QUESTION—To what does the phrase κατὰ τὸ εὐαγγέλιόν μου 'according to my gospel' relate?

1. This prepositional phrase is dependent on the entire statement of the verse and means that Paul's gospel teaches that God will judge through Christ

Jesus [AB, Ho, ICC1, ICC2, Mor, Mu, NAC, NICNT, NTC, SSA, St, TH; CEV, NCV, NIV, NLT, NRSV, REB, TEV]: it is through Christ Jesus that God will judge, as my gospel teaches. The teaching about God's judgment is a part of the gospel [Mor, NTC, St]. The gospel of grace does not dispense with judgment [Mu]. Paul's gospel teaches that all people will be judged by Jesus Christ according to their obedience to the law [BECNT]. The good news of salvation shines brightly against the backdrop of impending divine judgment [St].

2. This relates to the clause κρίνει ὁ θεός 'God will judge' [WBC; GW]. God will use the good news to make the judgment [GW]. Paul is expounding the gospel in terms of Jew-Gentile relations, and wants to undercut the exclusivity of the Jews who assumed that the Gentiles would fare poorly in the final judgment because they did not have the law. Here he is saying that this gospel will replace the law as the criterion for the judgment. His gospel operates in broader terms than the law, and while faith in Christ is the fuller and more normative expression of responsiveness to God as creator, it is not the exclusive expression of it, and a less well-defined responsiveness will be treated as equivalent to such faith in Christ. [WBC].

3. It relates to the phrase τὰ κρυπτὰ τῶν ἀνθρώπων 'the hidden things of people', meaning that, according to Paul's gospel, God will judge the secret things of the heart, the personal faith that someone has before God [HNTC].

QUESTION—To what does the phrase διὰ Χριστοῦ Ἰησοῦ 'through Christ Jesus' relate and what is the meaning?

This relates to the clause κρίνει ὁ θεός 'God will judge' [AB, BECNT, Gdt, Ho, ICC1, ICC2, Mor, Mu, NAC, NICNT, NTC, SSA, St, TH, WBC; CEV, GW, KJV, NASB, NCV, NIV, NRSV, REB, TEV]: it is through Christ Jesus that God will judge. Jesus himself said that God had entrusted all judgment to him, and regularly referred to his central role on the day of judgment [Ho, St]. This is consistent with Paul's teaching that all will stand before the judgment seat of Christ [NICNT]. This concept that Christ will judge, and that God gave him this role and will act through him, is familiar in the earliest Christian thought and in many NT texts [WBC].

QUESTION—What is meant by μου 'my' in the phrase τὸ εὐαγγέλιόν μου 'my gospel'?

1. Paul is not referring to some form of teaching particularly characteristic of himself, but rather to the gospel which is common to all Christians, and which God entrusted to Paul to proclaim [ICC2, NICNT]. He called it 'my gospel' because he loved the gospel that had been conveyed to him by the Lord [NTC]. It is the gospel Paul was commissioned to deliver [Ho], and was given to him by revelation from Jesus Christ [NAC]. By this phrase Paul reminds us that the gospel was committed to him, that he was separated unto it and he identified with it [Mu]. This phrase serves as a reminder that preaching the gospel to the Gentiles is Paul's particular call

[BECNT]. Paul is not referring to something particular in his expounding the gospel, but rather that he knows it, espouses it wholeheartedly, and has made it his own [Mor]. It means the gospel as he habitually taught it [ICC1], the gospel that he preached [SSA], his personal way of proclaiming it [AB].
2. It speaks of something unique in Paul's message [Gdt, HNTC, WBC]. This may refer to the fact that Paul's expounding the gospel in terms of Jewish-Gentile relations was unique [WBC]. Foundational to Paul's preaching, and which he has brought out most clearly, is the antithesis between the works of the law as something purely legal and external, and good works that are the fruit of faith and based on the truly moral principle of love [Gdt]. It refers to Paul's emphasis on judgment of the secret things, that God's judgment is not based on behavior that is visible or external, but on the secret things of the heart and the faith that a person holds before God [HNTC].

DISCOURSE UNIT: 2:17–3:31 [REB]. The topic is the Jews and their Law.

DISCOURSE UNIT: 2:17–3:8 [GNT, St, TNTC; CEV, KJV, NCV, NET]. The topic is God's wrath against self-confident Jews [St], the Jews and the Law [GNT; CEV], the condemnation of the Jew [NET], the Jew [TNTC], the Jews and the Law [NCV].

DISCOURSE UNIT: 2:17–29 [HNTC, Ho, ICC1, Mu, NAC, NICNT, TNTC; GW, NIV, NLT, TEV]. The topic is the just judgment of God and the Jew [Ho], God will judge Jewish people [GW], judgment and the Jew [HNTC], the Jews and the Law [NIV, NLT, TEV], the failure of the Jew [ICC1], the aggravation of the Jew's condemnation [Mu], authentic Jewishness is inward [NAC], the limitations of the covenant [NICNT], privilege brings responsibility [TNTC].

DISCOURSE UNIT: 2:17–24 [AB, Ho, ICC1, Mor, NICNT, WBC]. The topic is the transgression of the law by Jews [AB], the case of the Jews [Ho], the Jew's confidence and the Jew's failure [Mor], limitations of the covenant law [NICNT], profession and reality regarding the law [ICC1], favored status no security [WBC].

2:17 But[a] if[b] you call-yourself[c] (a) Jew

LEXICON—a. δέ (LN 89.124): 'but' [AB, BECNT, HNTC, ICC2, LN, WBC; NASB, NRSV, REB], 'on the other hand' [LN], 'now' [NICNT, NTC; NET, NIV], 'behold' [KJV], not explicit [CEV, GW, NCV, NLT, TEV].
  b. εἰ (LN 89.65) (BAGD I.1.a. p. 219): 'if' [BECNT, HNTC, ICC2, LN, NICNT, NTC, WBC; NASB, NET, NIV, NLT, NRSV], 'suppose' [AB], not explicit [GW, KJV, NCV, REB, TEV]. The word denotes a condition which is thought of as real [BAGD].
  c. pres. mid. indic. of ἐπονομάζω (LN 33.132) (BAGD p. 305): 'to call oneself' [AB, BAGD, BECNT, LN, NICNT, NTC; CEV, GW, NCV, NET, NIV, NRSV, TEV], 'to regard oneself' [LN], 'to classify oneself as'

[LN], 'to be called' [WBC; KJV], 'to bear the name of' [HNTC; NASB, REB], 'to be' [NLT], 'to have the name' [ICC2].

QUESTION—What is the function of the word εἰ 'if' in this clause?

1. It introduces the protasis or first part of a conditional sentence, the apodosis or answering part of which is not explicit [ICC2, Mor, NAC, NICNT, SSA, TH, WBC]. The first of three privileges for the Jew is mentioned in this clause, but the second part of the conditional sentence, the matching 'then' clause is not clearly evident [NICNT]. This word introduces a condition, but there is an anacoluthon, or change in the grammatical construction done for rhetorical effect, and the thought is left unfinished [WBC]. The use of this word with the indicative clauses that follow is equivalent in force to an affirmative statement: 'if, as is the case' [Mor, TH]. The construction is broken off at the end of 2:20 [ICC2, TH, WBC].

2. Εἰ 'if' introduces the protasis of the apodosis which begins in 2:21 [AB, BECNT, Ho, ICC1, Mu]. It introduces a set of premises in order to raise a rhetorical question in 2:21 that makes a statement: suppose you call yourself a Jew...then do you not teach yourself? [AB]. In 2:21–24 he describes the failure of the Jews to live up to the privileges described in 2:17–20 [Mu, NICNT].

3. It introduces two sets of four propositions, one set in 2:17–20, which describes the advantages the Jews had, and the other in 2:21–24, which contrasts the iniquities of their conduct with those advantages. It also introduces a transition from the principles discussed earlier in this chapter to their application to be discussed in the rest of the chapter, of which the conclusion is not explicitly stated but should be self-evident to the understanding of the readers [Gdt].

QUESTION—What is meant by σὺ Ἰουδαῖος ἐπονομάζῃ 'you call yourself a Jew'?

1. This is the first of 3 privileges that Jews of the time would have claimed as their own, namely, to be a member of the covenant people of Israel and thus to have a special and favored religious status distinct from all other peoples [NICNT]. Paul recognizes that having the Mosaic law and a special relationship with God were a distinct advantage for the Jews, but he wants to expose the error of placing confidence in those, since God's judgment will be based on their observance of the law, and not just their possession of it [AB]. Paul is speaking of the pride and self-confidence the Jewish person had in the honorable name of God's chosen people [St]. The term 'Jew' represented all the privileges that Jewish people prided themselves on, and which Paul goes on to describe [Mu]. This is part of the rhetoric of diatribe, and Paul probably has in mind the imaginary objector as representative of any Jews who believe they can be saved through the law, regardless of whether or not the particular accusations of 2:21–23 could be made against them specifically [SSA]. This is the first explicit indication that Paul is addressing the Jews, and he acknowledges

that they had a special status and mission relative to the rest of the world [ICC2]. The Jews were uniquely privileged, but many of them considered themselves better than everyone else [NTC]. The term calls attention to nationality, distinguishing the Jew as a member of the chosen people and as distinct from the heathen [ICC1].
2. There is a contrast here with the "true" Jew such as he describes in 2:29 [BECNT, HNTC, WBC]. The designation distinguishes Jews as being those people particularly favored by God, as distinct from Gentiles, but the chapter ends with Paul defining true Jewishness in spiritual rather than ethnic or racial terms, and where he stresses that any covenantal advantage of being a Jew is nullified if the law is disobeyed [BECNT]. Paul has in mind the typical Jew, aware of his distinctiveness from other nations and his special privilege in having the law, and the pride he took in distinguishing himself from Gentiles; however, in subsequent passages Paul raises the question about what constitutes true Jewishness [WBC].

and rely-on[a] (the)-law[b] and boast[c] in[d] God

LEXICON—a. pres. mid. (deponent = act.) indic. of ἐπαναπαύομαι (LN 31.83) (BAGD 2. p. 283): 'to rely on' [AB, BAGD, BECNT, ICC2, LN, NTC, WBC; GW, NASB, NET, NIV, NLT, NRSV, REB], 'to depend on' [LN; TEV], 'to trust in' [NCV], 'to put one's trust in' [HNTC, LN; CEV], 'to take pride in' [NICNT], 'to rest in' [KJV]. The phrase ἐπαναπαύῃ νόμῳ 'and rely-upon (the) law' is translated, 'you are relying on God's law for your special relationship with him' [NLT].

b. νόμος: 'law'. See this word at 2:13. This word, which lacks the definite article, is translated as having the article by AB, BECNT, HNTC, ICC2, NICNT, NTC, WBC; all versions. It is translated 'God's law' [NLT], 'the laws in Moses' teaching' [GW], 'the law of Moses' [NCV].

c. pres. mid. (deponent = act.) indic. of καυχάομαι (LN 33.368) (BAGD 1. p. 425): 'to boast' [AB, BAGD, BECNT, HNTC, LN, NICNT, WBC; KJV, NASB, NET, NLT, NRSV, TEV], 'to glory in (a person)' [BAGD, ICC2], 'to take pride in' [CEV, REB], 'to pride oneself in or about a person' [BAGD], 'to brag about' [NTC; GW, NIV], 'to make one's boast' [HNTC; KJV].

d. ἐν with dative object (LN 90.23): 'in' [BECNT, HNTC, ICC2, LN, NICNT, WBC; CEV, NASB, REB], 'about' [LN; GW, TEV], 'with regard to, with respect to, with reference to, concerning' [LN], 'of' [AB; KJV]. The phrase καυχᾶσαι ἐν θεῷ 'boast in God' is translated 'brag about your relationship to God' [NIV], 'boast of your relationship/relation to God' [NET, NRSV], 'you boast that all is well between yourself and God' [NLT], 'brag that you are close to God' [NCV].

QUESTION—What is meant by ἐπαναπαύῃ νόμῳ 'rely on the law'?

It means to lean on, to depend on, or to have confidence in the law [TH], which was a sign of divine favor [Gdt]. The Jews relied on their possession of the law to shield them from judgment [NICNT, St]. They thought they could fulfill the law in such a manner as to put God in their debt, or that merely possessing it gave security against judgment [ICC2]. The Jews were in danger of relying on the fact of their having the law for their acceptance before God, as opposed to observing what the law requires [AB]. The Jews of whom Paul spoke were guilty of thinking that mere possession of and instruction in the law provided security and superiority for them, and that their efforts to obey it could earn salvation for them [NTC]. The Jews' hopes for a secure standing before God and for salvation was based on having the law and on the promises made to their forefathers [HNTC]. It means that they were resting their hopes on the law, which was the basis for their national identity and of their unique relationship to God [NAC]. This same verb is used in Micah 3:11 where the prophet condemns the people for their reliance on God's presence among them despite their disobedience to him [Ho, ICC2, NICNT].

QUESTION—What is meant by καυχάομαι ἐν θεῷ 'to boast in God'?
1. It has a negative connotation and means to boast about their relationship to God [Ho, ICC2, NAC, NTC, St, TH, WBC]. They boast that God will save them and that they belong to him [SSA]. The Jews boasted about their unique relationship to God [NAC, NTC]. While it is not wrong to boast in God, it is wrong to brag as though one's relationship with God were a human attainment [NTC]. This is used here in the sense of 'brag' and refers to Jewish pride in monotheism and their supposed monopoly of God [St]. The Jewish boasting had to do with a nationalistic exclusiveness, as though God belonged to them alone [WBC]. This refers to the Jews' misplaced confidence that, because of God's promises to their forefathers, the Jews could be assured of salvation and would be in a position to pass sentence on others [HNTC]. Here it refers not to boasting in God himself, but rather in their particular relationship to him [TH]. While boasting in God is not wrong in itself, the Jews' boast that they alone had the favor of God, regardless of their character, and that all other nations were his enemies, was wrong [Ho].
2. It has a positive connotation and means to take pride in God [BECNT, Mor, NICNT; CEV, REB]. It is a deeply felt pride in the one God himself, whom the Jew felt he knew in contrast to others who did not know him; however, their mistake was in not giving full consideration to the character of God as the judge of all men. [Mor]. Paul does not criticize boasting in God, but he does say that failure to obey the law dishonors the God in whom they boast [BECNT]. The Jews' boasting in God was not wrong in and of itself, as there was a legitimate pride and joy in God for all he had given them [NICNT].

2:18 and you-know[a] the will[b]

LEXICON—a. pres. act. indic. of γινώσκω (LN 28.1, 32.16) (BAGD 6.a.α. p. 161): 'to know' [AB, BAGD, BECNT, HNTC, ICC2, LN (28.1), NICNT, NTC, WBC; all versions except CEV], 'to know about, to have

knowledge of, to be acquainted with' [LN (28.1)], 'to come to understand, to comprehend' [LN (32.16)], 'to learn how' [CEV].
  b. θέλημα (LN 25.2, 30.59) (BAGD 1.a., 1.c.γ., p. 354): 'will' [AB, BAGD, BECNT, HNTC, ICC2, LN (30.59), NICNT, NTC, WBC; KJV, NASB, NET, NIV, NRSV, REB], 'intent, purpose, plan' [LN (30.59)], 'desire' [LN (25.2)], 'God's will' [BAGD (1.a. p. 354)]. This noun is translated as a phrase: 'how God wants you to behave' [CEV], 'what he wants' [GW, NCV, NLT], 'what God wants you to do' [TEV]. This phrase with the definite article is specifically identified as being God's will: 'his will' [AB, BECNT, HNTC, ICC2, NICNT, NTC, WBC; KJV, NASB, NET, NIV, NRSV, REB].

QUESTION— Whose will is being referred to in this context by the phrase τὸ θέλημα 'the will'?

This refers to the will of God [AB, BECNT, Gdt, HNTC, Ho, ICC1, ICC2, Mor, Mu, NAC, NICNT, NTC, SSA, St, TNTC, WBC; CEV, TEV]. The article is possessive and refers to God, and the absolute use of the phrase 'the will' is a customarily Jewish way of referring to God's will [NICNT, TH, WBC]. While he does not criticize knowing God's will, the attitude Paul refers to is an assumption of a privileged knowledge of it by virtue of instruction in the law [WBC]. God's will is the absolute to which all others are relative [St].

and you-approve/discern[a] the-(things) being-valuable[b]

LEXICON—a. pres. act. indic. of δοκιμάζω (LN 27.45, 30.98, 30.114) (BAGD 1., 2.b. p. 202): 'to approve' [BAGD (2.b. p. 202), BECNT, LN (30.114), NICNT, NTC, WBC; KJV, NASB, NET, NIV], 'to judge' [HNTC, LN (30.114)], 'to discern' [ICC2], 'to discover' [BAGD (1. p. 202); CEV], 'to determine' [NRSV], 'to distinguish' [GW], 'to test, to examine' [LN (27.45)], 'to determine the genuineness of' [LN (27.45)], 'to judge to be genuine, to judge as good, to approve' [LN (30.114)], 'to regard as worthwhile, to think of as appropriate' [LN (30.98)], 'to know' [NCV, NLT, REB], 'to learn to choose' [TEV], 'to scrutinize' [AB].
  b. pres. act. participle of διαφέρω (LN 65.6) (BAGD 2.b. p. 190): 'to be valuable, to have worth' [LN], 'to be superior to' [BAGD; NET, NIV], 'to be excellent' [BECNT], 'to be more excellent' [KJV], 'to be best' [NICNT; NRSV], 'to be essential' [ICC2; NASB], 'to really matter' [AB, NTC, WBC; REB], 'to be right and good' [HNTC], 'to be right or wrong' [NLT], 'to be right' [CEV, TEV]. The phrase τὰ διαφέροντα 'the things being valuable' is translated 'right from wrong' [GW], 'what is right or wrong' [NLT], 'the things that really matter' [AB], 'what is important' [NCV].

QUESTION—What is meant by δοκιμάζω 'approve/discern'?
  1. It means to approve [BECNT, Ho, ICC1, Mor, Mu, NICNT, NTC, SSA; KJV, NET, NIV]: you approve of the things that are valuable. The law provides insight for the Jew into God's will and thus enables him to

approve of what is truly excellent [BECNT]. As a result of being taught in the law, the Jew would be able to approve things that really mattered and to rank essentials above non-essentials [NTC]. They are able to determine as well as to choose what is right [SSA].
2. It means to distinguish or discern, that is, to evaluate [AB, Gdt, HNTC, ICC2, NAC, WBC; CEV, NLT, NRSV, REB, TEV]: you distinguish which things are valuable. In this context it means to distinguish the things which matter or which are essential, such as the weightier things of the law mentioned in Matt. 23:23; the Jew who knows the law does discern such things, though often failing to act accordingly [ICC2]. It means to judge what is good and significant [HNTC]. Paul is saying the Jew could distinguish the things that were morally superior [NAC]. Because the Jew knows the will and law of God he is able to concentrate on and appreciate that which counts most in life [AB]. It is the process of evaluating priorities, to determine what is essential and what is not, but in the case of the Jews, resulted in too much priority being given to less important matters of Jewish distinctiveness, such as circumcision [WBC].
3. Both meanings are intended; they have the ability to discern what is right and to choose it [SSA, TH]. The law is the basis for being able to choose what is right [TH].

QUESTION—What is meant by τὰ διαφέροντα 'the things being valuable'?
1. It means things which are more valuable, excellent, or which really matter as compared with other things [AB, BECNT, HNTC, Ho, ICC1, ICC2, Mor, Mu, NAC, NICNT, NTC, SSA, TNTC, WBC; KJV, NET, NIV, NRSV, REB]. These things are the matters of life that are the most important [AB, NAC], the things that really matter [NTC, WBC]. In a context where no explicit comparison is made, the word is more likely to mean 'to excel' than to mean 'to differ' [NICNT]. The basic meaning is 'to differ', but when things differ one is taken to be better than the other, so the meaning here refers to what is excellent [Mor]. Paul is conceding all that the Jews claimed, given their superior knowledge, which is that they not only discern what is best, they approve it [Ho].
2. It refers to the difference between what is right and what is wrong [Gdt, TH; CEV, NLT, TEV]. This may be a reference to discussions of legal casuistry in which the rabbis sought to determine very precisely what the will of God was for the Jews [Gdt].

QUESTION—What is meant by δοκιμάζεις τὰ διαφέροντα 'you approve/ discern the things being valuable'?

It should be understood to mean approving those things which are best [BECNT, NICNT, NTC], or which are excellent [Ho, ICC1, Mor, Mu, TNTC]. More than simply knowing right from wrong, it is to approve of what is right, in keeping with their knowledge of God's will, as he has already mentioned [Mor]. They can both determine as well as choose that which excels [SSA]. It means to discern that which matters most, or which is essential [AB, ICC2, WBC], to discern what is significant and good

[HNTC], to distinguish what was morally superior [NAC]. It means to appreciate and concentrate on those matters of life which are most important [AB]. In the law, the Jews had a readily accessible guide to what is right and wrong, but the Jews often erred in understanding what God counts important because they paid too much attention to superficial things [WBC]. It means to discern precisely what is right and wrong, as exemplified by the legal casuistry in which Jewish schools excelled [Gdt].

being-taught[a] from[b] the law,

LEXICON—a. pres. pass. participle of κατηχέω (LN 33.225, 33.190) (BAGD 2.a. p. 423): 'to be taught' [LN; GW, NLT, REB], 'to be instructed' [AB, BAGD, BECNT, HNTC, ICC2, LN, NICNT, NTC, WBC; KJV, NASB, NET, NIV, NRSV], 'to be informed or told' [LN (33.190)]. The passive form is also translated actively: 'to learn' [NCV, TEV].

b. ἐκ with genitive object (LN 90.16) (BAGD 3.g.β. p. 235): 'from' [BAGD, LN, WBC; NET, TEV], 'by' [AB, BECNT, HNTC, LN, NICNT; NIV], 'out of' [BAGD, ICC2, NTC; KJV, NASB], 'in' [NRSV], not explicit [CEV, GW, NCV, NLT].

QUESTION—What relationship is implied by the use of the participle κατηχούμενος 'being instructed' ?

It indicates reason [AB, BECNT, NAC, NICNT, NTC, SSA, St; GW, NCV, NET, NIV, NLT, NRSV]: you know or approve or discern because you are taught by the law. The adverbial participle κατηχούμενος 'being taught' modifies both 'know' and 'approve' in the preceding clauses and gives the reason why the Jews both know God's will and approve of what is best, which is that they are instructed by the law [AB, BECNT, ICC2, NICNT, NTC, WBC]. The law is the source of their knowledge [Gdt, Ho; CEV, REB, TEV]. The reason the Jew has moral discernment is that he is instructed by the law [St]. The ability to know God's will and to rank essentials above non-essentials resulted from being taught in the law [NTC]. The law is the source of wisdom [AB].

2:19 and being-convinced[a] (that) you are (a) guide[b] of-blind[c] (persons),

LEXICON—a. perf. pass. participle of πείθω (LN 33.301) (BAGD 2.b. p. 639): 'to be convinced' [BAGD, BECNT, LN, NICNT, NTC; NET, NIV, NLT], 'to be persuaded' [AB, LN], 'to be certain' [BAGD], 'to be sure' [BAGD; CEV, NRSV, TEV], 'to be confident that' [HNTC, ICC2, WBC; GW, KJV, NASB, REB], 'to think' [NCV]. The perfect form of the participle should be understood with a present meaning [AB, BAGD, BECNT, Mor, NAC, NICNT, NTC, SSA, St]

b. ὁδηγός (LN **36.4**) (BAGD 2. p. 553): 'guide' [AB, BAGD, BECNT, HNTC, ICC2, **LN**, NICNT, NTC, WBC; all versions], 'leader' [BAGD, LN].

c. τυφλός (LN 32.42) (BAGD 2.b. p. 831): 'blind' [AB, BAGD, BECNT, HNTC, ICC2, LN, NICNT, NTC, WBC; all versions]. The word is used figuratively of mental and spiritual blindness [BAGD].

QUESTION—What relationship is indicated by τε 'and' ?

This verse is loosely connected to the preceding by the conjunction τε 'and', as Paul now begins to enumerate four prerogatives which the Jew has in relation to other people because of the five blessings that have just been listed, and which come from belonging to the covenant people of Israel [NICNT]. This is joined with what comes before it by τε 'and', which typically links clauses which have a close connection and relationship; here Paul turns from discussing the Jews' relationship to God to discussing their attitude toward other people [Mor, Mu]. The Jew is convinced that he is competent to teach others because of his having been instructed by the law [St]. These next verses present a fair characterization of what Paul clearly sees as typical of Jewish attitudes, which is that because they have the law, the very embodiment of knowledge and truth, they are able to fulfill Israel's task of being educator and guide to all others who are ignorant of it [WBC]. It introduces a four-part statement which forms the last of six claims the Jews made based on the fact that they possessed and were instructed in the law [SSA]. These verses begin a discussion of what the Jews considered to be the effects produced in them by the particular advantages they had [Ho]. Out of the special knowledge and faculties of discernment which the Jew has comes the role he claims to have in relation to others, and which Paul now describes [Gdt].

QUESTION—What is the implied tone of this passage?

Paul is using sarcasm [ICC1, NTC]. He offers a touch of ridicule for the pretentious self-assurance of the Jews [Gdt]. These metaphors describe the attitude of self-righteousness and superiority of the Jewish people, who fell short of what God intended for them and used the blessings of God to promote their own self-aggrandizement [NAC]. The Jews really were called to fulfill all these roles [HNTC, Mor, Mu, NAC, NICNT, NTC], but they fell far short of doing so [Mu, NAC, NICNT]. They should have done so with an attitude of humility, not of superiority [Mor]. Their vanity was not in thinking of themselves as having such a calling, for they did indeed have it, but in thinking that they had fulfilled it when in fact they had not [BECNT, Mu]. This is not merely irony, for the Jews not only had such a calling, they did actually fulfill it to some extent, but their inadequacy in doing so was clear before God [ICC2]. The Jews did have the responsibility to teach the knowledge of God to the Gentiles, and carried it out, but they did not live up to that knowledge [St]. Instead of being convicted of their responsibility toward the Gentiles, the Jews became convinced of their superiority over them; Paul implies that the Jews are not fulfilling their role but are instead misguided and mistaken in understanding God's will and their own priorities [WBC].

(a) light[a] of-the-(ones) in[b] darkness,[c]

LEXICON—a. φῶς (LN 14.36) (BAGD 3.b. p. 872): 'light' [AB, BAGD, BECNT, HNTC, ICC2, LN, NICNT, NTC, WBC; all versions except

NLT], 'beacon light' [NLT]. The word is used figuratively in reference to people who bear or bring the kind of 'light' that illumines the soul and spirit of man [BAGD].
  b. ἐν (LN 13.8): 'in' [AB, BECNT, HNTC, ICC2, LN, NICNT, NTC, WBC; all versions].
  c. σκότος (LN 88.125) (BAGD 2.b. p. 758): 'darkness' [AB, BAGD, BECNT, HNTC, ICC2, LN, NICNT, NTC, WBC; all versions except CEV, GW, NIV], 'the dark' [CEV, GW, NIV]. The word is figurative of religious and moral darkness [BAGD]. This has the sense of the realm of sin and evil, or the evil world [LN (88.125)].

QUESTION—What is being referred to by the metaphors in this section?
  The pagans, who are without the law, are those in darkness, and the Jews, instructed by the law, are those in the light [AB, Gdt, Ho, NTC, St]. Light was connected with the law and conversion from paganism to Judaism was often viewed as moving from darkness to light [NICNT]. Darkness and light are metaphors of ethical conduct [AB]. The light refers to the law which Israel had been given, and the task of God's servant is to open the eyes of the blind, and to be their guide; these biting phrases strike at the confidence of the Jews that they could be guides and educators for all the immature who did not have the law [WBC]. The two metaphors here are a doublet in which the Jews are presented as guides and instructors for Gentiles who are ignorant of or do not understand God's truth, in particular the law [SSA]. By virtue of having God's revelation in the law, they had the important task of teaching those who did not have it [Mor, Mu]. They were to fulfill their calling with gratitude and humility for what God had done, not with pride in their privileged position or with a sense of natural superiority [Mor].

2:20 (an) instructor[a] of-foolish[b] (persons),
LEXICON—a. παιδευτής (LN **33.244**) (BAGD p. 603): 'instructor' [BAGD, BECNT, HNTC, **LN**, NICNT, NTC, WBC; GW, KJV, NIV, REB, TEV], 'corrector' [AB; NASB, NRSV], 'teacher' [BAGD, LN], 'educator' [ICC2; NET]. This noun is also translated as a verb phrase: '(you think) you can instruct' [CEV, NLT], '(you think) you can show' [NCV]. The word denotes one who provides instruction in proper behavior [LN].
  b. ἄφρων (LN **32.52**) (BAGD p. 127): 'foolish' [AB, BAGD, BECNT, ICC2, **LN,** NICNT, NTC, WBC; KJV, NASB, NIV, NRSV, REB, TEV], 'ignorant' [BAGD; GW, NLT], 'senseless' [LN; NET], 'unwise' [LN]. This adjective is also translated as a noun: 'fools' [HNTC; CEV].

QUESTION—What is meant by παιδευτής 'instructor'?
  The word refers to training or teaching people [ICC2, Mor, NICNT, NTC], people who are like young children with regard to their religious understanding [NICNT]. It denotes one who considers himself to be thoroughly qualified to teach the ignorant and foolish [NTC]. Paul is thinking of the general influence of Jewish moral standards among Gentiles,

and in particular of moral guidance given by teachers of the law to proselytes [ICC2]. Here the word is equivalent to 'teacher' [TH].
1. The word includes connotations of discipline or correction [AB, ICC1, Mor, NAC, SSA, WBC]. The word means 'schoolmaster' and includes the ideas of discipline and correction as well as teaching [ICC1]. It is one who corrects and disciplines fools [AB].
2. The word has no connotations of discipline or correction [ICC2].

QUESTION—What is meant by ἄφρων 'foolish'?

It denotes those who are ignorant, untrained, or immature with respect to religious understanding, as the Jews commonly regarded the Gentiles [NICNT, WBC]. It does not mean those who are scornful of God's truth [NICNT]. This and the next phrase together refer to those who are spiritual babies, that is proselytes or converts [St]. The word means 'foolish', but here Paul is suggesting that Jews considered Gentiles to be foolish in the sense that they do not understand spiritual truth [SSA]. The word refers to moral, not intellectual, weakness here [ICC2, TH]. Paul is not contrasting the intelligence of Jews and Gentiles, but is thinking of those who lack spiritual perception [Mor]. It refers to those without moral intelligence and in need of instruction [NAC].

(a) teacher[a] of-children,[b]

LEXICON—a. διδάσκαλος (LN 33.243) (BAGD p. 191): 'teacher' [AB, BECNT, HNTC, ICC2, LN, NICNT, NTC, WBC; GW, KJV, NASB, NET, NIV, NRSV, REB, TEV], 'instructor' [LN]. This noun is also translated as a verb: 'to teach' [CEV, NCV, NLT].

b. νήπιος (LN **9.43**) (BAGD 1.b.α. p. 537): 'child' [LN; NLT, NRSV], 'small child' [LN], 'little child' [**LN;** NET], 'the young' [WBC], 'young person' [CEV], 'minor or very young child, infant' [BAGD; NIV], 'babe' [BECNT, HNTC; KJV], 'immature' [AB, ICC2, NICNT, NTC; NASB, REB], 'the ignorant' [TEV], 'those who know nothing' [NCV]. The word normally is used to denote a small child probably not more than three or four years of age, but here means 'the unlearned' [LN].

QUESTION—What is meant by νήπιος 'children'?

This word further defines what Paul means by 'foolish' in the preceding phrase, meaning those who are ignorant, untrained, or immature in their religious understanding [NICNT]. This term was used by Jews to describe proselytes [Gdt, St] and converts [NTC, St]. 'Children' is figurative of people who are spiritually immature [Mor, NAC, WBC] and need instruction about God [Mor], God's will [WBC], God's truth [SSA], life's priorities [WBC], issues of religious significance [NAC]. They need moral and religious instruction similar to what very small children would receive [Mor]. The term is used in a patronizing manner [NAC].

QUESTION—Is there a significant difference of the meaning between διδάσκαλος 'teacher' and παιδευτής 'instructor' earlier in this verse?

The two words are virtually synonymous [BECNT, NICNT, NTC, TH, WBC]. There may be some overtone of 'corrector' in the latter term, but the two phrases are essentially synonymous [WBC]. As contrasted with παιδευτής 'educator' this word διδάσκαλος 'teacher' may be taken as indicating somewhat more theoretical instruction [ICC2].

having the embodiment[a] of knowledge[b] and of-the truth[c] in the law;

LEXICON—a. μόρφωσις (LN **58.3**) (BAGD 1. p. 528): 'embodiment' [AB, BAGD, BECNT, HNTC, ICC2, LN, NICNT, NTC, WBC; NASB, NIV, NRSV, REB], 'full content' [LN; GW, TEV], 'the formulation of' [BAGD], 'the form of' [KJV], 'the essential features' [**LN**; NET], not explicit [CEV, NCV]. This noun is also translated as an adjective: 'complete' [NLT]. The word means the embodiment of the essential features and qualities of something [LN].
  b. γνῶσις (LN **28.17**) (BAGD 1. p. 163): 'knowledge' [AB, BAGD, BECNT, HNTC, ICC2, **LN,** NICNT, NTC, WBC; all versions except NCV]. The phrase 'having the embodiment of knowledge' is translated 'you think you know everything' [NCV].
  c. ἀλήθεια (LN 72.2) (BAGD 2.a. p. 35): 'truth' [AB, BAGD, BECNT, HNTC, ICC2, LN, NICNT, NTC, WBC; all versions].

QUESTION—What relation is signaled by the participle ἔχοντα 'having'?

The participle indicates the reason the Jews are able to instruct others, which is that they have in the law the embodiment of knowledge and truth [AB, BECNT, Ho, Mor, Mu, NTC, SSA, St, WBC; CEV, GW, NCV, NET, NIV, NLT, REB]. This statement forms something of a climax and explains the confidence expressed in 2:19, and is the basis on which the Jew was certain that he could fulfill the four roles just mentioned [ICC2]. Paul mentions here another of the benefits enjoyed by Jews who have the law [NICNT].

QUESTION—What is meant by μόρφωσις 'embodiment'?

The primary sense is completeness of content [AB, BECNT, Gdt, Ho, NAC, TH, WBC; GW, NCV, NLT, TEV] or sufficiency [NICNT]. Paul recognizes that the law encapsulates all knowledge and truth, and truly expresses God's will [AB]. Here it refers to the sufficiency of the law in that it contains knowledge and truth in a much more clear and detailed form than what is available to those without special revelation [NICNT]. The word means 'embodiment' or 'complete expression' and reflects the Jewish claim that knowledge and truth per se are embodied in the law; Paul has come to recognize that knowledge and truth could be encountered outside the boundaries marked by the law, and criticizes the notion that all one needed in terms of knowledge and truth was fully given in the form of the law [WBC]. The sense is to have the full content or to know completely [TH]. The Jew possesses in the law the precise sketch, outline, or rigorous formula by which he can convey truth to others [Gdt]. There is no suggestion here that the merely outward form is intended, rather Paul asserts that the law embodies knowledge and truth [BECNT]. It means that knowledge and truth are represented and expressed in the law [Ho]. They believed that the law held the essential features of knowledge and truth [NET]. There is also some emphasis on the written form of the law itself as an accurate representation of all truth and knowledge [Ho, ICC1, ICC2, Mor, Mu, SSA]. The law is the written expression of divine truth [Ho, SSA]. In the law the Jew really did have knowledge and truth in a form that is able to be clearly grasped and expressed [ICC2].

2:21 therefore[a] the-(one) teaching[b] another (person) do-you- not -teach yourself?

LEXICON—a. οὖν (LN 89.50): 'therefore' [LN, NICNT; KJV, NASB, NET], 'then' [AB, ICC2, LN, WBC; NIV, NRSV, REB], 'well then' [HNTC; NLT], 'therefore since' [BECNT], 'accordingly, consequently, so then' [LN], not explicit [CEV, GW, NCV, TEV].

b. pres. act. participle of διδάσκω (LN 33.224): 'to teach' [LN]. The phrase 'the one...teaching another' is translated 'you who teach another' [ICC2, NICNT, WBC; KJV, NASB], 'you who teach someone else' [NET], 'you who/that teach others' [NIV, NRSV], 'you who teach your neighbor' [HNTC], 'if you teach others' [NLT], 'you teach others' [BECNT; NCV, REB, TEV], 'as you teach others' [GW], 'you who would teach others' [AB], 'how can you teach others (when)' [CEV].

QUESTION—What relationship is indicated by οὖν 'therefore'?

1. It indicates a conclusion to the preceding verses [BECNT, Gdt, Ho, ICC1, Mu, SSA]. It introduces the conclusion or apodosis to the conditionals or protasis of 2:17–20 [Ho, Mu, SSA]. It resumes the argument of 2:17–20 and introduces what follows as a conclusion or apodosis of that section [ICC1]. The word ironically contrasts what their knowledge has actually produced in the Jews as compared to what it should have produced [Gdt].

2. This is probably resumptive, as Paul has not followed up his 'if' of 2:17 in strict grammatical sequence [Mor, NAC].

QUESTION—What is the function of the rhetorical questions of this section?

These rhetorical questions are in keeping with the diatribe style to which Paul has now returned [AB, NAC, NICNT, WBC]. They expose the Jew as being hypocritical, inconsistent, and disobedient, despite the boasts described in the previous sections [NICNT]. The questions advance the premise that they are guilty of hypocrisy [BECNT, ICC1]. Although these questions could be considered as direct statements, because of the style Paul is using these are best understood as taunting questions which allude to the Jewish conviction at that time that knowledge of and instruction in the law alone could make the nation holy [AB]. By use of these five rhetorical questions Paul turns the tables on the Jews to show that they do not live up to their knowledge, and points out their inconsistency [St]. In order to prove that the Jews stand condemned just as much as non-Jews Paul presents a series of five hard-hitting rhetorical questions with implied negative answers, and are semantically are accusations [SSA]. This is a series of four sentences which are accusatory rhetorical questions, and may be read as statements [ICC2]. These questions form a pointed rebuke to the hypocrisy of the Jew by selecting transgressions that go to the heart of the law in which the Jew gloried, and should arouse him from the complacency that a distorted view of his advantages had produced [Mu]. Clearly Paul asserts by these questions that the Jews are guilty of the sins described here [Ho].

QUESTION—How do the questions of this section relate to one another?

The first question regarding teaching oneself functions like a heading which is then further broken down into three specific examples [BECNT, NICNT], the first two of which are included in the Ten Commandments, and all of which evidence flagrant violations of the law by the Jews [NICNT]. The three questions that follow the first one clarify that hypocrisy is Paul's primary accusation here [BECNT]. The first question, 'you who teach, do you not teach yourself', is a general question, followed by three more questions regarding particular sins, and then followed up by the fifth and final general question [St]. The first question is generic, the next three are specific examples of condemnation related to it, and the last forms the conclusion [Mor, Mu, SSA]. The rhetorical style indicates that the four sentences following are intended as questions, and the scriptural proof of 2:24 should be taken as a statement of conclusion [WBC].

the-(one) preaching^a not to-steal^b do-you-steal?

LEXICON—a. pres. act. participle of κηρύσσω (LN 33.256) (BAGD 2.b.β. p. 431): 'to preach' [AB, BAGD, BECNT, HNTC, ICC2, LN, NICNT, WBC; all versions except NCV, NLT, REB], 'to proclaim' [BAGD; REB], 'to tell' [NCV, NLT]. The word means to publicly announce religious truths while urging people to accept and comply with them [LN].

b. pres. act. infin. of κλέπτω (LN 57.232) (BAGD p. 434): 'to steal' [BAGD, HNTC, ICC2, LN, WBC; CEV, KJV, NASB, NLT, REB, TEV]. The phrase μὴ κλέπτειν 'not to steal' is translated 'against stealing' [AB, BECNT, NICNT; GW, NET, NIV, NRSV], 'it is wrong to steal' [CEV].

2:22 the-(one) saying not to-commit-adultery^a do-you-commit-adultery?

LEXICON—a. pres. act. infin. of μοιχεύω (LN 88.276) (BAGD 2.a. p. 526): 'to commit adultery' [BAGD, BECNT, HNTC, ICC2, LN, NICNT, WBC; CEV, GW, KJV, NASB, NET, NLT, REB, TEV], 'to take part in adultery' [NCV]. The phrase ὁ λέγων μὴ μοιχεύειν 'saying not to commit adultery' is translated 'you forbid adultery' [AB; NRSV], 'speak against adultery' [BECNT], 'you say that adultery is forbidden' [NIV].

QUESTION—Should the word μοιχεύω 'adultery' be taken in a metaphorical or literal sense?

1. It should be understood in the literal sense [BECNT, Gdt, Ho, Mor, Mu, NAC, NICNT, NTC, SSA, St, TH, WBC]. This sin was widespread in the ancient world, even taken as normal for men in many places, and although

the Jews had higher standards than the Gentiles on this count, they were far from blameless [Mor].
2. It should be understood in a metaphorical sense [HNTC, ICC2]. It is certainly possible to find examples of this as well as the other sins mentioned, but this is somewhat beside the point as the argument would be lost if based only on comparatively unusual events; it is better to understand that all men are guilty of all these sins when they are strictly and radically understood along the lines of Mat. 5:21–48 [HNTC, ICC2].

the-(one) abhorring^a the idols^b do-you-rob-temples^c?

LEXICON—a. pres. mid. (deponent = act.) participle of βδελύσσομαι (LN 25.186) (BAGD p. 138): 'to abhor' [BAGD, BECNT, ICC2, LN, WBC; KJV, NASB, NET, NIV, NRSV], 'to detest' [BAGD, NICNT; TEV], 'to abominate' [AB, **LN;** REB], 'to regard as an abomination' [HNTC], 'to hate' [CEV, NCV], 'to condemn' [NLT], 'to treat with disgust' [GW]. 'to regard as an abomination' [HNTC].
 b. εἴδωλον (LN 6.97) (BAGD 2. p. 221): 'idol' [AB, BAGD, BECNT, HNTC, ICC2, LN, NICNT, WBC; all versions except NLT, REB], 'false gods' [BAGD; REB], 'idolatry' [NLT].
   c. pres. act. indic. of ἱεροσυλέω (LN **53.104, 57.241**) (BAGD p. 373): 'to rob temples' [AB, BAGD, BECNT, **LN** (57.241), NICNT; CEV, NET, NIV, NRSV, TEV], 'to steal from...temples' [NLT], 'to rob shrines' [REB], 'to commit sacrilege by damaging temples' [**LN** (53.104)], 'to commit sacrilege' [HNTC, ICC2, **LN** (53.104), WBC; KJV], 'to desecrate' [LN (53.104)].

QUESTION—What is meant by ἱεροσυλέω 'to rob temples'?
1. It means literally to rob temples [BAGD, BECNT, ICC1, Mu, NTC, SSA, St, WBC]. Both stealing and adultery are to be understood literally in the verse, so it is best to take 'to rob temples' literally as well, which is typically the meaning of the word used here, and presumably refers to the robbing of pagan temples [BECNT]. It is most likely that Paul is thinking of pagan temples here, and in all the sins mentioned he seems to have actions rather than thoughts in mind [St]. It is probable that he means the plundering of pagan temples and idols [WBC], or getting profit from things that had been stolen from temples [BECNT, NICNT, WBC]. It is possible that Paul could be arguing that using articles or precious metals stolen from pagan temples is a practice that should be seen as being in contradiction to abhorring idols [Gdt, Mu], though the Jews probably did not rob these temples themselves [Gdt]. There is some question as to whether he is referring to the theft itself or to profiting from the theft [SSA].
2. It means to commit sacrilege in a more general or symbolic sense, not literally robbing temples [AB, HNTC, Ho, ICC2; KJV].
  2.1 It used in the more general sense of 'committing sacrilege', both in overt sacrilegious behavior as well as in more subtle forms of it [ICC2].

2.2 Inscriptions and papyri conclusively show that the word has a wider meaning than the literal robbing of temples, and when the Jew sets himself up as judge over others he renders to himself a devotion that rightly belongs only to God, which is the fundamental problem with idolatry [HNTC].

2.3 This refers to the Jews elevating the law to a level of unwarranted devotion, importance, and permanence such that it was never intended to have, that Christ and his role in God's plan were excluded [AB].

2.4 It is not known whether the Jews robbed heathen temples, and it is unlikely that this would have been considered sacrilege or of the same nature as idolatry, which the context would seem to require. Consequently the essence of idolatry, the profaning of God, should be understood here in the sense of withholding from God his due, whether in withholding tithes and offerings, or in a more general irreverence for God and holy things [Ho].

2.5 The word refers to activity which damages or harms sacred objects in temples, thus desecrating them, and which is therefore considered a sacrilege [LN (53.104)].

QUESTION—Is Paul making the accusation that all Jews, or at least most Jews, were actually guilty of the sins mentioned in this section?

1. Paul does not intend to accuse all or even many Jews of actually committing these sins [BECNT, NICNT, SSA, WBC]. Rather he is using a rhetoric that takes particularly shocking examples to illustrate the principle that Jews violate the very law they preach [BECNT, WBC]. One rabbi of Paul's day bewailed the increase of all these evils in Jewish society [St]. Paul has in mind the imaginary objector as representative of any Jew who believes he can be saved through the law, regardless of whether or not he is personally guilty of the particular accusations of 2:21–23 [SSA]. Perhaps Paul's purpose was to use these sins to represent the theme of the contrast between words and works, between possessing and obeying the law, a condition which was pervasive in Judaism, and to highlight the equivalence between Gentile and Jewish sins [NICNT]. Paul is pointing out the sharp contrast between Jewish theology and doctrine on the one hand, and their life and practice on the other [NTC]. Paul's point is that Jewish pride in the law is misplaced, since the mere possession of the law does not save the Jew who violates it [WBC]. A disobedient Jew is no better than a Gentile [Gdt].

2. The specific committing of these sins is not the point being made, rather a broader understanding of them should be taken, the standard being that of Matt. 5:21–48, which focuses on the thought life and not outward conduct [HNTC, ICC2]. That isolated examples of these sins could be found among Jews is beside the point, because Paul implies that all Jews are guilty of the sins described [ICC2].

2:23 (You) who boast[a] in[b] (the) law,[c]
LEXICON—a. pres. mid. (deponent = act.) indic. of καυχάομαι (LN 33.368) (BAGD 1. p. 425): 'to boast' [AB, BAGD, BECNT, HNTC, LN, NICNT, WBC; KJV, NASB, NET, NLT, NRSV, TEV], 'to glory in' [BAGD, ICC2], 'to pride oneself in or about something' [BAGD], 'to take pride in' [CEV, REB], 'to be proud of' [NLT], 'to brag' [NTC; GW, NCV, NIV]. See this word also at 2:17
  b. ἐν with dative object (LN 90.23): 'in' [BECNT, HNTC, ICC2, LN, NICNT, WBC; CEV, NASB, NET, NRSV, REB], 'about' [LN; GW, NCV, NIV, TEV], 'of' [AB; KJV], 'of knowing' [NLT], 'to' [NET, NIV, NRSV], 'with respect to, with reference to, concerning' [LN].
  c. νόμος (LN 33.55): 'the law' [AB, BECNT, HNTC, ICC2, NICNT, NTC, WBC; KJV, NASB, NET, NIV, NLT, NRSV, REB], 'the Law' [CEV, NASB], 'God's law' [NCV, TEV], 'the laws in Moses' teachings' [GW]. See this word in 2:17.
QUESTION—Is Paul condemning any boasting in the law?
  Boasting in the law would be legitimate if the Jews consistently kept the law, but their violations of it show their boast in it to be meaningless [AB, BECNT, NICNT]. To boast of the law as a revelation of God's will is right, but to do so in order to obligate God to oneself or as a basis for having a condescending attitude towards others is wrong [AB, ICC2]. The Jew may boast in the law as a mark of God's favor, but this is open to criticism when this boast becomes reason to boast over those who don't have it [WBC]. It is obedience to the law that honors God, not boasting in it [NICNT].

by[a] the transgression[b] of-the law you-dishonor[c] God./do-you dishonor[c] God?
LEXICON—a. διά with genitive object (LN 89.76): 'by' [AB, HNTC, ICC2, LN; GW, NCV, NET, NIV, NLT, NRSV, REB, TEV], 'through' [BECNT, LN, NICNT, WBC; KJV, NASB], 'by means of' [LN], not explicit [CEV].
  b. παράβασις (LN **36.28**) (BAGD p. 611): 'transgression' [AB, BAGD, BECNT, LN, NICNT, WBC], 'disobedience' [LN], 'violation (of the law)' [BAGD]. This noun is translated as a participle: 'overstepping' [BAGD], 'breaking' [KJV, NASB, NCV, NIV, NLT, NRSV, REB, TEV], 'transgressing' [HNTC, ICC2, **LN**; NET], 'ignoring' [GW]; as a verb 'to disobey' [CEV]. It is a transgression of a revealed law or commandment [ICC2, NICNT].
  c. pres. act. indic. of ἀτιμάζω (LN 87.74) (BAGD p. 120): 'to dishonor' [AB, BAGD, BECNT, HNTC, ICC2, NICNT, WBC; all versions except CEV, NCV, TEV], 'to bring shame to/on (God)' [CEV, NCV, TEV], 'to cause to be dishonored' [LN], 'to insult' [BAGD].
QUESTION—Should this clause be considered a question or a statement?
  1. It is a statement [AB, BECNT, GNT, HNTC, ICC1, ICC2, Mu, NICNT, WBC; CEV, NCV, NET, NLT, REB]: you dishonor God. This may be

taken as a statement that sums up the position he has now reached [AB, BECNT, HNTC, ICC1, ICC2, Mu, WBC]. It provides the explicit conclusion to what has been implied in preceding verses [WBC]. It offers a decisive categorical answer to the four previous questions [Mu].
2. It is a question [LN (36.28), Mor, NAC, NTC, SSA, St; GW, KJV, NASB, NIV, NRSV, TEV]: do you dishonor God? This rhetorical question, like the preceding four, is used to make a statement [SSA].

2:24 For[a] the name[b] of God is-blasphemed[c] among[d] the Gentiles[e] because-of[f] you,

LEXICON—a. γάρ (LN 89.23) (BAGD 1.b. p. 151, 1.e. p. 152, 4. p. 152): 'for' [BAGD (1.b., 1.e.), BECNT, HNTC, ICC2, NICNT, WBC; KJV, NASB, NET, NRSV], 'indeed' [BAGD (4.)], not explicit [AB, NTC; CEV, GW, NCV, NIV, NLT, REB, TEV].
  b. ὄνομα (LN 33.126, 33.265) (BAGD I.4.b. p. 571): 'name' [AB, BAGD, BECNT, HNTC, ICC2, LN (33.126), NICNT, WBC; all versions except CEV, TEV], 'reputation' [LN (33.265)], not explicit [CEV, TEV].
  c. pres. pass. indic. of βλασφημέω (LN **33.400**) (BAGD 2.b.β. p. 142): 'to be blasphemed' [AB, BAGD, HNTC, LN, NICNT, WBC; KJV, NET, NIV, NLT, NRSV], 'to be reviled' [BECNT, **LN**], 'to be defamed' [LN], 'to be profaned' [REB], 'to have insulting things said about' [CEV], 'to be spoken evil of' [TEV].
  d. ἐν with dative object (LN 83.9, 90.6): 'among' [AB, BECNT, HNTC, ICC2, LN (83.9), NICNT, WBC; all versions except CEV, NLT, TEV], 'by' [LN (90.6)], not explicit [CEV, NLT, TEV].
  e. ἔθνος (LN 11.37): 'nation' [LN]. This plural noun is translated 'the Gentiles' [AB, BECNT, HNTC, ICC2, WBC; all versions except CEV, GW, NLT], 'nations' [NICNT; GW], 'foreigners' [CEV], 'the world' [NLT], 'heathen, pagans' [LN].
  f. διά with accusative object (LN 90.44) (BAGD B.II.1. p. 181): 'because of' [AB, BAGD, LN, NICNT; GW, NASB, NET, NIV, NLT, NRSV, REB, TEV], 'on account of' [BAGD, BECNT, LN], 'on your account' [HNTC, ICC2], 'through' [WBC; KJV]. This entire clause is translated 'You have made foreigners say insulting things about God' [CEV].

QUESTION—What relationship is indicated by γάρ 'for'?
  In indicates the ground for his preceding statement [BECNT, HNTC, Ho, ICC1, ICC2, Mor, NICNT, SSA, WBC]: it is true that you dishonor God because his name is blasphemed because of you.

just-as[a] **it-has-been-written.**[b]

LEXICON—a. καθώς (LN 64.14) (BAGD 1. p. 391) 'just as' [BAGD, BECNT, LN; CEV, NASB, NCV, NET], 'as' [AB, BAGD, HNTC, WBC; GW, KJV, NIV, NRSV, REB], 'even as' [ICC2, NICNT], not explicit [TEV].
  b. perf. pass. indic. of γράφω (LN 33.61) (BAGD 2.c. p. 166): 'to be written' [AB, BAGD, BECNT, LN, NICNT, WBC; KJV, NASB, NET, NIV, NRSV], 'to stand written' [AB]. This verb is also translated as a

phrase: 'Scripture says' [HNTC, ICC2; GW, REB, TEV], 'the Scripture says' [TEV], 'the Scriptures say' [NCV, NLT], 'the Scriptures tell us' [CEV].

QUESTION—What is the source of the quotation used here?

Note that there is a considerable amount of overlap possible between the positions listed below, and one does not rule out the other.

1. This is probably a quotation of Isaiah 52:5 [AB, BECNT, HNTC, ICC1, ICC2, Mu, NAC, NICNT, NTC, TH, TNTC]. It is an adaptation of the last part of Isaiah 52:5 from the LXX [HNTC, ICC1, ICC2, Mu, TH]. He is quoting from the LXX, which differs somewhat from the MT (Masoretic Hebrew text) [AB, NICNT]. In the MT, God's name is dishonored by those who scoff at the miserable lot of God's people in exile, and the LXX adds δι' ὑμᾶς 'because of you', meaning because of what happened to the people of Israel; here Paul applies the words 'because of you' to the Jewish transgression of boasting in the Mosaic law while continuing to disobey it, which then results in God's name being despised by those who don't know him [AB]. Although in Isaiah the blaspheming of God's name comes through the oppression of Israel by foreign powers, Paul makes an ironic switch in the application by saying here that the blasphemy comes via the disobedient lives of God's people, for it is the people of Israel, not the Gentiles, who are responsible for dishonoring God [NICNT]. The scandal that dishonored God came about because of Israel's inconsistency [ICC1]. Just as the past sins of the Jews were the cause of their captivity, so too their more current sins led to Gentiles speaking evil of God [Ho]. The misfortunes of the Jews in exile caused Gentiles to dishonor God by presuming he was unable to help his people, but here it is the misconduct of the Jews that causes the dishonor to the name of God [ICC2, NAC, TNTC]. Seen in its larger context, the Isaiah passage is quite applicable to this situation, because although the dishonoring of God's name occurred because of the oppression Israel suffered, the oppression they suffered was due to their own sin; Paul is saying here that the Jews' sin dishonors God and leads to judgment [BECNT]. While Ezekiel 36:17–23 is conceptually closer to what Paul is saying, the Isaiah passage is linguistically closer; Paul has simply used the wording of Isaiah to express his point [NICNT]. There is tragic irony in the fact that the Jewish nation became the instruments for provoking blasphemy instead of leading other nations in true worship [Mu]. In both the OT situation and in Paul's day, the nation failed to be the light for others in darkness, with the result that in both situations God's name was mocked among the pagans [NTC].

2. This is perhaps a combination of both Isaiah 52:5 and Ezekiel 36:17–23 [Gdt, Ho, Mor, SSA, St, WBC]. Though there are minor differences, the language is here close to that found in Isaiah, but is also resembles Ezek 36:20, 23 in that the thought of this context is closer to the Ezekiel passage [Gdt, Mor]. Paul probably has both Isaiah 52:5 and Ezekiel 36:22 in mind, since in both passages God's name is mocked because his people

have been defeated and enslaved; likewise in this passage, moral defeat brings discredit on God's name [St]. While this is a quote of Isaiah 52:5, Paul probably also has in mind Ezekiel 36:17–23, which is a clearer condemnation and allows him to lend a sharper, more accusatory tone to the Isaiah passage. In those passages it was Israel's sin which resulted in subjugation to pagans and caused God to be dishonored by those nations, and here Jewish transgression of the law results in dishonor to God [WBC].

DISCOURSE UNIT: 2:25–29 [AB, Ho, ICC1, Mor, NICNT, WBC]. The topic is that circumcision does not make the real Jew [AB], no exemption from judgment based on circumcision [Ho], limitations of the covenant circumcision [NICNT], profession and reality regarding the circumcision [ICC1], circumcision no guarantee [WBC], the inward and the outward [Mor].

2:25 For[a] circumcision[b] indeed/on-the-one-hand[c] is-of-value[d] if you-do[e] (the) law;

LEXICON—a. γάρ (LN 89.23) (BAGD 1.b. p. 151) (BAGD 4 p. 152): 'for' [BAGD (1.b.), BECNT, LN, NICNT, WBC; KJV, NASB, NET], 'because' [LN], 'to be sure, indeed' [BAGD (4.)], not explicit [AB, HNTC, NTC; CEV, GW, NCV, NIV, NLT, NRSV, REB, TEV].
  b. περιτομή (LN 53.51) (BAGD 2. p. 652): 'circumcision' [AB, BAGD, BECNT, HNTC, ICC2, LN, NICNT, NTC, WBC; all versions except CEV, NLT], 'the Jewish ceremony of circumcision' [NLT]. This noun is translated as a participial phrase: 'being circumcised' [CEV].
  c. μέν (LN 91.6, 91.3, 89.136) (BAGD p. 502): 'indeed' [AB, LN (91.6), NTC; NASB, NRSV], 'then' [LN (91.6)], 'and, so' [LN (91.3)], 'verily' [KJV], not explicit [WBC; CEV, GW, NCV, NET, NIV, NLT, REB, TEV]. The word is a weak affirmative particle [BAGD]. It is also possible that μέν functions together with other particles in the sentence; either with δέ 'but', or with γάρ 'for', or even together with both of these (μέν γάρ...δέ). See LN 89.136 and the next section below for this discussion. The phrase μέν γάρ is translated 'for example' [GW], 'this is what I mean' [HNTC].
  d. pres. act. indic. of ὠφελέω (LN 35.2, 68.33) (BAGD 2.b. p. 900): 'to have value' [AB; NET, NIV, REB], 'to be of value' [NASB, NRSV, TEV], 'to be valuable' [GW], 'to be of benefit' [BAGD, WBC], 'to profit' [BECNT, NTC; KJV], 'to be profitable' [HNTC, ICC2], 'to be of profit' [NICNT], 'to be worthwhile' [CEV], 'to be worth something' [NLT], 'to have meaning' [NCV], 'to be of use' [BAGD], 'to accomplish something (of value)' [BAGD, LN (68.33)].
  e. pres. act. subj. of πράσσω (LN 42.8) (BAGD 1.a. p. 698): 'to do' [BAGD, LN], 'to practice' [BECNT, HNTC, ICC2, NICNT, WBC; NASB, NET], 'to put into practice' [NTC], 'to observe' [AB, BAGD; NIV], 'to obey' [CEV, NLT, NRSV, TEV], 'to keep' [KJV, REB], 'to follow' [GW, NCV], 'to carry out' [LN].

ROMANS 2:25

QUESTION—What relationship is indicated by γάρ 'for'?
It relates this paragraph to an implied proposition, which is the Jewish belief that circumcision functions as a protection from the wrath God because it is the sign of being in a special covenant relationship with him [BECNT]. This indicates the connection with 2:25–29 with what precedes, which is to meet an objection based on one of the main grounds of Jewish confidence, which was circumcision [ICC2]. It refers this verse to the implied proposition that the Jew was indeed exposed to condemnation because circumcision is valuable only on the condition that one keeps the law [Ho]. The preposition relates this whole paragraph to an implied objection from Jews, which is that if circumcision marks them as belonging to God's chosen people, how can it be suggested that they will be treated the same as Gentiles and be in danger of experiencing God's wrath? [NICNT].

QUESTION—What is the value of circumcision if one obeys the law?
1. The profit in question is salvation [BECNT, NICNT]; Paul is arguing against the idea, held by many Jews, that circumcision was a guarantee of salvation [AB, Gdt, Ho, ICC2, Mor, NAC, NICNT, NTC, St, WBC]. The presumed value of circumcision, which Paul is contesting, is its ability to rescue from the tyranny of sin and from God's judgment [NICNT]. Paul is arguing that since the new covenant has arrived, salvation cannot be gained under the old covenant except by perfect obedience on the part of those who desire to live under it, because the death of Christ has made the old sacrificial system invalid [BECNT]. Circumcision admitted one to membership in the covenant people of God, but only benefited if the person lived like a member of the covenant people [Mor].
2. The value of circumcision is that it is a sign and seal of the covenant of grace, based on faith, that God established with Abraham and with any of his descendents who also had faith as Abraham did [Ho]. Circumcision was relevant only within the context of this covenant of grace [Mu]. Paul does not doubt the value of circumcision as appointed by God as a token of the covenant with him for the Jew who obeys the law [ICC2]. Circumcision points to a relation with God that is based not on legal observance but on faith [HNTC, SSA].

QUESTION—What is meant by ἐὰν νόμον πράσσῃς 'if you do the law', and is Paul suggesting that this is possible?
1. This means to have a right relationship with God through faith, to which the law points [HNTC, Ho, ICC2, Mu]. In Paul's view the circumstances of the new age call for a practice of the law that need not include the outward rite of circumcision [WBC]. Circumcision was the sign of the covenant of grace and promise to Abraham, so practicing the law cannot refer to a perfect fulfillment of the law in the legalistic sense, but rather to fulfilling the obligations and conditions of faith and obedience that belong to the covenant of grace [Mu]. To those Jews who had the faith of Abraham and kept the covenant of faith God established with him, circumcision was profitable as a sign and seal of that covenant

relationship; however, it had no inherent or magical efficacy for those who were destitute of the covenant of Abraham [Ho]. He is not referring to fulfilling all the law's demands perfectly, but to a genuine faith in God that is expressed in obedience [ICC2]. For Paul, doing what the law requires is not a matter of carrying out all the details of what is commanded in the Pentateuch, but fulfilling that relationship to God that the law is pointing toward, which is a matter of faith and not of legal obedience [HNTC].
2. This refers to obedience to and conformity with the letter of the law [AB, BECNT, NICNT, TNTC]. Being circumcised carried with it the obligation to keep the whole law, but if that was not done, the circumcised person has defaulted on his obligation and it brought no benefit [TNTC]. Throughout Romans Paul maintains a critical distinction between faith on the one hand, and works or doing the law on the other; this standard of perfect obedience to the law is one that no one can hope to meet, so circumcision alone is of no value to anyone for securing salvation. His purpose here is to convince the Jews that circumcision does not afford any automatic pardon from judgment [NICNT]. Paul argues that under a covenant of law, for which circumcision is a sign, only perfect obedience would qualify one for salvation, and that no one can meet that standard [BECNT]. Circumcision is a sign of the covenant, and the covenant requires obedience in order to be of benefit; here Paul insists that a combination of circumcision and obedience to the law are necessary for one to be a real Jew, since God cannot ignore transgressions of the law which break that covenant [AB].
3. Fulfilling the law meant living as a member of the covenant people; Paul frequently uses conditionals like this in his argumentation, but here it is very general and implies nothing as to whether the condition is fulfilled or not. [Mor].

but[a] if[b] you-are (a) transgressor[c] of-(the)-law,

LEXICON—a. δέ (LN 89.124, 89.94): 'but' [AB, BECNT, HNTC, ICC2, LN (89.124), NICNT, NTC, WBC; all versions except GW], 'on the other hand' [LN (89.124)]. There are various ways of seeing this particle in combination with others. One is to consider the construction μέν...δέ as marking items in contrast with one another, and having the meaning 'on the one hand...but on the other hand' [BAGD (1.a.α. p. 502), LN (89.136)], or as having the meaning 'indeed...but' [BAGD; NRSV], 'to be sure...but' [BAGD]. Another is to see the three particles as working together as the unit μέν γάρ...ἐάν δέ 'for indeed...but if' [BAGD (1.a.α. p. 502, 1.b. p. 151), ICC2], 'for...verily...but' [KJV]. The sentence would then be a concessive sentence, with the protasis introduced by μέν γάρ and the apodosis, with the contrast that is being emphasized, introduced by ἐάν δέ 'but if' [BAGD (1.a.α. p. 502)].

b. ἐάν (LN 89.65) (BAGD I.1.a. p. 211): 'if' [AB, BAGD, BECNT, HNTC, ICC2, LN, NICNT, WBC; all versions], 'only if' [NTC].

c. παραβάτης (LN **36.29**) (BAGD p. 612): 'transgressor' [AB, BAGD, BECNT, HNTC, ICC2, LN, NICNT, NTC, WBC; NASB], 'breaker' [KJV]. This noun is also translated as an active verb 'to break (the law)' [NCV, NET, NIV, NRSV, REB], 'to not obey' [CEV, NLT], 'to disobey' [TEV], 'to not follow (the laws)' [GW]. This word is a derivative of παραβαίνω 'to disobey, to break the law' (LN 36.28) and denotes a person who customarily breaks or disobeys the law [LN].

QUESTION—What is the function of the particle δέ 'but' in this verse?

It functions in correlation with the particle μέν in the first clause of the sentence and indicates a contrast between what is in the two clauses [ICC2, NICNT].

your circumcision has-become uncircumcision[a]

LEXICON—a. ἀκροβυστία (LN 11.52) (BAGD 2. p. 33): 'uncircumcision' [AB, BAGD, BECNT, HNTC, ICC2, NICNT, NTC, WBC; GW, KJV, NASB, NET, NRSV], 'being uncircumcised' [LN]. This noun is translated as a clause: 'people who are not circumcised' [CEV]. This entire clause is translated 'you have become as though you had not been circumcised' [NIV], 'your circumcision is as if it had never been' [NRSV], 'it is as if you were never circumcised' [NCV], 'you might as well never have been circumcised' [TEV] 'you are no better off than people who are not circumcised' [CEV], 'you are no better off than an uncircumcised Gentile' [NLT].

QUESTION—What is meant by ἡ περιτομή σου ἀκροβυστία γέγονεν 'your circumcision has become uncircumcision'?

Paul argues that transgressing the law has the effect of invalidating one's circumcision [AB, BECNT, HNTC, Ho, Mor, Mu, NAC, NICNT, St, TH, TNTC, WBC]. A Jew who transgresses the law has become equivalent to, or no better off than, an uncircumcised pagan [AB, NAC, NICNT, NTC, St]. In God's sight a Jewish person who did not keep the law was unsaved and not a part of God's people, and in that sense like the uncircumcised [BECNT]. Without obedience to the law, a Jewish person might as well never have been circumcised [TH]. There is an implied comparison in that the Jews considered circumcision to make them acceptable to God, thus the point of similarity is being 'useless' or 'no better than', the sense then being 'your circumcision is no better than uncircumcision' [SSA]. Transgression of the law by a circumcised Jew does not mean that his circumcision is annulled in God's sight, but that in heart he has become uncircumcised; that is, his heart is far from God and his life contradicts his membership in the covenant people, with the result that he is in a negative position relative to God's purposes and outside that 'Israel within Israel' referred to later in 9:6 [ICC2]. Circumcision alone cannot save those who are destitute of the faith Abraham had, since it is a sign and seal of a covenant relationship that is based on such faith, and it alone cannot prevent a transgressor from being treated as a transgressor, and as someone who had never been circumcised [Ho]. Circumcision had meaning only within the context of the covenant of promise and grace, a covenant which is fulfilled through faith and obedience, and not in the context of law and works in opposition to grace, so when these obligations of the covenant of grace, of which circumcision was a symbol, were violated or neglected, circumcision was meaningless [Mu].

2:26 **If therefore**[a] **the uncircumcision**[b] **keeps**[c] **the requirements**[d] **of-the law,**
LEXICON—a. οὖν (LN 89.50): 'therefore' [BECNT, LN, NTC; KJV, NASB, NET], 'then' [ICC2, LN, NICNT, WBC], 'so' [LN; GW, NRSV], 'in fact' [CEV], 'equally' [REB], 'this is what I mean' [HNTC], 'accordingly, consequently' [LN], not explicit [AB; GW, NCV, NIV, NLT, TEV].
  b. ἀκροβυστία (LN 11.53) (BAGD 2. p. 33): 'uncircumcision' [BAGD; KJV], 'uncircumcised person' [AB, HNTC, ICC2, LN, NTC, WBC; NET, NRSV, REB], 'uncircumcised man' [NASB], 'uncircumcised Gentile' [BECNT; TEV], 'person who is uncircumcised' [NICNT; NIV, NRSV], 'the Gentile, who is not circumcised' [TEV], 'the Gentiles' [LN; NLT], 'a man' [GW], 'people who are not Jews are not circumcised' [NCV].
  c. pres. act. subj. of φυλάσσω (LN 36.19) (BAGD 1.f. p. 868): 'to keep' [AB, BAGD, BECNT, HNTC, NTC, WBC; KJV, NASB, NET, NIV, NRSV, REB], 'to obey' [LN; CEV, NLT, TEV], 'to observe' [BAGD, ICC2], 'to follow' [BAGD], 'to guard' [NICNT], 'to do' [GW, NCV], not explicit [CEV].
  d. δικαίωμα (LN 33.334) (BAGD 1. p. 198): 'requirements' [BAGD, HNTC, ICC2, LN, NTC, WBC; NASB, NIV, NRSV], 'righteous requirements' [HNTC, ICC2; NET], 'regulations' [BAGD, LN], 'commandments' [BAGD], 'commands' [TEV], 'precepts' [AB; REB], 'ordinances' [BECNT, NTC], 'righteousness' [KJV], 'just decrees' [NICNT], 'what Moses' teachings demand' [GW], 'what the law says' [NCV], not explicit [CEV, NLT].
QUESTION—Who are 'the uncircumcision' in this clause and in what sense do they keep the law?
  1. Paul is referring to Gentile Christians who in some sense keep the law and are considered righteous [BECNT, Gdt, HNTC, ICC2, Mor, Mu, WBC]. The assertion of this verse and of 2:29, that these persons keep the requirements of the law refers to a level of fulfillment of the law that only Christians, by the enabling of the Spirit, could hope to attain [BECNT, Gdt]. These are converted Gentiles who exercise the faith and obedience which is the point of the law [Mu]. They meet the demands of the law in a qualitative sense by faith and life, though not in terms of all the ritual requirements [WBC]. These are uncircumcised Gentiles who have faith, and who thus are doing what the law requires in order to be righteous with God since this faith is what the eschatological activity of God in Christ points to; the result is that outward circumcision is irrelevant and God

treats them as circumcised and as full members of his people [HNTC]. This refers to Gentile Christians who exhibit a grateful and humble faith in God and whose lives are turned in the direction of obedience to him, with the result being that God considers them to be members of the people of Israel. Paul is not suggesting a perfect fulfillment of the law, which only Christ could accomplish [ICC2]. While this may well refer to Gentile Christians, Paul's statement is broad enough to include people such as Cornelius. Paul is not saying that these Gentiles merit salvation, but that by responding in faith and love to what God has made known that he wants of people, which is what real circumcision means, they are considered to have kept the requirements of the law [Mor]. Paul does not depict the Christian as being under obligation to the specific requirements of the Mosaic law, and clearly does not hold that salvation can be gained by anyone on the basis of obeying the law, for Jews will face the same standard of judgment for disobedience as the Gentiles, despite the Jews' covenant privileges. Rather, the Gentile believer is under the 'law of Christ' [NICNT].
2. The statement is hypothetical and refers to uncircumcised Gentiles [Ho, NICNT]. Hypothetically if they kept the law, they would be justified; however he explicitly denies than anyone can do so and this statement is only meant to make the point that circumcision alone cannot be the grounds for justification or condemnation [Ho]. No one is granted salvation by obedience to the law, since no one perfectly keeps the law; however, under the new covenant there will be a different sense in which they actually can do the law, when by faith and by the indwelling Spirit of God they can meet God's demands and so come into a relationship with him [NICNT].
3. The statement is to be understood literally and refers to uncircumcised pagans [AB, NTC]. These are uncircumcised pagans who, in following their conscience, obey some of the prescriptions of the law and will stand in judgment against Jews who violated it [AB]. It refers to those already mentioned in 2:14 who, in some sense, keeps God's law [NTC].

will- not his uncircumcision -be-regarded[a] as[b] circumcision?

LEXICON—a. fut. pass. indic. of λογίζομαι (LN 31.1) (BAGD 1.b. p. 476): 'to be regarded' [BAGD, LN, NTC; NASB, NET, NIV, NRSV, TEV], 'to be looked upon' [BAGD], 'to be considered' [BAGD, LN, NICNT; GW], 'to reckon' [AB, BECNT, ICC2, WBC], 'to be counted' [HNTC; KJV, REB], 'to be as good as' [CEV], 'to be (as if)' [NCV]. This entire clause is translated 'won't God give them all the rights and honors of being his own people?' [NLT]. The passive of this verb points in Semitic fashion to God as agent [HNTC]. See this word in 2:3.

c. εἰς (LN 13.62) (BAGD 8.a.γ. p. 230): 'as' [AB, BECNT, HNTC, ICC2, NICNT, NTC, WBC; NASB, NET, NIV, NRSV, REB], 'as if' [NCV], 'for' [LN; KJV], 'as though he were' [TEV], not explicit [GW, NLT].

This prepositional phrase is the equivalent of a predicate nominative [BAGD]. The word marks a change of state [LN].

QUESTION—When will this regarding of one's uncircumcision as circumcision take place, and by whom will it be regarded?

1. The future tense of the verb is temporal and implies that it will be done at the last day, and its passive form would imply that God is the one who will judge [BECNT, Gdt, WBC].
2. The future tense of the verb is logical [HNTC, ICC2, NTC]. If an uncircumcised Gentile has faith God counts him a full member of his people [HNTC]. In God's sight an uncircumcised person who, at least in some sense, obeys the law, is equal to a circumcised person [NTC]. It is not only a reference to the final judgment since 11:17ff indicates that God already considers Gentile believers to be his people [ICC2].
3. Since it is only hypothetical it does not actually happen [Ho, NICNT], though now that a new stage in salvation history has begun there is a different sense in which it actually will occur, based on a new understanding of what the covenant is and requires [NICNT].

2:27 **and the uncircumcision by^a nature^b keeping^c the law**

LEXICON—a. ἐκ with genitive object (LN 89.3, 90.16): 'by' [AB, HNTC, ICC2, LN (90.16), NICNT; KJV], 'from' [BECNT, LN (89.3, 90.16)], not explicit [NTC, WBC; CEV, GW, NASB, NCV, NET, NIV, NLT, NRSV, REB, TEV].

b. φύσις (LN 58.8) (BAGD 1. p. 869): 'nature' [AB, BAGD, LN, NICNT; KJV], 'birth' [BECNT, ICC2], 'race' [HNTC], not explicit [CEV, GW, NLT]. The phrase 'by nature' is translated 'physically' [NASB, NET, NRSV, REB, TEV], 'naturally' [WBC], 'in their bodies' [NCV]. The phrase καὶ...ἡ ἐκ φύσεως ἀκροβυστία 'and the uncircumcision by nature' is translated 'everyone who...has never been circumcised' [CEV], 'the man who is by virtue of his birth an uncircumcised Gentile' [ICC2]. See this word at 2:14.

c. pres. act. participle of τελέω (LN **36.20**) (BAGD 2. p. 811): 'to keep' [AB, BAGD, LN, NTC; NASB, NET, NLT, NRSV], 'to fulfill' [BAGD, BECNT, HNTC, ICC2, WBC; KJV, REB], 'to carry out' [BAGD; GW], 'to obey' [**LN**; CEV, NCV, NIV, TEV], 'to do' [**LN**], 'to complete' [NICNT].

QUESTION—What does the phrase ἐκ φύσεως 'by nature' modify in this verse?

This phrase modifies 'uncircumcision' [AB, BECNT, HNTC, Ho, ICC1, Mu, NAC, NICNT, SSA, WBC]. This qualification implies a contrast based on what a person is by birth [BECNT, NICNT], which in this case is the Gentile versus the Jew [NICNT]. The phrase means those who have not been circumcised from the time of their birth [SSA].

QUESTION—What is meant by ἐκ φύσεως ἀκροβυστία the 'uncircumcision by nature'?
This refers to Gentiles [AB, BECNT, Gdt, HNTC, Ho, Mor, Mu, NAC, NICNT, NTC, St, TH, TNTC, WBC]. This implies a contrast between the Jews and Gentiles based on one's birth [ICC1, NICNT]. This is a Gentile who is physically uncircumcised [ICC2, TH, TNTC]. This means a person who in his natural condition is still an uncircumcised Gentile pagan, not Gentile Christians [AB]. The phrase means those who have not been circumcised from the time of their birth [SSA]. It refers to those who by race are uncircumcised [HNTC], who belong by birth to a people group that did not practice circumcision [NAC]. This simply refers to Gentiles who remain uncircumcised [Mu]. Paul is speaking of Gentile Christians who are not physically circumcised [WBC]

will-judge[a] you the-(one) with[b] (the) written-(code)[c] and circumcision (who are a) transgressor[d] of-(the)-law.

LEXICON—a. fut. act. indic. of κρίνω (LN 56.30) (BAGD 4.b.β. p. 452): 'to judge' [BAGD, BECNT, HNTC, ICC2, LN (30.108), NICNT, NTC, WBC; KJV, NASB, NET], 'to condemn' [AB, LN, NTC; CEV, GW, NIV, NRSV, TEV], 'to sit in judgment upon' [BAGD], 'to pass judgment on' [WBC; REB], 'to judge as guilty' [LN], 'to show (you are) guilty' [NCV]. This entire clause is translated 'will be much better off than you Jews who are circumcised and know so much about God's law, but don't obey it' [NLT]. See this word at 2:16.

b. διά with genitive object (LN 89.76) (BAGD A.III.1.c. p. 180): 'with' [AB, BAGD, LN, NTC], 'through' [LN (89.76), WBC], 'by' [KJV]. This word is translated as a phrase 'that have' [NRSV], 'having the advantages of' [BECNT]. It is translated as introducing a concessive clause: 'for all your observance of' [HNTC], 'for all your possession of' [ICC2], 'for all your written code and your circumcision' [REB], 'though having' [NICNT], 'even though you have' [CEV, NIV, TEV], 'though provided with the written code' [BAGD, NTC], 'in spite of the fact that you are circumcised and have Moses' teachings' [GW], 'despite having the advantages of the letter of the law' [BECNT], 'despite the written code' [NET], 'even though you have it written down' [TEV], '(you who) for all your observance of the letter' [HNTC], '(you) who for all your possession of Scripture' [ICC2]. It is translated as expressing means: '(who) by the letter' [KJV]; as expressing attendant circumstance: '(you) with your written code' [AB], 'that have the written code' [NRSV], '(you) know so much about God's law' [NLT]. See this word also at 2:23.

c. γράμμα (LN 33.50) (BAGD 2.c. p. 165): 'the written code' [AB, BAGD (A.III.1.c. p. 180), NTC; NET, NIV, NRSV, REB], 'letter' [BAGD, HNTC, LN, NICNT, WBC; KJV], 'what has been written' [LN], 'Scripture' [ICC2], 'God's law' [NLT], 'the letter of the law' [BECNT; NASB], 'the written law' [NCV], 'the Law' [CEV], 'Moses' teachings in writing' [GW]. This noun is also translated as a clause: 'you have it written down' [TEV].

d. παραβάτης: 'transgressor'. See this word at 2:25.

QUESTION—What relationship is indicated by διά 'with'?
1. The preposition denotes attendant circumstances [AB, BAGD, BECNT, Gdt, Ho, ICC1, ICC2, Mor, Mu, NAC; NLT, NRSV]: you, the transgressor of the law, having the written code and being circumcised. The situation in which the Jew is disobedient is that of one who has both the Scriptures and circumcision [HNTC]. This denotes the state or circumstances in which an act is accomplished, in this case the Jew who possesses both the letter of the law and circumcision [Gdt].
2. The preposition denotes concession [BECNT, HNTC, Ho, ICC2, Mor, NAC, NICNT, NTC, SSA, TH; CEV, NET, NIV, REB, TEV]: you, the transgressor of the law, although having the written code and being circumcised. Paul is not blaming the law or circumcision for the disobedience of Jews, rather he says they disobey despite having these advantages [BECNT, NICNT]. The word denotes attendant circumstance as well as concession [BECNT, Ho, ICC2, Mor, NAC, NTC].
3. The preposition has an instrumental meaning and the sense is that it is through means of the letter and circumcision that the transgression has taken place; that is, understanding the law only superficially, and focusing too much on the level of outward ritual acts, and seeing these as marking Israel's identity as distinct from other nations, was itself a breach of the law, since it prevents God's purposes in the law from being fulfilled [WBC].

QUESTION—What is meant by γράμμα 'written (code)'?
1. It refers to the law [AB, BECNT, Ho, NICNT, St, TH]. It means the Scriptures, the law of Moses [ICC2, SSA]. It is the law and the commandments contained in it [BECNT]. It is the law as embodied in the Scriptures and viewed as written [Mu]. Paul is emphasizing the concreteness of the Scripture as being written, visible and tangible, and is aware of the external nature of the Jews' possession of the Scriptures [ICC2]. It emphasizes the law's physical and external form, just as circumcision emphasizes the physical and external form of membership in the covenant [Mor]. It does not refer to legalism, but does emphasize the externality of the law [BECNT]. The term is neutral [NICNT], and does not imply criticism of the content of the law [BECNT]. It is the law as that which has been written down in letters [NICNT].
2. The word connotes making a distinction between outward form and deeper meaning, here having a negative connotation and referring to a superficial understanding of the law and circumcision as being only on the level of outward ritual [WBC].

QUESTION—Should the statement of this verse regarding Gentiles judging Jews be taken as a hypothetical situation or as a real one?
1. It should not be taken literally [BECNT, ICC2, Mu, NICNT, SSA, TH]. This should not be understood to mean that Gentiles will literally have the role of judges, but rather that their obedience will be evidence against the Jew of what they could and ought to have been [BECNT, ICC2, Mu, SSA, TH]. This does not mean that the Gentiles will themselves condemn the Jews, but that the fact that they have obeyed the commands of the Law will serve as a basis for the Jews being condemned [TH]. This is probably not to be taken literally for it is God who will actually do the condemning; their example will show that God is right in condemning [SSA]. Paul's intent here is to emphasize the equality of Jew and Gentile with respect to judgment [NICNT].
2. It should probably be taken literally, meaning that believing Gentiles will stand up in the judgment and condemn unbelieving Jews [AB, Gdt, Mor]. This context speaks of Gentile Christians condemning Jews by their fulfillment of the law; it would be a bitter thing for the Jews to hear that they will not only be judged like the Gentiles, but also by them [Gdt].

2:28 For not the (one) in (what is) visible[a] is (a) Jew

LEXICON—a. φανερός (LN **24.20**) (BAGD 2. p. 852): 'the open' [BAGD], 'evident' [**LN**], 'clearly' [LN]. The phrase ἐν τῷ φανερῷ 'in (what is) visible' is translated 'outwardly' [BAGD, BECNT, NICNT; KJV, NASB, NET, NIV, NRSV], 'outward' [HNTC, ICC2], 'outside' [NTC; TEV], 'that which can be seen' [**LN**], 'that which is external' [LN], 'externals' [REB], 'outwardly only' [AB], 'only outwardly' [NIV], 'one visibly marked as such' [WBC], 'because of his appearance' [GW], 'born of Jewish parents' [NLT], 'in his physical body' [NCV]. This entire verse is translated 'Just because you live like a Jew and are circumcised does not make you a real Jew' [CEV].

QUESTION—What relationship is indicated by γάρ 'for'?
It introduces the grounds for making the claim of 2:27 [Mu, NICNT, SSA]. It introduces the reason that circumcision avails so little [Ho]. It introduces grounds for his claim that circumcision does not guarantee salvation nor does the lack of it bar from salvation [NICNT]. This preposition links 2:28–29 with 2:25–27, confirming that there is no salvific value to circumcision or having the law, and also showing that Gentile Christians are in view here, since Paul emphasizes that what counts in belonging to the people of God is being circumcised in heart, not having an outward sign or an ethnic connection [BECNT].

QUESTION—What is meant by ἐν τῷ φανερῷ 'in (what is) visible'?
Paul's statement here is very condensed and grammatically elliptical [ICC1, ICC2], even ambiguous [ICC1, Mor]. It means outwardly, externally, and physically, that which can be detected visibly by others [AB, ICC1, Mor, Mu, NAC, St]. It refers to external actions such as the performance of rituals

[SSA], specifically the external rite of circumcision [Ho]. The ceremonial activities of Judaism have to do with the outward appearance [NAC]. This does not simply mean the circumcised Jew, but rather the Jew who externalizes his religion and considers his membership in the people of God as a privilege he can parade before the world, with his circumcision being a kind of visible proof of that membership [HNTC]. It refers to being Jewish only with reference to physical or biological descent [NTC]. It refers to natural descent from Abraham, having the privileges that relation affords, and the physical mark of circumcision [Mu]. In view of the contrast which exists in Romans 2:28–29 between ἐν τῷ φανερῷ 'in the open' and ἐν τῷ κρυπτῷ 'in secret', it is better to represent the contrast as 'that which can be seen' and 'that which cannot be seen' [LN (24.20)]. The basic contrast of these verses is 'outer/inner' and is between what can be physically seen and the inner transformation and changed heart that ultimately only God can see [NICNT]. This refers to circumcision as a visible mark in the flesh, in contrast to that which is inward, or in secret, what God knows of the hidden truth about a person's heart [WBC]. Paul is referring to one who is to all outward appearances a Jew as distinct from one who is inwardly a Jew in the special sense he goes on to define [ICC2].

nor (is) circumcision in (what is) visible[a] in flesh,[b]
LEXICON—a. φανερός (LN **24.20**) (BAGD 2. p. 852): 'the open' [BAGD], 'outward' [HNTC, ICC2, NICNT; KJV, NASB, NET, NIV], 'evident' [**LN**], 'external' [AB, NTC; NRSV]. This adjective is also translated as an adverb: 'outwardly' [BAGD], 'clearly' [LN], 'visibly' [WBC]; as a phrase 'an external mark' [REB], 'an outward matter' [BECNT], 'on the outside of' [NCV], 'merely outward' [NIV], 'something external' [NTC; NRSV]; as a clause 'that which is performed visibly' [WBC], 'that which can be seen' [**LN**], 'how (the body) looks' [GW], not explicit [TEV].
b. σάρξ (LN **8.63**) (BAGD 1. p. 743): 'flesh' [BAGD, LN], 'the flesh' [AB, BECNT, ICC2, NICNT, WBC; KJV, NASB, NET, REB], 'a physical thing' [TEV], 'the body' [GW, NCV]. This noun is also translated as an adjective: 'physical' [BAGD, NTC; NIV, NRSV], 'fleshly' [HNTC].

2:29 but[a] the (one) in[b] the secret[c] (place) (is a) Jew,
LEXICON—a. ἀλλά (LN 89.125) 'but' [BECNT, HNTC, ICC2, NICNT, NTC, WBC; CEV, KJV, NASB, NET, REB, TEV], 'rather' [AB; GW, NET, NRSV, TEV], 'no' [HNTC; NIV, NLT], not explicit [NCV, NLT, REB].
b. ἐν (LN 83.13): 'in' [AB, BECNT, LN (13.8, 83.13), NICNT, WBC], not explicit [HNTC, ICC2, NTC; GW, KJV, NASB, NCV, NET, NIV, NLT, NRSV, REB, TEV].
c. κρυπτός (LN **24.20**, **26.1**, 28.69) (BAGD 2.b. p. 454): 'secret' [AB, BECNT, HNTC, LN (28.69), NICNT], 'hidden' [LN (28.69)], 'inward' [ICC2]. The phrase ἐν τῷ κρυπτῷ 'in the secret place' is translated 'in secret' [AB, BAGD, BECNT], 'in a hidden place' [BAGD], 'in a hidden way' [WBC], 'that which cannot be seen' [**LN** (24.20)], 'inwardly'

[BAGD, **LN** (26.1), NTC; GW, KJV, NASB, NET, NIV, NRSV, REB], 'in the heart' [**LN** (26.1)], 'inside' [NCV], 'on the inside' [TEV]. The entire phrase ὁ ἐν τῷ κρυπτῷ Ἰουδαῖος 'the one in the secret place is a Jew' is translated, 'he is a Jew who is one inwardly' [**LN** (26.1); KJV], 'the Jew who is one inwardly' [BAGD], 'it is the inward Jew who is a Jew in the fullest sense' [ICC2]. This entire clause is translated 'To be a real Jew you must obey the Law' [CEV], 'a true Jew is one whose heart is right before God' [NLT].

QUESTION— What is meant by the phrase ὁ ἐν τῷ κρυπτῷ 'the one in the secret place'?

It means 'inwardly' [AB, Gdt, Ho, ICC2, Mu, NAC, NICNT, NTC, SSA, St, WBC], and is used adverbially [SSA]. This refers to the inward circumcision of the heart [AB, BECNT, Gdt, Ho, ICC2, TH, WBC], which was a well known concept in the OT and in Judaism [NAC, NICNT]. It is an idiom referring to the inner intellectual, emotional, and spiritual aspects of a person, in contrast to the purely physical aspects [LN (26.1)]. This refers to the transformation of the heart which ultimately only God can see, the inner reality of a person's heart relationship to God as contrasted with that which can only be seen outwardly [NICNT]. It speaks of the inner motivation of human actions [AB], the hiddenness of the real person, as opposed to the immediate perception of an onlooker [WBC]. This refers to what is in the recesses of one's heart as contrasted with external profession [Mu]. Authentic Jewishness is inward and spiritual [NAC].

and circumcision (is) of-heart[a] in[b] Spirit/spirit[c] not letter,[d]

LEXICON—a. καρδία (LN 26.3) (BAGD 1.b.δ. p. 404): 'heart' [AB, BAGD, BECNT, HNTC, ICC2, LN, NICNT, NTC, WBC; all versions], 'inner self' [LN]. The word generally refers to the center of one's inner life including thinking, feeling and volition, and here more specifically of the moral life [BAGD]. It denotes the inner, psychological life of a person [LN]. The word is a dead figure here standing for one's inner being or nature [SSA]. See this word also at 2:15.

b. ἐν (LN 13.8, 89.5, 83.13): 'in' [HNTC, LN (13.8, 89.5, 83.13), NICNT, WBC; KJV], 'with regard to' [LN (89.5)], 'of' [AB], 'by' [BECNT, NTC; NET, NIV], not explicit [GW, NRSV, REB]. The phrase ἐν πνεύματι 'in Spirit/spirit' is translated 'by the Spirit' [BECNT, NTC; NCV, NET, NIV], 'wrought by the Spirit' [ICC2], 'produced by God's Spirit' [NLT], 'the work of God's Spirit' [TEV], 'in the Spirit' [NICNT], 'in Spirit' [WBC], 'in the spirit' [KJV], 'is spiritual' [GW, NRSV, REB]. The phrase καρδίας ἐν πνεύματι 'of heart, in spirit' is translated 'something that happens deep in your heart' [CEV].

c. πνεῦμα (LN 12.18, 26.9) (BAGD 5.g.γ. p. 677): 'Spirit' [BECNT, ICC2, LN (12.18), NICNT, NTC, WBC; NCV, NET, NIV], 'God's Spirit' [NLT, TEV], 'spirit' [AB, BAGD, HNTC, LN (26.9), WBC; KJV, REB], 'inner being, spiritual nature' [LN (26.9)]. This noun is also translated as an adjective: 'spiritual' [NRSV].

d. γράμμα (LN 33.35, 33.50) (BAGD 2.c. p. 165): 'letter' [AB, BECNT, HNTC, LN (33.35), NICNT, WBC; KJV], 'writing' [BAGD, LN (33.50)]. This noun is translated as a phrase: 'the letter of the law' [ICC2], 'the written code' [NTC; NET, NIV], 'the written Law' [TEV], 'the written law' [NCV], 'a written rule' [GW], not explicit [NLT, NRSV, REB]. The phrase οὐ γράμματι 'not letter' is translated 'not of the letter' [AB], 'not the letter' [BECNT], 'not in letter' [NICNT, WBC], 'not in the letter' [KJV], 'not of the written Law' [TEV] 'not merely…the letter of the law' [ICC2], 'not by the written code' [NTC; NET, NIV], 'not literal' [NRSV, REB]. The phrase περιτομή…οὐ γράμματι 'circumcision…not letter' is translated 'true circumcision is not a cutting of the body' [NLT], 'circumcision is…not literal' [REB]. This entire clause is translated 'it is circumcision of the heart (wrought by the Spirit and not merely a matter of fulfillment of the letter of the law) which is circumcision in the fullest sense' [ICC2], 'circumcision is of the heart, in Spirit, not in letter' [WBC]. See this word also in 2:27.

QUESTION—What is meant by the phrase καὶ περιτομὴ καρδίας 'circumcision is of the heart'?

This means a change of heart brought about by the work of the Holy Spirit [BECNT, Ho, ICC2, Mu, NAC, NTC, SSA, St, TH, WBC]. It is an eschatological reality, one in which God writes his law on the heart and puts his spirit within, and from which obedience flows [BECNT]. This concept occurs regularly in the OT [AB, Mor, Mu, St, WBC]. It is having the motivation for all one's conduct purified [AB]. He is referring to the removal of evil from the heart [NTC], to the cutting away of the old sinful nature [NAC], to that which cleanses the heart [Gdt]. In OT terms this refers to the renewal and purification of the heart [Mu]. This refers here to man's humble response to God's gracious love and election as also in Deut. 10:16, and also to repentance, as in Jer. 4:4 [HNTC].

QUESTION—What is the meaning of the phrase ἐν πνεύματι 'in Spirit/spirit' in this verse?

1. The preposition ἐν 'in' signals agency, meaning that circumcision of the heart is done by the Holy Spirit [BECNT, Gdt, Ho, ICC2, Mu, NAC, NTC, SSA, St, TH, WBC; NET, NIV, NLT, TEV]. The OT prophesied and anticipates the gift of the Holy Spirit for the new age, who would circumcise the heart and make obedience to the law a reality [BECNT]. The Spirit is the force which transforms the heart and produces true inward purification [Gdt].
2. It means in the sphere of the Spirit of God [AB, NICNT]. It is through the work of the Spirit of God who alone is able to bring about a change of heart that could be accurately referred to as a circumcision of the heart [NICNT]. The old dispensation of the law stands in contrast to the new dispensation of the Spirit of God [AB].

3. Circumcision is something of the heart, it is spiritual as opposed to a written rule [GW], it is spiritual, not literal [NRSV, REB]. It is in the spirit as opposed to being in the letter [KJV]. The meaning here is probably general and has the sense 'in a spiritual way' [HNTC].

QUESTION—What is the meaning of the word γράμμα 'letter' in this verse?

Paul is referring to the written law [AB, BECNT, Ho, Mu, NAC, NTC, St], and the commandments contained in it [BECNT], the mechanical observances of the written code [NAC], the rituals required by the law [SSA], obedience to the letter or prescriptions of the law [Ho]. For Paul this refers to the law, in particular the Decalogue, and is always in antithesis to Spirit [AB]. Paul means the written code or letter of the law [NTC, St], the written Torah [WBC]. This refers to the written law; Paul is exposing the mistake of Jewish presumption and confidence in merely possessing the law as embodied in Scriptures [Mu]. In this context the externality of the law is emphasized [BECNT, St]. This refers to the outward rule of the law which does not change either the heart or the will of a person [Gdt]. The contrast is between the fulfillment of the letter of the law's requirements and a work of God's Spirit [ICC2].

QUESTION—What is the significance of the contrast between Spirit and letter made in this verse?

It refers to the difference between the old and new covenants [AB, BECNT, Mu, NICNT, St]. This contrast is an important salvation-historical one in that 'letter' refers to the past era where the Mosaic law played a central role, and 'Spirit' to the new era where the Spirit of God is given in eschatological fullness [BECNT, NICNT]. This sums up the different realities of the old and new dispensations; the former is governed by the written code as an extrinsic norm to be observed, and the new is an intrinsic principle reshaping human beings through the gift of God's Spirit [AB]. Although both the law and circumcision are advantages for the Jews, there is no ability without the Spirit to obey the law, whereas, with the Holy Spirit and the circumcision of the heart, obedience to the law is possible; Paul considered this eschatological promise to have become a reality evidenced by some Gentiles obeying the law through the power of the Spirit [BECNT]. Paul is summing up the difference between the old covenant of external law and the new covenant in the gift of the Holy Spirit [NTC, St]. What matters is not ritual observance, but being changed inwardly by God's Spirit [NAC, SSA]. The contrast Paul is making is between the work of the Holy Spirit and the impotence of the law as externally administered, or mere possession of the law in the Scriptures when seen as sufficient for salvation; this is to make clear the folly of Jewish presumption and confidence in possessing the law [Mu]. This should not be understood simply as referring to inwardness of religion, an attack on ritualism, or promoting true morality over legalism. Rather, Paul challenges the fact that the Judaism of his day had become too much identified with one ethnic group, and too much in terms of physical characteristics and rituals. He is saying that what circumcision, the law, and

Judaism are really about have now been realized through the work of the Spirit in the hearts of both Gentiles and Jews [WBC].

of-whom the praise[a] (is) not from[b] people[c] but from God.

LEXICON—a. ἔπαινος (LN 33.354) (BAGD 1.a.α, β., p. 281): 'praise' [AB, BAGD, BECNT, ICC2, LN, NICNT, NTC, WBC; all versions except REB], 'approval' [BAGD], 'recognition' [BAGD], 'commendation' [REB], 'due' [HNTC]. The phrase οὗ ὁ ἔπαινος 'of whom the praise' is translated 'whose praise' [KJV], 'his praise' [AB, WBC], 'the praise for such a Jew' [BECNT], 'he is a Jew whose due' [HNTC], 'this man's praise' [ICC2], 'that Jew has praise' [NICNT], 'such a person's praise' [NTC], 'such a man's praise' [NIV], 'such a person receives praise' [NRSV, TEV], 'this person's praise' [NET]. The phrase οὗ ὁ ἔπαινος οὐκ ἐξ ἀνθρώπων 'of whom the praise is not from people' is translated 'such a person receives praise...not from human beings' [TEV].

b. ἐκ (LN 90.16) (BAGD 3.c. p. 235): 'from' [AB, BAGD, BECNT, HNTC, ICC2, LN, NICNT, NTC, WBC; all versions except KJV], 'by' [LN], 'of' [KJV]. The word denotes origin [BAGD]. The word marks the source of an activity [LN].

c. ἄνθρωπος (LN 9.1): 'human being' [LN]. This plural noun is translated 'people' [BECNT, LN; GW, NCV, NET, NLT], 'human beings' [AB, NICNT], 'men' [HNTC, ICC2, WBC; KJV, NIV, REB], 'humans' [CEV], 'others' [NRSV], 'man' [NTC; TEV], 'men' [NASB]. This entire clause is translated, 'besides, you should want praise from God and not from humans' [CEV], 'whoever has that kind of change seeks praise from God, not from people' [NLT], 'his praise comes not from human beings, but from God' [AB], 'such a person receives his praise from God, not from man' [TEV], 'the praise for such a Jew is not from people but from God' [BECNT], 'he is a Jew whose due comes not from men but from God' [HNTC], 'he receives his commendation not from men but from God' [REB], 'that person's praise will come from God, not people' [GW].

QUESTION—What praise is being referred to in this verse?

There is a play on words here, since 'Jew' is derived from 'Judah' which is related to and derived from the Hebrew word for 'praise' [AB, BECNT, Gdt, HNTC, ICC1, ICC2, Mor, Mu, NICNT, NTC, SSA, St, TNTC, WBC]. This should be understood eschatologically, and is a reference to the praise with which God will honor his people on the last day [BECNT, ICC2, NICNT], in keeping with the focus on judgment throughout this entire chapter [NICNT]. The eschatological reward of eternal life from God results for those who by the power of the Spirit have circumcised hearts, and thus are enabled to be obedient to the moral norms of the law [BECNT]. Paul is referring to God who will recognize and praise that person who is a real Jew by virtue of a circumcised heart [AB]. It is God's approval [NAC, St]. The internal excellence of the Christian is seen and acknowledged by God [Ho].

DISCOURSE UNIT: 3:1–20 [GW]. The topic is everyone is a sinner.

ROMANS 3:1 205

DISCOURSE UNIT: 3:1–8 [AB, Gdt, HNTC, Ho, ICC1, Mu, NAC, NICNT, TNTC]. The topic is refuting Jewish objections [Ho], the advantage of the Jew [HNTC], the faithfulness of God [Mu, NAC], God's faithfulness and the judgment of Jews [NICNT], what then of God's faithfulness [WBC], objections answered [TNTC], an answer to Jewish objections [ICC1], Jewish prerogative is no exemption from judgment [Gdt], objections to judgment for Jews [AB], God's faithfulness [NIV], God remains faithful [NLT].

3:1 What then[a] (is) the advantage[b] of-the Jew

LEXICON—a. οὖν (LN 89.50): 'then' [AB, HNTC, ICC2, LN, NICNT, NTC, WBC; KJV, NIV, NLT, NRSV, REB, TEV], 'therefore' [BECNT, LN; NET], 'so then' [LN; GW, NASB], 'so' [NCV], not explicit [CEV].

b. περισσός (LN **65.46**) (BAGD 1. p. 651): 'advantage' [AB, BAGD, ICC2, NICNT, NTC, SSA, WBC; all versions except CEV, NCV], 'special advantage' [**LN**], 'benefit' [BECNT], 'greater benefit' [LN]. This clause is translated 'What good is it to be a Jew?' [CEV], 'What does the Jew possess which others have not' [HNTC], 'So, do Jews have anything that other people do not have?' [NCV].

QUESTION—What is the function of the question introduced by τί οὖν 'what then'?

Paul frequently uses this expression to raise questions that further clarify his arguments [NICNT]. Since in chapter 2 he has just argued that one can be a true Jew without an ethnic connection and be truly circumcised without the physical rite, he now poses the question that would logically arise about whether there is any advantage to being an ethnic Jew or physically circumcised [AB, BECNT, Gdt, Ho, ICC1, ICC2, Mu, NAC, NICNT, NTC, St, TNTC, WBC]. This is nothing less than a question as to the credibility of God and the veracity of the OT, since God chose the Jews and the OT contains his promises to them [HNTC, ICC2, Mor]. This introduces a conclusion that Paul's critics might have drawn, or a false charge that they might have made [SSA]. The phrase Τί οὖν is part of an inclusio that begins here and concludes in 3:9 [AB].

QUESTION—Who is it that is raising this question?

1. Paul is using the diatribe rhetorical style or a modified form of it, in which opposing views that an opponent might voice are raised in order to present a refutation of those arguments [AB, BECNT, HNTC, ICC1, St, TH, TNTC]. He is debating an imaginary Jewish opponent [AB, St]. The imaginary objector actually leads the argument forward [BECNT]. These arguments were suggested by actual debates Paul had engaged in [HNTC]. While they are drawn from his own experience in controversies with Jews and Jewish Christians, Paul is giving the substance of debates he has experienced within his own thoughts [ICC1]. Paul continues on with the diatribe style, but the debate becomes increasingly personal as he deals with hard questions that are relevant to his own faith [WBC]. Paul's

opponent here is Paul himself, and he is remembering attitudes he himself had in his days as an unconverted Pharisee [St, WBC].
2. Paul's approach differs somewhat from the diatribe style, and Paul is the one posing the questions to his readers [Gdt, Mor, NAC, NICNT]. Paul himself senses objections that would naturally be raised to what he is saying [NAC, NTC]. While he has been influenced by his debates with the Jews, his questions here are largely ones that have come from within himself [Mor]. The dialogue is really a debate between Paul the Jew and Paul the Christian [NICNT].

QUESTION—What is meant by περισσός 'advantage'?

It means to have an advantage over another person [AB, BECNT, Gdt, Ho, Mor, Mu, NAC, NICNT, SSA, St, TH, TNTC, WBC]. The Jewish advantage includes preeminence, privilege, and superiority [Ho, ICC2]. In this context there is very little difference of meaning between this word and 'value' in the next clause; Paul is basically raising the question of whether or not being Jewish or being circumcised really matters if what he has just said is true [Mor]. Israel's privileges and honors, which primarily consisted in being the custodians of God's oracles, also entailed duties and responsibilities [NTC]. The advantage of the Jew is real, since he is first in election and is instructed out of the law, but that advantage is also a terrible one, since he is also first in judgment [HNTC]. It is the privilege that the Jews had over the Gentiles [Gdt].

or what (is) the value[a] of the circumcision?[b]

LEXICON—a. ὠφέλεια (LN **65.41**) (BAGD p. 900): 'value' [AB, NTC, WBC; GW, NASB, NET, NIV, NLT, NRSV, REB, TEV], 'profit' [BECNT, HNTC, NICNT; KJV], 'benefit' [ICC2, LN], 'advantage' [**LN**], 'use' [BAGD], 'good' [CEV], '(anything) special' [NCV].

b. περιτομή (LN 53.51) (BAGD 2. p. 652): 'circumcision' [BECNT, HNTC, ICC2, LN, NICNT, NTC, WBC; KJV, NASB, NET, NIV, NRSV, REB], 'the state of having been circumcised' [BAGD], 'being circumcised' [SSA;, GW, NCV, TEV]. This noun is translated as a verb: 'to be circumcised' [CEV]; as a phrase: 'the Jewish ceremony of circumcision' [NLT].

QUESTION—What is intended by this question?

Paul is raising the question of whether or not circumcision provides any advantage with respect to salvation [AB, BECNT], whether it saves one from condemnation [Gdt], makes a difference on the day of judgment [NICNT, St], or makes one acceptable before God [SSA]. He is asking whether there is any gain to be had from being Jewish and having the sign of the covenant [AB, Mor, WBC]. He is asking what profit there is in observing all the Jewish ordinances if they were to be reduced to the level of other nations [HNTC]. He wanted to ensure that his comments in chapter 2 would not be misunderstood to mean that being Jewish brought only liability and disadvantage [Mu].

3:2 Much[a] in[b] every way.[c]

LEXICON—a. πολύ (LN 59.11, 78.3): 'much' [AB, BECNT, HNTC, ICC2, LN (59.11, 78.3), NICNT, NTC, WBC; KJV, NIV, NRSV, TEV], 'great' [LN (59.11, 78.3); REB], 'many (advantages)' [NLT]. This pronominal adjective is translated as a phrase: 'there are many' [NET], 'much indeed' [TEV], 'it is good' [CEV].

    b. κατά with accusative object (LN 89.8) (BAGD II.5.b.α. p. 407): 'in' [AB, BAGD, BECNT, HNTC, ICC2, NICNT, NTC, SSA, WBC; CEV, NIV, NRSV, REB, TEV], not explicit [KJV, NLT].

    c. τρόπος (LN 89.83) (BAGD 1. p. 827): 'way' [AB, BAGD, HNTC, ICC2, LN, NICNT, SSA, WBC; CEV, KJV, NIV, NRSV, REB, TEV], 'respect' [BAGD, BECNT, NTC]. The phrase κατὰ πάντα τρόπον is translated 'in every way' [BAGD, HNTC, ICC2, NICNT, WBC; NRSV, REB], 'actually there are many advantages' [NET], 'in a lot of ways' [CEV], 'there are all kinds of advantages' [GW], 'much, indeed, in every way' [TEV].

QUESTION—What is meant by the statement πολὺ κατὰ πάντα τρόπον 'much in every way'?

It means that the advantage relates to a significant number of matters [Gdt, NICNT]. While only one advantage is listed here, that of having been entrusted with God's words, there are others listed in 9:4–5 [HNTC, ICC1, Mu, NAC, NICNT, NTC, St, TH]. Because of the way the question is posed and following what he has said in chapter 2, one might conclude there would be no advantage at all [BECNT, Mor, NAC, TNTC], but Paul accepts the fact that the OT does witness to the election of Israel with its special covenant relation to God, and to the fact that this election entails various advantages, though a more thorough discussion of it does not come until chapters 9–11 [BECNT, TNTC]. God had chosen the Jews to be the guardians of his revelation and custodians of his plan of redemption, but Paul does not elaborate further about other advantages until chapter 9 [NAC]. This does not mean that Jews surpass Gentiles in advantages of every imaginable sort, but that the privilege and priority the Jew has is in every respect great and important [ICC2]. The advantage is many-sided, though he only mentions one aspect here [Mor]. It helps very much in everything [TH]. Since in this verse only one advantage is listed, this may be taken as hyperbole [SSA].

First[a] that/because[b] they-were-entrusted-with[c] the messages[d] of-God.

TEXT—Some manuscripts include γάρ 'for' at the beginning of this sentence. GNT includes this word in brackets but does not give it a rating. It is included only by BECNT, NRSV.

LEXICON—a. πρῶτος (LN 60.46, 65.52): 'first' [ICC2, LN (60.46)], 'most important' [LN (65.52); NCV], 'chiefly' [KJV]. This adjective is translated as a phrase: 'first of all' [AB, BECNT, NICNT, NTC, SSA;

CEV, GW, NASB, NET, NIV, NLT], 'in the first place' [HNTC, WBC; NRSV, REB, TEV].
- b. ὅτι (LN 90.21, 89.33): 'because' [LN (89.66); KJV], 'that' [ICC2, LN (90.21); NASB], not explicit [AB, BECNT, HNTC, NICNT, NTC, WBC; all versions except KJV, NASB].
- c. aorist pass. indic. of πιστεύω (LN **35.50**) (BAGD 3. p. 662): 'to be entrusted with' [AB, BAGD, BECNT, HNTC, ICC2, **LN,** NICNT, NTC, WBC; GW, NASB, NET, NIV, NLT, NRSV, REB], 'to have something committed to someone' [KJV]. This passive verb is translated in the active voice: 'to entrust to' [LN], 'God trusted...to (the Jews)' [TEV], 'God trusted (the Jews) with' [NCV]. This entire clause is translated 'First of all, God's messages were spoken to the Jews' [CEV].
- d. λόγια (LN 33.97) (BAGD p. 476): 'messages' [LN; CEV], 'oracles' [AB, BECNT, HNTC, ICC2, LN, NICNT, NTC, WBC; KJV, NASB, NET, NRSV, REB], 'sayings' [LN], 'words' [GW], 'teachings' [NCV]. This plural noun is translated as singular: 'message' [LN; TEV]; as a phrase: 'the very words' [NIV], 'the whole revelation of' [NLT].

QUESTION—What is the meaning of πρῶτον 'first'?
1. It means first in a list or series [AB, BECNT, HNTC, Ho, ICC1, ICC2, Mor, NAC, NICNT, SSA, St, TH, WBC]. This refers to the first item in a list, but Paul's thought is distracted and the list is reduced here to a single item, the advantage of having been entrusted with the Scriptures [BECNT, HNTC, ICC1, NAC]. It means 'first of all', but although Paul probably intended to give a longer list, he was likely distracted by a concern about the Jews' response to 'the oracles of God', and did not list other advantages at this point [NICNT]. Paul does not go beyond stating the supreme privilege of having been entrusted with God's revelation to mankind [Mor]. Paul does list other privileges at 9:4–5 [AB, HNTC, ICC1, ICC2, St, TH, WBC].
2. It means 'the most important thing' [Gdt, Mor, NTC, TNTC]. It means that Paul wished to single out the single most important advantage among others [Gdt, NTC], the advantage that was of first importance [TNTC]. The advantage Paul chooses to mention is of the first rank, leading all the others and from which all the others flow [Gdt].

QUESTION—Who are the referents of the pronoun 'they'?
1. Paul is referring to Jews generally [AB, BECNT, Gdt, HNTC, Ho, ICC1, ICC2, Mor, Mu, NAC, NTC, St, TH, TNTC, WBC].
2. Paul is referring specifically to unbelieving Jews [NICNT].
3. This refers to 'our Jewish ancestors' since it was not to the Jews of Paul's time that these were entrusted [SSA].

QUESTION—To what does the phrase λόγια τοῦ θεοῦ 'messages of God' refer?
1. This refers to the entire OT generally [AB, HNTC, Ho, Mor, Mu, NAC, NTC, St, TH, TNTC, WBC]. This is not to be limited either to the messianic promises or to the Mosaic Law, but refers in the broadest sense

to all of the OT [AB, Ho, Mor, NTC, St]. This means the entire special revelation given to Israel consisting not only of commandments but also of predictions and promises [NTC], the revelation of God's will and purposes [TNTC]. It is the deposit of divine knowledge that distinguished them from every other nation [Ho].
2. It refers to the OT as a whole, but with special reference to the promises [BECNT, Gdt, NICNT]. Though this is a comprehensive way of referring to the OT Scriptures, the promises of salvation for Israel are uppermost in Paul's mind, not simply the possession of the Scriptures [BECNT]. It refers primarily to God's promises, since that is what is in view here [SSA]. The word is used here of God's promises to the Jews [BAGD]. It may also refer to those privileges that Paul will elaborate on in 9:4–5 [NICNT].
3. Paul seems to be focusing on those utterances which are most unmistakably divine, which are the Law of Moses and the promises relating to the Messiah [ICC1].
4. It should be understood in the widest sense of God's self-revelation given to the Jews, both in the OT and through all the gospel events [ICC2].

3:3 For what? If some did-not-believe/were-unfaithful,^a
LEXICON—a. aorist act. indic. of ἀπιστέω (LN 31.39, 31.97) (BAGD 2. p. 85): 'to not believe' [LN (31.39, 31.97); CEV, KJV, NASB, NET], 'to refuse to believe' [LN (31.97)], 'to prove to be unbelieving' [HNTC], 'to not have faith' [CEV, NIV], 'to disbelieve' [LN (31.39)], 'to fail to respond with faith' [ICC2], 'to be unfaithful' [AB, BAGD, BECNT, NICNT, NTC, WBC; GW, NLT, NRSV, REB, TEV], 'to not be faithful' [NCV].
QUESTION—How should this verse be punctuated so as to clarify the questions being posed and the identity of the questioner?
1. The verse should be divided into two substantive questions, the first being 'What if some were unfaithful?', and the second being 'Will their unfaithfulness nullify the faithfulness of God?' [BECNT, NAC, NTC; CEV, GW, KJV, NCV, NIV, NLT, NRSV, REB, TEV].
2. The verse should be divided with one short question 'For what then?', followed by a longer substantive question: 'Though some were unfaithful, their unfaithfulness will not nullify the faithfulness of God will it?' [AB, Gdt, HNTC, Ho, ICC1, ICC2, Mu, NICNT, SSA, WBC; NASB, NET]. The larger question may be seen as that of Paul himself [AB, ICC2, NICNT]. Paul is probably the questioner here, as indicated by the fact that he uses μή 'not', indicating the expectation of a negative answer as in 3:2, and that he uses a third person plural instead of a first person plural such as would be expected with another Jewish objector [NICNT]. The entire verse may be taken as Paul's own question [ICC2].

QUESTION—What is meant by the use of τινες 'some' in the phrase 'some were unfaithful'?

Even though he says 'some', Paul has the majority of Jews in mind [BECNT, Ho, ICC2, Mu, NICNT]. This wording is perhaps partly motivated by Paul's desire to lessen the offense to Jews, [ICC2, NICNT], though as chapters 9–11 show, he regards most of them as not having responded appropriately to God's word [NICNT]. Though not a blanket condemnation of all Jews, this denotes the bulk of Paul's contemporaries [WBC]. 'Some' simply means not all of them, even though they are actually many [Gdt]. He seems to be referring to most Jews, but graciously and tactfully uses the term 'some' [NTC]; the proportion is not indicated [Gdt, NTC]. Paul may be thinking of the fact that only a remnant (9:27, 11:5) accepted Christ [AB, Mor]. Paul is careful to indicate that not all Jews are unbelieving and disobedient [Mu], but many were [SSA].

QUESTION—What is the intended meaning of the verb ἀπιστέω?

Note that there is a considerable amount of overlap possible between the positions listed below, and one does not rule out the other.

1. This means to be unfaithful [AB, BECNT, Ho, NICNT, NTC, SSA, TH, TNTC, WBC; GW, NLT, NRSV, REB, TEV]. In this context he is discussing how Israel has been unfaithful to the trust committed to them [Ho, NTC, SSA, TNTC]. Paul is contrasting the Jews, who were unfaithful to the covenant, with God, who was faithful in keeping his agreement [NTC, SSA, TH, WBC]. Because of their unfaithfulness, they are under the same sin and exposed to the same condemnation as the Gentiles [Ho]. In this context he is talking about unfaithfulness, although that does not exclude unbelief [WBC].

2. This means to lack faith, to not believe [Gdt, HNTC, ICC1, ICC2, Mu, St; CEV, KJV, NASB, NET, NIV]. Here the meaning is that the Jews have failed to believe the words of God entrusted to them, but it is also true that this unbelief is also a matter of unfaithfulness to the covenant [ICC2]. The main point of the context is Jewish disbelief in the OT promises and their fulfillment in Christ, but the concept of unbelief includes unfaithfulness, and even suggests it [ICC1]. This refers to the unbelief of the Jews in Paul's day as shown in their rejecting Jesus as Messiah and therefore also rejecting the oracles of God referred to in 3:2 [Mu].

3. This means both to refuse to believe and to be unfaithful [AB, BECNT, Mor, NAC]. The context strongly favors the sense that while God was faithful, the Jewish people were unfaithful to their trust, yet there is also the sense that they did not believe, and Paul may not have intended to distinguish between the two senses [Mor]. The Jews did not believe Jesus to be the fulfillment of the OT promises, nor were they faithful to their covenant obligations [NAC]. The unfaithfulness of the Jews to the covenant included their refusal to believe in Christ [BECNT].

(certainly) their unbelief/unfaithfulness[a] will- not -nullify[b] the faithfulness[c] of God?

LEXICON—a. ἀπιστία (LN **31.89**, 31.97) (BAGD 1. p. 85): 'unbelief' [HNTC, LN (31.97); KJV, NASB, NET], 'unfaithfulness' [BAGD, BECNT, LN (31.89), NICNT, NTC, WBC; GW], 'lack of faithfulness' [LN (**31.89**)], 'lack of faith' [ICC2; NIV], 'infidelity' [AB], 'faithlessness' [NRSV, REB], 'this' [TEV], 'that' [NCV]. This noun is translated as an active clause 'they broke their promises' [NLT], 'to not have faith' [CEV].

b. fut. act. indic. of καταργέω (LN 76.26, 13.163, 13.100) (BAGD 1.b. p. 417): 'to nullify' [AB, BAGD, BECNT, NICNT, NTC; NASB, NET, NIV, NRSV], 'to make or render ineffective' [BAGD, ICC2, LN; KJV], 'to invalidate, to abolish, or to cause not to function' [LN (76.26)], 'to put a stop to, or to cause to cease' [LN (13.163)], 'to put an end to, or cause to become nothing' [LN (13.100)], 'to make void' [HNTC], 'to break (his promises)' [NLT], 'to do away with' [WBC], 'to cancel' [GW, REB], 'to not be faithful' [TEV], not explicit [CEV]. The phrase 'nullify the faithfulness of God' is translated 'stop God from doing what he promised' [NCV].

c. πίστις (LN **31.88,** 33.289) (BAGD 1.a. p. 662): 'faithfulness' [BAGD, BECNT, HNTC, ICC2, **LN,** NICNT, NTC, WBC; GW, NASB, NET, NIV, NRSV, REB], 'faithful' [TEV], 'trustworthiness, or dependability' [LN], 'fidelity' [AB], 'faith' [KJV], not explicit [NLT]. This entire clause is translated 'But does this mean that God cannot be trusted' [CEV].

QUESTION—In relation to what have some Jews exhibited ἀπιστία 'unbelief/unfaithfulness'?

Note that there is a certain amount of overlap possible between the positions listed below, and one does not necessarily rule out the other.

1. This refers primarily to the Jews' failure to meet their covenant obligations [Ho, NICNT, NTC, SSA, TH, TNTC, WBC]. This refers to the Jews' unfaithfulness or infidelity to the covenant entrusted to them, and that they did not do what they had promised within that covenant [SSA]. The Jews failed to obey the law, which he has discussed in chapter 2, but they also failed to embrace Jesus, the Messiah promised by the Scriptures [NICNT]. Jewish unfaithfulness was now being expressed by their failure to embrace the fulfillment in the gospel of what God had promised them [WBC]. This refers to Jewish unfaithfulness to the responsibilities entrusted to them of accepting, obeying, honoring, and transmitting to others the special revelation that God had given to them [NTC].

2. This refers to Jewish unbelief in God's promises, including the failure of Jews to believe in Christ as fulfilling the OT promises about the Messiah [Gdt, ICC1, ICC2, Mor, Mu, St]. In the NT the word most often has the sense of unbelief or disbelief, and interpreting it this way here is strengthened by taking τὰ λόγια 'the messages' to refer to God's

promises [Gdt, ICC1, ICC2]. This is Jewish unbelief in God's word, that is, the whole OT [HNTC].
3. This includes both the Jewish failure to believe in Christ and their transgressions of the law [AB, BECNT, NAC, NICNT]. The emphasis here is on disobedience to the law [BECNT]. His statement refers to the whole history of Israel, not just to the unbelief of his contemporaries [AB].

QUESTION—What is meant by the phrase τὴν πίστιν τοῦ θεοῦ 'the faithfulness of God'?
1. This refers to God's faithfulness, particularly his commitment to bless his people according to the terms of the covenant [AB, ICC2, NICNT, TH, WBC]. It refers to God's trustworthiness or faithfulness in relation to his promises [HNTC, ICC1, SSA, St]. It is God's fidelity to his covenant people [AB]. This is God's unchanging faithfulness to his word, his truth, his faith-keeping in contrast with man's unfaithfulness [Mu]. This refers to God keeping his word [ICC1]. It refers to God's faithfulness to his promise of eschatological salvation for the Jews [BECNT, Gdt]. This expression foreshadows chapters 9–11 and complements several others: God being true (in 3:4), the righteousness of God (in 3:5), and the truth of God (in 3:7), all of which relate to God's faithfulness to his covenant promises [BECNT]. Paul has in mind the harmony between God's words and deeds, and in particular that God will bring about the final salvation of the Jews after their partial rejection of Christ as Messiah [Gdt]. The thought here is the continuity of God's purpose in his covenant commitment to Israel [WBC].
2. This refers to God's faithfulness both to his promises of blessings as well as to his threats to judge the wicked [Ho, Mor, NAC, NTC]. At this time the Jews did not question that God's faithfulness guaranteed his blessings, but they had forgotten that he will also punish disobedience [NAC]. Lack of fidelity among the Jews is no grounds for assuming a lack of fidelity on God's part, nor is his condemnation of sinful Jews inconsistent with his promises [Ho]. God is faithful to his promises as well as to his threats [NTC].

QUESTION—What is meant by the word καταργέω 'nullify'?
It means to nullify [BECNT, NICNT, NTC, SSA, St, TH], to render something ineffective or inoperative [AB, ICC2, Mor, WBC], to invalidate [Gdt, Ho] or render invalid [ICC1], to cancel something out [NAC], or to make something void [HNTC]. Here the sense is to nullify or to render something powerless, since he asserts that the unfaithfulness of Israel cannot nullify the faithfulness of God [NICNT]. It means God's truthfulness is not annulled by unbelief, but remains inviolate [Mu].

3:4 Never may-it-be!ᵃ

LEXICON—a. aorist mid. (deponent = act.) optative of γίνομαι (LN 13.107) (BAGD I.3.a. p. 158): 'to come to be' [LN], 'to occur or to happen' [LN].

The phrase μὴ γένοιτο 'never may it be!' is translated 'may it never be!' [NASB], 'certainly not' [AB, BECNT; REB, TEV], 'absolutely not' [NET], 'of course not' [HNTC; NLT], 'by no means' [NICNT, NTC; NRSV], 'not at all' [WBC; NIV], 'God forbid' [KJV], 'that would be unthinkable!' [GW], 'No!' [NCV], 'No, indeed!' [CEV].

QUESTION—What is the significance of this expression?

This is a formula of emphatic rejection [BECNT, Ho, ICC2, Mor, NAC, NICNT, NTC, WBC]. Paul frequently uses this phrase in Romans to strongly refute a false conclusion or inference he fears may be drawn from something he has just said [BECNT, ICC1]. It is an emphatic repudiation of the very idea that God might be unfaithful [Mor]. Paul asserts with this strong negative that God will never break his covenant [NAC, St, TH]. This is often used after a question, and the sense here is that it is unthinkable that Jewish unbelief could render the faithfulness of God ineffective [Gdt, ICC2, WBC]. This strong expression indicates the apostle's abhorrence of the idea posed [Mu]. It expresses denial and strong aversion [Ho].

But let- God -be true,[a] even-if/and every man[b] a liar,[c]

LEXICON—a. ἀληθής (LN 72.1) (BAGD 1. p. 36): 'true' [AB, HNTC, ICC2, LN, NICNT, NTC, WBC; KJV, NASB, NET, NIV, NLT, NRSV, REB, TEV], 'truthful, righteous' [BAGD]. This whole clause is translated 'God tells the truth' [CEV], 'God is honest' [GW], 'God will continue to be true' [NCV].

b. ἄνθρωπος (LN 9.1, 9.24): 'man' [HNTC, LN (9.24), WBC; KJV, NASB, NIV], 'person' [LN (9.1), NICNT, NTC; NCV], 'human being' [AB, BECNT, LN (9.1)], 'individual' [LN]. This singular noun is translated as plural: 'men' [ICC2; REB], 'everyone' [NRSV]; as a phrase: 'everyone else' [CEV, GW], 'everyone else in the world' [NLT], 'all mankind' [NET], 'all human beings' [TEV].

c. ψεύστης (LN 33.255) (BAGD p. 892): 'liar' [AB, BAGD, BECNT, HNTC, LN, NICNT, NTC, WBC; CEV, GW, KJV, NASB, NIV, NLT, NRSV]. This singular noun is translated as a plural: 'liars' [ICC2; NET, REB, TEV]; as an adjective 'false' [NCV].

QUESTION—What is the meaning of the word ἀληθής 'true' in this context?

God is completely reliable [Mor, SSA], and he will do what he has promised [ICC1, Mor, SSA, TH]. The OT speaks of God as being true in the sense of reliability or trustworthiness, so that God is true to his word [Mu, NICNT, WBC]. Here it means that God is true both to his promise to bless his people as well as true and reliable when he carries out judgment on those who are disobedient, just as he said he would [BECNT, NICNT, NTC]. This word often refers to God's faithfulness to his covenant relationship with Israel, and this reaffirms the thought of 3:3 [BECNT]. It has the sense of faithfulness and of fidelity to his promises [AB, HNTC, ICC2, WBC], though given the contrast with 'liar' the idea of truthfulness is not excluded [AB, ICC2, WBC]. God is to be recognized as true to his word and faithful to his righteous character [NAC]. This refers to the truth and fidelity of God to his promises as well as in his condemning of sin [Ho]. It speaks of God's veracity and reliability [Gdt]. This refers to the veracity of God in contrast to the falsehood of men [Gdt].

QUESTION—What is the meaning of the third person imperative form γινέσθω 'let be' in this clause?

1. The meaning can be paraphrased as 'let God be recognized as true' [Gdt, HNTC, Ho, ICC1, Mor, NAC, NTC, WBC]. Paul prays that full recognition will be given to the veracity and truthfulness of God [NTC]. Paul is speaking of what comes to be seen, or becomes apparent to our apprehending it, not that it is not already the case [Mor]. The verb often denotes the transition from something being to becoming apparent, and here has the sense 'to prove to be, or be seen to be' [ICC1]. The meaning is that the truth or veracity of God is revealed to and recognized by man more and more in history by the new effects it produces [Gdt].

2. This form is equivalent to an indicative statement meaning 'God is true' [AB, BECNT, ICC2, Mu, NICNT, SSA, St]. This form is often used in the NT without its dynamic meaning and is to be understood as 'God is true', or 'we confess that God is true', an understanding that is consistent with the meaning of the second half of the verse which affirms that in fact they already are liars, not that they will become liars [NICNT]. The verb should not be understood dynamically as if God at some time in the future will act to fulfill his promises, but confessionally with the sense 'he remains true' to his promises [BECNT]. God is true and remains so, regardless of how false men are [St]. The imperative is equivalent to an indicative, signaling intensity, meaning that God always does what he promises [SSA]. This forefronts the faithfulness of God and his inviolate truthfulness [Mu]. The meaning may be expressed as 'God will be true'; his fidelity will shine forth though all humans will appear before God as liars [AB].

QUESTION—Should the last clause be understood as concessive?

1. It should be understood as concessive [AB, BECNT, Gdt, HNTC, ICC1, Mor, Mu, NAC, NICNT, SSA, St]: God is to be seen as true, even if all men are to be viewed as liars. Not only does God remain faithful when some are unfaithful, he is found to be true even if every other person is proven unreliable [Mor, NICNT]. It is translated as concessive by CEV, NASB, NLT, NRSV, REB, TEV.

2. The clause is not concessive [ICC2, WBC]: God is true, and men are false. This statement is a general characterization of men when compared with God [ICC2]. It seems to be a quotation from Psalm 116.11 [WBC]. It is translated as a statement: 'and' [GW, NET, NIV], 'even when' [NCV]. It is translated as a contrast: 'but' [KJV].

QUESTION—What is the meaning of the word ψεύστης 'liar' in this context?

This is a general characterization of men, which stands in contrast to God's truthfulness [ICC2, TNTC]. It means that people are liars [AB, BECNT,

HNTC, NAC, NTC]. It emphasizes the contrast between God, who is true, reliable, and faithful, and humans, who are liars, unreliable, and unfaithful [ICC2, Mor, Mu, NICNT, St]. It speaks of being unfaithful and untrustworthy [NTC]. It means the inward bad faith by which the human heart resists the moral good that it knows and understands [Gdt]. It means that some are liars by virtue of their asserting that God's promises have not been fulfilled [ICC1].

just-as it-is-written,[a]
LEXICON—a. perf. pass. indic. of γράφω (LN 33.61) (BAGD 2.c. p. 166): 'to be written' [BAGD, BECNT, LN, NICNT, NTC, WBC; KJV, NASB, NET, NIV, NRSV]. This phrase is translated 'the Scriptures say (about God)' [CEV], 'as the Scriptures say' [NCV, NLT], 'Scripture says' [GW, TEV], 'for we read in Scripture' [REB].
QUESTION—What is the function of this clause?
This is Paul's customary introductory formula often used before OT quotations [BAGD, ICC1, ICC2, Mor, NICNT, SSA, WBC]. It is used to substantiate Paul's point regarding the reliability and consistency of God [NICNT]. This is a formula for introducing quotations [BAGD, ICC2]. This introduces the quotation from Ps. 51:4 that follows [AB, HNTC, ICC1, Mor, NICNT, NTC, TNTC, WBC].

That you-might-be-justified[a] **in**[b] **your words**[c]
LEXICON—a. aorist pass. subj. of δικαιόω (LN **88.16**) (BAGD 3.d. p. 198): 'to be justified' [LN, NICNT, WBC; KJV, NASB, NET, NRSV], 'to be shown to be right' [LN; NCV, TEV], 'to be proved to be right' [BAGD, HNTC, LN, NTC; NIV, NLT], 'to be proven to be true' [CEV], 'to be vindicated' [AB, BECNT; REB], 'to be acknowledged as righteous' [ICC2]. This passive verb is also translated actively: 'you hand down justice' [GW].
  b. ἐν with dative object (LN 67.33, 90.23, 89.5): 'in' [AB, BECNT, ICC2, LN (90.23, 89.5), NICNT, NTC, WBC; KJV, NASB, NET, NLT, NRSV], 'when' [HNTC, LN (67.33); GW, NCV, NIV, REB, TEV], 'concerning, with respect to, or with reference to' [LN (90.23)], 'in, about, or with regard to' [LN (89.5)], not explicit [CEV].
  c. λόγος (LN 33.98, 33.99) (BAGD 1.b.α. p. 478): 'word' [BAGD, BECNT, ICC2, LN (33.98), NICNT, NTC, WBC; CEV, NASB, NET, NRSV], 'statement, saying, or message' [LN (33.98)], 'speech' [AB, LN (33.99)], 'speaking' [LN (33.99)], 'sayings' [KJV]. This noun is translated as a verb: 'when thou speakest' [HNTC], 'when you speak' [GW, NCV, NIV, REB, TEV], 'what he says' [NLT], 'what you have said' [SSA].
QUESTION—What relationship is indicated by the phrase ὅπως ἂν 'that you might (be)'?
  1. It indicates purpose [BECNT, Gdt, ICC2, Mor, Mu, NICNT].
    1.1 It relates to what is stated in 3:4a, 'Let God be true' [BECNT, Gdt]. That is, God remains true, including being true to his judging

righteousness, so that he will ultimately triumph and be vindicated when he judges sin [BECNT, NICNT]. God has revealed his truth clearly enough that if people sin in spite of this knowledge, God would be pure in the matter and the guiltiness would clearly belong the sinner, and not to God [Gdt].

1.2 It relates to 3:3b and 3:4a. Paul is saying that human sinfulness will not disestablish God's justice, but rather vindicates and establishes it since God's judgments against sin are always just; and if that is the case, then human faithlessness will not invalidate God's faithfulness [Mu].

1.3 The purpose clause relates to 3:3; sin is confessed as being a sin against God, so that through the confession God might be acknowledged as just [ICC2, NTC].

2. It expresses result [ICC1]. Just as the result of the Psalmist's sin is that what God has said is established when he judges, so also God will be shown to have fulfilled his promises, even if people refuse to believe it [ICC1].

QUESTION—What words are being referred to by the phrase ἐν τοῖς λόγοις σου 'in your words'?

1. This refers to the judging righteousness of God, since God's faithfulness and truth cannot be limited to his saving righteousness alone [BECNT, NICNT]. God is shown to be faithful, right, and true to his word when he judges sins [Gdt, Mor, NAC, NICNT, NTC, St, WBC]. God is just when he judges [ICC2]. In the process of judging and condemning sinners God is proved or declared to be right by means of what he says; his words are the means [Mor]. It refers to God's judgment of sin both in this passage as well as in the OT passage [SSA]. God judgments of men for sin are always just [Mu]. God will be proven right when he speaks in judgment [NAC]. God will be acknowledged as righteous both in the warnings he has given and in the sentence he pronounces for sin, which in this context is against Israel for their rejection [Gdt].

2. This refers to God's promises, to what he has said [AB, ICC1]. It refers to the sayings or promises just mentioned earlier, and God will be pronounced righteous in his judgment of mankind [ICC1]. It refers to God's promise in Ps. 89:35 that he would not be false to David [AB].

3. This refers to any time God speaks [Ho, TH]. The meaning is that the truthfulness of God will be seen and acknowledged under all circumstances [Ho].

and you-will-prevail[a] in[b] your judging/being-judged.[c]

TEXT—Instead of the future indicative νικήσεις 'you will prevail' some manuscripts read the aorist subjunctive νικήσῃς 'you may prevail'. GNT does not deal with this variant. This verb is translated as indicative [SSA, WBC; CEV, NET, NLT, REB]; as subjunctive [AB, BAGD, BECNT, HNTC, ICC2, NICNT, NTC; KJV, NIV, NRSV, TEV].

LEXICON—a. fut. act. indic. of νικάω (LN 39.57) (BAGD 1.b. p. 539): 'to prevail' [BAGD, NTC; NASB, NET, NIV, NRSV], 'to conquer' [BAGD, LN], 'to win out' [AB], 'to triumph' [BECNT, NICNT], 'to be a victor or victorious over' [HNTC, LN], 'to win' [BAGD, SSA; NLT], 'to win (one's) case' [CEV, GW, NCV, REB, TEV], 'to overcome' [ICC2, WBC; KJV]. The word refers to prevailing or winning in a legal action [BAGD].
  b. ἐν with dative object (LN 67.33, 90.23): 'in' [LN (90.23), NTC; CEV, GW, NLT, NRSV], 'concerning, with respect to, or with reference to' [LN (90.23)], 'when' [AB, BECNT, HNTC, ICC2, LN (67.33), NICNT, SSA, WBC; KJV, NASB, NET, NIV, REB, TEV], not explicit [NCV].
  c. pres. pass. infin. of κρίνω (LN 30.108) (BAGD 6.b. p. 452): 'to be judged' [AB, BAGD, LN; KJV, NASB, NET], 'to be criticized, condemned, or have fault found (against one)' [BAGD], 'to be on trial' [WBC], 'to be tried' [TEV]. This passive verb form is translated as middle with an active voice meaning: 'you judge' [BECNT, NICNT; NIV], 'you contend' [ICC2], 'to prevail (in your judging)' [NRSV], 'to win the case' [REB, TEV], 'you enter into judgment' [HNTC]; as a participle: 'thy judging' [NTC], 'your judging' [NRSV]. The whole clause is translated 'you will win your case' [NCV], 'and in court you will win your case' [CEV], 'and he will win his case in court' [NLT], 'and you win your case in court' [GW].
QUESTION—Is κρίνεσθαι to be understood as passive or middle voice?
  1. The verb should be understood as a middle form with an active meaning, having the sense 'when you judge' [BECNT, NAC, NICNT, NTC, St, TNTC; NIV, NRSV]. Paul is referring to the judging righteousness of God, not his saving righteousness [BECNT]. God will be proven right when he judges and will win when the world goes on trial [NAC].
  2. It has a middle voice meaning, indicating when you have a case at law [Gdt, HNTC], or when you contend [ICC2].
  3. The verb should be understood as passive, having the sense 'when you are judged' [AB, BAGD, Ho, ICC1, WBC; KJV, NASB, TEV], or 'when people accuse you' [SSA]. Paul follows the passive of the LXX, but in either case the sentiment is the same, which is that God is acknowledged to be just [Ho]. Paul probably has in mind an accusation which might be raised against God's faithfulness given the fact of Israel's unbelief and rejection, so the best sense is 'that you may win when you have a case at law' [Gdt]. It means that God will always win out against anyone who accuses him [TH]. Paul sees that an indictment of the unfaithfulness of the Jews might carry with it an indictment of the God who remains faithful to them, but is convinced that God's covenant purpose and faithfulness will be vindicated in the final judgment [WBC]. The word in this context refers to unfavorable human judgment directed against God [BAGD].
QUESTION—What is the connection between this quote and the context?
  1. As in the OT passage, God is seen to be righteous in his judging and condemning sinners, since his punishment of sin is part of his faithfulness,

not a contradiction of it [Mor, NAC]. Sin against God only causes his righteousness to be shown more clearly, and since human sin does not nullify God's righteousness, human unfaithfulness will not nullify God's faithfulness [Mu]. Paul cites David's acknowledgement that God will be seen as just in every circumstance [Ho]. Paul cites the Psalmist to support his contention that God is always shown to be faithful to what he has said, and that even human sin will magnify God's uprightness [AB]. Consistent with the OT passage Paul indicates that against the background of human sin, the righteousness of God in judging stands out even more clearly [NTC], and human unfaithfulness will cause God's faithfulness to stand out in bold relief [HNTC, NTC]. It speaks of God's righteousness in contrast to human sinfulness, but also of God's faithfulness in the face of grievous sin [ICC2]. God will be declared guiltless with respect to promises he has fulfilled, despite some people not believing that he has done so [ICC1]. The picture is one of God and man in court pleading against one another, a situation in which God will always be found to be right and where man's sin brings out God's righteousness and truth more clearly [HNTC].

2. Paul is showing that God's faithfulness to his word relates to both his promises and his judgments [BECNT, NICNT]. The truthfulness, reliability, and faithfulness of God are not confined to his saving righteousness since his promises also include his judgments of sin. Despite God's promises of salvation for the Jews, no individual can presume a guarantee of salvation, nor exclusion from judgment [BECNT, NICNT]. In 3:3 God's faithfulness is expressed more generally, and would likely be understood to mean his commitments to bless Israel, but in 3:4 Paul is showing that God's faithfulness must also be recognized in his judging sin as much as in fulfilling his promises of blessing, since his oracles include both [NICNT].

3:5 But if our unrighteousness[a] demonstrates[b] (the) righteousness[c] of-God, what shall-we-say?

LEXICON—a. ἀδικία (LN 88.21) (BAGD 2. p. 18): 'unrighteousness' [BAGD, BECNT, HNTC, ICC2, LN, NICNT, NTC, WBC; KJV, NASB, NET, NIV], 'wickedness' [AB, BAGD], 'wrongdoing' [TEV], 'what we do wrong' [GW, NCV], 'injustice' [NRSV, REB]. This singular noun is translated as a plural: 'evil deeds' [CEV], 'sins' [NLT].

b. pres. act. indic. of συνίστημι (LN 28.49) (BAGD I.1.c. p. 790): 'to demonstrate' [BAGD, BECNT, HNTC, LN, WBC; NASB, NET], 'to show' [BAGD, LN; CEV, GW, NCV], 'to bring out' [BAGD], 'to bring out more clearly' [NIV], 'to bring forth' [AB], 'to serve to confirm' [NRSV, REB], 'to serve to show up' [TEV], 'to serve a good purpose' [NLT], 'to show up' [ICC2], 'to commend' [NICNT; KJV], 'to confirm' [NTC].

c. δικαιοσύνη (LN 88.13) (BAGD 3. p. 197): 'righteousness' [BAGD, BECNT, HNTC, ICC2, LN, NICNT, NTC, WBC; KJV, NASB, NET, NIV], 'uprightness' [AB], 'justice' [NRSV, REB], 'goodness' [NLT]. This noun is translated as an adjective: 'how right God is' [CEV], 'God's doing right' [TEV], 'that God is fair' [GW], 'that God is right' [NCV].

QUESTION—What is meant by ἡ ἀδικία ἡμῶν 'our unrighteousness'?

1. This refers generally to human sinfulness [AB, Gdt, HNTC, Ho, ICC1, Mor, Mu, NTC, St, TH]. Human wickedness brings about the manifestation of God's uprightness [AB]. Paul imagines an objector who reasons that human wickedness of any sort can bring out God's righteousness more clearly [Mor]. It is wickedness, all that is the opposite of moral excellence [Ho]. This is human unrighteousness in general, but without doubt it has a special application to the Jewish unrighteousness from which the objection comes [Gdt]. This means 'doing wrong' and is in contrast with God's doing what is right [TH]. This includes unbelief [ICC1].
2. This refers to Jewish unfaithfulness [BECNT, ICC2, NAC, NICNT, SSA, WBC]. Paul is concerned throughout this section with Jewish disobedience; 'unrighteousness' parallels 'unfaithfulness', and 'liar' can be seen as referring to Jewish unfaithfulness to the covenant [NICNT]. Paul is speaking of the human inability of the Jews to keep the law [BECNT], and of Jewish wickedness [SSA]. This refers to the unrighteousness of unbelieving Jews [NAC]. The term includes the thought of Jewish unfaithfulness but treats it as part of universal human unrighteousness [WBC].

QUESTION—What is meant by θεοῦ δικαιοσύνη 'righteousness of God'?

1. This refers to God's righteousness in judgment [BECNT, NICNT, St]. This refers to God's faithfulness to his own person and promises, acting in accord with his own character and word [NICNT]. Paul has just spoken in 3:4b of God's judging righteousness and it is most likely that here he continues to develop the theme that God's judging is an integral part of his righteousness [BECNT]. This refers to the righteousness of God's character, but the reference to God as judge in 3:4 may be influencing Paul to speak here of his justice in making judgments [St].
2. This refers to God's attributes of righteousness, fairness, and justice [AB, Gdt, HNTC, Ho, Mor, NAC, NTC, SSA, TH]. This means that God acts in a just or righteous manner [SSA]. This refers to God's attribute of being right and doing what is right [TH]. This is an attribute of God referring to his fidelity and uprightness [AB]. This is the character of God as righteous and faithful in contrast to human sinfulness [HNTC, Mor, NAC, NTC]. This means God's rectitude, the attribute manifested in doing what is right [Ho]. It is God's perfection which prevents him from acting in any wrong manner towards any being [Gdt].
3. This refers to God's faithfulness to his covenant and promises [ICC1, ICC2, Mu, WBC]. This terminology recalls 'the faithfulness of God' in

3:3, and denotes God's actions in behalf of his people, or of people in general, despite their failure to respond as they should [WBC]. Paul has in mind the faithfulness of God to his promises [ICC1] or to his covenant [ICC2]. This means God's inherent equity and is synonymous with the truth or truthfulness of God as shown by his faithfulness in fulfilling his promises [Mu].

QUESTION—In what sense does man's unrighteousness demonstrate the righteousness of God?

1. Man's sin contributes to the glory of God by contrast, in that it brings out God's righteousness, truth, and faithfulness more clearly, or more conspicuously [AB, HNTC, Ho, Mor, Mu, NAC, NTC, St, TH, TNTC, WBC]. The more unrighteous the sinner is, the more righteous the judge appears, or possibly the more glorious the gospel appears [St]. Human sinfulness accentuates God's righteousness [NTC]. God is faithful even to the unfaithful, and shows goodness even to the unrighteous [WBC]. It is possible to argue from 3:3–4 that unrighteous conduct could serve to enhance or magnify the righteousness of God, but Paul denies this [NAC]. Human wickedness brings about the manifestation of God's uprightness [AB].
2. God's righteousness is demonstrated by the fact that he judges human sin [BECNT, NICNT]. When God judges sin and blesses obedience he is acting in line with his character and word [NICNT]. God's faithfulness and reliability are demonstrated in his judging of sin [BECNT].
3. The wickedness of the Jewish people shows the reason why God has not blessed them as he had promised [SSA].

QUESTION—Who is the 'we' posing the question of this verse?

1. It is Paul himself [AB, Gdt, ICC2, Mu, NAC, NICNT, WBC]. Paul is formulating this objection, as indicated by the transitional clause 'what shall we say', which he normally uses to introduce his own conclusions or questions, and by his use of the negating particle μή to indicate an expected negative response, and also by his apology for the 'human' way of asking the question [NICNT]. Paul realizes that his statements may result in false conclusions being drawn, so he introduces questions drawn from his own experience [AB]. The possible perversion of Paul's teaching about to be mentioned is one of which Paul has been accused [Mu]. Paul answers his own question based on an implication that might have been drawn from 3:3–4 [NAC].
2. It is the Jewish objector to Paul's teachings [BECNT, HNTC, Ho, Mor, St, TNTC]. The objector raises this question [NTC]. Paul is rephrasing in his own words some accusations he has often encountered [BECNT]. Paul is speaking as the objector but rhetorically classes himself with them [Mor]. This is a false inference which some Jews, who thought that they would not be exposed to condemnation regardless of their sins, were disposed to draw, since unrighteousness only serves to further display God's rectitude [Ho].

God, the-(one) inflicting^a the wrath,^b (is) not unjust^c (is he)?^d

LEXICON—a. pres. act. participle of ἐπιφέρω (LN **90.94**) (BAGD 4. p. 304): 'to inflict' [BAGD, BECNT, HNTC, ICC2, NICNT, NTC, WBC; NASB, NET, NRSV], 'to cause to experience' [**LN**], 'to bring upon' [AB, LN; NIV, REB], 'to impose upon' [LN], 'to take (vengeance)' [KJV], 'to vent (his anger)' [GW], not explicit [CEV, NCV, NLT, TEV].

b. ὀργή (LN **38.10**, 88.173) (BAGD 2.b. p. 579): 'wrath' [AB, BECNT, HNTC, ICC2, LN (88.173), NICNT, NTC, WBC; NASB, NET, NIV, NRSV], 'anger' [LN (88.173); GW], 'punishment' [BAGD, LN (38.10)], 'judgment' [BAGD], 'vengeance' [KJV], 'retribution' [REB]. The phrase 'inflicting wrath' is translated 'to punish' [**LN** (38.10); NCV, NLT, TEV], 'to become angry and punish' [CEV].

c. ἄδικος (LN **88.20**) (BAGD 1. p. 18): 'unjust' [AB, BAGD, HNTC, **LN**, NICNT, WBC; NIV, NRSV, REB], 'unrighteous' [BECNT, ICC2, LN, NTC; KJV, NASB, NET], 'not right' [BAGD, LN], 'unfair' [GW, NLT], 'wrong' [CEV, NCV, TEV].

d. These words are not in the Greek text, but are supplied in order to show that the question expects a negative answer. This question is variously posed: 'Is God...?' [AB, BECNT, HNTC, ICC2, WBC; GW, KJV], 'that God is...?' [NCV, NRSV], 'that God does...?' [TEV], 'God is not...is he?' [NICNT, NTC; NASB, NET], 'is it wrong for God...?' [CEV], 'is it unfair for God...?' [NLT], 'is it unjust of God...?' [REB].

QUESTION—What is the function of this question, and who is raising it?

1. It is put forth as a possible logical extension of or conclusion to the premise assumed in the previous question [BECNT, HNTC, Ho, ICC1, NICNT, NTC, St; NCV, NLT, NRSV, TEV].
2. Paul raises this rhetorical question as a negative answer to the previous question [Gdt, ICC2, Mor, NAC]. The particle μή assumes a negative answer, but an objector would not pose the question this way [ICC2, Mor].

QUESTION—What is the meaning of the word ἄδικος 'unjust'?

It means to be unjust [Gdt, HNTC, Ho, ICC2, Mor, NAC, St, WBC], or unfair [NTC]. It means to be unfair or to act against the principles of justice, and here it is in reference to the justness of God in condemning Jews for sins which ultimately manifest his righteousness [BECNT, NICNT]. It means to do wrong [TH].

QUESTION—What is the event referred to in the phrase ἐπιφέρων τὴν ὀργήν 'inflicting the wrath'?

1. This refers generally to God's bringing judgment and inflicting wrath on sinful human beings [HNTC, Ho].
2. This refers to the eschatological wrath or judgment that God will inflict on sinners in the final judgment [Gdt, ICC1, ICC2, NICNT, WBC]. The sense is primarily eschatological but also includes the wrath already being displayed, as mentioned in 1:18 and 2:5 [WBC]. Paul echoes a fundamental Jewish belief in God as the eschatological judge of all human

beings [AB, ICC1, ICC2]. Both for Paul and those Jews with whom he may be arguing, it is a fixed belief that in the end God will judge the world [NAC]. Although this question is framed in a very general way, it alludes to the day of wrath mentioned in 2:4–5 [Gdt].
3. The question is being posed as to whether God is unjust in bringing wrath on his own people the Jews [NAC, SSA, St].

I-speak according-to[a] **man.**[b]

LEXICON—a. κατά with accusative object (LN 89.8): 'according to' [LN], 'from' [BAGD, BECNT, NTC, WBC], 'in a…fashion' [NICNT], 'in a…way' [NRSV], 'as' [KJV, NCV].

b. ἄνθρωπος (LN 9.1) (BAGD 1.c. p. 68): 'man' [KJV], 'human being' [LN], 'humans' [GW], 'people' [NCV]. This noun is translated as a phrase: 'some people' [NLT], 'human arguments' [HNTC; NIV], 'a human way' [BAGD; NRSV], 'a human standpoint' [BAGD, NTC, WBC], 'a human point of view' [BECNT], 'human terms' [AB; NASB, NET, REB], 'human fashion' [NICNT]. This sentence is translated 'What a foolish thing to ask!' [CEV], 'this would be the natural question to ask' [TEV], 'I'm arguing the way humans would' [GW], 'I am speaking in human terms' [AB; NASB, NET], 'I speak of him in human terms' [REB], 'I am using a human argument' [NIV], 'that is actually the way some people talk' [NLT], 'forgive these human arguments' [HNTC], 'I am giving expression to thoughts which are very human' [ICC2].

QUESTION—What is the purpose of this statement 'I speak according to man'?

This is a parenthetic apology for the unacceptable idea of God being unjust [HNTC, ICC1, ICC2, Mor, NAC, SSA, St, TNTC, WBC]. That God might be unrighteous is so impossible that Paul apologizes for even mentioning it [Mor, TNTC]. Paul makes this apology to show that the previous objection was not his own argument, and even posed the rhetorical question in a form that expects a negative answer in order to show his reverence for God [HNTC]. Paul wants to distance himself from any suggestion that God might be unrighteous, thus indicating that the previous statement only represents a purely human perspective or view of things [Gdt, NICNT]. Paul is showing that he does not agree with the suggestion of unjust behavior on God's part, and wants to protect himself from seeming blasphemous [AB]. The thought is that in asking these questions he is accommodating himself to the human mode of interrogation and reasoning [Mu]. Paul is not here speaking his own thoughts in his own character as an apostle and Christian, but as expressing what others would think and say [Ho]. This represents the presumptive thought of man left to himself and his own reason, but which Paul finds revolting [Gdt]. Paul is saying parenthetically that such an argument is based on human wisdom [TH]. Paul is saying that such an idea is inappropriate for him as an apostle or even as a Christian to suggest [SSA]. It is embarrassing to Paul even to make the statement [St].

3:6 Never may-it -be!ᵃ

LEXICON—a. aorist mid. (deponent = act.) optative of γίνομαι (LN 13.107) (BAGD I.3.a. p. 158): 'to come to be' [LN], 'to occur, or happen' [LN]. The phrase μὴ γένοιτο 'never may it be!' is translated 'may it never be!' [NASB], 'by no means' [BAGD, NICNT, NTC; NRSV, TEV], 'far from it' [BAGD], 'God forbid' [BAGD, ICC2; KJV], 'certainly not' [AB, BECNT; NIV, REB], 'of course not' [HNTC; NLT], 'not at all' [WBC], 'absolutely not' [NET], 'But the answer is, "No"' [CEV], 'That's unthinkable!' [GW], 'No!' [NCV].

QUESTION—What is the function of this clause?

Paul is emphatically rejecting the notion of injustice with God [AB, Gdt, ICC2, Mor, Mu, NAC, NTC, TH]. This statement is always used to reject a false conclusion in Paul's writings, and indicates a strong rejection of the notion that God might act unjustly even in judging his own people [NICNT]. The objection previously made is inconsistent with the axiomatic belief for Paul that God will judge the world, and is rejected [ICC1]. The premise is absurd because one must reject what should be held as axiomatic, which is that God is the judge of all men [ICC2]. This is a categorical denial [St]. Paul is filled with holy indignation and crushes this type of wicked reasoning [NTC]. Paul frequently uses this strong negation with rhetorical questions, and uses it here to dismiss the sentiment just expressed, which appalls him [WBC]. Paul emphatically rejects the notion of cheap grace for Israel or of infidelity in God [AB].

For-otherwiseᵃ how (will) God judgeᵇ the world?ᶜ

LEXICON—a. ἐπεί (LN 89.32) (BAGD 2. p. 284); 'for otherwise' [BAGD; NET], 'otherwise' [AB, BECNT, HNTC, WBC; CEV, GW, NASB] 'for' [BAGD, LN], not explicit [NCV]. This conjunction is translated as a phrase: 'for in that case' [ICC2], 'for (how) then' [NICNT], 'for then (how)' [NTC; KJV, NRSV], 'if that were so' [NIV]; as a clause 'if God is not just' [NLT, TEV], 'if God were unjust' [REB].

b. fut. act. indic. of κρίνω (LN 56.20) (BAGD 4.b.α. p. 452): 'to judge' [AB, BAGD, BECNT, HNTC, ICC2, LN, NICNT, NTC, WBC; all versions]. The phrase πῶς κρινεῖ ὁ θεός 'how will God judge' is translated 'how is he qualified to judge' [NLT].

c. κόσμος (LN 9.23) (BAGD 5.a. p. 446): 'world' [AB, BAGD, BECNT, HNTC, ICC2, NICNT, NTC, WBC; all versions].

QUESTION—What is the significance of this question?

1. It points out that if God himself were unjust, he would not then be able to judge the world [HNTC, ICC1, ICC2, NICNT, NTC, St, TNTC, WBC]. If God were in fact unrighteous in his judging of sinful men, then this would impugn the moral government of the universe, as God would then have no way to punish sin and to vindicate truth, and consequently could not act as judge [HNTC, Mor, St, TNTC]. The question is meant to draw out the absurd and impossible consequences of God being considered unjust,

since if he were he could not then judge the world [NICNT, WBC]. Paul echoes a fundamental Jewish belief in God as the eschatological judge of all human beings [AB, ICC1, ICC2, Mu]. Paul says that if God really were unjust he could not judge the world, and to impugn his justice is to undercut his competence to judge and proves the absurdity of the question itself [ICC2, NTC, St]. The axiomatic belief that God is the final judge rules out the possibility of his being unjust [WBC]. Paul is saying that if God is qualified to judge the world, as is the case, then how could he be unjust [NTC].
2. The Jewish objection to the notion that they were open to condemnation was to plead the promise of God which their own unfaithfulness could not render ineffectual; Paul is answering this objection by saying that if the Jew were allowed such grounds for exclusion, the same would apply to everyone, and then God could not judge the world [Ho]. Paul reasons that because God will judge the world, there must of necessity be punishment; but if sinners could plead that their sins furthered God's purposes and thereby exempted them from punishment, there would then be no real judgment, a situation which cannot be if in fact God is going to judge the world, as everyone holds [Gdt, Mor].
3. Paul is saying that if it were unjust for God, who is just, to judge the Jews, then he would not do so, and thus would not be the judge of all people; but since he is admittedly the eschatological judge of all people, then it is not unjust for him to judge or punish the Jews [NAC, SSA].

QUESTION—What is the significance of using the term κόσμος 'world' in this question?

This indicates that Paul has in view God's judgment in the broadest possible sense [AB, Gdt, HNTC, Ho, ICC1, ICC2, Mor, NAC, NICNT, NTC, SSA, St, TH, TNTC]. Paul accepts as axiomatic that God is the universal judge [AB, Mor, St, WBC]. This refers to the belief that God is final judge of the totality of the universe and all of humankind [WBC]. The term 'world' is a metonymy representing 'anyone in the world' [SSA]. It means all people [ICC1, ICC2, TH]. Behind this may be the Jewish notion that God would judge Gentiles but save Jews despite their sins, but Paul argues that real judgment includes all sinners [Mor]. Paul means all mankind and is referring to the final judgment [TH].

3:7 But[a] if by[b] my falsehood[c] the truth[d] of-God abounded[e] to[f] his glory,[g]

TEXT—Instead of δέ 'but' some manuscripts read γάρ 'for'. GNT selects the reading δέ with a B rating, indicating that the text is almost certain. The reading γάρ 'for' is taken by KJV, NET.

LEXICON—a. δέ 'but' [HNTC, ICC2, Mor, WBC; NASB, NLT, NRSV, TEV], 'now' [BECNT], 'and' [NICNT], 'again' [AB; REB], not explicit [GW]. The argument of this verse is introduced by the clause 'some might object' [NTC], 'a person might say' [NCV], 'some might argue' [NIV], 'some might still argue' [NLT], 'you may ask' [CEV].

b. ἐν with dative object (LN 89.26, 89.76): 'by' [BECNT, HNTC, LN (89.76), WBC; NET], 'by means of' [ICC2, LN (89.76)], 'through' [AB, LN (89.76), NICNT, NTC; KJV, NASB, NRSV, REB], 'because of, on account of, or by reason of' [LN (89.26)], not explicit [CEV, GW, NCV, NIV, NLT, TEV].

c. ψεῦσμα (LN 33.254) (BAGD p. 892): 'falsehood' [BAGD, HNTC, **LN**, NTC; NIV, REB], 'lie' [BECNT, ICC2, **LN**, NICNT, WBC; GW, KJV, NASB, NET, NRSV], 'lying' [BAGD], 'untruthfulness' [AB, BAGD], 'untruth' [TEV], 'dishonesty' [NLT]. This singular noun is translated as a plural: 'lies' [CEV]. The noun is translated as a verb: '(when) I lie' [NCV].

d. ἀλήθεια (LN 72.2) (BAGD 1. p. 35): 'truth' [BECNT, HNTC, ICC2, LN, NICNT, WBC; KJV, NASB, NCV, NET, REB, TEV], 'truthfulness' [AB, BAGD, NTC; NIV, NLT, NRSV]. This noun is also translated as an adjective describing God: 'truthful' [CEV, GW].

e. aorist act. indic. of περισσεύω (LN 59.52) (BAGD 1.a.γ. p. 650): 'to abound' [BECNT, LN, NICNT; KJV, NASB, NRSV], 'to be more abundantly manifested' [ICC2], 'to show (something) to be supremely rich, great, or abundant' [BAGD], 'to overflow' [AB, WBC], 'to increase' [HNTC; GW], 'to enhance' [NTC; NET, NIV], 'to display to (his) greater (glory)' [REB], 'to make stand out more clearly' [TEV]. The clause 'if by my falsehood the truth of God abounded to his glory' is translated 'if my dishonesty highlights his truthfulness and brings him more glory' [NLT], 'since your lies bring great honor to God by showing how truthful he is' [CEV], 'when I lie, it really gives him glory, because my lie shows God's truth' [NCV], 'if my lie makes God's truth appear more glorious' [**LN**], 'if God's truth abounds to his glory because of my falsehood' [**LN**]. This verb is found only here in the NT.

f. εἰς with accusative object (LN 89.48): 'to' [AB, ICC2, NICNT, NTC, WBC; NASB, NRSV, REB], 'unto' [KJV], 'for' [BECNT], 'with the result that, or so that as a result, to cause' [LN], not explicit [CEV, GW, NCV, NET, NLT]. The phrase 'to his glory' is translated 'thereby increased his glory' [HNTC]. The clause 'the truth of God abounded to his glory' is translated 'serves God's glory by making his truth stand out more clearly' [TEV], 'enhances God's truthfulness and so increases his glory' [NIV].

g. δόξα (LN 33.357): 'glory' [AB, BECNT, HNTC, ICC2, LN, NICNT, NTC, WBC; all versions except CEV], 'honor' [CEV].

QUESTION—To what does ψεῦσμα 'falsehood' refer?

Note that there is a certain amount of overlap possible between the positions listed below, and one does not rule out the other.

1. This refers to human falsehood generally [HNTC, ICC2, Mu, NTC, TNTC]. This refers to the falsehood of man in denying the fulfillment of God's promises as in 3:4 [ICC1]. The lie referred to is the voluntary

ignorance of goodness in order to escape any obligation of doing it [Gdt]. It is human rejection of truth [NAC].
2. The sense is untruthfulness, unreliability, or unfaithfulness, especially to the covenant [BECNT, NICNT, SSA, TH]. In this context 'untruth' is parallel to 'doing wrong' in 3:5 and in this passage refers more to unrighteousness or sin than to speaking a lie [TH]. It means to fail to do what God has commanded, to be unfaithful or unreliable [SSA]. This refers to the Jewish objector's unrighteousness in being unfaithful to the covenant [NICNT]. This refers to the sinfulness of the Jews in their inability to keep the law and their not believing the gospel [BECNT]. It is a failure to be what God intended [Mor].
3. It refers both to Israel's unfaithfulness as well as general human falseness [WBC].

QUESTION—What is the meaning of the phrase ἡ ἀλήθεια τοῦ θεοῦ 'the truth of God'?
1. It means God's truthfulness, with emphasis on his reliability [AB, HNTC, Ho, ICC1, ICC2, Mor, Mu, NAC, NTC, SSA, TNTC, WBC]. The Hebrew concept of God's reliability underlies the Greek here and ties the thought back to the parallel expressions of 3:3, 5, 7 which are virtually equivalent; it refers to God's faithfulness to Israel as well as God's truth [WBC]. It means God's truthfulness in keeping his promises [Ho, ICC1]. It means God's truthfulness and complete reliability [Mor]. This refers to God's moral uprightness and recalls the discussion of 3:3–4 [Gdt].
2. This refers to God's faithfulness and truthfulness in judging sin [BECNT, NICNT]. It means God's faithfulness, but with a focus on truthfulness in judging sin; God's name and honor will be vindicated in his judgment of Jewish sinners [BECNT]. The contrasting words 'truth' and 'lie' are picked up from 3:4 and refer to God being reliable, trustworthy and true to his word, which applies both in blessing as well as in judgment of sin, as in this particular context [NICNT].
3. It means God's righteousness [Gdt, TH]. In this context the contrast is between the unrighteousness of man in doing wrong and the righteousness of God in doing what is right [TH]. It is the moral uprightness of God, as set against the voluntary ignorance of goodness on the part of men [Gdt].

why am-I- still[a] -being-judged[b] even-I as[c] a sinner?[d]

LEXICON—a. ἔτι (LN 67.128), (BAGD 2.c. p. 316): 'still' [AB, BAGD, BECNT, ICC2, LN, NTC, WBC; CEV, GW, NASB, NET, NIV, NRSV, TEV], 'yet' [LN, NICNT; KJV], 'any longer' [REB], 'actually' [HNTC], not explicit [NCV, NLT].
b. pres. pass. indic. of κρίνω (LN 56.30, 30.108) (BAGD 4.b.α. p. 452): 'to be judged' [BAGD, BECNT, HNTC, ICC2, LN (30.108), NICNT, WBC; GW, KJV, NASB, NCV, NET], 'to be condemned' [AB, LN (56.30), NTC; NIV, NRSV, REB, TEV], 'to be punished' [BAGD]. This passive

verb is translated as active: '(how can) God judge and condemn me' [NLT], 'God still says you are a sinner' [CEV].
- c. ὡς (LN **64.12**) (BAGD III.1.a. p. 898): 'as' [AB, BAGD, BECNT, ICC2, LN, NICNT, NTC, WBC; all versions except CEV, NCV], not explicit [CEV, NCV]. This conjunction is translated as a verb: 'to be' [HNTC].
- d. ἁμαρτωλός (LN 88.295): 'sinner' [AB, BAGD, BECNT, HNTC, ICC2, LN, NICNT, NTC, WBC; all versions].

QUESTION—What is the significance of the use of the first person singular?
1. This is a rhetorical device [Ho, ICC2, Mor, Mu, NAC, NICNT, St]. This is a rhetorical variant of the first person plural in 3:5, but Paul here speaks more as from the person of the objector himself than he did in 3:5 [NICNT]. As Paul continues the argument he impersonates the objector by using this pronoun [St]. It is the objector speaking [HNTC]. The first person singular stands for anyone [Ho]. Paul applies to himself what is really the case with his opponents [ICC1].
2. This refers to Paul, who is focusing the debate on himself, whom he indicts first and foremost. However, it applies to all people in general and to the Jew in particular, since the problem posed is not one from which the Jew can easily distance himself, both as a sinner as well as a recipient of God's saving righteousness [WBC].

QUESTION—What is the function of this verse?
1. This verse reads naturally as a restatement and elaboration of the same basic objection as is found in 3:5 [AB, BECNT, ICC1, ICC2, Mor, Mu, NAC, NICNT, NTC, TH]. Here it is given from man's viewpoint, who asks, If my sin brings God glory how is it fair that he still judges me? [ICC1, ICC2, NICNT]. This verse is parallel to 3:5 and repeats essentially the same argument as there, but this time in terms of falsehood and truthfulness; that is, if my falsehood shows how great God's truthfulness and reliability are, why should I be condemned for it? [Mor].
2. This and the following verse explain and amplify 3:6 [Gdt, Ho, Mor]. If it were unfair for God to punish sins that result in his greater glory, then anyone could come to God with that type of excuse, which would encourage sin [Gdt, Ho, Mor]. This kind of thinking says that the worse we are the better, since the more conspicuous God's mercy will be in pardoning us [Ho]. This verse is the confirmation of the answer given in 3:6, since if all sinners could be acquitted by claiming that their sin had contributed to God's glory, judgment would be brought to nothing [Gdt].
3. Paul continues and develops the previous argument from the position of the antinomian who rationalizes his lawlessness [St]. The objector can not quite let go the dilemma and implications raised by Paul in 3:4, and Paul apparently had to face the charge of teaching antinomianism or worse [HNTC].
4. The verse begins to turn the question away from the thought of God's final judgment back to the theme of Jewish condemnation of Gentiles, and so is not a mere repetition of 3:5 [WBC].

3:8 And not as we-are-defamed[a]

LEXICON—a. pres. pass. indic. of βλασφημέω (LN **33.400**) (BAGD 1. p. 142): 'to be defamed' [AB, BAGD, LN], 'to be reviled' [BAGD, **LN**], 'to be slanderously reported' [KJV, NASB, NIV]. This passive verb is translated as active: 'to say' [CEV] 'to allege' [HNTC], 'to slander' [GW, NET, NLT, NRSV], 'to insult' [TEV]. This verb is translated as an adverb: 'slanderously' [BECNT, ICC2, NICNT, NTC, WBC; REB]; as a verb clause: 'some people find fault with us' [NCV].

QUESTION—To what does βλασφημέω 'defamed' refer?
1. This refers to the slanderous accusation that Paul had been teaching that people should do evil that good may come [AB, BECNT, Gdt, HNTC, Ho, ICC1, ICC2, Mor, Mu, NAC, SSA, St, TH, TNTC]. By making this accusation some intended to discredit Paul and undermine his gospel [BECNT]. The accusation made by Paul's opponents refers to his teaching as well as practicing this false principle [Gdt].
2. There are elements of both a specific accusation of Paul teaching the doctrine just mentioned, as well as an impugning of the name and character of God (implicit in the accusation) by suggesting that he would act unjustly [NICNT].
3. This refers both to the slanderous accusation just mentioned, and to the fact that perhaps many of Paul's Jewish opponents thought him blasphemous for his insistence on the inclusion of the Gentiles, presumably because he had failed to recognize the special favor that God holds for Israel [WBC].

and as some report[a] us to-say

LEXICON—a. pres. act. indic. of φημί (LN 33.69) (BAGD 2. p. 856): 'to report' [NICNT, NTC, WBC; REB], 'to say' [LN; NLT, NRSV], 'to claim' [BECNT, NTC; CEV, GW, NIV], 'to charge' [AB], 'to allege' [HNTC, ICC2; NET], 'to accuse' [TEV], 'to affirm' [KJV, NASB]. This phrase is translated '(Some people…) say we teach this' [NCV].

QUESTION—Who are the ones leveling this accusation?
1. Paul is most likely referring to Jewish opponents [AB, BECNT, Ho, Mor, NICNT, SSA]. These opponents feel his gospel undermines morality [BECNT]. Paul has not mentioned the Jew specifically, and the language is general enough to include all, but the form of the expression and the type of objection made point strongly to the Jew being primarily in mind [Mor]. It is most likely that these would have been Paul's more legalistic opponents, who imputed to him this abuse by distorting the doctrine of grace he taught [Mu]. Paul is arguing against the ground of confidence on which the Jews rested their hopes of exemption from condemnation [Ho].
2. These objections would have been raised not only by Jewish people but perhaps from Jewish Christians [WBC]. The question was raised by Paul's Jewish contemporaries and perhaps even by certain Christians [HNTC].

QUESTION—Who are the referents of the plural pronoun ἡμᾶς 'us' that are being 'defamed'?
1. This refers to Paul [Gdt, HNTC, Ho, ICC1, ICC2, Mor, Mu, NAC, SSA, St, TH, TNTC, WBC; NLT, REB, TEV]. Since Paul's critics are viewed as making the objections, this can be taken as referring to Paul [SSA]. Paul says that reports of him teaching the antinomian idea that good will result from doing evil is slanderous [NAC]. These false accusations have been raised against Paul and his doctrine [Gdt].
2. This refers to Paul, but possibly to others also [AB, BECNT]. This refers to Paul, and perhaps to other apostles as well, being accused of promoting this doctrine [BECNT]. It refers to Paul, but possibly to Christians in general [AB].

Let-us-do evil[a] (things), so-that[b] good[c] (things) may-come?[d]
LEXICON—a. κακός (LN 88.106) (BAGD 1.c. p. 398): 'evil' [AB, BAGD, BECNT, HNTC, ICC2, LN, NICNT, NTC, WBC; all versions except CEV]. This plural adjective is translated as a singular: 'something evil' [CEV]. This is translated 'why not indeed do evil' [REB].
b. ἵνα (LN 89.59) 'so that' [BECNT, LN; CEV, GW, NCV, NET, NRSV, TEV], 'that' [AB, HNTC, ICC2, NTC, WBC; KJV, NASB, NIV, REB], 'in order that' [NICNT], not explicit [NLT].
c. ἀγαθός (LN 88.1) (BAGD 2.b.γ. p. 3): 'good' [AB, BAGD, BECNT, HNTC, ICC2, NTC, WBC; all versions except CEV, NLT], 'good things' [BAGD, LN, NICNT]. This plural adjective is translated as singular: 'something good' [CEV]. This clause is translated 'the more we sin the better it is' [NLT].
d. aorist act. subj. of ἔρχομαι (LN 13.50) (BAGD I.2.b. p. 311): 'to come' [AB, BAGD, BECNT, HNTC, ICC2, NICNT, WBC; CEV, KJV, NET, NRSV, REB, TEV], 'to result' [NTC; NIV].
QUESTION—Is Paul answering the objection raised in 3:7 in this verse?
Paul is not fully answering the objection here, but does so in 6:1ff [HNTC, ICC1, TNTC, WBC]. Paul simply rejects the allegation with a parenthetical aside [AB, ICC2]. Paul is responding to the specific accusation that his gospel undermines morality but his response is very brief [BECNT, TNTC]. Paul does not really answer the accusation and sees it as self-evidently perverse since no good results can justify encouraging evil [St]. Paul was not yet ready to fully discuss this issue, so to avoid getting off course he cuts the question off as slanderous [WBC]. Paul briefly repudiates the accusation here as being obviously unreal, but he also speaks of it further in chapter 6 [ICC1]. Paul briefly but firmly repudiates the accusation of these contemporaries [Mor].
QUESTION—What is the relation of this statement to 3:7?
1. This verse provides something of a rhetorical answer to the objection of 3:7 [AB, BECNT, Gdt, ICC1, ICC2, Mor, Mu, NAC, NICNT, NTC, St, TH, TNTC; CEV, GW, NASB, NCV, NET, NIV, NLT, NRSV, TEV],

and the form shows the rhetorical question expects a negative answer [ICC2]. Paul does not accept the conclusion drawn by his opponents in 3:7 and here affirms that they should be condemned [TH].
2. This verse is part of the objection introduced in 3:7, not Paul's reply; that is, the objector is saying that if the reasoning process described in 3:7 is true, then this is a further conclusion that would or could be drawn [HNTC, Ho, SSA; REB].

QUESTION—What is the 'good' that some would say could come from human sinfulness?

This refers to the notion that human sinfulness gives greater scope for God's saving activity and truth to be known, and human unreliability shows up the complete reliability of God, thus increasing God's glory [Mor]. This is a false and human notion that unrighteous conduct could enhance and magnify the righteous character of God, and that a person's rejection of the truth could serve to make the truthfulness of God more apparent, thus increasing his glory, a claim Paul says is slanderous [NAC]. Some say that if human unfaithfulness and wickedness are the means whereby God's faithfulness and mercy are made more conspicuous, then we ought not be punished for it, since God's mercy is made more obvious by human sinfulness [Ho]. Paul has pushed the refutation of the previous argument to the utmost by suggesting that some would say that sinning more freely only serves to give God further opportunities to do good [Gdt]. Some hold that someone's doing wrong causes people to recognize more clearly that God does right, that his truthfulness or righteousness is thereby made more conspicuous [TH]. The good would be that people will praise God for the fact that God keeps his promises, even if people are sinful [SSA]. The purported good would be that God's character would be shown and his glory thereby promoted [St].

of-whom the condemnation[a] is just.[b]

LEXICON—a. κρίμα (LN 56.30) (BAGD 4.b. p. 450): 'condemnation' [AB, BAGD, LN, NTC, WBC; NASB, NET, NIV, NRSV], 'God's condemnation' [BECNT], 'judgment' [LN, NICNT], 'damnation' [KJV], not explicit [HNTC]. This noun is translated as a passive verb: 'to be condemned' [ICC2; GW, NLT, TEV]; as an active verb: 'to condemn' [REB]. This clause is translated 'but God is fair and will judge them as well' [CEV], 'they are condemned, and that is what they deserve' [GW], 'they (are wrong) and deserve the punishment they will receive' [NCV], 'they will be condemned, as they should be' [TEV], 'to condemn such men as these is surely just' [REB].

b. ἔνδικος (LN **88.15**) (BAGD p. 263): 'just' [BAGD, BECNT, LN, NICNT; KJV, NASB, REB], 'surely just' [REB], 'not unjust' [AB], 'deserved' [BAGD, LN, NTC, WBC; NET, NIV, NRSV], not explicit [CEV]. This adjective is translated as an adverb: 'deservedly' [ICC2]; as a phrase: 'well deserved' [WBC], 'as (they) should be' [TEV], 'what they deserve' [HNTC; GW], 'they deserve' [NCV, NLT].

QUESTION—What is the identity of the antecedent of the pronoun ὧν 'of whom' in the statement ὧν τὸ κρίμα ἔνδικόν ἐστιν 'of whom the condemnation is just'?
   1. This refers in particular to some people who have slandered Paul [AB, BECNT, Gdt, HNTC, ICC2, NAC, NICNT, NTC, SSA, St, TH, TNTC, WBC].
      1.1 The referents are primarily Jewish [AB, BECNT, St, TH, WBC]. The context is addressing Jewish concerns and the people just mentioned who object that Paul's doctrine encourages sin; these opponents were probably Jewish [AB, BECNT, St]. This was probably a Jewish or Jewish Christian objection [WBC].
      1.2 The referents could be anyone who might raise objections such as those in 3:7–8 [HNTC, ICC2, Mu, NAC, NICNT, NTC]. They are those who claim they are unjustly condemned for a lie or for any sin that eventually glorifies God, as well as those who claim that Paul would teach or has taught such a doctrine [NICNT, NTC]. This refers to those who make the previous accusations, and may have been some of Paul's contemporaries who misrepresented his teachings or even members of some of his own churches who misunderstood them [HNTC]. This should not be restricted to those who slandered Paul but includes all who might draw this false inference from Paul's teaching and as a result promote immorality [Mu].
   2. This refers to people such as were mentioned in 3:7 who would say 'why am I still judged as a sinner?' [ICC1], or who would say 'Let us do evil that good may result' [Ho]. Paul reduces the reasoning of the Jews to a conclusion which is shocking to one's moral sense and thereby refutes it [Ho].
QUESTION—What is the meaning of the word κρίμα 'condemnation'?
   There is no doubt that a negative judgment is meant [Mor]. It means God's condemnation [AB, BECNT, Gdt, ICC1, ICC2, Mu, NAC, NICNT, NTC, SSA, St, TH, TNTC, WBC]. This refers to the justness of condemning the evil actions of people such as those just mentioned [NICNT]. Paul summarily rejects the charges of these opponents, and says they will face judgment and that their condemnation is just [BECNT]. Paul says the charge is self-condemned because it is a contradiction in terms [TNTC]. The sense is that this judgment is just and they are receiving a condemnation which they deserve [ICC1, NAC, WBC].

DISCOURSE UNIT: 3:9–31 [NET]. The topic is the condemnation of the world.

DISCOURSE UNIT: 3:9–20 [BECNT, Gdt, GNT, HNTC, Ho, ICC1, Mor, Mu, NAC, NICNT, NTC, St, TNTC, WBC; CEV, NCV]. The topic is the unrighteousness of all people [BECNT], universal condemnation is proclaimed in Scripture [Gdt], no one is justified by works of law [Ho], all have sinned [HNTC], Scripture illustrates universal failure to attain righteousness [ICC1], all people are guilty [NCV], universal sinfulness: proof from Scripture [Mor], the universality of sin and condemnation: conclusion [Mu], all people are unrighteous [NAC], the guilt of all humanity [NICNT], there is none righteous, not even one [NTC], God's wrath against the whole human race [St], all mankind found guilty [TNTC], God's judgment on all without exception [WBC], no one is good [CEV], there is none righteous [GNT], no one is righteous [NIV, TEV], all people are sinners [NLT].

3:9 What then?ᵃ Do-we-have-an-advantage?ᵇ Certainlyᶜ not;

TEXT—The phrase οὐ πάντως 'certainly not' does not occur in a few manuscripts. This variant is not mentioned by GNT and has weak manuscript support. It is omitted only by WBC.

LEXICON—a. The phrase τί οὖν is translated 'what then?' [ICC2, NICNT, NTC; KJV, NASB, NET, NRSV], 'what, then, is the situation?' [AB; GW], 'what then should we conclude?' [BECNT], 'what shall we conclude then?' [NIV], 'and what of that?' [HNTC], 'what does all this mean' [CEV], 'so' [NCV], 'well then' [NLT, REB, TEV].

b. pres. mid. or pass. indic. of προέχω (LN **65.47**) (BAGD 2. p. 705; 3. p. 306). This is translated as having an active intransitive meaning: 'to have an advantage' [BAGD, BECNT, ICC2, NICNT; GW], 'to have or experience an advantage superior (to someone), to have a greater benefit (than someone)' [LN], 'to be better off' [NTC; CEV, NET, NRSV, REB], 'to be better than' [KJV, NCV, NIV, NLT], 'to be in a better condition' [TEV], 'to be any better' [NTC; NASB], 'to stand on a higher plane' [HNTC]. It is possible to translate this as a passive verb with the sense 'to be in a worse position (than someone)' [BAGD], 'are we Jews at a disadvantage' [AB]. The phrase τί οὖν is translated in conjunction with the following verb: 'What then do we plead in our own defense', a rendering based on the omission of οὐ πάντως 'certainly not' in a few manuscripts [WBC].

c. πάντως (LN 71.16, 91.10) (BAGD 5.a. p. 609): 'certainly' [BECNT, LN (71.16, 91.10)], 'doubtless, no doubt' [LN (71.16)], 'indeed' [LN (91.10)]. The phrase οὐ πάντως is translated 'No, it doesn't!' [CEV], 'Not at all' [GW, NASB, NIV, TEV], 'No, in no wise' [KJV], 'No!' [NCV], 'Certainly not' [NET], 'No, not at all' [NLT, NRSV, REB].

QUESTION—What is the function of the question τί οὖν 'what then'?

The question asks what inference or conclusion is to be drawn from the discussion which has preceded it [Gdt, HNTC, Ho, ICC1, Mor, Mu, St, TH]. As Paul approaches the end of a lengthy argument he wraps it up with this summary question concerning what conclusion we should now reach, which is that the whole human race faces the condemnation of sin [St]. This is most often used where a new or concluding phase of an argument is introduced, and here it is the beginning of the conclusion in the first main section of the argument [WBC]. As a part of the diatribe style, this brief transitional phrase introduces a question that has been stimulated by what has just been said previously [AB, NICNT]. This probably forms the introduction to a new question that someone might ask at this point in Paul's argument [SSA]. With these two brief questions Paul is leading toward a summation of what he has been developing since 1:18, and which he states in 3:19–20, that all people are in bondage to sin [NICNT]. It introduces a brief pause in the argument for the purpose of reflecting on what has been said [Mor]. Paul now draws a logical conclusion to his argument [NAC].

QUESTION—Who is the subject of the verb προεχόμεθα 'do we have an advantage'?

1. The subject is the Jews [AB, BECNT, Gdt, HNTC, Ho, ICC1, ICC2, Mu, NAC, NICNT, NTC, SSA, St, TH, TNTC; CEV]. This passage is still focused on the Jews, and the implied comparison has to do with non-Jews [SSA]. Given the dismal picture Paul has just painted, the question now arises of whether the Jew was in any way better off than the Gentile [NAC].
2. The subject is Paul and, by implication, other Christians [Mor, NTC]. He is asking whether he and other Christians are by nature better off than any other people [NTC].
3. The subject is Paul and all other people. That is, what excuse can anyone offer in light of all that has now been said? No defense is possible for anyone [WBC].

QUESTION—How should the form of the verb προέχω 'to have an advantage' be understood, and what is its meaning?

1. The form should be understood as middle with an active meaning [AB, BECNT, Gdt, HNTC, Ho, ICC2, Mor, NTC, SSA, St, TH, WBC; CEV, KJV, NET, NIV, NLT, NRSV, REB, TEV].
1.1 The form is middle but the meaning is active, and 'we' refers to the Jews, meaning 'Do we Jews have an advantage'? [AB, BECNT, HNTC, Ho, ICC2, NICNT, SSA, St, TH, TNTC; CEV, NLT, REB, TEV]. In Hellenistic Greek the distinction between middle and active was sometimes blurred, with the middle being used for the active; Paul has mentioned the priority of the Jews with respect to the promises of salvation, but must point out that this priority does not exempt them from his judgment [BECNT]. This passage is still focused on the Jews, and it is not uncommon for verbs in the middle voice to have an active sense; here the question has to do with spiritual advantage [SSA]. The sense of the question is 'are we Jews any better off' [Ho, NTC, St].
1.2 The form is middle but the meaning is active, and 'we' refers to Paul and other Christians [Mor, NTC]. Paul is asking whether he and other Christians have any priority, holding a higher standing in the eyes of God concerning righteousness, to which the answer is 'No' [NTC]. Paul is asking whether Christians are able to make a defense as if claiming to be blameless [Mor].
1.3 The form is middle, the meaning is active, and the 'we' refers to all people generally. The verb means to put forward an excuse or defense,

so Paul is asking, 'What can we human beings put forward as a defense?' [WBC].
- 1.4 The form is middle, the meaning is active, and the 'we' refers to the Jews. The verb means to protect or shelter oneself, and Paul is asking, 'Do we Jews have any shelter or refuge under which we can regard ourselves as delivered from God's wrath'? [Gdt].
2. The form is passive with a passive meaning, the 'we' refers to the Jews, and the verb means 'Are we Jews at a disadvantage to others?' [AB, ICC1, Mu]. While some might conclude that the tables had been completely turned and the Gentiles now had an advantage over the Jews, Paul is saying that, in terms of the present moral condition of Jews and Gentiles, both are equally sinful [ICC1]. The verb should be taken as passive and the sense is most likely a question of whether the Jews are excelled or surpassed by others in some advantage with reference to the judgment of God, given the privilege which they possess which was mentioned in 3:1–2; because of the doctrine of universal human depravity, Paul denies any difference or advantage for anyone with respect to the condemnation that comes from sin [Mu].

QUESTION—How should the negative clause οὐ πάντως 'certainly not' be understood?

Note that ordinarily when the negative οὐ precedes πάντως it limits it, giving the meaning of 'not completely' or 'not absolutely', whereas if the word order were reversed, πάντως οὐ, the meaning would be 'absolutely not' or something similar.
1. It is an emphatic refusal meaning 'certainly not' [AB, BECNT, Gdt, HNTC, Ho, ICC1, Mor, Mu, NICNT, NTC, SSA, St, TH, TNTC, WBC; all versions].
   1.1 Paul is insisting categorically that despite the Jews having certain salvation and historical advantages, as alluded to in 3:1, they have no such advantages over others with regard to responsibility and accountability for sin and judgment before God [BECNT, Gdt, Ho, Mu, NICNT, St, TNTC]. When speaking of privilege in 3:1 Paul asserts that the Jews had advantage, but here with regard to any kind of favoritism he says they have none, for they will not be exempt from God's judgment [St]. Paul clarifies that while there is some advantage for the Jew, this does not do away with the charge that all men are under sin, and regarding that question, there is no advantage for anyone before God [HNTC]. Paul concludes that, because they are sinners, the Jews have no advantage over the Gentiles [Ho]. Although the Jews had the advantage of having God's message, they were no better off than Gentiles with regard to being under the power of sin [TH]. The advantage the Jew has is to know, based on Scripture, that no one has an advantage before God [HNTC]. Neither Jew nor Gentile had any advantage over the other, since both alike were sinful [ICC1].

1.2 Paul has already shown both Jews and Gentiles to be under sentence of condemnation for sin, and here decisively applies the same to all, including Christians, who belong to sin-laden humanity [NTC].
2. It is a qualified negative meaning 'not entirely', 'not altogether', or 'not in every respect'; although Paul concedes that Jews do have some advantages, he qualifies that statement here with regard to judgment for sin, saying that the Jews have no claim on God regarding any merit in the matter of sinfulness [ICC2].

for we-have-previously-accused^a both Jews and Greeks^b all to-be under^c sin,^{d}

LEXICON—a. aorist mid. (deponent = act.) indic. of προαιτιάομαι (LN 33.430) (BAGD p. 702): 'to accuse previously' [BECNT, LN], 'to accuse already' [NICNT], 'to charge already' [AB, BAGD, WBC; GW, NASB, NET, NIV, NRSV], 'to bring a charge' [HNTC], 'to lay a charge against' [ICC2], 'to previously make a charge' [NTC], 'to already draw up an indictment' [REB], 'to say' [CEV, NCV], 'to have before proved' [KJV], 'to show already' [NLT, TEV]. This word is found only here in the NT.
b. Ἕλλην (LN 11.40, 11.90) (BAGD 2.a. p. 252): 'Greek' [AB, BECNT, HNTC, ICC2, LN (11.40, 11.90), NICNT, NTC, WBC; GW, NASB, NET, NRSV, REB], 'Gentile' [BAGD, LN (11.40); CEV, KJV, NIV, NLT, TEV], 'non-Jew' [LN (11.40)], 'those who are not Jews' [NCV], 'pagan, heathen' [BAGD].
c. ὑπό with accusative object (LN 37.7) (BAGD 2.b. p. 843): 'under' [AB, BAGD, ICC2, LN, NICNT, WBC; KJV, NASB, NET, NIV], 'under the control of' [LN], 'under the power of' [AB, BAGD, BECNT, NTC; GW, NLT, NRSV, REB, TEV], 'under the rule or command of' [BAGD], 'under the dominion of' [HNTC]. The expression ὑφ'...εἶναι 'to be under' is translated 'are ruled by' [CEV], 'are guilty of' [NCV].
d. ἁμαρτία (LN 88.310): 'sin' [AB, BAGD, BECNT, HNTC, ICC2, LN, NICNT, NTC, WBC; all versions].

QUESTION—Who is the subject 'we' indicated in προῃτιασάμεθα 'we have already accused'?

It is Paul [AB, BECNT, Gdt, HNTC, Ho, ICC1, ICC2, Mor, Mu, NAC, NICNT, NTC, SSA, St, TH, WBC]. The first person plural 'we' is an editorial 'we', referring to what Paul has already written thus far in the epistle [NAC, SSA]. It is translated 'I' [SSA; CEV, TEV]. Paul states that he has already made the charge that all are sinners and thus without advantage or defense [Mor].

QUESTION—To what is Paul referring when he says this accusation of universal sin has already been made?

He is referring to the comprehensive indictment of all humanity in 1:18–2:29 [ICC1, ICC2, NICNT, St], or 1:18–2:24 [Mu]. Paul's thesis in 1:18–3:20 is that all mankind is guilty of sin, and this particular verse should dispel any doubt that such was his purpose [BECNT]. What Paul has said in 1:18–3:8

comes to a climax in this section [WBC]. In 1:18–3:9 Paul has described the deplorable status of both Gentiles and Jews [NTC]. The previous accusations referred to in 1:18–2:29 are an indictment of mankind as a whole as being sinful, Jews and Gentiles alike [HNTC, ICC2, WBC]. The apostle has just demonstrated that the Jews as well as the Gentiles are under God's wrath, and here confirms in summary that there is no shelter from God's wrath for the Jews [Gdt]. This states Paul's own comment about his purpose in the epistle up to this point, which is to show that all people are captives to the power of sin [NICNT].

QUESTION—What is meant by the phrase ὑφ' ἁμαρτίαν 'under sin'?

It means that all people are under the power of sin [AB, BECNT, Gdt, Ho, ICC2, Mor, Mu, NICNT, NTC, SSA, St, TH, WBC]. The phrase means to be under the control of sin or to be ruled by sin [SSA], to be under the dominion of sin [HNTC, ICC1], to be held fast by sin [TNTC]. According to Paul, all those who have not experienced the righteousness of God by faith are, without exception, helpless captives to the power of sin, enslaved under that power, and desperately in need of a new power to break in and set them free, a power which is found only in the gospel of Christ [NICNT]. Sin is a power ruling over all people, and manifesting itself as specific acts; it is described in Romans as reigning, enslaving, ruling, and exercising lordship, and the quotes of 3:10–18 confirm that people need to be freed from it [BECNT]. Paul personifies sin as a master who dominates the slave, since sin holds humans in bondage [AB]. Paul considers sin more as a power which has control over a person than as individual acts which he or she commits; here, as in other places, Paul personifies sin [ICC2]. Here Paul is talking not so much about being under the guilt of sin as under its power, which continues to reproduce and increase the guilt [Gdt]. Sin binds man to his own mortality and corruptibility, neutralizes whatever knowledge of God or concern for his will a person may have, and stirs up physical appetites to the point of forgetting the fact that he is a creature of God [WBC]. It means to be controlled by the desire to sin [TH]. They are under the condemnation of sin [NAC]. It means to be subject to condemnation before God by virtue of belonging to a sin-laden and guilt-burdened race [NTC].

DISCOURSE UNIT: 3:10–20 [AB]. The topic is all human beings alike are sinners.

3:10 **just-as it-is-written**[a]

LEXICON—a. perf. pass. indic. of γράφω (LN 33.61) (BAGD 2.c. p. 166): 'to be written' [AB, BAGD, BECNT, LN, NICNT, NTC, WBC; KJV, NASB, NET, NIV, NRSV]. This phrase is translated 'The Scriptures tell us' [CEV], 'even as Scripture testifies' [ICC2], 'as the Scriptures say' [NCV, NLT, TEV], 'Scripture says' [REB], 'as Scripture says' [GW], 'and this moreover is the verdict of Scripture. Hear these words of Scripture' [HNTC].

QUESTION—What is the purpose of the long string of OT quotes beginning in this verse and continuing through 3:18?

Paul quotes Scripture to prove his point that all are enslaved to sin and stand under God's wrath as sinners [AB, BECNT, Gdt, Ho, ICC2, Mor, Mu, NAC, NTC, SSA, St, TH]. Paul's purpose is to substantiate the accusation which he made in 3:9, that sin is universal and no one, even faithful Jews, may claim to be righteous [NICNT]. The Jews' belief that they were righteous was a misunderstanding of the meaning of their covenant privilege and responsibility [WBC]. By a common rabbinical practice of stringing a number of related passages together, Paul reinforces his point that all are sinners, and shows that Scripture consistently stresses this fact [Mor, NAC]. The central theme of these quotes is sin's universal hold on men, as expressed by the repetition of οὐκ ἔστιν 'there is not' six times and πάντες 'all' twice (3:9, 18) [ICC2].

QUESTION—Is there a discernable structure in this collection of OT quotes?

1. There are at least 3 major sections or 'strophes': 3:10–12, 3:13–14, and 3:15–18 [Gdt, Ho, ICC2, NAC, NTC, SSA]. 3:10 functions as a heading for what follows, and 3:18 returns to the same theme that 'there is no one', with the two verses framing what comes between them; 3:11–12 describes the universality of human sin generally, developing the theme introduced in 3:10 with a series of five generally synonymous repetitions of the thought that there are none righteous; 3:13–14 describes the sinfulness of human speech; and 3:15–17 focuses on sins of violence against others [NICNT]. The human depravity and suffering depicted in 3:15–17 arise from the lack of a fear of God mentioned in 3:18 [Gdt]. The second and third sections, by focusing on various parts of the human body, convey the idea that not only are all men sinners, but every part of every person is involved in sin [AB, ICC2, SSA]. The first section deals with the fact that, without exception, all men are sinners, the second with the sinfulness of man's speech, and the third with the violent and deadly character of men's conduct [ICC2]. The most general characteristics of human corruption are seen in 3:10–12, which emphasizes the universality of sin, and then two classes of the manifestation of this sinfulness are seen in 3:13–17 [AB, Gdt, Ho, ICC2, NTC].
2. Verses 3:10–12 depict the universality of sin, 3:13–14 focuses on the sins of speech, 3:15–17 portrays the results of sin as injurious to human society and conduct, and 3:18 makes clear that the ground and root cause of the sins previously described is failure to reckon rightly with God [BECNT].
3. The repetition of οὐκ ἔστιν 'there is not' in 3:10, 11, 12, and 3:18 forms the most recognizable structure [AB, WBC].

QUESTION—What are the sources of the quotations found in 3:10–18?

Although there are some changes in wording, Paul's quotes agree most closely with the LXX [BECNT, NICNT, WBC], most of the quotes being fairly literal translations from the Hebrew Masoretic text [AB, BECNT]. The lines in 3:10–12 are taken from Ps. 14:1–3 and 53:3; the lines of 3:13–14 are taken from Ps. 5:9 and Ps. 140:3; line 3:14 is from Ps. 10:7; the lines of 3:15–17 are from Isaiah 59:7–8; and 3:18 comes from Ps. 36:1 [AB, BECNT, Gdt, HNTC, Ho, ICC1, ICC2, Mor, Mu, NICNT, SSA, TH, TNTC, WBC], though 3:10 is closer to Eccl. 7:20 [AB, NAC, St, WBC] and 3:15–17 may draw from Pr. 1:16 [AB, HNTC, TH].

There-is not (a) righteous[a] (person), not-even one;
LEXICON—a. δίκαιος (LN 88.12) (BAGD 1.b. p. 195): 'righteous' [BAGD, BECNT, HNTC, ICC2, LN, NICNT, NTC, WBC; KJV, NASB, NET, NIV, NRSV, REB, TEV], 'just' [BAGD, LN], 'upright' [AB, BAGD], 'good' [NLT]. This clause is translated 'no one is acceptable to God' [CEV], 'not one person has God's approval' [GW], 'there is no one who always does what is right' [NCV].
QUESTION—What is the meaning of this clause?
It means that no one stands before God as righteous, all are guilty before God [BECNT, Ho, ICC2, Mu, NAC, NICNT, St, WBC]. Paul has edited the quote slightly by saying 'righteous' instead of 'good' as in the text of Psalms 14:1–3, and his choice of 'righteous' carries the specific nuance of forensic righteousness characteristic of Paul [BECNT, HNTC, Ho, ICC2, NICNT, TH]. The thought is that no one may claim to have righteous standing or moral righteousness before God [ICC2]. While there may be some hyperbole here, Paul's argument for the universality of sin is given greater impact by using the words and phrases 'all', 'not one', 'together', and 'not even one' in the section 3:10–12 [SSA].

3:11 there-is not one (who is) understanding,[a] there-is not one (who is) seeking[b] God.
LEXICON—a. pres. act. participle of συνίημι (LN 32.5, **32.26**) (BAGD p. 790): 'to understand' [BAGD, BECNT, LN (32.5, 32.26), NICNT, NTC, WBC; CEV, KJV, NASB, NCV, NET, NIV, REB], 'to be able to understand' [LN (**32.26**)], 'to be able to comprehend' [LN (32.26)], 'to comprehend, perceive, or have insight into' [LN (32.5)]. This verb is translated as a noun: '(to have) understanding' [AB, ICC2; GW, NRSV], 'to have real understanding' [NLT], 'with understanding' [HNTC]; as an adjective: '(who is) wise' [TEV].
b. pres. act. participle of ἐκζητέω (LN 27.35) (BAGD 1. p. 240): 'to seek' [BECNT, ICC2, LN, NICNT; NET, NIV, NLT, NRSV, REB], 'to seek out' [BAGD, WBC], 'to seek after' [HNTC; KJV], 'to seek for' [NASB], 'to search for' [AB, BAGD, NTC; CEV, GW], 'to worship' [TEV], 'to look (to God) for help' [NCV].
QUESTION—What doesn't anyone understand?
No one understand what is really right [TH], moral and religious truth [ICC1, ICC2], God's truth [SSA].

3:12 all have-turned-away,[a] together[b] they-have-become-worthless;[c]

LEXICON—a. aorist act. indic. of ἐκκλίνω (LN **31.99**) (BAGD p. 241): 'to turn away' [AB; CEV, GW, NCV, NET, NIV], 'to turn away from (God)' [BAGD, LN; NLT, TEV], 'to turn aside' [BAGD, BECNT, ICC2, NICNT, NTC, WBC; NASB, NRSV], 'to swerve aside' [REB], 'to fall away' [HNTC], 'to go out of the way' [KJV].
   b. ἅμα (LN 89.114) (BAGD 1.b. p. 42): 'together' [BAGD, BECNT, ICC2, LN, NICNT, NTC, WBC; GW, KJV, NASB, NCV, NET, NIV, NRSV], 'all' [AB, HNTC; NLT, TEV], 'all alike' [REB], not explicit [CEV].
   c. aorist pass. (deponent = act.) indic. of ἀχρειόω (LN **88.263**) (BAGD 2. p. 128): 'to be or become worthless' [BAGD, HNTC, NTC, WBC; CEV, NET, NIV, NRSV], 'to become depraved' [AB, BAGD], 'to become perverse' [LN], 'to become debased' [REB], 'to become unprofitable' [KJV], 'to become useless' [BECNT, ICC2; NASB, NCV], 'to become rotten to the core' [GW], 'to go wrong' [**LN**, NICNT; NLT, TEV]. This word is found only here in the NT.

QUESTION—What is meant by the phrase πάντες ἐξέκλιναν 'all have turned away'?
   It means that human beings have deliberately turned away from God and the paths in which he would have them walk, resulting in their own depravity [AB]. The verb implies deliberate avoidance [Mor]. People have turned away from God and his law [NTC]. People have turned away from God and have stopped obeying him [SSA]. This is not an accidental omission; people have deliberately turned away from God [NAC], they have voluntarily departed from the good [Gdt]. They are guilty of backsliding and apostasy, as is also described in 1:21, for in one way or another all men have turned away from the way of godliness [Mu]. People have turned from the way that God has prescribed and that leads to himself, and have moved into spiritual blindness and moral depravity [Ho]. It means to turn away from God or to no longer have him in mind [TH]. It means to turn from God to the worship of other gods [BECNT].

QUESTION—What is meant by 'worthless' in the clause ἅμα ἠχρεώθησαν 'together they have become worthless'?
   This should be understood in the ethical sense and means to become useless or unprofitable [Mor]. This expresses the fact that in the end their lives turn out to be useless and unprofitable [NAC]. In this quote from the psalm, the Greek verb emphasizes uselessness and the Hebrew emphasizes corruption; all men without exception are described as having gone bad, and are corrupted [Mu]. 'Worthless' does not mean that they have no value, but that they have become unfit for the purpose for which God made them [SSA]. This refers to the universal moral degradation and depravity of sinful men who have turned away from God [Ho]. It means unfit for good, to become spoiled [Gdt]. It refers to the depravity that results from turning away from God [AB]. This verb is a negated cognate of the noun χρηστότης 'good' in the next line, which indicates that which is good and useful [Mor].

there-is no-one doing good,[a] **there is not even**[b] **one.**

TEXT—Some manuscripts omit the second οὐκ ἔστιν 'there is not'. GNT includes these words in brackets with a C rating, indicating difficulty in deciding whether or not to place them in the text. These words are included by BECNT, HNTC, NICNT, NTC, WBC; CEV, NET, NRSV. They are omitted by AB, ICC2; KJV, NIV, TEV.

LEXICON—a. χρηστότης (LN **88.10**) (BAGD 1. p. 886): 'good' [BECNT, NICNT, WBC; KJV, NASB, NLT], 'anything good' [GW, NCV] 'kindness' [HNTC, ICC2; NET, NRSV, REB], 'right' [CEV], 'what is right' [BAGD, NTC; TEV]. The phrase ὁ ποιῶν χρηστότητα 'doing goodness' is translated '(none) that practices kindness' [HNTC], 'who shows kindness' [ICC2; NET, NRSV], '(no one) to show kindness' [REB], '(no one) does anything good' [GW, NCV].

b. ἕως (LN 59.21) (BAGD II.4. p. 335): 'even' [AB, BAGD, BECNT, HNTC, NICNT, NTC; GW, NASB, NCV, NET, NIV, NLT, NRSV, TEV], 'as much as' [ICC2, LN], 'so much as' [WBC], not explicit [CEV, KJV, REB].

3:13 **A grave**[a] **having-been-opened**[b] **(is) their throat,**[c]

LEXICON—a. τάφος (LN 7.75) (BAGD 2. p. 806): 'grave' [BAGD, BECNT, HNTC, ICC2, LN, NICNT, NTC, WBC; GW, NASB, NCV, NLT], 'tomb' [BAGD, LN], 'pit' [CEV], 'sepulchre' [KJV]. This singular noun is translated as a plural: 'graves' [AB; NET, NIV, NRSV], 'tombs' [REB], not explicit [TEV].

b. perf. pass. participle of ἀνοίγω (LN **79.110**) (BAGD 1.b. p. 71): 'to be opened' [LN]. This participle is translated as an adjective: 'open' [AB, BAGD, BECNT, HNTC, ICC2, LN, NICNT, NTC, WBC; all versions except NRSV, TEV], 'opened' [NRSV], not explicit [TEV].

c. λάρυγξ (LN **8.26**) (BAGD p. 467): 'throat' [BAGD, BECNT, HNTC, ICC2, LN, NICNT, NTC, WBC; GW, KJV, NASB, NCV]. This singular noun is translated as a plural: 'throats' [AB; NET, NIV, NRSV, REB], 'words' [CEV, TEV], 'talk' [NLT]. This clause is translated 'their speech is full of deadly deceit' [LN], 'their words are full of deadly deceit' [TEV]. This word occurs only here in the NT.

QUESTION—What is meant by λάρυγξ 'throat'?

It refers to human speech [AB, BECNT, Gdt, Ho, ICC2, Mor, Mu, NAC, NICNT, NTC, TH]. This is a metonymy for speech [SSA]. It refers to speaking, but perhaps the psalmist wanted to indicate a more deep-seated evil here [Mor].

QUESTION—What is the significance of comparing throats to an open grave?

1. This highlights the inner corruption of this wicked speech [AB, BECNT, Ho, ICC2, NAC, NICNT, St, TH], or possibly the deadly effects [BECNT, Ho, ICC2, NICNT, TH]. The comparison is to the offensive and diseased character of an open grave [Ho]. They are full of corruption and infection [St]. The metaphor signifies that just as a tomb emits a foul

smell when opened, so also when a sinner opens his mouth to speak he emits foul language [NAC, SSA]. It speaks of filth and contamination [AB]. This refers to the death caused by what evil men say [TH]. When a grave is opened it is so that it can be filled with a corpse that will corrupt it, and when the mouths of the wicked are opened it is to vent speech that is depraved [ICC1].
2. It speaks of how the brutal man would devour others [Gdt, Mu, NTC].

with their tongues[a] they-were-deceiving;[b]
LEXICON—a. γλῶσσα (LN 8.21) (BAGD 1.a. p. 162): 'tongue' [AB, BAGD, BECNT, HNTC, ICC2, LN, NICNT, NTC, WBC; all versions except NLT], 'speech' [NLT].
b. imperf. act. indic. of δολιόω (LN **88.154**) (BAGD p. 203): 'to deceive' [BAGD, BECNT, **LN,** WBC; NET, NRSV], 'to practice deceit' [AB, HNTC; NIV], 'to practice deception' [NTC], 'to use deceit' [KJV], 'to keep deceiving' [NASB], 'to trick, to be treacherous' [LN], 'to be filled with lies' [NLT], 'to be wont to deceive' [ICC2]. This verb is translated as an adverb: '(speak) deceptively' [NICNT]; as a noun: 'treachery' [REB], 'deception' [GW]. This clause is translated 'and their tongues are good only for telling lies' [CEV], 'they use their tongues for telling lies' [NCV], 'wicked lies roll off their tongues' [TEV], 'their speech is filled with lies' [NLT]. This word occurs only here in the NT.
QUESTION—To what does ἐδολιοῦσαν 'they were deceiving' refer?
This refers to the deceptive flatteries of those who intend to do evil [NICNT]. This denotes the falseness and flattery that permeate much of human speech, where even kind words can hide insidious purposes [BECNT]. This refers to flattery [Ho, ICC2, NTC] and smooth talk [Gdt, Mu]. This word implies treachery [Mor]. They are not dedicated to the truth [St]. They are practiced in fraud [ICC1]. The imperfect tense indicates repeated action [Gdt].

poison[a] of-asps[b] (is) under[c] their lips;[d]
LEXICON—a. ἰός (LN **8.74**) (BAGD 1.a. p. 378): 'poison' [AB, BAGD, BECNT, HNTC, ICC2, **LN,** NICNT, NTC; KJV, NASB, NCV, NET, NIV, NLT], 'venom' [LN, WBC; GW, NRSV, REB], not explicit [CEV]. This word is translated as a phrase: 'dangerous threats, like snake's poison' [TEV].
b. ἀσπίς (LN **4.53**) (BAGD p. 117): 'asp' [AB, BAGD, BECNT, HNTC, ICC2, **LN,** NICNT, WBC; KJV, NASB, NET], 'viper' [LN, NTC; NIV, NRSV], 'cobra' [LN], 'snake' [CEV, GW, NCV, TEV], 'deadly snakes' [NLT], 'adders' [REB]. This word occurs only here in the NT.
c. ὑπό with accusative object (LN 83.51) (BAGD 2.a.β. p. 843): 'under' [BAGD, BECNT, HNTC, ICC2, LN, NICNT, NTC, WBC; KJV, NASB, NET, NRSV], 'lies behind' [AB], 'is on' [NIV, REB], 'drips from' [NLT], 'roll from' [TEV], not explicit [CEV, GW, NCV].

d. χειλός (LN 33.74) (BAGD 1. p. 879): 'lip' [AB, BAGD, BECNT, HNTC, ICC2, LN, NICNT, NTC, WBC; all versions except CEV, NCV]. This clause is translated 'dangerous threats, like snake's poison, (roll) from their lips' [TEV], 'each word is as deadly as the fangs of a snake' [CEV], 'their words are like snake poison' [NCV].

QUESTION—What is Paul communicating with this clause?

The phrase highlights the destructive nature of sinful human communication [BECNT, ICC2, NTC, SSA]. Here Paul refers to the vicious and deadly things people say [AB]. Paul is emphasizing the manner in which people, acting from motives outside God's grace, try to destroy others; although the words may be flattering, they should not be trusted [NTC]. The metaphor is that sinful speech harms people spiritually in a way similar to the way a snake's venom harms people physically [SSA]. This description vividly characterizes the malignancy of their slander [ICC2]. The metaphor means that wicked people speak evil, poisonous things [Mor]. The way malignant lips give forth slander and deceit is compared to the way a snake infuses its poison [Gdt]. They are so malignant they delight in inflicting suffering [Ho].

3:14 whose mouth[a] is-full[b] of curse[c] and bitterness,[d]

LEXICON—a. στόμα (LN 8.19, 33.74): 'mouth' [BECNT, HNTC, ICC2, LN (8.19, 33.74), NICNT, NTC, WBC; GW, KJV, NASB, NCV, NIV], 'speech' [LN (33.74); TEV], not explicit [CEV]. This singular noun is translated as a plural: 'mouths' [AB; NET, NLT, NRSV, REB].

b. pres. act. indic. of γέμω (LN 59.41) (BAGD 1. p. 153): 'to be full of (something)' [AB, BAGD, BECNT, HNTC, ICC2, LN, NICNT, NTC, WBC; all versions except CEV], 'to say nothing but' [CEV].

c. ἀρά (LN **33.473**) (BAGD p. 103): 'curse' [BAGD, LN]. This singular noun is translated as plural: 'curses' [LN, NICNT, WBC; CEV, GW, TEV]; as a participle: 'cursing' [AB, BECNT, HNTC, ICC2, NTC; KJV, NASB, NCV, NET, NIV, NLT, NRSV, REB]. This word occurs only here in the NT.

d. πικρία (LN 79.40, **88.201**) (BAGD 2. p. 657): 'bitterness' [AB, BECNT, HNTC, ICC2, LN (79.40, 88.201), NICNT, NTC, WBC; KJV, NASB, NET, NIV, NLT, NRSV], 'spite' [LN (88.201)], 'hate' [NCV]. This noun is translated as an adjective: 'bitter' [LN; CEV, GW, REB, TEV]; as a phrase: 'bitter resentment' [LN (**88.201**)].

QUESTION—What is meant by saying that their mouths are ἀρᾶς καὶ πικρίας γέμει 'full of curse and bitterness'?

This refers to the pervasiveness of the sins of the tongue, that they are not just occasional [BECNT, TH]. Paul comments that this kind of speech is habitual with these people [Mor]. This refers to the overflow of the ungodly person's heart, and which displays his fallen nature when he speaks [NAC]. This refers to the fact that humans scoff even at God in their violent speech [AB]. This refers to the way some people will insincerely pronounce curses

3:15 Swift[a] (are) their feet[b] to-shed[c] blood,[d]

LEXICON—a. ὀξύς (LN **67.112**) (BAGD 2. p.574): 'swift' [AB, BAGD, BECNT, HNTC, ICC2, **LN,** NICNT, NTC, WBC; KJV, NASB, NET, NIV, NRSV], 'quick' [**LN;** NLT, TEV]. This adjective is translated as a verb: 'to hasten' [REB]; as an adverb: 'quickly' [CEV, GW]. This clause is translated 'they are always ready to kill people' [NCV].

b. πούς (LN 8.49) (BAGD 1.b. p. 696): 'feet' [AB, BAGD, BECNT, HNTC, ICC2, LN, NICNT, NTC, WBC; KJV, NASB, NET, NIV, NRSV, REB], not explicit [NCV, TEV]. The phrase ὀξεῖς οἱ πόδες αὐτῶν 'swift are their feet' is translated 'they are quick' [BAGD; NLT], 'these people quickly' [CEV], 'they run quickly' [GW]. The phrase οἱ πόδες αὐτῶν 'their feet' is a metonymy referring to the people themselves [LN (67.112)].

c. aorist act. infin. of ἐκχέω (LN **20.84**, 47.4) (BAGD 1. p. 247): 'to shed' [AB, BAGD, BECNT, HNTC, ICC2, NICNT, NTC, WBC; KJV, NASB, NET, NIV, NRSV, REB], 'to pour out' [BAGD, LN (47.4)]. The phrase ἐκχέαι αἷμα 'to shed blood' is an idiom translated 'to murder' [LN (20.84); GW], 'to commit a murder' [BAGD; NLT], 'to kill' [BAGD, LN (**20.84**); NCV], 'to hurt and kill' [TEV], 'to become violent' [CEV].

d. αἷμα (LN 8.64) (BAGD 2.a. p. 22): 'blood' [AB, BAGD, BECNT, HNTC, ICC2, LN, NICNT, NTC, WBC; KJV, NASB, NET, NIV, NRSV, REB], not explicit [CEV, GW, NCV, NLT, TEV].

QUESTION—What is he speaking of in this clause?

This refers to murder and violence [AB, BECNT, NTC, SSA, TH]. Human sinfulness is not confined to speech, and the barbarism to which the world often turns is expressed in society through murder and killing [AB, BECNT]. A long series of wars and murders proves that this is an ongoing reality [NTC]. The 'feet' is either a metonymy where the body part represents the associated action, or a synecdoche where the part represents the whole person; the meaning is that these people are eager to murder others [SSA]. The sense is not that such people would take desperate measures only if driven to it, but that they are eager for homicide [Mor]. The natural instincts of the unrighteous encourage them to kill [NAC]. It speaks of the sins of violence, as they will commit murder on the slightest provocation [Ho]. This describes the lifestyle of the wicked who act without concern for how they compromise the welfare or lives of others [Gdt]. These people are quick to hurt and kill others [TH].

3:16 ruin[a] and misery[b] (are) in their ways,[c]

LEXICON—a. σύντριμμα (LN **20.59**) (BAGD p. 793): 'ruin' [AB, BAGD, **LN,** NICNT, NTC, WBC; CEV, GW, NCV, NET, NIV, NRSV, REB, TEV], 'destruction' [BAGD, BECNT, ICC2, LN; KJV, NASB, NLT], 'affliction' [HNTC]. This word occurs only here in the NT.

b. ταλαιπωρία (LN **22.11**) (BAGD p. 803): 'misery' [BAGD, BECNT, ICC2, NICNT, NTC; KJV, NASB, NCV, NET, NIV, NLT, NRSV, REB], 'wretchedness' [AB, BAGD, HNTC, **LN,** WBC], 'distress, trouble' [BAGD], 'hardship' [LN], 'destruction' [CEV, TEV], 'suffering' [GW].
c. ὁδός (LN 1.99, 41.16) (BAGD 2.b. p. 554): 'way' [BAGD, ICC2, LN (1.99), NTC, WBC; KJV, NIV], 'path' [AB, BECNT, HNTC, NICNT; NASB, NET, NRSV], 'tracks' [REB], 'way of life' [LN (41.16)]. This word is translated as a clause: 'Wherever they go' [CEV, GW, NLT, TEV], 'everywhere they go' [NCV].

QUESTION—To what does σύντριμμα καὶ ταλαιπωρία 'ruin and misery' refer?

This refers to the ruin, misery, and destruction that these people cause wherever they go [AB, BECNT, Gdt, Ho, ICC2, SSA, TH]. They spread desolation all around themselves [Ho]. This is describing their characteristic way of life; 'ruin' denotes destructive activities, and 'misery', the wretchedness of the results [Mor]. They ruin things and make people miserable [SSA]. People behave violently and savagely, inflicting destruction and misery on others [BECNT]. Human wrath has brought about a long and continuing series of wars and murders [NTC]. Or, the desire of the wicked to prevail at any cost leads to suffering and disaster, as evil brings about its own collapse and personal retribution [NAC].

3:17 and (the) way[a] of-peace[b] they-have- not -known.[c]

LEXICON—a. ὁδός (LN 1.99, 41.16) (BAGD 2.a. p. 554): 'way' [BAGD, BECNT, HNTC, ICC2, LN (1.99), NICNT, NTC, WBC; KJV, NET, NIV, NRSV], 'path' [AB; NASB, REB, TEV], 'way of life' [LN (41.16)], 'road' [LN (1.99)], not explicit [CEV, GW, NCV, NLT].
b. εἰρήνη (LN 22.42, 25.248) (BAGD 1.b. p. 227): 'peace' [AB, BAGD, BECNT, HNTC, ICC2, LN (22.42, 25.248), NICNT, NTC, WBC; all versions], 'tranquility' [LN (22.42)], 'freedom from worry' [LN (25.248)]. This genitive noun means 'that leads to peace' [BAGD].
c. aorist act. indic. of γινώσκω (LN 27.2, 28.1, 32.16): 'to know' [AB, BECNT, HNTC, ICC2, LN (28.1), NICNT, NTC, WBC; KJV, NASB, NET, NIV, NLT, NRSV, TEV], 'to learn, to find out' [LN (27.2)], 'to perceive, to comprehend, to come to understand' [LN (32.16)], 'to know about, or to have knowledge of' [LN (28.1)], 'to know how to (live in peace)' [CEV, NCV].

QUESTION—What is meant by not knowing the way of peace?

1. It means these people have a lifestyle characterized by violence. Paul does not mean anxiety and emotional turbulence in the hearts of sinful people, but rather the violent, savage, and warlike lifestyle of these people [BECNT]. These people do not know the way of peace, since their interest is in destruction and bloodshed [Mor]. It means they do not know how to live peacefully with others [SSA]. They do not know how to establish true peace among themselves [ICC2]. In the most comprehensive sense, these

people neither approve nor frequent a way of life that leads to peace; the general prevalence of violence shows how depraved human nature is [Ho]. Paul means that people such as those he has just described do not know a life characterized by blessing from God [AB]. It means that these people never do anything to bring about peace with their fellow men [TH].
2. This means that these people's lives are marked by unrest and by the lack of genuine satisfaction of their deeper longings [NAC]. It means that these people do not know peace either in their own hearts or in their relationships with others [Gdt]. Their lives are not full and bounteous or characterized by the fullness of God's blessings [AB].

3:18 **There-is not fear[a] of-God before[b] their eyes.[c]**
LEXICON—a. φόβος (LN 53.59) (BAGD 2.b.α. p. 864): 'fear' [AB, BECNT, HNTC, ICC2, NICNT, NTC, WBC; KJV, NASB, NCV, NET, NIV, NLT, NRSV], 'reverence' [BAGD, LN; REB, TEV], 'awe' [LN], 'respect' [BAGD]. This clause is translated 'they don't even fear God' [CEV], 'they are not terrified of God' [GW]. The word denotes a reverence and respect towards God [BAGD], a profound respect and awe for deity [LN].
b. ἀπέναντι (LN 83.42) (BAGD 1.b. p. 84): 'before' [AB, BAGD, HNTC, ICC2, LN, NTC, WBC; KJV, NASB, NET, NIV, NRSV], 'in' [BECNT, NICNT], not explicit [CEV, GW, NCV, NLT, REB, TEV].
c. ὀφθαλμός (LN 8.23, 32.24): 'eye' [AB, HNTC, ICC2, LN (8.23, 32.24), NICNT, NTC, WBC; KJV, NASB, NET, NIV, NRSV], 'understanding' [LN (32.24)], 'their sight' [BECNT], not explicit [CEV, GW, NCV, NLT, REB, TEV]. The word can be used figuratively to refer to the capacity to perceive, or to understand as the result of perception [LN (32.24)].

QUESTION—What is meant by οὐκ ἔστιν φόβος θεοῦ 'there is not fear of God'?
1. It means they do not reverence God [AB, NAC, SSA, St, TH]. People like those just described are not motivated by reverence for God [AB]. It means that in the thinking of these people there is no reverence for God [SSA]. This means more than fright, it refers to an awesome respect for God [TH]. These people do not venerate or hold God in esteem, it does not even enter their thoughts [NAC].
2. It means that they do not fear God [ICC2, Mor]. These people do not fear God, they have no terror of him and feel no need to dread God's judgments [Mor]. It means that God is left out of man's thinking, and the fear of God has no part in directing his life [ICC2].
3. It means that both fear of and reverence for God are lacking [BECNT, Ho]. It means to reject God, and not to fear, reverence, or honor him [BECNT]. They have no proper regard for God and act as if there were no God to whom they will have to answer for their conduct [Ho].
4. It means they do not have a constant awareness of God [Gdt, Mu]. The fear of God means that God is constantly in the center of one's thoughts,

and that life is characterized by an all-pervasive consciousness of dependence on him and responsibility to him; the absence of this means that God is not at all in one's thoughts, but rather is excluded from one's reckoning altogether [Mu]. This describes what the OT refers to as piety, and it is the disposition in man in which he always has God and his will and judgment present in his heart; it is the inward view of God on which a person's moral conduct depends [Gdt].

3:19 Now[a] we-know that whatever the law[b] says
LEXICON—a. δέ (LN 89.124, 89.94): 'now' [AB, HNTC, NICNT, NTC, WBC; KJV, NASB, NET, NIV, NRSV, REB, TEV], 'but' [ICC2, LN (89.124)], 'and' [BECNT, LN (89.94)], 'obviously' [NLT], not explicit [CEV, GW, NCV].
  b. νόμος (LN 33.55, 33.333) (BAGD 3. p. 543; 4.b, p. 543): 'law' [AB, BAGD, BECNT, HNTC, ICC2, LN (33.333), NICNT, NTC, WBC; KJV, NCV, NET, NIV, NLT, NRSV, REB], 'Law' [LN (33.55); CEV, NASB, TEV], 'Moses' Teachings' [GW]. This phrase 'whatever the law says' is translated 'everything written in the Law' [CEV], 'all the words of the law' [REB].
QUESTION—What relationship is indicated by the use of the conjunction δέ 'now'?
  It has a loose consecutive function, and is used by Paul to draw out the implications of the previous quotations regarding the position of men before the divine judge [NICNT]. It signals that Paul is making a further point in his argument, and is referring to the Scriptures just cited [SSA].
QUESTION—What is the significance of the first person plural 'we' in the verb οἴδαμεν 'we know'?
  This refers to Paul and his readers, and indicates that this statement would be generally known and acknowledged by them [NICNT]. Paul assumes that all will agree with the statement that what the law says, it says to those in the realm of law [BECNT]. This is used to introduce something known and believed by all concerned [SSA]. Paul appeals to what everyone who was familiar with Jewish Scriptures would take for granted and he identifies himself with his own people as well as with all humankind who are under the power of sin [WBC]. Paul is appealing to what is common knowledge, to facts that are well known [Mor]. The phrase means that this statement is plain in itself and universally conceded [Ho]. Paul uses this to appeal to the common sense of his readers [Gdt].
QUESTION—What is meant by the first occurrence of ὁ νόμος 'the law'?
  It means the whole OT canon [AB, BECNT, Gdt, HNTC, Ho, ICC1, ICC2, Mor, Mu, NAC, NICNT, NTC, St, TH, TNTC]. Since the quotations just cited are drawn from the Psalms and Isaiah, the first reference to 'law' here does not denote the law of Moses, the Torah, as it usually does in Paul, but here means the entire OT canon [BECNT, HNTC, ICC2, Mor, Mu, NICNT, TH, TNTC]. This first occurrence of the word is wider than the Mosaic law

since the quotations given are not from the Pentateuch, but it is not necessary to draw too sharp a distinction since those called evil in the Psalms and Isaiah were evil precisely because they did not observe the Mosaic law [BECNT]. This clearly refers to the preceding collection of verses quoted from the Writings and Prophets, not the Pentateuch, so it must be taken as a reference to the OT as a whole [Ho, NAC].

QUESTION—Is there any significance to the shift from the verb λέγω 'to say' in this clause and the verb λαλέω 'to speak' in the following clause?
1. The first verb is used in reference to what the law says and the latter to the act of speaking [BECNT, Gdt, ICC1, ICC2, NICNT, NTC, TH].
2. There is no significance to this shift [HNTC, Mor].

it-speaks to-the-(ones) in[a] the law,
LEXICON—a. ἐν with dative object (LN 83.13) (BAGD I.5.d. p. 260): 'in' [LN, NICNT], 'under' [AB; CEV, GW, KJV, NASB, NET, NIV, NRSV, REB, TEV], 'subject to' [BAGD], 'within' [WBC]. This preposition is translated as a phrase: 'in the realm of' [BECNT], 'within the scope of' [HNTC], 'within the pale of' [NTC], '(those who) possess' [ICC2], '(those who) have' [NCV]. The whole clause is translated 'the law applies to those to whom it was given' [NLT].

QUESTION—Who are 'the ones in the law'?
1. This refers to the Jews [BECNT, HNTC, Ho, ICC1, ICC2, Mor, NAC, NICNT, SSA, St, TH, WBC]. Paul is referring to the Mosaic law and his intent is to say that the law was particularly directed to the Jews [BECNT]. The Jews are included in the judgment as well [St]. They are those who are subject to the law, the Jews [HNTC]. This means those who orient their lives and have their whole being by and in the law, that is, the Jews [Mor]. The point that really needed proving was that the Jews are guilty, since they were likely to explain away passages that condemned them [ICC1]. It has already been concluded that Gentiles are under condemnation, and here Paul shows that the Jews are also guilty in God's sight [TH]. The law was what marked the boundary between Jew and Gentile [WBC].
2. This refers to all people [Mu, NTC]. God's word has a message for all, authority over all, and is of concern for all, whether Jew or Gentile [NTC]. Paul is showing that sin is an all-inclusive universal condition for Jews and Gentiles alike [Mu].
3. It applies the Scripture passages first of all to the Jews, but then also to all humanity because all are sinners [AB].

QUESTION—What is meant by the phrase ἐν τῷ νόμῳ 'in the law'?
1. It means to live in subjection to, or under the jurisdiction of the law [BECNT, HNTC, Ho, Mor, NAC, NICNT, St, TH]. The phrase has a metaphorical spatial sense meaning that the Jews live within the sphere of the revelation of God given in the Scriptures [NICNT]. It refers to those who are in the realm of the law, which was directed in particular to the

Jews [BECNT]. It means those who possess and know the OT Scriptures, the Jews [ICC2]. It means those who are obliged to keep the law, or those who bind themselves to behave according to it [TH]. It means those who fall within the scope of the law and are thus subject to the law, which in this case is the law of Moses [HNTC, Mor]. It means those under the jurisdiction of the law, the Jews [NAC]. Paul is saying that the law speaks to those who are subject to it, who are within its orbit, not outside of it, namely, the Jews, who cannot rest on a false idea of security as if they will not come under the judgment of God [Mor]. The Jews cannot deny that the declaration that all men are under sin applies to them [Ho]. The Jews are those whose religion, ethnicity, and way of life is shaped by the Torah [WBC].

2. It means all for whom the law has something to say [AB, Mu, NTC]. God's word has a message for all, has authority over all, and is of concern for all, whether Jew or Gentile, and the immediate context of 3:19b–20 makes it clear that Paul's summary includes all people [NTC]. Paul is including both the Jew, who had been given the OT, as well as the Gentile, who did not have that or any specially revealed law, for he means all those who are living in the sphere within which the law has relevance, within the sphere of judgment pronounced in the OT, and who are without excuse and condemned in God's sight, which is the whole world [Mu]. The Jews fall under the law's indictment, but so do all other people [AB].

3. It means those directed by the law. The phrase is somewhat similar to 'under the law' but here 'directed by' the law is preferable, since here it lacks the component of compulsion to obey the law which is signaled by the phrase 'under the law' [SSA].

QUESTION—What is meant by this second occurrence of τῷ νόμῳ 'the law'?

1. It means the whole OT canon [Gdt, Ho, ICC1, ICC2, Mu, NAC, NTC, St, TH]. Since there is no reason to assume here that 'law' has its usual and more narrow sense, it can be understood to denote the whole OT just as in the earlier part of the verse [ICC1, ICC2]. Since Paul has not quoted from the Pentateuch, but only from Psalms, the Prophets, and the Writings, the term must refer to the OT as a whole [NAC, NTC].

2. It means the law of Moses [BECNT, HNTC, Mor, WBC]. The parallel phrase in 2:12, 'as many as are in the law', specifically distinguished Jews from Gentiles [BECNT].

3. Paul uses the term specifically of the Mosaic Law, but also generally of the entire OT [AB].

so-that[a] every mouth[b] may-be-stopped[c]

LEXICON—a. ἵνα 'so that' [AB, LN (89.59); NET, NIV, NRSV, REB], 'that' [NTC; KJV, NASB], 'in order to' [LN; TEV], 'in order that' [BECNT, ICC2, NICNT, WBC], 'to the intent that' [HNTC]. This conjunction is translated as a phrase: 'its purpose is to' [NLT], not explicit [CEV, GW, NCV].

b. στόμα (LN 8.19, **33.125**): 'mouth' [AB, BECNT, HNTC, ICC2, NICNT, NTC, WBC; KJV, NASB, NET, NIV, NRSV], not explicit [CEV, GW, NCV, NLT, REB, TEV]. This clause is translated 'in order to stop everyone from having anything to say' [LN (33.125)].

c. aorist pass. subj. of φράσσω (LN 68.45) (BAGD 1.b. p. 865): 'to be stopped' [BAGD, ICC2, LN, NICNT, WBC; KJV], 'to stop' [LN (33.125); CEV, NCV, TEV], 'to be silenced' [AB, NTC; NET, NIV, NRSV], 'to close' [BAGD, BECNT], 'to shut (the mouth)' [HNTC], 'to be closed' [NASB], not explicit [GW, NLT, REB].

QUESTION—What relationship is indicated by ἵνα 'so that'?

1. It indicates purpose [AB, BECNT, Gdt, HNTC, Ho, ICC1, ICC2, Mu, NICNT, NTC, TH, WBC; CEV, KJV, NASB, NET, NLT, NRSV, REB, TEV].
2. It indicates result [SSA; NCV].

QUESTION—What is the meaning of this clause?

It means that no one can offer any defense against his own guilt for sin [AB, BECNT, Gdt, HNTC, Ho, ICC2, Mor, Mu, NAC, NICNT, NTC, St, TH, WBC]. The terminology here reflects that of a courtroom scene where the defendant has no more to say in his own defense for the charges brought against him [NAC, NICNT]. It refers to the fact that the accused at trial has exhausted all possibility of refuting charges against himself, having no evidence left to plead in his defense, indicating that the whole world is liable to God's judgment and deserving of condemnation [BECNT]. It means that there can be no boasting or declaration of one's innocence before others or before God [AB], or being full of vain self-satisfaction [Gdt]. This evokes a picture of a defendant in court who, because of the weight of evidence against him, is speechless to defend himself further and can only await his sentencing [ICC2, St]. The accused have no answer to give to the charges because their guilt has been exposed [NTC]. No one, whether they are Jewish or non-Jewish, will be able to say anything to God in his own defense [SSA, WBC]. All men should be reduced to silence as they recognize that they have nothing to say against the charge of sin [Ho]. The law exists to stop all human excuses [TH].

QUESTION—Who is intended in the phrase πᾶν στόμα φραγῇ 'every mouth will be closed'?

This refers to all humanity [BECNT, Gdt, HNTC, Ho, ICC2, Mor, Mu, NAC, NICNT, NTC, SSA, St, TH, WBC]. If the Jews, who had the privilege of a covenantal relationship with God, could not keep the law, then it follows that no one else, including Gentiles, can do so either, all deserve condemnation and judgment [BECNT, ICC2]. If God's chosen people, the Jews, are under sin's tyranny, then surely also all others having no special claim on God's favor are also under sin [NICNT]. The Scriptures consign all to sin [AB], and all are without excuse, guilty and liable to God's judgment, such that no one can claim innocence before God [AB, St]. All the world without exception is answerable to God and all protest is silenced [WBC]. It speaks of both Jew and Gentile [Ho, NAC, SSA], both of whom are accountable to God and fall under his judgment [NAC].

and all the world^a may-become accountable^b to-God;

LEXICON—a. κόσμος (LN 9.23) (BAGD 5.a. p. 446): 'world' [AB, BECNT, HNTC, ICC2, NICNT, NTC, WBC; all versions], 'mankind' [BAGD], 'people of the world' [LN].

b. ὑπόδικος (LN **56.17**) (BAGD p. 844): 'accountable' [BAGD], 'answerable' [BAGD, BECNT, **LN**]. The phrase ὑπόδικος γένηται is translated 'to become accountable' [NASB], 'to be held accountable' [NICNT; NET, NIV, NRSV], 'to be accountable to' [AB], 'to be liable to judgment' [BAGD, LN, WBC], 'to be exposed to judgment' [NTC], 'to be brought under the judgment of' [GW], 'to bring under (God's) judgment' [NCV, TEV], 'to bring into judgment' [NLT], 'to be liable to punishment' [BAGD], 'to be brought to trial' [HNTC], 'to stand guilty before' [ICC2], 'to be exposed to (God's) judgment' [REB], 'to become guilty' [KJV]. The phrase 'and all the world may become accountable to God' is translated 'to let God show that the whole world is guilty' [CEV].

QUESTION—What is meant by the phrase ὑπόδικος...τῷ θεῷ 'accountable to God'?

1. It means to be judged and condemned as guilty [BECNT, Gdt, HNTC, Ho, ICC2, Mu, NAC, NTC, SSA, St, WBC]. In extra-biblical Greek, the word denotes one who has offended against law and is guilty and liable to punishment [Gdt, ICC2]. Here Paul presents God as both the one offended and as the one who will render judgment, pronouncing the deserved verdict of condemnation as all humanity stands before him and is proven guilty beyond any doubt of violating his will [ICC2]. They are unable either to refute the charges against them or to avert the condemnation and consequences that will follow [BECNT]. The OT citations show that the Jews as well as all others are without excuse, under accusation without possibility of defense, and are guilty and condemned before God [Mu, NAC, NTC, SSA, St, WBC]. It refers to one whom the judge has declared guilty and who owes satisfaction to the law; the whole world is guilty before God and is under his judgment [Gdt, TH].

2. It means to have to answer to someone [ICC1, NICNT], or to be liable to prosecution by someone [NICNT]. It means to be liable to judgment by God; all mankind, both pagan and Jew, is subject to God's judgment [AB]. It means to be answerable to God, but not exactly condemned as guilty before God yet; all men have offended against God and owe him satisfaction [ICC1]. They are liable to prosecution for their inexcusable violations of God's will, and waiting for the condemnation they deserve [NICNT].

3. The term conveys more than general liability to punishment but less than definitive condemnation [ICC2, Mor]. There is no doubt regarding their guilt, but they are still awaiting the condemnation to be pronounced

[ICC2]. It describes one who has exhausted all possibility of refuting the charge against him, or averting the condemnation that will follow. Paul is speaking of the Jew who felt that he would need to give account but would not be found guilty [Mor].

3:20 for[a] by[b] works[c] of-law[d] no flesh[e] shall-be-justified[f] before[g] him,

LEXICON—a. διότι (LN 89.26) (BAGD 3. p. 199): 'for' [BAGD, BECNT, HNTC, ICC2, NICNT, WBC; NET, NLT, NRSV, REB, TEV], 'since' [AB], 'because' [NASB, NCV], 'therefore' [NTC; KJV, NIV], not explicit [CEV, GW].
  b. ἐκ with genitive object (LN 89.77, 90.12) (BAGD 3.f. p. 235): 'by' [BECNT, HNTC, LN (90.12), NICNT, NTC, WBC; all versions except CEV], 'by means of' [LN (89.77)], 'by reason of' [BAGD], 'because of' [BAGD; CEV], 'as a result of' [BAGD, LN (90.12)], 'through' [AB], 'on the ground of' [ICC2].
  c. ἔργον (LN 42.11, 42.42) (BAGD 1.c.β. p. 308): 'work' [BECNT, HNTC, LN (42.42), NICNT, NTC, WBC; NASB, NET], 'act' [LN (42.11)], 'deed' [AB, BAGD, LN (42.11); KJV, NRSV]. This noun is translated as a verb phrase: 'having done what (the law) requires' [ICC2], 'obey (the law)' [CEV]; as a participle: 'observing' [NIV], 'keeping' [REB], 'doing what (his law) commands' [NLT], 'doing what (the law) requires' [TEV], 'following (Moses' Teaching)' [GW], 'by following (the law)' [NCV].
  d. νόμος (LN 33.55, 33.333) (BAGD 3. p. 542; 4.b. p. 542): 'law' [LN (33.333)], 'Law' [LN (33.55)]. This word, which lacks the definite article here, is translated 'law' [HNTC, NTC], 'the Law' [CEV, NASB, TEV], 'the law' [BECNT, ICC2, NICNT, WBC; KJV, NCV, NET, NIV, NRSV, REB], 'his law' [NLT], 'deeds prescribed by the law' [AB; NRSV], 'Moses' Teachings' [GW].
  e. σάρξ (LN 9.11) (BAGD 3. p. 743): 'flesh' [BECNT, HNTC, ICC2, LN, NTC, WBC; KJV, NASB], 'person' [BAGD; GW], 'human being' [AB, LN (9.11), NICNT; NRSV, REB]; this singular noun is translated as a plural: 'people' [LN (9.11); CEV], 'no one' [NCV, NET, NIV, NLT, TEV].
  f. fut. pass. indic. of δικαιόω (LN 34.46, 56.34) (BAGD 3.a. p. 197): 'to be justified' [AB, BAGD, BECNT, HNTC, ICC2, NICNT, NTC, WBC; KJV, NASB, NRSV, REB], 'to be pronounced and treated as righteous' [BAGD], 'to be declared righteous' [NET, NIV], 'to be put right with' [LN (34.46); TEV], 'to cause to be in a right relationship with' [LN (34.46)], 'to be made right' [NCV, NLT], 'to be acquitted' [BAGD, LN (56.34)], 'to have one's guilt removed, to be set free' [LN (56.34)], 'to be accepted (by God)' [CEV], 'to have God's approval' [GW]. The word may refer to causing someone to be in a proper relationship with another [LN (34.46)] or to the act of clearing someone of transgression [LN (56.34)]. Paul uses the word almost exclusively of God's action when he acquits or justifies people [BAGD].

g. ἐνώπιον with genitive object (LN 83.33, 90.20) (BAGD 3. p. 270): 'before' [AB, BECNT, HNTC, ICC2, LN (83.33), NICNT, WBC; NET]. This preposition is translated as a phrase: 'in the opinion of' [BAGD, LN (90.20)], 'in the judgment of' [BAGD, LN (90.20)], 'in the sight of' [LN (90.20), NTC; KJV, NIV, NLT, REB], 'in his sight' [NASB, NCV, NRSV], 'in God's sight' [TEV], not explicit [CEV, GW].

QUESTION—What is the meaning of the conjunction διότι 'for' and how does this indicate the function of this verse?

1. This indicates the reason that the whole world is accountable to God [AB, BECNT, Gdt, HNTC, Ho, ICC1, ICC2, Mor, Mu, NICNT, SSA, WBC]. It introduces the reason why no one will be justified by keeping the law, which is that no one keeps it completely [SSA]. This verse provides the reason for all of 3:19; that is, justification by law is ruled out because no one can keep what the law says [BECNT]. This verse delivers the final and fundamental reason for the whole world being answerable to God for its unrighteousness [WBC]. This verse gives the reason that every mouth is stopped and the whole world is condemned [Mu]. They will be silenced because no one can be justified by works [Ho]. Paul counters any hope of the Jew evading the force of 3:19 by explicitly denying that the law can offer any hope of defense regarding accountability to God for sin [NICNT]. It means 'for' rather than 'because', and is used to introduce a confirmation from Scripture about what he has just said in 3:19 [ICC2].

2. It introduces a conclusion to be drawn [NTC; KJV, NIV]: therefore. Because of what man is and says and does he stands condemned before God, and consequently is doomed because he can never attain the state of moral perfection the law demands [NTC].

QUESTION—Is this verse a quotation from OT Scriptures?

It is an allusion to Ps. 143:2, though not a quotation [AB, BECNT, Ho, ICC2, Mor, NAC, NICNT, NTC, WBC]. While Paul's comment resembles Ps. 143:2b, the lack of an introductory formula for the quote and the significant differences in what Paul says as compared with the text of that verse make it unlikely that this is a direct quotation [NICNT]. There is one significant addition to the quote from Ps. 143:2, which is 'by doing what the law requires' [TH]. Paul alludes to Ps. 143 and then makes the bold addition of 'through deeds of the law' as he applies the cry for justification to the specific problem of attaining uprightness through observing the law [AB]. This is a free quotation and amplification of Ps. 143:2, which Paul makes doubly applicable by adding 'works of the law' and 'no flesh' [WBC]. This is the thought of Ps. 143:2 in somewhat different phraseology [NTC]. It is from 143:2b but Paul introduces two modifications into it [HNTC].

QUESTION—What is the meaning of the phrase ἔργων νόμου 'the works of the law'?

1. This refers in general to things done in obedience to the law [AB, BECNT, Ho, ICC2, Mor, Mu, NAC, NICNT, SSA, St, TH]. They are what the law requires [BECNT, ICC2, NAC, NICNT, SSA]. The principle

Paul is presenting in this part of the book has universal application for all, which is that no one is capable of doing anything that can insure acceptance with God, but all must see faith in Christ as the only way to God [NICNT]. The expression most naturally denotes the whole law, that is, the actions and deeds required by the law, and should not be restricted to certain key observances which separated Jews from Gentiles [BECNT]. In the whole context Paul is attacking merit and self-salvation by reliance on moral works, and there is no indication that Paul meant only cultural and ceremonial works [St]. It is works of any kind which the law prescribes, whether done by us or wrought in us [Ho]. Paul is arguing that all are sinners, and none can be saved by any type of works of law at all [Mor]. This means works done in obedience to the law and which are regarded as a means of justification [HNTC]. The phrase means those things done in obedience to the law and which are looked on as a means of establishing a right relationship with God [TH]. The good works are the requirements of the moral law, not of the ceremonial law, and which would presumably be done in one's own strength and with no other help than from the law itself, which of course a sinful human being cannot do [Gdt]. People cannot fulfill the most basic requirement of the law, which is loving God with all one's heart and one's neighbor as oneself [NTC].

2. This means those actions performed on demand of the law, in service to the Torah, and which marked out and identified those who were the covenant people of the law as distinct from others, and which were necessary to maintain their status within the covenant, particularly such observances as circumcision, abstaining from certain foods, or hearing the law read [WBC].

QUESTION—What is the meaning and significance of the use of the word σάρξ 'flesh' here?

1. The word means simply 'human beings' [AB, BECNT, Gdt, HNTC, Ho, Mor, Mu, NAC, NICNT, SSA]. Flesh was a common OT way of referring to human beings which makes it improbable that Paul intends any negative nuance by the use of the word here [NICNT, NTC]. The phrase indicates that all people without exception are included in the universality of sin [Ho]. The phrase 'no flesh' is a Hebraism meaning 'nobody' [Mor]. Paul shows that no human being can be brought into right standing with God on the basis of doing what the law requires [NAC].

2. Paul intends a negative nuance in the use of this word [ICC1, ICC2, NTC, WBC]. No doubt Paul's point is to denote man in his weakness, corruptibility, dependence on this world, and as taking his sense of values from the world and its society and standards. Paul implies that the Jewish assumption of a special covenant prerogative that would assure acquittal on the day of judgment, and equating membership in the covenant with a physical rite or national kinship is to think and live with a fleshly or superficial understanding of the law [WBC]. Paul uses this frequent OT expression to refer to all humanity, in contrast to God, as considered in

their frailty and mortality [ICC2, NTC] and their insignificance [NTC]. It is man in his weakness and frailty [ICC1].

QUESTION—What is meant by the word δικαιόω 'justified'?

It is a forensic term [BECNT, Ho, ICC1, Mor, TH, WBC]. This refers to the final judgment and should be understood forensically; those who depend on the law for justification will not be vindicated on the last day, for righteousness cannot be obtained by works of the law [BECNT]. Paul shows that no human being can be brought into right standing with God on the basis of obedience to the law's requirements [NAC]. It does not mean pardon, nor does it mean to be made right, just, or good, but is a forensic term expressing a judicial act of declaring that a person is not to be punished, that there is no longer grounds for condemnation since the demands of justice have been satisfied [Ho]. This is not ethical in the sense of making someone morally upright, rather it indicates God's pronouncement that the person is acquitted and not guilty in his sight, and is put into right relationship with God [TH]. It is the verdict of acquittal when one finally stands before God [Mor, WBC], to be pronounced righteous [ICC1].

for through[a] law[b] (comes)[c] knowledge[d] of-sin.[e]

LEXICON—a. διά with genitive object (LN 89.76, 90.8) (BAGD A.III.1.d. p. 180): 'through' [AB, BAGD, BECNT, HNTC, ICC2, LN (89.76, 90.8), NICNT, NTC, WBC; NASB, NET, NIV, NRSV], 'by means of' [LN (89.76, 90.8)], 'by' [KJV], not explicit [GW, NCV, NLT]. This preposition is translated as a verb: 'to bring' [REB]. The phrase 'for through law' is translated 'all the law does' [CEV], 'what the law does' [TEV].

b. νόμος (LN 33.55, 33.333) (BAGD 3. p. 542): 'law' [LN (33.333)], 'Law' [LN (33.55)]. This word, which lacks the definite article here, is translated 'law' [NTC], 'the law' [AB, BECNT, ICC2, NICNT, WBC; KJV, NCV, NET, NRSV, REB], 'his law' [NLT], 'the Law' [CEV, NASB, TEV], 'Moses' Teachings' [GW].

c. There is no lexical entry for this verb in the Greek text, it is implied. It is represented in translation as 'comes' [AB, BECNT, HNTC, ICC2, NICNT, NTC, WBC; NASB, NET, NRSV], 'is' [KJV], 'we become (conscious)' [NLT], '(law) brings' [REB].

d. ἐπίγνωσις (LN 28.2, 28.18) (BAGD p. 291): 'knowledge' [BECNT, ICC2, LN (28.2, 28.18), NICNT, WBC; KJV, NASB, NET, NRSV], 'full, or definite knowledge' [LN (28.18)], 'knowledge about' [LN (28.2)], 'real knowledge' [AB], 'recognition of' [HNTC], 'consciousness of' [BAGD, NTC; REB]. This clause is translated 'For the more we know God's law, the clearer it is that we aren't obeying it' [NLT], 'all the law does is to point out our sin' [CEV], 'Moses' Teachings show what sin is' [GW], 'the law only shows us our sin' [NCV], 'what the Law does is to make man know that he has sinned' [TEV].

e. ἁμαρτία (LN 88.289, 88.310) (BAGD 1. p. 43): 'sin' [AB, BECNT, HNTC, ICC2, LN (88.289, 88.310), NICNT, NTC, WBC; all versions except CEV, NLT], 'guilt' [BAGD, LN (88.310)]. This noun is translated as a clause: 'we aren't obeying it' [NLT], 'he has sinned' [TEV].

QUESTION—To what does διὰ νόμου 'through' law refer?

It refers to the Jewish law [AB, BECNT, HNTC, Ho, ICC2, NAC, NTC, WBC].

QUESTION—What is meant by ἐπίγνωσις ἁμαρτίας 'the knowledge of sin'?

It means an experiential recognition that one is in fact a sinner [AB, BECNT, Gdt, Ho, ICC1, Mor, Mu, NAC, NICNT, NTC, SSA, St, TH, WBC]. It is as we fail to attain the demands of God as presented in the law that we recognize ourselves to be in bondage to the power of sin and justly condemned as sinners [NICNT, TH]. The law creates a dreadful and mortifying sense of sinfulness and a presentiment of complete and eternal doom [NTC]. It means a recognition of what sin is and that we are sinners [Mor, Mu]. It is an inward conviction involving both an intellectual apprehension of sin as well as a due sense of guilt for sin [Ho]. The law opens a person's eyes to his or her own sinful condition [ICC1]. Even the people of God should recognize that they are in continual need of grace no less than Gentiles were [WBC].

QUESTION—In what sense is the knowledge of sin διὰ νόμου 'through law'?

The law reveals the presence of sin, and imparts the knowledge of sin [Gdt, Ho, ICC2, Mor, Mu, NAC, NICNT, NTC, SSA, St, TH, WBC]. Through their failure to keep the law it is made experientially clear to people that sin is a power that holds everyone in bondage and which brings guilt and condemnation [NICNT]. The law demands moral and spiritual perfection, which no man in his own power can attain, so the law creates in a person a sense of sin and a presentiment of doom [NTC]. The function of the law is to reveal, expose, and condemn sin [Ho, St, WBC]. The phrase 'through the law' is a shortened form of expressing a reason; it is as a result of our knowing God's law that we know clearly that we are sinful [SSA]. The law serves to define what sin is [Gdt]. The law shows the true character of sin as a violation of God's expressed will and a powerful force in life, and makes people conscious of their condition [AB]. The law helps man discern the sin which reigns over him, to better see his own true corruption [Gdt].

DISCOURSE UNIT: 3:21–4:25 [CEV]. The topic is God's way of accepting people.

DISCOURSE UNIT: 3:21–8:39 [St]. The topic is the grace of God in the gospel.

DISCOURSE UNIT: 3:21–5:21 [Mor, NAC, TNTC, WBC]. The topic is justification [Mor], the righteousness only God can provide [NAC], the way of righteousness: universal need met [TNTC], God's saving righteousness by faith [WBC].

DISCOURSE UNIT: 3:21–5:11 [Gdt]. The topic is justification by faith acquired for the whole world.

DISCOURSE UNIT: 3:21–4:25 [BECNT, NICNT, St; CEV]. The topic is the saving righteousness of God [BECNT], justification by faith [NICNT], God's righteousness revealed and illustrated [St], God's way of accepting people [CEV].

DISCOURSE UNIT: 3:21–31 [AB, GNT, HNTC, Ho, ICC1, Mu, NAC, NTC, SSA, TNTC, WBC; GW, NCV]. The topic is God's righteousness comes to all through Christ by faith [AB], God gives us his approval as a gift [GW], how God makes people right [NCV], the gospel and justification [Ho], the righteousness of God [HNTC, Mu], exposition of the new system [ICC1], righteousness received through faith in Christ [NAC], a righteousness from God through faith in Christ [NTC], God's provision [TNTC], faith in Jesus Christ [WBC], righteousness through faith [GNT; NIV], God's way of accepting people [CEV], Christ took our punishment [NLT], how we are put right with God [TEV].

DISCOURSE UNIT: 3:21–26 [AB, BECNT, Gdt, ICC2, Mor, NICNT, SSA, WBC]. The topic is all share in the justification through Jesus [AB], God's righteousness in the death of Jesus [BECNT], that by which justification by faith is acquired [Gdt], righteousness from God manifested in the gospel [ICC2], justification effected by the death of Christ [Mor], justification and the righteousness of God [NICNT], God's righteousness demonstrated in the death of Jesus [WBC].

3:21 But now apart-from^a law^b (the) righteousness^c of-God has-been-revealed,^d

LEXICON—a. χωρίς with genitive object (LN 89.120) (BAGD 2.b.δ. p. 891): 'apart from' [BECNT, HNTC, ICC2, LN, Mor, NICNT, NTC, WBC; NASB, NET, NIV, NRSV], 'without regard to' [BAGD], 'without' [LN; KJV, NCV], 'independently of' [AB; REB], 'a way other than' [GW], 'a different way' [NLT], not explicit [CEV, TEV].

   b. νόμος (LN 33.55, 33.333) (BAGD 3. p. 542): 'law' [LN (33.333)], 'Law' [LN (33.55)]. This word, which lacks the definite article here, is translated 'law' [NTC; NIV, NRSV, REB], 'the law' [AB, BECNT, HNTC, ICC2, NICNT, WBC; KJV, NCV, NET], 'the Law' [CEV, NASB, NLT], 'the Law of Moses' [TEV], 'Moses' Teachings' [GW].

   c. δικαιοσύνη (LN 88.13) (BAGD 3. p. 197): 'righteousness' [BAGD, BECNT, HNTC, ICC2, LN, Mor, NICNT, NTC, WBC; KJV, NASB, NET, NIV, NRSV, REB], 'uprightness' [AB]. The phrase δικαιοσύνη δὲ θεοῦ, which lacks the definite article, is translated 'the righteousness of God' [BECNT, NICNT, WBC; KJV, NASB, NET, NRSV, REB], 'the uprightness of God' [AB], 'God's righteousness' [HNTC, ICC2], 'a righteousness from God' [NTC], 'God does make people acceptable to him' [CEV], 'God's approval' [GW], 'God has a way to make people

ROMANS 3:21

right with him' [NCV], 'God's way of putting people right with himself' [TEV], 'a way of being right in God's sight' [NLT].
d. perf. pass. indic. of φανερόω (LN **28.36**) (BAGD 1.b. p. 853): 'to be revealed' [BAGD, LN, NTC, WBC; TEV], 'to be made known' [**LN; NIV, REB**], 'to be made plain' [LN; GW], 'to be disclosed' [AB, LN; NET, NRSV], 'to be manifested' [BECNT, HNTC, ICC2; KJV, NASB], 'to be made manifest' [NICNT]. This passive verb is translated as active: 'now we see how' [CEV], 'he has now shown us' [NCV], 'now God has shown us...a different way' [NLT].

QUESTION—What is signaled by the phrase νυνὶ δέ 'but now'?
   1. This signals a temporal transition to a new phase of salvation history [AB, BECNT, Ho, ICC1, ICC2, NICNT, NTC, SSA, TNTC, WBC]. This denotes a transition in Paul's exposition of the gospel and of salvation history as he shifts focus from the old covenant era of sin's domination to the new covenant era of salvation, from those justly condemned, helpless under the power of sin, and powerless to escape God's wrath, to the new era for all those who respond in faith to God's intervention through the cross of Christ [NICNT]. This denotes a temporal shift in salvation-history as Jesus, who inaugurates the new era, has come and carried out his role [AB]. It is temporal, indicating a decisive shift to the new eschatological state of affairs brought about by Christ [WBC]. This marks the temporal contrast between the impossibility of justification by works of the law, and justification apart from the law made possible by the decisive event of God's free gift being manifested [ICC1, ICC2].
   2. This signals a logical shift in the argument [Gdt, NAC]. The shift represented here is logical and moral, not temporal, and the contrast is between the condemnation pronounced by the law in 3:20 and the righteousness acquired without the law here in 3:21 [Gdt]. The expression is perhaps more sequential than temporal and introduces God's answer to man's dilemma, the emphasis falling on the qualitative difference between God's remedy and human attempts to bridge the gap [NAC].
   3. This represents both a temporal and logical shift [HNTC, Mor, Mu, TH]. This may be seen as both moving to the next logical point in the argument and as temporal in shifting to the next point in time, as Paul contrasts what people knew before the coming of the gospel with what has been revealed in the gospel as the human predicament has been radically transformed because of the saving act of God in Christ [Mor]. Paul emphasizes not only the contrast between justification through works of the law with justification apart from the law, but he is also using this expression to emphasize that, in contrast with the past, the manifestation of God's righteousness has now come with the revelation of Christ [Mu]. For Paul all of time is divided into that which was before the revelation of the way in which God puts men right with himself and that which now follows [TH].

4. This has a threefold reference: logical in a shift of the developing argument, chronological as to the present time, and eschatological in that a new age has arrived [St].

QUESTION—With what is the phrase χωρὶς νόμου 'apart from law' connected?

Note that there is a certain amount of overlap possible between the positions listed below, and one does not necessarily rule out the other.

1. It goes with the phrase 'righteousness of God' [AB, Ho, ICC2, Mor, Mu, NAC, SSA, TH; CEV, KJV, NCV, NIV, NLT, TEV]: the righteousness of God, which is acquired apart from law, is manifested. Either is grammatically possible, but the phrase is better taken with the phrase 'righteousness of God' [Mor, NAC]. The righteousness of God is being manifested as something that has nothing to do with anything that has been earned by people fulfilling the law [ICC2]. Paul is showing that God's way of putting men right with himself has nothing to do with any kind of legal system [TH].

2. It goes with the verb [AB, Gdt, HNTC, ICC1, NICNT, St; GW, REB]: the righteousness of God has been manifested apart from the law. The text speaks of God's righteousness being made known apart from the law, indicating the aspect of its newness, though also representing it as a fulfillment of the OT Scriptures [St]. This manifestation of righteousness takes place apart from the law because, when manifested through the law, it only led to wrath, but now, manifested in a different way, leads to justification [HNTC]. This righteousness is apart from the Law as independent from it, as an alternative for it, and destined to supersede it [ICC1]. In this new era of salvation history God has acted apart from the law to deliver and vindicate his people [NICNT].

QUESTION—What is the meaning of the phrase χωρὶς νόμου 'apart from law'?

1. It means that God's righteousness is attained without any contribution from doing the 'works of the law' [AB, BECNT, Gdt, Ho, ICC1, ICC2, Mor, Mu, NAC, NICNT, NTC, SSA, TH, WBC]. This means 'without recourse to the law'; that is, the new manifestation of God's uprightness has nothing to do with deeds prescribed by the Mosaic law [AB, Gdt]. God's saving righteousness cannot be gained by keeping the law [BECNT]. God's righteousness was not and cannot be earned by man's obedience to God's law, and has nothing to do with human performance [NAC, NTC]. Since the method of works for justification has been shown to be impossible, this phrase means that God reveals another method of justification that is not based on the condition of obedience to law, but on the condition of faith [Ho]. It signals a shift in salvation history away from the old covenant system of law [BECNT, NICNT]. Under the old covenant the law as a system regulated the lives of God's people and revealed their sin, but now under the new covenant God's justifying activity, his saving righteousness, is being revealed in a way that is apart

ROMANS 3:21

from the law as a system, outside the confines of the old covenant [NICNT]. The word for law is general; no law, whether Jewish or otherwise, can bring salvation, it can do no more than point up the problem of sin [Mor].
2. It means outside the religious and national parameters of the Jews set by the law such as circumcision, food laws and the Sabbath. That is, it is without reference to the normal hallmarks of Jewishness, for Paul's purpose is to destroy the presumption that works of the law insure final vindication with God for the Jew, or that God's saving outreach is determined by being a Jew [WBC].

QUESTION—What is meant by the phrase δικαιοσύνη θεοῦ 'the righteousness of God'?
1. It means God's saving righteousness [BECNT, Gdt, Ho, Mor, Mu, NAC, NICNT, SSA, TH, WBC]. This has the same sense as in 1:17 and 3:22 and means the righteousness of God, but the aspect in view is the status of righteousness before God, which is his gift bestowed upon man: God's way of putting men right with himself [Gdt, ICC1, NAC, TH]. This refers to the eschatological justifying activity of God, both in intervening to deliver his people in fulfillment of his promises, and giving to man the status of acquittal, declaring him just [NICNT]. This denotes the saving righteousness of God; it is not an abstract attribute of God, nor does it refer to the judging righteous of God [BECNT]. It is the gracious gift of a righteous status before God [ICC2]. This has heavy covenantal overtones and means the righteousness of God revealed in terms of Christ, God's saving action on behalf of his people, his saving outreach achieved through Jesus Christ [WBC]. This is to be understood to mean God's declaration of righteousness for sinners and may be expressed 'God declares us freed from the guilt of sin' [SSA]. This means the right standing that comes from God, the status of being right and accepted before God [Mor]. It is the righteousness of God that leads to our justification and is brought to bear upon us to salvation [Mu]. In Pauline thought this word refers to the righteousness bestowed by God which is based on faith and closely approximates salvation [BAGD].
2. It means God's attribute of righteousness or uprightness whereby he acquits sinful people in a just judgment [AB].
3. It means both God's attribute of righteousness as well as his activity of saving righteousness [HNTC, St, TNTC]. As can be seen in combination with 3:24 where God's righteousness is identified with justification, this is a combination of God's righteous character, his saving initiative, and his gift to sinners of a righteous standing before him [St]. This means both God's personal characteristic of righteousness and the righteousness with which he justifies sinners on the grounds of faith [TNTC]. This righteousness has two aspects, God's quality of being right or righteous, and his activity of setting things and persons right [HNTC].

QUESTION—What is being referred to by πεφανέρωται 'has been revealed' in the phrase δικαιοσύνη θεοῦ πεφανέρωται 'the righteousness of God has been revealed'?

This refers in particular to the death of Christ [AB, BECNT, Gdt, Ho, ICC1, ICC2, Mor, Mu, NAC, St, TH, WBC]. It means that God has made known, or made public his uprightness in the passion, death, and resurrection of Christ [AB]. The perfect tense must refer to the historical death of Christ and its continuing consequences [BECNT, Gdt, Ho, NAC, St, TH, WBC]. This refers to the events of the gospel themselves, the decisive manifestation of the 'righteousness of God' in Christ [ICC2]. The verb is regularly used of the incarnation and all its accompaniments [ICC1]. Paul means that the revelation of the righteousness of God has a beginning, and is being revealed in the gospel and the eschatological events that it witnesses to [HNTC]. What has been revealed is that by the atonement God has now made known that the way of grace is how he planned to save people all along [Mor].

being-witnessed[a] by[b] the law and the prophets,[c]

LEXICON—a. pres. pass. participle of μαρτυρέω (LN 33.262) (BAGD 2.a. p. 493): 'to be witnessed' [BAGD, LN, NICNT; KJV, NASB], 'to have witness borne' [BAGD], 'to bear witness to' [AB, BECNT; REB], 'to give witness to' [TEV], 'to be attested' [HNTC, ICC2, NTC, WBC; NET, NRSV]. This passive verb is also translated as active: 'to testify to' [Mor; NIV], 'to tell how' [CEV]. The clause is translated 'Moses' Teachings and the Prophets tell us this' [GW], 'which the law and the prophets told us about' [NCV], 'by the way promised in the Scriptures long ago' [NLT].

b. ὑπό with genitive object (LN 90.1) (BAGD 1.a.β. p. 843): 'by' [BAGD, HNTC, ICC2, LN, NICNT, NTC, WBC; KJV, NASB, NET, NLT, NRSV], 'to which' [BECNT], not explicit [CEV, GW, NCV, NIV, REB, TEV].

c. προφήτης (LN 53.79) (BAGD 1. p. 723): 'prophets' [AB, BECNT, HNTC, ICC2, NICNT, NTC, WBC; all versions except NLT]. The phrase 'being witnessed by the law and the prophets' is translated 'promised in the Scriptures long ago' [NLT].

QUESTION—In what sense do the law and the prophets witness to the righteousness of God?

Paul is pointing out a continuity in salvation history in that the OT as a whole anticipates and predicts the work of God in Christ [Gdt, Ho, ICC1, Mor, Mu, NICNT, NTC, TH, TNTC, WBC]. Paul guards against the notion that the OT was an inferior revelation, for it acknowledged that the promise of salvation would not come to fruition under the Mosaic covenant, and often promises and looks forward to the time when God would completely fulfill his saving promises [BECNT]. This recalls 1:2, which tells of the promise of the gospel being in the prophets, and to other partial foretellings and foreshadowing in the law and prophets of the revelation of Christ; the old confirms the new, and the new fulfills the old [AB, Gdt, HNTC, ICC1, ICC2, NAC, St]. Paul wants to guard against a misunderstanding of 'apart from law', so he emphasizes the continuity of divine purpose, implying that the gospel is the continuation and completion of the law properly understood throughout the whole of Scripture [WBC]. Both the OT law and the prophets show that right standing comes from God [Mor]. What was once buried in the types and somewhat indistinct utterances of the Old Testament are now made clear and apparent in the gospel [Ho].

QUESTION—What is meant by τοῦ νόμου καὶ τῶν προφητῶν 'the law and the prophets'?

This phrase designates the OT as a whole [BECNT, Gdt, HNTC, Ho, ICC2, Mor, Mu, NAC, NICNT, NTC, SSA, St, TH, WBC]. Though this phrasing represents the customary division of the OT into the Pentateuch and 'everything else', the entire OT is meant [NICNT]. This phrase is familiar elsewhere as referring to the whole of Jewish sacred writings [WBC]. The phrase refers to the two parts of the OT [SSA]. Paul is using 'law' here in a different sense than in the first part of the verse; here it denotes the Pentateuch [AB].

3:22 even[a] (the) righteousness[b] of-God through[c] faith[d] (in)[e] Jesus Christ for[f] all the-(ones) believing.[g]

TEXT—Some manuscripts include καὶ ἐπὶ πάντας 'and upon all' after εἰς πάντας 'for all'. It is omitted by GNT with a B rating, indicating that the text is almost certain. It is included only by KJV.

LEXICON—a. δέ (LN 89.94): 'even' [LN; KJV, NASB], 'namely' [BECNT, ICC2, NTC; NET], 'that is' [WBC], 'yet' [HNTC], not explicit [AB, NICNT; CEV, GW, NCV, NIV, NLT, NRSV, REB, TEV].

  b. δικαιοσύνη (LN 88.13) (BAGD 3. p. 197): 'righteousness' [BAGD, BECNT, HNTC, ICC2, LN, Mor, NICNT, NTC, WBC; KJV, NASB, NET, NIV, NRSV], 'uprightness' [AB], 'it' [REB]. The phrase δικαιοσύνη δὲ θεοῦ, which lacks the definite article, is translated 'the righteousness of God' [BECNT, NICNT, WBC; KJV, NASB, NET, NRSV], 'the uprightness of God' [AB], 'God's righteousness' [HNTC], 'that righteousness from God' [ICC2], 'a righteousness from God' [NTC], 'God's approval' [GW], 'he accepts people' [CEV], 'God makes people right with himself' [NCV], 'God puts people right' [TEV], 'we are made right in God's sight' [NLT], not explicit [REB].

  c. διά with genitive object (LN 89.76) (BAGD A.III.1.d. p. 180): 'through' [AB, BAGD, BECNT, HNTC, ICC2, LN, NICNT, NTC, WBC; GW, NASB, NCV, NET, NRSV, TEV], 'by means of' [BAGD, LN], 'by' [LN; KJV]. This preposition is translated 'comes through' [NIV], 'when we (trust in)' [NLT], 'is effective through' [REB]. The phrase 'through faith' is translated 'because they have faith' [CEV].

  d. πίστις (LN 31.85) (BAGD 2.b.β. p. 663): 'faith' [AB, BAGD, BECNT, HNTC, ICC2, LN, NICNT, NTC, WBC; all versions except NET, NLT], 'trust' [LN], 'faithfulness' [NET]. This noun is translated as a verb: 'to trust in' [NLT].

e. There is no lexical entry for this preposition in the Greek text, the relationship between 'faith' and 'Jesus Christ' being expressed by the genitive case of 'Jesus Christ'. This is represented in translation by the preposition 'in' [AB, BECNT, HNTC, ICC2, NICNT, NTC, WBC; CEV, GW, NASB, NCV, NLT, NRSV, REB, TEV], 'of' [KJV, NET]. The phrase πίστεως Ἰησοῦ Χριστοῦ 'faith in Jesus Christ' is translated 'the faithfulness of Jesus Christ' [NET].

f. εἰς with accusative object (LN 90.41, 90.59): 'for' [BECNT, ICC2, LN (90.41, 90.59), NICNT; NASB, NCV, NET, NRSV, REB], 'to' [LN (90.59), WBC; NIV, TEV], 'toward' [AB], 'directed to' [HNTC], 'unto' [KJV], not explicit [CEV, GW, NLT].

g. pres. act. participle of πιστεύω (LN 31.102) (BAGD 2.b. p. 661): 'to believe' [AB, BAGD, BECNT, ICC2, Mor, NICNT, WBC; GW, KJV, NASB, NCV, NET, NIV, NRSV, TEV], 'to be a believer' [BAGD, LN], 'to be a Christian' [BAGD, LN], 'to have faith' [HNTC; CEV, REB], 'to exercise faith' [NTC], 'to trust (in Jesus Christ)' [NLT].

QUESTION—How should the genitive construction πίστεως Ἰησοῦ Χριστοῦ be understood in the phrase 'faith in Jesus Christ'?

1. The genitive is objective, meaning 'through faith in Jesus Christ' [AB, BECNT, Gdt, HNTC, Ho, ICC1, ICC2, Mu, NAC, NICNT, NTC, SSA, St, TH, TNTC, WBC; CEV, GW, NASB, NCV, NLT, NRSV, REB, TEV]. Paul is not drawing attention to Christ's faithfulness anywhere in Romans [AB, WBC], rather Christ is himself the manifestation of God's uprightness and people appropriate to themselves the effects of his work through faith in him [AB]. Paul indicates that the object of the faith is Jesus Christ [Mu, NTC]. The emphasis in the entire section is on the faith of the believer in contrast to 'works of the law' as the means through which God's righteousness comes to expression; this faith is directed towards Christ as the object [WBC]. The genitive should be taken as objective, since the thrust of the entire section is to further explicate 1:17, and the same construction in Gal 2:16 means 'believed in Christ Jesus' [SSA]. The righteousness in question is that which is received by means of faith in Christ, who is the object of the faith [ICC2]. The righteousness that God provides comes by means of faith in Christ, and is received and appropriated through the faith of which Christ alone is the object [Ho].

2. The genitive is subjective or possessive, meaning through the faithfulness of Jesus Christ [NET].

3. It could have both objective and subjective meanings, and Paul does not care to limit it to only one or the other; our faith is in Jesus Christ but is based on what he did in his faithfulness [Mor].

QUESTION—What is the significance of the phrase εἰς πάντας τοὺς πιστεύοντας 'for all the ones believing'?
1. This expresses the universal availability of God's righteousness to all people [AB, BECNT, Ho, ICC2, Mu, NICNT, SSA, St, TH, TNTC, WBC]. Paul wants to highlight the universal availability of God's righteousness, a conspicuous motif of the epistle and explicitly mentioned in 3:22–23; it is available only through faith in Christ, but it is available to anyone who has such faith [NICNT]. God's righteousness has a universal efficacy, for now the Gentiles are included as well [BECNT]. This expresses the universal destination of God's uprightness for all people; it is made known as his power for the justification of all [AB]. This indicates both that all people need this righteousness and it is offered to all, as well as the fact that it comes to all who believe [Ho, Mu, NTC, SSA, St]. This emphasizes the universal outreach of God's saving purpose and action, and the present tense of the verb denotes the continuing reliance on Christ as the basis for the relationship [WBC].
2. This refers to the fact that only those who have faith are restored to true relationship with God [Gdt, HNTC, Mor]. Faith is so important that it is emphasized by this phrase. From the human side, faith and faith alone is the only requirement for this righteousness, though is not itself a merit for earning salvation, but the means through which the gift is given [Mor]. The object that Paul has in view is to eliminate every other distinction except that of believing [Gdt].

For there-is no distinction,[a]
LEXICON—a. διαστολή (LN 58.42) (BAGD p. 188): 'distinction' [AB, BAGD, BECNT, HNTC, ICC2, LN, NICNT, NTC, WBC; NASB, NET, NRSV, REB], 'difference' [BAGD, LN, Mor; GW, KJV, NIV, TEV]. This clause is translated 'toward all, without distinction' [AB], 'because all people are the same' [NCV], 'no matter who we are or what we have' [NLT], 'God treats everyone alike' [CEV].
QUESTION—To what distinction does this statement refer?
1. This means that there is no difference among people regarding their condition of sin, or regarding the means of salvation offered to them [Gdt, Ho, ICC1, ICC2, Mu, NTC, SSA, St, TH, TNTC, WBC]. Differences of age, race, sex, and economic status are of no consequence in granting God's righteousness to true believers in Jesus, as all need it and can obtain it [NTC]. This explains both the preceding and following 'all' and means in particular that there is no distinction between Jew and Gentile; all have sinned and the basis of relationship with God is the same for all. With this shocking assertion Paul attacks the presumption and axiomatic nature of Jewish self-understanding that, as the people of God, they were different in having special prerogatives and defense before God [WBC]. This indicates that there is no distinction between Jew and Gentile, and though it is somewhat ambiguous, it probably means there is no difference with

regard to both sin and the method of salvation [SSA]. This statement denies any distinction regarding the righteousness of God, because all alike, Jew and Gentile, have sinned, and will receive righteousness only as an undeserved and free gift [ICC2]. The Jew has no advantage over the Gentile, for both alike need a righteousness which is not theirs, and both are offered God's righteousness on exactly the same terms [ICC1]. Paul has proved that since all people are under sin, there is no difference with regard to God's penal judgment of them, but also that whenever faith is operative, God's righteousness comes without distinction upon all who believe in Jesus Christ [Mu]. Paul means that there are not two ways by which one can be justified, for no one can be saved by obedience to the law; only the way of faith remains open [Gdt]. God's righteousness is offered to all because it is needed by all [St].

2. This refers to the universality of the offer of salvation [AB, BECNT]. Paul is supporting the idea that God's saving righteousness is not confined to the Jews, but is for all people [BECNT]. Paul means that God's righteousness is for both Jew and Greek, that the opportunity is given equally to all humanity [AB].

3. This means that with respect to sin, there is no difference between Jew and Gentile, all stand guilty before God [HNTC, Mor, NICNT].

3:23 for[a] **all have-sinned**[b] **and are-falling-short-of**[c] **the glory**[d] **of God,**

LEXICON—a. γάρ (LN 89.23): 'for' [AB, ICC2, LN, Mor, NICNT, WBC; KJV, NASB, NET, NIV, NLT, REB], 'because' [LN; GW, TEV], 'since' [BECNT, NTC; NRSV], not explicit [HNTC; CEV, NCV].

b. aorist act. indic. of ἁμαρτάνω (LN 88.289) (BAGD 1. p. 42): 'to sin' [AB, BAGD, BECNT, HNTC, ICC2, LN, NICNT, NTC, WBC; all versions], 'to transgress, to do wrong' [BAGD]. This aorist form is translated as perfect [AB, BECNT, HNTC, ICC2, NICNT, NTC, WBC; all versions]. The word refers to offenses against the moral law of God [BAGD].

c. pres. pass. indic. of ὑστερέω (LN 13.21) (BAGD 2. p. 849): 'to fall short of' [AB, BECNT, NICNT, NTC; CEV, GW, NASB, NET, NIV, NLT, NRSV], 'to come short of' [BAGD; KJV], 'to lack' [BAGD, HNTC, ICC2, WBC], 'to be far away from' [TEV], 'to be deprived of' [REB], 'to fail to attain' [LN], 'to be not good enough' [NCV].

d. δόξα (LN 79.18, 87.23) (BAGD 1.a. p. 203; 3. p. 204): 'glory' [AB, BAGD, BECNT, HNTC, ICC2, LN, NICNT, NTC, WBC; all versions except NLT, TEV], 'greatness' [LN (87.23)], 'honor' [BAGD (3.)], 'splendor' [BAGD (1.a.), LN (79.18)]. This noun is translated as an adjective: '(God's) glorious standard' [NLT]; as a phrase: 'God's saving presence' [TEV].

QUESTION—What is the significance of the aorist form of the verb ἥμαρτον 'have sinned'?

It is a summary aorist and refers to the sins of all people throughout the past viewed as in a single moment [Ho, ICC1, Mu, NAC, NICNT, St, WBC]. Everyone in the world has sinned individually [Ho, NTC, TNTC]. All people now stand before God as sinners [Ho]. This is a collective historical aorist, summing up the totality of evil deeds by man and expressing what is true generally, or at any given time, all seen together as expressing a past fact [ICC2, SSA]. It speaks of the sins of all people throughout the past as summarized into a single moment [NICNT]. Where there is no clear separation or interval between the present and a past fact or series of events an aorist verb is often translated as perfect tense in English [ICC1]. Sin is not just a matter of something that happened in the past [Mor]. The aorist is used as a general statement of the sins of all humanity, perhaps from the perspective of eschatological judgment, and is inclusive of the original historical act of Adam and the resulting predisposition to sin of all mankind [NAC]. It is used either because the perspective is that of the final judgment or that of the universality of man's fall in sin [WBC]. All men are equal with respect to the fact of sin, and the aorist takes no account as to whether the sin was once or more, for even once suffices to deprive men of being considered righteous [Gdt]. This aorist is used in the same sense as the English perfect tense [AB, BECNT, HNTC, ICC1, ICC2, NICNT, NTC, SSA, WBC; all versions].

QUESTION—What is the relationship between the two verbs of this clause?
1. The second is the consequence of the first; that is, because all have sinned all are falling short of God's glory [AB, BECNT, Gdt, Ho, NAC, NICNT, NTC, WBC]. Because of their sins, all human beings remain without a share in God's glory, lacking it or failing to reach it [AB]. Paul is thinking of Adam, who as a consequence of sin forfeited the glory he originally had and failed to reach the glory intended for him; the plight is the same for Jew and Gentile because all have sinned and all are missing out on the glory intended for them [WBC]. The sinning is represented as past and the present and abiding consequence of sin is the lack of the glory of God [Ho]. Man's sin deprives him of righteousness and as a consequence he experiences the lack of the glory of God, or is below the normal level of the state known as 'the glory of God' [Gdt]. Glory was lost when Adam sinned, and people continue to refuse to glorify God [BECNT].
2. The relationship is coordinate [Mor, Mu, SSA]. This indicates that all people have sinned, and that they continue always to fall short of God's glory, even including believers [Mor].

QUESTION—What is the meaning of the phrase ὑστεροῦνται τῆς δόξης τοῦ θεοῦ 'are falling short of the glory of God'?
1. It means a loss of the image or glory of God which man had at creation but lost through the fall [BECNT, Gdt, HNTC, ICC1, ICC2, Mor, Mu, NAC, NICNT, St, TNTC, WBC]. It means a diminishing of or a declining

from the image of God, from the condition of being like God in which humans were first made; it also involves not experiencing the magnificent presence of the Lord [NICNT]. Although they were made in the image and glory of God, they fail to live up to that [St]. People do not reflect God's glory in the sense of being conformed to his image [Mu]. As a result of sin, they no longer have the illumination of divine glory [ICC2]. The future glory will be the restoration of that original glory which has been lost [HNTC, NICNT], when they will experience a conformity to the image of Christ and exhibit that God-likeness for which they were created [NICNT]. This glory is being restored to those who believe in Christ, and will be completely restored when redemption is complete [BECNT, ICC1, ICC2]. It means that all fail to live up to God's image and glory in which they were created; no one even approaches God's standard [St]. Paul refers both to the glory lost to man in the fall as well as to its consequence, in that fallen man is still presently failing to reach the glory originally intended for him, including that of fellowship with God [WBC]. This probably refers to the likeness of God that each man is intended to bear, but which was forfeited because of sin [Gdt, Mu, NAC]. Not only has man lost the glory he possessed at creation, but all people also fail to give God the glory, honor, and praise he deserves [BECNT].
2. Paul is not here making reference to the glory Adam lost in the fall, but to a quality of man's being as a creature of God, and also of that condition which he was intended to experience eschatologically in God's presence. Because people are estranged from God by sin they lack that enhancing quality in this life as well as the eschatological condition intended for the next life [AB].
3. It means the lack or loss of God's approval, approbation or praise [Ho, NTC]. When man transgressed God's command he lost what he had before the fall, namely, the divine approval or approbation that was his, and hence freedom of access to God [NTC].
4. It means not achieving the glorious goals that God had set for people. The noun 'glory' is semantically the attribute 'glorious', and the verb means 'to miss or fail to reach' [SSA].

QUESTION—What is the significance of the present tense of the verb ὑστεροῦνται 'are falling short of'?

The verb with a following genitive means 'to come short of something', and the present tense suggests that Paul wants to say that people are regularly falling short of God's glory [BECNT, Mor, NICNT]. Even Christians fall short of that goal until they are transformed in the last day by God [Mor, NICNT]. Paul maintains that all human beings are presently in and remain in the condition of failing to attain, or lacking God's glory [AB, HNTC, Ho, ICC2, NTC, St]. Both the idea of forfeiting what one had and failing to attain or falling short of an intended goal are contained in this verb; it is the continuing hopelessness of man's self-achievements which make God's initiative indispensable [WBC]. The present tense is reflective of the sinful state or condition of all men, which arises from the fact of sin, past and present [Mu]. Believers do not yet experience that transcendent majesty of eschatological glory that will one day be theirs, though there is a relative glory that even now illumines their lives [ICC2].

3:24 being-justified^a freely^b (by)^c his grace^d

LEXICON—a. pres. pass. participle of δικαιόω (LN **34.46**, 56.34) (BAGD 3.a. p. 197): 'to be justified' [AB, BAGD, BECNT, HNTC, ICC2, Mor, NICNT, NTC, WBC; KJV, NET, NIV, NRSV, REB], 'to be put right' [LN (**34.46**); TEV], 'to be pronounced and treated as righteous' [BAGD], 'to cause to be in a right relationship with' [LN (34.46)], 'to be acquitted' [BAGD, LN (56.34)], 'to have one's guilt removed' [LN (56.34)], 'to declare to be not guilty' [NLT], 'to be set free' [LN (56.34)], 'to accept and set free from sins' [CEV]. The word may denote the act of causing someone to be in a proper relationship with another [LN (34.46)] or the act of clearing someone of transgression [LN (56.34)].

b. δωρεάν (LN 57.85) (BAGD 1. p. 210): 'freely' [AB, BECNT, ICC2, Mor, NICNT, NTC; CEV, GW, KJV, NET, NIV], 'as a free gift' [HNTC, LN], 'as a gift' [BAGD, WBC; NASB, NRSV], 'a free gift' [NCV], '(by) the free gift' [TEV], '(by) free (grace)' [REB], 'without cost or payment' [BAGD, LN].

c. There is no lexical entry for this preposition in the Greek text, the relationship between 'being justified' and 'grace' being expressed by the dative case of the noun 'grace'. It is represented in translation as 'by' [AB, BECNT, HNTC, ICC2, NICNT, NTC, WBC; GW, KJV, NASB, NCV, NET, NRSV, REB, TEV]. The phrase τῇ αὐτοῦ χάριτι 'by his grace' is translated 'God treats us much better than we deserve' [CEV], 'God in his gracious kindness' [NLT].

d. χάρις (LN 57.103, 88.66) (BAGD 2.a. p. 877): 'grace' [AB, BAGD, BECNT, HNTC, ICC2, LN (88.66), NICNT, NTC, WBC; all versions except CEV, GW, NLT], 'graciousness' [LN (88.66)], 'kindness' [LN (88.66); GW, NLT], 'gracious kindness' [NLT], 'gift, gracious gift' [LN (57.103)], not explicit [CEV].

QUESTION—What is the connection between the participle δικαιούμενοι 'being justified' and the context?

3:22b and 3:23 are a parenthetical comment, and δικαιούμενοι resumes the discussion of justification for those who believe that was begun in 3:21–22a [Gdt, ICC1, ICC2, Mu, NICNT, NTC, WBC]. 3:22b–3:23 is a parenthesis in which Paul expands on his statement in 3:22; that is, the righteous of God comes to all who have faith (3:22), there is no distinction, for all have the same condition of need (3:23), and all who believe are justified freely by grace (3:24) [NTC]. Although the πάντας 'all' in the phrase 'all the ones believing' is in the accusative case, δικαιούμενοι, which modifies it, is in the nominative case because of its distance from πάντας in the text as well as because of the fact that it introduces a new clause [NTC]. The participle δικαιούμενοι 'being justified' modifies the 'all' of 3:22, but is in the nominative case because of influence from the πάντες 'all' of 3:23, a clause with which it has a certain parallelism [ICC1, ICC2, NICNT]. The correspondence between 3:23 and 3:24 is that the participle δικαιούμενοι in 3:24 states the positive side of the negative statement in 3:23 that 'there is no distinction' in God's dealings, that God deals graciously with all alike, justifying freely by grace, while at the same time continuing and explaining his theme of righteousness by faith in 3:22 [NICNT]. The subject of δικαιούμενοι 'being justified' is the πάντας τοὺς πιστεύοντας 'all the ones believing' in 3:22b; it is only believers who will be justified [ICC1, Mu, NTC, SSA, TNTC, WBC]. Being justified freely by grace as he describes in 3:24 is the evidence for what he has said in 3:23, that all people are sinful and fall short of God's glory [Mor].

QUESTION—What is the meaning of πάντες 'all' in 3:23 in relation to the participle δικαιούμενοι 'being justified' of this verse?

He is saying that in God's dealings with people, without distinction all those who are justified are justified freely by grace through faith [Ho, ICC1, ICC2, Mor, Mu, NAC, NICNT, NTC, SSA, St, TNTC, WBC], and the participle δικαιούμενοι picks up and resumes the discussion of justification for those who believe that was begun in 3:21–22a [ICC1, ICC2, Mu, NICNT, NTC, WBC]. Paul is not suggesting universalism here [Mor, NAC, NICNT, NTC, SSA]. He is saying that justification is available to anyone, not that it is experienced by everyone [NICNT]. This does not mean 'all' universally, but means that all who believe are declared righteous [NAC, SSA]. The way of faith in Jesus is open to all who believe in him; we make what Christ has procured effectively our own by faith [TNTC].

QUESTION—What is the meaning of the participle δικαιούμενοι 'being justified'?

1. It means 'to be declared righteous' [BECNT, Gdt, HNTC, Ho, ICC2, Mor, Mu, NAC, NICNT, NTC, SSA, St, TH, TNTC]. Paul does not mean 'to be made righteous' in an ethical sense, nor 'to be treated as righteous' despite not really being so, but rather to receive a judicial verdict of acquittal by God from all charges that might be brought against someone due to their sin [NICNT]. It is not a legal fiction [HNTC, NICNT]. It means to be declared to be in right relation with God, not being made righteous or virtuous, and just as in 1:17, this means the status of righteousness before God, which is his gift [BECNT, Ho, ICC2, Mor, St, TH]. This is a legal or forensic term, the opposite of which is condemnation, and it is the declaration of a right status or acquittal in God's court [St]. It is in contrast to condemnation, and means that the sinner's guilt is imputed to Christ, and Christ's righteousness is imputed to the sinner [NTC]. In Paul it means to count or treat as righteous in the sense of being acquitted before God, and anticipates the verdict of the final judgment [HNTC]. It focuses on the final verdict of acquittal in the day of judgment, a verdict

which is already being delivered and the basis of which has already been established in the present, which is by grace, and through faith [WBC].
2. It means to achieve the status of uprightness through God's declaration of acquittal; the sinner is not only declared to be upright, but is also made to be upright [AB].

QUESTION—What is meant by the adjective δωρεάν 'as a free gift'?

This means that justification is a gift, and those who place their faith in Christ are put in right relationship with him by virtue of their faith in Christ and not on the basis of their own efforts [AB, BECNT, Gdt, HNTC, Ho, ICC1, ICC2, Mor, Mu, NAC, NTC, St, TH, TNTC, WBC]. This, along with the phrase 'by his grace', emphasizes the totally unmerited nature of God's act of justifying sinners, and that he is not predisposed to act, or constrained to any degree whatsoever, by anything we are or do [Mu]. It is not a matter of wages or payment [BECNT, Gdt, Ho, NTC, WBC], and involves no exchange in the sense of something given in return [TH].

QUESTION—What is the meaning of χάρις 'grace'?

It is God's free, unmerited favor and goodness towards people [Mor]. Paul uses this term to describe the way in which God has acted in Christ towards man, completely unconstrained by anything other than his own will to render a verdict of justification, supplying all that is necessary to put man right with himself, an action which is totally unmerited, and which must be received completely by faith [NICNT]. It is the merciful benevolence of God [AB]. It means that justification is an altogether gratuitous action, unmerited by those who receive it [Ho]. This refers to the absolutely free and undeserved favor of God, who in love comes to our rescue giving himself generously in and through Jesus Christ [St]. This refers to the unconditional character of God's action in providing his righteousness for man [Mu, WBC], and is implicitly in antithesis to the law and works [Mu, WBC]. Grace is that goodwill on the part of God that prompts him to bestow favor on sinful humanity [Gdt].

through[a] the redemption[b] in[c] Christ Jesus;

LEXICON—a. διά with genitive object (LN 89.76): 'through' [AB, BAGD, BECNT, HNTC, ICC2, LN, NICNT, NTC, WBC; all versions except CEV, NCV], 'by means of' [LN], not explicit [CEV, NCV].

b. ἀπολύτρωσις (LN 37.128) (BAGD 2.a. p. 96): 'redemption' [AB, BAGD, BECNT, ICC2, Mor, NICNT, NTC, WBC; KJV, NASB, NET, NIV, NRSV], 'deliverance, liberation' [LN], 'state of being redeemed' [BAGD]. This noun is translated as a phrase: 'the act of redemption' [HNTC], 'his act of liberation' [REB], 'the price...paid to set us free' [GW]; as a verb: 'who sets them free' [TEV], 'freed us by taking away' [NLT], 'he sets us free' [CEV], 'made free' [NCV].

c. ἐν with dative object (LN 90.6, 89.119) (BAGD III.1.b. p. 260): 'in' [LN (89.119); NRSV], 'that comes in' [AB], 'that is in' [BECNT, NICNT; KJV, NET], 'which is in' [WBC; NASB], 'that he performed in' [HNTC], 'accomplished in' [ICC2, NTC], 'in the person of' [REB], 'by' [LN

(90.6), Mor; NIV], 'through' [BAGD; NCV, NLT, TEV], not explicit [CEV, GW].

QUESTION—What is the meaning of ἀπολύτρωσις 'redemption'?

1. It means to be set free through the payment of a price [AB, BECNT, Gdt, Ho, ICC1, Mor, Mu, NAC, NICNT, NTC, SSA, St, TNTC]. This term was used historically to describe the payment of a price to gain release for prisoners of war or for someone under sentence of death, or to free slaves [Mor, NAC, NICNT], and the connotation here would be of Christ's death as a ransom or payment that takes the place of the penalty for sins by which all people are indebted to God [NICNT]. The word group from which this Greek term stems is used in the account of the exodus and liberation of Israel from Egypt [BECNT, St, TNTC, WBC]. Although the concept of a price being paid is not always specified in those LXX passages where the term is used, the idea of cost and effort is always present; moreover, the sacrificial character of this context also points to payment of a price; in addition, the fact that Christ's blood, which Paul elsewhere specifies was the price of redemption, is referred to in 3:25; all of these considerations lead to the conclusion that payment of a price is intended here [BECNT]. This means that by his death on the cross Christ has emancipated or ransomed man from bondage to sin [AB]. Jesus Christ bought us out of captivity to sin by shedding his blood as a ransom price [St]. It means deliverance from the guilt, punishment, and power of sin by means of the payment of a ransom [NTC]. This expression is a way of describing the death of Christ, by which believers are bought with a price [Gdt, ICC1]. Christ's work to secure our deliverance from the punishment of sin was effected by the payment of a ransom [Ho, SSA].

2. This word does not necessarily suggest the thought of a payment being made [ICC2, TH]. The word appears often in Paul and means to be set free, and even in its OT usage the emphasis is on the result accomplished, that of being set free, and not on the price paid [TH].

QUESTION—From what are people liberated or redeemed?

They are liberated from the guilt, punishment, and power of sin [HNTC, Ho, Mor, NTC], from bondage to sin [AB, Mu, NAC, St, WBC]. People need to be liberated from sin as an enslaving power [NICNT].

QUESTION—If redemption is understood to involve the payment of a price, to whom was it paid?

1. This metaphor should not be pressed so far as to ask who paid a ransom to whom [ICC1, ICC2, Mor, NICNT, SSA, WBC]. Certainly we are not to think of Christ's death as a payment which God made to Satan [Mor, NICNT]. Though 3:25 might be taken to imply that God as judge is the recipient of the ransom, it must be remembered that he is also the originator of the liberating process [NICNT]. Paul's point is that though a ransom was required for the acquittal to be given, it was provided by God alone at his initiative [WBC]. The appeasement of God's wrath is accomplished through the blood of his son [BECNT]. Jesus Christ shed

his blood as a ransom price and as a propitiation, appeasement, or placating of God's wrath [St].
2. The emphasis in the use of this word is not on the price paid, but on the result accomplished, that of being set free [TH].

QUESTION—What relationship is indicated by the preposition ἐν in the phrase ἐν Χριστῷ Ἰησοῦ 'in Christ Jesus'?

1. It is instrumental [HNTC, ICC2, Mor, Mu, NAC, SSA, St, TH]: the redemption accomplished by Christ. It was through Christ's sacrificial death on the cross in our place, and through his blood shed there that he bought us out of captivity to sin, ransoming us and making it possible for God to justify us [St]. This means that is was in and through the person and work of Christ that God accomplished his redeeming action [ICC2]. It is because of Christ's saving work which they have appropriated by faith that believers will be acquitted at the bar of God's justice [Mor]. While God is the primary agent, Christ is the secondary agent, for it is through Christ that men are put right with God [TH]. Redemption is through the costly price that Christ paid [Mu].
2. It means that redemption is made effective in relation to Christ; the price paid was the blood of Christ at the cross, and the redeeming work thus made possible is then applied to each person as they believe [NICNT].
3. It means both that redemption was accomplished by Christ, and that it is effective for those who are in him [BECNT, NTC, WBC]. It was accomplished in connection with Christ and by means of his death on the cross [NTC]. The ransom was accomplished by Christ, but only those in Christ enjoy the deliverance he accomplished [BECNT]. Paul is referring to the decisive act of Christ's death and resurrection by which the new salvation epoch was introduced, but also to the fact that those who are in Christ are participating in his death and new life, experiencing a power that effects a dying to sin and a rising to new life in the believer [WBC]. The ransom and redemption has already been achieved by Christ at his death and resurrection, but only those who are in Christ become partakers of it [AB].

3:25 whom God set-forth[a] (as an) expiation/propitiation[b]

LEXICON—a. aorist act. indic. of προτίθημι (LN **13.15**, 30.62) (BAGD 2.a. p. 722): 'to set forth' [NICNT, WBC; KJV], 'to publicly set forth' [BECNT, HNTC], 'to show' [GW], 'to display publicly' [BAGD; NASB, NET], 'to put forward' [NRSV], 'to present' [AB; NIV], 'to give' [NCV], 'to send' [CEV, NLT], 'to offer' [TEV], 'to bring forth, to cause to be' [LN (**13.15**)], 'to purpose' [ICC2, LN (30.62)], 'to intend, to plan beforehand' [LN (30.62)], 'to design…to be' [REB].
b. ἱλαστήριον (LN **40.12**) (BAGD p. 375): 'expiation' [LN, WBC]. This noun is translated as a phrase: 'that which expiates or propitiates' [BAGD], 'as a means of propitiation' [BECNT], 'as a propitiation' [NASB], 'a means of expiation' [BAGD], 'a propitiatory sacrifice' [ICC2,

NICNT], 'a wrath removing sacrifice' [NTC], 'a sacrifice of atonement' [NIV, NRSV], 'the means by which sins are forgiven' [**LN;** TEV], 'a way to forgive sins' [NCV], 'a means of expiating sin' [AB], 'the means of expiating sin by his death' [REB], 'to be a propitiation for…sins' [KJV], 'his sacrificial death as his means of dealing with sin' [HNTC], 'as a satisfaction for sin' [NET], 'to be our sacrifice' [CEV], '(showed that) Christ is the throne of mercy' [GW]. This word is translated as a clause: 'God sent Jesus to take the punishment for our sins and to satisfy God's anger against us' [NLT].

QUESTION—What is the meaning of προτίθημι 'set forth'?

1. It means to 'set forth' or 'display publicly' [AB, BECNT, HNTC, Ho, ICC1, Mor, Mu, NAC, NICNT, TH, TNTC, WBC]. This is the middle form of the verb προτίθημι and in this context the preferred sense is 'to display publicly' since this fits better the imagery in this context [ICC1, NICNT], and also because of the fact that this verb and its cognate noun are used in the LXX with reference to the showbread of the altar, where the verb means to 'set before' [AB, Mu, NICNT]. This sense is best because the immediate context is full of terms denoting public manifestation [ICC1, Mu]. It refers to the public nature of Christ's sacrifice, which also fits well with the use of 'demonstration' in 3:25–26, and 'manifested' in 3:21 [BECNT]. 'Mercy seat' is a metonymy for the atoning sacrifice of Christ, and whereas the former was hidden behind the curtain and seen only by the high priest, God puts forward the sacrifice of Christ in the open [TNTC]. It refers to the public crucifixion of Christ [AB]. The word evokes a set of related ideas including the public nature of Christ's crucifixion, and the use of sacrificial blood in the inner sanctum of the Temple on Atonement day as standing in contrast with the open and public nature of Christ's death as the decisive eschatological sin offering [WBC]. The verb means to set forth or to exhibit, not in the sense of a spectacle, but rather of opening a way to the public, a sense which is further supported by the use of ἔνδειξις 'showing forth' in 3:25–26 [SSA].

2. It means to plan, purpose, or design something [Gdt, ICC2, NTC]. In the middle voice this verb means to set before oneself for consideration; God intended or purposed for Christ to be the one through whom the plan of salvation would be realized [NTC]. In both other NT occurrences the meaning is 'purpose' and this is usually the meaning of the cognate noun as well [ICC2, NTC]. In this context Paul is less concerned with man being aware of God's righteousness and of the cross being a public event, than with God being righteous and that redemption has its origin in God's eternal purpose of grace [ICC2]. The context is strongly in favor of the sense of designing something beforehand; the fundamental idea of the passage is to contrast the time of God's forbearance with regard to sin with the decisive moment when he carried out expiation for sin, so it is

natural to emphasize that God had both foreseen this need and provided for it beforehand [Gdt].

QUESTION—Does ἱλαστήριον mean 'expiation' or 'propitiation'?

Note that in this discussion the term 'expiation' refers to making a covering for sin, that is, atonement, and 'propitiation' refers to an appeasing of divine wrath.

1. It means 'expiation' or wiping away sin and involves an allusion to the 'mercy seat' of the OT [AB, HNTC, NICNT, SSA, TH, WBC; CEV, GW, NCV, NET, NIV, NRSV, REB, TEV]. The sense 'a sacrifice of atonement' is to be understood here [NIV, NRSV]. The noun ἱλαστήριον alludes to the OT mercy seat which was the cover over the ark of the covenant, and onto which sacrificial blood was poured to make atonement for sin. This is the meaning of the word in the only other NT occurrence (Heb 9:5) and in 21 of 27 LXX occurrences. In referring to Christ as the mercy seat, Paul, is suggesting that Christ is the new covenant equivalent to the old covenant place of atonement, and, by extension, to the atonement itself, and now occupies the place the mercy seat once had in the OT economy as the focal point of God's provision of atonement for his people's sins. The verse further indicates that what was hidden from view by a veil in the OT has now been made public and has been fulfilled by Christ's once-for-all sacrifice [NICNT]. There is double metonymy here in that the mercy seat cover stands for the event of atonement by sprinkling blood there, and the event in turn stands for Christ, the person who was the means by which it was accomplished. However, the more focal idea here is atonement, which is to make amends, or to pay the penalty for wrongdoing, so 'expiation' is the better understanding, the idea being that in mercy God has expiated sin through the atoning death of Christ [SSA].

2. The term means 'propitiation' or 'propitiatory sacrifice', that is, a sacrifice for appeasing, averting, or placating the wrath of God against sin [Gdt, Ho, ICC2, Mor, Mu, NAC, NTC, St; KJV, NASB]. Romans is not cast in the sphere of Levitical symbolism [Gdt, St]. The term characteristically means the removal of wrath both in secular Greek literature and in the OT; Paul has gone to considerable lengths from 1:18 onwards to show that sinners are all subject to God's wrath, and now he indicates how that wrath is removed [Mor]. In the context Paul is describing not only sin, but also God's wrath on sin because of his holy character, yet he goes on to show that God, by his own initiative and out of his great love, propitiated his own wrath through the gift of his son who died for us [ICC2, St]. It is clear that for the sinner to be saved, the wrath of God must be removed, and in Christ's voluntary sacrifice in place of sinners he himself was this wrath-removing or propitiatory sacrifice [NTC]. The preferred sense is that of a propitiatory sacrifice, since the wrath of God is prominent in the preceding sections of Romans and the phrase 'his blood' indicates that a propitiatory sacrifice is what is in mind, but also because the idea of

averting wrath is basic to the word group in the OT and in secular Greek [ICC2]. It is the placating of God's wrath against sin, and this need not carry the negative connotations of human anger [NAC]. This means the provision of grace by which we are freed from liability to the wrath of God, and here Christ is said to have been the propitiatory sacrifice [Mu]. The word should be taken in a very wide sense as 'a means of propitiation' [Gdt].
3. The word means both the wiping away or removal of sin, expiation, as well as the satisfying of God's anger, or propitiation [BECNT, TNTC; NLT]. The death of Jesus both removed sin and satisfied God's anger, and probably refers to the mercy seat mentioned in Lev 16. What Jesus accomplished on the cross transcended and fulfilled previous categories, for Jesus functioned as priest, victim, and the place where the blood is sprinkled, making it possible for believers to meet with God [BECNT].

through[a] faith[b] in[c] his blood[d]

LEXICON—a. διά with genitive object (LN 89.76) (BAGD A.III.1.d. p. 180): 'through' [AB, BAGD, BECNT, HNTC, LN, NICNT, NTC, WBC; GW, KJV, NASB, NCV, NET, NIV, NRSV, REB, TEV], 'received through' [HNTC], 'by' [ICC2; CEV], 'by means of' [LN], not explicit [NLT].
b. πίστις (LN 31.85) (BAGD 2.b.β. p. 663): 'faith' [AB, BAGD, BECNT, HNTC, ICC2, LN, NICNT, NTC, WBC; all versions except NLT].
c. ἐν with dative object (LN 90.23): 'in' [BECNT, HNTC, LN, NICNT, WBC; CEV, GW, KJV, NASB, NCV, NIV, TEV], 'with respect to, or with reference to, concerning' [LN], 'by' [NET, NRSV, REB], not explicit [AB, NTC; NLT].
d. αἷμα (LN 8.64, 23.107) (BAGD 2.b. p. 23): 'blood' [AB, BAGD, BECNT, LN (8.64), NICNT, WBC; KJV, NET, NIV, NLT, NRSV, TEV], 'death' [LN (23.107)]. This noun is translated as a phrase: 'his death' [REB], 'his bloody...death' [HNTC], 'the shedding of his blood' [ICC2, NTC]. The phrase 'through faith in his blood' is translated 'Christ offered his life's blood, so that by faith in him' [CEV]. In this context the word refers to the blood of Jesus as a means of expiation [BAGD].

QUESTION—What relationship is indicated by διά 'through'?
It indicates the means by which individuals appropriate the benefits of Christ's sacrifice [AB, BECNT, Gdt, HNTC, Ho, ICC2, Mor, NICNT, TNTC, WBC]: through faith. To share in the benefits of what Christ did, one must exercise genuine faith [AB, ICC2, Mor, Mu, NTC]. The sense is that of a propitiation through faith or that is appropriated through faith [Ho]. It indicates the means of propitiation, the efficacy which was bound by the condition of faith from the beginning [Gdt].

QUESTION—To what is the phrase ἐν τῷ αὐτοῦ αἵματι 'in his blood' connected?
1. It is connected with ἱλαστήριον 'expiation' or 'propitiation' [BAGD, BECNT, Gdt, HNTC, ICC1, ICC2, Mor, Mu, NAC, NICNT, TNTC,

WBC; CEV, NASB, NET, NRSV, REB, TEV]: expiation or propitiation in his blood. Paul never makes Christ's blood the object of faith, and as in other NT passages, the phrase 'in his blood' singles out Christ's blood as the means by which God's wrath is propitiated or turned away, the means through which salvation is secured. Paul's purpose is to designate Christ's death as a sacrifice [NICNT]. The appeasing of God's wrath is accomplished through the blood of his Son Jesus Christ, that is through his death [BECNT, HNTC, Mor, Mu]. In Paul, the object of faith is a person, not a thing, so this should not be construed with 'faith' but rather with 'a propitiatory sacrifice' [NTC]. It was the divine purpose that by means of the shedding of his blood Christ was to be the propitiatory sacrifice, so this is to be connected to ἱλαστήριον 'propitiatory sacrifice' [ICC2]. In a passage entirely devoted to explaining propitiation Paul would not fail to indicate the manner in which it operates, so propitiation is qualified by two phrases: 'through faith' indicating the subjective condition on the part of the one saved, and 'in his blood' setting out the objective condition of the efficacy of the means of propitiation, namely the blood of the Savior [Gdt].
2. It is connected with πίστεως 'faith' and indicates the object of faith: 'faith in his blood' [Ho, SSA; CEV, GW, KJV, NCV, NLT]. 'Blood' here is metonymy for the event of Christ dying and shedding his blood on the cross as also in Eph 1:7 and Rom 5:9, so here this means trusting in what Christ has done on the cross, not simply blood as an object of faith [SSA]. 'Blood' represents the work and sufferings of Christ for our redemption, including his death, and it is the ground for the confidence expressed in one's faith; having faith in his blood means that we rely on Christ's propitiatory sacrifice [Ho].
3. It is connected with 'God presented him' [AB]: through his blood God presented him [AB].

for[a] a-demonstration[b] of- his -righteousness[c]

LEXICON—a. εἰς with accusative object (LN 89.57): 'for' [LN, NICNT], 'for the purpose of' [LN], 'in order to' [BECNT, HNTC, ICC2, LN; TEV]. This preposition is translated 'this was to be' [AB], 'this was to' [NASB, NET], 'God did this to' [NTC; CEV], 'he did this to' [NIV, NRSV], 'God meant by this' [REB], not explicit [WBC; GW, KJV, NCV, NLT].
  b. ἔνδειξις (LN 28.52) (BAGD 2. p. 262): 'demonstration' [LN, NICNT], 'proof' [LN], 'clear indication, evidence, or verification of' [LN], 'manifestation' [AB], not explicit [NLT]. This noun is translated as an infinitive verb: 'to demonstrate' [BECNT, NTC, WBC; NASB, NET, NIV, REB, TEV], 'to declare' [KJV], 'to show' [CEV, GW, NCV, NRSV], 'to prove' [ICC2].
  c. δικαιοσύνη (LN 88.13) (BAGD 3. p. 197): 'righteousness' [BAGD, BECNT, HNTC, ICC2, LN, NICNT, WBC; KJV, NASB, NET, NRSV], 'uprightness' [AB], 'justice' [NTC; NIV, REB]. This noun is translated as

an adjective '(he is) righteous' [TEV], 'right' [CEV], not explicit [GW]. This word is translated '(God) always does what is right' [NCV], '(God) was being entirely fair and just' [NLT].

QUESTION—What relationship is indicated by the use of the preposition εἰς 'for' in this verse?

It introduces a purpose clause [AB, BECNT, Gdt, HNTC, Ho, ICC1, ICC2, Mu, NAC, NICNT, NTC, SSA, TH, WBC; CEV, NASB, NET, NRSV, REB, TEV]. God set forth Christ as a sacrifice of atonement in order to show that he is righteous [NICNT]. The preposition should be taken as indicating purpose here since the restatement of the same thought in 3:26 using the preposition πρός clearly expresses purpose [SSA]. The justice of God in the justification of sinners is the end to which this demonstration of righteousness is directed, and the exigency in view is [Mu].

QUESTION—What is the meaning of the word ἔνδειξις 'demonstration'?

1. It means 'to show or demonstrate' [AB, BECNT, Gdt, Ho, Mor, Mu, NAC, NICNT, SSA; CEV, GW, NASB, NCV, NET, NIV, NRSV, REB, TEV]. The term means a demonstration or public revelation [St]. In light of the word 'to publicly display' earlier in 3:25, emphasis should be placed on the sense 'showing' or 'demonstrating' [NICNT]. This may be expressed 'in order to show that' [SSA]. The saving act did many things, one of which was to show that God is just [Mor]. The purpose or end of Christ's work as stated here was to declare or vindicate God's righteousness to men because of his having passed by sins previously [Ho].
2. It means 'to prove' [ICC2]. If God were to simply pass over sins indefinitely, this would not only call his righteousness into question, it would seem to condone evil, and would be contrary to his nature. However it was his intention all along to deal with sin decisively and finally through the cross, and thereby establish his righteousness, his goodness, and his mercy [ICC2].
3. It means both 'to demonstrate' and 'to prove' [HNTC, ICC1, TH, WBC]. It means to show forth as well as to prove by the showing forth; God reveals his righteousness and thereby proves that it exists [HNTC]. 'To demonstrate' includes in its meaning the idea of 'to prove' [TH]. It means 'to indicate, prove, or demonstrate' [WBC].

QUESTION—What is the meaning of the term δικαιοσύνη 'righteousness' in this verse?

1. It refers to an attribute or aspect of God's character [AB, ICC2, Mor, Mu, NICNT, SSA, St, TNTC].
1.1 This means God's own attribute of righteousness [AB, ICC2, NICNT, NTC, St, TNTC]. This refers to God's justice and impartiality, and his always acting in complete accordance with his own character for his own glory, which is the same sense it has in 3:26 [NICNT]. This refers to God having justified sinners through Christ's substitutionary death in a way that is worthy of himself and that did not violate his truth,

condone or treat sin lightly, and which justly punished sin [St]. This is an attribute or quality of God, referring to his uprightness by which he actively acquits sinful people, manifesting towards them his power and gracious activity in a just judgment because of what Christ has done for them [AB].

1.2 It means God's attribute of justice [Gdt, Ho, Mor, Mu, NAC, NTC, SSA]. Jesus' sacrifice was to demonstrate or prove that God had not been unjust when in forbearance he overlooked sins in the past [NTC]. For God not to punish sin would show him to be unjust and to condone evil and sin, but the cross shows us that God's inflexible righteousness is the means by which sin is forgiven [Mor]. The term here means the justice of God, for it is this very attribute of God which seemed to be in conflict with his passing by the sins of the past without punishing them; his justice required vindication and public exhibition, and the death of Jesus Christ satisfied that justice [Ho].

2. It refers to the activity of God [BECNT, WBC].

2.1 It is God's saving action on behalf of those to whom he has pledged himself, and is expressed in terms of the covenant he established with them to save and sustain them. God's work in Christ is the fulfillment of the covenant promises in that Christ is now put forth as the means by which sins are forgiven and the promises of salvation can be realized [WBC].

2.2 It refers to God's activity both in terms of his judging as well as his saving righteousness, though it also includes his being righteous. The meaning of this term must include God's judging righteousness, since there is a close connection between God's righteousness and his wrath, and his justice is specifically mentioned in 3:5, 26; in the death of Jesus, both the saving and judging righteousness of God meet [BECNT].

QUESTION—In what sense does God's bringing forth Christ demonstrate his own righteous character?

1. In the past God allowed many sins to go unpunished, not because he was ignoring them, but because he intended to satisfy his own justice by punishing them through Christ's sacrificial death [Mor, NAC, SSA, St]. In the past God had overlooked sins, but for God's righteousness to be vindicated, action had to be taken [HNTC]. Those sins which had been previously committed had to be punished in order to satisfy God's justice [Gdt, Ho]. God's forbearance in the past should not be interpreted as his being indifferent to the claims of justice, because he has now provided a propitiation that fully satisfies his justice [Mu]. God vindicates his righteousness in the cross, satisfying his wrath by sending his son as a substitute and atonement for sin, thus showing that he did not ignore former sins, but was looking forward to the death of Christ as atonement for them, and that it was his fixed purpose to fully and justly punish these sins in the death of his son [BECNT, ICC2, NTC]. God's past restraint in not having fully and severely punished sins under the old covenant calls

into question his impartial justice and creates the need to satisfy his justice, which has been demonstrated by the sacrifice of Christ as the propitiatory sacrifice for sins [NICNT]. The death of Christ demonstrates the impossibility of simply passing over sins and is a sacrifice that satisfies the conditions that a righteous God requires [ICC1].
2. God demonstrates his saving faithfulness by providing a sacrifice that fulfills the terms of the covenant he established with Israel [WBC].
3. God demonstrates how he puts men right with himself, which is through faith in what Christ has done [TH]. The death of Christ publicly shows God's bountiful acquittal of sinners, an event which, having long been foreseen, has guided all God's dealings with humanity throughout history [AB].

on-account-of[a] **the passing-over**[b] **of-the previously-committed**[c] **sins**[d]

LEXICON—a. διά with accusative object (LN 89.26) (BAGD B.II.1. p. 181): 'on account of' [ICC2, LN], 'because of' [BECNT, HNTC, LN, NICNT, NTC], 'because' [NASB, NET, NIV, NRSV, REB], 'by reason of' [LN], 'for' [AB; KJV], 'in' [WBC], not explicit [CEV, GW, NCV, NLT, TEV]. This preposition is translated 'this was necessary on account of' [ICC2].

b. πάρεσις (LN **30.49**) (BAGD p. 626): 'passing over' [BAGD, BECNT, LN, NICNT, WBC; NET]. This noun is translated as a verb: 'to pass over' [NASB, NRSV], 'to overlook' [REB, TEV], 'to purposely pay no attention to, to disregard' [LN], 'to let go unpunished' [BAGD], 'to leave unpunished' [NIV], 'to not punish' [NLT], 'to pass over without punishment or remission' [HNTC], 'the remission of (sins)' [KJV], 'to pardon' [AB], 'to be patient and forgive' [CEV], 'to wait to deal' [GW], 'to treat with indulgence' [NTC]; as a participle: 'overlooking' [ICC2, LN]. This word is translated 'he was patient and did not punish' [NCV]. This word occurs only here in the NT.

c. perf. act. participle of προγίνομαι (LN **13.114**) (BAGD p. 703): 'previously committed' [BECNT; NASB, NET, NRSV], 'committed beforehand' [NICNT; NIV], 'to occur formerly, to happen previously' [LN], 'to happen before' [BAGD, LN], 'to be committed in former times' [BAGD, WBC], 'to sin in former times' [NLT], 'to commit in days gone by' [HNTC]. This participle is translated as an adjective: 'former' [**LN**], 'past' [AB, ICC2, NTC; KJV, REB]; as a phrase: 'in the past' [CEV, GW, NCV, TEV]. This word occurs only here in the NT.

d. ἁμάρτημα (LN **88.290**) (BAGD p. 42): 'sin' [AB, BAGD, BECNT, HNTC, ICC2, LN, NICNT, NTC, WBC; GW, KJV, NASB, NCV, NET, NIV, NRSV, REB], 'people's sins' [TEV], 'transgression' [BAGD], 'wrong doing' [LN], 'sinners' [CEV]. This noun is translated as a verb: 'to sin' [NLT].

QUESTION—What relationship is indicated by the preposition διά 'on account of'?

1. It causal, and the sense is 'because of the passing over of former sins' [BECNT, Gdt, HNTC, Ho, ICC1, ICC2, Mu, NICNT, NTC, SSA, St, TNTC, WBC; NASB, NET, NIV, NRSV, REB]. The preposition has its more usual sense of 'on account of' here, which is supported by the mention of God's forbearance [ICC2]. In 3:25 we are told the reason that this demonstration of God's righteousness, which is his just character, was necessary [Mu]. Because God had overlooked or pardoned previous sins, it was necessary that there be this exhibition of God's righteousness in the death of Christ [Ho]. Because of all the sins that had been being committed throughout the world's history, God judged it necessary to manifest his justice in the death of Jesus, who bore the punishment that all such sinners would have otherwise deserved to undergo themselves [Gdt].
2. It is prospective, indicating purpose; what God did through Christ was for the purpose of pardoning all the sins committed in the past [AB].

QUESTION—What is the meaning of πάρεσις 'passing over'?

1. It means to postpone punishment, to overlook, to pass over, or to leave unpunished [BECNT, Gdt, HNTC, ICC1, ICC2, Mor, Mu, NAC, NICNT, SSA, St, TH, TNTC, WBC; CEV, GW, NASB, NCV, NET, NLT, NRSV, REB, TEV]. When applied to legal charges or sins the word means to postpone or to neglect prosecution; Paul means that God postponed the full penalty due for sins during the old covenant, allowing people to stand before him even though an adequate satisfaction of the demands of his justice had not yet been provided [NICNT]. Paul's point is that God did not exact a full and immediate punishment for sins in former times, but passed over or tolerated them only because he looked forward to his Son being the atonement for them, fully paying for them and thus satisfying his justice [BECNT, NTC, St]. It does not mean to disregard, but rather 'to let go unpunished', for while the past sacrificial system was a legitimate way of dealing with sin at that time, it did not constitute an adequate or final answer to the sin problem that only Christ's sacrifice could give [WBC]. The noun expresses an event of disregarding or allowing to pass [SSA]. It means to temporarily suspend inflicting a punishment until a later date [ICC1].
2. It means to pardon [AB, Ho; KJV].

QUESTION—What is referred to by the phrase τῶν προγεγονότων ἁμαρτημάτων 'the previously committed sins'?

1. It refers to sins committed in the ages before Christ, during the period of God's forbearance [Gdt, HNTC, Ho, ICC1, ICC2, Mu, TNTC], to sins occurring during the era before the cross and the new age of salvation [NICNT], during the Mosaic era [BECNT]. This refers to the sins of former generations, which God overlooked and left unpunished [NAC, NTC, St, TH]. It refers to the sins committed up until the time of the decisive act of Christ on the cross [HNTC, ICC2]. It means the former

280   ROMANS 3:25

times up until the coming of Jesus Christ during which time, although sinful humans were subject to God's wrath, that wrath did not always manifest itself because of the eschatological nature of the punishment of sin in God's plan of salvation [AB].
2. It refers both to the sins of people in the days before Christ as well as to sins that Christians have committed in the past, since what Paul says is true of both. The perfect tense indicates sins which took place at an earlier time, but which also still persist through having made those who committed them sinners [Mor].

3:26 in[a] the forbearance[b] of God,

LEXICON—a. ἐν with dative object (LN 89.26) (BAGD I.4.d. p. 259): 'in' [BECNT, HNTC, ICC2, NICNT, NTC, WBC; NASB, NET, NIV, NRSV, REB], 'because of, on account of, by reason of' [LN], 'through' [KJV], not explicit [CEV, GW, NCV, NLT, TEV].
  b. ἀνοχή (LN 25.171) (BAGD 2. p. 72): 'forbearance' [AB, BAGD, BECNT, HNTC, ICC2, NICNT, NTC, WBC; KJV, NASB, NET, NIV, NRSV, REB], 'patience' [LN], not explicit [CEV, NCV, NLT]. This noun is translated as a verb: 'to be patient' [TEV], 'to wait' [GW]. This word occurs only here and at 2:4 in the NT.

QUESTION—What is being referred to by τῇ ἀνοχῇ τοῦ θεοῦ 'the forbearance of God'?

It refers to God's delay in punishing with full severity the sins committed in the Mosaic era under the old covenant; this does not mean that God completely failed to punish sins or just overlooked sins before Christ, but that he tolerated them as he looked forward to the atoning death of his son as the true sacrifice for sins that would fully satisfy his justice [AB, BECNT, Mor, Mu, NICNT, WBC]. In his patience God withheld punishment when he might have inflicted it, which is a problem eventually resolved by the cross of Christ [Gdt, HNTC, Ho, ICC2, Mor, NAC, TH]. God left unpunished and overlooked the sins of previous generations because he intended to punish them fully through Christ's death [ICC1, ICC2, Mu, NAC, NTC, St, TNTC].

for[a] the demonstration of-his righteousness[b] in[c] the now[d] time,[e]

LEXICON—a. πρός with accusative object (LN **89.60**) (BAGD III.3.a. p. 710): 'for' [BAGD, NICNT; NASB], 'for the purpose of' [BAGD, LN], 'for the sake of' [LN], 'in order to' [ICC2, **LN**; TEV], 'to' [BECNT, HNTC, NTC, WBC; KJV, NCV, NRSV, REB], not explicit [AB; CEV, GW, NLT]. This word is translated as a clause: 'he did this' [NIV], 'this was also to' [NET],
  b. δικαιοσύνη (LN 88.13) (BAGD 3. p. 197): 'righteousness' [BAGD, BECNT, HNTC, ICC2, LN, NICNT, WBC; KJV, NASB, NET, TEV], 'uprightness' [AB], 'justice' [NTC; GW, NIV, REB]. This adjective is translated as a verb phrase: 'God is right' [CEV], 'he does what is right' [NCV], 'he is entirely fair and just' [NLT], 'he himself is righteous' [NRSV].

c. ἐν with dative object (LN 67.136): 'in' [BECNT, HNTC, ICC2, NTC, WBC; NET, NLT, REB, TEV], 'at' [AB, NICNT; GW, KJV, NASB, NIV, NRSV], 'during, within, for' [LN], not explicit [CEV, NCV].
d. νῦν (LN 67.38) (BAGD 3.a. p. 546): 'now' [LN], 'present' [AB, BAGD, BECNT, HNTC, ICC2, NICNT, NTC, WBC; GW, NASB, NET, NIV, NLT, NRSV, REB, TEV], 'this' [KJV], not explicit [CEV, NCV].
e. καιρός (LN 67.145) (BAGD 1. p. 394): 'time' [AB, BAGD, BECNT, HNTC, ICC2, NICNT, NTC, WBC; GW, KJV, NASB, NET, NIV, NLT, NRSV, TEV], 'period of time' [BAGD, LN], 'age, era' [LN], not explicit [CEV, REB]. The phrase 'now time' is translated 'today' [NCV].

QUESTION—What relationship is indicated by the preposition πρός 'for'?

It indicates purpose [BECNT, Gdt, HNTC, Ho, ICC1, Mor, Mu, NAC, NICNT, SSA, TNTC, WBC]. The shift from εἰς in 3:25 is purely stylistic; both indicate purpose [NICNT]. The goal intended in the demonstration of God's righteousness was to show both that God was righteous in himself and also that he justified the person who relied on faith [HNTC]. This indicates the goal aimed at with conscious purpose [Mor]. This preposition, like εἰς 'for' in 3:25, expresses the design, object, or purpose for which something is done [Ho].

1. It is parallel to εἰς ἔνδειξιν 'for demonstration' in 3:25 and expresses the additional point that the demonstration of God's righteousness has significance for the present age as well as for the past [AB, BECNT, Gdt, HNTC, Ho, ICC2, Mor, Mu, NICNT, NTC, WBC]. There is a contrast between what God is doing in the present time and the forbearance he showed in the past [HNTC, Mor, Mu]. The phrase about what God is doing in the present time balances the comment about what God did in the past [WBC].
2. It is connected with the clause just before it, and means that God's forbearance in punishing sins in the past was for the purpose of demonstrating his righteousness now [ICC1].

QUESTION—What is meant by ἐν τῷ νῦν καιρῷ 'in the now time'?

It stands in contrast to the time of God's forbearance [Gdt, HNTC, Ho, Mu, NTC, WBC]. It means the time period after Christ's coming as the climactic, eschatological age of salvation history [NICNT]. It means the present era of salvation history [BECNT]. It means the present time [AB, TH], the eschatological now [AB]. While the sins were committed earlier, the demonstration of God's righteousness is in the present [Mor]. It speaks of the contrast between the time of God's forbearance of sins in the past, which made God appear unjust, and the punishment of those sins on the cross [St]. There is a contrast between the old dispensation, under which the sins of the past had been committed, and the new dispensation; Christ's atonement reaches backward as well as forward to both dispensations [NTC]. This embraces both the period of the gospel events themselves, beginning with the coming of Christ, as well as the proclamation of them in the ongoing preaching of the gospel [ICC2]. This shows the significance of the historical epoch in which God gave this demonstration of his justice, as contrasted with past generations during which he exercised forbearance [Mu]. Formerly it looked as though God was neither just nor justifying, but now he shows that he is both [SSA]. The death of Christ vindicated the justice of God in forgiving the sins in all ages of the world, since they were all punished in the work of Christ [Ho]. This is in contrast both with the previous time of God's past forbearance as well as with the eschatological future, in the sense that the manifestation of righteousness that will characterize the last judgment has been brought forward even into the present [HNTC]. The phrase means more than just the present, it also means the appointed time, the time of opportunity, the actions and decisions of which will determine the future; Christ's death is a pivotal point in human history, having effect both for the past as well as for the future [WBC].

for[a] him to-be just[b] and (the one) justifying[c] the-(one) of[d] faith in-Jesus.
LEXICON—a. εἰς (LN 89.48, 89.57) (BAGD 4.e. p. 229): 'for the purpose of, in order to' [LN (89.57)], 'in order that' [BECNT, NICNT], 'so that' [BAGD, HNTC, ICC2; NET], 'so' [NCV], 'so that as a result, with the result that' [LN (89.48)], 'that' [KJV, NASB], not explicit [NLT, NRSV]. The articular infinitive phrase εἰς τὸ εἶναι 'for him to be' is translated 'so as to be' [NIV], 'that he might be' [NTC, WBC], 'in this way he shows' [TEV], 'showing that' [REB], 'to show that' [AB], 'this also shows' [CEV], 'this shows that' [GW].

b. δίκαιος (LN 88.12) (BAGD 2. p. 196): 'just' [BECNT, LN, NICNT, NTC, WBC; KJV, NASB, NET, NIV, REB], 'righteous' [BAGD, HNTC, ICC2, LN; NRSV, TEV], 'upright' [AB, BAGD], 'right' [CEV], 'entirely fair and just' [NLT]. This word is translated as an adverb: '(judge) rightly' [NCV]; as a phrase: 'a God of justice' [GW].

c. pres. act. participle of δικαιόω (LN 34.46) (BAGD 3.b. p. 197): 'to justify' [AB, HNTC, ICC2; NRSV, REB], 'to cause to be in a right relationship' [LN], 'to put right' [LN; TEV], 'to acquit to pronounce and treat as righteous' [BAGD], 'to accept people' [CEV], 'to approve' [GW], 'to declare to be right in his sight' [NLT], 'to make right' [NCV]. This participle is translated as a noun: 'justifier' [BECNT, NICNT; KJV, NASB, NET]; as a phrase: 'the one who justifies' [NTC, WBC; NIV].

d. ἐκ with genitive object (LN 89.3) (BAGD 3.d. p. 235). The phrase τὸν ἐκ πίστεως Ἰησοῦ 'the one of faith in (Jesus)' is translated 'those who have (faith in)' [BAGD; NIV], 'the one who has faith in' [BECNT; NRSV], 'the person who has faith in' [NICNT, NTC], 'people who have faith in' [CEV], 'the one who has faith in' [NASB], 'any person who has faith in' [NCV], 'those who put faith in' [AB], 'anyone who puts his faith in' [REB], 'him/those who believe in' [WBC; GW, KJV], 'the man who believes in' [ICC2], 'everyone who believes in' [TEV], 'the one who lives because of (Jesus)' faithfulness' [NET], 'the man who relies on faith' [HNTC], 'they believe in' [NLT].

QUESTION—What relationship is indicated by the articular infinitive phrase εἰς τὸ εἶναι 'for him to be'?
  1. It indicates purpose [AB, BECNT, HNTC, ICC2, Mor, NICNT, NTC, WBC].
    1.1 It relates to the clause just before it and indicates the purpose of God's righteousness being manifested: God's righteousness is manifested in order to show that he is both just and the justifier [AB, BECNT, Gdt, HNTC, ICC1, Mor, NICNT]. God did this so that he would be just and also so that he might be seen to be just [Mor]
    1.2 It relates to the sentence begun in 3:25 and indicates the purpose for which God set forth Christ [Ho, ICC2, NTC, SSA, WBC; NCV, NRSV]: God set forth Christ as a propitiation or expiation in order to demonstrate his justice *and* in order to be just and the justifier. God put forth Christ as propitiation so that he might be righteous, not just be seen as righteous [ICC2].
  2. It is translated as indicating result [CEV, GW, REB, TEV]: this shows that he is just, etc.
QUESTION—What is the meaning of the word δίκαιος 'just' in the phrase εἶναι αὐτὸν δίκαιον 'him to be just'?
  Note that there is a certain amount of overlap possible between the positions listed below, and one does not necessarily rule out the other.
  1. It means 'just' [Gdt, HNTC, Ho, Mor, Mu, NTC, SSA, St]. It refers to God acting as judge according to strict justice; although formerly he might have been considered unjust, by the death of Christ he shows himself to be acting justly [SSA]. The crucifixion shows God's abhorrence of sin and his righteous judgment on it [HNTC], and as a result the Judge of all the earth is seen to do right [Gdt, St]. By putting all sin past, present, and future onto Christ, God demonstrated that he is just, as he always has been and always will be [NTC]. This expresses the idea that sin must be punished and the demands of the law and justice must be met, and that Christ was set forth as a sacrifice to manifest that God is just in this regard [Ho]. In 3:25 and 3:26 the righteousness of God is his inherent justice [Mu]. God would not be just unless he showed himself to be so [Gdt].
  2. It refers to God's attribute of righteous character [AB, BECNT, ICC1, ICC2, NAC, NICNT, TNTC], but specifically to his judging righteousness [BECNT, NICNT]. Paul realizes that what was really at stake was not only God being shown to be righteous, but in fact actually being righteous, since he would not be righteous if he neglected to show himself as being so [ICC2]. The propitiatory sacrifice of Christ, which provided full satisfaction for the demands of God's justice, enabled God to show that he is maintaining his righteous character even though he had postponed the punishment of past sins [NICNT]. The righteousness with which Paul is concerned cannot be confined only to his saving activity, but includes the attribute of righteousness as well, since the display of his righteousness in the work of Christ is an expression of his own righteous

character and nature [BECNT]. The process of acquitting humanity and making people upright before God flows from God's own inherent uprightness [AB].
3. It means 'just' as well as 'righteous'; God demonstrates his righteous nature by doing what justice requires [NAC].
4. It means God's saving activity or saving righteousness, not his attribute of justness. God's righteousness is his fulfilling of his covenant obligation to save and sustain Israel, and Christ's death does with effective finality what the earlier sacrificial system had done only in part [WBC].

QUESTION—In this verse what is the relationship between the adjective δίκαιον 'just' and the participle δικαιοῦντα 'justifying'?
1. The relationship is coordinate [HNTC, ICC1, Mor, Mu, NAC, NTC, SSA, St, TH, TNTC, WBC]: he is just and justifying. Paul sees the whole process of God's acquitting humanity and rendering it upright as something that proceeds from what God is in himself; he demonstrates his own uprightness in the work of Christ and justifies those who put their faith in Jesus [Mu]. By punishing sin in the death of his son, God could simultaneously be just himself, and be the one who justifies those who have faith in Jesus [HNTC, St, WBC]. Since God has demonstrated that he is just, no one can deny that he alone has the right to be the justifier of those who trust in Jesus [NTC]. In the offering of Christ, God's righteousness is vindicated and the believing sinner is justified [TNTC]. Christ's death on the cross satisfies the righteous nature of God and demonstrates that he is both just and the justifier of those who have faith in Jesus [NAC].
2. The relationship is concessive [BECNT, Gdt, Ho, ICC2, NICNT]: he is just, although he justifies. Paul is making the point that God is able to maintain his righteous character even while justifying sinners because it is Christ as propitiatory sacrifice that provides full satisfaction of the demands of God's justice [BECNT, NICNT]. It means that God is righteous even in justifying; that is, he can justify righteously without compromising his own righteous character, and achieve a forgiveness worthy of his character and righteousness because he bears the burden of evil himself in the person of his son [ICC2]. The concessive sense of this conjunction is well attested by other passages, and in this instance ought to be rendered 'and yet', or 'although' [Ho]. God is just, even while justifying, and justifies, even while remaining just [Gdt].
3. It expresses grounds; God's intervention in human history in which he acquits human beings shows or proves that he is upright [AB].

QUESTION—What is the meaning of the phrase τὸν ἐκ πίστεως ᾽Ιησοῦ 'the one of faith in Jesus'?
It means the one who believes, who relies on faith in Jesus [AB, BECNT, Gdt, HNTC, Ho, ICC1, Mor, Mu, NAC, NICNT, NTC, SSA, St, TH, WBC]. The expression is rare in the NT, but the singular 'one' has the sense of the generic 'everyone', and the preposition ἐκ here means 'characterized by',

and therefore 'everyone who'; the entire phrase may be expressed as 'everyone who trusts in what Jesus has done' [SSA]. This shows that the object of God's justifying is the person who believes in Jesus [ICC2]. This is the person of faith, meaning not only the person who has faith in Jesus, but the person whose characteristic is faith, whose position proceeds from faith and is not mixed with law [Mor]. The expression means the faith of which Jesus is the object; the man who relies on Jesus as propitiatory sacrifice is justified by God, and justly so [Ho]. This must be interpreted in accord with Paul's usage elsewhere in which Jesus Christ is always the object of the faith referred to [Mu].

DISCOURSE UNIT: 3:27–31 [AB, BECNT, Gdt, ICC1, ICC2, Mor, NICNT, SSA, WBC]. The topic is a polemical development of the theme [AB], righteousness by faith for Jews and Gentiles [BECNT], justification and the true meaning of the law [Gdt], boasting excluded [ICC1], all glorying is excluded [ICC1, ICC2], justification effected by faith [Mor], by faith alone: initial statement [NICNT], consequences for self-understanding by Jewish people [WBC].

3:27 Where then^a (is) boasting?^b It-is-excluded.^c

LEXICON—a. οὖν (LN 89.50) (BAGD 1.c.α. p. 593): 'then' [AB, BAGD, BECNT, ICC2, LN, NICNT, NTC, WBC; KJV, NASB, NET, NIV, NLT, NRSV, REB, TEV], 'so' [LN; GW, NCV], 'so then, consequently, accordingly' [LN], not explicit [CEV]. This inferential particle is translated as a clause functioning as the protasis of a conditional sentence: 'if this is what the manifestation of righteousness, and justification mean' [HNTC].

b. καύχησις (LN 33.368) (BAGD 1. p. 426): 'boasting' [AB, BAGD, BECNT, HNTC, LN, NICNT, NTC, WBC; KJV, NASB, NET, NIV, NLT, NRSV], 'glorying' [ICC2], 'human pride' [REB]. This word is translated as a verb: 'to brag' [CEV, GW, NCV], 'to boast' [TEV].

c. aorist pass. indic. of ἐκκλείω (LN **13.143**) (BAGD 2. p. 240): 'to be excluded' [BAGD, BECNT, HNTC, ICC2, LN, NICNT, NTC, WBC; KJV, NASB, NET, NIV, NRSV, REB], 'to be not allowed' [**LN**], 'to be ruled out' [AB], 'to be eliminated' [BAGD, LN; GW], 'to be without basis (for boasting)' [LN]. It is also possible to understand the word in this context as meaning that there is no basis for boasting; in other words, there is nothing that one can boast about [LN], 'Not a thing!' [CEV], 'No!' [NCV, NLT], 'Nothing!' [TEV].

QUESTION—What relationship is indicated by οὖν 'then'?

It draws a conclusion from what has been said in 3:21–26 [BECNT, ICC2, Mu, NICNT, SSA], or from 3:23–26 [Gdt], or possibly from 1:18–3:26 [ICC2]. It draws a conclusion from what has been said in 3:21–26, that boasting has been ruled out because righteousness is obtained by faith in Christ and not by obeying the law [BECNT]. Boasting is ruled out because of the death of Christ [WBC], because righteousness is obtained by faith and not by the works of the law [BECNT].

QUESTION—What καύχησις 'boasting' is Paul referring to?

1. Paul has in view the contrast between faith and works in general, and the pride of accomplishment as a basis on which a relationship with God could be established or maintained [BECNT, Gdt, HNTC, Ho, ICC2, Mor, Mu, NICNT, NTC, SSA]. Paul means human pride in accomplishments as a basis for relationship with God, but he is also probably thinking in particular of Jews and their boasting as shown by his elaboration on the term 'law', by his return to the diatribe style with an imagined Jewish opponent, and by his focus on Jew and Gentile in 3:29–30 [NICNT]. Boasting based on human works is ruled out since Paul shows that a right relationship with God is based on the atonement of Christ and faith in him, and 3:28 provides the explicit grounds for the present verse by stating that righteousness is by faith, apart from works of law [BECNT]. Paul is referring to the human tendency to rely on one's own power or merit to achieve justification in God's sight [AB], or to the fact of having been given the law, or the degree to which one had kept the law [Mor]. The implied referent of boasting is 'about being declared righteous by God' and the implied means is 'by obeying the law' [SSA]. The context and the next verse show that in particular it this means the pretension to justify oneself by one's own works; perhaps particularly Jews [Gdt, ICC2]. Boasting is excluded in direct proportion to the degree that justification by faith is affirmed [Gdt].

2. Paul is referring to the pride the Jews held in the law, and in their special covenant relationship with God [NAC, WBC]. Paul is speaking of the understandable pride of the Jewish nation for being the chosen people of God [NAC]. This is a clear allusion to 2:17, 23 which speaks of Jewish pride in the law as indicating God's commitment to his people, and bragging about their relationship to God as his chosen ones. It is the Jewish overconfidence in their privileged status he has in view, not boasting in one's own achievements [WBC].

3. This refers in general to sinners boasting in self-exaltation before God, and while it does not refer specifically to Jews boasting over Gentiles, it does include that [Ho].

QUESTION—What is implied by the tense and voice of this passive verb?

God is the implied agent of the passive verb [AB, BECNT, ICC2, NAC, WBC], and the possibility is excluded decisively once and for all [ICC1, Mor, Mu, NAC, WBC].

By[a] what-sort-of[b] law?[c] Of works?[d]

LEXICON—a. διά with genitive object (LN 89.76) (BAGD A.III.1.d. p. 180): 'by' [BAGD, HNTC, ICC2, LN, WBC; KJV, NASB, NET, NRSV], 'by means of' [LN], 'through' [BECNT, LN, NICNT], 'on' [AB, NTC; GW, NIV, REB], 'because' [CEV], not explicit [NCV, NLT, TEV].

b. ποῖος (LN 58.30) (BAGD 1.a. β. p. 684): 'what sort of' [LN], 'what kind of' [BAGD, HNTC, ICC2, LN, WBC; NASB], 'what' [AB, NICNT, NTC; GW, KJV, NET, NIV, NRSV, REB], not explicit [NCV, NLT, TEV]. This phrase is translated 'Is it because we obeyed some law?' [CEV].

c. νόμος (LN 33.333) (BAGD 1. p. 542): 'law' [BAGD, BECNT, HNTC, ICC2, LN, NICNT, WBC; CEV, KJV, NASB, NCV, NRSV, TEV], 'principle' [AB; NET, NIV, REB], 'basis' [NTC; GW]. This noun is translated a verb: 'to be based on' [NLT].

d. ἔργον (LN 42.11): 'work' [BECNT, HNTC, ICC2, LN, NICNT, NTC, WBC; KJV, NASB, NET, NRSV], 'deed' [AB, LN], 'effort' [GW]. This plural genitive noun is translated as a phrase: 'the principle of deeds' [AB], 'a law based on works' [HNTC], 'based on our good deeds' [NLT], 'the keeping of the law' [REB], 'observing the law' [NIV], 'the way of trying to obey' [NCV]. This word is translated as a complete sentence: 'Is it because we obeyed some law?' [CEV], 'Is it that we obey the Law?' [TEV].

No, but through^a (the) law of-faith.^b

LEXICON—a. διά with genitive object (LN 89.76): 'through' [BECNT, LN, NICNT], 'by means of' [LN], 'by' [HNTC, ICC2, WBC; KJV, NASB, NET, NRSV], 'on' [AB, NTC; GW, NIV, NLT], 'because of' [CEV], not explicit [REB, TEV]. This word is translated 'It is (the way of)' [NCV].

b. πίστις (LN 31.85) (BAGD 2.d.α. p. 663): 'faith' [AB, BAGD, BECNT, ICC2, LN, NICNT, NTC, WBC; all versions except TEV]. This genitive noun is translated as a phrase: 'a law based on faith' [HNTC]; as a clause: 'we believe' [TEV].

QUESTION—What is the meaning of the word νόμος 'law' in this verse?

1. Here it is used in a somewhat different sense than normally and refers to a principle, standard, or rule [AB, Gdt, Ho, ICC1, Mor, Mu, NTC, SSA, St]. Whether Paul had in mind ceremonial works of the law or moral ones having to do with obeying commandments, boasting on that basis is excluded not on the principle of observing law, but on that of faith, for sinners are justified by faith alone [St]. It is used here in a figurative sense [AB], referring to a basis, norm, standard, or principle [NTC]. In this context the word refers to the basis or means for being declared righteous [SSA]. It refers to a system as the constituted order of things, and the essence of the system under discussion here that it is a system of faith [ICC1]. Here it is a rule of action [Ho]. There is a contrast here between two orders of things [Mu].

2. The word is partly metaphorical, referring to a principle or rule, and is partly a play on words referring to the Mosaic Law [AB, BECNT, NICNT]. The word has the general sense of a rule or system of demands, but in Romans is connected so often to works that it would naturally bring to mind the Torah or Law of Moses here as well. [NICNT]. The 'law of

works' refers to the Mosaic law, but the play on words is such that readers will understand that the law teaches righteousness by faith if it is correctly understood [BECNT]. By 'the law of works' Paul understands the Mosaic law, understood as a demand for individual acts, but here is playing on a figurative sense meaning 'principle' [AB].
   3. The word refers to the law of Moses, the law of the Old Testament [ICC2, WBC]. The phrase the 'law of works' can only be a reference to the Torah and its characteristic obligations, and the question posed has to do with the proper kind of understanding of the law [WBC]. In asking 'what kind of law' he is raising the question of how the law should be characterized or understood; the OT law is intended to be as that which summons men to faith, not as that which prompts them to seek to be justified as a reward for their works [ICC2].
   4. The word does not simply mean the Jewish law, but refers to the religious system of Judaism. His argument is that if we accept the religion of faith, then by definition there are no works and no grounds for boasting [HNTC].

QUESTION—In excluding boasting, is Paul contrasting two different perspectives on the same law, the law of Moses, or is he contrasting two different 'laws' or principles altogether, that of works and that of faith?
   1. Paul is contrasting two different 'laws', that of works and that of faith [AB, BECNT, Gdt, HNTC, Ho, ICC1, Mor, Mu, NAC, NICNT, NTC, SSA, St, TH]. Paul's explanation for the exclusion of any boasting rests on the contrast between works or achievements, and the kind of faith that gains standing with God that is explicitly described as being apart from the Mosaic law. This distinction is reflected in the entire passage as well as throughout Romans, and in his larger teachings about the law [NICNT]. In both 3:27 and 3:28 there is a marked contrast between 'faith' and the 'law of works' [BECNT]. Paul uses an oxymoron to contrast law and faith, and insists that the uprightness that comes by virtue of faith in Christ in no way depends on human merit, coming purely as a grace from God [AB]. Observing the law might give a person some sense of a grounds for boasting, but faith attributes salvation entirely to Christ and so eliminates all boasting [St]. Paul shows that boasting and faith are mutually exclusive, since a person who boasts of his own deeds cannot trust God's act of redemption [HNTC]. The contrast is between an order of things in which works are the medium of justification and one in which justification is exclusively by faith [Mu]. The sense of the word is a general one meaning 'mode of action', or a rule or principle to which one is subject or that determines one's conduct [Gdt].
   2. Paul is contrasting two different perspectives on the same law, the law of Moses, whether understood in terms of faith or simply in terms of works, which could lead to boasting [ICC2, WBC]. This refers to the law of the OT, God's law, but not misunderstood as directing men to seek justification as a reward for works, but as summoning men to faith

[ICC2]. The contrast here is a view of law in terms of works, with particular emphasis on Jewish identity markers, versus looking at it in terms of faith, which opens it up to Gentiles. The law understood in terms of works functioning to document Jewish membership in the chosen people of God, and in which the Jew can take pride, is not excluded, but the kind of boasting as is referred to in 2:17 and 2:23 is excluded by the law when the law is understood in terms of faith. If the law is seen only as marking off Jew from Gentile, it makes God only the God of the people of the law, but when the law is understood in terms of faith, it means that God can be God of both Jew and Gentile, and that his righteousness is extended to all who believe [WBC].

QUESTION—What is meant by the phrase νόμου πίστεως 'law of faith'?
1. It means a principle or rule pertaining to faith such that a person is justified by faith apart from the law [AB, Gdt, Ho, ICC1, Mor, Mu, NICNT, NTC, SSA, St, TH]. This refers to the Mosaic law, and the play on words here is intended to show that the law, if correctly understood, teaches righteousness by faith; relationship with God is based on faith in the atonement of Christ, not on human works [BECNT]. 'Law of faith' is an oxymoron, since faith is not a law at all; now faith is what God has ordained as the way to salvation [AB]. What is meant is Christian faith, faith in Christ [ICC1]. Paul sees faith as a principle, but it is also possible that he means that the law and the prophets point to faith and the righteousness that comes by faith [Mor].
2. It means the OT law, the Torah, but Paul does not mean the law as bearing witness to faith, or summoning people to faith, or as in reference to the ministry of Christ, but he means the whole law as understood in terms of its faith character, such that its distinctive Jewish character is not the primary focus and the distinctively Jewish works such as circumcision become secondary and may be disregarded by Gentiles. It is the law as addressed to faith and fulfilled through faith [WBC]. It means the OT law, but should be understood as God's law, which by its very nature summons men to faith [ICC2].
3. He is contrasting a religion based on faith, which affords no grounds for boasting, with a religion based on moral and ceremonial works, of which boasting could be made [HNTC].

3:28 For[a] we-consider[b] (a) person to-be-justified[c] by[d] faith[e]

TEXT—Instead of γάρ 'for', some manuscripts have οὖν 'therefore'. GNT selects the reading γάρ 'for' with a B rating, indicating that the text is almost certain. The reading οὖν 'therefore' is taken by KJV only.

LEXICON—a. γάρ (LN 89.23): 'for' [AB, BECNT, HNTC, ICC2, NICNT, NTC, WBC; NASB, NET, NIV, NRSV, REB, TEV], 'so' [NLT], not explicit [CEV, GW, NCV].
  b. pres. mid. (deponent = act.) indic. of λογίζομαι (LN 31.1) (BAGD 3. p. 476): 'to consider' [LN; NET], 'to hold' [BAGD; NRSV], 'to maintain

that' [AB, NTC; NASB, NIV], 'to reckon' [BECNT, HNTC, ICC2, NICNT, WBC], 'to see that' [CEV], 'to conclude that' [GW, KJV, TEV], not explicit [NCV, NLT]. This is translated 'our argument is' [REB].
   c. pres. pass. infin. of δικαιόω (LN 34.46) (BAGD 3.a. p. 197): 'to be justified' [AB, BAGD, BECNT, HNTC, ICC2, NICNT, NTC, WBC; KJV, NASB, NIV, NRSV, REB], 'to be put right with God' [LN; TEV], 'to be made right with God' [NCV, NLT], 'to be acceptable to God' [CEV], 'to be declared righteous' [NET], 'to have God's approval' [GW].
   d. There is no lexical entry for the word 'by' in the Greek text, but it is used in translation to express the relation to the verb indicated by the dative case of the noun 'faith'. This relation is translated 'by' [AB, BAGD, BECNT, HNTC, ICC2, LN, NICNT, NTC, WBC; KJV, NASB, NET, NRSV, REB], 'through' [NCV, NLT], 'only through' [TEV], 'because they have (faith)' [CEV], 'because of (faith)' [GW].
   e. πίστις (LN 31.85) (BAGD 2.d.α. p. 663): 'faith' [AB, BAGD, BECNT, HNTC, ICC2, LN, NICNT, NTC, WBC; all versions].
QUESTION—What relationship is indicated by the conjunction γάρ 'for'?
   1. It indicates grounds [AB, BECNT, Gdt, HNTC, Ho, ICC1, ICC2, Mor, Mu, SSA, TH]. This verse is the grounds for all of 3:27 by confirming that righteousness is by faith and not of works, thus excluding any boasting [BECNT, HNTC]. This verse supports 3:27 as a whole, not only saying that glorying is excluded, but specifically that it is excluded by the law of faith [ICC1, ICC2, SSA]. The connection indicates a supporting argument for what has just been said, giving a reason for the argument of 3:27 and not a conclusion drawn from it [Gdt, Ho, Mor, Mu, SSA]. It gives the grounds for 3:27b, and introduces a summary of 1:15–3:26 [HNTC].
   2. It introduces an explanation in which he explains the rule of faith [NICNT].
QUESTION—Who are the intended referents of the plural form of the verb λογιζόμεθα 'we consider'?
   1. It includes both Paul and his readers [AB, ICC2, Mor, NICNT, WBC]. Most likely it refers to Paul and his readers, whom he assumes would agree with his assessment on this point [NICNT]. The basis of the assertion that Paul is making would not have seemed strange to his readers, and so he includes them in his use of this word [AB]. Paul means to indicate that this conviction is common to all believers [ICC2, WBC]. This introduces a contention of Paul's own, but the plural loosely associates Christians in general with him, and is not just an individual opinion [Mor].
   2. It is an apostolic plural and refers to Paul alone [BECNT].

apart-from[a] works[b] of-law.[c]
LEXICON—a. χωρίς (LN 89.120) (BAGD 2.b.δ. p. 891): 'apart from' [AB, BECNT, ICC2, LN, NTC, WBC; NASB, NET, NIV, NRSV], 'without' [LN; KJV], 'having no relationship to, independent of' [LN],

'without regard to' [BAGD], 'to the exclusion of' [HNTC], 'not because of' [GW], 'not through' [NCV], 'not by' [NLT, TEV], 'quite apart from any question of' [REB], not explicit [CEV].
   b. ἔργον (LN 42.11) (BAGD 1.c.β. p. 308): 'work' [BECNT, HNTC, ICC2, NICNT, NTC, WBC; NASB, NET, NRSV], 'deed' [AB, BAGD, LN; KJV], '(his own) efforts' [GW]. This noun is translated as a verb: 'to obey' [CEV, NCV, NLT], 'to observe' [NIV], 'to keep' [REB]; as a participle: 'doing' [TEV].
   c. νόμος (LN 33.55, 33.333): 'law' [LN (33.333)], 'Law' [LN (33.55)]. This word, which lacks the definite article here, is translated 'law' [HNTC, NTC], 'the law' [AB, BECNT, ICC2, NICNT, WBC; KJV, NCV, NET, NIV, NLT, NRSV, REB], 'the Law' [CEV, NASB, TEV]. The phrase ἔργων νόμου 'works of law' is translated 'deeds prescribed by the law' [AB], 'works prescribed by the law' [NRSV], 'law works' [NTC], 'his own efforts' [GW], 'obeying the law' [NCV, NLT], 'observing the law' [NIV], 'any question of keeping the law' [REB], 'doing what the Law commands' [TEV].

QUESTION—What is the meaning of the phrase ἔργων νόμου 'works of the law'?

1. It means obedience specifically to the Mosaic law, or the Jewish legalistic trust in and reliance on keeping the law [AB, BECNT, NTC, SSA, St, TH, WBC]. This term embraces all that is contained in the Mosaic law, and Paul shows that since no one can obey the whole law, boasting is out of the question, and further that righteousness cannot be obtained through the Mosaic covenant, but only through faith in the death of Jesus Christ. Paul fundamentally rules out righteousness by any works [BECNT]. Paul means the prescriptions of the Mosaic law, and is saying that uprightness has now been manifested to men apart from any need to observe these prescriptions [AB]. Paul may mean either ceremonial rules for diet and Sabbath observance, or he may mean moral works of obeying God's commands, but neither can gain God's favor or forgiveness [St]. This means obeying the law, which it is impossible to do [SSA]. The word 'law' is to be understood as a reference to the Jewish Law [TH]. It means the law regarded as exclusively and distinctively Jewish and marking the boundary between the Jew and the Gentile [WBC].
2. It means more generally anything a person does [HNTC, Ho, ICC2, Mor, Mu, NICNT, TNTC]. The phrase means anything someone does, whether in obedience to the law, or, by extension, anything at all that a person does, since no matter what the nature or motivation of works, they can play no part in making a sinner right with God [NICNT]. Here the proposition is general, referring to moral law, including works done on the basis of natural conscience, which applies as much to Gentiles as to Jews [Ho]. The phrase does not mean works done in obedience to the law in a legalistic spirit, and regarded as in themselves a means of justification, but rather means that there are no works, no obedience to God's requirements,

which can provide sufficient grounds for justifying man in God's sight [ICC2]. Since Paul contrasts two religious systems, one based on works and the other based on faith, 'works of law' refers here to Jewish religious works, whether moral or ceremonial [HNTC]. The phrase means works performed in obedience to divine commandment, and Paul insists that any works in performance of any commandment avail nothing in justification [Mu]. Justification occurs apart from any kind of law works [Mor].

3:29 Or (is he) the God of-Jews only? (Is he) not (the God) of-Gentiles also? Yes,[a] of-Gentiles also,

LEXICON—a. ναί. The clause ναὶ καὶ ἐθνῶν is translated 'yes, he is the God of the Gentiles also' [BECNT, NICNT], 'yes, of the Gentiles also' [KJV], 'Yes, of the Gentiles too' [NET, NIV], 'Yes, of Gentiles also' [NRSV], 'of course he is' [HNTC; NLT, TEV], 'yes even of Gentiles' [AB], 'yes he is' [CEV], 'most certainly of the Gentiles also' [ICC2], 'Certainly, of Gentiles also' [NTC; REB].

QUESTION—What is the purpose or function of these questions?

Paul is taking advantage of the Jewish conviction that God is the God of all humans and using it to his own purpose to corroborate the teaching about excluding all boasting and to support the equal standing of Jew and Gentile [AB, Mor, WBC]. No Jew would have questioned that God is the God of all men in the sense of being their creator, Ruler, and Judge [HNTC, ICC2, NAC, WBC], but this question indicates what would be true if it were not true that, as 3:28 states, all men are justified by faith apart from works of law, and goes on to insist that God's purpose is gracious and merciful for all men [ICC2]. Paul adds to this common belief of Jews the notion that Jew and Gentile are equal before God, that no one can boast, and that all will be justified by faith [HNTC]. Paul alludes to the fact that Israel's own Psalter and prophets recognized that all nations are called upon to praise God, and that he is also their God [AB]. The Jews insisted there was but one God, so Paul reasons that since that is true, it is unthinkable that the approach to him could only be possible for small proportion of all those he has created [Mor]. Paul exploits the tension in the thought of the Jews between their national self-consciousness as the people of God, distinct from other nations, and their recognition of God as creator and lord of all nations [WBC]. He appeals to the unity of God as the basis for his argument; if God is indeed one, he is God of Gentile as well as Jew, and therefore will not operate in two different modes in justifying people [Mu]. Paul gives the alternative to the principle just stated in 3:28 [BECNT, ICC1, ICC2, NICNT, NTC, SSA]. If justification is by works of the law then only those in the law, the Jews, could be justified, Gentiles living apart from the law could have no chance to be saved, and God would be God of the Jews only [NTC]. By the form of the second question, which implies a positive answer, Paul rejects the alternative he has just presented that God is God of the Jews alone, and then goes on to state the case explicitly that he is also God of the Gentiles [NICNT]. Paul is introducing a fresh argument here in support of justification by faith [BECNT, SSA].

3:30 if-indeed[a] God (is) one

LEXICON—a. εἴπερ (LN 89.66) (BAGD VI. 11. p. 220): 'if indeed' [BAGD, HNTC, LN; NASB, REB], 'since' [BAGD, NICNT; NET, NIV, NRSV], 'since after all' [WBC], 'for' [AB], 'seeing that' [BECNT, ICC2, NTC], 'seeing' [KJV], not explicit [TEV]. This clause is translated 'There is only one God' [CEV, NLT], 'for God…is one' [AB], 'since there is only one God' [NIV], 'since God is one' [NET], 'since it is the same God' [GW], 'because there is only one God' [NCV], 'seeing it is one God' [KJV]. This word is an emphatic marker of condition [LN].

QUESTION—What is the meaning of the word εἴπερ 'if indeed'?

It introduces a reason for what has been stated, and means 'since' or 'seeing that' [AB, BAGD, Gdt, ICC2, Mor, NAC, NICNT, SSA, TH]. It introduces the necessary and sufficient condition for what he has just affirmed [WBC]. It expresses certainty [TH], meaning 'if, as is indeed true' [ICC2].

who will-justify[a] (the) circumcision[b] by[c] faith[d] and (the) uncircumcision[e] through[f] faith.

LEXICON—a. fut. act. indic. of δικαιόω (LN 34.46) (BAGD 3.b. p. 197): 'to justify' [AB, BECNT, HNTC, ICC2, LN, NICNT, NTC, WBC; KJV, NASB, NET, NIV, NRSV, REB], 'to put right' [LN; TEV], 'to make right with' [NCV, NLT], 'to accept' [CEV], 'to approve' [GW].

b. περιτομή (LN 53.51) (BAGD 4.a. p. 653): 'circumcision' [LN], 'those who are circumcised' [BAGD], 'circumcised people' [GW], 'Jews' [CEV, NCV, NLT]. This noun, which lacks the definite article, is translated as having the article: 'the circumcision' [HNTC, ICC2, LN, NICNT, WBC; KJV], 'the circumcised' [AB, BECNT, NTC; NASB, NET, NIV, NRSV, REB], 'the Jews' [BAGD; TEV]; as not having the definite article: 'circumcision' [WBC].

c. ἐκ with genitive object (LN 89.77) (BAGD 3.f. p. 235): 'by' [BECNT, HNTC, NTC; KJV, NASB, NCV, NET, NIV, REB], 'only by' [NLT], 'by means of' [LN], 'by reason of' [BAGD], 'as a result of' [BAGD], 'because of' [BAGD; CEV, GW], 'in virtue of' [AB], 'on the ground of' [ICC2; NRSV], 'on the basis of' [NICNT; TEV], 'from' [WBC].

d. πίστις (LN 31.85) (BAGD 2.d.α. p. 663): 'faith' [AB, BAGD, BECNT, HNTC, ICC2, LN, NICNT, NTC, WBC; all versions].

e. ἀκροβυστία (LN 11.53) (BAGD 3. p. 33). This noun, which lacks the definite article, is translated 'uncircumcision' [WBC; KJV], 'the uncircumcision' [HNTC, ICC2, NICNT], 'the uncircumcised' [AB, BECNT, LN, NTC; NASB, NET, NIV, NRSV, REB], 'uncircumcised people' [GW], 'Gentiles' [LN; CEV, NLT], 'the Gentiles' [BAGD; TEV], 'those who are not Jews' [NCV].

f. διά with genitive object (LN 89.76) (BAGD A.III.1.d. p. 180): 'through' [AB, BAGD, BECNT, HNTC, ICC2, LN, NICNT, NTC, WBC; all versions except CEV, NLT], 'by' [LN; NLT], 'by means of' [LN], 'because of' [CEV].

QUESTION—What is the significance of the future tense of the verb in the phrase ὃς δικαιώσει 'who will justify'?

1. This is a logical future, that is, used to express a logical conclusion [AB, ICC2, NICNT]. While it may be seen as eschatological, expressing an action that will happen in the future, here it is gnomic, expressing a norm [AB, NICNT].
2. This future should be understood to refer to every case of justification yet to be accomplished, and does not refer to the final judgment [Gdt, Ho, Mu]. The future speaks not of the final judgment, but expresses permanent purpose [Ho].
3. This future is in reference to the final judgment [BECNT, WBC]. Justification is a matter both of the present, as in 3:28, as well as of the future, for the declaration of justification in the future seals the present reality [BECNT]. This is not just a logical future; having one God, Creator, and Judge in view it looks forward to the final judgment [WBC].

QUESTION—Is there any significance in the variation between the prepositions ἐκ 'by' and διά 'through' in Paul's descriptions of faith?

1. The change in prepositions is simply a stylistic variation and there is no significant difference in meaning indicated [AB, BECNT, HNTC, Ho, ICC2, Mor, Mu, NAC, NICNT, SSA, TH, WBC]. Although no other clear examples of rhetorical variations of these two prepositions can be found in the NT, none of the suggested distinctions based on this variation make much sense, and it is probably just a stylistic variation [NICNT]. This is simply a matter of style and rhetoric since it would be incredible to have different nuances signaled in this way in a context where Paul is emphasizing that Jews and Gentiles alike are justified on the same basis [AB, BECNT, WBC]. That there is but one way to salvation, through faith alone, is the foundation of Paul's argument [HNTC]. Paul freely uses both prepositions elsewhere with 'faith', and both in relation to the Jews, so there is no significant difference of meaning here; God requires faith of both Jew and Gentile [Mor].
2. There is some significance in the change of prepositions [Gdt, ICC1]. Paul uses ἐκ to imply that the Jews' justification is 'from the source' of faith, but διά means 'with the attendant circumstances' (of circumcision). For the Jew the force at work is faith, and the channel through which it works is circumcision. For the Gentile faith is the one thing needed for justification [ICC1]. Since the Jew laid claim to a righteousness arising from or out of works, Paul uses ἐκ because he wants to describe a righteousness that arises from or out of faith; because the Gentile had no means at all of obtaining righteousness, he uses διά because he wants to describe faith as the way or means that they may now receive this unexpected righteousness [Gdt].

QUESTION—What is the significance of the article τῆς 'the' in the phrase διὰ τῆς πίστεως 'through the faith'?

The article is anaphoric, pointing back to the previously mentioned faith in the first phrase; that is, Gentiles are justified by the same faith as are the Jews [ICC1, Mor, NICNT, NTC]. Paul strongly emphasizes that there is only one God, and one way of salvation for all, which is by faith and faith alone [NAC, NTC]. The article indicates that faith is the well-known means [Gdt]. This is translated 'through that faith' [NICNT], 'through that same faith' [Mor, NTC; NIV], 'the same faith', or 'the faith just mentioned' [ICC1], 'in the same way…trust in him (Christ)' [SSA].

3:31 Therefore[a] do-we-invalidate[b] (the) law through[c] faith?

LEXICON—a. οὖν (LN 89.50): 'therefore' [BECNT, LN], 'so' [LN; NCV], 'consequently, so then' [LN], 'well then' [NLT], 'then' [AB, HNTC, ICC2, NICNT, NTC, WBC; KJV, NASB, NIV, NRSV], not explicit [CEV, GW, NET, REB, TEV].

b. pres. act. indic. of καταργέω (LN 76.26, 13.100) (BAGD 1.b. p. 417): 'to invalidate' [ICC2, LN (76.26), NTC], 'to make invalid' [BAGD, WBC], 'to make void' [KJV], 'to nullify' [AB, BECNT, NICNT; NASB, NET, NIV], 'to abolish' [LN (76.26); GW], 'to put an end to' [LN (13.100)], 'to do away with' [HNTC; TEV], 'to overthrow' [NRSV], 'to undermine' [REB], 'to destroy' [CEV, NCV], 'to forget about' [NLT].

c. διά with genitive object (LN 89.76) (BAGD A.III.1.d. p. 180): 'through' [BAGD, BECNT, ICC2, LN, NICNT, NTC, WBC; KJV, NASB, NET], 'by means of' [LN], 'by' [AB; CEV, GW, NCV, NIV, NRSV, TEV]. This preposition is translated as a phrase: 'by this insistence upon' [HNTC], 'through our insistence on' [NTC]; by a clause: 'if we emphasize (faith)' [NLT], 'by using (faith)' [REB].

QUESTION—In what sense could faith nullify or invalidate the law?

It would be to rob the law of the role it should rightfully have [NAC]. Paul is emphasizing the inadequacy of works and the passing importance of the Mosaic law so much that his argument takes on an 'anti-law' flavor, but he quickly denies that the law is invalidated and affirms a continuing role for it [NICNT]. Paul draws a conclusion from his teaching about faith that some might wish to dismiss the Mosaic law, and expresses this as a possible objection from his imaginary interlocutor; however this is a position Paul refuses by affirming that it is through faith that the law is fulfilled, not nullified [AB]. By 'law' the Jews meant the Mosaic legislation, and they would think that Paul was setting faith and law in opposition to one another, exalting faith at the expense of law by saying that works of the law could not possibly provide a satisfactory basis for God's acceptance. This conclusion that faith thus nullifies law is one Paul denies [NTC, St]. The Jew held a strong conviction that the law came from God and showed his chosen people the way of salvation, so for Paul to assert that only faith is required of either Gentile or Jew would seem, to the Jew, to imply that the law is done away with and has no function [Mor]. Because for the Jew the law was closely bound up with his identity and distinctiveness, Paul's argument would seem destructive of the law and undermining of the special link between Israel and the law, but Paul says this is so only if the law is wrongly understood as the boundary and identity marker of the Jews, but not when understood as a 'law of faith', which then establishes and confirms its validity [WBC]. None of the moral requirements of the OT have been weakened or penalty disregarded [Ho]. Paul is accused of making the law void by advancing a gospel that sets aside legal works as a way of being made right with God [Gdt].

Never may-it-be![a] On-the-contrary,[b] we uphold[c] (the) law.

LEXICON—a. aorist mid. (deponent = act.) optative of γίνομαι (LN 13.107) (BAGD I.3.a. p. 158): 'to happen' [LN], 'to occur, or to come to be' [LN]. The phrase μὴ γένοιτο is translated 'may it never be!' [NASB], 'by no means' [BAGD, NICNT, NTC; NRSV, REB], 'far from it, may it not be' [BAGD], 'not at all' [WBC; CEV, NIV, TEV], 'God forbid' [BAGD, ICC2; KJV], 'certainly not' [AB, HNTC], 'of course not' [BECNT; NLT], 'absolutely not' [NET], 'No!' [NCV], 'that's unthinkable!' [GW].

b. ἀλλά (LN 89.125) (BAGD 1.a. p. 38): 'on the contrary' [BECNT, HNTC, LN, NTC, WBC; NASB, NRSV], 'rather' [AB, BAGD, ICC2, NICNT; GW, NIV], 'instead' [LN; NET, TEV], 'yea' [KJV], 'in fact' [NLT], not explicit [CEV, NCV, REB].

c. pres. act. indic. of ἵστημι (LN **76.20**) (BAGD I.2.a. p. 382): 'to uphold' [AB, ICC2, **LN,** NTC; NET, NIV, NRSV, REB, TEV], 'to establish' [BAGD, BECNT, HNTC, NICNT, WBC; KJV, NASB], 'to confirm' [BAGD], 'to support' [GW], 'to make more powerful' [CEV], 'to truly fulfill' [NLT], 'to accept the validity of, to maintain' [LN]. The clause 'we uphold the law' is translated 'faith causes us to be what the law truly wants' [NCV].

QUESTION—What is the meaning of the word νόμος 'law' in the phrase νόμον ἱστάνομεν 'we uphold the law'?

1. It means specifically the Jewish or Mosaic law, not the OT in a general sense [AB, BECNT, ICC1, Mu, NICNT, NTC, SSA, St, TH, WBC]. The 'law' ultimately means the Pentateuch [ICC1]. The term 'law' by itself refers to the commands of the law, the Mosaic prescriptions [BECNT, Mu]. When he uses this term by itself Paul usually means the commands given by God through Moses, and this is consistent with his use of it later in the book when he further discusses the continuing validity of the Mosaic law [NICNT]. It is primarily the moral requirements of the OT, but is not limited to that [Ho].
2. It means both the Jewish law and law in general, and the lack of the article in the verse does not indicate any difference in the meaning of the term elsewhere in the passage [Mor].

3. It does not simply mean the OT, but means both the written record of God's revelation of himself in the OT as well as that whole system of religious thought and practice based upon it, which is called Judaism [HNTC]. It is the whole religious system of Judaism, which is visibly embodied in the OT [TH].

QUESTION—What is the meaning of Paul's assertion that νόμον ἱστάνομεν 'we uphold the law'?

Note that there is a certain amount of overlap possible between the positions listed below, and one does not necessarily rule out the other.

1. Paul means that the demands of the law are fulfilled through our faith in Christ [AB, ICC2, NICNT, St]. Paul's stress on faith as establishing the law suggests that through our faith in Christ the law is fulfilled in us in the sense that our relationship to Christ by faith provides for the full satisfaction of the demands of God's law [AB, NICNT]. Those who are justified by faith and who live according to the Spirit will fulfill the righteous requirements of the law [St]. Paul is responding to the kind of critic who would suggest that by declaring justification to be by faith, he is thereby encouraging disobedience and antinomianism, so here he is stressing that justified believers who live according to the Spirit fulfill the righteous requirements of the law [St]. He means that believers fulfill or uphold the law in the same way that Abraham did through his receiving God's gift of righteousness by faith [TNTC]. Paul means that what he has been saying about faith is completely consonant with the law and is confirmed by the law; the law, rightly understood, supports and confirms the doctrine of faith [ICC2]. The moral requirements of the OT are strengthened by new and stronger motives within the believer [Ho]. Christianity accomplished all that the law had failed to accomplish [ICC1].
2. Paul means 'law' as a broad reference to the OT Scriptures, which he says is in harmony with his teaching of justification by faith in the gospel, and the gospel is in harmony with the true meaning of the law. Thus faith establishes the law by maintaining its spirit in the new dispensation of the righteousness of faith [Gdt]. The 'law' is not simply the OT, or the written record of God's revelation, but the whole system of religious thought and practice based on this revelation, that is, the religion of Judaism which Paul believes to be fulfilled in the person of Jesus Christ and understood in the gospel [HNTC]. Paul is talking about the Jewish law, but by universalizing it and seeing it as directed to faith rather than to works, he confirms or establishes it in its proper function and role in the eschatological age, which is to bring all mankind under the Creator's rule, not to divide Israel off from other nations [WBC].
3. Paul means that Christians are obliged to continue to obey the moral demands of the law [BECNT, Mu]. When speaking of the testimony of the OT to the truth of justification by faith, Paul never uses 'law' by itself, but rather uses 'law and prophets' or 'the Scriptures'. In Paul's letters the

phrase 'the law and prophets' embraces all of Scripture, whereas the term 'law' focuses on the prescriptions of the Mosaic law. The idea is that those who have faith in Christ will keep the law, for righteousness apart from the law does not mean that the moral norms of the law can be dispensed with, because they are still the authoritative will of God for the believer [BECNT].
4. Both alternatives 1 and 2 above are meant [Mor]. The divine plan for salvation in the atoning death of Christ was the working out of and fulfillment of what the law really means, and was attested to in the law and the prophets. Those who receive the Holy Spirit by faith are enabled by his power to live according to the standards of which the law speaks. To see the role of the law and the outworking of it this way is to establish the law [Mor].
5. Paul is saying that it is through the law that the consciousness of sin comes that causes someone to call out for help, and that deliverance is then fully supplied whenever a sinner surrenders his life to God in faith. Consequently salvation by faith and the usefulness of the law coincide [NTC].

DISCOURSE UNIT: 4:1–25 [AB, BECNT, Gdt, ICC1, ICC2, Mor, Mu, NAC, NICNT, NTC, WBC; GW]. The topic is the justification of Abraham by faith not deeds [AB], Abraham as the father of Jews and Gentiles [BECNT], faith the principle of Abraham's justification [Gdt], the relation of this new system to the OT: The crucial case of Abraham [ICC1], the case of Abraham: glorying excluded [ICC2], justification proved from Abraham [Mor], corroboration from the Old Testament [Mu], Abraham the great example of faith [NAC], by faith alone: Elaboration regarding Abraham [NICNT], we have God's approval because of faith [GW], justification by faith is scriptural [NTC], Abraham as a test case [WBC]; the illustration of justification [NET], Abraham justified by faith [NIV], the faith of Abraham [NLT], Abraham's faith [REB].

DISCOURSE UNIT: 4:1–17 [Ho]. The topic is arguments for justification by faith.

DISCOURSE UNIT: 4:1–12 [GNT, HNTC, NTC; CEV, NCV, TEV]. The topic is the example of Abraham [GNT, NTC; CEV, NCV, TEV], Abraham justified by faith [HNTC].

DISCOURSE UNIT: 4:1–8 [AB, ICC1, Mor, NICNT, TNTC]. The topic is Abraham justified by faith [AB], Abraham's acceptance by faith, not works [ICC1], God's way is grace [Mor], faith and works [NICNT], two Old Testament precedents [TNTC].

4:1 **What then shall-we-say (that) Abraham, our forefather[a] according-to[b] flesh[c] to-have-found?[d]**

TEXT—Instead of προπάτορα 'forefather' some manuscripts read πατέρα 'father'. GNT selects the reading προπάτορα 'forefather' with a B rating, indicating that the text is almost certain. Προπάτορα 'forefather' is read by [AB, BECNT, ICC2, NICNT, NTC, WBC].

TEXT—Some manuscripts omit εὑρηκέναι 'to have found'. GNT includes this word with a B rating, indicating that the text is almost certain. It is included by [AB, BECNT, HNTC, ICC2, NICNT, NTC, WBC; NET, NIV]. It is omitted by [CEV].

LEXICON—a. προπάτωρ (LN **10.20**) (BAGD p. 709): 'forefather' [AB, BAGD, BECNT, ICC2, LN, NICNT, NTC; NASB, NIV], 'father' [KJV, TEV], 'ancestor' [HNTC, LN; CEV, GW, NET, NRSV, REB], 'the founder (of our Jewish nation)' [NLT], 'the father of our race' [TEV]. The word refers to a person several preceding generations removed from the reference person [LN]. This word is used only here in the NT.

b. κατά with accusative object (LN 89.4) (BAGD II.6. p. 407): 'according to' [AB, BAGD, BECNT, ICC2, NICNT, NTC, WBC; NASB, NET, NRSV], 'with respect to' [BAGD], 'with regard to, in relation to' [LN], 'pertaining to' [KJV], 'by' [REB]. The phrase κατὰ σάρκα 'according to flesh' is translated 'physically' [BAGD], 'on human terms' [HNTC], 'by natural descent' [REB], not explicit [CEV, GW, NCV, NIV, NLT, TEV]. See this word at 3:5.

c. σάρξ (LN 58.10, 9.12, 8.63) (BAGD 4. p. 743): 'flesh' [AB, BECNT, ICC2, LN (8.63), NICNT, NTC, WBC; KJV, NET, NRSV], 'human nature' [BAGD, LN (58.10, 9.12)], 'mortal nature' [BAGD], 'physical nature' [LN (58.10, 9.12)], 'earthly descent' [BAGD], 'natural descent' [REB], 'human terms' [HNTC], 'humanly speaking' [NLT], not explicit [CEV, GW, NIV, TEV]. See this word at 3:20.

d. perf. act. infin. of εὑρίσκω (LN 27.1): 'to find' [AB, BECNT, HNTC, ICC2, LN, NICNT; KJV, NASB], 'to find out' [LN, WBC], 'to learn' [LN; NCV], 'to discover' [LN, NTC; GW, NET, NIV], 'to be gained by' [NRSV], not explicit [CEV, REB]. The question 'what shall we say…to have found' is translated 'what was his experience' [TEV], 'what were his experiences concerning this question of being saved by faith' [NLT]. This word refers to learning something previously not known and frequently involves an element of surprise [LN].

QUESTION—What is the function of this question for this chapter?

It connects this chapter in a general way with the previous discussion of 3:27-31 [BECNT, HNTC, Ho, ICC2, Mor, Mu, NAC, NICNT, NTC, SSA, St, TNTC, WBC]. This question establishes a general connection to the previous discussion and the chapter goes on to elaborate through the history of Abraham each of the key points of the passage 3:27-31 [NICNT]. Paul has argued that righteousness is by faith and not by works, and this question asks whether or not Abraham is a case that validates that position [BECNT, Mor]. Paul has explained and defended the gospel of justification by faith and now supplies an OT precedent and example for it in the case of Abraham, supplemented by the case of David, to show that it has been proclaimed in and is consistent with the OT [St]. Paul wants to prepare for the position he is about to present by implying that Abraham's standing before God was an act of grace from the outset and that this grace determined his standing with God from then on [WBC]. It introduces evidence that supports the principle stated in 3:21–16 and calls the reader to consider how the life of Abraham illustrates justification by faith [HNTC, SSA]. Abraham is the person that Jews would be most likely to consider as having attained salvation by merit, so Paul uses his story to confirm the truth of what he has just said about justification by faith [ICC2, NTC]. The questions Paul has been discussing in chapter 3 regarding the advantage of the Jew and boasting, he now narrows down to the crucial case of Abraham who would have been central to the Jewish position, but whom he shows had no grounds to boast before God [ICC1]. It is critical to Paul's argument to show that the way of salvation by grace is not an innovation, but supported by a right understanding of the OT and proven by the case of Abraham [Mor, NAC]. Paul has taught that justification is by faith, and now in anticipation of a Jewish objection he raises the case of Abraham in order to confirm the doctrine [Ho]. It elaborates on the previous discussion by showing through the case of Abraham that this principle of justification by faith was already operating in the OT and that Abraham is the type for those who are upright through faith, not an example of uprightness achieved by observing the law [AB].

QUESTION—Who are the referents of the plural pronoun ἡμῶν 'our'?
1. 'Our' refers to Jewish people, who are physically descended from Abraham [AB, HNTC, Ho, ICC1, ICC2, Mor, NAC, NICNT, SSA, TH, TNTC].
2. 'Our' refers to Christians, who are spiritually descended from Abraham [Gdt].

QUESTION—What is the meaning of the word εὑρίσκω 'to find' here?
1. It refers to what Abraham discovered [Mor, NAC, NICNT, NTC, SSA, WBC; KJV, NASB, NCV, NET, NIV]. It means what he discovered by experience [NICNT] or what he found to be the case [NICNT, WBC]. Paul is asking his readers to contemplate what Abraham has found to be the case with regard to the matter at hand, which is faith apart from works [NICNT], about being declared righteous [NTC, SSA]. The answer to the question Paul raises is that Abraham found justification by faith, through God's grace [TNTC]. The word is used here in the sense of intellectual discovery [Mor].
2. It refers to what Abraham attained [Ho], gained [NRSV], or found to be of some advantage [Gdt]. Paul is asking whether Abraham had secured justification through the flesh [Ho]. Paul is asking whether Abraham found some advantage with regard to salvation [Gdt].
3. It refers to what the readers have discovered [GW]: 'What can we say that we have discovered about Abraham?' [GW].

QUESTION—What is the antecedent to the phrase κατὰ σάρκα 'according the flesh'?
1. It modifies the phrase τὸν προπάτορα ἡμῶν 'our forefather' [AB, BECNT, HNTC, ICC1, Mor, Mu, NAC, NICNT, NTC, SSA, St, TH, TNTC, WBC; GW, NASB, NCV, NET, NIV, NLT, NRSV, REB, TEV]. This is intended to limit the phrase 'our forefather' to the Jews, referring to their physical relationship with Abraham [NICNT]. Paul recalls the traditional Jewish understanding of Abraham as the father of all those circumcised, who are Jews according to the flesh, and the fact that descent from Abraham was a source of pride for Jews [AB]. Abraham is naturally appealed to as father of the race in view of his place in salvation history, and as a decisive test case [WBC]. That is, Abraham is ancestor by natural descent [St], the physical progenitor of the Jewish race [Mor, Mu], the ancestor of the Jews on human terms [HNTC]. It is connected to ἡμῶν 'us', meaning that he is the forefather of us who are Jews according to the flesh; he also has other children in another, different sense [ICC2].
2. It refers to the verb εὑρηκέναι 'to have discovered' and the question posed is what Abraham has discovered by his own fleshly efforts [Gdt, Ho]. Paul uses the this expression as equivalent to 'by works' and refers to such external, physical things as rites, ceremonial works, and all forms of personal righteousness as opposed to that which is internal and spiritual [Ho]. It refers to what Abraham would have found by his own labor and specifically to circumcision [Gdt].

QUESTION—Is σάρξ 'flesh' used in a pejorative sense?
1. There is a pejorative sense [Gdt, Ho]. Paul uses the word to refer to all forms of personal righteousness, of external works of human effort and merit after the manner of man versus the righteousness of God [Ho].
2. There is something of a pejorative sense [BECNT, NICNT, WBC]. There is something of a pejorative sense here because Abraham's paternity in relation to the Jews is not only limited by physical descent, but also by the perspective of that older era, since in the new era Abraham is to be seen as spiritually the father of all believers, both Jew and Gentile [NICNT]. As usual, the phrase has a somewhat negative and slightly pejorative sense [WBC]. That he is forefather according to the flesh is not a criticism of Abraham, but there is the implication that simply being descended from Abraham physically is not enough [BECNT].
3. Here it only refers to the paternity of Abraham in terms of natural generation and is not used in a pejorative sense [Mu].

4:2 For if Abraham was-justified[a] by[b] works,[c]

LEXICON—a. aorist pass. indic. of δικαιόω (LN 34.46, 56.34) (BAGD 3.a. p. 197): 'to be justified' [AB, BAGD, HNTC, ICC2, NICNT, NTC, WBC; KJV, NASB, NIV, NRSV, REB], 'to be put right with God' [LN (34.46); TEV], 'to be acquitted or pronounced righteous' [BAGD], 'to be declared righteous' [NET], 'to be made right' [NCV]. This passive verb is translated as active: 'he became acceptable to God' [CEV], 'God accepted him' [NLT], 'had God's approval' [GW], 'was righteous' [BECNT]. See this word at 3:30.

b. ἐκ (LN 89.77, 90.12) (BAGD 3.f. p. 235): 'by' [AB, BECNT, LN (90.12), NICNT; KJV, NASB, NCV, NET, NIV, NRSV, REB, TEV], 'by means of' [LN (89.77)], 'by reason of' [BAGD], 'because of' [BAGD; CEV, GW, NLT], 'on the grounds of' [HNTC, ICC2], 'on the basis of' [NTC], 'as a result of' [BAGD, LN (90.12)], 'from' [WBC]. See this word used in this sense at 3:20.

c. ἔργον (LN 42.11, 42.42) (BAGD 1.c.β. p. 308): 'work' [BECNT, HNTC, ICC2, LN (42.42), NICNT, NTC, WBC; KJV, NASB, NIV, NRSV], 'deed' [AB, BAGD, LN (42.11)], 'act' [LN (42.11)]. This word is translated by a phrase: 'that which is done' [LN (42.11)], 'what he did' [CEV], 'the things he did' [NCV, TEV], 'something he did' [GW], 'anything he did' [REB], 'works of the law' [NET], 'his good deeds' [NLT]. See this word at 3:28.

QUESTION—What is the relationship between this verse and 4:1?

1. This verse gives the reason for raising the question in 4:1 [BECNT, Gdt, HNTC, Ho, ICC2, Mor, NICNT]. Paul explains in this verse why he asked about Abraham's experience in 4:1, since if Abraham could boast that he was justified by works, then the claim of 3:27–28 that all boasting is excluded would not be true [Gdt, NICNT]. The question of 4:1 assumes a negative answer, and this verse introduces the reason for that negative answer [Ho]. This verse explains the relevance of the question concerning Abraham to Paul's purpose in the section by confirming the truth of the statement of 3:27, that boasting has been excluded [ICC2, NTC]. In diatribe style, the case of Abraham is invoked by a Jewish objector and Paul now moves to prove from Scripture that, contrary to the perspective of some Jews, Abraham was not justified on the basis of works and thus has no reason to boast before God [HNTC]. Paul cannot accept the view, widely held among the Jews, that Abraham was justified by works, so he attempts to prove it wrong and show instead that Abraham was justified freely by grace [Mor].

2. This verse introduces the content of something that Paul wants his readers to think about regarding Abraham's justification; semantically it does not seem to fit as grounds for 4:1 [SSA].

QUESTION—What is the meaning of the argument introduced by εἰ 'if'?

The εἰ 'if' is used to introduce an idea for the sake of argument which Paul will then refute; that is, if such-and-such were the case, this is what we might conclude [BECNT, Mor, Mu, NAC, NICNT, WBC]. Jews of Paul's day generally believed that Abraham was in fact accepted before God because of his good works [AB, ICC2, Mor, NAC, NICNT, WBC], which is what he must refute from the Genesis passage.

QUESTION—What is the meaning of ἔργον 'works' here?
This is parallel with the usage in 3:20, 27–28 and means works of the law [WBC]. Many Jews saw Abraham as one who had kept the provisions of the Law even before it was given [HNTC, ICC1, Mor, NAC, WBC]. Paul is not talking about 'good works', but about faithful obedience to what God requires, and he is attacking the widely accepted way of thinking about Abraham among Jews as the model of a devout Jew who had kept God's commandments and observed the law even in its unwritten state [WBC]. Abraham's faith and obedience were considered meritorious works [NICNT]. This means 'doing good things' and the phrase 'by works' is an event that expresses a reason: 'because of doing good works' [SSA].

he-has (a) boast,[a] but[b] not before[c] God.

LEXICON—a. καύχημα (LN 33.372) (BAGD 1. p. 426): 'something to boast about' [BAGD, HNTC, NTC, WBC; CEV, NASB, NET, NIV, NLT, NRSV, TEV], 'the right to boast' [LN], 'reason to boast' [AB, NICNT], 'a reason for boasting' [BECNT], 'a reason to brag' [GW, NCV], 'a right to glory' [ICC2], 'whereof to glory' [KJV], 'grounds for pride' [REB].

b. ἀλλά (LN 89.125): 'but' [AB, BECNT, ICC2, LN, NICNT, NTC, WBC; all versions], 'but in fact' [HNTC]. This word marks a more emphatic contrast than δέ. See this word at 3:31.

c. πρός with accusative object (LN 90.20, 89.112): 'before' [AB, HNTC, LN (90.20, 89.112), NICNT, WBC; NET, NIV, NRSV], 'in the opinion of, in the judgment of' [LN (90.20)], 'in the eyes of' [REB], 'from the point of view of' [NTC; NLT], 'in the sight of' [TEV]. This phrase is translated 'but he has no reason…in God's presence' [BECNT], 'but this is not how God sees him' [ICC2], 'but in fact before God he has no such ground of boasting' [HNTC], 'but from God's point of view, he has no reason (to boast)' [NTC], 'he would never be able to brag about it to God' [CEV], 'from God's point of view Abraham had no basis at all for pride' [NLT].

QUESTION—How is the word καύχημα 'boast' used here?
This noun emphasizes the ground or reason for boasting [BECNT, Gdt, ICC1, Mor, NICNT], while the similar word καύχησις, which is used in 3:27, refers to the act of boasting itself [BECNT, Mor, NICNT]. The distinction is not always maintained, but this form denotes the object of the boasting or what is said in boasting, and here means that Abraham could take credit for his justification before God by his own efforts [Mor]. While this word can signify a justifiable boast, the Jewish boasting that Paul criticizes here tended towards nationalistic exclusiveness, or a boasting based on outward evaluation, physical relationship, and faithfulness in those obligations marking Jews as covenant people and which were considered to establish one's righteousness before God [WBC].

QUESTION—What is the purpose of the phrase ἀλλ' οὐ πρὸς θεόν 'but not before God'?

This recognizes that the conditional clause is not correct and rejects boasting altogether in relation to justification [AB, BECNT, HNTC, Ho, ICC2, Mor, Mu, NICNT, St, WBC]: if Abraham was justified by works, he would have reason to boast about it, but (since his faith, not his works, justified him,) he never could have reason to boast before God. This statement rejects the logic stated in the conditional sentence and rejects the possibility of boasting altogether, because when God's viewpoint is considered, there is no right to boast at all [NICNT, WBC]. In theory perhaps there could be reason for Abraham to boast before people, but even this idea is eventually rejected by Paul who aligns Abraham with the rejection of boasting in 3:27, since his upright status before God was from God's grace and favor [AB]. Paul repudiates the notion that Abraham may have been justified by works on the grounds that this would have given him reason to boast, and he rejects any possibility of humans boasting before God [St]. Paul does not imply by this statement that Abraham had something to boast about before men, and no contrast between boasting before men and boasting before God is in mind [Mor]. Paul is not suggesting that Abraham could boast in any self-achieved attainment or was justified by works [Mu]. Paul's point is that Abraham did not have works sufficient to be able to boast before God, but that does not mean that he had reason to boast before people [BECNT].

4:3 For what says the Scripture[a]?

LEXICON—a. γραφή (LN 33.10, 33.53) (BAGD 2.b.β. p. 166): 'Scripture' [AB, BECNT, ICC2, LN, NICNT, NTC, WBC; all versions], 'Scripture passage' [LN (33.53)], 'passage' [LN (33.10)], 'the passage of Scripture' [HNTC]. This singular noun is translated as a plural: 'Scriptures' [CEV]. See this word at 1:2.

QUESTION—What is the Scripture quoted here and what is its significance for Paul's argument?

The quotation is from Gen 15:6 and it provides a further reason or grounds for arguing that there is no boasting before God with respect to justification [AB, BECNT, HNTC, Ho, ICC2, Mor, Mu, NAC, NICNT, NTC, SSA, St, TNTC, WBC]. The basis for Abraham's relationship to God was his faith or trust in God, not his works [BECNT, TH, TNTC]. This provides the reason for the previous assertions that before God there is no reason for boasting by linking believing with attaining righteousness and it ties Abraham, the father of Israel and recipient of God's promises, to this principle [NICNT]. Paul focuses on this passage since it is the only one in the accounts about Abraham which speaks specifically of Abraham's faith and which shows righteousness to be something attributed by God [WBC]. In using this passage in defense of justification by faith Paul makes use of the very passage his opponents would have used to support the opposite view, since many Jews considered the faith of Abraham to be a meritorious act on his part; Paul uses this passage instead to demonstrate that God bestowed righteousness on Abraham as a free gift and not on the basis of works [ICC2]. When understood properly, this passage is actually proof of the opposite conclusion, that justification is by faith [NAC]. Paul makes the point that the Scripture makes clear that no one is justified by his works, for if Abraham was not justified by works, then clearly no one else could be [Mor].

And Abraham believed[a] God, and it-was-reckoned[b] to-him as[c] righteousness.[d]

LEXICON—a. aorist act. indic. of πιστεύω (LN **31.85**) (BAGD 1.b. p. 661): 'to believe' [BAGD, ICC2, LN, NTC, WBC; all versions except CEV, REB], 'to believe in' [BECNT, NICNT], 'to have faith in' [AB, HNTC, LN; CEV], 'to put one's faith in' [AB; REB], 'to trust in' [LN]. The phrase ὠπίστευσεν δὲ ᾿Αβραὰμ τῷ θεῷ 'and Abraham believed God' is translated 'because Abraham had faith in God' [CEV]. See this word at 3:22.

b. aorist pass. indic. of λογίζομαι (LN 57.227) (BAGD 1.a. p. 476): 'to be reckoned to' [BAGD, ICC2, NICNT, NTC, WBC; NASB, NRSV], 'to be credited to' [AB, BAGD; NET, NIV], 'to be accounted, to be taken into account' [BAGD], 'to be put into (one's) account' [LN], 'to be counted to' [BECNT, HNTC; KJV, REB], 'to be regarded (by God)' [LN; GW]. This passive verb is translated as active with God as the subject: 'to accept' [CEV, NCV, TEV], 'to declare to be' [NLT]. See this word at 2:26, 3:28.

c. εἰς (LN **13.62**) (BAGD 8.a.γ. p. 230): 'as' [AB, BECNT, HNTC, NICNT; NASB, NET, NIV, NRSV, REB, TEV], 'for' [ICC2, LN, NTC, WBC; KJV], not explicit [CEV, GW, NCV, NLT].

d. δικαιοσύνη (LN 88.13) (BAGD 3. p. 197): 'righteousness' [BAGD, BECNT, HNTC, ICC2, LN, NICNT, NTC, WBC; KJV, NASB, NET, NIV, NRSV, REB], 'righteous' [TEV], 'uprightness' [AB]. This noun is translated as a verb phrase: 'to be righteous' [NLT], 'to be right' [NCV], '(God's) approval of' [GW], not explicit [CEV]. In Pauline thought this word refers to the righteousness bestowed by God, which is based on faith and closely approximates salvation [BAGD]. See this word at 3:21.

QUESTION—What does the phrase ἐλογίσθη αὐτῷ εἰς δικαιοσύνην 'it was accounted to him as righteousness' mean?

His faith was not a righteous act or an act that merited righteousness; rather the righteousness that was accounted to him did not inherently belong to him [BECNT, NICNT], and this was based on Abraham's trust and reliance on God, not on works [BECNT]. The term 'was reckoned' is a bookkeeping term meaning to 'credit or put to someone's account' and is used figuratively here [AB, ICC1, Mu, NAC, St]. The verb means to impute something to someone [Ho, Mu], and then treat him accordingly [Ho]. On the basis of Abraham's faith God reckoned or considered or counted this ungodly person to be something that, in and of himself, he was not, namely righteous [AB, Gdt, Mor, NTC]. It means that he was declared to be or considered to be righteous because he trusted in God [ICC2, SSA, TH]. It is an accounting metaphor and means 'to set down on the credit side', and in the LXX this verb frequently has the legal sense of imputation of guilt or innocence; in this case it means that one quality, faith, is credited to the individual as equivalent to or in place of another quality, righteousness [ICC1]. Abraham held God's promise for the reality itself, and God in turn held Abraham's faith as righteousness itself, though it was not that [Gdt]. Righteousness is a status accorded by God to people; it is acceptance by God, as opposed to being acceptable to God [WBC].

4:4 Now[a] to the-(one) working[b] the wage[c] is- not -reckoned[d] according-to[e] favor[f] but according-to[g] debt,[h]

LEXICON—a. δέ: 'now' [AB, BECNT, ICC2, NICNT, NTC, WBC; KJV, NASB, NET, NIV, NRSV, REB], not explicit [HNTC; CEV, GW, NCV, NLT, TEV].

b. pres. mid. (deponent = act.) participle of ἐργάζομαι (LN 42.41) (BAGD 1. p. 307): 'to work' [BECNT, LN, NICNT, NTC, WBC; GW, NASB, NCV, NET, NIV, NLT, NRSV, TEV], 'to do a piece of work' [REB], 'to labor' [AB]. This participle is translated as a noun: 'workman' [BAGD]; as a plural noun: 'works' [HNTC, ICC2], 'workers' [CEV]. The phrase τῷ...ἐργαζομένῳ 'to the one working' is translated 'to a man who does works' [HNTC], 'to him that worketh' [KJV], 'if a man does have works to his credit' [ICC2]. See this word also at 2:10.

c. μισθός (LN 38.14, 57.173) (BAGD 2.a. p. 523): 'wages' [AB, BAGD, BECNT, ICC2, LN (57.173), NICNT, NTC; NASB, NIV, NLT, NRSV, REB, TEV], 'pay' [HNTC, LN (57.173); GW, NCV, NET], 'money paid' [CEV], 'recompense, reward' [LN (38.14), WBC; KJV].

d. pres. pass. indic. of λογίζομαι (LN **57.227**) (BAGD 1.a. p. 476): 'to be reckoned' [ICC2, NICNT, NTC, WBC; KJV, NASB, NRSV], 'to be credited' [AB, BAGD; NET, NIV], 'to be credited to one's account' [**LN**], 'to be put into one's account' [LN], 'to be regarded' [LN; GW, TEV], 'to be counted' [BECNT, HNTC; REB], 'to be given' [NCV], 'to be' [CEV], not explicit [NLT]. See this word above at 4:3.

e. κατά with accusative object (LN 89.4): 'according to' [LN, NICNT], 'as' [AB, BECNT, NTC, WBC; NIV, NRSV, TEV], 'as a matter of' [HNTC, ICC2], 'as a' [GW, NASB, NCV], 'to be a' [REB], 'of' [KJV], 'due to' [NET], not explicit [CEV, NLT]. See this word at 4:1.

f. χάρις (LN 25.89, 88.66) (BAGD 2.a. p. 877): 'favor' [AB, BAGD, LN, NTC, WBC; NASB], 'goodwill' [BAGD, LN], 'kindness' [LN (88.66)], 'grace' [HNTC, ICC2, LN (88.66), NICNT; KJV, NET], 'gift' [BECNT; CEV, NCV, NIV, NLT, NRSV, REB, TEV]. The phrase κατὰ χάριν 'according to favor' is translated 'as a gift' [CEV, GW], 'not a gift' [NLT]. See this word at 1:7 and 3:24.

g. κατά with accusative object (LN 89.4, 89.8): 'according to' [LN (89.8), NICNT], 'as' [AB, BECNT, HNTC, ICC2, NTC, WBC; NASB, NCV, NIV, NRSV], 'due to' [NET], not explicit [GW, KJV, REB].
h. ὀφείλημα (LN **57.221, 71.26**) (BAGD 1. p. 598): 'debt' [BAGD, BECNT, ICC2, LN (57.221), NTC, WBC; KJV], 'what is owed to (one)' [LN (**57.221**)], '(one's) due' [HNTC; NASB, REB], 'obligation' [LN (**71.26**), NICNT; NET, NIV]. This noun is translated as a phrase 'something due' [NRSV], 'what is due' [AB], 'something they earn' [CEV], 'something that has been earned' [NCV, TEV], 'something they have earned' [GW]. The phrase ἀλλὰ κατὰ ὀφείλημα 'according to debt' is translated 'It is something they earn by working' [CEV], 'workers earn what they receive' [NLT].

QUESTION—What is the point Paul is making here?

If a person works, the wages that person receives are a matter of obligation or of something owed, and not a matter of something given freely [NICNT]. Paul is contrasting the way of works not just with the way of faith, which Jews of his day would have understood as a meritorious work, but with the way of grace [Mor]. Paul is saying that faith and works are opposites; faith is not a meritorious work, so when Abraham had righteousness 'counted' to him on the basis of his faith, he was the recipient of grace [HNTC, Mor, St]. Paul is intending to show that the Scripture passage he has quoted means that to justify by faith is to justify gratuitously and thus denies that works were the grounds of Abraham being accepted [Ho]. The contrast is not just between the worker and the non-worker, but between the worker and the non-worker who believes on the one who justifies the ungodly [Mu]. Working is a matter of a person's own capabilities and involves doing, but believing is a matter of relying on someone else, and the genius of belief is receiving [BECNT]. Paul is posing two opposite alternatives: work is reckoned as a debt owed, but faith is reckoned as favor given [WBC].

QUESTION—What is the meaning of the phrase οὐ λογίζεται κατὰ χάριν 'not credited according to favor'?

It means that it is a matter of obligation, a debt that is owed [BECNT, Ho, Mor, Mu, NAC, NICNT, St, TNTC, WBC]. The laborer has a right to the profit of his labor; it is a matter of justice [AB]. In business and commerce the reward or payment for work done is a matter of contractual obligation [WBC]. Wages come to workers because they have worked to earn them [NAC].

4:5 but to the-(one) not working[a] but believing[b] on[c] the-(one) justifying[d] the ungodly,[e]

LEXICON—a. pres. mid. (deponent = act.) participle of ἐργάζομαι (LN 42.41) (BAGD 1. p. 307): 'to work' [BECNT, LN, NICNT, NTC, WBC; GW, KJV, NASB, NET, NIV, NLT], 'to labor' [AB]. This participle is translated as a noun: 'work' [ICC2], 'workman' [BAGD, LN]; as a plural noun: 'works' [HNTC; NRSV]. The phrase τῷ...μὴ ἐργαζομένῳ 'the one not working' is translated 'the man who has no work to his credit' [ICC2], 'one without works' [NRSV], 'without any work to his credit' [REB], 'those who depend...not on deeds' [TEV]. This clause is translated 'But people cannot do any work that will make them right with God.' [NCV]. This entire verse is translated 'But you cannot make God accept you because of something you do. God accepts sinners only because they have faith in him' [CEV], 'people are declared righteous because of their faith, not because of their work' [NLT]. See this word above at 4:4.

b. pres. act. participle of πιστεύω (LN 31.85) (BAGD 2.a.δ. p. 661): 'to believe' [BAGD, BECNT, LN, NICNT, WBC; GW, KJV, NASB], 'to believe in' [BAGD, ICC2; NET, TEV], 'to put faith in' [AB; REB], 'to have faith' [HNTC], 'to rest (one's) faith in' [NTC], 'to trust' [BAGD; NCV, NIV, NRSV], 'to have faith in' [LN; CEV]. This verb is translated as a noun '(their) faith' [NLT]. See this word above at 4:3.

c. ἐπί with accusative object (LN 90.57): 'on' [BECNT, LN, NICNT, NTC, WBC; KJV], 'in' [AB, HNTC, ICC2; CEV, NASB, NCV, NET, REB, TEV], not explicit [GW, NIV, NLT, NRSV]. See this word at 2:9.

d. pres. act. participle of δικαιόω (LN 34.46, 56.34) (BAGD 3.b. p. 197): 'to justify' [AB, BECNT, HNTC, ICC2, NICNT, WBC; KJV, NASB, NIV, NRSV], 'to acquit' [LN (56.34); REB], 'to remove guilt' [LN (56.34)], 'to accept' [CEV], 'to declare righteous' [NET], 'to approve' [GW], 'to declare innocent' [TEV], 'to make right' [NCV], 'to put right with' [LN (34.46)]. See this word above at 4:2.

e. ἀσεβής (LN 53.11) (BAGD 1. p. 114): 'ungodly' [BECNT, HNTC, ICC2, LN, NICNT, NTC, WBC; KJV, NASB, NET, NRSV], 'ungodly people' [GW], 'godless' [AB, BAGD], 'impious' [BAGD; NIV], 'wicked' [BAGD], 'sinners' [CEV], 'evil people' [NCV], 'guilty' [TEV], 'wrongdoer' [REB]. The entire last clause τὸν δικαιοῦντα τὸν ἀσεβῆ 'the one justifying the ungodly' is not translated by NLT. The word refers to living without regard for religious belief or practice [LN].

QUESTION—Does the statement about 'not working' mean that the believer need not be concerned about producing good works?

Paul did not rigidly separate faith and obedience to the point that obedience was unimportant to him and while criticizing works motivated by human pride, he praised works that resulted from faith [BECNT]. Paul is emphasizing that one should not depend on good works for one's standing before God, not that a Christian need not have concern for producing good works [Mor, NICNT]. Paul has no intention of discouraging the doing of good works, but simply wants to assert that they don't constitute any claim upon God [ICC2]. Paul is not contrasting the worker with the non-worker, but rather one who trusts in his works as opposed to one who trusts in God [Mor].

QUESTION—What is the meaning of the phrase τὸν δικαιοῦντα τὸν ἀσεβῆ 'the one justifying the ungodly'?

Whereas the OT use of 'justify' had to do with a declaration about some existing situation, what Paul has in mind here is justification as a creative act in which a new status is given, and it emphasizes the loving and giving nature of God, who is not under obligation to any human being [NICNT]. It means to acquit the guilty, or declare innocent the guilty person who, having no claim of merit, reaches out in faith for God's good gift [Mor]. God counted Abraham as righteous, even though he was a sinner [BECNT, ICC2]. God has acquitted the ungodly in a divine act that is a paradox of mercy and grace [HNTC]. The word 'ungodly' is a strong one, and the whole phrase is meant to show the magnificence and extent of the gospel of grace, for God's justifying judgment is exercised not simply on the unrighteous but on the ungodly [Mu]. The word 'ungodly' is more forceful, and he uses it here so that even the most sinful people will recognize that they are not excluded from the privilege of being justified by faith [Gdt].

QUESTION—Is Paul saying that Abraham was ungodly?

1. It does not refer specifically to Abraham [AB, Gdt, ICC1, Mu, NAC]. What he says in 4:4–8 is a general statement that compares believing with working and does not necessarily refer specifically to Abraham [NAC]. While Abraham believed in the God who justifies the ungodly, the phrase 'the one justifying the ungodly' is a description of God, not of Abraham, because at the specific time that Abraham believed God he had already been called by God and had responded [AB]. He was not saying that Abraham, a man of outstanding piety and righteousness, was ungodly, but states this principle of justification by grace and not works as something that applies equally to those who are ungodly [TNTC]. This word is not intended to describe Abraham specifically, but makes a general statement about the method of grace [Ho, Mu]. Paul is generalizing from Abraham's case to apply the principle to people of his own day [ICC1]. Paul would certainly not have called Abraham ungodly, although his works were insufficient for Abraham to have been justified by them [Gdt].

2. The phrase 'justifying the ungodly' is applied to Abraham [BECNT, ICC2, Mor, NTC, WBC]. Before being counted righteous Abraham was an ungodly individual, a sinner [NTC]. Paul is stating a general principle, but he applies it specifically to the case of Abraham [WBC], whom the Jews of Paul's day believed to have become the first proselyte by turning from idolatry to the worship and service of God [Mor, WBC].

his faith[a] is-reckoned[b] as[c] righteousness;[d]

LEXICON—a. πίστις (LN 31.85, 31.102) (BAGD 2.a. p. 662): 'faith' [AB, BAGD, BECNT, HNTC, ICC2, LN (31.85, 31.102), NICNT, NTC, WBC; all versions except CEV]. This noun is translated as a verb 'to have faith' [CEV]. See this word also at 3:31.

b. pres. pass. indic. of λογίζομαι (LN 57.227) (BAGD 1.a. p. 476): 'to be reckoned' [ICC2, LN, NICNT, NTC, WBC; NASB, NRSV], 'to be regarded' [LN; GW], 'to be credited' [AB, BAGD; NET, NIV], 'to be put into (one's) account' [LN], 'to be counted' [BECNT, HNTC; REB], 'for' [KJV], 'to be declared' [NLT], not explicit [CEV, TEV]. This clause is translated 'Then God accepts their faith' [NCV]. See also at 4:4 above.

c. εἰς (LN 13.62): 'as' [AB, BECNT, HNTC; GW, NASB, NET, NIV, NRSV, REB], 'for' [ICC2, LN, NICNT, NTC, WBC; KJV], not explicit [CEV, NCV, NLT]. The phrase 'his faith is reckoned as righteousness' is translated 'it is his faith that God takes into account in order to put him right with himself' [TEV]. See above at 4:3.

d. δικαιοσύνη (LN 88.13) (BAGD 3. p. 197): 'righteousness' [BAGD, BECNT, HNTC, ICC2, LN, NICNT, NTC, WBC; KJV, NASB, NET, NIV, NRSV, REB], 'righteous' [NLT], 'uprightness' [AB], 'God's approval' [GW]. This noun is translated as a verb phrase: 'to make right (with him)' [NCV], 'to put right with (himself)' [TEV], 'God accepts sinners' [CEV]\. See this word at 4:3.

QUESTION—What is the meaning of the word λογίζεται 'is reckoned'?

It means that something, in this case righteousness, is granted to a person which they do not have or which is not inherent to them, but is granted or reckoned to them by God's grace [BECNT, NTC]. A righteous status was credited to his account by God [Mor]. It is not a matter of God making a sinner righteous at this point but rather of counting him as righteous, of imputing righteousness to him [St]. The fact that Abraham's righteousness was reckoned or counted to him means that is was a matter of grace, and not because of something Abraham did, and it was a forensic acquittal, not a matter of making him ethically righteous [HNTC]. For Paul, the expression 'it was reckoned to him as righteousness' and 'God reckoned righteousness to him' are to be considered equivalent to 'God justified him' [Mu, NICNT].

4:6 just-as David also speaks-of[a] the blessedness[b] of-the person to-whom God reckons[c] righteousness[d] apart-from[e] works,[f]

LEXICON—a. λέγω (LN 33.69): 'to speak of' [BECNT, HNTC, WBC; NASB, NIV, NLT, NRSV, REB, TEV], 'to speak regarding' [NET], 'to say' [LN; CEV, NCV], 'to speak' [LN; GW], 'to utter' [AB], 'to pronounce' [ICC2, NICNT, NTC], 'to describe' [KJV, NLT].

b. μακαρισμός (LN 25.118) (BAGD p. 487): 'blessedness' [BAGD, WBC; KJV, NET, NIV, NRSV], 'blessing' [BAGD, BECNT, HNTC, ICC2, NICNT, NTC; GW, NASB], 'happiness' [LN; NLT, REB, TEV], 'a beatitude' [AB]. This singular noun is translated as a plural: 'blessings' [CEV]. It is translated as a verb 'to be blessed' [NCV]. The phrase Δαυὶδ λέγει τὸν μακαρισμὸν 'David speaks of the blessedness' [WBC; NIV, NRSV] is also translated 'David pronounces a blessing' [NICNT, NTC], 'David pronounces the blessing' [ICC2], 'David utters a beatitude' [AB],

'David speaks of the blessing' [BECNT, HNTC], 'David talks about the blessings' [CEV], 'David spoke of the happiness' [TEV].
- c. pres. act. indic. of λογίζομαι (LN 57.227) (BAGD 1.a. p. 476): 'to reckon' [BAGD, ICC2, NICNT, NTC, WBC; NASB, NRSV], 'to credit' [AB, BAGD; NET, NIV], 'to credit to (one's) account, to put into (one's) account' [LN], 'to count' [BECNT, HNTC; REB], 'to impute' [KJV], 'to make right' [NCV], 'to declare to be' [NLT], 'to accept as' [TEV], not explicit [CEV, GW]. See this word at 4:4.
- d. δικαιοσύνη (LN 88.13) (BAGD 3. p. 197): 'righteousness' [BAGD, BECNT, HNTC, ICC2, LN, NICNT, NTC, WBC; KJV, NASB, NET, NIV, NRSV], 'uprightness' [AB]. This noun is also translated as an adjective: 'righteous' [NLT, REB, TEV]. The phrase ᾧ ὁ θεὸς λογίζεται δικαιοσύνη 'to whom God reckons righteousness' is translated '(people) who are acceptable to God' [CEV], 'God approves of a person' [GW], 'makes people right with himself' [NCV]. See above at 4:3.
- e. χωρίς (LN **89.120**) (BAGD 2.b.δ. p. 891): 'apart from' [AB, BECNT, HNTC, ICC2, LN, NICNT, NTC; NASB, NET, NIV, NRSV, REB, TEV], 'without' [LN, WBC; GW, KJV, NCV], 'without paying attention to' [NCV], 'without regard to' [BAGD], 'independent of' [LN], not explicit [CEV, NLT]. See this word at 3:28.
- f. ἔργον (LN 42.42) (BAGD 1.c.β. p. 308): 'works' [BECNT, HNTC, ICC2, LN, NICNT, NTC, WBC; KJV, NASB, NET, NIV, NRSV], 'good works' [REB], 'deeds' [AB, BAGD], 'anything one does' [TEV]. The phrase χωρὶς ἔργων 'apart from works' is translated 'even though they don't do anything to deserve (those blessings)' [CEV], 'without that person's earning it' [GW], '(without paying attention to) good deeds' [NCV], 'apart from anything that person does' [TEV], 'undeserving sinner' [NLT]. See this word at 3:28.

QUESTION—What is meant by λέγει τὸν μακαρισμόν 'speaks of the blessedness'?
1. He speaks about the blessed condition [BECNT, HNTC, NAC, SSA, WBC; KJV, NASB, NCV, NET, NIV, NLT, NRSV, REB, TEV].
2. He pronounces a benediction [Gdt, ICC1, ICC2, NICNT, NTC; GW]. He declares that such a person is blessed [Ho, Mu].

QUESTION—What is the significance of Paul's use of this quoted material from Psalm 32:1–2a?

Paul is using a Jewish method of interpretation whereby a word occurring in one passage is used to interpret another passage where the same word occurs [AB, Mor, NICNT, TH, TNTC, WBC]. He uses the similarities of thought between the Psalm 32 passage and the Genesis 15 passage, particularly the use of λογίζομαι, to say that not reckoning sin is the same as forgiving acts of lawlessness or covering sin [WBC]. The link between the two passages is that where the Genesis passage spoke of crediting faith as righteousness this passage speaks of sins not being credited because of forgiveness [Mor]. He spoke of God having credited Abraham's faith as righteousness, and now speaks of crediting righteousness in place of evil deeds [St]. He uses the Psalm 32 passage to confirm the point made in the case of Abraham about justification, but here the reckoning of righteousness consists of remitting or not imputing sin [Mu]. He uses this passage to show that justification involves not imputing sins to the person; forgiveness is an essential component of justification [NICNT]. In linking Abraham and David he is showing that all people stand unworthy before God [NAC]. Paul uses this passage to show that in the case of both Abraham and of David the OT supports his thesis of God's gracious justification through faith [AB]. Both David and Abraham are recipients of God's grace apart from works [NTC]. The non-imputation of sin is the same as the imputation of righteousness or the declaration of acquittal [TNTC]. Paul cites these two passages in which λογίζομαι appears in order to show that it was while Abraham was still uncircumcised that he was credited with uprightness and became the father of believing pagans as well as believing Jews [AB]. It strengthens and elaborates on the argument from the Genesis passage [TH]. In discussing the relation of works to justification he first cites the example of Abraham, who did not perform any works that would enable him to boast before God, and he gives further evidence from the example of David, who even though he was a sinner and lacked works was counted righteous [BECNT]. The passage about Abraham spoke of the blessing that faith confers, while this passage speaks of the evil that it removes, and thus the two passages complement one another [Gdt].

4:7 Blessed[a] (are) (they)-of-whom the lawlessnesses[b] have-been-forgiven[c]

LEXICON—a. μακάριος (LN 25.119) (BAGD 1.b. p. 486): 'blessed' [AB, BAGD, BECNT, HNTC, ICC2, NICNT, NTC, WBC; GW, KJV, NASB, NET, NIV, NRSV], 'happy' [BAGD, LN; NCV, REB, TEV], 'fortunate' [BAGD]. It is translated as a phrase: 'God blesses people' [CEV], 'Oh what joy for (those who)' [NLT]. See the related noun above in 4:6.

b. ἀνομία (LN 88.139) (BAGD 2. p. 72): 'lawlessness' [LN], 'lawless deeds' [BAGD, BECNT, WBC; KJV, NET, REB], 'lawless acts' [NICNT], 'transgressions' [BAGD, NTC; NIV], 'sins' [CEV, NCV], 'iniquities' [AB, HNTC, ICC2; KJV, NRSV], 'wrongs' [TEV], 'disobedience' [GW, NLT].

c. aorist pass. indic. of ἀφίημι (LN 40.8) (BAGD 2. p. 126): 'to be forgiven' [AB, BECNT, HNTC, ICC2, LN, NICNT, NTC, WBC; all versions], 'to be pardoned' [BAGD, LN], 'to be canceled, to be remitted' [BAGD].

QUESTION—What is the meaning of the word μακάριος 'blessed' as it is used here?

This refers to the happiness of those who are conscious of receiving a great blessing from God which is undeserved and unexpected [BECNT]. This technical expression sums up the happy status of those who have been acquitted by God and find themselves in right relationship to him [AB]. The person who is so blessed is conscious of having been pardoned and rejoices in God's acceptance and pardon [NTC]. It means to be privileged to have received divine favor [WBC]. It speaks of the happiness of the person whose sins God forgives and whom God accepts as righteous [TH]. In this verse this word refers to the fact that God is pleased with people whose sins have been forgiven, but in 4:6 the related word μακαρισμός speaks of the happiness of a person blessed by God [SSA]. This 'blessedness' means the epitome of divine favor on those whose iniquities are forgiven and whose sins are covered [Mu].

QUESTION—Is there any significant difference in the meaning of the terms ἀνομία 'lawlessnesses' and ἁμαρτία 'sins'?

1. The first means to step over a known boundary, 'to transgress', and the second means to fall short of a known standard, 'to sin' [St]. 'Lawlessness' means transgressions or violations of the law, acts of lawlessness [NTC]. Lawlessness is a deliberate rebellion against God [ICC2, NAC].
2. There is no significant difference, they are used more or less synonymously [AB, BECNT, Mor, NICNT, SSA, TH, WBC]. This would designate the actions characteristic of those who are outside the law and the covenant: lawlessness and sins [WBC]. There is no significant difference in meaning between the phrases 'lawlessnesses were forgiven' and 'sins were covered' [SSA]. While it is true that 'lawlessnesses' depicts evil as a lack of conformity to God's law, the strict sense should not be insisted on here and the term is parallel to 'sins' [Mor].

and of-whom the sins[a] have-been-covered;[b]

LEXICON—a. ἁμαρτία (LN 88.289): 'sin' [AB, BECNT, HNTC, ICC2, LN, NICNT, NTC, WBC; all versions except CEV, NCV], 'evil deed' [CEV], 'wrongs' [NCV]. See this word at 3:20.
  b. aorist pass. indic. of ἐπικαλύπτω (LN **40.11**) (BAGD p. 294): 'to be covered' [AB, BAGD, BECNT, HNTC, ICC2, NICNT, NTC, WBC; KJV, NASB, NET, NIV, NRSV], 'to be forgiven' [LN], 'to be forgotten' [CEV], 'to be pardoned' [GW, NCV, TEV], 'to be put out of sight' [NLT], 'to be blotted out' [REB].

QUESTION—What is the meaning of the phrase ἐπεκαλύφθησαν αἱ ἁμαρτίαι 'the sins have been covered'?

To be covered is another way of saying that the sins are forgiven [AB, ICC2, Mu, NAC], they have been put out of sight by God [AB, NAC]. However, it does not mean that they remain and are simply covered over by God's benevolence [AB] or are being concealed [NTC]. Being covered is the same as being pardoned and the opposite of being imputed or reckoned [St]. It means for sin to be blotted out [NTC, TH], to be removed or forgiven [TH]. To reckon as righteous, to not reckon sin, and to forgive lawless acts are synonymous with covering sins [SSA, WBC]. Covering sins is a figurative way of saying that God has decided to forget them [SSA]. Saying that the sins are covered is a figurative way of saying that they are not visible to God because they have been forgiven or put away [Mor].

4:8 blessed[a] (is the) man[b] whose sin[c] (the) Lord by-no-means[d] will reckon.[e]

LEXICON—a. μακάριος (LN 25.119) (BAGD 1.b. p. 486): 'blessed' [AB, BAGD, BECNT, HNTC, ICC2, NICNT, NTC, WBC; GW, KJV, NASB, NET, NIV, NRSV], 'happy' [LN; NCV, REB, TEV]. This adjective is translated as a phrase: 'The Lord blesses people' [CEV], 'what joy for (those who)' [NLT]. See also at 4:7.

b. ἀνήρ (LN **9.1**, 9.24) (BAGD 6. p. 67): 'man' [AB, BAGD, HNTC, ICC2, LN (9.24), NTC; KJV, NASB, NIV, REB], 'person' [BECNT, LN (9.1), NICNT; GW, NCV, TEV], 'the one' [WBC; NET, NRSV]. This singular noun is translated as plural: 'people' [CEV], 'those' [NLT].

c. ἁμαρτία (LN 88.289, 88.310) (BAGD 1. p. 43): 'sin' [AB, BAGD, BECNT, HNTC, ICC2, LN (88.289, 88.310), NICNT, NTC, WBC; all versions except GW, NCV], 'guilt' [LN (88.310)]. This noun is also translated as an adjective: 'sinful' [GW], 'guilty' [NCV]. Here sin is considered as a debt [BAGD]. See this word at 3:20 and above at 4:7.

d. οὐ μή (LN 69.5) (BAGD D.1.a. p. 517): 'by no means' [LN, WBC], 'certainly not' [LN], 'does not' [AB, NICNT; NCV, NET, REB], 'will not' [BECNT, HNTC; KJV, NASB, NRSV, TEV], 'in no wise' [ICC2], 'never' [GW], 'will never' [NTC; NIV], 'no longer' [NLT], not explicit [CEV]. This is an emphatic negative [AB, Mor, NAC], and means 'never, ever, by no means' [NAC]. The double negative strengthens the negation [BAGD].

e. aorist mid. (deponent = act.) subj. of λογίζομαι (LN 29.4, 57.227) (BAGD 1.a. p. 476): 'to reckon' [ICC2, NICNT, WBC; NRSV], 'to reckon (against him)' [NTC], 'to count (something) against' [BAGD, BECNT; NET, NIV, NLT, REB], 'to count' [HNTC], 'to take into account' [NASB], 'to keep an account' [TEV], 'to keep a record, to remember, to bear in mind' [LN (29.4)], 'to put into (one's) account, to regard' [LN (57.227)], 'to credit' [AB], 'to consider' [GW, NCV], 'to impute' [KJV], not explicit [CEV]. The phrase 'will by no means reckon' is translated 'are erased from his book' [CEV]. See this word at 4:6.

DISCOURSE UNIT: 4:9–25 [TNTC]. The topic is the faith of Abraham.

DISCOURSE UNIT: 4:9–12 [AB, ICC1, Mor, NICNT]. The topic is faith and circumcision [ICC1, Mor, NICNT], Abraham justified before he was circumcised [AB].

4:9 (Is) then[a] this blessing[b] on[c] the circumcision[d] (only)[e] or on[f] the uncircumcision[g] also?

LEXICON—a. οὖν (LN 89.50): 'then' [AB, HNTC, ICC2, LN, NTC, WBC; KJV, NASB, NET, NRSV], 'therefore' [BECNT, LN, NICNT], 'so then' [LN], 'now then' [NLT], not explicit [CEV, GW, NCV, NIV, REB, TEV].

b. μακαρισμός (LN 25.118) (BAGD p. 487): 'blessing' [BAGD, BECNT, HNTC, ICC2, NICNT, NTC; CEV, NASB, NCV], 'blessedness' [WBC; KJV], 'happiness' [LN; REB], 'beatitude' [AB]. This noun is translated as a verb, 'to be blessed' [GW]. See this word at 4:6.
c. ἐπί with accusative object (LN 90.57) (BAGD III.1.b.ζ. p. 289): 'on' [BAGD, LN], 'upon' [KJV, NASB], 'meant for' [CEV], 'to' [LN], '(confined) to' [REB], 'over' [AB], 'apply to' [BECNT, ICC2], 'valid for' [HNTC], 'given to' [NICNT], '(pronounced) upon' [NTC], 'come on' [WBC], not explicit [GW, NCV].
d. περιτομή (LN 53.51) (BAGD 4.a. p. 653): 'circumcision' [BECNT, HNTC, ICC2, LN; KJV], 'the circumcised' [AB, NTC, WBC; NASB, NCV, REB]. This singular noun is also translated as a plural: 'circumcised people' [CEV, GW], 'Jews' [BAGD]. See this word at 3:30.
e. There is no lexical entry in the Greek text for this word, but it is implied by the presence of καί 'also' at the end of the sentence. It is represented in translation as 'only' [AB, BECNT, HNTC, ICC2, NTC; GW, KJV, NCV, NIV, NLT, NRSV, TEV], 'confined to' [REB]. The question is presented as a limited versus an unlimited choice; that is, for the circumcised only or also for the uncircumcised [AB, BECNT, HNTC, ICC2, NTC; all versions except CEV]. It is presented as a simple either/or question; that is, for the circumcised or for the uncircumcised [WBC; CEV].
f. ἐπί with accusative object (LN 90.57) (BAGD III.1.b.ζ. p. 289): 'on' [BAGD, LN], 'upon' [KJV, NASB], 'for' [CEV, REB], 'to' [LN], not explicit [GW, NCV]. See above.
g. ἀκροβυστία (LN 11.53) (BAGD 3. p. 33): 'uncircumcision' [BECNT, HNTC, ICC2, LN; KJV], 'the uncircumcised' [AB, LN, NICNT, NTC, WBC; GW, NASB, REB]. This singular noun is also translated as a plural: 'those who are not circumcised' [CEV, NCV], 'Gentiles' [BAGD, LN], 'heathenism' [BAGD]. See this word at 3:30.

QUESTION—What relationship is indicated by οὖν 'then'?

It is inferential and asks a conclusion from what has just been said about the relation between blessedness and the state of circumcision [BECNT, Mor]. It introduces 4:9–12 as his third argument on this issue [Ho]. It resumes the discussion of the relation between blessedness and the state of circumcision [Gdt].

QUESTION—What relationship is indicated by ἐπί 'on'?
1. It indicates for whom it was intended [BECNT, Gdt, HNTC, ICC2, NAC, NICNT, St; CEV]: it was intended for, or meant for, or valid for, or applicable to.
2. It indicates an action taken.
2.1 It assumes the implied aorist verb λέγεται 'was pronounced (over)' [AB, Ho, ICC1, ICC2, Mu, NTC].
2.2 It assumes the implied aorist verb δίδοται 'was bestowed (on)' [NICNT], or the implied verb 'came upon' [WBC]. It indicates whom the blessing comes to [Mor].

For we say, Faith^a was-reckoned^b to-Abraham for^c righteousness.^d

LEXICON—a. πίστις (LN 31.85) (BAGD 2.a. p. 662): 'faith' [AB, BAGD, BECNT, HNTC, ICC2, LN, NICNT, NTC, WBC; all versions]. This noun with the definite article is translated as not having the article [AB, BECNT, HNTC, ICC2, NICNT, NTC, WBC; all versions]. It is translated as indicating possession: 'his' faith [HNTC, ICC2, NTC; NLT, TEV], 'Abraham's faith' [GW, NCV, NIV, REB]. See above at 4:5.

b. aorist pass. indic. of λογίζομαι (LN 57.227) (BAGD 1.a. p. 476): 'to be reckoned' [ICC2, NICNT, NTC, WBC; KJV, NASB, NRSV], 'to be credited' [AB, BAGD; NET, NIV], 'to be declared' [NLT], 'to be regarded' [LN; GW], 'to be put into (one's) account, to be charged to (one's) account' [LN], 'to be counted to' [BECNT, HNTC], 'to be counted as' [REB]. This passive verb is translated as active: 'to accept as' [TEV]. This entire phrase is translated 'Well, the Scriptures say that God accepted Abraham because Abraham had faith in him' [CEV], 'We have already said that God accepted Abraham's faith and that faith made him right with God' [NCV]. See above at 4:8.

c. εἰς (LN 89.57): 'for' [ICC2, LN, NICNT, NTC, WBC], 'as' [AB, BECNT, HNTC; REB]. See above at 4:5.

d. δικαιοσύνη (LN 88.13) (BAGD 3. p. 197): 'righteousness' [BAGD, BECNT, HNTC, ICC2, LN, NICNT, NTC, WBC; KJV, NASB, NET, NIV, NRSV], 'uprightness' [AB], 'God's approval' [GW]. This sentence is translated 'God accepted Abraham because Abraham had faith in him' [CEV], 'God accepted Abraham's faith and that faith made him right with God' [NCV], 'he was declared righteous by God because of his faith' [NLT], 'because of his faith God accepted him as righteous' [TEV]. See this word above at 4:6.

QUESTION—What relationship is indicated by γάρ 'for'?

It introduces a digression in which Paul reminds the readers of the OT text he is citing in order to set the stage for the answer he will give to the question raised at the beginning of this verse [NICNT]. It introduces the quote from Gen 15:6 as the key to interpreting the quote from Psalm 32 [BECNT, ICC2]. It reinforces the link between the two OT passages, and shows that the Psalm 32 passage was drawn in to help explicate Gen 15:6 [WBC]. It reintroduces Gen 15:6 to show that God has always saved people by the way of grace, that it is not an innovation [Mor]. It implies the unstated answer 'and on the uncircumcised' to the question posed at the beginning of the verse, and appeals to Gen 15:6 to interpret Psalm 32 [ICC2]. It implies the unstated answer 'it is not spoken concerning the circumcised as such' [Ho].

4:10 How then was-it-reckoned?^a

LEXICON—a. aorist pass. indic. of λογίζομαι (LN 57.227) (BAGD 1.a. p. 476): 'to be reckoned' [ICC2, NICNT, NTC, WBC; KJV, NASB, NRSV], 'to be credited' [AB, BAGD; NET, NIV], 'to be regarded' [LN;

GW], 'to be put into (one's) account' [LN], 'to be counted to' [BECNT, HNTC]. See this word above at 4:9.

Being in[a] circumcision[b] or in uncircumcision?[c]

LEXICON—a. ἐν (LN 13.8): 'in' [LN, WBC; KJV], 'in a state of' [HNTC, LN]. The phrase ἐν...ὄντι 'being in' is translated 'while he was' [AB, BECNT; NASB], 'when he was' [ICC2, NICNT, WBC], not explicit [CEV, GW, NCV, NET, NIV, NLT, NRSV, REB, TEV].
  b. περιτομή (LN 53.51) (BAGD 2. p. 652): 'circumcision' [HNTC, LN, WBC; KJV, NASB, NCV, NET, NIV, NLT, NRSV, REB, TEV], 'the state of having been circumcised' [BAGD], 'circumcised' [AB, BECNT, ICC2, NICNT]. The phrase 'being in circumcision or in uncircumcision?' is translated 'was it before or after Abraham was circumcised?' [CEV], 'Was he circumcised or was he uncircumcised at that time?' [GW], 'Did God accept Abraham before or after he was circumcised?' [NCV], 'Was he circumcised or not?' [NET], 'Was it after he was circumcised, or before?' [NIV], 'Was he declared righteous only after he had been circumcised, or was it before he was circumcised?' [NLT], 'Was it before or after he had been circumcised?' [NRSV], 'Was he circumcised at the time or not?' [REB], 'Was it before or after Abraham was circumcised?' [TEV]. See above at 4:9.
  c. ἀκροβυστία (LN 11.52) (BAGD 2. p. 33): 'uncircumcision' [HNTC, LN, WBC; KJV], 'uncircumcised' [BECNT; GW, NASB], 'not yet circumcised' [AB], 'still uncircumcised' [ICC2], 'was yet uncircumcised' [NICNT], not explicit [CEV, NCV, NET, NIV, NLT, NRSV, REB, TEV]. This entire clause is omitted in NTC.

QUESTION—What is the function of the participle ὄντι 'being'?
  It is temporal with relation to Abraham's state of uncircumcision; that is, before he was circumcised or after [AB, BECNT, Gdt, Ho, ICC2, Mu, NICNT, St, WBC; CEV, NASB]. It focuses particularly on Abraham's condition or status relative to circumcision at the time he was accepted by God [Mor, Mu].

Not in[a] circumcision[b] but in[c] uncircumcision;[d]

LEXICON—a. ἐν (LN 13.8): 'in' [LN, WBC; KJV], 'in a state of' [HNTC, LN], 'while' [BECNT; NASB]. See this word above. The phrase 'not in' is translated 'not after he had been' [NTC], 'he was not' [AB; NET], 'not when he was' [ICC2], 'it was not when he was' [NICNT]. This entire phrase is translated 'Of course, it was before' [CEV], 'He had not been circumcised' [GW], 'It was before his circumcision' [NCV], 'It was not after, but before' [NIV], 'The answer is that God accepted him first, and then he was circumcised later' [NLT], 'It was not after, but before he was circumcised' [NRSV], 'He was not yet circumcised, but uncircumcised' [REB], 'It was before, not after.' [TEV].
  b. περιτομή (LN 53.51) (BAGD 2. p. 652): 'circumcision' [HNTC, LN, WBC; KJV, NCV], 'the state of having been circumcised' [BAGD],

'circumcised' [AB, BECNT, ICC2, NICNT, NTC; GW, NASB, NET, REB]. See this word above.
c. ἐν (LN 13.8): 'in' [LN, WBC; KJV], 'in a state of' [HNTC, LN]. This preposition is translated 'was still' [AB], 'while he was' [BECNT; NASB], 'while he was still' [NTC], 'when he was still' [ICC2], 'when he was' [NICNT], not explicit [NET, NIV, NLT, NRSV, REB, TEV]. See this word above.
d. ἀκροβυστία (LN 11.52) (BAGD 2. p. 33): 'uncircumcision' [BAGD, HNTC, WBC; KJV], 'uncircumcised' [AB, BECNT, ICC2, LN, NICNT, NTC; NASB, NET, REB]. This singular noun is translated as a phrase: 'while he was still uncircumcised' [NTC], 'was still uncircumcised' [WBC], 'he had not been circumcised' [GW], 'And then he was circumcised later!' [NLT], 'It was before his circumcision' [NCV], 'but before he was circumcised' [NRSV], 'it was before, not after' [TEV], not explicit [CEV, NIV]. See this word above.

4:11 **and he-received (the) sign**[a] **of-circumcision (as a) seal**[b] **of-the righteousness**[c] **of-faith**[d] **the –(one)**[e] **(he-had) in**[f] **uncircumcision,**[g]
LEXICON—a. σημεῖον (LN 33.477) (BAGD 1. p. 748): 'sign' [AB, BECNT, HNTC, ICC2, LN, NICNT, NTC, WBC; KJV, NASB, NET, NIV, NLT, NRSV, REB, TEV], 'mark' [BAGD; GW]. The phrase '(the) sign of circumcision' is translated 'Abraham let himself be circumcised to show' [CEV], 'the circumcision ceremony was a sign' [NLT], 'his circumcision was a sign to show that' [TEV], 'Abraham was circumcised to show that' [NCV].
b. σφραγίς (LN 73.9) (BAGD 2.a. p. 796): 'seal' [AB, BECNT, HNTC, ICC2, LN, NICNT, NTC, WBC; GW, KJV, NASB, NET, NIV, NRSV], 'hallmark' [REB], 'something that confirms' [BAGD], 'certification, validation, proof, evidence of genuineness' [LN], not explicit [TEV]. This noun is translated as a phrase: 'to show that' [CEV, TEV]. The phrase σφραγῖδα τῆς δικαιοσύνης τῆς πίστεως 'as a seal of the righteousness of faith' is translated 'to show that he had been accepted because of his faith' [CEV], 'to show that he was right with God' [NCV], 'that God had already accepted him and declared him to be righteous' [NLT].
c. δικαιοσύνη (LN 88.13) (BAGD 3. p. 197): 'righteousness' [BAGD, BECNT, HNTC, ICC2, LN, NICNT, NTC, WBC; KJV, NASB, NET, NIV, NRSV, REB], 'uprightness' [AB]. The phrase δικαιοσύνης τῆς πίστεως 'the righteousness of faith' is translated 'that righteousness that faith had given him' [REB], 'because of his faith God had accepted him as righteous' [TEV], 'that he had been accepted (because of his faith)' [CEV], '(Abraham's faith) was regarded as God's approval' [GW], 'that he was right with God (through faith)' [NCV], 'that (God) declared him to be righteous' [NLT].

d. πίστις (LN 31.85) (BAGD 2.a. p. 662): 'faith' [AB, BAGD, BECNT, HNTC, ICC2, LN, NICNT, NTC, WBC; all versions]. See this word at 4:5.
e. The phrase 'the (one)' represents the definite article τῆς, which would stand in apposition to one of the nouns immediately preceding, probably to the noun 'righteousness', though possibly to the noun 'faith'. It is represented in translation as 'that was his' [BECNT, NICNT], 'which he had' [ICC2, NTC, WBC; KJV, NASB], 'that he had' [NET, NIV, NRSV], 'he had' [HNTC], 'which faith had given him' [REB].
f. ἐν (LN 13.8, 67.136): 'in' [LN (13.8), WBC], 'in a state of' [LN (13.8)], 'during' [LN (67.136)]. This preposition is translated as indicating a temporal relation: 'while' [AB, BECNT, HNTC, ICC2, NTC; GW, NASB, NET, NIV, NRSV, REB], 'when' [NICNT], 'when he was' [NICNT], '(even) before he was' [CEV, NCV, NLT], 'being (uncircumcised)' [KJV], 'before he had been' [TEV]. See this word above at 4:10.
g. ἀκροβυστία (LN 11.52) (BAGD 2. p. 33): 'uncircumcision' [BAGD, WBC], 'uncircumcised' [AB, BECNT, HNTC, ICC2, LN, NICNT, NTC; KJV, NASB, NET, NIV, NRSV, REB], 'being uncircumcised' [LN], not explicit [GW]. The phrase ἐν τῇ ἀκροβυστίᾳ 'in the uncircumcision' is translated 'while he was still uncircumcised' [AB; NET, NIV, NRSV, REB], 'while uncircumcised' [BECNT], 'while still uncircumcised' [HNTC, ICC2, NTC], 'even before he was circumcised' [CEV, NLT], 'before he was circumcised' [NCV, TEV], 'in his uncircumcision' [WBC]. See this word above at 4:10.

QUESTION—How much later was it after Abraham was justified by his faith that he was circumcised?

It was probably at least 14 years [Gdt, ICC2, NTC, St, TNTC]. The rabbis held that it was 29 years later [NICNT, NTC, St]. It was almost 30 years [WBC].

QUESTION—How are the nouns related in the genitive construction σημεῖον...περιτομῆς 'the sign of circumcision'?

'Of circumcision' is epexegetic of sign, that is, it stands in apposition to it, indicating that circumcision is the sign [AB, BECNT, Gdt, Ho, ICC1, ICC2, Mor, NAC, NTC, TH, WBC]. Circumcision is the sign of the covenant [AB, Mu]. Abraham was circumcised to show that God had accepted him [SSA].

QUESTION—What did circumcision signify?

The sign indicated God's acceptance of Abraham as righteous [Ho, ICC1, ICC2, Mor, SSA, TH, TNTC]. It symbolized the removal of sin and guilt [NTC]. It was the outward, visible sign of God's covenant with Abraham and entitled the Jewish people (or proselytes from among the Gentiles) to all the privileges of the covenant [TNTC]. It was the sign of the covenant with God [AB, ICC2, Mu], the sign of the covenant between God and his people [Gdt], of the covenant with Abraham and his descendents [ICC2]. But as such it also signified faith and the justification by faith that Abraham experienced, and without which the covenant was meaningless [Mu]. It signified that God had accepted the circumcised person and that he was a member of the covenant; Abraham's circumcision ratified the fact that God had accepted him [WBC]. It identified Abraham's descendents as God's covenant people, the justified people of God [St].

QUESTION—What is the relationship between the terms 'sign' and 'seal'?
1. Sign and seal are used more or less synonymously [AB, BECNT, Ho, NICNT, SSA, TNTC, WBC]. They stand in apposition [NICNT, SSA, TH]. He uses both terms to show more clearly that circumcision is not intrinsic to or essential to faith, but is used to confirm, ratify, authenticate, and document the right standing with God that Abraham already had by virtue of his faith [BECNT]. In giving the sign of circumcision God set his seal on or attests to the righteousness that was imputed to Abraham [Mor]. The seal was to authenticate a state that was already existing, which is righteousness based on faith [ICC1, ICC2].
2. There is some distinction between the terms [Gdt, Mu, NAC, NTC]. Circumcision as a sign symbolized the removal of sin and guilt and as a seal it was a guarantee that God's promises were trustworthy; however, neither signs nor seals actually save [NTC]. While the term 'sign' relates to the material thing itself, 'seal' relates to the religious significance of it [Gdt]. The seal confirms, guarantees and authenticates the faith Abraham had [Mu]. As a sign it represents and as a seal it authenticates the righteousness Abraham had by faith [NAC]. The sign identifies them as God's covenant people and the seal authenticates them as the justified people of God [St].

QUESTION—How are the nouns related in the genitive construction τῆς δικαιοσύνης τῆς πίστεως 'the righteousness of faith'?

Faith is the source or cause or basis of the righteousness [AB, BECNT, HNTC, Ho, ICC1, ICC2, NICNT, SSA, TH, WBC; REB]. Abraham's righteousness depended solely on believing [WBC]. God declared him righteous because he trusted in God [SSA].

QUESTION—To what does the definite article τῆς 'the' in the phrase τῆς ἐν τῇ ἀκροβυστίᾳ 'the (one) in uncircumcision' stand in apposition?
1. It is in apposition to τῆς δικαιοσύνης, which is the righteousness he had while still uncircumcised [BECNT, ICC1, ICC2, Mor, NICNT, NTC, WBC; NCV, NET, NIV, NRSV].
2. It is in apposition to τῆς πίστεως, which is the faith that he had while still uncircumcised [AB, Gdt, HNTC, Mu, TH; KJV, NASB, REB].

QUESTION—What is the relation of this clause to the context?
1. It amplifies what Paul is saying at the end of 4:10 and shows the relationship between Abraham's justification based on faith and his being circumcised later [BECNT, ICC2, NICNT, NTC, WBC]. In other words, Abraham was counted as justified when he was uncircumcised and consequently received circumcision as a sign, all so that he could be the father of all those who have faith, whether circumcised or not.

2. The argument from the end of 4:10 picks up again in 4:11b, so that 11a is a parenthesis that answers the question about why Abraham was circumcised [HNTC]. In other words, Abraham was counted as justified when he was uncircumcised so that he might be the father of all who have faith, whether circumcised or not; and as to the question of why he was circumcised, it was as a sign or seal.
3. This statement, along with the one immediately preceding it in 4:10c 'not in circumcision but in uncircumcision' are given as reasons for Abraham's becoming the father of all who believe (4:11–12), which in turn is the justification for his claim in 4:9 that the blessing of right standing with God is for non-Jews as well as Jews [SSA]. That is, we can say that right standing with God is for non-Jews as well as Jews (4:9) because Abraham is the father or founder of all those who believe, whether circumcised or not (4:12), which fact we know to be true because Abraham was declared to have right standing with God while still uncircumcised (4:10) and he was circumcised to show that right standing (4:11a) [SSA].

for[a] him to-be father[b] of-all the-(ones) believing[c] during[d] uncircumcision,

LEXICON—a. εἰς (LN 89.48, 89.57): 'for, for the purpose of' [LN (89.57)], 'the purpose was to' [NRSV], 'as a result' [LN (89.48)], 'so that as a result' [LN (89.48)], 'so that' [BECNT, ICC2, NTC; NET] 'that' [KJV, NASB], 'with the result that' [LN (89.48)], 'thus' [AB], 'in order that' [HNTC, NICNT, WBC], 'so then' [NIV], 'so' [NCV, NLT], 'it follows that' [REB], 'and so' [TEV], 'therefore' [GW]. The phrase εἰς τὸ εἶναι αὐτὸν πατέρα 'for him to be father' is translated 'this makes Abraham the father' [CEV]. See this word above at 4:9.

b. πατήρ (LN **58.64**, 10.14, 10.20) (BAGD 2.f. p. 635): 'father' [AB, BAGD, BECNT, HNTC, ICC2, LN (10.14, **58.64**), NICNT, NTC, WBC; CEV, GW, KJV, NCV, NET, NIV, NLT, REB], 'forefather' [LN (10.20)], 'ancestor' [LN (10.20); NRSV], 'archetype' [LN (58.64)], 'spiritual father' [LN (58.64); TEV]. The 'fatherhood' may consist in the fact that the one so called is the prototype of a group or the founder of a class of persons [BAGD].

c. pres. act. participle of πιστεύω (LN 31.85) (BAGD 2.b. p. 661): 'to believe' [AB, BAGD, BECNT, ICC2, LN, NICNT, WBC; KJV, NCV, NET, NIV, NRSV, TEV], 'to have faith' [HNTC, NTC; NLT, REB]. The phrase τῶν πιστευόντων 'the ones believing' is translated 'because of their faith' [CEV], 'all who believe' [AB; NASB], 'all those who believe' [ICC2], 'every believer' [GW], 'all who have faith' [HNTC, NTC]. See this word at 4:5.

d. διά with genitive object (LN 67.136) (BAGD A.III.1.c. p. 180): 'during' [LN], 'in a state of' [BAGD, HNTC, ICC2], 'through' [BAGD, WBC], 'when' [AB; REB], 'while' [NICNT]. The meaning of the word here is closely related to its meaning or sense of denoting attendant circumstances [BAGD]. The phrase πιστευόντων δι' ἀκροβυστίας 'believing during uncircumcision' is translated 'the uncircumcised who believe' [BECNT], 'those who believe while not circumcised' [NICNT], 'who have faith but have not been circumcised' [NTC], 'those who believe but have never been circumcised' [NET], 'believe but have not been circumcised' [NIV], 'believe without being circumcised' [NRSV], 'even though they are not circumcised' [CEV, TEV], 'have faith but have not been circumcised' [NLT], '(every believer) who is not circumcised' [GW], 'though they be not circumcised' [KJV], 'without being circumcised' [NASB], 'but are not circumcised' [NCV].

QUESTION—Does the phrase εἰς τὸ εἶναι 'for him to be' indicate purpose or result?

1. It indicates purpose [AB, BECNT, Gdt, HNTC, Ho, ICC1, ICC2, Mor, Mu, NICNT, NTC, St, TH, WBC]. It is translated as indicating purpose by KJV, NASB, NET. It indicates purpose, but that does not exclude result as well [NTC]. The purpose is God's purpose [Gdt].
2. It indicates result [SSA]. It is translated as indicating result by CEV, GW, NCV, NIV, NLT, REB, TEV.

for[a] to-be-reckoned[b] to-them also righteousness,[c]

TEXT—Some manuscripts omit καί 'also'. GNT includes this word a with a C rating, indicating difficulty in deciding whether or not to place it in the text. This word is omitted by AB, BECNT, HNTC, ICC2, NTC; CEV, NIV, NLT, REB, TEV, although the decision about including or omitting it may be due to stylistic concerns rather than textual concerns. It is included by NICNT, WBC; NET, NRSV and translated 'also' [NICNT], 'as well' [WBC], 'too' [NET], 'and' [NRSV].

LEXICON—a. εἰς (LN 89.48, 89.57): 'for, for the purpose of' [LN (89.57)], 'as a result, so that as a result, with the result that' [LN (89.48)], 'so that' [AB, BECNT, ICC2, NICNT], 'that' [HNTC, WBC; KJV, NASB, NET], 'in order that' [NTC; NIV], 'because of' [CEV], 'thus' [NRSV], 'and so' [REB], not explicit [GW, NCV, NLT, TEV]. See this word above.

b. aorist pass. infin. of λογίζομαι (LN 57.227) (BAGD 1.a. p. 476): 'to be reckoned' [ICC2, NICNT, NTC, WBC; NASB, NRSV], 'to be credited' [AB, BAGD; NET, NIV], 'to be put into (one's) account' [LN], 'to be imputed' [KJV], 'to be regarded' [LN], 'to be counted to one' [BECNT, HNTC; GW, REB], 'to be made (right)' [NLT], 'to be accepted as' [NCV, TEV], not explicit [CEV]. See this word above at 4:10.

c. δικαιοσύνη (LN 88.13) (BAGD 3. p. 197): 'righteousness' [BAGD, BECNT, HNTC, ICC2, LN, NICNT, NTC, WBC; KJV, NASB, NET, NIV, NRSV, REB, TEV], 'uprightness' [AB], 'God's approval (of them)' [GW], '(being) right with God' [NCV]. This entire phrase is translated 'who are acceptable to God' [CEV], 'they are made right with God' [NLT], 'and are accepted as righteous by him' [TEV]. See this word above at 4:11.

QUESTION—Does the phrase εἰς τὸ λογισθῆναι [καὶ] αὐτοῖς 'for to be credited to them also' indicate purpose or result?
1. It indicates purpose [AB, BECNT, Gdt, HNTC, Ho, ICC1, Mor, Mu, NTC, St, WBC]. However this does not exclude result [NTC]. The purpose is that of the person who believes; there is a desire in faith, which in this case is the desire for righteousness to be imputed to them as well [Gdt]. This clause is explanatory of the previous purpose clause, so that 'for him to be father' and 'for them to be credited righteousness' are more or less synonymous [Ho].
2. It indicates result [ICC2, NICNT, SSA].

4:12 and father[a] of-circumcision[b] to-the-(ones) not from[c] circumcision only
LEXICON—a. πατήρ (LN 10.14, 10.20, 58.64) (BAGD 2.f. p. 635): 'father' [AB, BAGD, BECNT, HNTC, ICC2, LN (10.14, 58.64), NICNT, NTC, WBC; all versions except NLT], 'forefather' [LN (10.20)], 'ancestor' [LN (10.20); NRSV], 'spiritual father' [LN (58.64); NLT]. See this word above at 4:11.
b. περιτομή (LN 53.51) (BAGD 4.a. p. 653): 'circumcision' [HNTC, ICC2, LN, WBC; KJV, NASB], 'the circumcised' [BECNT, NICNT; NET, NIV, NRSV, REB]. This noun is translated by a phrase 'the Jews' [BAGD], 'those circumcised' [AB], 'those who have been circumcised' [NCV, NLT], 'those circumcised people' [NTC], 'those who are circumcised' [GW, TEV], 'everyone who is circumcised' [CEV]. See this word above at 4:11.
c. ἐκ (LN 89.77, 90.16) (BAGD 3.d. p. 235): 'from' [LN (89.77, 90.16)], 'of' [WBC; KJV, NASB], 'belong to' [ICC2]. The phrase τοῖς οὐκ ἐκ περιτομῆς μόνον 'to the ones not from circumcision only' is translated 'the circumcision party' [BAGD], 'who are not only such' [AB], 'who are not only circumcised' [BECNT, NICNT, NTC; GW, NET, NIV, NRSV], 'who are not of the circumcision only' [KJV], 'who do not rely on circumcision only' [HNTC], 'who not only belong to the circumcision' [ICC2], 'who not only are of the circumcision' [NASB], 'provided they are not merely circumcised' [REB], 'who are not only men of circumcision' [WBC], 'who in addition to being circumcised also' [TEV], not explicit [CEV, NCV, NLT]. See this word at 4:2.

but also to-the-(ones) following[a] the footprints[b] of-the in uncircumcision faith[e] of-the father[f] of-us Abraham.
LEXICON—a. pres. act. participle of στοιχέω (LN 41.12, **41.47**) (BAGD p. 769): 'to follow' [BAGD, HNTC, WBC; GW, NASB, NCV, NRSV, REB], 'to imitate, or to do as others do' [LN (41.47)], 'to live' [LN (41.12); TEV], 'to behave in accordance with, to conduct (oneself) in accordance with' [LN (41.12)], 'to hold to or agree with' [BAGD], 'to walk in' [AB, BECNT, ICC2, NICNT, NTC; KJV, NET, NIV]. The phrase τοῖς στοιχοῦσιν τοῖς ἴχνεσιν τῆς...πίστεως 'to the ones following the footprints of the...faith' is translated 'because they live the

same life of...faith' [LN (**41.47**); TEV]. This entire phrase is translated 'but only if they have the same kind of faith Abraham had before he was circumcised' [NLT], 'and has faith in God, as Abraham did before he was circumcised' [CEV].
   b. ἴχνος (LN **41.47**) (BAGD p. 384). This plural noun is translated 'footprints' [BAGD], 'footsteps' [BAGD, HNTC, NTC, WBC; GW, NET, NIV], 'steps' [BECNT, ICC2, NICNT; KJV, NASB], 'example' [NRSV], 'footsteps in the path' [AB], 'that path' [REB], not explicit [CEV, NCV, TEV]. The word is used only figuratively in this literature [BAGD].
   c. ἐν (LN 13.8, 67.136): 'in' [LN, WBC], 'in a state of' [LN (13.8)], 'during' [LN (67.136)], 'while' [AB, BECNT; NASB], 'while still' [HNTC, ICC2, NICNT; REB], 'even before' [NTC], 'before he was' [CEV, NCV, NIV, NRSV, TEV], 'when he was still' [NET], not explicit [GW, KJV, NLT]. See this word above at 4:11.
   d. ἀκροβυστίᾳ (LN 11.52) (BAGD 2. p. 33): 'uncircumcision' [BAGD, WBC], 'uncircumcised' [AB, BECNT, HNTC, ICC2, NICNT; KJV, NASB, NET, REB]. This noun is translated as a verb phrase 'before he was circumcised' [NTC; CEV, GW, NCV, NIV, NLT, NRSV, TEV]. See this word above at 4:11.
   e. πίστις (LN 31.85) (BAGD 2.a. p. 662): 'faith' [AB, BAGD, BECNT, HNTC, ICC2, LN, NTC, WBC; all versions]. This noun is translated as a verb phrase 'who believed' [NICNT]. See this word at 4:5.
   f. πατήρ (LN 10.14, 10.20, 58.64) (BAGD 2.e. p. 635): 'father' [AB, BAGD, BECNT, HNTC, ICC2, LN (10.14, 58.64), NICNT, NTC, WBC; KJV, NASB, NCV, NET, NIV, REB, TEV], 'forefather' [LN (10.20)], 'ancestor' [LN (10.20); NRSV], not explicit [CEV, NLT]. See this word above at 4:11.

QUESTION—What contrast is being expressed in the construction οὐκ μόνον...ἀλλὰ καί 'not only...but also'?
   1. It refers to Jewish believers, who not only are circumcised but who also follow Abraham's faith [BECNT, Gdt, HNTC, Ho, ICC1, ICC2, Mor, Mu, NICNT, SSA, TH, WBC].
   2. It refers to two groups of people for whom Abraham is father and who are spiritually circumcised; that is, he is father not only of all those Jewish believers who are physically circumcised, but also of all who have faith, whether Jewish or not [AB].

DISCOURSE UNIT: 4:13–25 [AB, GNT, HNTC, NTC; CEV, NCV]. The topic is the promise realized through faith [GNT], faith and promise [HNTC], God's promise through faith not works [NTC], as with Abraham, the promise comes only to the people of faith [AB], the promise is for all who have faith [CEV], the promise is received through faith [TEV], God keeps his promise [NCV].

DISCOURSE UNIT: 4:13–22 [NICNT]. The topic is faith, promise, and law.

DISCOURSE UNIT: 4:13–17 [ICC1, Mor]. The topic is faith and law [Mor], promise and law [ICC1].

4:13 For not through[a] law[b] (was) the promise[c] to-Abraham or/and[d] to-his seed,[e]

LEXICON—a. διά with genitive object (LN 89.76, 90.8) (BAGD A.III.1.d. p. 180): 'through' [AB, BAGD, BECNT, LN (89.76, 90.8), NICNT, NTC, WBC; KJV, NASB, NCV, NET, NIV, NRSV, REB], 'by' [LN (89.76); GW], 'by means of' [LN (89.76, 90.8)], 'because' [CEV, TEV]. This preposition is translated by a phrase 'in the context of' [HNTC], 'on the basis of' [ICC2], 'based on' [NLT]. See this word above at 4:11.

b. νόμος (LN 33.333, 33.55) (BAGD 3. p. 542): 'law' [BAGD, LN (33.333)], 'the Law' [LN (33.55)]. This word, which does not have the definite article here, is translated as having the definite article: 'the law' [AB, BECNT, ICC2, NICNT, NTC, WBC; KJV, NET, NRSV], 'the Law' [NASB, TEV], 'Moses' Teachings' [GW], 'God's law' [NLT]. It is translated as not having the article: 'law' [HNTC; NIV, REB], 'a law' [CEV]. The phrase οὐ γὰρ διὰ νόμου 'for not through law' is translated '(This promise) was not made because Abraham had obeyed a law' [CEV], 'not on the basis of fulfillment of the law' [ICC2]. See this word also at 3:31.

c. ἐπαγγελία (LN 33.288, 33.280) (BAGD 2.a. p. 280): 'promise' [AB, BAGD, BECNT, HNTC, ICC2, LN (33.288), NICNT, NTC, WBC; GW, KJV, NASB, NCV, NET, NIV, NRSV, REB], 'God's promise' [NLT], 'agreement' [LN (33.280)]. The phrase ἡ ἐπαγγελία τῷ ᾽Αβραὰμ ἢ τῷ σπέρματι αὐτοῦ 'the promise to Abraham or to his seed' is translated 'God promised Abraham and his descendants' [CEV, TEV].

d. ἤ (LN 89.139): 'or' [AB, HNTC, ICC2, LN, NICNT, NTC; GW, KJV, NASB, NET, NRSV], 'and' [BECNT, WBC; CEV, NCV, NET, NIV, NLT, REB, TEV].

e. σπέρμα (LN 10.29) (BAGD 2.b. p. 761): 'seed' [BAGD, HNTC, ICC2, LN, NICNT, NTC, WBC; KJV], 'descendants' [BAGD, BECNT, LN; all versions except KJV, NIV], 'children' [BAGD], 'offspring' [LN; NIV], 'posterity' [AB, BAGD, LN]. See this word at 1:3.

QUESTION—What relationship is indicated by γάρ 'for'?

It serves to link 4:9–12, which shows that Abraham is the father of both Jews and Gentiles by faith, with 4:13–22, which shows that the promise is actualized not by law but by the righteousness of faith [BECNT]. It introduces 4:13–15 as an explanation for why Paul does not mention the law in tracing Abraham's spiritual descendents, since the Jews believed that God's blessing of Abraham was because of Abraham's faithfulness to the law and that a person could only be a child of Abraham by taking upon himself the yoke of the law [NICNT]. It introduces grounds for his statement that Abraham was the father of those who believe [ICC1, Mor], which is that he acted in conformity to faith, not law [Mor]. It introduces another aspect of his argument that justification is by faith and that Abraham is the father of all who believe [Mu]. It introduces a response to an anticipated objection, which is that the descendents of Abraham who will inherit the world are specifically those descended from Isaac, the one who was named to be heir of Canaan as well as of the covenant that was marked by circumcision; Paul rejects this reasoning on the grounds that the promise was granted to Abraham by faith, not by law [Gdt]. It introduces additional grounds for his basic premise about justification by faith; just as Abraham was not justified by circumcision, neither was he justified by obedience to the law [Ho]. It introduces 4:13 as part of the argument for the premise in 4:16 that what God promised is guaranteed to all who believe as Abraham did; that is, it was not through law but through faith that Abraham was declared righteous, and so all people can receive similar blessings because they trust in God [SSA].

QUESTION—What relationship is indicated by διά 'through'?
1. It is instrumental [BECNT, Ho, ICC2, NICNT, SSA]. It means through anything done in obedience to the law of Moses [NICNT]. It means becoming an heir on the basis of practicing the law [BECNT] or on condition of obedience to the law [Ho].
2. It indicates attendant circumstance; that is, he is asking if the promise falls within the context or domain of law or within that of the righteousness that comes through faith [HNTC].

QUESTION—Does νόμος refer to the Mosaic law, or more generally to law as a principle?
1. It refers to the Mosaic law [AB, BECNT, Gdt, ICC2, NICNT, NTC, SSA, WBC; GW, KJV, NASB, NET, NLT, NRSV].
2. It refers to law more generally [HNTC, ICC1, Mu, St; NIV, REB]. It refers to law as law, as that which demands obedience and stands in contrast to promise [Mu]. It refers to law generally, as well as to the particular form of law found in the law of Moses [Ho].

(that) he be the heir[a] of-(the)-world,[b]

LEXICON—a. κληρονόμος (LN 57.133) (BAGD 2.b. p. 435): 'heir' [BAGD, BECNT, HNTC, ICC2, LN, NTC, WBC; KJV, NASB, NIV]. This adjective is translated as a verb phrase 'that he would inherit' [AB; GW, NET, NRSV], 'to give (the whole earth)' [NLT]. This phrase is translated 'that he would give them the world' [CEV], 'that they would get the whole world' [NCV], 'that they should be the heirs' [NICNT], 'that the world should be their inheritance' [REB], 'that the world would belong to him' [TEV].
b. κόσμος (LN 1.39) (BAGD 4.a. p. 446): 'world' [AB, BAGD, BECNT, HNTC, ICC2, LN, NICNT, NTC, WBC; all versions except NLT], 'earth' [NLT]. See this word at 3:19.

QUESTION—What is implied in the term 'heir'?
To inherit means to obtain something as a gift [NTC]. This word does not necessarily imply that a death must occur for the inheritance to be received,

as in normal English usage [TH], it simply refers to the securing of possessions regardless of how they are gained [Mor]. It refers to a secure possessor, since possessions gained by inheritance were considered more secure than those gained by purchase [Ho]. An heir is someone who receives something that has been promised [SSA].

QUESTION—In what sense would Abraham be 'heir' of the world?

The phrase 'inherit the world' is drawn from Gen 22:17–18 where it mentions 'all the nations' (v.18) and where 'shall possess' (v.17) is translated 'shall inherit' in the LXX [HNTC, TH], wording which Paul uses to summarize the content of the promise [HNTC]. This statement summarizes several promises given to Abraham: that he would inherit the land (that is, Canaan), that he would have many descendents embracing many nations, that through him God would bless all the peoples of the earth [Gdt, ICC2, NICNT, NTC], as well as that his descendents would possess the gates of their enemies [NICNT]. There was also the general promise of the universal supremacy of the messianic kingdom, which the people of Israel tended to think of more in political terms than in religious terms [Gdt]. This also refers generally to all that God promised his people [NICNT]. It also includes the promise of ultimate restoration of man's inheritance that was lost through sin (see Gen 1:27) to Abraham and his descendents [ICC2]. The merging of all the elements of the promise, that Abraham would have descendents, that he would be given the land of Canaan, and that all nations would be blessed through him, leads to the conclusion that his descendents will inherit the world [BECNT]. God's guarantee of universal blessing for all peoples through Abraham means that God will reclaim the world that was lost because of Adam's sin [BECNT]. Based on the universality inherent in the promise that all the families of the earth would be blessed through Abraham, Jewish tradition expanded that to include inheriting the world [AB]. This statement refers to the various promises in Genesis (12:3, 18:18 and 22:18) about the families and nations of the world being blessed or blessing themselves through Abraham [TNTC]. This comes from the promise in Genesis that all nations would be blessed through Abraham's descendents, coupled with the fact that the messiah would exercise a universal dominion [St]. It refers to all the spiritual blessings, prosperity, and happiness that believers experience through redemption, as well as to the ultimate establishment of the universal kingdom of Christ and the part believers will have in that reign [Ho]. The promise was that all the people in the world would be blessed through Abraham [SSA]. The promise made to Abraham and to his descendents is that through one of Abraham's descendents the whole world would be blessed, and that all the rest of Abraham's descendents would enjoy world-wide messianic rule or dominion through him [ICC1]. It is the worldwide dominion promised to Christ and to the spiritual descendents of Abraham in Christ [Mu].

but through^a (the) righteousness^b of-faith.^c

LEXICON—a. διά with genitive object (LN 89.76, 90.8) (BAGD A.III.1.d. p. 180): 'through' [AB, BAGD, BECNT, LN (89.76, 90.8), NICNT, NTC, WBC; GW, KJV, NASB, NCV, NET, NIV, NRSV, REB], 'because' [CEV, TEV], 'by' [LN (89.76)]. This preposition is translated by a phrase: 'in the context of' [HNTC], 'on the basis of' [ICC2], not explicit [NLT]. See this word above at 4:11.

  b. δικαιοσύνη (LN 88.13) (BAGD 3. p. 197): 'righteousness' [BAGD, BECNT, ICC2, LN, NICNT, NTC, WBC; KJV, NASB, NET, NIV, NRSV, REB], 'uprightness' [AB]. The phrase 'righteousness of faith' is translated 'uprightness that came from faith' [AB], 'righteousness that is by faith' [BECNT], 'faith-righteousness' [HNTC], 'righteousness of faith' [ICC2, NICNT, WBC], 'righteousness resulting from faith' [NTC], 'his faith in God made him acceptable' [CEV], 'God's approval of his faith' [GW], 'being right with God' [NCV], 'the new relationship with God (that comes by faith)' [NLT], '(he believed and) was accepted as righteous (by God)' [TEV]. This word, which does not have the definite article here, is translated as though having the definite article [AB, BECNT, ICC2, NICNT, WBC; KJV, NASB, NET, NIV, NRSV]; as not having the definite article [NTC; REB]. See this word above at 4:11.

  c. πίστις (LN 31.85) (BAGD 2.a. p. 662): 'faith' [AB, BAGD, BECNT, ICC2, LN, NICNT, NTC, WBC; all versions except CEV, TEV], 'faith in God' [CEV], '(because) he believed' [TEV]. See this word above at 4:12.

QUESTION—How are the nouns related in the genitive phrase δικαιοσύνης πίστεως '(the) righteousness of faith'?

  1. Faith is the source or cause of the righteousness [AB, BECNT, Ho, NTC, SSA; CEV, NCV, NET, NIV, NLT, REB]. The righteousness of faith is that relationship with God of which faith is the basis and expression [WBC]. He was accepted by God as righteous because he believed [SSA, TH].

  2. Abraham's faith is something which God approves [GW].

4:14 **For if the-(ones) of^a law^b (are) heirs,^c**

LEXICON—a. ἐκ (LN 89.77, 90.12, 90.16) (BAGD 3.d. p. 235): 'of' [BAGD, BECNT, NICNT; KJV, NASB], 'by' [LN (90.12, 90.16); NET, NIV], 'from' [LN (89.77, 90.16)], 'by means of' [LN (89.77)], 'as a result of' [LN (90.12)]. The phrase οἱ ἐκ νόμου 'the ones of law' is translated 'those who hold to the law' [AB], 'those who hold by the law' [REB], 'those who rely on the law' [HNTC], 'those who live by law' [NTC], 'the people of the law' [WBC], 'those who have a claim on the basis of their fulfillment of the law' [ICC2], 'because they had obeyed a law' [CEV], 'those who obey Moses' Teachings' [GW], 'adherents of the law' [NRSV], not explicit [NCV, NLT, TEV]. See this word above at 4:12.

  b. νόμος (LN 33.333) (BAGD 3. p. 542): 'law' [AB, BAGD, BECNT, HNTC, ICC2, LN, NICNT, NTC, WBC; all versions except GW, NLT],

'Moses' Teachings' [GW], 'God's law' [NLT]. This word does not have the definite article here. See this word above at 4:13.
  c. κληρονόμος (LN 57.133, 57.139) (BAGD 2.b. p. 435): 'heir' [AB, BAGD, BECNT, HNTC, ICC2, LN (57.133, 57.139), NICNT, NTC, WBC; GW, KJV, NASB, NET, NIV, NRSV, REB]. This noun is also translated as a verb phrase: 'could receive (what God promised)' [NCV], '(what God promises) is to be to be given to' [TEV], 'were given (this promise)' [CEV], '(God's promise) is for' [NLT]. See this word above at 4:13.

QUESTION—What relationship is indicated by γάρ 'for'?

It introduces grounds for the statement made in 4:13, that the promised inheritance becomes a reality through the righteousness of faith and not by law [BECNT, ICC2]. It introduces an explanation for the statement in 4:13 that the promise can't be attained by the law [NICNT]. It introduces an explanation of the terms he has just used in 4:13 as a justification for the statements made there [HNTC]. It introduces grounds for his statement in 4:13 that Abraham was declared righteous by God because he trusted God to keep his promise [SSA].

QUESTION—What relationship is indicated by εἰ 'if'?

He raises a possibility which is not actually true in order to show what the consequences would be if it were true [NICNT].

QUESTION—What is meant by the phrase οἱ ἐκ νόμου 'the ones of law'?

It means those who keep or attempt to keep the law [BECNT, TH]. They are partisans of the law [BAGD]. They are those who adhere to or are governed by the law [SSA]. They base their hope for inheriting the blessings promised to Abraham on the law, that is, their status as Jews [NICNT]. It means those who attempt to obey the law in all its details in order to be saved [NTC]. He is speaking of legalists [Ho, Mor], who seek justification by the works of the law [Ho], those for whom law is the central thing [Mor]. It is those who would have a claim to the inheritance on the basis of fulfilling the law, which of course would be no one, since no one can do that [ICC2]. The Jews are vassals of a legal system, depending on law [ICC1]. The continuing existence of the Jewish people not only arises out of the law, but the law determines their character and distinctiveness as God's people [WBC]. It contrasts those whose religion has law as its guiding and determining principle with those whose religion has faith as the fundamental principle [Mu].

faith[a] is-made-invalid[b]

LEXICON—a. πίστις (LN 31.85, 31.102): 'faith' [AB, BECNT, HNTC, ICC2, LN (31.85, 31.102), NICNT, NTC, WBC; all versions]. Although this word has the definite article here it is translated without it by all commentaries and versions. See this word above at 4:13.
  b. perf. pass. indic. of κενόω (LN 76.27) (BAGD 2. p. 428): 'to be made invalid' [BAGD], 'to be rendered invalid' [WBC], 'to be deprived of its

value' [NTC], 'to be caused to lose power, to be caused to be emptied of power, to be deprived of (its) power, to be made powerless' [LN], 'to be emptied of meaning' [AB, HNTC], 'to be emptied' [NICNT], 'to be made of no effect' [BECNT], 'to be rendered vain' [ICC2], 'to mean nothing' [CEV, TEV], 'to be useless' [GW, NLT], 'to be made void' [KJV, NASB], 'to be worthless' [NCV], 'to be empty' [NET], 'to have no value' [NIV], 'to be null' [NRSV], 'to become pointless' [REB].

and the promise^a is-made-ineffective;^b

LEXICON—a. ἐπαγγελία (LN 33.288, 33.280) (BAGD 2.a. p. 280): 'promise' [AB, BAGD, BECNT, HNTC, ICC2, LN (33.288), NICNT, NTC, WBC; all versions except NCV, TEV], 'God's promise' [NCV, TEV], 'agreement' [LN (33.280)]. See this word above at 4:13.

    b. perf. pass. indic. of καταργέω (LN 76.26) (BAGD 1.b. p. 417): 'to be made ineffective' [BAGD], 'to be invalidated' [LN], 'to be nullified' [AB, BAGD, BECNT, NICNT, WBC; NASB, NET], 'to be brought to nothing' [HNTC], 'to be made of none effect' [KJV], 'to be abolished' [LN], 'to be annulled' [ICC2], 'to be rendered worthless' [NTC]. This passive verb is translated as intransitive active: 'to be worthless' [CEV, GW, NCV, NIV, TEV], 'to be meaningless' [NLT], 'to be void' [NRSV], 'to go for nothing' [REB]. See this word also at 3:31.

QUESTION—In what sense is faith made invalid and the promise made ineffective if only the ones of the law are heirs?

If receiving the inheritance were based on fulfilling the requirements of the law, there would be no heirs because no human being can fulfill all that the law requires, and consequently the promise would go unfulfilled and their exercise of faith in this regard would have failed to attain its end [NICNT]. If observing the law is decisive in receiving the inheritance, then faith and the promise play no role in it [BECNT] and have no meaning [HNTC]. Since no sinner is able to render perfect obedience, salvation would be impossible and the promise would be worthless because it could never be fulfilled [Gdt, NTC, TNTC]. Faith and works are exclusive of one another, just as are law and promise [Mu]. The Jewish understanding of the covenant as being based on Abraham's obedience would make Abraham's faith, which was reckoned by God as righteousness, empty and ineffective and it would nullify the promise by denying that it was given by God and accepted by Abraham then and there as a commitment God had taken upon himself [WBC]. Since the original condition of fulfillment was faith, it would break the covenant to substitute another condition [Ho].

4:15 for the law^a brings-about^b wrath;^c

LEXICON—a. νόμος (LN 33.333) (BAGD 3. p. 542): 'law' [AB, BAGD, BECNT, HNTC, ICC2, LN, NICNT, NTC, WBC; KJV, NCV, NET, NIV, NLT, NRSV, REB], 'Law' [CEV, NASB, TEV]. This word, which has the definite article, is translated without the definite article: 'law' [NIV, REB]. See this word above at 4:14.

b. pres. mid. (deponent = act.) indic. of κατεργάζομαι (LN **13.9**) (BAGD 2. p. 421): 'to bring about' [BAGD, **LN,** WBC; GW, NASB], 'to bring' [AB; NCV, NET, NIV, NLT, NRSV, REB], 'to bring down' [TEV], 'to effect, to result in' [LN], 'to produce' [BAGD, BECNT, HNTC, NICNT, NTC], 'to create' [BAGD], 'to work' [ICC2; KJV], not explicit [CEV]. See this word at 2:9.

c. ὀργή (LN 38.10, 88.173) (BAGD 2.b. p. 579): 'wrath' [AB, BAGD, BECNT, HNTC, ICC2, NICNT, NTC, WBC; KJV, NASB, NET, NIV, NRSV], 'anger' [LN (88.173); NCV], 'punishment' [LN (38.10); NLT], 'retribution' [REB]. This noun is translated as a phrase 'God's anger' [GW, TEV], 'God becomes angry' [CEV]. See this word at 3:5.

QUESTION—What relationship is indicated by γάρ 'for'?

It introduces grounds for the statement of 4:14 that the inheritance cannot be gained through law, which is that law only produces wrath [BECNT, Gdt, Ho, ICC2, NICNT] and brings death [Ho]. It introduces a second justification for the dogmatic statement made in 4:13 about law, promise and faith [HNTC]. It introduces additional grounds for what is stated in 4:13 that the promise did not come through law, which is that law only brings wrath [Mu, SSA]. It introduces 4:15 as a parenthesis that proves what he has said in the previous verse, that law and promise are incompatible [ICC1]. The reason that law makes both faith and promise void is that law evokes the wrath of God and it does not bring the favor which faith and promise presuppose [Mu].

QUESTION—What is the logic of this statement?

God's wrath is activated by the law because people fail to keep it; even though all people are guilty of sin, even those without the law, a transgression of the law is even more serious because it is a conscious violation of a known standard [BECNT]. The actual effect of the law, as opposed to what people who trust in it hope to gain by it, is to bring God's wrath on them because it turns their sin into conscious transgression, making it more exceedingly sinful [ICC2]. The law invariably imposes penalty for failure to conform to it [TNTC]. Law is so bound up with sin, stimulating and increasing that which naturally brings God's wrath and showing how sinful it is, that it would be unthinkable that it should be the basis of God's promise [HNTC, NAC]. It is ironic that the very thing the Jews depended on to make them acceptable before God actually highlights their sinfulness [NAC]. Paul anticipates an objection that raises the question about the role of the law, and he wants to link the Torah with God's wrath instead of God's promise [WBC]. This statement is a parenthetical comment, meaning that wherever there is law, there will be disobedience [SSA].

but/and[a] where (there) is no law[b] neither (is there) transgression.[c]

TEXT—Instead of δέ 'but/and' some manuscripts read γάρ 'for, because'. GNT reads δέ with a B decision, indicating that the text is almost certain. The reading γάρ 'for, because' is taken only by KJV, NET.

LEXICON—a. δέ (LN 89.124, 89.94): 'but' [AB, ICC2, LN (89.124), NTC; CEV, GW, NASB, NCV, NRSV, TEV], 'and' [BECNT, HNTC, LN (89.94), NICNT, WBC; NIV, REB], not explicit [NLT].
  b. νόμος (LN 33.333): 'law' [AB, BAGD, BECNT, HNTC, ICC2, LN, NICNT, NTC, WBC; all versions]. This word does not have the definite article here. See this word above.
  c. παράβασις (LN 36.28) (BAGD p. 612): 'transgression' [AB, BAGD, BECNT, HNTC, ICC2, LN, NICNT, NTC, WBC; KJV, NET, NIV], 'violation' [NASB, NRSV]. The phrase οὐδὲ παράβασις 'neither is there transgression' is translated 'it cannot be broken' [CEV], 'they can't be broken' [GW], 'there can be no breach of law' [REB], 'there is nothing to disobey' [NCV], 'there is no disobeying of the law' [TEV]. This entire clause is translated 'the only way to avoid breaking the law is to have no law to break' [NLT]. See this word at 2:23.
QUESTION—What does he mean that there is no transgression?
  Transgression is the sin of violating specific commands, and the law, which defines transgression, renders people even more accountable for their sin by defining it more clearly [BECNT, ICC2, NICNT]. He is not saying that there is no sin apart from the law; the law turns sin into overt transgression as a conscious violation of it [BECNT]. Evil is vaguely apprehended apart from law, but is not regarded as transgression [AB]. Direct breach of a known boundary is far more serious than accidental or unconscious wrongdoing [ICC1]. When God gave the promise to Abraham the law had not been given and transgression of it was impossible, so the promise had ample room to function [NTC]. Apart from law sin still exists, but cannot be called specific transgression of law; law turns people into conscious sinners [NAC]. The law gives people the recognition of sin, and if understood rightly would not distinguish Jew from Gentile but would put both in need of the grace of God [WBC].

4:16 Because of this[a] (it is) from[b] faith,[c]
LEXICON—a. διά with accusative object (LN 89.26): 'on account of' [LN]. The phrase διὰ τοῦτο 'because of this' [LN, NICNT] is also translated 'for this reason' [AB, ICC2, NTC, WBC; NASB, NET, NRSV], 'therefore' [BECNT, HNTC; GW, KJV, NIV], 'so that's why' [NLT], 'and so' [TEV], 'so' [NCV], not explicit [CEV, REB].
  b. ἐκ (LN 89.77, 90.16): 'from' [LN (89.77, 90.16)], 'by' [BECNT, LN, NTC; NASB, NCV, NET, NIV], 'by means of' [LN (89.77)], 'on the basis of' [ICC2], 'based on' [GW], 'on the ground of' [REB], 'of' [NICNT, WBC; KJV], not explicit [NLT]. This preposition is translated by a verb: 'made to rest upon' [HNTC], 'depends on' [AB; CEV, NRSV], 'is based on' [TEV]. This clause is translated 'everything depends on having faith in God' [CEV], 'so that's why faith is the key' [NLT], 'so people receive God's promise by having faith' [NCV]. See this word above at 4:14.

c. πίστις (LN 31.85) (BAGD 2.a. p. 662): 'faith' [AB, BAGD, BECNT, HNTC, ICC2, LN, NICNT, NTC, WBC; all versions]. See this word above at 4:13.

QUESTION—What relationship is indicated by διὰ τοῦτο 'therefore'?
  1. It refers forward to the purpose clause 'in order that it might be in accordance with grace' which immediately follows; that is, the reason the promised inheritance is received by faith is so that it might be a matter of grace [BECNT, ICC2, NAC, NICNT, NTC]: For this reason it is from faith, namely that it might be in accordance with grace.
  2. It refers backward and draws a conclusion from what has been stated [AB, Gdt, HNTC, Ho, ICC1, Mor, Mu, SSA, TH; GW, KJV, NCV, NIV, NLT]. It refers backward to 4:14, and insists that promise, faith, and grace belong together inseparably [HNTC]. It refers backward to 4:13; since law and promise are incompatible, it has to be by faith [AB]. It refers backward to the impossibility of salvation by law [Mor] or that the divine plan could be achieved by law [ICC1]. Law and the promised inheritance are contradictory, since law knows no grace, so the inheritance must therefore be of faith and by grace [Mu]. Because the law only brings wrath, the fulfillment of the promise had to be on the basis of faith and grace [Gdt, Ho]. It draws a conclusion from all that is stated in 4:13-15; that is, because God's blessings to Abraham were given because he believed God and not because of obeying law, we can conclude that we will receive what God has promised because we trust in him [SSA].

QUESTION—What is it that is from faith and in accordance with grace, and which is the implied subject of this sentence?
  1. The implied subject is the promise [AB, BECNT, Gdt, Ho, Mu, NAC, NICNT, NTC, SSA, TH, WBC].
    1.1 It is the promised inheritance [AB, BECNT, Gdt, Ho, NAC, NICNT, SSA].
    1.2 It is the promise of salvation [NTC].
  2. The implied subject is God's plan of salvation [HNTC, ICC1, ICC2], or justification [St].

in-order-that[a] (it might be) in-accordance-with[b] grace,[c]
LEXICON—a. ἵνα (LN 89.59): 'in order that' [BECNT, HNTC, ICC2, NICNT, NTC, WBC; NRSV, REB, TEV], 'that (it might be)' [AB; KJV, NASB], 'so that' [LN; CEV, GW, NET, NIV], '(this happens) so' [NCV], not explicit [NLT].
  b. κατά with accusative object (LN 89.4, 89.8): 'in accordance with' [LN (89.8), WBC; NASB], 'according to' [BECNT, ICC2, NICNT], 'by' [KJV, NET, NIV], 'with regard to' [LN (89.4)], 'in relation to' [LN (89.4, 89.8)], 'a matter of' [AB, HNTC, NTC; REB], 'as' [TEV]. The prepositional phrase κατὰ χάριν 'in accordance with grace' is translated 'is given to us as a free gift' [NLT], 'may rest on grace' [NRSV], '(God's

promise) is assured by his great kindness' [CEV], 'it can be a gift' [GW], '(the promise) can be a free gift' [NCV]. See this word at 4:4.
  c. χάρις (LN 25.89, 88.66) (BAGD 2.a. p. 877): 'grace' [AB, BECNT, HNTC, ICC2, LN (88.66), NICNT, NTC, WBC; KJV, NASB, NET, NIV, NRSV], 'favor' [BAGD, LN (25.89)], 'goodwill' [BAGD, LN (25.89)], 'gift' [GW], 'great kindness' [CEV], 'a free gift' [NCV, NLT], 'God's free gift' [TEV], 'sheer grace' [REB]. This entire clause is translated 'so that God's promise is assured by his great kindness' [CEV], 'God's promise is given to us as a free gift' [NLT]. See this word at 4:4.

so-that[a] the promise[b] be certain[c] to-all the descendants,[d]

LEXICON—a. εἰς (LN 89.57): 'so that' [BECNT, HNTC, ICC2, NICNT], 'in order that' [NTC; NASB], 'that' [WBC; REB], 'for the purpose of' [LN], 'so as' [AB], 'with the result that' [NET], 'consequently' [GW], 'to the end' [KJV], not explicit [CEV, NCV, NIV, NLT, NRSV, TEV]. See this word above at 4:11.
  b. ἐπαγγελία (LN 33.288, 33.280) (BAGD 2.a. p. 280): 'promise' [AB, BAGD, BECNT, HNTC, ICC2, LN (33.288), NICNT, NTC, WBC; CEV, GW, KJV, NASB, NCV, NET, NLT, TEV], 'agreement' [LN (33.280)], not explicit [NIV, NRSV, REB]. See this word above at 4:14.
  c. βέβαιος (LN **71.15**) (BAGD 2. p. 138): 'certain' [BAGD, **LN**, WBC; NASB, NET, NLT], 'sure' [LN; KJV], 'reliable' [BAGD], 'dependable' [BAGD], 'confirmed' [BECNT, NICNT], 'valid' [AB; REB], 'secure' [HNTC], 'guaranteed' [GW, NIV, NRSV, TEV]. This adjective is translated as a phrase: 'certain of fulfillment' [ICC2, NTC], 'to be for' [CEV], 'can have' [NCV]. The phrase εἰς τὸ εἶναι βεβαίαν 'so that...to be certain' is translated 'we are certain to receive it' [NLT].
  d. σπέρμα (LN 10.29) (BAGD 2.b. p. 762): 'descendants' [BAGD, BECNT, LN; CEV, GW, NASB, NET, NRSV, REB, TEV], 'children' [BAGD; NCV], 'offspring' [LN; NIV], 'posterity' [AB, BAGD, LN], 'the seed' [HNTC, ICC2, NICNT, NTC, WBC; KJV], 'we' [NLT]. It refers to Abraham's spiritual sons, those who have faith like his [BAGD]. The phrase παντὶ τῷ σπέρματι 'to all the descendants' is translated 'for all Abraham's posterity' [AB]. See this word above at 4:13.

QUESTION—What relationship is indicated by εἰς in the phrase εἰς τὸ εἶναι 'so that...to be'?
  1. It indicates purpose [Gdt, HNTC, ICC1, ICC2, Mor, Mu, NICNT, NTC, WBC; NASB].
  2. It indicates result [AB, SSA; NET].

QUESTION—What is emphasized in this clause?
  1. It emphasizes the idea of the promise being made certain [ICC2, NAC]. God's plan is by faith and according to grace so that it will be sure of fulfillment, because if it were by law it would never be fulfilled [ICC2]. If it were on the basis of human achievement it would not be sure at all [NAC].

2. It emphasizes the idea of the promise being for all the descendents [HNTC, Mu, St, WBC].
3. It has a two-fold emphasis; it is being made firm in the sense of coming to fruition, and it is for all Abraham's descendents [BECNT, Gdt, NICNT]. Because the promise is secured by God's grace, it is guaranteed for all Abraham's descendents [BECNT]. It is made sure, in contrast to being made ineffective (4:14), and it is for all Abraham's descendents, whether Jew or Gentile [Gdt].

not to-the-(one who is) of[a] the law[b] only
LEXICON—a. ἐκ with genitive object (LN 89.3, 89.77, 90.12) (BAGD 3.d. p. 235): 'of' [BAGD, BECNT, ICC2, NICNT, WBC; KJV, NASB, NIV, NRSV]. This preposition is translated as a verb 'to adhere to' [AB; NRSV], 'to be under' [NET], 'to rely on' [HNTC], 'to live by' [NTC], 'to live under' [NCV], 'to obey' [TEV], 'to have' [CEV], 'to follow (Jewish customs)' [NLT]. The phrase τῷ ἐκ τοῦ νόμου 'the one who is of the law' is translated 'partisans of the law' [BAGD], 'that part of the seed which is able to rely on the law' [HNTC], 'those who hold by the law' [REB], 'who have the Law' [CEV], 'by obeying Moses' Teachings' [GW]. See this word above at 4:16.

b. νόμος (LN 33.333): 'law' [AB, BAGD, BECNT, HNTC, ICC2, LN, NICNT, NTC, WBC; KJV, NET, NIV, NRSV], 'Law' [CEV, NASB, REB, TEV], 'Jewish customs' [NLT], 'Moses' Teachings' [GW], 'the law of Moses' [NCV] This phrase is translated 'whether or not we follow Jewish customs' [NLT]. This word, which has the definite article here, is translated as having the definite article by all versions except GW and NLT, both of which also refer specifically to Moses' law [GW] or to Jewish customs [NLT]. See this word at 4:15.

but also to-the-(one) of[a] (the) faith[b] of-Abraham,
LEXICON—a. ἐκ (LN 89.3, 89.77, 90.12) (BAGD 3.d. p. 235): 'of' [ICC2, WBC; KJV, NASB, NIV]. See above. The phrase τῷ ἐκ πίστεως 'the (one) of (the) faith' is translated 'the one who has faith' [BAGD], 'those who have the faith' [NET], 'those who have (Abraham's) faith' [REB], 'those who share (his) faith' [AB], 'those who share the faith' [NRSV], 'those who are of the faith' [BECNT, NICNT; NIV], 'those who live by the faith' [NTC], 'that which relies on the faith' [HNTC], 'if we have faith' [NLT], 'anyone who lives with faith (like…)' [NCV], 'because they have faith' [CEV], 'by believing as (Abraham did)' [GW], 'those who believe as' [TEV].

b. πίστις (LN 31.85) (BAGD 2.a. p. 662): 'faith' [AB, BAGD, BECNT, HNTC, ICC2, LN, NICNT, NTC, WBC; all versions except GW, TEV], 'trust, confidence' [BAGD]. This noun is translated as a verb 'to believe' [GW, TEV]. This entire phrase is translated 'those who believe as Abraham did' [TEV]. See this word above at 4:14.

QUESTION—What contrast is being expressed in the construction οὐ...μόνον ἀλλὰ καὶ 'not only...but also'?
1. God's promises are not only for believers from among the Jews, they are for all those who have faith, including believers from among the Gentiles [AB, BECNT, Gdt, Ho, ICC1, ICC2, Mor, Mu, NAC, NICNT, SSA]. Gentiles who are saved by faith are just as saved as believing Jews are [Mor]. Paul is arguing for the equality of Gentile and Jewish believers [AB].
2. God's promises are not just limited to the Jews, they are for all those who accept the same grace as Abraham did, whether Jew or Gentile [St, WBC].
3. God's promises are certain to be fulfilled for all Abraham's true descendents, who are people who, while honoring the law, rest their faith in God as Abraham did [NTC].

QUESTION—What is meant by someone being 'of the faith of Abraham'?
It refers specifically to Gentile Christians [NICNT]. It applies to any who share the faith of Abraham, to both Jewish Christians as well as Gentile Christians [BECNT]. They trust God just as Abraham did [SSA]. Abraham is the father of all who live by faith [NAC].

who is (the) father[a] of-us all,

LEXICON—a. πατήρ (LN 10.14, 10.20) (BAGD 2.f. p. 635): 'father' [AB, BAGD, BECNT, HNTC, ICC2, LN (10.14), NICNT, NTC, WBC; all versions except CEV, TEV], 'forefather' [LN (10.20)], 'the ancestor' [LN (10.20); CEV]. This noun is translated as a phrase 'the spiritual father' [TEV]. This clause is translated 'Abraham is the father of all who believe' [NLT]. This word, which lacks the definite article here, is translated as having the definite article by all versions and by all commentaries except AB. See this word above at 4:12.

DISCOURSE UNIT: 4:17–25 [ICC1]. The topic is Abraham's faith: a type of the Christian's.

4:17 just-as it-is-written,[a] (The) Father[b] of-many nations[c] I-have-made[d] you,

LEXICON—a. perf. pass. indic. of γράφω (LN 33.61) (BAGD 2.c. p. 166): 'to be written' [AB, BECNT, HNTC, NICNT, NTC, WBC; KJV, NASB, NCV, NET, NIV, NRSV]. This is a formula introducing OT quotations [BAGD]. This verb is translated as a phrase: 'the Scriptures say' [CEV], 'even as scripture says' [ICC2], 'as Scripture says' [GW, REB], 'as the scripture says' [TEV]. This clause is translated 'that is what the Scriptures mean when God told him' [NLT]. See this word at 3:10.
b. πατήρ (LN 10.14, 10.20) (BAGD 2.f. p. 635): 'father' [AB, BAGD, BECNT, HNTC, ICC2, LN, NICNT, NTC, WBC; all versions], 'forefather' [LN (10.20)], 'ancestor' [LN (10.20); CEV]. See this word above at 4:16.

c. ἔθνος (LN 11.55): 'nation' [AB, BECNT, ICC2, LN, NICNT, NTC, WBC; all versions], 'people' [LN], 'Gentiles' [HNTC]. This word, which lacks the definite article here, is translated as having the definite article [AB, BECNT, NICNT; CEV, NET, NLT, NRSV]. See this word at 3:29.

d. perf. act. indic. of τίθημι (LN **13.9**) (BAGD I.2.a.α. p. 816): 'to make to be' [AB, BAGD, ICC2, LN, NTC, WBC; all versions except CEV, REB], 'to cause to be' [LN], 'to appoint' [BECNT, HNTC, NICNT; REB]. The phrase τέθεικά σε 'I have made you' is translated 'that Abraham would become' [CEV].

QUESTION—What is the relation of this clause to the context?

The statement 'just as it is written, (the) Father of many nations I have made you' is a parenthesis expanding on 4:16b [AB, BECNT, HNTC, Ho, ICC2, Mu, NAC, NICNT, TNTC; KJV, NASB, NCV, REB, TEV]. The parenthetical comment includes the statement in 4:16b 'who is father of us all' [NAC, NTC; NRSV, REB, TEV]. While this comment is parenthetical, it is not an aside in Paul's argument since it corroborates his statement that Abraham is the father of us all, and both those statements taken together reiterate what is said in 4:11–12 about Abraham being the father of all believers [Mu]. It provides evidential grounds for the premise in 4:16 that what God promises is guaranteed to all people who trust him; this premise is supported by what is written in the Scriptures that God would appoint Abraham to be the ancestor of many ethnic groups [SSA].

in-the-sight-of[a] God, whom he-believed,[b]

LEXICON—a. κατέναντι with genitive object (LN 90.20) (BAGD 2.b. p. 421): 'in the sight of' [AB, BAGD, BECNT, LN; NASB, NIV, TEV], 'before' [BAGD, HNTC, ICC2, NICNT, WBC; KJV, NCV], 'in the opinion of' [LN], 'in the judgment of' [LN], 'in the presence of' [NTC; GW, NET, NRSV, REB], not explicit [NLT]. This word marks a participant whose viewpoint is relevant to an event [LN]. This entire phrase is translated 'this promise was made to Abraham because he had faith in God' [CEV], 'this happened because Abraham believed in the God who…' [NLT], 'the promise was good in the sight of God in whom Abraham believed' [TEV].

b. aorist act. indic. of πιστεύω (LN 31.85) (BAGD 1.b. p. 661): 'to believe' [BAGD, BECNT, HNTC, ICC2, LN, NICNT, WBC; all versions except CEV, REB], 'to trust' [LN], 'to have faith in' [LN; CEV], 'to have faith' [REB], 'to put one's faith in' [AB], 'to rest one's faith in' [NTC]. See this word above at 4:11.

QUESTION—How does the phrase 'in the sight of God, whom he believed' relate to the context?

1. The phrase 'in the sight of God' picks up again from what is said in 4:16b about Abraham being father of us all. That is, in God's sight Abraham is the father of us all [AB, Ho, ICC2, Mu, SSA, St; NCV, NET, NIV], or in God's sight Abraham already was the father of all [Gdt]. In his omniscience God looked upon Abraham as surrounded by many nations

of children [Ho]. Abraham is the father of us all, and his fatherhood has validity and sanction because God instituted it and has recognized it [Mu]. The phrase 'before God' indicates that God guarantees the promise [SSA].
2. It refers to the promise of blessing mentioned in 4:16a; it is in God's sight that the promise is valid or guaranteed or made certain to all Abraham's spiritual posterity [NAC, TNTC; TEV].
3. It was in the presence of God that Abraham exercised faith [BECNT, ICC1, NICNT, NTC, WBC; GW, REB]. It was in the presence of God that the promise about things not yet existing was given by God and accepted in faith by Abraham [NICNT]. It was the presence of God or a vision of God that inspired Abraham's faith [BECNT, NTC]. What sustained Abraham's faith was a vision of God who could do the impossible [BECNT]. Abraham had a vivid experience of the presence of God [NTC]. Abraham stood in God's presence and conversed with him [ICC1].

the-(one) making-alive[a] the dead[b]

LEXICON—a. pres. act. participle of ζῳοποιέω (LN **23.92**) (BAGD 1. p. 341): 'to make alive' [BAGD, LN; NET, REB], 'to make live, to cause to live' [LN], 'to raise to life' [LN; CEV], 'to bring to life' [BAGD; NLT, TEV], 'to give life to' [AB, BAGD, BECNT, NICNT, WBC; GW, NASB, NCV, NIV, NRSV], 'to be able to make alive' [**LN**], 'to impart life to' [NTC], 'to quicken' [HNTC, ICC2; KJV].
  b. νεκρός (LN 23.121) (BAGD 2.a. p. 535): 'dead' [AB, BAGD, BECNT, HNTC, ICC2, LN, NICNT, NTC, WBC; all versions except GW], 'dead people' [GW]. See this word at 1:4.
QUESTION—To what does this statement refer?
  It refers to God granting Abraham the ability to beget and Sarah the ability to conceive [BECNT, Gdt, ICC2, NICNT, NTC, TNTC, WBC]. It refers to the fact that they will beget a son in their old age [NAC]. It refers to God's life-giving creative power [WBC]. The bodies of Abraham and Sarah were dead in terms of childbearing [BECNT]. It is a reference to God's supernaturally enabling the dead womb of Sarah to conceive [AB]. It also has some reference to 4:14 which mentions Jesus' resurrection from the dead [ICC1, ICC2, NICNT]. It refers to the spiritual deadness of the Gentiles, to Abraham's and Sarah's infertility, and to the raising of Jesus from the dead [Mor]. Humanly speaking the fulfillment of God's promise that Abraham and Sarah would have a child was as impossible as raising the dead [Mu]. It refers to resurrection from the dead; the birth of Isaac was at the same time an act of creation (with reference to Isaac) as well as of resurrection (with reference to Abraham) [St].

and calling[a] the-(things) not existing[b] as existing[c];

LEXICON—a. pres. act. participle of καλέω (LN 33.131) (BAGD 2. p. 399): 'to call' [AB, HNTC, ICC2, NICNT, NTC, WBC; GW, KJV, NASB, NIV, NRSV, REB], 'to speak of' [BECNT], 'to summon' [NET], 'to bring'

[NLT]. This participle is translated as a noun '(whose) command' [TEV]. This entire phrase is translated 'and creates new things' [CEV], 'who creates something out of nothing' [NCV].
  b. pres. participle of εἰμί (LN **13.69**) (BAGD I.1. p. 223): 'to exist' [AB, BAGD, BECNT, HNTC, WBC; NET, NLT, NRSV, TEV], 'to be' [NICNT, NTC; KJV, NIV, REB]. This clause is translated 'whose command brings into being what did not exist' [**LN;** TEV], 'who brings into existence what didn't exist before' [NLT], 'and calls into being the things which do not exist' [HNTC], 'and calls into being the things that exist not' [AB], 'calls things which are not into being' [ICC2; REB], 'who creates something out of nothing' [NCV], 'calls things which have no existence into existence' [WBC], 'calls into existence the things that do not exist' [NRSV], 'who raises the dead to life' [CEV], 'calls into existence nations that do not even exist' [GW], 'calls into being that which does not exist' [NASB], 'calleth those things which be not as though they were' [KJV], 'calls those things that are not as though they were' [NICNT, NTC; NIV], 'who speaks of things not existing as if they existed' [BECNT], 'summons the things that do not yet exist as though they already do' [NET].
  c. pres. participle of εἰμί (LN **13.69**) (BAGD I.1. p. 223): 'to exist' [BAGD, BECNT, WBC; GW, NASB, NLT, NRSV], 'to be' [NICNT, NTC; KJV, NIV, REB], 'to come into being' [AB, HNTC], 'to bring into being' [LN; TEV], 'to create new things' [CEV], 'creates something out of nothing' [NCV]. The phrase ὡς ὄντα 'as existing' is translated 'as though they do' [NET].

QUESTION—What is meant by the phrase 'calling the things not existing as existing'?
  1. It refers to the fact that God summons or calls things that do not yet exist as though they already existed [BECNT, Gdt, Ho, ICC1, Mu, NICNT, SSA, TNTC]. Abraham trusted that God could call these things into existence even though they did not exist at that time [BECNT]. God describes to Abraham the nations that will come from him even before they existed [NICNT]. These are things that God has determined should come to pass, which have not yet done so but which will surely happen [Mu]. To call means to invite someone or something to appear; here God calls to appear before Abraham's view those nations that do not yet exist [Gdt]. God calls things that don't exist as though they do, and thereby causes them to come into existence [TNTC]. The actual as well as the possible are equally under the command of God, to whom all things are present to his view and under his control [Ho]. The things not existing at that point were the children of Abraham not yet born [SSA].
  2. It refers to the fact that God created everything out of nothing, summoning things that did not yet exist into existence [AB, HNTC, ICC2, Mor, NAC, NTC, St, TH, WBC]. It refers to God's creative activity during the week of creation [NTC]. He speaks the non-existent into

existence [NAC]. He creates new spiritual life out of the nothingness of people's lives [WBC]. Here it refers to Isaac, who was not yet born [AB, NAC], as well as to the many Gentiles who would be called into being as Abraham's children [AB, Mor].

DISCOURSE UNIT: 4:18–25 [Mor]. The topic is faith and Abraham.

4:18 who contrary-to[a] hope[b] on-the-basis-of[c] hope believed[d]

LEXICON—a. παρά with accusative object (LN 89.137) (BAGD III.6. p. 611): 'contrary to' [BAGD, LN], 'opposed to or not in accordance with' [LN], 'against' [AB, BECNT, HNTC, ICC2, NICNT, NTC, WBC; KJV, NASB, NET, NIV, NRSV]. The word marks that which is contrary to what should be or to what is expected [LN]. The clause 'who contrary to hope on the basis of hope believed' is translated 'hoping against hope he believed' [AB, HNTC; NRSV], 'in hope against hope he believed' [NASB], 'he in hope against all hope believed' [ICC2], 'who against hope believed in hope' [KJV], 'against hope Abraham believed in hope' [NET], 'against all hope, Abraham in hope believed' [NIV], 'when it all seemed hopeless, Abraham still had faith in God' [CEV], 'when hope seemed hopeless' [REB], 'when there was nothing left to hope for, Abraham still hoped and believed' [GW], 'there was no hope' [NCV], 'Abraham believed and hoped, even when there was no reason for hoping' [TEV], 'Abraham believed him...even though such a promise seemed utterly impossible' [NLT], 'when hope seemed hopeless, his faith was such' [REB], 'There was no hope that Abraham would have children. But Abraham believed God and continued hoping' [NCV].

b. ἐλπίς (LN 25.59) (BAGD 1. p. 252): 'hope' [AB, BECNT, HNTC, ICC2, LN (25.59), NICNT, NTC, WBC; GW, KJV, NASB, NCV, NET, NIV, NRSV, REB], 'expectation' [BAGD]. This noun is translated as a verb: 'to hope' [TEV].

c. ἐπί with dative object (LN 89.27) (BAGD II.1.b.γ. p. 287): 'on the basis of' [BAGD, LN, NICNT], 'in' [BECNT, NTC, WBC; KJV, NASB, NET, NIV], 'because of' [LN], not explicit [AB, HNTC, ICC2; CEV, GW, NCV, NLT, NRSV, REB, TEV].

QUESTION—What is meant by the phrase παρ' ἐλπίδα ἐπ' ἐλπίδι 'contrary to hope on the basis of hope'?

There was no hope from a purely human standpoint, but because of God's promise Abraham did have hope [NICNT, WBC]. His hope was God-given, independent of human calculations and possibilities and contrary to all human expectation [ICC2]. Contrary to all human expectation Abraham believed anyway, confident in God's promise [AB]. Despite the fact that it appeared impossible that his hope for the child God had promised him could be born, Abraham was persuaded that God would be faithful to his promise, so he continued to trust God, with the result that the hope was fulfilled [NTC]. When he had no natural reason to hope, he still hoped because of what God had promised [Mor]. These contrasting prepositional phrases describe the paradoxical nature of Abraham's faith [NAC]. His faith expressed itself in hope in a situation that presented no grounds for hope [Gdt]. 'Against hope' considers the circumstances and their possibility of fulfillment in terms of human resources, but 'in hope' involves the calculations of faith, which focus on the omnipotence and faithfulness of God [Mu]. The phrase ἐπ' ἐλπίδι means 'confidently' [Ho, Mu, SSA].

so-that[a] he became[b] father[c] of-many nations[d]
LEXICON—a. εἰς (LN 13.62, 89.48) (BAGD 4.e. p. 229): 'so that' [BAGD, BECNT, ICC2, NICNT, NTC], 'so that as a result' [LN (89.48)], 'that' [KJV, NRSV, REB], 'so as to' [AB, HNTC], 'in order that' [WBC; NASB], 'with the result that' [LN (89.48); NET], 'as a result' [GW], 'and so' [NCV, NIV, TEV], 'to, for' [LN (13.62)], not explicit [CEV, NLT].
  b. aorist mid. (deponent = act.) infin. of γίνομαι (LN 13.48) (BAGD I.4.a. p. 159): 'to become' [AB, BAGD, BECNT, HNTC, ICC2, LN, NICNT, NTC, WBC; all versions].
  c. πατήρ (LN 10.14, 10.20): 'father' [AB, BAGD, BECNT, HNTC, ICC2, LN (10.14), NICNT, NTC, WBC; all versions except CEV], 'ancestor' [LN (10.20); CEV], 'forefather' [LN (10.20)]. This word, which lacks the definite article here, is translated as having the definite article [AB, BECNT, HNTC, ICC2, NICNT, NTC; all versions except GW, NASB, REB]; as not having the definite article [WBC; GW, NASB, REB]. See this word above at 4:17.
  d. ἔθνος (LN 11.55): 'nation' [AB, BAGD, BECNT, HNTC, ICC2, LN, NICNT, NTC, WBC; all versions], 'Gentiles' [HNTC], '(a) people' [LN]. See this word at 4:17.
QUESTION—What is the function of the prepositional phrase εἰς τὸ γενέσθαι αὐτὸν 'so that he became'?
  1. It introduces the result or consequence of an action [AB, BAGD, HNTC, ICC1, ICC2, Mor, NICNT, NTC; CEV, GW, NCV, NET, NIV, REB, TEV]: he believed, and consequently became the father of many nations. This result was of course God's purpose [ICC1]. Though it is difficult to say whether this construction indicates purpose or result, it can be said that what was a purpose according to God's design was seen as a result from Abraham's viewpoint [BECNT].
  2. It introduces purpose [Gdt, Ho, Mu, WBC; KJV, NASB]: 'in order that'. It was Abraham's purpose; he believed so that he could experience the fulfillment of the promise [Gdt]. It was clearly purpose on God's part, but that does not mean that it was not also Abraham's purpose as well [Mu].
  3. It introduces the content of the belief [SSA; NLT, NRSV]: he believed that he would be the father of many nations.

according-to[a] the-(thing) said,[b] Thus shall-be your descendants;[c]
LEXICON—a. κατά with accusative object (LN 89.8) (BAGD II.5.a.α. p. 407): 'according to' [AB, BAGD, BECNT, HNTC, ICC2, LN, NICNT; KJV, NASB, NET, NRSV], 'in accordance with' [BAGD, LN, WBC], 'in

agreement with' [NTC], 'in fulfillment of' [REB], 'just as' [NIV, TEV], 'as' [GW], not explicit [CEV, NCV, NLT].
b. perf. pass. participle of λέγω (LN 33.69) (BAGD 4. p. 226): 'to be said' [AB, BECNT, LN, NICNT; NIV, NRSV], 'to be written' [BAGD], 'to be spoken' [ICC2; KJV, NASB], 'to be told' [NTC; GW]. This passive participle is translated as an active finite verb: 'the Scripture says' [TEV], 'God had also said' [NLT], 'as God told him' [NCV]; as a noun: 'promise' [REB], 'pronouncement' [NET]; as a phrase: 'the scripture word' [HNTC]. This entire phrase is translated 'God promised Abraham a lot of descendants' [CEV]. See this word at 3:5.
c. σπέρμα (LN 10.29) (BAGD 2.b. p. 762): 'descendants' [BAGD, BECNT, LN; all versions except KJV, NIV], 'seed' [HNTC, ICC2, NICNT, NTC, WBC; KJV] 'offspring' [LN; NIV], 'children' [BAGD], 'posterity' [AB, BAGD, LN]. The phrase Οὕτως ἔσται 'thus shall be' is translated 'So numerous ...shall be' [NLT], 'so shall...be' [NIV, REB], 'so will be' [NET], 'will be as many as the stars' [TEV]. See this word at 4:16.

4:19 and not having-weakened[a] in faith[b] he-considered[c] his-own body already having-become-dead,[d]

TEXT—Some manuscripts add οὐ 'not' before κατενόησεν 'he considered'. GNT rejects this addition with a C rating, indicating difficulty in deciding whether or not to include it in the text. The reading οὐ κατενόησεν 'he did not consider' is taken only by KJV.

TEXT—Some manuscripts omit ἤδη 'already'. It is included by GNT with a C rating, indicating difficulty in deciding whether or not to place it in the text. Ἤδη 'already' is read by [AB, BECNT, NICNT, WBC; NRSV, TEV]. It is omitted by [HNTC, ICC2, NTC; CEV, NET, NIV, NLT, REB].

LEXICON—a. aorist act. participle of ἀσθενέω (LN 74.26) (BAGD 2. p. 115): 'to weaken' [AB, BECNT, HNTC, ICC2, NICNT, NTC, WBC; GW, NIV, NLT, NRSV, REB, TEV], 'to be weak' [BAGD, LN; KJV, NET], 'to become weak' [CEV, NASB, NCV].
b. πίστις (LN 31.85): 'faith' [AB, BAGD, BECNT, HNTC, ICC2, LN, NICNT, NTC, WBC; all versions]. See this word above at 4:16.
c. aorist act. indic. of κατανοέω (LN **30.4, 32.12**) (BAGD 2. p. 415): 'to consider' [AB, BAGD, BECNT, HNTC, ICC2, WBC; KJV, NET, NRSV, REB], 'to consider carefully' [LN (**30.4**)], 'to consider closely, to think about very carefully' [LN (30.4)], 'to think of' [TEV], 'to think about (all this)' [NCV], 'to be thoroughly aware' [LN (**32.12**)], 'to understand completely, to perceive clearly' [LN (32.12)], 'to observe' [NICNT], 'to take note of the fact' [NTC], 'to face the fact' [NIV], 'to know' [CEV, NLT], 'to regard' [GW], 'to contemplate' [NASB].
d. perf. mid. participle of νεκρόω (LN 68.48) (BAGD p. 535): 'to be dead' [NICNT, WBC; KJV, NET], 'to be as good as dead' [AB, BECNT, HNTC, ICC2, NTC; GW, NASB, NIV, NRSV, REB], 'to be practically dead' [TEV], 'to be almost dead' [CEV]. The phrase τὸ ἑαυτοῦ

σῶμα...νενεκρωμένον 'his own body...having become dead' is translated 'his worn-out body' [BAGD], 'he was too old to be a father' [NLT], 'much past the age for having children' [NCV].

QUESTION—What is the main verb in this verse?
1. It is translated with the participial phrase μὴ ἀσθενήσας 'not having weakened' expressing the main thought and with the finite verb κατενόησεν 'he considered' expressing the subordinate thought [AB, BECNT, NAC, NICNT; NRSV, REB, TEV]: he did not weaken when he considered.
2. It is translated with the finite verb κατενόησεν 'he considered' expressing the main thought and with the participial phrase μὴ ἀσθενήσας 'not having weakened' expressing the subordinate thought [Gdt, HNTC, ICC1, ICC2, NTC, WBC; KJV, NASB, NET, NIV]: without weakening he considered. Or, accepting the textual variant οὐ, since Abraham was not weak in faith he did not give much consideration to the apparent impossibility of the circumstances, but believed instead [Ho].
3. It is translated as a concessive statement [SSA; NCV, NLT]: Even though he considered, he did not weaken.
4. It is translated as two coordinate expressions [CEV, GW]: he did not weaken; he considered.

being about[a] (a) hundred-years[b] (old) and the deadness[c] of-the womb[d] of-Sarah;

LEXICON—a. που (LN **78.40**) (BAGD 2. p. 696): 'about' [AB, BAGD, HNTC, ICC2, LN, NICNT, NTC, WBC; GW, KJV, NASB, NET, NIV, NRSV, REB], 'approximately' [BAGD], 'almost' [**LN**; NCV, TEV], 'nearly' [BECNT, LN; CEV]. The phrase που ὑπάρχων 'being about' is translated 'at the age of' [NLT], 'for he was' [CEV, NET, NIV, REB].
  b. ἑκατονταετής (LN **67.173**) (BAGD p. 237): 'hundred years' [LN], 'a hundred years old' [AB, BAGD, HNTC, ICC2, **LN,** NICNT, NTC; CEV, GW, KJV, NASB, NCV, NIV, NRSV, REB], 'one hundred years old' [BECNT, WBC; NET, TEV], 'at the age of one hundred' [NLT]. This word occurs only here in the NT.
  c. νέκρωσις (LN **23.57**) (BAGD 2.a. p. 535): 'deadness' [AB, BAGD, BECNT, ICC2, NICNT, WBC; KJV, NASB, NET, REB], 'barrenness' [**LN**; NRSV]. This noun is translated as a phrase 'the dead state' [HNTC]; as a verb 'to be dead' [NTC; NIV]. This entire phrase is translated 'and of the fact that Sarah could not have children' [**LN**], 'and that his wife Sarah could not have children' [CEV], 'that Sarah's womb was also dead' [NTC; NIV], 'Sarah could not have children' [NCV, TEV], 'Sarah had never been able to have children' [NLT], 'and Sarah was unable to have children' [GW]. The word is a figurative extension of 'death' and is used to denote the state of not being able to bear children as the result of having passed through menopause [LN].

d. μήτρα (LN 8.69) (BAGD p. 520): 'womb' [AB, BECNT, HNTC, ICC2, NTC, WBC; KJV, NASB, NET, NIV, NRSV, REB], not explicit [CEV, GW, NCV, NLT, TEV]. The phrase 'of Sarah's womb' is translated 'of the mother Sarah' [NICNT].

4:20 but[a] with-respect-to[b] the promise[c] of-God he- did-not -waver[d] in-unbelief[e]

LEXICON—a. δέ (LN 89.124): 'but' [LN; CEV], 'yet' [AB, NTC; NASB, NIV], 'and yet' [ICC2], 'rather' [HNTC], not explicit [BECNT, NICNT, WBC; GW, KJV, NCV, NET, NLT, NRSV, REB, TEV].
  b. εἰς (LN 90.23) (BAGD 6.a. p. 230): 'with respect to' [LN, NTC; NASB], 'with regard to' [ICC2], 'regarding' [NIV], 'concerning' [LN; NRSV], 'about' [AB, LN; NET], 'looking to' [HNTC], 'at' [BAGD; KJV], not explicit [BECNT, NICNT, WBC; CEV, GW, NCV, NLT, REB, TEV].
  c. ἐπαγγελία (LN 33.288) (BAGD 2.a. p. 280): 'promise' [AB, BECNT, HNTC, ICC2, NICNT, NTC, WBC; all versions]. See this word also at 4:13.
  d. aorist pass. (deponent = act.) indic. of διακρίνω (LN 31.37) (BAGD 2.b. p. 185): 'to waver' [AB, BAGD, HNTC, ICC2, NTC; NASB, NET, NIV, NLT, NRSV], 'to doubt' [BAGD, BECNT, LN, NICNT, WBC; CEV, GW, REB, TEV], 'to be uncertain about something' [LN], 'to be at odds with oneself' [BAGD], 'to stagger (at)' [KJV]. The phrase οὐ διεκρίθη τῇ ἀπιστίᾳ 'he did not waver in unbelief' is translated 'Abraham never doubted or questioned' [CEV], 'Abraham never wavered in believing' [NLT], 'no distrust made him waver' [NRSV], 'no distrust made him doubt' [REB], 'he never doubted' [NCV], 'he staggered not at the promise' [KJV].
  e. ἀπιστία (LN 31.97) (BAGD 2.b. p. 85): 'unbelief' [BECNT, HNTC, ICC2, LN, NICNT, NTC; KJV, NASB, NET, NIV], 'disbelief' [AB, BAGD, WBC], 'distrust' [NRSV, REB], 'lack of faith' [GW]. This noun is translated as a verb: 'to question' [CEV]. The phrase οὐ διεκρίθη τῇ ἀπιστίᾳ 'he did not waver in unbelief' is translated 'never wavered in believing' [NLT], 'his faith did not leave him' [TEV], 'he never stopped believing' [NCV]. This word signifies not just a lack of faith but an active rejection of faith, the positive refusal to believe what God has promised [ICC2, WBC]. See this word also at 3:3.

QUESTION—What is expressed by the dative noun τῇ ἀπιστίᾳ 'in unbelief'?
  1. It is causal [BECNT, Gdt, Ho, ICC1, NICNT]: he did not waver because of unbelief.
  2. It expresses an attendant state or condition [AB, HNTC, ICC2, NTC, WBC]: in unbelief.
  3. The two phrases 'did not waver' and 'in unbelief' are an intensification of the one concept of doubting: he did not doubt at all [SSA].

but he-was-enabled[a] in-faith,[b]

LEXICON—a. aorist pass./pass. (deponent = act.) indic. of ἐνδυναμόω (ἐνδυναμόομαι) (LN **74.6**, 74.7) (BAGD 2.b. p. 263): 'to be enabled' [LN (**74.6**)], 'to be empowered, to be given the capability to' [LN (74.6)], 'to filled with power' [TEV], 'to become able or capable' [LN (74.7)], 'to grow strong' [BAGD, BECNT, HNTC, NICNT; NASB, NCV, NLT, NRSV], 'to be strengthened' [AB, ICC2, LN (74.6), NTC, WBC; NET, NIV], 'to become strong' [GW], 'to be strong' [KJV, REB]. The phrase ἐνεδυναμώθη τῇ πίστει is translated 'his faith made him strong' [CEV], 'his faith filled him with power' [TEV].

b. πίστις (LN 31.85) (BAGD 2.a. p. 662): 'faith' [AB, BAGD, BECNT, HNTC, ICC2, LN, NICNT, NTC, WBC; all versions]. The relation indicated by the dative case of this word is translated 'in faith' [AB, BECNT, HNTC, ICC2, NICNT, NTC, WBC; KJV, NASB, NET, REB], 'in his faith' [NCV, NIV, NRSV], 'because of faith' [GW]. It is translated as being the subject of the action: 'his faith (made him strong)' [CEV], 'his faith (filled him with power)' [TEV], 'his faith (grew stronger)' [NLT].

QUESTION—How is the verb ἐνεδυναμώθη to be understood here?

1. It is passive; Abraham was strengthened [AB, Ho, ICC1, ICC2, Mor, NAC, NTC, WBC; CEV, NET, NIV, TEV]. God is the agent of the action [ICC2, Mor, NAC].
2. It is intransitive active; Abraham grew strong or was strong [BECNT, Gdt, NICNT; GW, KJV, NASB, NCV, NLT, NRSV, REB].

QUESTION—What is expressed by the dative case of τῇ πίστει in the phrase ἐνεδυναμώθη τῇ πίστει 'he was strengthened in faith'?

1. It is a dative of reference [AB, BECNT, HNTC, ICC2, Mu, NICNT, NTC; KJV, NASB, NCV, NET, NIV, NRSV, REB]: he grew strong or was made strong in faith [AB, BECNT, HNTC, ICC2, NICNT, NTC, WBC; KJV, NASB, NCV, NET, NIV, NRSV, REB], or his faith grew strong [NLT].
2. It is causal [ICC1, LN (74.6), Mor; CEV, GW, TEV]. He became strong because of faith [GW], his faith made him strong [CEV, TEV].
3. The dative construction τῇ πίστει goes with the participle that follows: he was strengthened, and by his faith gave glory to God [Gdt].

having-given glory[a] to-God

LEXICON—a. δόξα (LN 33.357, 87.23) (BAGD 3. p. 204): 'glory' [AB, BAGD, BECNT, HNTC, ICC2, LN (87.23), NICNT, NTC, WBC; KJV, NASB, NET, NIV, NLT, NRSV, REB], 'praise' [BAGD, LN; NCV, TEV], 'honor' [GW], 'all the credit' [CEV]. In conjunction with the verb 'to give' it means to glorify [LN (33.357)]. This phrase is translated 'he gave glory to God' [AB; NIV, NRSV, REB], 'he gave God the glory' [HNTC], 'by giving glory to God' [BECNT], 'giving glory to God'

[ICC2, NICNT, NTC, WBC; NET], 'in this he brought glory to God' [NLT], 'he gave praise to God' [TEV].

QUESTION—What is meant by 'having given glory to God'?

Abraham did what man in his primal sin failed to do, which is to live in total trust and dependence on God; by giving the proper response of a creature to the creator, which is trust, he glorified God [WBC]. Acknowledging God's truthfulness and goodness and submitting to his authority glorifies God [ICC2, NAC]. This phrase describes Abraham's response of grateful recognition to God [AB]. Abraham glorified God when he had the men of his household circumcised [Mor, NTC], as a sign of the covenant God would establish through Isaac [Mor]. It is to take him for what he truly is, almighty and faithful, being fully convinced that he is able to do and will do what he promised [Ho]. Abraham glorified God by having the conviction that God would do what he promised [Gdt]. To give glory to God is to acknowledge what he is and rely on his power and faithfulness, and is coordinate with the action of being fully persuaded of God's ability to fulfill his promise [Mu]. It means that he praised God for how he was going to fulfill the promise [SSA].

QUESTION—What is the temporal sense of the aorist participle 'having given'?

1. The action is viewed as related to or coincidental with his being strong in faith, but also comes as a result of having grown strong in faith; as he grew strong in faith, he glorified God because of it [NICNT]. Glorifying God is a further description of what it means to live in faith; by living in unconditional trust Abraham glorified God [WBC]. By trusting Abraham glorified God [AB]. Abraham glorified God by acknowledging God's truthfulness and goodness [ICC2]. Because his faith was strengthened, he gave glory to God by being fully persuaded that God was able to do and would do what he had promised [Ho]. Being fully persuaded of God's ability to fulfill his promise is coordinate with giving glory to God; both describe the state of mind and actions which were involved in Abraham's faith [Mu].

2. The aorist tense of this participle and the one in the following clause indicates action that happened previously and which then caused Abraham's faith to become strong. That is, because he glorified God and was confident that God could fulfill his promise, his faith became strong [BECNT]. Because he glorified God by obeying God's command to circumcise all the men in his household, he grew strong in faith [NTC].

4:21 and having-become-fully-convinced[a] that what he-had-promised[b] he-was able[c] also to-do.[d]

LEXICON—a. aorist pass. (deponent = act.) participle of πληροφορέω (LN **31.45**) (BAGD 2. p. 670): 'to be fully convinced' [AB, BAGD, HNTC, NICNT, WBC; NET, NRSV], 'to be absolutely convinced' [NLT], 'to be convinced' [REB], 'to be absolutely sure' [**LN;** TEV], 'to feel sure' [NCV], 'to be certain' [LN; CEV], 'to be fully assured or certain'

[BAGD, BECNT; NASB], 'to be fully persuaded' [ICC2, NTC; KJV, NIV], 'to be confident' [GW].
  b. perf. pass. (deponent = act.) indic. of ἐπαγγέλλομαι (LN 33.286) (BAGD 1.b. p. 281): 'to promise' [AB, BAGD, BECNT, HNTC, ICC2, LN, NICNT, NTC, WBC; all versions].
  c. δυνατός (LN 74.2) (BAGD 1.a.β. p. 208): 'able' [BAGD, LN, NICNT, NTC, WBC; KJV, NASB, NCV, NET, NLT, NRSV, REB, TEV], 'can' [LN; CEV], 'capable indeed' [AB], 'to have the power to do (something)' [HNTC, ICC2; NIV]. The phrase δυνατός ἐστιν καὶ ποιῆσαι 'he was able also to do' is translated 'God could do' [BECNT; CEV], 'God would do' [GW], 'he (God) had the power also to do' [HNTC], 'he had the power to do' [ICC2].
  d. aorist act. infin. of ποιέω (LN 42.7, 13.9): 'to do' [AB, BECNT, HNTC, ICC2, LN (42.7), NICNT, WBC; all versions except KJV, NASB], 'to perform' [LN (42.7), NTC; KJV, NASB], 'to carry out, to accomplish' [LN (42.7)], 'to bring about' [LN (13.9)].
QUESTION—What is the relation of the aorist participle to the previous verse?
Note that there is a certain amount of overlap possible between the positions listed below, and one does not rule out the other.
  1. The action of being fully convinced repeats and further describes the action of growing strong [NICNT].
  2. 'Being fully convinced' is a further description of Abraham's faith [AB, ICC2, WBC]. Abraham's faith was not just in what had been promised, but in God who had promised it [ICC2, WBC].
  3. It is coordinate to the action of giving glory to God; that is, being confident that God could fulfill his promise and glorifying God caused Abraham's faith to grow strong [BECNT].
  4. Because his faith was strengthened Abraham glorified God by believing his promise [Ho]. Abraham glorified God by being fully convinced that he would do what he had promised [Gdt].
  5. Giving glory to God and being fully persuaded are coordinate, and define the ways in which the strengthening of Abraham's faith was expressed [Mu].
  6. Because he was 'fully convinced' that God's promise would be fulfilled, he glorified God by circumcising all the males of his household as a sign of the covenant even long before Isaac was conceived [Mor].

4:22 Therefore also it-was-reckoned[a] to-him as[b] righteousness.[c]

TEXT—The word καί 'also' does not occur in some manuscripts. It is included by GNT with a C rating, indicating difficulty in deciding whether or not to place it in the text. It is included only by NICNT; KJV, NASB, NET, NLT. It is translated as 'also' [NICNT; NASB], 'and' [KJV, NLT], 'indeed' [NET]. The decision about including or omitting it may be due to stylistic concerns rather than textual concerns.

LEXICON—a. aorist pass. indic. of λογίζομαι (LN 57.227) (BAGD 1.a. p. 476): 'to be reckoned to' [ICC2, NICNT, NTC, WBC; NASB, NRSV], 'to be credited' [AB, BAGD; NET, NIV], 'to be credited to (one's) account, to be put to (one's) account' [LN], 'to be imputed (to him)' [KJV], 'to be regarded' [LN; GW], 'to be counted to' [BECNT, HNTC; REB], 'to be accepted as' [CEV, TEV]. This passive verb is also translated actively: 'So God accepted him' [CEV], 'God accepted Abraham's faith' [NCV], 'God declared him to be (righteous)' [NLT]. See this word at 4:11.

b. εἰς (LN 13.62): 'as' [AB, BECNT, NTC; NASB, NET, NIV, NRSV, REB, TEV], 'for' [HNTC, ICC2, LN (13.62), NICNT, WBC; KJV], not explicit [CEV, GW, NCV, NLT].

c. δικαιοσύνη (LN 88.13, 34.46) (BAGD 3. p. 197): 'righteousness' [BAGD, BECNT, HNTC, ICC2, LN (88.13, 34.46), NICNT, NTC, WBC; KJV, NASB, NET, NIV, NLT, NRSV, REB, TEV], 'uprightness' [AB], 'righteous, just, doing what God requires, or what is right' [LN (88.13)], 'to put right with, or to cause to be in a right relationship with' [LN (34.46)], 'to be accepted (by God)' [CEV], 'God's approval (of him)' [GW], 'to be made right with God' [NCV]. See this word also at 4:13.

QUESTION—What relationship is indicated by διό 'therefore'?

It draws a conclusion from 4:17–21; because Abraham had the kind of faith described here, he was reckoned as righteous before God [BECNT, SSA]. It draws a conclusion from the whole exposition from 4:3 on [WBC]. It draws a conclusion from 4:21, which is that because Abraham was fully convinced of God's faithfulness, God credited that to him as righteousness [Gdt]. It draws a conclusion primarily from the immediately preceding verses concerning Abraham's faith, but also from the discussion of Gen 15:6 that began in 4:3 [NICNT]. It draws a conclusion from the preceding section in which he has described the nature of Abraham's faith, and concludes that, because Abraham's faith was of this nature, God credited it to him as righteousness [ICC2, Mor]. Because Abraham's faith expected everything from God and trusted so completely, it was credited to him as righteousness [NTC]. It introduces a conclusion to his analysis of Abraham's faith given in the previous verses [Mu]. It draws a conclusion from what is said in 4:21; because he was fully persuaded that God was able to do what he promised, Abraham's faith was credited as righteousness [St].

DISCOURSE UNIT: 4:23–25 [NICNT]. The topic is the faith of Abraham and of the Christian.

4:23 Now[a] it-was- not -written[b] for-the-sake-of[c] him only that it-was-reckoned[d] to-him,

LEXICON—a. δέ (LN 89.124, 89.94): 'now' [BECNT, HNTC, NTC; KJV, NASB, NLT, NRSV], 'but' [HNTC, LN (89.124); CEV, GW, NET], 'and' [LN (89.94), NICNT], not explicit [AB; NCV, NIV, REB, TEV].

b. aorist pass. indic. of γράφω (LN 33.61) (BAGD 2.c. p. 166; 2.c. p. 167): 'to be written' [AB, BAGD, BECNT, HNTC, ICC2, LN, NICNT, NTC, WBC; all versions except NLT, NRSV, REB]. This clause is translated 'now this wonderful truth' [NLT], 'now the words…were written' [NRSV], 'the words' [REB]. See this word also at 4:17.

c. διά with accusative object (LN 90.38): 'for the sake of' [AB, BECNT, ICC2, LN, WBC; KJV, NASB, NET, NRSV], 'for the benefit of' [LN; NLT], 'for' [LN, NICNT, NTC; CEV, GW, NCV, NIV, TEV], 'on his account' [HNTC], 'on behalf of' [LN]. This preposition is translated as a verb 'to be meant to apply to' [REB]. See this word also at 4:16.

d. aorist pass. indic. of λογίζομαι (LN 57.227) (BAGD 1.a. p. 476): 'to be reckoned to' [ICC2, NICNT, NTC, WBC; NASB, NRSV], 'to be credited' [AB, BAGD; NET, NIV], 'to be credited to (one's) account, to be put to (one's) account' [LN], 'to be regarded' [LN; GW], 'to be counted to' [BECNT, HNTC; REB], 'to be imputed' [KJV], 'to be declared (to be righteous)' [NLT], 'to be accepted (as righteous)' [TEV], 'to be accepted' [NCV], not explicit [CEV]. See this word above at 4:22.

4:24 but also for-the-sake-of[a] us, to-whom it-is-going[b] to-be-reckoned,[c]

LEXICON—a. διά with accusative object (LN 90.38): 'for the sake of' [BECNT, ICC2, LN], 'on behalf of, for the benefit of' [LN], 'for' [AB, LN, NICNT, NTC, WBC; CEV, GW, KJV, NCV, NET, NLT, NRSV, TEV], '(to apply) to' [REB]. This phrase is translated 'but on ours also' [HNTC], 'but for ours also' [NRSV], 'but for our sakes also' [ICC2; NASB], 'but also for our sake' [NET], 'it was also for us' [NIV], 'it was for us too' [NLT]. See this word above at 4:23.

b. pres. act. indic. of μέλλω (LN 67.62) (BAGD 1.c.δ. p. 501): 'to be going to' [AB, LN, NICNT], 'to be about to' [LN], 'to be destined, must, will certainly be' [BAGD], 'to be' [HNTC, ICC2, NTC, WBC; CEV, GW, KJV, NASB, NET, NIV, NRSV, REB, TEV], 'must' [BAGD], '(those who) will be' [BECNT], not explicit [NCV, NLT].

c. pres. pass. infin. of λογίζομαι (LN 57.227) (BAGD 1.a. p. 476): 'to be reckoned to' [ICC2, NICNT, NTC, WBC; NASB, NRSV], 'to be credited' [AB, BAGD; NET], 'to be credited to (one's) account' [LN], 'to be put to (one's) account' [LN], 'to be regarded' [LN], 'to be counted to' [HNTC; REB], 'to be accepted' [CEV, TEV], 'to be imputed' [KJV]. This passive verb is translated as active with God as the subject: 'to count as' [BECNT], 'to accept' [NCV], 'to credit' [NIV], 'to declare to be (righteous)' [NLT]. This clause is translated 'since we will also be accepted' [CEV], '(Our faith) will be regarded (as God's approval)' [GW]. See this word above at 4:23.

QUESTION—How is the verb 'it is going (to be)' used here?

1. It is temporal; that is, at the future judgment righteousness will be credited to us [AB, HNTC, TH, WBC].

2. It is logical; whenever the condition is fulfilled the crediting of righteousness occurs [Gdt, Ho, ICC2, Mor, NICNT]. This justification is certain because it is based on a divine decision, and is a fact which Christians are to assume as the basis for their day to day living [ICC2]. Righteousness is appointed to be imputed to those who believe, just as it was to Abraham [Ho].

to-the-(ones) believing[a] on[b] the-(one) having-raised[c] Jesus our Lord from-(among)[d] dead (ones),[e]

LEXICON—a. pres. act. participle of πιστεύω (LN 31.85) (BAGD 2.a.δ. p. 661): 'to believe' [AB, BAGD, BECNT, HNTC, ICC2, LN, NICNT, NTC, WBC; all versions except GW, REB], 'to have faith in' [LN], 'to trust' [BAGD, LN], 'to rest one's faith on' [NTC]. The phrase τοῖς πιστεύουσιν 'to the ones believing' is translated 'because of our faith' [CEV], 'if we believe in God' [NLT], 'of us who believe' [GW], 'our faith too…faith in (the God)' [REB]. See this word at 4:18.

b. ἐπί with accusative object (LN 90.23) (BAGD III.1.b.ε. p. 289): 'on' [BAGD, ICC2, NTC; KJV], 'in' [AB, BAGD, BECNT, HNTC, LN, NICNT, WBC; all versions except KJV], 'with reference or respect to, concerning' [LN].

c. aorist act. participle of ἐγείρω (LN 23.94) (BAGD 1.a.β. p. 214): 'to raise' [AB, BAGD, BECNT, HNTC, ICC2, NICNT, NTC, WBC; all versions except CEV, GW, NLT], 'to raise to life' [BAGD, LN; CEV], 'to make live again' [LN], 'to bring back' [NLT]. The phrase 'having raised…from (among) dead (ones)' is translated 'brought…back to life' [GW]. The word means to cause someone to live again after having once died [LN].

d. ἐκ (LN 84.4): 'from' [AB, BECNT, HNTC, ICC2, LN, NICNT, NTC, WBC; all versions except CEV, GW], 'out from, out of' [LN], not explicit [CEV, GW].

e. νεκρός (LN 23.121): 'dead' [AB, BECNT, HNTC, ICC2, LN, NICNT, NTC, WBC; all versions except CEV, GW, TEV], 'death' [TEV]. The phrase ἐκ νεκρῶν 'from (among) dead ones' is not explicit [CEV, GW]. See this word also at 4:17.

4:25 who was-handed-over[a] because-of[b] our transgressions[c]

LEXICON—a. aorist pass. indic. of παραδίδωμι (LN 37.111) (BAGD 1.b. p. 615): 'to be handed over' [AB, BAGD, LN, NICNT, WBC; NRSV], 'to be handed over to die' [NLT], 'to be handed over to death' [GW], 'to be given over' [NET], 'to be given over to die' [TEV], 'to be given to die' [NCV], 'to be given up to death' [REB], 'to be delivered for' [KJV], 'to be delivered up' [BECNT, HNTC, ICC2, NTC; NASB], 'to be delivered over' [NIV], 'to be turned over to' [LN]. This clause is translated 'God gave Jesus to die for our sins' [CEV]. See this word also at 1:24.

b. διά with accusative object (LN 89.26, 90.44) (BAGD B.II.1. p. 181): 'because of' [BAGD, BECNT, HNTC, LN (89.26, 90.44), NICNT; GW,

NASB, NET, NLT, TEV], 'on account of' [LN (89.26, 90.44)], 'for' [AB, ICC2, NTC, WBC; CEV, KJV, NCV, NIV, NRSV, REB]. See this word above at 4:24.

    c. παράπτωμα (LN **88.297**) (BAGD 2.b. p. 621): 'transgression' [BAGD, **LN,** WBC; NASB, NET], 'sin' [BAGD, HNTC, LN; CEV, NCV, NIV, NLT, TEV], 'trespass' [AB, BECNT, ICC2, NICNT, NTC; NRSV], 'failure' [GW], 'offence' [KJV], 'misdeed' [REB]. This noun is translated 'sins we had committed' [HNTC].

QUESTION—Who is the agent of the passive verb παρεδόθη 'was handed over'?

The agent is God the Father [AB, BECNT, Gdt, Ho, ICC2, Mu, NICNT, St, TH, TNTC, WBC]. Both passive verbs are divine passives [AB, WBC], both the death and resurrection are attributed to the initiative of the father [St]. While he does not say here who delivered Jesus over, he does say in 8:32 that the Father did so [Mor]. It reflects the language and thought of Is 52:13–53:12 [BECNT, Gdt, Ho, ICC2, NAC, NICNT, NTC, TH, TNTC, WBC].

and was-raised[a] because-of[b] our justification.[c]

LEXICON—a. aorist pass. indic. of ἐγείρω (LN 23.94): 'to be raised' [AB, BECNT, ICC2, LN, NICNT, NTC, WBC; KJV, NASB, NCV, NET, NRSV], 'to be raised up' [HNTC], 'to be raised to life' [LN; CEV, NIV, REB, TEV], 'to be made to live again' [LN], 'to be raised from the dead' [NLT], 'to be brought back to life' [GW]. This passive verb is translated as active: 'he raised him to life' [CEV]. See this word above at 4:24.

    b. διά with accusative object (LN 90.44) (BAGD B.II.1. p. 181): 'because of' [BAGD, BECNT, HNTC, LN; NASB], 'on account of' [LN], 'for' [AB, ICC2, NICNT, NTC, WBC; KJV, NIV, NRSV, REB], 'for the sake of' [NET], 'so that' [CEV, GW], 'in order to' [LN; TEV]. The relation indicated by this preposition is expressed in translation by the use of the infinitive verb: 'to (make us right with)' [NCV, NLT].

    c. δικαίωσις (LN **34.46**) (BAGD p. 198): 'justification' [AB, BAGD, BECNT, HNTC, ICC2, NICNT, NTC; KJV, NASB, NET, NIV, NRSV, REB], 'acquittal' [BAGD], 'vindication' [BAGD, WBC]. The phrase διὰ τὴν δικαίωσιν ἡμῶν 'because of our justification' is translated 'so that we would be made acceptable to God' [CEV], 'because of the justification that was to be granted to us' [HNTC], 'in order to put us right with God' [**LN;** TEV], 'so that we would be made acceptable to God' [CEV], 'to make us right with God' [NCV, NLT], 'so that we could receive God's approval' [GW]. This word occurs only here and in 5:18 in the NT.

QUESTION—What relationship is indicated by διά 'because of' in this second clause?

    1. Christ was raised for the sake of our justification, that is, because of the need for it [AB, ICC1, ICC2, Mu, NAC, NICNT, St, WBC], or in order to

insure it [NTC]. It is used here in order to correspond rhetorically with the first half of the verse [AB, WBC].

- 1.1 In the first clause διά indicates cause or reason, but here it indicates purpose [AB, ICC2, NAC, NICNT, NTC, WBC]. This preposition has a retrospective function in the first line, looking back to our transgression as that which necessitated Christ's death, but in this line is has a prospective function, looking forward to the purpose to be achieved by his death [NAC, NICNT, NTC, St].
- 1.2 Both clauses are prospective, looking forward to the expected result of the action; he was handed over in order to atone for our sins and raised in order that we could be justified [Ho, Mu, TNTC].
- 2. Christ's resurrection was the result of his having procured our justification; once his death procured the expiation of our sins, we were justified, and by virtue of our solidarity with him, our justification transformed his death into life, his resurrection being the incarnation, as it were, of our justification [Gdt].
- 3. Christ was raised because what he had done had secured our justification and because God wanted to prove that fact to us. God wanted to show that he had accepted Christ's sacrificial death as the grounds for declaring us righteous [SSA].

QUESTION—What is the significance of connecting Christ's crucifixion with our transgressions and his resurrection with our justification?

- 1. His statement is structured this way for rhetorical balance [AB, NAC, WBC]. This is common in Hebrew poetic parallelism [Mor]. Both effects, forgiveness and justification, are to be ascribed to both actions [AB, NAC]. The use of διά in both clauses makes the parallelism of the two clauses clear [AB]. The resurrection is not the only cause of our justification [Mor]. Christ's death and resurrection are inseparably bound together, his death providing the basis for acquittal and his resurrection proving the redemptive reality of his death [NAC]. It does not mean that the resurrection had nothing to do with the atonement or that the crucifixion had nothing to do with justification [TNTC]. In Paul's thinking the death and resurrection of Christ are inseparable events, brought about mightily by God, by which we are brought into a right relationship with himself and by which our sins are forgiven [TH].
- 2. There is some distinction intended between the two clauses [ICC2, Mu, NICNT, NTC]. Paul is making a theological connection between the resurrection and our justification; the resurrection vindicated Christ and freed him from the influence of sin forever, thus providing for continuing victory over sins for those in union with Christ [NICNT]. We have union with Christ, but that only has efficacy if he is a living Christ [Mu]. Our sins made it necessary for him to be handed over, but he was raised up in order to assure us of the forgiveness of those sins and of our righteous status before God [NTC]. There is no rigid separation between the function of Christ's death and that of his resurrection, yet the distinction

ROMANS 4:25   353

between these two clauses is not strictly rhetorical because while Christ's atoning death was necessitated by our sins, it would not have secured our justification if not for the resurrection [ICC2]. Christ's death was necessary to satisfy divine justice and his resurrection was necessary to prove that this satisfaction had occurred, that his victory over sin was complete [Ho]. Christ's death is the payment of my debt, and his resurrection is the proof that the justification has occurred [Gdt].

DISCOURSE UNIT: 5:1–8:39 [AB, BECNT, ICC2, NICNT, NTC; CEV]. The topic is a new life for God's people [CEV], hope as a result of righteousness by faith [BECNT], the love of God further assures salvation to those justified by faith [AB], the life promised for those who are righteous by faith [ICC2], the assurance provided by the gospel: the hope of salvation [NICNT], justification by faith is effective, producing the desired results [NTC].

DISCOURSE UNIT: 5:1–6:23 [St]. God's people united in Christ.

DISCOURSE UNIT: 5:1–21 [ICC1, ICC2, NAC, NICNT, WBC; REB]. The topic is the results of faith [NAC], effects of righteousness by faith [ICC1], a life characterized by peace with God [ICC2], the hope of glory [NICNT], first conclusions: the new perspective of faith in relation to the individual and to humanity large [WBC], life in Christ [REB].

DISCOURSE UNIT: 5:1–11 [AB, BECNT, Gdt, GNT, HNTC, Ho, ICC2, Mor, Mu, NICNT, NTC, TNTC, WBC; CEV, GW, NCV, NET, NIV, NLT, NRSV, TEV]. The topic is the results of justification [GNT; NRSV], what it means to be acceptable to God [CEV], we are at peace with God because of Jesus [GW], peace with God [ICC2], right with God [NCV, TEV], the expectation of justification [NET], peace and joy [NIV], faith brings joy [NLT], assurance of hope [BECNT], justified Christians are reconciled to the God of love; they will be saved through hope of a share in the risen life of Christ [AB], the certainty of final salvation for believers [Gdt], peace with God and future glory [Ho], justification and salvation [HNTC], the effects of justification [Mor], the fruits of justification [Mu], from justification to salvation [NICNT], peace and assurance of complete salvation [NTC], new perspective on the believer's present and future [WBC], the blessings which accompany justification: peace, joy, hope, love [TNTC].

DISCOURSE UNIT: 5:1–8 [NAC]. The topic is peace and hope.

5:1 Therefore[a] having-been-justified[b] because-of[c] faith[d]

LEXICON—a. οὖν (LN 89.50) (BAGD 1.a. p. 593): 'therefore' [AB, BAGD, BECNT, LN, NICNT, NTC, WBC; KJV, NASB, NET, NIV, NLT, NRSV, REB], 'consequently, accordingly, so' [BAGD, LN], 'so then' [LN], 'then' [BAGD, HNTC, ICC2, LN], not explicit [CEV, GW, NCV, TEV].

   b. aorist pass. participle of δικαιόω (LN 34.46, 56.34) (BAGD 3.a. p. 197): 'to be justified' [AB, BAGD, BECNT, HNTC, ICC2, NICNT, NTC,

WBC; KJV, NASB, NIV, NRSV, REB], 'to be put right' [LN (34.46)], 'to be put right with God' [TEV], 'to be made right in God's sight' [NLT], 'to be acquitted' [LN (56.34)], 'to be declared righteous' [NET], 'to be made acceptable to God' [CEV], 'to have God's approval' [GW]. The sense of this passive participle relative to the clause is translated 'having been' [ICC2, NICNT, NTC, WBC; NASB], 'now that we are' [AB], 'now that we have (God's approval)' [GW], 'now that we have been' [REB], 'since we have been' [BECNT, HNTC; NCV, NET, NIV, NLT], 'since we are' [NRSV], 'being' [KJV], 'we have been' [CEV].

c. ἐκ with genitive object (LN 89.77, 90.12): 'because of' [GW], 'on the basis of' [HNTC, ICC2], 'by' [BECNT, LN (90.12), NICNT, NTC; CEV, KJV, NASB, NCV, NET, NLT, NRSV], 'by means of' [LN (89.77)], 'from' [LN (89.77), WBC], 'as a result of' [LN (90.12)], 'through' [AB; NIV, REB, TEV].

d. πίστις (LN 31.85, 31.102) (BAGD 2.d.α. p. 663): 'faith' [BAGD, LN (31.85, 31.102); all versions except NCV], 'our faith' [NCV].

QUESTION—What relationship is indicated by οὖν 'therefore'?

It marks a transition to a new section, one in which he introduces the consequences of justification [AB, Mor]. It introduces a conclusion about peace with God based on the fact of reconciliation [Ho]. It introduces his recapitulation of 4:22–24 about justification [WBC]. It introduces conclusions based on what he has said in the first four chapters [ICC2, NAC, NICNT, NTC], but particularly in 3:21–4:25 [Mu, NTC, SSA].

QUESTION—What relationship is expressed by the participle δικαιωθέντες 'having been justified'?

It expresses the reason for the following clause [AB, BECNT, HNTC, Ho, NAC, SSA, TH; NCV, NET, NIV, NLT, NRSV]: because we have been justified we therefore have peace with God.

QUESTION—Does the aorist participle primarily reflect a past action or present status?

It refers to the past action by which God has accepted believers into their current relationship and status [WBC]. Justification is a once-for-all act of acquitting a sinner that brings him into a new and permanent status [NICNT]. Those who have received justification enjoy the benefit of it now [NTC].

QUESTION—What relationship is indicated by ἐκ 'because of'?

It indicates the reason God has justified us [HNTC, ICC2, SSA, TH, WBC; GW]: we have been justified because we have faith. This refers to faith in what Jesus Christ has done [SSA]. Many translate this as though it indicates the means by which we have received justification [AB, BECNT, ICC1; all versions except GW]: we have been justified by faith. However the implied subjects of the events are different, i.e., God justifies us and we believe, so 'by' probably implies reason also.

we-have peace[a] with[b] God because-of/through[c] our Lord Jesus Christ,
LEXICON—a. εἰρήνη (LN 22.42) (BAGD 3. p. 227): 'peace' [AB, BAGD, BECNT, HNTC, ICC2, LN, NICNT, NTC; all versions].
  b. πρός with accusative object (LN **89.112**) (BAGD III.4.b. p. 710): 'with' [AB, BAGD, BECNT, HNTC, ICC2, **LN**, NICNT, NTC; all versions], 'toward' [BAGD], 'before' [BAGD, LN].
  c. διά with genitive object (LN 90.4): 'because of' [CEV, GW, NLT], 'through' [AB, BECNT, HNTC, ICC2, LN, NICNT, NTC; all versions except CEV, GW, NLT].
QUESTION—Does εἰρήνη 'peace' represent an objective reality or a subjective one?
It is primarily the objective state of not being at enmity with God, although subjective peace is not excluded [AB, BECNT, Ho, ICC2, Mor, NAC, NTC] and in fact follows [Ho]. It refers to a harmonious relationship between people and God [SSA, TH] and is the result of being reconciled with God [BECNT, NICNT, NTC, TH, TNTC] and being restored to his favor [NTC]. It implies the positive qualities of the Hebrew word *shalom*, which is the fullness of right relationship with God [AB, NICNT, WBC] and the salvation God will bring his people in the last days [NICNT, TH, WBC]. It is primarily objective, but must also include the resultant subjective experience as well [BECNT].
QUESTION—Does διά mean 'because of' or 'through' Jesus Christ?
  1. It indicates the reason peace has been provided [TH; CEV, GW, NLT]: we have peace because of our Lord Jesus Christ. We have peace with God because of what Jesus Christ has done [CEV, GW, NLT]. Jesus died and returned to life to make this peace possible [St]. Jesus Christ caused us to be at peace with God [TH].
  2. Many translate this proposition as 'through', which seems to indicate the means of providing peace [AB, BECNT, HNTC, ICC2, LN, NICNT, NTC, SSA; all versions except CEV, GW, NLT]: we have peace with God brought about by our Lord Jesus Christ. This does not indicate what we do as a means of obtaining peace with God, so probably an event is implied with Jesus Christ as the actor. 'We have a peaceful relationship restored with God by what our Lord Jesus Christ has done for us' [SSA].

5:2 **through[a] whom also we-have[b] access[c]**
LEXICON—a. διά with genitive object (LN 90.4): 'through' [AB, BECNT, HNTC, ICC2, LN, NTC, WBC; GW, NASB, NET, NIV, NRSV], 'by' [LN; KJV], not explicit [CEV, NCV, NLT, REB].
  b. perf. act. indic. of ἔχω (LN 57.1): 'to have' [BECNT, LN, NICNT, WBC; KJV], 'to gain' [AB, HNTC, NTC; NIV], 'to obtain' [ICC2; NASB, NET, NRSV], not explicit [CEV, NCV, NLT, REB]. This perfect form is translated as indicating a present condition: 'we have' [BECNT, NICNT, WBC]; as a past event: 'we have gained' [AB, HNTC, NTC; NIV], 'we have obtained' [ICC2; NASB, NET, NRSV].

c. προσαγωγή (LN 33.72) (BAGD p. 711): 'access' [AB, BAGD, BECNT, ICC2, LN, NICNT, NTC, WBC; KJV, NET, NIV, NRSV, REB], 'our access' [HNTC], 'our introduction' [NASB], 'approach' [BAGD, LN]. The phrase τὴν προσαγωγὴν ἐσχήκαμεν 'we have access' is translated '(Christ) has introduced us' [CEV], 'has brought us (into)' [NCV, NLT, TEV], 'we can approach God' [GW]. The implication of this word is not just that we have access, but that Christ introduces us [ICC1, Mor, SSA, St, TNTC].

QUESTION—What is indicated by the perfect tense of the verb ἐσχήκαμεν?

The perfect refers to the continuing situation [NICNT] or current condition of the believer [AB]. It refers to the initial experience of coming into God's presence as well as its ongoing availability and outworking [WBC]. The perfect tense signifies that they have peace because they have already had access [Ho].

by[a]-faith into[b] this grace[c] in[d] which we-stand[e]

TEXT—Some manuscripts omit the phrase τῇ πίστει 'by faith'. GNT includes it with a C rating, indicating difficulty in deciding whether or not to place it in the text. The phrase is omitted by HNTC, NICNT; CEV, GW, NCV, NRSV, REB.

LEXICON—a. There is no lexical entry in the Greek text for the preposition 'by', the relationship being indicated by the dative case of πίστις 'faith'. It is represented in translation as 'by (faith)' [BECNT, ICC2, NTC, WBC; KJV, NASB, NET, NIV, TEV], 'in (faith)' [AB], 'because of (our faith)' [NLT].

b. εἰς with accusative object (LN 84.22): 'into' [BECNT, LN, NICNT, NTC, WBC; KJV, NASB, NCV, NET, NIV, NLT, TEV], 'to' [AB, HNTC, ICC2; CEV, NRSV, REB], not explicit [CEV, GW].

c. χάρις (LN 88.66) (BAGD 3.b. p. 878): 'grace' [AB, BAGD, BECNT, HNTC, ICC2, LN, NICNT, NTC, WBC; KJV, NASB, NET, NIV, NRSV, REB], 'experience of God's grace' [TEV], 'blessing of God's grace' [NCV], 'kindness' [LN], 'undeserved kindness' [CEV], 'favor' [GW], 'place of highest privilege' [NLT].

d. ἐν with dative object (LN 13.8, 83.13): 'in' [AB, BECNT, HNTC, ICC2, LN (13.8, 83.13), NICNT, NTC, WBC; GW, NASB, NET, NIV, NRSV, REB, TEV], 'on' [CEV], not explicit [NCV]. The phrase 'in which' is translated 'wherein' [KJV], 'where' [NLT].

e. perf. act. indic. of ἵστημι (LN **13.29**, 17.1) (BAGD II.2.c.β. p. 382): 'to stand' [AB, BAGD, BECNT, HNTC, ICC2, LN (17.1), NICNT, NTC, WBC; GW, KJV, NASB, NET, NIV, NLT, NRSV], 'to take one's stand' [CEV], 'to remain firmly' [**LN** (13.29)], 'to live' [REB, TEV]. The phrase ἐν ᾗ ἑστήκαμεν 'in which we stand' is translated 'that we now enjoy' [NCV]. This perfect tense verb is translated as a present tense by AB, BECNT, HNTC, ICC2, NICNT, NTC, WBC, and all versions. It is translated with the temporal adverb 'now' by AB, HNTC, NIV, NLT.

QUESTION—How is the term 'grace' used here?

It is the realm or sphere of grace [BECNT, NICNT, St, WBC], the state of grace [HNTC, Ho, Mu, NTC], the state of being the objects of God's favor [ICC2]. Here 'grace' represents a state determined by the grace of God [HNTC, ICC1]. This state of grace is the state of justification [Ho, ICC2, Mu, NTC]. It is a status of high favor with God [TNTC]. It is the privileged position of being accepted by him [St]. It is the realm of grace but also implies power [BECNT]. It denotes the realm or sphere marked out by God's grace as well as the status characterized by his grace [WBC]. Access to grace is access to God, because grace is God's gracious giving of himself [Mor]. Grace represents an event, the experience of God's acting graciously toward us [SSA, TH].

QUESTION—What is indicated by the perfect tense of the verb ἵστημι 'to stand'?

The perfect tense has a present tense meaning and indicates the current condition or experience of the Christian [AB, BECNT, Gdt, HNTC, Mor, Mu, NICNT, SSA, St, TH; all versions]. It speaks of the fact that conversion results in a settled and established relationship with God as well as a settled and sustained commitment on the part of the one standing in that relationship [WBC].

and we-boast[a] in[b] hope[c] of-the glory[d] of God.

LEXICON—a. pres. mid. (deponent = act.) indic. of καυχάομαι (LN 33.368) (BAGD 1. p. 425): 'to boast' [AB, BAGD, LN, NICNT, WBC; NRSV, TEV], 'to brag' [GW], 'to exult' [BECNT, HNTC, ICC2, NTC; NASB, REB], 'to rejoice' [KJV, NET, NIV], 'to be happy' [CEV, NCV]. The phrase 'we boast in hope of the glory of God' is translated 'we confidently and joyfully look forward to sharing God's glory' [NLT].

b. ἐπί with dative object (LN 89.27) (BAGD II.1.b.γ. p. 287): 'in' [BECNT, HNTC, ICC2, NICNT, NTC, WBC; KJV, NASB, NET, NIV, NRSV, REB], 'on the basis of' [LN], 'because of' [LN; GW, NCV], 'of' [AB; TEV], not explicit [CEV, NLT].

c. ἐλπίς (LN 25.59) (BAGD 2.b. p. 253): 'hope' [AB, BAGD, BECNT, HNTC, ICC2, LN, NICNT, NTC, WBC; all versions except CEV, GW, NLT], 'confidence' [GW]. The phrase ἐπ' ἐλπίδι 'in hope' is translated 'we look forward to sharing in' [CEV, NLT]. This noun is translated with the definite article: 'the hope' [BECNT, NICNT, NTC; NCV, NET, REB, TEV]; without the definite article: 'hope' [ICC2, WBC; KJV, NASB]; with a possessive pronoun: 'our hope' [AB, HNTC; NRSV], 'our confidence' [GW]. For Paul, hope implies certainty [Mor, TNTC] and confidence [St]. It is a confident expectation in regard to something that will happen in the future [SSA].

d. δόξα (LN 79.18, 87.4) (BAGD 1.a. p. 203; 3. p. 204): 'glory' [AB, BAGD, BECNT, HNTC, ICC2, LN (79.18), NICNT, NTC, WBC; all versions], 'honor' [BAGD, LN (87.4)]. The genitive phrase 'of the glory' is translated 'for the glory' [AB], 'that we will receive glory' [GW], 'of sharing the glory' [NRSV], 'of sharing (God's) glory' [NCV, TEV], 'to sharing in the glory' [CEV], 'to sharing (God's) glory' [NLT], 'glory that is to be ours' [REB].

QUESTION—What relationship is indicated by καί 'and'?

It coordinates the phrases 'we have peace' and 'we exult' [AB, BECNT, Gdt, ICC2, Mor, Mu, NICNT].

QUESTION—In what sense do they 'boast'?

It means to have joyful confidence [HNTC, NICNT] or jubilation [ICC2], to exult [BECNT, HNTC, Ho, ICC2, Mor, NTC, St, WBC; NASB, REB], to rejoice [Gdt, Ho, Mu, NAC, SSA, TH; KJV, NET, NIV]. They have a confident hope within themselves [AB]. Boasting in the Lord is the truest form of worship [BECNT].

QUESTION—What is meant by the genitive construction ἐλπίδι τῆς δόξης τοῦ θεοῦ 'hope of the glory of God'?

The glory of God is the object they hope for [AB, BECNT, HNTC, Ho, ICC2].

1. Glory is the attribute possessed by God [BECNT, Ho, St, TH, TNTC; CEV, NCV, NLT, NRSV, REB, TEV]: we hope to share in the glory possessed by God. They expect to share in God's likeness and in his divine qualities and attributes [TH]. The glory spoken of refers to the full manifestation of God's own glory, and which will be reflected in his people [Mu].

2. Glory describes the glory God gives to us [HNTC, ICC1, ICC2, NAC, NICNT, NTC, TH, TNTC, WBC]: we hope to receive the glory God gives us. Fallen humanity may now be restored to the glory from which it fell [HNTC, ICC2, NAC, NICNT, TNTC, WBC]. God will transfigure man's whole being with his glory when we enter his presence [ICC1]. They expect to share in God's likeness and in his divine qualities and attributes [TH]. They expect future bliss [NTC].

5:3 And not only (this),[a] but we-boast[b] also in[c] tribulations,[d]

LEXICON—a. The phrase οὐ μόνον δέ is translated 'and not only this' [NICNT, NTC; NASB], 'not only this' [NET], 'yet not only that' [AB], 'and not only that' [BECNT; NRSV], 'and not only so' [ICC2; KJV], 'not only so' [WBC; NIV], 'further' [HNTC], 'but that's not all' [CEV, GW], 'more than this' [REB], not explicit [NCV, NLT, TEV].

b. pres. mid. (deponent = act.) indic. of καυχάομαι (LN 33.368) (BAGD 1. p. 425): 'to boast' [BAGD, LN], 'to glory' [BAGD], 'to pride oneself' [BAGD]. The indicative and subjunctive forms of this verb are identical. Here it is translated as indicative [BECNT, HNTC, ICC2, NICNT, NTC, WBC; all versions]: we boast. It is also translated as a hortatory subjunctive [AB]: let us boast. This entire clause is translated 'we gladly suffer' [CEV]. See this word in 5:2.

c. ἐν with dative object (LN 13.8, 89.5): 'in' [BECNT, HNTC, ICC2, LN (13.8, 89.5), NICNT, NTC, WBC; KJV, NASB, NET, NIV, NRSV, REB], 'about' [LN (89.5)], 'of' [AB; TEV], 'with (our)' [NCV], not explicit [CEV]. The phrase 'in tribulations' is translated 'when we are suffering' [GW], 'when we run into problems' [NLT].
d. θλῖψις (LN 22.2) (BAGD 1. p. 362): 'tribulation' [BAGD, NICNT; KJV, NASB], 'affliction' [AB, BAGD, BECNT, HNTC, ICC2, WBC], 'suffering' [LN, NTC; NET, NIV, NRSV], 'present suffering' [REB], 'trouble' [NCV, TEV], 'trouble and suffering' [LN], 'oppression' [BAGD], 'persecution' [LN], 'problems and trials' [NLT]. This noun is also translated as a verb: 'to suffer' [CEV, GW]. The plural definite article ταῖς is translated as the possessive pronoun 'our' [AB, BECNT, HNTC, NICNT, NTC; NASB, NCV, NIV, NRSV, REB].

QUESTION—What is the referent to the phrase 'and not only this'?

It refers to their boast or confidence [AB, BECNT, HNTC, Ho, ICC2, Mu, NAC, NICNT, SSA]: not only do we boast the hope of the glory of God, but we also boast in tribulations. Not only do they have this confidence, they do so even in the face of affliction [AB]. Not only do they glory in what they hope for in the future, they glory in the tribulations of the present [Mu].

QUESTION—What relationship is indicated by ἐν 'in'?

1. It indicates the basis for boasting [AB, BECNT, Gdt, Ho, ICC2, Mor, NAC, NICNT, NTC, St, TH, TNTC, WBC]: we boast because we experience tribulations. We understand that suffering is the path to glory in the future and to maturity in the present [St]. Afflictions are the object of our boasting because we regard them to be the grounds for confidence in our redeemed status [NICNT].
2. It indicates the situation within which the exulting takes place [SSA]: we boast even when we have tribulations.
3. It indicates the basis for boasting as well as the situation within which the boasting takes place [NICNT, NTC]: we boast because of and when we experience tribulations.

QUESTION—Are the 'tribulations' persecution because of Christian faith or difficulty in general?

1. It refers to troubles in general [AB, BECNT, Mor, NICNT, WBC]. All the suffering that Christians experience occurs because Satan dominates this present age [NICNT]. It refers to the sufferings characteristic of the end time [HNTC, TH, WBC].
2. It is tribulation for Christ and the gospel [Ho, Mu, NTC, St]. The tribulation is due to the opposition and persecution of those who are hostile to God's people [St].
3. It refers to all trouble, including but not limited to suffering because of one's faith in Christ [SSA].

knowing[a] **that tribulation produces**[b] **endurance,**[c]

LEXICON—a. perf. (with pres. meaning) act. participle of οἶδα (LN 28.1, 32.4): 'to know' [AB, BECNT, HNTC, ICC2, LN (28.1), NICNT, NTC, WBC; all versions], 'to understand' [LN (32.4)]. This perfect participle is translated as indicating a causal relation: 'because we know' [BECNT, HNTC, NTC; CEV, NCV, NIV, REB, TEV], 'since we know' [AB], 'for we know' [NLT].

b. pres. mid. (deponent = act.) indic. of κατεργάζομαι (LN 13.9, 42.17) (BAGD 2. p. 421): 'to produce' [BAGD, BECNT, HNTC, NICNT, WBC; NCV, NET, NIV, NRSV, TEV], 'to bring about' [BAGD, LN (13.9), NTC; NASB], 'to accomplish' [LN (42.17)], 'to work' [ICC2; KJV], 'to create' [GW], 'to make for' [AB], 'to be a source of' [REB]. The phrase ὑπομονὴν κατεργάζεται 'produces endurance' is translated 'helps us to endure' [CEV], 'help us learn to endure' [NLT].

c. ὑπομονή (LN 25.174) (BAGD 1. p. 846): 'endurance' [AB, BAGD, BECNT, HNTC, ICC2, LN, NICNT; GW, NET, NRSV, REB, TEV], 'patience' [BAGD, WBC; KJV, NCV], 'perseverance' [BAGD, NTC; NASB, NIV], 'fortitude' [BAGD], 'steadfastness' [BAGD]. This noun is translated as a verb: 'to endure' [CEV, NLT]. It refers to holding out under trials [ICC1]. It is the spiritual fortitude that bears up under suffering [NICNT].

QUESTION—What relationship is expressed by the participle εἰδότες 'knowing'?

It expresses the reason we boast in tribulation [AB, BECNT, Gdt, HNTC, NICNT, NTC, SSA, TH; CEV, NCV, NIV, NLT, REB, TEV]: we boast in tribulations because we know that tribulations lead to the following qualities. The reasons for boasting are fourfold: development of endurance (5:3), proven character (5:4), hope (5:4), and not being disappointed (5:5) [SSA].

5:4 **and endurance (produces) proven-character,**[a] **and proven-character hope.**[b]

LEXICON—a. δοκιμή (LN 65.12) (BAGD 1. p. 202): 'proven character' [NICNT, NTC; NASB], 'tested character' [BECNT], 'tried character' [HNTC], 'strength of character' [NLT], 'character' [AB, BAGD, WBC; CEV, GW, NCV, NET, NIV, NRSV], 'provedness' [ICC2], 'experience' [KJV], 'approval' [REB], 'God's approval' [TEV]. This word is used only by Paul in the NT, and its use is unknown prior to Paul. It is associated with the verb δοκιμάζω 'to test' [Mor]. It is the quality of being approved [BAGD, SSA]. Both testing and approving are involved and it is one's character that is approved [TH]. It refers to a character that results from enduring trials [ICC1]. It is God who approves [SSA, TH].

b. ἐλπίς (LN 25.59) (BAGD 2.b. p. 253): 'hope'. See this word at 2.5.

QUESTION—What is this hope?

It is the same hope of God's glory that is mentioned in 5:3 [BECNT, Gdt, Ho, ICC2, NTC, SSA, WBC]. It is hope in God, in the fulfillment of his promises, and of his glory [ICC2]. It is the hope of eternal blessing [NICNT].

5:5 And hope does- not -disappoint,[a]

LEXICON—a. pres. act. indic. of καταισχύνω (LN 25.194) (BAGD 3.a. p. 410): 'to disappoint' [AB, BAGD, NTC; all versions except GW, KJV, REB], 'to put to shame' [HNTC, ICC2, LN, NICNT, WBC], 'to make ashamed' [KJV], 'to shame (someone)' [BECNT]. This clause is translated 'we're not ashamed to have this confidence' [GW], 'such hope is no fantasy' [REB]. This verb form could have either a present tense or a future tense meaning, depending on how it is accented. It is translated as a present tense by AB, HNTC, ICC2, NTC, WBC; GW, KJV, NASB, NET, NIV, NRSV, REB, TEV; as a future tense by BECNT, NICNT, as well as by CEV, NCV, NLT, though possibly for stylistic reasons only.

QUESTION—Does καταισχύνω 'disappoint' focus on the believer's embarrassment or shame before others or on the believer's own disappointment?

1. It is the shame or embarrassment of having one's hope disappointed [AB, BECNT, HNTC, Ho, ICC2, Mor, Mu, SSA, TNTC, WBC]: this hope is so sure that we will never be embarrassed by having hoped in something false. Christians would be put to shame if what they built their lives and hope for eternal blessing upon should turn out to be inadequate [NICNT].
2. It is the disappointment of having one's hope proven to be baseless [Gdt, ICC1, NAC, NICNT, NTC, St, TH]: this hope is so sure that we will never be disappointed by not having it turn out. The hope is not illusory [ICC1, St].

because the love of God has-been-poured-out[a] **into**[b] **our hearts**[c]

LEXICON—a. perf. pass. indic. of ἐκχέω (LN **90.89**) (BAGD 2. p. 247): 'to be poured out' [AB, BAGD, BECNT, HNTC, ICC2, **LN**, NICNT, NTC, WBC; NASB, NET], 'to be poured' [GW, NRSV], 'to be shed abroad' [KJV]. This passive verb is translated actively with God as the actor and love as the object: 'God has poured out his love' [NCV, NIV, TEV]; with God's love as the actor and hearts as the object: 'God's love has flooded our hearts' [REB]. This entire phrase is translated 'our hearts have been made to fully experience the love of God' [**LN**]. This phrase is translated with the one following as 'because God has given us the Holy Spirit, who fills our hearts with his love' [CEV], 'for we know how dearly God loves us, because he has given us the Holy Spirit to fill our hearts with his love' [NLT].

b. ἐν with dative object (LN 83.13): 'into' [AB, BECNT, NICNT, NTC; GW, KJV, NIV, NRSV, TEV], 'in' [HNTC, ICC2, LN, WBC; NET], 'within' [NASB], not explicit [CEV, NCV, NLT, REB].

c. καρδία (LN 26.3) (BAGD 1.b.θ. p. 404): 'heart' [AB, BAGD, BECNT, HNTC, ICC2, LN, NICNT, NTC, WBC; all versions].

362   ROMANS 5:5

QUESTION—What relationship is indicated by ὅτι 'because'?
  This is proof for the preceding clause [AB, Gdt, Ho, ICC2, NAC, NICNT, SSA, WBC]: hope does not disappoint us because God's love has been poured out into our hearts. The fact that God loves us is a proof of the security of our hope [ICC2]. The certainty of God's love is the guarantee of Christian hope [AB]. Hope is rewarded by a fresh awareness of God's great love [NAC]. The revelation of God himself and of his love is the source of hope [Gdt].

QUESTION—What relationship is indicated by the genitive τοῦ θεοῦ in the phrase ἡ ἀγάπη τοῦ θεοῦ 'the love of God'?
  It refers to the love God has for people [AB, BECNT, Gdt, HNTC, Ho, ICC1, ICC2, Mor, Mu, NICNT, NTC, SSA, TH, WBC; CEV, GW, NCV, NIV, NLT, NRSV, REB, TEV].

QUESTION—What is meant by God's love for us being poured into our hearts?
  It means that we are made deeply aware that God loves us [St], we have a sense of God's love for us [ICC1]. God has shown us how much he loves us [TH], he has communicated to us that he loves us [SSA]. It is an act of revelation that leaves a permanent impression of being loved by God [Gdt]. The Holy Spirit brings an inner subjective certainty of being loved by God [NICNT]. The verb 'pour out' indicates that it is done lavishly or in abundance [Ho, ICC2, Mor, NICNT, NTC].

through[a] (the) Holy Spirit the-(one) having-been-given[b] to-us.
LEXICON—a. διά with genitive object (LN 90.4) (BAGD A.III.2.b.δ. p. 180): 'through' [AB, BAGD, BECNT, HNTC, ICC2, LN, WBC; NET, NRSV, REB], 'by' [LN, NTC; GW, KJV, NASB, NIV], 'by means of' [BAGD; TEV], not explicit [CEV, NLT].
  b. aorist pass. participle of δίδωμι (LN 57.71): 'to be given' [AB, BECNT, HNTC, ICC2, LN, NTC, WBC; GW, KJV, NASB, NET, NRSV]. This passive verb is translated as active: 'God has given' [CEV, NCV], 'he has given' [NIV, NLT, REB]. The phrase 'the Holy Spirit the one having been given to us' is translated 'the Holy Spirit, who is God's gift to us' [TEV].

QUESTION—What is the relation between the action of pouring out of God's love and the Holy Spirit?
  The preposition διά 'through' indicates the means by which God pours out his love into our hearts [NTC]. The Spirit is the secondary agent [TH]. The Holy Spirit is the one who causes us to be aware of God's love [ICC2, NICNT, St]. The Spirit causes us to recognize and rejoice in God's love [ICC2]. This is shown in the translations 'God has given us the Holy Spirit, who fills our hearts with his love' [CEV], 'we know how dearly God loves us, because he has given us the Holy Spirit to fill our hearts with his love' [NLT]. The Holy Spirit both fills people with the love of God and communicates it [BECNT, Ho, Mu, St]. God communicates his love to us by his Spirit working within us to assure us that God loves us [SSA].

QUESTION—What is the significance of adding that the Holy Spirit has been given to us?

The aorist tense 'has been given' refers to consequence of justification at the time of conversion [St]. Because believers have received the Holy Spirit they are enabled to experience and become aware of the love of God [HNTC, ICC1, ICC2, SSA, WBC]. The giving of the Holy Spirit is the proof of God's love as well as the medium of its outpouring [AB].

5:6 **For while-ᵃ we- stillᵇ -being helpless,ᶜ at (the right)-timeᵈ Christ died forᵉ ungodlyᶠ (persons).**

TEXT—Instead of ἔτι γάρ 'for still' some manuscripts read εἴ γε 'if indeed' and other manuscripts read εἰς τί γάρ 'for, for what?' GNT selects the reading ἔτι γάρ 'for still' with a C rating, indicating difficulty in deciding which variant to place in the text. It is not clear which, if any, of the versions or commentaries take the variant reading.

LEXICON—a. There is no lexical entry for this word in the Greek text, the temporal element being implied by the presence of ἔτι 'still' with the present participle ὄντων 'being' in the genitive absolute construction ὄντων ἡμῶν ἀσθενῶν 'we being helpless'. It is represented in translation as 'while' [AB, BECNT, HNTC, NICNT, NTC, WBC; GW, NASB, NET, NRSV, REB], 'when' [ICC2; KJV, NCV, NIV, NLT, TEV], 'at a time when' [CEV].

b. ἔτι (LN 67.128) (BAGD 1.a.β. p. 315): 'still' [AB, BAGD, BECNT, HNTC, ICC2, LN, NICNT, NTC, WBC; GW, NASB, NET, NIV, NRSV, REB, TEV], 'yet' [BAGD, LN; KJV], not explicit [CEV, NCV, NLT]. This word actually occurs both at the beginning and at the end of the first clause, possibly for emphasis [AB, BECNT, ICC2, Mor, NAC, NTC]. It is translated only once by all versions and commentaries.

c. ἀσθενής (LN **22.3**, 79.69, **88.117**) (BAGD 2.b. p. 115): 'weak' [BAGD, BECNT, LN (79.69), NICNT, WBC; NRSV], 'helpless' [AB, **LN** (22.3); CEV, GW, NASB, NET, REB, TEV], 'utterly helpless' [NLT], 'powerless' [HNTC, ICC2, NTC; NIV], 'without strength' [KJV], 'without moral strength' [LN (88.117)], 'morally weak' [BAGD, **LN** (88.117)] 'unable to help ourselves' [NCV].

d. καιρός (LN 67.1) (BAGD 1., 2. p. 395): 'time' [BAGD, LN; CEV], 'right time, proper time' [BAGD]. The phrase κατὰ καιρόν is translated 'at the right time' [BECNT; GW, NASB, NET, NRSV], 'at just the right time' [NICNT; NIV, NLT], 'at the appointed time' [AB, ICC2, NTC; REB], 'at the time that God chose' [TEV], 'at that time' [WBC], 'in due time' [KJV], 'at the due moment' [HNTC], 'at the moment of our need' [NCV]. The temporal adverb ἔτι 'still' is conflated with the phrase κατὰ καιρόν and translated 'at a time when' [CEV].

e. ὑπέρ with genitive object (LN 90.36) (BAGD 1.a.ε. p. 838): 'for' [AB, BAGD, BECNT, HNTC, ICC2, LN, NICNT, NTC, WBC; all versions].

f. ἀσεβής (LN **53.11**) (BAGD 1. p. 114): 'ungodly' [BECNT, LN, NTC, WBC; KJV, NASB, NET, NIV, NRSV], 'ungodly men' [ICC2], 'us ungodly men' [HNTC], 'many ungodly people' [GW], 'godless' [AB, BAGD], 'godless people' [NICNT], 'wicked' [REB, TEV], 'us sinners' [NLT]. This word is translated as a phrase: 'we were living against God' [NCV]. The phrase ὄντων ἡμῶν ἀσθενῶν…ὑπὲρ ἀσεβῶν 'while we were helpless…for godless persons' is translated 'at a time when we were helpless and sinful' [CEV].

QUESTION—What relationship is indicated by γάρ 'for'?

It introduces his argument in 5:6–8 for the absolute and abundant love of God just discussed in 5:5 [Gdt, HNTC, Ho, NICNT]. It gives the objective grounds in 5:6–8 for the subjective experience of the love of God described in 5:5 [BECNT, NTC]. It introduces 5:6–8 as grounds for the hope spoken of in 5:1–5 [WBC]. It introduces 5:6 as an explanation and confirmation concerning what he said about the love of God in 5:5 [Mu].

QUESTION—Does ἀσθενής refer to human weakness in general or specifically to moral weakness?

It is a moral helplessness to do anything to save oneself [AB, BAGD, HNTC, ICC1, ICC2, Mor, NTC, SSA, St, TH] and is translated 'helpless' [AB, **LN** (22.3); CEV, GW, NASB, NET, NLT, REB, TEV]. It is parallel to 'godless' in this verse and 'sinners' in 5:8 [BECNT, Mu, NICNT]. It is the total incapacity for good [Gdt]. It primarily refers to weakness in contrast to the might of the creator, but it is also the first of a string of four words which increasingly refer to moral weakness [WBC]. It is the weakness of sinfulness and the inability to do what is spiritually good [Ho].

QUESTION—What is the phrase κατὰ καιρόν 'at the right time' connected with?

It is connected with ἀπέθανεν 'died' [AB, BAGD, BECNT, HNTC, Ho, ICC2, Mor, NTC, SSA]: Christ died at the right or appointed time.

QUESTION—Does καιρός 'time' indicate an appointed time or an opportune time?

1. It is the appointed time [AB, HNTC, Ho, ICC2, NTC, SSA, TH; TEV]. It was the time appointed by God for him to die [Ho, SSA].
2. It is the opportune time in the sense of being a time of great need on the part of sinful people [ICC1, NICNT, TNTC; CEV, NCV]. Christ chose the right time in the world's history [ICC1]. It was the very time when we were weak [ICC1, NICNT; CEV, NCV].
3. It is both appointed as well as opportune [BECNT, Gdt, Mor, Mu, NAC, WBC]. It was the last hour, when the time of God's patience was at its limit and he must either judge or pardon [Gdt].

5:7 For hardly[a] will- someone -die for[b] (a) righteous[c] (person);

TEXT—Instead of μόλις 'hardly' some manuscripts read μόγις 'with difficulty'. GNT does not deal with this variant. Μόγις 'with difficulty' is read by TEV.

LEXICON—a. μόλις (LN 78.41) (BAGD 2. p. 526): 'hardly' [BAGD, LN; NASB, REB], 'hardly ever' [NICNT], 'seldom' [BECNT], 'scarcely' [BAGD, HNTC, ICC2, LN, NTC; KJV], 'not readily' [BAGD], 'rarely' [NET, NRSV], 'very rarely' [NIV], 'only rarely' [BAGD, WBC], 'it is rare' [GW], 'rare indeed is it' [AB]. The phrase μόλις...τις ἀποθανεῖται 'hardly...someone will die' is translated 'no one is really willing to die' [CEV], 'very few people will die' [NCV], 'no one is likely to die' [NLT]. Μόλις indicates how rare this happens [NICNT]. TEV takes the variant μόγις: 'it is a difficult thing'.
  b. ὑπέρ with genitive object (LN 90.36) (BAGD 1.a.ε. p. 838): 'for' [AB, BAGD, BECNT, HNTC, ICC2, LN, NICNT, NTC, WBC; all versions except NCV], 'to save the life of' [NCV].
  c. δίκαιος (LN 88.12) (BAGD 1.a. p. 195): 'righteous' [BAGD, BECNT, HNTC, ICC2, LN, NICNT, NTC, WBC; KJV, NASB, NET, NIV, NRSV], 'upright' [AB], 'godly' [GW], 'good' [NLT], 'just' [LN; TEV], 'honest' [CEV], not explicit [NCV].
QUESTION—What relationship is indicated by γάρ 'for'?
  It indicates a further amplification of the subject of Christ dying for the ungodly [SSA]. It explains how dying for sinners is proof of God's love [ICC1, NICNT].

though^a for^b the good^c (person) perhaps^d someone even would-dare^e to-die;
LEXICON—a. γάρ (LN 89.23) (BAGD 4. p. 152): 'though' [AB, NTC; CEV, NASB, NET, NIV, NLT, NRSV, REB], 'although' [BECNT, NICNT; NCV], 'for' [HNTC, LN, WBC], 'yet' [KJV], 'it may even be that' [TEV], 'but' [BAGD], not explicit [ICC2; GW].
  b. ὑπέρ with genitive object (LN 90.36) (BAGD 1.a.ε. p. 838): 'for' [AB, BAGD, BECNT, ICC2, LN, NICNT, NTC, WBC; all versions], 'on behalf of' [HNTC, LN].
  c. ἀγαθός (LN 88.1) (BAGD 1.b.α. p. 3): 'good' [BAGD, BECNT, HNTC, LN, NICNT, NTC, WBC; all versions except CEV, NLT], 'really good' [AB], 'truly good' [CEV], 'especially good' [NLT], 'benefactor' [ICC2]. This word refers to good moral qualities [BAGD, LN].
  d. τάχα (LN **71.12**) (BAGD p. 806): 'perhaps' [BAGD, BECNT, ICC2, LN, WBC; NASB, NCV, NET], 'possibly' [BAGD, LN], 'maybe' [LN; GW], 'peradventure' [KJV], 'it may be' [**LN**], 'conceivably' [AB], 'even' [HNTC]. The uncertainty suggested by this word is conveyed through the use of an adverb or adverbial phrase: 'might' [NICNT; TEV], 'might possibly' [NTC; NIV], 'perhaps...might possibly' [NET], 'conceivably might' [AB], 'might actually' [NRSV, REB], 'might (be willing)' [CEV, NLT].
  e. pres. act. indic. of τολμάω (LN 25.161) (BAGD 1.a. p. 821): 'to dare' [BAGD, BECNT, HNTC, LN, NICNT, NTC, WBC; KJV, NASB, NET, NIV, NRSV, TEV], 'to have the courage' [AB, BAGD; GW], 'to bring

oneself to do something' [ICC2], 'to brave (death)' [REB], 'to be willing' [CEV, NLT], not explicit [NCV].

QUESTION—What relationship is expressed by γάρ 'though'?

It expresses concession [AB, BECNT, NICNT, NTC, SSA, St; CEV, NASB, NCV, NET, NIV, NLT, NRSV, REB]: though. The conjunction γάρ does not in itself mean 'though' but here the context demands the idea of concession [SSA, St]. Or, Paul virtually repeats himself with another γάρ 'for' [HNTC, WBC].

QUESTION—Does Paul imply any contrast between the 'righteous' person and the 'good' person?

1. There is a contrast [AB, BECNT, Ho, ICC1, ICC2, Mor, NAC, SSA, St, TH, WBC]. The righteous person has a cold, unattractive uprightness [St], he merely commands respect [Ho]. The 'good' person is a benefactor [AB, BECNT, ICC2], someone with a warms and appealing goodness [St] and people respond to him with affection [Ho]. The good person's actions cause him to be held in higher esteem than the righteous person [SSA]. There is a distinction, but 'the good' refers not to a good person but to a good or noble cause [Gdt].
2. They are used more or less synonymously [Mu, NTC, TNTC]. Perhaps there are a few righteous or good people for whom one might die [TNTC].

5:8 but[a] God demonstrates[b] his-own love for[c] us,

LEXICON—a. δέ (LN 89.124): 'but' [BECNT, HNTC, ICC2, LN, NICNT, NTC, WBC; all versions], 'yet' [AB], not explicit [GW].

b. pres. act. indic. of συνίστημι (LN **28.49**) (BAGD p. 790; I.1.c. p. 790): 'to demonstrate' [BAGD, BECNT, LN, NTC, WBC; GW, NASB, NET, NIV], 'to show' [BAGD, **LN**; CEV, NCV, NLT, TEV], 'to show forth' [AB], 'to prove' [HNTC, ICC2; NRSV], 'to commend' [NICNT; KJV]. This verb is translated as a noun: 'that is God's proof' [REB].

c. εἰς with accusative object (LN **90.59**) (BAGD 4.c.β. p. 229): 'for' [AB, BECNT, HNTC, ICC2, LN, NICNT, NTC; GW, NCV, NET, NIV, NLT, NRSV, REB], 'toward' [**LN**; KJV, NASB], 'to' [LN, WBC]. The phrase τὴν ἑαυτοῦ ἀγάπην εἰς ἡμᾶς 'his own love for us' is translated 'how much he loved us' [CEV, TEV].

QUESTION—With which word is εἰς ἡμᾶς 'for us' to be taken?

1. It is to be taken with 'love' [AB, BECNT, HNTC, ICC2, Mor, NICNT, NTC, SSA, St, TH, WBC; all versions]: his love for us.
2. It is to be taken with 'demonstrates' [ICC1]: he demonstrates to us his love.

(in) that[a] while[b] we- still -being sinners[c] Christ died for[d] us.

LEXICON—a. ὅτι (LN 91.15) (BAGD 1.c. p. 589): 'in that' [AB, BAGD, BECNT, NICNT, WBC; KJV, NASB, NET, NRSV], 'that' [LN; TEV], 'in this' [NIV], 'in this, that' [NTC], 'in this way' [NCV], 'by the fact that' [HNTC, ICC2], 'namely that, namely, that is' [LN], not explicit [GW]. The phrase συνίστησιν...ὅτι 'demonstrates...in that' is translated

ROMANS 5:8   367

'that is God's proof' [REB]. The phrase ὅτι...Χριστὸς ὑπὲρ ἡμῶν ἀπέθανεν 'that...Christ died' is translated 'by having Christ die' [CEV], 'by sending Christ to die' [NLT].

b. There is no lexical entry in the Greek text for this word, the temporal element 'while' being implied, as in 5:6, by ἔτι 'still' and the present participle ὄντων 'being' in the genitive absolute phrase ἔτι ἁμαρτωλῶν ὄντων ἡμῶν 'while we still being sinners'. This temporal element is represented in translation as 'while' [AB, BECNT, HNTC, NICNT, NTC, WBC; all versions except CEV], 'when' [NTC], not explicit [CEV].

c. ἁμαρτωλός (LN 88.294, 88.295) (BAGD 2. p. 44): 'sinner' [AB, BAGD, BECNT, HNTC, ICC2, LN (88.295), NICNT, NTC, WBC; all versions except CEV], 'sinful' [LN (88.294); CEV].

d. ὑπέρ with genitive object (LN 90.36) (BAGD 1.a.ε. p. 838): 'for' [AB, BECNT, HNTC, ICC2, LN, NICNT, NTC, WBC; all versions].

QUESTION—What relationship is indicated by the preposition ὑπέρ 'for'?

1. It speaks of a substitutionary or vicarious action [AB, Ho, NTC, St]: he died in our place.
2. It contains the idea of representation as well as of substitution [BECNT, Mor, NICNT].
3. It means that Christ died for the sake of [TH] or on behalf of sinners [Gdt, ICC2, SSA]. It neither implies nor excludes the idea of substitution [Gdt].

DISCOURSE UNIT: 5:9–11 [NAC]. The topic is reconciliation.

5:9 Much more[a] therefore now having-been-justified[b] by[c] his blood[d]

LEXICON—a. The phrase πολλῷ...μᾶλλον is translated 'much more' [BAGD, HNTC, ICC2, NTC; KJV, NASB, NET], 'how much more' [NICNT, WBC; NIV, TEV], 'certainly' [NLT], 'all the more certainly' [AB; REB], 'we are even more certain' [GW], 'surely' [NCV], 'much more surely' [NRSV]. The phrase πολλῷ οὖν μᾶλλον 'therefore much more' is translated 'it surely follows, therefore' [BECNT], 'but there is more!' [CEV]. The dative πολλῷ expresses degree of difference [BAGD].

b. aorist pass. participle of δικαιόω (LN 34.46, 56.34) (BAGD 3.a. p. 197): 'to be justified' [AB, BAGD, BECNT, HNTC, ICC2, NICNT, NTC, WBC; GW, KJV, NASB, NIV, NRSV, REB], 'to be put right' [LN (34.46)], 'to be put right with God' [TEV], 'to be made right with God' [NCV], 'to be made right in God's sight' [NLT], 'to be declared righteous' [NET], 'to be acquitted' [LN (56.34)]. This passive participle is also translated as an active verb phrase: 'God has accepted us' [CEV]. This participle is translated as indicating a logical relationship: 'since' [AB, BECNT, HNTC, ICC2, NTC; GW, NIV, NLT, REB], 'because' [NCV, NET].

c. ἐν with dative object (LN 89.76) (BAGD III.1.a. p. 260): 'by' [AB, BAGD, BECNT, ICC2, LN, NTC, WBC; all versions except CEV, GW], 'through' [NICNT], 'at the cost of' [HNTC], not explicit [GW]. The

phrase ἐν τῷ αἵματι αὐτοῦ 'by his blood' is translated 'because Christ sacrificed his life's blood' [CEV].
  d. αἷμα (LN 8.64, **23.107**) (BAGD 2.b. p. 23): 'blood' [AB, BAGD, BECNT, HNTC, ICC2, LN (8.64), NICNT, NTC, WBC; GW, KJV, NASB, NET, NIV, NRSV], 'the blood of Christ' [NLT], 'blood of Christ's death' [NCV], '(his) life's blood' [CEV], 'death' [**LN** (23.107)], 'sacrificial death' [REB, TEV].

QUESTION—What relationship is indicated by οὖν 'therefore'?
  It introduces the conclusion drawn from 5:6–8 that because God shows his love by sending Christ to die for sinners, he will preserve them safely till the end [BECNT]. It introduces the conclusion based on the greatness of God's love that the believer will ultimately be saved [Ho]. It introduces a conclusion about the future based on the fact of justification mentioned in 5:1 [HNTC, Mor]. It draws a conclusion from 5:6–8 [Gdt, ICC2], and introduces the reasons given in 5:9–10 for the fact that their hope will not be disappointed [Gdt, ICC2, NTC].

QUESTION—What relationship is expressed by the participle δικαιωθέντες 'having been justified'?
  It expresses reason [AB, BECNT, HNTC, ICC2, Mor, NTC, SSA; GW, NCV, NET, NIV, NLT, REB]: because we have been justified we shall be saved through him.

QUESTION—How is it possible to be justified by Christ's blood?
  The noun 'blood' is used as a metonymy standing for Christ's death [LN (23.107); NCV] and 'his blood' is synonymous with 'the death of his Son' in 5:10 [TNTC]. Blood is appropriately used to represent Christ's death in connection with the Jewish sacrificial system [SSA, TH] and some translate this 'his sacrificial death' [REB, TEV]. We are reconciled by means of 'what Christ accomplished for us when he shed his blood when he died on the cross' [SSA].

we-shall-be-saved[a] through[b] him from[c] wrath.[d]

LEXICON—a. fut. pass. indic. of σῴζω (LN 21.27) (BAGD 2.b. p. 798): 'to be saved' [AB, BAGD, BECNT, HNTC, ICC2, LN, NICNT, NTC, WBC; all versions except CEV, GW, NLT], 'to be kept safe' [CEV]. This passive verb is translated as active: '(Christ/he) will save us' [GW, NLT].
  b. διά with genitive object (LN 90.4) (BAGD A.III.2.b.γ. p. 180): 'through' [BAGD, BECNT, HNTC, ICC2, LN, NICNT, NTC, WBC; KJV, NASB, NCV, NET, NIV, NRSV, REB], 'by' [AB, LN; TEV]. The phrase δι' αὐτοῦ 'through him' is not explicit [CEV, GW, NLT].
  c. ἀπό with genitive object (LN 89.122): 'from' [AB, BECNT, HNTC, ICC2, LN, NICNT, NTC, WBC; all versions].
  d. ὀργή (LN 38.10) (BAGD 2.b. p. 579): 'wrath' [BAGD], 'judgment' [BAGD], 'punishment' [LN]. This noun with the definite article is translated 'wrath' [BECNT, NICNT, WBC; KJV], 'the wrath' [ICC2], 'the wrath of God' [NASB, NRSV], 'God's wrath' [HNTC, NTC; NET,

NIV], 'the wrath to come' [AB], 'God's anger' [CEV, GW, NCV, TEV], 'final retribution' [REB], 'God's judgment' [NLT].

QUESTION—What is the focus of 'we shall be saved'?

It is eschatological, referring to the final outworking of salvation [AB, BECNT, NICNT, WBC], of being saved in the judgment [Gdt, HNTC, ICC1, ICC2, Mor, Mu, NTC, SSA, TH, TNTC]. It also refers to being rescued from the cycle of independence from God and dependence on sinful passions, which merit the wrath of God even now [WBC]. God will complete his work and ultimately glorify those whom he has justified [Ho].

QUESTION—How are we saved from God's wrath through Christ?

This is explained more fully in the next verse in the phrase 'by his life' [AB, ICC1, ICC2, NICNT], although 'by his life' includes his death as well as the resurrection and exaltation [ICC2]. It is being in union with the living Christ that saves one from final judgment [ICC1]. Sharing the life of the risen Christ is salvation [AB]. We will be saved from final judgment through the mediation of the risen Christ who has been appointed Son-of-God-in-power through his resurrection [NICNT]. He saves us by his providence, his Spirit, and his intercession [Ho]. The death of Christ saves us both from the guilt of our sins and from God's judgment on our sins [St]. God's wrath was outpoured in the death of Jesus, and will not have to be endured by those who have identified with Christ in his death [NTC, WBC].

5:10 **For if, being enemies,[a] we-have-been-reconciled[b] to-God through[c] the death[d] of his Son,**

LEXICON—a. ἐχθρός (LN **39.11**) (BAGD 2.b.α. p. 331): 'enemy' [AB, BAGD, BECNT, HNTC, ICC2, LN, NICNT, NTC, WBC; all versions]. The present participle ὄντες 'being' implies a temporal element: 'when we were enemies' [AB, HNTC, ICC2, WBC; CEV, KJV, NIV, REB], 'while we were enemies' [BECNT, NICNT, NTC; GW, NASB, NCV, NET, NLT, NRSV], not explicit [TEV].

b. perf. pass. indic. of καταλλάσσω (LN 40.1) (BAGD 2.a. p. 414): 'to be reconciled' [AB, BAGD, BECNT, HNTC, ICC2, LN, NICNT, NTC, WBC; KJV, NASB, NET, NIV, NRSV, REB], 'to be restored to friendship' [NLT]. The phrase κατηλλάγημεν τῷ θεῷ 'we have been reconciled to God' is translated 'he made peace with us' [CEV], 'he made friends with us' [NCV], 'he made us his friends' [TEV], '(the death of his son) restored our relationship with God' [GW].

c. διά with genitive object (LN 90.8) (BAGD A.III.1.a. p. 180): 'through' [AB, BAGD, BECNT, HNTC, ICC2, LN, NICNT, NTC, WBC; NASB, NCV, NET, NIV, NRSV, REB, TEV], 'by means of' [BAGD, LN], 'by' [KJV, NLT], 'because' [CEV], not explicit [GW].

d. θάνατος (LN 23.99) (BAGD 1.b.β. p. 351): 'death' [AB, BAGD, BECNT, HNTC, ICC2, LN, NICNT, NTC, WBC; all versions except CEV]. The phrase διὰ τοῦ θανάτου τοῦ υἱοῦ αὐτοῦ 'through the death of his Son' is translated 'because his Son died for us' [CEV].

QUESTION—What relationship is indicated by γάρ 'for'?
It introduces a restatement of 5:9 [BECNT]. It is an amplification of 5:9 [SSA].

QUESTION—Does the term 'enemy' refer to human hostility toward God, divine hostility toward humans, or both?
1. It refers to mutual hostility between God and men [AB, BECNT, Ho, ICC1, ICC2, NAC, NICNT, SSA, St, WBC]. Our hostile acts towards God makes us enemies [SSA]. This interpretation is supported by the fact that reconciliation has to be mutual [ICC1].
2. It refers to God's hostility toward people [Gdt, Mor, Mu, NTC]. It is primarily divine hostility toward people, but there is also a human hostility toward God [Gdt].
3. It refers to human hostility toward God [HNTC, TH, TNTC]. It means that we hated God and would have nothing to do with him [TH].

much more[a] having-been-reconciled[b] we-shall-be-saved[c] by[d] his life;[e]

LEXICON—a. The phrase πολλῷ μᾶλλον is translated 'much more' [BAGD, HNTC, ICC2, NTC; KJV, NASB], 'how much more' [NICNT, WBC; NET, NIV, REB, TEV], 'surely' [NCV], 'much more surely' [NRSV], 'it surely follows that' [BECNT], 'certainly' [NLT], 'all the more certainly' [AB], 'we are even more certain that' [GW], 'yet something even greater than friendship is ours' [CEV].

b. aorist pass. participle of καταλλάσσω (LN 40.1) (BAGD 2.a. p. 414): 'to be reconciled' [AB, BAGD, BECNT, HNTC, ICC2, LN, NICNT, NTC, WBC; KJV, NASB, NET, NRSV, REB], 'to be restored to friendship' [NLT]. The phrase 'having been reconciled' is translated 'because of this restored relationship' [GW], 'now that we are God's friends' [TEV], 'now that we are his friends' [NCV], 'now that we are at peace with God' [CEV]. The tense of the participle in its logical aspect is shown in translation by such phrases as 'having been (reconciled)' [ICC2, NTC, WBC; NASB, NIV, NRSV], 'being (reconciled)' [NICNT; KJV], 'because of' [GW], 'now that' [AB, HNTC; CEV, NCV, REB, TEV], 'since' [BECNT; NET].

c. fut. pass. indic. of σῴζω (LN 21.27) (BAGD 2.b. p. 798): 'to be saved' [AB, BAGD, BECNT, HNTC, ICC2, LN, NICNT, NTC, WBC; all versions except GW, NCV, NLT], 'to be delivered from eternal punishment' [NLT]. This passive verb is translated as active: 'to save' [GW, NCV].

d. ἐν with dative object (LN 90.10) (BAGD I.4.d. p. 259): 'by' [AB, BECNT, HNTC, ICC2, LN, WBC; all versions except GW, NCV, NIV], 'through' [NICNT, NTC; NCV, NIV], not explicit [GW].

e. ζωή (LN 23.88) (BAGD 1.a. p. 340): 'life' [AB, BAGD, BECNT, HNTC, ICC2, LN, NICNT, NTC, WBC; all versions]. The phrase 'we shall be saved by his life' is translated 'the life his Son lived will save us' [GW].

QUESTION—What correlation is there between 'justified' in 5:9 and 'reconciled' in this verse?

They are different metaphors describing the same reality [HNTC, TH], the first referring to a state of legal guilt and the second to a state of enmity [HNTC]. 'Justification' in 5:9 is legal language and speaks of right standing with God, whereas 'reconciliation' in this verse has to do with a personal relationship with him [ICC2, NAC, NICNT]. Justification leads to reconciliation, which is essentially social [AB]. Reconciliation is integral to God's justification of sinners, though not explicitly suggested by the word 'justification' [ICC2]. Sinners are justified and enemies are reconciled [Ho]. Although the two terms are parallel, justification refers to the removal of condemnation while reconciliation refers to the removal of God's wrath [Gdt]. Both are forensic in nature [Mu].

QUESTION—What does 'saved' refer to in this verse?

It refers to being saved from the wrath of God in the future, at the judgment [BECNT, Gdt, HNTC, ICC2, Mor, NICNT, SSA, St; NLT]. It is sharing in the risen life of Christ [AB, St]. It is eschatological as well as a daily deliverance from sin's power and dominion [NAC]. It is preservation from evil and apostasy [Ho].

QUESTION—Does 'life' refer to the power of his current resurrected state and existence, or to the life that he lived while on earth?

1. It refers to his resurrection life [AB, HNTC, Ho, Mor, Mu, NAC, NTC, SSA, St, TH, TNTC, WBC]. It designates what his resurrection accomplished with regard to salvation [BECNT] as well as his current intercessory ministry [BECNT, Ho, Mu, NAC]. The new life Christ won and in which believers share is what will save them on judgment day [NICNT]. The exaltation life of Christ guarantees our final salvation [Mu].
2. It refers to the life he lived on earth [GW].

5:11 and[a] not only (this),[b] but also[c] we-are-boasting[d] in/because-of[e] God through[f] our Lord Jesus Christ,

LEXICON—a. δέ (LN 89.94, 89.124): 'and' [BECNT, HNTC, ICC2, LN (89.94), NICNT, NTC; CEV, KJV, NASB, NCV], 'but' [LN (89.124); NRSV, REB, TEV], 'yet' [AB], not explicit [WBC; GW, NIV, NLT].
  b. The phrase οὐ μόνον is translated 'not only this' [BECNT, ICC2, NICNT, NTC; NASB, NET], 'not only that' [AB; NCV], 'not only so' [WBC; KJV], 'not only is this so' [NIV], 'not only (have we this hope)' [HNTC], 'in addition' [GW], 'in addition to everything else' [CEV], 'more than that' [NRSV], 'that is not all' [REB, TEV], not explicit [NLT].
  c. καί (LN 89.93): 'also' [BECNT, ICC2, LN, NICNT, NTC, WBC; KJV, NASB, NCV, NET, NIV, REB], 'even' [HNTC; NRSV], 'and, and also' [LN], not explicit [AB; CEV, GW, NLT, TEV].
  d. pres. mid. (deponent = act.) participle of καυχάομαι (LN 33.368) (BAGD 1. p. 425): 'to boast' [AB, BAGD, LN, NICNT; NRSV], 'to exult'

[BECNT, HNTC, ICC2, NTC; NASB, REB], 'to glory' [BAGD], 'to brag' [GW], 'to rejoice' [NET, NIV, NLT, TEV], 'to joy' [KJV], 'to be very happy' [NCV]. This present participle is translated as a finite indicative verb [AB, HNTC, ICC2, NICNT, NTC, WBC; all versions]. This and the following phrase are translated 'we are happy because God sent our Lord Jesus Christ to make peace with us' [CEV]. It means to exult or rejoice about something [AB, BECNT, Gdt, HNTC, ICC1, ICC2, Mor, Mu, NAC, NICNT, NTC, St].

e. ἐν with dative object (LN 89.5): 'in' [BECNT, HNTC, ICC2, LN, NICNT; all versions except CEV, GW, NLT, TEV], 'in our wonderful new relationship with (God)' [NLT], 'about' [LN, SSA; GW], 'of' [AB], 'because of' [TEV], 'because' [CEV].

f. διά with genitive object (LN 90.4): 'through' [AB, BECNT, HNTC, ICC2, LN, NICNT, NTC, WBC; all versions except CEV, GW, NLT]. The phrase 'through our Lord Jesus Christ' is translated 'all because of what our Lord Jesus Christ has done for us' [NLT], '(God) sent our Lord Jesus Christ to make peace with us' [CEV], 'our Lord Jesus Christ lets us (continue to brag about God)' [GW].

QUESTION—To what does the phrase 'and not only this' refer?

1. It refers to salvation in the previous verse; not only will we be saved, but we also boast or exult in God himself [AB, Gdt, Ho, ICC1, ICC2, NAC, NICNT, NTC, SSA].
2. It refers backwards to all that precedes from 5:2 on; not only do we exult in hope and in our difficulties, we also exult in God [BECNT].
3. It is his way of indicating that he has more to say, especially focusing on the words 'boast' and 'reconciliation' in 5:1–10, about which he wants to say more [WBC].

QUESTION—Does the preposition ἐν mean 'in' God or 'because of' God?

1. The preposition specifies the content of boasting [AB, BECNT, HNTC, Ho, ICC2, NICNT, NTC, SSA, St, WBC; all versions except CEV, TEV]: we boast about God. To boast about a person implies that some event or quality of that person are part of the reason and here it implies what God has done for us [SSA]. They boast about God's love and favor towards them [Ho].
2. The preposition indicates the reason for boasting [CEV, TEV]: we boast because of what God has done for us [TEV], because he has sent Christ to make peace [CEV].

QUESTION—What does it mean that they boast in God διά 'through' Jesus Christ?

1. It indicates the reason they boast about God [SSA]: we boast about what God has done because of what Christ accomplished. Christ's death for us is the basis for God's blessings that we experience [SSA]. What Christ has done is the reason for boasting [Gdt, ICC2, Mor, NICNT, TH].
2. It indicates the means by which God blessed us [Ho, NAC, NICNT, TH]: we boast about what God has done by means of Christ. God caused this

by means of Christ [TH]. What Christ has done enables the relationship with God in which they rejoice [Ho, NAC]. Everything God has given us is through Christ [NICNT].
3. Christ is the mediator of offering their thanks to God [WBC]. 'We boast in God, doing this through Christ.' This is similar to the sense of the phrase in 1:8, 'I thank my God *through* Jesus Christ', and it means that we express thanksgiving to God through Christ's mediation made possible by his death and risen life [WBC].

through[a] whom now we-have-received[b] reconciliation.[c]
LEXICON—a. διά with genitive object (LN 90.4): 'through' [AB, BECNT, HNTC, ICC2, LN, NICNT, NTC, WBC; GW, NASB, NCV, NET, NIV, NRSV, REB], 'by' [LN; KJV], not explicit [CEV, NLT, TEV].
 b. aorist act. indic. of λαμβάνω (LN 57.125) (BAGD 2. p. 465): 'to receive' [AB, BAGD, BECNT, HNTC, ICC2, LN, NICNT, NTC, WBC; KJV, NASB, NET, NIV, NRSV], 'to have' [GW], not explicit [CEV, NCV, NLT, TEV]. This active verb is translated as passive: 'to be granted' [REB]. This aorist verb is translated as a perfect tense: 'we have received' [AB, NICNT], 'we have now received' [BECNT, WBC; KJV, NASB, NIV, NRSV], 'we have now already received' [ICC2, NTC], 'we have here and now received' [HNTC], 'we have now been granted' [REB]. It is translated as a present tense verb: 'we now have' [GW], 'we are now (God's friends)' [NCV].
 c. καταλλαγή (LN **40.1**) (BAGD p. 414): 'reconciliation' [AB, BAGD, BECNT, HNTC, ICC2, LN, NICNT, NTC, WBC; NASB, NET, NIV, NRSV, REB], 'restored relationship' [GW], 'atonement' [KJV]. The phrase νῦν τὴν καταλλαγὴν ἐλάβομεν 'now we have received reconciliation' is translated 'we were reconciled (with God)' [**LN**], 'we are now God's friends again' [NCV], 'in making us friends of God' [NLT], '(Jesus Christ) has now made us God's friends' [TEV]. The definite article with this verb is translated as implying something specific: 'this (reconciliation)' [NICNT, WBC; NET], 'our (reconciliation)' [NTC], 'this restored relationship' [GW]. The phrase 'boasting in God through our Lord Jesus Christ, through whom we have now received reconciliation' is translated 'we are happy because God sent our Lord Jesus Christ to make peace with us' [CEV].
QUESTION—What relationship is indicated by διά 'through'
Christ is the agent who made us God's friends [TH]. It is on the basis of Christ dying for us and reconciling us to God that God has done that for which we boast [SSA]. Salvation is a gift from both the Father and the Son [BECNT].

DISCOURSE UNIT: 5:12–8:13 [AB]. New Christian life brings a threefold liberation and is empowered by the Holy Spirit.

DISCOURSE UNIT: 5:12–21 [AB, GNT, HNTC, Ho, ICC2, Mor, Mu, NAC, NICNT, NTC, WBC; CEV, GW, NCV, NET, NIV, NLT, NRSV, TEV]. The topic is freedom from the power of death and sin [AB], a new perspective on God's righteous purpose for humankind [WBC], the universality of salvation in Christ proved by the universality of death in Adam [Gdt], Adam and Christ [GNT, HNTC, Ho, ICC2; CEV, NRSV, TEV], solidarity in Adam and Christ [Mor], Adam and Christ compared [GW, NCV], Adam and Christ contrasted [NLT], the analogy [Mu], the amplification of justification [NET], death through Adam, life through Christ [NIV], the gift of righteousness [NAC], the reign of grace and life [NICNT], the certainty of salvation confirmed by the parallel Adam: Christ [NTC].

5:12 Therefore,[a] just-as through[b] one man sin entered into[c] the world[d]

LEXICON—a. διὰ τοῦτο: This phrase is translated 'therefore' [AB, HNTC, WBC; NASB, NIV, NRSV], 'wherefore' [ICC2, NTC; KJV], 'for this reason' [BECNT], 'because of this' [NICNT], 'so' [GW], 'so then' [NET], not explicit [CEV, NCV, NLT, TEV]. The logical relation expressed by this word is translated 'what does this imply?' [REB].

b. διά with genitive object (LN 90.4): 'through' [AB, BECNT, HNTC, ICC2, LN, NICNT, NTC, WBC; GW, NASB, NET, NIV, NRSV, REB, TEV], 'by' [LN; KJV], not explicit [CEV, NLT]. The phrase 'through one man' is translated 'because of what one man did' [NCV].

c. εἰς with accusative object (LN 84.22): 'into' [BECNT, LN, NICNT, WBC; CEV, GW, KJV, NASB, NCV, NRSV]. The phrase 'entered into' is translated simply 'entered' [AB, HNTC, ICC2, NTC; NET, NIV, NLT, REB].

d. κόσμος (LN 1.39, 9.23) (BAGD 5.a. p. 446): 'world' [AB, BAGD, BECNT, HNTC, ICC2, LN (1.39), NICNT, NTC, WBC; all versions except NLT], 'people of the world' [LN (9.23)], 'the entire human race' [NLT]. Here the word refers to mankind in general [BAGD, ICC2]. It is the world of human existence and experience [AB, BAGD, BECNT, HNTC, ICC2, Mor, Mu, NICNT, St, WBC; NLT], the world of human beings as opposed to creation [WBC].

QUESTION—What relationship is indicated by the phrase διὰ τοῦτο 'therefore'?

1. The phrase διὰ τοῦτο introduces a conclusion drawn from 5:1–11 [AB, BECNT, ICC1, ICC2, NTC, SSA, TH]. Justification and the certainty of salvation (mentioned in 5:1–11) is the basis of our hope, as evidenced by Christ's having conquered sin and death [AB]. The basis of hope is that Christ has reversed the consequences of Adam's sin [BECNT, Mor]. Because believers are reconciled we may conclude that something has occurred that is as universal in its consequence as the sin of the first man; Paul infers Christ's significance for all people based on what he sees that Christ means for believers [ICC2]. It introduces an application for the doctrine of justification by faith [SSA].

2. It indicates that 5:12-21 functions as a conclusion to all that he has argued about justification so far [Gdt, Ho, SSA, WBC], which would be from 1:18 on [WBC].
3. It introduces a conclusion based on what has preceded, especially in 5:11, that Christ's reconciliation has reversed the evil brought about by Adam [Mor].
4. Instead of the phrase διά τοῦτο meaning 'because of this' it has the sense of 'for the sake of this', with τοῦτο 'this' referring to the promise of salvation in 5:9-10. Thus 5:12-21 is the grounds for what he has said in 5:1-11, that is, for the sake of the certainty of salvation (mentioned in 5:9-11) God has brought about a life-giving union between Christ and believers that is more powerful than the death-giving union they had with Adam [NICNT].
5. It is a particle of transition, marking a loose relation between 5:1-11 and what follows [HNTC, NAC].

QUESTION—What would be the 'so also' conclusion that the ὥσπερ 'just as' construction in this verse introduces?

It is an anacoluthon (that is, there is something lacking in the logical sequence) in which Paul begins a comparison but digresses, and does not state the conclusion until 5:18-19 [BECNT, Gdt, Ho, ICC2, Mor, NAC, NICNT, NTC, SSA, St, TNTC, WBC].

1. The idea is reintroduced in 5:18-19 [BECNT, Gdt, Ho, ICC2, NAC, NICNT, NTC, SSA, St, WBC]: just as condemnation came through the sin of one man, so also righteousness comes through the obedience of one man. The first part of 5:18 is virtually a restatement of this clause [SSA].
2. The conclusion is implied in the last clause of 5:14, which states that Adam was a type of Christ [AB]: just as through one man sin and death entered and spread to all, so also....
3. The comparison is completed in 5:15 where he says 'but not as the transgression, so also the free gift' [Mu]: just as the transgression of one man affected all, so also the free gift of the one man Jesus affected the many.

QUESTION—How could sin enter the world through one man?

The sin of Adam is the cause of all people being sinful [SSA]. The coming of sin refers to the beginning of sin in the human race and the first man, Adam, is responsible because of his disobedience [NICNT]. Although Eve committed the first sin, Adam is referred to because Paul holds him to be responsible [St]. Sin is treated as a power that rules over all humanity [NICNT]. Sin and death are personified here [Ho, ICC1, NICNT, SSA, WBC].

and through[a] sin death,[b]

LEXICON—a. διά with genitive object (LN 89.76): 'through' [AB, BECNT, HNTC, ICC2, LN, NTC, WBC; GW, NASB, NET, NIV, NRSV, REB],

'by means of' [LN], 'by' [LN; KJV], 'with' [NCV], not explicit [CEV, NLT, TEV].
- b. θάνατος (LN 23.99) (BAGD 1.b.γ. p. 351): 'death' [AB, BAGD, BECNT, HNTC, ICC2, LN, NTC, WBC; all versions]. An implied verb is added to this phrase, of which 'death' would be the subject: death 'came' [HNTC, ICC2; GW, NCV, NRSV], death 'entered' [BECNT]. The word 'death' is also translated as being the object of an implied verb: sin 'brought death' [CEV, NLT, TEV]. It refers to natural death as divine punishment [BAGD]. The word 'death' is stated as being specifically the death of Adam [HNTC]: 'through sin came that man's death'.

QUESTION—In what sense does he use the term θάνατος 'death'?
1. It is death in all its physical and spiritual aspects [AB, BECNT, Ho, Mor, NAC, NICNT, St], as a penalty incurred for sin [NICNT]. Physical death is the sign and symbol of spiritual death [Mor].
2. It is physical death [BAGD, Gdt, ICC1, Mu, NTC].

QUESTION—What is meant by death entering the world through sin?
According to Genesis 2:17 and 3:19 the penalty of sin was death [St]. Adam died because he sinned [SSA]. Adam's sin resulted in death coming into the human race [AB, HNTC, ICC2, NICNT, NTC, TH]. Death followed sin like a shadow [ICC2].

and thus death spread[a] to all people,[b]

LEXICON—a. aorist act. indic. of διέρχομαι (LN 15.32) (BAGD 2. p. 194): 'to spread' [AB, BECNT, NICNT, NTC; GW, NASB, NET, NLT, NRSV, TEV], 'to come' [BAGD, HNTC, ICC2, WBC; NIV], 'to pervade' [REB], 'to pass through' [LN], 'to pass upon' [KJV]. This entire phrase is translated 'and so everyone must die' [CEV], 'this is why everyone must die' [NCV].
- b. ἄνθρωπος (LN 9.1) (BAGD 1.b. p. 68): 'person' [LN], 'human being' [BAGD, LN], 'man' [BAGD]. This plural noun is translated 'people' [BECNT, NICNT; NET], 'men' [HNTC, ICC2, WBC; KJV, NASB, NIV], 'mankind' [NTC], 'human beings' [AB], 'the human race' [REB, TEV], not explicit [NRSV]. The phrase 'all people' is translated 'everyone' [CEV, GW, NCV, NLT], 'the whole human race' [REB, TEV], 'all' [NRSV].

QUESTION—What relationship is indicated by οὕτως 'thus'?
It correlates the manner that death came into the world, which is through sin, with the manner that it spread to all, which is also through sin [NICNT]. It correlates the way in which sin and death entered the world with the way they became universal, which is that Adam sinned and with sin came death, which permeated the whole human race because in Adam all sinned [Gdt, Mu]. There is a fatal connection between sin and death, which is that everyone sins and everyone dies, a pattern first established by Adam [WBC]. It indicates the relationship between sin and death: Adam brought sin and consequently death on all [Ho]. Through Adam's sin comes death, and as a

consequence death spread to all because of the corrupt nature inherited from Adam [ICC2]. Through Adam's sin and through their own sin, death comes to all [AB].

QUESTION—In what way did death spread to all people?

Death made its way to every individual of the human race [ICC1] and all must die [TH]. When Adam sinned, the consequence was that he died, and the same thing happens to all others so that when they sin they also must die [St]. As a result of the entrance into the human race of sin, followed by death, death reached everyone because everyone sins [ICC2].

on-the-basis-of[a] the-fact-that all have-sinned;[b]

LEXICON—a. ἐπί with dative object (LN 89.13, 89.27) (BAGD II.1.b.γ. p. 287): 'on the basis of' [LN (89.13, 89.27)], 'because of' [LN (89.27)], 'in view of' [LN (89.13)]. The phrase ἐφ' ᾧ 'on the basis of the fact that' is the equivalent of ἐπὶ τοῦτο ὅτι 'because/for the reason that' [BAGD]. It is translated 'because' [HNTC, ICC2, NICNT; GW, NASB, NCV, NET, NIV, NRSV, TEV], 'for' [NLT], 'since' [NTC], 'in that' [WBC], 'inasmuch as' [REB], 'for that' [KJV], 'on the basis of (this death)' [BECNT], 'with the result that' [AB], not explicit [CEV]. The logical relation between sin and death expressed by this phrase is translated 'everyone has sinned, so everyone must die' [CEV].

b. aorist act. indic. of ἁμαρτάνω (LN 88.289) (BAGD 1. p.42): 'to sin' [AB, BAGD, BECNT, HNTC, ICC2, LN, NICNT, NTC, WBC; all versions].

QUESTION—What relationship is indicated by the phrase ἐφ' ᾧ 'on the basis of the fact'?

1. It indicates the reason that all died [Gdt, Ho, ICC1, ICC2, Mor, Mu, NICNT, SSA, St, TH, TNTC; CEV, GW, NCV]: death came to all persons because all persons sinned.

    1.1 All people sinned corporately in Adam when he sinned and die as a consequence of Adam's sin [Gdt, Ho, Mor, Mu, NICNT, SSA, St, TNTC]. Adam was the both head and representative of all his descendants so that his act of sin was attributed to all his descendants [Ho, St], and therefore on judicial grounds death passed to all people since they were regarded as sinners on account of Adam's sin [Ho]. There is such a connection between the one man and the all, that the sin of the one is at the same time regarded as the sin of all [NICNT]. It is not that all people sinned together at some specific time, rather it is as though all people sinned when Adam sinned [SSA].

    1.2 All people sin individually and die as a consequence of their individual sins [ICC1, ICC2, TH; CEV, GW, NCV]. All people sin in their own persons as a result of the corrupt nature inherited from Adam [ICC1, ICC2]. The fall gave them the predisposition to sin [ICC1].

2. It indicates the result of sin and death entering the world [AB, BECNT, NAC, NTC]: Adam's sin and consequent death brought the same fate to all his descendants That is, people experience death because they sin but

they also sin because they are born in a state of spiritual death, of alienation from God [BECNT]. The consequence of what Adam did spread to all people, with the result that all sinned [NAC].
3. The syntax here is vague and may not be pressed for a clear decision on a point which Paul does not appear to have intended to clarify. However, he is asserting that no one is exempt from the partnership of sin and death, established initially by Adam and now followed by all people, all of whom sin and all of whom die [WBC].

5:13 for until^a law^b sin was in (the) world,^c

LEXICON—a. ἄχρι with genitive object (LN 67.119) (BAGD 1.a. p. 128): 'until' [BAGD, BECNT, HNTC, LN, WBC; KJV, NASB], 'up to the time of' [AB]. The phrase ἄχρι νόμου 'until law' is translated 'before the law' [NICNT; NRSV], 'before the law was given' [BAGD, ICC2, NTC; NET, NIV, NLT, TEV], 'before the Law came' [CEV], 'before there were any laws' [GW], 'before the law of Moses' [NCV], 'before there was law' [REB].

b. νόμος (LN 33.55, 33.333) (BAGD 3. p. 542): 'law' [BAGD, LN (33.333)], 'Law' [LN (33.55)]. This noun, which lacks the definite article, is translated as having the definite article: 'the law' [AB, BECNT, HNTC, ICC2, NICNT, NTC, WBC; CEV, KJV, NASB, NET, NIV, NLT, NRSV, TEV], 'the law of Moses' [NCV]; as without the definite article: 'law' [REB], 'any laws' [GW].

c. κόσμος (LN 1.39) (BAGD 5.a. p. 446): 'world' [AB, BAGD, BECNT, HNTC, ICC2, LN, NICNT, NTC, WBC; all versions except NLT]. The phrase 'sin was in the world' is translated 'people sinned' [NLT].

QUESTION—What relationship is indicated by γάρ 'for'?
It introduces what follows as a support for what has just been said [Ho, Mor, NICNT, WBC]. It introduces 5:13–14 as an additional argument to support 5:12a–c [NICNT, WBC], which serves to clarify the role of the law [WBC]. It introduces 5:13–14 as an explanatory note to what he has said in 5:12 about the fact that all sinned [Mu, NTC].

QUESTION—What 'law' is he speaking of here?
It is the Mosaic law [AB, BECNT, Gdt, HNTC, Ho, ICC1, ICC2, Mor, Mu, NAC, NICNT, NTC, SSA, WBC; NCV].

but sin is- not -accounted,^a (there) not (yet) being^b law,^c

LEXICON—a. pres. pass. indic. of ἐλλογέω (LN **33.45**) (BAGD p. 252): 'to be accounted' [AB, BAGD, WBC], 'to be taken into account' [HNTC, NTC; NIV], 'to be reckoned' [BECNT, NICNT; NRSV], 'to be imputed' [KJV, NASB], 'to be counted against someone' [NCV], 'to be charged to (one's) account' [BAGD], 'to be recorded' [LN], 'to be registered with full clarity' [ICC2]. The phrase 'sin is not accounted' is translated 'there is no accounting for sin' [NET], 'no account is kept of sins' [**LN**; TEV], 'no reckoning is kept of sin' [REB], 'no record of sin was kept' [CEV], 'no record of sin can be kept' [GW], 'there was no law to break' [NLT].

b. pres. act. participle of εἰμί. The participial phrase μὴ ὄντος νόμου is translated 'when there is no law' [AB, BECNT, NICNT, NTC; KJV, NASB, NCV, NET, NIV, NRSV], 'when there are no laws' [GW], 'where there is no law' [HNTC; TEV], 'in the absence of the law' [ICC2, WBC], 'because there was no law' [CEV], 'before there was law' [REB], 'since it had not yet been given' [NLT].
c. νόμος (LN 33.55, 33.333) (BAGD 3. p. 542): 'law' [AB, BAGD, BECNT, HNTC, LN (33.333), NICNT, NTC; all versions except CEV], 'the law' [ICC2, WBC], 'Law' [LN (33.55); CEV]. This noun lacks the definite article here.

QUESTION—What does he mean that sin is not accounted?
1. Prior to the giving of the Mosaic law human sin was not a matter of transgressing specific commands, though it was still sin [BECNT, Gdt, HNTC, ICC1, ICC2, Mu, NAC, NICNT, SSA, St, TH, TNTC, WBC]. In the absence of the law it was not as sharply defined or apparent, but it was still sin, as proved by the fact that everyone died [ICC2]. Because people sin they stand condemned before God, although the guilt incurred is not for having broken specific laws [SSA]. He is saying that while they had not violated specific clear commands as Adam did, they all shared in Adam's sin through their corporate solidarity in him, and that sin was imputed to them [Gdt, Mu].
2. He means that sin was not recorded in the heavenly books prior to the giving of the Mosaic law [AB].
3. The statement is a hypothetical objection that he raises in order to refute, which he does in the next verse by pointing out that the fact that people died indicates that there really must have been law, though not Mosaic law, and that sin must have been being taken into account after all [NTC].

QUESTION—What law is he referring to?
It is the Mosaic law [AB, HNTC, Ho, ICC1, NICNT, SSA, WBC].

5:14 nevertheless[a] death[b] reigned[c] from[d] Adam until[e] Moses

LEXICON—a. ἀλλά (LN 91.2, 89.125): 'nevertheless' [NTC, WBC; KJV, NASB, NIV], 'yet' [AB; CEV, GW, NET, NRSV], 'and yet' [LN (91.2)], 'all the same' [HNTC], 'but' [BECNT, ICC2, LN (89.125), NICNT; NCV, TEV], not explicit [NLT, REB].
b. θάνατος (LN 23.99) (BAGD 1.f. p. 351): 'death' [AB, BAGD, BECNT, HNTC, ICC2, LN, NICNT, NTC, WBC; all versions except NCV, NLT]. This noun is translated as a verb: 'to die' [NCV, NLT]. Death here is personified [BAGD].
c. aorist act. indic. of βασιλεύω (LN **37.22**) (BAGD 1.c. p. 136): 'to reign' [BECNT, HNTC, ICC2, **LN**, NICNT, NTC, WBC; KJV, NASB, NET, NIV], 'to rule' [BAGD; GW, TEV], 'to exercise dominion' [NRSV], 'to have power' [CEV], 'to hold sway' [AB; REB]. The phrase 'death reigned' is translated 'everyone had to die' [NCV], 'they all died' [NLT].

c. ἀπό with genitive object (LN 67.131) (BAGD II.2.b. p. 87): 'from' [AB, BAGD, BECNT, HNTC, ICC2, LN, NICNT, WBC; KJV, NASB, NET, NRSV, REB], 'from the time of' [NTC; CEV, GW, NCV, NIV, TEV], not explicit [NLT].

d. μέχρι with genitive object (LN 67.119) (BAGD 1.b. p. 515): 'until' [AB, BAGD, BECNT, LN, NICNT, WBC; NASB, NET], 'to' [ICC2; KJV, NRSV, REB], 'up to' [HNTC], 'to that of' [NTC], 'to the time of' [CEV, GW, NCV, NIV, TEV], not explicit [NLT].

QUESTION—Does 'Moses' refer to Moses the man or to the law of Moses?

He is referring to the time when Moses lived [SSA; CEV, GW, NCV, TEV]: from the time of Adam until the time of Moses. The point of naming Moses is that he wrote the law that changed things [BECNT, ICC2]: from the time of Adam until the time of the giving of the law by Moses.

QUESTION—To what does 'death' refer?

1. As in 5:12 it refers to physical and spiritual death [BECNT, Ho, NICNT, WBC].
2. It refers primarily to physical death [Gdt, NTC, St].

QUESTION—What is meant by 'death reigned'?

Death is personified in this metaphor [ICC1, SSA, WBC] and it means that death was in complete control; that is, death is what all had to experience [SSA, TH]. No person could escape the power of death [WBC]. Death was universal [ICC1, NICNT] and inescapable [NICNT].

QUESTION—What relationship is indicated by ἀλλά 'nevertheless'?

It introduces a contrast what was just said in 5:13b: despite the fact that sin is not accounted unless there is law, death ruled anyway [Gdt, Ho, ICC2, Mor, NICNT, NTC].

even over[a] the (ones) not having-sinned in the likeness[b] of-the transgression[c] of-Adam,

LEXICON—a. ἐπί with accusative object (LN 37.9) (BAGD III.1.b.α. p. 288): 'over' [AB, BAGD, BECNT, HNTC, ICC2, LN, NICNT, NTC, WBC; all versions except NCV, NLT], not explicit [NCV, NLT].

b. ὁμοίωμα (LN 64.3) (BAGD 1. p. 567): 'likeness' [BAGD, LN], 'similarity' [LN]. The phrase ἐπὶ τῷ ὁμοιώματι 'in the likeness (of)' [BECNT, NICNT; NASB] is also translated 'like' [NRSV], 'in a way similar to' [AB], 'in the same way' [ICC2; GW, NET, TEV], 'in the very manner of' [WBC], 'after the similitude of' [KJV], 'in such a way as to produce (a transgression)' [HNTC], 'by (transgressing)' [NTC], 'as (Adam did)' [CEV, NIV, NLT, REB], 'as (Adam had)' [NCV].

c. παράβασις (LN 36.28) (BAGD p. 611): 'transgression' [AB, BAGD, BECNT, HNTC, LN, NICNT, WBC; KJV, NRSV], 'transgression of a direct commandment' [ICC2], 'transgressing an express command' [NTC], 'offense' [NASB]. The phrase 'in the likeness of the transgression of Adam' is translated 'in the same way Adam did when he disobeyed' [GW], 'in the same way Adam did when he disobeyed God's command'

[TEV], 'in the same way as Adam...transgressed' [NET], 'by breaking a command, as Adam had' [NCV], 'by breaking a command, as did Adam' [NIV], 'disobey an explicit commandment of God, as Adam did' [NLT], 'as Adam did, by breaking a direct command' [REB], 'disobeyed a direct command from God, as Adam did' [CEV].

QUESTION—Is παράβασις 'transgression' different from ἁμαρτία 'sin' (5:13)?

Transgression is sin involving the violation of a clear commandment [AB, BECNT, ICC2, Mor, NICNT, WBC]. Sin is a disposition of rebellion and exalting the self against God, but it becomes visible and assessable as transgression only when law is given [HNTC].

QUESTION—What is Paul's argument here about the relation between sin and death?

1. Paul is arguing that even though the people who lived before the Mosaic law could not be accused of transgressing a clear written code, the fact that they still died indicated that they were experiencing the consequence of sin [AB, BECNT, Gdt, HNTC, Ho, ICC2, Mor, NAC, NICNT, SSA, WBC]. The sin for which they experienced the consequences was the sin of Adam, in which they shared by their solidarity with him [Mu].
2. Paul is arguing that even though the people who lived before Moses could not be accused of transgressing the Mosaic law, the fact that they still died indicated that they were violating law and experiencing the consequence of sin [NTC]. He is then refuting the hypothetical objection 'but sin is not accounted, (there) not (yet) being law' by saying 'obviously there was law, because they experienced death, which is the penalty of sin' [NTC].

who is a type[a] of-the-(one) coming.[b]

LEXICON—a. τύπος (LN **58.63**) (BAGD 6. p. 830): 'type' [AB, BAGD, BECNT, HNTC, ICC2, NICNT, NTC, WBC; NASB, NET, NRSV], 'pattern' [NIV], 'figure' [**LN**; KJV, TEV], 'image' [GW], not explicit [NLT]. This phrase is translated 'In some ways Adam is like Christ who came later' [CEV], 'Adam was like the One who was coming in the future' [NCV], 'Adam foreshadows the man who was to come' [REB]. What comes first in time is called the type and what comes afterwards is the antitype [ICC1]. In a religious sense a type is not a mere incidental similarity, but a designed resemblance so that the type is intended to prefigure the antitype [Ho].

b. pres. act. participle of μέλλω (LN 67.62) (BAGD 2. p. 501): 'to come' [AB, BAGD, BECNT, HNTC, ICC2, NICNT, NTC, WBC; all versions]. It refers to Christ as the coming one [BAGD].

QUESTION—In what sense was Adam a type of Christ?

Their lives corresponded in some ways [SSA]. Adam prefigures Christ in the sense that what he did had universal consequences for other people [BECNT, Ho, ICC2, NICNT, SSA, St], Adam in his effectiveness for ruin and Christ in his effectiveness for salvation [ICC2, NAC]. Both are a corporate head of a race of people [Ho, Mor, NAC], archetypes of humanity [TNTC], each drawing after him all mankind [Gdt]. Adam prefigures Christ as the head of humanity [AB, St]. Adam and Christ each began an epoch characterized by their respective actions [WBC]. They are the respective heads of two ages [St]. They were in similar circumstances with similar temptations, though responding differently, and their acts brought consequences of similar scope [HNTC]. Both Adam and Christ imparted to those who were their own that which belonged to them [NTC]. Since the effects produced by the actions of each are so opposite, the clause is translated 'what a contrast between Adam and Christ who was yet to come' [NLT].

5:15 **But not as the trespass,[a] thus also (is) the gracious-gift;[b]**

LEXICON—a. παράπτωμα (LN 88.297) (BAGD 2.a.α. p. 621): 'trespass' [NICNT, NTC, WBC; NIV, NRSV], 'transgression' [AB, BAGD, BECNT, LN; NASB, NET], 'sin' [LN; CEV, NCV, NLT, TEV], 'act of sin' [HNTC], 'misdeed' [ICC2], 'failure' [GW], 'offence' [KJV], 'wrongdoing' [REB].

b. χάρισμα (LN 57.103): 'gracious gift' [LN, NICNT; NET], 'gift' [AB, LN, NICNT; CEV, NIV], 'free gift' [NTC; KJV, NASB, NRSV], 'God's free gift' [NCV, TEV], 'God's gift' [GW], 'God's generous gift' [NLT], 'God's act of grace' [REB], 'act of grace' [BECNT, HNTC], 'effect of grace' [WBC]. This word is translated 'the gift that God was kind enough to give' [CEV].

QUESTION—What is the difference between παράπτωμα 'trespass' here and παράβασις 'transgression' in 5:14?

1. The two are almost synonyms [TH, WBC]. Both refer to an act of sin while ἁμαρτία 'sin' in 5:13 is a more generic term [TH]. Both refer to Adam's disobedience [WBC].
2. There is a difference [Gdt, ICC1, ICC2, NICNT, NTC]. Here παράπτωμα 'trespass' does not focus on a transgression of a commandment like παράβασις 'transgression' does, but on a false step, a misdeed that broke Adam's relationship with God [ICC1, ICC2]. Παράπτωμα 'trespass' is a deviation from the path, a fault, whereas παράβασις is the transgression of a specific command [NTC]. It is similar to ἁμαρτία 'sin' [ICC1, ICC2, NICNT]. Παράπτωμα may have been chosen for phonetic similarity to other words he has been using [Gdt, NAC].

QUESTION—What is the 'gracious gift'?

1. It is Christ's act or work, which is a work of grace [BECNT, HNTC, NICNT], his self sacrifice [St], which results in righteousness [BECNT, NICNT]. It is what Christ graciously did for humanity [AB]. Christ's act is an embodiment of as well as a concrete enactment of God's generous outreach to humanity [WBC].
2. It is the gift of our standing before God [Ho, ICC2, SSA]. It is the gift of justification as seen in 3:24 and 5:15-21 [SSA]. It is the status of a right

standing with God [ICC2, SSA], the gift of righteousness (5:17) [Ho, ICC1]. It is either the gift of righteous (5:17) or the gift of the Spirit (5:5) [WBC].

for if by-the trespass of-the one[a] (person) the many[b] died,[c]
LEXICON—a. εἶς (LN 60.10): 'one' [BECNT, HNTC, ICC2, LN, NICNT, NTC, WBC; KJV, NASB], 'one man' [AB; NCV, NET, NIV, NRSV, REB, TEV], 'one man, Adam' [NLT], 'one person' [GW]. The phrase 'the trespass of the one' is translated 'that one sin' [CEV].
   b. πολύς (LN 59.1) (BAGD I.2.a.β. p. 688): 'many' [AB, BAGD, BECNT, HNTC, ICC2, LN, NICNT, NTC, WBC; KJV, NASB, NET, NIV, NLT, NRSV], 'many people' [NCV, TEV], 'many others' [CEV], 'so many' [REB], 'humanity' [GW].
   c. aorist act. indic. of ἀποθνῄσκω (LN 23.99): 'to die' [AB, BECNT, HNTC, ICC2, LN, NICNT, NTC, WBC; GW, NASB, NCV, NET, NIV, NRSV, TEV], 'to be dead' [KJV]. This entire phrase is translated 'that one sin brought death to many others' [CEV], 'for this one man, Adam, brought death to many through his sin' [NLT], 'the wrongdoing of that one man brought death upon so many' [REB].
QUESTION—What is the function of the clause introduced by εἰ 'if'?
It expresses grounds for a conclusion to be drawn [AB, Mor, NAC, SSA, TH]: since it is true. This clause is translated as a fact without using 'if' [SSA; CEV, NCV, NLT, TEV], and two emphasize the fact with 'it is true that' [TEV], 'it is certain that' [SSA].
QUESTION—Who are 'the many' who died, and in what sense did they die?
It is all humanity [AB, BECNT, Gdt, HNTC, Ho, ICC1, ICC2, Mor, NTC, SSA, TH, TNTC, WBC]. Here 'many' refers to all people since the effects of sin have spread to all people, but Paul uses 'many' to parallel the 'many' in the other half of the comparison where 'many' does not include all people [SSA]. Their death is both physical and spiritual [BECNT, WBC] in that it is separation from God [BECNT]. In using this word Paul is not intending to delimit but to contrast, though the scope of the 'many' who die is the same as the 'all men' of 5:12 and 18 [Mu].

much more[a] the grace of-God and the gift[b] in[c] grace the (grace) of-the one man Jesus Christ abounded[d] to[e] the many.
LEXICON—a. The phrase πολλῷ μᾶλλον is translated 'much more' [HNTC, ICC2, NTC; KJV, NASB], 'how much more' [AB, BECNT, NICNT, WBC; NET, NIV], 'much more surely' [NRSV], 'it is certainly true' [GW]. The phrase 'much more the grace of God' is translated 'but the grace from God was much greater' [NCV], 'the grace of God was much greater' [TEV], 'and what a difference between our sin and God's generous gift of forgiveness' [NLT]. This entire clause is translated 'Yet in an even greater way, Jesus Christ alone brought God's gift of kindness to many people' [CEV], 'its effect is vastly exceeded by the grace of God and the gift that came to so many by the grace of the one man, Jesus

Christ' [REB]. The dative πολλῷ (literally 'by much') expresses degree of difference [BAGD].

b. δωρεά (LN 57.84) (BAGD p. 210): 'gift' [AB, BAGD, BECNT, HNTC, ICC2, LN, NICNT, NTC, WBC; all versions except NCV, NRSV, TEV], 'free gift' [NRSV, TEV], 'gift of life' [NCV].

c. ἐν with dative object (LN 89.76) (BAGD IV.4.b. p. 261): 'in' [BECNT, NICNT; NRSV], 'by' [LN; KJV, NASB, NCV, NET], 'by means of' [LN], 'through' [TEV], 'because of' [AB]. The phrase ἐν χάριτι 'in grace' stands for the genitive χάριτος 'of grace' [BAGD]. It is translated 'which has come by the grace' [ICC2], 'that came by the grace' [NTC; NIV, REB], 'gracious' [HNTC], 'bountiful' [NLT], 'of kindness' [CEV], 'given through the kindness' [GW].

d. aorist act. indic. of περισσεύω (LN 59.52) (BAGD 1.a.β. p. 650): 'to abound' [BECNT, HNTC, ICC2, LN, NICNT; KJV, NASB, NRSV], 'to overflow' [AB, NTC, WBC; NIV], 'to be showered on' [GW], 'to multiply' [NET], 'to be vastly exceeded by' [REB], 'to be available in great abundance' [BAGD], 'to be much greater' [TEV], not explicit [CEV]. The phrase 'the gift...abounded to/for the many' is translated 'many people received God's gift of life' [NCV], 'brought forgiveness to many' [NLT].

e. εἰς with accusative object (LN 90.59): 'to' [AB, LN, NTC, WBC; CEV, NASB, NET, NIV, NLT, REB, TEV], 'unto' [ICC2; KJV], 'for' [BECNT, HNTC, LN, NICNT; NRSV], 'on' [GW], not explicit [NCV].

QUESTION—What is the meaning of πολλῷ μᾶλλον 'much more' in the argument?

1. It refers to greater certainty [Gdt, Ho, ICC1, SSA; GW, NRSV]: the sin of Adam caused many to die, but it is much more certain that because of what Jesus did many abundantly experienced God's grace.
2. It refers to the greater achievements of God's grace [NICNT; CEV, NCV, REB, TEV]: the sin of Adam caused many to die, but God's grace and the gift by the grace of Jesus Christ accomplished much more for many.

QUESTION—What is 'the grace of God' that abounded to the many?

This refers to God acting graciously toward them [SSA, WBC]. It is God's manner of showing grace [TH]. Grace describes God's motive and the manner in which he acts [NICNT]. It is God's benevolent favor [AB].

QUESTION—How is 'the gift in grace' related to 'the (grace) of the one man Jesus Christ'?

'The gift' refers to the gift from God that has come 'by the grace' displayed by Christ [ICC2, NICNT, SSA, TH]. The gift refers to χάρισμα 'gracious gift' in the first part of the verse and 'in grace' refers to Christ acting graciously toward them, [ICC2, SSA]. This gift is righteousness [Ho, ICC2, NICNT, SSA]. This is translated 'and the gift given through the kindness of...Christ' [GW], 'and the gift by the grace of...Christ' [NASB], 'many people received God's gift of life by the grace of...Christ' [NCV]. 'and the gift by the grace of…Christ' [NET], 'and the gift that came to so many by the grace of…Christ' [REB].

QUESTION—Who are 'the many' to whom grace abounded?
1. It refers to all people [AB, Gdt, ICC1, ICC2], to the mass of mankind [HNTC], to humanity in that age in the mass [WBC].
2. It refers to all believers [BECNT, Ho, Mor, NICNT], to all those who belong to Christ [NTC]. They are the ones 'receiving the abundance of grace' mentioned in 5:17, that is, those who respond to the offer of the gospel [BECNT, NICNT].

5:16 And the gift[a] (is) not like (what comes) through[b] (the) one having-sinned;

LEXICON—a. δώρημα (LN 57.84) (BAGD p. 210): 'gift' [BAGD, LN]. See entry above.
b. διά with genitive object (LN 90.4): 'through' [LN]. The phrase 'what comes through' is translated 'the result of' [AB, HNTC, NTC; NIV, NLT], 'that which resulted from' [BECNT], 'the result that followed' [HNTC], 'that which came through' [NASB], 'the effect of' [NRSV], '(in) its effect (with)' [REB], 'as it was by' [KJV], not explicit [NICNT, WBC; CEV, GW, NCV, NET, TEV]. This clause is translated 'and the gift is not like the one who sinned' [NICNT; NET], 'and not as the one who sinned, the gift' [WBC], 'there is a difference between God's gift and the sin of one man' [TEV], 'there is a lot of difference between Adam's sin and God's gift' [CEV], 'there is also no comparison between God's gift and the one who sinned' [GW], 'after Adam sinned once, he was judged guilty. But the gift of God is different' [NCV].

QUESTION—What is being compared in this clause?
He is comparing the gift that comes through Christ with the condemnation that comes through Adam that is mentioned in the next verse [AB, BECNT, ICC2, NICNT, TNTC]. He is contrasting Adam's effectiveness for evil with Christ's influence for good [NTC]. He is summing up the contrast in epochs in terms of their beginnings and ends: one beginning in sin and resulting in condemnation, and the other beginning with a gracious act and resulting in acquittal [WBC]. This verse emphasizes the contrast between the one and the many both in terms of judgment as well as grace [Mu].

for the verdict[a] from[b] one (trespass)[c] results-in[d] condemnation,[e]

LEXICON—a. κρίμα (LN 30.110, **56.24**) (BAGD 4.a. p. 450): 'verdict' [BAGD, LN (**56.24**); GW], 'judicial verdict' [NICNT], 'judicial action' [REB], 'judgment' [AB, BECNT, ICC2, LN (30.110, 56.24), NTC, WBC; KJV, NASB, NET, NIV, NRSV, TEV], 'the process of judgment' [HNTC], 'sentence' [LN (56.24)], 'condemnation' [NLT], not explicit [CEV]. This noun is translated as a verb phrase: 'to be judged guilty' [NCV].
b. ἐκ with genitive object (LN 90.16): 'from' [BECNT, HNTC, LN, NICNT, WBC; NASB], 'resulting from' [AB; NET], 'following' [NRSV],

'following on' [REB], 'followed' [ICC2, NTC; GW, NIV], 'by' [LN; KJV], not explicit [CEV, NCV, NLT, TEV]. This entire clause is translated 'That one sin led to punishment' [CEV], 'after Adam sinned once, he was judged guilty' [NCV], 'the verdict which followed one person's failure condemned everyone' [GW], 'the judgment was by one to condemnation' [KJV], 'Adam's sin led to condemnation' [NLT], 'after the one sin came the judgment of guilty' [TEV].

c. There is no lexical entry for this word in the Greek text. It is implied by the presence of παράπτωμα 'trespass' in the following clause with which it stands in balanced contrast. It is represented in translation as 'transgression' [NASB, NET], 'act of transgression' [HNTC], 'sin' [BECNT, NICNT, NTC; CEV, NIV, NLT, TEV], 'trespass' [AB; NRSV], 'misdeed' [ICC2], 'offence' [REB], 'failure' [GW], not explicit [WBC; KJV]. The phrase 'one (transgression)' is translated 'Adam sinned once' [NCV].

d. εἰς with accusative object (LN 89.48): 'resulting in' [NASB, REB], 'to' [WBC; KJV]. This preposition is variously translated: 'resulted in' [BECNT, NICNT], 'with the result that' [LN], 'which leads to' [HNTC], 'led to' [CEV, NET, NLT], 'to cause' [LN], 'became' [AB], 'issued in' [ICC2], 'brought' [NTC; NIV, NRSV], not explicit [GW, NCV, TEV].

e. κατάκριμα (LN **56.31**) (BAGD p. 412): 'condemnation' [AB, BECNT, HNTC, ICC2, LN, NICNT, NTC, WBC; KJV, NASB, NET, NIV, NLT, NRSV], 'a verdict of condemnation' [REB], 'punishment' [BAGD; CEV], 'doom' [BAGD]. This noun is translated as a verb: 'condemned (everyone)' [GW]; as an adjective 'guilty' [NCV, TEV].

QUESTION—What is ἑνός 'one' connected with?

In view of the rhetorical variation in the next clause, this could refer to Adam, Adam's transgression, or both [WBC]. It is difficult to distinguish which ἑνός refers to, but because there is a unity of person and act in Paul's thinking, he is in effect talking about the one trespass of the one man [Mu].

1. It modifies an understood παράπτωμα 'trespass' [AB, BAGD, BECNT, HNTC, Ho, ICC2, Mor, NICNT, NTC; CEV, NASB, NCV, NET, NIV, NRSV, REB, TEV]: the verdict from one trespass.
2. It refers to the one person, Adam [Gdt, SSA; GW, KJV]: the verdict from one person's trespass.

but[a] the gracious-gift[b] from[c] many trespasses[d] results-in[e] justification.[f]

LEXICON—a. δέ: 'but' [BECNT, HNTC, ICC2, NICNT, NTC, WBC; all versions], 'whereas' [AB]. This particle is the second member of the μέν...δέ construction which posits a balanced contrast similar to the English construction 'on the one hand this, but on the other hand that'. The particle μέν occurs in the previous clause in the phrase τὸ μὲν γὰρ κρίμα 'for the condemnation' but is not translated in any of the versions or commentary translations due to considerations of normal English style.

b. χάρισμα (LN 57.103) (BAGD 1. p. 879): 'gracious gift'. See this word at 5:15.
c. ἐκ with genitive object (LN 90.16): 'from' [LN, WBC; NET], 'by' [LN], 'of' [KJV]. This preposition is translated 'arose from' [NASB], 'following' [NRSV], 'following on' [REB], 'following upon' [AB], 'followed' [ICC2, NTC; NIV], 'after' [GW, TEV], 'came after' [NICNT; NCV], 'that came after' [BECNT], 'wrought in the context of' [HNTC], not explicit [CEV, NLT].
d. παράπτωμα (LN 88.297) (BAGD 2.b. p. 621): 'trespass'. See this word at 5:15. This noun is translated as a verb: 'we have sinned' [CEV].
e. εἰς with accusative object (LN 89.48): 'resulting in' [NASB], 'unto' [KJV]. This preposition is translated as a past tense verb or verb phrase: 'brought' [AB, NTC; GW, NIV], 'resulted in' [BECNT; REB], 'led to' [NET], 'issued in' [ICC2]; as a present tense verb or verb phrase: 'leads to' [HNTC], 'brings' [NRSV]; not explicit [CEV, NCV, NLT, TEV].
f. δικαίωμα (LN **56.34**) (BAGD 3. p. 198): 'justification' [AB, BECNT, HNTC, ICC2, NICNT, NTC, WBC; KJV, NASB, NET, NIV, NRSV], 'acquittal' [LN; REB], 'God's approval' [GW]. The concept of justification is communicated by a phrase: 'being accepted by God' [NLT], '(makes people) right with God' [NCV], 'to be acceptable to him' [CEV], '(the undeserved gift of) 'Not guilty' [TEV].

QUESTION—What relationship is indicated by ἐκ 'from'?
1. It indicates the time after which or the situation from which justification came [AB, BECNT, Gdt, HNTC, ICC2, NICNT, NTC, St, TH, TNTC; NASB, NCV, NIV, NRSV, REB]. The many trespasses were the occasion that called God's mercy forth [Mor].
2. It is causal [SSA]: what God freely did because many people trespassed.
3. It indicates that for which they are forgiven in Christ's justifying act: he procures our justification from our own innumerable offenses [Ho].

5:17 For if by-the trespass[a] of-the one (person) death[b] reigned[c] through[d] the one,

LEXICON—a. παράπτωμα (LN 88.297) (BAGD 2.a.α. p. 621): 'trespass'. See this word at 5:15. The phrase εἰ...τῷ τοῦ ἑνὸς παραπτώματι 'if by the transgression of the one person' is translated 'because Adam had sinned' [CEV], 'one man sinned' [NCV].
b. θάνατος (LN 23.99) (BAGD 1.f. p. 351): 'death' [AB, BAGD, BECNT, HNTC, ICC2, LN, NICNT, NTC, WBC; all versions].
c. aorist act. indic. of βασιλεύω (LN 37.22) (BAGD 1.c. p. 136): 'to reign'. See this word at 5:14.
d. διά with genitive object (LN 90.4): 'through' [AB, BECNT, HNTC, ICC2, LN, NICNT, NTC, WBC; NASB, NET, NIV, NRSV, REB], 'by' [LN; KJV], 'because of' [GW, NCV, TEV], not explicit [NLT]. The phrase διὰ τοῦ ἑνός 'through the one' is translated 'because Adam had sinned' [CEV].

QUESTION—What relationship is indicated by γάρ 'for'?

It introduces 5:17 as the grounds for 5:16 [BECNT, Gdt, Ho, ICC2]. It introduces another claim following the one made in the previous verse [SSA].

QUESTION—What relationship is expressed by the clause introduced by εἰ 'if'?

It expresses grounds for a conclusion to be drawn [AB, BECNT, Mor, SSA, TH; CEV]: if, as is true.

QUESTION—To what does ἑνός 'one' in the phrase διὰ τοῦ ἑνός 'through the one' refer?

It is masculine and refers to the one person, Adam [AB, BECNT, Gdt, HNTC, Ho, ICC2, Mu, NICNT, NTC, SSA, WBC; KJV, NASB, NCV, NET, NIV, NRSV, REB, TEV].

much more[a] the (ones) receiving[b] the abundance[c] of-grace[d] and of-the gift[e] of-righteousness[f]

LEXICON—a. The phrase πολλῷ μᾶλλον is translated 'much more' [HNTC, ICC2, NTC; KJV, NASB, REB], 'how much more' [AB, BECNT, NICNT, WBC; NET, NIV], 'much more surely' [NRSV], 'surely' [NCV], 'it is even more certain' [GW], 'how much greater' [TEV], not explicit [NLT]. See this phrase at 5:15.

b. pres. act. participle of λαμβάνω (LN 57.125) (BAGD 2. p. 465): 'to receive' [AB, BAGD, BECNT, HNTC, ICC2, LN, NICNT, NTC, WBC; all versions except CEV, NCV], 'to accept' [NCV], not explicit [CEV].

c. περισσεία (LN 59.53) (BAGD p. 650): 'abundance' [AB, BAGD, BECNT, ICC2, LN, NICNT, WBC; KJV, NASB, NET, NRSV], 'excess' [HNTC], 'overflowing' [GW], 'overflowing fullness' [NTC], not explicit [CEV]. This noun is translated as an adjective: 'abundant' [NIV, TEV], 'full' [NCV]; as a phrase: 'in far greater measure' [REB]. The phrase 'the abundance of grace and of the gift' is translated 'God's wonderful, gracious gift' [NLT]. This word stresses God's generosity [Mor].

d. χάρις (LN 88.66) (BAGD 3.b. p. 878): 'grace' [AB, BAGD, BECNT, HNTC, ICC2, LN, NICNT, NTC, WBC; KJV, NASB, NCV, NET, NRSV, REB, TEV], 'provision of grace' [NIV], 'kindness' [LN; GW], not explicit [CEV]. This noun is translated as an adjective: 'gracious' [NLT]. This entire phrase is translated 'But that cannot compare with what Jesus Christ has done. God has been so kind to us, and he has accepted us because of Jesus.' [CEV].

e. δωρεά (LN 57.84) (BAGD p. 210): 'gift' [BAGD, LN]. See this word at 5:15.

f. δικαιοσύνη (LN 88.13) (BAGD 3. p. 197): 'righteousness' [BAGD, BECNT, HNTC, ICC2, LN, NICNT, NTC, WBC], 'uprightness' [AB], '(his) approval' [GW]. This noun is also translated as a verb: 'to be made right with (him)' [NCV], 'to be put right with (him)' [TEV], 'to accept us' [CEV].

QUESTION—What is the relationship between the nouns in the genitive phrase τὴν περισσείαν τῆς χάριτος 'the abundance of grace'?
1. 'Abundance' describes how generously grace is given [ICC1, Mor, Mu, SSA], or how great God's unmerited love is [Ho]. The word 'abundance' modifies both 'grace' and 'free gift', and 'grace' describes the disposition which bestows it [Mu].
2. 'Grace' is epexegetic of 'abundance', as is 'gift of righteousness' which follows [HNTC, NICNT]; the abundance is due to or consists of God's grace and his gift, which is the result of that grace [NICNT].

QUESTION—What is the relationship between the nouns in the genitive phrase τῆς δωρεᾶς τῆς δικαιοσύνης 'the gift of righteousness'?

'Righteousness' is epexegetic of 'gift'; the gift consists of righteousness [AB, BECNT, Gdt, Ho, ICC1, ICC2, Mor, Mu, NICNT, NTC, TH, WBC]. The gift of righteousness is God's action of freely declaring them to be righteous [SSA]. God's acceptance is a gift given, not by passing it from God's hands but by drawing the receiver into his arms [WBC].

shall-reign[a] in[b] life[c] through[d] the one (man) Jesus Christ.

LEXICON—a. fut. act. indic. of βασιλεύω (LN 37.22, 37.64) (BAGD 1.b.δ. p. 136): 'to reign' [AB, BECNT, HNTC, ICC2, LN (37.22, 37.64), NICNT, NTC, WBC; KJV, NASB, NET, NIV, REB], 'to rule' [BAGD, LN (37.64); GW, NCV, TEV], 'to exercise dominion' [NRSV], 'to be king' [BAGD]. The phrase 'shall reign in life' is translated 'shall live and reign' [REB], 'we will live and rule like kings' [CEV], 'will surely have true life and rule' [NCV], 'will live in triumph over sin and death' [NLT].

b. ἐν with dative object (LN 13.8, 83.13): 'in' [AB, BECNT, HNTC, ICC2, LN (13.8, 83.13), NICNT, NTC, WBC; GW, KJV, NASB, NET, NIV, NRSV, TEV], not explicit [CEV, NCV, NLT, REB].

c. ζωή (LN 23.88) (BAGD 2.b.β. p. 341): 'life' [AB, BAGD, BECNT, HNTC, ICC2, LN, NICNT, NTC, WBC; GW, KJV, NASB, NET, NIV, NRSV, TEV], 'true life' [NCV]. This noun is translated as a verb: 'to live' [CEV, NLT, REB].

d. διά with genitive object (LN 90.4) (BAGD A.III.2.b.γ. p. 180): 'through' [AB, BAGD, BECNT, HNTC, ICC2, LN, NICNT, NTC, WBC; NASB, NCV, NET, NIV, NLT, NRSV, REB, TEV], 'by' [LN; KJV], 'because of' [CEV, GW].

QUESTION—What implied difference is there between his two uses of the word 'reign'?

The two clauses are not exactly parallel with regard to the subject of the verb 'reign'; those who were ruled by death will themselves rule in life [HNTC, Mor, Mu, NTC, St, WBC], that is, in the life of the eschatological future after their final vindication [WBC]. In the first clause people are involuntarily subject to the fate of death, though not as a consciously chosen destiny, but in the second clause they experience the reign of life through a personal decision [NICNT]. Those who were slaves under the tyranny of death become kings with Christ, with death under their feet [St].

5:18 Therefore then as through[a] one/of-one[b] trespass, for[c] all people[d] (the result was) for[e] condemnation,[f]

LEXICON—a. διά with genitive object (LN 89.76, 90.8): 'through' [AB, HNTC, LN (89.76, 90.8), NICNT; GW, NASB], 'by' [LN (89.76); KJV], 'by means of' [LN (89.76, 90.8)], 'because' [CEV], 'as the result of' [ICC2; NIV, REB]. This preposition is translated as a verb: 'brought' [BECNT; NCV, NLT], 'came through' [NET], 'resulted in' [NTC], 'led to' [NRSV], 'condemned' [TEV].
- b. εἷς (LN 60.10): 'one' [LN]. This cardinal numerical adjective could modify either the noun παράπτωμα, as in 'one trespass', or an implied actor, as in 'one man'. It is translated as modifying 'trespass' [AB, HNTC, NTC; GW, NASB, NCV, NET, NIV, NLT, REB, TEV]; as modifying 'man' [BECNT, ICC2, NICNT, WBC; CEV, KJV, NRSV].
- c. εἰς with accusative object (LN 90.59): 'for' [HNTC, ICC2, LN, NTC; NET, NIV, NRSV, REB], 'to' [BECNT, LN, NICNT, WBC; NASB, NCV], 'upon' [AB; KJV, NLT], not explicit [CEV, GW, TEV].
- d. πάντας ἀνθρώπους: 'all people' [BECNT, NICNT; NCV, NET, NLT, REB], 'all men' [HNTC, ICC2, NTC, WBC; KJV, NASB, NIV], 'all' [AB; NRSV], 'all mankind' [TEV], 'everyone' [CEV, GW].
- e. εἰς with accusative object (LN 89.48): 'to' [WBC; KJV], 'as a result, with the result that, to cause' [LN]. The phrase εἰς κατάκριμα 'the result was for condemnation' is translated 'resulted in condemnation' [NTC], 'there resulted condemnation' [NASB], 'the result was condemnation' [HNTC; NIV, REB], 'the result...has been...for condemnation' [ICC2], 'brought condemnation' [BECNT; NLT], 'led to condemnation' [NRSV], 'condemnation came' [AB, NICNT; NET].
- f. κατάκριμα (LN 56.31) (BAGD p. 412): 'condemnation' [AB, BECNT, HNTC, ICC2, LN, NICNT; KJV, NASB, NET, NIV, NLT, NRSV, REB], 'punishment' [BAGD], 'punishment of death' [NCV], 'doom' [BAGD]. This noun is translated as a verb: 'to condemn' [TEV], 'to be condemned' [GW].

QUESTION—What relationship is indicated by ἄρα οὖν 'therefore then'?
1. It introduces the apodosis or conclusion of the argument begun in 5:12 [BECNT, Gdt, ICC1, Mor, NTC, TH, WBC]. It introduces what follows in 5:18–21 as a summary to his argument comparing Adam and Christ in 5:12–17 [NICNT]. The phrase also introduces a conclusion to be drawn from 5:15–17 [BECNT].
2. It introduces a new claim, related to but not exactly the same as those in 5:15–17 [SSA].
3. It introduces an inference from all that has been said in the epistle up to this point, as in 5:12, which is that, as we are condemned for the offence of one man, so also are we justified by the righteousness of one man [Ho].

4. It introduces a resumption of what has been argued in the immediately preceding verses [Mu].

QUESTION—What relationship is indicated by ἑνός 'one'?

1. It modifies 'trespass' and is in the genitive case because of the preposition διά [AB, Gdt, HNTC, ICC1, Mu, NTC, SSA; GW, NASB, NCV, NET, NIV, NLT, REB, TEV]: through one trespass. Semantically it refers to the one sin of the one man, Adam [SSA].
2. It is translated as a masculine substantive referring to Adam, the genitive case indicating possession [BECNT, ICC2, NICNT, TNTC, WBC; CEV, KJV, NRSV]: the trespass of one man.

thus also through one/of-one[a] righteous-act,[b] for all people (the result was) for[c] justification/righteousness[d] of-life;[e]

LEXICON—a. εἷς (LN 60.10): 'one' [LN]. This cardinal numerical adjective could modify either the noun δικαίωμα, as in 'one righteous act', or an implied actor, as in 'one man'. It is translated as modifying 'righteous act' [AB, HNTC, NTC; GW, NASB, NCV, NET, NIV, NLT, REB, TEV]; as modifying 'man' [BECNT, ICC2, NICNT, WBC; CEV, KJV, NRSV].

b. δικαίωμα (LN **88.14**) (BAGD 2. p. 198): 'righteous act' [LN, NICNT, WBC; NET, REB, TEV], 'act of righteousness' [BECNT, HNTC, NTC; NASB, NIV, NLT, NRSV], 'act of uprightness' [AB], 'righteous deed' [BAGD], 'righteous conduct' [ICC2], 'good act' [NCV], 'verdict' [GW], 'righteousness' [KJV]. This entire clause is translated 'But because of the good thing that Christ has done, God accepts us and gives us the gift of life' [CEV].

c. εἰς: 'to' [NICNT]. This preposition is translated as a verb: 'to come' [AB, NICNT; KJV, NET], 'to bring' [BECNT], 'to result in' [NTC], 'to lead to' [NRSV]; as a verbal phrase: 'the result was' [HNTC; NIV], 'the result is' [ICC2; REB], 'there resulted' [NASB]; not explicit [CEV, GW, NCV, NLT, TEV].

d. δικαίωσις (LN **56.34**) (BAGD p. 198): 'justification' [AB, HNTC, ICC2, NTC; KJV, NASB, NIV, NRSV], 'acquittal' [BAGD, LN; REB], 'righteousness' [BECNT, NICNT; NET], 'approval' [GW]. This noun is also translated as a verb phrase: 'to be made right with God' [NCV], 'to make right in God's sight' [NLT]. The phrase εἰς πάντας ἀνθρώπους εἰς δικαίωσιν ζωῆς 'for all persons for justification of life' is translated 'sets all people/mankind free and gives them life' [**LN**; TEV].

e. ζωή (LN 23.88) (BAGD 2.b.β. p. 341): 'life' [AB, BAGD, LN, WBC; KJV, NASB, NRSV]. The genitive ζωῆς 'of life' is translated 'that leads to life' [BECNT], 'which leads to life' [HNTC], 'leading to life' [NET], 'resulting in life' [ICC2], 'issuing in life' [NTC], 'that brings life' [NIV], 'that brings true life' [NCV], 'gives us the gift of life' [CEV], 'and gives them life' [NLT, TEV]. The phrase εἰς δικαίωσιν ζωῆς 'for justification of life' is translated 'life-giving approval' [GW], 'justification and life' [NRSV], 'acquittal and life' [REB].

QUESTION—What is the function of ἑνός 'one'?
1. It modifies δικαιώματος 'righteous deed' [AB, Gdt, HNTC, ICC1, Mu, NTC, SSA; CEV, GW, NASB, NCV, NET, NIV, NLT, REB, TEV]: through one righteous deed. Semantically it is the one supreme righteous act of the one man, Christ, which was his substitutionary death [SSA].
2. It is translated as modifying the implied masculine noun 'person' [AB, BAGD, BECNT, Ho, ICC2, NICNT, TNTC, WBC; KJV, NRSV]: through the righteous deed of one person.

QUESTION—What is the meaning of δικαίωμα 'righteous act'?
1. It refers to Jesus' righteous act [AB, BECNT, HNTC, Ho, ICC2, Mu, NICNT, NTC, SSA, TH, TNTC, WBC; CEV, KJV, NASB, NCV, NET, NIV, NLT, NRSV, REB, TEV]: through the righteous act of the one man, Jesus.
1.1 It is his work on the cross [BECNT, HNTC, TNTC, WBC], his substitutionary death [SSA]. His voluntary death on the cross is representative of and the climax to his entire sacrificial earthly ministry [NTC], the crowning act of a life-long obedience [TNTC].
1.2. It is the obedience of his life as a whole [Ho, ICC2, Mu].
2. It refers to God's verdict of justification [Gdt, ICC1, Mor; GW]: through God's act of pronouncing people righteous.

QUESTION—What people are included in the phrase πάντας ἀνθρώπους 'all persons'?
1. It refers to all believers [BECNT, Ho, Mu, NICNT, NTC, SSA, St], to all those in Christ [Mor, NAC]. Terms such as 'many' and 'all people' may be used imprecisely for the sake of the rhetorical balance found throughout this passage [NICNT, SSA]. He uses this strong expression to emphasize that it includes both Jews as well as Gentiles [NTC]. The parallelism is in the manner of operation of condemnation and justification, not the numerical extent of their effects [Mu].
2. It refers to all people [AB, Gdt, ICC1, ICC2, TH, WBC].
2.1 It is an offer available to all, but that does not mean that all will take it [Gdt, ICC1, ICC2, NAC]. It is extended potentially to all, but each person must embrace the redemption offered to them [ICC1].
2.2 It refers to all people of this epoch without respect to ethnicity, that is, to Gentiles as well as Jews, but Paul is not clear about whether or not the 'all' is universal [WBC].

QUESTION—How are the nouns related in the genitive construction δικαίωσιν ζωῆς 'justification/righteousness of life'?
1. It is a justification that leads to life [AB, Gdt, ICC1, Mor, Mu, SSA, TNTC] or includes life [AB].
2. It is a righteousness that leads to life [BECNT, ICC2, Mu, NAC, NICNT, NTC].

3. The genitive may have various meanings, none of which is necessarily excluded, so the ambiguity leaves a richer sense of meaning. That is, δικαίωσιν ζωῆς can mean any and all of the following: life which is righteousness, life which comes from righteousness, and life which results in righteousness [WBC].

QUESTION—What is meant by 'life'?

It refers to eschatological salvation [BECNT], to salvation from wrath in the eschatological future [NICNT], to eternal life [SSA]. 'Life' is explained more fully in chapter 8 [AB]. It is the fullness of everlasting resurrection life described in 2:7 [NTC]. It is spiritual life and the re-establishing of holiness, and ultimately the restoration and glorification of the body itself [Gdt].

5:19 for just-as[a] through[b] the disobedience[c] of-the one man the many[d] were-made[e] sinners,[f]

LEXICON—a. ὥσπερ (LN 64.13) (BAGD 1. p. 899): 'just as' [AB, BAGD, BECNT, LN, NICNT, NTC; NET, NIV, NRSV, TEV], 'as' [HNTC, ICC2, LN, WBC; KJV, NASB, REB], not explicit [CEV, GW, NCV, NLT].

b. διά with genitive object (LN 89.76): 'through' [AB, BECNT, HNTC, ICC2, LN, NICNT, NTC, WBC; GW, NASB, NET, NIV, REB], 'by' [LN; KJV, NRSV], 'as a result of (the fact that)' [TEV], 'because (one person disobeyed God)' [NLT], not explicit [CEV, NCV].

c. παρακοή (LN **36.27**) (BAGD p. 618): 'disobedience' [AB, BAGD, BECNT, HNTC, ICC2, LN, NICNT, NTC, WBC; all versions except CEV, NCV, NLT]. This noun is translated as a verb: 'to disobey' [CEV, NCV, NLT], 'to refuse to listen' [**LN**].

d. πολύς (LN 59.1) (BAGD I.2.a.β. p. 688): 'many' [AB, BAGD, BECNT, HNTC, ICC2, LN, NICNT, NTC, WBC; KJV, NASB, NCV, NET, NIV, NRSV, REB], 'many people' [NLT], 'many others' [CEV], 'all people' [TEV], 'humanity' [GW].

e. aorist pass. indic. of καθίστημι (LN **13.9**) (BAGD 3. p. 390): 'to be made' [AB, BAGD, BECNT, HNTC, ICC2, **LN**, NICNT, NTC, WBC; KJV, NASB, NET, NIV, NRSV, REB, TEV], 'to be caused to be' [LN]. This passive verb is translated as an active intransitive verb: 'to become' [BAGD; GW, NCV, NLT]; as an active transitive verb: 'to cause to be' [CEV]. This means 'to be constituted', that is, to be placed into the class or condition of being a sinner [ICC1].

f. ἁμαρτωλός (LN 88.295) (BAGD 2. p. 44): 'sinner' [AB, BAGD, BECNT, HNTC, ICC2, LN, NICNT, NTC, WBC; all versions except GW]. This noun is translated as an adjective: 'sinful' [GW].

QUESTION—What is meant by many people being made sinners?

1. Once sin entered human life through Adam's sin, all people lived sinful lives [ICC2, SSA, TH]. They became those who sin [SSA]. It does not mean that they are condemned for Adam's sin [ICC2, TH]. Every

descendant of Adam is born into a race of people who are already separated from God [TH]. Here 'many' means all people [SSA].
2. When Adam sinned, his sin was the ground for all people being placed in the category of sinners [Ho, ICC1, NICNT]. This action was apart from anything they chose or decided [ICC1].

so[a] also through the obedience[b] of-the one the many shall-be made[c] righteous.[d]

LEXICON—a. οὕτως (LN 61.9) (BAGD 1.a. p. 597): 'so' [AB, BAGD, BECNT, HNTC, ICC2, LN, NICNT, NTC, WBC; KJV, NASB, NET, NIV, NRSV, REB], 'thus' [LN], not explicit [CEV, NLT]. The phrase 'so also' is translated 'in the same way' [NCV, TEV].
   b. ὑπακοή (LN 36.15) (BAGD 1.b. p. 837): 'obedience' [AB, BAGD, BECNT, HNTC, ICC2, LN, NICNT, NTC, WBC; all versions except CEV, NCV, NLT]. This noun is translated as a verb: 'to obey' [CEV, NCV, NLT].
   c. fut. pass. indic. of καθίστημι (LN 13.9) (BAGD 3. p. 390). See entry above.
   d. δίκαιος (LN 34.47, 88.12) (BAGD 1.b. p. 195): 'righteous' [BAGD, BECNT, HNTC, ICC2, LN (88.12), NICNT, NTC, WBC; KJV, NASB, NET, NIV, NRSV, REB], 'upright' [AB], 'right' [NCV], 'in a right relation with God' [LN (34.47)], '(put) right with God' [LN (34.47); TEV], 'acceptable to God' [CEV], 'right in God's sight' [NLT]. The phrase 'shall be made righteous' is translated 'will receive God's approval' [GW].

QUESTION—What is meant by many being made righteous?
   Unlike the use of 'many' in the previous clause, where it means 'all people', this refers to many since not all are made righteous [SSA]. Christ's obedience made it possible for every person to be put right with God [TH]. This refers to their legal standing before God of being acquitted of all charges, not to being morally upright [ICC1, NICNT]. They are constituted righteous, a status which Christ in his perfect obedience alone has deserved [ICC2]. 'Righteous' is used in the forensic sense of having right standing before God [AB, Gdt, Ho, ICC1, ICC2, Mor, Mu, NAC, NICNT, TH, WBC]. It is used primarily in the forensic sense, but never without the expectation that forensic righteousness will result in ethical righteousness [BECNT, NTC].

QUESTION—What is to be understood from the use of the future tense 'shall be made'?
   1. It is a logical future [AB, BECNT, ICC2, Mu, NAC, NICNT].
   1.1 Their being constituted righteous was in the future from the time of Christ's act of obedience and this refers to the continual acts of making individual people righteous when they believe [ICC1, NICNT].

1.2 Their justification is something present as well as in the eschatological future [AB]. God's grace is now and will continually be being expressed through all future generations [ICC1, Mu].
1.3 The righteousness is their justification, which has already occurred [BECNT, NAC]. It refers to the present life of believers [ICC2].
2. It is a real future, referring to the final judgment [Gdt, WBC].

5:20 Now^a law^b slipped-in,^c in-order-that^d the trespass^e might-increase;^f

LEXICON—a. δέ (LN 89.124, 89.94): 'now' [BECNT, NICNT; NET], 'moreover' [NTC; KJV], 'and' [LN (89.94); NASB], 'but' [ICC2, LN (89.124); NRSV], not explicit [AB, HNTC, WBC; CEV, GW, NCV, NIV, NLT, REB, TEV].

b. νόμος (LN 33.55, 33.333) (BAGD 3. p. 542): 'law' [BAGD, LN (33.333); NRSV, REB, TEV], 'the law' [AB, BECNT, HNTC, ICC2, NICNT, NTC, WBC; KJV, NCV, NET, NIV], 'the Law' [LN (33.55); CEV, NASB], 'God's law' [NLT], 'rules' [GW]. It refers to the Mosaic law [BAGD]. This noun lacks the definite article here.

c. aorist act. indic. of παρεισέρχομαι (LN 34.30) (BAGD 1. p. 624): 'to slip in' [AB, BAGD], 'to slip into' [LN], 'to intrude into this process' [REB], 'to enter' [BECNT; KJV], 'to come in' [BAGD, NICNT, WBC; NASB, NET, NRSV], 'to come in besides' [NTC], 'to come' [CEV, NCV], 'to take a subordinate place' [HNTC], 'to come in as a new feature of the situation' [ICC2]. This active verb is also translated as passive: 'to be added' [GW, NIV], 'to be given' [NLT], 'to be introduced' [TEV].

d. ἵνα (LN 89.59, 89.49): 'so that' [LN; CEV, NET, NIV, NLT], 'that' [AB, BECNT; KJV, NASB], 'in order that' [HNTC, ICC2, NTC], 'to (with infinitive)' [NICNT, WBC; GW, NCV, REB], 'in order to' [LN (89.59); TEV], 'with the result that' [LN (89.49); NRSV].

e. παράπτωμα (LN 88.297) (BAGD 2.a.β. p. 621): 'trespass' [AB, NICNT, NTC, WBC; NIV, NRSV], 'transgression' [BAGD, BECNT, HNTC, LN; NASB, NET], 'misdeed' [ICC2], 'sin' [BAGD, LN; CEV, NCV], 'failure' [GW], 'offense' [KJV], 'law-breaking' [REB], 'wrongdoing' [TEV], not explicit [NLT]. This noun with the definite article is translated as having the definite article by ICC2, NICNT, NTC, WBC; GW, KJV, NASB, NET, NIV, NRSV. It is translated without it by AB, BECNT, HNTC; REB, TEV.

f. aorist act. subj. of πλεονάζω (LN 59.67) (BAGD 1.a. p. 667): 'to increase' [AB, BAGD, BECNT, ICC2, LN, NICNT, NTC, WBC; GW, NASB, NET, NIV, TEV], 'to abound' [KJV], 'to make worse' [NCV], 'to multiply' [HNTC, LN; NRSV, REB]. This clause is translated 'the Law came, so that the full power of sin could be seen' [CEV], 'God's law was given so that all people could see how sinful they were' [NLT].

QUESTION—What 'law' is he referring to here?
1. It is the Mosaic law [AB, BECNT, Gdt, HNTC, ICC1, ICC2, Mu, NAC, NICNT, SSA, TH, TNTC, WBC]. It is the entire OT economy and its institutions [Ho].
2. It probably refers to law in general [Mor].

QUESTION—What is implied in the verb παρεισέρχομαι 'to slip in'?

It indicates that the law comes in addition to or alongside what is already there, and occupies a subordinate place [BAGD, BECNT, HNTC, Ho, ICC1, Mor, NTC, TH]. Sin and death had entered the world (5:12) and now the law is set alongside them [ICC2, WBC]. It was introduced into the situation that was brought about by sin [TH]. It entered into and became a factor in human existence [AB]. It is a parenthetic dispensation in God's dealings with humanity [ICC1, TNTC], entering with Moses and ending with Christ [ICC1]. This statement does not describe the whole purpose of the law, only that purpose relevant to the current discussion [Mu]. Paul uses a word with a negative connotation to indicate the relative unimportance of the law in salvation history, that it has no power to alter the situation in which it was added [NICNT]. The law is personified and the nonfigurative meaning is that God introduced the law [SSA]. Many translate this word as meaning entered without the idea of slipping in or being subordinate: it entered [BECNT; KJV], it came [NICNT, WBC; CEV, NASB, NCV, NET, NRSV], it was given [NLT], it was introduced [SSA; TEV].

QUESTION—How does law cause trespasses to increase?

It multiplies sin in that it increases the awareness of transgression [AB, HNTC, Mor, NAC, NTC, SSA]. It has the effect of defining sin and describing it as transgression against the revealed will of God [ICC1, ICC2, NICNT], thus intensifying the seriousness of it [NICNT]. It increases the awareness of transgression but also stimulates evil desires in rebellious hearts through its prohibitions [Ho, Mu, St, TH, TNTC]. It increases awareness of sin through defining it as transgression of specific rules, but it also increased the sin of the Jewish people in that they became prideful and blind to their sinfulness, and came to depend on their keeping of the law to make them righteous above and beyond the rest of sinful humanity [WBC]. The law became allied with sin and death to bring people under bondage. It increases both the seriousness and the frequency of sinning [BECNT].

but where sin[a] increased, grace[b] abounded-even-more,[c]

LEXICON—a. ἁμαρτία (LN 88.289): 'sin' [AB, BECNT, HNTC, ICC2, LN, NICNT, NTC, WBC; all versions except NLT]. The phrase 'where sin increased' is translated 'as people sinned more and more' [NLT].
b. χάρις (LN 88.66) (BAGD 2.a. p. 877): 'grace' [AB, BAGD, BECNT, HNTC, ICC2, LN, NICNT, NTC, WBC], 'God's grace' [TEV], 'God's kindness' [CEV, GW], 'God's wonderful kindness' [NLT].
c. aorist act. indic. of ὑπερπερισσεύω (LN **59.49, 78.34**) (BAGD 1. p. 841): 'to abound even more' [LN (59.49)], 'to abound all the more' [AB,

HNTC; NASB, NRSV], 'to abound much more' [KJV], 'to increase all the more' [BECNT, NICNT, NTC; NIV], 'to increase even more' [GW], 'to increase much more' [TEV], 'to increase' [NCV], 'to be even more' [LN (78.34)], 'to be even more powerful' [CEV], 'to superabound' [ICC2], 'to overflow in abundance' [WBC], 'to become more abundant' [NLT], 'to multiply all the more' [NET], 'to be even more powerful' [CEV], 'to immeasurably exceed' [REB].

QUESTION—What is he referring to when he says 'where sin increased'?

It refers to Israel in its response to the law [BECNT, Gdt, ICC2, NICNT, WBC]. The law radicalized sin, intensifying its seriousness [BECNT, ICC2, NICNT], as well as increasing the number of transgressions [BECNT]. The ultimate 'increase' of sin is the rejection of the Messiah [Gdt, ICC2, St].

QUESTION—In what way did grace abound even more?

God's grace immeasurably exceeded the extent of human sin [NAC]. His grace is so much more effective and efficacious than evil [Ho, Mor]. Where the law intensified the gravity and occurrences of sin, grace increased to conquer the sin that had been aided and abetted by the law [BECNT]. God's grace has more than matched the intensification of sin caused by the law in the old epoch, and provided a sure promise of life beyond death in the new epoch, something the law could never do [WBC]. Paul is speaking of salvation history; the law's negative purpose of radicalizing sin for Israel by intensifying its seriousness has been more than fully met by the provisions of God's grace [NICNT]. The climax of the increase of sin was the rejection of Christ at the crucifixion, but it was in the cross that God's grace abounded even more [Gdt, ICC2, St], where sin was submerged, as it were, under a flood of pardon [Gdt]. God's grace is victorious over man's rebellion [HNTC].

5:21 so-that^a just-as sin^b reigned^c in^d death,^{e}

LEXICON—ἵνα (LN 89.59, 89.49): 'so that' [AB, LN (89.59, 89.49); NCV, NET, NIV, NRSV], 'in order that' [BECNT, HNTC, ICC2, NICNT, NTC, WBC; REB], 'so' [NLT], 'so then' [TEV], 'that' [KJV, NASB], not explicit [CEV, GW]. When this word is translated 'so that' the phrase could be understood either as a marker of purpose (LN 89.59) or as a marker of result (LN 89.49). Its use as a marker of purpose is shown by the use of conditional terms: 'might reign' [AB; NIV], 'might exercise dominion' [NRSV], 'could rule' [NCV]. Its use as a marker of result is shown by the use of a future indicative verb phrase: 'so that…grace will reign' [NET]. Result is also indicated by a present indicative verb phrase: 'so then…grace rules' [TEV], 'so…God's wonderful kindness rules instead' [NLT].

b. ἁμαρτία (LN 88.289): 'sin' [AB, BAGD, BECNT, HNTC, ICC2, LN, NICNT, NTC, WBC; all versions].

c. aorist act. indic. of βασιλεύω (LN 37.22) (BAGD 1.c. p. 136): 'to reign' [LN], 'to rule' [BAGD]. See this word at 5:14, 17.

d. ἐν with dative object (LN 13.8, 83.13, 89.48, 89.76, 90.10): 'in' [AB, BECNT, HNTC, ICC2, LN (13.8, 83.13), NICNT, NTC, WBC; NASB, NET, NIV, NRSV], 'by' [LN (89.76, 90.10)], 'by bringing' [GW], 'by means of' [LN (89.76); CEV, TEV], 'by way of' [TEV], 'to cause' [LN (89.48)], 'to bring to' [NLT], 'with the result that' [LN (89.48)], 'unto' [KJV]. The phrase 'sin reigned in death' is translated 'sin used death to rule us' [NCV].

e. θάνατος (LN 23.99): 'death' [AB, BECNT, HNTC, ICC2, LN, NICNT, NTC, WBC; all versions].

QUESTION—What relationship is indicated by ἵνα 'so that'?

1. It indicates purpose [AB, BECNT, HNTC, Ho, ICC2, Mor, Mu, NICNT, NTC, SSA, WBC; NCV, NET, NIV, NRSV, REB]: grace abounded even more in order that grace might reign through righteousness.
2. It indicates a result [NLT, TEV]: grace abounded even more. So then, grace reigns through righteousness.

QUESTION—In what sense does sin reign 'in' death?

1. Sin is preeminent in the sphere or dominion of death [BECNT, Ho, ICC1, NICNT; NCV], which is humanity as determined and dominated by Adam [BECNT, NICNT]. The subjects over whom sin rules are people who are as good as dead [ICC1].
2. Sin used death to rule people [HNTC, NTC; CEV, NCV, TEV].
3. Sin ruled over people and brought death [ICC2, SSA; GW, NLT]. It rules along with death and results in death [ICC2]. All inevitably sin with the result that they all die [SSA].
4. Sin's rule over people is characterized by and summed up in the death it causes [WBC].

thus also grace[a] might-reign[b] through[c] righteousness[d]

LEXICON—a. χάρις (LN 88.66) (BAGD 2.a. p. 877): 'grace' [AB, BAGD, BECNT, HNTC, ICC2, LN, NICNT, NTC, WBC], 'God's grace' [REB, TEV], 'kindness' [LN; CEV, GW], 'God's wonderful kindness' [NLT].

b. aorist act. subj. of βασιλεύω (LN 37.22) (BAGD 1.c. p. 136): 'to reign' [LN], 'to rule' [BAGD; CEV]. See entry above.

c. διά with genitive object (LN 89.76) (BAGD A.III.2.b.γ. p. 180): 'through' [AB, BAGD, BECNT, HNTC, ICC2, LN, NICNT, NTC, WBC; KJV, NASB, NET, NIV, NRSV], 'in' [REB], 'by means of' [BAGD, LN; TEV], 'by (bringing)' [GW], 'by (making)' [NCV], not explicit [CEV, NLT].

d. δικαιοσύνη (LN 88.13) (BAGD 3. p. 197): 'righteousness' [BAGD, BECNT, HNTC, ICC2, LN, NICNT, NTC, WBC; KJV, NASB, NET, NIV, REB, TEV], 'uprightness' [AB], 'justification' [NRSV]. The phrase διὰ δικαιοσύνης 'through righteousness' is translated 'and God has accepted us' [CEV], 'by bringing us his approval' [GW], 'by making people right with him' [NCV], 'giving us right standing with God' [NLT].

QUESTION—In what sense does grace 'reign'?
It manifests its rule by conquering sin [BECNT, NTC]. Where grace has dominion and is in control the outcome is life [NICNT]. Through Christ grace rules, thus making possible the righteousness that leads to eternal life [HNTC]. Grace triumphs and overthrows death [Mor]. It is abundantly and effectively displayed [Ho]. God's grace rules us by putting us into right relationship with himself and by leading us to eternal life [TH].

QUESTION—What relationship is indicated by the preposition διά 'through'?
1. It is instrumental [BECNT, HNTC, ICC1, Mor, NTC, TH]. Through the gift of right standing before God, grace reigns in the sense of bringing eternal life [ICC1, ICC2, SSA, TH]. Grace, through righteousness leads to eternal life [HNTC, Mor, NTC]. By conquering sin, grace demonstrates that people are in right standing with God and not condemned [BECNT]. Righteousness is the means through which grace achieves its effect as well as being the effect itself [WBC]. It is through the righteousness of Christ that grace triumphs [Ho].
2. It indicates the sphere or dominion where grace rules; righteousness is the gateway to life [NICNT].

resulting-in[a] life eternal[b] through[c] Jesus Christ our Lord.

LEXICON—a. εἰς with accusative object (LN 89.48, 89.57): 'resulting in' [BECNT; NLT], 'leading to' [NICNT; NRSV], 'leading us to' [TEV], 'to' [WBC; NASB, NET], 'unto' [ICC2; KJV], 'for the purpose of' [LN (89.57)], 'with the result that' [LN (89.48)]. This preposition is translated as an infinitive: 'to cause' [LN (89.48)], 'to bring' [AB, NTC; NIV]. It is translated as a phrase: 'this results in' [GW], 'and (might) result in' [REB], 'and this brings' [NCV], 'this means that we will have' [CEV], 'with (eternal life) as its goal' [HNTC].
  b. αἰώνιος (LN 67.96) (BAGD 3. p. 28): 'eternal' [AB, BAGD, BECNT, HNTC, ICC2, LN, NICNT, WBC; CEV, KJV, NASB, NET, NIV, NLT, NRSV, REB, TEV], 'everlasting' [NTC]. The phrase 'life eternal' is translated 'our living forever' [GW], 'life forever' [NCV].
  c. διά with genitive object (LN 90.4) (BAGD A.III.2.b.γ. p. 180): 'through' [AB, BAGD, BECNT, HNTC, ICC2, LN, NICNT, NTC, WBC; NASB, NCV, NET, NIV, NLT, NRSV, REB, TEV], 'by' [LN; KJV], 'because of' [CEV, GW].

DISCOURSE UNIT: 6:1–8:39 [ICC1, Mor, NAC, TNTC, WBC]. The topic is progressive righteousness in the Christian [ICC1], the way of godliness [Mor], the righteousness in which we are to grow [NAC], the outworking of the gospel in relation to the individual [WBC], the way of holiness [TNTC].

DISCOURSE UNIT: 6:1–7:25 [Gdt]. The topic is sanctification.

DISCOURSE UNIT: 6:1–7:6 [Gdt; GW]. The topic is the principle of sanctification contained in justification by faith [Gdt], no longer slaves to sin, but God's servants [GW].

DISCOURSE UNIT: 6:1–23 [AB, BECNT, ICC2, Mor, Mu, NAC, NICNT, TNTC, WBC; REB]. The topic is the triumph of grace over the power of sin [BECNT], freedom from self through union with Christ [AB], a life characterized by sanctification [Mor], the sanctifying effects [Mu], no longer slaves to sin [NAC], freedom from bondage to sin [NICNT], freedom from sin [TNTC], does grace encourage sin? [WBC], baptism into Christ [REB].

DISCOURSE UNIT: 6:1–14 [Gdt, HNTC, ICC2, Mor, NAC, NICNT, NTC; CEV, NET, NIV, NLT, NRSV, TEV]. The topic is sanctification in Christ dead and risen [Gdt], shall we continue to sin in order that grace may abound? [Mor], free from sin [HNTC], dead to sin, alive to God [ICC2], dead to sin, alive in Christ [NAC], dead to sin through union with Christ [NICNT], holiness [NTC], dead to sin but alive because of Christ [CEV], the believer's freedom from sin's domination [NET], sin's power is broken [NLT], dead to sin but alive in union with Christ [NIV, TEV], dying and rising with Christ [NRSV].

DISCOURSE UNIT: 6:1–11 [AB, Ho, Mu, WBC]. The topic is freedom from sin and self through baptism [AB], freedom from sin through union with Christ [Ho], the abuse of grace exposed [Mu], the believer has died to sin [WBC].

DISCOURSE UNIT: 6:1–2 [TNTC]. The topic is a supposed objection.

6:1 What then shall-we-say? Should-we-continue[a] in-sin,[b]

LEXICON—a. pres. act. subj. of ἐπιμένω (LN 68.11) (BAGD 2. p. 296): 'to continue' [BAGD, BECNT, ICC2, LN; KJV, NASB, NCV, NRSV, TEV], 'to remain in' [LN, NICNT], 'to keep on' [LN; CEV, NLT], 'to persist' [AB, BAGD, WBC; GW, REB], 'to go on' [HNTC, NTC; NIV].

b. ἁμαρτία (LN 88.289): 'sin' [BECNT, HNTC, ICC2, LN, NICNT, WBC; GW, KJV, NASB, NET, NRSV, REB]. The phrase τῇ ἁμαρτίᾳ 'in sin' is translated 'sinning' [AB, NTC; CEV, NCV, NIV, NLT]. It has also been expanded to include a verb 'to live in sin' [TEV].

QUESTION—What relationship is indicated by τί οὖν 'what then'?

Paul is attempting to anticipate and answer questions that could be raised in objection to his statements about sin, law, and grace in 5:20–21 [BECNT, HNTC, Ho, ICC1, ICC2, Mor, NAC, NICNT, TH], and especially his statement in 5:20b that where sin abounded grace abounded even more [ICC1, Mor, NAC, NICNT, TH]. He is attempting to answer questions that could be raised about his statements in 5:12–21 [AB]. He anticipates an objection to what he has written in the section 3:21–5:21 [SSA], or to the doctrine of justification expounded in the entire epistle up to this point [Gdt]. It asks what is to be concluded from the doctrine of justification by faith apart from works [Ho, SSA].

QUESTION—What does 'in sin' here refer to?

It refers to a state of sin [BECNT, Gdt, ICC1, Mor, Mu, NICNT, WBC; KJV, NASB, NET, NRSV, REB, TEV]: should we continue to live in sin. It is a realm or sphere in which the believer no longer lives [Mu]. Sin is a power, one which is expressed through specific sinful acts [BECNT]. It is a state of continuing to sin [NAC, TH]. It refers to sinners refusing to change from their habitual sin, and instead staying where they are [Mor]. It refers to the lordship or control of sin over the individual discussed in 5:21 [WBC]. Many translate it so that it refers simply to the action of sinning [SSA; CEV, GW, NCV, NLT]: should we continue to sin. It means to continue to sin habitually [SSA].

in-order-that grace[a] may-increase?[b]

LEXICON—a. χάρις (LN 88.66) (BAGD 2.a. p. 877): 'grace' [AB, BAGD, BECNT, HNTC, ICC2, LN, NICNT, NTC, WBC; KJV, NASB, NCV, NET, NIV, NRSV, REB, TEV], 'favor' [BAGD], 'kindness' [LN; GW], '(God's) wonderful kindness' [CEV], 'kindness and forgiveness' [NLT]

b. aorist act. subj. of πλεονάζω (LN 59.67) (BAGD 1.a. p. 667): 'to increase' [BAGD, BECNT, ICC2, LN, NICNT, NTC, WBC; GW, NASB, NET, NIV, TEV], 'to abound' [AB; KJV, NRSV], 'to grow, to become more, to be present in abundance' [BAGD], 'to increase considerably, to multiply, to become more and more' [LN], 'to be more' [BAGD, HNTC], 'to show up even better' [CEV]. This phrase is translated, 'so that God will give us even more grace' [NCV], 'so that God can show us more and more grace' [NLT], 'there may be all the more' [REB]. It refers to grace being conspicuously displayed [Ho]. See this word at 5:20 where trespasses increase.

QUESTION—What is the function of this rhetorical question?

This is the question and answer style that Paul has already used as a pedagogical device 3:1-9, 27-37; 4:1-12 [NICNT]. This question is a hypothetical objection to what Paul has written in 3:21-5:2a and posed so that Paul can give an answer to what is wrong with such an argument [SSA]. This question might be changed into a statement that shows that this is not Paul's belief: 'Someone might say in reply to what I have written that perhaps we should continue to sin in order that he may continue to act even more graciously toward us and keep on forgiving us' [SSA]. This question might be transformed into a statement that gives the forgone conclusion: 'We should by no means continued to sin in our lives just so that God's showing grace will be greater and greater' [TH].

6:2 Never may-it-be![a]

LEXICON—a. aorist mid. (deponent = act.) optative of γίνομαι (LN 13.107) (BAGD I.3.a. p. 158): 'to come to be, to happen' [LN]. The phrase μὴ γένοιτο 'never may it be!' is translated 'No, we should not!' [CEV], 'by no means' [BAGD, NICNT, NTC; NIV, NRSV], 'far from it' [BAGD], 'God forbid' [BAGD, ICC2; KJV], 'Certainly not!' [AB, BECNT, WBC; REB, TEV], 'That's unthinkable!' [GW], 'Of course not' [HNTC; NLT], 'May it never be!' [NASB], 'No!' [NCV], 'Absolutely not!' [NET]. See this expression also at 3:4, 6, 31, and 6:15.

(We) who have-died[a] to-sin,[b]

LEXICON—a. aorist act. indic. of ἀποθνῄσκω (LN 23.99, **74.27**) (BAGD 1.b.γ. p. 91): 'to die' [AB, BAGD, BECNT, HNTC, ICC2, LN (23.99, **74.27**), NICNT, NTC, WBC; all versions except CEV, KJV], 'to be dead to' [LN (74.27); CEV, KJV], 'not to respond to, to have no part in' [LN (74.27)]. The emphasis is on the past event of having died, not the ongoing state of being dead [Ho, Mor, Mu].

  b. ἁμαρτία (LN 88.289): 'sin' [LN]. This word is translated by the phrase 'our old sinful lives' [NCV]

QUESTION—How does he use the relative pronoun οἵτινες 'we who'?

It indicates a quality [Gdt, ICC1, ICC2, Mor, Mu, NICNT]: we who are of the sort or of such a nature.

QUESTION—In what sense have believers 'died' to sin?

They have died to sin in the sense that they are no longer subject to its power [BECNT, NICNT, SSA, TH, WBC]. Sin's reign and control over them is ended [Mor, NAC]. Sin lost its power over believers when they accepted Christ as their savior [Ho]. They died to sin in the sense that when they were converted, professed their faith, and were baptized, they renounced allegiance to their sinful selves and the enticements of this world [NTC]. Their identity is definitively different now such that they no longer live in the realm or sphere of sin [Mu]. Christ's death broke the ruling power of sin and through sharing in his death and resurrection Christians are set free from sin's dominion and enter into the realm of Christ's glorious resurrection life [AB]. Or, they died to sin in God's sight in the juridical sense that God sees them as having died in Christ's death [ICC2]. When a believer takes Christ's expiatory death for himself, it becomes in him the sentence of death to his own sin and an absolute breaking with sin occurs in his will and conscience [Gdt].

how shall-we- still[a] -live[b] in[c] it?

LEXICON—a. ἔτι (LN 67.128) (BAGD 1.b.β. p. 315): 'still' [BAGD, BECNT, ICC2, LN, WBC; GW, NASB, NET], 'yet' [BAGD, LN, NICNT], 'any longer' [NTC; KJV, NIV, REB]. The temporal aspect of this adverb is translated in conjunction with the verb ζάω 'live' as 'go on (living)' [AB, HNTC; NRSV, TEV], 'go on (sinning)' [CEV], 'continue (living)' [NCV], 'continue (to live)' [NLT].

  b. fut. act. indic. of ζάω (LN 23.88) (BAGD p. 336; 3.a. p. 336): 'to live' [AB, BAGD, BECNT, HNTC, ICC2, LN, NICNT, NTC, WBC; all versions except CEV], 'to go on' [CEV].

  c. ἐν with dative object (LN 83.13): 'in' [AB, BECNT, HNTC, ICC2, LN, NICNT, NTC, WBC]. The phrase 'to still live in it' [NASB, NET, NIV] is also translated 'to continue to live in it' [NLT], 'to go on living in it' [NRSV, TEV], 'to live in it any longer' [REB], 'to still live under sin's influence' [GW], 'to continue living with sin' [NCV], 'to live any longer therein' [KJV], 'to go on sinning' [CEV]. 'In sin' means to continue to sin [TH], to live in its realm and under its authority [WBC].

QUESTION—What is the function of this rhetorical question?

It is a moral appeal to avoid living in sin [ICC2, NICNT], although it is based on the fact of having been freed from the dominating power of sin [NICNT]. He is saying that acquiescence to sin is incompatible with being a Christian [Ho, Mor, NTC, St]. Continuing to live in sin is an impossibility for a believer, and if one lives in sin he is not a believer [Ho, Mu, NAC]. They have not actually become dead to sin in the sense of no longer feeling the desire to sin, but the exhortation means that they should begin to consider themselves unresponsive to sinful desires [SSA]. The death is the death of Adam spoken of in 5:12–21, and those who are in Christ have been transferred from being in Adam and his epoch [WBC].

DISCOURSE UNIT: 6:3–14 [TNTC]. The topic is the meaning of baptism.

6:3 **Or do-you-not-know**[a] **that as-many-as we-were-baptized**[b] **into**[c] **Christ Jesus,**

LEXICON—a. pres. act. indic. of ἀγνοέω (LN 28.13, 32.7) (BAGD 1. p. 11): 'to not know' [AB, BAGD, BECNT, HNTC, LN (28.13), NTC; CEV, GW, KJV, NASB, NET, NIV, NRSV, TEV], 'to be unaware' [LN (28.13), WBC], 'to not understand, to fail to understand' [LN (32.7)], 'to be ignorant' [BAGD, ICC2, LN (28.13), NICNT], 'to forget' [NCV, NLT, REB].

b. aorist pass. indic. of βαπτίζω (LN 53.41) (BAGD 2.b.β. p. 132): 'to be baptized' [AB, BAGD, BECNT, HNTC, ICC2, LN, NICNT, NTC, WBC; all versions]. The phrase 'as many as we were baptized into Christ Jesus' is translated 'all who share in Christ Jesus by being baptized' [CEV].

c. εἰς with accusative object (LN 90.23): 'into' [LN]. The phrase 'to be baptized into Christ Jesus' [AB, BECNT, HNTC, ICC2, NICNT, NTC, WBC; GW, KJV, NASB, NET, NIV, NRSV] is also translated 'to be baptized into union with Christ Jesus' [REB, TEV], 'to become part of Christ when we are baptized' [NCV], 'to share in Christ Jesus by being baptized' [CEV], 'to be baptized to become one with Christ Jesus' [NLT].

QUESTION—What is implied by the question 'do you not know'?

He is asserting that they really do know this [AB, ICC2, Mor, NICNT, NTC, TH]. Translated as a statement it would be 'certainly you know that when we were baptized...' [TH]. They not only know this, it was their whole purpose in turning to Christ initially [Ho]. The Roman Christians already knew the reality of what he is saying from their own experience [NICNT]. The content of what he is about to state belonged to the common tradition of the church in that day [ICC2]. He is appealing to what is already familiar to them to draw a conclusion that should be obvious once he states it [WBC]. Or, they may or may not know this, but it is something he wants them to remember [SSA]. He is stating that an antinomian attitude is the result of ignorance about the meaning of conversion and baptism [St].

QUESTION—What is meant by being baptized 'into' Christ?
1. 'Into' indicates being put into union with Christ [AB, BECNT, Ho, ICC1, Mor, Mu, NAC, NICNT, St, TH, TNTC, WBC; REB, TEV]. They then are united with his death [BECNT, Mu, NAC, NICNT], as well as with his burial and resurrection [BECNT]. They are put into close personal relation to him [NTC]. It describes the initial movement of incorporation by which a person comes into life in Christ [AB].
2. They have been baptized 'into' his name [HNTC, ICC2]. This means they have received Christian baptism, indicating they have made a personal decision concerning a relationship with Christ [ICC2]. It indicates they have become Christ's [HNTC]. They have been baptized in relation to the name of Christ Jesus, whose property they became at that point [Gdt].

QUESTION—Is he speaking of the specific act of baptism or of the wider reality of everything involved in conversion?

He is referring to the act of baptism itself, which is an event that signifies death to a whole way of life [Mor]. Baptism is a symbol of the entire redemptive event which Christ's death brings about and which is brought to completion in the believer's faith [NAC]. In baptism they are incorporated into him and through their union with him by faith they share in his crucifixion, burial, resurrection, and exaltation [TNTC]. In speaking of baptism as he does, he is actually speaking of the believer's saving union with Christ that baptism signifies, and assumes for the sake of the discussion that there is genuine faith on the part of those who have been baptized [Ho].

we-were-baptized[a] into[b] his death?[c]

LEXICON—a. aorist pass. indic. of βαπτίζω (LN 53.41) (BAGD 2.b.β. p. 132): 'to be baptized' [AB, BAGD, BECNT, HNTC, ICC2, LN, NICNT, NTC, WBC; GW, KJV, NASB, NET, NIV, NRSV, REB, TEV]. The phrase 'we were baptized into his death' is translated 'by being baptized also share in his death' [CEV], 'we shared his death in our baptism' [NCV], 'we died with him' [NLT].

b. εἰς with accusative object (LN 90.23): 'into', [AB, BECNT, HNTC, ICC2, LN, NICNT, NTC, WBC; GW, KJV, NASB, NET, NIV, NRSV, REB], 'into union with' [TEV], 'with respect to' [LN], 'with reference to' [LN]. This preposition is also translated as a verb phrase: 'to share (his death)' [NCV], 'to share in (his death)' [CEV], not explicit [NLT].

c. θάνατος (LN 23.99) (BAGD 1.b.β. p. 351): 'death' [AB, BAGD, BECNT, HNTC, ICC2, LN, NICNT, NTC, WBC; all versions except NLT]. This word is translated as a verb: 'to die' [NLT]

QUESTION—What is meant by being baptized 'into' Christ's death?

It means that they share in the effects of Christ's death [NICNT]. Baptism points to and is a pledge of their death to sin which, in God's sight has already occurred [ICC2]. In receiving baptism, believers testify that they have personally appropriated the benefits of Christ's death [Gdt, Ho, ICC2, SSA]. Through baptism they have union with Christ in his suffering and dying and as a result, victory over sin [AB]. Through baptism they participated in Christ's death and resurrection, and this anticipates the affliction and resurrection they will have to go through before entering the age to come [HNTC]. Christ's death to sin becomes their death to sin [NAC]. It means that bringing people into close personal relationship with Christ makes his death become meaningful to them as that which removes their guilt and gives them power to fight the pollution of sin [NTC].

6:4 Therefore we-were-buried-with[a] him through[b] baptism[c] into[d] death,[e]

LEXICON—a. aorist pass. indic. of συνθάπτω (LN **52.8**) (BAGD p. 789): 'to be buried with' [AB, HNTC, LN, NTC, WBC; all versions except GW], 'to be buried together with' [BAGD, BECNT, ICC2, LN, NICNT], 'to be placed into the tomb with' [GW].

b. διά with genitive object (LN 89.76, 90.8): 'through' [AB, BECNT, HNTC, ICC2, LN (89.76, 90.8), NICNT, NTC, WBC; NASB, NET, NIV], 'by' [LN (89.76); KJV, NLT, NRSV, REB, TEV], 'by means of' [LN (89.76, 90.8)], not explicit [CEV, GW, NCV]

c. βάπτισμα (LN 53.41) (BAGD 2. p. 132): 'baptism' [AB, BAGD, BECNT, HNTC, ICC2, LN, NICNT, NTC, WBC; KJV, NASB, NET, NIV, NLT, NRSV, REB, TEV]. The phrase διὰ τοῦ βαπτίσματος 'through baptism' is translated 'when we were baptized' [CEV, GW, NCV].

d. εἰς with accusative object (LN 84.22): 'into' [AB, BECNT, HNTC, ICC2, LN, NTC, WBC; GW, KJV, NASB, NET, NIV, NRSV, REB], 'unto' [NICNT], not explicit [CEV, NCV, NLT, TEV].

e. θάνατος (LN 23.99) (BAGD 1.b.β. p. 351): 'death' [BAGD, BECNT, LN, NICNT, NTC, WBC; KJV, NASB, NET, NIV, NRSV]. The phrase εἰς τὸν θάνατον 'into death' is translated 'into his death' [HNTC, ICC2; GW, REB], 'we shared his death' [NCV, TEV], 'we died' [CEV, NLT], 'in order that we would be unresponsive to sinful desires' [SSA].

QUESTION—What relationship is indicated by οὖν 'therefore'?

It draws the inference from 6:3 that because we are baptized into his death we are also joined with him in his burial [BECNT, Gdt, ICC2, Mor, Mu, NICNT, SSA]. It draws an inference from 6:3 to confirm what he has said in 6:2 that those who are dead to sin can't live in it any more [Ho].

QUESTION—Why does he mention burial?

Burial confirms and validates the fact that death has occurred [BECNT, Gdt, ICC1, ICC2, Mu, NAC, TNTC]. It emphasizes the completeness and finality of death [Mor]. Burial symbolizes the fact that Christians delve down so deeply into the meaning of Christ's death, even bury themselves in it, that they see its marvelous benefits for them [NTC]. It is burial that gives meaning to resurrection [Mu]. Burial symbolizes being cut off from the world [Ho].

QUESTION—What relationship is indicated by διά 'through'?

Baptism is the instrument through which believers are buried with Christ, though a believer's association with Christ's death and burial occurs in a way that cannot be precisely defined with respect to time or nature [NICNT]. Believers are buried with Christ when they are baptized [TH; CEV]. Baptism is a decisive event in which God powerfully and unequivocally lays claim to a person's life [ICC2]. Because of their having been baptized and by reflecting on its meaning they comprehend the significance of Christ's self-sacrificial death [NTC].

QUESTION—With what action is 'into' to be taken?

It is to be taken with 'baptized' death [AB, BECNT, Gdt, HNTC, ICC2, Mor, Mu, NICNT, NTC, WBC; GW]: we were baptized into.

in-order-that just-as Christ was-raised[a] from[b] dead[c] (persons) through[d] the glory[e] of-the Father,

LEXICON—a. aorist pass. indic. of ἐγείρω (LN 23.94) (BAGD 2.c. p. 215): 'to be raised' [AB, BAGD, BECNT, HNTC, ICC2, LN, NICNT, NTC, WBC; all versions except GW], 'to be raised to life, to be caused to live again' [LN], 'to be brought back from (death)' [GW].

b. ἐκ with genitive object (LN 84.4): 'from' [AB, BECNT, HNTC, ICC2, LN, NICNT, NTC, WBC; all versions except CEV, GW], 'out from, out of' [LN]. The phrase ἐκ νεκρῶν 'from among dead persons' is translated '(raised) to life' [CEV], '(brought back) from death to life' [GW].

c. νεκρός (LN 23.121) (BAGD 2.a. p. 535): 'the dead' [AB, BAGD, BECNT, HNTC, ICC2, LN, NICNT, NTC, WBC; KJV, NASB, NCV, NET, NIV, NLT, NRSV, REB], 'death' [GW, TEV]. The phrase 'was raised from dead' is also translated 'was raised to life' [CEV].

d. διά with genitive object (LN 89.76, 90.8): 'through' [BECNT, ICC2, LN (89.76, 90.8), NTC, WBC; NASB, NET, NIV], 'by' [AB, LN (89.76), NICNT; CEV, GW, KJV, NCV, NLT, NRSV, REB, TEV], 'by means of' [LN (89.76, 90.8)], 'in a manifestation of' [HNTC].

e. δόξα (LN **76.13**, 79.18) (BAGD 1.a. p. 203): 'glory' [AB, BECNT, HNTC, ICC2, LN (79.18), NICNT, NTC, WBC; CEV, KJV, NASB, NET, NIV, NRSV], 'glorious power' [LN (**76.13**); GW, NLT, REB, TEV], 'wonderful power' [NCV], 'amazing might' [LN (76.13)].

QUESTION—What relationship is indicated by ἵνα 'in order that'?

It indicates purpose [AB, BECNT, Gdt, Ho, ICC2, Mor, Mu, NTC, WBC]. The purpose for believers' participation in Christ's death, burial and resurrection is that they might live differently; this purpose clause is almost imperatival in its effect [BECNT]. We share his death in order to partake in his life [Ho].

QUESTION—What relationship is indicated by ὥσπερ 'just as'?

It is comparative, but also has a causal sense in that the newness of life that Christians experience is based on the resurrection of Christ [BECNT, Ho, Mu, NICNT, NTC, WBC].

QUESTION—What is meant by Christ being raised ἐκ νεκρῶν 'from dead (persons)'?
1. It means that he was raised from among those who are dead [ICC1, ICC2, NICNT, WBC; KJV, NASB, NCV, NET, NIV, NLT, NRSV, REB].
2. It is translated as his having been raised from death without reference to other dead persons [SSA, TH; CEV, GW, TEV]. He was resurrected [SSA], raised to life [CEV].

QUESTION—What does δόξα 'glory' represent here?
It refers to God's power [AB, BECNT, ICC2, NICNT, SSA, TH], to his glorious or majestic power [NTC, TNTC]. It is the power of God gloriously exercised or manifested [ICC1, ICC2, Mor, NAC, NICNT, St]. It is God's omnipotent power gloriously manifested in the resurrection [Ho]. Christ's resurrection manifested the glory of the father [HNTC, Mu].

thus also we might-walk[a] in[b] newness[c] of-life.[d]

LEXICON—a. aorist act. subj. of περιπατέω (LN 41.11) (BAGD 2.a.δ. p. 649): 'to walk' [BAGD, BECNT, ICC2, NICNT, NTC, WBC; KJV, NASB, NET, NRSV], 'to live' [BAGD, LN; CEV, GW, NCV, NIV, NLT, TEV], 'to conduct (oneself)' [AB, BAGD], 'to exist' [HNTC], 'to set out (on)' [REB]. This verb reflects the fact that the life is not so much a possession as an activity engaging the believer [Mu, NAC].
b. ἐν with dative object (LN 13.8), 'in' [AB, BECNT, HNTC, ICC2, LN, NICNT, NTC, WBC; KJV, NASB, NET, NRSV], '(to set out) on' [REB], not explicit [CEV, GW, NCV, NIV, NLT, TEV].
c. καινότης (LN **58.70**) (BAGD p. 394): 'newness' [BECNT, ICC2, LN, NICNT, NTC, WBC; KJV, NASB, NRSV]. The phrase καινότητι ζωῆς 'newness of life' is translated, 'a new life' [BAGD, HNTC; CEV, GW, NCV, NET, NIV, NLT, REB, TEV], 'a new way (of life)' [AB]. This word occurs only here and in 7:6 in the NT.
d. ζωή (LN 23.88) (BAGD 2.b.α. p. 340): 'life' [AB, BAGD, BECNT, HNTC, ICC2, LN, NICNT, NTC, WBC; all versions]

QUESTION—How are the nouns related in the genitive construction καινότητι ζωῆς 'newness of life'?
1. It is attributive: the life is new [AB, BECNT, Gdt, HNTC, Ho, ICC1, ICC2, SSA, St, TH, TNTC], lived in a new way [ICC2, TH], or lived according to a new principle [ICC1]. It is the new resurrection life [HNTC], a new mode or quality of life [TNTC]. It is life that is new and springs from a new source, as compared with that which is natural and original [Ho]. This unusual expression emphasizes the quality of newness [Mor, NTC], and connotes something extraordinary [Mor]. To speak of newness of life instead of new life gives prominence to the new nature of the life [Gdt].
2. It is objective: it is the newness or new age that gives life [NICNT].
3. It is epexegetic: it is the newness that is life [Mu], a new sphere which is life [NAC].

6:5 For if we-have-become joined-with[a] the likeness[b] of-his death,[c]

LEXICON—a. σύμφυτος (LN **89.117**) (BAGD p. 780): 'joined with' [HNTC, NICNT; NCV], 'united with' [NTC; GW, NASB, NET, NIV, NLT, NRSV], 'knit together' [WBC], 'grown together' [BAGD], 'grown into union' [AB], 'united together' [BECNT], 'one with' [LN; TEV], 'conformed to' [ICC2], 'like' [LN], 'planted together' [KJV], 'identified with' [REB]. This entire clause is translated 'If we shared in Jesus' death by being baptized' [CEV]. This word does not occur elsewhere in the NT.

b. ὁμοίωμα (LN **64.3**) (BAGD 1. p. 567): 'likeness' [BAGD, BECNT, LN, NICNT, WBC; KJV, NASB, NET], 'similarity' [LN], not explicit [ICC2; NLT, REB]. The phrase τῷ ὁμοιώματι τοῦ θανάτου αὐτοῦ 'in the likeness of his death' is translated 'in dying as he died' [**LN**; TEV], 'through a death like his' [AB], 'in a death like his' [NTC; GW, NRSV], '(united with him) like this in his death' [NIV], 'by means of the image of his death' [HNTC]. This entire clause is translated as 'If we shared in Jesus' death by being baptized' [CEV], 'Christ died, and we have been joined with him by dying too' [NCV].

c. θάνατος (LN 23.99) (BAGD 1.b.β. p. 351): 'death' [AB, BAGD, BECNT, HNTC, ICC2, LN, NICNT, NTC, WBC; all versions except NCV, TEV], '(joined with him) by dying too' [NCV], 'in dying (as he did)' [TEV].

QUESTION—What relationship is indicated by γάρ 'for'?

It introduces a validation of what was said in the previous verse [Gdt, HNTC, ICC2, Mu, TH, WBC]. It indicates the reason for what is stated in 6:4, which is that believers are to walk in newness of life because they share in Christ's death and resurrection [BECNT, Gdt, Mu, SSA]. It shows the close connection between this verse and the two preceding it [NTC].

QUESTION—What relationship is indicated by εἰ 'if'?

It introduces a true statement as the basis for reasoning [Mor, NAC, NICNT, SSA, WBC; NCV, NLT, TEV]: since we have become joined with the likeness of his death.

QUESTION—What is meant by σύμφυτος 'united'?

It means to be united with [BECNT, Gdt, ICC2, Mor, NAC, NICNT, TH], to be in an intimate union with [Ho]. It signifies growing together in a close union [AB, ICC1, Mor, Mu], such as in grafting [AB, Gdt, ICC1, Mor], or in the fusing of the edges of a wound or a broken bone growing together [WBC].

QUESTION—What is the object of σύμφυτος 'united'?

1. The implied object is 'with him'; they have been united with him in the likeness of his death [AB, Gdt, Mor, NAC, NTC, TH].
2. The object is τῷ ὁμοιώματι 'the likeness'; they have been joined with the likeness of his death [Ho, ICC1, ICC2, Mu, NICNT, WBC]. In baptism they have become conformed to the pattern of his death [ICC2]. The fusion with the likeness of Christ's death is equivalent to a fusion with Christ in his death [WBC].

3. The object is 'his death'; they have been joined with his death through the act of baptism [AB, HNTC].

QUESTION—What relationship is indicated by the dative case of ὁμοίωμα 'likeness'?

1. It indicates manner; that is, in the likeness of his death [BECNT, ICC2, NAC], or in a death like his [NTC].
2. It is instrumental, indicating means [Gdt, HNTC]. That is, joined by means of the image of his death, which is baptism [HNTC], or joined by means of the likeness of his death, which is the inner experience by which Christ's death is reproduced within the believer [Gdt].
3. It indicates that 'likeness' is the object of the verb phrase σύμφυτοι γεγόναμεν 'we have become joined with': we have become joined with the likeness of his death [ICC1, ICC2, Mu, NICNT, WBC]. Being fused together with the likeness of Christ's death means to be fused with Christ in his death, a death which ends the old epoch and breaks sin's dominion [WBC].

QUESTION—What is meant by the phrase τῷ ὁμοιώματι τοῦ θανάτου αὐτοῦ 'in the likeness of his death'?

It expresses similarity, referring to dying as Christ died [AB, ICC1, ICC2, LN, NAC, TH]. It refers to sharing in the death of Jesus [BAGD; CEV], undergoing a death like his [ICC1]. They have been joined together in a similar death [Ho]. 'Likeness' means that there is a sharing or participation in Christ's death, but their experience of death is not exactly the same as his in every respect [BECNT, Mor, NAC]. Through union with Christ believers experience a death to sin that corresponds to but is not identical with his own death [Mu]. Believers' union with Christ means they are united with Christ in a death like his, such that his death enables them to die to constantly living in sin [NTC]. The theme of the paragraph is separation from sin, and this phrase uses the metaphor of death to show the finality of that separation [SSA]. In some way believers actually share or participate in the death that Christ died, though the time and nature of that is not clearly defined, and they will also evidence a conforming to the pattern of Christ's death throughout their lives [NICNT]. It refers to baptism as something representing or being the image of his death [AB, HNTC]. It refers to the believer's being fused together to the reality of Christ's epoch-ending and sin-defeating death in the here and now [WBC]. It refers to the initial act of faith in which Christ's death is reproduced in the believer as a death to sin [Gdt].

certainly[a] also we-shall-be (joined with-the likeness)[b] of-the resurrection;[c]

LEXICON—a. ἀλλά (LN **91.11**) (BAGD 4. p. 38). The phrase ἀλλὰ καί 'certainly…also' is translated 'certainly' [BAGD, **LN**, NTC; GW, NRSV], 'certainly also' [NTC, WBC; GW, NASB, NET, NIV], 'also' [AB, BECNT, HNTC, ICC2, NICNT; KJV, NCV, NLT, REB]. This

clause is translated 'we will be raised to life with him' [CEV], not explicit [TEV]. There is a considerable ellipsis in the text [**LN**].
- b. There is no lexical entry in the Greek text for the phrase 'joined with the likeness', but is carried forward anaphorically from the first clause in this verse because of the conditional sentence structure and the parallelism of the two clauses [AB, BECNT, ICC2, NICNT, NTC, WBC; GW, KJV, NASB, NCV, NET, NIV, NRSV, REB, TEV].
- c. ἀνάστασις (LN 23.93) (BAGD 2.a. p. 6): 'resurrection' [AB, BAGD, BECNT, HNTC, ICC2, LN, NICNT, NTC, WBC; KJV, NASB, NET, NIV, NRSV, REB]. This entire phrase has been translated 'raised to life' [CEV, TEV], 'come back to life' [GW], 'by rising from the dead' [NCV], 'raised (as he was)' [NLT].

QUESTION—What is the function of the phrase ἀλλὰ καί?

It stresses the certainty of what is expressed in the second clause [BECNT, Gdt, Mu, NAC, NICNT, WBC]. It points to the sharp contrast between Christ's death and his resurrection [Mor, Mu].

QUESTION—Does the future tense verb ἐσόμεθα 'we shall be' indicate a real future or a logical future?
- 1. It indicates a real future [BECNT, HNTC, NICNT, TH, TNTC, WBC], though there are significant implications for the present life as well [BECNT, NICNT, WBC]. Christ's death and resurrection are historical events as well as eschatological events that transcend time, and which have power to affect the life of Christians in the present [BECNT]. Their identifying with Christ and being knit together in the ongoing reality of Christ's death and resurrection enables them to show the effect of his death and resurrection in their present lives and gives them hope that they will share in the resurrection of the body [WBC].
- 2. It indicates a logical future [AB, Gdt, Ho, Mu, NAC, NTC, SSA, St]. It expresses a logical sequence to what is said in the first part of the verse, and describes the share that the Christian already enjoys in the risen life of Christ here and now [AB]. This statement of fact is used in a hortatory sense [Gdt]. It refers to being conformed in the moral life to Christ [ICC2, NAC, St], to walking in newness of life [Mu, NTC]. Paul is primarily concerned that the believer experience the resurrection now in his moral life, but there is also a view to the future in that he will experience it fully at the resurrection of the dead [Ho, Mor]. The future tense is used to indicate certainty [Ho, Mu].

6:6 **knowing this, that our old[a] man[b] was-crucified-together-with[c] (him),**

LEXICON—a. παλαιός (LN **58.75**) (BAGD 2. p. 605): 'old' [AB, BAGD, BECNT, HNTC, ICC2, LN, NICNT, NTC, WBC; all versions except CEV, GW]. It implies being inferior, obsolete, and unsatisfactory [LN]. The phrase ὁ παλαιὸς ἡμῶν ἄνθρωπος 'our old man' is translated 'the persons we used to be' [CEV, GW].

b. ἄνθρωπος (LN 9.24, 41.43) (BAGD 2.c.β. p. 68): 'man' [BAGD, LN, NICNT, NTC, WBC; KJV, NET], 'person' [CEV, GW]. The phrase παλαιὸς...ἄνθρωπος 'old man' is translated 'old self' [AB, HNTC, ICC2, LN; NASB, NIV], 'old sinful selves' [NLT], 'old pattern of life' [LN], 'old person' [BECNT], 'old life' [NCV], 'old humanity' [REB], 'old being' [TEV].

c. aorist pass. indic. of συσταυρόω (LN 20.78) (BAGD 2. p.795): 'to be crucified together with' [BAGD, BECNT, LN], 'to be crucified with' [AB, HNTC, ICC2, NICNT, NTC, WBC; GW, KJV, NASB, NET, NIV, NLT, NRSV, REB], 'to be nailed to the cross with' [CEV], 'to be put to death with' [TEV], 'to die with' [NCV].

QUESTION—What relationship is indicated by the participle γινώσκοντες 'knowing'?

1. It introduces support for the argument stated in the previous verse [Mu]. It introduces in 6:6–7 a restatement and elaboration of what has been said in 6:4–5, which is that we know that our old man was crucified with Christ to render it powerless so we would no longer serve sin [NICNT].
2. It introduces 6:6–8 as a second basis, following the first in 6:2–5, for the two appeals to be made in 6:9–11 and in 6:12–14 [SSA].
3. The knowing is the means or condition of the resurrection mentioned in the previous verse, since the believer participates in Christ's resurrection through the moral cooperation of the act of knowing or recognizing [Gdt].

QUESTION—What is meant by ὁ παλαιὸς ἡμῶν ἄνθρωπος 'our old man'?

Note that there is a considerable amount of overlap possible between the positions listed below, and one does not rule out the other. Some commentators see 'the old man' as being essentially the same as the unregenerate nature or 'the flesh', while others distinguish between them, seeing 'the old man' as the Adamic human nature which passes away at conversion and baptism, and 'the flesh' as that part of human nature which is inclined toward sin and which remains until physical death, even in the Christian.

1. It refers to the whole fallen human nature, which comes under God's condemnation [ICC2]. It is the sinful nature we had prior to conversion [Gdt, Ho, SSA], the self as the radical principle of being, the corrupt nature as opposed to the new nature brought about by regeneration [Ho]. It is the old self or ego, the unregenerate man in his entirety as contrasted with the new, regenerate man in his entirety [Mu]. It refers to the kind of people we used to be before conversion [AB, TH, TNTC], the old self that belonged to the old aeon and was dominated by sin and subject to wrath [AB]. It is the person we once were, considered apart from grace [NTC].
2. It is a term that describes humanity in the old era, a corporate structure to which believers once belonged through their connection to Adam and as part of the old age of sin and death [BECNT, NICNT, WBC]. This is true both in a corporate sense as well as individually [BECNT, NICNT]. It is the Adamic self, the person as being in union with Adam, who is the old

man, as opposed to the person in union with Christ, the new man [HNTC, Mor, NAC]. It is not the old nature but the person we used to be in Adam, the whole of us in our pre-conversion past [St].

QUESTION—At what point in time does this co-crucifixion with Christ occur?
1. It occurred at the time of Christ's crucifixion, since by virtue of their solidarity with him they were present in Christ at his crucifixion [NAC, NTC, TNTC].
2. It occurs when the believer is baptized in the sense that baptism is the sign and seal of the fact that by God's gracious decision the fallen nature was crucified with Christ at Golgotha [ICC1, ICC2]. The effect of Christ's death enters into their experience at their baptism [WBC].
3. It transcends temporal categories and is not related to a point in time [NICNT].

in-order-that the body^a of-sin^b might-be-made-ineffective,^{c}

LEXICON—a. σῶμα (LN 8.1, **9.8**) (BAGD 1.b. p. 799): 'body' [AB, BECNT, HNTC, ICC2, LN (8.1), NICNT, NTC, WBC; CEV, GW, KJV, NASB, NET, NIV, NRSV], 'physical being' [**LN** (9.8)], 'self' [LN (9.8); REB, TEV], 'selves' [NCV]. The entire clause is translated 'so that sin might lose its power in out lives' [NLT]. It refers to the mortal body [BAGD].

b. ἁμαρτία (LN 88.289) (BAGD 3. p. 43): 'sin' [BAGD, BECNT, ICC2, LN, NICNT, NTC, WBC; GW, KJV, NASB, NET, NIV, NRSV], 'sin-dominated' [HNTC]. The genitive phrase τῆς ἁμαρτίας 'of sin' is translated 'sinful' [AB; CEV, NCV, NLT, REB, TEV], 'prone to sin' [LN (**9.8**)].

c. aorist pass. subj. of καταργέω (LN 13.100, 76.26) (BAGD 2. p. 417): 'to be abolished' [HNTC, LN (76.26)], 'to be done away with' [BAGD, WBC; NASB, NIV], 'to be put an end to' [LN (13.100); GW], 'to be invalidated' [LN (76.26)], 'to be rendered powerless' [AB, NICNT], 'to lose its power' [NLT], 'to be nullified' [BECNT], 'to be destroyed' [ICC2, NTC; KJV, NRSV, TEV], not explicit [CEV, NCV]. The entire clause is translated 'for the destruction of the sinful self' [REB], 'so that the body of sin would no longer dominate us' [NET].

QUESTION—What relationship is indicated by ἵνα 'so that'?
It indicates that the purpose for our old man being crucified together with Christ was to destroy or render ineffective the 'body of sin' [BECNT, Ho, Mor, NICNT, SSA, St], which is to release believers from the slavery of sin [BECNT, NICNT, St].

QUESTION—What is meant by the 'body of sin'?
1. It refers to the whole person enslaved by sin [AB, BECNT, ICC2, NAC, NICNT, NTC, TH], the sinful human nature [HNTC, St], the old man [Ho]. 'Body' refers to the whole person [NICNT, TH, WBC], especially with regard to the person's interaction with the world [NICNT]. 'Body' refers to the whole person, including the physical body which constitutes him as a social being, but it also denotes humanity in solidarity with

Adam and as belonging to the old era of sin's domination [WBC]. When Paul refers to the body as being sin-dominated he is really speaking of human nature in its domination by sin [HNTC]. It refers to the sin-dominated unregenerate nature [TNTC]. It is the whole person as being inclined toward sin and oriented to this world and not to the things of God and of the Spirit [AB]. It is human nature apart from regenerating grace, the whole person viewed as controlled by sin [NTC]. The body is the emblem of the sin that dominates those in Adam as well as the means by which sin is actually carried out [BECNT]. The phrases 'the body of sin' and 'our old man' are synonymous, except that 'body' gives more emphasis to the sinful man as an individual [ICC2]. He uses the term 'body of sin' figuratively, with sin being personified as a body, something that can be crucified [Ho].

2. It refers primarily to the body, which is so subject to the pull of sin [Mor]. It is the body as conditioned and controlled by sin [Mu]. It refers to the sinful inclinations of the body [SSA]. It is the body as the seat of sin, of which sin has taken possession and which is subject to its carnal impulses [ICC1].

3. It refers to the use of the body as its instrument by the sinful, corrupt will [Gdt].

QUESTION—In what sense could it be said that the 'body of sin' is made ineffective or destroyed?

It refers to making ineffective the pull of the sinful nature on our bodies to commit sin [SSA, TNTC]. The influence of the power of sin over the whole person, as represented by the body, is taken away and the person can interact with the world apart from the domination of sin [NICNT]. In baptism the sinful self is crucified and dies in God's estimation, so that in practical living we can cease being enslaved to sin [ICC2]. Believers are not free from sin's presence, since they still sin, but they are freed from its dominion and mastery in that they now have the choice not to sin [BECNT]. Death to sin through baptism is the first step toward ending the pattern of servitude to sin [HNTC]. It means that by the working of the Holy Spirit the person no longer desires to be controlled by sin [NTC]. The body is an integral part of the personality, and since the old man has been crucified, resulting in the radical transformation of the entire person, the body of the believer is no longer conditioned and controlled by sin [Mu]. The sinful nature is stripped of its power [NAC]. The pull of carnal impulses on the body as the seat of sin is reduced to a state of impotence [ICC1]. Christians no longer need focus their sights on sin [AB]. A decisive step has been taken to put the power of sin and death out of action and rendered powerless, enabling the believer to live under the lordship of grace, though with the final ultimate victory yet to come [WBC]. The inward power or principle of evil is destroyed, giving us spiritual freedom [Ho]. The sinful nature is deprived of power [Gdt, St].

(that) we no-longer be-slaves[a] to-sin;[b]
LEXICON—a. pres. act. infin. of δουλεύω (LN **37.25**) (BAGD 2.c. p. 205): 'to be a slave to' [AB, BECNT, HNTC, ICC2, LN, NTC; GW, NASB, NCV, NIV, NLT, REB], 'to be the slaves of' [CEV, TEV], 'to be enslaved to' [NET, NRSV], 'to serve' [BAGD, NICNT, WBC; KJV], 'to obey' [BAGD], 'to be controlled by' [LN].

b. ἁμαρτία (LN 88.289) (BAGD 3. p. 43): 'sin' [AB, BAGD, BECNT, HNTC, ICC2, LN, NICNT, NTC, WBC; all versions].

QUESTION—What relationship is indicated by the genitive articular infinitive τοῦ μηκέτι δουλεύειν 'that we no longer be slaves'?
1. It expresses purpose [HNTC, ICC1, ICC2, LN, Mor, Mu, NICNT, SSA, TH, WBC]: in order not to be slaves. It is a second purpose for our old man being crucified together with Christ [SSA].
2. It expresses result [AB]: rendering the sinful body powerless results in freedom from sin.

6:7 **for the (one) having-died[a] is-freed[b] from[c] sin.[d]**
LEXICON—a. aorist act. participle of ἀποθνῄσκω (LN 23.99) (BAGD 1.b.β. p. 91): 'to die' [AB, BAGD, BECNT, ICC2, LN, NICNT, NTC, WBC; GW, NASB, NCV, NET, NIV, NLT, NRSV, TEV], 'to be dead' [KJV]. The phrase 'the one having died' is translated 'a dead man' [HNTC], 'dead people' [CEV], 'death' [REB].

b. perf. pass. indic. of δικαιόω (LN **37.138**) (BAGD p. 197; 3.c. p. 197): 'to be freed' [BAGD, NTC; GW, KJV, NASB, NET, NIV, NRSV], 'to be set free' [LN; NLT, TEV], 'to be made free' [NCV], 'to be declared free' [WBC], 'to be justified' [BECNT, ICC2, LN, NICNT], 'to be released' [LN], 'to be acquitted' [AB]. The phrase 'to be freed from sin' is translated 'to be clear from sin,' [HNTC], 'sin doesn't have power over' [CEV], 'death cancels the claims of sin' [REB].

c. ἀπό with genitive object (LN 89.122): 'from' [HNTC, ICC2, LN, NICNT, NTC, WBC; all versions except CEV, REB], 'separated from' [LN], 'of' [AB, BECNT], not explicit [CEV, REB].

d. ἁμαρτία (LN 88.289): 'sin' [AB, BECNT, HNTC, ICC2, LN, NICNT, NTC, WBC; all versions except NCV, TEV], 'sin's control' [NCV], 'power of sin' [TEV].

QUESTION—What relationship is indicated by γάρ 'for'?
1. It indicates the reason for the proposition in 6:6 that believers should not be slaves of sin, which is their participation in the death of Christ through baptism [AB, BECNT, Mor, NICNT]. It confirms what was said in 6:6 that believers cannot serve sin any longer because they have been justified from it [Ho].
2. It indicates an amplification the statement in 6:6 concerning the body of sin being made ineffective [SSA].

QUESTION—What area of meaning of the verb δικαιόω is intended in this verse?

Note that there is a certain amount of overlap possible between the positions listed below, and one does not rule out the other.
1. It is forensic and means to be justified or acquitted from the guilt of sin [AB, BECNT, HNTC, Ho, ICC1, ICC2, Mor, Mu, NTC, St]. It also implies growth in personal sanctification [BECNT], of becoming free from sin's power [HNTC, NTC]. The believer is free because of having been justified [Ho, Mu, NTC, TNTC]. In 6:18 and 22 he uses a different verb to signify being freed, whereas in all the other uses of this word in Romans and the NT it means 'to justify' [St].
2. It means to be liberated or freed from sin [BAGD, Gdt, NAC, NICNT, SSA, TH, WBC]. It is to be free from blame in the event of disobedience [Gdt].

6:8 But[a] if[b] we-died[c] with[d] Christ,

LEXICON—a. δέ (LN 89.94, 89.124): 'but' [AB, HNTC, ICC2, LN (89.124), NICNT, WBC; NRSV, REB], 'and' [LN (89.94); NLT], 'as surely as' [CEV], not explicit [BECNT, NTC; GW, KJV, NASB, NCV, NET, NIV, TEV].
  b. εἰ (LN **89.30**) (BAGD III. p. 219): 'if' [AB, BAGD, BECNT, HNTC, ICC2, LN, NICNT, NTC, WBC; GW, KJV, NASB, NCV, NET, NIV, NRSV, REB], 'since' [**LN**; NLT, TEV], 'because' [LN], 'as surely as' [CEV].
  c. aorist act. indic. of ἀποθνῄσκω (LN 23.99) (BAGD 1.b.β. p. 91): 'to die' [AB, BAGD, BECNT, HNTC, ICC2, LN, NICNT, NTC, WBC; all versions].
  d. σύν (LN 89.107) (BAGD 2.b. p. 781): 'with' [AB, BAGD, BECNT, HNTC, LN, NICNT, NTC, WBC; all versions].

QUESTION—What relationship is indicated by δέ 'but'?
1. It indicates a contrast [AB, HNTC, ICC1, ICC2, LN (89.124), NICNT, WBC; NRSV, REB]: but. It implies, 'but there is another side to the process of dying to sin, that of living with him' [ICC1].
2. It indicates a continuation [Gdt, Ho, Mor, SSA; NLT; probably BECNT, NTC; GW, KJV, NASB, NCV, NET, NIV, TEV]: and/now. It adds to 6:7 another amplification for the statement in 6:6 concerning the body of sin being made ineffective [SSA]. Union with Christ not only delivers us from the penalty and power of sin, it also enables us to share his life [Gdt, Ho, Mor].

QUESTION—How is εἰ 'if' to be understood here?

It introduces a true statement as the basis for reasoning [AB, BAGD, BECNT, ICC2, LN, Mu, NICNT, SSA, WBC]: since we have died with Christ, we conclude that we will live with him.

we-believe[a] **that also we-shall-live-with**[b] **him,**

LEXICON—a. pres. act. indic. of πιστεύω (LN 31.35) (BAGD 1.a.β. p. 660): 'to believe' [AB, BAGD, BECNT, HNTC, ICC2, LN, NICNT, NTC, WBC; all versions except NCV, NLT], 'to know' [NCV, NLT]

b. fut. act. indic. of συζάω (LN 23.96) (BAGD p. 775): 'to live with' [BAGD, HNTC, ICC2, LN, NICNT, NTC, WBC; all versions except NLT], 'to live together with' [BECNT, LN], 'to come to life with' [AB], 'to share his new life' [NLT].

QUESTION—Does συζήσομεν αὐτῷ refer primarily to the eschatological future or to the present experience?

1. It refers primarily to the present experience of new life in Christ, but there is also a reference to the future life [Ho, ICC2, Mor, Mu, NAC, NTC, SSA, TH]. Since the life with him is permanent and eternal, it applies to the body as well as to the soul [Ho].

2. It refers primarily to the eschatological future [AB, Gdt, HNTC, ICC1, NICNT, WBC]. The use of 'believe', which shows that this is an object of faith as opposed to a present experience, indicates that 'live' primarily has a future meaning [NICNT]. However, this future expectation has significant implications for how life is lived in the present [NICNT, TH]. It does not refer exclusively to the future, for they participate in the resurrection life of Christ here and now [AB, Mu].

3. Paul would not have distinguished between sharing Christ's life now and sharing his resurrection on the last day; life now is resurrection anticipated and resurrection will be life consummated [St].

6:9 knowing that Christ having-been-raised[a] **from**[b] **dead**[c] **(persons) no-longer dies,**

LEXICON—a. aorist pass. participle of ἐγείρω (LN 23.94) (BAGD 2.c. p. 215): 'to be raised' [AB, BAGD, BECNT, HNTC, ICC2, LN, NICNT, NTC, WBC; KJV, NASB, NCV, NET, NIV, NRSV, REB, TEV], 'to be raised to life' [LN; CEV], 'to be brought back to life' [GW], 'to rise' [BAGD; NLT].

b. ἐκ with genitive object (LN 84.4): 'from' [AB, BECNT, HNTC, ICC2, LN, NICNT, NTC, WBC; all versions except CEV, GW], not explicit [CEV, GW].

c. νεκρός (LN 23.121): 'dead' [AB, BECNT, HNTC, ICC2, LN, NICNT, NTC, WBC; KJV, NASB, NCV, NET, NIV, NLT, NRSV, REB], 'death' [TEV]. The phrase 'to be raised from dead persons' is translated 'to be raised to life' [CEV], 'to be brought back to life' [GW]. See this phrase at 6:4.

QUESTION—What relationship is indicated by the participle εἰδότες 'knowing'?

1. It is causal, giving the grounds for what was just said in the previous clause [Gdt, Ho, Mor, NICNT]. The participle is translated with a causal

ROMANS 6:9

conjunction: 'since' [AB, HNTC, NTC]; 'because' [BECNT]; 'for' [NIV, TEV].
2. It introduces grounds for the following exhortation in 6:11 [SSA].
3. It introduces another thought relevant to what has just been said [ICC2].
4. It is translated as an independent verb, presumably a participle of attendant circumstance [CEV, GW, NCV, NET, NLT, NRSV]: we know that death has no power over Christ.

QUESTION—What relationship is indicated by the participle ἐγερθείς 'having been raised'?

It is causal [NICNT, SSA, WBC]: because Christ was raised, he no longer will die.

death[a] no-longer rules[b] him.
LEXICON—a. θάνατος (LN 23.99) (BAGD 1.f. p. 351): 'death' [BAGD, LN].
  b. pres. act. indic. of κυριεύω (LN 37.50) (BAGD 2. p. 458): 'to rule' [BAGD, BECNT, LN; TEV], 'to reign over' [LN], 'to have power over' [CEV, GW, NCV, NLT], 'to be lord' [BAGD], 'to be master' [BAGD; NASB], 'to have mastery over' [NET, NIV], 'to have sway over' [AB] 'to have dominion over' [HNTC; KJV, NRSV], 'to be under the dominion of' [REB], 'to exercise lordship over' [ICC2, NICNT, NTC, WBC].

QUESTION—What is meant by death no longer ruling Christ?

His resurrection means there is a final and decisive break with death and its power [NICNT]. Death has power through sin, but when Christ died for the sins of mankind, he was set free from the power of sin forever [ICC1]. Christ no longer will be subject to dying [Gdt, SSA]. Christ's resurrection can never be undone, Christ is supreme [Mor]. Just as Jesus' resurrection, which cannot be negated or repeated, assures an irreversible victory over death, so also the Christian's participation in Christ's resurrection cannot be suspended or interrupted; dying and rising with Christ are definitive and decisive [Mu]. The perpetuity of Christ's life is the ground of assurance of the perpetuity of the life of believers; because his life is perpetual he is the source of life for his people in all ages [Ho]. Christ's death is an eschatological event, anticipating the resurrection of the coming age; consequently he cannot die again [HNTC]. If the crucifixion was sin's final move, the resurrection was God's checkmate, and the game is over with sin in final defeat [NAC].

6:10 For that-which[a] he-died,
LEXICON—a. ὅς (LN 92.27) (BAGD I.7.c. p. 584): 'that which' [LN], 'whereas' [LN], 'what' [BAGD]. This relative pronoun gains its content from what immediately follows [BAGD]. The phrase ὃ ἀπέθανεν 'that which he died' is translated 'the death he died' [BECNT, TNTC, WBC; NET, NIV, NRSV], 'the death which he died' [ICC2], 'the death that he died' [NICNT; NASB], 'in dying as he did' [AB], 'whereas he died' [HNTC], 'when Christ died' [CEV, NCV], 'when he died' [GW, REB], 'in that he died' [KJV], 'because he died' [TEV], 'he died' [NLT].

QUESTION—What relationship is indicated by γάρ 'for'
1. It introduces the grounds for his statement in 6:9 that death has no power over Christ, which is that he has died to sin [ICC2, NICNT]. Christ can never die again because he has died once for all [Ho].
2. It introduces a further reason for the statement in 6:7 that the dominion of death has ended [BECNT].
3. It introduces an amplification of what is said about Christ's death in 6:9 [SSA, TH].

QUESTION—What does the neuter relative pronoun ὅ 'that which' refer to?
1. This neuter pronoun is translated as if its antecedent is the masculine noun θάνατος 'death' [AB, BAGD, BECNT, Gdt, ICC2, Mor, NICNT, NTC, TNTC, WBC; NASB, NET, NIV, NRSV]: the death he died.
2. It is used adverbially, referring to the fact of his death [HNTC, Mu; CEV, GW, KJV, NCV, REB]: whereas he died [HNTC, Mu], when he died [CEV, GW, NCV, REB], in that he died [KJV].

he-died to-sin[a] once-for-all;[b]

LEXICON—a. ἁμαρτία (LN 88.289): 'sin' [AB, BECNT, HNTC, ICC2, LN, NICNT, NTC, WBC; CEV, KJV, NASB, NET, NIV, NRSV, REB]. The phrase 'he died to sin' is translated 'he died…to sin's power' [GW], 'he died to defeat the power of sin' [NCV], 'he died…to defeat sin' [NLT], 'because he died sin has no power over him' [TEV].
b. ἐφάπαξ (LN **60.68**) (BAGD 2. p. 330): 'once for all' [BAGD, BECNT, HNTC, NICNT, NTC; NASB, NET, NIV, NRSV, REB], 'once and for all' [AB, ICC2, **LN,** WBC; CEV, GW], 'once' [KJV, NLT] 'once and never again' [LN], 'one time—enough for all time' [NCV], not explicit [TEV].

QUESTION—What relationship is indicated by the dative construction τῇ ἁμαρτίᾳ 'to sin'?
It is a dative of disadvantage, meaning that Christ has adversely affected sin by his death [BECNT, ICC2, TNTC]. His death destroyed the power of sin and death [AB, BECNT]. His death condemned sin by taking the penalty of sin upon himself [ICC2]. It is a dative of reference, meaning that with reference to sin Christ died to expiate and destroy it [Gdt]. In identifying with his people he was subject to the power of sin and death which had dominated them [WBC]. It indicates that his death is a release from the realm of sin as a ruling power in the old age [NICNT]. Christ was set free from this realm of existence where sin dominates people [TH]. He died to sin in that he bore its penalty [St]. At his death the liability to sin and death, and the pressure of the human sin which he bore and which wreaked its effect on him, ceased to have any claim upon him [ICC1]. He was separated from sin by death and has ended once and for all any relationship with sin [NAC]. His life on earth was conditioned by the sin of his people and the fact of having to carry the burden of his people's sin [NTC]. He died to sin in that he died sinless, he died rather than sin, and he died in a context of sin [HNTC]. He

came into a sinful world and died a death that put sin away, which meant an end of being in the realm of sin and of his whole relationship with sin [Mor]. Just as death ruled over him until he broke its power, so also his incarnate state was conditioned by the sin with which he was vicariously identified; having destroyed the power of sin and death he entered the resurrection state that was not conditioned by sin [Mu]. He freed himself from the burden of the sin which he had assumed and bore on the cross, and he is now separated from it [Ho].

and that-which[a] he-lives, he-lives to-God.

LEXICON—a. ὅς (LN 92.27) (BAGD I.7.c. p. 584): 'that which' [LN], 'whereas' [LN], 'what' [BAGD]. This relative pronoun gains its content from what immediately follows [BAGD]. The phrase ὅ ζῇ 'that which he lives' is translated 'the life he lives' [NET, NIV, NRSV], 'the life that he lives' [NASB, REB], 'now he lives' [GW, NLT], 'now he is alive' [CEV], 'he now has a new life' [NCV], 'now he lives his life' [TEV], 'in that he lives' [KJV]. Compare with the phrase ὅ ἀπέθανεν 'that which he died' at the beginning of this verse.

QUESTION—What is meant by the statement ζῇ τῷ θεῷ 'he lives to God'?

He lives for God [BECNT, WBC] and for his glory [BECNT, NICNT]. The resurrection has given him new power to fulfill God's will and purpose [NICNT]. Christ left this sinful world and entered a world where he enjoys uninterrupted fellowship with God [NAC, TH]. He has left sin's realm and is no longer focused on the negative aspects of putting away sin, and now he lives singly devoted to God and for his glory [Mor]. After accomplishing the work of redemption he was then enabled to live to God in an unhampered manner in the sense of no longer being affected by the sins of his people which he bore [NTC]. His resurrection state is in no way conditioned by the sin which he vicariously bore [Mu]. His life belongs preeminently to God and as a consequence is everlasting [ICC2]. He continues to live to God only, in complete obedience to and dependence upon God; he never lived otherwise [HNTC]. He lives in order to honor God [SSA], solely to manifest and serve him [Gdt], seeking his glory [St]. He enjoys a new relationship to the Father [AB]. He lives only for God and no other power has any influence over him [ICC1]. This expression stands in contrast to the previous statement that he died to sin, and is used primarily to indicate the analogy between Christ and believers, who like Christ must be freed from sin and devoted to God [Ho].

6:11 Thus you also, consider[a] yourselves to-be dead[b] to-sin[c]

TEXT—Some manuscripts omit the infinitive εἶναι 'to be'. GNT brackets this word, indicating doubt about including it, but does not mention it as a variant in the apparatus. This word is omitted either for textual or stylistic reasons by most versions except KJV and NASB. NCV translates this word as 'being'.

LEXICON—a. pres. mid. (deponent = act.) impera. of λογίζομαι (LN 31.1) (BAGD 1.b. p. 476): 'to consider' [AB, BAGD, BECNT, HNTC, LN, NICNT, NTC; GW, NASB, NET, NLT, NRSV], 'to regard' [LN; REB], 'to recognize' [ICC2], 'to reckon' [WBC; KJV], 'to think of' [CEV, TEV], 'to count' [NIV], 'to see (yourselves as)' [NCV]. This is Paul's first use of the imperative as exhortation in Romans [AB, NAC].
  b. νεκρός (LN 23.121) (BAGD 1.b.α. p. 534): 'dead' [AB, BAGD, BECNT, HNTC, ICC2, LN, NICNT, NTC, WBC; all versions].
  c. ἁμαρτία (LN 88.289): 'sin' [AB, BECNT, HNTC, ICC2, LN, NICNT, NTC, WBC; KJV, NASB, NET, NIV, NLT, NRSV, REB], 'the power of sin' [CEV, NCV], 'sin's power' [GW], 'so far as sin is concerned' [TEV].

QUESTION—What relationship is indicated by οὕτως 'thus'?
  1. It is inferential [BECNT, ICC2, NICNT, NTC]. It draws the conclusion from what is stated in 6:1–10, that because believers have died with Christ to sin and have experienced the power of the resurrection, they should live as though they are dead to sin and alive to God [BECNT, NICNT].
  2. It indicates a comparison ('in the same way') between Christ's dying and living and Christians' attitudes about themselves [Gdt, Mor, NAC, NICNT, WBC].

QUESTION—What is implied by the use of the verb λογίζομαι 'consider'?
They are to consider it to be true because in fact it really is true [AB, BECNT, Gdt, Ho, ICC2, Mor, Mu, NAC, NICNT, St, TNTC, WBC]. The present tense indicates that it is something that must continually be done [NAC, NICNT]. It is an eschatological reality that is not necessarily visibly apparent [HNTC]. They must regard themselves as they are in Christ, not as they used to be in themselves [Gdt]. The fact that they are in principle dead to sin and alive to Christ must become the abiding conviction of mind and heart, because they are no longer what they used to be [NTC]. Their acceptance of the fact helps them become more and more aware of that union psychologically [AB].

QUESTION—In what sense are they 'dead' to sin?
Here sin is conceived of as a power, one whose mastery and dominion over those in Christ has come to an end [BECNT]. They are dead in terms of sin having no power over them [TH], and they are free from its penalty and dominion [Ho]. In God's estimation it is as though they died with Christ in his crucifixion [ICC2]. By faith those belonging to Christ have passed through death and resurrection and have come to be alive to God [HNTC]. They died with Christ who died to sin [Mor, NTC], and though they are not immune to sinning, they have been set free from the dominion of sin [Mor]. They have died to sin through union with Christ in the efficacy of his death [Mu]. They should not respond to sin's stimulus [SSA]. Their entire perspective has been so radically changed that they should consider themselves dead to its appeal and power [NAC]. The part of them that used to be under the dominion of sin is dead [ICC1]. They are no longer living in relation to the power of sin and are in that sense dead to it [WBC]. The new

nature is wholly consecrated to God and has broken with sin, and it is this identity that the believer must regard as his true self [Gdt].

but/and^a living^b to-God in^c Christ Jesus.

TEXT—Some manuscripts add τῷ κυρίῳ ἡμῶν 'our Lord' following Ἰησοῦ 'Jesus'. GNT omits this phrase with an A decision, indicating that the text is certain. This phrase is added only by KJV.

LEXICON—a. δέ (LN 89.124, 89.94): 'but' [AB, BECNT, HNTC, ICC2, LN (89.124), NTC; CEV, GW, KJV, NASB, NET, NIV, TEV], 'and' [LN (89.94), NICNT, WBC; NCV, NLT, NRSV, REB].

b. pres. act. participle of ζάω (LN 23.88) (BAGD 2.a. p. 336; 3.b. p. 337): 'to live' [BAGD, LN]. The phrase 'to be living to God' is translated 'to live for God' [CEV, GW], 'alive to God' [NASB, NET, NIV, NRSV, REB], 'alive unto God' [KJV], 'alive with God' [NCV], 'living in fellowship with God' [TEV], 'to be able to live for the glory of God' [NLT].

c. ἐν with dative object (LN 83.13, 89.119) (BAGD I.5.d. p. 259): 'in' [AB, BAGD, BECNT, HNTC, ICC2, LN (83.13, 89.119), NICNT, NTC, WBC; NASB, NET, NIV, NRSV], 'in union with' [LN (89.19); REB], 'through' [KJV, NCV, NLT, TEV]. The phrase 'in Christ Jesus' is translated 'in the power Christ Jesus gives you' [GW], 'Christ Jesus has given life to you' [CEV]. The preposition refers to a close personal relation [BAGD].

QUESTION—What is meant by the phrase 'in Christ Jesus'?

It speaks of the union that believers have with Christ [AB, Gdt, Ho, Mor, NAC, NTC]. Christ is the representative head over the new age or realm, and those who belong to that realm are incorporated into him and experience whatever has taken place with him [NICNT]. Paul normally uses the phrase 'with Christ' to refer to actions (such as dying and rising) in which believers participate in Christ's experience, and 'in Christ' to refer to ongoing conditions such as being dead to sin or alive to God that they experience through him [NICNT]. It refers to God's decision to accept Christ's death as having been our death, such that in God's sight we died in his death and were raised up in his resurrection [ICC2]. Those who belong to Christ by faith are 'in Christ' and they are transferred from this age to the one to come through his death and resurrection, which were events of eschatological significance and scope [HNTC]. Through their union with him his blessings come to them, and they also have union with each other [Mor]. Through the Holy Spirit they have a union with Christ's risen body and share in the vitality of his life in glory [AB]. The Christian has his being in Christ just as a fish lives in the water, a creature in the air, or a plant in the earth [ICC1]. Through their identification with Christ in his death they derive their vital energies and motivations from God in Christ [WBC]. This phrase may mean that their experience of union with Christ is the means by which they are alive to God, and 'in' may also indicate the circumstances accompanying being alive to God, or it may explain what being alive to God means [TH].

DISCOURSE UNIT: 6:12–23 [AB, Mu, WBC]. The topic is freedom for commitment [AB], the imperatives for the sanctified [Mu], the believer should therefore live to God [WBC].

6:12 Therefore sin should- not -rule[a] in[b] your mortal[c] body

LEXICON—a. pres. act. impera. of βασιλεύω (LN 37.22) (BAGD 1.c. p. 136): 'to rule' [BAGD, WBC; GW], 'to reign' [BECNT, HNTC, LN, NICNT, NTC; KJV, NASB, NET, NIV, REB], 'to control completely' [LN], 'to control' [NCV, NLT]. This third person singular imperative is translated 'don't let sin rule' [CEV], 'sin must not rule' [TEV], 'do not, then, let sin hold sway' [AB], 'do not let sin exercise dominion' [NRSV], 'stop, then, allowing sin to reign' [ICC2]. Even though this is a third person imperative, it is a command to believers: don't let sin rule [AB, BECNT, Gdt, HNTC, ICC2, Mu, NAC, NICNT, TH; CEV].

b. ἐν with dative object (LN 83.13): 'in' [BECNT, HNTC, ICC2, LN, NICNT, NTC, WBC; KJV, NASB, NET, NIV, NRSV, REB, TEV], 'over' [AB], not explicit [CEV, GW, NCV, NLT].

c. θνητός (LN **23.124**) (BAGD p. 362): 'mortal' [AB, BAGD, BECNT, HNTC, ICC2, LN, NICNT, NTC, WBC; KJV, NASB, NET, NIV, NRSV, REB, TEV], 'physical' [GW]. This adjective is translated as a verbal phrase: '(your body) is bound to die' [CEV]. The phrase 'your mortal body' is translated 'your life here on earth' [NCV], 'the way you live' [NLT].

QUESTION—What relationship is indicated by οὖν 'therefore'?

It is inferential, drawing a conclusion from 6:11 [BECNT, Gdt, Ho, ICC2, NAC]: since you are dead to sin and alive to God, sin must not rule over you. It draws a conclusion from the whole argument in 6:1–11 [WBC].

QUESTION—What is implied by the present tense of the third person imperative βασιλευέτω 'should (not) rule'?

1. Paul is telling them that they should never let sin rule [BECNT, HNTC, ICC2, Mu, NICNT]. The negated present imperative does not necessarily imply that they are letting sin rule and should stop doing so [BECNT, NICNT]. It is because of the fact that sin does not rule them that Paul urges them not to begin to let it rule [Mu].
2. Paul is telling them to stop allowing sin to rule [AB, Gdt, ICC2, NAC]. They should not continue to let sin reign unopposed in their lives as they always did before [ICC2]. The believer must challenge the authority that sin previously exercised in his or her life [NAC].

QUESTION—In what sense does he use the designation 'your mortal body'?

The body represents the whole person, including, but not limited to, the physical body [BECNT, NAC, NICNT]. The body represents the entire person in contact with this world and is the means of interaction with it [NICNT]. It is the whole man in his fallen condition [ICC2], man as a whole belonging to this world [WBC]. He is referring not just to bodily passions but to all sinful desires and intentions [ICC2, TH]. It refers to our bodies and our personalities as conditioned by the present age, bodies within which sin is ever at hand and personalities within which sinful desires are naturally engendered [HNTC]. The body is the organ through which sin expresses itself [Ho, Mor]. Evil passions are often associated with the body and its functions, and in the fallen state the body tends toward sin and death [NTC]. The lusts mentioned are those specifically associated with the body [Mu]. It is mortal in that it participates in the weakness and frailty of this age [NAC]. 'In your mortal body' is equivalent to saying 'in you' [Ho]. The body with its instincts and passions is destined to die, and therefore should not rule the personality of the believer [Gdt]. It is the physical body, which sin is able to use as a bridgehead through which to govern us [St].

so-as[a] to-obey[b] its desires,[c]

LEXICON—a. εἰς with accusative object (LN 89.48, 89.57) (BAGD 4.e. p. 229): 'so that' [AB, BAGD, HNTC; GW, NASB, NCV, NET, NIV, TEV], 'so that as a result, to cause' [LN (89.48)], 'with the result that' [BECNT, LN (89.48)], 'that' [KJV], 'in order to' [LN (89.57), NICNT], 'for the purpose of' [LN (89.57)], 'in such a way that' [ICC2], 'so (don't obey)' [CEV], not explicit [WBC; NLT]. This preposition is also translated with a verb phrase: 'to make you (obey)' [NTC; NRSV], 'exacting (obedience)' [REB].
  b. pres. act. infin. of ὑπακούω (LN 36.15) (BAGD 1. p. 837): 'to obey' [AB, BAGD, BECNT, HNTC, ICC2, LN, NICNT, NTC, WBC; CEV, GW, KJV, NASB, NET, NIV, NRSV, TEV], 'to give in to' [NLT], 'to follow, to be subject to' [BAGD]. This infinitive is also translated as a finite verb 'you obey' [AB, BECNT, HNTC, ICC2; GW, NET, NIV].
  c. ἐπιθυμία (LN 25.12) (BAGD 3. p. 293): 'desire' [BAGD, BECNT, HNTC, ICC2, LN, WBC; CEV, GW, NET, NIV, NLT, REB, TEV], 'lusts' [AB; KJV, NASB], 'passions' [NICNT, NTC; NRSV], 'what your sinful self wants to do' [NCV].

QUESTION—What relationship is indicated by εἰς 'so as'?

1. It expresses the result of allowing sin to reign [AB, BAGD, BECNT, HNTC, ICC2, Mor, NICNT; GW, NASB, NCV, NET, NIV, TEV]: with the result that you would obey.
2. It introduces purpose [NICNT, TH]. It also has a causative relation: so as to cause you to obey [TH].

QUESTION—What is the antecedent of αὐτοῦ 'its' in the phrase 'its desires'?

The possessive pronoun αὐτοῦ 'its' is neuter and refers to the neuter noun σῶμα 'body', the desires and passions of which should not be obeyed, and not to ἁμαρτία 'sin', which is a feminine noun [BECNT, Gdt, HNTC, Ho, ICC2, Mor, NAC, NICNT, NTC, SSA; CEV, NCV, NRSV, REB, TEV]. The body represents the sinful self [ICC2; TEV].

QUESTION—What is meant by ἐπιθυμία 'desire'?

It refers to evil desires [Mor], to cravings that come from sin [AB], to desires that are in conflict with the will of God [NICNT, TH]. They are lusts associated with the body [Mu]. It is all the lusts of the fallen nature, not just bodily desires [ICC2]. It represents the instincts and appetites of the body which act on the soul to bring it into passions and sin [Gdt]. They are the sinful desires that are naturally engendered in a personality belonging to this age, and which must not be obeyed [HNTC]. It is a dependency on having one's needs satisfied that becomes slavery [WBC].

6:13 nor be-yielding[a] your members[b] to-sin[c] (as) instruments[d] of-unrighteousness,[e]

LEXICON—a. pres. act. impera. of παρίστημι (LN **13.11**) (BAGD 1.a. p. 627): 'to yield' [BAGD; KJV], 'to give control' [WBC], 'to put at (sin's) control' [REB], 'to cause to serve as' [**LN**], 'to put (at sin's) disposal' [AB], 'to present' [BECNT, NICNT; NASB, NET, NRSV], 'to offer' [HNTC, NTC; GW, NCV, NIV], 'to place at the disposal of' [ICC2], 'to surrender' [TEV], 'to let (sin) control' [NLT], 'to let become' [CEV]. See this word also at 6:16, 6:19, and 12:1.

b. μέλος (LN 8.9) (BAGD 1. p. 501): 'member' [AB, BAGD, BECNT, HNTC, ICC2, LN, NICNT; KJV, NASB, NRSV], 'part of one's body' [LN, NTC; CEV, GW, NCV, NIV, NLT, REB], 'part of one's self' [TEV], 'what you are or do' [WBC]

c. ἁμαρτία (LN 88.289): 'sin' [AB, ICC2, LN, WBC; all versions except GW, NLT], 'sin's power' [GW]. The phrase τῇ ἁμαρτίᾳ is translated 'for sin' [NICNT], 'to be used for sinning' [NLT].

d. ὅπλον (LN **6.3**) (BAGD 1. p. 575): 'instrument' [**LN**; KJV, NASB, NIV, NRSV], 'tool' [BAGD, ICC2, LN; NLT], 'means' [LN], 'weapon' [AB, BECNT, HNTC, NICNT, NTC, WBC]. The phrase 'as instruments of' is translated 'be used to do' [GW], 'to be used for' [TEV], 'as things to be used in doing' [NCV], 'as instruments to be used for' [NET], 'as an implement for doing' [REB], 'become a slave of' [CEV].

e. ἀδικία (LN 88.21) (BAGD 2. p. 18): 'unrighteousness' [BAGD, BECNT, HNTC, ICC2, LN, NICNT, WBC; KJV, NASB, NET], 'unjust deed' [LN], 'wickedness' [AB, NTC; NIV, NLT, NRSV], 'any ungodly thing' [GW], 'evil' [CEV], 'wrong' [REB], 'wicked purposes' [TEV].

QUESTION—In what sense does he use the term 'members'?

1. Whereas 'mortal body' represents the entire person in contact with the world [NICNT], 'members' represents the various natural capacities of the person [HNTC, ICC2, NICNT, St], or human faculties [Gdt, Ho, WBC]. It refers to every part that makes up the person [Mor], including bodily members [St].
2. It refers to parts of the physical body such as eyes, hands, and feet [Mu, SSA].

QUESTION—What is meant by the term ὅπλον 'instrument'?

1. It is a reference to instruments in general [Gdt, Ho, LN, Mor, SSA, TH; KJV, NASB, NET, NIV, NRSV] or tools [ICC2; NLT].

2. It is a military reference to weapons [AB, BECNT, HNTC, ICC1, Mu, NICNT, NTC, WBC].

QUESTION—How are the nouns related in the genitive phrase ὅπλα ἀδικίας 'instruments of unrighteousness'?

It indicates purpose; they must not yield their members to the power of sin as weapons for the purpose of acting unrighteously [BECNT, ICC2, NAC, NICNT], to promote or effect unrighteousness [AB, Ho, Mor], or in the service of unrighteousness [HNTC].

but yield[a] yourselves to-God as[b] those-alive[c] from[d] dead[e] (persons)

LEXICON—a. aorist act. impera. of παρίστημι (LN 13.11) (BAGD 1.a. p. 627): 'to yield'. See this word in the first clause of this verse.

b. ὡσεί (LN 64.12) (BAGD 1. p. 899): 'as' [AB, BAGD, BECNT, HNTC, ICC2, LN, NICNT, NTC, WBC; all versions except NLT, REB]. The phrase 'as those alive from dead persons' is translated as 'since you have been given new life' [NLT]. This word is also translated as a phrase: 'think of yourselves as' [REB].

c. pres. act. participle of ζάω (LN 23.88, 23.93) (BAGD 2.a. p. 336): 'to live' [LN (23.88), NICNT], 'to live again' [LN (23.93)], 'to rise to life again' [LN (23.93)], 'to be alive' [BAGD, BECNT, ICC2, WBC; KJV, NASB, NET]. This active participle is translated as passive: 'to be raised to life' [CEV, REB, TEV], 'to be brought from death to life' [NTC; NIV, NRSV]. The phrase ὡσεὶ ἐκ νεκρῶν ζῶντας 'as those alive from dead persons' is translated 'those who have come to life from death' [AB], 'as dead men brought to life' [HNTC], 'as people who have come back from death' [GW], 'people who have died and now live' [NCV], 'since you have been given new life' [NLT].

d. νεκρός (LN 23.121) (BAGD 2.a. p. 535): 'dead'. See the phrase ἐκ νεκρῶν 'from dead persons' at 6:4.

QUESTION—Is there any significance in the use of the aorist imperative 'yield yourselves' in this clause as opposed to the present imperative in the previous clause?

The present imperative of the previous clause indicates something they must stop doing, and the aorist imperative of this clause represents something they must do once for all [Gdt, ICC1, Mor, Mu, NAC, NTC, TH]. The aorist imperative calls for a decisive and resolute action [ICC2, St, WBC], a once-for-all event [Ho, SSA], resulting in an immediate change to a new state [Gdt]. The present tense in the first clause indicates that the prohibition continually remains in force [NICNT, St]. The aorist tense here does not necessarily denote urgency, frequency, or duration, but because the prohibition in the first clause remains in force throughout the life of the believer this related command does also [NICNT]. Or, the forms are used more or less synonymously here [AB, BECNT].

QUESTION—What relationship is indicated by ὡσεί 'as'?
1. It means to yield yourselves as you really are, not as you used to be [NAC]. It indicates a reality [Gdt, Mor], not just a supposition [Mor]. Because they have in one sense been raised with Christ it has the effect of saying 'as in fact you are', but because they have not yet experienced the final resurrection it also has the effect of saying 'as if you were' [HNTC].
2. It indicates the reason they are to yield themselves [BECNT, ICC2, NAC, NICNT]. They should do this because they are alive from the dead by having participated in the power of Christ's resurrection [BECNT, ICC2, NAC, NICNT].

and (yield) your members[a] (as) instruments[b] of righteousness[c] to-God.

LEXICON—a. μέλος (LN 8.9) (BAGD 1. p. 501): 'member' [AB, BAGD, BECNT, HNTC, ICC2, LN, NICNT; KJV, NASB, NET, NRSV], 'body part' [LN], 'bodily parts' [NTC], 'every part of your body' [CEV], 'parts of your body' [GW, NCV, NIV], 'your whole body' [NLT], 'bodies' [REB], 'your whole being' [TEV], 'what you are and do' [WBC].

b. ὅπλον (LN 6.3) (BAGD p. 575): 'instrument' [LN; KJV, NASB, NET, NIV, NRSV], 'tool' [BAGD, ICC2, LN; NLT], 'implement' [REB], 'weapon' [AB, BAGD, BECNT, HNTC, NICNT, NTC, WBC], 'a slave' [CEV]. This noun is also translated as a verb phrase: 'use them (to do)' [GW], 'to be used in' [NCV], 'to be used for' [TEV].

c. δικαιοσύνη (LN 88.13) (BAGD 2.b. p. 196; 3. p. 197): 'righteousness' [BECNT, HNTC, ICC2, LN, NICNT, NTC, WBC; KJV, NASB, NET, NIV, NRSV], 'uprightness' [AB, BAGD], 'righteous purposes' [TEV]. This noun is also translated as a verb phrase: 'to do right' [REB], 'to do what is right' [NLT], 'to do good' [NCV], 'to do everything that God approves of' [GW]. The phrase ὅπλα δικαιοσύνης 'instruments of righteousness' is translated 'instruments to be used for righteousness' [NET], 'implements for doing right' [REB], 'a tool to do what is right' [NLT], 'to be used for righteous purposes' [TEV]. The phrase ὅπλα δικαιοσύνης τῷ θεῷ 'instruments of righteousness to God' is translated 'a slave that pleases God' [CEV], 'a tool to do what is right for the glory of God' [NLT].

QUESTION—How are the nouns related in the genitive phrase ὅπλα δικαιοσύνης 'instruments of righteousness'?
They must yield their members to God as weapons for the purpose of righteousness [BECNT, Mor, NICNT, TH], for the service of righteousness [HNTC], for the promotion of righteousness [Mu], for doing righteous things [SSA], by which righteousness might be effected [Ho].

QUESTION—What area of meaning is intended by the term δικαιοσύνη 'righteousness'?
Here it refers to moral behavior that is pleasing to God [AB, Gdt, HNTC, ICC2, NAC, NICNT, NTC, TH], not to a forensic righteousness [NICNT]. It refers to God's righteous purposes [Mor].

QUESTION—What relationship is indicated by the dative construction τῷ θεῷ 'to God'?
1. It is the indirect object of the implied verb παρίστημι 'yield' [AB, BECNT, HNTC, Ho, ICC2, Mor, Mu, NAC, NTC, SSA, TH, WBC; GW, NCV, NET, NIV, NRSV, REB, TEV, and probably those who translate τῷ θεῷ as 'to God': KJV, NASB]: yield your members to God as instruments of righteousness.
2. It indicates the purpose of the instruments or weapons, that they are instruments of righteousness for the service of God [Gdt, NICNT; CEV, NLT]: yield your members as instruments of righteousness for God.

6:14 For sin[a] shall- not -rule[b] you;

LEXICON—a. ἁμαρτία (LN 88.289): 'sin' [AB, BECNT, HNTC, ICC2, LN, NICNT, NTC, WBC; all versions].
   b. fut. act. indic. of κυριεύω (LN 37.50) (BAGD 2. p. 458): 'to rule' [BAGD, BECNT, LN], 'to reign over' [LN], 'to control' [BAGD], 'to have sway (over)' [AB], 'to dominate (over)' [HNTC], 'to be lord (over)' [ICC2, NTC], 'to have lordship (over)' [NICNT], 'to exercise lordship (over)' [WBC]. This future indicative verb is translated as a present indicative: 'sin is no longer your master' [NLT]; as a future indicative: 'sin will not be your master' [NCV], 'for sin will have no mastery over you' [NET], 'sin will have no dominion over you' [NRSV], 'sin shall not be master' [NASB], 'sin shall not be your master' [NIV], 'sin shall no longer be your master' [REB], 'sin shall not have dominion' [KJV]; as a simple imperative: 'don't let sin keep ruling (your lives)' [CEV], 'sin shouldn't have power (over you)' [GW], 'sin must not be your master' [TEV].

QUESTION—What relationship is indicated by γάρ 'for'?
It gives grounds for the imperatives in 6:12–13 [Ho, ICC2, Mu, NICNT, SSA]. It gives a reason or basis for the command just given; they are to yield themselves and their members to God because sin cannot rule over them [BECNT, Ho, Mor].

QUESTION—What is intended by the use of the future tense of κυριεύω 'rule'?
1. It indicates a promise [BECNT, Gdt, Ho, Mor, Mu, NAC, NICNT, NTC, St, WBC; probably all versions except CEV, GW, TEV]: sin shall not rule you. This promise is one that is valid for the present and the future [NICNT]. It refers to the eschatological future era [BECNT, HNTC], although that era has also broken into and become a reality in the present [BECNT]. It is a promise that although sin will always have an influence on them in this life, it is no longer their lord and master and they are free to fight against it and show their true allegiance to Christ [ICC2]. It means that sin's lordship and ownership over the believer has been destroyed and the believer is now able to offer himself in service to God [NTC]. It asserts something that is true now, not just in the future [Mu]. The

struggle against sin is one in which the victory is certain [Ho]. Sin has no right or power to rule over them [NAC]. It is a promise of grace to live now as one who will live with Christ in the future [WBC].
   2. It is an implied imperative [AB, TH; CEV, GW, TEV]: don't let sin rule over you. It is a matter of permission [TH].

for you-are not under^a law^b but under grace.^c

LEXICON—a. ὑπό with accusative object (LN 83.51) (BAGD 2.b. p. 843): 'under' [AB, BAGD, BECNT, HNTC, ICC2, LN, NICNT, NTC, WBC; KJV, NASB, NCV, NET, NIV, NRSV, REB, TEV]. The phrase οὐ...ἐστε ὑπό 'you are not under' is translated 'you are not ruled by' [CEV], 'you're not controlled by' [GW], 'you are no longer subject to' [NLT].

b. νόμος (LN 33.55, 33.333) (BAGD 3. p. 542): 'law' [AB, BAGD, LN (33.333), NICNT, NTC; NASB, NCV, NET, NIV, NRSV, REB, TEV], 'the Law' [LN (33.55); CEV], 'the law' [BECNT, ICC2, WBC; KJV, NLT], 'the reign of law' [HNTC], 'laws' [GW]. This noun lacks the definite article here.

c. χάρις (LN 88.66) (BAGD 3.b. p. 878): 'grace' [AB, BECNT, ICC2, LN, NICNT, NTC, WBC; KJV, NASB, NCV, NET, NIV, NLT, NRSV, REB, TEV], 'kindness' [LN], 'God's kindness' [CEV], 'the reign of grace' [HNTC], 'God's favor' [GW].

QUESTION—What relationship is indicated by γάρ 'for'?
   It gives a reason for the assertion in 6:14a that sin shall not rule them, which is that they are not under law but under grace [BECNT, Mor, Mu, NICNT, SSA]. It is a reason why they should not let sin rule them [TH].

QUESTION—What is meant by 'law' here?
   1. It refers to the Mosaic law and covenant [AB, BECNT, ICC2, Mor, NICNT, SSA, St, WBC]. This statement occurs within the larger context of his discussion of salvation history and the respective roles of the Mosaic law and the era of grace; to live under law, that is, the Mosaic economy, is to live under the power of sin [BECNT, NICNT]. It refers to the law in its function of condemning sinners [ICC2, St]. It refers to the Mosaic law's social function of creating a distinction between Jews and Gentiles [WBC].
   2. It refers to law in general [Gdt, Ho, Mu]. To be under law means to be a slave to sin; law can only accentuate and confirm that bondage, never relieve it [Mu]. 'Law' here means not just the Mosaic legislation but the sense of duty to all the law of God as that which binds the conscience to do the will of God [Ho]. While 'law' is primarily the Mosaic law, here he is referring more specifically to law *as* law [Gdt].

QUESTION—What does it mean to be under law or under grace?
   Note that there is a considerable amount of overlap possible between the positions listed below, and one does not rule out the other.
   1. To be under law means being subject to the law as a means of salvation [HNTC, Ho, Mor, NTC, SSA], and thereby subject to the curse of the law

for failure to fulfill its demands [NTC, St]. To be under law means to be subject to its power or rule; the inability of those who are under law to keep the law perfectly means they are also subject to sin [Mor]. To be under law is to be a slave to sin because law actually incites more sin and accentuates and confirms bondage to it; but to be under grace means to have all the resources of redeeming and renewing grace to deliver from sin's bondage [Mu]. The law demands obedience but being under grace liberates because it gives the desire and ability to obey [TNTC]. To be 'under' law or grace means to be subject to an imperious and efficacious power [Gdt].
2. To be 'under' law or grace refers to one's relation to the two eras of salvation history [BECNT, NAC, NICNT, WBC], the era of the Mosaic covenant and the new age of grace begun by Christ's death and resurrection [BECNT]. To be under law is to be subject to the system of the old era of salvation history, a system that can only strengthen sin and bring condemnation for sin; to be under grace is to be subject to the new era in which there is liberation from sin's power [NICNT]. In the new era the power to overcome sin is readily attainable [NAC].
3. It means to be subject either to God's condemnation or to his gracious favor [ICC2, St]. Law and grace are the opposing principles of the old and new orders, of Adam and Christ; to be under grace means acknowledging our dependence on Christ's work to save us, which justifies and frees us [St].
4. Law here symbolizes man's striving to put himself right with God by his own effort [HNTC, TH]. It represents mans' attempt to enthrone himself as God and the upward striving of human religion and morality, which are affected by sin [HNTC].

DISCOURSE UNIT: 6:15–7:6 [Mor]. The topic is the question, Shall we sin because we are under grace, not law?

DISCOURSE UNIT: 6:15–23 [Gdt, HNTC, ICC2, Mor, NAC, NICNT, NTC; CEV, NET, NIV, NLT, TEV]. The topic is the power of the new principle of sanctification to deliver from sin [Gdt], a choice between two masters [ICC2], we are not slaves [Mor], in bondage to righteousness [HNTC], slaves to righteousness [GNT, NAC; NIV, NRSV, TEV], freed from sin's power to serve righteousness [NICNT], who is your master? Sin or God? [NTC], slaves who do what pleases God [CEV], the believer's enslavement to God's righteousness [NET], freedom to obey God [NLT].

6:15 What then?[a] Should-we-sin,[b] because we-are not under law but under grace? Never may-it-be![c]

LEXICON—a. τί οὖν: This phrase is translated 'what then?' [HNTC, ICC2, NICNT, NTC, WBC; KJV, NASB, NET, NIV, NRSV, REB], 'what, then?' [TEV], 'what, then, does this mean?' [AB], 'what then should we conclude?' [BECNT], 'what does all this mean?' [CEV], 'then what is the

implication?' [GW], 'so what should we do?' [NCV], 'so...does this mean?' [NLT].
   b. aorist act. subj. of ἁμαρτάνω (LN 88.289): 'to sin' [AB, BECNT, HNTC, ICC2, LN, NICNT, NTC, WBC; all versions except NLT], 'to go on sinning' [NLT].
   c. aorist mid. (deponent = act.) optative of γίνομαι (LN 13.107) (BAGD I.3.a. p. 158): 'to happen' [LN], 'to occur' [LN]. The phrase μὴ γένοιτο 'never may it be' is translated 'certainly not' [AB, BECNT, HNTC, WBC; CEV], 'by no means!' [BAGD, NICNT, NTC; NIV, NRSV, TEV], 'far from it' [BAGD], 'God forbid!' [BAGD, ICC2; KJV], 'that's unthinkable!' [GW], 'may it never be!' [NASB], 'no!' [NCV], 'absolutely not!' [NET], 'of course not!' [NLT, REB]. See this expression also at 3:4, 6, 31; 6:2.

QUESTION—What relationship is indicated by τί οὖν 'what then'?
   Paul is attempting to anticipate and answer questions that could be raised in objection to his statements about law and grace in 6:14 [BECNT, HNTC, ICC2, Mor, Mu, NICNT, NTC, TH]. It gives rhetorical flourish and is designed to keep the argument moving [WBC].
   1. Paul is saying that even though believers are no longer subject to the Mosaic covenant, that does not mean they are free to live in sin [ICC2, Mor, Mu, NICNT, NTC, TH]. Although they are free from the law as a means of salvation, that does not mean that they are under no obligation to God [HNTC].
   2. Paul is saying that believers are free from the power of sin, which is indissolubly connected with the Mosaic law, and are now able because of grace to keep the moral norms of the law [BECNT].

6:16 Do-you- not -know that to-whom you-yield[a] yourselves as slaves[b] for[c] obedience,[d] you-are slaves (of-him) whom you-obey,[e]

LEXICON—a. pres. act. indic. of παρίστημι (LN 13.11) (BAGD 1.a. p. 627): 'to yield' [BAGD; KJV], 'to put yourself at anyone's disposal' [AB], 'to present (yourself)' [BECNT, NICNT; NASB, NET, NRSV], 'to offer (yourself)' [HNTC, NTC; NIV], 'to offer to be (someone's slave)' [GW], 'at whose disposal you place (yourselves)' [ICC2], 'to give control of (yourself)' [WBC], 'to give (yourself)' [NCV], 'to choose to obey' [NLT], 'to bind yourself to obey' [REB], 'to surrender yourself (as a slave)' [TEV], not explicit [CEV]. See this word also at 6:13, 19, and 12:1.
   b. δοῦλος (LN 37.3) (BAGD 3. p. 205): 'slave' [BAGD, BECNT, HNTC, ICC2, NICNT, NTC, WBC; CEV, GW, NASB, NCV, NET, NIV, NRSV, TEV], 'servant' [KJV], '(if you bind yourselves) to obey a master' [REB], not explicit [NLT]. This pertains to a state of being completely controlled by something, to be subservient to it [LN]. The phrase 'yield yourselves as slaves' is translated 'put yourselves at anyone's disposal' [AB].

c. εἰς with accusative object (LN 89.48, 89.57) (BAGD 4.e. p. 229): 'to' [BAGD, HNTC, ICC2, NTC, WBC; KJV, NCV, NIV, NLT, REB, TEV], 'in' [AB], 'with the result that' [LN (89.48)], 'which results in' [TEV], 'for' [BECNT, NICNT; NASB], 'for the purpose of' [LN (89.57)]. The phrase 'for obedience' is translated 'of anyone you obey' [CEV], not explicit [GW, NET, NRSV].

d. ὑπακοή (LN 36.15) (BAGD 1.a. p. 837): 'obedience' [BAGD, BECNT, LN, NICNT; NASB]. This word is also translated as a verb: 'to obey' [AB, HNTC, ICC2, NTC, WBC; CEV, GW, KJV, NCV, NIV, NLT, REB, TEV]; as an adjective: 'obedient' [NET, NRSV].

e. pres. act. indic. of ὑπακούω (LN 36.15) (BAGD 1. p. 837): 'to obey' [AB, BAGD, BECNT, HNTC, ICC2, LN, NICNT, NTC, WBC; all versions except GW, NLT], not explicit [NLT]. The phrase 'you are slaves of him whom you obey' is translated 'you must obey your master' [GW].

QUESTION—Does Paul's statement mean that obedience indicates slavery, or that it constitutes or leads to slavery?

1. Obedience leads to or constitutes slavery [AB, Gdt, Ho, ICC2, NAC, NICNT, NTC, SSA, St]. You are the slave of whatever power you choose to obey [ICC2, Mu].
2. Our obedience indicates whose slaves we are [Mor].

whether (slaves) of-sin^a leading-to^b death^c

LEXICON—a. ἁμαρτία (LN 88.289): 'sin' [AB, BECNT, HNTC, ICC2, LN, NICNT, NTC, WBC; all versions]. Here sin is spoken of both as a power and as specific acts of disobedience [BECNT].

b. εἰς with accusative object (LN 89.48) (BAGD 4.e. p. 229): 'which leads to' [AB], 'to' [BAGD, NICNT, NTC; NIV, NLT, NRSV], 'unto' [KJV], 'resulting in' [BECNT, WBC; NASB, NET], '(with death) as the consequence' [ICC2], 'ends in (death)' [HNTC], not explicit [CEV, NCV, REB].

c. θάνατος (LN 23.99) (BAGD 2.b. p. 351): 'death' [AB, BAGD, BECNT, HNTC, ICC2, LN, NICNT, NTC, WBC; all versions except CEV], '(sin and) die' [CEV].

QUESTION—What relationship is indicated by εἰς 'leading to'?

It indicates the result or consequence of the slavery [AB, HNTC, ICC2, Mor, NAC, NICNT, NTC, SSA, TH, WBC].

QUESTION—What is the 'death' to which he refers?

It refers to eternal death [BAGD, Ho, ICC2, SSA], a spiritual and eternal death [Gdt, Ho]. It involves both physical and eternal death [BECNT, Mor, NICNT, St]. It is primarily eternal death, but also refers to present spiritual death [NICNT]. It is spiritual, physical, and everlasting death [NTC], death in all its aspects [Mu].

or (slaves) of-obedience[a] to[b] righteousness?[c]

LEXICON—a. ὑπακοή (LN 36.15) (BAGD 1.b. p. 837): 'obedience' [AB, BAGD, BECNT, HNTC, ICC2, LN, NICNT, NTC, WBC; GW, KJV, NASB, NET, NIV, NRSV, REB, TEV]. This noun is translated as an adjective: 'obedient' [CEV]; as a verb: 'obey' [NCV, NLT].

b. εἰς with accusative object (LN 89.48) (BAGD 4.e. p. 229): 'to' [AB, BAGD, NICNT, NTC; GW, NIV, NRSV], 'leads to' [GW], 'unto' [KJV], 'resulting in' [BECNT, WBC; NASB, NET], 'results in' [TEV], 'with (righteousness) as the consequence' [ICC2], not explicit [HNTC; CEV, NCV, NLT, REB].

c. δικαιοσύνη (LN 88.13) (BAGD 3. p. 197): 'righteousness' [BAGD, BECNT, HNTC, ICC2, LN, NICNT, NTC, WBC; KJV, NASB, NET, NIV, NRSV, REB], 'uprightness' [AB], 'God's approval' [GW, NLT]. The phrase εἰς δικαιοσύνην 'to righteousness' is translated 'and be acceptable to him' [CEV], 'makes you right with him' [NCV], 'being put right with God' [TEV].

QUESTION—What is the nature of the righteousness spoken of here?

1. It is forensic justification [ICC2, Mor, St, TH, TNTC]. It refers to final justification and acquittal [ICC2]. It is justification that comes from obedience to the call of the gospel [Mor].
2. It is moral righteousness, conduct that pleases God [AB, Gdt, Ho, NAC, NICNT, SSA, WBC]. It is personal growth in spiritual maturity [NAC].
3. The righteousness is forensic as well as ethical and experiential [BECNT]. It is a righteousness both of state and condition [NTC]. Both 'death' and 'righteousness' are viewed eschatologically [BECNT].
4. It is righteousness in all its aspects and culminating in the consummated righteousness of the new heavens and earth [Mu].

6:17 But[a] thanks[b] to-God that you-were slaves[c] of-sin[d]

LEXICON—a. δέ (LN 89.124): 'but' [AB, BECNT, ICC2, LN, NICNT, NTC, WBC; all versions except NLT, REB], not explicit [HNTC; NLT, REB]

b. χάρις (LN 33.350) (BAGD 5. p. 878): 'thanks' [AB, BAGD, BECNT, HNTC, ICC2, LN, NICNT, NTC, WBC; NASB, NET, NIV, NRSV, TEV]; translated as a verb: 'I thank' [CEV, GW], '(but God) be thanked' [KJV]. The phrase 'thanks to God' is translated 'thank God' [NCV, NLT, REB].

c. δοῦλος (LN 37.3) (BAGD 3. p. 205): 'slave' [AB, BAGD, BECNT, HNTC, ICC2, NICNT, NTC, WBC; all versions except KJV], 'servant' [KJV]. The phrase 'that you were slaves' is translated 'you who were once slaves' [AB, ICC2], 'that even though you were slaves' [BECNT], 'you were indeed slaves' [HNTC], 'because you were slaves' [NICNT], 'you were slaves' [NTC; GW], 'that when you were slaves' [WBC], 'you used to be slaves' [CEV, NIV], 'that though you were slaves' [NASB], 'In the past you were slaves' [NCV], 'once you were slaves' [NLT, REB], 'that you, having once been slaves' [NRSV], 'for though at one time you were slaves' [TEV].

d. ἁμαρτία (LN 88.289) (BAGD 3. p. 43): 'sin' [AB, BAGD, BECNT, HNTC, ICC2, LN, NICNT, NTC, WBC; all versions].

QUESTION—What relationship is indicated by δέ 'but'?

It is adversative [AB, BECNT, ICC2, LN, NICNT, NTC, WBC; all versions except NLT, REB]. While his comments in 6:16 speak of a choice about whether to serve either sin or righteousness, he asserts here that the Christian is not neutral in such a battle [BECNT].

QUESTION—What is the relationship of the clause ὅτι ἦτε δοῦλοι τῆς ἁμαρτίας 'that you were slaves of sin' to the clause that follows?

This clause is concessive; although you were slaves [BECNT, HNTC, ICC2, Mu, NAC, NICNT, SSA; NASB, TEV]. It is the second clause that contains the subject of his thanksgiving, not the first [Gdt].

but you-obeyed[a] from[b] (the) heart[c] (the) pattern[d] of-teaching[e] to[f] which you-were-given-over,[g]

LEXICON—a. aorist act. indic. of ὑπακούω (LN 36.15) (BAGD 1. p. 837): 'to obey' [BAGD, LN, NICNT, NTC; CEV, KJV, NCV, NET, NIV, NLT, TEV], 'to become obedient to' [AB, BECNT, ICC2; GW, NASB, NRSV], 'to give one's obedience to' [HNTC, WBC], 'to yield obedience to' [REB], 'to be subject to' [BAGD].

b. ἐκ with genitive object (LN 90.16) (BAGD 3.g.γ. p. 235): 'from' [BAGD, BECNT, HNTC, ICC2, LN, NICNT, WBC; KJV, NASB, NET, NRSV], 'out of' [BAGD], 'with all' [CEV, NLT, TEV], not explicit [AB, NTC; GW, NCV, NIV, REB].

c. καρδία (LN 26.3) (BAGD 1.b.α. p. 403): 'heart' [BAGD, BECNT, HNTC, ICC2, LN, NICNT, WBC; KJV, NASB, NET, NRSV], 'your heart' [CEV, NLT, TEV], 'mind, inner self' [LN]. The phrase 'from (the) heart' is translated 'wholeheartedly' [AB, NTC; GW, NCV, NIV, REB]

d. τύπος (LN 58.59) (BAGD 4. p. 830): 'pattern' [BAGD, BECNT, ICC2, NICNT, NTC, WBC; NET, REB], 'standard' [AB], 'form' [KJV, NASB, NIV, NRSV], not explicit [HNTC; CEV, GW, NCV, NLT, TEV].

e. διδαχή (LN 33.224) (BAGD 2. p. 192): 'teaching' [AB, BAGD, BECNT, ICC2, LN, NICNT, NTC, WBC; CEV, GW, NASB, NET, NIV, NRSV, REB, TEV], 'doctrine' [HNTC; KJV]. The phrase, 'pattern of teaching' is translated 'the things you were taught' [NCV], 'the new teaching God has given you' [NLT], 'the truths found in the teaching you received' [TEV].

f. εἰς with accusative object (LN 84.16): 'to' [AB, BECNT, HNTC, ICC2, LN, NICNT, NTC, WBC; NASB, NET, NIV, NRSV, REB], not explicit [CEV, GW, KJV, NCV, NLT, TEV].

g. aorist pass. indic. of παραδίδωμι (LN 33.237, 57.77) (BAGD 1.b. p. 615): 'to be given over' [BAGD, LN (57.77)], 'to be given' [GW], 'to be handed over' [HNTC, LN (57.77), NICNT, WBC], 'to be instructed' [LN (33.237)], 'to be taught' [LN (33.237)], 'to be entrusted' [AB; NET,

NIV, NRSV], 'to be transferred' [BECNT], 'to be delivered' [ICC2, NTC; KJV], 'to be committed' [NASB], 'to be made subject' [REB]. The phrase εἰς ὃν παρεδόθητε 'to which you were given over' is translated 'which you received from me' [CEV], 'that you were taught' [NCV], 'God has given you' [NLT], '(teaching) you received' [TEV].

QUESTION—What relationship is indicated by δέ 'but'?

It introduces the apodosis of a concessive statement: although you were slaves of sin, you obeyed [BECNT, HNTC, ICC2, Mu, NAC, NICNT; NASB, TEV].

QUESTION—What is the obeying he refers to here?

It is a reference to their conversion [Gdt, Mor, NICNT].

QUESTION—What is the τύπον διδαχῆς, 'pattern of teaching'?

1. It refers to Christian doctrine [HNTC, SSA], to accepted, authentic Christian teaching [Mor], to sound doctrine [NTC]. It refers to a pattern of teaching as an authoritative code, which in this case is being contrasted to the pattern or form of Jewish teaching, the Law [NICNT]. It refers to the gospel [Gdt, Ho, NTC]. It is gospel teaching, but with an emphasis on its ethical implications [Mu], on how their lives are to be lived [ICC2]. It was apostolic teaching which included both gospel instruction as well as ethics [St].
2. It is a summary of the ethical teaching of Jesus which new converts were taught [NAC, TNTC]. It refers primarily to their obeying the ethical teaching of the gospel, not to a formulated creed [TH].

QUESTION—What is implied by his statement that they were given over to the pattern of teaching?

In the imagery of a slave transfer, God has transferred them from one master to another [BECNT, ICC2, NTC, SSA, WBC], the new master being the teaching [BECNT]. Once Christ is received he becomes the new master in place of the old one [Gdt]. Becoming a Christian meant being placed under the authority of Christian teaching as the expression of God's will for them [NICNT]. They must be in subjection to the teaching God has given them [Mor]. Their devotion to the gospel was total, and their subjection to it was not optional [Mu]. They are subject to the word of God which created them [HNTC, NAC, St]. The pattern of Christian ethical teaching was embodied in Christ to whom they now belonged [TNTC].

6:18 and having-been-freed[a] from[b] sin[c] you-became-enslaved[d] to-righteousness.[e]

LEXICON—a. aorist pass. participle of ἐλευθερόω (LN 37.135) (BAGD 2. p. 251): 'to be freed' [AB, BAGD; GW, NASB, NET], 'to be set free' [BAGD, BECNT, ICC2, LN, NICNT, NTC, WBC; CEV, NIV, NRSV, TEV], 'to be made free' [KJV, NCV], 'to be free' [NLT], 'to be emancipated' [REB], 'to be released' [LN], 'to be liberated' [HNTC].

b. ἀπό with genitive object (LN 89.122): 'from' [AB, BECNT, HNTC, ICC2, LN, NICNT, NTC, WBC; all versions].

c. ἁμαρτία (LN 88.289): 'sin' [AB, BECNT, HNTC, ICC2, LN, NICNT, NTC, WBC; all versions]. Sin is spoken of as a power, but the ethical dimension is not to be excluded [BECNT].
d. aorist pass. indic. of δουλόω (LN 87.82) (BAGD 2. p. 206): 'to become enslaved' [WBC; NET], 'to be enslaved' [BAGD, BECNT, LN, NICNT], 'to be made a slave' [BAGD, HNTC, ICC2, LN; GW], 'to become a slave' [AB; NASB, NIV, NLT, NRSV, REB, TEV], 'to be a slave' [CEV, NCV], 'to enter the service of' [NTC], 'to become the servant of' [KJV].
e. δικαιοσύνη (BAGD, LN 88.13) (BAGD 3. p. 197): 'righteousness' [LN]. The phrase τῇ δικαιοσύνῃ 'to righteousness' is translated 'who please God' [CEV].

QUESTION—What does being enslaved to righteousness mean?
It refers to their conversion [NICNT]. They became slaves of God to do what is right [TH]. They are freed from sin so they can give themselves over completely to worthwhile causes [Mor]. They entered the service of righteousness [NTC]. They have become obligated to live righteously [NAC, SSA]. Man exists only in a relation of dependency on a superior power, either to God or to sin [WBC].

6:19 I-speak humanly[a] on-account-of[b] the weakness[c] of-your flesh.[d]

LEXICON—a. ἀνθρώπινος (LN 9.6) (BAGD 1. p. 67): 'humanly' [BECNT], 'human' [LN], 'after the manner of men' [KJV], 'in a human way' [NICNT; GW], 'in a very human way' [ICC2], 'in human terms' [AB, BAGD, NTC, WBC; NASB, NET, NIV, NRSV], 'in a human illustration' [HNTC]. It refers to speaking as people do in daily life [BAGD]. The phrase 'I speak humanly' is translated 'I am using these everyday examples' [CEV], 'I use everyday language' [TEV], 'I use this example' [NCV], 'to use language that suits your human (weakness)' [REB], 'I speak this way, using the illustration of slaves and masters' [NLT].
b. διά with accusative object (LN 89.26): 'on account of' [LN, WBC], 'because of' [AB, BECNT, HNTC, ICC2, LN, NICNT, NTC; GW, KJV, NASB, NET, NRSV, TEV], 'because' [CEV, NCV, NIV, NLT], not explicit [REB].
c. ἀσθένεια (LN 74.23) (BAGD 2. p. 115): 'weakness' [BAGD, BECNT, ICC2, LN, NICNT, NTC, WBC; GW, NASB, NET], 'limitation' [LN; NRSV], 'incapacity' [LN], 'weak (human nature)' [AB], 'infirmity' [KJV]. The phrase 'on account of the weakness of your flesh' is translated 'because your understanding is only human' [HNTC], 'because in some ways you are still weak' [CEV], 'because this is hard for you to understand' [NCV], '(to use language) that suits your human weakness' [REB], 'because of the weakness of your natural selves' [TEV], 'because you are weak in your natural selves' [NIV], not explicit [NLT].
d. σάρξ (LN 26.7, 58.10) (BAGD 7. p. 744): 'flesh' [BAGD, BECNT, ICC2, NICNT, NTC, WBC; KJV, NASB, NET], 'physical nature' [LN (58.10)], 'human nature' [AB, LN (26.7, 58.10)], 'corrupt nature' [GW],

'natural selves' [NIV, TEV], 'natural limitations' [NRSV]. This whole sentence is translated as 'I am giving all this in a human illustration because your understanding is only human' [HNTC], not explicit [CEV, NCV, NLT, REB].

QUESTION—What does Paul mean by 'the weakness of your flesh'?
1. It refers to natural limitations [TNTC]. Human nature is too frail to grasp divine truth without the use of analogies [HNTC, NAC, TH]. It is a reference to the weakness of human nature, but not of the sinful human nature [SSA]. Because of weak human nature he wants to make sure his discussion of Christian liberty is not misunderstood [AB]. It refers to weakness in judgment [BAGD].
2. Here 'flesh' refers to what it means to be human apart from God and his Spirit [NICNT], to their nature as being unspiritual and corrupt [Ho], their love of ego which makes them morally weak [Gdt]. Fallen human nature makes it hard to understand spiritual things [ICC2, St]. Man as 'flesh' is subject to corruption and human desires, and blind to God's truth and his own creaturely status [WBC]. Paul refers to a weakness of human understanding as a characteristic of the present evil age resulting from sin [BECNT]. It is a weakness of understanding that is natural in this life [Mor]. It was a difficulty in understanding resulting from lack of spiritual experience [ICC1]. Though they had made much progress in spiritual growth, they were far from mature and needed these kinds of analogies because of their weakness to grasp great spiritual truths [NTC].

QUESTION—What is the relation of σάρξ 'flesh' here to 'body of sin' in 6:6 and 'mortal body' in 6:12?
1. In all three passages he is speaking generally about the fallen nature or condition [Gdt, Ho, ICC1, NICNT, WBC].
    1.1 In 6:6 it refers to the corrupt nature, in 6:12 to the body as the organ through which sin expresses itself, and in 6:19 to the unspiritual and corrupt nature [Ho].
    1.2 It 6:6 he speaks of the sinful nature prior to conversion, in 6:12 of the body as pulled by its instincts and passions and which is destined to die, and here of the moral weakness of the ego [Gdt].
    1.3 All three expressions refer to man as a whole and as being subject to the pull of this world and of the fallen nature [NICNT]. In 6:6 he speaks of the whole person enslaved by sin, in 6:12 of the body as representing the whole person, and in 6:19 'flesh' refers to what it means to be human apart from God and his Spirit. This description of 'flesh' does not view it as positively sinful, but neither is it entirely neutral [NICNT].
    1.4 In 6:6 and 6:12 he speaks of the man as a whole with reference to his belonging to this world and being subject to the pull of sin. In 6:19 he uses 'flesh' to speak of being prone to weakness and corruption as though still ruled by the desires of the mortal body [WBC].
2. In all three passages he is speaking about the body, and emphasizes the concrete and practical demands of holiness [Mu].

3. Whereas in 6:6 and 6:12 he was speaking of the body, here he refers to human nature [AB, Mor, SSA], though not specifically to the sinful nature [Mor, SSA].

For just-as you-yielded[a] **your members**[b] **(as) slaves**[c] **to-impurity**[d] **and to-lawlessness**[e] **for**[f] **lawlessness,**

LEXICON—a. aorist act. indic. of παρίστημι (LN 13.11) (BAGD 1.a. p. 627): 'to yield' [BAGD; KJV, REB], 'to present' [BECNT, NICNT; NASB, NET, NRSV], 'to offer' [HNTC; GW, NCV, NIV], 'to put' [AB], 'to place' [ICC2], 'to enlist' [NTC], 'to hand over' [WBC], 'to surrender' [TEV], 'to let…be (slaves)' [CEV, NLT]. See this word also at 6:13, 16, and 12:1.

b. μέλος (LN 8.9) (BAGD 1. p. 501): 'member' [AB, BAGD, BECNT, HNTC, ICC2, LN, NICNT; KJV, NASB, NET, NRSV], 'body part' [LN], 'bodily parts' [NTC]. This plural is translated 'the parts of your body' [NCV, NIV], 'the different parts of your body' [CEV], 'all the parts of your body' [GW], 'your bodies' [REB], 'yourselves' [TEV], 'what you are and do' [WBC], not explicit [NLT].

c. δοῦλος (LN **37.3**) (BAGD p. 205): 'slave' [BECNT, HNTC, ICC2, NICNT, WBC; CEV, GW, NASB, NCV, NET, NLT, NRSV], 'in slavery' [BAGD; NIV, TEV], 'subservient to' [LN], 'in the service of' [NTC], 'to the service of' [REB], 'servant' [KJV], 'controlled by' [LN]. This noun is translated as an adverb: 'slavishly' [AB].

d. ἀκαθαρσία (LN 88.261) (BAGD 2. p. 28): 'impurity' [AB, LN, NTC; NASB, NET, NIV, NLT, NRSV, REB, TEV], 'immorality' [BAGD, LN], 'filthiness' [LN], 'uncleanness' [BECNT, HNTC, ICC2, NICNT, WBC; KJV], 'sexual perversion' [GW], 'sin' [NCV]. This word is conflated with the following phrase and translated 'of your evil thoughts' [CEV]. See this word also at 1:24.

e. ἀνομία (LN 88.139) (BAGD 1. p. 71): 'lawlessness' [BAGD, BECNT, ICC2, LN, NICNT, NTC, WBC; NASB, NET, NLT, REB], 'lawless living' [LN], 'iniquity' [AB, HNTC; KJV, NRSV], 'evil' [NCV] 'disobedience' [GW], 'wickedness' [NIV, TEV], not explicit [CEV]. See this word also at 4:7.

f. εἰς with accusative object (LN 78.51, 89.48, 89.57): 'for' [ICC2, LN (89.57), NTC; TEV], 'for the purpose of' [LN (89.57)], 'with the result that' [LN (89.48)], 'resulting in' [BECNT; NASB], 'with the result of (producing iniquity)' [HNTC], 'which results in' [WBC], 'leading to' [NICNT; NET], 'unto' [KJV]. This preposition is translated as a verb phrase: 'which led to' [AB; GW], 'you lived only for (evil)' [NCV], 'making for (moral anarchy)' [REB], not explicit [CEV, NIV, NLT, NRSV].

QUESTION—What relationship is indicated by εἰς 'for' in the phrase 'for lawlessness'?

1. It indicates result [AB, HNTC, ICC2, NICNT, SSA, TH, WBC; GW, NASB, REB]: you yielded your members as slaves to impurity and to lawlessness and as a result you did more unlawful things. That is, living as a slave to lawlessness leads to more lawlessness [AB, HNTC, ICC2, NICNT]. It indicates an emphatic amplification of 'lawlessness' and 'holiness' [TH]. There is a progressive deterioration [WBC].
2. It indicates purpose [Ho, LN (37.3), Mor, NAC, NTC; TEV]: you yielded your members as slaves to impurity and to lawlessness in order to do more unlawful things. That is, don't give yourselves to wickedness for wicked purposes, but to righteousness with a view to sanctification [Ho, Mor, NAC]. Impurity and lawlessness promote lawlessness, and righteousness promotes holiness [NTC].

thus now yield[a] your members[b] (as) slaves[c] to-righteousness[d] for[e] holiness.[f]

LEXICON—a. aorist act. impera. of παρίστημι (LN 13.11) (BAGD 1.a. p. 627): 'to yield' [BAGD; KJV, REB], 'to present' [BECNT, NICNT; NASB, NET, NRSV], 'to offer' [HNTC; GW, NIV], 'to put' [AB], 'to place' [ICC2], 'to enlist' [NTC], 'to hand over' [WBC] 'to make...serve' [CEV], 'to give' [NCV], 'to choose (to be slaves)' [NLT], 'to surrender' [TEV].

b. μέλος (LN 8.9) (BAGD 1. p. 501): 'member' [BAGD, BECNT, HNTC, ICC2, LN, NICNT; KJV, NASB, NET, NRSV], 'them' [AB, NTC; NIV, REB], 'body part' [LN], 'all the parts of your body' [GW], 'what you are and do' [WBC], 'yourselves' [NCV, TEV], not explicit [NLT]. This plural noun is translated 'every part of your body' [CEV].

c. δοῦλος (LN 37.3) (BAGD p. 205): 'slave' [BAGD, BECNT, HNTC, ICC2, NICNT, WBC; GW, NASB, NCV, NET, NIV, NLT, NRSV, TEV], 'in slavery' [NIV], 'subservient, controlled by' [LN], 'service' [NTC; REB, TEV], 'servant' [KJV, NASB]. This noun is translated as an adverb: 'slavishly' [AB]. The phrase δοῦλα τῇ δικαιοσύνῃ εἰς ἁγιασμόν 'as slaves to righteousness for holiness' is translated 'serve God, so that you will belong completely to him' [CEV].

d. δικαιοσύνη (LN 88.13): 'righteousness' [BECNT, HNTC, ICC2, LN, NICNT, NTC, WBC; KJV, NASB, NET, NIV, NLT, NRSV, REB, TEV], 'uprightness' [AB], 'what God approves of' [GW], 'goodness' [NCV], not explicit [CEV].

e. εἰς with accusative object (LN 89.48, 89.57): 'for' [ICC2; NRSV, REB, TEV], 'for the purpose of' [LN (89.57)], 'which leads to (holiness)' [AB], 'leading to' [NICNT; NET, NIV], 'this leads you' [GW], '(resulting) in' [BECNT; NASB], 'with the result that' [LN (89.48)], 'the result of this will be' [HNTC], 'which results in' [WBC], 'for the promotion of' [NTC], 'unto' [KJV], 'so that' [NLT], not explicit [CEV, NCV].

f. ἁγιασμός (LN 53.44) (BAGD p. 9): 'holiness' [AB, BAGD, NTC; KJV, NIV], 'consecration' [BAGD, LN, WBC], 'dedication' [LN], 'sanctification' [BAGD, BECNT, HNTC, ICC2, NICNT; NASB, NET, NRSV], 'holy life' [GW, REB], 'holy lives' [CEV], not explicit [NCV]. This noun is also translated as a verb phrase: 'to be holy' [NLT]. The phrase 'for holiness' is translated 'so that you will become holy' [NLT], 'for holy purposes' [TEV].

QUESTION—What is meant by ἁγιασμός 'holiness'?

1. It refers to the process of sanctification, of becoming more and more holy [BECNT, HNTC, ICC1, ICC2, Mor, NICNT, SSA, St]. It refers to a holy manner of living rather than a state of holiness [SSA].
2. It refers to the state of holiness and consecration that is brought about by conversion [Gdt, Ho, Mu, WBC], to the quality and condition of holiness [NTC]. It means a consecration in which they have been set apart for God, to be holy, and which they must also live out in their day to day lives [AB]. It speaks of being set aside or dedicated to God for achieving his holy purposes or living a holy life [TH].

QUESTION—What relationship is indicated by εἰς 'for' in the phrase 'for holiness'?

1. It indicates result [AB, BECNT, Gdt, HNTC, Ho, ICC2, NICNT; GW, NASB, NCV, NET, NIV, REB]: yield your members as slaves to righteousness with the result that you will be holy. Serving righteousness leads to holiness [AB, HNTC, ICC2, NICNT].
2. It indicates purpose [ICC1, Mor, Mu, SSA; CEV, NLT, TEV]: yield your members as slaves to righteousness in order to be holy.

6:20 For when you-were slaves[a] of-sin,[b] you-were free[c] (with-respect-to)[d] righteousness.[e]

LEXICON—a. δοῦλος (LN 37.3) (BAGD 3. p. 205): 'slave' [AB, BAGD, BECNT, HNTC, ICC2, NICNT, NTC, WBC; all versions except KJV], 'servant' [KJV], 'subservient to' [**LN**], 'controlled by' [LN].

b. ἁμαρτία (LN 88.289) (BAGD 3. p. 43): 'sin' [AB, BAGD, BECNT, HNTC, ICC2, LN, NICNT, NTC, WBC; all versions].

c. ἐλεύθερος (LN 37.134) (BAGD 2. p. 250): 'free' [AB, BECNT, HNTC, ICC2, LN, NICNT, NTC, WBC; GW, KJV, NASB, NET, NIV, NRSV, REB, TEV]. This clause is translated 'you didn't have to please God' [CEV], 'goodness did not control you' [NCV], 'you weren't concerned with doing what is right' [NLT].

d. There is no lexical entry for the phrase 'with respect to', the dative case being used to express the relation between the adjective ἐλεύθερος 'free' and the noun δικαιοσύνη 'righteousness'. This relation is translated 'with respect to' [NICNT], 'in relation to' [ICC2, WBC], 'with reference to' [BECNT], 'in regard to' [NASB, NRSV], 'with regard to' [NET], 'in respect of' [HNTC], 'from' [AB; GW, KJV, TEV], 'from the control of' [NTC; NIV, REB], not explicit [CEV, NCV, NLT].

e. δικαιοσύνη (LN 88.13): 'righteousness' [BECNT, HNTC, ICC2, LN, NICNT, NTC, WBC; KJV, NASB, NET, NIV, NRSV, REB, TEV], 'uprightness' [AB], 'goodness' [NCV], not explicit [CEV]. This word is translated by the phrase 'doing what God approves of' [GW], 'doing what is right' [NLT]. This righteousness is ethical righteousness, referring to behavior and not to a forensic status [NICNT].

QUESTION—What relationship is indicated by γάρ 'for'?

It introduces the grounds for the imperative in 6:19b [BECNT, Ho, ICC2, NICNT, SSA]. The grounds for the imperative is found in 6:20–23 [BECNT, NICNT], or 6:20–22 [Ho, SSA], or 6:20–21 [ICC2]. They must yield their members to righteousness because the only other option is slavery to sin, as they know from experience [BECNT]. It introduces a confirmation of what has just been said [Ho].

QUESTION—What does it mean to be 'free' with respect to righteousness?

Being free from righteousness means being a slave to sin [BECNT, NICNT]. Sin, not righteousness, was their master then [Ho, TNTC]. As slaves of sin they were unconcerned and carefree about any demands of righteousness [Mu]. They were not at all annoyed by any convictions regarding what is righteous, nor did they let it hamper their course of life [Gdt]. It refers to license [St]. The statement is ironic; they were not subject to the power and influence of conduct that pleases God [NICNT]. They were not under obligation to live righteously [HNTC, SSA, TH], or to do what God required [TH]. One cannot be the slave of sin and of righteousness at the same time, so if they were slaves to sin they could not be slaves to righteousness and thus were free in regard to righteousness [ICC2, NTC, WBC]. They were not subject to the rule of righteousness [Ho, Mor] and saw no compulsion to do right; such a freedom, however, is a grim freedom [Mor]. It is a play on the words 'slave' and 'free', emphasizing that the two ways of life are not compatible [AB].

6:21 Therefore[a] what fruit[b] were-you-having then[c]

LEXICON—a. οὖν (LN 89.50): 'therefore' [NASB], 'then' [AB, BECNT, ICC2, NTC; KJV, NASB, NET], 'so' [LN; NET, NRSV], 'so then, accordingly, therefore, consequently' [LN], not explicit [HNTC, NICNT, NTC, WBC; CEV, GW, NCV, NIV, NLT, REB, TEV].

b. κάρπος (LN 43.15) (BAGD 2.a. p. 405): 'fruit' [BECNT, HNTC, ICC2, LN, NICNT, WBC; KJV], 'outcome' [BAGD], 'benefit' [AB, NTC; NASB, NET, NIV], 'good' [CEV], 'advantage' [NRSV], 'gain' [REB, TEV], not explicit [GW, NCV, NLT].

c. τότε (LN 67.47): 'then' [ICC2, LN, NICNT, WBC; KJV, NASB], 'at that time' [NIV], not explicit [AB, BECNT, HNTC, ICC2; CEV, NCV, NET, NLT, REB, TEV]. The temporal element of this adverb is expressed by the phrase 'what you used to do' [GW].

QUESTION—What relationship is indicated by οὖν 'therefore'?
It has a temporal function and is not inferential; in 6:21 he clearly articulates what is implied in 6:20, which is that their current slavery to righteousness is much better than their former slavery to sin. [BECNT]. It is adversative; you were 'free' from righteousness, nevertheless, you got nothing good out of that way of living [SSA].

in[a] (things) which now[b] you-are-ashamed-of?[c]
LEXICON—a. ἐπί with dative object (LN 89.27, 90.23) (BAGD II.1.b.γ. p. 287): 'in, about, with reference to, with respect to' [LN (90.23)], 'because of' [LN (89.27)], 'of which' [AB, BECNT, HNTC, ICC2, NICNT, NTC, WBC; NASB], 'what' [GW], 'whereof' [KJV], 'that' [NET, REB, TEV], 'from' [NIV, NRSV], not explicit [CEV, NCV, NLT].
  b. νῦν (LN 67.38): 'now' [AB, BECNT, HNTC, ICC2, LN, NICNT, NTC, WBC; all versions except CEV, GW], not explicit [CEV, GW].
  c. pres. mid. (deponent = act.) indic. of ἐπαισχύνομαι (LN **25.193**) (BAGD 2. p. 282): 'to be ashamed' [AB, BAGD, BECNT, HNTC, ICC2, LN, NICNT, NTC, WBC; all versions except CEV, REB], 'to make (one) ashamed' [REB]. This phrase is translated 'all you have to show for them is your shame' [CEV].
QUESTION—How are these two clauses related?
  1. The first clause asks the question 'What fruit were you having?' and the second clause answers 'the fruit was in things you are now ashamed of' [Gdt, GNT, HNTC, Ho, ICC2, Mor, NAC, NICNT, NTC, TNTC, WBC; CEV, REB].
  2. Both clauses comprise a single question expecting a negative answer: 'What fruit were you having in the things you are now ashamed of? Things that result in death!' [AB, BECNT, ICC1, LN, Mu, SSA; KJV, NASB, NET, NRSV, TEV].

For the end[a] of-those-things (is) death.[b]
LEXICON—a. τέλος (LN 67.66, **89.40**) (BAGD 1.c. p. 811): 'end' [BAGD, HNTC, ICC2, LN (67.66, 89.40), NICNT; KJV, NET, NRSV, REB], 'result' [LN (**89.40**); TEV], 'end result' [WBC], 'outcome' [BAGD, BECNT, LN (89.40), NTC; NASB]. The phrase τὸ γὰρ τέλος ἐκείνων 'for the end of those things is' is translated 'things that result in' [AB], 'those things result in' [NIV], 'and they lead to' [CEV], 'things that end in' [NLT], 'it ended in' [GW], 'those things only bring' [NCV].
  b. θάνατος (LN 23.99) (BAGD 2.b. p. 351): 'death' [AB, BAGD, BECNT, HNTC, ICC2, LN, NICNT, NTC, WBC; all versions except NLT], 'eternal doom' [NLT].
QUESTION—What relationship is indicated by γάρ 'for'?
  1. It introduces additional grounds for the statement implied by the rhetorical question in the first clause of this verse; nothing good comes from those shameful things you once did, for they only result in death [BECNT].

2. It introduces additional grounds for the answer given in 6:21b to the rhetorical question in 6:21a; the fruit you got from that way of life was shame, and such shameful behavior leads to death [ICC2, NICNT].

QUESTION—What is the 'death' to which he is referring here?

It is eternal and eschatological death [BECNT, ICC2, Mu, SSA, St], eternal separation from God [Gdt, NICNT], eternal death of the soul [Ho], death in its fullest sense [AB, NAC].

6:22 **But now having-been-freed^a from^b sin^c and having-been-enslaved^d to-God**

LEXICON—a. aorist pass. participle of ἐλευθερόω (LN 37.135) (BAGD 2. p. 251): 'to be freed' [AB, BAGD, HNTC, NTC; GW, NASB, NET, NRSV, REB], 'to be set free' [BAGD, BECNT, ICC2, LN, NICNT, WBC; CEV, NIV, TEV], 'to be released' [LN], 'to be made free' [KJV], 'to be free' [NCV, NLT].

b. ἀπό with genitive object (LN 89.122): 'from' [AB, BECNT, HNTC, ICC2, LN, NICNT, NTC, WBC; all versions].

c. ἁμαρτία (LN 88.289) (BAGD 3. p. 43): 'sin' [AB, BAGD, BECNT, HNTC, ICC2, LN, NICNT, NTC, WBC; all versions except NLT, REB], 'the power of sin' [NLT], 'the commands of sin' [REB].

d. aorist pass. participle of δουλόω (LN 87.82) (BAGD 2. p. 206): 'to be enslaved' [BAGD, BECNT, LN, NICNT, WBC; NASB, NET, NRSV], 'to be made a slave' [BAGD, ICC2, NTC], 'to become a slave' [AB, HNTC; NCV, NIV, NLT], 'to become God's slaves' [GW], 'to become servants' [KJV]. This phrase is translated 'and you are God's slaves' [CEV], 'bound to the service of God' [REB], 'you…are the slaves of God' [TEV].

you-have your fruit^a to^b holiness,^c

LEXICON—a. καρπός (LN 43.15) (BAGD 2.a. p. 405): 'fruit' [BECNT, HNTC, ICC2, LN, NICNT, WBC; KJV], 'benefit' [AB, NTC; NASB, NET, NIV], 'advantage' [NRSV], 'gain' [REB, TEV], 'outcome' [BAGD]. This clause is translated 'this will make you holy' [CEV], 'this results in a holy life' [GW], 'this brings you a life that is only for God' [NCV], 'now you do those things that lead to holiness' [NLT].

b. εἰς with accusative object (LN 89.48): 'to, with the result that, so that as a result' [LN], 'unto' [ICC2; KJV], 'resulting in' [BECNT; NASB], 'results in' [WBC; GW], 'to cause' [LN], 'leading to' [NICNT; NET], 'lead to' [AB, NTC; CEV, NIV, NLT, REB], 'proves (to be)' [HNTC], not explicit [NCV, NRSV, TEV].

c. ἁγιασμός (LN 53.44) (BAGD p. 9): 'holiness' [AB, NTC; KJV, NIV, NLT, REB], 'a holy life' [GW], 'sanctification' [BECNT, HNTC, ICC2, NICNT; NASB, NET, NRSV], 'consecration' [BAGD, LN, WBC], 'dedication' [LN]. This phrase is translated 'this will make you holy' [CEV], 'a life that is only for God' [NCV], 'a life fully dedicated to him' [TEV].

QUESTION—What is meant by ἁγιασμός 'holiness'?
1. As in 6:19, it refers to the process of sanctification, of becoming more and more holy [BECNT, ICC2, Mor, NAC, NICNT, TNTC].
2. As in 6:19 it refers to a state of holiness [Gdt, Mu, NTC]. Being enslaved to God involves a consecration or dedication to God that leads to holiness [AB, WBC], which is withdrawing from the sinful and profane [AB]. It means full dedication to God [TH].

and the result[a] (is)[b] life eternal.
LEXICON—a. τέλος (LN 67.66, 89.40) (BAGD 1.c. p. 811): 'result' [HNTC, LN (89.40); NIV, TEV], 'outcome' [BAGD, BECNT, LN (89.40), NTC; NASB], 'end' [ICC2, LN (67.66, 89.40), NICNT; KJV, NET, NRSV, REB], 'end product' [WBC]. The phrase τὸ...τέλος 'the result' is translated 'will lead you to' [CEV], '(and) result (in)' [NLT], 'which results in' [AB], 'this gives you' [NCV], not explicit [GW].
b. There is no lexical entry in the Greek text for the phrase 'is', the accusative case of 'life' implying that the preposition εἰς is carried forward anaphorically from the previous clause. This implied relation is translated 'is' [BECNT, NICNT, NTC, WBC; NET, NIV, NRSV, REB, TEV], 'will be' [HNTC], 'to lead you to' [CEV, GW], '(result) in' [AB]. '(results) in' [NLT], not explicit [ICC2; KJV, NASB, NCV].

QUESTION—What is it that results in eternal life?
Note that there is a certain amount of overlap possible between the positions listed below, and one does not rule out the other.
1. Eternal life is the result of holiness [Mu, NICNT, WBC], of dedication to God [AB, TH].
2. Eternal life is the result that comes from their slavery or service to God [Gdt, Ho, ICC2, NAC], from their inward obedience of faith [HNTC]. The fruit of being freed from sin is sanctification, and it is sanctification that gives assurance of eternal life to come [Mor]. Eternal life, like sanctification, results from having been freed from sin [St].

6:23 **For the wages[a] of-sin (is) death, but the gracious-gift[b] of-God (is) eternal life in[c] Christ Jesus our Lord.**
LEXICON—a. ὀψώνιον (LN **89.42**) (BAGD 2. p. 602): 'wages' [AB, BECNT, HNTC, ICC2, LN, NICNT, NTC, WBC; KJV, NASB, NIV, NLT, NRSV], 'compensation' [BAGD], 'result' [LN], 'reward' [GW], 'payoff' [NET]. The phrase τὰ γὰρ ὀψώνια τῆς ἁμαρτίας 'for the wages of sin is' is translated 'sin pays off with' [CEV], 'they earn what sin pays' [NCV], 'for sin pays a/its wage' [REB, TEV].
b. χάρισμα (LN **57.103**) (BAGD 1. p. 879): 'gracious gift' [LN, WBC], 'gift' [AB, BAGD, BECNT, LN, NICNT; CEV, GW, KJV, NET, NIV, REB], 'free gift' [ICC2, NTC; NASB, NCV, NLT, NRSV, TEV], 'gift freely given' [HNTC].
c. ἐν with dative object (LN 83.13, 89.119, 90.6) (BAGD I.5.d. p. 259): 'in' [AB, BECNT, HNTC, ICC2, LN (83.13, 89.119), NICNT, NTC, WBC;

GW, NASB, NET, NIV, NRSV, REB], 'in union with' [LN (89.119); TEV], 'by' [LN (90.5)], 'given by' [CEV], 'through' [KJV, NCV, NLT]. It indicates a close personal relationship [BAGD].

QUESTION—What relationship is indicated by γάρ 'for'?

It gives the grounds for his statements relating sin to death and holiness to eternal life in 6:21–22 [BECNT]. It introduces a clarification of 6:21–22 and a solemn conclusion to this section as a whole [ICC2]. It introduces a summary conclusion of his present topic begun in 6:15 [SSA].

QUESTION—How are the nouns related in the genitive construction τὰ ὀψώνια τῆς ἁμαρτίας 'the wages of sin'?

1. Sin pays the wages [AB, BECNT, Gdt, ICC2, Mor, Mu, NAC, NICNT, St, TH, WBC]. Sin is pictured as a commanding officer paying a wage to a soldier [AB, BECNT, Mor, Mu, NAC, NICNT, NTC] or as a slave owner paying an allowance to a slave [ICC2], or an agent who pays wages [TH].
2. God pays the wages to the one who commits sin [SSA]. Here 'sin' is a metonymy representing the person who commits sin; what a sinner receives for sinning is eternal death [SSA].

QUESTION—What relationship is indicated by ἐν 'in'?

It is in Jesus Christ that God gives the gift of eternal life [Ho, ICC2, NICNT]. It indicates that union with Christ is the means by which eternal life is made possible [SSA, TH], but it also refers to the qualitative nature of the life, that it is lived in union with him [TH]. Eternal life is bound up with the person and work of Jesus Christ [AB, Mor]. It is in intimate union with him that everlasting life is experienced [NTC]. It is in union with Christ that all the blessings of the Father are experienced and bestowed [Mu]. It is in communion of life with Christ that the communication of God's mercy takes place [Gdt]. Being personally united to Christ by faith is the only condition of receiving the gift of eternal life [St].

DISCOURSE UNIT: 7:1–8:17 [BECNT]. The topic is the triumph of grace over the power of the law.

DISCOURSE UNIT: 7:1–25 [AB, ICC2, NAC, NICNT, St, TNTC, WBC; NET, REB]. The topic is freedom from the Law [AB, TNTC], freedom from bondage to the law [NICNT], a life characterized by freedom from the law's condemnation [ICC2], no longer condemned by law [NAC], what role does the law play in all this? [WBC], God's law and Christian discipleship [St], the believer's relationship to the law [NET], the role of the law [REB].

DISCOURSE UNIT: 7:1–16 [Gdt, HNTC, ICC2, NTC]. The topic is emancipation from the Law [Gdt], liberty: freedom from the law [NTC], free from the law [HNTC], freedom from the law's condemnation [ICC2].

DISCOURSE UNIT: 7:1–6 [AB, Mor, Mu, NICNT, TNTC, WBC; CEV, NCV, NIV, NLT, NRSV, TEV]. The topic is an analogy from marriage [TNTC; NRSV], an example from marriage [CEV, NCV], an illustration from marriage

[Mor; NIV, TEV], freedom from the law by the death of Christ [AB], no longer bound to the law [NLT], released from the law, joined to Christ [NICNT], the believer has been released from the law which condemned him to death [WBC], death to the law [Mu].

7:1 Or do-you-not-know,ᵃ brothers,ᵇ

LEXICON—a. pres. act. indic. of ἀγνοέω (LN 28.13) (BAGD 1. p. 11): 'to not know' [BAGD, BECNT, LN, NTC, WBC; KJV, NASB, NET, NIV, NLT, NRSV], 'to be unaware' [AB, LN], 'to be ignorant' [BAGD, NICNT], 'to be ignorant of' [LN]. In this rhetorical question the verb is translated 'surely you know' [NCV], 'you surely cannot fail to know' [HNTC], 'don't you realize' [GW], 'you must be aware' [REB], 'certainly you will understand' [TEV], 'you surely (understand enough about law) to know' [CEV].

b. ἀδελφός (LN 11.23): 'Christian brother, fellow believer' [LN]. This plural noun is translated 'brothers' [AB, NTC, WBC; NIV], 'my brothers' [TEV], 'brothers and sisters' [BECNT, NICNT; GW, NCV, NET, NRSV], 'dear brothers and sisters' [NLT], 'brethren' [HNTC, ICC2; KJV, NASB], 'my friends' [CEV, REB]. The use of this word here indicates that he is about to introduce a sensitive subject [WBC], or that he is becoming emotionally involved [Mor], or that he is about employ a more familiar mode of teaching than he has used prior to this [Gdt].

QUESTION—To what previous issue is he returning with this question?

It refers to what he said in 6:14 about not being under law, but under grace [Gdt, HNTC, Ho, ICC2, Mor, Mu, NICNT, NTC, TNTC]. It refers back to the questions raised in 6:14–15 about the role of law in the life of a Christian [AB, NTC]. It returns to the discussion in 6:9 and 14 where the same verb 'to rule' was used of sin and death [WBC]. It also carries a step further the argument concerning Christian freedom and the law, which was introduced in 6:15–23 [BECNT, HNTC, NICNT].

for I-speak to-(ones)-knowingᵃ (the) law,ᵇ

LEXICON—a. pres. act. participle of γινώσκω (LN 28.1) (BAGD 3.a. p. 161): 'to know' [AB, BAGD, BECNT, HNTC, ICC2, LN, NICNT, NTC, WBC; KJV, NASB, NET, NIV, NRSV], 'to know about' [TEV], 'to have knowledge of' [LN], 'to have some knowledge of' [REB], 'to be acquainted with' [LN], 'to be familiar with' [GW, NLT], 'to understand' [NCV], 'to understand enough (to know that)' [CEV].

b. νόμος (LN 33.55, 33.333) (BAGD 1., 3., p. 542): 'law' [LN (33.333)], 'Law' [LN (33.55)]. This noun lacks the definite article here. It is translated without the definite article: 'law' [AB, BAGD, LN (33.333), NTC; CEV, REB, TEV]; as though having the definite article 'the law' [HNTC, ICC2, NICNT, WBC; KJV, NASB, NET, NIV, NLT, NRSV]; as though referring specifically to the Torah: 'the law of Moses' [NCV], 'the Mosaic law' [BECNT], 'Moses' teachings' [GW].

QUESTION—Is νόμος 'law' a reference to the Mosaic law or to law in general?
1. It is a reference to the Mosaic law [AB, BAGD, BECNT, Gdt, HNTC, Ho, ICC2, Mu, NICNT, NTC, WBC; GW, NCV]. All the previous references to the law have been to the Jewish Law and the readers would take this to be the same [WBC]. This statement would apply only to Jewish law [AB, HNTC, WBC], since Roman law allowed women to initiate divorce. The idea is a general one and not necessarily limited only to the Mosaic law, but here he speaks of the Mosaic law considered as revelation of the Jewish moral law [Ho].
2. It refers to law in general [ICC1, Mor, NAC, SSA, TH; CEV, REB, TEV]. He will articulate a general axiom that death clears all scores [Mor]. He is speaking of Jewish law certainly, but probably also Roman law as well [St].

QUESTION—Is Paul addressing only Jewish Christians?
Although the reference is to the Mosaic law, his comments are addressed to both Jewish and non-Jewish Christians [AB, BECNT, Gdt, HNTC, Ho, ICC2, Mu, NICNT, NTC, WBC]. It is likely that many, if not most, of the Gentile converts in Rome had been adherents of a synagogue prior to conversion and therefore knew the Jewish law [WBC]. At this stage of the argument he is not concerned with any specifically Jewish laws about marriage, but with a general principle that applies in all cultures [NICNT, TNTC], so it does not matter if the readers knew the Mosaic law or not [TNTC].

that the law[a] rules-over[b] the person[c] for[d] as-long-as[e] he-lives?
LEXICON—a. νόμος (LN 33.55, 33.333) (BAGD 3. p. 542): 'law' [BAGD, LN (33.333)], 'the law' [AB, BECNT, HNTC, ICC2, NICNT, NTC, WBC; KJV, NASB, NCV, NET, NIV, NLT, NRSV, REB, TEV], 'Law' [LN (33.55)]. This singular noun is translated as a plural: 'laws' [CEV, GW]. Here it has the definite article.
  b. pres. act. indic. of κυριεύω (LN 37.50) (BAGD 2. p. 458): 'to rule over' [BECNT, NICNT; NCV, TEV], 'to rule' [BAGD, LN], 'to have dominion over' [HNTC; KJV], 'to govern, to reign over' [LN], 'to have authority over' [AB, ICC2, NTC; NIV], 'to be lord over' [NET], 'to exercise lordship over' [WBC], 'to have power over' [CEV, GW], 'to have jurisdiction over' [NASB], 'to apply to' [NLT], 'to be binding on' [NRSV]. The phrase 'the law rules over the person' is translated 'a person is subject to the law' [REB].
  c. ἄνθρωπος (LN 9.1, 9.24) (BAGD 3.b. p. 69): 'person' [BECNT, LN (9.1), NICNT, NTC; NASB, NET, NLT, NRSV, REB], 'man' [BAGD, HNTC, ICC2, LN (9.24), WBC; KJV, NIV], 'human being' [AB, BAGD, LN]; this singular (generic) noun is translated as a plural: 'people' [CEV, GW, NCV, TEV]. This noun with the definite article is translated as not having the article, that is, in the generic sense [AB, BAGD, BECNT,

HNTC, ICC2, NICNT, NTC, WBC; all versions]. Because this noun has the definite article here it is used in a generic sense [BAGD].
- d. ἐπί with accusative object (LN 67.136) (BAGD III.2.b. p. 289): 'for' [HNTC, LN], not explicit [AB, BECNT, ICC2, NICNT, NTC, WBC; all versions].
- e. ὅσος (LN **59.19**, 67.139) (BAGD 1. p. 586): 'as long as' [LN (**59.19**, 67.139)]. The phrase ἐφ' ὅσον χρόνον 'for as long as' is translated 'as long as' [AB, BAGD, BECNT, NICNT, NTC; GW, KJV, NASB, NET, NIV, REB, TEV], 'so long as' [ICC2, WBC], 'for such time' [HNTC], 'while' [NCV]. This entire phrase is translated 'who are alive' [CEV], 'a person who is still living' [NLT], 'during that person's lifetime' [NRSV].

QUESTION—What happens when a person dies?

The word 'only' is implied since death ends the rule of the law over a person [AB, HNTC, ICC1, ICC2, NICNT, NTC, SSA, St, TNTC; CEV, GW, NCV, NIV, NLT, NRSV, REB, TEV]: the law rules over the person *only* as long as he lives. The authority of the law is limited to our lifetime and this axiom is universally accepted [St].

7:2 For[a] the married[b] woman is-bound[c] to-the-living[d] husband by-law;[e]

LEXICON—a. γάρ (LN 89.23): 'for' [ICC2, LN, NICNT, WBC; KJV, NASB, NET], 'thus' [AB; NRSV], 'for example' [NTC; CEV, GW, NCV, NIV, REB, TEV], 'for (to take an example)' [HNTC], 'for instance' [BECNT], 'let me illustrate' [NLT].
- b. ὕπανδρος (LN **34.75**) (BAGD p. 837): 'married' [AB, BAGD, BECNT, HNTC, ICC2, LN, NICNT, NTC, WBC; GW, NASB, NET, NIV, NRSV, REB, TEV], 'which hath an husband' [KJV], 'subject to a man, under the power of a man' [BAGD], not explicit [CEV, NCV, NLT]. This entire clause is translated 'For example, the Law says that a man's wife must remain his wife as long as he lives' [CEV], 'a woman must stay married to her husband as long as he is alive' [NCV], 'when a woman marries, the law binds her to her husband as long as he is alive' [NLT].
- c. perf. pass. indic. of δέω (LN **37.45**) (BAGD 3. p. 178): 'to be bound' [AB, BAGD, BECNT, HNTC, ICC2, NICNT, NTC, WBC; GW, KJV, NASB, NET, NIV, NRSV, REB, TEV], not explicit [CEV, NCV]. The phrase 'a woman is bound…by law' is translated 'the law binds her' [NLT]. The phrase τῷ…ἀνδρὶ δέδεται νόμῳ 'is bound to the… husband by law' is translated 'is under the law of her husband' [LN]. It refers to the binding of a wife to her husband by law and duty [BAGD].
- d. pres. act. participle of ζάω (LN 23.88) (BAGD 1.a.α. p. 336): 'to live' [BAGD, LN]. The phrase τῷ ζῶντι ἀνδρὶ 'to the living husband' is translated 'while he is alive' [AB], 'while he lives' [BECNT, WBC; REB], 'while he is living' [NASB], 'for such time as he is alive' [HNTC], 'as long as he is living' [ICC2], 'as long as he is alive' [NTC; GW, NCV, NIV, NLT], 'as long as he lives' [NICNT; CEV, NET, NRSV, TEV], 'so long as he liveth' [KJV].

e. νόμος (LN 33.55, 33.333) (BAGD 3. p. 542): 'law' [AB, BAGD, BECNT, HNTC, LN (33.333), NTC; GW, NASB, NET, REB], 'Law' [LN (33.55)], not explicit [NCV, NIV]. This word, which does not have the definite article here, is translated as having the definite article: 'the law' [ICC2, NICNT, WBC; CEV, KJV, NLT, NRSV, TEV], 'the Law' [CEV]; as not having the definite article [AB, BECNT, HNTC, NTC; GW, NASB, NET, NIV, REB].

QUESTION—What relationship is indicated by the conjunction γάρ 'for'?

It indicates an example of the principle stated in 7:1 [Gdt, Ho, ICC2, NICNT, SSA, St, WBC; CEV, GW, NCV, NIV, NLT, REB, TEV]. This example illustrates the general principle about law made in the previous verse [NICNT, SSA]. It is a confirmatory illustration [Ho]. The illustration now given proves the truth of the principle in 7:1 [ICC1].

but if the husband dies, she-is-released^a from the law^b about the husband.

LEXICON—a. perf. pass. indic. of καταργέω (LN **37.136**) (BAGD 3. p. 417): 'to be released' [AB, BAGD, BECNT, ICC2, LN, NICNT, NTC, WBC; NASB, NET, NIV, REB], 'to be loosed' [KJV], 'to be discharged' [NRSV], 'to be freed' [LN]. This passive verb is translated as an intransitive active verb: 'to be free' [**LN**; CEV, NCV, TEV], 'to be done with' [HNTC]. The phrase 'she is released from the law about the husband' is translated 'that marriage law is no longer in effect for her' [GW], 'she is free to marry' [CEV], 'the laws of marriage no longer apply to her' [NLT], 'she is done with the law, as she is done with her husband' [HNTC].

b. νόμος (LN 33.55, 33.333, **33.341**) (BAGD 3. p. 542): 'law' [BAGD, LN (33.333)], 'Law' [LN (33.55)]. Here it has the definite article. The phrase τοῦ νόμου τοῦ ἀνδρός 'the law about the husband' is translated 'the law of her husband' [WBC; KJV], 'the law regarding her husband' [AB], 'the law concerning the husband' [NASB, NRSV], 'the law relating to her husband' [NICNT], 'the law that binds her to her husband' [BECNT], 'the law that bound her to him' [TEV], 'the law in so far as it binds her to her husband' [ICC2, NTC], 'the marriage bond' [REB], 'marriage law' [LN (33.341); GW], 'the law of marriage' [NCV, NIV], 'the law of the marriage' [NET], 'the laws of marriage' [NLT], not explicit [CEV].

QUESTION—What is the νόμου τοῦ ἀνδρός 'law about the husband'?

1. It is the law by which a wife was bound to her husband [BECNT, ICC2, Mor, NAC, NTC, SSA, TNTC, WBC], marriage law [TH]. It is the law concerning or relating to the husband [Ho, ICC1, St]. Under the Mosaic law, the wife had no right to divorce her husband [AB, BECNT, WBC]. It refers to the law about remaining married to a husband [SSA], the law that commands a married woman to stay with her husband [TH].
2. It is the legal power that the husband has in relation to his wife [Gdt].

3. 'Husband' is in apposition to 'law', since in the analogy as a whole the husband represents the law; that is, she is done with the law because she is done with her deceased husband [HNTC].

QUESTION—In what way does this text address questions of divorce and remarriage?

This passage is not intended to give a full discussion of that topic and does not address that question in any detail [BECNT, NICNT].

7:3 **So then,**[a] **(while)**[b] **the husband (is) living, she-will-be-called**[c] **an-adulteress**[d] **if she-becomes**[e] **(joined)**[f] **to-another-man;**

LEXICON—a. ἄρα (LN 89.46) (BAGD 4. p. 104): 'so, consequently' [BAGD, LN], 'as a result' [BAGD], 'then' [LN]. The phrase ἄρα οὖν is translated 'so then' [ICC2, NTC; KJV, NASB, NET, TEV], 'so' [GW, NLT], 'accordingly' [AB, WBC; NRSV], 'therefore' [BECNT, NICNT; REB], 'see what this means' [HNTC], 'for example' [NIV], not explicit [CEV, NCV].

b. There is no lexical entry for this word, the temporal aspect being implied by the present active participle in the genitive absolute phrase ζῶντος τοῦ ἀνδρός 'while the husband is living'. It is translated 'while' [AB, BECNT, HNTC, ICC2, NICNT, NTC, WBC; all versions except REB]. The phrase 'while the husband is living' is translated 'in her husband's lifetime' [REB].

c. fut. act. indic. of χρηματίζω (LN 33.127) (BAGD 2. p. 885): 'to bear the name'. This active verb is also translated passively: 'to be called' [AB, BAGD, BECNT, LN, NICNT, NTC; GW, KJV, NASB, NET, NIV, NRSV, TEV], 'to be named' [BAGD, WBC], 'to be said to be' [CEV], 'to be styled' [HNTC], 'to be accounted' [ICC2], 'to be held to be' [REB]. The phrase 'she will be called an adulteress' is translated 'the law says she is guilty of adultery' [NCV], 'she would be committing adultery' [NLT]. The future tense here is a gnomic future [AB, WBC] making a statement about the nature of things, not of an action at a future point in time.

d. μοιχαλίς (LN **88.278**) (BAGD 1. p. 526): 'adulteress' [AB, BAGD, BECNT, HNTC, ICC2, LN, NICNT, NTC, WBC; KJV, NASB, NET, NIV, NRSV, REB, TEV], 'adulterer' [GW], 'unfaithful' [CEV], not explicit [NCV, NLT].

e. aorist mid. (deponent = act.) subj. of γίνομαι (LN 57.2) (BAGD II.3. p. 160): 'to become' [ICC2, WBC], 'to belong to' [BAGD, LN (57.2)], 'to have' [LN (57.2)]. See next entry.

f. There is no lexical entry for the word 'joined', but is implied by the verb γένηται 'becomes' followed by ἀνδρὶ ἑτέρῳ 'to another man', the dative case of which indicates possession and reflects a corresponding Hebrew construction in several OT passages [AB, NICNT]. This grammatical relation is translated 'joined to' [NICNT; NASB, NET], 'marries' [AB, NTC; GW, NCV, NIV], 'married' [NLT], 'be married' [KJV], 'gives herself to' [AB, HNTC; REB], 'goes off with' [CEV], 'lives with'

[NRSV, TEV]. The phrase γένηται ἀνδρὶ ἑτέρῳ is translated 'becomes another man's' [ICC2, WBC].

QUESTION—What relationship is indicated by ἄρα οὖν 'so then'?

It introduces the conclusion drawn from 7:2 that what would not be legitimate during the husband's lifetime is legitimate if he has died [BECNT, Gdt, Ho, Mor].

but if the husband dies, she-is free[a] from[b] the law,[c] so-that she will- not -be an adulteress, (by) having-become[d] (joined) to-another man.

LEXICON—a. ἐλεύθερος (LN 37.134) (BAGD 2. p. 250): 'free' [AB, BECNT, HNTC, ICC2, LN, NICNT, NTC, WBC; all versions except NIV], 'released' [NIV]. The phrase ἐλευθέρα...ἀπό 'free from' is translated 'no longer bound by' [BAGD].

b. ἀπό with genitive object (LN 89.122): 'from' [BECNT, HNTC, ICC2, LN, NICNT, NTC, WBC; all versions except CEV, REB, TEV], 'of' [AB; REB], not explicit [CEV, TEV].

c. νόμος (LN 33.333): 'law' [LN (33.333)]. This word with the definite article is translated 'the law' [BECNT, HNTC, ICC2, NICNT, NTC, WBC; NASB, REB], 'this law' [GW], 'that law' [AB; KJV, NET, NIV, NLT, NRSV], 'the law of marriage' [NCV], not explicit [CEV, TEV]. The phrase 'she is free from the law' is translated 'she is legally a free woman' [TEV], 'she is free to marry' [CEV]. This 'law' is the law relating to the husband in the previous verse, but he does not qualify it as such in order to apply the analogy more effectively [NICNT].

d. aorist mid. (deponent = act.) participle of γίνομαι (LN 57.2) (BAGD II.3. p. 160): 'to belong to' [BAGD, LN], 'to have' [LN]. This relation implied by the aorist participle is translated 'when (she remarries)' [NLT], 'by (giving herself)' [REB], 'to (marry)' [CEV]. It is also translated as expressing a conditional statement: 'if' [AB, HNTC, ICC2, NICNT, NTC, WBC; GW, NCV, NET, NRSV, TEV], 'even if' [BECNT], 'though' [KJV, NASB], 'even though' [NIV].

7:4 Therefore, my brothers, you also have-been-put-to-death[a] to-the law[b] through[c] the body[d] of-Christ,

LEXICON—a. aorist pass. indic. of θανατόω (LN 20.65) (BAGD 2.b. p. 351): 'to be put to death' [BAGD, HNTC, NICNT, WBC], 'to be killed' [LN], 'to be made to die' [NASB], 'to be made dead' [ICC2, NTC]. This passive verb is translated as an intransitive active verb: 'to be dead' [CEV], 'to become dead' [KJV], 'to die' [AB, BECNT; GW, NCV, NET, NIV, NLT, NRSV, REB, TEV]. The passive is a divine passive; God is the agent of the action of putting to death [ICC2, Mor, NAC, WBC].

b. νόμος (LN 33.55, 33.333) (BAGD 3. p. 542): 'law' [BAGD, LN (33.333)], 'Law' [LN (33.55); CEV]. It has the definite article here. The phrase τῷ νόμῳ is translated 'to the law' [AB, BECNT, ICC2, NICNT, NTC; KJV, NET, NIV, NRSV, REB], 'to the Law' [NASB], 'in relation to the law' [WBC], 'with reference to the law' [HNTC], 'to the power of

the Law' [CEV], 'to its power' [NLT], 'to the laws in Moses' teachings' [GW]. The phrase 'you have been put to death to the law' is translated 'your old selves died, and you became free from the law' [NCV], 'as far as the Law is concerned, you also have died' [TEV].
- c. διά with genitive object (LN 89.76, 90.8) (BAGD A.III.1.a. p. 180): 'through' [AB, BAGD, BECNT, HNTC, ICC2, LN (89.76, 90.8), NICNT, NTC, WBC; GW, NASB, NCV, NET, NIV, NRSV, REB], 'by' [LN (89.76); KJV], 'by means of' [BAGD, LN (89.76, 90.8)]. This entire clause is translated 'you are now part of the body of Christ and are dead to the power of the Law' [CEV], 'the law no longer holds you in its power, because you died to its power when you died with Christ on the cross' [NLT], 'as far as the Law is concerned, you also have died because you are part of the body of Christ' [TEV].
- d. σῶμα (LN 8.1) (BAGD 1.b. p. 799): 'body' [AB, BAGD, BECNT, HNTC, ICC2, LN, NICNT, NTC, WBC; all versions except NLT], not explicit [NLT]. It refers to Christ's earthly body [BAGD].

QUESTION—What relationship is indicated by ὥστε 'therefore'?

It introduces a conclusion drawn from 7:1–3 that believers are released from bondage to the Mosaic law and freed to be joined to Christ [AB, BECNT, Gdt, ICC1, ICC2, Mor, NICNT, WBC]. He draws a conclusion from the principle stated in 7:1 and illustrated in 7:2–3 [ICC2, WBC]. It is an expanded application of the principle that a person is freed from being required to obey the law after he dies, applying the principle to the person who has died with Christ [SSA].

QUESTION—What does it mean that they have been 'put to death to the law'?

They are released from the authority of the Mosaic law [AB, BECNT, Gdt, SSA, WBC]. The relation of bondage to the law has been broken by a death [HNTC]. They have been severed from bondage to the law as a system that will condemn but cannot save or enable obedience [NICNT]. They are no longer under the condemnation of the law [ICC2, St] or the penalty of the law [Ho]. They are released from the law's condemnation as well as its power to provoke sin in human beings [BECNT]. All indebtedness to the law has been paid off [NTC]. They are released from law as a method of salvation [Ho, Mor, SSA], and from all forms of legalism [Mor]. Christ's punishment for us set him and us free from the jurisdiction of the law, granting us glorious liberty in to a higher life in communion with God [Gdt]. All the virtue of Christ's death in meeting the law's demands are met through our union with Christ, thus freeing us from the bondage to the power of sin to which the law had committed us [Mu].

QUESTION—How do the various elements in Paul's analogy (such as the wife, the husband, the law) relate to the conclusion he draws?

In the illustration in 7:2–3 the wife does not die to be free from the law, but here the believer dies (through Christ's death) to be free from the law, so a strict allegorical identification is not intended here [WBC]. He does not intend a point-for-point correspondence [AB, BECNT, HNTC, ICC2, NAC,

NICNT, NTC, TNTC]. Paul reasons from the specific to the generic [AB] and primarily intends to illustrate that death changes one's relation to the law [AB, BECNT, Gdt, Ho, Mu, St, TNTC]. Death breaks the bond between wife and husband and similarly the death of the believer through his death with Christ breaks his bond to law, enabling him to be joined with Christ [NICNT, TNTC]. The death of either spouse changes the wife's standing as a married wife [Gdt]. There is also the analogy of the new relationship being a union that follows a death [NICNT, TH, TNTC]. The analogy is intended to show that death ends the lordship of the law and frees the believer to live in union with Christ; no more is intended [HNTC, Mor, NTC, WBC]. The illustration extends the axiom of 8:1 to apply not only to the obligations of the dead person but to the obligations of the survivor who had a contract with the person who died [St].

QUESTION—How did the body of Christ effect this death to the law?

Through their union with Christ in his bodily death they 'died' with him to the law's condemnation [AB, BECNT, ICC2, NAC, St]. Christ's death on the cross was also the believer's death to the law as well as to sin [HNTC, Mor, Mu, NICNT, WBC]. We died in the sense that when Christ was crucified he died in our behalf and in our stead [Ho]. Christ's crucifixion paid their debt to the law [NTC]. Christ's body formed the bond between him and the theocratic Jewish nation, and when that bond was broken by his death it was also broken in the case of believers who draw their life from him [Gdt]. They died with Christ when he was crucified [Ho, SSA]. They died because they are a part of the body of Christ [HNTC; TEV]. 'You also have died because you are a part of the body of Christ' [TEV].

in-order-that[a] you may-become[b] (joined) to-another (person),

LEXICON—a. εἰς followed by articular infinitive (LN 89.57) (BAGD 4.e. p. 229): 'so that' [BAGD], 'for the purpose of, in order to' [LN]. The relation indicated by εἰς followed by the articular infinitive is translated 'that you might' [AB, HNTC; NASB, NIV], 'so that you might' [ICC2, NICNT, NTC; NCV], 'so that you may' [NRSV], 'so that you could' [BECNT; NET], 'in order that you might' [WBC], 'that ye should' [KJV], not explicit [CEV, GW, NLT, REB, TEV].

b. aorist mid. (deponent = act.) infin. of γίνομαι (LN 57.2) (BAGD II.3. p. 160): 'to belong to' [BAGD, LN]. This verb in conjunction with the dative case of the pronoun that follows is translated 'to be joined to' [NICNT; NASB, NET], 'to belong to' [ICC2, NTC; CEV, GW, NCV, NIV, NRSV, TEV], 'to give yourselves to' [AB, HNTC; REB], 'to be married to' [BECNT; KJV], 'to be united with' [NLT].

QUESTION—Does this phrase employ the metaphor of marriage or of a slave transfer?

1. It continues the metaphor of marriage [AB, BECNT, Gdt, HNTC, Ho, ICC2, Mu, NICNT, NTC, SSA, TNTC, WBC; KJV].
2. It presents a new metaphor of a slave transfer [Mor].

to-the-(one) having-been-raised[a] from-(among)[b] dead[c] (persons),
LEXICON—a. aorist pass. participle of ἐγείρω (LN 23.94): 'to be raised' [AB, BECNT, HNTC, ICC2, LN, NICNT, NTC, WBC; all versions except GW, REB], 'to be brought back (to life)' [GW]. This aorist participle is also translated as an active verb: 'to rise' [REB].
  b. ἐκ with genitive object (LN 84.4): 'from' [AB, BECNT, HNTC, ICC2, LN, NICNT, NTC, WBC; all versions except CEV, GW], 'out from' [LN], not explicit [CEV, GW].
  c. νεκρός (LN 23.121) (BAGD 2.a. p. 535): 'dead' [AB, BAGD, BECNT, HNTC, ICC2, LN, NICNT, NTC, WBC; all versions except CEV, GW, TEV]. The phrase ἐκ νεκρῶν ἐγερθέντι 'having been raised from among dead persons' is translated 'raised from death' [TEV], 'raised to life' [CEV], 'brought back to life' [GW].

in-order-that we-might-bear-fruit[a] for God.
LEXICON—a. aorist act. subj. of καρποφορέω (LN 23.199) (BAGD 2. p. 405): 'to bear fruit' [AB, BAGD, BECNT, ICC2, LN, NICNT, NTC, WBC; NASB, NET, NIV, NRSV, REB], 'to bear offspring' [HNTC], 'to bring forth fruit' [KJV], 'to yield fruit' [BAGD]. The phrase 'bear fruit for God' is translated 'serve God' [CEV], 'be used in service to God' [NCV], 'be useful in the service of God' [TEV], 'do what God wants' [GW], 'produce good fruit, that is, good deeds for God' [NLT].
QUESTION—How is the metaphor of bearing fruit to be understood?
  1. It refers generally to the idea of an appropriate moral outcome, not of childbearing [ICC2, Mu, TNTC, WBC]. The fruit of the union with Christ is a holy life [Ho, St], a reformed life dedicated to God [AB], the new life characterized by good works [NAC], a life that honors God [SSA], a life that is useful to God [TH]. Believers are to produce character traits that glorify God [NICNT]. They live a life pleasing to God; it is conceptually similar to 6:4 where he speaks of walking in newness of life [BECNT]. The fruit born of this new union consists of good attitudes, aspiration, words, and work directed to the glory of God [NTC]. The fruit is the fruit of the Holy Spirit in Gal 5:22–23 [Mor]. It is good works, the fruit unto holiness mentioned in 6:22 [TNTC], holy works done in God's service [Gdt].
  2. The idea is a continuation of the marriage metaphor in which the believers are married to Christ to bear children [HNTC, ICC1]. This continues the metaphor of marriage and the Christian is wedded to Christ to bear the fruit of a reformed life [ICC1].

7:5 For when we-were in[a] the flesh,[b]
LEXICON—a. ἐν with dative object (LN 13.8): 'in' [BECNT, HNTC, ICC2, LN, NICNT, NTC, WBC; KJV, NASB, NRSV], 'in a state of' [LN], 'on the level of' [REB], 'according to' [TEV], not explicit [AB; CEV, GW, NCV, NET, NIV, NLT].

b. σάρξ (LN 26.7) (BAGD 7. p. 744): 'flesh' [BECNT, HNTC, ICC2, NICNT, NTC, WBC; KJV, NASB, NET, NRSV], 'human nature' [LN], 'unregenerate state' [BAGD]. The phrase ἦμεν ἐν τῇ σαρκί 'we were in the flesh' is translated 'we were living merely natural lives' [AB], 'we thought only of ourselves' [CEV], 'we were living under the influence of our corrupt nature' [GW], 'we were ruled by our sinful selves' [NCV], 'we were controlled by the sinful nature' [NIV], 'we were controlled by our old nature' [NLT], 'we lived on the level of mere human nature' [REB], 'we lived according to our human nature' [TEV].

QUESTION—What relationship is indicated by γάρ 'for'?

It introduces 7:5–6 as a further explanation of what he says in 7:4 [BECNT, Gdt, Ho, ICC2, Mor, NICNT, SSA]. This explains why it is necessary to be freed from the law [NICNT].

QUESTION—In what sense does he use the term σάρξ 'flesh'?

Note that there is a certain amount of overlap possible between the positions listed below, and one does not rule out the other.

1. It refers to a state of existence prior to being in Christ [AB, HNTC, ICC2, WBC], when they were unregenerate [TNTC], when they were controlled by sin [Mu]. It was a state in which they were dominated by sin, death, and law [HNTC, NAC], a state characterized by the weaknesses and appetites of this life [AB, WBC]. It means that the basic direction of their lives was controlled and governed by the fallen nature [ICC2]. It also represents the failure of the Jewish people when they trusted in circumcision done in the flesh, that is, the physical body [WBC].

2. It is the sinful human nature [NTC, SSA, TH], life lived apart from the control of the Holy Spirit, according to one's human nature, and subject to the law, sin, and death [TH]. The body, as the seat of painful and pleasant sensations, represents the natural man under the dominion of love of pleasure and fear of pain and inclined to self-satisfaction [Gdt]. It refers to a way of life that succumbs to temptations and is dominated by the lower part of human nature [Mor]. Living under the control of the sinful human nature does not necessarily refer only to the unregenerate state [SSA].

3. It is a redemptive-historical category in which 'flesh' represents the power of the old age, with its human and worldly principles and values as set in opposition to the Spirit [NICNT].

4. It refers to the old era of redemption history, but also refers to the sinful aspect of human beings [BECNT]. It refers to their former unregenerate state as well as their former legal state of being subject to external rites, ceremonies and commands [Ho].

the passions[a] of sins, the-ones through[b] the law,[c] were-working[d] in[e] our members,[f]

LEXICON—a. πάθημα (LN **25.30**) (BAGD 2. p. 602): 'passion' [BAGD, LN]. The phrase τὰ παθήματα τῶν ἁμαρτιῶν is translated 'the passions of sins' [BECNT], 'sinful passions' [AB, ICC2, NICNT, NTC, WBC; GW,

NASB, NIV, NRSV, REB], 'the passions bound up with sins' [HNTC], 'sinful desires' [CEV, NET, NLT, TEV], 'sinful things' [NCV], 'motions of sins' [KJV].

b. διά with genitive object (LN 89.76, 90.8) (BAGD A.III.1.d. p. 180): 'through' [BECNT, LN (89.76, 90.8), NICNT], 'engendered through' [HNTC], '(which) operate through' [WBC], 'by' [LN (89.76); KJV], 'aroused by' [AB, BAGD; NASB, NET, NIV, NRSV], 'evoked by' [REB], 'stimulated by' [ICC2, NTC], 'stirred up by' [GW, TEV], not explicit [CEV, NCV]. The phrase διὰ τοῦ νόμου 'through the law' is translated 'the Law made us have (sinful desires)' [CEV], 'the law made us want (to do)' [NCV], 'the law aroused' [NLT]. The preposition διά indicates a means relationship here and needs some event word to be supplied, such as 'sins stimulated, excited, kindled, or aroused by (knowing) God's law' [SSA].

c. νόμος (LN 33.55, 33.333) (BAGD 3. p. 542): 'law' [BAGD, LN (33.333)], 'Law' [LN (33.55)]. This noun, which has the definite article here, is translated 'the law' [AB, BECNT, HNTC, ICC2, NICNT, NTC; KJV, NCV, NET, NIV, NLT, NRSV, REB], 'the Law' [CEV, NASB, TEV], 'Moses' laws' [GW].

d. imperf. mid. indic. of ἐνεργέω (LN 42.3) (BAGD 1.b. p. 265): 'to work' [HNTC, LN, NICNT; KJV], 'to be at work' [AB, BAGD, LN; GW, NASB, NIV, NLT, NRSV, TEV], 'to be active' [ICC2, NTC; NET, REB], 'to be effective' [WBC]. This middle voice is translated as passive: 'to be stimulated' [BECNT]. The phrase ἐνεργεῖτο ἐν τοῖς μέλεσιν ἡμῶν 'were working in our members' is translated 'it made every part of our bodies into slaves' [CEV], 'it made us want to do sinful things that controlled our bodies' [NCV].

e. ἐν with dative object (LN 83.13): 'in' [AB, BECNT, HNTC, ICC2, LN, NICNT, NTC, WBC; KJV, NASB, NRSV, REB, TEV], 'within' [NLT], 'throughout' [GW], not explicit [CEV, NCV, NET, NIV].

f. μέλος (LN 8.9) (BAGD 1. p. 501): 'member' [AB, BAGD, BECNT, HNTC, ICC2, LN, NICNT, NTC; KJV, NRSV], 'body part' [LN]. This plural noun is translated 'bodies' [GW, NCV, NIV, REB, TEV], 'members of our body' [NASB, NET], 'every part of our bodies' [CEV], 'what we are and do' [WBC], 'us' [NLT].

QUESTION—How are the nouns related in the genitive phrase τὰ παθήματα τῶν ἁμαρτιῶν 'the passions of sins'?

1. The genitive τῶν ἁμαρτιῶν 'of sins' is descriptive [AB, ICC2, Mu, NICNT, NTC, TH, WBC; CEV, GW, NASB, NCV, NET, NIV, NLT, NRSV, REB, TEV]: the sinful passions. Sinful passions are the inclination to sin, following strong sensory impressions [AB]. They are the desires mentioned in 7:7 that the law forbids [NICNT]. The passions are bound up with sins, that is, arising from and leading to sins [HNTC]. The plural here means that he is speaking of concrete acts of sin as opposed to sin as a condition or principle [ICC2].

2. The passions produce or lead to sin [Gdt, Mor, NAC, SSA].

QUESTION—What is he saying about the relation between the law and sinful passions?

The law's prohibitions actually stimulate sin in sinful human nature [AB, BECNT, Gdt, HNTC, Ho, ICC2, Mor, NICNT, St, TH, WBC]. Passions are inflamed by God's law [ICC2, Mor]. The law causes dormant instincts to become active and even violent [Gdt]. In the absence of the Spirit, the law causes such passions in the heart to become inflamed even more [ICC2]. Sin lies dormant apart from the specific commandment [NTC]. The law incites sin to action [NAC].

QUESTION—What is meant by μέλεσιν ἡμῶν 'our members'?

1. It refers to the various natural human capacities including, but not limited to, the body [BECNT, Ho, ICC2]. These natural capacities become the sphere where the sinful passions are at work [ICC2]. It includes emotional and cognitive faculties in addition to the physical ones [NICNT]. They are the faculties and organs of the human nature [HNTC]. 'Members' refers to their very beings [AB]. These are emotions and passions of the heart and mind, but they are often expressed through physical members [NTC].
2. He is speaking of the parts of our bodies [Gdt, Mor]. Every evil instinct has a member of the body as its corresponding agent [Gdt].
3. It is a synecdoche in which the part, the member, refers to the whole, the body [SSA; GW, NCV, NIV, REB, TEV].

so-as-to[a] bear-fruit[b] for-death;[c]

LEXICON—a. εἰς followed by articular infinitive (LN 89.48): 'so as to' [AB, WBC], 'so that' [BECNT, ICC2, LN, NTC; NIV], 'so' [NCV], 'with the result that' [NICNT], 'as a result' [LN], 'to cause' [LN], not explicit [CEV, GW, NLT, REB, TEV]. This preposition is conflated with the infinitive that follows and translated 'to' [KJV, NASB, NET, NRSV]. It is also translated as indicating purpose: 'that we might' [HNTC].

b. aorist act. infin. of καρποφορέω (LN 13.86) (BAGD 2. p. 405): 'to bear fruit' [AB, BECNT, ICC2, NICNT, NTC, WBC; NASB, NET, NIV, NRSV, REB], 'to yield fruit' [BAGD], 'to bring forth fruit' [KJV], 'to bear offspring' [HNTC], 'to produce' [LN], 'that result in' [GW], 'resulting in' [NLT]. This entire phrase is translated 'who are doomed to die' [CEV], 'they did things that result in death' [GW], 'so the things we did were bringing us death' [NCV], 'and all we did ended in death' [TEV].

c. θάνατος (LN 23.99) (BAGD 2.b. p. 351): 'death' [AB, BAGD, BECNT, HNTC, ICC2, LN, NICNT, NTC, WBC; all versions except CEV]. This noun is also translated as a verb: 'to die' [CEV]. It refers to eternal death [BAGD].

QUESTION—What relationship is indicated by εἰς with the articular infinitive in the phrase εἰς τὸ καρποφορῆσαι 'so as to bear fruit'?
1. It indicates result [HNTC, Ho, ICC2, Mor, NICNT, NTC, SSA; GW, NCV, NLT, TEV].
2. It indicates purpose [Gdt, WBC]. God's purpose is that sin be terminated by death; sin, stirred up by the law, is judged and brought to an end in death [WBC]. It indicates result as well as purpose; there is a secret aspiration after death in the affections of the flesh [Gdt].

QUESTION—What is the meaning of the metaphor he is using?
1. Such passions lead to actions which in turn lead to death or are worthy of death [Ho, Mor, Mu, NICNT, SSA, TNTC]. When man is 'under' law outside the sphere of grace, the passions resulting from the union of man and law lead to in death [HNTC]. He is talking about living in a way that is the opposite of what is expected of a Christian [AB].
2. The law stimulates sinful passions with a view to their work of producing death [WBC].

7:6 but now we-have-been-released^a from^b the law,^c

LEXICON—a. aorist pass. indic. of καταργέω (LN 37.136) (BAGD 3. p. 417): 'to be released' [AB, BAGD, BECNT, ICC2, LN, NICNT, NTC, WBC; NASB, NET, NIV, NLT, REB], 'to be discharged from' [NRSV], 'to be free' [TEV], 'to be freed' [LN], 'to be made free' [NCV], 'to be delivered' [KJV], 'to be done with' [HNTC]. This clause is translated 'but the Law no longer rules over us' [CEV], 'but now we have died to those laws that bound us' [GW].
b. ἀπό with genitive object (LN 89.122): 'from' [AB, BECNT, ICC2, LN, NICNT, NTC, WBC; all versions except CEV, GW], not explicit [HNTC; CEV, GW].
c. νόμος (LN 33.55, 33.333) (BAGD 3. p. 542): 'law' [BAGD, LN (33.333)], 'Law' [LN (33.55)], 'the law' [AB, BECNT, HNTC, ICC2, NICNT, NTC, WBC; KJV, NCV, NET, NIV, NLT, NRSV, REB], 'the Law' [CEV, NASB, TEV], 'those laws' [GW]. This word has the definite article here.

QUESTION—To what does the term νυνί 'now' refer?
1. It has temporal force [AB, BECNT, Gdt, Ho, ICC2, Mu, NICNT, St, WBC]. 'Now' contrasts with 'when' in 7:5 [Ho, TH]. It refers to the time when they first believed as the beginning of their present state as believers [ICC2, WBC], as well as to their being in a new eschatological era [AB, WBC]. The contrast of this 'but now' with 7:5 corresponds with the contrast 'when you were' and 'but now' in 6:20 and 22 [Gdt, St]. It refers to the new aeon of the Christian dispensation [AB, WBC]. It refers to what is true of believers, who have now passed from bondage to law into serving in the newness that comes from the Spirit [BECNT, NICNT, WBC].
2. It has logical force [ICC1]: 'as it is'.

3. The contrast is both logical and temporal [HNTC, Mor].

having-died^a (to-that) by^b which we-were-being-bound,^c

LEXICON—a. aorist act. participle of ἀποθνῃσκω (LN 23.99) (BAGD 1.b.γ. p. 91): 'to die' [AB, BECNT, HNTC, ICC2, LN, NICNT, NTC, WBC; GW, NASB, NCV, NET, NIV, NLT, REB, TEV], 'to be dead' [BAGD; KJV, NRSV]. This entire phrase is translated 'We are like dead people, and it cannot have any power over us' [CEV], 'that being dead wherein we were held' [KJV].

    b. ἐν with dative object (LN 13.8): 'by' [BECNT, HNTC, ICC2, NTC, WBC; NASB], 'in' [LN, NICNT], 'with' [LN], not explicit [CEV, GW, KJV, NCV, NLT, NRSV, REB, TEV]. The phrase ἐν ᾧ '(to that) in which' is translated 'to what' [AB; NET, NIV].

    c. imperf. pass. indic. of κατέχω (LN 37.17) (BAGD 1.d.α. p. 423): 'to be bound' [BAGD, BECNT; NASB], 'to be held captive' [AB, NICNT], 'to be held fast' [HNTC, NTC], 'to be held' [ICC2; KJV], 'to be confined' [WBC], 'to be kept' [LN]. This passive verb is translated as an active verb: 'to bind' [GW, NIV], 'to hold one bound' [REB], 'to hold captive' [NRSV], 'to control' [NET], 'to hold (as) prisoner' [NCV, TEV]. This entire phrase is translated 'We are like dead people, and it cannot have any power over us' [CEV], 'we died with Christ, and we are no longer captive to its power' [NLT].

QUESTION—What relationship is indicated by the participle ἀποθανόντες 'having died'?

    1. It expresses reason [AB, BECNT, HNTC, Ho, Mor, NICNT, SSA, TNTC, WBC]: we have been released because we have died. Their vicarious death in Christ brought about their deliverance from the law [Ho].

    2. It expresses means [Mu, NTC]: we have been released by means of our death to sin.

QUESTION—What is the antecedent to ἐν ᾧ 'to that in which'?

    1. They have died to the law [AB, BECNT, Gdt, HNTC, Ho, ICC2, Mor, NICNT, NTC, SSA, TH, WBC].

    2. They have died to the flesh, the old sinful state [ICC1].

QUESTION—What does it mean that believers have 'died' to the law?

They have freedom from it [HNTC, NICNT], they are released from its power [BECNT], redeemed from its bondage [Ho]. There is no link between the believer and the law since salvation is not due to the law; believers have been made null and void so far as the law is concerned [Mor]. They have been discharged from the liability under law that they once held [TNTC].

so-as^a to-serve^b in^c newness^d of-Spirit/spirit^e

LEXICON—a. ὥστε (LN 89.52, 89.61) (BAGD 2.a.β. p. 900): 'so that' [AB, BAGD, BECNT, HNTC, ICC2, LN (89.52, 89.61), NICNT, NTC, WBC; GW, NASB, NET, NIV, NRSV], 'that' [KJV], 'so' [NCV], 'so then' [LN (89.52)], 'and so' [LN (89.52)], 'as a result' [LN (89.52)], 'in order to'

[LN (89.61)], not explicit [CEV, NLT, REB, TEV]. It indicates an actual result [BAGD].
  b. pres. act. infin. of δουλεύω (LN 37.25, 87.79) (BAGD 1.b. p. 205): 'to serve' [AB, BECNT, HNTC, ICC2, NICNT, NTC, WBC; all versions except NRSV], 'to be a slave' [BAGD, LN (37.25, 87.79); NRSV]. The phrase ὥστε δουλεύειν 'so that you might serve' is translated as indicating purpose or potential: 'so that we might serve' [AB, NICNT, WBC], 'that we should serve' [KJV], 'so that we may serve' [NET]. It is translated as indicating effect or result: 'so that we serve' [BECNT, HNTC, ICC2, NTC; NASB, NIV], 'so now we serve' [NCV], 'now we can serve' [CEV, NLT], 'we serve' [TEV], 'we are serving' [GW], 'we are slaves' [NRSV].
  c. ἐν with dative object (LN 13.8, 89.84): 'in' [AB, BECNT, HNTC, ICC2, LN (13.8), NICNT, NTC, WBC; all versions], 'with' [LN (13.8, 89.84)].
  d. καινότης (LN 58.70, **67.101**) (BAGD p. 394): 'newness' [BECNT, ICC2, LN (58.70, **67.101**), NICNT, NTC, WBC; KJV, NASB]. This noun is translated as an adjective: 'new' [AB, BAGD; all versions except KJV, NASB]. The phrase ἐν καινότητι πνεύματος 'in newness of Spirit' is translated 'in a new way of the Spirit' [AB], 'in the new way of the Spirit' [NIV, TEV], 'in a new way by obeying his Spirit' [CEV], 'in a new way with the Spirit' [NCV], 'in a new spiritual way' [GW], 'in a new life marked by the gift of the Spirit' [HNTC], 'in the new life of the Spirit' [NET], 'in the new way, by the Spirit' [NLT], 'in the new life of the Spirit' [NRSV], 'in a new way, the way of the spirit' [REB].
  e. πνεῦμα (LN 12.18, 26.9) (BAGD 5.g.γ. p. 677): 'Spirit' [AB, BAGD, BECNT, HNTC, ICC2, LN (12.18), NICNT, NTC, WBC; CEV, NASB, NCV, NET, NIV, NLT, NRSV, TEV], 'spirit' [LN (26.9); KJV, REB]. This noun is translated as an adjective: 'spiritual' [GW].

QUESTION—What relationship is indicated by ὥστε 'so as'?
  1. It indicates result [BAGD, BECNT, HNTC, ICC2, Mor, Mu, NICNT, NTC, SSA, TH, WBC; CEV, GW, NASB, NCV, NIV, NLT, NRSV, TEV]: we have been released from the law, with the result that we serve in newness of Spirit.
  2. It indicates purpose [AB, ICC1, NAC, WBC; KJV, NET]: we have been released from the law in order that we might serve in newness of Spirit.

QUESTION—In what sense is the term πνεῦμα 'Spirit/spirit' used in the phrase καινότητι πνεύματος 'newness of Spirit/spirit'?
  1. It refers to the Holy Spirit [AB, BAGD, BECNT, HNTC, Ho, ICC1, ICC2, Mu, NAC, NICNT, NTC, SSA, St, TNTC, WBC; CEV, NASB, NCV, NET, NIV, NLT, NRSV, TEV]. It fulfills the OT promise that the new covenant would give people power to keep the law [BECNT].
  2. It refers to the spiritual as opposed to the fleshly or non-spiritual dimension: 'the spirit' [GW, KJV, REB]. We serve in a new spiritual way [GW], in a way of the spirit in contrast to the old way of the written law [REB].

3. The service is a thing of the human spirit, but is only possible because of the help of the Spirit of God [Mor].

QUESTION—How are the nouns related in the genitive phrase καινότητι πνεύματος 'newness of spirit/Spirit'?

1. 'Of Spirit' indicates the source of the newness [AB, BECNT, Gdt, HNTC, Ho, Mu, NICNT, NTC, SSA, TH, WBC]: a newness that is produced by the Holy Spirit. It is a newness that comes from the Holy Spirit [BECNT, Mu, NTC], or which is determined by the Spirit [AB, NICNT], or which is characterized by the gift of the Spirit [HNTC]. There is a new way of serving God which the Spirit effects or makes possible [SSA, TH]. There is a new and holy state which the Spirit has produced [Ho], into which the believer is introduced by the Holy Spirit [Gdt]. It is a newness resulting from the work of the Spirit and a new epoch marked by the Spirit [WBC], with the Spirit as the new dynamic principle [AB].
2. 'Of Spirit' is in apposition to newness [ICC1, ICC2]: newness, that is, the Holy Spirit. The newness is the power of God's Spirit dwelling within [ICC2]. The newness is a new way of serving, which is serving in the Spirit [NAC].
3. 'Of spirit' indicates the kind of new way to serve [Mor; GW, REB]: we serve in a new way, the way of the spirit. It is a new way of service that is a thing of the human spirit [Mor], in a new spiritual way [GW], in a way of the spirit, not the old way of the written law [REB].

and not (in) oldness[a] **of-letter.**[b]

LEXICON—a. παλαιότης (LN **58.74, 67.100**) (BAGD p. 606): 'oldness' [BECNT, ICC2, LN (67.100), NICNT, NTC; KJV, NASB], 'being obsolete' [LN (67.100)], 'old way' [AB, LN (**58.74, 67.100**); CEV, GW, NCV, NIV, NLT, REB, TEV], 'old life' [HNTC], 'old (written code)' [BAGD; NET, NRSV].

b. γράμμα (LN 33.50) (BAGD 2.c. p. 165): 'letter' [BECNT, ICC2, NICNT, NTC; KJV, NASB], 'writing' [BAGD, LN], 'written law' [HNTC; TEV], 'written Law' [CEV], 'written code' [AB; NET, NIV, NRSV, REB], 'written words' [GW]. This word in the genitive case is translated 'by obeying the written Law' [CEV], 'which was marked only by observance of the written law' [HNTC], 'dictated by written words' [GW], 'with written rules' [NCV], 'by obeying the letter of the law' [NLT].

QUESTION—What does 'letter' refer to?

1. It refers to the Mosaic law [SSA], to the OT as the legislation of the old covenant [AB], to their subservience to the requirements of the letter of the law [HNTC]. It refers to the commands of the law, which could not produce the righteousness they required [BECNT]. It refers to law as something written [Ho, Mu]. It is strict adherence to the written Mosaic law as a way of obtaining salvation [NTC]. Paul uses γράμμα 'letter' to refer to the legal authority that has now been replaced; this is in contrast with how he uses γραφή to speak of the positive and lasting effects of

Scripture [Mor]. It refers to strait-laced interpretation [NAC]. It is the moral obligation of the written code which is imposed on man as something foreign to his true inward dispositions [Gdt].
2. It refers to the old age of the Mosaic covenant with its external code [NICNT].
3. It refers to living in the mode of the old epoch in which law is seen as letter only, that is, observed at a too superficial level, the level of the flesh, particularly with regard to circumcision [WBC]. 'Letter' refers to the perverse way of legalism, misunderstanding and misusing God's law [ICC2].

QUESTION—How are the nouns related in the genitive phrase παλαιότητι γράμματος 'oldness of letter'?

1. It indicates apposition [AB, HNTC, ICC1, ICC2, NTC]: oldness, that is, the letter. The old way was the way of the written code [AB, Gdt, Mor, NAC], the way made possible by the written law or spelled out by the written law [TH], and characterized by subservience to its requirements [HNTC]. The oldness is the old and perverse way of legalism as a misuse and misunderstanding of God's law [ICC2].
2. It indicates source [BECNT, Ho, NICNT]: the old state determined by the letter [NICNT], or that stems from the letter [BECNT]. It is the old state of which the law is the source [Ho].

QUESTION—What is meant by the contrast 'newness of Spirit/spirit and not in oldness of letter'?

It signifies the disjunction between the two covenants [BECNT, NICNT] or between the two epochs [WBC]. It is a difference between the two covenants and epochs, but also between pre-conversion and post-conversion life [St]. It is the difference between serving a written code and serving God himself with the new dynamic principle of the Holy Spirit [AB]. Service in the new epoch does not depend on consultation of the written text but is motivated and directed immediately from the Spirit within [WBC]. It contrasts life characterized by the fruit of the Spirit as opposed to subservience to the letter of the law [HNTC]. It is a contrast of life lived by the power of God's indwelling Spirit as opposed to misusing and misunderstanding God's law legalistically [ICC2]. It contrasts the attempt to be saved by strict adherence to the Mosaic law to living lives of gratitude for salvation received as a divine gift [NTC]. It contrasts the way of legal authority with the kind of wholehearted service that is spiritual and enabled by God's Spirit [Mor]. It is a contrast between submission to an external code and a internal regulative principle that comes from the Spirit [TNTC]. The old state was one in which moral obligation was imposed from without and contrary to the inclination within, whereas the new state is one in which moral obligation and the inclination of the heart are in harmony [Gdt]. It is the contrast between serving in the servitude that law brings as opposed to serving in the newness of the liberty that the Holy Spirit brings [Mu].

DISCOURSE UNIT: 7:7–25 [Gdt, GNT, HNTC, ICC2, WBC; CEV, NIV]. The topic is the powerlessness of the law to sanctify man [Gdt], the problem of indwelling sin [GNT], the battle with sin [CEV], struggling with sin [NIV], the law and sin [HNTC], a necessary clarification of what has been said concerning the law [ICC2], the law is still exploited by sin and death as experience demonstrates [WBC].

DISCOURSE UNIT: 7:7–13 [AB, Mu, NTC, TNTC; GW, NCV, NLT, TEV] The topic is our fight against sin [NCV], law and sin [NRSV, TEV], the role of the Law in human life [AB], God's law reveals our sin [NLT], Moses' laws show what sin is [GW], transitional experience [Mu], the dawn of conscience [TNTC], the sinner's relation to God's law in the light of Paul's own experience and that of others like him [NTC].

DISCOURSE UNIT: 7:7–12 [Mor, NICNT]. The topic is the coming of the law [NICNT], is the law sin? [Mor].

7:7 What then shall-we-say? (Is) the law[a] sin?[b]

LEXICON—a. νόμος (LN 33.55, 33.333) (BAGD 3. p. 542): 'law' [BAGD, LN (33.333)], 'Law' [LN (33.55)], 'the law' [AB, BECNT, HNTC, ICC2, NICNT, NTC, WBC; KJV, NCV, NET, NIV, NRSV, REB], 'the Law' [CEV, NASB, TEV], 'Moses' laws' [GW], 'the law of God' [NLT]. This word has the definite article here.

b. ἁμαρτία (LN 88.289) (BAGD 1. p. 43): 'sin' [AB, BECNT, HNTC, ICC2, LN, NICNT, NTC, WBC; KJV, NASB, NCV, NET, NIV, NRSV, REB]. This noun is translated as an adjective: 'sinful' [CEV, GW, TEV], 'evil' [NLT]. The phrase 'is the law sin?' is translated 'is the law identical with sin?' [REB], 'that the Law itself is sinful?' [TEV], 'that sin and the law are the same thing' [NCV].

QUESTION—How is the question 'Is the law sin' to be taken?

He is raising the rhetorical question of whether or not the Mosaic law is sinful or evil [AB, Gdt, Ho, ICC1, ICC2, Mor, Mu, NAC, NICNT, St, TH, WBC]. Paul then denies that it is sinful while admitting that it incidentally does produce sin [Ho]. He is raising the rhetorical question of whether the law is the origin of sin and death [St]. The question asks whether we are to infer from the preceding statements that the law is evil because it arouses our sinful desires [SSA]. Those who read what Paul wrote about law, sin, and death might get the impression that Paul thought that the law was responsible for sin and death [St]. Paul now deals with this possible false conclusion [ICC2]. Many Jews and Jewish Christians must have accused Paul of holding such an opinion and the Roman Christians would have learned of their accusations [NICNT].

Never may-it-be;[a]

LEXICON—a. aorist mid. (deponent = act.) optative of γίνομαι (LN 13.107) (BAGD I.3.a. p. 158): 'to happen, to occur' [LN]. The phrase μὴ γένοιτο is translated 'may it never be!' [NASB], 'certainly not!' [AB, BECNT,

HNTC, WBC; CEV, NIV], 'absolutely not!' [NET], 'of course not!' [REB, TEV], 'of course not! The law is not sinful' [NLT], 'not at all!' [NTC], 'by no means!' [BAGD, NICNT; NRSV], 'far from it' [BAGD], 'God forbid!' [BAGD, ICC2; KJV], 'that's unthinkable!' [GW], 'that is not true' [NCV]. This phrase is punctuated by an exclamation point by all except HNTC and KJV. See this phrase also at 3:4, 6, 31; 6:2, 15.

but[a] I-did- not -know[b] sin[c] except[d] through[e] law;[f]

LEXICON—a. ἀλλά (LN 89.125, 91.2) (BAGD 1.a. p. 38): 'but' [ICC2, LN (89.125), NICNT; CEV, NCV, NLT, TEV], 'on the contrary' [LN (89.125), NTC; NASB], 'nevertheless' [BECNT, WBC], 'yet' [AB, HNTC, LN (91.2); NRSV, REB], 'nay' [KJV], 'in fact' [GW], 'certainly' [NET], 'indeed' [NIV].

b. aorist act. indic. of γινώσκω (LN 28.1, **32.16**) (BAGD 1.a. p. 160): 'to know' [BAGD, LN (28.1); CEV], 'to come to know' [BAGD], 'to have knowledge of' [LN (28.1)], 'to understand' [**LN (32.16)**]. The aorist οὐκ ἔγνων 'I did not know' is translated as the consequence of a conditional statement: 'I would not have known sin' [AB, BECNT, NICNT, WBC; NET, NRSV], 'I would not have known what sin was' [NIV], 'I would not have known what sin is really like' [CEV], 'I would not have come to know sin' [NTC; NASB], 'I should not have come to know sin' [ICC2], 'I should never have become acquainted with sin' [REB], 'I wouldn't have recognized sin' [GW], 'I would not have experienced sin' [WBC]. It is also translated as a positive statement: 'I had not known sin' [KJV], 'I came to know sin' [HNTC]. The whole clause is translated 'the law was the only way I could learn what sin meant' [NCV], 'it was the law that showed me my sin' [NLT], 'it was the Law that made me know what sin is' [TEV].

c. ἁμαρτία (LN 88.289) (BAGD 1. p. 43): 'sin' [AB, BAGD, BECNT, HNTC, ICC2, LN, NICNT, NTC, WBC; all versions].

d. εἰ μή (LN 89.131, BAGD VI.8.a. p 220): 'except, if not' [BAGD], 'except that, but only' [LN]. The phrase εἰ μὴ διά is translated 'except through' [BECNT, NICNT, WBC; NASB, NET, NIV], 'but by' [KJV], 'it is only through' [HNTC], 'if it were not for' [AB], 'had it not been for' [REB], 'had it not been through' [NTC], 'if it had not been for' [CEV, NRSV], 'if (those laws) hadn't' [GW], not explicit [NCV, NLT, TEV].

e. διά with genitive object (LN 89.76, 90.8): 'through' [BECNT, HNTC, LN (89.76, 90.8), NICNT, NTC, WBC; NASB, NET, NIV], 'by' [KJV], 'by means of' [LN (90.8)], not explicit [AB; CEV, GW, NCV, NLT, NRSV, TEV].

f. νόμος (LN 33.55, 33.333) (BAGD 3. p. 542): 'law' [BAGD, LN (33.333)], 'Law' [LN (33.55)], 'the law' [AB, BECNT, HNTC, ICC2, NICNT, NTC, WBC; KJV, NCV, NET, NIV, NLT, NRSV, REB], 'the Law' [CEV, NASB, TEV], 'those laws' [GW]. This word lacks the definite article here.

QUESTION—What relationship is indicated by ἀλλά 'but'?
1. It is adversative and indicates the contrast of what follows to the idea that the law is sin. That is, the law is not sin or the cause of sin; on the contrary law is that which causes us to know how our lives lack conformity to the law [Ho, ICC1, ICC2, Mor, Mu, SSA, WBC].
2. It is restrictive, and indicates the relation of what follows to μὴ γένοιτο 'never may it be', which rejects the idea that the law is sin [BECNT, Gdt, HNTC, NICNT]: the law is not sin, nevertheless it is true that there is some relationship to sin since the laws brings the knowledge of sin. The law is not sin, but it is impossible to deny that there is some relationship [HNTC].

QUESTION—In what sense did he come to 'know' sin through the law?

He came to understand sin for what it really is [BECNT, HNTC, NICNT, SSA, WBC], both because the law more clearly defined it and because the law stimulated a desire for the very thing it prohibited [BECNT, HNTC, NICNT, St, WBC]. The law reveals sin in its true character [NTC]. It is not that a person has no knowledge of right and wrong apart from the law, it is that the law exposes sin as a transgression of the will of God [AB]. Here the verbs for knowing mean experiential knowledge [NAC, TH]. He felt a sense of conviction and a consciousness of guilt [Ho]. While a moral code is nearly universal in that all people have a sense of right and wrong, it takes the law of God to show that wrongdoing is sin against God [Mor]. Sin can only emerge in a recognizable and measurable way when there are divine commands; but not only does the law reveal sin, it actually acts as a catalyst to aid or initiate human sin in that it stimulates man's inherent rebellion against his creaturely status [HNTC]. Sin can only be defined with respect to violating concrete commands, so when Paul became conscious of having rejected specific commands he became conscious of himself as a sinful person [TH]. The law enabled him to recognize evil instincts within himself [Gdt]. It revealed the nature and fact of sin, and it also brought subjective conviction that he was sinful [Mu].

QUESTION—Is Paul speaking of a recognition of sinfulness as a condition or of recognizing particular acts as being sinful?

He came to know his own state and character as a sinner [Ho]. He was convicted of sin and sinfulness [Mu]. Through revealing the sinfulness of particular acts the law brings the knowledge of the nature and power of sinfulness as a condition [BECNT, NICNT]. He is speaking of experiencing sin as particular sinful acts as well as a force [WBC]. It is particularly the tenth commandment with its focus on the desires of the heart that revealed to Paul his sinful condition [Gdt, NTC].

for I-was- not -knowing[a] coveting[b]

LEXICON—a. pluperfect (with imperfect meaning) act. indic. of οἶδα (LN 28.1) (BAGD 1.b. p. 555): 'to know' [BAGD, LN], 'to know about, to have knowledge of' [LN]. This verb exists only in the perfect stem

system, the perfect tense having a present meaning and the pluperfect tense having an imperfect meaning. This negated imperfect verb is translated 'I would not have known' [AB, BECNT, NICNT, NTC; CEV, GW, NASB, NET, NIV, NRSV, TEV], 'I would never have known' [NCV, NLT], 'I should never have known' [REB], 'I should not know' [HNTC, ICC2], 'I had not known' [KJV]. He is saying that a person would not otherwise know that coveting is sinful [SSA].
  b. ἐπιθυμία (LN 25.12, 25.20) (BAGD 3. p. 293): 'coveting' [ICC2; NASB], 'covetousness' [NICNT, WBC], 'desire' [BAGD, HNTC, LN (25.12, 25.20)], 'longing' [BAGD], 'craving' [BAGD], 'lust' [LN (25.20); KJV]. The phrase τὴν…ἐπιθυμίαν 'the coveting' is translated 'what it was to covet' [AB; REB], 'what it is to covet' [NRSV], 'what coveting was' [BECNT], 'what coveting really was' [NIV], 'what it meant to covet' [NTC], 'that coveting is wrong' [NLT], 'that some desires are sinful' [GW], 'what it means to want something that belongs to someone else' [CEV], 'what it means to want to take something belonging to someone else' [NCV], 'what it means to desire something belonging to someone else' [NET], 'to desire what belongs to someone else' [TEV].
QUESTION—Is there any implied difference between the two words for knowing used in this verse?
  In classical usage the verb γινώσκω usually indicates a more personal acquaintance with something or someone, usually by experience, whereas οἶδα typically refers to a more rational knowledge [NICNT, WBC].
  1. Their use here is near synonymous, but γινώσκω inclines more toward experience 'I did not experience' and οἶδα simply means 'to know' [ICC1, WBC].
  2. There is no difference in meaning intended [BECNT, Mor, NAC, NICNT, TH]. Both reflect an experiential knowledge [NAC].
QUESTION—Does the pluperfect tense of οἶδα indicate a continuance of the knowing?
  1. It indicates that the knowledge began and continues [ICC2, Mor, WBC].
  2. There is no nuance of continued activity intended [BECNT, Gdt, HNTC, NICNT, TH]. There is no aorist form for οἶδα that Paul could have used [NICNT].
QUESTION—What is meant by the term ἐπιθυμία 'coveting'?
  It refers generally to any and all strong desire [BECNT, Gdt, HNTC, Ho, NICNT, WBC], including coveting material goods as well as lust [BECNT]. It refers to the evil desires of the heart [NTC], to any and all evil desire or desire for evil things [Mor], to all illicit desire [ICC1, St]. It is really an exalting of the ego or self over all else [HNTC, Mor]. It is whatever people selfishly desire for themselves, including the desire to usurp the place of the creator [HNTC, NICNT]. Paul follows a common Jewish viewpoint which speaks of the sequence of desire, sin, and death [TH].

except-that[a] **the law**[b] **was-saying, You-shall- not -covet.**[c]

LEXICON—a. εἰ μή (LN 89.131, BAGD VI.8.a. p 220): 'unless' [BECNT, WBC; CEV], 'if...had not' [AB, NICNT, NTC; GW, NASB, NCV, NET, NIV, NLT, NRSV, REB, TEV], 'if...did not' [HNTC], 'except' [KJV], 'had not' [ICC2].

  b. νόμος (LN 33.55, 33.333) (BAGD 3. p. 542): 'law' [BAGD, LN (33.333)], 'Law' [LN (33.55)], 'the law' [AB, BECNT, HNTC, ICC2, NICNT, NTC, WBC; KJV, NCV, NET, NIV, NLT, NRSV, REB], 'the Law' [CEV, NASB, TEV], 'Moses' teachings' [GW]. This word has the definite article here.

  c. fut. act. indic. of ἐπιθυμέω (LN 25.12, 25.20) (BAGD p. 293): 'to covet' [AB, BECNT, ICC2, LN (25.20), NICNT, NTC, WBC; KJV, NASB, NET, NIV, NLT, NRSV, REB], 'to desire' [BAGD, HNTC, LN (25.12)], 'to desire what belongs to someone else' [TEV], 'to long for' [BAGD, LN (25.12)], 'to lust' [LN (25.20)], 'to have wrong desires' [GW], 'to take your neighbor's things' [NCV], not explicit [CEV].

7:8 **But sin, having-taken**[a] **opportunity**[b] **through**[c] **the commandment,**[d]

LEXICON—a. aorist. act. participle of λαμβάνω (LN 18.1) (BAGD 1.a. p. 464): 'to take' [BECNT, NICNT; GW, KJV, NASB, NLT, NRSV], 'to seize' [AB, HNTC, WBC; NET, NIV], 'to find' [BAGD; NCV, REB, TEV], 'to obtain' [ICC2], 'to grasp' [BAGD, NTC], not explicit [CEV].

  b. ἀφορμή (LN **22.46**) (BAGD p. 127): 'opportunity' [AB, BAGD, BECNT, HNTC, **LN**, NICNT, NTC; GW, NASB, NET, NIV, NRSV, REB], 'advantage' [NLT], 'a base for its operations' [ICC2], 'a way to use' [NCV], 'occasion' [LN; KJV], 'chance' [TEV]. This entire phrase is translated 'It was sin that used this command as a way' [CEV]. This noun represents a starting point from which a military attack is launched, a bridgehead, or base of operations [HNTC, Mor, NAC, St, TNTC].

  c. διά with genitive object (LN 89.76, 90.8) (BAGD A.III.1.d. p. 180): 'through' [BAGD, BECNT, HNTC, ICC2, LN (89.76, 90.8), NICNT, WBC; NASB, NET, REB], 'in' [NRSV], 'by' [KJV], 'by means of' [LN (90.8); TEV], 'provided by' [GW], 'afforded by' [NTC; NIV], 'using' [AB]. The phrase 'taking opportunity through the commandment' is translated 'used this command' [CEV], 'found a way to use that command' [NCV], 'took advantage of this law' [NLT].

  d. ἐντολή (LN 33.330) (BAGD 2.a.α. p. 269): 'commandment' [AB, BECNT, ICC2, LN, NICNT, NTC; GW, KJV, NASB, NET, NIV, NRSV, REB, TEV], 'command' [CEV, NCV], 'law' [BAGD, HNTC; NLT].

QUESTION—In what sense did sin 'take opportunity'?

Sin used what should have been its mortal enemy to achieve its own purpose [AB]. This is a description of the tactics of the serpent in the garden who is personified here as sin; he was unable to tempt until after the commandment had been given, but when it had, he used the opportunity to deceive and seduce Eve into sinning [WBC]. Sin aimed an attack at man through the law that the law never intended [HNTC]. Sin exists, but apart from the law it can't produce guilt [ICC1]. The prohibition causes the object desired to be desired even more strongly [Gdt]. Instead of using this personification of sin, it is translated 'because I desired to sin I took the opportunity to covet in many ways' [SSA].

QUESTION—What does the phrase διὰ τῆς ἐντολῆς 'through the commandment' modify?

1. It modifies ἀφορμὴν δὲ λαβοῦσα 'taking opportunity' [AB, BECNT, HNTC, NICNT, NTC, SSA; CEV, GW, KJV, NASB, NCV, NET, NIV, NLT, NRSV, REB]: sin took opportunity through the commandment.
2. It modifies the phrase κατειργάσατο ἐπιθυμίαν 'brought about... coveting' [Gdt, Ho, ICC1, ICC2, Mor, Mu, NAC, WBC]: sin brought about coveting through the commandment.

QUESTION—Does διὰ τῆς ἐντολῆς 'through the commandment' refer generally to the Law or specifically to the tenth commandment about coveting?

It refers to the specific commandment about coveting [AB, BECNT, Gdt, HNTC, ICC1, NICNT, NTC, TH]. In this case the part stands for the whole, the specific commandment about coveting illustrating and representing the entire moral law [Ho].

brought-about[a] in[b] me all-kinds-of[c] coveting;[d]

LEXICON—a. aorist mid. (deponent = act.) indic. of κατγεργάζομαι (LN 13.9) (BAGD 2. p. 421): 'to bring about, to cause to be' [LN], 'to produce' [AB, HNTC, NICNT, NTC; NASB, NET, NIV, NRSV, REB], 'to work' [BECNT, ICC2; KJV], 'to call forth' [BAGD], 'to stir up' [WBC; TEV], 'to arouse' [NLT], 'to make (me have)' [CEV, GW], 'to cause (me to want)' [NCV]. See this word at 1:27; 2:9; 4:15; 5:3.

b. ἐν with dative object (LN 83.13) (BAGD I.5.a. p. 259): 'in' [BAGD, LN]. The phrase ἐν ἐμοί 'in me' is translated 'me' [CEV].

c. πᾶς (LN 58.28): 'all kinds of' [NICNT; CEV, GW, NCV, NET, NLT, NRSV, REB, TEV], 'every kind of' [BECNT, HNTC, LN; NASB, NIV], 'all sorts of' [LN], 'every sort of' [AB], 'all manner of' [ICC2, WBC; KJV], 'of every variety' [NTC].

d. ἐπιθυμία (LN 25.12, 25.20) (BAGD 3. p. 293): 'coveting' [BECNT, NICNT, NTC; NASB], 'covetousness' [AB, ICC2, WBC; NRSV], 'covetous desire' [NIV], 'desire' [BAGD, HNTC, LN (25.12, 25.20); CEV], 'wrong desires' [GW, NET, REB], 'forbidden desires' [NLT], 'selfish desires' [TEV], 'concupiscence' [KJV], 'longing, craving' [BAGD], 'lust' [LN (25.20)], 'to want things I should not want' [NCV].

QUESTION—Is Paul dealing primarily with this one commandment about coveting, or does the principle of law stimulating what it forbids apply to other sins as well?

The mention of coveting is a specific example of the general effect law has [AB]. He is primarily dealing with wrong desire, which in Jewish thinking was considered to be at the heart of all sin [WBC]. It primarily has to do with the commandment about coveting [TNTC].

QUESTION—What does he mean by saying that the law 'brought about' the sin of coveting?

In addition to defining sin, the commandment actually stimulates the multiplying of sin in rebellious human nature [AB, BECNT, Gdt, HNTC, Mor, Mu, NICNT, SSA]. The law actually gives sin the opportunity to goad the ego into open and flagrant rebellion [AB]. The commandment to Adam gave the opportunity for desire to turn him inward upon himself instead of on God, and became the means of corrupting what should have been a strong positive force in his life [WBC]. Humans tend to want things even more when what they want is forbidden [TNTC]. The law defined the sin of evil desire and showed it for what it is, thus bringing about the possibility of a multitude of ways it can be transgressed [NTC].

for apart-from^a law^b sin (is) dead.^c

LEXICON—a. χωρίς with genitive object (LN 89.120) (BAGD 2.b.γ. p. 890): 'apart from' [BAGD, BECNT, HNTC, LN, NICNT; NASB, NET, NIV, NRSV, TEV], 'without' [LN; CEV, GW, KJV, NCV], 'in the absence of' [AB, ICC2, NTC, WBC; REB], 'if there were no (law)' [NLT].

b. νόμος (LN 33.55, 33.333) (BAGD 3. p. 542): 'law' [AB, BAGD, HNTC, LN (33.333), NTC; NIV, NLT, REB, TEV], 'laws' [GW], 'the law' [BECNT, ICC2, NICNT, WBC; KJV, NCV, NET, NRSV], 'Law' [LN (33.55)], 'the Law' [CEV, NASB]. This word lacks the definite article here.

c. νεκρός (LN 23.121) (BAGD 1.b.β. p. 535): 'dead' [BAGD, BECNT, HNTC, ICC2, LN, NICNT, NTC, WBC; CEV, GW, KJV, NASB, NET, NIV, NRSV], 'a dead thing' [TEV], 'as good as dead' [AB], 'devoid of life' [REB]. The phrase 'sin (is) dead' is translated 'sin has no power' [NCV], 'sin would not have that power' [NLT].

QUESTION—What does it mean that sin is 'dead' apart from law?

1. The law not only brought sin to light, it even aroused it [Ho]. In the years before the giving of the Mosaic law sin was not as powerfully active as it was afterwards [NICNT]. The law becomes sin's agent in killing people, provoking the very desire it forbids [WBC]. Sin has no power apart from the law [TH; NCV]. The law created the conditions within which inordinate desire could operate [HNTC]. Sin existed, but it was the law that caused it to awaken within him [Gdt, Mu]. Filled out, the metaphor is that without the law prohibiting sin, one's desire to sin is unable to be aroused just like a dead person is unable to be aroused [SSA].

2. Sin is dead apart from law in the sense that, because it is undefined, it cannot be designated as sin [NAC]. Sin is dormant until the law shows how many ways desire can be evil [NTC]. Without the law, even in their wickedness people were not in open rebellion against God [AB].

QUESTION—What is the tense of the implied verb 'to be' in this clause?
1. It is present tense, expressing a general truth [AB, BECNT, Gdt, HNTC, Ho, ICC1, ICC2, NICNT, NTC, SSA, TH, WBC; all versions except KJV]: apart from the law sin is dead. It is a generic statement applicable to anyone in such a condition [SSA].
2. It is past tense, expressing an historical truth, presumably either for Paul, or for Israel, or possibly for the human race [Mu; KJV]: apart from the law sin was dead.

7:9 And[a] once[b] I was-alive[c] apart-from[d] law[e]

LEXICON—a. δέ: 'and' [BECNT, HNTC, ICC2, NICNT, WBC; NASB, NET], 'indeed' [AB], not explicit [NTC; CEV, GW, KJV, NIV, NLT, NRSV, REB, TEV].
b. ποτέ (LN 67.9) (BAGD 1. p. 695): 'once' [AB, BAGD, HNTC, ICC2, NTC; KJV, NASB, NET, NIV, NRSV, TEV], 'once upon a time' [WBC], 'formerly' [BAGD, BECNT], 'at one time' [NICNT; GW], 'there was a time when' [REB], 'at some time' [LN]. It conveys an indefinite reference to time [LN]. This phrase is translated 'before I knew about the Law, I was alive' [CEV], 'I was alive before I knew the law' [NCV], 'I felt fine when I did not understand what the law demanded' [NLT].
c. imperf. act. indic. of ζάω (LN 23.88) (BAGD 2.a. p. 336): 'to be alive' [BAGD, HNTC, ICC2, LN, NICNT, NTC, WBC; all versions except NLT, REB], 'to be fully alive' [REB], 'to feel fine' [NLT], 'to live' [AB, BECNT, LN].
d. χωρίς with genitive object (LN 89.120) (BAGD 2.b.γ. p. 890): 'apart from' [BAGD, BECNT, HNTC, LN, NICNT, NTC; NASB, NET, NIV, NRSV, TEV], 'without' [LN; GW, KJV], 'in the absence of' [AB, ICC2, WBC; REB]. The phrase χωρίς...ποτέ 'apart from...once' is translated 'before I knew about' [CEV], 'before I knew' [NCV], 'when I did not understand' [NLT].
e. νόμος (LN 33.55, 33.333) (BAGD 3. p. 542): 'law' [AB, BAGD, HNTC, LN (33.333), NTC; NIV, REB, TEV], 'any laws' [GW], 'Law' [LN (33.55)], 'the law' [BECNT, ICC2, NICNT, WBC; KJV, NCV, NET, NRSV], 'the Law' [CEV, NASB]. This word does not have the definite article here. It is translated as a phrase: 'what the law demanded' [NLT].

QUESTION—What does ἔζων χωρὶς νόμου 'I was alive apart from law' mean?
1. Εζων refers qualitatively to being 'alive' in the sense of having a certain quality of life prior to understanding the law's prohibitions [Gdt, HNTC, Ho, ICC1, ICC2, Mor, Mu, NAC, NICNT, NTC, SSA, St, TH, WBC].
1.1 Paul was alive in the sense that his life was unimpeded [NICNT] or untroubled by consciousness of sin or dread of punishment [Ho, ICC1]. He had not died as a result of a confrontation with the law of God [Mor]. He saw himself as faultless before the law prior to his conversion and prior to his grasping the full scope and power of what the law demanded

[NAC]. He thought he was living successfully until he recognized the full implication of the law's demands and he then recognized what a great sinner he was [Mor, NTC]. His manner of life was complacent, self-righteous, and unperturbed before he realized what the law required [Mu, SSA]. As a child, and before his coming of age and accepting the responsibility to be a 'son of the Torah', he was experiencing the beginning of a life in God, but when he accepted the responsibility to keep the law at his coming of age his moral consciousness awakened and he recognized sin in his heart [Gdt]. He had not yet come under the condemnation of the law [St].

1.2 It describes the experience of Adam in the garden, but also that of all other people and himself as well; after coming to know the law in greater depth as a young man Paul realized his sinfulness more fully [HNTC, TNTC]. He is speaking primarily as representing Adam, who is the only one of whom these statement could be fully true. However, Paul's personal experience is not entirely lacking either in the sense that the law only ties the individual, as it did with Adam and Israel, more tightly to the sin-and-death nexus that characterizes the old epoch, and of which a person becomes more keenly aware as he develops a deeper knowledge of the true meaning of the law [WBC].

1.3 It refers to the experience of Israel prior to the giving of the Mosaic law, and Paul speaks as being in solidarity with them [NICNT].

2. It refers to the simple fact of having lived for a time prior to having the law or prior to having a full sense of awareness of the law's demands [AB, BECNT].

2.1 Before the coming of the law, even though people were not living in union with God, they were ignorant of the true nature of their evil conduct because it had not yet been formalized as transgression [AB].

2.2 There was a time in Paul's own life when he lacked a full consciousness of his own sin, but after becoming more fully aware of his sin and the law's condemnation of it he sensed a separation from God which he describes here as death [BECNT].

but the commandment[a] having-come, sin sprang-to-life,[b]

LEXICON—a. ἐντολή (LN 33.330) (BAGD 2.a.α. p. 269): 'commandment' [AB, BECNT, HNTC, ICC2, LN, NICNT, NTC, WBC; GW, KJV, NASB, NET, NIV, NRSV, REB, TEV], 'law' [BAGD], 'the law's command' [NCV], not explicit [NLT]. The phrase ἐλθούσης τῆς ἐντολῆς 'the commandment having come' is translated 'as soon as I heard that command' [CEV]. The definite article with this word is translated 'this (commandment)' [GW].

b. aorist act. indic. of ἀναζάω (LN 23.93, **42.6**) (BAGD 1.b. p. 53): 'to spring to life' [AB, BECNT, HNTC, ICC2, LN (**42.6**), NTC; NIV, REB, TEV], 'to spring to life again' [NICNT], 'to come to life' [CEV], 'to become alive' [BAGD; GW, NASB, NET], 'to begin to live' [NCV], 'to revive' [LN (23.93); KJV, NRSV], 'to come back to life, to live again' [LN (23.93)], not explicit [NLT]. It may imply suddenness of action [LN (42.6)].

QUESTION—To what event does the 'coming' of the commandment refer?
1. It refers a time in Paul's life prior to his conversion when he became more fully aware of the full scope and power of what the law demands [HNTC, Ho, ICC1, NAC, NTC, SSA, TNTC]. Paul's experience parallels Adam's experience in dealing with the prohibited fruit [HNTC, TNTC]. It refers to his coming of age and accepting the responsibility to keep the commandments [Gdt, HNTC]. It refers to his coming to realize the full meaning of the tenth commandment [Mu].
2. It refers to the giving of the Mosaic law at Sinai [AB, NICNT]. The tenth commandment referred to in 7:7 here represents the whole of the Mosaic law [NICNT].
3. It refers primarily to Adam and the commandment given him by God. However, it also applies to Israel as well as to Paul or any individual who becomes aware of the requirements of God [WBC].

QUESTION—What does he mean by saying when the commandment came sin became 'alive'?

Sin existed, but it was not as powerful and active before the law came as it was afterward [BECNT, NICNT]. Sin slumbered until the law stimulated it to action [BECNT]. When he understood the law's demands he realized that he was sinning [SSA]. When Paul more fully understood the demands of the law sin was roused to action [Ho]. When the commandment came home to him in the sense of fully understanding it he could not longer ignore the presence of sin in his life [Mor]. It sprang to life in the sense that the law aroused sin to activity; desire became coveting and the pursuit of coveting became a revolt against God [AB]. In Paul's own experience the fuller realization of the import of God's law was accompanied by a strengthening of the power of sin, such that he realized he was condemned to death [NAC]. The increased activity of sin gave him an increased awareness of sin [Ho]. It was only within the context of the prohibition given to Adam that sin became possible and the serpent had opportunity to deceive and seduce [WBC]. Sin sprang to life in the sense that when Paul recognized his guilt it became an unbearable burden [NTC]. When he began seriously to put the law fully into practice at his coming of age, the tenth commandment became a problem to him [Gdt]. At his coming of age, when Paul assumed responsibility for abiding by the law, he began to desire those things which the law had forbidden and to be independent of God, who had placed such restraint upon him [HNTC]. Sin is dormant until there is a specific prohibition, at which point it becomes an active power for mischief [ICC1]. The prohibition actually aroused the innate depravity to more open and virulent activity [Mu].

QUESTION—What area of meaning is intended by the verb ἀναζάω?
1. It means to become alive or spring to life [AB, BECNT, Gdt, HNTC, Ho, ICC1, ICC2, LN, Mor, NAC, NTC, TH, WBC; CEV, GW, NASB, NCV, NET, NIV, REB, TEV]. It was aroused from a dormant state [BECNT, Ho]. Sin was dormant prior to the giving of the law in comparison to its influence after the law was given [BECNT].
2. It means to revive [NICNT; KJV, NRSV]. After working through the commandment given in the garden of Eden sin lay dormant, in a certain sense, only to be revived and come back with increased strength at the giving of the law at Sinai [NICNT].

7:10 and I died,^a

LEXICON—a. aorist act. indic. of ἀποθνῄσκω (LN 74.27) (BAGD 1.b.α, p. 91): 'to die' [AB, BAGD, HNTC, ICC2, LN, NICNT; all versions except GW, NLT], 'to result in (one's) death' [BECNT], 'to bring death' [NTC; GW], 'to prove a means of death' [WBC]. This phrase is translated 'I...was doomed to die' [NLT]. It is included as part of v.9 by KJV, NASB, NIV, REB.

QUESTION—What is meant by the statement 'I died'?
1. This describes Paul's subjective experience when he realized that he was condemned by the law [BECNT, Gdt, Ho, ICC1, Mor, Mu, NTC, SSA, TH]. As a child Paul was taught the law, but was living without recognizing how this commandment applied to him; however, when he did understand clearly he recognized his sinfulness [BECNT, Ho, ICC1], and felt separation from God [BECNT, SSA]. His greater understanding of his own guiltiness disturbed his sense of security and goodness and brought him a sense misery and of being in danger [Ho]. Paul's experience is paradigmatic of what happens to everyone under the law [BECNT]. His experience is typical of persons as well as nations before they are restrained by an express command [ICC1]. When he realized his real guilt his sense of moral self-satisfaction and self-confidence died [Mor, NTC]. His desire to gratify himself and be independent of the God who placed restraints upon him was death [HNTC]. It refers to being under God's sentence of death because of sin [ICC2]. He could no longer be at rest in his former complacency and self-assurance [Mu].
2. Paul is using personal terms to speak of what happened to Israel at the giving of the Mosaic law [NICNT]. The law turned sin into actual transgression, strengthening and radicalizing that state of spiritual death that is natural to all Adam's descendants [NICNT]. Human conduct became recognized as rebellion, putting humanity under the domination of death as a consequence of violating law [AB].
3. He is using first person pronouns to describe what happened to Adam and all people, who come under the sway of death because of sin [WBC].

ROMANS 7:10

and the commandment^a the-(one) for^b life^c this was-found^d for^e death^f to-me;

LEXICON—a. ἐντολή (LN 33.330) (BAGD 2.a.α. p. 269): 'commandment' [AB, BECNT, HNTC, ICC2, LN, NICNT, NTC, WBC; GW, KJV, NASB, NET, NIV, NRSV, REB, TEV], 'command' [CEV, NCV], 'law' [BAGD; NLT]. The phrase ἡ ἐντολή...αὕτη 'the commandment...the one' is translated 'the very commandment' [HNTC, NTC; NET, NIV, NRSV], 'the very command' [CEV], 'this very commandment' [BECNT], 'this commandment' [NASB].
  b. εἰς with accusative object (LN 89.57): 'intended for' [WBC], 'that was meant for' [AB], 'that was meant to bring' [TEV], 'meant to bring' [NCV], 'that/which was intended to bring' [BECNT, NTC; GW, NET, NIV], 'that was supposed to bring' [CEV], 'which was intended to produce' [HNTC], 'which was ordained to' [KJV], 'which was to result in' [NASB], 'which was supposed to show the way of' [NLT], 'that promised' [NRSV], 'which should have led to' [REB], 'unto' [ICC2, NICNT], 'for the purpose of' [LN].
  c. ζωή (LN 23.88) (BAGD 2.b.α. p. 340): 'life' [AB, BAGD, BECNT, HNTC, ICC2, LN, NICNT, NTC, WBC; all versions].
  d. aorist pass. (deponent = act.) indic. of εὑρίσκω (LN **13.7**, 27.1) (BAGD 2. p. 325): 'to be found to be' [AB, LN (**13.7**)], 'to be discovered to be' [LN (13.7)], 'to be discovered' [LN (27.1)], 'to be found out' [LN (27.1)], 'to turn out to be' [LN (13.7)], 'to prove to be' [BAGD, ICC2, WBC; NRSV], 'to prove' [NASB, REB], not explicit [BECNT, HNTC, NICNT, NTC; CEV, GW, NCV, NET, NIV, NLT, TEV]. This is translated as deponent: 'to find' [KJV].
  e. εἰς with accusative object (LN 89.48): 'unto' [ICC2, NICNT; KJV], 'a means to' [WBC], 'brought' [NTC; CEV, GW, NCV, NET, NIV, TEV], 'gave' [NLT], 'to lead to' [REB], 'to result in' [NASB], 'resulted in' [BECNT], 'resulted for' [HNTC], 'with the result that, so that as a result' [LN], not explicit [AB; NRSV].
  f. θάνατος (LN 23.99) (BAGD 2.a. p. 351): 'death' [AB, BAGD, BECNT, HNTC, ICC2, LN, NICNT, NTC, WBC; all versions except NLT], 'the death penalty' [NLT].

QUESTION—What relationship is indicated by the first εἰς 'for (life)'?

It indicates purpose: the commandment was intended to bring life [AB, Gdt, HNTC, ICC2, Mu, NICNT, NTC, TH], and it would have given life if it had been perfectly obeyed [AB, Gdt, Mor, NICNT, NTC]. God, however, knowing human sinfulness, never intended it to become a means of salvation [NICNT]. It refers to the prohibition given to Adam, who would have had free access to the tree of life if he had lived according to the commandment [WBC]. In man's original estate law would have directed and regulated him in such a way as to guard and promote life [Mu]. 'Life' and 'death' are figurative terms; the law was designed to bring happiness and holiness but became the cause of misery and sin [Ho]. The purpose was Paul's purpose, not God's; that is, Paul presumed he would be able to live eternally because of the commandment [SSA].

7:11 **for sin, having-taken opportunity[a] through the commandment[b] deceived[c] me,**

LEXICON—a. ἀφορμή (LN 22.46) (BAGD p. 127). This word is used in a military sense to represent a bridgehead or base of operation [BECNT, ICC2, NICNT]. See 7:8.
- b. ἐντολή (LN 33.330): 'commandment' [AB, BECNT, HNTC, ICC2, LN, NICNT, NTC, WBC; GW, KJV, NASB, NET, NIV, NRSV, REB, TEV], 'command' [CEV, NCV], 'law' [NLT]. This word with the definite article is translated 'this command' [CEV], 'this commandment' [GW], 'the good law' [NLT].
- c. aorist act. indic. of ἐξαπατάω (LN 31.12) (BAGD p. 273): 'to deceive' [AB, BAGD, BECNT, HNTC, ICC2, LN, NICNT, NTC, WBC; GW, KJV, NASB, NET, NIV, NRSV, TEV], 'to seduce' [REB], 'to mislead' [LN], 'to trick' [CEV], 'to fool' [NCV, NLT].

QUESTION—In what sense did sin 'deceive' him?
1. Paul was deceived into thinking that he could achieve righteousness by living in strict obedience to God's law [NTC]. He was deceived in that the law had the opposite effect from what he expected; he expected life but found death [Mu]. Paul was deceived into expecting life, happiness, holiness, and blessedness from obeying the law but instead received misery and corruption because the law can only aggravate his guilt and misery [Ho]. One does not expect God's commandment to be the occasion of death [Mor]. Those who depend on law and religion to bridge the separation between them and God are misusing religion and are deceived [HNTC]. His own sinful inclinations urged him on into aggravated and unthinking transgression [SSA]. Although this is Paul's own experience, it also alludes to the temptation in the garden of Eden wherein God's motives were impugned by the serpent and his commandments falsely represented as being that which denied life [Gdt]. Sin deceives in the sense of promising what it cannot deliver [St].
2. Paul speaks as representing Israel, and says that because the law promised life for those who obeyed, Israel was deceived into thinking that they could obtain life through the law [NICNT].
3. It is referring to the deception of Adam and Eve by the serpent in the garden [AB, ICC2, WBC], although it also applies to Israel as well [ICC2]. The serpent took the prohibition as an opportunity to deceive them about God's motives and the potential outcome of rebellion [ICC2, WBC]. Just as the serpent used God's command as an opportunity to deceive Adam and Eve, so sin used the law as an opportunity to deceive the human ego into seeking autonomy and make itself 'like God' when confronted with God's demand for submission [AB].

QUESTION—With which action is the phrase διὰ τῆς ἐντολῆς 'through the commandment' to be taken?
1. It is to be taken with ἀφορμὴν λαβοῦσα 'took opportunity' [AB, BECNT, NICNT, NTC, WBC; CEV, GW, KJV, NASB, NET, NIV, NLT, NRSV, REB]: sin took opportunity through the commandment.
2. It is to be taken with ἐξηπάτησέν με 'deceived me' [Gdt, HNTC, Ho, ICC1, ICC2; TEV]: sin deceived him through the commandment.
3. His own desire to sin deceived him into thinking he could have eternal life by obeying the commandment [SSA].

and through[a] it killed[b] (me).
LEXICON—a. διά with genitive object (LN 89.76, 90.8): 'through' [AB, BECNT, ICC2, LN (89.76, 90.8), NICNT, NTC, WBC; NASB, NET, NIV, NRSV, REB], 'by' [KJV], 'by means of' [HNTC, LN (89.76, 90.8); TEV], 'because of' [CEV], not explicit [GW, NCV]. The phrase δι' αὐτῆς 'through it' is translated 'used it to' [NLT].
b. aorist act. indic. of ἀποκτείνω (LN 20.61) (BAGD 1.b. p. 94): 'to kill' [AB, BAGD, BECNT, HNTC, ICC2, LN, NICNT, NTC, WBC; GW, NASB, NRSV, REB, TEV], 'to slay' [KJV], 'to make (someone) die' [NCV], 'to make (someone) guilty of death' [NLT], 'to put to death' [NIV]. This verb is translated as intransitive: 'I died' [CEV, NET].

7:12 So-then[a] on-the-one-hand the law[b] (is) holy[c]
LEXICON—a. ὥστε (LN 89.52) (BAGD 1.a. p. 899): 'so then' [HNTC, ICC2, LN, NTC; NASB, NET, NIV, REB, TEV], 'so' [BAGD; GW, NCV, NRSV], 'and so' [LN], 'therefore' [BAGD, BECNT, LN, NICNT], 'wherefore' [KJV], 'so that' [LN, WBC], 'yet' [AB], 'still' [CEV], 'but still' [NLT].
b. νόμος (LN 33.55, 33.333) (BAGD 3. p. 542): 'law' [BAGD, LN (33.333)], 'Law' [LN (33.55)], 'the law' [AB, BECNT, HNTC, ICC2, NICNT, NTC, WBC; KJV, NCV, NET, NIV, NLT, NRSV], 'the law itself' [NLT, TEV], 'the law in itself' [REB], 'the Law' [CEV, NASB], 'Moses' teachings' [GW]. This word has the definite article here.
c. ἅγιος (LN 88.24) (BAGD 1.a.β. p. 9): 'holy' [AB, BAGD, BECNT, HNTC, ICC2, LN, NICNT, NTC, WBC; all versions].
QUESTION—What relationship is indicated by ὥστε 'therefore'?
1. It introduces the conclusion to be drawn from what has been said before [Gdt, Ho, ICC2, Mor, Mu, NICNT, SSA, TH, WBC]. It introduces the conclusion from 7:7–11 that the law is holy [Mu]. It introduces the conclusion to be drawn from the previous verses [ICC2]. The conclusion is to be drawn from the true role of the law in the history he has summarized in 7:7b–11 [NICNT]. It introduces the conclusion to be drawn from the preceding answer to the question in 7:7 'is the law sin?' [Mor, SSA, TH, WBC].
2. It introduces a contrast; sin killed him through the law, but the law in itself was good and never actually commanded anyone to do evil [AB].

QUESTION—What relationship is indicated by μέν 'on the one hand'?

There is an implied contrast between the law and sin [Gdt, ICC1, ICC2, Mor, NICNT, WBC]. The holiness of the law is not questioned [Gdt].

and the commandment^a (is) holy^b and righteous^c and good.^d

LEXICON—a. ἐντολή (LN 33.330): 'commandment' [AB, BECNT, HNTC, ICC2, LN, NICNT, NTC, WBC; GW, KJV, NASB, NET, NIV, NRSV, REB, TEV], 'command' [CEV, NCV], not explicit [NLT].

b. ἅγιος (LN 88.24) (BAGD 1.a.β. p. 9): 'holy' [AB, BAGD, BECNT, HNTC, ICC2, LN, NICNT, NTC, WBC; all versions].

c. δίκαιος (LN 88.12) (BAGD 4. p. 196): 'righteous' [BAGD, BECNT, HNTC, ICC2, LN, NTC; NASB, NET, NIV], 'upright' [AB], 'right' [GW, NCV, NLT, TEV], 'just' [LN, NICNT, WBC; KJV, NRSV, REB], 'correct' [CEV].

d. ἀγαθός (LN 88.1) (BAGD 1.b.β. p. 3): 'good' [AB, BAGD, BECNT, HNTC, ICC2, LN, NICNT, NTC, WBC; all versions].

QUESTION—Is any distinction implied between νόμος 'law' and ἡ ἐντολή 'the commandment'?

1. Both refer to the law of Moses [NAC, NICNT, NTC, WBC]. The specific commandment discussed in 7:7 represents the whole law [NAC, NICNT, WBC]. The commandment represents the law archetypically just as Adam represents humankind as a whole archetypically [WBC].

2. 'Law' refers to the whole law, and 'commandment' to any of the particular commandments that comprise it [Gdt, HNTC, ICC1, ICC2, TH, TNTC]. 'Law' represents the whole law, and 'commandment' refers to the specific commandment about coveting [Ho, Mu, SSA], although that commandment represents all the others [SSA].

QUESTION—In what sense is the law 'holy'?

It comes from a holy source, which is God himself [HNTC, ICC1, NAC, NICNT, TH]. It is God's law, expressing God's power and purposes [WBC]. It reflects God's character and will, which are holy [Mor, Mu, TNTC]. It reflects God's holiness, righteousness, and goodness and tries to promote those qualities in people [NTC]. Its requirements are holy [St]. It reveals the holiness of God, and in itself is right and good and excellent [Ho]. Although he rejects the law as a way of salvation, Paul is just as firm in his acceptance of it for its intended purposes, in that it is equitable and makes no unfair demands [Mor]. It is holy in that it requires consecration to God [Gdt].

DISCOURSE UNIT: 7:13–25 [Mor, NICNT]. The topic is life under the law [NICNT], did the good law cause death? [Mor].

7:13 (Did) the good^a then^b become death^c to-me?^d

LEXICON—a. ἀγαθός (LN 88.1) (BAGD 2.a.α. p. 3): 'good' [BAGD, LN; CEV]. The phrase τὸ ἀγαθόν 'the good' is translated 'what was good' [AB], 'what is good' [NRSV, TEV], 'the good thing' [BECNT, NICNT], 'this good thing' [REB], 'that which is good' [ICC2, NTC, WBC; KJV,

NASB, NET, NIV], 'that which in itself is good' [HNTC], 'something good' [CEV, GW], 'something that is good' [NCV], 'which is good' [NLT].
b. οὖν (LN 89.50): 'then' [AB, HNTC, ICC2, LN, NTC, WBC; KJV, NET, NIV, NRSV], 'therefore' [BECNT, LN, NICNT; NASB], 'now' [GW]. The logical relation indicated by this word is translated 'am I saying that' [CEV], 'does this mean that' [NCV, TEV], 'but how can that be' [NLT], 'are we therefore to say' [REB].
c. θάνατος (LN 23.99) (BAGD 2.a. p. 351): 'death' [AB, HNTC, ICC2, LN, NICNT, NTC, WBC; all versions except NASB, NLT], 'a cause of death' [BECNT; NASB], 'doom' [NLT].
d. ἐγώ. The dative ἐμοί is the indirect object of ἐγένετο 'become' [AB, BECNT, HNTC, ICC2, NICNT, NTC, WBC; all versions]. The dative case relation is translated 'to me' [ICC2, NTC, WBC; NET, NIV, NRSV], 'unto me' [KJV], 'for me' [AB; NASB], 'in me' [NICNT], 'in my case' [HNTC], 'my (death)' [BECNT; CEV, GW, REB, TEV], 'my (doom)' [NLT].

Never may-it-be![a]
LEXICON—a. aorist mid. (deponent = act.) optative of γίνομαι (LN 13.107) (BAGD I.3.a. p. 158): 'to happen' [LN], 'to occur' [LN]. The phrase μὴ γένοιτο is translated 'certainly not!' [AB, BECNT, WBC; CEV], 'by no means!' [BAGD, NICNT; NIV, NRSV, TEV], 'no indeed' [HNTC], 'not at all!' [NTC], 'of course not!' [NLT, REB], 'absolutely not!' [NET], 'far from it' [BAGD], 'God forbid!' [BAGD, ICC2], 'God forbid' [KJV], 'that's unthinkable!' [GW], 'may it never be!' [NASB], 'no!' [NCV]. This phrase is punctuated with an exclamation point by all except HNTC, KJV. See this phrase also at 3:4, 6, 31; 6:2, 15; 7:7.

But[a] sin,[b] in-order-that it-might-appear[c] sin,
LEXICON—a. ἀλλά (LN 89.125) (BAGD 1. a. p. 38): 'but' [BAGD, BECNT, ICC2, LN, NICNT, NTC, WBC; KJV, NET, NIV], 'rather' [AB, BAGD; GW, NASB], 'the fact is that' [HNTC], not explicit [CEV, NCV, NLT, NRSV, REB, TEV].
b. ἁμαρτία (LN 88.289): 'sin' [AB, BECNT, HNTC, ICC2, LN, NICNT, NTC, WBC; all versions].
c. aorist mid. (deponent = act.) subj. of φαίνω (LN **28.36**) (BAGD 2.e. p. 852): 'to appear' [KJV], 'to appear as' [WBC], 'to stand out as' [NTC], 'to expose its true character' [REB], not explicit [CEV, NLT]. This active verb is translated as a passive verb: 'to be unmasked as' [AB], 'to be manifested as' [BECNT], 'to be manifest as' [ICC2], 'to be shown to be' [NASB, NET, NRSV], 'to be shown up as' [HNTC], 'to be made fully and clearly known' [**LN**], 'to be revealed' [LN; TEV], 'to be recognized as' [BAGD; GW, NIV]. This clause is translated 'this happened so that I could see what sin is really like' [NCV].

QUESTION—What is the function of ἀλλά 'but'?

It is adversative, introducing Paul's counter assertion that it was not the law but sin that cause his death [AB, Gdt, Ho, Mor, NICNT, SSA].

through the good bringing-about[a] death to-me,[b]

LEXICON—a. pres. mid. (deponent = act.) participle of κατεργάζομαι (LN 13.9) (BAGD 2. p. 421): 'to bring about' [BAGD, LN; NLT, REB], 'to bring' [NCV, TEV], 'to bring forth' [HNTC], 'to produce' [AB, NICNT, NTC, WBC; NET, NIV], 'to effect' [BECNT; NASB], 'to work' [ICC2; KJV, NRSV]. The phrase μοι κατεργαζομένη θάνατον 'bringing about death to me' is translated 'that killed me' [CEV], '(my death) was caused' [GW].

b. ἐγώ. The dative μοι is the indirect object of κατεργάζομαι. The dative case relation is translated 'for me' [AB, HNTC, ICC2, WBC], 'in me' [NICNT, NTC; KJV, NET, NIV, NRSV], 'to me' [NCV, TEV], '(killed) me' [CEV], 'my (death)' [GW, NASB, REB], 'my (condemnation)' [NLT], not explicit [BECNT].

in-order-that sin might-become[a] exceedingly[b] sinful[c] through[d] the commandment.[e]

LEXICON—a. aorist mid. (deponent = active) subj. of γίνομαι (LN 13.48) (BAGD II. 1. p. 160): 'to become' [AB, BECNT, ICC2, LN, NICNT, NTC, WBC; GW, KJV, NASB, NET, NIV, NRSV, REB,], 'to be shown to be' [TEV], 'to be' [BAGD], not explicit [CEV, NCV, NLT]. This entire clause is translated 'Now we can see how terrible and evil sin really is' [CEV], 'through a/the commandment sin became more sinful than ever' [GW, REB], 'the command was used to show that sin is very evil' [NCV], 'so we can see how terrible sin really is' [NLT].

b. ὑπερβολή (LN 78.33) (BAGD p. 840). The phrase καθ' ὑπερβολήν is translated 'exceedingly' [BECNT, HNTC, NICNT], 'exceeding' [KJV], 'beyond measure' [BAGD, ICC2], 'beyond all measure' [AB], 'utterly' [WBC; NASB, NET, NIV], 'thoroughly' [NTC], 'more than ever' [GW, REB], 'even more' [TEV]. The phrase 'might become exceedingly sinful' is translated 'sin is very evil' [NCV], 'how terrible and evil sin is' [CEV], 'how terrible sin is' [NLT], 'be shown to be even more terribly sinful' [TEV].

c. ἁμαρτωλός (LN 88.294) (BAGD 1. p. 44): 'sinful' [AB, BAGD, BECNT, HNTC, ICC2, LN, NICNT, NTC, WBC; GW, KJV, NASB, NET, NIV, NRSV, REB, TEV], not explicit [CEV, NCV, NLT].

d. διά with genitive object (LN 89.76) (BAGD A.III.1.d. p. 180): 'through' [AB, BAGD, BECNT, ICC2, LN, NICNT, NTC, WBC; GW, NASB, NET, NIV, NRSV, REB], 'by means of' [HNTC, LN], 'by' [BAGD, LN; KJV], not explicit [CEV, NCV, NLT].

e. ἐντολή (LN 33.330): 'commandment' [AB, BECNT, HNTC, ICC2, LN, NICNT, NTC, WBC; KJV, NASB, NET, NIV, NRSV, REB, TEV], 'God's good commandment' [NLT], 'command' [NCV], not explicit

[CEV]. This noun with the definite article is translated as not having the article: 'a commandment' [GW].

QUESTION—In what sense does sin become exceedingly sinful through the commandment?

The commandment reveals it for what it is [BECNT, HNTC, ICC1, Mor, NICNT, TH], that it is pernicious and hideous [ICC1], that it is something evil and demonic and utterly in enmity against God [Mor]. The commandment shows how contrary to God and to goodness sin really is [TNTC]. He realized that sin is exceedingly detestable [SSA]. By clearly defining sin, the law turns sin into conscious and deliberate rebellion against God and his will [AB, NICNT]. The purity of the law makes the blackness of sin stand out all the more [NTC]. The law did not cause the death of the ego, but became the occasion of that death [AB]. Because sin uses something good, the law, to bring about death, it shows how truly sinful it is [Gdt, Ho, NAC, NTC, St]. Because sin contradicts and even abuses the commandment to produce an evil effect it not only demonstrates its sinfulness but actually aggravates the gravity of sin beyond measure [Mu].

DISCOURSE UNIT: 7:14–25 [AB, Mu, NTC, TNTC; GW, NCV, NIV, NLT, NRSV, TEV]. The topic is the war within us [NCV], God's standards are at war with sin's standards [GW], struggling with sin [NLT], the wretched man's struggle and victory [NTC], complaint and cry of human beings enslaved by the Law [AB], the conflict within us [TNTC; TEV], the inner conflict [NRSV], struggling with sin [NIV], the contradiction in the believer [Mu].

7:14 **For we-know that the law^a is spiritual,^b**

TEXT—Instead of οἴδαμεν 'we know', some manuscripts have οἶδα μέν 'for I know'. GNT selects the reading 'we know' with an A rating, indicating that the text is certain. Only GW takes the reading 'for I know'.

LEXICON—a. νόμος (LN 33.55, 33.333) (BAGD 3. p. 542): 'law' [BAGD, LN (33.333)], 'Law' [LN (33.55)], 'the law' [AB, BECNT, HNTC, ICC2, NICNT, NTC, WBC; KJV, NCV, NET, NIV, NLT, NRSV, REB], 'the Law' [CEV, NASB, TEV], 'God's standards' [GW]. This word has the definite article here.

b. πνευματικός (LN 26.10) (BAGD 2.a.β. p. 679): 'spiritual' [AB, BAGD, BECNT, HNTC, ICC2, LN, NICNT, NTC, WBC; all versions except NLT], 'good' [NLT].

QUESTION—What relationship is indicated by γάρ 'for'?

It introduces the grounds for his assertion in 7:13: it is sin, not the law, that causes death [BECNT, ICC2, NICNT]. It introduces a confirmation of the whole preceding argument from 7:5 on, which is that it is sin and not the law that works death, as the problem is in us and not the law [Ho]. It introduces what follows as the answer to an implied question which may arise in someone's mind about the goodness of the law [HNTC]. It introduces the claim in 7:14b about how he is influenced by his sinful nature [SSA]. It introduces a transition from Paul's historical experience described in 7:7–13 to the description of the real moral nature of his previous state described in 7:14–25 [Gdt].

QUESTION—What is meant by calling the law πνευματικός 'spiritual'?

He is saying that the law has a divine origin [AB, BECNT, HNTC, ICC1, ICC2, Mor, Mu, NAC, NICNT, SSA, TH] and character [HNTC, ICC1, ICC2, Mor, Mu], and it expresses the holiness of God's character [NAC]. Its divine origin means it has divine authority, character and effectiveness [ICC2]. It belongs to the sphere of God and has the purpose of leading people to life and to God [AB]. The Holy Spirit is the author [SSA]. Its origin is from the Holy Spirit [BECNT]. It is inspired by the Spirit, embodies and manifests the Spirit, and was intended to address at the level of the Spirit [WBC]. The law is divine and partakes of the nature of its author, the Holy Spirit [Ho]. The law is consistent with the Holy Spirit's nature and leading; what the law commands is the same thing that the Holy Spirit works in the heart which he indwells [Gdt].

QUESTION—What is indicated by the shift from the past tense in 7:6–13 to the present tense in 7:14–25 regarding what he says about his experience with the law?

1. The earlier passage described Paul's life prior to conversion using past tense verbs, and the second passage, which uses present tense verbs, describes his present life experience as a believer [Mor, Mu, NTC, TNTC].
2. The earlier passage uses past tense verbs to describe Paul's life prior to conversion using past tense verbs, and the second passage uses present tense verbs to describe the real moral nature of his spiritual condition at that time [Gdt].
3. In the earlier passage Paul was primarily describing the fall of Adam as well as the experience of Israel under the law, whereas in this passage he is using his own experience to describing the weakness of believers [ICC2].
4. In the earlier passage Paul is telling his own story, but it is also everybody's story, and applies as well to Adam and to Israel at Sinai. Then in 7:14–25 he is describing the regenerate person who lacks the power of the indwelling Spirit, especially those Jewish Christians who are still living under the law [St].
5. 7:6–13 was a confession, whereas 7:14–25 is an apology for the law itself; Paul is saying that the problem is not with the law, but with the human condition [AB]. The shift is used to depict his spiritual condition while being under the law and as a captive to the power of sin [BECNT]. It sharpens the note of personal existential involvement [WBC].

but I am fleshly,[a] sold[b] under[c] sin.

LEXICON—a. σάρκινος (LN 26.8, 41.42, 79.4) (BAGD 2. p. 743): 'fleshly' [BAGD, BECNT, NICNT, WBC], 'of flesh' [AB; NASB], 'of the flesh' [NRSV], 'a man of flesh' [HNTC], 'carnal' [ICC2, NTC; KJV], 'a mortal

man' [TEV], 'human' [LN (26.8, 79.4)], 'merely a human' [CEV], 'unspiritual' [NET, NIV], 'not spiritual' [NCV], 'worldly' [LN (41.42)], 'natural' [LN (79.4)]. The phrase ἐγὼ δὲ σάρκινός εἰμι 'but I am fleshly' is translated 'but I am not' [REB], 'but I have a corrupt nature' [GW], 'the trouble is not with the law but with me' [NLT].
   b. perf. pass. participle of πιπράσκω (LN **57.186**) (BAGD p. 659): 'to be sold' [AB, BAGD, BECNT, HNTC, LN, NICNT, NTC, WBC; all versions except NCV], not explicit [ICC2; NCV].
   c. ὑπό with accusative object (LN 37.7) (BAGD 2.b. p. 843): 'under' [BAGD, BECNT, LN, NICNT, WBC; KJV], 'under the control of' [LN], 'under the power of' [BAGD, ICC2, LN], 'as a slave so as to be under the power of' [HNTC], 'in/into bondage to' [AB; NASB], 'into slavery to' [NET], 'as a slave to' [NTC; CEV, GW, NIV, REB, TEV], 'into slavery under' [NRSV], 'a slave under' [ICC2]. The phrase πεπραμένος ὑπὸ τὴν ἁμαρτίαν 'sold under sin' is translated 'sold into slavery, with sin as my master' [NLT], 'sin rules me as if I were its slave' [NCV].
QUESTION—Who does the 'I' represent in this chapter?
   1. Paul is speaking from his own experience prior to becoming a Christian as representing the experience of unregenerate people [AB, Gdt, NICNT].
      1.1 It represents Paul in corporate solidarity with the people of Israel under the law and prior to Christ; while the 'I' represents Paul himself, he did not personally experience all the events narrated here, but relates Israel's experience as his own through his solidarity with his nation [NICNT].
      1.2 Paul is using first person pronouns as a rhetorical device to describe an historical and corporate reality, namely, the experience of unregenerate humanity when confronted with the Mosaic law [AB].
   2. In verses 7–12 Paul is speaking from his own experience prior to becoming a Christian as a paradigm of the history of the human race, including the experience both of Adam in the garden and of Israel since the giving of the law at Sinai. Then in verses 13–25 he is describing the state of anyone still living under law [BECNT, St], including Christians who somehow lack the enabling help of the Holy Spirit [St]. In the first section he examines his pre-Christian experience retrospectively from the standpoint of having become a Christian [BECNT].
   3. Paul is speaking of his own experience as a Christian [HNTC, Ho, ICC2, Mor, Mu, NAC, NTC, SSA, TH, TNTC]. Verse 7–13 describe Paul's pre-conversion experience, and the rest of the chapter describes his experience as a believer [Mu]. He uses his experience as an illustration of the experience of regenerate people struggling with the power of sin [Mu, NAC, SSA]. Paul's experience is similar to the experience of Adam, but can apply to anyone in any period of history [TH]. Paul also uses the first person as a rhetorical device to illustrate the general condition of all people, and especially of the believer [NAC]. He writes in the first person not to represent any particular individual or group, but to depict the situation of people in the absence of law and then in the presence of law

[ICC2]. This passage is autobiographical, but it also reflects the experience of all people who turn to God for salvation by grace alone and cease trusting in human merit [NTC]. He is describing his own confrontation with the law, but doing so as representing all people [Mor]. He is revealing the difficulty of meeting the radical demands of the Christian faith and the inevitability of spiritual defeat apart from the help of God's spirit [NAC]. These insights are Christian insights, and concern human nature on earth and not in heaven, written from within a Christian perspective to account for the role of religion in human experience [HNTC]. He is using his own experience to describe the nature and extent of the weakness of believers [ICC2].
   4. Paul uses the first person to describe the experience of Adam and 'everyman', and now broadens that to include 'everyman' in the present [WBC]. Paul's account is autobiographical but is also the autobiography of 'everyman' and of the human race as well, and parallels the temptation and fall of Adam in the garden. Paul is the Adam of his own soul [TNTC].

QUESTION—What is meant here by σάρκινος 'fleshly'?

It means to be subject to and under the influence of this world [NICNT]. It means to belong to the sphere of flesh, not oriented to God, and inclined toward the earthbound; flesh is not evil in itself, but is powerless to do good [AB]. 'Flesh' emphasizes the weak and transitory nature of human existence which, though not evil in itself, has a fatal inclination toward what is opposed to God's will and nature [NAC]. It is the individual in his condition of belonging to the realm of the epoch of Adam, which is subject to the dominion of sin and death, and living in and through that corruptible condition that is destined to return to dust [WBC]. It means to be carnal in the sense of being imperfect and unspiritual because of the sinful human nature that a believer still has, but that is not the same as being 'in the flesh' and controlled by the sinful human nature as an unbeliever is [NTC]. It is to be subject to the power of the flesh, which is our whole nature as fallen and corrupt, and which retains much of its original power even in mature believers [Ho]. He is influenced by his self-directed and sinful human nature [SSA]. It is that attitude even within regenerate humanity that seeks to be independent of God [TNTC]. It is the fallen human nature that, even in a Christian, is inclined toward sin [Mor]. It is that proclivity toward sin that affects all people [HNTC]. It is to be exposed to all the temptations that are expressed through the body [ICC1]. He has within him an element that is radically opposed to God [ICC2]. It is his self-seeking and corrupt sinful nature [Gdt]. It means to be under the control of the twisted, self-centered nature [St].

QUESTION—What does it mean to be 'sold under sin'?

   1. It refers to all people, whether regenerate or not [BECNT, NAC, WBC]. It means being enslaved by the power of sin when relying on one's own devices and operating under the influence of the old nature [NAC]. It refers to those who are still part of the old epoch, the epoch of Adam and

the realm of flesh [WBC]. It means to be enslaved by the control of sin, which applies to anyone who lives under the law or who tries to have spiritual life by means of the law, because the law is inherently unable to transform [BECNT].
2. It refers to the struggle of the regenerate person [HNTC, Ho, ICC2, Mor, Mu, NTC, SSA]. Paul is still subject to his sinful human nature, even though not controlled by it, living in an era in which the two ages overlap; there was a time when he was exclusively a sinner and there will be a time when he will be exclusively a saint, but for now he is both [NTC]. He is speaking of believers and their continuing struggle against the sinful nature with its lack of faith, hardness of heart, love of the world and pride, all representing a power from which he would long to be fully free [Ho]. The fleshly nature has been destroyed in principle but that process of destruction must be brought to completion in experience [HNTC]. Even within the Christian there is that which is inclined to continuing sinfulness [ICC2]. 'Sold' is a metonymy, with the cause (selling) representing the effect or condition of being a slave [SSA]. He is not fully under the control of his own will, but is subject to an alien power [Mu].
3. It refers to the unregenerate person, and means being enslaved by the power of sin prior to becoming a Christian [AB, Gdt, NICNT]. The flesh is the seller and sin is the buyer [Gdt].

QUESTION—Whose experience is being described in this verse and through the end of the chapter?
1. It is Paul's experience prior to his conversion [BECNT, Gdt]. However, this experience is paradigmatic of all people who live under the law, whether converted or not [BECNT].
2. It is Paul's experience even after his conversion [HNTC, Ho, Mor, Mu, NAC, NTC, SSA, TH, TNTC].
3. Paul describes the experience of the ego of flesh, dominated by sin, when confronted with the spiritual law of God [AB].
4. It is the experience of unregenerate Israel, represented by Paul, under the law of Moses, and by extension, other non-Christians [NICNT]. Paul contrasts the status and condition of unregenerate Israel after the giving of the law (7:7–12) who were thereby 'sold under sin' (7:14), with the condition of the regenerate, who have been freed from sin (6:18, 22) [NICNT].
5. It is the experience of Adam, but also of every man, when confronted by the demands of law and living in the realm of flesh, of the Adamic epoch; there is a clear element of Paul's personal testimony as well [WBC].

7:15 For what I-do[a] I- do-not –understand/acknowledge;[b]

LEXICON—a. pres. mid. (deponent = act.) indic. of κατεργάζομαι (LN 42.17) (BAGD 1. p. 421): 'to do' [AB, BAGD, BECNT, HNTC, WBC; GW, KJV, NASB, NCV, NET, NIV, TEV], 'to do thoroughly' [LN], 'to accomplish' [BAGD, LN, NTC], 'to perform successfully' [BAGD, LN],

'to work' [ICC2], 'to produce' [NICNT], not explicit [NLT]. The phrase ὃ...κατεργάζομαι 'what I practice' is translated 'the works I do' [HNTC], 'why I act the way I do' [CEV], 'my own actions' [NRSV, REB]. This entire clause is translated 'I don't understand myself at all' [NLT]. See this word at 1:27; 2:9; 4:15; 5:3; 7:8, 13.
  b. pres. act. indic. of γινώσκω (LN 28.1, 32.16) (BAGD 6.1.α. p. 161): 'to understand' [AB, BECNT, LN (32.16); CEV, NASB, NCV, NET, NIV, NLT, NRSV, TEV], 'to know' [BAGD, LN (28.1), NICNT, WBC], 'to comprehend' [LN (32.16)], 'to acknowledge' [ICC2], 'to acknowledge as one's own' [REB], 'to approve of' [NTC], 'to realize' [GW], 'to allow' [KJV]. The phrase 'I do not understand' is translated 'are incomprehensible to me' [HNTC].

QUESTION—What relationship is indicated by γάρ 'for'?
  It introduces the grounds for the assertion in 7:14 that he is fleshly, sold under sin [BECNT, Ho, ICC2, Mor, NICNT]. It introduces 7:15-23 as an explanation for the assertion in 7:14 that he is sold under sin [ICC2].

QUESTION—What area of meaning is intended by the term γινώσκω 'understand/acknowledge'?
  1. It means to understand [AB, BECNT, Gdt, HNTC, NAC, SSA, TH; CEV, NASB, NCV, NET, NIV, NLT, TEV]: I can't fully comprehend my own actions. He doesn't recognize the depth of sin in himself [BECNT]. He doesn't realize what he is doing [GW]. The statement is hyperbolic in the sense that it is only some of the time that this is the case, not all the time [SSA]. He acts, as it were, from blind instinct [Gdt].
  2. It means to approve or acknowledge [HNTC, Ho, ICC1, ICC2, NICNT, NTC, TNTC; REB]: I do what I disapprove of.
  3. It means both to understand and to acknowledge [Mu, WBC]. He does not approve of his behavior, and is even bewildered by what he does [Mu].

for not what I-want[a] this I-practice,[b]

LEXICON—a. pres. act. indic. of θέλω (LN 25.1) (BAGD 2. p. 355): 'to want' [AB, BAGD, LN, NTC, WBC; GW, NCV, NET, NIV, NRSV], 'to wish' [BAGD, HNTC, LN], 'to desire' [BECNT], 'to will' [BAGD, ICC2, NICNT]. The phrase ὃ θέλω 'what I want' is translated 'what I want to do' [REB], 'what I would like to do' [NASB, TEV], 'what I would' [KJV], 'what I know is right' [CEV], 'I really want to do what is right' [NLT].
  b. pres. act. indic. of πράσσω (LN 42.8) (BAGD 1.a. p. 698): 'to practice' [BECNT, HNTC, ICC2, NICNT, NTC; NASB], 'to do' [AB, BAGD, LN; all versions except NASB], 'to carry out' [LN], 'to commit' [BAGD, WBC].

QUESTION—What is the function of γάρ 'for'?
  It introduces a specific example or an amplification of 7:15a [SSA].

QUESTION—Does οὐ 'not' go with the verb 'practice' or the verb 'want'?
1. It goes with 'practice' [AB, BECNT, HNTC, Ho, ICC2, SSA; CEV, GW, KJV, NASB, NCV, NET, NIV, NLT, TEV]: I do not practice what I want.
2. It goes with 'want' [WBC; REB]: I practice what I do not want.
3. He is quoting what amounts to a proverb to the effect of 'it's not what I will, this I do, but what I hate, this I practice' [NICNT, NTC].

but what I-hate[a] this I-do.[b]
LEXICON—a. pres. act. indic. of μισέω (LN 88.198) (BAGD 2. p. 523): 'to hate' [BECNT, HNTC, ICC2, LN, NICNT, WBC; all versions except REB], 'to detest' [AB, BAGD, LN; REB], 'to loathe' [NTC].
  b. pres. act. indic. of ποιέω (LN **42.7**) (BAGD I.1.b.ε. p. 681): 'to do' [AB, BAGD, BECNT, HNTC, ICC2, **LN**, NICNT, NTC, WBC; all versions], 'to carry out' [LN], 'to bring about' [BAGD].

7:16 But if what I-do- not -want[a] this I-do,[b]
LEXICON—a. pres. act. indic. of θέλω (LN 25.1) (BAGD 2. p. 355): see previous verse. The phrase ὃ...θέλω 'what...I want' is translated 'what I know is right' [CEV].
  b. pres. act. indic. of ποιέω (LN 42.7) (BAGD I.1.b.ε. p. 681): see previous verse.

I-agree-with[a] the law[b] that (it is) good.[c]
LEXICON—a. pres. act. indic. of σύμφημι (LN **31.16**) (BAGD p. 780): 'to agree (with)' [BAGD, BECNT, HNTC, ICC2, **LN**, NICNT, WBC; NASB, REB], 'to agree (that)' [AB, NTC; CEV, GW, NCV, NET, NIV, NLT, NRSV, TEV], 'to consent unto' [KJV], 'to assent to' [LN]. This word is found only here in the NT.
  b. νόμος (LN 33.333, 33.55) (BAGD 3. p. 542): 'law' [LN (33.333)], 'Law' [LN (33.55)], 'the law' [AB, BECNT, HNTC, ICC2, NICNT, NTC, WBC; KJV, NCV, NET, NIV, NLT, NRSV, REB], 'the Law' [CEV, NASB, TEV], 'God's standards' [GW]. This word has the definite article here.
  c. καλός (LN 88.4) (BAGD 2.b. p. 400): 'good' [AB, BECNT, ICC2, LN, NICNT, NTC; all versions except REB, TEV], 'right and good' [HNTC], 'right' [TEV], 'admirable' [WBC; REB], 'morally unobjectionable' [BAGD].

7:17 But[a] now[b] no-longer[c] I am-doing[d] it but the sin dwelling[e] in[f] me.
LEXICON—a. δέ (LN 89.124, 89.94): 'but' [AB, HNTC, ICC2, LN (89.124), NICNT, NTC, WBC; NCV, NET, NLT, NRSV], 'and' [BECNT, LN (89.94)], not explicit [CEV, GW, KJV, NASB, NIV, REB, TEV].
  b. νυνί (LN 67.38) (BAGD 2.a. p. 546): 'now' [BAGD, BECNT, LN, NICNT, WBC; NET]. The relationship expressed by this word is translated 'now then' [KJV], 'so now' [NASB], 'so' [CEV, GW, TEV], 'this being so' [ICC2], 'then' [ICC2], 'this being so, then' [NTC], 'this means' [REB], 'what in fact is happening' [HNTC], 'as it is' [AB; NIV],

'in fact' [NRSV], not explicit [CEV, NCV, NLT]. As it is used here this word may be taken to express a logical and not a temporal relationship [BAGD].
c. οὐκέτι (LN 67.130) (BAGD 2. p. 592): 'no longer' [AB, BECNT, LN, NICNT, WBC; GW, NASB, NET, NIV, NRSV, REB], 'no more' [KJV], 'not (I)' [HNTC, ICC2, NTC; CEV, NCV, TEV], not explicit [NLT]. As it is used here, this word may be taken to express a logical and not a temporal relationship [BAGD].
d. pres. mid. (deponent = act.) indic. of κατεργάζομαι (LN 42.17) (BAGD 1. p. 421): 'to do' [AB, BAGD, BECNT, WBC; CEV, GW, KJV, NASB, NCV, NET, NIV, NRSV], 'to accomplish' [LN, NTC], 'to produce' [NICNT], 'to perform' [REB], 'to do thoroughly' [LN]. The phrase κατεργάζομαι αὐτό 'doing it' is translated 'I that do my works' [HNTC], 'I who work that which I do' [ICC2], 'I am…doing the things I hate' [GW], 'doing these hated things' [NCV], '(that makes me) do these hated things' [NLT], '(who) perform the action' [REB], '(who) does this thing' [TEV]. See this word at 1:27; 2:9; 4:15; 5:3; 7:8, 13, 15.
e. pres. act. participle of οἰκέω (LN **85.73**): 'to dwell' [AB, BECNT, HNTC, ICC2, NICNT, NTC, WBC; KJV, NRSV, REB], 'to reside' [**LN**], 'to live' [LN; CEV, GW, NCV, NET, NIV, TEV]. The phrase οἰκοῦσα ἐν 'dwelling in' is translated 'to indwell' [NASB], 'to be within' [NLT]. See this word at 7:18, 20.
f. ἐν with dative object (LN 83.13) (BAGD I.5.a. p. 259): 'in' [AB, BAGD, BECNT, HNTC, ICC2, LN, NICNT, NTC; all versions except NLT, NRSV], 'within' [WBC; NLT, NRSV].

QUESTION—What relationship is indicated by νυνὶ δέ 'but now'?

It indicates a logical relationship, not a temporal one [AB, BAGD, BECNT, Gdt, HNTC, Ho, ICC1, ICC2, Mor, Mu, NICNT, NTC, SSA, TH]. It introduces a logical conclusion based on 7:15 [Ho] or 7:16 [NTC]. In light of 7:15–16, it must be concluded that it is not Paul (alone) who is doing these things he hates, but sin at work in him [BECNT, NICNT]. It expresses a contrast between what he wants and what he actually does [AB]. The conjunction δέ moves the argument along and introduces the conclusion of the argument begun in 7:16a [SSA]. It indicates a logical relationship but there is also an eschatological element present [WBC].

QUESTION—What is meant by the statement that he is no longer the one doing it?

He is not denying personal responsibility [Ho, ICC2, Mu, NTC, WBC], for the 'I' that sins is also the 'I' of the inner man, but there is another force, sin, that exercises great compulsion on the individual [WBC]. He is acknowledging the extent to which sin that still lives within the Christian can usurp control in his life [ICC2]. It is not properly and fully his true self that is acting [Ho, ICC1], certainly not his renovated nature [Ho]. He is saying sin lives within him as an unwelcome intruder or squatter, making it impossible for him to do the good he wants to do [Mor, NTC]; however, he is not rejecting responsibility for his own sins, since they come from his own sinful nature [NTC]. Even if he initially does not want to act in this way, as soon as he agrees to do it, he really is the one responsible [TNTC]. The sin living within him is not the real Paul, as sin is always out of character for the believer [Mor]. He is making a distinction between the true self, the 'I', and the flesh which is dominated by sin and does not carry out his better intentions [HNTC]. He does not do it because he wills it, but because the desire to sin that so permeates his nature causes him to [SSA]. He is speaking from the standpoint of the pain of the experience, not of moral responsibility and culpability; he is miserable and humiliated that he is not the master of his own behavior [Gdt]. Paul distinguishes between his determinate will, in which he agrees with the law of God, and his flesh, in which there is nothing good, but which is just as much a part of him [Mu].

7:18 **For I-know that (there does) not dwell[a] in me, that is, in my flesh,[b] (any) good;[c]**

LEXICON—a. pres. act. indic. of οἰκέω (LN 85.73) (BAGD 1. p. 557): 'to dwell' [AB, BAGD, BECNT, HNTC, ICC2, NICNT, NTC, WBC; KJV, NASB, NRSV, REB], 'to live' [BAGD, LN; GW, NCV, NET, NIV, TEV], 'to reside' [LN]. This and the following phrase are translated 'I know that my selfish desires won't let me do anything that is good' [CEV], 'I know I am rotten through and through so far as my old sinful nature is concerned' [NLT]. See this word at 7:17, 20.

b. σάρξ (LN 26.7, 58.10) (BAGD 7. p. 744): 'flesh' [AB, BAGD, BECNT, HNTC, ICC2, NICNT, NTC, WBC; KJV, NASB, NET, NRSV], 'physical nature' [LN (58.10)], 'human nature' [LN (26.7, 58.10); TEV], 'sinful nature' [NIV], 'old sinful nature' [NLT], 'the part of me that is earthly and sinful' [NCV], 'selfish desires' [CEV], 'corrupt nature' [GW], 'unspiritual self' [REB].

c. ἀγαθός (LN 88.1): 'good' [AB, BECNT, ICC2, LN, NICNT, NTC; GW, NASB, NCV, NET, NIV, NRSV, REB, TEV], 'good thing' [HNTC, WBC; KJV], 'anything that is good' [CEV], not explicit [NLT].

QUESTION—What does Paul mean by 'the flesh' in this verse?

1. It refers to that aspect of our being which refuses to submit to God [TH]. It is the human self as dominated by sin and opposed to God and his will [AB]. It refers to the whole self in its fallenness [NAC]. It refers to the fallen human nature of a Christian apart from the sanctifying activity of the Holy Spirit [Ho, ICC2]. It is the sinful nature that a Christian still has within him [NTC], the self-directed sinful human nature [SSA]. It is man as fallen [Mor]. It is the self as attached to the present age, but is not identical with the pre-Christian state [WBC]. It is that element in human nature which is radically evil and so completely under the power of sin that it corrupts all human activity [HNTC]. It is the lower nature, which is easily made the instrument of evil, as opposed to the higher nature [ICC1]. It is not just the lower self as a part of his nature, but the whole

fallen nature as such, everything that is in him apart from the sanctification of the Holy Spirit [ICC2]. It is that within an unregenerate person that gives the active impulse to behavior, as contrasted with the ego, which is able to contemplate the good but not to achieve it [Gdt].

2. It refers to the material body, which is the part or aspect of a person most susceptible to sin, as opposed to the 'mind' which by contrast can want to do good [NICNT].

for to-want[a] is-present-with[b] me,

LEXICON—a. pres. act. infin. of θέλω (LN 25.1) (BAGD 2. p. 355): 'to want' [BAGD, LN; NCV, NET, NLT], 'to will' [BECNT, ICC2; KJV, NRSV], 'to wish' [BAGD, HNTC], 'to desire' [AB, LN]. This articular infinitive is translated 'the will' [REB], 'the willing' [NICNT, WBC], 'the wishing' [NASB], 'the desire' [NTC; GW, NIV, TEV]. This phrase is translated 'Even when I want to do right' [CEV].

b. pres. mid. (deponent = act.) indic. of παράκειμαι (LN 85.23): 'to be present with' [NICNT; KJV], 'to be present in' [BECNT; NASB], 'to be present' [LN], 'to be in' [TEV], 'to be there' [REB], 'to be at hand' [LN], 'to lie ready to (my) hand' [WBC], not explicit [AB, HNTC, ICC2, NTC; CEV, GW, NCV, NET, NIV, NLT, NRSV]. The phrase θέλειν παράκειταί μοι 'to want is present with me' is translated 'I can desire' [AB], 'I have the desire' [NTC; GW, NIV], 'I can always wish' [HNTC], 'I can will' [ICC2; NRSV], 'I want' [CEV, NCV, NET, NLT]. This word occurs in the Bible only here and in 7:21.

QUESTION—What relationship is indicated by γάρ 'for'?

It introduces grounds for the statement in the first part of the verse that nothing good dwells in his flesh, which is that he can wish to do good but not carry it out [BECNT, Ho].

but to-do[a] the good[b] (is) not;

TEXT—Instead of οὐ 'not', some manuscripts read οὐχ εὑρίσκω 'I do not find', and other manuscripts read οὐ γινώσκω 'I do not know'. GNT reads οὐ 'not' with a B decision, indicating that the text is almost certain. The reading 'I find not' is taken only by KJV.

LEXICON—a. pres. mid. (deponent = act.) infin. of κατεργάζομαι (LN 42.17) (BAGD 1. p. 421): 'to do' [GW, NCV, NET, NRSV, TEV], 'to accomplish' [BAGD, LN, NTC], 'to perform' [KJV], 'to perform successfully' [LN], 'to carry out' [AB, BECNT; NIV], 'to achieve' [HNTC], 'to work' [ICC2]. This articular infinitive is translated 'the producing' [NICNT], 'the doing' [WBC; NASB], 'the ability to effect it' [REB]. This phrase is translated 'I cannot' [CEV], 'but I can't' [NLT]. See this word at 1:27; 2:9; 4:15; 5:3; 7:8, 13, 15, 17.

b. καλός (LN 88.4) (BAGD 2.b. p. 400): 'good' [LN], 'morally good' [BAGD]. This articular adjective is translated 'good' [REB, TEV], 'the good' [BECNT, NICNT; NASB, NET], 'what is good' [AB; NIV], 'that which is good' [ICC2; KJV], 'the things that are good' [NCV], 'a really good work' [HNTC], 'what is admirable' [WBC], 'what is right' [GW, NRSV], 'right' [CEV, NLT], not explicit [NTC].

7:19 for I- do-not -do^a that good^b I-want^c

LEXICON—a. pres. act. indic. of ποιέω (LN 42.7): 'to do' [AB, BECNT, HNTC, ICC2, LN, NICNT, NTC, WBC; all versions], 'to carry out' [LN], 'to accomplish' [LN].
  b. ἀγαθός (LN 88.1): 'good' [AB, BECNT, HNTC, ICC2, LN, NICNT, NTC, WBC; all versions except CEV, NCV], 'good things' [NCV], 'right' [CEV].
  c. pres. act. indic. of θέλω (LN 25.1) (BAGD 2. p. 355): 'to want' [BAGD, LN, NTC; GW, NCV, NET, NIV, NLT, NRSV, REB, TEV], 'to wish' [BAGD, HNTC, WBC; NASB], 'to will' [ICC2, NICNT], 'to desire' [AB, BECNT, LN]. 'I want' is translated 'I would' [KJV]. This phrase is translated 'Instead of doing what I know is right' [CEV].

QUESTION—What relationship is indicated by γάρ 'for'?
  It introduces an amplification of what is stated in the last part of 7:18 and a restatement of 7:15 [SSA].

but that evil^a I- do-not -want^b this I-practice.^c

LEXICON—a. κακός (LN 88.106) (BAGD 1.c. p. 398): 'evil' [AB, BAGD, BECNT, HNTC, ICC2, LN, NICNT, NTC, WBC; GW, KJV, NASB, NET, NIV, NRSV, TEV], 'wrong' [CEV, NLT, REB], 'bad' [LN], 'bad things' [NCV].
  b. pres. act. indic. of θέλω (LN 25.1) (BAGD 2. p. 355). This clause is translated 'instead of doing what I know is right, I do wrong' [CEV].
  c. pres. act. indic. of πράσσω (LN 42.8) (BAGD 1.a. p. 698): 'to practice' [BECNT, HNTC, ICC2, NICNT, NTC; NASB], 'to do' [BAGD, LN; all versions except NASB], 'to commit' [WBC], not explicit [AB].

7:20 But if what I-do- not -want this I do,^a no-longer^b (do) I do^c it but the sin dwelling^d in me.

LEXICON—a. pres. act. indic. of ποιέω (LN 42.7) (BAGD I.1.b.ε. p. 681): 'to do' [BAGD, LN]. See above.
  b. οὐκέτι (LN 67.130) (BAGD 2. p. 592): 'no longer' [AB, BECNT, LN, NICNT, NTC, WBC; CEV, GW, NASB, NET, NIV, NRSV, REB, TEV], 'no more' [KJV]. The relationship indicated by οὐκέτι ἐγώ 'no longer I' is translated 'that shows that it cannot be I' [HNTC], 'then in these circumstances it is not I' [ICC2], 'I am not the one' [NCV, NLT], 'clearly it is no longer I' [REB], 'this means that I am no longer the one' [TEV]. As it is used here this word may be taken to express a logical and not a temporal relationship [BAGD].
  c. pres. mid. (deponent = act.) indic. of κατεργάζομαι (LN 42.17) (BAGD 1. p. 421): 'to do' [BAGD]. See above. See this word at 1:27; 2:9; 4:15; 5:3; 7:8, 13, 15, 17, 18.

d. pres. act. participle of οἰκέω (LN 85.73) (BAGD 1. p. 557): 'to dwell' [BAGD, LN], 'to live' [BAGD, LN], 'to reside' [LN]. See this word at 7:17, 18.

QUESTION—What relationship is indicated by οὐκέτι 'no longer'?
1. It is logical, not temporal [BAGD, BECNT, HNTC, Ho, ICC1, ICC2, SSA, TH]. It introduces the conclusion drawn from 7:18–19 that because I will to do good but cannot, it is not I doing the evil but sin acting in me [BECNT].
2. It is temporal [Mor]: formerly he had done this.

QUESTION—What difference, if any, is there between the verbs κατεργάζομαι, πράσσω, and ποιέω in this section of the epistle?
1. There is considerable overlap of meaning and little significant difference in their use [NICNT]. The two verbs πράσσω and ποιέω are synonymous here [BECNT, HNTC, TH]. It is possible that κατεργάζομαι might have a somewhat stronger connotation than the other two [NICNT]. In 7:15b Paul uses πράσσω for the doing of evil and ποιέω for the doing of good, whereas in 7:19 he does exactly the opposite [NICNT, WBC].
2. The verb πράσσω tends to denote activity in process, whereas ποιέω tends to focus on that which is accomplished as a result [Gdt].
3. Κατεργάζομαι means to put into effect or execution, πράσσω to act as a moral and responsible being, and ποιέω to produce some result without reference to the moral nature of it [ICC1].
4. Κατεργάζομαι and ποιέω refer to the effectiveness or completion of an action that is undertaken, whereas πράσσω is more indefinite and is used with reference to an inconclusive activity, usually one that is not approved of [ICC2].

7:21 I-find[a] therefore[b] the law,[c]

LEXICON—a. pres. act. indic. of εὑρίσκω (LN 27.1) (BAGD 2. p. 325): 'to find' [BAGD, BECNT, NICNT, WBC; KJV, NASB, NET, NIV, NRSV, TEV], 'to find out' [LN], 'to discover' [AB, LN, NTC; GW, REB], 'to learn' [LN; NCV], 'to prove by experience' [ICC2]. The phrase 'I find then the law' is translated 'it seems to be a fact of life that' [NLT], 'what then does this amount to? That there is imposed upon me...a law' [HNTC]. This entire verse is translated 'The Law has shown me that something in me keeps me from doing what I know is right' [CEV].
b. ἄρα (LN 89.46) (BAGD 1. p. 103): 'therefore' [BECNT, NICNT], 'then' [HNTC, LN, WBC; KJV, NASB, REB], 'so' [AB, LN, NTC; GW, NCV, NET, NIV, NRSV, TEV], 'so then' [ICC2], 'consequently' [LN], not explicit [CEV, NLT]. This word marks inference from what has preceded [LN].
c. νόμος (LN 33.333, 33.55) (BAGD 2. p. 542): 'law' [LN (33.333)], 'Law' [LN (33.55)], 'principle' [BAGD], 'rule' [LN (33.333)]. This noun with its definite article is translated 'this principle' [AB; REB], 'the principle' [NASB], 'this rule' [NCV], 'this truth' [GW], 'a fact of life' [NLT], 'a

law' [HNTC, NICNT, NTC; KJV, NRSV], 'the law' [BECNT, ICC2, WBC; NET], 'this law' [NICNT, NTC; NIV, TEV], 'the Law' [CEV].

QUESTION—What relationship is indicated by ἄρα 'therefore'?

It introduces in 7:21–25 a logical conclusion drawn from 7:14–20 [BECNT].

QUESTION—What is meant by the term νόμος 'law'?

1. It means 'principle' [AB, Gdt, Ho, ICC1, ICC2, Mor, Mu, NAC, NICNT, NTC, St, TH; GW, KJV, NASB, NCV, NIV, NLT, NRSV, REB, TEV]. The principle is the fact or presence of sin [NICNT]. It is a governing or controlling principle [Gdt, Ho], a coercion of the will [ICC1]. It is the 'other law' of 7:23, the law of sin [ICC2, Mu]. It is that power, authority and control that sin exercises over the believer [ICC2], the presence and rule of evil as a principle that demands action in opposition to the determinate will to do good [Mu]. This principle is stated as a fact of life, as being what always happens [SSA; NLT].
2. It refers to the Mosaic law [BECNT, WBC; CEV]. The accusative case is translated not as a direct object, 'I find the law', but as an accusative of reference, 'I find with reference to the law' [BECNT]. That is, with reference to the requirements of the Mosaic law, he finds that he wants to do the good it requires but can't because of sin within [BECNT].
3. It refers to a law-like rule, which is in effect a counterfeit or base imitation of the true law of Moses, and arises through the perversion and abuse of the law of Moses by men who use Moses' law for self-glorification instead of being taught by it to live in a state of humble dependence before God [HNTC].

to-me the-(one) wishing[a] to-do[b] the good,[c]

LEXICON—a. pres. act. participle of θέλω (LN 25.1) (BAGD 2. p. 355): 'to wish' [BAGD], 'to desire' [LN], 'to want' [BAGD, LN]. See above. The phrase τῷ θέλοντι ἐμοί 'to me the one wishing' expresses a circumstantial relation: when I wish [SSA].

b. ποιέω. See above.

c. καλός (LN 88.4) (BAGD 2.b. p. 400): 'good' [BECNT, LN, NTC; KJV, NASB, NCV, NET, NIV], 'the good' [NICNT, WBC], 'morally good' [BAGD], 'what is good' [ICC2; NRSV, TEV], 'right' [AB; REB], 'what is right' [NLT], 'what is good and right' [HNTC], 'what I know is right' [CEV], 'what God's standards say is good' [GW].

that with-me[a] the evil[b] is-present;[c]

LEXICON—a. ἐγώ. The dative form of this pronoun is translated 'with me' [NICNT; GW, KJV, NCV, NET, NIV], 'in me' [BECNT; NASB], 'for me' [WBC], not explicit [AB; CEV, NLT, NRSV, TEV]. It is also translated in conjunction with the verb παράκειμαι 'to be present': 'within my (reach)' [ICC2; REB], '(attends) me' [HNTC].

b. κακός (LN 88.106) (BAGD 1.c. p. 397): 'evil' [AB, BAGD, BECNT, HNTC, ICC2, LN, NICNT, NTC, WBC; GW, KJV, NASB, NCV, NET,

NIV, NRSV], 'what is evil' [TEV], 'wrong' [REB], 'what is wrong' [NLT], not explicit [CEV].

c. pres. mid. (deponent = act.) indic. of παράκειμαι (LN **85.23**): 'to be present' [BECNT, **LN**, NICNT; GW, KJV, NASB, NET], 'to be at hand' [AB, LN], 'to lie close at hand' [NTC; NRSV], 'to lie ready to hand' [WBC], 'to be there' [NCV], 'to be right there' [NIV], 'to be within reach' [ICC2; REB], 'to attend (me)' [HNTC], not explicit [CEV, NLT, TEV].

7:22 for[a] I-agree-with[b] the law[c] of-God with-respect-to[d] the inner[e] person,[f]

LEXICON—a. γάρ (LN 89.23): 'for' [AB, BECNT, HNTC, ICC2, LN, NICNT, NTC, WBC; KJV, NASB, NET, NIV, NRSV], 'because' [LN], not explicit [CEV, GW, NCV, NLT, REB, TEV].

b. pres. mid. (deponent = act.) indic. of συνήδομαι (LN **25.127**) (BAGD p. 789): 'to agree with' [BECNT, HNTC; CEV], 'to agree with joyfully' [BAGD], 'to joyfully concur' [NASB], 'to delight in' [AB, ICC2, **LN**, NTC; KJV, NET, NIV, NRSV, REB, TEV], 'to rejoice in' [LN, NICNT, WBC], 'to take pleasure in' [GW], 'to be happy with' [NCV], 'to love' [NLT]. This verb is used only here in the NT.

c. νόμος (LN 33.333, 33.55) (BAGD 3. p. 542): 'law' [BAGD, LN (33.333)], 'Law' [LN (33.55)]. The phrase τῷ νόμῳ τοῦ θεοῦ is translated 'the law of God' [BECNT, NICNT, WBC; CEV, KJV, NASB, NET, NRSV, REB, TEV], 'God's law' [AB, HNTC, ICC2, NTC; NCV, NIV, NLT], 'God's standards' [GW].

d. κατά with accusative object (LN 89.4) (BAGD II.6. p. 407): 'with respect to' [BAGD], 'in' [AB, BECNT, HNTC; GW, NASB, NCV, NET, NIV, NRSV, REB], 'in so far as' [ICC2], 'so far as…is concerned' [WBC], 'according to' [NICNT, NTC], 'with regard to' [LN], 'with' [CEV, NLT], 'after' [KJV], not explicit [TEV].

e. ἔσω (LN 26.1, 83.13) (BAGD 2. p. 314): 'inner' [BAGD], 'inside' [LN (83.13)]. The phrase τὸν ἔσω ἄνθρωπον is translated 'the inner person' [NICNT], 'the inner man' [ICC2, WBC; NASB], 'the inward man' [KJV], 'the inner being' [LN (**26.1**)], 'the inmost being, inwardly' [LN (26.1)], 'my inner person' [BECNT], 'my inner self' [HNTC], 'my inner being' [NTC; GW, NET, NIV, TEV], 'my inmost self' [AB; NRSV, REB], 'my whole heart' [CEV], 'all my heart' [NLT], 'my mind' [NCV].

f. ἄνθρωπος (LN 9.1) (BAGD 2.c.α. p. 68): 'person' [LN], 'man' [BAGD]. See entry above.

QUESTION—What relationship is indicated by γάρ 'for'?

It introduces a further explanation of what he says about the principle of indwelling sin in 7:21 [BECNT, Ho, ICC2, NICNT, SSA]. It introduces 7:22–23 as an explanation of the situation described in 7:21 [ICC2].

QUESTION—What is the 'law of God' that he refers to here?

It is the Mosaic law [AB, BECNT, HNTC, Ho, ICC2, NAC, NICNT, TNTC, WBC]. It is the system of moral principles that are summarized in the ten commandments, and which for the believer becomes the ruling principle for expressing his gratitude, though not a means of salvation [NTC]. Or, it is the objective moral law, whether written or unwritten [Gdt].

QUESTION—What is the ἔσω ἄνθρωπος 'inner man' of which he speaks here?

- 1. It refers to the mind [AB, BECNT, Gdt, HNTC, ICC1, ICC2, Mu, NAC, NICNT, TH]. It is the thinking and reasoning part of him [ICC1], that part of the soul that can distinguish between true and false, bad and good [Gdt]. It is the same as the mind in 7:23 and 7:25, and the renewed mind in 12:2, which represents the working of God's spirit within the Christian [ICC2]. It is his 'true self', reflecting what he really prefers [Mu, NAC, TH], the 'I' that wants to do good [HNTC, TH].
  - 1.1 It denotes the mental or spiritual aspect of a person, which corresponds with 'wishing' or 'willing' in previous verses, as opposed to the outer or bodily aspect of the person, which corresponds to 'flesh', 'members', and 'doing' in previous verses [NICNT].
  - 1.2 It is the deepest and inmost self-determination, the mind, and which is contrasted with the outward man, the body; however, that contrast does not mean that there is a metaphysical or ethical distinction between spirit and body, mind and matter, because the principle called 'flesh' is not identical with the body [Mu].
- 2. It is the new nature in Christ [SSA, TNTC], that nature which is being renewed in the image of God the creator [TNTC]. The inner man is that aspect of the believer that is already united with Christ in his death and sharing in his resurrection life [WBC]. It is the heart and the new principle of life that the Holy Spirit implanted in it when Paul became a new man, a man who is now being transformed into the image of Christ [NTC]. It refers to the renewed soul of a believer [Ho], the real, regenerate self [St]. It is the real Paul, who has been regenerated and enlightened by the working of the Spirit of God within him [Mor].
- 3. It is the mind or reason, even of unregenerate humanity, and which recognizes the ideal that God's law proposes [AB].

7:23 but I-see[a] another[b] law[c] in[d] my members[e]

LEXICON—a. pres. act. indic. of βλέπω (LN 32.11) (BAGD 7.b. p. 143): 'to see' [AB, BECNT, ICC2, LN, NICNT, NTC, WBC; GW, KJV, NASB, NCV, NET, NIV, NRSV, TEV], 'to observe' [HNTC], 'to perceive' [**LN**; REB], 'to find' [BAGD], 'to discover' [CEV]. Βλέπω 'I see' is translated 'there is' [NLT].

b. ἕτερος (LN 58.37, 58.36) (BAGD 2. p. 315): 'another' [AB, BECNT, HNTC, LN (58.37), NICNT, WBC; KJV, NCV, NIV, NLT, NRSV], 'different' [BAGD, ICC2, LN (58.36), NTC; GW, NASB, NET, REB, TEV]. The phrase 'another law' is translated 'something' [CEV].

c. νόμος (LN 33.333) (BAGD 2. p. 542): 'law' [AB, BECNT, HNTC, ICC2, LN, NICNT, NTC, WBC; all versions except CEV, GW], 'principle' [BAGD], 'standard' [GW], not explicit [CEV].
d. ἐν with dative object (LN 83.13): 'in' [AB, BAGD, BECNT, HNTC, ICC2, LN, NICNT, NTC, WBC; CEV, KJV, NASB, NET, NRSV, REB], 'working in' [NCV], 'at work in' [NIV, TEV], 'at work within' [NLT], 'throughout' [GW].
e. μέλος (LN 8.9) (BAGD 1. p. 501): 'member' [BAGD, LN], 'body part' [LN]. This plural noun is translated 'members' [AB, BECNT, HNTC, ICC2, NICNT; KJV, NASB, NET, NRSV], 'bodily members' [NTC], 'members of (my) body' [NIV], 'body' [GW, NCV, TEV], 'constituent parts' [WBC], 'every part of me' [CEV], 'me' [NLT], '(my) outward actions' [REB].

QUESTION—What is the 'other law' he speaks of here?

1. It is sin as a governing principle [AB, Gdt, Ho, ICC1, ICC2, Mor, Mu, NICNT, NTC, SSA, TH]. It is the authority and power of sin, which is opposed to God's law [AB, NICNT, NTC]. It is the power exercised over us by sin [ICC2], a force or principle of action at work in our lives [SSA]. Using the term 'law' makes the point that the power that sin exercises over us is a grotesque parody of the rightful authority over us that God's law should exercise [ICC2]. It is the instinctive self-centeredness that has ruled over people since the fall [Gdt].
2. It is the Mosaic law [BECNT, WBC]. It is the Mosaic law in alliance with sin, with the result that he is not able to obey the Mosaic law [BECNT]. It is the same as 'the law of sin', which is the Mosaic law as used by sin to deceive and kill [WBC].
3. It is the usurping and perverting of the Mosaic law by sin in the form of human religion, which cannot meet God's standards and from which there is no human means of escape [HNTC].

QUESTION—In what sense is the term μέλος 'members' used here?

'Members' refers to the flesh, that aspect of his nature through which indwelling sin is expressed [NICNT]. It is the same as 'flesh' in 7:18 [Ho]. It is the physical body in which sin exerts itself, though not the body as distinct or separated from the whole person [BECNT]. It is the various members of his physical body, though this does not rule out his spiritual part of his being [NTC]. As in 6:13 it refers to constituent parts as well as natural capacities and faculties [WBC]. While he does not view the body as evil, the forces of evil do work through it [Mor] and it is the battlefield where the struggle against desire, sin, and death is fought [TH]. It is his various faculties, his corporeal existence in this age and as determined by the conditions of this life [HNTC]. It is his human nature in its condition of being subject to the usurping authority of sin [ICC2]. It means 'in my body', which is a synecdoche for 'in me' [SSA]. The self-centered instincts attached to the members of the body seek gratification through those members [Gdt]. The law of sin expresses itself in concrete ways using the members of the body as agents and instruments of its power, but it is the whole person and not just the physical members that are in captivity to sin [Mu].

warring-against[a] the law[b] of-my mind[c]

LEXICON—a. pres. mid. (deponent = act.) participle of ἀντιστρατεύομαι (LN 39.2) (BAGD p. 75): 'to war against' [KJV], 'to wage war against' [BECNT, ICC2, NTC; NASB, NET, NIV], 'to make war against' [NCV], 'to make war upon' [HNTC], 'to battle against' [AB], 'to be at war with' [BAGD, WBC; GW, NLT, NRSV], 'to fight against' [NICNT; CEV, REB, TEV], 'to oppose' [**LN**]. This word occurs only here in the NT.

b. νόμος (LN 33.333) (BAGD 2. p. 542): 'law' [AB, BECNT, HNTC, ICC2, LN, NICNT, NTC, WBC; KJV, NASB, NCV, NET, NIV, NRSV, REB, TEV], 'principle' [BAGD], 'standard' [GW], not explicit [CEV, NLT].

c. νοῦς (LN 26.14) (BAGD 2. p. 544): 'mind' [AB, BAGD, BECNT, HNTC, ICC2, LN, NICNT, NTC, WBC; all versions], 'intellect' [BAGD]. The phrase τοῦ νοός μου 'of my mind' is translated 'that my mind acknowledges' [AB], 'that my mind accepts' [NCV], 'that my mind approves' [REB], 'which my mind approves of' [TEV], 'which rules my mind' [HNTC], 'my mind sets' [GW], 'my mind' [CEV, NLT].

QUESTION—In what sense is the term νόμος 'law' used here?

1. It means 'principle' [Ho, Mor, Mu, NAC]. It is the principle of rational thought, by which Paul knew the right thing to do [NAC]. It is the principle that is at work in his rational nature [Mor]. It is the same as the 'inner person' of the previous verse [Ho, SSA]. It is the rational part of conscience which decides between right and wrong [ICC1]. It is the subjective moral sense in man, which perceives the objective law of God and makes it the rule of the individual [Gdt]. It is God's law which regulates the mind and which the mind serves [Mu].

2. It is the Mosaic law, which his mind approves of or acknowledges [AB, BECNT, HNTC, ICC2, WBC]. God's law is the one which his inner self approves [HNTC].

and making- me -captive[a] to[b] the law[c] of sin[d] the-(one) being in my members.[e]

LEXICON—a. pres. act. participle of αἰχμαλωτίζω (LN 37.29, 55.24) (BAGD 2. p. 27): 'to make (one) captive' [AB, LN (55.24); NET, NRSV], 'to make (one) a prisoner' [BAGD, ICC2, NTC, WBC; CEV, NASB, NCV, NIV, REB, TEV], 'to take (one) captive' [BECNT, LN (55.24); GW], 'to take (one) a prisoner' [HNTC], 'to hold (one) captive' [NICNT], 'to bring (one) into captivity' [KJV]. The phrase καὶ αἰχμαλωτίζοντά με 'and making me captive' is translated 'wins the fight and makes me a slave' [NLT].

b. ἐν with dative object (LN 13.8, 89.5): 'to' [AB, BECNT, HNTC, WBC; GW, KJV, NET, NLT, NRSV, TEV], 'of' [ICC2, NTC; CEV, NASB,

NIV], 'in' [LN (13.8, 89.5), NICNT], 'under' [REB], 'with' [LN (13.8)], 'with regard to' [LN (89.5)], not explicit [NCV].
   c. νόμος (LN 33.333, 33.55) (BAGD 2. p. 542): 'law' [LN (33.333)], 'Law' [LN (33.55)], 'principle' [BAGD]. This noun with the definite article is translated 'the law' [AB, BECNT, HNTC, ICC2, NICNT, NTC, WBC; KJV, NASB, NCV, NET, NIV, NRSV, REB, TEV], 'standards' [GW]. The phrase τῷ νόμῳ τῆς ἁμαρτίας 'the law of sin' is simply translated 'sin' [NLT]. The phrase τῷ νόμῳ τῆς ἁμαρτίας τῷ ὄντι ἐν τοῖς μέλεσίν μου 'the law of sin the one being in my members' is translated 'sin that controls everything I do' [CEV], 'sin which controls my conduct' [REB], 'sin's standards which still exist throughout my body' [GW], 'a slave to the sin that is still within me' [NLT].
   d. ἁμαρτία (LN 88.289) (BAGD 3. p. 43): 'sin' [AB, BAGD, BECNT, HNTC, ICC2, LN, NICNT, NTC, WBC; all versions].
   e. μέλος (LN 8.9) (BAGD 1. p. 501): 'member' [BAGD, LN], 'body part' [LN]. This plural noun is translated 'members' [AB, BAGD, BECNT, HNTC, ICC2, LN, NICNT, NTC; KJV, NASB, NET, NIV, NRSV], 'constituent parts' [WBC], 'body' [GW, NCV, TEV], 'me' [NLT], 'my conduct' [REB], 'everything I do' [CEV].

QUESTION—In what sense is the term νόμος 'law' used here?
   1. It is a principle or rule [Gdt, Ho, ICC2, Mor, Mu, NAC, NTC, SSA, TNTC]. It is the propensity toward sin the comes from the lower nature [NAC]. It is sin as a controlling power, and is the same as the 'other law' in the previous clause [Ho, ICC2, Mu]. It is the subjective organ by which the individual falls under the law or rule of sin [Gdt].
   2. It refers to the Mosaic law [AB, BECNT, WBC]. Even though the law itself is good, the alliance of sin in the unregenerate person with the Mosaic law actually results in disobedience to the law [BECNT]. It is the Mosaic law that occasions sin, though not actually causing it, and which is being used by sin to entice the ego [AB]. It is the Mosaic law, which was used by sin to deceive and kill [WBC].
   3. It is the 'other law' mentioned above, which is a sinful perversion and abuse of the Mosaic law [HNTC].

7:24 Wretched[a] man (am) I; who will-rescue[b] me from[c] this body[d] of-death?[e]

LEXICON—a. ταλαίπωρος (LN **22.12**) (BAGD p. 803): 'wretched' [BAGD, BECNT, HNTC, ICC2, LN, NICNT, NTC, WBC; KJV, NASB, NET, NIV, NRSV, REB], 'miserable' [CEV, GW, NCV, NLT], 'unhappy' [TEV]. The phrase ταλαίπωρος ἄνθρωπος 'wretched man' is translated 'wretch' [AB]. This word or its cognates is a strong term used in the LXX and the NT to describe the distress that will accompany the judgment of God [NICNT].
   b. fut. mid. (deponent = act.) indic. of ῥύομαι (LN **21.23**) (BAGD p. 737): 'to rescue' [AB, **LN**, NTC; CEV, GW, NET, NIV, NRSV, REB, TEV],

'to deliver' [BECNT, HNTC, ICC2, LN, NICNT, WBC; KJV], 'to set free' [BAGD; NASB], 'to free' [NLT], 'to save' [NCV].
  c. ἐκ with genitive object (LN 84.4): 'from' [AB, BECNT, HNTC, ICC2, LN, NICNT, NTC, WBC; all versions].
  d. σῶμα (LN 8.1) (BAGD 1.b. p. 799): 'body' [AB, BAGD, BECNT, HNTC, ICC2, LN, NICNT, NTC, WBC; all versions except NLT, REB], 'life' [NLT], 'state' [REB].
  e. θάνατος (LN 23.99) (BAGD 2.a. p. 351): 'death' [BAGD, BECNT, HNTC, ICC2, LN, NICNT, NTC, WBC; KJV, NASB, NCV, NET, NIV, NRSV, REB, TEV]. The phrase τοῦ θανάτου 'of death' is translated 'dying' [GW], 'doomed' [AB], 'that is doomed to die' [CEV], 'that brings me death' [NCV], 'that is taking me to death' [TEV]. The phrase 'this body of death' is translated 'this life that is dominated by sin' [NLT], 'this state of death' [REB].

QUESTION—What does this cry of despair represent?
  1. It represents the Christian's longing for liberation from the inclination of his human nature to sin [Ho, ICC1, ICC2, Mor, Mu, NAC, NTC, TNTC]. It represents the Christian's longing for resurrection [Mu]. It is an expression of grief over not being able to serve God as completely and wholeheartedly as he would like [NTC]. This impassioned cry echoes the experience of a soul in anguish until it is finally perfected in holiness [TNTC]. Spiritual depth is shown in a sensitive conscience and a genuine sorrow for sin [Mor]. It is a cry of anguish, but not of despair [ICC2, Mu, St], arising from the justified man who deeply desires to respond to the claims that the gospel makes upon his life [ICC2]. The term 'wretched' is not so much a state as how he feels about himself in the situation he has just been describing [SSA].
  2. It represents the non-Christian's recognition of the need to be rescued from spiritual failure and condemnation [Gdt, NICNT].
  3. It represents the cry of frustration of anyone, whether Christian or non-Christian, who lives under the law and who relies on the law as a means for transformation and liberation from the power of sin [BECNT]. It represents the desperate cry for help of the ego, weighted down by sin and unable to help itself. It also represents the tension between existence in Adam and existence in Christ, between the old aeon and the new, that lasts throughout life [AB].
  4. It represents the cry of the Christian resulting from the eschatological tension of living between the two epochs of Adam and Christ, of death and life. It is also a cry for escape from an age dominated by sin and death, and an expression of the frustration of trying to live the new life in the Spirit while still a man of flesh [WBC].

QUESTION—What is the demonstrative τούτου 'this' connected with?
  1. It is connected with σώματος 'body' [AB, HNTC, ICC2, NICNT, NTC, SSA; CEV, NET, NIV, NRSV, TEV]: this body of death.

2. It is connected with θανάτου 'death' [Gdt, Ho, ICC1, Mu, WBC; KJV, NASB]: the body of this death.

QUESTION—What does 'body of death' refer to?

It refers to the ego with its limited natural resources, and which cannot deliver from the spiritual death that is the natural outcome of sin [AB]. It is the physical death that is intrinsic to and results from the bondage to sin [Mu]. He is like a man who is tied to a corpse, which represents the sinful nature clinging on and interfering with the impulses of the higher nature [NAC]. It is a variation on 'body of sin' (6:6), 'this mortal body' (6:12), 'my flesh' (7:18), and 'my members' (7:23), and refers more or less to the fleshly nature [WBC]. 'Body of death' is used in a figurative sense to represent the heavy burden that the sinful nature is to the soul [Ho]. It is the body as subject to sinful inclinations and death [NTC]. It is his body or human nature under hostile occupation by the power of sin [TNTC]. It is his body, which is mortal, and in which sin operates to bring death [Mor]. It is the body or human nature which has fallen under the dominion of death [HNTC]. The body involves him in sin and thus in mortality and eternal death [ICC1]. It is the condition of life in this body under the occupation of sin and which must die because of sin [ICC2]. It represents the struggle against the sinful things the body desires [SSA]. The body is the instrument which sin uses to enslave the soul and bring it to death [Gdt]. The body is the sphere and instrument where the law of sin operates to bring about captivity to sin [Mu].

7:25 But thanks[a] (be) to-God through[b] Jesus Christ our Lord.

TEXT—Instead of χάρις δὲ τῷ θεῷ 'but thanks (be) to God' some manuscripts read εὐχαριστῶ τῷ θεῷ 'I thank God'. GNT reads χάρις δὲ τῷ θεῷ 'but thanks (be) to God' with a B decision, indicating that the text is almost certain. GW, KJV, and NCV read 'I thank God' and CEV and NLT read 'Thank God', although it is not clear whether it is because of the variant or for stylistic reasons.

LEXICON—a. χάρις (LN 33.350) (BAGD 5. p. 878): 'thanks' [AB, BAGD, BECNT, HNTC, ICC2, LN, NICNT, NTC, WBC; NASB, NET, NIV, NRSV, REB, TEV], 'gratitude' [BAGD]. The phrase χάρις δὲ τῷ θεῷ 'but thanks to God' (or possibly εὐχαριστῶ τῷ θεῷ) is translated 'I thank God' [GW, KJV, NCV], 'Thank God!' [CEV, NLT].

b. διά with genitive object (LN 90.4) (BAGD A.III.2.a. p. 180): 'through' [AB, BAGD, BECNT, HNTC, ICC2, LN, NICNT, NTC, WBC; KJV, NASB, NET, NIV], 'by' [LN]. The phrase διὰ Ἰησοῦ Χριστοῦ 'through Jesus Christ' is translated 'Jesus Christ will rescue me' [CEV], 'Jesus Christ rescues me' [GW], 'for saving me through Jesus Christ' [NCV], 'the answer is in Jesus Christ' [NLT], 'who does this through Jesus Christ' [TEV].

QUESTION—What relationship is indicated by διά 'through'?
1. In answer to the question of the previous clause, it is through Christ that freedom is gained [AB, BECNT, Gdt, HNTC, ICC1, Mor, NAC, NTC, SSA, TH, TNTC; CEV, GW, NCV, NIV, NLT, TEV].
2. It is through Christ that thanks are given to God [KJV, NASB, NET, NRSV, REB].
3. It stresses Christ's mediatorial role in giving thanks to God as well as his role as God's agent in bringing final deliverance [Ho, WBC].

So[a] then on-the-one-hand I myself[b] serve[c] (the) law[d] of-God with-the-mind,[e]
LEXICON—a. ἄρα (LN 89.46) (BAGD 4. p. 104): 'so, consequently' [BAGD, LN], 'as a result' [BAGD], 'then' [LN]. The phrase ἄρα οὖν is translated 'so then' [AB, BAGD, ICC2, NTC, WBC; KJV, NASB, NET, NIV, NRSV], 'so' [CEV, GW, NCV], 'therefore' [BECNT], 'to sum up then' [HNTC; REB], 'now then' [NICNT], 'so you see how it is' [NLT], 'this then is my condition' [TEV].
b. The phrase αὐτὸς ἐγώ is translated 'I myself' [AB, BECNT, HNTC, ICC2, NTC, WBC; KJV, NASB, NET, NIV], 'I' [NICNT; CEV, GW, NCV, NLT, NRSV], 'left to myself' [REB], 'on my own' [TEV].
c. pres. act. indic. of δουλεύω (LN 35.27) (BAGD 2.c. p. 205): 'to serve' [BAGD, BECNT, HNTC, ICC2, LN, NICNT, NTC, WBC; CEV, KJV, NASB, NET, REB, TEV], 'to obey' [BAGD], 'to be a slave to' [AB; NCV, NIV, NRSV], 'to be obedient to' [GW]. The phrase 'I serve the law of God with the mind' is translated 'in my mind I really want to obey God's law' [NLT].
d. νόμος (LN 33.333, 33.55) (BAGD 3. p. 542): 'law' [BAGD, LN (33.333)], 'Law' [LN (33.55); CEV]. The phrase νόμῳ θεοῦ, which lacks the definite article, is translated 'the law of God' [BECNT, ICC2, NICNT, NTC, WBC; KJV, NASB, NET, NRSV], 'the Law of God' [CEV], 'God's law' [AB, HNTC; NCV, NIV, NLT, REB, TEV], 'God's standards' [GW].
e. νοῦς (LN **26.14**) (BAGD 2. p.544): 'mind' [AB, BAGD, BECNT, HNTC, ICC2, LN, NICNT, NTC, WBC; all versions]. The relation indicated by the dative case of this noun is translated 'with' [BECNT, HNTC, ICC2, NTC, WBC; CEV, GW, KJV, NASB, NET, NRSV, REB, TEV], 'in' [AB, NICNT; NCV, NIV, NLT]. This noun is translated as though having the possessive pronoun 'my' [AB, BECNT, HNTC, ICC2, LN, NICNT, NTC, WBC; all versions except KJV].

QUESTION—What relationship is indicated by ἄρα οὖν 'therefore then'?
It is inferential, drawing a conclusion from what has been said previously [BECNT, Gdt, Ho, ICC2, Mor, NICNT, SSA, TH, TNTC]. It introduces a summary conclusion for the paragraph of 7:14–25 [SSA]. It introduces a summary and restatement of what Paul says about the inner struggle in 7:15–23 [BECNT, NICNT] or in 7:14–24 [TNTC]. It introduces a conclusion to what he has said from 7:14 on about the impotence of the law

[Ho]. It sums up his entire argument [NTC]. It sums up the anguish and tension the Christian feels for as long as he is in this life [ICC2, Mor]. He now summarizes the elements of the antithesis described from 7:14 on, which are the law of God versus the law of sin, and the mind versus the flesh [Mu].

but with-the flesh[a] (the) law[b] of-sin.[c]

LEXICON—a. σάρξ (LN 26.7, 58.10) (BAGD 7. p. 744): 'flesh' [AB, BAGD, BECNT, HNTC, ICC2, NICNT, NTC, WBC; KJV, NASB, NET], 'human nature' [LN (26.7, 58.10); TEV], 'corrupt nature' [GW], 'unspiritual nature' [REB], 'sinful nature' [NIV, NLT, NRSV], 'sinful self' [NCV], 'selfish desires' [CEV]. The relation indicated by the dative case of this noun is translated 'with' [BECNT, HNTC, ICC2, NTC, WBC; GW, KJV, NASB, NET, NRSV, REB, TEV], 'in' [AB, NICNT; NCV, NIV], 'because of' [NLT], not explicit [CEV]. This noun is translated as though having the possessive pronoun 'my' [AB, BECNT, ICC2, NICNT, NTC, WBC; all versions except KJV, NIV].

b. νόμος (LN 33.333) (BAGD 3. p. 542): 'law' [AB, BAGD, BECNT, HNTC, ICC2, LN, NICNT, NTC, WBC; all versions except GW, NLT], 'standards' [GW]. The phrase δουλεύω...νόμῳ ἁμαρτίας 'I serve...the law of sin' is translated 'I am a slave to sin' [NLT].

c. ἁμαρτία (LN 88.289) (BAGD 3. p. 43): 'sin' [AB, BAGD, BECNT, HNTC, ICC2, LN, NICNT, NTC, WBC; all versions].

DISCOURSE UNIT: 8:1–39 [Gdt, ICC2, Mor, Mu, St, TNTC, WBC; NET, REB]. The topic is the believer's relationship to the Holy Spirit [NET], life through the Spirit [REB], life in the Spirit [Mu], living in the Spirit [WBC], a life characterized by the indwelling of God's Spirit [ICC2], the work of the Holy Spirit [Gdt], the Holy Spirit in the believer [Mor], God's Spirit in God's children [St], freedom from death [TNTC].

DISCOURSE UNIT: 8:1–30 [NICNT, NTC, WBC]. The topic is the eschatological tension and fulfillment of God's purpose through the Spirit [WBC], the assurance of eternal life in the Spirit [NICNT], no condemnation for those in Christ Jesus [NTC].

DISCOURSE UNIT: 8:1–17 [GNT, TNTC; CEV, GW, NCV, NIV, NLT, NRSV, TEV]. The topic is life in the Spirit [GNT, TNTC; NLT, NRSV, TEV], life through the Spirit [NIV], living by the power of God's Spirit [CEV], God's Spirit makes us his children [GW], be ruled by the Spirit [NCV].

DISCOURSE UNIT: 8:1–13 [AB, NICNT]. The topic is Christian life empowered by the Spirit of God [AB], the Spirit of life [NICNT].

DISCOURSE UNIT: 8:1–11 [Gdt, HNTC, ICC2, Mor, WBC]. The topic is the victory over sin and death [Gdt], life in the Spirit [HNTC], the indwelling of the Spirit [ICC2], the Spirit of sonship [WBC], the opposition of flesh and spirit [Mor].

8:1 Therefore (there is) now no condemnation[a] to-those in[b] Christ Jesus.

TEXT—Following Ἰησοῦ 'Jesus', some manuscripts add μὴ κατὰ σάρκα περιπατοῦσιν ἀλλὰ κατὰ πνεῦμα 'not walking according to (the) flesh but according to (the) Spirit'. It is omitted by GNT with an A rating, indicating that the text is certain. Only KJV includes it.

LEXICON—a. κατάκριμα (LN 56.31) (BAGD p. 412): 'condemnation' [AB, BECNT, HNTC, ICC2, LN, NICNT, NTC, WBC; all versions except CEV, GW, NCV], 'punishment, doom' [BAGD]. This noun is translated as a verb: 'to be condemned' [GW], 'to be judged guilty' [NCV], 'to be punished' [CEV]. See this word also at 5:16, 18.

b. ἐν with dative object (LN 83.13, 89.119) (BAGD I.5.d. p. 259): 'in' [AB, BAGD, BECNT, HNTC, ICC2, LN (83.13, 89.119), NICNT, NTC, WBC; KJV, NIV, NRSV], 'one with, in union with' [LN (89.119)], 'who live in union with' [TEV], 'who are united with' [REB], 'who belong to' [NLT], 'who are believers in' [GW].

QUESTION—What relationship is indicated by ἄρα 'therefore'?

The combination ἄρα νῦν 'now therefore' is emphatic, showing that a significant conclusion follows [NICNT]. It draws a conclusion from, and restates and elaborates on, what has been discussed in chapters 5, 6, and 7, but especially in 5:12–21 concerning how those in Christ have eternal life instead of the condemnation and death that those in Adam have [NICNT]. It draws a conclusion from chapters 5, 6, and 7, but especially 5:18–21 [AB]. It introduces a conclusion to be drawn from 7:1–6 [ICC2]. It introduces a conclusion to be drawn from the discussion of sanctification in 6:1 through 7:6; that is, since they are dead to sin, alive to God, subject to grace and freed from the law, they are not under condemnation [Gdt]. It draws a conclusion based on the premise of 7:6, that believers are not under condemnation because they are no longer under the domination of the law [BECNT, HNTC], and also on the exclamation of victory in 7:24–25, which is linked to 7:6 [BECNT]. It draws a conclusion from the premise in 7:25 that through Christ's atoning work God has provided the means of freedom from the sinful nature, so that there is no condemnation for those in Christ [NAC, NTC]. The law is both the means used by sin to fasten its grip on people as well as the basis for God's judgment, but because Christians have died to the law through union with Christ they escape judgment [HNTC]. It draws a conclusion based on the discussion about the enslaving power of sin in chapters 6 and 7 [Mu, NTC]. It draws a conclusion from all that has been said in the epistle, but especially from chapters 3, 4, and 5 about salvation through Christ's death and resurrection [St]. It draws a conclusion from all that has already been said in the epistle concerning justification [Ho, NTC], and especially in chapters 5, 6 and 7, which is that because of Christ's sacrifice, believers have been released from the curse of the law [NTC]. It introduces a restatement of the major theme of the epistle [WBC]. It draws a conclusion from all that has been said in the epistle about Christ's debt-removing sacrifice of himself, especially in chapters 6 and 7, and most particularly in 7:25 [NTC].

QUESTION—To what does νῦν 'now' refer?

1. It is temporal, and refers to the new era in salvation history [AB, BECNT, Gdt, NAC, NICNT, St, WBC], the eschatological 'now' [AB], the era begun by the death and resurrection of Christ [NICNT], and in which God's covenant promises are fulfilled [BECNT]. It initiates a contrast between someone dominated by his human nature and someone under the control of the Holy Spirit [TH]. The new epoch replaces the previous dispensation of condemnation [NAC]. They have passed into the age to come because through their union with Christ they have shared in his death and resurrection [HNTC]. It is the present time, as opposed to the time prior to having justification in Christ; it also speaks of the time to come when salvation will be fully realized, though for now we rejoice in experiencing all that 'no condemnation' means [Mor]. This salvation is ours if we are in Christ, as opposed to being in Adam [St].
2. It is logical, and points toward a conclusion to be drawn in consequence of the fact of being in Christ Jesus, which is that there is no condemnation [NTC]. Since men cannot be justified by works, being sinners, and since by the obedience of one man many are made righteous, and since deliverance from the power of sin has come through Christ, not law, there is therefore no condemnation [Ho].
3. It is both logical and temporal, drawing a conclusion from the fact of what has happened in the gospel events themselves; that is, now that Christ has died and has been raised from the dead, this is true [ICC2].

QUESTION—What condemnation is he speaking of?

It is the penalty attached to the condition of being lost and separated from God [NICNT]. It is the penalty that follows the sentence of 'guilty' [BAGD, TNTC]. It refers to the results of the curse [AB, BECNT], being under the tyranny of sin [Mu]. It is the condemnation for sin brought by the law [HNTC]. Believers are released from the curse of the law [NTC]. It is the judgment of God against sin, as well as the execution of that judgment [Mor, NAC, SSA]. It is the condemnation spoken of in 5:12–21 [WBC]. It is the condemnation for being under the domination of sin [Gdt]. The condemnation that once was directed toward the sinner now falls upon sin [ICC1].

8:2 For the law^a of the Spirit^b of life^c

LEXICON—a. νόμος (LN **33.333**) (BAGD 5. p. 543): 'law' [AB, BAGD, BECNT, HNTC, ICC2, LN (**33.333**), NICNT, NTC, WBC; all versions except GW, NLT], 'religion' [HNTC], 'standards' [GW], 'power' [NLT]. The reference is to basic principles [LN]. The phrase ὁ γὰρ νόμος τοῦ πνεύματος τῆς ζωῆς 'For the law of the Spirit of life' is translated 'The Holy Spirit will give you life' [CEV].

b. πνεῦμα (LN 12.18) (BAGD 5.e. p. 677): 'Spirit' [AB, BAGD, BECNT, HNTC, ICC2, LN, NICNT, NTC, WBC; all versions except CEV], 'the Holy Spirit' [CEV].

c. ζωή (LN 23.88) (BAGD 2.b.α, p. 340): 'life' [AB, BAGD, BECNT, HNTC, ICC2, LN, NICNT, NTC, WBC; all versions]. The phrase 'of life' is translated 'life-giving' [HNTC; NET, NLT, REB], 'who gives life' [GW], 'that brings life' [NCV], 'which brings us life' [TEV], 'will give you life' [CEV]

QUESTION—What relationship is indicated by γάρ 'for'?

It introduces 8:2 as the grounds for the statement made in 8:1 [BECNT, HNTC, Ho, Mor, Mu, NAC, NICNT, St, TH], which is that Christians are freed from condemnation by being freed from the law [HNTC], or from the law of sin and death [St]. It continues and develops the thought of 8:1, which draws a conclusion from 7:1–6 [ICC2]. It introduces Paul's reason for the assurance expressed in 8:1 that there is no condemnation for the Christian, which is that one of the two laws mentioned in 7:22–23 is stronger than the other [WBC].

QUESTION—How is the term 'law' used in this verse?

1. It refers to a power, a principle, or a binding authority [AB, Gdt, HNTC, ICC2, LN, Mor, NAC, NICNT, NTC, SSA, TH, TNTC; GW, NLT]. It is the authority and constraint that the Holy Spirit exercises in the life of believers [ICC1, ICC2]. In using the term 'law' with 'Spirit' Paul employs an oxymoron [AB]. It is used in the sense of 'standard' by which a person may live [GW]. It is a ruling factor [NTC], the rule that governs his conduct [Mor]. It is the principle that the power of sin is broken in the life of believers only by union with Christ [NAC].

2. In both instances 'law' represents the respective approaches to religion: the religion of the life-giving Spirit and the old religion, Judaism, which is abused by sin and death [HNTC].

3. It is the gospel, the 'law' of which the life-giving Spirit is the author, has delivered me from the law [Ho].

4. It refers to the Mosaic law [BECNT, St, WBC]. The law of Moses operates either under the power of the Holy Spirit, restoring and reviving the godly, or the power of sin and death [BECNT]. God's law is not sin, but it occasioned both sin and death [St].

5. The term 'law of the Spirit' is a metonymy for 'Holy Spirit' and 'law of sin and death' is a metonymy for 'sin and death' [CEV].

QUESTION—How is the term 'spirit' used here?

It refers to the Holy Spirit [AB, BECNT, Gdt, HNTC, Ho, ICC1, ICC2, Mu, NAC, NICNT, NTC, SSA, St, TH, TNTC, WBC; all versions].

QUESTION—How is the genitive phrase τῆς ζωῆς 'of life' related to the preceding noun phrase τοῦ πνεύματος 'the Spirit'?

1. Τῆς ζωῆς 'of life' tells what the Holy Spirit gives [AB, BECNT, HNTC, Ho, ICC1, ICC2, Mor, Mu, NICNT, NTC, SSA, TH, WBC; CEV, GW,

NCV, NET, NLT, REB, TEV]: the Spirit who gives life. He is the author of life and he is life [ICC1, Mu].
2. It describes both cause and effect; the Spirit proceeds from the life that is Jesus himself, and causes or produces life in the believer [Gdt].
3. Τῆς ζωῆς 'of life' describes τοῦ πνεύματος 'of the Spirit' [BAGD, WBC]: the Spirit of Life. The terms 'Spirit' and 'life' represent two aspects of the same dynamic outpouring of life from the creator to his creatures, reflecting man's total dependence on the creator for breath/spirit of life.

QUESTION—What is the 'law of the Spirit of life'?
1. It is the authority and power of the Spirit of God that liberates from the old age and confers life [ICC1, ICC2, Mor, Mu, NICNT, SSA, TH, TNTC]. It is the power of the life-giving Spirit [NLT]. It is the forceful and effective operation of the Holy Spirit at work in the lives of God's people [NTC]. It is the principle of new life in the Spirit [AB]. The power of the Spirit produces life in the believer [Gdt].
2. It is the Mosaic law, appropriated and used by faith in the realm of the Holy Spirit, reviving and restoring, since the result of the Spirit's work is life [BECNT]. It is the law in its eschatological expression, understood in its proper function and empowered by the Holy Spirit to be lived out in the lives of believers [WBC].
3. It is the gospel [Ho, St]. It is the new religion brought by Christ [HNTC].

in[a] Christ Jesus has-freed[b] you from[c] the law[d] of sin[e] and of death.[f]

TEXT—Instead of σε 'you', some manuscripts read με 'me'. GNT selects the reading σε 'you' with a B decision, indicating that the text is almost certain. The reading με 'me' is taken by NTC; KJV, NIV, TEV.

LEXICON—a. ἐν with dative object (LN 83.13, 89.119): 'in' [AB, BECNT, ICC2, LN (83.13, 89.119), WBC; KJV, NASB, NET, NRSV, REB], 'made possible in' [HNTC], 'in union with' [LN (89.119); TEV], 'through' [NICNT, NTC; GW, NCV, NIV, NLT], 'that comes from' [CEV].

b. aorist act. indic. of ἐλευθερόω (LN 37.135) (BAGD 2. p. 251): 'to free' [BAGD; NLT], 'to set free' [AB, BAGD, BECNT, ICC2, LN, NICNT, NTC, WBC; CEV, GW, NASB, NET, NIV, NRSV, REB, TEV], 'to make free' [KJV, NCV], 'to release' [LN], 'to liberate' [HNTC].

c. ἀπό with genitive object (LN 89.122): 'from' [AB, BECNT, HNTC, ICC2, NICNT, NTC, WBC; all versions].

d. νόμος (LN **33.333**, 33.55) (BAGD 2. p. 542): 'law' [AB, BAGD, BECNT, ICC2, LN (**33.333**), NICNT, NTC, WBC; all versions except GW, NLT], 'the Law' (meaning Torah) [LN (33.55)], 'old religion' [HNTC], 'standards' [GW], 'principle' [BAGD], 'power' [NLT], not explicit [CEV]. The phrase 'the law of sin and death' is translated 'sin and death' [CEV].

e. ἁμαρτία (LN 88.289) (BAGD 3. p. 43): 'sin' [AB, BAGD, BECNT, HNTC, ICC2, NICNT, NTC, WBC; all versions].

f. θάνατος (LN 23.99): 'death' [AB, BECNT, HNTC, ICC2, NICNT, NTC, WBC; all versions].

QUESTION—With what should the phrase 'in Christ Jesus' be taken?
1. It should be taken with the verb that follows [AB, BECNT, Ho, ICC1, ICC2, Mu, NICNT, NTC, SSA, WBC]: it has set you free through or in union with Christ Jesus.
2. It should be taken with 'life' [TH; CEV]: the life is in Christ Jesus, who is the source of the life.
3. It should be taken with 'law' [Gdt, HNTC]. It is in Christ that the new law or religion is made possible [HNTC]. The reign of the Spirit was inaugurated by Christ [Gdt].

QUESTION—What area of meaning is intended by the term νόμος 'law' here?
1. It refers to the Mosaic law [BECNT, Gdt, HNTC, Ho, LN, St, WBC]. The Mosaic law was a way of life and a religion for the Jewish people, but sin seized and perverted it, leading the people into death [HNTC]. It is the law in its baneful effect over those who still belong to the old epoch [WBC].
2. It refers to a principle or governing power [AB, BAGD, ICC1, ICC2, Mor, Mu, NAC, NICNT, NTC, SSA, TH].

QUESTION—How do the genitives τῆς ἁμαρτίας καὶ τοῦ θανάτου 'of sin and death' relate to the noun νόμος 'law'?
1. 'The law of sin and death' refers to the binding authority and power of sin, which leads to death [AB, Gdt, ICC1, Mu, NAC, NICNT, NTC, SSA; NLT]. The law uses sin to bind human weakness to death [WBC]. The words 'sin' and 'death' are combined to form the antithesis of 'life' [Gdt].
2. The two genitives apply separately to νόμος 'law': the law of sin and the law of death. The law may be used in the realm of the Spirit, resulting in life, or in the realm of sin and of death [BECNT].
3. The religion of the law of Moses is abused by sin and leads to death [HNTC]. God's law provokes sin in fallen people and thus brings about death [St].

8:3 For the impossible[a] (thing) of-the Law,

LEXICON—a. ἀδύνατος (LN 71.3, 74.22) (BAGD 2.b. p. 19): 'impossible' [BAGD, LN (71.3)], 'incapable, not capable, unable' [LN (74.22)]. The phrase τὸ ἀδύνατον τοῦ νόμου 'the impossible thing of the Law' is translated 'the Law of Moses cannot do this' [CEV], 'which/what the law could not do' [BECNT, NICNT, NTC; KJV, NASB, NET, NRSV, REB, TEV], 'which/what the law was unable to do' [ICC2, WBC], 'what the law was powerless to do' [AB; NIV], 'the law was without power' [NCV], 'which the law could never effect' [HNTC], 'it is impossible to do what God's standards demand' [GW], 'the law of Moses could not save us' [NLT].

QUESTION—What was it that the law could not do?
1. The law could not free people from the power of sin and death [AB, Ho, NICNT, NTC], it could not overcome the power of sin and put people right with God [AB]. It could not save people [HNTC; NLT], or give eschatological life [NICNT], it could not deal with sin [WBC], conquer sin [NAC], or get rid of sin [ICC1]. The law could not condemn sin in the flesh [Gdt, ICC2, Mu]. It could not produce righteousness, the fulfillment of the law [BECNT]. It could not justify or sanctify [St].
2. This is a personification and really refers to what we cannot do, which is to be saved by obeying the law of God [SSA; GW]: what was impossible for us to do by trying to obey the Law.
3. The new religion frees from the old religion, which the law could not do [HNTC].

in that[a] it-was-weak[b] through[c] the flesh,[d]

LEXICON—a. ἐν ᾧ (LN 89.26) (BAGD IV.6.d. p. 261): 'in that' [BECNT, NICNT; KJV, NIV], 'because' [BAGD, HNTC, ICC2, LN, NTC; CEV, NCV, NET, REB, TEV], 'because of' [GW, NLT]. The phrase ἐν ᾧ ἠσθένει 'in that it was weakened' is translated 'weak as it was' [NASB], 'weakened (by)' [AB; NRSV].
b. imperf. act. indic. of ἀσθενέω (LN **74.26**) (BAGD 1.b. p. 115): 'to be weak' [BECNT, HNTC, ICC2, LN, NTC, WBC; KJV, NASB, TEV]. 'to be weakened' [AB, BAGD, NICNT; NET, NIV, NRSV], 'to be made weak' [NCV], not explicit [NLT]. This entire clause is translated 'because our selfish desires make the Law weak' [CEV], 'because of the weakness our human nature has' [GW], 'because human weakness robbed it of all potency' [REB].
c. διά with genitive object (LN 89.76, 90.8) (BAGD A.IV. p. 181): 'through' [BECNT, HNTC, ICC2, LN (89.76, 90.8), NTC, WBC; KJV, NASB, NET], 'by' [AB, LN (89.76), NICNT; NCV, NIV, NRSV], 'by means of' [LN (89.76)], 'because of' [BAGD], not explicit [CEV, GW, NLT, REB, TEV].
d. σάρξ (LN 26.7) (BAGD 7. p. 744): 'flesh' [AB, BAGD, BECNT, HNTC, ICC2, NICNT, NTC, WBC; KJV, NASB, NET, NRSV], 'sinful nature' [NIV, NLT], 'human nature' [LN; GW, TEV], 'human weakness' [REB], 'our selfish desires' [CEV], 'our sinful selves' [NCV].

QUESTION—What relationship is indicated by ἐν ᾧ 'in that'?
1. It indicates reason [AB, BECNT, Gdt, HNTC, Ho, ICC2, Mor, NICNT, NTC, SSA, WBC; all versions]: it was impossible because it was weak.
2. It is modal [ICC1]: in which it was weak, or its weakness being this.

QUESTION—What area of meaning is intended by the term σάρξ 'flesh'?
It is sinful human nature [Mu, NTC; GW, NCV, NIV, NLT, REB], unregenerate human nature [BECNT], the self-directed sinful nature [SSA], the fallen, selfish nature [St]. It is the focus on this world that all people

naturally have [NICNT]. It is human depravity [Ho], the depraved instinct, human self-complacency [Gdt].

QUESTION—What is the relation of the first two clauses in 8:3 to the rest of the sentence?
1. There is an anacoluthon or broken construction in which these two clauses require an implied predicate expressing what the main idea would be: *he did*. That is, God did what the law could not do in that it was weak through the flesh [AB, Gdt, HNTC, Mor, Mu, NAC, NICNT, NTC, SSA, St, WBC; NASB, NET, NIV, NRSV, REB, TEV].
2. These clauses are parenthetical to and explanatory of the main thought, which is that God condemned sin in the flesh (which the law couldn't do because it was weak) [ICC1, ICC2; GW, NCV], or that God saved us, which the law could not do, etc. [NLT].

God, having-sent[a] his-own Son in[b] (the) likeness[c] of-flesh[d] of-sin[e] and for[f] sin,[g]

LEXICON—a. aorist act. participle of πέμπω (LN 15.66) (BAGD 1. p. 642): 'to send' [AB, BAGD, BECNT, HNTC, ICC2, NICNT, NTC, WBC; all versions].
  b. ἐν with dative object (LN 13.8) (BAGD I.4.d. p.259): 'in' [AB, BECNT, HNTC, ICC2, LN, NICNT, NTC, WBC; KJV, NASB, NET, NIV, NLT, NRSV, REB], 'with (a nature)' [TEV], not explicit [CEV, GW, NCV].
  c. ὁμοίωμα (LN 64.3) (BAGD 4. p. 567): 'likeness' [BECNT, ICC2, LN, NTC, WBC; KJV, NASB, NET, NIV, NRSV, REB], 'very likeness' [WBC], 'form' [HNTC], 'form like that (of)' [AB]. The phrase ἐν ὁμοιώματι σαρκὸς ἁμαρτίας 'in likeness of flesh of sin' is translated 'to be like us sinners' [CEV], 'to have a human nature as sinners' [GW], 'with the same human life that others use for sin' [NCV], 'in a human body like ours, except that ours are sinful' [NLT], 'with a nature like man's sinful nature' [TEV].
  d. σάρξ (LN 8.4, 26.7) (BAGD 7. p. 744): 'flesh' [AB, BAGD, BECNT, HNTC, ICC2, NICNT, NTC, WBC; KJV, NASB, NET, NRSV], 'sinful man' [NIV], 'sinful nature' [REB], 'human nature' [LN (26.7); GW, TEV], 'human life' [NCV], 'human body' [NLT], 'physical body, body' [LN (8.4)], not explicit [CEV].
  e. ἁμαρτία (LN 88.289): 'sin' [LN]. This genitive noun is translated as an adjective: 'sinful' [AB, BECNT, ICC2, NICNT, NTC, WBC; KJV, NASB, NET, NIV, NLT, NRSV, REB, TEV]; as a noun: 'like us sinners' [CEV], 'as sinners' [GW], 'that others use for sin' [NCV]; as a descriptive phrase: 'which had passed under sin's rule' [HNTC].
  f. περί with genitive object (LN 89.6) (BAGD 1.g. p. 644): 'for' [LN, NTC; KJV], 'to deal with' [HNTC, ICC2; NRSV, REB], 'concerning' [LN, NICNT; NET], 'to pay for' [GW], 'as a sacrifice for' [NLT], 'as an offering for' [NASB], 'an offering to pay for' [NCV], 'for the sake of' [AB], 'to take away, to atone for' [BAGD], not explicit [BECNT, WBC].

The phrase 'for sin' is translated 'as a sin offering' [BECNT, WBC], 'to be a sin offering' [NIV], 'to be a sacrifice for our sin' [CEV], 'to do away with sin' [TEV].

g. ἁμαρτία (LN 88.289): 'sin' [AB, BECNT, HNTC, ICC2, NICNT, NTC, WBC; all versions]. This singular noun is translated in the plural: 'our sins' [NLT].

QUESTION—What is meant by the verb 'sent'?
1. It focuses on the incarnation [AB, HNTC, Ho, ICC1, NTC, St]. It implies his preexistence [AB, Gdt].
2. It focuses mainly on the redemptive aspect of his death, though not excluding a reference to the incarnation [Mor, NICNT].
3. It means that Christ's ministry and message were authorized by God, but this does not necessarily imply that Christ was preexistent [WBC].

QUESTION—What is meant by the term ὁμοίωμα 'likeness'?
Christ participated fully in the same flesh that sinful men had [AB, BECNT, HNTC, ICC2, NAC, WBC], though without participating in sin itself [AB, BECNT, NICNT, SSA]. Christ's body was like ours because it too was a body of flesh, but it was only *like* ours because his body was not sinful as ours are [ICC2]. He had a body or human nature that was like the body or human nature of people who sin [SSA]. He participated fully in the old age of the flesh in that his body was subject to the powers of the old age, such as sickness and death [BECNT, WBC]. He took on such flesh without ceasing to be what he had always been [ICC2]. Christ came in the closest relation to sinful humanity that was possible without actually being sinful himself, and the word 'likeness' guards the truth of his sinlessness [Mu]. His nature was susceptible of pain, weariness, and sorrow, but not sinful [Ho]. His humanity was real, but sinless [St, TNTC].

QUESTION—What area of meaning is intended by the preposition περί 'for'?
1. It has the general meaning 'concerning' sin [AB, Gdt, HNTC, ICC2, Mor, Mu, NICNT, NTC; NET]: having sent his own Son concerning sin. He came to deal with sin [AB, ICC2, Mor].
2. It has the specific meaning 'as a sin offering' [BECNT, Ho, NAC, NICNT, SSA, St, TNTC, WBC; CEV, GW, NASB, NCV, NIV, NLT, TEV]: having sent his own Son *as an offering* for sin. Some event is required with the phrase 'and for sin' so that this means that God sent his Son in order that his Son might atone for our sin [SSA]. He came as a sin offering, but there is also a more general sense in which he came to deal with sin [ICC1].

condemned[a] the sin[b] in[c] the flesh,[d]

LEXICON—a. aorist act. indic. of κατακρίνω (LN 56.31) (BAGD p. 412): 'to condemn' [AB, BAGD, BECNT, HNTC, ICC2, NICNT, NTC, WBC; all versions except NCV, NLT, REB], 'to destroy' [NCV, NLT], 'to pass judgment against' [REB], 'to pronounce sentence on' [BAGD]. This phrase is translated 'God used Christ's body to condemn sin' [CEV].

b. ἁμαρτία (LN 88.289) (BAGD 3. p. 43): 'sin' [AB, BAGD, BECNT, HNTC, ICC2, NICNT, NTC, WBC; all versions except NLT], 'sin's control' [NLT].
c. ἐν with dative object (LN 83.13): 'in' [AB, BECNT, HNTC, ICC2, NICNT, NTC, WBC; all versions except CEV, NCV, NLT], 'within' [REB], not explicit [CEV, NCV, NLT].
d. σάρξ (LN 8.4, 26.7) (BAGD 4. p. 743): 'flesh' [AB, BECNT, HNTC, ICC2, NICNT, NTC, WBC; KJV, NASB, NET, NRSV], 'physical body' [LN (8.4)], 'human nature' [BAGD, LN (26.7); TEV], 'mortal nature' [BAGD]. The phrase 'in the flesh' is translated as referring to Christ's body (LN 8.4), focusing on where the condemnation took place: 'Christ's body' [CEV], 'a human life' [NCV]. It is also translated as referring to the sinful human nature (LN 26.7), focusing on where the sin was that was condemned: 'our corrupt nature' [GW], 'within that very nature' [REB], 'sinful man' [NIV]. The phrase 'sin in the flesh' is translated 'sin's control over us' [NLT].

QUESTION—What does it mean that he 'condemned sin in the flesh'?
1. God executed his judgment on sin through Christ's death [AB, BECNT, HNTC, Ho, ICC1, Mor, Mu, NAC, NICNT, NTC, St, TNTC]. In Christ God also broke the power of sin [AB, ICC2, Mu, WBC].
2. Christ's sinless life represents a living condemnation of sin, that it is unworthy of existing in humanity [Gdt].

QUESTION—With what does ἐν τῇ σαρκί 'in the flesh' go?
1. It goes with 'condemned'; that is, in the human body of Jesus as he was on the cross God condemned sin [AB, BECNT, Ho, ICC1, ICC2, Mor, Mu, NAC, NICNT, NTC, SSA, St, TNTC, WBC; CEV, NCV]. It implies the humanity of Christ but also the sphere of human weakness into which Christ entered to do his work [NICNT].
2. It goes with condemned, but refers to the life Jesus lived in the flesh, not his sacrificial death [Gdt]. That is, in Jesus' earthly life lived in human flesh he condemned sinfulness as unworthy of existing in humanity.
3. It goes with 'sin' [TH; GW, NIV, NLT, REB]: he condemned the sin that was in fleshly human nature.

8:4 in-order-that the righteous-requirement[a] of-the Law might-be-fulfilled[b] in[c] us

LEXICON—a. δικαίωμα (LN 33.334) (BAGD 1. p. 198): 'righteous requirement' [ICC2, NICNT, NTC; NET], 'righteous requirements' [NIV], 'requirement' [AB, BAGD, HNTC, LN, WBC; NASB, NLT], 'righteous demands' [TEV], 'righteous decree' [BAGD, LN], 'just requirement' [NRSV], 'righteousness' [KJV], 'ordinance' [BECNT], 'commandment' [REB], 'what the Law commands' [CEV], 'God's standards' [GW]. This entire phrase is translated 'so that we could be the kind of people the law correctly wants us to be' [NCV], 'so that we would

do what the Law commands' [CEV]. This word represents one harmonious divine will, as opposed to a series of commandments [Mor].
  b. aorist pass. subj. of πληρόω (LN **59.33**) (BAGD 4.b. p. 671): 'to be fulfilled' [BAGD, BECNT, HNTC, ICC2, NICNT, WBC; KJV, NASB, NET, NRSV], 'to be fully met' [AB, NTC; NIV], 'to be completely met' [**LN**], 'to be fully accomplished' [NLT], 'to be fully satisfied' [TEV], 'to be made complete' [**LN**], not explicit [CEV]. This entire phrase is translated 'so that we may do all that the Law requires' [**LN**], 'so that we may do everything the Law requires' [**LN**], 'so that the commandment of the law may find fulfillment in us' [REB], 'therefore we are able to meet God's standards' [GW], 'so we could be the kind of people the law correctly wants us to be' [NCV].
  c. ἐν with dative object (LN 83.13): 'in' [AB, BECNT, HNTC, ICC2, NICNT, NTC, WBC; KJV, NASB, NET, NIV, NRSV, REB, TEV], 'for' [NLT], not explicit [CEV, GW, NCV].
QUESTION—What relationship is indicated by ἵνα 'in order that'?
  1. It indicates the purpose for which God condemned sin in the flesh [AB, Gdt, HNTC, Ho, Mu, NICNT, St, TH, WBC].
  2. It indicates both the purpose and the result of Christ's work of redemption [ICC2, Mor, NTC].
QUESTION—In what sense is the righteous decree of the Law fulfilled?
  1. God met the requirement through the death of Christ [AB, Ho, NAC, NICNT]. The righteousness required by the law is forensically applied to the believer through Christ's obedience and death [NICNT].
  2. The believer's life and conduct are transformed so that he fulfills the law by living as the law rightly requires [BECNT, Gdt, ICC1, ICC2, Mor, Mu, NTC, SSA, St, TH, TNTC, WBC; CEV, GW, NCV]. By means of the working of the Holy Spirit within them they fulfill the law's requirements in their living [NTC]. Only Christ has completely fulfilled the law's requirements, but in Christ and through the indwelling of the Holy Spirit we begin to live the kind of life God wants, for justification and sanctification are never to be separated [Mor]. It is not fulfilled perfectly, but is fulfilled in the sense that their lives are turned in the direction of obedience [ICC2]. The Holy Spirit enables them to do God's will spontaneously [TNTC].

the-(ones) walking[a] not according-to[b] (the) flesh[c] but according-to (the) Spirit/spirit.[d]

LEXICON—a. pres. act. participle of περιπατέω (LN 15.227, **41.11**) (BAGD 2.a.δ. p. 649): 'to walk' [BECNT, ICC2, LN (15.227), NICNT, NTC, WBC; KJV, NASB, NET, NRSV], 'to live' [LN (**41.11**); GW, NCV, NIV, TEV], 'to behave' [LN (41.11)], 'to conduct oneself' [AB], 'to follow' [NLT]. This word refers to lifestyle and daily conduct [NICNT], the walk of life [BAGD]. The phrase 'the ones walking not according to' is translated 'whose lives are determined not by' [HNTC], 'whose conduct is no longer controlled by' [REB]. This entire phrase is translated 'by obeying the Spirit instead of our own desires' [CEV].

b. κατά with accusative object (LN 89.8) (BAGD II.5.a.γ. p. 407): 'according to' [AB, BAGD, BECNT, ICC2, NICNT, NTC; NASB, NET, NIV, NRSV, TEV], 'in accordance with' [BAGD, LN, WBC], 'by' [GW], 'determined by' [HNTC], 'following' [NCV], '(who) follow' [NLT], 'in conformity with' [BAGD], 'after' [KJV]. The phrase 'who walk not according to' is translated 'who no longer follow' [NLT], 'whose conduct is no longer controlled by' [REB], 'instead of (obey) our own desires' [CEV].

c. σάρξ (LN 26.7) (BAGD 7. p. 744): 'flesh' [AB, BAGD, BECNT, HNTC, ICC2, NICNT, NTC, WBC; KJV, NASB, NET, NRSV], 'the old nature' [REB], 'human nature' [LN; TEV], 'our corrupt nature' [GW], 'the sinful nature' [NIV], 'our sinful nature' [NLT], 'our sinful selves' [NCV], 'our own desires' [CEV]. This word lacks the definite article in the Greek but is translated as having the article [AB, BECNT, HNTC, ICC2, NICNT, NTC, WBC; KJV, NASB, NET, NIV, NRSV].

d. πνεῦμα (LN 12.18, 26.9) (BAGD 5.g.α. p. 677): 'Spirit' [AB, BAGD, BECNT, HNTC, ICC2, LN (12.18), NICNT, NTC, WBC; all versions except GW], 'Holy Spirit' [LN (12.18)], 'our spiritual nature' [GW], 'spirit, inner being' [LN (26.9)].

QUESTION—What relationship is indicated by the participial phrase 'the ones not walking according to the flesh'?

1. It is descriptive: the righteous requirement of the law is fulfilled in Christians, who are people who don't live according to the flesh [BECNT, Mor, Mu, NAC, NICNT, NTC, WBC]. This passage is descriptive, describing the essential nature and source of Christian living, not hortatory [BECNT, NICNT]. However, it does give a hint about the obligation expressed in 8:12–13 [NTC]. Those in whom this has been met show the fruit of it in the kind of life they live [NAC].
2. It is conditional: it is fulfilled by imputation, provided we don't live according to the flesh [AB, Ho]. It describes the class of people who are entitled to appropriate Christ's justification [Ho].
3. It is instrumental: it is fulfilled by our walking according to Spirit instead of according to the flesh [Gdt, ICC2, SSA, St]. Holiness, which was God's purpose, consists of fulfilling what the law requires [St].

QUESTION—What area of meaning is intended by the term πνεῦμα 'Spirit/spirit'?

1. 'Spirit' is the Holy Spirit [AB, BECNT, Gdt, HNTC, Ho, ICC1, ICC2, Mu, NICNT, NTC, SSA, St, TH, TNTC, WBC; all versions except GW]. 'Flesh' and 'Spirit' are redemptive-historical categories representing the two realms of salvation history [NICNT] and the governing power of the two eras in salvation history [BECNT], but they are also ontological categories, describing the being or nature of a person by which behavior is determined [BECNT].

2. The word 'spirit' refers to the spiritual aspect of humanity, 'our spiritual nature' [GW].

8:5 For those being[a] according-to[b] (the) flesh[c] set-their-mind-on[d] the-things of-the flesh,

LEXICON—a. pres. participle of εἰμί (LN 13.1) (BAGD III.6.b. p. 225): 'to be' [LN], 'to live' [BAGD]. This participle is translated as a finite verb: '(those who) live' [AB, NTC; GW, NCV, NET, NIV, NRSV, REB, TEV], '(who) exist' [WBC], '(those who) are' [BECNT, NICNT; NASB], '(they that) are' [KJV], not explicit [HNTC, ICC2; CEV, NLT].

b. κατά with accusative object (LN 89.8): 'according to' [AB, BECNT, LN, NICNT, NTC; NASB, NET, NIV, NRSV], 'by' [GW], 'in accordance with' [LN], 'in terms of' [WBC], 'on the level of' [REB], 'following' [NCV]. The phrase οἱ...κατὰ...ὄντες 'those being according to' is translated 'those whose lives are determined by' [HNTC, ICC2], 'people who are ruled by' [CEV], 'those who are dominated by' [NLT], 'who live as (their human nature) tells them to' [TEV].

c. σάρξ (LN 8.63, 26.7) (BAGD 7. p. 744): 'flesh' [BAGD, LN (8.63)], 'the flesh' [AB, BECNT, HNTC, ICC2, NICNT, NTC, WBC; KJV, NASB, NET, NRSV], 'human nature' [LN (26.7); TEV], 'the old nature' [REB], 'the corrupt nature' [GW], 'the sinful nature' [NIV, NLT], 'their sinful selves' [NCV], 'their desires' [CEV].

d. pres. act. indic. of φρονέω (LN 31.1) (BAGD 2. p. 866): 'to set (one's) mind on' [BAGD, HNTC, NTC; NASB, NIV, NRSV], 'to have one's mind set on' [NICNT], 'to mind' [KJV], 'to think on' [BECNT], 'to think about' [NCV, NLT], 'to be concerned about' [AB], 'to have the attitude of' [GW], 'to have one's outlook shaped by' [NET], 'to have one's outlook formed by' [REB], 'to have one's mind controlled by' [TEV], 'to be intent on' [BAGD], 'to regard' [LN (31.1)]. The phrase τὰ τῆς σαρκὸς φρονοῦσιν 'set their minds on the things of the flesh' is translated 'are on the flesh's side' [ICC2], 'take the side of the flesh' [WBC], 'think only of themselves' [CEV].

QUESTION—What relationship is indicated by γάρ 'for'?

1. It introduces grounds for what is stated in 8:4 [AB, BECNT, Ho, ICC2, Mor], which is about walking according to the Spirit instead of the flesh [AB, ICC2], or about how those who live by the Spirit are able to fulfill the law [BECNT].

1.1 The grounds for 8:4 includes 8:5–6 [Ho]. That is, men must be holy because sin is death, but holiness is life and peace.

1.2 The grounds for 8:4 includes 8:5–8 [AB, Mor].

1.3 The grounds for 8:4 includes 8:5–11 [BECNT, ICC2, WBC].

2. It introduces the following argument in which he explains why the flesh brings death and the spirit brings life [NICNT].

3. It introduces the definition of living in the flesh and living in the Spirit [HNTC].

4. It introduces a further description of the two classes of people mentioned in 8:4, which are those who live according to the Spirit and those who live according to the flesh [NTC]. It introduces confirmation and explanation of the contrast between 'flesh' and 'spirit' at the end of 8:4 [Mu].

QUESTION—What does it mean to 'set one's mind on' the things of the flesh or the Spirit?

It means to set the will to adopt an entire way of thinking and living based on the essential nature of a person, whether unregenerate or regenerate [BECNT]. It means to have the basic disposition or direction of one's life either on God's side or on the side of the sinful human nature [NTC]. It means to take the side of someone or something, and allow that person or thing to determine the direction of one's life [ICC2, NAC]. It means to have one's very being dominated by the unregenerate nature [AB]. To set one's mind on something means to have a settled way of understanding or to maintain a particular attitude [WBC]. It is to look at things totally from that one viewpoint [Mor]. To set one's mind on something includes thinking, willing, and aspiring [Gdt], reason, will, and affections [ICC1, TH]. It means that the thoughts, interests, affections, and purpose are absorbed by that object [Mu, St].

but the-(ones) according-to Spirit/spirit[a] the-(things)[b] of-the Spirit/spirit.

LEXICON—a. πνεῦμα (LN 12.18, 26.9) (BAGD 5.d.β. p. 677): 'the Spirit' [AB, BAGD, BECNT, HNTC, ICC2, LN (12.18), NICNT, NTC, WBC; all versions except GW, REB], 'Holy Spirit' [LN (12.18); CEV], 'the spirit' [REB], 'spiritual nature' [GW], 'spirit, inner being' [LN (26.9)].

b. The phrase τὰ τοῦ πνεύματος is translated 'the (things) of the Spirit' [BECNT, NICNT, NTC; KJV, NASB, NET, NRSV], 'things of the Spirit' [AB], 'the affairs of the Spirit' [HNTC], 'the things the Spirit wants them to do' [NCV], 'what the Spirit wants' [TEV], 'what the Spirit desires' [NIV], 'the things that please the Spirit' [NLT], '(are on) the Spirit's side' [ICC2], 'the side of the Spirit' [WBC], 'spiritual things' [CEV], 'the spiritual nature's attitude' [GW], 'the spiritual outlook' [REB].

QUESTION—What are the 'things of the Spirit/spirit'?

It refers to what the Holy Spirit desires in our behavior [SSA; NCV, NIV, NLT]. It refers to having one's mind focused on God, the invisible one who gives meaning and authority to existence [HNTC]. It refers to those things that are dear to the Spirit of God [NTC]. It refers to the fruit of the Spirit [NAC]. It refers to the promptings of the Spirit; their aspirations are changed and their lives manifest the fruit of the Spirit [AB]. It is a contemplation of what the Spirit does when he chooses to move, and is the opposite of a focus on oneself, including one's own Christian service [Mor].

2. It refers to the attitude of one's spiritual nature [GW], its outlook [REB].

QUESTION—How does this verse relate to the overall argument of this section?

1. He is speaking in ontological terms, saying that believers, who by nature are of the Spirit, will consequently walk or live according to the Spirit [AB, BECNT, St]. He is defining what it means to be in the Spirit, which is to have one's life focused on God and what God wants [HNTC]. The nature determines the mindset, which then determines the pattern of conduct and also results in a spiritual state, whether of life and peace, or death and enmity [St].
2. He is speaking in behavioral terms, saying that the behavior of believers may be governed by either nature, by the Spirit or by the flesh [ICC2, NTC, WBC].

8:6 For the mind-set[a] of-the flesh (is/brings)[b] death,[c]

LEXICON—a. φρόνημα (LN **26.15**) (BAGD p. 866): 'mind-set' [BAGD, BECNT], 'mind' [ICC2, NICNT, NTC; CEV, NIV, NLT, NRSV], 'outlook' [LN; NET, REB], 'way of thinking' [BAGD, LN, WBC], 'thinking' [NCV], 'concern' [AB], 'attitude' [GW], not explicit [TEV]. This noun is translated as a verb phrase: 'to have one's mind set on' [HNTC]. The phrase τὸ φρόνημα τῆς σαρκός 'the mind-set of the flesh' is translated 'the mind set on the flesh' [NASB], 'to set the mind on the flesh' [NRSV], 'to those whose outlook is formed by their human nature' [**LN**], 'if our minds are ruled by our desires' [CEV], 'to be carnally minded' [KJV], 'if people's thinking is controlled by the sinful self' [NCV], 'if your sinful nature controls your mind' [NLT], 'to be controlled by human nature' [TEV]. This word connotes mental processes as well as the will and the affections [NICNT].

b. There is no lexical entry for this word in the Greek text. The implied verb is translated 'is' [AB, ICC2, NICNT, NTC, WBC; KJV, NASB, NET, NIV, NRSV], 'leads to' [GW], 'results in' [BECNT, HNTC; TEV], '(that) spells' [REB], not explicit [CEV]. This clause is translated as a conditional statement: 'if people's thinking is controlled by the sinful self, there is death' [NCV], 'if your sinful nature controls your minds, there is death' [NLT], 'if our minds are ruled by our desires we will die' [CEV].

c. θάνατος (LN 23.99) (BAGD 2.a. p. 351): 'death' [AB, BAGD, BECNT, HNTC, ICC2, LN, NICNT, NTC, WBC; all versions except CEV]. This noun is translated as a verb phrase 'we will die' [CEV]. It refers to spiritual death [BAGD].

QUESTION—What relationship is indicated by γάρ 'for'?

It continues the argument begun in the previous verse [BECNT, Ho, Mor, NICNT; NIV, NRSV]. It introduces an amplification in 8:6–8 of what was begun in 8:5 [SSA]. It introduces the grounds for an implied affirmation of the absoluteness of the opposition of flesh and Spirit; the opposition of flesh and Spirit is absolute because the mind determined by the flesh leads to death and the mind determined by the Spirit leads to life [HNTC]. It introduces an explanation of the conflict between the Spirit and the flesh in the previous verse [ICC2, Mor]. It introduces an explanation of the moral necessity of what he has just described, which is that the inward moral state always leads to aspiration, aspiration leads to action, which in turn leads to an inevitable end, whether life or death [Gdt]. It introduces 8:6 as an explanation of 8:5 [Mu].

QUESTION—What is the nature of this 'death'?

It is death in the fullest sense, eternal eschatological judgment [AB, BECNT, Gdt, NICNT, SSA, WBC]. It is to be cut off from God, the source of life itself [HNTC, Mu]. It is the doom awaiting the world [NTC]. It is the destruction that is set in contrast to eternal life [NAC]. It is to be cut off from the life that is truly life [Mor]. It is a death in the present, as well as eventual death of body and soul [ICC1]. It is spiritual death [BAGD, Ho], being cut off from spiritual life [Ho].

but the mind-set of-the Spirit/spirit,[a] life[b] and peace;[c]

LEXICON—a. φρόνημα (LN 26.15) (BAGD p. 866): 'mind-set' [BAGD], 'outlook' [LN], 'way of thinking' [BAGD, LN]. The phrase τὸ... φρόνημα τοῦ πνεύματος 'the mind-set of the Spirit/spirit' is translated 'if our minds are ruled by the Spirit' [CEV], 'the spiritual nature's attitude leads to life and peace' [GW].

b. πνεῦμα (LN 12.18, 26.9): 'Spirit' [LN (12.18); CEV, NASB, NCV, NET, NIV, NRSV, TEV], 'Holy Spirit' [LN (12.18); NLT], 'spirit, inner being' [LN (26.9)], 'the level of the spirit' [REB], 'the spiritual nature' [GW]. The phrase 'mind-set of the Spirit' is translated 'to be spiritually minded' [KJV].

c. ζωή (LN 23.88) (BAGD 2.b.α. p. 340): 'life' [AB, BAGD, BECNT, HNTC, ICC2, LN, NICNT, NTC, WBC; all versions].

d. εἰρήνη (LN 22.42) (BAGD 3. p. 227): 'peace' [AB, BAGD, BECNT, HNTC, ICC2, LN, NICNT, NTC, WBC; all versions].

QUESTION—Is this peace primarily objective or subjective?

1. It refers to a subjective inner peace [Gdt, Mor, Mu, NAC, NTC, SSA, TH]. It is the enjoyment of all that being reconciled to God means [Mor]. It is the inward feeling of tranquility that accompanies Christian faith and living, and which is shown in the fact of not being subject to the fear of death and judgment [Gdt]. There is a sense of being at one with God that brings tranquility of heart and mind [Mu].

2. It primarily refers to the objective reality of salvation that the believer has entered into [NICNT]. It is friendship with God [AB]. It is future eschatological blessing [WBC].

3. It is both a subjective experience as well as an objective relationship with God [HNTC]. It is the state of reconciliation as well as a comprehensive sense of harmony and tranquility resulting from that reconciliation [ICC1].

8:7 because the mind-set of-the flesh (is) enmity^a toward^b God,
LEXICON—a. ἔχθρα (LN 39.10) (BAGD p. 331): 'enmity' [BAGD, BECNT, HNTC, ICC2, LN; KJV, REB], 'hostility' [AB, NTC, WBC], 'hostile attitude' [GW]. This noun is translated as an adjective: 'hostile' [NICNT; NASB, NET, NIV, NLT, NRSV]; as a phrase: 'being an enemy of' [LN]. The phrase 'enmity toward God' is translated 'at enmity against God' [BECNT], 'in a state of enmity against God' [HNTC], 'they are against God' [NCV]. This clause is translated 'our desires fight against God' [CEV], 'a person becomes an enemy of God when he is controlled by his human nature' [TEV].
  b. εἰς with accusative object (LN 90.23, 90.59) (BAGD 4.c.α. p. 229): 'toward' [ICC2, LN (90.59), NICNT; GW, KJV, NASB], 'against' [BAGD, BECNT, HNTC; CEV, NCV], 'to' [AB, LN (90.59), NTC; NET, NIV, NLT, NRSV], 'with' [REB], 'with respect to' [LN (90.23)], not explicit [TEV].
QUESTION—What relationship is indicated by διότι 'because'?
  1. It introduces grounds, elaborated in 8:7–8, for the statement in 8:6 about why the mindset of the flesh leads to death [Gdt, Mor, NICNT, NTC, SSA; GW]. It introduces grounds for the statement made in 8:6a about the mind of the flesh resulting in death, which is that it is hostile to God and cannot submit to his law [ICC1, Mu, TH].
  2. It introduces grounds for the claims made in 8:5–6 about why those who are 'according to the flesh' are destined for death, which is that they are unable to submit to God's law [BECNT, ICC2].
  3. It introduces grounds for the statement made in the second half of this verse: the reason that the flesh cannot submit to God's law is because it is hostile to God [AB].
QUESTION—What is the 'mindset of the flesh'?
  It is a total life-direction that is according to the principle and power of this godless world [NICNT]. Their mindset is directed against the things of God [BECNT, SSA]. It is a mind from which God is excluded [HNTC]. It is the state of being self-centered and hostile toward God [NTC]. It is being in a condition of enmity and hostility against God [AB]. It is selfishness as a ruling, determining influence [WBC]. It is hostility to God, being in the opposite camp, refusing to be subject to his law, being dominated by the fallen state [Mor]. It is the outlook, assumptions, values, and desires of the fallen human nature, which is prompted by his self-centeredness [ICC2]. It is an aspiration, a way of thinking and willing according to the impulses of the natural man [Gdt]. It is a disposition underlying all activity of opposition to and hatred of God [Mu].

for to-the law^a of-God it-is- not -subject,^b
LEXICON—a. νόμος (LN 33.333) (BAGD 3. p. 542): 'law' [AB, BAGD, BECNT, HNTC, ICC2, LN, NICNT, NTC, WBC; all versions except

GW]. This singular noun is translated as a plural: 'laws' [CEV, NLT], 'standards' [GW]. This word has the definite article here.
   b. pres. pass./pass. (deponent = act.) indic. of ὑποτάσσω (LN 36.18, 37.31) (BAGD 1.b.β. p. 848): translated as a deponent: 'to be subject to' [BECNT, ICC2; KJV, NET, REB], 'to be submissive to' [AB], 'to obey' [BAGD, LN (36.18); CEV, TEV], 'to submit to' [LN (36.18), NICNT, NTC; NIV, NRSV], 'to obey' [NCV, NLT], 'to place oneself under the authority of' [GW]; translated as a middle voice: 'to subject (oneself)' [BAGD; NASB], 'to submit oneself to' [WBC].
QUESTION—What 'law of God' is referred to here?
   1. It refers specifically to the law of Moses [BECNT, WBC].
   2. It refers generally to God's righteous demands [NICNT, TH].
   3. It refers to true religion as opposed to perverted religion [HNTC].

for it-is- not -able;[a]
LEXICON—a. pres. mid. (deponent = act.) indic. of δύναμαι (LN 74.5) (BAGD 2. p. 207): 'to be able' [BAGD, BECNT, LN; NASB, NCV, NET]; as an irregular verb: 'can' [AB, BAGD, HNTC, ICC2, LN, NICNT, NTC, WBC; CEV, GW, KJV, NIV, NRSV, REB]. 'It is not able' is translated 'it never will' [NLT].

8:8 and[a] those being[b] in (the) flesh are- not -able to-please[c] God.
LEXICON—a. δέ (LN 89.94): 'and' [BECNT, ICC2, LN, NTC, WBC; NASB, NRSV], 'so' [AB], 'now' [NICNT], 'it follows that' [HNTC], 'so then' [KJV], 'that's why' [NLT], not explicit [CEV, GW, NCV, NET, NIV, REB, TEV].
   b. pres. participle of εἰμί (LN 13.1) (BAGD III.4. p. 225): 'to be' [LN], 'to live' [AB, BAGD; REB]. This participle is translated as a finite verb: '(those who) are' [BECNT, HNTC, ICC2, NICNT, NTC, WBC; GW, NASB, NET, NLT, NRSV], '(those people who) are' [NCV], '(they that) are' [KJV]. The phrase οἱ δὲ ἐν σαρκί ὄντες 'and the ones being in (the) flesh' is translated 'If we follow our desires' [CEV], 'those controlled by the sinful nature' [NIV], 'those who obey their human nature' [TEV].
   c. aorist act. infin. of ἀρέσκω (LN 25.90) (BAGD 2.a. p. 105): 'to please' [AB, BAGD, BECNT, HNTC, ICC2, LN, NICNT, NTC, WBC; all versions], 'to be pleasing to' [BAGD].
QUESTION—What relationship is indicated by δέ 'and'?
   1. It indicates a logical conclusion is being drawn from what precedes [AB, HNTC; KJV, NLT].
   2. It continues the thought of the previous verse [BECNT, ICC1, ICC2, LN, Mor, NTC, WBC].
   3. It is adversative, stating the other side of the enmity; the flesh rebels against God, but neither is God pleased with the flesh [Gdt].
QUESTION—What does 'being in (the) flesh' mean here?
   1. It is referring to the unregenerate state [BECNT, HNTC, NICNT, NTC, St]. It is being unable to please God because it is dominated by indwelling

sin [AB, NAC]. They are those whose interests are limited to the earthly, wholly involved in this life [Mor]. Attachment to self and enmity toward God are the essential nature of the flesh [Gdt]. It is to be under the government of the corrupt nature, the original nature of fallen man, and destitute of the grace of God, which is the case with all unrenewed persons [Ho].

2. It is referring to behavior that comes from the sinful nature, which even believers might engage in [ICC2, SSA, WBC].

8:9 But^a you are not in (the) flesh but in (the) Spirit/spirit,^b

LEXICON—a. δέ: (LN 89.124): 'but' [BECNT, HNTC, ICC2, LN, NICNT; GW, KJV, NCV, NLT, NRSV, REB, TEV], 'yet' [AB], 'however' [NTC, WBC; NASB, NET, NIV], not explicit [CEV].

b. The phrase ἐν πνεύματι is translated 'in (the) Spirit' [AB, BECNT, HNTC, ICC2, NICNT, NTC, WBC; KJV, NASB, NET, NRSV], 'controlled by the Spirit' [NIV, NLT], 'ruled by the Spirit' [NCV], 'ruled by God's Spirit' [CEV], 'live as the Spirit tells you to' [TEV], 'under the control of your spiritual nature' [GW], 'live by the spirit' [REB].

QUESTION—What relationship is indicated by δέ 'but'?

It is adversative [AB, BECNT, Gdt, HNTC, ICC2, Mor, NICNT, NTC, WBC; GW, KJV, NASB, NCV, NET, NIV, NLT, NRSV, REB, TEV]. The ὑμεῖς 'you' is emphatic [Mor, NAC, NICNT, SSA]: but you are different. He assures them that they are in the Spirit [BECNT]. He assures them that they don't have to be under the control of the sinful nature [SSA]. He is speaking of the contrast of two ways of life [TH].

QUESTION—How is the preposition ἐν 'in' used here?

Being 'in' one or the other means to have the direction of the life controlled by that influence [ICC2, Mu, TH], to be subject to one current or the other [Gdt], to be under the domination of one or the other [ICC1]. It means to be determined by or under the control of either the flesh or the Spirit [HNTC, NTC]. If the Holy Spirit is in a person that person is said to be 'in' the Spirit [BECNT, NICNT]. A person is 'in' the flesh or spirit in the sense of belonging to the respective age or realm characterized by flesh and spirit [NICNT]. 'In' refers to a mindset, a conditioned pattern of thinking and behaving [WBC]. Being in the flesh means to be bound to and characterized by the flesh [Mor]. The Spirit is the element in which they live [Ho].

QUESTION—What do 'flesh' and 'Spirit/spirit' connote here?

1. 'Flesh' and 'Spirit' connote belonging respectively to the old age of sin and death or to the new age of righteousness and life [BECNT, NICNT]. By definition a Christian is in the Spirit, not the flesh [AB, BECNT, NAC, NICNT, NTC]. The believer is in the Spirit and the Spirit is in the believer [Mu]. Being in the flesh means living to please oneself instead of God, but Christians are people whose lives are directed from a source that is beyond themselves [HNTC]. Here they represent those who are worldly and those who are believers, in whom the Holy Spirit dwells [Mor].

2. They connote influences that may even influence and control a believer's behavior [ICC2, SSA, WBC]. They represent conditioned patterns of thinking and acting, of orientation and of motive, either as belonging to this world or as belonging to God [WBC].
3. They are the two different aspects of human nature, the lower being 'flesh' and the higher being 'spirit' [ICC1; GW, REB], which is that aspect which holds communion with God and which is subject to the influence of God's Spirit [ICC1].

if-indeed[a] (the) Spirit of-God dwells[b] in you.
LEXICON—a. εἴπερ (LN 89.66) (BAGD VI. 11. p. 220): 'if indeed' [BAGD, LN; NASB, NET], 'if in fact' [AB; TEV], 'if' [NICNT; GW, NIV, NLT], 'if so be' [KJV], 'if...really' [NCV], 'if, as is indeed the case' [HNTC], 'seeing that' [ICC2, NTC], 'assuming that' [WBC], 'since' [BAGD; CEV, NRSV, REB], 'provided that' [BECNT]. The phrase εἴπερ πνεῦμα θεοῦ οἰκεῖ ἐν ὑμῖν 'if indeed the Spirit of God dwells in you' is translated 'God's Spirit, who lives in you' [CEV].
b. pres. act. indic. of οἰκέω (LN **85.73**) (BAGD 1. p. 557): 'to dwell' [BAGD, **LN**; KJV, NASB, NRSV, REB], 'to live' [LN; CEV, GW, NCV, NET, NIV, NLT, TEV]. This verb connotes a settled residency [NICNT].

QUESTION—What relationship is indicated by εἴπερ 'if'?
1. Paul assumes that the Holy Spirit is in them [BECNT, HNTC, ICC1, ICC2, Mor, NAC, NICNT, NTC, SSA; CEV, NRSV, REB]. He uses this word because he wants them to reflect on the matter and to conclude, as he does, that the Spirit actually does dwell in them [BECNT]. He is not expressing doubt about their condition, but is trying to stimulate them to vigilance; if their profession is serious, this should be the result, and they can verify the validity of their professed faith [Gdt]. When Paul is making a positive statement (as in this sentence) he assumes that his readers do have the Spirit, but when speaking of the negation of the same idea (as in the next sentence in this verse) he speaks in a more general and vague form and uses εἰ 'if' [ICC1].
2. Paul is establishing a criterion or definition as the grounds upon which the previous clause was based; if the Spirit lives in you then by definition you are a believer, and are not in the flesh [Ho, Mu]. Paul is unsure if the Holy Spirit is really in them, as not all those hearing the epistle being read would necessarily be believers [WBC].

But if anyone has not (the) Spirit of-Christ, this-(one) is[a] not his.
LEXICON—a. pres. indic. of εἰμί (LN 13.1) (BAGD IV.2. p. 225): 'to be' [HNTC, LN; KJV], 'to belong to' [AB, BAGD, BECNT, ICC2, NICNT, NTC, WBC; all versions except KJV, NLT]. This sentence is translated 'those who do not have the Spirit of Christ living in them are not Christians at all' [NLT].

8:10 But[a] if Christ (is) in[b] you,

LEXICON—a. δέ: (LN 89.124, 89.94): 'but' [AB, BECNT, ICC2, LN (89.124), NICNT, NTC; CEV, NET, NIV, NRSV, REB, TEV], 'however' [GW], 'and' [LN (89.94), WBC; KJV, NASB], not explicit [NLT].
  b. ἐν with dative object (LN 83.13, 89.119) (BAGD I.5.a. p. 259): 'in' [AB, BAGD, BECNT, HNTC, ICC2, LN (83.13, 89.119), NICNT, NTC, WBC; all versions except NLT], 'within' [NLT], 'in union with' [LN (89.119)]. It indicates a very close connection [BAGD]. The phrase 'is in you' is translated 'lives in you' [CEV, GW, TEV], 'lives within you' [NLT].

QUESTION—What relationship is indicated by εἰ 'if'?
  It expresses grounds for what follows based on an assumed condition [HNTC, ICC2, Mor, NAC, NICNT, NTC, SSA, St, WBC; CEV, NLT]: since Christ is in you.

QUESTION—What is implied by his alternately using 'Spirit of God' and 'Spirit of Christ', and shifting from the indwelling of the Spirit in 8:9 to the indwelling of Christ in this verse?
  There is no distinction intended between the indwelling of Christ and the indwelling of the Spirit [HNTC]. Christ and the indwelling Spirit are distinguishable, but inseparable [NAC, NICNT]. Christ and the Spirit are inseparable with respect to the saving benefit they communicate to believers [BECNT, NICNT]. If the Spirit indwells someone, then so does Christ, who does so by his Spirit [Gdt, HNTC, Ho, SSA]. This shows that in Paul's thinking Christ is fully divine [NTC]. 'Spirit of God' and 'Christ' are used synonymously here, because they are perceived in Christian experience as one; Christ is known only through the Spirit [WBC]. There is little difference between the indwelling of Christ and that of the Spirit [Mor]. It is through the indwelling Spirit that Christ dwells in the believer [ICC2]. It underlines the intimacy of the relation of the persons of the trinity without blurring the distinctions [Mu]. The persons of the trinity are eternally distinct in their personal modes of being, but they are inseparable because they share the same divine essence and will [St].

the body[a] (is) dead[b] because-of[c] sin,[d]

LEXICON—a. σῶμα (LN 8.1, 9.8) (BAGD 1.b. p. 799): 'body' [AB, BAGD, BECNT, HNTC, ICC2, LN (8.1), NICNT, NTC, WBC; all versions], 'physical being' [LN (9.8)]. The definite article 'the' is translated as 'your' [CEV, GW, NET, NIV, NLT, TEV].
  b. νεκρός (LN 23.121) (BAGD 1.b.β. p. 535): 'dead' [AB, BAGD, BECNT, HNTC, LN, NICNT, NTC, WBC; all versions except CEV, NLT], 'mortal' [ICC2]. This adjective is translated as a verb phrase: 'must die' [CEV], 'will die' [NLT].
  c. διά with accusative object (LN 89.26): 'because of' [AB, BECNT, ICC2, LN, NICNT, NTC, WBC; all versions], 'on account of' [HNTC, LN], 'by reason of' [LN].

d. ἁμαρτία (LN 88.289): 'sin' [AB, BECNT, HNTC, ICC2, LN, NICNT, NTC, WBC; all versions]; this singular noun is translated as a plural: 'sins' [CEV]. It is translated as indicating possession: 'your' [ICC2; CEV].

QUESTION—What does it mean that the body is dead?
1. It refers to the certainty of physical death still to be experienced by the believer as the penalty of sin [BECNT, Gdt, Ho, ICC1, ICC2, Mor, Mu, NAC, NICNT, NTC, SSA, St, TH, TNTC; NLT, TEV].
2. It refers to a baptized person's death to sin [HNTC].
3. It refers to the lack of spiritual life and vitality that the unbeliever has apart from Christ, and which is changed when a person becomes a believer [AB].
4. 'Body' is the 'body of sin' spoken of in 6:6 and the 'body of death' spoken of in 7:24, and refers not to the individual but to humanity as embodied in its environment in this age, which is still under sin and death; people in this age live in a state of deadness that has resulted from sin; sin and death still have a grip on the mortality of a believer, and the sway of sin, though diminishing, still lasts while the body lasts [WBC].

QUESTION—What is the relation of this clause to the one that follows?
The two clauses are connected by the μέν...δέ construction, which posits two ideas in some form of contrast to one another, often concessive. This construction is translated as two contrasting ideas: 'on the one hand this...but on the other hand that' [HNTC]; as a statement followed by a contrasting statement: '(statement)...but' [NICNT, WBC; GW, KJV, NCV, NET], '(statement)...yet' [NIV]; as concessive: 'though...(statement)' [AB, BECNT, ICC2; NRSV], 'even though...(statement)' [CEV, NLT, TEV], 'though...yet' [NTC; NASB], 'although ...yet' [REB].

the Spirit/spirit[a] (is)[b] life[c] because-of[d] righteousness.[e]
LEXICON—a. πνεῦμα (LN 12.18, 26.9) (BAGD 5.g.β. p. 677): 'Spirit' [BECNT, HNTC, ICC2, LN (12.18), NICNT, NTC, WBC; KJV, NCV, NET, NRSV, REB, TEV], 'spirit' [AB, BAGD, LN (26.9); GW, NIV, NLT], 'inner being' [LN (26.9)], 'you' [CEV]. The possessive pronoun 'your' is added to distinguish between the Holy Spirit and the spirit of the believer: 'your spirit' [GW, NIV, NLT]. It refers to the divine Spirit [BAGD]. The phrase τὸ δὲ πνεῦμα ζωή 'the spirit is life' is translated 'So you are alive' [CEV].
b. There is no lexical entry for this implied verb in the Greek text. It is represented in translation as 'is' [BECNT, ICC2, NICNT, NTC, WBC; KJV, NASB, NET, NIV, NLT, NRSV, REB], 'is (life) for you' [TEV], '(your spirits) are' [GW], 'gives' [NCV], 'is at work giving' [HNTC], 'has' [AB], not explicit [CEV].
c. ζωή (LN 23.88) (BAGD 2.b.α. p. 340): 'life' [AB, BAGD, BECNT, HNTC, ICC2, LN, NICNT, NTC, WBC; KJV, NCV, NET, NRSV, REB,

TEV], 'alive' [CEV, GW, NASB, NIV, NLT]. This noun is translated with the possessive pronoun: 'your life' [NET, REB].
   d. διά with accusative object (LN 89.26): 'because of' [AB, BECNT, ICC2, LN, NICNT, NTC, WBC; KJV, NASB, NET, NIV, NRSV], 'because' [HNTC; CEV, GW, NCV, NLT, REB, TEV], 'on account of' [LN], 'by reason of' [LN].
   e. δικαιοσύνη (LN 88.13) (BAGD 3. p. 197): 'righteousness' [BAGD, BECNT, LN, NICNT, WBC; KJV, NASB, NET, NIV, NRSV], 'uprightness' [AB], '(your) justification' [ICC2, NTC]. The phrase διά δικαιοσύνη 'on account of righteousness' is translated 'because God has accepted you' [CEV], 'because you are (righteous)' [HNTC], 'because you have God's approval' [GW], 'because Christ made you right with God' [NCV], 'because you have been made right with God' [NLT], 'because you have been put right with God' [TEV], 'because you have been justified' [REB].

QUESTION—What does it mean that the Spirit/spirit is life?
   1. The word πνεῦμα refers to the spirit of the believer, and means that the person is alive or will live [AB, Gdt, Ho, ICC1, NAC, SSA, St; CEV, GW, NASB, NIV, NLT]. Without the Spirit a person is like a lifeless corpse, but in union with Christ the human spirit has life and vitality [AB].
   2. The word πνεῦμα refers to the Holy Spirit [BAGD, BECNT, HNTC, ICC2, Mor, Mu, NICNT, NTC, TH, TNTC, WBC; KJV, NCV, NET, NRSV, REB, TEV]. The Spirit will overcome death through the resurrection of the body [BECNT, ICC2, NICNT, WBC]. The Holy Spirit, who conveys spiritual life in the present to the believer in the form of deliverance from condemnation, will in the future convey resurrection life to the body itself [NICNT]. The Spirit is continually giving life to the believer in the form of all the graces of the Christian life that accrue because of justification [HNTC]. Although the believer cannot escape this body of death or the death of the body in this life, nevertheless God's acceptance, life, and power which are brought by the Holy Spirit triumph over sin and death, and when sin plays death as its last card the Holy Spirit will trump it [WBC].

QUESTION—What does 'life' mean here?
   1. Their resurrection to eternal life will take place because of the imputed righteousness of Christ resulting in justification [BECNT, ICC1, ICC2, NICNT, SSA, WBC]. The vista of life which the Spirit is giving also includes the resurrection [HNTC]. Through the agency of the Spirit who is life, God will give life to them on the day of resurrection [Mu, NTC]. 'Life' is to be taken in a broad sense, but with a primary focus on the eternal life of the future [ICC1]. There is a principle of life in the soul because of regeneration which is the beginning of eternal life [Ho].

2. They have spiritual life because of the imputed righteousness of Christ [AB, NAC, SSA, St]. Because of union with the Spirit of God the spirit of the believer not only has life as an attribute, but as its very nature [Gdt].
3. God's acceptance brings spiritual life and vitality as well as the eventual resurrection of the body [WBC].

8:11 But[a] if the Spirit of-the-(one) having-raised[b] Jesus from-(among) dead (persons)[c] dwells[d] in[e] you,

LEXICON—a. δέ LN (89.124, 89.94): 'but' [ICC2, LN (89.124), WBC; KJV, NASB], 'yet' [CEV], 'and' [AB, HNTC, LN (89.94), NICNT, NTC; NIV], 'moreover' [NET, REB], 'now' [BECNT], not explicit [GW, NCV, NLT, NRSV, TEV].
  b. aorist act. participle of ἐγείρω (LN 23.94) (BAGD 1.a.β. p. 214): 'to raise' [AB, BAGD, BECNT, ICC2, NICNT, NTC, WBC; all versions except GW, KJV], 'to raise up' [BAGD, HNTC; KJV], 'to raise to life, to cause to live again' [LN], 'to bring back (to life)' [GW].
  c. νεκρός (LN 23.121) (BAGD 2.a. p. 535): 'the dead' [AB, BAGD, BECNT, HNTC, ICC2, LN, NICNT, NTC, WBC; KJV, NASB, NCV, NET, NIV, NLT, NRSV, REB], 'death' [TEV]. The phrase ἐγείραντος τὸν Ἰησοῦν ἐκ νεκρῶν 'having raised Jesus from (among) dead (persons)' is translated 'God raised Jesus to life' [CEV], 'who brought Jesus back to life' [GW].
  d. pres. act. indic. of οἰκέω (LN 85.73) (BAGD 1. p. 557): 'to dwell' [AB, BAGD, BECNT, HNTC, ICC2, LN, NICNT, NTC, WBC; KJV, NASB, NRSV, REB], 'to live' [BAGD, LN; CEV, GW, NET, NLT, TEV], 'to be living' [NIV]. This entire clause is translated 'Yet God raised Jesus to life! God's Spirit now lives in you' [CEV].
  e. ἐν with dative object (LN 83.13, 89.119) (BAGD I.5.a. p. 259): 'in' [AB, BAGD, BECNT, HNTC, ICC2, LN (83.13, 89.119), NICNT, NTC, WBC; all versions], 'in union with, joined closely to' [LN (89.119)].

QUESTION—What relationship is indicated by δέ 'but'?
1. It is resumptive [BECNT, Gdt, NTC]. 8:11 recapitulates and elaborates on 8:10b [BECNT]. Not only does the life of Jesus penetrate the spirit, it takes hold of the body as well [Gdt].
2. It is adversative [ICC2, Mor, WBC; KJV, NASB]: it contrasts the ongoing state described in 8:10 with the Christian's expectation for the future [WBC].

QUESTION—What is implied by his use of εἰ 'if'?
Paul assumes the condition he states, which is that the Spirit actually does dwell in them [BECNT, HNTC, Mor, NAC, NICNT, NTC, SSA, St, WBC].

the-(one) having-raised Christ from-(among) dead (persons) will-make-alive[a] your mortal[b] bodies[c] also

LEXICON—a. fut. act. indic. of ζῳοποιέω (LN 23.92) (BAGD 1. p. 341): 'to make alive' [BAGD, LN; GW, NET], 'to give life to' [AB, BAGD, NICNT, WBC; NASB, NCV, NIV, NLT, NRSV, TEV], 'to give new life to' [REB], 'to grant life to' [BECNT], 'to impart life to' [NTC], 'to quicken' [HNTC, ICC2; KJV], 'to raise to life' [LN; CEV]. The phrase 'will make alive your mortal bodies' is translated 'he will raise you to life' [CEV].

b. θνητός (LN 23.124) (BAGD p. 362): 'mortal' [AB, BAGD, BECNT, HNTC, ICC2, LN, NICNT, NTC, WBC; all versions except CEV, NCV], 'that die' [NCV]. The phrase καὶ τὰ θνητὰ σώματα ὑμῶν 'your mortal bodies also' is translated 'you' [CEV]. Whereas in 8:10 he spoke of the fact of death, here in 8:11 he speaks of the quality of being mortal [Gdt].

c. σῶμα (LN 8.1) (BAGD 1.b. p. 799): 'body' [AB, BAGD, BECNT, HNTC, ICC2, LN, NICNT, NTC, WBC; all versions except CEV], not explicit [CEV]. This plural noun is translated as singular 'body' [NLT].

QUESTION—To what does the verb ζῳοποιέω 'to make alive' refer?

It refers to the future bodily resurrection [AB, BECNT, Gdt, Ho, ICC2, Mor, Mu, NAC, NICNT, NTC, SSA, St, TH, WBC]. At the resurrection not only will our bodies be made alive, they will no longer be subject to death again [Mor]. It also refers to the life-giving activity of the Holy Spirit working in every stage in the period between Christ's resurrection and the final resurrection [HNTC]. The Holy Spirit also gives spiritual life and vitality to people here and now [AB].

QUESTION—What correlation is indicated by καί 'also'?

1. It correlates Jesus' resurrection with their own eventual resurrection; that is, just Christ was made alive, so also will their bodies be made alive. [BECNT, Ho, ICC2, Mor, Mu, NICNT, WBC; NLT].
2. It correlates their being made alive spiritually with their bodies being made alive physically in the future resurrection; that is, the power of new life extends even to your mortal bodies [AB, Gdt, HNTC, ICC1, NAC; GW]. Even the mortal body is transformed and quickened [HNTC].
3. It correlates Jesus' resurrection with their own as well as their being made alive spiritually with their being made alive physically in the resurrection [St].

QUESTION—What is the relation between the 'mortal body' and previous references to the body?

1. 'Mortal body' is the physical body, whereas 'body of sin' (in 6:6) and 'body of death' (in 7:24) are metaphorical, representing the sinful nature or the struggle against or susceptibility to the sinful nature [AB, HNTC, Ho, ICC2, Mor, NAC, SSA, TNTC, WBC]. 'Body of sin' and 'body of death' speak of the body as subject to the dominating influences of sin and death [AB, TNTC], and 'mortal body' refers to the body itself that can be thus dominated by them [AB]. The mortal and corruptible body is humanity's embodiment in this age in its most obvious and characteristic expression [WBC]. The 'mortal body' is the physical body which will die and also be resurrected, 'the body of sin' is human nature in its domination by sin, and 'body of death' is the body or human nature which has fallen under the dominion of death [HNTC]. 'Mortal body' is the

physical body, whereas 'body of sin' speaks of the whole man as controlled by sin, and 'body of death' is the condition of life in this body which is under the occupation of sin and which must die because of sin [ICC2]. 'Mortal body' speaks of the certainty of physical death, whereas 'body of sin' refers to the sinful inclinations of the body, and 'body of this death' represents the struggle against the sinful things the body desires [SSA]. This passage speaks of physical mortality, but in 6:6 and 7:24 he is speaking of the body as that which the corrupt sinful nature uses [Gdt]. Here the term is used concretely of the body, but in the two other passages it is used figuratively to speak of the sinful nature [Ho]. Here he speaks of the body as subject to death; in 6:6 he speaks of the body as subject to the domination by sin, and in 7:24 the body is that in which sin operates to brings us death [Mor].
2. 'Mortal body' refers to the physical body which is subject to death as well as to resurrection, whereas the 'body of sin' (6:6) refers to the whole person in his interaction with this world, and 'body of death' (7:24) refers to the status of an unsaved person as condemned and bound for hell [NICNT].
3. All three passages refer to the physical body, subject as it is to mortality and death [Mu]. 'Mortal body' is the body that will die, 'body of sin' is the body as the seat of sin and subject to its impulses and pull, and 'body of death' speaks of the body as that which leads to mortality and eternal death through sin [ICC1].

through[a] his Spirit the-(one) indwelling[b] in you.

LEXICON—a. διά with genitive object (LN 89.76): 'through' [AB, BECNT, HNTC, ICC2, LN, NICNT, NTC, WBC; NASB, NCV, NET, NIV, NRSV, REB], 'by' [LN; CEV, GW, KJV, NLT, TEV], 'by means of' [LN].
b. pres. act. participle of ἐνοικέω (LN 85.73) (BAGD p. 267): 'to indwell' [BECNT; NASB, REB], 'to dwell (in)' [AB, BAGD, HNTC, ICC2, LN, NICNT, NTC, WBC; KJV, NRSV], 'to live in' [LN; GW, NCV, NET, NIV], 'to be living within' [NLT], not explicit [CEV, TEV]. The phrase τοῦ ἐνοικοῦντος αὐτοῦ πνεύματος ἐν ὑμῖν 'his Spirit the one indwelling in you' is translated 'his indwelling Spirit' [REB], 'the presence of his Spirit in you' [TEV], not explicit [CEV].

DISCOURSE UNIT: 8:12–30 [HNTC]. The topic is the hope of glory.

DISCOURSE UNIT: 8:12–17 [Gdt, Mor, WBC]. The topic is adoption [Gdt], the Spirit of sonship [WBC], the family of God [Mor].

DISCOURSE UNIT: 8:12–16 [ICC2]. The topic is the indwelling of the Spirit—the establishment of God's law.

8:12 Therefore then,[a] brothers, [b]

LEXICON—a. ἄρα οὖν: 'therefore then' [BECNT], 'therefore' [NICNT, NTC; KJV, NIV], 'so then' [AB, ICC2, WBC; NASB, NET, NRSV, TEV], 'so' [GW, NCV, NLT], 'in consequence of this' [HNTC], 'it follows' [REB], not explicit [CEV].

b. ἀδελφός (LN 11.23): 'Christian brother, fellow believer' [LN]. This plural noun is translated 'brothers' [AB, ICC2, NICNT, NTC, WBC; NIV], 'my brothers' [TEV], 'brothers and sisters' [BECNT; GW, NET, NRSV], 'my brothers and sisters' [NCV], 'brethren' [HNTC; KJV, NASB], 'my friends' [REB], 'my dear friends' [CEV], 'dear Christian friends' [NLT].

QUESTION—What relationship is indicated by ἄρα οὖν 'therefore then'?

It is inferential [AB, BECNT, Gdt, HNTC, Ho, ICC2, Mor, Mu, NICNT, NTC, SSA, TH, WBC; NET]. It is emphatic and inferential [NICNT; NET], drawing a conclusion from what has been stated about the Spirit living in them [NICNT] or about Christ giving life to believers [Mor]. It draws a conclusion based on what has been stated in 8:1–11 [AB, HNTC, ICC2, Mu, TH], or in 8:5–11 [BECNT], or in 8:7–11 [ICC1]. It draws a conclusion from what he says about the nature and tendency of the flesh in 8:5–11 [Ho]. It draws the conclusion from 8:2 that since they have been freed from the law of sin and death, they should not place themselves back under that curse again [Gdt]. The section it introduces is primarily hortatory [ICC1, ICC2, NTC, SSA, WBC], or at least with hortatory implications [BECNT, Mu].

we-are debtors,[a] not to-the flesh to-live according-to (the) flesh,[b]

LEXICON—a. ὀφειλέτης (LN 57.222) (BAGD 2.b. p. 598): 'debtor' [BECNT, ICC2, LN, NICNT; KJV, NRSV], 'indebted' [AB], 'under obligation' [BAGD, HNTC, WBC; NASB, NET], '(to have) an obligation' [NTC; GW, NIV, NLT, TEV], 'obligated' [BAGD]. This entire phrase is translated 'we must not live to satisfy our desires' [CEV], 'we must not be ruled by our sinful selves' [NCV], 'our old nature has no claim over us' [REB].

b. σάρξ (LN 8.63, 26.7) (BAGD 7. p. 744): 'flesh' [BAGD], 'human nature' [LN (26.7)]. The phrase κατὰ σάρκα ζῆν is translated 'to live according to the flesh' [BECNT, ICC2, NICNT; NASB, NET, NRSV], 'to live in accordance with the flesh' [WBC], 'to have to live according to it' [AB], 'to live according to its standard' [NTC], 'to live after the flesh' [KJV], 'to allow our lives to be determined by it' [HNTC], 'to live in that way' [REB], 'to live to satisfy our desires' [CEV], 'to live the way our corrupt nature wants us to live' [GW], 'to live the way our sinful selves want' [NCV], 'to the sinful nature, to live according to it' [NIV], 'to live as our human nature wants us to' [TEV], 'to do what you sinful nature wants you to do' [NLT].

QUESTION—What relationship is indicated by the infinitive phrase τοῦ...ζῆν 'to live'?

'To live' is epexegetic to τῇ σαρκί 'to the flesh' [AB, BECNT, HNTC, Mor, NAC, NICNT, SSA, TH, WBC]: to the flesh, that is, to live according to its dictates.

QUESTION—In what sense are they not debtors to the flesh?

Their daily life is no longer subject to the domination of the power of the old age that lives in rebellion against God [BECNT, NAC, NICNT]. They are not compelled to live as the sinful nature directs [AB, NTC, SSA]. Even though they belong inescapably to the realm of the flesh, that does not mean that they are obligated to live by the flesh [WBC]. The implied contrast is that they are obligated to the Holy Spirit [Ho, Mor]. The first and most important obligation of the natural man is to take care of his own person, but once the Spirit takes possession of someone this obligation is should not be paid or even acknowledged [Gdt]. They are no longer to be governed by the complex of sinful desires, motives, affections, principles, and purposes [Mu].

8:13 for if you-are-living according-to (the) flesh, you-are-destined[a] to-die;

LEXICON—a. pres. act. indic. of μέλλω (LN 71.36) (BAGD 1.c.δ. p. 501): 'to be destined' [BAGD], '(one) must' [BAGD, LN], '(one) has to' [LN], '(one) will certainly' [BAGD]. This clause is translated 'you will die' [AB, BECNT, NICNT; CEV, NET, NIV, NRSV], 'you will die spiritually' [NCV], 'you will certainly die' [ICC2, WBC], 'you must die' [NASB, REB], 'you are doomed to die' [NTC], 'you are doomed to death' [HNTC], 'you are going to die' [GW, TEV], 'ye shall die' [KJV], 'we will die' [CEV], 'you will perish' [NLT].

QUESTION—What relationship is indicated by γάρ 'for'?

It introduces grounds for the expressed and implied assertions of 8:12 [Mu, SSA]. It is explanatory; although he tells them they have no obligation to live according to the flesh, he warns them of what will happen if they succumb to the flesh [BECNT].

QUESTION—What sense of ἀποθνῄσκω 'to die' is intended here?

It is eschatological death, eternal separation from God [AB, BECNT, HNTC, Mu, NICNT, SSA]. It is spiritual death [NCV], the final death [TH]. There is a kind of living that is really death, and there is a kind of dying that is really life [Mor, St]. They will die without hope of life with God [ICC2].

but if by[a] (the)-Spirit/spirit[b] you-put-to-death[c] the deeds[d] of-the body[e] you-will-live.[f]

LEXICON—a. There is no lexical entry for this word in the Greek text, the relationship being indicated by the dative case of the word πνεῦμα. This relation is translated 'by' [BECNT, HNTC, ICC2, NICNT, NTC, WBC; NASB, NET, NIV, NRSV, REB, TEV], 'by the help of' [CEV], 'through' [AB; KJV], 'through the power of' [NLT], 'you use' [GW, NCV].

b. πνεῦμα (LN 12.18, 26.9) (BAGD 5.g.α. p. 677): 'Spirit' [AB, BAGD, BECNT, HNTC, ICC2, LN (12.18), NICNT, NTC, WBC; all versions except CEV, GW, NLT], 'Holy Spirit' [LN; NLT], 'God's Spirit' [CEV], 'your spiritual nature' [GW], 'spirit' [LN (26.9)].

c. pres. act. indic. of θανατόω (LN **68.48**) (BAGD 2.c. p. 351): 'to put to death' [AB, BAGD, BECNT, HNTC, ICC2, **LN**, NTC, WBC; GW, NET, NIV, NRSV, REB, TEV], 'to be putting to death' [NICNT; NASB], 'to mortify' [KJV], 'to completely cease to do' [**LN**], 'to stop doing' [NCV], 'to say "No" to' [CEV], 'to turn from' [NLT]. The present tense signifies the need for continual action [NAC].

d. πρᾶξις (LN 42.8) (BAGD 4.b. p. 698): 'deed' [AB, BECNT, LN, WBC; KJV, NASB, NET, NRSV], 'disgraceful deed' [BAGD, NTC], 'evil deed' [BAGD; NLT], 'evil activity' [GW], 'activity' [HNTC, ICC2], 'practice' [NICNT], 'misdeed' [NIV], 'base pursuit' [REB], 'wrong things you do' [NCV], 'what (one) has done' [LN]. The phrase τὰς πράξεις τοῦ σώματος 'the deeds of the body' is translated 'your desires' [CEV], 'your sinful actions' [TEV].

e. σῶμα (LN 8.1, 9.8) (BAGD 1.b. p. 799): 'body' [AB, BECNT, HNTC, ICC2, LN (8.1), NICNT, NTC, WBC; GW, KJV, NASB, NET, NIV, NRSV, REB], 'living body' [BAGD], 'self, physical being' [LN (9.8)], not explicit [CEV, NLT, TEV]. It is used here with the same meaning as σάρξ 'flesh' [BAGD]. The phrase 'the deeds of the body' is translated 'the wrong things you do with your body' [NCV].

f. fut. mid. (deponent = act.) indic. of ζάω (LN 23.88) (BAGD 2.b.α. p. 336): 'to live' [BAGD, LN]. This future tense verb is translated 'you will live' [AB, BECNT, HNTC, NICNT, NTC, WBC; all versions except KJV, NCV], 'you will have true life' [NCV], 'you shall live' [ICC2], 'ye shall live' [KJV].

QUESTION—What are 'the deeds of the body'?

It refers to the influence of the flesh expressing itself in deeds worked out through the body [BECNT, Gdt, NICNT; CEV, NCV, NLT, TEV]. Here body is used as an equivalent to 'sinful flesh' [AB, ICC2, NAC, WBC], or of 'body of death' from 7:24 [Mor]. The deeds of the body are disgraceful [NTC]. They are attempts to satisfy merely human appetites and ambitions [WBC]. The body is the instrument of the fleshly nature [Gdt]. The 'deeds of the body' are sinful actions [TH], any use of the body which serves ourselves instead of God and other people [St]. This phrase indicates the concreteness and practicality of what is expected of the believer [Mu]. It is the inclination to indulge the license of the flesh [ICC1]. The deeds of the body are deeds performed by the body as the organ of sin, and the expression represents all sinful deeds, not just those of the body [Ho].

DISCOURSE UNIT: 8:14–39 [AB]. The topic is Christian life, lived in freedom bestowed by the indwelling Spirit, having its destiny in glory.

DISCOURSE UNIT: 8:14–17 [AB, NICNT]. The topic is through the Spirit the Christian becomes a child of God, destined for glory [AB], the spirit of adoption [NICNT].

8:14 For as-many-as are-being-led[a] by-(the)-Spirit of-God, these are sons[b] of-God.

LEXICON—a. pres. pass. indic. of ἄγω (LN **36.1**) (BAGD 3. p. 14): 'to be led' [AB, BAGD, BECNT, ICC2, **LN**, NICNT, WBC; CEV, KJV, NET, NIV, NLT, NRSV, REB, TEV], 'to be being led' [NTC; NASB], 'to allow (oneself) to be led' [BAGD, HNTC], 'to be guided' [GW], 'to be directed' [LN]. The phrase 'are being led by the Spirit of God' is translated 'who let God's Spirit lead them' [NCV].

b. υἱός (LN 9.4, 36.39) (BAGD 1.c.γ. p. 834): 'son' [HNTC, ICC2, LN (9.4), NICNT, NTC, WBC; KJV, NASB, NET, NIV, REB, TEV], 'child' [AB, BECNT; CEV, GW, NCV, NLT, NRSV], 'person (of)' [LN (9.4)], 'follower' [LN (36.39)]. It is used in a figurative sense, implying being bound by close, non-material ties [BAGD].

QUESTION—What relationship is indicated by γάρ 'for'?

It clarifies and restates what has been said in 8:13 [BECNT, ICC2]. It clarifies 8:13 by changing the imagery [St]. It indicates the grounds for what he has said in 8:13 [Mu, NICNT, NTC], which is that putting the misdeeds of the body to death by the Spirit will bring eschatological life [NICNT], or that eternal life is the certain outcome of sonship [Ho, Mu], or that they are able to put to death the deeds of the body because they are sons of God and therefore led by the Spirit of God [NTC]. It introduces an amplification of what is stated in 8:13 (and implied in 8:12) about living by the Spirit and not by the flesh [SSA]. It introduces the grounds for the statement 'you will live' in the previous verse [Mor]. It draws a conclusion from the promise 'you shall live', which is that if they let themselves be led by the Spirit, they are sons of God and thus have life by being sons of him who is life [Gdt].

QUESTION—Does ὅσοι 'as many as' have an inclusive or exclusive meaning?

1. It is inclusive [AB, Gdt, ICC2, Mor, NICNT, NTC]: all who are led are sons.
2. It is exclusive [Mu, NAC]: only those who are led are sons.
3. Both are true, considered from different aspects [BECNT]. It may be deliberately ambiguous [WBC].

QUESTION—What does it mean to be 'led' by the Spirit of God?

It refers not so much to guidance but to the overall governing and directing of one's life by the Spirit, including the 'putting to death' of 8:13 [BECNT, HNTC, ICC2, Mu, NICNT, NTC]. It is a distinguishing sign of being a son of God [Mor, Mu, NICNT]. The Spirit leads believers into truth and shows them the way in that sense [Mor]. It is similar to the relation between a shepherd and his sheep in that the Holy Spirit is their guide and protector [NAC]. It refers to the active influence of the Spirit in the Christian life [AB]. There is a degree of emotional intensity and even enthusiasm involved in this [WBC]. It means to be subject to the government of the Spirit [Ho]. There is a certain holy violence involved here, as the Spirit takes a person where the flesh would not want to go [Gdt]. It means to give voluntary submission to the Holy Spirit's leadership [TH]. It means to be enlightened and persuaded by the Spirit, as well as to be prompted to put to death the misdeeds of the body [St].

8:15 For you-received[a] not a Spirit/spirit[b] of-slavery[c] (leading)-to[d] fear[e] again,

LEXICON—a. aorist act. indic. of λαμβάνω (LN 57.125, 90.63): 'to receive' [AB, BECNT, HNTC, ICC2, LN (57.125, 90.63), NICNT, NTC, WBC; all versions except CEV, NLT, TEV], not explicit [CEV, NLT]. This entire clause is translated 'God's Spirit doesn't make us slaves who are afraid of him' [CEV], 'the Spirit that God has given you does not make you slaves and cause you to be afraid' [TEV], 'you should not be like cowering, fearful slaves' [NLT].

b. πνεῦμα (LN 12.18, 26.9, 30.6): 'Spirit' [HNTC, LN (12.18); NCV, REB, TEV], 'Holy Spirit, Spirit of God' [LN (12.18)], 'God's Spirit' [CEV], 'spirit' [AB, BECNT, ICC2, LN (26.9), NICNT, NTC, WBC; GW, KJV, NASB, NET, NIV, NRSV], 'disposition, attitude, way of thinking' [LN (30.6)], not explicit [NLT].

c. δουλεία (LN **37.26**) (BAGD 2. p. 205): '(of) slavery' [BAGD, BECNT, ICC2, LN, NICNT, NTC, WBC; NET, NRSV, REB], '(of) slaves' [GW], 'that enslaves you' [**LN**], 'that makes you a slave' [NIV], 'enslaving you' [AB], '(of) bondage' [KJV], 'one which brings into bondage' [HNTC]. The phrase οὐ...ἐλάβετε πνεῦμα δουλείας 'not...you received Spirit/spirit of slavery' is translated 'the Spirit that God has given you does not make you slaves' [LN (**37.36**); TEV], 'God's Spirit doesn't make us slaves' [CEV], 'the Spirit we received does not make us slaves' [NCV], 'you should not be like cowering, fearful slaves' [NLT].

d. εἰς with accusative object (LN 89.48) (BAGD 4.e. p. 229): 'to' [AB, BAGD; KJV, NASB, NCV, NET, NIV], 'unto' [NICNT], 'into' [BAGD; GW], 'which reduces you to' [HNTC], 'leading you back into' [REB], 'to lead you into' [ICC2], 'to fall back into' [NRSV], 'falling back into' [WBC], 'to fill you with' [NTC], 'resulting in' [BECNT], 'with the result that, to cause' [LN], not explicit [CEV, NLT, TEV].

e. φόβος (LN 25.251) (BAGD 2.a.β. p. 863): 'fear' [AB, BECNT, ICC2, LN, NICNT, WBC; GW, KJV, NASB, NCV, NET, NIV, NRSV], 'a state of fear' [HNTC], 'a life of fear' [REB], 'dread' [NTC]. The phrase εἰς φόβον 'leading to fear' is translated 'to cause you to fear' [BAGD]. The phrase 'of slavery leading to fear' is translated 'slaves who are afraid of him' [CEV], 'to make you slaves and cause you to be afraid' [TEV].

QUESTION—What relationship is indicated by γάρ 'for'?

It introduces grounds for his statement in 8:14 [AB, BECNT, ICC2, SSA], which is about believers being God's children [BECNT]. It introduces an explanation for the relationship between being in the Spirit and sonship [NICNT]. It introduces 8:15–16 as that which fills out the contextual rationale in a believer's life of what was stated in 8:14 about being sons of

God [WBC]. It introduces 8:14 as additional confirmation of the thought expressed in 8:13–14 that sonship is the guarantee of eternal life [Mu].

QUESTION—What is the 'receiving' of the Spirit he is referring to?

It refers to the time of conversion [BECNT, ICC2, Mor, St, WBC], or of baptism [ICC1].

QUESTION—To what does the adverb πάλιν 'again' refer?

It refers to the sense of fear in which they once lived, not to a second reception of a spirit of fear [BECNT, Gdt, HNTC, Ho, ICC1, ICC2, Mu, NAC, NICNT, NTC, TH, WBC]. When they received the Holy Spirit they did not need to go back into the slavish bondage they had as non-believers [Gdt, Mu]. The Spirit will not lead them back into the bondage to sin, which inevitably leads to fear, in which they once lived [Mor]. It refers to the sense of anxiety and dread of judgment because of their sins they had prior to conversion, and from which the Spirit frees them [BECNT, Ho, NICNT]. They no longer need to be subject to anxiety about death or to have the kind of fearful mindset that a slave would have [AB]. It contrasts the difference between living in the old epoch and the new [WBC]. They were slaves of fear before receiving God's spirit, but now the Spirit has released them from fear [TH]. The servile temper is a fearful slavery to the Law [ICC1].

but[a] you-received[b] a Spirit/spirit[c] of-adoption[d]

LEXICON—a. ἀλλά (LN 89.125): 'but' [AB, ICC2, LN, NICNT, NTC, WBC; KJV, NASB, NET, NIV, NRSV, REB], 'instead' [LN; CEV, GW, NLT, TEV], 'no, (it was)' [HNTC], not explicit [NCV].

b. aorist act. indic. of λαμβάνω (LN 57.125, 90.63): 'to receive' [AB, LN (57.125, 90.63)]. This verb is translated as a past tense: 'you received' [AB, NICNT, NTC, WBC; NET, NIV]; as a perfect tense: 'you have received' [BECNT, ICC2; GW, KJV, NASB, NRSV], not explicit [HNTC; CEV, NCV, NLT, REB, TEV].

c. πνεῦμα (LN 12.18, 26.9, 30.6) (BAGD 5.e. p. 677): 'Spirit' [BAGD, BECNT, HNTC, ICC2, LN (12.18), NICNT, NTC, WBC; KJV, NCV, NET, NIV, REB, TEV], 'God's Spirit' [CEV], 'Holy Spirit, Spirit of God' [LN (12.18)], 'disposition, attitude, way of thinking' [LN (30.6)], 'spirit' [AB, LN (26.9); GW, NASB, NRSV], not explicit [NLT]. The phrase πνεῦμα υἱοθεσίας 'Spirit/spirit of adoption' is translated 'the Spirit which anticipates our adoption' [HNTC], 'the Spirit makes you God's children' [TEV], 'God's Spirit doesn't make us slaves...instead we become his children' [CEV], 'The Spirit...does not make us slaves...it makes us children of God' [NCV], 'the spirit of God's adopted children' [GW].

d. υἱοθεσία (LN 35.53) (BAGD 2. p. 833): 'adoption' [BAGD, BECNT, ICC2, LN, NICNT, NTC, WBC; KJV, NASB, NET, NRSV, REB], 'which anticipates our adoption' [HNTC], 'God's adopted children' [GW], 'God's very own children, adopted' [NLT], 'sonship' [AB; NIV], not explicit [CEV, NCV, TEV].

QUESTION—What is meant by πνεῦμα 'Spirit/spirit'?
1. It refers to the Holy Spirit [AB, BECNT, Gdt, HNTC, Ho, ICC2, LN (12.18), Mor, Mu, NICNT, NTC, SSA, TH, WBC; CEV, KJV, NCV, NET, NIV, REB, TEV].
2. It refers to an inner disposition or sense, to the human spirit [ICC1, NAC; GW, NASB, NRSV]. It is the consciousness of having become God's adopted children [ICC1, NAC].

QUESTION—Does υἱοθεσία 'adoption' refer primarily to the act of adoption or the status of sonship conferred by that act?
1. Here the focus is primarily on the act of adopting [NICNT].
2. The focus is primarily on the status of sonship that results from adoption [Gdt, Ho, Mor, NAC, WBC]. It is the consciousness of being in God's family as adopted sons [ICC1].
3. He is asserting the fact of adoption for those who have received the Spirit [BECNT].
4. The focus is on the anticipation of final adoption as sons which the Holy Spirit within us anticipates [HNTC].

QUESTION—How is the contrast between the Spirit/spirit of slavery and the Spirit/spirit of adoption used in this verse?
1. The contrast is used rhetorically to describe what the Holy Spirit does not do, or the attitude or experience he does not bring [AB, HNTC, Ho, ICC2, Mor, NICNT, NTC; CEV, NCV, REB, TEV]. That is, the Holy Spirit, which you have received, is not one that brings a sense of anxiety and dread of judgment before God, but a sense of adoption [Ho, ICC2, NICNT]. They are not in bondage to sin and the sense of anxiety and dread of judgment before God as they would have had under the law, but instead the Holy Spirit produces a sense of peace and security before God, our heavenly father [NICNT]. It is a play on words in which he contrasts an attitude of slavery to what happens when a person has the Spirit of God; they do not have a servile mentality as of a slave who fears his master, because the Holy Spirit brings freedom [AB]. The sentence does not imply that there is a spirit of slavery, just that the Holy Spirit is not like that, but is a Spirit of adoption instead [ICC2]. You are no longer oppressed with fear as you once were, but you have receive the Holy Spirit who transforms slaves into children and fills you with joy and confidence [NTC]. The Holy Spirit is not one of bondage, but of sonship; that is, he does not make people slaves, but sons [Mor].
2. The contrast is used rhetorically to highlight the difference between the new age of the Spirit and the old age under the law [BECNT, WBC]. The spirit of slavery is the slavery to sin and the fear of eschatological punishment brought about by sin which characterized the old age [BECNT].
3. The contrast is anthropological and refers to a servile temper or temperament such as they once had, as opposed to the new attitude or temperament they now have as believers [ICC1, NAC]. The spirit they

received was the consciousness of being God's adopted children [NAC]. This state, habit or temper of the human spirit is often due to supernatural influence [ICC1].

QUESTION—How does the genitive noun υἱοθεσίας 'of adoption' relate to the noun πνεῦμα 'Spirit/spirit'?
1. It indicates that the Spirit anticipates or pledges adoption [HNTC].
2. The Spirit effects adoption or sonship [Gdt, Ho, Mor, TH, WBC]. It indicates that the Holy Spirit bestows, reveals, and confirms the believer's status as a son of God [NICNT]. It is through the Spirit's work in the new birth that we are adopted [SSA]. The Holy Spirit brings about adoption through uniting people with Christ and causing them to share in Christ's sonship [ICC2]. Adoption is the effect of the Holy Spirit being present [BECNT]. Receiving the Spirit is what constitutes adoption as a son of God [AB]. The Spirit confirms our status as God's children [NTC]. He creates in the children of God the filial love and confidence by which they may call God 'father' and exercise their rights as his children [Mu]. The Spirit adopts, makes believers the sons of God, produces in believers the feelings that children have, and produces the character of sons in them [Ho].
3. It indicates their awareness of having been adopted as God's children [ICC1, NAC].
4. Those who have the Spirit of God and are led by him are sons of God [TNTC].

QUESTION—Is the adoption a future event or past event?
1. It is a future eschatological event [HNTC].
2. It refers to the reception of the Spirit at conversion [AB, Gdt, Ho, ICC2, Mor, Mu, NAC, NTC], or to the consciousness of having become a member in God's family that came about through baptism [ICC1]. Believers have the assurance that they are truly God's children, as well as of the certainty of final salvation [Ho].
3. Adoption is an 'already-not yet' phenomenon [BECNT, NICNT, WBC]. Believers have already received adoption but await the consummation and completion of it in the eschatological future [BECNT, NICNT].

by[a] which we-cry,[b] Abba[c], Father.

LEXICON—a. ἐν with dative object (LN 13.8, 90.6): 'by' [LN (90.6), WBC; GW, NASB, NET, NIV], 'in' [AB, BECNT, HNTC, LN (13.8), NICNT], 'whereby' [KJV], not explicit [CEV, NLT]. The phrase 'by which we cry' is translated 'by the Spirit's power we cry out' [TEV], 'by whose enabling we cry' [ICC2], 'enabling us to cry' [REB], 'who moves us to cry' [NTC], 'with that Spirit we cry' [NCV], 'when we cry' [NRSV], 'in whom we cry' [NICNT], 'by whom we cry' [WBC].
   b. pres. act. indic. of κράζω (LN 33.83) (BAGD 2.b.α. p. 448): 'to cry' [AB, BAGD, BECNT, HNTC, NICNT, NTC, WBC; KJV, NET, NIV, NRSV, REB], 'to cry out' [ICC2; NASB, NCV], 'to cry out to God' [TEV], 'to

call' [BAGD; CEV, NLT], 'to call out' [BAGD; GW], 'to shout' [LN]. This clause is translated 'and call him our Father' [CEV].
  c. ἀββά (LN 12.12) (BAGD p. 1): 'Abba' [AB, BAGD, HNTC, ICC2, NICNT, NTC, WBC; GW, KJV, NASB, NET, NIV, NRSV, REB], 'Father' [LN; CEV], 'father' [BAGD], not explicit [CEV, NCV]. The phrase 'Abba, Father' is translated 'Father, dear Father' [NLT], 'Father, my Father' [TEV].

QUESTION—What is the antecedent of ᾧ 'which' in the phrase 'in which'?
  It refers to the Holy Spirit [AB, Gdt, HNTC, ICC2, Mor, NICNT, NTC, TH, WBC; NCV, TEV].

QUESTION—What is the emotional and relational content of the term 'Abba'?
  It indicates the very personal and intimate spiritual connection between a Christian and God [NTC]. It indicates intimacy [Mor, NAC, WBC], and the opposite of fear [NAC]. It indicates warmth and confidence [Mu]. It was remembered by Christians as being the term of address that Jesus used in prayer; their use of it identified them as also being God's sons [WBC]. That Jesus authorized his disciples to use this term in prayer shows that he was granting them a share in his relationship to God [ICC2, St]. It was the word from his native language most ready to Paul in expressing his filial feelings toward God [Ho]. When Christians address God as Jesus did it shows that they have the same Spirit that he had [TNTC].

QUESTION—What is implied by the verb κράζω 'cry'?
  It indicates truth that is felt deeply and experienced intensely [BECNT, NICNT]. It is fervent prayer [Mor]. It is prayer in which believers acknowledge their adoption [BECNT, HNTC]. It indicates enthusiastic or inspired ecstatic speech [WBC], or Spirit-inspired prayer [HNTC]. It represents urgent and sincere prayer [ICC2]. It represents the profound emotion with which the believing heart expresses its adoration [Gdt]. It is the cry of childlike assurance, as opposed to the attitude of a servant [St].

QUESTION—What is the relationship of this phrase to the context?
  1. It goes with what precedes it [AB, BECNT, Gdt, HNTC, ICC1, ICC2, Mor, NICNT, NTC, SSA, TH, WBC; all versions except NRSV]: the spirit of adoption by which we cry Abba, Father.
  2. It goes with what follows it [St; NRSV]: when we cry Abba, Father, it is the Spirit bearing witness.

8:16 The Spirit himself bears-witness-with[a] our spirit that we-are children[b] of-God.

LEXICON—a. pres. act. indic. of συμμαρτυρέω (LN 33.266) (BAGD p. 778): 'to bear witness with' [AB, BAGD, HNTC, NICNT, NTC, WBC; KJV, NASB, NRSV], 'to bear witness to' [NET], 'to testify with' [BAGD; GW, NIV], 'to testify together with' [BECNT], 'to join with' [NCV], 'to affirm to' [REB], 'to confirm' [BAGD], 'to assure' [ICC2], 'to make (us) sure' [CEV], 'to testify in support' [BAGD, LN], 'to support by testimony, to provide supporting evidence' [LN]. This sentence is translated 'For his

Holy Spirit speaks to us deep in our hearts and tells us that we are God's children' [NLT], 'God's Spirit joins himself to our spirits to declare that we are God's children' [TEV]. See this word also at 2:15.
   b. τέκνον (LN 10.36) (BAGD 2.e. p. 808): 'child' [AB, BAGD, BECNT, HNTC, ICC2, LN, NICNT, NTC, WBC; all versions].

QUESTION—What is the force of the preposition συν- with the verb μαρτυρέω 'bears witness'?
  1. It has intensive force [Ho, ICC2, Mor, St; CEV, NET, NLT, REB]: the Spirit bears witness to and assures our spirit.
  2. It has the sense of accompaniment or 'bearing joint witness with' [AB, BECNT, Gdt, ICC1, Mu, NICNT, NTC, WBC; GW, NCV, NIV]. The Spirit adds his testimony to the believer's inner witness that he is God's child [Mu, SSA]. The Spirit concurs with Christians as they acknowledge that God is their Father [AB].
  3. It has both functions; the Holy Spirit witnesses to the regenerated spirit as well as witnessing with it, strengthening and confirming the inward conviction we have with the Spirit's powerful testimony [Gdt, NAC]. The dative τῷ πνεύματι ἡμῶν indicates that it is 'to our spirit' that the Holy Spirit conjointly bears witness along with our own spirit, which also bears witness [Gdt].

QUESTION—Is there any difference of connotation between τέκνον 'child' and υἱός 'son'?
  1. The difference is purely stylistic [BECNT, Mu, NICNT, TH, WBC]. There is no difference in meaning intended [Mor, NAC, TNTC].
  2. 'Son' connotes the dignity or honor involved in representing a family, whereas 'child' connotes the inner sense of relationship [Gdt]. 'Son' implies status and legal privileges, whereas 'child' denotes the natural relationship of a child to a parent [ICC1].

DISCOURSE UNIT: 8:17–30 [ICC2]. The topic is the indwelling of the Spirit—the gift of hope.

8:17 And if[a] children,[b] heirs[c] also;
LEXICON—a. εἰ (LN 89.30, 89.65) (BAGD I.1.a. p. 219): 'if' [AB, BAGD, BECNT, HNTC, ICC2, LN (89.30, 89.65), NICNT, NTC, WBC; all versions except CEV, NLT, TEV], 'since' [LN (89.30); NLT, TEV], 'because' [LN (89.30)], not explicit [CEV].
  b. τέκνον (LN 10.36) (BAGD 2.e. p. 808): 'child' [BAGD, LN (10.36)].
  c. κληρονόμος (LN 57.133, 57.139) (BAGD 2.b. p. 435): 'heir' [AB, BAGD, BECNT, HNTC, ICC2, LN (57.133, 57.139), NICNT, NTC, WBC; GW, KJV, NASB, NET, NIV, NRSV, REB]. This word is translated as a phrase: 'we will share his treasures' [NLT], 'we will possess the blessings he keeps for his people' [TEV]. This and the two following phrases are translated 'His Spirit lets us know that together with Christ we will be given what God has promised' [CEV], 'we will receive blessings from God together with Christ' [NCV].

heirs of-God, and fellow-heirs[a] of-Christ,

LEXICON—a. συνκληρονόμος (LN **57.134**) (BAGD p. 774): 'fellow heir' [BAGD, BECNT, ICC2, LN, NICNT, NTC; NET, REB], 'joint-heir' [HNTC; KJV, NRSV], 'co-heir' [AB; NIV], 'heir together with' [WBC; GW]. The phrase 'fellow-heirs with Christ' is translated 'together with Christ we will be given what God has promised' [CEV], 'we will receive blessings together with Christ' [NCV], 'we will also possess with Christ what God has kept for him' [TEV], 'everything God gives to his Son, Christ, is ours, too' [NLT].

QUESTION—How are the nouns related in the genitive construction 'heirs of God'?

1. The genitive is subjective; they will inherit what God has promised [AB, HNTC, Ho, ICC1, NAC, NICNT, NTC, SSA, TH, WBC]. The inheritance is eschatological life [NICNT]. They have a position of privilege because of their membership in God's family [Mor].
2. The genitive is objective; they will inherit God himself [BECNT, Gdt, ICC2, Mu, St]. They have God's life [ICC2], they have God as their God [BECNT]. He enriches his sons by imparting his life to them [Gdt].

QUESTION—What does it mean that they are fellow-heirs of Christ?

1. It is through Christ that inheriting the promised blessings becomes a reality [BECNT, HNTC, ICC2, NICNT]. Our sonship and status as heirs depend on our relationship to him [ICC2].
2. They receive the same privileges that Christ received from the Father [AB, Gdt, Ho, NAC, SSA, TNTC, WBC; CEV, NCV, NLT, TEV]. The inheritance consists of riches they will possess in connection with Christ [NTC], and they will share in the glory of Christ [AB, NTC, TNTC]. They enter into the possession bestowed upon them jointly with Christ, and share with him the glory of his exaltation [Mu]. They receive the good which Christ also receives, as he shares his throne and kingdom with them [Ho].
3. It is a title of dignity, assuring them that they have a place in the heavenly family of which he is the son and heir [Mor].

if-indeed[a] we-suffer-with[b] (him)

LEXICON—a. εἴπερ (LN 89.66) (BAGD VI.11. p. 220): 'if indeed' [BAGD, LN, NICNT; NASB, NET, NIV], 'if, in fact' [NRSV], 'if' [AB; GW, TEV], 'if so be that' [KJV], 'if after all' [BAGD, LN], 'provided that' [BECNT, WBC], 'since' [BAGD], 'because' [CEV], 'seeing that' [ICC2]. This is an emphatic marker of condition [LN]. The phrase 'if indeed we suffer with him' is translated 'since the fact that we are now sharing in his sufferings means that' [NTC], 'because we have suffered with him' [CEV], 'but we must suffer as Christ suffered' [NCV], 'but we must also share his suffering' [NLT, REB].

b. pres. act. indic. of συμπάσχω (LN 24.84) (BAGD p. 779): 'to suffer with' [AB, BAGD, HNTC, ICC2, NICNT, WBC; CEV, KJV, NET, NRSV], 'to

ROMANS 8:17

suffer together' [LN], 'to suffer together with' [BECNT], 'to suffer as' [NCV], 'to share in (his) suffering/sufferings' [NTC; GW, NIV, NLT, REB, TEV].

QUESTION—What relationship is indicated by εἴπερ 'if indeed'?
1. It states a condition that is assumed to be true [HNTC, ICC2, Mor, NAC, NTC, SSA, TH; CEV]: since we are suffering. They know they will inherit blessings because they are suffering as Christ did [SSA]. They share both in the trials of life as well as the benefits [NAC].
2. It states a possible condition that must be met for the promise to be fulfilled [AB, BECNT, Mu, NICNT, WBC; NCV, NLT]: if we suffer.

in-order-that we-may-be-glorified-with[a] **(him).**

LEXICON—a. aorist pass. subj. of συνδοξάζω (LN **87.10**) (BAGD 2. p. 785): 'to be glorified with' [AB, BAGD, HNTC, ICC2, NICNT, WBC; NASB, NET, NRSV], 'to be glorified together with' [BECNT; KJV], 'to be honored together with, to be exalted together with' [LN]; translated as a deponent: 'to share in (someone's) glory' [BAGD; CEV, NIV], 'to share (his) glory' [NTC; GW, NLT, REB, TEV], 'to receive honor together with' [**LN**]. This phrase is translated 'to have glory as Christ has glory' [NCV].

QUESTION—What relationship is indicated by ἵνα 'in order that'?
It indicates God's intended goal or outcome for these sufferings [HNTC, Ho, NICNT, WBC]. The glory is as sure as the suffering [HNTC], and the suffering is the indispensable prelude to the glory [TNTC]. It emphasizes the divinely ordained connection between suffering for Christ now and being glorified with him later [ICC2]. It indicates that the sure outcome of such suffering is sharing in his glory [Mor, NAC, NTC].

DISCOURSE UNIT: 8:18–39 [BECNT]. The topic is assurance of hope.

DISCOURSE UNIT: 8:18–30 [Gdt, GNT, NICNT, TNTC, WBC; CEV, NCV, NLT, NRSV, TEV]. The topic is the glory that is to be [GNT], the glory to come [TNTC], the future glory [NLT, TEV], our future glory [NCV, NRSV], a wonderful future for God's people [CEV], the spirit of glory [NICNT], the completion of salvation [Gdt], the spirit as firstfruits [WBC].

DISCOURSE UNIT: 8:18–27 [GW, NIV]. God's spirit helps us [GW], future glory [NIV].

DISCOURSE UNIT: 8:18–25 [Mor]. The topic is the glorious future.

DISCOURSE UNIT: 8:18–23 [AB]. The topic is creation groaning in travail testifies to this new destiny.

8:18 For I-consider[a] that the sufferings[b] of-the now[c] time[d]

LEXICON—a. pres. mid. (deponent = act.) indic. of λογίζομαι (LN 31.1) (BAGD 3. p. 476): 'to consider' [AB, BECNT, HNTC, LN, NICNT, NTC; GW, NASB, NET, NIV, NRSV, TEV], 'to reckon' [ICC2, WBC;

KJV, REB], 'to regard' [LN], 'to be sure' [CEV], 'to think, to believe, to be of the opinion' [BAGD], not explicit [NCV, NLT].
  b. πάθημα (LN 24.78) (BAGD 1. p. 602): 'suffering' [AB, BECNT, HNTC, ICC2, LN, NICNT, NTC, WBC; all versions except CEV, NLT, TEV], 'what (one) suffers' [BAGD; CEV, NLT, TEV]. This word is used here in a very different sense than in 7:5.
  c. νῦν (LN 67.38) (BAGD 3.a. p. 546): 'now' [AB, LN; CEV, NCV, NLT, REB], 'present' [BAGD, BECNT, HNTC, ICC2, NICNT, NTC, WBC; GW, KJV, NASB, NET, NIV, NRSV, TEV].
  d. καιρός (LN 67.78) (BAGD 1. p. 394): 'time' [BAGD, BECNT, HNTC, ICC2, LN, NICNT, NTC, WBC; KJV, NASB, NRSV, TEV]. The phrase τοῦ...καιροῦ 'of the...time' is not explicit [AB; CEV, GW, NCV, NET, NIV, NLT, REB].

QUESTION—What relationship is indicated by γάρ 'for'?
  It introduces what follows as an elaboration of the sequence of suffering and glory from the previous verse [Ho, NICNT]. He can say that they are heirs because the fact of suffering is not inconsistent with their being God's children or heirs; they will be glorified with Christ, for these sufferings are not worthy of thought [Ho]. It introduces an explanation of how the suffering and glory in 8:17 are related to each other [ICC1, ICC2]. It introduces what follows as an explanation of why suffering promotes hope instead of destroying it [BECNT]. It introduces what follows as grounds for the assertion that glory is as sure as the suffering [HNTC]. It introduces what follows as grounds for encouragement for those who are suffering [Mu, NAC]. It introduces a new topic, which is a theological statement based on Paul's own faith and hope [TH].

QUESTION—Are the sufferings general in nature or more specifically related to Christian faith?
  1. They include both general human difficulties as well as persecutions [Gdt, Mor, NICNT, NTC, St]. The sufferings include imperfections and unsatisfied aspirations [ICC1].
  2. It refers specifically to persecution or suffering as a Christian [HNTC, ICC2, NAC].

QUESTION—What period of time does τοῦ νῦν καιροῦ 'of the now time' refer to?
  1. It refers generally to the present evil age [Mor, Mu, NAC, NICNT, NTC, TH]. It is the present age that extends to the time of Christ's future coming [NTC]. It is the present time in contrast to the conditions of the new world which is to come [Gdt, St, TH].
  2. It refers specifically to the period between the incarnation and Christ's return [ICC2], or between the resurrection and Christ's return [AB, WBC]. It is the present eschatological moment which anticipates and precedes the future glory [HNTC].

(are) not worthy[a] to-be-compared-with[b] the glory[c] (that) is-going[d] to-be-revealed[e] in/to[f] us.

LEXICON—a. ἄξιος (LN **65.17**) (BAGD 1.a. p. 78): 'worthy' [HNTC, ICC2, LN, NTC; KJV, NASB], 'worth (comparing)' [AB, BECNT, NICNT; NIV, NRSV], 'comparable, of comparable value' [LN], not explicit [WBC]. The phrase οὐκ ἄξια '(are) not worthy' is translated 'cannot compare' [CEV], 'cannot be compared' [NET, TEV], 'bear no comparison' [REB], 'insignificant' [GW], 'nothing' [NCV, NLT].

b. πρός with accusative object (LN **64.17**) (BAGD III.5.d. p. 710): 'to be compared with' [HNTC, ICC2, **LN**, NTC, WBC; KJV, NASB, TEV], 'to be compared to' [BAGD, LN; NET], 'compared to' [GW, NCV, NLT], 'comparing to' [BECNT], 'in comparison with' [BAGD, LN], '(bear no) comparison with' [REB], 'comparing with' [AB, NICNT; NIV, NRSV], 'compare with' [LN; CEV]. This word conveys the classic idea of comparison [NICNT].

c. δόξα (LN 79.18, 87.23) (BAGD 1.b.β. p. 203): 'glory' [AB, BECNT, HNTC, ICC2, LN (79.18, 87.23), NICNT, NTC, WBC; all versions], 'glorious greatness' [LN (87.23)], 'splendor' [BAGD, LN (79.18)], 'radiance' [BAGD].

d. pres. act. participle of μέλλω (LN 67.62) (BAGD 1.b.α. p. 501): 'to be about to be' [BAGD, LN], 'will be' [CEV]. This unusual verb refers to what is going to happen (future tense), is about to happen (is imminent), or is destined to happen. It is translated 'that is going to be' [AB; TEV], 'that is about to be' [NRSV], 'that shall be' [BECNT, NICNT; KJV], 'that will be' [CEV, NCV, NET, NIV], 'that will soon be' [GW], 'that is to be' [HNTC, NTC; NASB], 'which is to be' [ICC2], 'to be' [WBC], 'later' [BECNT], not explicit [HNTC]. See this word also at 4:24; 5:14; 8:13.

e. aorist pass. infin. of ἀποκαλύπτω (LN 28.38) (BAGD 4. p. 92): 'to be revealed' [BAGD, HNTC, ICC2, LN, NICNT, NTC, WBC; GW, KJV, NASB, NIV, NRSV, TEV], 'to be disclosed' [LN], 'to be shown' [CEV, NCV, NET], not explicit [BECNT; NLT]. The phrase 'that is going to be revealed' is translated 'that he will give us later' [NLT], 'as yet unrevealed, which is in store for us' [REB]. This refers to an event that will occur, as opposed to an intellectual perception [NICNT].

f. εἰς with accusative object (LN 90.59): 'to' [LN, NICNT, WBC; CEV, GW, NASB, NCV, NET, NRSV, TEV], 'in' [AB, ICC2, NTC; KJV, NIV], 'in and for' [HNTC], not explicit [BECNT; NLT, REB].

QUESTION—What is the glory he speaks of?

It is a quality of existence characteristic of heaven, which includes transformation of the body [WBC]. It is participating in Christ's own glorious eschatological state, which includes the transformation of the body [NICNT]. It is the inheritance of believers that he has already referred to [BECNT]. It is the resurrection [NTC]. It is all that is involved in our being sons of God [Mor]. It is the glory that now belongs to Christ [Mu], the heavenly brightness that will be seen when he appears [ICC1]. It is the unutterable splendor of the eternal, immortal, and incorruptible God [St].

QUESTION—What is implied about the act of revealing by the participle μέλλουσαν 'is going (to be)'?

1. It emphasizes the certainty of the future glory [ICC1, Mor, NICNT]: it is certain to be revealed.
2. It speaks both of certainty as well as imminence [NAC, WBC].
3. It emphasizes the fact that the revelation is in the future [ICC2].

QUESTION—What relationship is indicated by εἰς 'to (us)'?

1. It will be revealed in the believers [Ho, ICC2, NTC; KJV, NIV]. It will come to them, enter them, fill them, envelope them, and then be revealed in them, and they will be a part of that glory, seeing it in each other [NTC]. In them God will display the divine glory to others [Ho].
2. It will be revealed to the believers [Mor, WBC; CEV, GW, NASB, NCV, NET, NRSV, TEV], as well as about them [WBC], or in them [Mor].
3. It will be revealed in them as well as for them [Gdt, HNTC].
4. It is a state in store for the believers [BECNT, NICNT; REB]. It will be revealed to them and bestowed upon them such that they become partakers of it [BECNT, Mu]. It will be revealed to them and will include them in its radiance [ICC1]. The sons of God will be manifested in glory [TNTC].

8:19 For the eager-expectation[a] of-the-creation[b] awaits[c] the revealing[d] of-the-sons[e] of-God.

LEXICON—a. ἀποκαραδοκία (LN **25.64**) (BAGD p. 92): 'eager expectation' [BAGD, ICC2, NICNT, WBC; NIV, REB], 'anxious expectation' [AB], 'earnest expectation' [KJV], 'anxious longing' [NASB], 'eager longing' [BECNT; NRSV, TEV], 'eager expectancy, eager desire, what (one) eagerly expects' [LN]. This is translated as modifying the verb that follows: 'eagerly' [HNTC; CEV, GW, NET, NLT], 'with excitement' [NCV], 'with eager expectation' [NIV, REB], 'with eager longing' [NRSV, TEV]. The phrase ἡ...ἀποκαραδοκία τῆς κτίσεως 'the eager expectation of the creation' is translated 'the eagerly awaiting creation' [BAGD], 'all creation...eagerly' [CEV], 'with outstretched head...eagerly' [NTC]. This is a personification [BECNT]. This word intensifies and adds emphasis to the verb ἀπεκδέχομαι [SSA]: very eagerly awaits.

b. κτίσις (LN 1.4, 42.38) (BAGD 1.b.β. p. 456): 'creation' [AB, BECNT, ICC2, LN (1.4, 42.38), NICNT, NTC, WBC; CEV, NASB, NET, NIV, NRSV], 'all creation' [CEV, GW, NLT, TEV], 'everything God made' [NCV], 'the created world' [HNTC], 'the created universe' [REB], 'universe' [LN (1.4)], 'creature' [LN (42.38); KJV]. This word in 8:19–22 probably refers to the whole of animate and inanimate creation below the human level [BAGD].

c. pres. mid. (deponent = act.) indic. of ἀπεκδέχομαι (LN **25.63**) (BAGD p. 83): 'to await' [LN, NICNT, WBC], 'to await eagerly' [BAGD], 'to wait for' [AB, BECNT, ICC2; CEV, GW, KJV, NASB, NCV, NET, NIV, NLT, NRSV, REB, TEV], 'to look forward eagerly' [HNTC, LN, NTC], 'to await expectantly' [LN].

d. ἀποκάλυψις (LN **28.38**) (BAGD 3. p. 92): 'revealing' [BAGD; NASB, NRSV], 'revelation' [AB, BECNT, ICC2, NICNT, NTC, WBC; NET], 'disclosure' [HNTC], 'manifestation' [KJV]. This noun is translated as a passive verb: 'to be revealed' [NIV, REB]. The phrase τὴν ἀποκάλυψιν τῶν υἱῶν τοῦ θεοῦ 'the revealing of the sons of God' is translated 'for God to show who his children are' [CEV], 'for God to reveal who his children are' [GW], 'God will reveal who his children are' [NLT], 'for God to reveal his sons' [TEV], 'for God to show his children's glory completely' [NCV].

e. υἱός (LN 9.46) (BAGD 1.c.γ. p. 834): 'son' [BAGD, LN (9.46)]. This word implies being bound to a person by close non-material ties [BAGD]. The plural form is translated 'sons' [HNTC, ICC2, NICNT, NTC, WBC; KJV, NASB, NET, NIV, REB, TEV], 'sons and daughters' [BECNT], 'children' [AB; CEV, GW, NCV, NLT, NRSV].

QUESTION—What relationship is indicated by γάρ 'for'?

It introduces additional support and development in 8:19-25 for what he says in 8:18 about the future glory, which is that Christians presently suffer with a sense of incompleteness and frustration and long for the fulfillment and transformation that will come [NICNT]. It introduces what follows in 8:19-30 as support for what he says in 8:18 about future glory [Ho, ICC2, Mor]. It introduces what follows in 8:19-27 as a continuation of the discussion of future glory begun in 8:18, and as the subject of the longing or groaning of creation, believers, and the Spirit [NTC]. It explains and demonstrates the suffering mentioned in the previous verse [Gdt]. It gives reasons for the endurance that 8:18 implies is needed [Mu].

QUESTION—What aspect of creation does he mean?

It refers to the subhuman creation [AB, BAGD, BECNT, Gdt, Ho, ICC1, ICC2, Mor, Mu, NAC, NICNT, NTC, St, TNTC, WBC].

QUESTION—In what sense are the sons of God to be revealed?

1. It means that God will reveal who his sons are [Mor, SSA; CEV, GW, NLT, TEV].
2. God will reveal who his children are as well as the glorious state to which he has transformed them [St, WBC].
3. God will reveal something about his children [AB, Gdt, Mu, NICNT, NTC; NCV]. It refers to the unveiling of the true nature of Christians, whose real status will be made known and brought to its final stage at the last day [NICNT]. Their full privilege and status as sons will be revealed to themselves and others [Mu]. He will reveal their glory [ICC1; NCV]. God will reveal how much he loves them and how richly he rewards them [NTC]. God will reveal their glorious destiny and status [AB]. Their true

character and glory as his sons will be revealed [Ho]. It refers to the appearing of the sons of God in their true sanctified nature [Gdt].
4. It refers to the experiential realization of their glorious future [NAC].

8:20 **For to-futility[a] the creation[b] was-subjected,[c] not willingly,[d]**
LEXICON—a. ματαιότης (LN 65.37) (BAGD p. 495): 'futility' [BECNT, LN, NTC, WBC; NASB, NET, NRSV], 'frustration' [AB, BAGD, NICNT; GW, NIV, REB], 'vanity' [ICC2; KJV], 'a vain life under inferior spiritual powers' [HNTC]. The phrase 'to futility the creation was subjected' is translated 'creation is confused' [CEV], 'everything God made was changed to become useless' [NCV], 'for creation was condemned to lose its purpose' [TEV], 'everything on earth was subjected to God's curse' [NLT].
b. κτίσις (LN **1.4**) (BAGD 1.b.β. p. 456): 'the creation' [BECNT, HNTC, ICC2, NICNT, NTC; NASB, NET, NIV, NRSV], 'creation' [AB, **LN**, WBC; CEV, GW, TEV], 'the creature' [KJV], 'everything God made' [NCV], 'everything on earth' [NLT], 'the created universe' [REB], 'the universe' [LN]. This word in 8:19–22 probably refers to the whole of animate and inanimate creation below the human level [BAGD].
c. aorist pass. indic. of ὑποτάσσω (LN 37.31) (BAGD 1.b.α. p. 848): 'to be subjected' [AB, BECNT, HNTC, ICC2, LN, NICNT, NTC, WBC; GW, NASB, NET, NIV, NLT, NRSV], 'to become subject' [BAGD], 'to be made subject' [KJV, REB], 'to be brought under control' [LN], not explicit [CEV, NCV, TEV]. This passive verb is translated as active with the agent made explicit: 'God made it this way' [CEV]. This is a divine passive, God being the agent [WBC; CEV, NET].
d. ἑκών (LN 25.65) (BAGD p. 247): 'willingly' [LN], 'of (one's) own free will' [LN]. The phrase οὐχ ἑκοῦσα is translated 'not willingly' [WBC; NET], 'against its will' [NLT], 'against its own will' [BAGD], 'not of its own will' [ICC2, NICNT; NRSV, TEV], 'not of its own choice' [AB, BECNT; REB], 'not by its own choice' [NTC; GW, NIV], 'not (creation's) own choice' [HNTC], 'not of its own wish' [NCV], 'not because it wants to' [CEV].
QUESTION—What relationship is indicated by γάρ 'for'?
It gives the reason that creation awaits the revelation, which is that it was subjected to frustration [ICC2, Mor]. It introduces 8:20–21 as an explanation for why the creation waits for the revealing of the sons of God mentioned in 8:19 [ICC2].
QUESTION—In what sense is the creation subjected to futility?
1. It is unable to achieve the purpose for which it was made [AB, BECNT, ICC1, ICC2, Mor, Mu, NAC, NICNT, NTC, SSA, WBC]. It was also futile when it was subjected to uses for which it was not made, as in those cases when people either abused nature for their own purposes or deified it [WBC]. It is subject to decay and arrested development [NTC]. It is

subject to frailty, death, decay, and barrenness [Gdt]. It was subjected to a frail, dying, miserable condition because of human sin [Ho].
2. It was subjected to malignant powers [TNTC], to inferior celestial or spiritual powers [HNTC].

QUESTION—What is the sense of the adverbial phrase οὐχ ἑκοῦσα 'not willingly'?

The focus is not on will, but on fault; that is, it's not whether or not the creation could exercise will, but that what happened was not the fault of creation. That is, creation was drawn into the consequences of Adam's failure [AB, BECNT, Ho, ICC1, ICC2, NAC, NTC, WBC]. Creation has always remained under the control of God, who is supreme [HNTC].

but because-of[a] the-(one) having-subjected[b] (it),

LEXICON—a. διά with accusative object (LN 90.44) (BAGD B.II.4.b. p. 181): 'because of' [ICC2, LN, NICNT, NTC; NASB], 'because of God' [NET], 'on account of' [LN], 'by' [AB, BAGD, HNTC; NRSV], 'by the will of' [NIV, REB], 'through the choice of' [BECNT], not explicit [GW, NLT]. This phrase is translated 'God made it this way' [CEV], 'because God wanted it' [NCV], 'because God willed it to be so' [TEV].
  b. aorist act. participle of ὑποτάσσω (LN 37.31) (BAGD 1.a. p. 848): 'to subject' [BAGD, LN], 'to subordinate' [BAGD], 'to bring under control' [LN]. See above.

QUESTION—Who subjected creation to futility?
  1. God subjected it [AB, HNTC, Ho, ICC1, ICC2, Mor, Mu, NAC, NICNT, NTC, SSA, St, TH, TNTC, WBC; CEV, NASB, NCV, NET, NLT, TEV].
  2. Satan dragged it into its current miserable state [Gdt].

in[a] hope[b]

LEXICON—a. ἐπί with dative object (LN 89.13) (BAGD II.1.b.γ. p. 287): 'in' [BECNT, ICC2, NICNT, NTC, WBC; CEV, GW, KJV, NASB, NET, NIV, NRSV], 'with' [AB; REB], 'on the basis of' [BAGD, LN], 'and qualified by' [HNTC]. This phrase ἐφ' ἐλπίδι 'in hope' is translated 'and because all along there was this hope' [NCV], 'yet there was this hope' [TEV], '(all creation) anticipates the day' [NLT]. The preposition indicates the condition in which the action occurred [NICNT].
  b. ἐλπίς (LN 25.59) (BAGD 1. p. 252; 2.a, 2.b. p. 253): 'hope' [BAGD, HNTC, ICC2, LN, NICNT, NTC, WBC; KJV, NASB, NCV, NET, NIV, REB], 'the hope' [BECNT; CEV, GW, TEV]. This noun is also translated as a verb: 'to anticipate' [NLT].

QUESTION—What previous phrase is this phrase connected with?
  1. It is connected with the verb phrase ἡ κτίσις ὑπετάγη 'the creation was subjected' [HNTC, Ho, ICC1, ICC2, Mu, NAC, NICNT, NTC]: it was subject to futility, but within the context of a hope that it would eventually be liberated.
  2. It is connected with the immediately preceding participial phrase τὸν ὑποτάξαντα 'the one having subjected it' [AB; CEV].

    2.1 God, who subjected it, had the hope of it being eventually liberated [CEV].
    2.2 God, who subjected it, gave it the hope of it being eventually liberated [AB].
QUESTION—Who is the subject of the hoping?
(Note that it is possible that this passage speaks objectively of what is hoped for without reference to the subject who hopes.)
    1. God is the one who hopes [TH; CEV]. God acted in hope when he subjected it [Mor]. The present condition of the creation is not the end of God's dealings but a stage in his larger purpose of drawing out and destroying the self-destructiveness of sin, so that creation can be restored as the context within which God's restored children live [WBC].
    2. The creation hopes [AB, BECNT, Gdt, Ho, ICC1, ICC2, Mu, NICNT], creation being personified in this passage [BECNT]. The phrase 'in hope' indicates an attendant condition, a context within which this hope is extended [Mu, NICNT]. That is, when God cursed people and the earth in Genesis 3 he also extended the promise to Eve that one day her seed would bruise the serpent's head [BECNT, NICNT]. Creation's current condition is not final or hopeless [AB, Mu], as it occurred within the context of God's purpose of ultimate deliverance [Mu], which is freedom from corruption and decay because of its association with the destiny of believers [AB].
    3. Believers are the ones who actually have the hope [SSA].

8:21 that/because^a the creation itself will-be-freed^b from^c the slavery^d of decay^e

LEXICON—a. ὅτι (LN 90.21, 89.33): 'that' [BECNT, LN (90.21), NICNT; CEV, GW, NASB, NET, NIV, NRSV, REB, TEV], 'because' [AB, HNTC, ICC2, LN (89.33), NTC, WBC; KJV], not explicit [NLT].
    b. fut. pass. indic. of ἐλευθερόω (LN 37.135) (BAGD 2. p. 251): 'to be freed' [AB, BAGD; REB], 'to be set free' [BAGD, BECNT, ICC2, LN, NICNT, NTC, WBC; CEV, GW, NASB, NCV, NET, NRSV, TEV], 'to be liberated' [HNTC; NIV], 'to be released' [LN]. This passive verb is translated as active: 'to join in glorious freedom' [NLT].
    c. ἀπό with genitive object (LN **13.62**): 'from' [AB, BECNT, HNTC, ICC2, LN, NICNT, NTC, WBC; all versions].
    d. δουλεία (LN 37.26) (BAGD 2. p. 205): 'slavery' [BAGD, BECNT, LN, WBC; GW, NASB, TEV], 'bondage' [AB, HNTC, ICC2, NICNT, NTC; KJV, NET, NIV], 'the shackles of' [REB], 'subservience' [LN], not explicit [CEV, NCV, NLT].
    e. φθορά (LN **23.205**) (BAGD 1. p. 858): 'decay' [AB, BAGD, ICC2, **LN**, NICNT, NTC; CEV, NET, NIV, NRSV, TEV], 'death and decay' [NLT], 'corruption' [BECNT, WBC; KJV, NASB], 'ruin' [NCV], 'mortality' [REB]. This noun is translated as an adjective: 'corrupting' [HNTC]. The phrase τῆς φθορᾶς is translated 'of decay' [ICC2; NET], 'of corruption'

[WBC; KJV], 'of mortality' [REB], 'to decay' [AB, NICNT, NTC; GW, NIV, TEV], 'to corruption' [NASB], 'resulting from corruption' [BECNT]. The phrase τῆς δουλείας τῆς φθορᾶς 'the slavery of decay' is translated 'the shackles of mortality' [REB].

QUESTION—What relationship is indicated by ὅτι 'that/because'?
1. ὅτι is translated 'that' and states the content of ἐλπίδι 'hope' in the preceding clause [BECNT, ICC1, NAC, NICNT, SSA, TH; CEV, GW, NASB, NET, NIV, NRSV, REB, TEV]: in hope that creation will be freed.
2. ὅτι is translated 'because' and indicates the reason why creation was subjected to futility [AB, Gdt, HNTC, ICC2, NTC, WBC; KJV]: it was subjected to futility because creation will be freed.

QUESTION—How are the nouns related in the genitive construction τῆς δουλείας τῆς φθορᾶς 'the slavery of decay'?
1. The genitive is objective.
   1.1 It denotes a slavery to decay or corruption [AB, BAGD, Gdt, Ho, ICC1, Mor, NAC, NICNT, NTC, SSA, St, TH; CEV, GW, NASB, NCV, NIV, NLT, NRSV, TEV]. Slavery to decay means that decay is inevitable and inescapable [SSA]. It is a slavery to a state of frailty and degradation [Ho].
   1.2 It denotes a slavery to corrupt powers, which, in turn, leads to corruption [HNTC].
2. The genitive is subjective, and denotes a slavery not only to decay, but which also comes from decay [ICC2].
3. It is appositional or epexegetic and denotes the slavery that is decay [BECNT, Mu, WBC]. It is the decay and death apparent everywhere in the physical world [Mu].

into[a] the freedom[b] of-the glory[c] of-the children[d] of-God.

LEXICON—a. εἰς with accusative object (LN 84.22) (BAGD 7. p. 230): 'into' [ICC2, LN, NICNT, WBC; KJV, NASB, NET], 'to' [BECNT, LN], 'and come to' [BAGD], 'and brought to' [AB], 'and brought into' [NIV], 'and would share' [TEV], 'and would share in' [CEV], 'so as to share' [NTC], 'in order to share' [GW], 'to attain' [HNTC], 'and will obtain' [NRSV], 'to have' [NCV], 'and is to enter upon' [REB], not explicit [NLT].
  b. ἐλευθερία (LN 37.133) (BAGD p. 250): 'freedom' [AB, BAGD, BECNT, HNTC, LN, NICNT; CEV, all versions except KJV, REB], 'liberty' [ICC2, NTC, WBC; KJV, REB].
  c. δόξα (LN 79.18) (BAGD 1.b.β. p. 203): 'glory' [LN], 'splendor' [BAGD, LN]. This genitive noun is translated as a common genitive: 'of the glory' [BECNT, ICC2, NICNT, WBC; NASB, NRSV]; as a genitive of source: 'which springs from the glory' [HNTC]; as an adjective modifying 'freedom': 'glorious' [AB, NTC; CEV, GW, KJV, NET, NIV, NLT, REB, TEV]. The genitive phrase τὴν ἐλευθερίαν τῆς δόξης 'the freedom of

the glory' is translated 'the freedom and glory' [NCV]. It refers to the radiance or glory of the next life [BAGD].
   d. τέκνον (LN 10.36) (BAGD 2.e. p. 808): 'child' [AB, BAGD, BECNT, HNTC, ICC2, LN, NICNT, NTC, WBC; all versions]. It refers to those who are adopted by God [BAGD].
QUESTION—How are the nouns related in the genitive construction τὴν ἐλευθερίαν τῆς δόξης 'the freedom of the glory'?
  1. It indicates association or possession [BECNT, Gdt, HNTC, Mu, NAC, NICNT, SSA, St]: the freedom is associated with or pertains to the state of glory that belongs to the children of God. The freedom comes from the eschatological glory [HNTC]. Paul's main focus in this passage is the contrast between glory and decay, not between freedom and slavery [ICC1, SSA]. Liberty is one of the aspects of the glory which the children of God will experience, and is the only aspect of that glory that creation will experience [Gdt].
  2. It is qualitative or descriptive [AB, NTC; CEV, GW, KJV, NET, NIV, NLT, REB, TEV]: the glorious freedom. Freedom is a characteristic of eschatological glory [AB].
  3. It is epexegetic or appositional: the freedom consists of the glory that belongs to the children of God [Ho, Mu, WBC]. It is the liberty which consists in or is associated with the glory that is the goal of redemption [Ho].
  4. It indicates source [HNTC, ICC2]: the freedom that springs from the glory. Liberty results from and must necessarily accompany the revealing of the glory of God's children [ICC2].

8:22 **For we-know that all the creation[a] groans-together[b] and suffers-agony-together[c] until[d] now;[e]**

LEXICON—a. κτίσις (LN 1.4) (BAGD 1.b.β. p. 456): 'creation' [BAGD, LN], 'universe' [LN]. The phrase πᾶσα ἡ κτίσις is translated 'all creation' [AB; CEV, GW, NLT], 'all of creation' [TEV], 'the whole creation' [BECNT, HNTC, ICC2, NICNT, NTC, WBC; KJV, NASB, NET, NIV, NRSV], 'the whole created universe' [REB], 'everything God made' [NCV]. This word in 8:19–22 probably refers to the whole of animate and inanimate creation below the human level [BAGD].
  b. pres. act. indic. of συστενάζω (LN **25.145**) (BAGD p. 795): 'to groan together' [BAGD, BECNT, **LN**, NICNT, WBC; KJV, NET], 'to groan' [AB; CEV, GW, NIV, NLT, NRSV, TEV], 'to groan with one consent' [HNTC], 'to groan with one accord' [ICC2, NTC], not explicit [NCV]. The phrase 'all the creation groans together' is translated 'the whole created universe in all its parts groans' [REB]. This word occurs only here in the NT.
  c. pres. act. indic. of συνωδίνω (LN **24.88**) (BAGD p. 793): 'to suffer agony together' [BAGD], 'to suffer together' [LN; NET], 'to suffer birth pangs' [BECNT], 'to suffer birth pangs together' [NICNT], 'to suffer the

pains of childbirth together' [WBC; NASB], 'to labor in pain' [AB], 'to travail' [HNTC, ICC2], 'to travail in pain together' [KJV], 'to be in pain like a woman about to give birth' [CEV]. The phrase συστενάζει καὶ συνωδίνει 'groans together and suffers agony together' is translated 'with one consent groans and travails' [HNTC], 'groans and travails with one accord' [ICC2], 'has been groaning with/as in the pain of childbirth' [GW, NIV], 'groans as if in the pangs of childbirth' [REB], 'groans with pain, like the pain of childbirth' [TEV], 'has been groaning in labor pains' [NRSV], 'has been waiting in pain, like a woman ready to give birth' [NCV]. This word occurs only here in the NT.

d. ἄχρι with genitive object (LN 67.119) (BAGD 1.a. p. 128): 'until' [BAGD, BECNT, LN; KJV, NASB, NCV, NET, NRSV], 'even until' [ICC2], 'up till' [WBC], 'up to' [AB, HNTC, NICNT; GW, NIV, REB, TEV], 'right up to' [NLT].

e. νῦν (LN 67.38) (BAGD 3.b. p. 546): 'now' [BAGD, BECNT, ICC2, LN, WBC; KJV, NASB, NCV, NET, NRSV], 'this moment' [HNTC], 'the present time' [AB, NICNT; GW, NIV, NLT, TEV], 'the present' [REB]. The phrase ἄχρι τοῦ νῦν 'until now' is translated 'is still' [CEV], 'and still is' [NTC].

QUESTION—What is the groaning and suffering that the creation is doing?

It refers metaphorically to the current state of distress as well as to the yearning and anticipation of the fulfillment of all things at the eschaton [Gdt, NICNT]. This groaning is both the expression and proof of the unnatural state to which nature is now subject [Gdt]. It reflects suffering and hope; there is a lack of peace and harmony, but there will one day be concord and harmony everywhere [NTC]. It describes the period of turmoil and anguish even for the non-human creation which will issue in a new order of things [WBC]. This is a vivid way of saying that nature is in a troubled state [Mor]. It conveys the thought of severe distress that will ultimately result in a happy and worthwhile outcome [ICC2]. It is the pains of birth, and not of death [Ho].

8:23 **and not only,[a] but (we) ourselves also having the firstfruits[b] of-the Spirit,**

LEXICON—a. The phrase οὐ μόνον δέ 'and not only' is translated 'not only so' [NIV], 'not only that' [AB], 'and not only does (the creation groan)' [BECNT], 'and not (the creation) only' [HNTC], 'and not only (creation)' [WBC; NRSV], 'however, not only (creation) groans' [GW], 'but it is not just creation alone (which groans)' [TEV], 'not only the world' [NCV], 'and not only this' [ICC2, NICNT; NASB], 'not only this' [NTC; NET], 'and not only they' [KJV], 'what is more' [REB], 'and even we Christians' [NLT], not explicit [CEV].

b. ἀπαρχή (LN **57.171**) (BAGD 1.β. p. 81): 'firstfruits' [AB, BAGD, BECNT, HNTC, ICC2, NICNT, NTC, WBC; KJV, NASB, NET, NIV, NRSV, REB], 'foretaste' [LN; NLT], 'foretaste and pledge' [**LN**]. The term 'the firstfruits of the Spirit' is translated 'the Spirit as the first of God's gifts' [GW, TEV], 'the Spirit as the first part of God's promise' [NCV], 'the Holy Spirit within us as a foretaste of future glory' [NLT]. This entire phrase is translated 'The Spirit makes us sure about what we will be in the future' [CEV].

QUESTION—What contrast is indicated by the phrase οὐ μόνον 'not only'?

1. Not only does non-human creation groan, but believers do as well [BECNT, Gdt, HNTC, Ho, ICC1, ICC2, Mor, Mu, NICNT, NTC, SSA, St, TH, WBC; GW, NCV, NRSV, TEV].
2. Not only does creation bear testimony to the destiny of believers, but believers themselves do so also by their hope [AB].

QUESTION—What relationship is indicated by the participle ἔχοντες 'having'?

1. It expresses a concession [AB, Gdt, ICC1, NTC; NLT]: although we have…we groan.
2. It is causal [BECNT, Mu, NICNT, WBC], or partly causal [Mor]: because we have…we groan.
3. It is attributive [HNTC, Ho, ICC2, SSA; KJV, NET, NIV, NRSV, REB, TEV]: we, who have…groan.

QUESTION—What is meant by ἀπαρχή 'firstfruits'?

This word conveys the idea that the redemptive and transforming work God has begun will be completed, and the gift of the Holy Spirit is the pledge guaranteeing that [BECNT, NICNT; CEV]. The Holy Spirit is the pledge guaranteeing future glory [SSA; NLT]. The Holy Spirit is the anticipation of final and full salvation [HNTC, NTC]. The Spirit is the foretaste of the future [AB, NAC], much more is yet to come [ICC2, Mor]. The Spirit is given as a pledge or earnest assuring the believer of all that is yet to be received [Ho], a pledge of the fullness of the Spirit to be given at the resurrection [Mu]. The firstfruits are of a piece with the whole, and the use of this word indicates a continuity between the gift of the Holy Spirit, the Spirit's work in believers, and the eventual resurrection [WBC]. In this world Christians receive a beginning of the fullness of the Spirit which will be given in entirety above [Gdt]. The charismata and moral and spiritual gifts bestowed upon the church at Pentecost serve to quicken a sense of and longing for greater gifts to come, chief of which will be the transformation of the body [ICC1].

QUESTION—How are the nouns related in the genitive phrase τὴν ἀπαρχὴν τοῦ πνεύματος 'the firstfruits of the Spirit'?

1. It is epexegetic or appositional [AB, BECNT, Gdt, HNTC, Ho, ICC2, Mor, NAC, NICNT, NTC, SSA, St, TH, WBC; GW, NCV, NLT, REB, TEV]: the firstfruits, which is the Spirit, or the Spirit's present work.
2. It is portative [ICC1, Mu]: the first portion of the Spirit in token of the fullness yet to be given, or the first gifts of the Spirit in token of all the rest that will be given.

we ourselves also groan[a] within[b] ourselves eagerly-awaiting[c] adoption,[d]

TEXT—Some manuscripts omit υἱοθεσίαν 'adoption'. GNT retains this word with an A decision, indicating that the text is certain. It is omitted by AB.

LEXICON—pres. act. indic. of στενάζω (LN 25.143) (BAGD p. 766): 'to groan' [AB, BECNT, HNTC, ICC2, LN, NICNT, NTC, WBC; all versions except NCV], 'to sigh' [BAGD, LN]. The phrase 'we ourselves also groan within ourselves' is translated 'we also have been waiting with pain inside us' [NCV].

b. ἐν with dative object (LN 83.13): 'within' [ICC2, LN, NTC, WBC; GW, KJV, NASB, NLT, TEV], 'in' [BECNT, LN, NICNT], 'inside' [NCV]. The phrase ἐν ἑαυτοῖς 'within ourselves' is translated 'inwardly' [AB, HNTC; NET, NIV, NRSV, REB], 'silently' [CEV].

c. pres. mid. (deponent = act.) participle of ἀπεκδέχομαι (LN 25.63) (BAGD p. 83): 'to await eagerly' [BAGD, NTC, WBC; NET], 'to await' [NICNT], 'to wait for' [AB, BECNT, ICC2; CEV, KJV, NCV, NRSV, TEV], 'to wait eagerly for' [GW, NASB, NIV], 'to wait anxiously for' [NLT], 'to look forward to' [HNTC], 'to look forward eagerly' [LN; REB]. This participle is translated as indicating a temporal relationship: 'while (we await)' [BECNT, HNTC, SSA; CEV, NRSV, REB]; 'as (we await)' [AB; GW, NET, NIV, TEV].

d. υἱοθεσία (LN 35.53) (BAGD 2. p. 833): 'adoption' [BAGD, BECNT, HNTC, ICC2, LN, NICNT, NTC, WBC; GW, KJV, NASB, NET, NRSV, REB], 'adoption as sons' [NIV]. This word is translated as a phrase: 'for God to show that we are his children' [CEV], 'for God to finish making us his own children' [NCV], 'that day when God will give us our full rights as his children' [NLT], 'for God to make us his sons' [TEV]. The possessive pronoun 'our' is added by HNTC, ICC2, NTC; GW, NASB, NET, NIV, REB: 'our adoption'.

QUESTION—What does the groaning express or indicate?

These non-verbal groans indicate an attitude of frustration at the moral and physical weakness characterizing our lives in the present age, as well as a sense of entreaty to God for deliverance [NICNT]. It is the metaphor of birth pangs; creation and believers alike long for future glory just as a mother groaning with labor pains longs for the birth of the baby [SSA]. It is another way of expressing the sufferings spoken of in 8:18 [AB]. The groaning expresses frustration, though not despair, on the part of believers, who must live with the tension of being caught in the overlap between the two ages [WBC]. It expresses deep sorrow about our current circumstances [Mor]. There is a groaning that comes from the fact that the outward man has not entered into the privilege of the new world that the inward man has entered into [Gdt]. It expresses the burdensome nature of this imperfect present age as well as a longing for the future glory to be revealed [Mu]. It is an anxious and painful longing to have our physical bodies transformed and delivered from all the evils that beset them [ICC1]. We groan for our body to be transformed and for our fleshly nature to be destroyed [St].

the redemption^a of-our body.^b

LEXICON—a. ἀπολύτρωσις (LN 37.128) (BAGD 2.a. p. 96): 'redemption' [AB, BAGD, BECNT, HNTC, ICC2, NICNT, NTC, WBC; KJV, NASB, NET, NIV, NRSV], 'liberation' [LN; REB], 'deliverance' [LN], 'the freeing...from sin' [GW]. This noun is translated as a verb phrase: 'and set (our whole being) free' [TEV]. The phrase τὴν ἀπολύτρωσιν τοῦ σώματος ἡμῶν 'the redemption of our bodies' is translated 'This means that our bodies will also be set free' [CEV], 'which means our bodies will be made free' [NCV], 'including the new bodies he has promised us' [NLT].

b. σῶμα (LN 8.1): 'body' [LN; all versions except REB, TEV]. This singular word is translated in the plural: 'our bodies' [AB, BECNT, ICC2, NICNT, NTC; CEV, GW, NCV, NET, NIV, NRSV], 'new bodies' [NLT]. The phrase 'the redemption of our bodies' is translated 'our liberation from mortality' [REB], 'set our whole being free' [TEV].

QUESTION—What is the relation between this phrase and the noun υἱοθεσία 'adoption'?

1. It is appositional, defining the nature of the adoption [BECNT].
2. The transformation of the body will be the final phase of the adoption process [BECNT, Gdt, ICC1, ICC2, Mor, Mu, NICNT, NTC, SSA, St]. The redemption of the body is a part of what is meant by adoption, but the adoption includes far more [Ho]. The redemption of the body is the resurrection, and the adoption will be the full and final manifestation of the status of God's children when they are fully invested as his sons and daughters [TNTC].

DISCOURSE UNIT: 8:24–25 [AB]. The topic is the fact of Christian hope testifies to this new destiny.

8:24 **For in-hope^a we-were-saved;^b**

LEXICON—a. ἐλπίς (LN 25.59) (BAGD 1. p. 253): 'hope' [BAGD, LN], 'expectation' [BAGD]. There is no lexical entry in the Greek text for the word 'in', the relation between 'hope' and the verb being indicated by the dative case of the word 'hope'. The phrase τῇ ἐλπίδι is translated 'in hope' [AB, BECNT, ICC2, NTC; NASB, NET, NRSV], 'in this hope' [HNTC; NIV], 'in terms of hope' [WBC], 'with hope' [NICNT], 'it was with this hope' [REB], 'with this hope in mind' [GW], 'by hope' [KJV, TEV]. This clause is translated 'and this hope is what saves us' [CEV], 'we were saved, and we have this hope' [NCV], 'now that we are saved, we eagerly look forward to this freedom' [NLT]. It means not yet in reality, 'only in expectation' [BAGD].

b. aorist pass. indic. of σῴζω (LN 21.27) (BAGD 2.b. p. 798): 'to be saved' [AB, BAGD, BECNT, HNTC, ICC2, LN, NICNT, NTC, WBC; all versions]. The aorist tense is translated as a perfect tense: 'we have been saved' [AB, BECNT; NASB]; as a past tense: 'we were saved' [HNTC,

ICC2, NICNT, NTC; GW, NCV, NET, NIV, NRSV, REB, TEV]; as a present tense: 'we are saved' [WBC; KJV, NLT], 'saves us' [CEV].

QUESTION—What relationship is indicated by γάρ 'for'?

It gives grounds for what was just said in the previous verse [Ho, Mor]. It introduces grounds for, and further explanation of, the eschatological focus of 8:23, since what believers hope for is still future [BECNT, ICC2], and the need to wait patiently should not be surprising [NICNT]. It introduces an amplification relating back to 8:19 [SSA]. Believers don't need to be discouraged by their afflictions because having such afflictions is necessary and does not at all mean that they are not God's children [Ho].

QUESTION—What relationship is indicated by the dative τῇ ἐλπίδι 'in hope'?

1. The dative is modal, meaning we are saved 'in hope' [AB, Gdt, HNTC, Ho, ICC1, ICC2, Mor, Mu, NAC, NTC, St, TNTC, WBC; NASB, NET, NIV, NRSV], or associative, meaning we are saved with hope or always having hope [BECNT, NICNT]. That is, the present experience of salvation has always been understood to be incomplete and that something more is to be experienced in the future.
2. It is instrumental [TH; CEV, KJV, TEV]: we are saved by hope. In this view hope is seen as an aspect of faith or as a synonym for faith.

QUESTION—What does it mean that we were saved 'in hope'?

There is an element of incompleteness in our salvation and we must be content to hope for the completion of the process [AB, BECNT, Gdt, HNTC, Ho, ICC1, ICC2, Mor, Mu, NICNT, NTC, SSA, St, WBC]. Hope is inseparable from salvation [BECNT]. This hope is a confidence about a future reality [HNTC].

but hope[a] being-seen[b] is not hope;[c]

LEXICON—a. ἐλπίς (LN **25.61**) (BAGD 4. p. 253): 'hope' [LN], 'what is hoped for' [**LN**], '(a) thing hoped for' [BAGD]. This clause is translated 'But if we already have what we hope for' [CEV]. Here the noun refers to the object of hope.

b. pres. pass. participle of βλέπω (LN 24.7) (BAGD 1.a. p. 143): 'to be seen' [AB, BAGD, BECNT, ICC2, LN, NICNT, NTC, WBC; KJV, NASB, NET, NIV, NRSV, REB]. This passive participle is translated as active: '(if) we see' [TEV], '(a hope) you can see' [HNTC], '(if) we already have' [CEV], 'you already have' [NLT], '(something) we already see' [GW], '(if) we see' [NCV].

c. ἐλπίς (LN 25.59, 25.61) (BAGD 4. p. 253): 'hope' [LN], 'what is hoped for' [LN (25.61)], 'looking forward with confidence' [LN (25.59)]. Here the noun probably refers to the subjective experience of hope, which one exercises only with respect to what he does not yet see.

QUESTION—In what sense is 'hope' used here?

Hope is used in two senses: one use, concerning what 'is seen', is the objective sense, indicating the object one hopes for [Gdt, ICC2, NICNT, NTC, SSA], and the other sense is the subjective attitude of hope regarding something not yet visible [Gdt, NICNT]. By definition hope is exercised with regard to things not yet seen [WBC].

for who hopes[a] (for) what he-sees?[b]
TEXT—Instead of τίς 'who?', some manuscripts read τις, τί 'anyone, why?'; other manuscripts read τις, τί καί 'anyone, why also?' giving the clause the meaning, 'for what anyone sees, why does he/she also hope for?' GNT reads τίς 'who?' with a B decision, indicating that the text is almost certain. The reading τις, τί 'anyone sees, why' is taken by HNTC; KJV, NASB.
TEXT—Instead of ἐλπίζει 'who hopes', some manuscripts read ὑπομένει 'he endures patiently'. GNT reads ἐλπίζει 'he hopes' with a B decision, indicating that the text is almost certain. The reading ὑπομένει 'he endures patiently' is taken only by HNTC.
LEXICON—a. pres. act. indic. of ἐλπίζω (LN 25.59) (BAGD 2. p. 252): 'to hope' [AB, BAGD, BECNT, ICC2, LN, NICNT, NTC, WBC; all versions], 'to hope for' [BAGD, LN]. This clause is translated 'there is no need to keep on hoping' [CEV].
  b. pres. act. indic. of βλέπω (LN 24.7) (BAGD 1.a. p. 143): 'to see' [AB, BAGD, BECNT, HNTC, ICC2, LN, NICNT, NTC, WBC; GW, KJV, NASB, NET, NRSV, REB, TEV]. The phrase 'what he sees' is translated 'what can be seen' [GW], 'something they/you already have' [NCV, NLT], 'what he already has' [NIV]. This verb, occurring twice in this verse, is translated by a single verb phrase 'if we already have' [CEV].

8:25 But if what we-see not we-hope-for, with[a] patience[b] we-await (it).
LEXICON—a. διά with genitive object (LN 89.76, 90.8) (BAGD A.III.1.c. p. 180): 'with' [AB, BAGD, BECNT, HNTC, ICC2, LN (90.8), NICNT, NTC, WBC; GW, KJV, NASB, NET, NRSV, REB, TEV], 'through' [BAGD, LN (89.76, 90.8)], 'by' [LN (89.76)], 'by means of' [BAGD, LN (89.76, 90.8)], not explicit [CEV, NCV, NIV, NLT].
  b. ὑπομονή (LN 13.28, 25.174) (BAGD 1. p. 846): 'patience' [BAGD, WBC; KJV, NRSV, REB, TEV], 'steadfast patience' [ICC2], 'endurance' [AB, BECNT, LN, NICNT; NET], 'patient endurance' [HNTC, NTC], 'perseverance' [GW, NASB]. The phrase δι' ὑπομονῆς 'with patience' is translated 'patiently' [CEV, NCV, NIV], 'patiently and confidently' [NLT].
QUESTION—What relationship is indicated by εἰ 'if'?
  1. It is conditional, introducing an 'if–then' statement [AB, BECNT, HNTC, Ho, NICNT, WBC; GW, KJV, NASB, NET, NIV, NLT, NRSV, REB, TEV]. That is, if we don't see what we hope for, we must wait patiently.
  2. It is factual, introducing a 'since–then' statement that is presumed to be true [ICC1, ICC2, NTC, SSA; CEV, NCV]. That is, because we don't yet see what we hope for, we wait patiently.
QUESTION—What relationship is indicated by διά 'with'?
  It indicates manner [AB, BECNT, Gdt, HNTC, Ho, ICC1, ICC2, NICNT, NTC, SSA, WBC; all versions]: patiently, with patience or endurance.

DISCOURSE UNIT: 8:26–27 [AB, Mor]. The topic is even the Spirit testifies to this new destiny [AB], the Spirit's intercession [Mor].

8:26 And in-the-same-way[a] the Spirit also helps-together[b] with-our weakness;[c]

LEXICON—a. ὡσαύτως (LN 64.16) (BAGD p. 899): 'in the same way' [BAGD, HNTC, LN, NICNT, NTC, WBC; NASB, NET, NIV, REB, TEV], 'likewise' [BAGD, BECNT; KJV, NRSV], 'in like manner' [ICC2, LN], 'similarly' [AB, BAGD], 'at the same time' [GW], 'and' [NLT], 'also' [NCV], 'in certain ways' [CEV].

b. pres. mid. (deponent = act.) indic. of συναντιλαμβάνομαι (LN **35.5**) (BAGD p. 784): 'to help together' [BAGD], 'to help' [BAGD, HNTC, ICC2, NTC, WBC; GW, KJV, NASB, NCV, NET, NIV, NLT, NRSV], 'to come to the aid' [AB, BECNT, NICNT; REB], 'to come to help' [TEV], 'to join in helping' [LN], 'to be here to help us' [CEV]. The prefix συν- has intensive force, meaning that the Spirit gives the help that believers need, not that he joins in helping [BECNT].

c. ἀσθένεια (LN 74.23) (BAGD 2. p. 115): 'weakness' [AB, BECNT, HNTC, ICC2, LN, NICNT, NTC, WBC; GW, NASB, NCV, NET, NIV, NRSV, REB], 'infirmities' [KJV], 'distress' [NLT], 'limitation, incapacity' [LN]. The phrase τῇ ἀσθενείᾳ ἡμῶν 'with our weakness' is translated 'weak as we are' [TEV], 'in certain ways we are weak' [CEV].

QUESTION—What relationship is indicated by ὡσαύτως 'and in the same way'?
1. It relates to hope [BECNT, Ho, Mu, NAC, NICNT, SSA, St]: just as our hope helps and sustains us, so the Spirit also helps us.
2. It relates to the inner groaning [AB, Gdt, ICC1, ICC2, NTC, TH, WBC]: just as we groan inwardly, the Spirit also prays with unexpressed sighs or groanings. Creation groans, we groan, and the Spirit groans [TH].
3. It relates to the Spirit; just as we have the Spirit as firstfruits while we await what is to come, so also the Spirit helps us in our weakness [Mor].

QUESTION—What is the weakness in which the Spirit helps?
1. It is the whole of our human weakness [Ho, Mor, Mu, NICNT, NTC, WBC]. It also includes suffering [Ho].
2. It has to do with not knowing what to pray for [AB, BECNT, HNTC, ICC1, ICC2, NAC, St, TH]. It also involves a general weakness in trusting God [TH].
3. It is weakness in enduring difficult suffering [Gdt].
4. It is weakness in our spirits [SSA]. It refers to lack of religious insight [BAGD].

for the what we-should-pray[a] as it-is-proper,[b] we-know not,[c]

LEXICON—a. aorist mid. (deponent = act.) subj. of προσεύχομαι (LN 33.178) (BAGD p.714): 'to pray' [AB, LN, NICNT, NTC; NASB, NCV, NET, NRSV, REB, TEV], 'to pray for' [BAGD, BECNT, ICC2, WBC; CEV,

GW, KJV, NIV, NLT]. The phrase 'what we should pray as it is proper' is translated 'the proper prayers to offer' [HNTC].
- b. pres. act. indic. of the irregular verb δεῖ (LN 71.21) (BAGD 6. p. 172): 'to be proper' [BAGD], 'should' [LN], 'ought' [LN]. The phrase καθὸ δεῖ 'as it is proper' is translated 'we should' [NET, NLT], 'as we should' [BECNT, WBC; KJV, NCV], 'we ought' [NTC; NIV, REB, TEV], 'as we ought' [KJV, NRSV], 'as it is necessary' [NICNT], 'what it is right (to pray for)' [ICC2], 'the proper (prayers)' [HNTC], 'what we need' [GW], not explicit [AB; CEV].
- c. perf. (with pres. meaning) act. indic. of the irregular verb οἶδα (LN 28.1): 'to know' [AB, BECNT, HNTC, ICC2, LN, NICNT, NTC, WBC; all versions].

QUESTION—What is the unknown element here?
1. They do not know what to pray for [BECNT, ICC2, Mu, NICNT, NTC, SSA, TH, WBC; CEV, NIV]. They may not know what to pray for in specific situations, despite knowing the will of God in general [NTC].
2. They do not know how to pray for what they need [GW], how they should word their prayers [ICC1].
3. They don't know what to pray for or how to pray [AB, Gdt, Ho, Mor, NAC; NLT]. The spirit teaches them what to desire and pray for, gives them faith in prayer, and helps them know how to express it [Ho].

but the Spirit himself pleads-for[a] (us) with[b] unexpressed[c] groanings;[d]

TEXT—Some manuscripts add ὑπὲρ ἡμῶν 'for us' following ὑπερεντυγχάνει 'pleads for'. GNT omits this phrase with an A decision, indicating that the text is certain. This phrase is included, either for stylistic reasons or by accepting the textual addition, by AB, BECNT, HNTC, ICC2, NTC, WBC; CEV, KJV, NASB, NET, NIV, NLT, REB, TEV.

LEXICON—a. pres. act. indic. of ὑπερεντυγχάνω (LN **33.348**) (BAGD p. 840): 'to plead for' [BAGD; REB, TEV], 'to intercede' [AB, BAGD, BECNT, HNTC, ICC2, **LN**, NICNT, NTC, WBC; GW, NASB, NET, NIV, NRSV], 'to intercede on behalf of' [LN], 'to make intercession for' [KJV], 'to pray for' [CEV, NLT], 'to speak to God for' [NCV].
- b. There is no lexical entry in the Greek text for the preposition 'with', the dative case of the noun στεναγμός being used to express the relation between it and the verb. This relation is translated 'with' [AB, BECNT, HNTC, ICC2, NTC, WBC; KJV, NASB, NCV, NET, NIV, NLT, NRSV], 'along with' [GW], 'in' [NICNT; CEV, TEV], 'through' [REB].
- c. ἀλάλητος (LN **33.96**) (BAGD p. 34): 'unexpressed' [BAGD], 'that words cannot express' [NICNT; NIV, TEV], 'that cannot be expressed in words' [LN; GW, NLT], 'that cannot be put into words' [CEV], 'that cannot be uttered' [KJV], 'that do not need expression in speech' [HNTC], 'inexpressible' [NET], 'ineffable' [AB], 'unspeakable' [BECNT], 'too deep for words' [BAGD; NASB, NRSV], 'unspoken' [ICC2, NTC], 'that words cannot explain' [NCV], 'inarticulate' [WBC; REB].

d. στεναγμός (LN 25.143) (BAGD p. 766): 'groaning' [BAGD, BECNT, ICC2, NTC; KJV, NASB, NET, NLT], 'groan' [BAGD, HNTC, LN, NICNT, WBC; GW, NIV, REB, TEV], 'sigh' [AB, BAGD, LN; NRSV], 'deep feeling' [NCV], 'ways' [CEV].

QUESTION—Whose are the groans unexpressed?
1. They are the sighings or groanings of the Holy Spirit as he intercedes directly to God for us [AB, Gdt, ICC1, ICC2, NAC, NICNT, NTC, St, TH]. The groanings are imperceptible to the Christians themselves [ICC2]. These groanings are more elevated, holy, and intense than what the believer is capable of by himself [Gdt].
2. They are the sighings or groanings of believers [BECNT, Ho, Mor, Mu, SSA, WBC]. Their groanings are the medium of the Holy Spirit's intercession [Mor, Mu]. They are the inexpressible longings to know and do God's will that arise in every believer's heart, and which have their source in the Holy Spirit [BECNT]. It is the Spirit who prompts the groanings of the believer as he prays, working within them desires about what to pray for and faith by which to pray [Ho].
3. The Holy Spirit identifies with the groans of believers and he intercedes with unspoken groanings, the Spirit and believers groaning together [St]. The Holy Spirit intercedes along with or through the groans of believers [TNTC; GW, REB].

QUESTION—Are the sighs inexpressible or merely unexpressed?
1. They are unexpressed, they are not put into words [BECNT, HNTC, ICC2, NICNT, NTC, St].
2. They are inexpressible, they cannot be put into words [AB, Gdt, Ho, Mor, Mu, NAC, SSA, TH, TNTC, WBC]. They transcend and bypass articulation and expression [Mu]. Some emotions are too big for utterance [Ho]. They cannot be put into human terms [AB, NAC]. Believers sometimes don't know what to say in prayer and can only express themselves in anguished frustration in this period of eschatological tension [WBC].

8:27 **and the-(one) searching[a] the hearts[b] knows what the mind[c] of-the Spirit (is),**

LEXICON—a. pres. act. participle of ἐραυνάω (LN 27.34) (BAGD p. 306): 'to search' [AB, BAGD, BECNT, HNTC, ICC2, LN, NICNT, NTC, WBC; GW, KJV, NASB, NET, NIV, NRSV, REB], 'to see' [NCV, TEV], 'to know' [NLT]. The phrase 'the one searching the hearts' is translated 'All of our thoughts are known to God' [CEV].
  b. καρδία (LN 26.3) (BAGD 1.b.α. p. 403): 'heart' [AB, BAGD, BECNT, HNTC, ICC2, LN, NICNT, NTC, WBC; all versions except CEV, REB], 'mind' [LN], 'thoughts' [CEV], 'inmost being' [REB].
  c. φρόνημα (LN 26.15) (BAGD p. 866): 'mind' [AB, NICNT; CEV, KJV, NASB, NCV, NET, NIV, NRSV], 'thought' [TEV], 'way of thinking' [LN, WBC], 'intention' [BECNT, ICC2, NTC]. The phrase 'the mind of

the Spirit' is translated 'what the Spirit means' [HNTC; REB], 'what the Spirit has in mind' [GW], 'what the Spirit is saying' [NLT].

QUESTION—What is implied by the phrase 'the one searching the hearts'?
1. He is saying that God sees into a believer's inner being where the Holy Spirit's ministry of intercession occurs [AB, BECNT, HNTC, Ho, Mu, NAC, NICNT, NTC, SSA, WBC]. Here 'heart' means inner feelings [SSA].
2. He is saying that if God can know the hearts of men, how much more does he know the intent of the Holy Spirit as he intercedes [ICC1, ICC2, Mor].

because/that[a] in-accordance-with[b] God he-pleads[c] for[d] (the) saints.[e]

LEXICON—a. ὅτι (LN 89.33, 90.21): 'because' [AB, LN (89.33), WBC; KJV, NASB, NCV, NET, NIV, NRSV, REB, TEV], 'for' [HNTC, LN (89.33), NICNT; NLT], 'that' [ICC2, LN (90.21), NTC], 'namely, that' [BECNT], not explicit [CEV, GW].
  b. κατά with accusative object (LN 89.8) (BAGD II.5.a.α. p. 407): 'in accordance with' [BAGD, LN], 'in conformity with' [BAGD]. The phrase κατὰ θεόν 'in accordance with God' is translated 'in accordance with his will' [AB; TEV], 'in accordance with the will of God' [NICNT], 'in accordance with God's will' [NIV], 'according to God's will' [BECNT, ICC2; NET], 'according to the will of God' [KJV, NASB, NRSV], 'as God would have it' [WBC], 'the way God wants him to' [GW], 'in the way God wants' [NCV], 'as God himself wills' [HNTC; REB], 'in harmony with God's will' [NTC], 'in harmony with God's own will' [NLT], not explicit [CEV].
  c. pres. act. indic. of ἐντυγχάνω (LN **33.169**, 33.347) (BAGD 1. p. 270): 'to plead' [LN **(33.169)**; NLT, REB, TEV], 'to intercede' [AB, BECNT, HNTC, ICC2, LN (33.347), NICNT, NTC, WBC; GW, NASB, NET, NIV, NRSV], 'to make intercession' [KJV], 'to speak to God (for)' [NCV], 'to appeal' [BAGD], 'to appeal to' [LN (33.169)], 'to petition' [BAGD, LN (33.169)], 'to pray' [CEV]. This verb conveys a feeling of urgency and intensity [LN (33.169)].
  d. ὑπέρ with genitive object (LN 90.36): 'for' [AB, BECNT, HNTC, ICC2, LN, NICNT, NTC; all versions except NET, TEV], 'on behalf of' [LN, WBC; NET, TEV].
  e. ἅγιος (LN11.27, 53.46, 88.24) (BAGD 2.d.β. p. 10): 'holy' [LN (53.46, 88.24)]. This plural adjective is translated 'saints' [BAGD, BECNT, HNTC, ICC2, NICNT, NTC, WBC; KJV, NASB, NET, NIV, NRSV], 'God's people' [LN (11.27); CEV, GW, REB], 'God's dedicated people' [AB], 'his people' [NCV, TEV], 'us believers' [NLT]. See this word also at 1:7.

QUESTION—What relationship is indicated by ὅτι 'because/that'?
1. It is causal, meaning 'because' [AB, Gdt, HNTC, Ho, NICNT, WBC; KJV, NASB, NCV, NET, NIV, NLT, NRSV, REB, TEV]: God knows the

mind of the Spirit because the Spirit intercedes in accordance with God's will.
2. It is explicative, meaning 'that' [BECNT, ICC1, ICC2, NAC, NTC, SSA]: God knows the mind of the Spirit, that he intercedes in accordance with God's will.

DISCOURSE UNIT: 8:28–39 [NIV]. The topic is more than conquerors.

DISCOURSE UNIT: 8:28–30 [AB, Mor]. The topic is the Christian called and destined for glory [AB], the purpose of God [Mor].

DISCOURSE UNIT: 8:28–29 [GW]. The topic is that nothing can separate us from God's love.

8:28 And we-know that to-the-(ones) loving God all (things) works-together[a] for[b] good,[c]

TEXT—Some manuscripts add ὁ θεός 'God' following συνεργεῖ 'works together', making 'God' the subject of συνεργεῖ and 'everything' the object of 'works together': 'God works everything together'. GNT rejects this addition with a B decision, indicating that the text is almost certain. It is also possible even without the variant to take God as the implied subject and 'everything' as the object of συνεργεῖ 'he works everything'. 'God' is taken as the subject of the verb by CEV, NASB, NCV, NIV, NLT, TEV, whether because of accepting the variant, or by assuming 'God' as the implied subject of συνεργεῖ, or for stylistic reasons. REB has 'he' as the subject of the verb, apparently referring to the Spirit.

LEXICON—a. pres. act. indic. of συνεργέω (LN 42.15) (BAGD p. 787): 'to work together' [AB, BECNT, NICNT, NTC; GW, KJV, NASB, NET, NLT, NRSV], 'to work' [NCV, NIV], 'to work with' [TEV], 'to be at work' [CEV], 'to cooperate' [HNTC; REB], 'to contribute toward' [WBC], 'to prove advantageous' [ICC2].

b. εἰς with accusative object (LN 89.48, 89.57) (BAGD 5. p. 230): 'for' [AB, BAGD, BECNT, HNTC, ICC2, NICNT, NTC, WBC; all versions], 'for the purpose of' [LN (89.57)], 'to cause' [LN (89.48)], 'with respect to, with reference to' [BAGD]. LN 89.48 indicates outcome or result, while LN 89.57 indicates intent or purpose.

c. ἀγαθός (LN 65.20, 88.1) (BAGD 2.a.β. p. 3): 'good' [BAGD, BECNT, HNTC, LN (65.20, 88.1), NICNT, NTC, WBC; KJV, NASB, NET, NRSV, REB, TEV], 'the good' [AB; CEV, GW, NCV, NIV, NLT], 'their true good' [ICC2].

QUESTION—What relationship is indicated by δέ 'and'?

It is not translated by AB; CEV, GW, NCV, NRSV, TEV.
1. It continues what was being said before [BECNT, HNTC, Ho, ICC1, ICC2, Mu, NICNT, NTC, SSA, WBC; KJV, NASB, NET, NIV, NLT, REB]: the Spirit helps us, and we know.
2. It is adversative [Gdt]: we groan and suffer, not knowing how to pray, but we do know that all things work together for good.

QUESTION—Is the 'we' of 'we know' inclusive or exclusive?

It includes the readers [ICC2, NICNT, St, TH, WBC]. They would know this truth from what they know about God and have experienced in their lives [NICNT]. He knows it is generally recognized as true [ICC2]. This knowledge was the corporate experience of the people of God [WBC]. It was a fact of common knowledge [TH].

QUESTION—What is the subject of συνεργεῖ 'works together'?

In Greek neuter plural nouns use a third person singular verb, so either πάντα 'all things' or 'he' (that is, God) could be the subject of the singular verb συνεργεῖ. In addition, the neuter plural nominative and accusative have the same form, so πάντα 'all things' could be either the subject or the object of the verb: 'all things (subject) work together' or 'he works all things (object) together'.

1. Πάντα 'all things' is the subject of συνεργεῖ and there is no object [AB, BECNT, Gdt, HNTC, Ho, ICC2, NICNT, NTC, WBC; GW, KJV, NET, NRSV]: all things work together.
2. 'He' (God) is the subject of συνεργεῖ 'works' [ICC1, Mor, SSA, St, TH; CEV, NASB, NCV, NIV, NLT, TEV]. God is the agent of the action [SSA, St].
2.1 πάντα is the object of the verb: God works all things together [Mor, St, TH; CEV, NIV, NLT, TEV], or causes all things to work together [ICC1; NASB, NLT].
2.2 πάντα describes the sphere within which God works [St; NIV, TEV] in all things God works.
3. The Spirit is the subject [TNTC; probably REB]: the Spirit cooperates for good for those who love God.

QUESTION—What relationship is indicated by the dative case of the phrase τοῖς ἀγαπῶσιν τὸν θεόν 'the ones loving God'?

1. It indicates that they are the recipients of the action [AB, BECNT, HNTC, Ho, ICC1, ICC2, NICNT, NTC, St, WBC; CEV, GW, KJV, NASB, NCV, NET, NIV, NLT, NRSV]: works for good to or for those who love God.
2. It is related to the prefix συν- 'with' in συνεργεῖ 'works together' [Gdt, TH; REB, TEV].
2.1 It indicates that God works for good with those who love him [TH; REB, TEV].
2.2 It indicates that all things work for good with those who love God as well as for them [Gdt].

to-those being called-(ones)[a] according-to[b] (his) purpose.[c]

LEXICON—a. κλητός (LN 33.314) (BAGD p. 436): 'called' [BAGD, LN; KJV]. The phrase τοῖς...κλητοῖς 'to those being called ones' is translated 'They are the ones God has chosen' [CEV], 'they are the people he called' [NCV]. This adjective is translated as a verb by all versions and commentary translations, with the prepositional phrase κατὰ πρόθεσιν 'according to his purpose' taken as referring to the calling: they were called according to his purpose.

b. κατά with accusative object (LN 89.8): 'according to' [BECNT, ICC2, NICNT, NTC, WBC; GW, KJV, NASB, NET, NIV, NLT, NRSV, REB, TEV], 'in accordance with' [AB, HNTC, LN], 'for' [CEV], not explicit [NCV].

c. πρόθεσις (LN 30.63) (BAGD 2.b. p. 706): 'purpose' [AB, BAGD, BECNT, HNTC, ICC2, LN, NICNT, NTC, WBC; all versions except GW, NCV, NLT], '(his) purpose for them' [NLT], 'plan' [LN; GW, NCV], 'will' [AB].

QUESTION—What is the relation between the phrases 'the ones being called' and 'in accordance with his purpose'?

His purpose was to call them to salvation [AB, HNTC, Ho, NTC, TH, WBC; NCV], to save them [St], which he does in order to show love and mercy to them [ICC2]. It is the divine plan of election from all eternity [AB]. God's purpose was to save them [Gdt, Mor], which is why he called them [Gdt]. They were effectually called to salvation [Mor, TNTC]. His eternal purpose was to call them to salvation and ultimately to glory [Mu]. If men are called according to God's eternal purposes their salvation is secure [Ho].

8:29 For[a] (those) whom he-knew-beforehand,[b]

LEXICON—a. ὅτι: 'for' [BECNT, ICC2, NICNT, NTC, WBC; KJV, NASB, NIV, NLT, NRSV, REB], 'because' [NET], 'this is true because' [GW], not explicit [AB, HNTC; CEV, NCV, TEV].

b. aorist act. indic. of προγινώσκω (LN 28.6, **30.100**) (BAGD p. 703): 'to know beforehand' [LN (28.6, 30.100), WBC], 'to foreknow' [AB, BECNT, HNTC, ICC2, NICNT, NTC; KJV, NASB, NET, NIV, NRSV], 'to know in advance' [NLT], 'to select in advance' [LN (30.100)], 'to choose beforehand' [BAGD, LN (**30.100**)]. The phrase οὓς προέγνω 'those whom he knew beforehand' is translated 'he has always known who his chosen ones would be' [CEV], 'he already knew his people' [GW], 'God knew them before he made the world' [NCV], 'those whom God knew before ever they were' [REB], 'those whom God had already chosen' [TEV].

QUESTION—What relationship is indicated by ὅτι 'for'?

1. It gives grounds for what has just been stated [AB, BECNT, Gdt, ICC1, ICC2, Mor]. It gives grounds for 8:28 as a whole [BECNT, ICC2]. It gives grounds for the promise that all things work together for good [Gdt, ICC1, Mor].

2. It explains the word πρόθεσις 'purpose'; God's purpose that guides all things is that believers become conformed to his son's image [HNTC, Mu, NICNT]. God's purpose and the process of bringing it about are described in 8:29–30 [HNTC].

3. It gives grounds for the promise that all things work together for good, but also explains the word πρόθεσις 'purpose', which is God's intent that

believers become conformed to Christ's image [Ho, NICNT]. Believers are called according to God's purpose, and all things work together for their good, for God's predestined plan cannot fail [Ho].

QUESTION—In what sense is the verb προγινώσκω 'know beforehand' used here?

1. It means that God foresaw their faith [Gdt, SSA].
2. It means that God chose them [AB, HNTC, Ho, ICC2, Mor, Mu, NAC, NICNT, NTC, St, TH, TNTC, WBC; TEV]. Before the foundation of the world God knew them intimately and chose them [NICNT, NTC], or loved them specially and chose them [Ho]. God's foreknowledge involves his ordaining; the history of the Church and who is a part of it is not a result of arbitrary human will or chance, but God's plan. On the other hand, he is not espousing a determinist philosophy [HNTC]. His use of this word has the nuance of personal and intimate knowledge [AB, NAC]. The knowing here has the Hebraic sense of a relationship experienced and acknowledged [WBC]. God knew and loved them beforehand [Mu, St].

he-predestined[a] also (to be) similar-in-form[b] to-the likeness[c] of-his Son,

LEXICON—a. aorist act. indic. of προορίζω (LN 30.84) (BAGD p. 709): 'to predestine' [AB, BAGD, BECNT, NICNT; NASB, NET, NIV, NRSV], 'to predestinate' [KJV], 'to decide beforehand' [LN], 'to decide upon beforehand' [BAGD], 'to decide' [CEV, NCV], 'to determine ahead of time' [LN], 'to predetermine' [WBC], 'to foreordain' [HNTC, ICC2, NTC], 'to ordain' [REB], 'to appoint' [GW], 'to choose' [NLT], 'to set apart' [TEV].

b. σύμμορφος (LN **58.5**) (BAGD p. 778): 'similar in form' [**LN**], 'of the same form' [LN], 'like' [BAGD]. The phrase συμμόρφους τῆς εἰκόνος 'to be similar in form to the likeness' is translated 'to be conformed to the image' [AB, BECNT, ICC2, NICNT, NTC, WBC; KJV, NASB, NET, NRSV], 'to be conformed to the likeness' [NIV], 'to share the likeness' [REB], 'to bear the same image as' [HNTC], 'to have the same form as' [GW], 'to let them become like' [CEV], 'to be like' [NCV], 'to become like' [NLT, TEV].

c. εἰκών (LN 58.35) (BAGD 2. p. 222): 'likeness' [LN; NIV, REB], 'image' [AB, BECNT, HNTC, ICC2, NICNT, NTC, WBC; KJV, NASB, NET, NRSV], 'appearance' [BAGD], 'same form' [LN; GW], 'be/become like' [CEV, NCV, NLT, TEV].

QUESTION—In what sense will they be 'similar in form to the likeness of his Son'?

This is a fulfillment of God's intent expressed in Gen 1:26 where people were made in the image of God [TNTC].

1. The focus is eschatological: they are predestined to enjoy in the future the glory of resurrected and transformed bodies that Christ now has [BECNT, HNTC, Mu, NICNT, WBC].
2. They will be like him in character [Mor, NAC, SSA].

3. They will share his glory [TH].
4. They are being conformed to his image in this life through the process of sanctification, and in the next life will be transformed to share in his glorious state [Gdt, Ho, ICC1, ICC2, NTC, St]. They also conform to him in enduring sufferings in this life [Ho].

for[a] him to-be firstborn[b] among[c] many brothers;[d]

LEXICON—a. εἰς with accusative object (LN 89.48, 89.57): 'for, for the purpose of' [LN (89.57)], 'to cause' [LN (89.48)]. This preposition is translated 'that (he might/should be)' [AB, BECNT, WBC; KJV, NASB, NIV], 'so that (he might be)' [HNTC, ICC2, NICNT, NTC; REB], 'in order that (he might be)' [NRSV], 'so that (Jesus would be)' [NCV], 'that (his Son would be)' [NET], 'so that (his/the Son would be)' [CEV, NLT, TEV], 'therefore His Son is' [GW].

b. πρωτότοκος (LN 10.43) (BAGD 2.a. p. 726): 'firstborn' [AB, BAGD, BECNT, ICC2, LN, NICNT, NTC, WBC; GW, KJV, NASB, NCV, NET, NIV, NLT, NRSV], 'first' [CEV, TEV], 'eldest' [HNTC; REB]. This noun lacks the definite article, but is translated as having the definite article by all commentaries and versions.

c. ἐν with dative object (LN 83.9): 'among' [AB, BECNT, ICC2, LN, NICNT, NTC, WBC; GW, KJV, NASB, NET, NIV, REB, TEV], 'in (a large company of)' [HNTC], 'of' [CEV, NCV], 'with' [NLT], 'within (a large family)' [NRSV].

d. ἀδελφός (LN 10.49) (BAGD 2. p. 16): 'brother' [BAGD, LN]. This plural noun is translated 'brothers' [AB, HNTC, ICC2, NICNT, NTC, WBC; NCV, NIV, TEV], 'brothers and sisters' [BECNT; NET, NLT], 'brethren' [KJV, NASB], 'children' [CEV, GW], 'family' [NRSV], 'family of brothers' [REB].

QUESTION—What is meant by πρωτότοκος 'firstborn'?

It signifies the fact that he is the first to be physically raised from death, to be followed later by believers [BECNT, ICC1, NICNT]. It signifies Christ's preeminence over, as well as his solidarity with, all humanity, and believers will rule with him [BECNT]. It expresses his preeminence as well as his humility and his marvelous love for people [NTC]. He is the one who fulfills what was God's intent for humanity from the beginning, which involves the glory of being in God's image and having dominion over all things [WBC]. His status and rank is compared to the highest rank given to a firstborn son in a family, but believers will also have privilege and status similar to the younger sons in a family [SSA]. He is the oldest of a group of joint-heirs and brothers who share his inheritance [HNTC]. It speaks of his preeminence, but also implies that others will share in his sonship [AB, Mor, NAC, St]. It focuses on his priority and his supremacy [Mu]. He has priority in time and primacy in rank [NAC]. He is the head of a multitude of brothers who have been made sons of God in him and through him [ICC2]. He precedes believers to glory, but also has superiority over them all [Gdt]. He is the head and chief of the great multitude who are made sons of God through him [Ho]. Christ is the firstborn of all creation in the old order because all things were made by him and for him, and by his resurrection he is head of a new order of brothers who inherit eternal life in him [TNTC].

8:30 and (those) whom he-predestined, these also he-called[a]; and (those) whom he-called, these also he-justified[b]; and (those) whom he-justified, these also he-glorified.[c]

LEXICON—a. aorist act. indic. of καλέω (LN 33.307) (BAGD 2. p. 399): 'to call' [AB, BAGD, BECNT, HNTC, ICC2, LN, NICNT, NTC, WBC; all versions except CEV, NLT], 'to call to come to him' [NLT], not explicit [CEV].

b. aorist act. indic. of δικαιόω (LN 34.46, 56.34) (BAGD 3.b. p. 197): 'to justify' [AB, BAGD, BECNT, HNTC, ICC2, NICNT, NTC, WBC; KJV, NASB, NET, NIV, NRSV, REB], 'to put right with' [LN (34.46); TEV], 'to make right with' [NCV], 'to give right standing with' [NLT], 'to acquit' [BAGD, LN (56.34)], 'to accept' [CEV], 'to approve' [GW].

c. aorist act. indic. of δοξάζω (LN 87.24) (BAGD 2. p. 204): 'to glorify' [AB, BAGD, BECNT, HNTC, ICC2, LN, NICNT, NTC, WBC; KJV, NASB, NCV, NET, NIV, NRSV, REB], 'to give glory to' [GW], 'to share (his) glory with' [CEV, TEV], 'to promise (them his) glory' [NLT], 'to clothe in splendor' [BAGD].

QUESTION—What is the function of τούτους καί 'these also' in this verse?

It shows the exact correspondence between those who were predestined and those who were called, those who were justified, and those who were glorified [NICNT]. Even though two of the actions were eternal and three occur in time, all five actions are co-extensive, as indicated by repetition of the verbs and by the conjunction 'also' [Mu]. It implies knowledge of those individuals whom God foreknew would believe, and that they were present in his mind when he decreed the height to which he intended to raise them [Gdt].

QUESTION—To what does 'he called' refer?

It refers to the moment in time when God brought them to himself through the gospel [AB, BECNT, HNTC, ICC2, NTC, WBC]. It refers to the effectual call [Ho, Mor, NTC, St], by which people respond in faith and conversion, brought about by the Holy Spirit [Ho, NTC]. The call is the outward invitation through preaching and the inward drawing by the Holy Spirit [Gdt].

QUESTION—What relation does the action of being glorified have with the predestining, calling, and justifying?

1. From the standpoint of the believer's experience the predestining, calling, and justifying all occurred in the past, and the glorifying will occur in the future [BECNT, HNTC, ICC2, Mu, NICNT, SSA, WBC]. The aorist tense is used because from God's standpoint it is past in the sense that it has already been decreed that it should occur [BECNT, Ho, NICNT]. It is

spoken of as future because of certainty that it will occur [HNTC, Mor, NAC, SSA, St, TNTC]. It is a prophetic past tense [St, TNTC]. Their glorification has already occurred through their union with the glorified Christ, but it has not yet been revealed in history [ICC2]. Since Christ as their head is already glorified, they are glorified as well [Gdt]. It is proleptic, indicating certainty that it will happen [Mu].
2. The process of glorification begins in this life and is completed in the next [AB, NAC]. Sanctification is glory begun, and glory is sanctification completed [St, TNTC].

DISCOURSE UNIT: 8:31–39 [AB, Gdt, GNT, HNTC, ICC2, Mor, NICNT, NTC, TNTC, WBC; CEV, NCV, NLT, NRSV, TEV]. The topic is God's love [GNT; CEV], God's love in Christ Jesus [NCV, NRSV, TEV], nothing can separate us from God's love [NLT], the Christian's triumph song [Mor], hymn to the love of God made manifest through Christ Jesus [AB], hymn of assurance of salvation [Gdt], the triumph of God—his faithfulness and the assurance of faith [WBC], assurance [HNTC], conclusion to 8:1–39 and to the entire forgoing argument of the epistle [ICC2], the believer's security celebrated [NICNT], being more than conquerors [NTC], the triumph of faith [TNTC].

8:31 What therefore shall-we-say[a] to[b] these (things)?
LEXICON—a. fut. act. indic. of λέγω (LN 33.69) (BAGD 1. p. 226): 'to say' [AB, BAGD, BECNT, HNTC, ICC2, LN, NICNT, NTC, WBC; all versions].
  b. πρός with accusative object (LN 90.25): 'to' [BECNT, LN; KJV, NASB], 'about' [AB, LN; CEV, GW, NCV, NET, NLT, NRSV], 'in view of' [ICC2, NICNT, WBC; TEV], 'in response to' [NTC; NIV], 'of' [HNTC], 'with all this in mind' [REB].
QUESTION—To what does ταῦτα 'these things' refer?
  1. It includes all that has been said in the epistle so far [Gdt, ICC2, Mor, NTC, WBC], particularly from 1:16 on [WBC]. It refers to all that has been said, but especially to 8:18 and following [NTC].
  2. It refers to his discussion of Christian assurance in chapters 5–8 [BECNT, HNTC, NICNT], especially 8:18–30 [NICNT]. It refers to 8:18–30, if not to chapters 5–8 as a whole [AB]. It refers specifically to 8:18–30, but since that section summarizes and rounds off chapters 6–8, it refers more generally to that larger section as well [WBC].
  3. It refers to all that has been said in chapter 8 so far. That is, if God has delivered us from the law of sin and death, granted us renewal by his indwelling Spirit, makes us his children, and predestines us to holiness and glory, what do we have to fear for the future, and whom do we need to fear? [Ho].
  4. It refers to what he has been saying in the immediately preceding verses, particularly 8:15 and following [NAC] or from 8:18 and following [Mu], or in 8:30 [probably TNTC].

5. It refers to his five convictions expressed in 8:28 and the five affirmations of 8:29-30, to which he adds these five unanswerable questions in 8:31-39 [St].

QUESTION—What relationship is indicated by οὖν 'therefore'?

It introduces the rhetorical question that invites the reader to draw a conclusion from all that has been said before [Gdt, Ho, Mor, Mu, NICNT, SSA, WBC], probably from 3:21 on, about all that God does for them [SSA], or from all the blessings mentioned in chapter 5 through 8 [NICNT], or from chapter 8 [Ho], or from the whole letter [Mor].

If God (is) for[a] us, who (is/can be) against[b] us?

LEXICON—a. ὑπέρ with genitive object (LN 90.36) (BAGD 1.a.δ. p. 838): 'for' [AB, BAGD, BECNT, ICC2, LN, NICNT, NTC, WBC; all versions except CEV, NCV, REB], 'with' [NCV], 'on (someone's) side' [BAGD, HNTC; CEV, REB].

b. κατά with genitive object (LN 90.31) (BAGD I.2.b.γ. p. 406): 'against' [AB, BAGD, BECNT, HNTC, ICC2, LN, NICNT, NTC, WBC; all versions].

QUESTION—What relationship is indicated by εἰ 'if'?

It introduces the rhetorical question, but there is no doubt that God is actually for them [BECNT, Gdt, HNTC, ICC2, Mor, Mu, NICNT, NTC, SSA, WBC]. 'If' means 'since it is so' [WBC].

QUESTION—How is the preposition ὑπέρ 'for' used here?

It means that God is on their side [AB, Gdt, HNTC, NAC, NTC, St; CEV, REB], and is acting in their behalf [ICC2, NICNT, SSA]. It means no legal charge will be brought against them at the judgment [BECNT]. The statement 'God is for us' is a concise statement of the gospel [ICC2]. As judge he is satisfied, as our father he loves us, as the almighty who controls all things he has determined to save us, and as a being of unchanging and infinite love he does not allow anything to separate us from himself [Ho].

QUESTION—What is the sense of this rhetorical question?

While many are in fact against them in the present moment, no one can harm them in the ultimate sense [BECNT, NICNT]. It doesn't mean that they have no opposition [Gdt, Mor, Mu], just that no one will prevail against them [Gdt, Mor, SSA, TH]. Exposure to perils and pains of every kind will not endanger their salvation [HNTC]. They have nothing to fear, for they will certainly have victory [NTC]. It doesn't matter who is against them if God is for them [NAC]. The forces which oppose us cannot prevail, and what they do only works for our good [AB]. With the creator of all things being for us, all other opposition, however terrible it may seem now, is as nothing [WBC]. They do in fact have enemies who can cause grievous suffering, but they need not fear them [ICC2]. Even if all the powers of hell oppose us they can never prevail [St].

ROMANS 8:32

8:32 (He) who indeed[a] spared[b] not his-own Son but gave- him -up[c] for[d] us all,

LEXICON—a. γέ (LN 91.6) (BAGD 2. p. 152): 'indeed' [LN, WBC; NET], '(did not) even' [NICNT; NLT, TEV], not explicit [AB, BECNT, HNTC, ICC2, NTC; CEV, GW, KJV, NASB, NCV, NIV, NRSV, REB]. This intensive particle adds emphasis [NICNT].

b. aorist mid. (deponent = act.) indic. of φείδομαι (LN 22.28) (BAGD 1. p. 854): 'to spare' [AB, BAGD, BECNT, HNTC, ICC2, LN, NICNT, NTC; all versions except CEV, NRSV, TEV], 'to withhold' [NRSV], 'to keep back' [CEV, TEV].

c. aorist act. indic. of παραδίδωμι (LN 57.77) (BAGD 1.b. p. 615): 'to give (someone) up' [BAGD, ICC2, NTC, WBC; NET, NIV, NLT, NRSV, REB], 'to give over' [LN], 'to give' [CEV, NCV], 'to hand over' [AB, BAGD, LN, NICNT], 'to hand over to death' [GW], 'to deliver (someone) up' [BECNT, HNTC; KJV, NASB], 'to offer (someone)' [TEV].

d. ὑπέρ with genitive object (LN 90.36) (BAGD 1.a.ε. p. 838): 'for' [AB, BAGD, BECNT, ICC2, LN, NICNT, NTC, WBC; all versions], 'on behalf of' [HNTC, LN], 'in behalf of' [BAGD].

QUESTION—What is the function of ὅς γέ 'who indeed'?

1. It is intensive, adding emphasis to what is being said [BAGD, Gdt, ICC1, ICC2, NICNT, NTC, WBC]. Emphasis is also added by the fact that 'his own son' precedes the verb [SSA].
2. It is causal, explaining why believers can have confidence that God is for them and nothing can defeat them [BECNT].

QUESTION—In what sense is ὑπέρ 'for' used?

1. Because of its use in conjunction with παραδίδωμι 'to give up' the preposition ὑπέρ 'for' has the sense of vicarious substitution, 'in the place of' [AB, Ho, Mor, Mu, WBC].
2. It means that Christ's death is for their benefit [BECNT, ICC2].

QUESTION—Who is encompassed in the phrase ἡμῶν πάντων 'us all'?

It refers to all the believers [BECNT, Gdt, ICC1, ICC2, Mor, Mu, NICNT, NTC, SSA, WBC]. Gentiles are included as well as Jews [BECNT, ICC2, NTC, WBC].

how shall-he- not also with[a] him -freely-give[b] us all (things)?[c]

LEXICON—a. σύν with dative object (LN 89.105, 89.107) (BAGD 4.a. p. 782): 'with' [BAGD, BECNT, HNTC, ICC2, LN (89.105, 89.107), NICNT, NTC, WBC; KJV, NASB, NCV, NRSV], 'along with' [AB; GW, NET, NIV], 'together with' [LN (89.105, 89.107)], not explicit [CEV, NLT, REB, TEV].

b. fut. mid. (deponent = act.) indic. of χαρίζομαι (LN **57.102**) (BAGD 1. p. 876): 'to give freely' [BAGD, NICNT; CEV, KJV, NASB, NET, TEV], 'to give graciously' [**LN**, NTC; NIV], 'to give graciously as a favor' [BAGD], 'to give' [AB, ICC2, LN, WBC; GW, NCV, NLT, NRSV], 'to grant' [LN], 'to grant graciously' [BECNT], 'to bestow' [HNTC], 'to bestow generously' [LN], 'to lavish' [REB].

c. πᾶς (LN 59.23): 'everything' [GW], 'everything else' [AB; CEV, NLT, NRSV], 'all things' [BECNT, HNTC, ICC2, NICNT, NTC, WBC; KJV, NASB, NCV, NET, NIV, TEV], 'every other gift' [REB], 'every, all' [LN].

QUESTION—What relationship is indicated by the prefix σύν 'with'?

God gives everything along with Christ, who has already been given [ICC2, NICNT, St]. All possible gifts are included in the gift of his Son [Gdt, Ho]. God has given Christ; he will also give all things in addition, in keeping with Christ's role as representing Adam, to whom all things were originally entrusted in the original dominion mandate [WBC]. Since Christ is the greatest possible gift, the granting of lesser gifts is thereby guaranteed [BECNT, Mu, NAC]. God gave the greatest gift in Christ, but he also gives everything else needed as well [NTC]. The prefix indicates that believers receive God's gifts because of their union with the crucified Christ [Mor].

QUESTION—What is the scope of the τὰ πάντα 'all things' that God gives?

1. It refers to all the spiritual and material blessings we need as we progress to final salvation [NICNT, NTC]. It refers to the fullness of salvation and all gifts and grace necessary for salvation [Ho, ICC1, ICC2, Mor, Mu]. It is everything needed for eschatological salvation [AB]. It refers to all that we need to be able to live for him [SSA]. It is all the blessings previously mention [Gdt].
2. They will share in Christ's lordship over all creation as a fulfillment of the dominion mandate given to Adam [WBC].
3. It refers to all things comprehensively [BECNT].

8:33 Who shall-bring-a-charge[a] against[b] God's chosen-ones?[c]

LEXICON—a. fut. act. indic. of ἐγκαλέω (LN 33.427) (BAGD p. 215): 'to bring a charge' [AB, HNTC, NICNT, NTC; NASB, NET, NIV, NRSV, REB], 'to bring charges' [BAGD, LN, WBC; CEV], 'to bring an accusing charge' [BECNT], 'to lay a charge' [ICC2], 'to lay (anything) to the charge' [KJV], 'to accuse' [BAGD; GW, NCV, NLT, TEV].

b. κατά with genitive object (LN 90.31) (BAGD I.2.b.β. p. 405): 'against' [AB, BAGD, BECNT, HNTC, ICC2, LN, NICNT, NTC, WBC; CEV, NASB, NET, NIV, NRSV, REB], not explicit [GW, KJV, NCV, NLT, TEV].

c. ἐκλεκτός (LN 30.93) (BAGD 1.b. p. 242): 'chosen' [AB, BAGD, LN; CEV], 'elect' [BECNT, HNTC, ICC2, NICNT, NTC, WBC; KJV, NASB, NET, NRSV]. This word is translated 'God's chosen people' [TEV], 'the people God has chosen' [NCV], 'those whom God has chosen' [GW, NIV, REB], 'us whom God has chosen for his own' [NLT].

QUESTION—How is 8:33-34 to be punctuated?

1. 8:33 and 8:34 each begin with a rhetorical question followed by assertions that answer the question [BECNT, Gdt, GNT, Ho, ICC1, ICC2, Mor,

NICNT, NTC, SSA, TH, WBC; GW, NASB, NCV, NET, NIV, NRSV, REB, TEV]: 'Who will bring a charge? It is God who justifies. Who will condemn? Christ died, etc.
2. The question 'who will condemn?' is a rhetorical question that logically follows the statement 'it is God who justifies', and the question 'who shall separate us from the love of Christ?' follows from the three previous questions, 'who is against us', 'who shall bring a charge', and 'who will condemn' [Mu].
3. Each of the four clauses contains a rhetorical question followed by another question which proposes an answer to the first one which will obviously be rejected [AB, HNTC]. That is, 'Who will bring a charge? God who justifies? Who will condemn? Christ who died?

God (is) the-(one) justifying;[a]
LEXICON—a. pres. act. participle of δικαιόω (LN 34.46, 56.34) (BAGD 3.b. p. 197): 'to justify' [AB, BAGD, BECNT, HNTC, ICC2, NICNT, NTC, WBC; KJV, NASB, NET, NIV, NRSV], 'to acquit' [LN (56.34); REB], 'to declare not guilty' [TEV], 'to put right with, to cause to be in a right relation with' [LN (34.46)], 'to make right' [NCV]. This phrase is translated 'If God says...are acceptable to him' [CEV]. The present participle is translated as a perfect tense verb: 'God has approved (of them)' [GW], 'has given right standing with himself' [NLT]; as a simple present tense verb by all commentaries and versions except GW, NLT.
QUESTION—What is the sense of the present tense of the participle 'justifying'?
1. The present tense is gnomic, without reference to time, simply indicating that it God is the one who justifies [AB, BECNT, Mor, NAC, NICNT, NTC].
2. It indicates that justification is an on-going action by God [WBC].

8:34 who will-be-condemning?[a]
LEXICON—a. fut. act. participle of κατακρίνω (LN 56.31) (BAGD p. 412): 'to condemn' [AB, BAGD, BECNT, HNTC, ICC2, LN, NICNT, NTC, WBC; all versions except NCV, REB], 'to pronounce judgment' [REB]. This phrase is translated 'who can say God's people are guilty?' [NCV].
QUESTION—Is this a future participle or a present participle?
Depending on how it is accented the participle could be either a present participle (κατακρίνων) or a future participle (κατακρινῶν). Since ancient manuscripts usually lack accents, the decision is more an interpretive and exegetical decision than a textual one. This participle is translated as present tense by NTC; KJV, NASB, NCV, NIV, and as future tense by GW, NET, NLT, REB, TEV, though possibly for stylistic reasons only.
1. It is future and refers to the judgment [AB, BECNT, ICC2, Mor, NICNT, WBC].
2. It is present [HNTC, ICC1].

Christ Jesus (is) the-(one) having-died, or rather[a] having-been-raised,[b]
TEXT—Some manuscripts omit Ἰησοῦς 'Jesus'. GNT includes this word in brackets with a C decision, indicating difficulty in deciding whether or not to place it in the text. This word is omitted by CEV, GW, KJV, NET, REB.
LEXICON—a. μᾶλλον (LN 89.126): 'but rather' [LN]. The phrase μᾶλλον δέ introduces a statement that supplements the previous one [SSA]. It is translated 'or rather' [AB, HNTC; REB, TEV], 'rather' [WBC], 'yea rather' [KJV], 'yes' [NRSV], 'but...also' [NCV], 'and more' [NICNT], 'and more importantly' [GW], 'and even more' [BECNT], 'more than that' [ICC2; NIV], 'and more than that' [NET], 'what is more' [NTC], 'and' [CEV, NLT].
b. aorist pass. (or pass. deponent = act.) participle of ἐγείρω (LN 23.94) (BAGD 2.c. p. 215): 'to be raised' [AB, BAGD, BECNT, HNTC, ICC2, LN, NICNT, NTC, WBC; NASB, NET, NRSV], 'to be raised from the dead' [NCV], 'to be raised to life' [LN; CEV, NIV, NLT, TEV], 'to be brought back to life' [GW], 'to be risen' [KJV]. This passive participle form is translated as a deponent: 'to rise' [BAGD], 'to rise again' [REB]. This aorist form is translated as perfect: 'has been raised' [BECNT]; as present: 'is risen' [KJV].

who is also at[a] (the) right-(hand)[b] of God, who also[c] intercedes[d] also for[e] us.
LEXICON—a. ἐν with dative object (LN 83.23): 'at' [AB, BECNT, HNTC, ICC2, LN, NICNT, NTC, WBC; all versions except GW, NCV], 'on' [NCV], not explicit [GW].
b. δεξιός/δεξιά (LN 8.32, 82.8) (BAGD 2.a. p. 174): 'right' [BAGD, LN (82.8)], 'right side' [LN (82.8); CEV, NCV, TEV]. This word is translated as an adjective modifying the understood feminine noun χειρί 'hand' [BAGD]; it is translated as a feminine noun δεξιά 'right hand' [AB, BECNT, HNTC, ICC2, LN (8.32), NICNT, NTC, WBC; KJV, NASB, NET, NIV, NRSV, REB]. The phrase 'who is also at the right hand of God' is translated 'Christ has the highest position in heaven' [GW], 'is sitting at the place of highest honor next to God' [NLT].
c. καί (LN 89.93): 'also' [BECNT, ICC2, LN, NICNT, NTC, WBC; GW, KJV, NASB], 'and' [LN; REB], 'and now' [NCV], 'and also' [LN; NET, NIV], 'even' [AB], 'and who actually (is)' [HNTC], not explicit [CEV, NLT, NRSV, TEV].
d. pres. act. indic. of ἐντυγχάνω (LN 33.169, **33.347**) (BAGD 1. p. 270): 'to intercede' [AB, BECNT, HNTC, ICC2, LN (33.347), NICNT, NTC, WBC; GW, NASB, NET, NIV, NRSV], 'to make intercession' [KJV], 'to plead, plead for' [BAGD, LN (33.169); NLT, TEV], 'to plead one's cause' [REB], 'to beg' [NCV], 'to petition' [LN (33.169)], 'to speak to (someone)' [CEV].
e. ὑπέρ with genitive object (LN 90.36): 'for' [AB, BECNT, ICC2, LN, NICNT, NTC; all versions except REB], 'on behalf of' [LN], 'in (our)

behalf' [HNTC], 'on (our) behalf' [WBC], 'for the sake of' [LN], not explicit [REB].

QUESTION—What status is implied in being at God's right hand?

Jesus is the vice-regent of the universe who also intercedes for us as high priest in God's own presence [NICNT]. He has the place and role of highest honor [Mor, SSA; GW, NLT], the place of honor and authority [TH]. He is the judge who intercedes [HNTC]. He was exalted to the place of honor, power. and authority as a reward for the mediatorial work he accomplished [NTC]. It speaks of the enthronement and majestic power of the exalted Christ [AB]. The right hand represents power, and the seat at the right hand is a place of honor [WBC]. It signifies the outpouring of the Holy Spirit as well as the fact that the government of the world and the direction of all the events of our life are put into his hands [Gdt]. It means that he is invested with sovereignty and dominion and crowned with glory [Mu]. He is exalted to universal dominion and is the director of all events and of all worlds [Ho]. At God's right hand he occupies the place of highest honor, exercises his authority to save, and awaits his final triumph; his position there is also the evidence that his work of atonement is complete [St].

8:35 **Who will-separate^a us from the love^b of-Christ?**

LEXICON—a. fut. act. indic. of χωρίζω (LN **63.29**) (BAGD 1. p. 890): 'to separate' [AB, BAGD, BECNT, HNTC, ICC2, LN, NICNT, NTC, WBC; all versions].

b. ἀγάπη (LN 25.43) (BAGD I.2.a. p. 6): 'love' [AB, BAGD, BECNT, HNTC, ICC2, LN, NICNT, NTC, WBC; all versions].

QUESTION—What relationship is indicated by the genitive phrase τοῦ Χριστοῦ 'of Christ'?

It is subjective [AB, BECNT, Gdt, HNTC, Ho, ICC1, ICC2, Mu, NAC, NICNT, NTC, SSA, TH, WBC; GW, NCV, NLT]: Christ's love for us.

QUESTION—What is the relation of this question to the statements in 8:34 beginning with 'Christ Jesus...'?

1. This begins a new question, parallel to the question that begins 8:34 [AB, BECNT, HNTC, ICC1, ICC2, Mor, NICNT, NTC, WBC; all versions except NLT, REB, TEV].
2. It draws a conclusion from the statements immediately preceding it in 8:34 [NLT, REB, TEV]: since Christ died and was raised, etc., then who will separate us?
3. This states the second of two conclusions that are to be drawn from all that he has said in 8:1–30; the first is in 8:31b, that nothing can prevail against us, and this second conclusion asserts that nothing can separate us from God's love [SSA].
4. The question 'who shall separate us from the love of Christ?' follows from the three previous questions, 'who is against us', 'who shall bring a charge', and 'who will condemn' [Mu]. It is the last step and highest point

in the argument; no one can accuse, no one can condemn, no one can separate us from Christ's love [Ho].

(Shall) tribulation[a] or distress[b] or persecution[c] or hunger[d] or nakedness[e] or peril[f] or sword?[g]

LEXICON—a. θλῖψις (LN 22.2) (BAGD 1. p. 362): 'tribulation' [BAGD, NICNT; KJV, NASB], 'affliction' [BAGD, BECNT, HNTC, ICC2, NTC, WBC; REB], 'trouble' [CEV, GW, NET, NIV, NLT, TEV], 'troubles' [NCV], 'trouble and suffering' [LN], 'suffering' [LN], 'hardship' [NRSV], 'distress' [AB].

b. στενοχωρία (LN 22.10) (BAGD p. 766): 'distress' [BAGD, BECNT, LN, NICNT, NTC, WBC; GW, KJV, NASB, NET, NRSV], 'difficulty' [BAGD, LN], 'anguish' [AB, BAGD, HNTC, ICC2], 'suffering' [CEV], 'problems' [NCV], 'hardship' [NIV, REB, TEV], 'calamity' [NLT], 'trouble' [BAGD].

c. διωγμός (LN 39.45) (BAGD p. 201): 'persecution' [AB, BAGD, BECNT, HNTC, ICC2, LN, NICNT, NTC, WBC; all versions except CEV, NCV, NLT], 'sufferings' [NCV], 'hard times' [CEV]. This noun is translated as a phrase: 'if we are persecuted' [NLT].

d. λιμός (LN 23.31, 23.33) (BAGD 1. p. 475): 'hunger' [BAGD, LN (23.33), WBC; CEV, GW, NCV, REB, TEV], 'famine' [AB, BECNT, HNTC, ICC2, LN (23.33), NICNT, NTC; KJV, NASB, NET, NIV, NRSV], 'considerable hunger, lack of food' [LN (23.31)]. This noun is translated as a phrase: 'if we are hungry' [NLT].

e. γυμνότης (LN **49.23**) (BAGD 2. p. 168): 'nakedness' [AB, BECNT, HNTC, ICC2, **LN**, NICNT, NTC, WBC; CEV, GW, KJV, NASB, NCV, NET, NIV, NRSV, REB], 'poverty' [TEV], 'lack of sufficient clothing' [BAGD], 'destitution' [BAGD]. This noun is translated as a phrase: 'if we are cold' [NLT]. In this passage this word refers to poverty [LN].

f. κίνδυνος (LN **21.1**) (BAGD p. 432): 'danger' [AB, BAGD, BECNT, HNTC, **LN**, WBC; CEV, GW, NCV, NET, NIV, NLT, REB, TEV], 'peril' [ICC2, LN, NICNT, NTC; KJV, NASB, NRSV], 'risk' [BAGD, LN]. This noun is translated as a phrase: 'if we are in danger' [NLT].

g. μάχαιρα (LN 6.33, **20.68**) (BAGD 2. p. 496): 'sword' [AB, BECNT, HNTC, ICC2, LN (6.33), NICNT, NTC, WBC; KJV, NASB, NET, NIV], 'death' [LN (**20.68**); CEV], 'violent death' [BAGD; GW, NCV]. This noun is translated as a participle: 'being killed' [LN (20.68)]; as a phrase: 'if we are threatened with death' [NLT].

QUESTION—What difference is there between θλῖψις 'tribulation' and στενοχωρία 'distress'?

The two together represent the fearsome tribulation of the end time [WBC].
1. They are a doublet with essentially the same meaning [SSA].
2. 'Tribulation' refers to outward circumstances and 'distress' to an inward or subjective state produced by the outward pressure [Gdt, ICC2, NTC].

QUESTION—What does γυμνότης 'nakedness' represent?

It refers to not having adequate clothing [BAGD, Mor, NTC, SSA, St], to poverty [LN, WBC; TEV]. Hunger and nakedness describe human deprivation [WBC].

QUESTION—What does μάχαιρα 'sword' represent?

This word here represents violent death [BAGD, Gdt, Mor, NTC, TH, WBC; GW, NCV], such as being executed [Gdt, Mor, SSA] or being murdered [SSA]. The sword represents capital punishment [Gdt,].

8:36 Just-as it-is-written[a] that For-the-sake-of[b] you we-are-killed[c] all the day;[d]

LEXICON—a. perf. pass. indic. of γράφω (LN 33.61) (BAGD 2.c. p. 166): 'to be written' [BAGD, LN]. The phrase καθὼς γέγραπται is translated 'just as it is written' [BECNT; NASB], 'as it is written' [NTC, WBC; KJV, NET, NIV, NRSV], 'as it is written in the Scriptures' [NCV], 'even as it is written' [NICNT], 'even as it is written in Scripture' [ICC2], 'as it stands written' [AB], 'the Scriptures say' [CEV], 'even the Scriptures say' [NLT], 'it is exactly as the Scriptures say' [CEV], 'as Scripture says' [GW, REB], 'as the scripture says' [TEV], 'these things are foretold as our lot, as it is written' [HNTC]. This quote is from Psalm 44:22.

b. ἕνεκεν (LN 90.43) (BAGD p. 264): 'for the sake of, because of' [BAGD, LN], 'on account of' [BAGD]. The phrase Ἕνεκεν σοῦ is translated 'for your sake' [AB, BECNT, NICNT, WBC; NET, NIV, NLT, NRSV, REB, TEV], 'for thy sake' [HNTC, ICC2, NTC; KJV, NASB], 'for you' [CEV, NCV], 'because of you' [GW].

c. pres. pass. indic. of θανατόω (LN 20.65) (BAGD 1. p. 351): 'to be killed' [BAGD, LN, WBC; GW, KJV], 'to be put to death' [AB, HNTC, NICNT, NTC; NASB, NLT, NRSV], 'to suffer death' [BECNT], 'to be done to death' [ICC2; REB], 'to be in danger of death' [BAGD; NCV, TEV]. This passive verb is translated as active: 'to face death' [CEV, NIV], 'to encounter death' [NET].

d. ἡμέρα (LN 67.178) (BAGD 2. p. 346): 'day' [BAGD, LN]. The phrase ὅλην τὴν ἡμέραν 'all the day' is translated 'all day long' [AB, BECNT, NICNT; CEV, GW, NET, NIV, NRSV, REB], 'all the day long' [ICC2, NTC; KJV, NASB], 'all the day' [WBC], 'all the time' [NCV], 'at all times' [TEV], 'every day' [HNTC; NLT].

QUESTION—What relationship is indicated by καθώς 'just as'?

It gives the grounds for the assertion that none of these difficulties are able to separate the believer from God's love, which is that the Scripture teaches that these things happen even to the godly [BECNT, HNTC, NICNT].

QUESTION—How can we be killed 'all the day'?

The phrase 'all the day' is a Hebraism meaning that there is no escape [WBC]. To die every day obviously means to face death every day [TH]. We are in danger of being killed [CEV, NCV, NIV, TEV].

we-have-been-considered[a] **as sheep of-slaughter.**[b]

LEXICON—a. aorist pass. indic. of λογίζομαι (LN 31.1) (BAGD 1.b. p. 476): 'to be considered' [AB, BAGD, BECNT, LN, NICNT, NTC; NASB, NET, NIV], 'to be regarded' [LN], 'to be reckoned' [HNTC, ICC2, WBC], 'to be thought of' [GW], 'to be accounted' [KJV, NRSV], 'to be looked upon as' [BAGD], 'to be treated like' [REB, TEV], not explicit [NLT]. This passive verb is also translated as active: '(people) think' [NCV], 'we are (like)' [CEV].

b. σφαγή (LN **20.72**) (BAGD p. 795): 'slaughter' [BAGD]. This noun in the genitive case is translated 'to be slaughtered' [AB, BAGD, BECNT, ICC2, NTC; GW, NASB, NET, NIV, NRSV], 'that are to be slaughtered' [LN], 'that are going to be slaughtered' [TEV], 'to be killed' [NCV], 'for slaughter' [NICNT, WBC; REB], 'for the slaughter' [KJV], 'due for slaughter' [HNTC], 'on (their) way to be butchered' [CEV]. This clause is translated 'we are being slaughtered like sheep' [NLT].

8:37 **But**[a] **in**[b] **all these (things) we-have-complete-victory**[c] **through**[d] **the-(one) having-loved**[e] **us.**

LEXICON—a. ἀλλά (LN 89.125) (BAGD 3. p. 38): 'but' [BAGD, BECNT, ICC2, NICNT, WBC; NASB, NCV], 'true; but' [HNTC], 'yet' [AB], 'and yet' [REB], 'no' [NTC; NET, NIV, NLT, NRSV, TEV], 'nay' [KJV], not explicit [CEV, GW].

b. ἐν with dative object (LN 83.13): 'in' [AB, BECNT, HNTC, ICC2, LN, NICNT, WBC; all versions except NLT, REB]. The phrase ἐν τούτοις πᾶσιν is translated 'in all these things' [BECNT, HNTC, ICC2, NICNT, NTC, WBC; KJV, NASB, NCV, NET, NIV, NRSV, TEV], 'in everything' [CEV], 'in all of it' [AB], 'in all these difficulties' [GW], 'despite all these things' [NLT], 'throughout it all' [REB].

c. pres. act. indic. of ὑπερνικάω (LN **39.58**) (BAGD p. 841): 'to have complete victory' [**LN**; NET, TEV], 'to have full victory' [NCV], 'to be more than conquerors' [BECNT, HNTC, ICC2, NICNT, NTC; KJV, NIV, NRSV], 'to be more than victors' [AB], 'to win more than a victory' [CEV], 'to overwhelmingly conquer' [NASB], 'to prevail completely' [WBC], 'to win a most glorious victory' [BAGD], 'to be completely victorious' [LN]. The phrase 'we have complete victory' is translated 'overwhelming victory is ours' [NLT, REB], '(he) gives us an overwhelming victory' [GW].

d. διά with genitive object (LN 90.4) (BAGD A. III. 2.b.γ. p. 180): 'through' [BAGD, BECNT, HNTC, ICC2, LN, NICNT, NTC, WBC; KJV, NASB, NCV, NET, NIV, NLT, NRSV, REB, TEV], 'because of' [AB; CEV]. The phrase 'through the one having loved us' is made the subject of the sentence: 'the one who loves us gives us an overwhelming victory' [GW].

e. aorist act. participle of ἀγαπάω (LN 25.43) (BAGD 1.b.α. p. 4): 'to love' [AB, BAGD, BECNT, HNTC, ICC2, LN, NICNT, NTC, WBC; all versions]. The aorist tense probably refers to the love expressed on the cross, which shows what love really is [Mor, SSA], but there is no implication that his love has ceased [SSA].

QUESTION—What relationship is indicated by ἀλλά 'but'?
  1. It gives a 'no' answer to the question raised in 8:35 about whether such things can separate from God's love [BAGD, BECNT, HNTC, ICC2, Mor, NICNT, NTC, St, TH; NET, NIV, NLT, NRSV, TEV].
  2. It introduces a concessive statement that amplifies the assertion of 8:35 [AB, ICC1, SSA]: even if all these things happen to us, we have complete victory.

QUESTION—What relationship is indicated by ἐν 'in'?
  1. It marks attendant circumstance; that is, even in the midst of these things happening we prevail [ICC2, Mu, NTC, SSA, St, TH, WBC]. Such sufferings are the scene of the overwhelming victory Christ gives [HNTC].
  2. It is a Hebraism and means 'despite' all these things [TNTC].

QUESTION—To whom does he refer in the phrase 'the one having loved us'?
  1. It refers to Christ [AB, BECNT, Gdt, HNTC, Ho, ICC1, ICC2, Mu, NICNT, SSA, St, TH; CEV, NLT].
  2. It refers to God [WBC; NCV]. It is God's love expressed in the gift of his son, which outweighs even the worst that can happen to us [WBC].

8:38 For I-am-persuaded^a that neither death nor life nor angels nor rulers^b

LEXICON—a. perf. pass. indic. of πείθω (LN **31.46**) (BAGD 4. p. 640): 'to be persuaded' [BECNT, ICC2, LN, NICNT; KJV], 'to be convinced' [AB, BAGD, LN, NTC, WBC; GW, NASB, NET, NIV, NLT, NRSV, REB], 'to be confident' [HNTC], 'to be certain' [BAGD, LN; TEV], 'to be sure' [CEV, NCV]. This perfect tense verb is translated in the present tense [AB, BECNT, HNTC, ICC2, NICNT, NTC, WBC; all versions]: I am convinced, etc.

  b. ἀρχή (LN 12.44, 37.56) (BAGD 3. p. 112): 'ruler' [BAGD, BECNT, LN (12.44, 37.56), NICNT, WBC; GW, NET, NRSV], 'heavenly ruler' [TEV], 'principality' [AB, ICC2, NTC; KJV, NASB], 'prince' [HNTC], 'authority' [BAGD], 'spirit' [CEV], 'ruling spirit' [NCV], 'demon' [NIV, NLT]. The phrase 'angels nor rulers' is translated 'in the realm of spirits or superhuman powers' [REB].

QUESTION—What relationship is indicated by γάρ 'for'?
  1. It introduces grounds for his statement in 8:37: we have victory because nothing can separate us from God's love [ICC2, NICNT]. It introduces 8:38 as grounds in a greater-to-lesser argument for what has just been said in the previous context; we don't fear those things already mentioned because even in the whole universe there is nothing to be feared [Gdt].
  2. It introduces a restatement and amplification of what was said in 8:35 about not being separated from Christ's love [SSA].

QUESTION—What does θάνατος 'death' refer to?
1. It refers to physical death in general [AB, HNTC, Ho, ICC2, Mor, NICNT, NTC, SSA]. Death represents the fullest expression of sin's hostile power in this age [WBC].
2. It refers specifically to martyrdom [Gdt].

QUESTION—To what does ζωή 'life' refer?
It refers generally to life in rhetorical balance to 'death' as encompassing every human state and condition [NICNT, WBC], but carries no further significance [NICNT]. It refers to distractions, cares, trials, or problems of this life [AB, Gdt, Ho, ICC2, Mor, NTC, SSA]. Life in this age is one of suffering [WBC]. It refers to the dangers and temptations of life [AB], or its blandishments and trials [Ho], its calamities [St].

QUESTION—What distinction is there between 'angels' and 'rulers'?
1. He probably uses 'angels' to denote those spirit beings that are not fallen, and 'rulers' to denote those that are fallen [Gdt, Mu, NICNT, NTC, SSA; NIV, NLT]. His intent is to cover hypothetically the entire range of created things, not to assert that they would try to separate believers from God's love [Mu]. Even angels, whether good or evil, real or imagined, can't separate God's people from God's love in Christ [NTC]. Paul's intent is to say that no spiritual cosmic power, whether good or evil, can separate them from God's love [ICC2]. The rulers are the demons [SSA; NIV, NLT].
2. Both refer to fallen spirit beings, demons [BECNT, TH, WBC], since only they would try to separate believers from the Lord [BECNT].
3. The distinction here is not clear [AB], or it has only a general meaning with no distinction intended [Ho]. The couplet is indefinite and seems intended to include all superhuman powers [St].

nor (things)-being-present[a] nor (things)-going-to-be[b] nor powers[c]

TEXT—Some manuscripts place οὔτε δυνάμεις 'nor powers' at the beginning of this phrase. It is placed at the end of the phrase by GNT with an A rating, indicating that the text is certain. Only KJV and TEV place it at the beginning.

LEXICON—a. perf. act. participle of ἐνίστημι (LN 67.41) (BAGD 1. p. 266): 'to be present' [BAGD, LN]. This plural participle is translated 'the present' [AB; CEV, NIV, TEV], 'things present' [BECNT, HNTC, ICC2, NTC, WBC; KJV, NASB, NRSV], 'things that are present' [NET], 'present things' [NICNT], 'anything in the present' [GW], 'the world as it is' [REB], 'nothing now' [NCV], 'our fears for today' [NLT]. (This participle is in the perfect tense because in the present tense it can denote those things which are impending or are coming, and thus, in the perfect tense, those things which have come.)

b. pres. act. participle of μέλλω (LN 67.62) (BAGD 2. p. 501): 'to be going to be, to be about to (be)' [LN]. The plural is translated 'things to come' [BAGD, BECNT, HNTC, ICC2, NICNT, NTC, WBC; KJV, NASB,

NET, NRSV], 'the future' [AB; CEV, NIV, TEV], 'anything in the future' [GW], 'the world as it shall be' [REB], 'nothing in the future' [NCV], 'our worries about tomorrow' [NLT].
   c. δύναμις (LN 12.44, **37.61**) (BAGD 6. p. 208): 'power' [BAGD, BECNT, ICC2, LN (12.44), NICNT, NTC, WBC; KJV, NASB, NCV, NET, NIV, NRSV, TEV], 'power above' [CEV], 'spiritual power' [HNTC], 'ruler' [LN (37.61)], not explicit [CEV]. This plural noun is translated 'forces or powers' [GW], 'the forces of the universe' [REB]. The phrase 'power, nor height nor depth' is translated 'powers of hell' [NLT]. It refers to a supernatural spirit or angel [BAGD].
QUESTION—What are the things present and the things going to be?
   1. It refers generally to all circumstances or events, whether present or future [Gdt, Ho, ICC2, NICNT, SSA, WBC], including the eschatological future [ICC2], and including also the agents of such events [SSA]. Neither the problems of the present nor the forebodings for the future can separates us from God's deep love [NTC]. It speaks of the instability of the present age and the uncertainty of the future [AB]. It includes the dimension of time itself in his list, with the inexorable processes of change and decay [WBC]. It speaks of the present and the future, whether the future age or simply hazards which may yet happen in this life [TNTC].
   2. It refers to astrological powers [TH].
QUESTION—What is meant by 'powers'?
   1. They are spiritual beings, angelic powers [BAGD, BECNT, HNTC, Ho, ICC2, Mor, Mu, NICNT, NTC, SSA, TH, WBC; CEV, NLT, REB].
   2. They are human rulers [LN (37.61)], although it is also possible to take this to mean supernatural powers [LN (12.44)].

8:39 **nor height[a] nor depth[b] nor any other created-thing[c]**
LEXICON—a. ὕψωμα (LN **1.13**, 12.46) (BAGD 1. p. 851): 'height' [AB, BAGD, BECNT, ICC2, NTC, WBC; KJV, NASB, NET, NIV, NRSV], 'heights' [REB], 'the world above' [LN (1.13); TEV], 'power in the world above' [LN (**12.46**)], 'forces or powers in the world above' [GW], '(spiritual powers) above the level of the earth' [HNTC], 'powers above' [CEV], 'power of the world above' [LN (12.46)], '(nothing) above us' [NCV], 'whether we're high above the sky' [NLT]. It refers to the space above the earth's horizon [BAGD].
   b. βάθος (LN **1.18**, **12.47**, 81.8) (BAGD 1. p. 130): 'depth' [AB, BAGD, BECNT, ICC2, LN (81.8), NICNT, NTC, WBC; KJV, NASB, NET, NIV, NRSV], 'depths' [REB], '(spiritual powers) below the level of the earth' [HNTC], 'the world below' [LN (1.18); TEV], 'power in the world below' [LN (12.47)], 'forces or powers in the world below' [GW], 'powers below' [CEV], '(nothing) below us' [NCV], 'in the deepest ocean' [NLT]. This word can refer to the celestial space below earth's horizon from which the stars arise, but with the preceding ὕψωμα 'height' it probably refers to astral spirits [BAGD].

c. κτίσις (LN 42.38) (BAGD 1.b.α. p. 455): 'created thing' [BECNT, HNTC, ICC2, NICNT, NTC; NASB], 'creature' [AB, BAGD, LN, WBC; KJV], 'creation' [LN], 'what has been created' [LN]. The phrase 'nor any other created thing' is translated 'nothing in all creation' [CEV, NLT, REB, TEV], 'anything else in creation' [GW], 'anything else in the whole world' [NCV], 'anything else in creation' [NET], 'anything else in all creation' [NIV, NRSV]. The English term 'creature' normally refers to animals, but a more generic meaning is intended here [SSA].

QUESTION—To what do 'height' and 'depth' refer?
1. They are spatial terms encompassing the whole universe [BECNT, Ho, ICC2, NICNT, WBC; NLT], representing heaven and earth [Ho], or heaven and hell [ICC2, NICNT]. They complete the picture begun by his references to time: neither time nor space can separate from God's love [Mu, NTC]. In this verse he covers the full sweep of space and time [WBC].
2. They are astronomical terms used here to represent celestial spiritual powers [AB, BAGD, HNTC, SSA, TH]. His reference to the full sweep of the physical heavens also would include all astrological powers which might be thought to influence human destiny [WBC]. They are powers of the invisible world [Gdt]. They are powerful beings above the horizon and below the horizon [SSA]. While these were technical terms in astrology, referring to celestial powers that controlled the planets and thus the destinies of men, that does not mean Paul used them in that sense; nevertheless he is saying that fate, whether real or imagined, has no ability to separate believers from God's love [TNTC].

will-be-able to-separate[a] us from[b] the love of-God which (is) in[c] Christ Jesus our Lord.

LEXICON—a. aorist act. infin. of χωρίζω (LN 63.29) (BAGD 1. p. 890): 'to separate' [AB, BAGD, BECNT, HNTC, ICC2, LN, NICNT, NTC, WBC; all versions].
  b. ἀπό with genitive object (LN 89.122): 'from' [AB, BECNT, HNTC, ICC2, LN, NICNT, NTC, WBC; all versions].
  c. ἐν with dative object (LN 83.13) (BAGD I.5.d. p. 259): 'in' [AB, BAGD, BECNT, HNTC, ICC2, LN, NICNT, NTC, WBC; all versions except GW, NLT, TEV], 'through' [TEV]. The phrase 'which is in Christ Jesus our Lord' is translated 'which is ours through Christ Jesus our Lord' [TEV], 'which Christ Jesus our Lord shows us' [GW], 'that is revealed in Christ Jesus our Lord' [NLT]. This word indicates a close personal relationship [BAGD].

QUESTION—Does the 'nothing' that can separate believers from God's love also include believers themselves?
1. The 'who' in 8:35 includes also the believer [BECNT, Ho, NICNT]: no one, not even the believer can separate himself or herself from the love of God in Christ. Since salvation delivers from the guilt and power of sin, it

means that believers are preserved from apostasy and deadly sins, as this is the end and essence of salvation [Ho].
2. The believer may decide to separate himself from the love of God in Christ [Gdt].

QUESTION—What is meant by the qualifying phrase 'in Christ Jesus our Lord'?

God's love is revealed through Christ and experienced in relation to him [Gdt, ICC1, ICC2, NICNT]. God's love and Christ's love are synonymous and should not be distinguished from one another [BECNT]. The preposition ἐν 'in' introduces a means proposition which is an event, hence it refers to what Christ has done for us [SSA]. Christ, who is the lord over all powers both present and future, is the one in whom God elected us in love, and it is with him that we will enter into future glory and through him that we know and trust God [HNTC]. What Christ has done for humanity manifests God's love in a concrete way [AB]. God's love is not known apart from Christ, and it is the cross that shows what God's love really is [Mor]. Jesus embodies and mediates God's love [WBC]. This section, comprising chapters 5 through 8, ends as it begins with the reference to Christ Jesus as Lord, in whom the saints experience the love of God [NTC]. God expresses his love through Christ, and Christ causes us to experience God's love [TH]. It is only in Christ that the love of God exists, is manifest, is operative, and can be known and embraced [Mu]. God's unchangeable love is extended to us because of our connection with Christ [Ho]. God reveals his love through Christ [St]. God's love is secured to us through Christ [TNTC].

www.ingramcontent.com/pod-product-compliance
Lightning Source LLC
Chambersburg PA
CBHW052012040526
R18239600001BA/R182396PG44108CBX00008BA/15